The Literature of
AUTOBIOGRAPHICAL NARRATIVE

ST. JAMES PRESS
A part of Gale, Cengage Learning

Detroit • New York • San Francisco • New Haven, Conn • Waterville, Maine • London

The Literature of Autobiographical Narrative
Thomas Riggs, Editor
Andrea Kovacs Henderson, Project Editor

Artwork and photographs for *The Literature of Autobiographical Narrative* covers were reproduced with the following kind permission.

Volume 1
For foreground painting "Chief Geronimo, 1899" by Elbridge Ayer Burbank. © Butler Institute of American Art, Youngstown, OH USA/Museum Purchase 1912/The Bridgeman Art Library.

For background image of a band of Apache Indian prisoners, 1886. The Art Archive/National Archives Washington DC.

Volume 2
For foreground portrait "Anne Frank, 1960" (coal with pastel on paper) by Ilya Glazunov (b. 1930). Private Collection/The Bridgeman Art Library.

For background image of 263 Prinsengracht in Amsterdam, the house where Anne Frank and her family spent two years in hiding during the German occupation of The Netherlands during World War II. The Art Archive/Culver Pictures.

Volume 3
For foreground "May the Whole Country from the Mountains to the Rivers be a Sea of Red, 1960" (colour litho). Private Collection/© The Chambers Gallery, London/The Bridgeman Art Library.

For background image of detail of Political Relief Sculpture in Tiananmen Square. © Brian A. Vikanders/CORBIS.

© 2013 Gale, Cengage Learning

ALL RIGHTS RESERVED. No part of this work covered by the copyright herein may be reproduced, transmitted, stored, or used in any form or by any means graphic, electronic, or mechanical, including but not limited to photocopying, recording, scanning, digitizing, taping, Web distribution, information networks, or information storage and retrieval systems, except as permitted under Section 107 or 108 of the 1976 United States Copyright Act, without the prior written permission of the publisher.

For product information and technology assistance, contact us at
Gale Customer Support, 1-800-877-4253.
For permission to use material from this text or product,
submit all requests online at www.cengage.com/permissions.
Further permissions questions can be emailed to
permissionrequest@cengage.com.

While every effort has been made to ensure the reliability of the information presented in this publication, Gale, a part of Cengage Learning, does not guarantee the accuracy of the data contained herein. Gale accepts no payment for listing; and inclusion in the publication of any organization, agency, institution, publication, service, or individual does not imply endorsement of the editors or publisher. Errors brought to the attention of the publisher and verified to the satisfaction of the publisher will be corrected in future editions.

Library of Congress Cataloging-in-Publication Data

The literature of autobiographical narrative / Thomas Riggs, editor.
  volumes cm
  Includes bibliographical references and indexes.
  ISBN 978-1-55862-870-0 (set : alk. paper) -- ISBN 978-1-55862-871-7 (vol. 1 : alk. paper) -- ISBN 978-1-55862-872-4 (vol. 2 : alk. paper) -- ISBN 978-1-55862-873-1 (vol. 3 : alk. paper)
  1. Autobiography. 2. Biography as a literary form. 3. Authors--Biography--History and criticism. 4. Literature--History and criticism. I. Riggs, Thomas, 1963-
  CT25.L58 2013
  920.02--dc23
                                                  2013002574

Gale
27500 Drake Rd.
Farmington Hills, MI, 48331-3535

ISBN-13: 978-1-55862-870-0 (set)   ISBN-10: 1-55862-870-3 (set)
ISBN-13: 978-1-55862-871-7 (vol. 1)   ISBN-10: 1-55862-871-1 (vol. 1)
ISBN-13: 978-1-55862-872-4 (vol. 2)   ISBN-10: 1-55862-872-X (vol. 2)
ISBN-13: 978-1-55862-873-1 (vol. 3)   ISBN-10: 1-55862-873-8 (vol. 3)

This title will also be available as an e-book.
ISBN-13: 978-1-55862-881-6 ISBN-10: 1-55862-881-9
Contact your Gale, a part of Cengage Learning, sales representative for ordering information.

Printed in the United States of America
1 2 3 4 5 6 7 17 16 15 14 13

Advisory Board

CHAIR

Richard Bradford
Research Professor of English and Senior Distinguished Research Fellow, University of Ulster, Ulster, Northern Ireland. Author of *A Brief Life of John Milton* (2013); *The Odd Couple: The Curious Friendship between Kingsley Amis and Philip Larkin* (2012); *Martin Amis: The Biography* (2011); *The Life of a Long-Distance Writer: The Authorized Biography of Alan Sillitoe* (2008); *First Boredom, Then Fear: The Life of Philip Larkin* (2005); and *Lucky Him: The Life of Kingsley Amis* (2001). Editor of *Life Writing: Essays on Autobiography, Biography and Literature* (2010).

ADVISORS

Lynn Abram
Professor of Gender History, University of Glasgow, Glasgow, Scotland. Author of *Oral History Theory* (2010); *Myth and Materiality in a Woman's World: Shetland 1800–2000* (2005); *The Making of Modern Woman: Europe, 1789–1918* (2002); and *The Orphan Country: Children of Scotland's Broken Homes from 1800 to the Present Day* (1998). Series editor of Manchester University Press Gender in History series (2003–).

Suzanne Bunkers
Professor of English, Minnesota State University, Mankato, Mankato, Minnesota. Author of *In Search of Susanna* (1996). Coauthor, with Frank W. Klein, of *Good Earth, Black Soil* (1981). Editor of *Diaries of Girls and Women: A Midwestern American Sampler* (2001); *A Pioneer Farm Girl: The Diary of Sarah Gillespie, 1877–1878* (2000); *"All Will Yet Be Well": The Diary of Sarah Gillespie Huftalen, 1873–1952* (1993); and *The Diary of Caroline Seabury, 1854–1863* (1991). Coeditor, with Cynthia Huff, of *Inscribing the Daily: Critical Essays on Women's Diaries* (1996).

Cynthia Huff
Professor of English, Illinois State University, Normal, Illinois. Editor of *Towards a Geography of Women's Life Writing and Imagined Communities* (2005). Coeditor, with Suzanne Bunkers, of *Inscribing the Daily: Critical Essays on Women's Diaries* (1996). Contributor to the journals *Biography* and *a/b: Auto/Biography Studies*. Editorial board member of *a/b*.

Geneva Cobb Moore
Professor of English, University of Wisconsin-Whitewater, Whitewater, Wisconsin. Contributor to *Inscribing the Daily: Critical Essays on Women's Diaries* (1996), edited by Suzanne Bunkers and Cynthia Huff; and to *The Oxford Companion to African American Literature,* edited by William L. Andrews, Frances Smith Foster, and Trudier Harris (1997). Contributor of essays on Africa, Zora Neale Hurston, Alice Walker, Harriet Jacobs, Toni Morrison, and Danzy Senna to journals including the *Southern Literary Journal,* the *Black Scholar,* and the *Western Journal of Black Studies.* Former Fulbright Scholar of American and African American Literature at the University of Ghana, West Africa. Recipient of grants and awards from the National Endowment for the Humanities and the Paul W. Mellon Foundation.

Harry Ross
Associate Professor of Secondary Education, National Louis University, Chicago, Illinois. Coauthor of *13 Steps to Teacher Empowerment: Taking a More Active Role in Your School Community* (2009). National presenter on life writing, multicultural literature, urban teacher preparation, and teacher collaboration and leadership. Lead scholar on a National Endowment for the Humanities grant to teach the life stories written by the 1930s Federal Writers' Project authors.

Amanda Rust
English and Theatre Librarian, Northeastern University, Boston, Massachusetts.

Sharon Cadman Seelig
Roe/Straut Professor in the Humanities, Smith College, Northampton, Massachusetts. Author of *Autobiography and Gender in Early Modern Literature: Reading Women's Lives, 1600–1680* (2006); *Generating Texts: The Progeny of Seventeenth-Century Prose* (1996); and *The Shadow of Eternity: Belief and Structure in Herbert, Vaughan, and Traherne* (1981). Editorial board member of *English Literary Renaissance.*

Eugene Stelzig
Distinguished Teaching Professor of English, State University of New York at Geneseo, Geneseo, New York. Author of *Henry Crabb Robinson in Germany: A Study in Nineteenth-Century Life Writing* (2010); *The Romantic Subject in Autobiography: Rousseau and Goethe* (2000); *Herman Hesse's Fictions of the Self: Autobiography and the Confessional Imagination* (1988); and *All Shades of Consciousness: Wordsworth's Poetry and the Self in Time* (1975). Contributor to journals in the areas of Romantic studies and autobiography studies. Editor of *Romantic Autobiography in England* (2009).

Editorial and Production Staff

Associate Publisher
Marc Cormier

Product Manager
Philip J. Virta

Project Editor
Andrea Kovacs Henderson

Editorial Support
Rebecca Parks

Editorial Assistance
Laura Avery, Lisa Kumar, Michelle Lee, Margaret Mazurkiewicz, Tracie Moy

Art Director
Kristine Julien

Composition and Imaging
Evi Seoud, John Watkins

Manufacturing
Wendy Blurton

Rights Acquisition and Management
Kimberly Potvin, Margaret Chamberlain-Gaston

Technical Support
Luann Brennan, Mike Weaver

Table of Contents

Introduction xiii

Editor's Note xvii

Contributors xix

Academic Reviewers xxi

Adversity and Resistance

The Autobiography of W. E. B. Du Bois: A Soliloquy on Viewing My Life from the Last Decade of Its First Century by W. E. B. Du Bois 3

The Diving Bell and the Butterfly by Jean-Dominique Bauby 6

Dust Tracks on a Road by Zora Neale Hurston 9

Eighty Years and More, Reminiscences 1815–1897 by Elizabeth Cady Stanton 12

Hunger of Memory: The Education of Richard Rodriguez by Richard Rodriguez 15

I Know Why the Caged Bird Sings by Maya Angelou 18

Lakota Woman by Mary Crow Dog 21

Let My People Go by Albert Luthuli 24

The Long Walk to Freedom by Nelson Mandela 27

Mein Kampf by Adolf Hitler 30

Narrative of the Life of Frederick Douglass by Frederick Douglass 33

Rosa Parks: My Story by Rosa Parks and Jim Haskins 37

The Story of My Life: An Afghan Girl on the Other Side of the Sky by Farah Ahmedi 40

The Story of My Life: Helen Keller by Helen Keller 43

This Boy's Life by Tobias Wolff 47

Up from Slavery by Booker T. Washington 50

The Way to Rainy Mountain by N. Scott Momaday 54

Between Cultures

The Abandoned Baobab: The Autobiography of a Senegalese Woman by Ken Bugul 61

The Autobiography of Charles Darwin by Charles Darwin 65

Chona: The Autobiography of a Papago Woman by Maria Chona and Ruth Underhill 69

The Color of Water: A Black Man's Tribute to His White Mother by James McBride 72

A Cross and a Star: Memoirs of a Jewish Girl in Chile by Marjorie Agosín 75

Dreams from My Father: A Story of Race and Inheritance by Barack Obama 78

The Interesting Narrative of the Life of Olaudah Equiano, or Gustavus Vassa, the African, Written by Himself by Olaudah Equiano 81

A Long Way from Home by Claude McKay 84

Meatless Days by Sara Suleri 87

Memoirs of an Arabian Princess from Zanzibar by Emily Ruete 90

My Life Story by Fadhma Aïth Mansour Amrouche 93

Prison Writings: My Life Is My Sun Dance by Leonard Peltier 96

Rites: A Guatemalan Boyhood by Victor Perera 99

Ten Thousand Sorrows: The Extraordinary Journey of a Korean War Orphan by Elizabeth Kim 102

The Travels of Marco Polo by Marco Polo 105

When I Was Puerto Rican by Esmeralda Santiago 108

The Wonderful Adventures of Mrs. Seacole in Many Lands by Mary Seacole 111

The Worlds of a Maasai Warrior: An Autobiography by Tepilit Ole Saitoti 114

TABLE OF CONTENTS

Coming of Age

Angela's Ashes by Frank McCourt   119

Black Boy by Richard Wright   122

A Child's Christmas in Wales by Dylan Thomas   125

The Dark Child: The Autobiography of an African Boy by Camara Laye   128

The Education of Henry Adams by Henry Adams   132

An Egyptian Childhood by Taha Hussein   135

Fun Home: A Family Tragicomic by Alison Bechdel   139

Incidents in the Life of a Slave Girl, Written by Herself by Harriet A. Jacobs   142

Life on the Mississippi by Mark Twain   146

My Life Story by David Unaipon   149

My Revolutionary Years: The Autobiography of Madame Wei Tao-Ming by Cheng Yu-hsiu   152

Persepolis by Marjane Satrapi   155

Red Azalea by Anchee Min   158

Red Scarf Girl: A Memoir of the Cultural Revolution by Ji-li Jiang   161

Stop-Time by Frank Conroy   164

Under My Skin: Volume One of My Autobiography, to 1949 by Doris Lessing   167

The Unwanted by Kien Nguyen   170

The Woman Warrior: Memoirs of a Girlhood among Ghosts by Maxine Hong Kingston   173

Contemplation and Confession

The Autobiography of Ben Franklin by Benjamin Franklin   179

The Autobiography of Giambattista Vico by Giambattista Vico   183

The Autobiography of Malcolm X by Malcolm X   186

The Book of Margery Kempe by Margery Kempe   189

A Confession by Leo Tolstoy   193

Confessions by Augustine   196

Confessions by Jean-Jacques Rousseau   200

Darkness Visible by William Styron   204

Infidel by Ayaan Hirsi Ali   207

The Life by Teresa of Ávila   211

The Man Died: Prison Notes of Wole Soyinka by Wole Soyinka   214

The Meditations of the Emperor Marcus Aurelius Antoninus by Marcus Aurelius   218

Memoirs by Pablo Neruda   222

A Mountainous Journey: A Poet's Autobiography by Fadwa Tuqan   225

A True Relation of My Birth, Breeding, and Life by Margaret Cavendish   229

Walden; or, Life in the Woods by Henry David Thoreau   233

Theories

The Autobiographical Pact by Philippe Lejeune   239

An Autobiography, or The Story of My Experiments with Truth by Mohandas Gandhi   242

Autobiography: Essays Theoretical and Critical by James Olney   246

Bone Black: Memories of Girlhood by bell hooks   249

An Experiment in Autobiography by H. G. Wells   252

In the Presence of Absence by Mahmoud Darwish   255

Memories of a Catholic Girlhood by Mary McCarthy   258

"My Furthest-Back Person—'The African'" by Alex Haley   261

Praeterita by John Ruskin   264

Roland Barthes by Roland Barthes   267

Speak, Memory: An Autobiography Revisited by Vladimir Nabokov   270

To Be Young, Gifted and Black: An Informal Autobiography of Lorraine Hansberry by Lorraine Hansberry   273

Truth and Fiction Relating to My Life by Johann Wolfgang von Goethe   276

The Writing Life by Annie Dillard   279

War Experiences

An Arab-Syrian Gentleman and Warrior in the Period of the Crusades: Memoirs of Usāmah ibn Munqidh by Usāmah ibn Munqidh   285

An Autobiography, with Musings on Recent Events in India by Jawaharlal Nehru   289

Barefoot Gen: A Cartoon Story of Hiroshima by Keiji Nakazawa   293

Exiled Memories: A Cuban Childhood by Pablo Medina   296

Farewell to Manzanar by Jeanne Wakatsuki Houston and James D. Houston   299

Geronimo: His Own Story by Geronimo and S. M. Barrett 302

Golden Bones: An Extraordinary Journey from Hell in Cambodia to a New Life in America by Sichan Siv 306

The Invisible Thread by Yoshiko Uchida 309

A Long Way Gone: Memoirs of a Boy Soldier by Ishmael Beah 312

The Memoirs of Lady Anne Halkett by Lady Anne Halkett 315

Night by Elie Wiesel 318

Paekpom Ilchi: The Autobiography of Kim Ku by Kim Ku 322

The Sovereignty and Goodness of God by Mary Rowlandson 325

Testament of Youth by Vera Brittain 329

Wars I Have Seen by Gertrude Stein 332

When Heaven and Earth Changed Places: A Vietnamese Woman's Journey from War to Peace by Le Ly Hayslip and Jay Wurts 335

A Woman Soldier's Own Story by Xie Bingying 338

Subject Index 341

Author Index 451

Title Index 455

INTRODUCTION

An autobiographical narrative is an account by the teller of some aspect of his or her life. Yet beneath this overarching definition lie myriad variations upon a theme. For the modern reader the best-known manifestations of the genre are book-length memoirs or autobiographies. Their authors usually feel that they have something significant to say about their private experiences or that their role as witnesses to moments in history merits permanent record. Classic instances, covered in the *Autobiography and Memoir* volume of *The Literature of Autobiographical Narrative,* include Rosa Parks's *My Story* (1992). Parks propelled herself into fame in 1955 when she, an African American, refused to give up her bus seat to a white passenger. As a resident of Montgomery, Alabama, she was subject to the legally legitimatized system of segregation enforced in virtually all parts of the southern states of the United States. Her memoir covers that incident and also offers an account of her early life of subjection and injustice and provides readers with an insight into the growth of the civil rights movement, in which she became an activist.

Generically, Vladimir Nabokov's *Speak, Memory* (1951) belongs in the same category as Parks's book, but it is difficult to conceive of two more contrasting volumes. Nabokov is best known for *Lolita* (1955), a controversial novel narrated by a self-confessed pedophile who spends most of the book reflecting upon his obsession with the eponymous schoolgirl, but *Speak, Memory,* ostensibly at least, is not concerned with its author's career as a novelist. It covers the first four decades of his life, in which he witnessed some of the key transformative events in European history, notably, as a child, the Bolshevik Revolution (1917) in his native Russia. In this respect Nabokov and Parks might seem, as autobiographers, similarly motivated. Despite the significance of what they experienced, however, they differ radically in the telling of their stories. As an author, Parks is largely unobtrusive and transparent, allowing where possible the events of her life to bear witness to their political and emotional resonance. For Parks, memory and history are indistinguishable. Nabokov, on the other hand, writes about his life in much the same way that, as a novelist, he would describe the worlds of his inventions. At one point he tells of how the Russian Imperial Minister of War, Aleksey Kuropatkin, a friend of the Nabokov family, would amuse young Vladimir with a trick involving a match box; Nabokov then connects this anecdote with the story of Kuropatkin, now in disguise and on the run from the Bolsheviks, surreptitiously asking his father for a light. Nabokov does not alter the facts; rather, he believes that memory should be treated as a series of episodes that depend as much upon the impressions of their perceiver for significance as upon objective description.

Maya Angelou's autobiography *I Know Why the Caged Bird Sings* (1969) should, we might assume, have more in common with Parks's than Nabokov's book: it is the searingly honest story of her own experiences of racist violence and oppression in the American South. However, it is celebrated as much for its formal literary qualities as for its revelations. Angelou's manner of relating her shared history lends the latter a special degree of vividness and durability, and in this respect Angelou invites comparison with Nabokov. Like both, Tepilit Ole Scitoti, in *The World of a Maasai Warrior* (1986), wraps an emotionally charged autobiography—specifically its author's crossing of the boundary between precolonial African tribal existence and Western society—in a text that bears a close resemblance to what we expect of fiction: dialogue, historical narrative and myth are blended in a less than predictable manner.

Such variations in manner and theme reflect the richness and diversity of autobiography as a genre, in terms of both its informative, even educational, power and its strength as a literary form in its own right. How, then, should we classify Adolf Hitler's *Mein Kamf* (1925) in relation to the books so far mentioned? In order to qualify for inclusion and coverage in these volumes, a work must at least enlighten us as to the mindset of its author and the circumstances that led to its composition. The fact is that were it not for Hitler's hideous acts and legacy subsequent to the publication of *Mein Kamf* the book would have disappeared from the landscape of twentieth century history of writing. It is poorly written, its author is at time deranged in his avowed worship of the Aryan race, and its purely autobiographical passages are littered with stories that have since been proved to be exaggerations at best and often outright falsehoods. Its endurance as a "significant" autobiographical work has been ensured by events that no sane or decent person would have wished upon those affected by them. Here we come upon the uniqueness and importance of autobiographical narrative. Hitler's book might well be a compendium of half-truths and evil avocations, but it adds something to our knowledge of how a particularly foul individual came to power and wreaked havoc on the world. Like every work covered in these volumes, it carries a trace of our past and in particular the imprint of its author's involvement therein.

The second volume of *The Literature of Autobiographical Narrative* covers diaries and letters. The most obvious difference between these and autobiography is that while virtually all of the latter are addressed to a general readership, the former are works generally underpinned by a notion of confidentiality, privacy or intimacy. In this regard the diary is a particularly troubling genre. It is, by its nature, a record—often a day-to-day record—of its author's activities, some of them utterly mundane, that typically contains observations on the events and moods of his or her world. The motive or impulse behind the keeping of a diary remains a matter for speculation, but most would agree that it is a private endeavor with the author also its single reader (though intimate friends or family members have on occasions been allowed access to entries). We might, therefore, expect from such documents a different level of candor than is generally found in autobiographies intended for publication. It is not that authors of the latter deliberately set out to mislead—with the exception of figures such as Hitler—but rather that, even in unadorned acts of truth-telling such as Parks's *My Story*, there is a degree of performance. Honesty might be maintained but consideration is also given to the experience of the reader. Diaries, being designed for self-consumption, carry no such responsibilities.

Two of the best-known early-modern examples of the form are *The Diary of John Evelyn* (1818) and *The Diary of Samuel Pepys* (1825). Both are treated an invaluable insights into the events and mannerisms of mid-to-late seventeenth-century Britain. The period involved momentous occurrences, most notably the Civil War, the execution of Charles I, the establishment of the first modern European republic and the Restoration of the Monarchy. The printing press was more than a century old, and for the first time in history an abundance of documents, including government statements, manifestos, and declarations by individuals with an interest in the future of society, became available for later scrutiny by historians. Evelyn and Pepys provide an invaluable supplement to the largely impersonal evidence of print, taking us on a tour of their particular worlds, from what they wore and ate to their encounters with epoch-making events; Evelyn's account of the return of the monarch, Charles II, to London contains everything from the minutiae of the floral decorations to his own understated reflections on the significance of the day. Diaries bridge the divide between introspective impressionistic records of a time and a state of mind—so often lacking in works intended for publication—and a more objective conception of a historical milieu. Diaries and notebooks are immensely important too in our broader appreciation of how writers work. Even if in, for instance, Joseph Conrad's *Congo Diary* (1952), there is little direct reference to how his experience influenced his fiction, the implied connections are self-evident.

We should, however, deal cautiously with the commonplace assumption that the diary is always an impeccably candid record of its author's thoughts and impressions. That Evelyn's and Pepys's works did not go into print until over a century after they had been completed would seem to testify to both men's sense of them as private documents. Yet it is possible to imagine that Anne Frank, hiding from the Nazis, harbored a sense of duty to those who would later try to document the horrors of World War II. Even if, as she feared, she would not live to adulthood, perhaps she hoped that her words would survive as a record of a fate she shared with so many others. The same can be said of Victor Klemperer as he composed his *Diary of the Nazi Years* (1995). In a different context George Gissing, who was at the center of the thriving cultural and literary life of Victorian England, was surely not so naïve as to believe that his *Diary* would remain forever untouched and unpublished.

The letter involves a different level of candor in that, once the piece is dispatched, the recipient is trusted as its sole reader, but in this respect correspondence can be just as revealing as the private diary or notebook. Sylvia Plath's *Letters Home* (1975), mostly addressed to her mother, tells us more about her state of distress and her sense of vocation as a writer than anything primarily intended for publication.

The third volume of *The Literature of Autobiographical Narrative* covers oral histories, and the best introduction to this complex means of recording and preserving the past is Lynn Abrams's *Oral History Theory* (2010). Abrams examines the tendentious issues that surround the collecting of oral histories, principally the implicit tension between a voluntary spoken testimony and the role of the person who asks questions, edits, and coordinates this material: how much does the latter impose upon the former? One of the most famous nonacademic examples of the form is Ronald Blythe's *Akenfield: Portrait of an English Village* (1969), in which Blythe attempts to capture life in a fictionalized rural English community through a set of interviews with individuals such as farmworkers and blacksmiths who have known of little more than their immediate environment since the nineteenth century. Blythe's *Akenfield* is not a real village but a fictionalized composite based on interviews with residents of various villages. Although he does his best to remain in the background, Blythe's editorial approach has led critics to wonder to what extent the "Portrait" carries something of his influence.

Oral histories that are more rigorous than Blythe's in their maintenance of objectivity include Jeremy Seabrook's *Working-Class Childhood* (1982), in which Seabrook, as interviewer, refrains from any prompts and directions in his recordings of British working-class individuals during the late 1970s and early 1980s. As Lynn Abrams argues, however, it is virtually impossible to claim that an exercise in oral history can be a purely objective record, unaffected by the presence of the interviewer or coordinator. For example, Rhoda Lewin's *Witnesses to the Holocaust* (1991) is composed of her interviews with sixty survivors and liberators of the Nazi concentration camps. While Lewin scrupulously avoids leading her interviewees, the fact that they were all then residents of Minnesota suggests that their testimonies may have been skewed by a shared experience of the postwar years. Similarly, in Alison Baker's *Voices of Resistance: Oral Histories of Moroccan Women* (1998), women involved in the Moroccan independence movement speak freely of their personal lives, but this material is embedded in contextual information on Moroccan society, history, and politics and quotations from songs and poems, largely for the benefit of Western readers unfamiliar with the region. In this respect, then, Baker's choice and use of contextual material will in some way inevitably affect the reader's impression of the women themselves.

Esteban Montejo's *Autobiography of a Runaway Slave* (1993) originates from a series of interviews given by Montejo in 1963 to Miguel Barnet, who subsequently transcribed them as a book with the former as first-person narrator. Montejo, then aged 103, was thought to be the last surviving ex-slave on the island of Cuba; his testimony provided one final opportunity to record this period in Caribbean history. The book blurs the distinction between autobiography and oral history. One assumes that it is placed in the latter category because, without Barnet's act of recording the oral testimony, it would not exist, yet its potential status as a hybrid form makes it all the more intriguing. Once again questions arise about the concepts of fact and truth and the extent to which they are influenced by oral testimony and conventional notions of writing.

Oral history is the most complex of the three categories of autobiographical narrative and for this reason it is one of the most richly rewarding. For all of its variety, at its heart is the quintessential notion of a voice unsullied by the formalities and conventions of writing and print.

Only a few pieces covered in these three volumes predate the history of the printing press, notably St. Augustine's *Confessions* (397 CE) and Marcus Aurelius's *Meditations* (180 CE). Some, such as Marco Polo's *Travels* (c. 1300) and King Henry VI's *Literary Remains* (1549), found their way into print well within a century of their composition, but the vast majority of the pieces were either spoken, recorded, written or published during or after the seventeenth century. Autobiographical narrative, including oral history, will always owe something to the mechanism of print, including its recent electronic form, but its value as a means of understanding the human condition and permutations through ethnicity, region, history, and culture remains uncorrupted by this.

These three volumes will stand as an invaluable tool for researchers who wish to locate a starting point for a detailed scrutiny of a place, an event, or a state of mind. Their structure, including the subclassification of each of the three forms according to context and frame of reference, will assist greatly in its function as a basis for curriculum building. Each volume can serve numerous and often overlapping disciplinary roles. Writers' autobiographies, diaries, and notebooks offer invaluable insights into the relationship between private inspiration and the unfolding of literary history. Throughout, students of history, politics, and society will find testimonies to personal experience that underpin and illuminate a broader perception of our pasts and differences.

It is a unique enterprise, gathering seemingly disparate elements within a space to which all human beings will at some point commit themselves: speaking or writing to someone, even to ourselves, of our lives and experiences.

Richard Bradford

 Editor's Note

The Literature of Autobiographical Narrative, a three-volume reference guide, provides critical introductions to 300 autobiographies, memoirs, diaries, letters, and oral histories. All the works are based on the lives of the authors, but a wide variety of interests and ambitions, from the personal and artistic to the historical and political, motivated writers to share their intimate and exceptional memories.

An early memoir covered in the guide is *The Travels of Marco Polo,* which recounts the journey of the Venetian explorer in the 1290s to the Far East and the court of Kublai Khan. In 1298, three years after returning from Asia, Marco Polo was captured in a battle against the Genoese. Over several months in prison, with the help of his cellmate, Rustichiello of Pisa, he wrote his travelogue, filled with exotic tales set in a faraway land, which fascinated his European audience. Other works discussed in the guide had more private goals. Edgar Allan Poe's "Letter to Maria Clemm," written to his Aunt Maria on August 29, 1835, declares his love for her thirteen-year-old daughter, Virginia, and offers financial assistance to them both. Kept from publication for more than a century by Poe's family, the letter—in particular the passionate desire Poe expresses for his young cousin (later his wife)—is fundamental to the modern understanding of Poe as a transgressor of moral boundaries. *Japanese War Brides in America* (1998), an oral history of nineteen Japanese women who married American soldiers during the post-World War II occupation of Japan, is an example of an autobiographical work for which the motivation to publish was less an author's desire for self-expression than an outsider's interest in another person's story.

The structure and content of *The Literature of Autobiographical Narrative* was planned with the help of the project's advisory board, chaired by Richard Bradford, Professor of English and Senior Distinguished Research Fellow, University of Ulster, Northern Ireland. His introduction explains some of the concerns behind the development of the guide and provides a brief overview of autobiographical genres.

ORGANIZATION
All entries share a common structure, providing consistent coverage of the works and a simple way of comparing basic elements of one text with another. Each entry has six parts: overview, historical and literary context, themes and style, critical discussion, sources, and further reading. Entries also have either an excerpt from the original text or a sidebar discussing a related topic, such as the life of the author.

The Literature of Autobiographical Narrative is divided into three volumes, each with 100 entries organized into subject-oriented sections. The sections in volume 1, *Autobiographies and Memoirs,* are Adversity and Resistance, Between Cultures, Coming of Age, Contemplation and Confession, Theories, and War Experiences. Among the works representing "adversity" is *The Story of My Life* (1903), by Helen Keller, who describes her experience being a blind and deaf child in late-nineteenth-century Alabama. Her efforts to express herself and become educated came at a time when many disabled children in the United States were considered a lost cause and institutionalized. Volume 2, *Diaries and Letters,* includes the sections Adversity and Resistance, Historical Perspectives, Literary Lives, Theories, Travel and Exploration, War Experiences, and Work and Family Life. Under "Historical Perspectives" is *Jemima Condict,* the diary of young New Jersey maid during the American Revolution who records thoughts about her family, community life, and newly independent country. The works discussed in volume 3, *Oral Histories,* stand apart from the books in the other volumes in their absence of a premeditated written structure. The volume is divided into the sections Adversity and Resistance, Communities, Culture and Tradition, Theories, War Experiences, Witnessing History, and Work and Family Life. Covered in the latter section is *Soviet Baby Boomers* (2012), in which sixty men and women from two elite Russian schools discuss their lives in the late twentieth century; a major theme of the book is remembering things from the past that state propaganda tried to conceal.

Among the criteria for selecting entry topics were the importance of the work in university and high school curricula, the genre, the region and country of the author and text, and the time period. Entries can be looked up in the author and title indexes, as well as in the subject index.

ACKNOWLEDGMENTS

Many people contributed time, effort, and ideas to *The Literature of Autobiographical Narrative.* At Gale, Philip Virta, manager of new products, developed the original plan for the book, and Andrea Henderson, senior editor, served as the in-house manager for the project. *The Literature of Autobiographical Narrative* owes its existence to their ideas and involvement.

We would like to express our appreciation to the advisors, who, in addition to creating the organization of *The Literature of Autobiographical Narrative* and choosing the entry topics, identified other scholars to work on the project and answered many questions, both big and small. We would also like to thank the contributors for their accessible essays, often on difficult topics, as well as the scholars who reviewed the text for accuracy and coverage.

I am grateful to Greta Gard, project editor, and Erin Brown, senior project editor, especially for their work with the advisors and on the entry list; Mary Beth Curran, associate editor, who oversaw the editing process; David Hayes, associate editor, whose many contributions included organizing the workflow; and Hannah Soukup, assistant editor, who identified and corresponded with the academic reviewers. Other important assistance came from Mariko Fujinaka, managing editor; Anne Healey, senior editor; and Janet Moredock and Lee Esbenshade, associate editors. The line editors were Cheryl Collins, Chuong-Dai Vo, Constance Israel, Donna Polydoros, Harrabeth Haidusek, Holli Fort, Jane Kupersmith, Jill Oldham, Joan Hibler, Kathy Wilson Peacock, Kerri Kennedy, Laura Gabler, Lisa Trow, Natalie Ruppert, Tony Craine, and Will Wagner.

Thomas Riggs

Contributors

DAVID AITCHISON
Aitchison is a PhD candidate in literary studies and a university instructor.

GREG BACH
Bach holds an MA in classics and is a freelance writer.

KATHERINE BARKER
Barker has an MA in English literature.

CRAIG BARNES
Barnes holds an MFA in creative writing and has been a university instructor and a freelance writer.

KATHERINE BISHOP
Bishop is a PhD student in English literature and has been a university instructor.

ALLISON BLECKER
Blecker is a PhD candidate in Near Eastern languages.

WESLEY BORUCKI
Borucki holds a PhD in American history and is a university professor.

GERALD CARPENTER
Carpenter holds an MA in U.S. intellectual history and a PhD in early modern French history. He is a freelance writer.

ALEX COVALCIUC
Covalciuc is a PhD candidate in English literature. He has been a university instructor and a freelance writer.

JENNY DALE
Dale holds an MFA in creative writing and has been a university instructor.

FARNOOSH FATHI
Fathi has a PhD in English literature and creative writing and has been a university instructor.

JEN GANN
Gann holds an MFA in creative writing and has been a university instructor.

DAISY GARD
Gard is a freelance writer with a background in English literature.

GRETA GARD
Gard is a PhD candidate in English literature and has been a university instructor and a freelance writer.

TINA GIANOULIS
Gianoulis is a freelance writer with a background in English literature.

CYNTHIA GILES
Giles holds an MA in English literature and a PhD in interdisciplinary humanities. She has been a university instructor and a freelance writer.

KRISTEN GLEASON
Gleason holds an MFA in creative writing and has been a university instructor.

NICOLE GRANT
Grant holds an MA in English and has been a university instructor.

QUAN MANH HA
Ha holds a PhD in American literature and is a university professor.

IRENE HSIAO
Hsiao has a PhD in literature and has been a university instructor.

FRANKLIN HYDE
Hyde holds a PhD in English literature and is a university instructor.

ANNA IOANES
Ioanes is a PhD student in English language and literature and has been a university instructor.

LAURA JOHNSON
Johnson holds a PhD in English and has been a university instructor.

EMILY JONES
Jones holds an MFA in creative writing and has been a university instructor.

ALICIA KENT
Kent holds a PhD in English literature and is a university professor.

KRISTIN KING-RIES
King-Ries holds an MFA in creative writing and has been a university instructor.

LISE LALONDE
LaLonde holds MAs in English literature and translation and has been a university instructor.

GREGORY LUTHER
Luther holds an MFA in creative writing and has been a university instructor and freelance writer.

KATIE MACNAMARA
Macnamara holds a PhD in English literature and has been a university instructor.

MAGGIE MAGNO
Magno has an MA in education. She has been a high school English teacher and a freelance writer.

xix

CONTRIBUTORS

ABIGAIL MANN
Mann holds a PhD in English literature and is a university professor.

EMILY MANN
Mann has an MA in library and information science.

THEODORE MCDERMOTT
McDermott holds an MFA in creative writing and has been a university instructor and a freelance writer.

LISA MERTEL
Mertel holds an MA in library science and an MA in history.

RACHEL MINDELL
Mindell holds an MFA in creative writing and has been a freelance writer.

JIM MLADENOVIC
Mladenovic holds an MS in clinical psychology and is pursuing an MA in library science.

KATHRYN MOLINARO
Molinaro holds an MA in English literature and has been a university instructor and a freelance writer.

CAITIE MOORE
Moore holds an MFA in creative writing and has been a university instructor.

ROBIN MORRIS
Morris holds a PhD in English literature and has been a university instructor.

JANET MULLANE
Mullane is a freelance writer and has been a high school English teacher.

ELLIOTT NIBLOCK
Niblock holds an MTS in the philosophy of religion.

KATRINA OKO-ODOI
Oko-Odoi is a PhD candidate in Spanish language and literature and a university instructor.

JAMES OVERHOLTZER
Overholtzer holds an MA in English literature and has been a university instructor.

IOANA PATULEANU
Patuleanu holds a PhD in English literature and has been a university instructor.

EVELYN REYNOLDS
Reynolds is pursuing an MA in English literature and an MFA in creative writing and has been a freelance writer.

CHRIS ROUTLEDGE
Routledge holds a PhD in English literature and is a university lecturer and a freelance writer.

REBECCA RUSTIN
Rustin holds an MA in English literature and is a freelance writer.

ANTHONY RUZICKA
Ruzicka is pursuing an MFA in poetry and has worked as a university instructor.

CATHERINE E. SAUNDERS
Saunders holds a PhD in English literature and is a university professor.

CARINA SAXON
Saxon is a PhD candidate in English literature and has been a university instructor and a freelance editor.

JACOB SCHMITT
Schmitt holds an MA in English literature and has been a freelance writer.

NANCY SIMPSON-YOUNGER
Simpson-Younger is a PhD candidate in literary studies and a university instructor.

CLAIRE SKINNER
Skinner holds an MFA in creative writing and is a university instructor.

ROGER SMITH
Smith has an MA in media ecology and has been a university instructor and a freelance writer.

NICHOLAS SNEAD
Snead is a PhD candidate in French language and literature and has been a university instructor.

SARAH STOECKL
Stoeckl holds a PhD in English literature and is a university instructor and a freelance writer.

PAMELA TOLER
Toler has a PhD in history and is a freelance writer and former university instructor.

GRACE WAITMAN
Waitman is pursuing a PhD in educational psychology. She holds an MA in English literature and has been a university instructor.

ALLYNA WARD
Ward holds a PhD in English literature and is a university professor.

JENNA WILLIAMS
Williams holds an MFA in creative writing and has been a university instructor and a freelance writer.

Academic Reviewers

Barbara Allen
Associate Professor of History, La Salle University, Philadelphia, Pennsylvania.

Khaled Al-Masri
Assistant Professor of Arabic, Swarthmore College, Swarthmore, Pennsylvania.

Holly Arrow
Professor of Psychology, Institute of Cognitive and Decision Sciences, University of Oregon, Eugene.

Stephen Behrendt
George Holmes Distinguished Professor of English, University of Nebraska-Lincoln.

William Belding
Professorial Lecturer, School of International Service, American University, Washington, D.C.

Amy Bell
Associate Professor of History, Huron University College, London, Ontario, Canada.

Alan L. Berger
Raddock Family Eminent Scholar Chair in Holocaust Studies; Professor of Jewish Studies, English Department; Director, the Center for the Study of Values and Violence after Auschwitz, Florida Atlantic University, Boca Raton.

Moulay-Ali Bouânani
Professor of Africana Studies, Binghamton University-State University of New York, Vestal.

Claire Boyle
Lecturer in French, University of Edinburgh, United Kingdom.

Michael Breen
Associate Professor of History and Humanities, Reed College, Portland, Oregon.

Gerry Canavan
Assistant Professor of English, Marquette University, Milwaukee, Wisconsin.

Nathan Clarke
Assistant Professor of History, Minnesota State University Moorhead.

William Clemente
Professor of Literature, Peru State College, Peru, Nebraska.

Marc Conner
Ballengee Professor of English, Washington and Lee University, Lexington, Virginia.

Jane Crawford
Faculty, History and Political Science Department, Mount St. Mary's College, Los Angeles, California.

Sonja Darlington
Professor of Education and Youth Studies, Beloit College, Beloit, Wisconsin.

Gabriele Dillmann
Associate Professor of German, Denison University, Granville, Ohio.

Jeanne Dubino
Professor of English and Global Studies, Appalachian State University, Boone, North Carolina.

Elizabeth Duquette
Associate Professor of English, Gettysburg College, Gettysburg, Pennsylvania.

Breanne Fahs
Associate Professor of Women and Gender Studies, Arizona State University West, Glendale.

Danine Farquharson
Associate Professor of English, Memorial University of Newfoundland, St. John's.

Luanne Frank
Associate Professor of English, University of Texas at Arlington.

Gregory Fraser
Professor of English, University of West Georgia, Carrollton.

James Gigantino
Assistant Professor of History, University of Arkansas at Fayetteville.

Quan Manh Ha
Assistant Professor of American Literature and Ethnic Studies, University of Montana, Missoula.

Kevin J. Hayes
Professor of English, University of Central Oklahoma, Edmond.

Richard Higgins
Lecturer in English, Franklin College, Franklin, Indiana.

Nels Highberg
Associate Professor and Chair of Rhetoric and Professional Writing Department, University of Hartford, West Hartford, Connecticut.

ACADEMIC REVIEWERS

WALTER HÖLBLING
Professor of American Studies, Karl-Franzens-Universität Graz, Austria.

FRANKLYN HYDE
Adjunct Professor of English, University of Manitoba, Winnipeg.

PETER IVERSON
Regents' Professor of History, Arizona State University, Tempe.

KELLY JEONG
Assistant Professor of Comparative Literature and Korean Studies, University of California, Riverside.

A. YEMISI JIMOH
Professor of African American Literature and Culture, University of Massachusetts Amherst.

JEFFREY W. JONES
Associate Professor of History, University of North Carolina at Greensboro.

ALICIA A. KENT
Associate Professor of English, University of Michigan-Flint.

CHRISTOPHER KNIGHT
Professor of English, University of Montana, Missoula.

LEAH KNIGHT
Associate Professor of Literature, Brock University, St. Catharines, Ontario.

MARY LARSON
President of Oral History Association; Head of Oklahoma Oral History Research Program, Oklahoma State University, Stillwater.

CHANA KAI LEE
Associate Professor of History and of the Institute for African American Studies, University of Georgia, Athens.

WEIJING LU
Associate Professor of History, University of California, San Diego, La Jolla.

CAROL MACKAY
Professor of English, University of Texas at Austin.

BRIDGET MARSHALL
Associate Professor and Associate Chair of English Department, University of Massachusetts Lowell.

MARIA DEL CARMEN MARTINEZ
Assistant Professor of English, University of Wisconsin-Parkside.

LUCINDA MCCRAY
Professor and Chair of History Department, Appalachian State University, Boone, North Carolina.

CAROL MCFREDERICK
Adjunct Instructor of English, Florida International University, Miami.

GORDON MCKINNEY
Professor Emeritus, Berea College, Berea, Kentucky.

LAURIE MERCIER
Professor of History, Washington State University, Vancouver.

DANIEL METRAUX
Professor of Asian Studies, Mary Baldwin College, Staunton, Virginia.

GENEVA COBB MOORE
Professor of English and Women's Studies, University of Wisconsin-Whitewater.

EARL MULDERINK
Professor of History, Southern Utah University, Cedar City.

SHAKIR MUSTAFA
Visiting Associate Professor of Arabic, Northeastern University, Boston, Massachusetts.

SEIWOONG OH
Professor and Chair of English Department, Rider University, Lawrenceville, New Jersey.

MICHEL PHARAND
Director of the Disraeli Project, Queen's University, Kingston, Ontario, Canada.

JANET POWERS
Professor Emerita of Interdisciplinary Studies and Women, Gender, and Sexuality Studies, Gettysburg College, Gettysburg, Pennsylvania.

JOHN R. REED
Distinguished Professor of English, Wayne State University, Detroit, Michigan.

PATRICIO RIZZO-VAST
Instructor of Spanish and Portuguese, Northeastern Illinois University, Chicago.

ASHRAF RUSHDY
Professor and Chair of African American Studies Program; Professor of English, Wesleyan University, Middletown, Connecticut.

ANDRE SIMIĆ
Professor of Anthropology, University of Southern California, Los Angeles.

CARL SMELLER
Associate Professor of English and Humanities, Texas Wesleyan University, Fort Worth.

MARY ZEISS STANGE
Professor of Women's Studies and Religion, Skidmore College, Saratoga Springs, New York.

REBECCA JANE STANTON
Assistant Professor of Russian, Barnard College, New York, New York.

RICHARD STOFFLE
Professor of Anthropology, University of Arizona, Tucson.

BILINDA STRAIGHT
Professor of Anthropology, Western Michigan University, Kalamazoo.

GWEN TARBOX
Associate Professor of English, Western Michigan University, Kalamazoo.

BARBARA TRUESDELL
Assistant Director of the Center for the Study of History and Memory, Indiana University, Bloomington.

CHUONG-DAI VO
Visiting Scholar, Foreign Language and Literatures, Massachusetts Institute of Technology, Cambridge.

ALLYNA E. WARD
Assistant Professor of English, Booth University College, Winnipeg, Manitoba.

RICHARD WEIKART
Professor of History, California State University-Stanislaus, Turlock.

ACADEMIC REVIEWERS

DOROTHY WILLS
Professor of Anthropology, California State Polytechnic University, Pomona.

MICHAEL WILSON
Associate Professor of English, University of Wisconsin-Milwaukee.

SIMONA WRIGHT
Professor and Director of Italian Program, The College of New Jersey, Ewing.

PRISCILLA YBARRA
Assistant Professor of English, University of North Texas, Denton.

GERALD ZAHAVI
Professor of History; Director of Documentary Studies Program, University at Albany-State University of New York.

PIERANTONIO ZANOTTI
Adjunct Professor of Japanese Language, Università Ca' Foscari Venezia, Italy.

Adversity and Resistance

The Autobiography of W. E. B. Du Bois: A Soliloquy on Viewing My Life from the Last Decade of Its First Century by W. E. B. Du Bois	3
The Diving Bell and the Butterfly by Jean-Dominique Bauby	6
Dust Tracks on a Road by Zora Neale Hurston	9
Eighty Years and More, Reminiscences 1815–1897 by Elizabeth Cady Stanton	12
Hunger of Memory: The Education of Richard Rodriguez by Richard Rodriguez	15
I Know Why the Caged Bird Sings by Maya Angelou	18
Lakota Woman by Mary Crow Dog	21
Let My People Go by Albert Luthuli	24
The Long Walk to Freedom by Nelson Mandela	27
Mein Kampf by Adolf Hitler	30
Narrative of the Life of Frederick Douglass by Frederick Douglass	33
Rosa Parks: My Story by Rosa Parks and Jim Haskins	37
The Story of My Life: An Afghan Girl on the Other Side of the Sky by Farah Ahmedi	40
The Story of My Life: Helen Keller by Helen Keller	43
This Boy's Life by Tobias Wolff	47
Up from Slavery by Booker T. Washington	50
The Way to Rainy Mountain by N. Scott Momaday	54

The Autobiography of W. E. B. Du Bois
A Soliloquy on Viewing My Life from the Last Decade of Its First Century

W. E. B. Du Bois

OVERVIEW

First published in 1968, *The Autobiography of W. E. B. Du Bois: A Soliloquy on Viewing My Life from the Last Decade of Its First Century* follows the civil rights leader from his childhood in Massachusetts in the late nineteenth century through his travels in the late 1950s to the Soviet Union, China, and Ghana. In between, readers see descriptions of his studies, his teaching career, his role in the establishment of the National Association for the Advancement of Colored People (NAACP), his travels throughout Europe as he organized several Pan-African Congresses, and his prosecution in the United States as an alleged foreign agent. Throughout the narrative, he explains his gradual realization of racism's pervasiveness in the United States and his esteem of communism as a means to uplift the oppressed.

Published five years after Du Bois's death, his autobiography can be seen as an apologia for the author's involvement with the Communist Party, which he formally joined in 1961. Because American sensitivity about communism was heightened at the time due to the escalation of the Vietnam War and allegations against the loyalties of civil rights leader Martin Luther King Jr., the release of the book in early 1968 provoked mixed reactions. Historian Herbert Aptheker, also a communist, edited Du Bois's manuscript for publication, stating it had been preserved in Ghana, where Du Bois lived the last three years of his life. Although arguably one of Du Bois's least appreciated works, the autobiography nevertheless illuminates the life and beliefs of one of America's most important civil rights leaders.

HISTORICAL AND LITERARY CONTEXT

The Autobiography of W. E. B. Du Bois provides a scathing attack of U.S. race relations and the exploitation of labor by Western industrial powers. As African and Asian nations became independent of colonial powers such as Britain and France in the 1940s and 1950s, the United States and the Soviet Union, embroiled in the Cold War, jockeyed for international support. American propaganda argued that communism threatened these countries' newly gained freedom while Soviet propaganda cited America's history of abuses against blacks. As the civil rights movement advanced in the United States, Du Bois witnessed several important victories, such as the U.S. Supreme Court decisions about housing discrimination and school segregation, many of which were argued by the NAACP's legal department. However, Du Bois died before the triumphs of the Civil Rights Act of 1964 and the Voting Rights Act of 1965.

The first edition of *The Autobiography of W. E. B. Du Bois* features a preface by Aptheker in which he points out that the "full and final accounting" of Du Bois's life is "an indispensable volume for all to whom Life itself has any meaning." Although the autobiography was published in shortened versions in the Soviet Union, China, and East Germany in 1964 and 1965, the 1968 edition was the first complete version published in English. In the tense atmosphere of the Cold War, Du Bois points out to his American readers that "we can learn" from the Soviet Union, which he visited in 1959.

Du Bois's autobiography was the last of three works that can be considered, at least in part, autobiographical. The first two, *Darkwater: Voices from within the Veil* (1920) and *Dusk of Dawn* (1940), combine autobiographical notes with essays and, in the case of the former, poetry. Booker T. Washington, Du Bois's primary ideological rival, set the standard for successful African American autobiography in the twentieth century with *Up from Slavery* (1901). Fellow participants in the Harlem Renaissance—on which Du Bois is strangely silent in his autobiography—also published autobiographies, including Zora Neale Hurston's *Dust Tracks on a Road* (1942), Langston Hughes's *The Big Sea* (1940) and *I Wonder as I Wander* (1954), and Richard Wright's *Black Boy* (1945).

Du Bois's goals to contribute to the "triumph of communism" and to highlight condescending and exploitive tendencies among American whites inspired other African American communists to publish their life experiences. Georgia native Hosea Hudson, who had worked since the 1930s to organize African Americans in the South to register to vote and form labor unions, published *Black Worker in the Deep South: A Personal Record* in 1972, followed in 1979 by *The Narrative of Hosea Hudson: The Life and Times of a Black Radical,* which was composed by Nell Irvin

❖ Key Facts

Time Period:
Mid-20th Century

Relevant Historical Events:
Growth of the civil rights movement; decolonization of Africa

Nationality:
American

Keywords:
civil rights; decolonization; communism

W. E. B. Du Bois photographed in 1919.
© GL ARCHIVE/ALAMY

Painter after oral interviews with Hudson. Likewise, Nebraska-born Harry Haywood describes his attempts to foster African American racial solidarity in *Black Bolshevik: Autobiography of an Afro American Communist* (1978).

THEMES AND STYLE

The central theme of Du Bois's work is the universality of racism in the West, which manifests itself at a personal level in condescension. The author recounts several points in his life when such racism thwarted his goals. For example, he blames Florence Read, the president of Spelman College at Atlanta University, for defeating his plans for a "systematic study of the Negro problem" in the 1930s because she wanted to "placate the white South" and keep "radical influences" out of the university. Du Bois describes economic racism in the exploitation of black workers through low wages and limited educational opportunities. He stresses through his observations and opinions of communist nations such as the Soviet Union and China that workers there are happier than in the United States. Further, the U.S. government's prosecution of Du Bois as an alleged unregistered foreign agent in 1959 following his participation in a World Peace Conference in the Soviet Union serves as a prominent example of whites' arbitrariness in power and one of the reasons he joined the Communist Party.

While Du Bois sets out to defend communism in his autobiography, he also praises his own contributions toward the advancement of African Americans' rights and racial consciousness. Of his time as editor of the *Crisis* for the NAACP, he writes, "I think I may say without boasting that in the period from 1910 to 1930 I was a main factor in revolutionizing the attitude of the American Negro toward caste." He cites other scholars' praise, as when one professor characterized his commencement address on Jefferson Davis as a "ten-strike." Du Bois admits that he faced an intensifying philosophical "dilemma": as the NAACP pushed for an end to discrimination in housing and desegregation of public facilities, he also championed a spirit of black nationalism and independence from whites. Another dilemma for Du Bois is his love of country and recognition that in race relations the United States lags behind even the imperialist nations of Western Europe.

Du Bois structures the text by placing descriptions of his years as a student and teacher in the second part between accounts in the first and third parts of his travels to Eastern Europe and China and his subsequent prosecution as an alleged "foreign principle." His initial trips to Ghana at the invitation of president Kwame Nkrumah appear in the conclusion of the book, where he expresses a hopefulness for the future of newly independent African states. His closing statements focus on the flaws of U.S. democracy: "I know the United States. It is my country and the land of my fathers. It is still a land of magnificent possibilities…. But it is selling its birthright."

CRITICAL DISCUSSION

Even with its posthumous release, *The Autobiography of W. E. B. Du Bois* did not receive universal praise. One critic, Martin Duberman, writing in the *New Republic* in 1968, states that Du Bois is "a prophet" for calling for an "inner cooperative movement" several years before the Black Panthers' emergence. However, Duberman notes that he, like others, could not understand Du Bois's "mindless defenses" of communism. Because of the book's spirited defense of communism, critic Truman Nelson wonders if Aptheker embellished the work. Critics were also disappointed by the fact that the autobiography did not reveal much about Du Bois's character, though the author does reveal that his dedication to his work compromised the happiness in his first marriage and that his childhood relationships were not as affected by racial stereotypes as his earlier works had suggested.

As David L. Dudley points out in his profile of Du Bois in *African American Autobiographers: A Sourcebook,* the autobiography has been somewhat eclipsed by *Dusk of Dawn* primarily because the former largely repeats information from the latter and does not clearly contribute to new understandings of the author's intellectual development. Du Bois's *The Souls of Black Folk* (1903), his meditation on race in the United States, also tends to command more scholarly attention. Nevertheless, academics have found value in the autobiography in recent years, particularly as it illuminates Du Bois's methods and overall views toward the United States. William E. Cain, writing for *Black American Literature Forum,* analyzes the autobiography as an underappreciated work and points out how, with Du Bois's unabashed use of propaganda in support of communism, his choice of the word "soliloquy" in his subtitle suggests a lack of concern about his audience's views.

More recently scholars have been struck by Du Bois's fusion of history and philosophy into a study of sociology of race. Anthony Monteiro in a 2008 essay for *Journal of Black Studies* examines Du Bois's description of how he "conceived the idea of applying philosophy to an historical interpretation of race relations … [his] first steps toward sociology as the science of human action." In a 2006 piece for *Callaloo,* Rumiana Velikova writes how Du Bois identified his birth date, February 23, 1868, not with George Washington's birthday of February 22 but with Andrew Johnson's impeachment in 1868, highlighting the unfulfilled democracy of the slave-owning founders and the unfulfilled hopes of Reconstruction.

BIBLIOGRAPHY

Sources

Cain, William E. "W. E. B. Du Bois's *Autobiography* and the Politics of Literature." *Black American Literature Forum* 24.2 (1990): 299–313. Print.

Duberman, Martin. "Du Bois as Prophet." *New Republic* 23 (1968): 36–39. Print.

Du Bois, William Edward Burghardt. *The Autobiography of W. E. B. Du Bois: A Soliloquy on Viewing My Life from the Last Decade of Its First Century.* New York: International Publishers, 1968. Print.

Dudley, David L. "W. E. B. Du Bois." *African American Autobiographers: A Sourcebook.* Ed. Emmanuel Sampath Nelson. Westport, Conn.: Greenwood, 2002. 110–19. Print.

Monteiro, Anthony. "W. E. B. Du Bois and the Study of Black Humanity: A Rediscovery." *Journal of Black Studies* 38.4 (2008): 600–21. Print.

Velikova, Rumiana. "Replacing the Father: W. E. B. Du Bois' Reflections on George Washington's Birthday." *Callaloo* 29.2 (2006): 658–79. Print.

Further Reading

Blau, Judith R., and Eric S. Brown. "Du Bois and Diasporic Identity: The Veil and the Unveiling Project." *Sociological Theory* 19.2 (2001): 219–33. Print.

Gordon, Lewis R. "Du Bois's Humanistic Philosophy of Human Sciences." *Annals of the American Academy of Political and Social Science* 568 (2000): 265–80. Print.

DU BOIS'S FINAL NOVELS

Late in his life, W. E. B. Du Bois described institutionalized racism and unseemly politics in his final novels, the Black Flame trilogy, which includes *The Ordeal of Mansart* (1957), *Mansart Builds a School* (1959), and *Worlds of Color* (1961). The trilogy follows the trials and challenges of Manuel Mansart, who in the second novel becomes president of the black-only Georgia State Agricultural and Mechanical School. In the books, he sees his children harmed by racism. Son Bruce, an intelligent football star for the school, "was never again the same person" after police beat him for looking at a white girl after a football game. Son Revels is unjustly courtmartialed during World War I, and his marriage to a white woman fails due to incessant public scorn. Daughter Sojourner is a promising musician, but her marriage to a minister sours when white community leaders dash his plans for creating a large church.

Historical parallels make the stories poignant. One student comes to Macon after his father, a sharecropper, is killed in the 1919 Elaine, Arkansas, riots. Du Bois also mentions Herman Talmadge, who rose to Georgia's governorship by appealing to working-class whites' fear of job competition from African Americans. Nevertheless, Du Bois depicts the hope that working-class whites might recognize common interests with African Americans. For example, the character Joe Scroggs, a racist Populist state school board member, accepts Huey Long's advice to trust African Americans as political allies.

Horne, Gerald. *Black and Red: W. E. B. Du Bois and the Afro-American Response to the Cold War, 1944–1963.* Albany: State University of New York Press, 1986. Print.

Howe, Irving. "Remarkable Man, Ambiguous Legacy." *Harper's* 236 (1968): 146–49. Print.

Lewis, David Levering. *W. E. B. Du Bois: Biography of a Race, 1868–1919.* New York: Holt, 1993. Print.

———. *W. E. B. Du Bois: The Fight for Equality and the American Century, 1919–1963.* New York: Holt, 2000. Print.

Rebaka, Reiland. "The Souls of Black Radical Folk: W. E. B. Du Bois, Critical Social Theory, and the State of Africana Studies." *Journal of Black Studies* 36.5 (2006): 732–63. Print.

———. "W. E. B. Du Bois's Evolving Africana Philosophy of Education." *Journal of Black Studies* 33.4 (2003): 399–449. Print.

Wesley Borucki

THE DIVING BELL AND THE BUTTERFLY

Jean-Dominique Bauby

✦ Key Facts

Time Period:
Late 20th Century

Relevant Historical Events:
Bauby becomes a quadriplegic and suffers from locked-in syndrome

Nationality:
French

Keywords:
quadriplegia; locked-in syndrome; disability

OVERVIEW

Originally published in French in 1997, *Le scaphandre et le papillon* (*The Diving Bell and the Butterfly*) tells the story of Jean-Dominique Bauby's struggles as a quadriplegic following a massive stroke he suffered in December 1995. The stroke left Bauby, the former editor-in-chief of the fashion magazine *Elle,* a victim of "locked-in syndrome," which causes complete paralysis of the body while consciousness is preserved. There is usually no loss of cognitive function, and Bauby did retain movement of his left eyelid. By establishing a system of blinks, he was able to narrate his memoir, which he composed and edited in his head, to his amanuensis, Claude Mendibil. The text offers lyrical descriptions of the freedom of the imagination and harrowing details about the confinement of paralysis.

During much of the book's composition, doctors were uncertain of but hopeful for Bauby's slow recovery. In March 1997, however, just days after the publication of his memoir, Bauby died of heart failure. The book was immediately popular with readers, who were as amazed by the method of composition as with the lyrical simplicity of the prose. A decade after its publication, screenwriter Ronald Harwood adapted the book for the screen, and Julian Schnabel's directorial vision, also titled *The Diving Bell and the Butterfly,* garnered the award for best director at the 2007 Cannes Film Festival and 2008 Golden Globes, along with four 2008 Academy Award nominations.

HISTORICAL AND LITERARY CONTEXT

The Diving Bell and the Butterfly is one of the only firsthand accounts of a patient suffering from locked-in syndrome. Early sufferers of the condition were often considered unconscious or in a vegetative state. It was only three decades prior to Bauby's stroke that Fred Plum and Jerome B. Posner published the seminal work *Diagnosis of Stupor and Coma,* which recognizes locked-in syndrome as a legitimate medical condition defined as "quadriplegia, lower cranial nerve paralysis, and mutism with preservation of consciousness, vertical gaze, and upper eyelid movement." However, in a 1987 article from the *British Medical Journal,* Plum and Posner suggest that the mention of such a condition in French literature makes it likely "the syndrome was already recognized medically in 19th century France."

The Diving Bell and the Butterfly is unique in that the process of the book's composition is of as much interest as the text itself. French film director Jacques Beineix produced a short movie, *House Arrest* (1997), that documents the writing of the book. In the film Bauby's amanuensis, Mendibil, slowly recites a modified alphabet to Bauby, who, because of his paralysis, can only signal which letter he wants by blinking his left eye. It was this painstaking process that gave the book its final shape. The French version of *The Diving Bell and the Butterfly* was published on March 7, 1997, and Bauby died of heart failure two days later at age forty-four.

Bauby's memoir makes explicit reference to its earliest literary antecedent, Alexandre Dumas's novel *The Count of Monte Christo* (1844), which contains the first known reference to locked-in syndrome. The novel mentions a character named Nortier de Villefort. According to Bauby, Dumas describes him as "a living mummy, a man three-quarters of the way into the grave…. He spends his life slumped in a wheelchair, able to communicate only blinking his eye: one blink means yes; two means no." Nineteenth-century French literature also saw the publication of another novel containing a character with locked-in syndrome: in Émile Zola's *Thérèse Raquin* (1867), Madame Raquin suffers a stroke and is completely paralyzed, except for her eyes.

Only a month after the publication of *The Diving Bell and the Butterfly,* Julia Tavalaro published the second memoir to document the experience of locked-in syndrome, though it is highly unlikely that Bauby's book served as a model or an inspiration. *Look up for Yes* tells the story of Tavalaro, who suffered two strokes in 1967, emerged from a coma, and spent six years trying to gain recognition as a conscious but paralyzed individual. A decade after the publication of Bauby's memoir, Schnabel's film version of *The Bell and the Butterfly* garnered a broad audience and considerable critical praise.

THEMES AND STYLE

The central theme of *The Diving Bell and the Butterfly* is that despite even a bodily constraint such as locked-in syndrome, life carries on through memory and the imagination. Throughout the text Bauby offers examples of his mental freedom in the face of his paralysis,

The autobiography *The Diving Bell and the Butterfly* was adapted as a film directed by Julian Schnabel in 2007. Actor Mathieu Amalric, left, played author Jean-Dominique Bauby. © ETIENNE GEORGE/CORBIS

which he characterizes as a "diving bell": "My diving bell becomes less oppressive, and my mind takes flight like a butterfly. There is so much to do. You can wander off in space or in time, set out for Tierra del Fuego or King Midas's court." The text also emphasizes the memory as a place, or a freedom that can be accessed through the mind. This mental freedom is made more palpable through the descriptions of his physical suffering and paralysis. "My hands, lying curled on the yellow sheets, are hurting, although I can't tell if they are burning hot or ice cold."

Bauby's book reveals an intense personal desire for continued communication. Locked-in syndrome does not paralyze the vocal cords, but it renders the sufferer incapable of controlling the breath in order to vibrate those vocal cords and speak. In order for Bauby to communicate, and indeed narrate his memoir to Mendibil, someone needed to read him a modified alphabet, arranged according to frequency of occurrence in the French language. "It is a simple enough system," writes Bauby. "You read off the alphabet … until I stop you at the letter to be noted. This process continues until whole sentences and ideas are transcribed, a method that makes communication frustrating and difficult with all except for the most 'meticulous' people." The difficulty of narrating an entire memoir through this belabored process attests to Bauby's considerable desire to regain a "voice."

Stylistically, *The Diving Bell and the Butterfly* is notable for its lyricism and collage-like structure. In her 2001 essay in *Literature and Medicine,* Valerie Raoul claims that the book is "neither a novel nor an autobiography, but a collage of 29 fragments with styles ranging from relatively straightforward narrative to lament, and from dream sequence to whimsical flights of fancy." Bauby's restrained lyricism lends a particular poetic force to these vignettes and the evocation of his physical paralysis, such as when he describes himself as "a hermit crab dug into his rock."

CRITICAL DISCUSSION

Upon its publication, *The Diving Bell and the Butterfly* was both a critical and commercial success. Beineix's short documentary aired on French television in 1997, and it may have contributed to the book's popularity. *The Diving Bell and the Butterfly* went on to be translated into twenty-three languages. In one passage Bauby describes a meal that he is "simmering" in his memories, which prompted Thomas Mallon, writing for the *New York Review of Books,* to write, "It's as if [Bauby] reversed the most famous moment in Proust and used memory to bring back the madeleine."

Bauby's memoir continues to increase awareness of locked-in syndrome. Following his stroke in 1996, he set up the Association du Locked-in Syndrome (ALIS) for patients and families who suffer from the affliction. A similar group, LIS Organization, was founded in Germany in 2000 with the goals of optimal therapy for sufferers, education on the disease, and greater documentation of patients and medical developments. In 2011 the British newspaper *The Telegraph* reported on a study published in the *British Medical*

DISABILITY STUDIES

The Diving Bell and the Butterfly is a text one might find in a class on disability studies, a relatively new field in literary criticism that originated, according to the scholar Taylor Hagood in her essay "Disability Studies and American Literature," "in the wake of the civil rights movement of the 1960's." This iteration of identity politics views the disabled as a marginalized group oppressed by what has been deemed the "able-bodied," and it strives to establish that the concept of a perfectly able body is, in itself, a fiction—a socially constructed ideal against which any real body will fail to measure up.

This theoretical lens has been applied to a broad range of literary texts, from classic Greek literature to characters in Charles Dickens. American literature has proved to be a rich vein of inquiry for scholars working in disability studies, with studies focusing on characters such Herman Melville's Captain Ahab, Ernest Hemingway's Jake Barnes, William Faulkner's Benjy Compson, and Flannery O'Conner's Hulga Hopewell. The publication of anthologies of the literature of the disabled further attests to the growing academic trend. The anthology *With Wings: An Anthology of Literature by Women with Disabilities* (1989) focuses on some of the lesser-known voices in the field, while *An Anthology of Disability Literature* (2011) encompasses U.S. and international writers from Leo Tolstoy to Jumpha Lahiri.

Journal suggesting that the majority of people suffering from locked-in syndrome are happy. Along with scholarly inquiry that has focused on the syndrome itself, Bauby's memoir has been the subject of a small body of criticism that has studied the text's importance in the literature of disability.

The Diving Bell and the Butterfly is often read beside other pieces of "disability literature," such as Wilfred Owen's war poem "Disabled" (1917), in an attempt to, as the scholar Henry C. Stewart puts it in his piece "In the Blink of an Eye," expose readers "to a variety of literary texts, representing disparate genres, which either demanded scrutiny of disabled authors or disabled characters." James Overboe articulates the mutability of readings in his 2001 piece in *Literature and Medicine,* arguing that most nondisabled readers see Bauby's account "either as a story of triumph over adversity through writing or as a personal tragedy of disability." However, Overboe's perspective as a "disabled person" allows him to read it "as an attempt to validate [Bauby's] presence as a human being by managing to communicate an experience that is usually considered incommunicable."

BIBLIOGRAPHY
Sources

Bauby, Jean-Dominique. *The Diving Bell and the Butterfly.* New York: Alfred A. Knopf, 1997. Print.

Di Giovanni, Janine. "OWM: The Real Love Story behind the Diving Bell and the Butterfly." *Observer* 30 Nov. 2008. *LexisNexis Academic.* Web. 17 Oct. 2012.

Hagood, Taylor. "Disability Studies and American Literature." *Literature Compass* 7.6 (2010): 387–96. *Wiley Online Library.* Web. 17 Oct. 2012.

Mallon, Thomas. "In the Blink of an Eye." *New York Review of Books* June 1997. *EBSCOhost.* Web. 17 Oct. 2012.

Plum, Fred, and Jerome Posner. "Points: The Locked in Syndrome." *British Medical Journal* 294.6580 (1987): 1163. *JSTOR.* Web. 18 Oct. 2012.

Raoul, Valerie; Connie Canam; Gloria Onyeoziri; James Overboe; and Carla Paterson. "Narrating the Unspeakable: Interdisciplinary Readings of Jean-Dominique Bauby's *The Diving Bell and the Butterfly.*" *Literature and Medicine* 20.2 (2001): 183–208. *University of Montana Libraries.* Web. 17 Oct. 2012.

Stewart, Henry C. "In the Blink of an Eye: Teaching Bauby's *The Diving Bell and the Butterfly* while Learning from Eye Blinks." *Journal of Literary and Cultural Disability Studies* 4.1 (2010): 90–98. *Project MUSE.* Web. 17 Oct. 2012.

Tomlin, Anne, and Barbara Hoffbert. "LOOK up for Yes." *Library Journal* 22.2 (1997): 8. *Academic Search Elite.* Web. 19 Oct. 2012.

Further Reading

Christine, Gerard. "The Diving Bell & the Butterfly by Jean Dominique Bauby." *English Review* 18.1 (2007): 16. Print.

Laird, Kerry. "A Critical Analysis of Wilfred Owen's 'Disabled.'" *Disabled Studies Quarterly* 40.1 (2005). *MLA International Bibliography.* Web. 17 Oct. 2012.

Owen, Wilfred. *Collected Poems of Wilfred Owen.* London: Chatto & Windus, 1963. Print.

Smith, Eimear, and Mark Delargy. "Locked-in Syndrome." *British Medical Journal* 330.7488 (2005): 406–09. *JSTOR.* Web. 17 Oct 2012.

Stewart, Henry C. *Questioned Consciousness in the Memoirs of Jean-Dominique Bauby, Julia Tavalaro and Phillipe Vigand: Unlocking and Teaching the Locked-in Writings of the Written Off.* Indiana: Indiana University of Pennsylvania, 2012. Print.

Greg Luther

Dust Tracks on a Road
Zora Neale Hurston

OVERVIEW

Dust Tracks on a Road (1942), the autobiography of anthropologist, folklorist, and author Zora Neale Hurston, explores her life from her childhood in the rural South to her education and early career to her prominence in the Harlem Renaissance. The latter was a movement that encouraged black Americans to produce literature, music, and art as a means of challenging racism, and Hurston was a leading force in it. In her autobiography, she meets life optimistically and, through notably imaginative passages, discusses her mother's death, coping with loneliness, and the mystic sphere she had encountered through prophetic visions.

Dust Tracks on a Road won the Anisfield-Wolf Book Award in 1943 for its contributions to the improvement in race relations, a prize it may not have been awarded had the attack on Pearl Harbor not catalyzed Hurston and her editors to excise her critiques of the United States from her book. Her content and style were heavily edited, and Hurston was accused of pandering to a white audience by some reviewers but recognized as a creative writer innovating the field of autobiography by others. Today, *Dust Tracks on a Road* has been reclaimed as an important artifact that resists traditional valuations of the individual over the community and of formal writing over oral and folk narrations.

HISTORICAL AND LITERARY CONTEXT

Written at the height of Hurston's career—after the cultural explosion that was the Harlem Renaissance had faded but before the emergence of the civil rights movement—*Dust Tracks on a Road* earned commercial but not critical success. One reason for the lack of positive critical response was that, except for the chapter "My People, My People," Hurston writes little of race, which greatly disappointed many readers. She had taken up the subject to some extent in "Seeing the World as It Is," a chapter she and her publishers agreed must be cut, as they feared her criticism of the United States and the military would alienate readers and be seen as "unpatriotic," especially during wartime.

Hurston produced her autobiography—her sixth book in eight years—at her publisher's insistence, in fact writing it instead of a planned novel. As the patronage she had enjoyed earlier in her career had dried up during the Great Depression, she followed orders but struggled with the form, creating an often fictive and highly manipulated product that some have called her best fiction. Others, like Claudine Raynaud, have found Hurston's imaginative play and aberrations from fact focal points of resistance to editorial censorship.

A protégé of Franz Boas, the famed anthropologist, Hurston worked alone and with other researchers to record cultural traditions threatened by social and technological changes. In the 1930s she collaborated with ethnomusicologist Alan Lomax to capture blues and folk songs in the United States and recorded "religious ecstasy" in southern churches with her colleague Margaret Mead. In 1935, after she had spent six years in the field collecting material, Hurston's *Mules and Men* was released, the first volume of black American folklore published by an African American. Also predating *Dust Tracks on a Road* were the novels *Jonah's Gourd Vine* (1934); *Their Eyes Were Watching God* (1937); *Moses, Man of the Mountain* (1939); and a memoir of her time collecting research in the field in Haiti and Jamaica, *Tell My Horse* (1939). In *Dust Tracks on a Road* she veers away from preconceptions of what her autobiography should be—just as she deviates from what others seem to believe she should be—using nonstandard language, almost entirely ignoring the issue of race, and repeatedly pointing to the mutability of perception and identity rather than viewing the self as a fixed "statue." Several critics have suggested that *Dust Tracks on a Road* might be best appreciated if considered in the context of the "lying sessions" she watched during her childhood in Eatonville, Florida, when men gathered on the porch of the general store to construct and perform stories; Hurston recalls these performances as important to her hometown community and to her development as an artist.

According to Hurston's biographer Robert Hemenway, her publisher foresaw *Dust Tracks on a Road* as the first volume in a series on her life, but the series never came to pass. Hemenway posits that the work did more harm than good to Hurston's reputation despite her Anisfield-Wolf Award. After *Dust Tracks on a Road* appeared, she wrote only one more novel, *Seraph on the Suwanee* (1948), which was generally panned, though she produced articles for various newspapers and periodicals. Still, Hurston's autobiography has risen again and influenced later works, such as Audre Lorde's "biomythography" *Zami: A New Spelling of My Name* (1982), a mixture of autobiography, fiction, history, and myth.

❖ *Key Facts*

Time Period:
Mid-20th Century

Relevant Historical Events:
Harlem Renaissance

Nationality:
American

Keywords:
coming-of-age; race; ethnicity

Cast members of Zora Neale Hurston's play *Polk County*, during a dress rehearsal at the Arena Stage in Washington, D.C., in 2002. From left to right: Ida Elrod Eustics as Bunch, Sherri LaVie Linton as Maudella, Gabriele Goyette as Laura B, and Harriet D. Foy as Big Sweet. Copyrighted in 1944, the play was not published or performed professionally until after its discovery in the Library of Congress in 1997. © AP IMAGES/SCOTT SUCHMAN, ARENA STAGE

THEMES AND STYLE

In her autobiography, Hurston faces the impossibility of being the self that pleases her as well as the self that pleases. She writes that "people are prone to build a statue of the kind of person that it pleases them to be. And few people want to be forced to ask themselves, 'What if there is no me like my statue?'" Denying others the chance to dismiss her as too poor to be educated or too much of a woman to fight, Hurston styles her autobiography loosely on the mythic heroes she so loved as a child. She approaches challenges such as sexual harassment and poverty with equanimity in her quest to follow her mother's advice to "jump at de sun," acknowledging that "we might not land on the sun, but at least we would get off the ground."

Though Hurston bowed to her publisher's desires in writing the autobiography, she took the opportunity to set the record straight on several issues, such as a misunderstanding she had had with Charles Johnson and his wife; to pay homage to her supporters, such as the novelist Fannie Hurst and the singer Ethel Waters; and to promote herself as both an average person and as a unique individual. In her essay in "Race, Gender, and Cultural Context in Zora Neale Hurston's *Dust Tracks on a Road*," in *Life/Lines: Theorizing Women's Autobiography* (1988), Nellie McKay notes, "In the tradition of black women's autobiographies, *Dust Tracks* is a transitional text, in which Hurston makes a radical break with rhetorical patterns in the slave narrative and opens the way for even bolder experiments with form and content."

Hurston's evasions, misrepresentations, and inaccuracies of details such as her true birthdate keep the reader at a distance, and her decision to positively portray her struggles prevent the work from becoming a polemic. She portrays life's mutability in her shifting tone and jumping anecdotes; for example, she notes that "nothing that God ever made is the same thing to more than one person.... There is no single face in nature, because every eye that looks upon it, sees it from its own angle." Extending this concept of individual perception, Hurston writes that "the tune is the unity of the thing," meaning that the overall sense of a story or a song matters more than accurately recording its details. With comments such as this she validates the artistic license she takes with her autobiography and displays her belief that the truest representations do not always come from the most factual ones.

CRITICAL DISCUSSION

The ambivalence with which *Dust Tracks on a Road* was met did not prevent it from being a commercial success. Representing those who lamented its publication, Harold Preece, writing in *Tomorrow* in 1943, finds that *Dust Tracks on a Road* is "the tragedy of a gifted mind, eaten up by an egocentrism fed on the patronizing admiration of the dominant white world." Conversely, in the *New York Times Book Review* in November of the same year, Beatrice Sherman gushes, "Here is a thumping story, though it has none of the horrid earmarks of the [Horatio] Alger-type climb.... Her story is forthright and without frills. Its emphasis lies on her fighting spirit in the struggle to achieve the education she felt she had to have." The more neutral Edward Farrison reports in the *Journal of Negro History* that Hurston's experiences are "interestingly presented, whether fact or fancy, and there is much of both in it."

When Hurston died, impoverished, in 1960, her books were no longer in print. She remained largely forgotten until 1975, when Alice Walker published a groundbreaking article in *Ms.* magazine on Hurston and her impact on oral and folklore narratives in African American literature, reopening the discussion about Hurston's intents and effects. Whether Hurston was playing a trickster narrator too slippery to be held or was indeed pandering to a white audience as her detractors suggested is a point of scholarly contention. Interest in her work has revitalized attention to form as well as struggles over authorial and editorial control in African American autobiographies.

Dust Tracks on a Road is frequently read as a means of examining how identity is constructed in the autobiographical genre. Concentrating on the differences between the manuscript and the final document, Raynaud argues that the excisions from *Dust Tracks* left cracks that "act as positive loci of resistance" that can "be read as pockets of resistance to form, to the final ideal product." McKay argues that Hurston's "'unfixing of identity' could … be said to challenge the ways we have of describing the subject's specificity and historical locatedness, without necessarily denying their ultimate importance." Along similar lines, Françoise Lionnet, in her piece in *Autobiographical Voices: Race, Gender, Self-Portraiture* (1989), maintains that *Dust Tracks* is an "autoethnographic" self-portrait more than an autobiography, as the "book amounts to a kind of 'figural anthropology' of the self" that defines "one's subjective ethnicity as mediated through language, history, and ethnographical analysis."

BIBLIOGRAPHY

Sources

Bachan, Kyle. "Still Searching Out Zora Neale Hurston." *Ms. Blog*. Ms. Magazine, 2 Feb. 2011. Web. 6 Dec. 2012.

Farrison, Edward W. Rev. of *Dust Tracks on a Road,* by Zora Neale Hurston. *Journal of Negro History* 28.3 (1943): 352–55. *JSTOR*. Web. 20 Nov. 2012.

Hemenway, Robert. *Zora Neale Hurston: A Literary Biography.* Urbana: University of Illinois Press, 1977. Print.

Lionnet, Françoise. "Autoethnography: The An-Archic Style of *Dust Tracks on a Road*." *Autobiographical Voices: Race, Gender, Self-Portraiture.* Ithaca, NY: Cornell University Press, 1989. 97–129. Print.

McKay, Nellie. "Race, Gender, and Cultural Context in Zora Neale Hurston's *Dust Tracks on a Road*." *Life/Lines: Theorizing Women's Autobiography.* Ed. Bella Brodzki and Celeste Schneck. Ithaca: Cornell University Press, 1988. 178–88. Print.

Preece, Harold. Rev. of *Dust Tracks on a Road,* by Zora Neale Hurston. *Tomorrow* 1 (1943): 58–59. *Zora Neale Hurston Digital Archive*. Web. 21 Nov. 2012.

HURSTON'S IMPROVISATIONAL LIFE

Born in 1891, Zora Neale Hurston spent many of her formative years in the first incorporated black community in the United States—Eatonville, Florida—where her father would become mayor. Her mother died in 1904, an event that, coupled with her father's subsequent remarriage, impacted Hurston's education and forced her to search for work. After taking various positions, including serving as a maid for a singer in a Gilbert and Sullivan troupe, Hurston decided to continue her education. However, at age twenty-six she was too old to attend a publicly funded high school, so she lopped ten years off her age for good, allowing her to enter; she graduated in 1918 from the Morgan Academy in Baltimore. She went on to study at Howard University and Columbia University's Barnard College, attracting the attention of anthropologist Franz Boas and beginning her field research in the American South.

Besides conducting her anthropological work, Hurston wrote plays, memoirs, novels, and dozens of short stories and essays. She is best remembered for the novel *Their Eyes Were Watching God,* which she wrote in seven weeks in 1937 while she was on a Guggenheim fellowship–funded research trip to Haiti to study *obeah,* West Indian sorcery. She wrote more on her research trip in *Tell My Horse* (1938). Hurston died in obscurity in 1960; her grave remained unmarked until author Alice Walker purchased a tombstone for it in 1973.

Raynaud, Claudine. "'Rubbing a Paragraph with a Soft Cloth'? Muted Voices and Editorial Constraints in *Dust Tracks on a Road*." *De/Colonizing the Subject: The Politics of Gender in Women's Autobiography.* Ed. Sidonie Smith and Julia Watson. Minneapolis: University of Minnesota Press, 1992. 34–64. Print.

Sherman, Beatrice. "Zora Hurston's Story." *New York Times.* 29 Nov. 1942: BR 44. *ProQuest.* Web. 21 Nov. 2012.

Further Reading

Fox-Genovese, Elizabeth. "To Write My Self: The Autobiographies of Afro-American Women." *Feminist Issues in Literary Scholarship.* Ed. Shari Benstock. Bloomington: Indiana University Press, 1987. Print.

Raynaud, Claudine. "Autobiography as a 'Lying' Session: Zora Neale Hurston's *Dust Tracks on a Road*." *Studies in Black American Literature.* Vol. 3. Ed. Joe Weixlmann and Houston Baker. Greenwood, Fla.: Penkevill, 1988. 110–38. Print.

Rayson, Ann L. "*Dust Tracks on a Road:* Zora Neale Hurston and the Form of Black Autobiography." *Negro American Literature Forum* 7.2 (1973): 39–45. *JSTOR.* Web. 24 Oct. 2012.

Wall, Cheryl A. "Dust Tracks on a Road." *The Concise Oxford Companion to African American Literature.* Ed. William L. Andrews, Frances Smith Foster, and Trudier Harris. 2001. *Oxford Reference.* Web. 7 Nov. 2012.

Katherine Bishop

Eighty Years and More, Reminiscences 1815–1897

Elizabeth Cady Stanton

❖ **Key Facts**

Time Period:
Late 19th Century

Relevant Historical Events:
Seneca Falls Convention; growth of women's rights movement

Nationality:
American

Keywords:
women's rights; suffrage; activism

OVERVIEW

Composed by Elizabeth Cady Stanton, *Eighty Years and More, Reminiscences 1815–1897* (1898) relates the story of Stanton's personal life and career as a pioneering women's rights activist. The book shares her views on the women's rights movement in the United States, motherhood, the role of religion in American society, and her friendship with fellow women's rights activist Susan B. Anthony. *Eighty Years and More* is structured chronologically around different episodes in Stanton's life, beginning with her childhood in New York and progressing through her marriage, early activism, and leadership role in the National American Women's Suffrage Association (NAWSA). The book culminates with Stanton's reflections on her eightieth birthday. While she ostensibly places the focus of *Eighty Years and More* on her personal life, her personal relationships receive less emphasis in the text than the successes of her activist career.

Published four years before Stanton died, *Eighty Years and More* also serves as a retrospective of the nineteenth-century U.S. women's rights movement at large and speaks to Stanton's concerns about the NAWSA's decision to narrow the focus of the movement to achieving women's suffrage. *Eighty Years and More* had a limited impact on the direction of the women's rights movement at the time of its publication and was overshadowed by the controversial publication of *The Woman's Bible* (1895), also primarily authored by Stanton, a work that advocated a radical reassessment of women's roles in the American religious community to better reflect gender equality.

HISTORICAL AND LITERARY CONTEXT

The historical roots of *Eighty Years and More* lay in the broader history of the nineteenth-century women's rights movement in the United States, beginning with the Seneca Falls Convention of 1848. Stanton drafted *The Declaration of Sentiments* (1848) for the convention, a document based on the U.S. Declaration of Independence that called for gender equality before the law, in education, in employment, and in the right to vote. In 1866 Stanton and Anthony advocated for women's suffrage through the Fourteenth and Fifteenth Amendments but were resisted by the abolitionist community. In response, Stanton and Anthony formed the National Woman Suffrage Association in 1869, effectively splitting the women's rights movement into two factions, with Stanton emerging as the leader of the newer, more radical group. Unlike the more conservative American Woman Suffrage Association, Stanton's National Woman Suffrage Association advocated not only women's suffrage but also broader political, social, and economic reform to reflect universal equality between the genders. These organizations reunited in 1890 to form the NAWSA, with Stanton serving as the organization's first president.

By 1897 Stanton's health had deteriorated to the point she was confined to her apartment in New York City, but she continued to write speeches for Anthony to deliver at NAWSA events, along with numerous editorials, columns, and letters of support. In 1898 Anthony alienated Stanton by nominating Stanton's political rival, Carrie Chapman Catt, to succeed Stanton as president of the NAWSA. Stanton disagreed with Catt's—and by extension Anthony's—decision to abandon Stanton's broader gender equality agenda in favor of a concentrated pursuit of women's suffrage. Despite Stanton's objection, Catt was elected president of the NAWSA. Within this historical context, *Eighty Years and More* can be read as a defense of Stanton's broader gender equality focus throughout her activist career.

Stanton read biographies of George Elliot, William Lloyd Garrison, Alfred Tennyson, and George Washington before composing *Eighty Years and More*. Much of the book material originally appeared as Stanton's serialized reminiscences in Clara Colby's *Women's Tribune*. *Eighty Years and More* reflects a variety of literary sources, including Stanton's own work. As an autobiography, the work has been compared to Frederick Douglass's *Narrative of the Life of Frederick Douglass, an American Slave* (1845) and also has been identified as a companion piece to *The Woman's Bible*. Many of the themes present in *Eighty Years and More, Reminiscences 1815–1897* also appear in *History of Woman Suffrage* (1881–1922), which Stanton composed along with Anthony, Ida Husted Harper, and other women's rights activists throughout her life.

Eighty Years and More is one of Stanton's lesser-known works and has had minor literary influence in comparison to her speeches, histories of the women's rights movement, and journalistic work. James Weldon Johnson's autobiography *Along This Way* (1933) parallels many of the themes present in the work through Johnson's descriptions of his efforts to promote equality for African Americans in the United States. Stanton's children revised and reissued *Eighty Years and More* in 1922 in response to the 1920 passage of the Nineteenth Amendment, which granted American women the right to vote. *Eighty Years and More* has been republished in several subsequent editions, the most recent in 1993.

THEMES AND STYLE

The central theme of *Eighty Years and More* is Stanton's ability to overcome a variety of personal and professional challenges to advance the cause of women's rights. Her focus falls more heavily on her professional challenges, although in the opening of the book she identifies herself primarily as a "wife … an enthusiastic housekeeper … and the mother of seven children." She includes accounts of events in her life that pushed her toward activism, including a memory of her father, New York Judge Daniel Cady, saying, "What a pity it is she's a girl!" upon the birth of Stanton's sister. She also recounts the time she used scissors to cut the misogynistic laws out of her father's law books. In addition to reiterating her pro-gender-equality positions on divorce, theology, and social reform, she asserts that the "love of protection," often assumed by men, "too often degenerates into downright tyranny" and worries about the toll an isolated domestic life may take on mothers.

Stanton's purpose in *Eighty Years and More* is to defend herself against contemporary charges of radical elitism by humanizing her personal story and to emphasize her many successes as a women's rights activist. To these ends, she portrays her husband, Henry Stanton, and her father as largely sympathetic and supportive of her goals, although historical evidence suggests greater conflict in their relationships. She also downplays the personal and political conflicts she experienced as a leader of the U.S. women's rights movement and omits the radical/conservative movement schism of 1869 and her censure by the NAWSA in 1896 for publishing *The Woman's Bible*. More generally, she avoids attacking the contemporary woman's rights movement for championing women's domesticity but undercuts this position with anecdotes of domestic oppression.

The structure of *Eighty Years and More* is episodic and follows the chronology of Stanton's life. Her tone, while occasionally lyrical with Victorian rhetorical flourishes, is often practical, with directive diction that casts Stanton in the role of a friendly adviser. One example is Stanton's advice to a congressman's wife in 1854 regarding how to handle the anticipated irritation of her husband upon finding that she had purchased a new stove without his permission. She writes, "Remember every time you speak in the way of defense, you give him a new text on which to branch out again. If silence is ever golden, it is when a husband is in a tantrum."

Elizabeth Cady Stanton in 1900, shortly after the publication of her memoir *Eighty Years and More*. © TIME & LIFE PICTURES/ GETTY IMAGES

CRITICAL DISCUSSION

Eighty Years and More received little critical attention at the time of its publication. By 1898 popular focus was shifting to a new generation of women's rights activists that was more closely associated with Anthony than Stanton. Stanton scholar Ann D. Gordon notes in her 1993 afterword to *Eighty Years and More* that what initial critical attention the book received largely focused on the material related to Stanton's personal life, despite the book's marked emphasis on her activist career. In addition to republishing *Eighty Years and More* in 1922, Stanton's children, Harriot and Theodore, published an accompanying work, *Elizabeth Cady Stanton as Revealed in Her Letters, Diary and Reminiscences* in 1922.

Twentieth-century critics have focused on the relationship of *Eighty Years and More* to *The Woman's Bible*, with Elisabeth Griffith noting in her 1984 biography of Stanton that after the uproar caused by the publication of *The Woman's Bible*, "Stanton's autobiography was her apologia." Griffith argues that Stanton chose not to include materials in the book where she was challenged or where she might appear in a negative light in order to reinforce "the image she had created of herself as benign, nurturing, good humored, smart, respectable, and self reliant." In this regard, *Eighty Years and More* "lacked the introspection of her

THE ISOLATED HOUSEHOLD VERSUS COLLECTIVE LIVING

One of Stanton's more radical arguments in *Eighty Years and More, Reminiscences 1815–1897* is that in order for women to achieve their full potential, collective living arrangements are necessary. Stanton believed that isolated households centered on the nuclear family trapped women in domestic bondage through the necessity of performing housework and childcare. Regarding this issue, she writes, "I now fully understand the practical difficulties most women had to contend with in the isolated household, and the impossibility of woman's best development if in contact, the chief part of her life, with servants and children."

To this end, Stanton experimented with living at Brook Farm, an early experiment in communal living in New England, in the 1840s and was associated with the utopian community of New Harmony, Indiana, through Robert Dale Owen. She also lived for a period in a French convent. Her views on the benefits of communal living for gender equality influenced later women's rights activists such as Charlotte Perkins Gilman.

best speeches and the candor of her correspondence." Other scholars have noted Stanton's failure in the narrative to address the plight of women of different economic levels and race.

More-recent scholarship has focused on Stanton's use of the autobiographical form to advance her activist cause. In a 1991 article in *Communication Studies*, Martha Solomon classifies *Eighty Years and More* as an "oratorical autobiography" because the book is "characterized by a desire to show one's life as in some way an idealized pattern of human behavior" with the main theme being vocation and life's work rather than personal life. For Solomon, Stanton falls into this category as a proponent of the women's rights movement. Estelle C. Jelmek notes that details of Stanton's personal life in *Eighty Years and More* serve only to provide relief for the primary goal of advancing the suffrage movement. Jelmek notes that Stanton's false ordinariness would not have troubled sympathetic readers who would only see another side of an admirable woman.

BIBLIOGRAPHY

Sources

Griffith, Elisabeth. *In Her Own Right: The Life of Elizabeth Cady Stanton*. New York: Oxford University Press, 1984. Print.

Solomon, Martha. "Autobiographies and Rhetorical Narratives: Elizabeth Cady Stanton and Anna Howard Shaw as 'New Women.'" *Communication Studies* 42.4 (1991): 354–70. *Taylor & Francis Online*. Web. 20 Nov. 2012.

Stanton, Elizabeth Cady. *Eighty Years and More, Reminiscences 1815–1897*. New York: Schocken Books, 1971. Print.

"Stanton, Elizabeth Cady 1815–1902." *Encyclopedia of Life Writing: Autobiographical and Biographical Forms*. Ed. Margaretta Jolly. London: Routledge, 2001. *Credo Reference*. Web. 20 Nov. 2012.

Further Reading

Banner, Lois W. *Elizabeth Cady Stanton: A Radical for Women's Rights*. Boston: Little, Brown, 1980. Print.

Blatch, Harriot Stanton, and Theodore Stanton, eds. *Elizabeth Cady Stanton as Revealed in Her Letters, Diary and Reminiscences*. 2 Vols. New York: New York Times, 1969. Print.

Dubois, Ellen Carol, ed. *Elizabeth Cady Stanton, Susan B. Anthony Correspondence, Writings, Speeches*. New York: Schocken Books, 1981. Print.

Dubois, Ellen Carol, and Richard Candida Smith, eds. *Elizabeth Cady Stanton, Feminist as Thinker: A Reader in Documents and Essays*. New York: New York University Press, 2007. Print.

Engbers, Susanna Kelly. "With Great Sympathy: Elizabeth Cady Stanton's Innovative Appeals to Emotion." *Rhetoric Society Quarterly* 37.3 (2007): 307–32. *Literature Online*. Web. 21 Nov. 2012.

Ginzberg, Lori D. *Elizabeth Cady Stanton: An American Life*. New York: Hillard Wang, 2009. Print.

Craig Barnes

Hunger of Memory
The Education of Richard Rodriguez
Richard Rodriguez

OVERVIEW

Hunger of Memory: The Education of Richard Rodriguez (1982) is the intellectual autobiography of Mexican American writer Richard Rodriguez. The book comprises a prologue and six chapters that Rodriguez himself describes as "essays impersonating an autobiography." He uses the story of his development from Catholic grammar school pupil in Sacramento, California, to graduate researcher in London's British Museum to comment publicly on race politics in the U.S. education system. Reflecting on his experience of growing up during the civil rights era as a second-generation Mexican American assimilating into the dominant white culture, Rodriguez argues openly against bilingual education and affirmative action as credible responses to social inequality.

During the 1960s—the decade in which Rodriguez completed his bachelor's degree at Stanford (1967) and master's at Columbia (1969) and began his graduate studies at the University of California at Berkeley (1969–75)—affirmative action became a component of U.S. policy. The original purpose was to prohibit discrimination on the basis of "race, color, religion, sex, or national origin" and to offer positive remedies to those minority groups who were economically and culturally disadvantaged due to past discrimination. In this new climate, students such as Rodriguez were often compensated with generous offers of placement and funding based on "minority" status. Rodriguez, while acknowledging the support he received, criticizes the policy as misbegotten and having lost sight of class discrepancies by focusing on race differences. Although the autobiography was heavily praised for its eloquence and honesty, its politics caused a stir, with detractors accusing Rodriguez of being too white and betraying his Mexican American heritage.

HISTORICAL AND LITERARY CONTEXT

Rodriguez first published portions of *Hunger of Memory* as early as 1973, when he was a Fulbright fellow and approaching the end of his graduate studies at Berkeley. He had, at that point, come a long way since his school days when, as a child of Mexican immigrants in a household where only Spanish was spoken, he could barely speak English and was afraid to raise his voice in front of his white classmates. He recalls the pain of assimilating: losing the shared intimacies of the home sphere and coming to be embarrassed about his parents as he learned more and more to assert himself in English. Ultimately, however, he was grateful for that forced passage into what he calls public society, where the English language dominated. Rodriguez came to defend assimilation precisely during a period when activists were making a point of critiquing it as a mechanism that robbed Chicanos and other minorities of their identities and made them vulnerable to oppression.

Hunger of Memory was published during a period in which the importance of cultural studies as an academic discipline grew; it was strongly influenced by the Marxist critique of culture but also by the identity politics of the 1960s and 1970s. Exposing the forces of ideology and hegemony prevailing within modern society, the discipline became increasingly invested in minority identities as sites of resistance to oppression. It is against this background that Rodriguez's story becomes controversial to the extent that it speaks of acculturating to norms rather than celebrating differences and of succeeding precisely by opting into the orthodox structures rather than resisting them. As true as this might be, Rodriguez's aversion to identity thinking is precisely because it distracts us from thinking about class inequalities, or so he claims.

Rodriguez's overarching story of a Mexican American who finds success in the white public world by educating himself is reminiscent of what is perhaps the best-known African American autobiography, Booker T. Washington's *Up from Slavery* (1901). As an autobiography describing acculturation into the mainstream United States, *Hunger of Memory* can also be compared with *Barrio Boy,* by labor activist Ernesto Galarza (1971), a Mexican immigrant who, like Rodriguez, graduated from Stanford and Columbia. Rodriguez himself has claimed to see *Hunger of Memory* "in the tradition of *The Education of Henry Adams,*" an early-twentieth century autobiography similarly meditating on educational policies and practices.

Hunger of Memory continues to be Rodriguez's best-known and most contentious work, lending itself to conversations that, though begun in the mid- to late twentieth century, continue. His resistance in particular

Key Facts

Time Period:
Late 20th Century

Relevant Historical Events:
Civil rights movement; rise of cultural studies in academia

Nationality:
American

Keywords:
assimilation; immigration; ethnicity

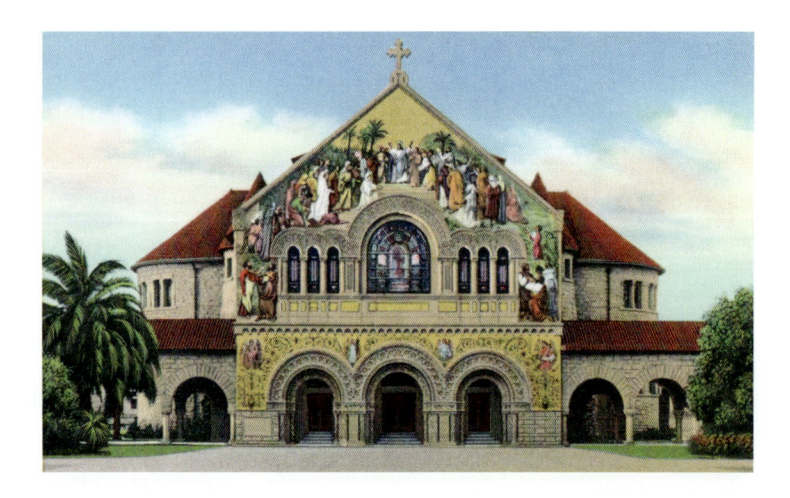

Memorial Chapel, located on the campus of Stanford University, Palo Alto, California. Richard Rodriguez earned degrees from Stanford University, Columbia University, and the University of California at Berkeley. © LAKE COUNTY MUSEUM/CORBIS

to teaching ethnic languages in the classroom, precisely because it preserves ethnic identity and prevents students from fully entering public society, speaks to heated debates over the legacy of multiculturalism and minority quotas—as in Walter Benn Michaels's *The Trouble with Diversity: How We Learned to Love Identity and Ignore Inequality* (2006), another book that angered many on the left with its critique of identity politics.

THEMES AND STYLE

Rodriguez's main theme is the way language determines public identity, a theme reflected in the story he tells of his childhood as a Mexican American growing up in a Sacramento neighborhood dominated by white people. Recognizing early on that "at home they [his family] spoke Spanish" while English was the language of "public society," he came to identify Spanish as an obstacle to public life. Hence the importance he attributes to his assimilation under the nuns who taught him, which he describes not as a loss of ethnic identity but as the gain of cultural prestige in the wider world. Deliberately giving up Spanish for English, however, proved bittersweet, like all rites of passage: it drove a wedge between Rodriguez and his family, who spoke only broken English and thus failed to enter into the public life Rodriguez sought.

In *Hunger of Memory*, Rodriguez relies on standard autobiographical themes of "education" and "schooling" to reveal how affirmative action benefits someone supposedly "socially disadvantaged" such as Rodriguez himself—but who never was discriminated against in any significant way and, as such, was never at risk. Claiming that other individuals, regardless of racial identity, were far more deserving of intervention and support, he insists class, not race, should be considered. He does not deny that his assimilation was painful, in the sense it distanced him culturally from his parents. As he says, "This is what matters to me: the story of the scholarship boy who returns home one summer from college to discover bewildering silence, facing his parents. This is my story." His point, however, is that his is not an ethnic story; it is, rather, "an American story"; while race and complexion figure heavily in his imagination, also important are his reflections on his social mobility, his Catholic faith, and his profession as a writer and scholar.

A distinctive element of *Hunger of Memory* is the way Rodriguez shifts from intensely personal memories of childhood and adulthood into blunt polemical expressions on the nature of education. Thus, in the first essay, "Aria," after recalling how as a child he would lovingly listen for the sounds of Spanish speakers, he begins a fresh passage, writing, "Today I hear bilingual educators say that children lose a degree of 'individuality' by becoming assimilated into public society." This consciously academic tone continues in the second essay, "The Achievement of Desire," in which he quotes extensively from Richard Hoggart's *The Uses of Literacy* (1957), a foundational study of culture and class in Britain read by Rodriguez in the course of his graduate research. At these moments, Rodriguez consciously maps his story on to intellectual debates over experiences much like his own.

CRITICAL DISCUSSION

Upon its release, *Hunger of Memory* drew substantial praise from commercial papers, including the *Boston Globe*, *New York Times*, and *Washington Post*, which described it variously as "a delicate, nuanced meditation," rendered in "exquisite clarity" and "affecting" in its "honesty, hauntingly so." When the work was republished in the early 1990s, critics acknowledged what remained "controversial views" on "Catholicism, complexion, bilingual education, civil rights, and affirmative action" while applauding the book's "courageous" treatment of Mexican American cultural and linguistic detachment. One *English Journal* critic predicted that "as the United States' Hispanic population grows in the next century," Rodriguez's autobiography would continue to raise "important questions for students and teachers alike."

Despite Rodriguez's popular appeal, many activists and reformers on the left have taken exception to his critiques of bilingual education and affirmative action, indicting him as a "conservative minority." As Paul Guajardo notes in *Chicano Controversy: Oscar Acosta and Richard Rodriguez* (2002), Rodriguez has come to be regarded as a "whipping boy" for some on the left. Guajardo represents a growing number of scholars willing to reappraise Rodriguez and draw him into Chicano studies, taking his story to be an exemplary narrative for understanding identities formed at the crossroads of separate cultures.

Scholarship on *Hunger of Memory* has revolved around the central category of identity, especially the ways Rodriguez positions himself in relation to Mexican and American cultures. Thus, scholars such as Nidesh Lawtoo and Henry Staten examine the book in terms of both the advantages and disadvantages of the "borderland" or "in-between" identity of the "subaltern subject." Spencer Herrera, David William Foster, and Yaakov Perry, meanwhile, take interest in the sexual subtexts of Rodriguez's work, reading it for encrypted gay (focusing on same-sex relations) and "queer" (focusing on difference and alienation) desires. The book has also been the subject of studies on the genre of autobiography. Lea Ramsdell, for example, in her essay in *Journal of Modern Literature*, undertakes a comparative study of what she calls "linguistic autobiographies" by Latino authors, in which "language choice" is understood as a "political act" articulated in relation to power structures in society. Petra Fachinger, writing for *MELUS*, explores how the concept of "ethnic" works with and against the conventions of autobiography.

BILINGUAL EDUCATION

Bilingual education for minority-language students was a hot topic for educators and policy makers alike in the decades leading up to the publication of *Hunger of Memory*. On one side of the debate were those who thought children in school should be educated in both English and the language of their parents; on the other were those who—like Richard Rodriguez—advocated immersion in English alone. Legislation passed in the United States in the 1970s, intended to ensure that non-English-speaking students would not be educationally disadvantaged, led the U.S. Department of Education to issue guidelines promoting a bilingual curriculum. The Office for Civil Rights enforced compliance with the guidelines.

By the end of the 1970s, however, detractors were claiming that not only was the bilingual curriculum ineffectual but that it led to divisiveness among different ethnic groups. Consequently, the Bilingual Education Act was amended, and bilingual education was demoted to a "transitional" (and so not strictly bilingual) role. Rodriguez's insistence in *Hunger of Memory* that by no means should Spanish be brought into the classroom was, in this light, guaranteed to stir up a storm.

BIBLIOGRAPHY

Sources

Fachinger, Petra. "Lost in Nostalgia: The Autobiographies of Eva Hoffman and Richard Rodriguez." *MELUS* 26.2 (2001): 111–27. Print.

Guajardo, Paul. *Chicano Controversy: Oscar Acosta and Richard Rodriguez*. New York: Peter Lang, 2002. Print.

Herrera, Spencer R. "Performing the Chicano (Homo) Erotic in Richard Rodriguez's *Hunger of Memory*." *Utah Foreign Language Review* 18 (2010): 10–18. Print.

Lawtoo, Nidesh. "Dissonant Voices in Richard Rodriguez's *Hunger of Memory* and Luce Irigaray's *This Sex Which Is Not One*." *Texas Studies in Literature and Language* 48.3 (2006): 220–49. Print.

Paisley, Lynn. Rev. of *Hunger of Memory: The Education of Richard Rodriguez, An Autobiography*, by Richard Rodriguez. *English Journal* 82.7 (1993): 83. Print.

Perry, Yaakov. "Metaphors We Write By: Desire's (Dis) Orientation and the Border in Richard Rodriguez's *Hunger of Memory*." *MELUS* 34.3 (2009): 155–82. Print.

Ramsdell, Lea. "Language and Identity Politics: The Linguistic Autobiographies of Latinos in the United States." *Journal of Modern Literature* 28.1 (2004): 166–76. Print.

Staten, Henry. "Ethnic Authenticity, Class, and Autobiography: The Case of *Hunger of Memory*." *PMLA* 113:1 (1998): 103–16. Print.

Further Reading

Christopher, Renny. "Rags to Riches to Suicide: Unhappy Narratives of Upward Mobility: *Martin Eden, Bread Givers, Delia's Song,* and *Hunger of Memory*." *College Literature* 29.4 (2002): 79–108. Print.

De Gregorio, Eduardo. "Language and Male Identity Construction in the Cultural Borderlands: Richard Rodriguez's *Hunger of Memory*." *Literature and Ethnicity in the Cultural Borderlands*. Ed. Jesús Benito and Anna María Manzanas. Amsterdam: Rodopi, 2002. Print.

Durán, Isabel. "Latino Autobiography, the Aesthetic, and Political Criticism: The Case of *Hunger of Memory*." *Nor Shall Diamond Die: American Studies in Honour of Javier Coy*. Ed. Carme Manuel and Paul Scott Derrick. Valencia: Universitat de València, 2003. Print.

Foster, David William. "Other and Difference in Richard Rodriguez's *Hunger of Memory*." *Postcolonial and Queer Theories: Intersections and Essays*. Ed. John C. Hawley. Westport, Conn.: Greenwood, 2001. Print.

Márquez, Antonio C. "Richard Rodriguez's *Hunger of Memory* and New Perspectives on Ethnic Autobiography." *Teaching American Ethnic Literatures: Nineteen Essays*. Ed. John R. Maitino and David R. Peck. Albuquerque: University of New Mexico Press, 1996. Print.

Marzán, J. A. "The Art of Being Richard Rodriguez." *Bilingual Review* 27.1 (2003): 45–64. Print.

David Aitchison

I Know Why the Caged Bird Sings
Maya Angelou

✤ **Key Facts**

Time Period:
Mid-20th Century

Relevant Historical Events:
Success of the civil rights movement; segregation and lynchings in the American South

Nationality:
American

Keywords:
oppression; racism; civil rights movement

OVERVIEW

Published by Maya Angelou in 1969, *I Know Why the Caged Bird Sings* is one of the best-known autobiographies of a black woman published in the post–civil rights era. The author's first volume of autobiography traces Angelou's emotional and personal growth during her childhood in the South in the 1930s and 1940s, including her parents' abandonment of Angelou and her brother when she was young, her experiences of racism at her grandmother's store, and her brutal rape by her mother's boyfriend when Angelou was eight years old. Despite the incredible hardship she endured, throughout *Caged Bird* she continuously stresses the need to celebrate humanity and community bonds against seemingly insurmountable adversity. In the text the recollection of dark moments in the author's life bears witness to and brings about reconciliation with Americans' collective past.

When *Caged Bird* was published, Angelou was best known as an actress and a performer, especially for her Emmy-nominated performance in the televised version of Alex Haley's *Roots*. She was also active in the civil rights movement and served as the northern coordinator of the Southern Christian Leadership Conference (SCLC) in the 1960s. Her book emerged in the immediate aftermath of the civil rights era, following the passage of groundbreaking antidiscrimination legislation in the mid-1960s. Immediately popular with the mainstream U.S. public, the text remained on the *New York Times* best-seller list for two years following its initial publication. Today the work is considered a classic of twentieth-century African American literature.

HISTORICAL AND LITERARY CONTEXT

Caged Bird constructs a powerful portrait of the reality of growing up poor and black in Stamps, Arkansas, during the 1930s and 1940s. Among the harshest experiences that Angelou recreates from her youth are the examples of virulent racism against blacks in the South. During the late 1920s and early 1930s, lynching of blacks in the American South continued—albeit in lesser numbers than in previous decades—despite the repeated attempts of the National Association for the Advancement of Colored People (NAACP) to pass anti-lynching legislation. Racial tensions in Arkansas specifically continued to run high during Angelou's childhood, in the aftermath of such brutal, racially charged events as the 1919 Elaine Massacre, in which more than 200 blacks were killed, and the 1927 lynching of John Carter.

Angelou composed *Caged Bird* after friends encouraged her to write about her past, though she was not convinced that a literary career was for her. Nevertheless, Angelou told Carol Neubauer in a 1987 interview that "by the time I was half finished with *Caged Bird* I knew I loved the form—that I wanted to try to see what I could do with the form." She continued, "I love the idea of the slave narrative, using the first person singular, really meaning always the third person plural." Angelou's use of narrative voice in the work reflects a sense of collectivity within the black community that emphasizes its resilience in the face of racial oppression. Her text reflects the communal solidarity that formed the basis of the civil rights movement, in which Angelou played a significant role.

Angelou's work is part of a growing body of black women's autobiography that emerges out of the tradition of female slave narratives, such as *Incidents in the Life of a Slave Girl* (1861) by Harriet Jacobs. Like Jacobs's narrative, Angelou's autobiography challenges and subverts a fear of the black woman's body present in American society, which hypersexualizes black women. In an interview for the documentary *Zora Neale Hurston: Jump at the Sun*, Angelou indicates that she found inspiration for *Caged Bird* in Hurston's autobiography *Dust Tracks on a Road* (1942), echoing Hurston's lyricism and attention to black female identity. W. E. B. Du Bois's autobiography *A Soliloquy on Viewing My Life from the Last Decade of Its First Century* (1968) also inspired Angelou for the narration of the numerous adversities Du Bois overcame as an African American at the turn of the twentieth century and his commitment to early civil rights activism.

The overwhelming success of Angelou's first autobiography led to a productive literary career, which included the publication of five subsequent volumes of autobiography, the most recent of which is *A Song Flung Up to Heaven* (2002). She has influenced numerous African American female writers, including Alice Walker, whose novel *The Color Purple* (1982) addresses similar issues as those found in *Caged Bird*, including rape, abandonment, and racism. Walker's collection of autobiographical stories *The Way Forward*

Is with a Broken Heart (2000) demonstrates the evolution in black women's autobiography since Angelou's first volume. Autobiographical accounts of resistance, such as *Rosa Parks: My Story* (1992), also reflect Angelou's influence in their candid portrayal of black women confronting and challenging racial adversity. Toni Morrison's depiction of racial self-hatred in *The Bluest Eye* (1970) demonstrates a similar concern with the self-image of young black girls as that reflected in *Caged Bird*.

THEMES AND STYLE

Angelou's work can perhaps be summed up best as a message of resilience and perseverance in the face of daunting adversity. The purpose of narrating a string of debilitating, traumatizing events from her childhood is not to dwell on the pain but to bear witness to her past in a way that demonstrates her personal and emotional growth and the path that led her to become the mature woman who narrates the autobiography. After describing her grandmother's stoic passivity in the face of taunts and insults from three white girls, the narrator recalls, "She was beautiful. Something had happened out there, which I couldn't completely understand, but I could see that she was happy…. Whatever the contest had been out front, I knew Momma had won." Through her resilient attitude in the face of blatant racism, Angelou's "momma"—what she calls her grandmother—reveals a different form of resistance to the young girl.

After Angelou began *Caged Bird,* writing quickly assumed a new role in her life. Reflecting on autobiographical writing in an interview with Joanne Braxton (1999), Angelou explains, "Anything I write, I write because I have to write. And I have to tell the truth about it, not just facts about it." Braxton notes that this drive to tell the truth, no matter how painful, moved Angelou to write about her rape. Angelou states that she thought to herself, "'You write so that … people who have not been raped might understand something, and people who have been raped might forgive themselves.'" To achieve this end, Angelou recreates the most painful moments of her rape in order to bear witness to and bring about healing for her audience. The narrator remembers "the pain. A breaking and entering when even the senses are torn apart. The act of rape on an eight-year-old body is a matter of the needle giving because the camel can't." Angelou's willingness to share the dark moments in the recesses of her memory evidences a courageousness that is present throughout the text.

The narration in *Caged Bird* achieves a balanced voice between the distanced perspective of the adult narrator and that of a young Angelou. The adult Angelou interjects insight into her younger counterpart's story that puts her childhood experiences into perspective. After narrating the humiliation she experienced when singing at an Easter Sunday service, she concludes, "If growing up is painful for the Southern Black girl, being aware of her displacement is the rust on the razor that threatens the throat. It is an unnecessary insult." Braxton argues that, evocative of the interplay between memory and history, this dichotomy communicates a "transcendent awareness through the agency of memory" that functions as a "point of consciousness" for Angelou's readers.

Author Maya Angelou circa 1970, shortly after the publication of *I Know Why the Cage Bird Sings.* © BETTMANN/CORBIS

CRITICAL DISCUSSION

Caged Bird became an immediate success upon its publication in 1969, earning noteworthy reviews from prominent national periodicals, including *Newsweek,* the *New York Times,* and the *Wall Street Journal.* Braxton cites review of the text in *Newsweek* (1970), in which Robert Gross declares that *Caged Bird* "quietly and gracefully portrays and pays tribute to the courage, dignity and endurance of the small, rural Southern Black community in which [Angelou] spent most of her early years." Numerous critics regarded the work as beginning a new era in African American literary consciousness and the tradition of black female autobiography.

THE SOUTHERN CHRISTIAN LEADERSHIP CONFERENCE AND THE CIVIL RIGHTS MOVEMENT

The Southern Christian Leadership Conference (SCLC) was founded in 1957 under the leadership of Dr. Martin Luther King Jr., with the goal of uplifting "the soul of America" through nonviolent resistance. The Montgomery bus boycott of 1955 served as inspiration for the group's formation. The SCLC operated as an umbrella organization that coordinated the action of different activist groups throughout the South, including the Nashville Christian Leadership Council and the Montgomery Improvement Association. Founded on Christian ideals, the SCLC had the backing of influential black religious leaders and churches across the region. Maya Angelou became involved with the SCLC after hearing King speak at a Harlem church in early 1960. She organized a highly successful revue called "Cabaret for Freedom" that raised funds for the SCLC.

Angelou became the new director of the SCLC's New York office in 1960 after Bayard Rustin left the position. The organization participated in voter registration drives across the South and played a pivotal role in the March on Washington, bringing national attention to the civil rights struggle. The group's efforts were invaluable to the passage of the Civil Rights Act of 1964 and the Voting Rights Act of 1965. Despite growing tensions in the late 1960s between the SCLC and more militant organizations, as well as the terrible blow the group received upon King's assassination in 1968, the SCLC remained influential. It persists as a nationwide organization that continues its commitment to bring about justice through nonviolent action.

While the popularity of Angelou's first autobiography continues, it has elicited censorship and sparked controversy because of its frank portrayal of rape, racism, and teen pregnancy. The book has faced at least thirty-nine public challenges or bans since 1983 and is one of the most frequently challenged books of the twenty-first century. Parents demanding the book's exclusion from school curricula cite its explicit sexual depictions as justification for censorship. Despite the controversy, however, *Caged Bird* has undoubtedly increased Angelou's readership and public stature. After the author recited her poem "On the Pulse of the Morning" at the 1993 inauguration of President Bill Clinton, sales of *Caged Bird* increased by almost 500 percent, and Bantam was forced to reprint the book. Scholarly approaches to the text range from studies on censorship, autobiography, history and memory, and somatophobia (hatred of the body) and the black woman to the book's place within the African American literary tradition.

Angelou's work is often examined in relation to literary form and the genre of autobiography. Characteristic of such scholarship is "Racial Protest, Identity, Words, and Form in Maya Angelou's *I Know Why the Caged Bird Sings*" (1993), in which Pierre Walker analyzes the text's formal structure. Walker notes that Angelou "shaped the material of her childhood and adolescent life story in *Caged Bird* to present Maya's first sixteen years, much as a bildungsroman would, as a progressive process of affirming identity." Other scholars examine *Caged Bird* within the African American literary tradition. For example, in *The Autobiographical Works of Maya Angelou* (1990), Dolly McPherson points out that "Maya Angelou, like other black autobiographers, describes the Southern black community as one that nurtures its members and helps them to survive in such an antagonistic environment."

BIBLIOGRAPHY

Sources

Angelou, Maya. *I Know Why the Caged Bird Sings*. New York: Random House, 1969. Print.

Braxton, Joanne. "Symbolic Geography and Psychic Landscapes: A Conversation with Maya Angelou." *Maya Angelou's* I Know Why the Caged Bird Sings *: A Casebook*. Ed. Joanne Braxton. New York: Oxford University Press, 1999. 3–20. Print.

McPherson, Dolly A. *The Autobiographical Works of Maya Angelou*. New York: Peter Lang, 1990. Print.

Neubauer, Carol. "Maya Angelou with Carol E. Neubauer." *Massachusetts Review* 28.2 (1987): 286–92. Print.

Walker, Pierre A. "Racial Protest, Identity, Words, and Form in Maya Angelou's *I Know Why the Caged Bird Sings*." *College Literature* 22.3 (1993): 91–108. Print.

Further Reading

Lupton, Mary Jane. "Singing the Black Mother: Maya Angelou and Autobiographical Continuity." *Black American Literature Forum* 24.2 (1990): 257–76. Print.

Moore, Opal. "Learning to Live: When the Bird Breaks from the Cage." *Censored Books: Critical Viewpoints*. Ed. N. Karolides, L. Burress, and J. Kean. Metuchen, N.J.: Scarecrow, 1993. Print.

Tate, Claudia. *Black Women Writers at Work*. New York: Continuum, 1983. Print.

Vermillion, Mary. "Reembodying the Self: Representations of Rape in *Incidents in the Life of a Slave Girl* and *I Know Why the Caged Bird Sings*." *Biography: An Interdisciplinary Quarterly* 15.3 (1992): 243–60. Print.

Katrina White

Lakota Woman

Mary Crow Dog

OVERVIEW

Published in 1990 under her married name, Mary Crow Dog, Mary Brave Bird's *Lakota Woman* provides an account of the life of a Lakota Sioux woman who was swept up in, and deeply affected by, Native American activism in the early 1970s. Written in collaboration with Austrian-born author Richard Erdoes from tapes recorded in the late 1970s, *Lakota Woman* describes Brave Bird's impoverished childhood on South Dakota's Rosebud Reservation; an adolescence of rage and disconnection; and, finally, the experience of finding her place as an activist and a woman amid the turbulence of the Red Power movement.

By the time Brave Bird's autobiography reached shelves, many of the key players in the narrative had mellowed and moved on to other pursuits. Public interest in their stories remained high, however, and *Lakota Woman* won substantial readership, as well as mostly favorable treatment by critics. While contemporary scholars have raised questions about the nature of collaborations between Native Americans and writers from outside their culture, Brave Bird's text stands as an important portrait of the struggles faced by contemporary American Indian women in a society where economic conditions and the shift away from traditional social structures have contributed to fraught relationships between generations and between the sexes.

HISTORICAL AND LITERARY CONTEXT

Lakota Woman describes the difficult life on Indian reservations in the mid- to late twentieth century and the galvanizing effect of the nascent American Indian Movement (AIM) on Brave Bird's generation. AIM, which was founded in 1968, advocated for recognition of Native American rights, especially in relation to land treaties and to the preservation of traditional Indian culture and spirituality in the face of assimilating forces such as the U.S. government and the Roman Catholic Church. In 1972 AIM activists spearheaded the Trail of Broken Treaties Caravan to Washington DC, which ended in the occupation of the Bureau of Indian Affairs and a promise from then-president Richard Nixon to respond to AIM's twenty demands within a month. The following year, for ten weeks, a group of Lakota activists and AIM members occupied the town of Wounded Knee on the Pine Ridge Reservation in South Dakota—where, in 1890, U.S. troops massacred 200 Sioux men, women, and children, an event that symbolically ended the Indian wars—to protest cronyism and corruption in tribal politics. The siege exposed the rift between the traditionalism of tribal elders and AIM members and the views of those who saw outside institutions as the path out of reservation poverty.

Published nearly twenty years after the events at Wounded Knee, *Lakota Woman* is Brave Bird's recounting of the birth of her awareness as a Sioux woman, acknowledging the ways in which she has made peace with this identity. She started writing as a teenager, her first work appearing in a mimeographed "newspaper" that she and her friends titled the *Red Panther*. Inspired by reports of the Black Power movement and early activism among urban Indians, "It was the kind of writing," she recalls in the book, "which foamed at the mouth, but which also lifted a great deal of weight from one's soul." *Lakota Woman* began as a collaboration with Erdoes during a period spent living off the reservation and campaigning for the release from prison of her husband, Lakota spiritual leader Leonard Crow Dog. While the text acknowledges some gains made by Native American activism in the 1970s, it also retains a measure of this anger.

Lakota Woman continues a tradition of Indian life stories that began as oral narratives and were shaped into autobiography by, or in collaboration with, non–Native American writers, who are often credited as "editor." *Black Elk Speaks* (1932), the best-known and most discussed work in the genre, describes the life of Nicolas Black Elk (1863–1950) as his people fought to maintain their way of life in the face of increasing incursions by white settlers. Also detailing Sioux religious practices and their visionary underpinnings, *Black Elk Speaks* became a model for works that would follow.

The success of *Lakota Woman* spurred Brave Bird to continue her story in *Ohitika Woman* (1993), which details her life from 1977 onward, focusing on her battles with alcoholism and the renewal she found after joining the Native American church. While reviews of *Ohitika Woman* were more mixed than those of its predecessor, both books are regarded as important accounts of the challenges faced by contemporary Native American women.

❖ *Key Facts*

Time Period:
Late 20th Century

Relevant Historical Events:
Birth of the American Indian movement; occupation of Wounded Knee; growth of the Red Power movement

Nationality:
American

Keywords:
Native American; Red Power; civil rights

ADVERSITY AND RESISTANCE

Detail of a costume of a woman Lakota dancer. Lakota activist and writer Mary Crow Dog discusses her life and native American issues in *Lakota Woman.* © PRISMA BILDAGENTUR AG/ALAMY

THEMES AND STYLE

Lakota Woman centers on Brave Bird's struggle to define herself in terms of her "Indianness" and with regards to her experience as a woman. Beginning with the book's title, which claims these two key elements of her identity, her story addresses the difficulties of growing up in a culture that has largely been stripped of its defining characteristic—a connection to the land, which is both spiritually significant and a proving ground to develop prowess as horseman, warrior, and hunter. "There is not much rep," she writes, "in putting a can of Spam or an occasional rabbit on the table." While Brave Bird sympathizes with the plight of Native American men, her real solidarity is with Indian women, who often bear the brunt of these male frustrations—beaten by their husbands, raped, and faced with persecution by the white establishment, which included forced sterilization in hospitals following the birth of a baby.

Throughout *Lakota Woman,* Brave Bird demonstrates a reverence for storytelling as a way to make meaning out of present circumstances and as an essential part of the struggle for autonomy by Native American people. She writes angrily of the tourist view of Indian culture exemplified by the Gildersleeve Trading Post at Wounded Knee, which became one of the central sites of the occupation in 1973. "Some of the postcards ... showed our slaughtered men and women frozen stiff in grotesque attitudes," she laments, expressing anger at the for-profit exploitation of Lakota history. At the same time, Brave Bird makes clear that being defined exclusively by identification with Sitting Bull or Crazy Horse is not the answer either. "You can't wear their eagle feathers, freeload off their legends. You have to make your own legends now." Indeed, in *Lakota Woman,* Brave Bird immortalizes women like Lizzy Fast Horse, a great-grandmother who fought her way to the top of Mount Rushmore, "reclaiming the Black Hills for their rightful owners," only to be dragged back down by police. Women like this, and Brave Bird counts herself among them, "made Mr. White Man realize that there were other Indians besides the poor human wrecks who posed for him for a quarter." As a portrait of her life, *Lakota Woman* seems calibrated to perform this same function.

Lakota Woman is marked by its frankness and by the cyclical structure of the narrative, in which stories from Lakota history are interwoven with the events of Brave Bird's life, echoing, as commentators have noted, the typical structure of traditional Indian storytelling and ceremonial practices. The siege at Wounded Knee, which is the central event in the narrative, opens the first chapter but is not treated in-depth until the middle of the book. Brave Bird's description of the event focuses as much on the physical details of her pregnancy and the birth of her son, Pedro—which occurred at Wounded Knee—as it does on details of the fighting and strategizing found in other accounts of the siege. She recounts, for instance, at nine months pregnant, her preoccupation with "getting to the toilet safely." Her anecdotes often include such mundane female experiences, which, while they lack the glamor of armed resistance, still connect to the larger struggle. With Pedro's first cries, which were accompanied by the "highest-pitched trembling brave-heart yell" of nearby women, Brave Bird recalls the feeling "that I had accomplished something for my people."

CRITICAL DISCUSSION

Lakota Woman garnered critical acclaim upon publication and was awarded the 1991 American Book Award. Writing in a 1990 edition of the *Chicago Tribune*, Edward Hower calls the book "powerful" and, quoting Brave Bird's assessment of the U.S. government's attempts to erase traces of Wounded Knee ("They cannot extinguish the memory in our hearts, a memory we will pass on to generations still unborn"), asserts that "*Lakota Woman* is an important part of that legacy." Mixed or negative reviews tended to focus on the circuitous nature of the narrative or on Brave Bird's vitriolic treatment of white America.

While Brave Bird has not written additional books since *Ohitika Woman*, her dual autobiographies continue to attract readers and remain important works in Native American studies. Writing on the author's reception in his classroom, Professor Christopher Wise refers to the "regenerative effect" of her work on his students and of their eagerness to unpack the complexities of "as told to" works of Native American autobiography.

Little scholarship has been published on *Lakota Woman*, perhaps in part because of the complicating role of Erdoes in Brave Bird's books. In a 1998 interview with Christopher and R. Todd Wise published in *Studies in American Indian Literatures*, Brave Bird said of their collaboration, "Like some of the stuff, [Erdoes] would reword it. I would say, 'Gee whiz, I don't talk like this.'" Ultimately, however, Brave Bird concludes, "Like I said, it's all right, just as long as it gets read." Other scholars affirm this view. Gretchen Bataille, in her 1996 review of *Lakota Woman*, points out that Erdoes's collaboration with holy man and AIM participant Lame Deer, which she considers a complement to Brave Bird's narrative, is written in a different voice than the one in *Lakota Woman*, suggesting that "much of what has been written is presented as Mary Crow Dog related it."

BIBLIOGRAPHY

Sources

Bataille, Gretchen. "Search for an Indian Self." *Mary Brave Bird (1953–). Contemporary Literary Criticism*. Ed. Brigham Narins, Deborah A. Stanley, and George H. Blair. Vol. 93. Detroit: Gale Research, 1996. *Literature Criticism Online*. Web. 21 Oct. 2012.

Crow Dog, Mary, and Richard Erdoes. *Lakota Woman*. New York: Grove, 1990. Print.

Hower, Edward. "A Woman of the Sioux Tribe Eloquently Narrates Her Life." *Chicago Tribune*. Chicago Tribune, 22 Apr. 1990. Web. 20 Oct. 2012.

Rice, Julian. "A Ventriloquy of Anthros: Densmore, Dorsey, Lame Deer and Erdoes." *American Indian Quarterly* 18.2 (1994): 169+. *Literature Resource Center*. Web. 19 Oct. 2012.

RICHARD ERDOES AND HIS COLLABORATIVE AUTOBIOGRAPHIES

Richard Erdoes was born in Austria in 1912 and fled to the United States after Nazi leader Adolf Hitler came to power. Originally an artist and illustrator, Erdoes made the transition to writing when forced to cover for a sick colleague with whom he had been working on assignment. According to his son Erich, Erdoes had always been fascinated with other cultures. Erdoes's visits to the Pine Ridge Reservation, where he saw a Sun Dance in 1967, would be influential in his undertaking a number of books on Native American history and culture, including a series of collaborative autobiographies on AIM activists Lame Deer, Crow Dog, and Dennis Banks, in addition to his work with Brave Bird.

While Erdoes's work was well received by the Lakota community and by general readers, some scholars have raised questions about his methodology and the authenticity of the American Indian voices in his autobiographical works. In the essay "A Ventriloquy of Anthros: Densmore, Dorsey, Lame Deer and Erdoes," Julian Rice criticizes Erdoes on several counts, including his alleged mining of earlier anthropological works for stories to put in the mouths of his coauthors. "Speaking to the mass-market, Euroamerican consumer community," Rice opines, "Richard Erdoes speaks less to enlighten than to preserve the illusion of a heroic presence with whom everyone will identify and whose wisdom everyone will buy."

Wise, Christopher, and R. Todd Wise. "Mary Brave Bird Speaks: A Brief Interview." *Studies in American Indian Literatures* 10:4 (1998): 1–8. Print.

———. "A Conversation with Mary Brave Bird." *American Indian Quarterly* 24:3 (2000): 482–93. Print.

Further Reading

Banks, Dennis, and Richard Erdoes. *Ojibwa Warrior: Dennis Banks and the Rise of the American Indian Movement*. Norman: University of Oklahoma Press, 2004. Print.

Brave Bird, Mary, and Richard Erdoes. *Ohitika Woman*. New York: Grove, 1993. Print.

Crow Dog, Leonard, and Richard Erdoes. *Crow Dog: Four Generations of Sioux Medicine Men*. New York: Harper, 1995. Print.

Matthiessen, Peter. *In the Spirit of Crazy Horse*. New York: Penguin, 1991. Print.

McCluskey, Sally. "'Black Elk Speaks': And So Does John Neihardt." *Western American Literature* 6.4 (1972): 231–42. Rpt. in *Twentieth-Century Literary Criticism*. Ed. Paula Kepos. Vol. 33. Detroit: Gale Research, 1989. *Literature Resource Center*. Web. 20 Oct. 2012.

Rielly, Edward. *Legends of American Indian Resistance*. Santa Barbara: ABC-CLIO, 2011. Print.

Rios, Theodore, and Kathleen Mullen Sands. *Telling a Good One: The Process of a Native American Collaborative Biography*. Lincoln: University of Nebraska Press, 2000. Print.

Daisy Gard

Let My People Go

Albert Luthuli

❖ **Key Facts**

Time Period:
Mid-20th Century

Relevant Historical Events:
Apartheid; drafting of the ANC's Freedom Charter; growth of apartheid resistance

Nationality:
South African

Keywords:
apartheid; civil rights; race

OVERVIEW

In *Let My People Go* (1962), Chief Albert Luthuli tells of living under South African apartheid. Born in 1898 to a line of chiefs and going on to work as an educator, an organizer, and the president of the African National Congress (ANC), Luthuli describes how life for nonwhite South Africans went from one of dignity to humiliation during the eras of segregation and apartheid. He traces the rise of land and education reform for those South Africans who were pushed out of cities and white-collar jobs toward farms and manual labor. When apartheid became the nation's official policy in 1948, Luthuli began to organize militant, nonviolent protests. A devout Christian, he recognized the benefits that came to South Africa from Europe, particularly Christianity and the ideas of the Enlightenment, but in his autobiography, he decries the "slave system" that outlawed protests, voting, and traveling without a "pass" for nonwhite South Africans.

Written with the help of a pastor, Charles Hooper, and his wife Sheila Hooper, *Let My People Go* appeared after Luthuli was already a leader in South Africa and known internationally as a nonviolent activist. At the start of apartheid, he had traveled to the United States to speak out against the oppressive laws and the growing segregation of South Africa. By the time he wrote the book, he was banned by the Nationalist government from entering any major city, attending any gathering, and having contact with the ANC. The autobiography, published just five years before his death under suspicious circumstances in 1967, is useful for its perspectives on preapartheid South Africa and the collective black struggle for liberation.

HISTORICAL AND LITERARY CONTEXT

Let My People Go exposes the racism of the National Party, which came to power in 1948. The policies regarding the separation of the nonwhite and white populations became more severe in the 1950s with laws such as the Group Areas Act (1950), which exiled nonwhites from desirable real estate, and the Pass Laws Act (1952), which required nonwhites to carry a pass whenever they traveled in the newly designated "white" areas. Any white person could demand that a nonwhite produce a pass for inspection. These pieces of legislation led to massive boycotts and strikes throughout the country, serving to galvanize the growing black political movement.

Before Luthuli began writing his autobiography, he had been acquitted of charges of high treason for his part in drafting the Freedom Charter for the People's Congress in 1955. Other antiapartheid leaders, including Nelson Mandela, with whom Luthuli was jailed, had received life sentences. The Treason Trials, begun in 1956, marked a change, as Europeans, Indians, and Africans were arrested *en masse*. Luthuli remarks in *Let My People Go* that "the resistance has long ceased to be a matter of race—it is not the dark skin versus the light, but a loose confederation of people of all classes." This insight prompted him to begin organizing with and speaking to large groups of white apartheid resisters, which, in turn, led to his arrest again in 1959. Upon release, Luthuli was confined to his home in Groutville for five years, banned from travel and public speaking. His autobiography was written during this exile.

Luthuli was a proponent of Mohandas Gandhi's theories of faith-based nonviolent resistance, and his autobiography goes the way of Gandhi's *An Autobiography, or The Story of My Experiments with Truth* (written in installments in the 1920s) by telling the political history of his country via his own experience and activism. However, Luthuli is more egalitarian than his predecessor, focusing on collective gains and commending the organizational work done by women.

After Luthuli's book was published, other antiapartheid autobiographical literature conformed to his

Albert Luthuli at his home in Groutville, Natal Province, South Africa, in 1961. © AP IMAGES

attention to political details as well as his emphasis on the collective struggle. Among these works are novelist Richard Rive's *Writing Black: An Author's Notebook* (1981) and Mandela's *Long Walk to Freedom* (1995). Although Luthuli did not write another book, he published numerous articles and forewords, including "Our Struggles for Progress" and "We Don't Want Crumbs," both of which appeared in the South African journal *New Age* in 1962.

THEMES AND STYLE

Let My People Go sheds light on the many ways the apartheid system worked to oppress nonwhites in South Africa. Frequently pausing to explain events at which he was not present but helped to organize across the country, Luthuli provides a picture of black South Africans' desperation to be free of oppressive laws. The nonviolent resistance to this oppression centered on mass disregard for "Europeans Only" postings, which were "found across the length and breadth of the country," everywhere from train stations to doctors' offices. Nonwhites were also required to have permission to travel in public spaces such as towns or roadsides and to carry their pass. Luthuli burned his pass in protest in 1960, and he writes that many others also "voluntarily destroyed the symbol of bondage … spontaneously, without urging."

Luthuli's objective was to use the autobiographical form to tell the collective story of South Africa and its struggle. *Let My People Go* begins with a story of the Zulu nation leader Shaka, who permitted whites to settle near his people. This unconventional opening, which situates Luthuli's life in a South Africa committed to multiculturalism, proves to be the rule for the rest of the text. While much of the focus is on nonwhites, whose struggles often resulted in police brutality, poverty, and starvation, Luthuli also makes constant note of solidarity among whites and blacks. He writes that "more significant than the colour bar in South Africa now, is the bar which stands between those who place their faith in rule by force and violence, and those who repudiate the police state."

Luthuli maintains a humble tone throughout his text. He "accuses" himself "of having contributed too little," singling out instead the unnamed activists across the country for bringing about change. He includes the Freedom Charter in the appendix, a collectively written document by activist leaders across South Africa, in keeping with this sentiment. The Charter opens by declaring that "South Africa belongs to all who live in it, black and white" and goes on to call for voting rights, equal representation in government, fair trials, and an end to indentured servitude.

CRITICAL DISCUSSION

Luthuli's text was warmly received upon its publication, perhaps garnering extra attention because he had won the 1960 Nobel Peace Prize. Early reviews highlighted the timeliness of *Let My People Go* as well as

THE SHARPEVILLE SHOOTINGS IN SOUTH AFRICA

In 1960 in South Africa, the African National Congress (ANC), led by Chief Albert Luthuli, planned a nationwide nonviolent protest against the Reference Books, or "passes." The idea was to stage a large movement that captured the national imagination while sustaining few casualties. However, the radical left-wing Pan African Congress (PAC) and its leader, Robert Sobukwe, called for all nonwhite citizens to leave their passes at home and go to the police, openly declaring that they had done so. This resulted in demonstrations across South Africa; in the Sharpeville township the police responded with gunfire, killing sixty-nine people on March 21.

Luthuli responded to the police actions by calling for a national day of mourning on March 28. He recounts in *Let My People Go* how he "asked people to stay home, and treat it as a day of prayer." Striving to "be rid" of his "shackles," Luthuli publicly burned his Reference Book, with others following suit. He was arrested for inciting riots, and a State of Emergency was issued. In April both the ANC and the PAC were banned under the Unlawful Organizations Act (1960). The Pass Laws Act would not be repealed until 1986. The ANC ban was lifted in 1990, which was one of the key events signaling the end of apartheid.

Luthuli's persistent humility. African studies scholar Violaine Junod commented in the September 1962 issue of *Africa Today* that *Let My People Go* "serves to remind us all that Africa is not yet free; that there remain important pockets of white resistance to black men's emergence." Bishop Ambrose Reeves also viewed the book as something of an educational tool. In a review in *International Affairs* in October of that same year, he remarked that Luthuli's text was ideal for those "anxious to understand the struggle for liberation in South Africa."

After Luthuli's death in 1967, his autobiography received less attention than his legacy of nonviolent organizing. Luthuli scholar Dorothy C. Woodson has drawn extensively on *Let My People Go* to repair the details of his life as well as those of South African activism. She argues in her 1986 bio-bibliography in *History in Africa* that "a re-evaluation" of Luthuli's autobiography, in addition to his other writings and speeches, does not reveal him to be "too passive," as was sometimes the criticism directed at him in his lifetime. Instead, Woodson notes, "Luthuli was militant" in his nonviolence and "his increasing impatience with the government." Subsequent scholars have followed Woodson's lead and used *Let My People Go* as a guide to a time when manipulation of historical events was the rule for state-controlled media.

Scholars have turned to Luthuli's autobiography for a reliable analysis of the events in South Africa between 1900 and 1960. Stephen Zunes, in his 1999 article in the *Journal of Modern African Studies,* cites *Let My People Go* at length to support his argument that the white South African "government felt threatened by the use of massive, disciplined non-violent resistance." Scholars Jabulani Sithole and Sibongiseni Mkhize support this view of Luthuli's text. In their 2000 article in *History and Theory,* they demonstrate that Luthuli has been used by both the extreme right and radical left to further projects of state or guerrilla warfare. Sithole and Mkhize refer to *Let My People Go* for the most authoritative representation of Luthuli as a politician and organizer.

BIBLIOGRAPHY

Sources

Junod, Violaine. "He Stopped Waiting for a Change of Heart." Rev. of *Let My People Go,* by Albert Luthuli. *Africa Today* 9.7 (1962): 11–12. *JSTOR.* Web. 18 Nov. 2012.

Luthuli, Albert J. *Let My People Go.* New York: McGraw, 1962. Print.

Reeves, Ambrose. Rev. of *Let My People Go,* by Albert Luthuli. *International Affairs* 38.4 (1962): 520. *JSTOR.* Web. 18 Nov. 2012.

Woodson, Dorothy C. "Albert Luthuli and the African National Congress: A Bio-Bibliography." *History in Africa* 13 (1986): 345–62. *JSTOR.* Web. 18 Nov. 2012.

Zunes, Stephen. "The Role of Non-Violent Action in the Downfall of Apartheid." *Journal of Modern African Studies* 37.1 (1999): 137–69. *JSTOR.* Web. 18 Nov. 2012.

Further Reading

Luthuli, Albert J. "South Africa Shall Have Its Freedom." *Africa Today* 3.5 (1956): 2–5. *JSTOR.* Web. 18 Nov. 2012.

Mandela, Nelson. *Long Walk to Freedom: An Autobiography of Nelson Mandela.* Boston: Back Bay, 1995. Print.

Marx, Shula. Rev. of *Let My People Go,* by Albert Luthuli. *Journal of African History* 4.1 (1963): 145–46. *JSTOR.* Web. 18 Nov. 2012.

Reeves, Ambrose. *Shooting at Sharpeville: The Agony of South Africa.* London: Houghton, 1961. Print.

Sithole, Jabulani, and Sibongiseni Mkhize. "Truth or Lies? Selective Memories, Imagings, and Representations of Chief Albert John Luthuli in Recent Political Discourses." *History and Theory* 39.4 (2000): 69–85. *JSTOR.* Web. 18 Nov. 2012.

Caitlin Moore

The Long Walk to Freedom
Nelson Mandela

OVERVIEW

Nelson Mandela's autobiography *The Long Walk to Freedom* (1994) is an account of the author's struggle to end the rule of South Africa's minority white government and its apartheid policies. The work traces Mandela's life from a childhood spent in poverty through his early political activity, his leadership of the African National Congress (ANC), and the twenty-seven years he spent in prison after being convicted of sabotage and conspiracy. As he relates the story of his life, Mandela constructs a narrative of his country in the twentieth century, reminding readers of South Africa's history of injustice and expressing hope for the future.

Published shortly after Mandela assumed the presidency of South Africa, *The Long Walk to Freedom* is a statement of his continued commitment to the struggle for freedom and equality. The book was well reviewed by critics and readers, who celebrated the success of the worldwide movement to secure his freedom. Although he served just one term as president of his country, his legacy as a leader in the fight against an unjust system remains significant. Today *The Long Walk to Freedom* is notable as both a historical record of apartheid and as a portrait of human perseverance in the face of injustice.

HISTORICAL AND LITERARY CONTEXT

Mandela's story is inextricably bound to the history of apartheid, which was rooted in the practice of racial segregation common in the European colonies through the early twentieth century. Apartheid became law in South Africa after Daniel François Malan's National Party came to power in 1948 and the government enacted multiple bills ensuring apartness of the races, starting with the Prohibition of Mixed Marriages Act in 1949. In addition to passing laws enforcing separate housing, education, and medical facilities, the government suppressed growing resistance to apartheid. The Suppression of Communism Act (1950) outlawed the Communist Party of South Africa (later SACP), using language broad enough to apply to most organized resistance activities regardless of whether they were based in communist ideology. Following the banning of the SACP, many antiapartheid constituents shifted their activities to the ANC and the militant group Umkhonto we Sizwe (MK). An active member of MK, Mandela was arrested; convicted of conspiracy; and sent to prison in 1962, where he remained for twenty-seven years.

Over the course of his imprisonment, local, and later international, pressure was increasingly brought to bear on the South African government to free him. He began writing his autobiography in 1975 and composed much of *The Long Walk to Freedom* in secret during his imprisonment. The book was finished following his release in 1990 and published in 1994, the year after he assumed the presidency of South Africa. As the title suggests, the book focuses on Mandela's struggle for freedom—particularly for other black South Africans. That he was willing to sacrifice his personal freedom in service of the cause adds credence to his work.

Mandela's autobiography is an important text in the literature of twentieth-century South Africa, much of which documents the suffering of black South Africans under apartheid and their struggle for racial equality and freedom, which was sometimes aided by antiapartheid Afrikaners, or white South Africans. Both fictional and nonfiction works have offered portraits of the privations suffered by black South Africans under apartheid. Alan Paton's classic *Cry, the Beloved Country,* published in 1948 just before apartheid became institutionalized, is a protest against the devastation wrought by forces of urbanization and the unjust social policies of the white government. Writers J. M. Coetzee, Nadine Gordimer, and André Brink have also made significant semiautobiographical contributions to the genre.

The Long Walk to Freedom was followed by several biographies of Mandela's life. *Mandela: An Authorized Biography* (1999) by Mandela's friend Anthony Sampson touches on several issues not dealt with in *The Long Walk to Freedom,* including the implication that South African president Frederik Willem de Klerk had interfered with Mandela's attempts to start peace talks with the government. In 2010 Mandela published *Conversations with Myself,* a collection of diary entries, calendar pages, letters, and transcripts of his conversations with author Richard Stengel, who ghostwrote the political prisoner's autobiography. Commentators have praised *Conversations with Myself* for filling in the gaps left by the autobiography and for providing insight into Mandela's family life;

❖ **Key Facts**

Time Period:
Late 20th Century

Relevant Historical Events:
End of apartheid; Mandela's incarceration; Mandela's assumption of South African presidency

Nationality:
South African

Keywords:
apartheid; incarceration; civil rights

Nelson Mandela, a painting by Cheik Ledy (1990). Activist and politician Mandela recounts his life in *The Long Walk to Freedom*. © CONTEMPORARY AFRICAN ART COLLECTION LIMITED/CORBIS

personal philosophies; and relationship with his ex-wife, Winnie, a controversial figure in South African public life for her alleged participation in violations of human rights.

THEMES AND STYLE

Central to Mandela's book is his conception of freedom: "To be free is not merely to cast off one's chains, but to live in a way that respects and enhances the freedom of others." Throughout the text, he describes ways in which the people of South Africa were not free under apartheid. Most obviously, black South Africans were forced to live in designated areas with little access to education and no voice in the governance of their country. However, those participating in apartheid, or following its racist tenants, were likewise not free: "A man who takes away another man's freedom is a prisoner of hatred, he is locked behind the bars of prejudice and narrow-mindedness." For Mandela, hate is merely learned; therefore, he is optimistic that wise and responsible leadership can bring out the inherent goodness of South Africans and fundamentally change the nature of their lives.

The Long Walk to Freedom was written under the aegis of the ANC as a way to build political capital for Mandela's new antiapartheid government and its supporters. While ostensibly the story of the South African president's life, it is also a history of his country. Indeed, he explicitly creates this linkage, for example, by describing his realization that "my hunger for the freedom of my own people became a hunger for the freedom of all people, white and black." He acknowledges that his struggle for freedom did not end with his release from prison. Alluding to his new role in leading the country, he writes, "I have taken a moment here to rest, to steal a view of the glorious vista that surrounds me, to look back on the distance I have come. But I can rest only for a moment, for with freedom comes responsibilities, and I dare not linger, for my long walk is not yet ended."

As the autobiography of a resistance leader and prisoner for decades, Mandela's book diplomatically engages with political issues. In a 1994 review for the *New York Times*, Bill Keller notes, "Mr. Mandela has been well served by his collaborator, Richard Stengel, a contributor to *Time* magazine, who preserved the unmistakable voice of Mr. Mandela—polite, good-humored—while curbing his tendency to speak in the collective voice of the movement." Although the book reveals some details of the author's personal life, it is not confessional in nature. Rather, it balances personal stories with the wisdom the author has gained through his experiences: "I learned that courage was not the absence of fear, but the triumph over it. The brave man is not he who does not feel afraid, but he who conquers that fear."

CRITICAL DISCUSSION

The Long Walk to Freedom received almost universally positive reviews when it was published. Mandela's imprisonment had garnered significant international attention in the preceding decade, and critics and the reading public were intensely interested in an autobiographical account of his life and his vision for the future of South Africa. Chris Goodrich, writing in the *Los Angeles Times* in 1995, calls the book "a page turner," adding, "One finishes the book with a single regret—that Mandela fails to indicate his willingness, once he's through straightening out South Africa, to emigrate to [the United States] and start anew." Keller's review, while largely positive, notes, "The candor of the book is less than complete," citing Mandela's failure to meaningfully address the ANC's violence against civilians and allegations of murder against Winnie.

Mandela's autobiography has been regarded as an important record of apartheid and as a living document that provides a model of committed, pragmatic leadership, particularly for other African countries attempting to transition to a more equitable democratic government. Scholar Zodwa Motsa, in a 2009 essay for the *Journal of Literary Studies,* suggests, "The heroic qualities of selflessness, bravery, humanness and responsible leadership that are mirrored in the epic provide a good model for a young nation like South Africa, particularly after the proclamation of its regeneration identity."

The Long Walk to Freedom has largely been treated as a historical document and has yet to attract significant critical attention. While some commentators have pointed out issues that Mandela ignores or glosses over in his account of events, his stature as a Nobel Prize–winning freedom fighter and honorable leader remains largely uncontested. As Keller notes in his review, "Mandela comes swaddled in myth."

BIBLIOGRAPHY

Sources

Goodrich, Chris. "Agitating for Equality: A Political Activist Who Exchanged a Prison Cell for the President's Office." *Los Angeles Times Book Review* 8 Jan. 1995: 3. *Literature Resource Center.* Web. 16 Nov. 2012.

Keller, Bill. "The Practical Mr. Mandela." *New York Times Book Review* 18 Dec. 1994: 1. *Literature Resource Center.* Web. 16 Nov. 2012.

SOUTH AFRICA'S PRESIDENCY AFTER MANDELA

When Nelson Mandela finished his single term as president of South Africa in June 1999, he largely retired from political life. Thabo Mbeki, who had served as Mandela's deputy, assumed the office and served until 2008. Mbeki was praised for fostering economic growth and for his diplomatic work, including his role in brokering an end to political violence in Zimbabwe. However, he was the subject of a number of controversies—most prominently his position that AIDS was caused by factors such as poverty and not by HIV. This position led to disastrous policies and many unnecessary deaths.

Mbeki became embroiled in a power struggle with former deputy Jacob Zuma, and after losing the support of the ANC, he resigned in 2008. Zuma assumed office following the 2009 elections. However, his presidency has been marred by charges of corruption and questions about financial improprieties. Concerns have also been raised about the remilitarization of the police and about legislation such as the Protection of State Information Bill, which limits freedom of expression, one of the fundamental rights that Mandela sought to secure.

Mandela, Nelson. *The Long Walk to Freedom.* New York: Back Bay, 1994. Print.

Motsa, Zodwa. "*Long Walk to Freedom* and the Mutating Face of the Epic." *Journal of Literary Studies* 25.2 (2009): 7. *Literature Resource Center.* Web. 16 Nov. 2012.

Further Reading

Clark, Nancy, and William Worger. *South Africa: The Rise and Fall of Apartheid.* 2nd ed. Harlow: Pearson Education, 2004. Print.

Lodge, Tom. *Nelson Mandela: A Critical Life.* Oxford: Oxford University Press, 2001. Print.

Mandela, Nelson. *Conversations with Myself.* New York: Farrar, Straus and Giroux, 2010. Print.

Mathbane, Mark. *Kaffir Boy: An Autobiography: The True Story of a Black Youth's Coming of Age in Apartheid South Africa.* New York: Touchstone, 1986. Print.

Sampson, Anthony. *Mandela: The Authorized Biography.* New York: Vintage, 2000. Print.

Daisy Gard

Mein Kampf
Adolf Hitler

Key Facts

Time Period:
Mid-20th Century

Relevant Historical Events:
German defeat in World War I; Treaty of Versailles; formation of the Nazi Party

Nationality:
German

Keywords:
Nazism; Hitler; fascism

OVERVIEW

Published in 1925, as Germany still staggered under the disastrous repercussions of World War I, *Mein Kampf* ("My Struggle") is the autobiography and political manifesto of the future German dictator and Nazi leader Adolf Hitler. Originally titled *Four and a Half Years of Struggle against Lies, Stupidity, and Cowardice,* the book is composed of two parts: "A Reckoning," which describes the author's life and the development of his political philosophy, and "The National Socialist Movement," published in 1927, which outlines the history of the Nazi party. Though there is much evidence indicating that several other people had a hand in creating the manuscript of *Mein Kampf,* the book represents Hitler's attempt to redefine himself in heroic terms while presenting his own ethnic hatreds and nationalistic dreams as a glorious plan for the future of the German state and people.

Written in 1923–24, while its author was imprisoned for his militant political activities, Hitler's autobiography emerged during a period of economic chaos and cultural depression in post–World War I Germany. *Mein Kampf* was received with enthusiasm by those Germans who sought scapegoats for their nation's loss of glory and with some trepidation by those who disagreed with his ultra-nationalist agenda. The first English translation was published in 1939, and foreign response to Hitler's plans for the restoration of German power varied from dismissive ridicule to apprehensive horror.

HISTORICAL AND LITERARY CONTEXT

The devastating effects of the First World War engendered vengeful feelings among Germany's enemies. Many blamed German aggression for the war, and they pressured their leaders to enforce punitive measures to ensure that Germany would not rise again with the same might. The Treaty of Versailles, negotiated in June 1919, not only disarmed the German nation by drastically reducing its military, but it also stripped Germany of many provincial lands and foreign colonies. In addition, the treaty required Germany to take full responsibility for causing the war and pay extensive reparations. Though these harsh measures assuaged Allied anger somewhat, they fueled German resentment.

In 1923 France invaded the industrialized Ruhr Valley in an attempt to separate the entire western Rhineland from Germany. At the same time, in the southern region of Bavaria, a movement for secession was gaining strength. Exorbitant reparations led to ruinous inflation of the German economy and increasing desperation among the populace. Feeling the time was right for a dramatic move, Hitler, already a leader in the newly formed National Socialist German Workers' Party, organized a takeover of a meeting of Bavarian leaders in Munich on November 8, 1923. The so-called "Beer Hall Putsch" was successful at first, but Nazi leaders failed to implement the next steps of their plan to take power, and Hitler was arrested and imprisoned in the Bavarian fortress of Landsberg. He remained there for just over a year, using the time to construct his famous autobiography and political vision.

Hitler's autobiographical writing fit into the historically German genre of bildungsroman, a form of personal storytelling describing the growth and development of the protagonist through experience. *Wilhelm Meister's Apprenticeship,* written by Johann Wolfgang von Goethe in 1795–1796, is the prototypical bildungsroman. The end of World War I saw the publication of a number of autobiographies and memoirs, including that of fighter pilot and German hero Baron Manfred von Richthofen, *The Red Air Fighter,* published in 1917. Hitler may have been influenced by the works of American industrialist Henry Ford, who, in addition to his anti-Semitic pamphlets published in the 1920s as *The International Jew,* also wrote an inspirational autobiography titled *My Life and Work* in 1922.

Though it achieved only modest sales in the years immediately following its publication, *Mein Kampf* became increasingly popular alongside the prominence of its author. In 1942 seven million copies were sold, and municipalities were ordered to present a copy to every newly married couple. Though some experts question how many people actually read Hitler's text, the book itself, as a representation of the life of the German leader, became a sort of bible for Germany's Third Reich. Following the defeat of Germany in World War II and the ultimate failure of Hitler's Nazi regime, *Mein Kampf* has generally been viewed with horror and disgust as the testament of a monster, though it continues to be revered as a sacred text by some members of modern right-wing movements.

Adolf Hitler gives the Nazi salute during the Reichsparteitag (Reich national party convention) in 1938. These annual events, commonly called the Nuremberg Rallies, enhanced Hitler's status as a national savior and unified the German people in their allegiance to the Nazi cause. © MEIN KAMPF/ EVERETT COLLECTION

THEMES AND STYLE

The major focus of *Mein Kampf* is the assault on Germany from neighboring nations and from non-Aryan people within, along with Hitler's plans to reestablish a powerful, racially pure state under one strong leader. Embedded in the author's grandiose theses of Aryan superiority and the destructive force of Jewish culture are darker themes of revenge and hate. He extols the Germanic contribution to civilization: "Every manifestation of human culture, every product of art, science and technical skill, which we see before our eyes today, is almost exclusively the product of Aryan creative power." He then gives a grim warning: "If he (the Aryan) should be exterminated or subjugated, then the dark shroud of a new barbarian era would enfold the earth." Even the Jews, in Hitler's view, are focused on Aryan supremacy: "Jewish youth lies in wait for hours on end satanically glaring at and spying on the unconscious girl whom he plans to seduce, adulterating her blood … and thus lowering its cultural and political level so that the Jew might dominate."

The autobiographical sections of Hitler's work do not strictly adhere to fact; rather, he constructs the tale of a glorious leader, changing facts when necessary to the story he wishes to tell. For example, he transforms a reasonably comfortable period in Vienna to a time of toil as a laborer. Hitler uses the device of sharing, or appearing to share, personal stories to build a credible background for the beliefs he intends to impart to his readers: "I am grateful that I was thrown into a world of misery and poverty and thus came to know the people for whom I was afterwards to fight." He uses this same personal experience to introduce the dominant theme of anti-Semitism: "Thus I finally discovered who were the evil spirits leading our people astray."

Hitler was better known as a compelling orator than a writer, and *Mein Kampf*'s style is awkward and stiff, with grammatical and spelling errors in the original text. His tone is frequently harsh and strident, and his reasoning is often confusing: "Only after subjugated races were employed as slaves was a similar fate allotted to animals and not vice-versa…. At first it was the conquered enemy who had to draw the plow and only afterwards did the ox and horse take his place. Nobody else but puling pacifists can consider this a sign of human degradation." He repeatedly lapses into grandiosity as well, with such statements as, "The Goddess of Fate clutched me in her hands and often threatened to smash me, but the will grew stronger as the obstacles increased, and finally the will triumphed."

CRITICAL DISCUSSION

Hitler's nationalistic diatribe found a ready audience in post–World War I Germany, and his rise to power, as chancellor in 1933 and soon thereafter as dictator, increased the popularity and sales of his autobiography. In a 1958 article in *Jewish Social Studies*, C. Caspar quotes a German school textbook of the time that refers to *Mein Kampf* as the "new bible of the people," although Caspar contends that some of Hitler's closest supporters admitted never having read it. Though Germans living in the Third Reich would

THE LIBEL THAT WILL NOT DIE: THE PROTOCOLS OF THE ELDERS OF ZION

In a chapter of his autobiography titled "Race and People," Adolf Hitler draws on the authority of a document called *The Protocols of the Elders of Zion* as proof of a Jewish conspiracy to undermine Aryan culture. Surfacing in Europe around the turn of the twentieth century, *The Protocols* purports to be the product of a gathering of Jewish leaders in a Basil, Switzerland, cemetery in 1897. Twenty-four protocols, or procedures, outline various aspects of an international Jewish plan for world domination. First published in Russian in 1903, *The Protocols* was translated into German, French, and English in 1920. Henry Ford's anti-Semitic pamphlets, *The International Jew*, were derived from the work.

Scholars and critics immediately questioned the authenticity of *The Protocols*. In 1921 the *Times* of London declared the document a forgery, and in 1935 a Swiss court fined Nazi activists for distributing them. However, in spite of continuing refutations and evidence of their illegitimacy, including denunciations by a Russian court in 1993 and the U.S. Department of State in 2004, neo-Nazis and other right-wing groups continue to cite *The Protocols* as evidence of a dangerous worldwide conspiracy of Jews. These groups use the document much as Hitler did in *Mein Kampf* to channel societal frustration, legitimize racism, and provide a simplistic scapegoat for economic and political problems.

have been unlikely to offer criticism of their leader's writing, the foreign press was not so constrained. John Chamberlain, writing for the *New York Times* in 1933, called it "turgid and intensely soporific" with "flashes of shrewdness." M. S. Call warned, in a 1939 edition of *World Affairs*, "Perhaps it is good for the Democracies to study that which caused Hitler."

Few works of literature have had such an immediately disastrous impact as Hitler's *Mein Kampf*. Considered by many to be a virtual blueprint of Hitler's plan for world domination and the extermination of Jews and others he considered "defective," the book has continued to have a profound societal effect almost a century after its publication. Translated into sixteen languages before the end of World War II, *Mein Kampf* has served as both inspiration for later extreme rightist movements and a reminder of the potential outcome of racist ideology. Scholars and political analysts continue to examine *Mein Kampf* in an effort to unearth deeper levels of meaning in the text that might work to explain Hitler's motivations and the extraordinarily destructive events he orchestrated.

One of the topics debated among analysts of *Mein Kampf* is how much of the text was actually written by Hitler himself. Many critics, including Caspar, confidently assert that large parts of the manuscript were conceived or at least revised by Hitler supporters such as Rudolph Hess, Father Bernhard Staempfle, and Karl Haushofer. However, in a 2006 German study, Othmar Plöckinger debunks this idea, claiming that the work is Hitler's alone. In *New German Critique* (2011), Eva Horn and Joel Golb describe the work as a "self-stylizing autobiography," stating, "*Mein Kampf*… is a narrative of self-transformation, the invention of a political identity and the rhetorical staging of self-affection: the story of a man discovering his mission in his hatred for Jews and creating national unity by sharing this hatred with others."

BIBLIOGRAPHY

Sources

Call, M. S. Rev. of *Mein Kampf*, by Adolf Hitler. *World Affairs* 102.2 (1939): 119–20. Print.

Caspar, C. "Mein Kampf: A Best Seller." *Jewish Social Studies* 20.1 (1958): 3–16. Print.

Chamberlain, John. "Books of the Times." Rev. of *Mein Kampf*, by Adolf Hitler. *New York Times (1923-Current file)* 11 Oct. 1933: 21. *ProQuest Historical Newspapers: The New York Times (1851–2008)*. Web. 15 Oct. 2012.

Horn, Eva and Joel Golb. "Work on Charisma: Writing Hitler's Biography." *New German Critique: Narrating Charisma* 114 (2011): 95–114. Print.

Weikart, Richard. "Cutting through the Legends Surrounding *Mein Kampf*." Rev. of *Geschichte eines Buches: Adolf Hitler's "Mein Kampf" 1922–1945*, by Othmar Plöckinger. *Hnet: Humanities and Social Services Online*. Web. 17 Oct. 2012.

Worthington, Jay. "Mein Royalties." *Cabinet*. Cabinet Magazine, Spring 2003. Web. 16 Oct. 2012.

Further Reading

Burke, Kenneth. "The Rhetoric of Hitler's 'Battle.'" *The Philosophy of Literary Form: Studies in Symbolic Action*. 3rd ed. Berkeley: University of California Press, 1973. 191–220. Rpt. in *Literature Resource Center*. Web. 17 Oct. 2012.

Hamann, Brigitte. *Hitler's Vienna. A Dictator's Apprenticeship*. Trans. Thomas Thornton. Oxford: Oxford University Press, 1999. Print.

Kershaw, Ian. *Hitler: 1889–1936 Hubris*. New York: Norton, 2000. Print.

Webman, Esther, ed. *The Global Impact of the Protocols of the Elders of Zion*. New York: Routledge, 2011. Print.

Werchmeister, O. K. "Hitler the Artist." *Critical Inquiry* 23.2 (1997): 270–97. Rpt. in *Literature Resource Center*. Detroit: Gale, 2012. *Literature Resource Center*. Web. 16 Oct. 2012.

Tina Gianoulis

Narrative of the Life of Frederick Douglass

Frederick Douglass

OVERVIEW

First published in 1845, *Narrative of the Life of Frederick Douglass* is one of the best-known slave narratives to emerge from antebellum America. In it, Douglass traces his early memories as a Maryland slave, his struggles with abusive masters, his realization of the importance of education as a means of liberating himself both literally and figuratively from slavery, his escape to New York in 1838, and the beginnings of his career as a public speaker and abolitionist. Throughout the text, Douglass is unwavering in his indictment of the corrupting influences of slavery on all whom it touches. Published two decades before the Thirteenth Amendment (1865) officially ended slavery, the autobiography offers impassioned descriptions of the evils of the institution, but it withholds the names of those who helped Douglass educate himself and escape, out of the author's fear that "were I to give a minute statement of all the facts, it is not only possible, but quite probable, that others would thereby be involved in the most embarrassing difficulties."

When Douglass's autobiography was published, he was already a prominent speaker on the lecture circuit organized by abolitionist William Lloyd Garrison. The work was penned in part as a means of further disseminating Douglass's story in aid of the abolitionist cause, and in part to silence skeptics who questioned how an African American, much less a former slave, could speak so eloquently. Immediately popular with abolitionist audiences hungry for details of slave life, the text helped to elevate Douglass to celebrity status within abolitionist circles and further stirred the passions of those already devoted to the cause. Today the work is one of the best-known slave narratives and is considered among the most important and influential works of nineteenth-century American literature.

HISTORICAL AND LITERARY CONTEXT

Narrative of the Life of Frederick Douglass offers a biting critique of the institution of slavery, which was flourishing in the American South at the time of the book's publication in 1845. Although the United States had banned the international slave trade in 1807, and although the spread of slavery westward had been largely prevented by the Missouri Compromise of 1820, the Southern economy remained dependent on slave labor, and resistance to abolition was strong in the South. In the North, however, the movement to immediately and permanently abolish slavery had gained momentum in the 1830s. This new wave was fueled in part by the efforts of Garrison and his pioneering newspaper the *Liberator*, which began circulating in 1831, and in part by the work of the American Anti-Slavery Society, which was established in 1833.

When Douglass's autobiography was published, it included a preface by Garrison, in which the abolitionist discusses the "fortunate, most fortunate occurrence" of having first met Douglass at an abolitionist gathering. It also includes a letter from abolitionist Wendell Phillips attesting to the strength and power of Douglass's work. The sponsorship of Garrison and Phillips was perceived to grant credibility to Douglass's story, while the fugitive slave's testimony was in turn seen to add credibility to existing accounts of the horrors of slavery, while counteracting common defenses of the institution by demonstrating the intelligence and humanity of enslaved peoples. The work also, however, drew the attention of the owner from whom Douglass had escaped, and rumors circulated that he would be captured and returned to slavery. In order to prevent such an occurrence, Douglass's supporters collected the funds necessary to purchase his freedom in 1846. Following the success of the autobiography, Douglass remained active in the abolitionist movement, becoming increasingly militant. He aided in the planning of John Brown's ill-fated raid on Harper's Ferry in 1859, and later he helped recruit African American soldiers to serve in the Union Army. After the Civil War, he used his influence in service of a number of other progressive causes, including racial equality and women's suffrage.

Douglass's autobiography is part of a broad tradition of antislavery writings that flourished in the years leading up to the American Civil War, one that notably includes Harriet Beecher Stowe's influential 1852 novel *Uncle Tom's Cabin*. Among the immediate predecessors of Douglass's text was *American Slavery as It Is* (1838), a collection of firsthand accounts of slavery authored by Theodore Weld and published by the American Anti-Slavery Society. In his autobiography, Douglass makes reference to *The Columbian Orator* (1797),

Key Facts

Time Period:
Mid-19th Century

Relevant Historical Events:
slavery (abolished 1865)

Nationality:
American

Keywords:
slavery; abolition; personal history; literacy

ADVERSITY AND RESISTANCE

Frederick Douglass in England, describing his former life as a slave in the United States. Hand-colored woodcut. © NORTH WIND PICTURE ARCHIVES/ALAMY

a collection of texts edited by Caleb Bingham that was widely used in education. He describes having been moved by a dialogue between master and slave in which "the whole argument in behalf of slavery was brought forward by the master, all of which was disposed of by the slave." He also remembers having been affected by "one of [Richard Brinsley] Sheridan's mighty speeches on and in behalf of Catholic emancipation," which he describes as offering "a bold denunciation of slavery and a powerful vindication of human rights" that inspired his own life and work. Douglass's text is also part of a tradition of slave narratives that also includes Olaudah Equiano's *The Interesting Narrative of the Life of Olaudah Equiano* (1789), which helped drive the abolition of the slave trade in the British Empire in 1807.

The success of Douglass's autobiography, coupled with growing interest in the lives and experience of slaves, led to a proliferation of slave narratives. Among the most prominent of these are Harriet Jacobs's *Incidents in the Life of a Slave Girl* (1861), which offers insight into the unique (and often sexual) perils of slavery for women. Douglass published two additional autobiographical works. *My Bondage and My Freedom* (1855) offers a further discussion of his path from slavery to political activism, although, like its predecessor, it suppresses information considered unsafe for publication. These suppressed details would not emerge fully until *Life and Times of Frederick Douglass* (1881), the most complete portrait of Douglass's experiences. A revised edition of the latter was published in 1892, three years before his death.

THEMES AND STYLE

The central theme of Douglass's autobiography is that slavery is an immoral and unchristian practice that destroys the enslaved and corrupts even good-hearted masters. Throughout the text, Douglass offers examples of the brutal acts committed against both male and female slaves, including the fatal beating of a female slave after the young woman fell asleep and failed to hear the cries of the infant in her care. The text also challenges common misperceptions used to justify slavery. Douglass records, for example, his surprise at learning that in the North, people "speak of the singing among slaves, as evidence of their commitment and happiness," going on to assert that "it is impossible to conceive of a greater mistake." He also details the effects of slavery on slave owners. He describes how Mrs. Auld, the mistress who gave him his first reading lessons, had her "heavenly smiles" and "kind heart" destroyed by the "fatal poison of irresponsible power," and details the hypocrisy of masters who attempt to use Biblical scripture to justify their decidedly unchristian treatment of their slaves.

Although Douglass's reason for writing his autobiography was ostensibly political, the text also reveals an intense personal desire to claim the history and autonomy that have been denied to him. In the opening pages of the text, he explains that "I have no accurate knowledge of my age, never having seen any authentic record containing it." Addressing rumors that his master was his father, Douglass notes that "of the correctness of this opinion, I know nothing; the means of knowing was withheld from me." As his story unfolds, he depicts his growing awareness that the withholding of information and education are powerful tools through which masters oppress and control their slaves. He describes how he began to seize control of his life, first through self-education, and later by standing up to the brutal Mr. Covey, famously noting of their struggle, "you have seen how a man was made a slave; you shall see how a slave was made a man." Although the autobiography represents Douglass's attempts to claim the power and authority to tell his own story, the necessity of suppressing details demonstrates the degree to which that story continued to be determined by external forces. Douglass's ongoing use of autobiography to reclaim those details reveals the importance that he placed on self-determination and self-narration.

Stylistically, *Narrative of the Life of Frederick Douglass* is notable for its first-person narration, intellectual tenor, and often poetic style. Robert B. Stepto argues in his 1979 book *From Behind the Veil* that Douglass "fashions language as finely honed and balanced as an aphorism or Popean [written by Alexander Pope] couplet." In one particularly noteworthy passage, Douglass relates an incident in which watching ships in the nearby Chesapeake Bay occasioned an address to those vessels, "You are loosed from your moorings, and are free; I am fast in my chains, and am a slave! You move merrily before the gentle gale, and I sadly before the bloody whip! You are freedom's swift-winged angels, that fly round the world; I am confined in bands of iron!"

CRITICAL DISCUSSION

Upon publication, *Narrative of the Life of Frederick Douglass* was an immediate success, selling well and drawing extensive commentary. Its popularity has been attributed in part to the fact that it was considered more authentic than many other slave narratives of the day, which, due to the illiteracy of their subjects, were transcribed and often altered by white abolitionists. The text was particularly well reviewed in Garrison's *Liberator*, which described it in a May 30, 1845, article as "the most thrilling work which the American press ever issued—and the most important," asserting that "if it does not open the eyes of this people, they must be petrified into eternal sleep."

In the years following the Civil War and the abolition of slavery, slave narratives lost much of their popular appeal. Although his political activism kept Douglass in the public eye, his later autobiographies failed to achieve the critical acclaim of the first. Despite the relative obscurity of his later autobiographies, *Narrative of the Life of Frederick Douglass* continues to attract considerable critical attention. Scholars have approached the work through a wide range of analytical frameworks, considering the value not only of its historical testimony, but also of its insights into nineteenth-century racial and gender politics, its literary qualities, and its construction as autobiography.

Douglass's text is often read alongside Jacobs's *Incidents in the Life of a Slave Girl*, as a means of examining the gendering of the slave experience. Typical of such scholarship is Winifred Morgan's 1994 *American Studies* article, in which she argues that Douglass "emphasizes his ability to speak in public as well as to read and write," an emphasis she associates with conventions of masculinity, while Jacobs, by contrast, "emphasizes her womanliness" by highlighting personal relationships. Scholars have also been interested in how Douglass constructs selfhood through his autobiography. Writing in the *Mississippi Quarterly*, Vince Brewton traces "two competing authorial personae: the fugitive slave who seeks to transform himself into the slave's opposite, the free man; and the de facto free man regarding his former life as a slave from the safe distance of the memoirist."

THE WPA AND SLAVE AUTOBIOGRAPHIES

During the Great Depression the Works Progress Administration (WPA) undertook as a project the compiling of autobiographies of former slaves. Between 1936 and 1938, more than two thousand former slaves were interviewed—and in many cases photographed—by WPA journalists. Some of the interviews were recorded. The interviewees were drawn from a wide swath of the American South.

The men and women who told their stories related diverse experiences of slavery and its aftermath. Among them were house slaves, field hands, and enslaved tradesmen. Some had experienced brutality firsthand; others had merely witnessed it. Many described the sexual abuse of female slaves by their masters and the frequency with which masters fathered the children of their slaves. They recalled their daily lives as slaves, discussing their working conditions, diet, and family lives. Many of the former slaves had fathers or other relatives who had fought in the Civil War. Some recalled vivid memories of the war, emancipation, and the transition to freedom. Following the war, many had gone on to improve their educations, buy land, and establish careers in a variety of fields.

During the 1970s the stories were collected as *The American Slave: A Composite Autobiography* (1972–79) under the editorship of George P. Rawick. Although scholars have identified a potential for bias arising from the fact that the interviews were conducted by white journalists during a period of social segregation, the collection remains one of the most comprehensive accounts of slave life.

BIBLIOGRAPHY

Sources

Brewton, Vince. "'Bold Defiance Took Its Place'— 'Respect' and Self-Making in *Narrative of the Life of Frederick Douglass, an American Slave*." *Mississippi Quarterly* 58.3–4 (2005): 703–17. Print.

Douglass, Frederick. *Narrative of the Life of Frederick Douglass, an American Slave. Autobiographies: Narrative of the Life of Frederick Douglass, an American Slave; My Bondage and My Freedom; Life and Times of Frederick Douglass.* Ed. Henry Louis Gates Jr. New York: Library of America, 1996. 1–102. Print.

"Frederick Douglass." Rev. of *Narrative of the Life of Frederick Douglass*, by Frederick Douglass. *Liberator* 30 May 1845: 86. Print.

Morgan, Winifred. "Gender-Related Difference in the Slave Narratives of Harriet Jacobs and Frederick Douglass." *American Studies* 35.2 (1994): 73–94. Print.

Stepto, Robert B. *From Behind the Veil: A Study of Afro-American Narrative.* Urbana: University of Illinois Press, 1979. Print.

Further Reading

Andrews, William L., and Henry Louis Gates Jr., eds. *Slave Narratives*. New York: Penguin, 2000. Print.

Berlin, Ira. *Generations of Captivity: A History of American Slaves*. New York: Viking, 2010. Print.

———. *Many Thousands Gone: The First Two Centuries of Slavery in North America*. Cambridge, Mass.: Belknap, 1998. Print.

Butterfield, Stephen. *Black Autobiography in America*. Amherst: University of Massachusetts Press, 1974. Print.

Davis, Charles T., and Henry Louis Gates Jr. *The Slave's Narrative*. New York: Oxford University Press, 1985. Print.

McBride, Dwight A. *Impossible Witnesses: Truth, Abolitionism, and Slave Testimony*. New York: New York University Press, 2001. 151–72.

McFeely, William S. *Frederick Douglass*. New York: W. W. Norton, 1995. Print.

Rawick, George P., ed. *The American Slave: A Composite Autobiography*. Westport, Conn.: Greenwood, 1972–79. Print.

Weld, Theodore Dwight. *American Slavery as It Is: Testimony of a Thousand Witnesses*. New York: American Anti-Slavery Society, 1839. Print.

Greta Gard

Rosa Parks
My Story
Rosa Parks, Jim Haskins

OVERVIEW

Rosa Parks: My Story, written by civil rights activist Rosa Parks with Jim Haskins and published in 1992, is a memoir of Parks's life and the development of her political ideals. Propelled into fame by an act of courage in 1955 when she refused to give up her seat on a Montgomery, Alabama, bus to a white passenger, Parks became a symbol and a heroine of the burgeoning civil rights movement. In *My Story* she goes beyond the mythology about her famous protest and presents a portrait of a committed activist, from her roots growing up in a system of racial injustice and learning to question that system to the pragmatic realities of working within a movement for social change.

At a time of conservative attacks on many of the gains of the civil rights movement, Parks's memoir was welcomed by people of color and white progressives as a reminder of the courage and determination required to challenge injustice. *My Story* was almost universally hailed for its quiet dignity and the powerful simplicity of its descriptions of the segregated South and the ordinary people who refused to accept their degradation. Aimed primarily at young readers, the work soon became a standard text for those studying the history of the civil rights movement.

HISTORICAL AND LITERARY CONTEXT

Government-sanctioned racial discrimination had its roots in the 1896 Supreme Court decision *Plessy v. Ferguson,* which permitted black passengers to be barred from first-class railway cars and laid the groundwork for an institutionalized system of segregation. "Separate but equal" became the doctrine that legitimized the relegation of blacks to inferior accommodations in almost every public venue in the southern United States and some in the North as well. African Americans had struggled against racial injustice from the time of their enslavement, and a new wave of protest began in the mid-1940s. Blacks who had served their country during World War II found it difficult to return to second-class status as civilians. Those who did not leave the South launched organizations and campaigns of action to promote black electoral power and black equality.

Though Parks's memoir is set during the early moments of the civil rights movement of the 1950s and 1960s, it was published during a period of backlash to that movement. The 1980s saw a number of challenges to progressive policies such as affirmative action, which had been implemented in an effort to offset decades of racial inequality. The rise of vocal white supremacist organizations and a number of well-publicized instances of racially motivated attacks on black Americans led to a feeling of discouragement and pessimism among many people of color and their progressive allies. At the same time a new generation of activists continued to work to give legitimacy to the pioneers who fought segregation. In 1983 President Ronald Reagan signed a bill creating a national holiday celebrating the birthday of civil rights leader Martin Luther King Jr. Parks, always uncomfortable with her fame as the patron saint of the civil rights movement, chose this moment to write her story, which puts a very human face on her contribution to the movement she helped launch.

The autobiography had been a staple of African American literature since the slave narratives of the 1800s. Writers such as Booker T. Washington (*The Story of My Life and Work,* 1901) and Sojourner Truth (*Narrative of Sojourner Truth,* 1884) had written the stories of their lives to explain their choices and to promote social change. Writers such as Langston Hughes (*I Wonder as I Wander,* 1956) and Paul Robeson (*Here I Stand,* 1958) continued this tradition at the dawn of the civil rights movement, recounting their experiences of segregation and the choices they made to challenge the racist system. The feminist movement of the late 1960s and 1970s led to an increased interest in the stories of women's lives, such as Anne Moody's 1968 memoir *Coming of Age in Mississippi* and Audre Lorde's 1982 autobiography *Zami: A New Spelling of My Name.* In addition to Parks's book, a number of other memoirs of the Montgomery boycott were published during the 1980s and 1990s, including Jo Ann Gibson Robinson's *The Montgomery Bus Boycott and the Women Who Started It* (1987) and Fred Gray's *Bus Ride to Justice* (1994).

My Story helped introduce a new generation to the struggles and sacrifices of those who combated the racial prejudice and discrimination that was the legacy of slavery in the United States. Adult readers who had admired Parks as a pioneer of the movement

❖ Key Facts

Time Period:
Late 20th Century

Relevant Historical Events:
Civil rights movement; Parks's refusal to obey Jim Crow laws

Nationality:
American

Keywords:
civil rights; Jim Crow; racism

Rosa Parks has her fingerprints taken during her arrest for protesting segregation on a public bus in 1955. © PICTORIAL PRESS LTD/ALAMY

greeted her personal revelations enthusiastically and encouraged their children and grandchildren to read her memoir. Parks followed *My Story* with two more memoirs: *Quiet Strength* (1994), which focuses on her spiritual philosophy, and *I Am Rosa Parks* (1997), written for younger children.

THEMES AND STYLE

My Story aims to instruct readers about the injustice of racism and the resistance to that injustice that has been a central part of the African American community. Parks understands this struggle from an early age: "From the time I was a child, I tried to protest against disrespectful treatment." She views her own courage and sense of justice as the result of the influence and inspiration of her family and friends. She reserves her greatest respect for those who dedicate their lives to justice, describing her husband as someone who "was always interested in and willing to work for things that would improve life for his race, his family, and himself." Her personal history of activism begins with her grandfather, who "instilled in my mother and sisters, and in their children, that you don't put up with bad treatment from anybody. It was passed down almost in our genes."

Parks's purpose in *My Story* is to present a picture of her life and civil rights work that is more complete than her status as an icon of the struggle. Emphasizing that the decisive act of protest for which she became famous was not an isolated personal incident but arose out of an organized political movement, she debunks the popular myth that she refused to give up her seat on the bus because her feet hurt. "People always say that I didn't give up my seat because I was tired but that isn't true.... No, the only tired I was, was tired of giving in." Even-handed and measured, Parks's prose counters her depictions of white hatred and violence with her awareness, even as a child, that all white people did not share racist attitudes: "There had been a few times in my life when I had been treated by white people like a regular person, so I knew what that felt like." She chooses to focus her story on her early life and her work in the movement, such as the Montgomery bus boycott organized around her act of protest. Her life after the 1960s is summed up in a chapter titled "The Years Since," in which she expresses concern over the "resurgence of reactionary attitudes" and her efforts to "keep hope alive."

Parks tells her story in a plainspoken, conversational style, as if she is speaking to a family friend, and the simplicity of her writing adds to the poignancy of observations such as "like millions of black children, before me and after me, I wondered if 'White' water tasted different from 'Colored' water." She begins the book with "How It All Started," which, briefly but dramatically, describes the moment in December when Parks refused to give up her seat on the bus. "Two white policemen came. I asked one of them, 'Why do you push us around?' He answered, 'I don't know, but the law is the law and you're under arrest.'" Going back in time, she then proceeds to describe her family roots, beginning with the portentous sentence, "For half my life there were laws and customs in the South that kept African Americans segregated from Caucasians and allowed white people to treat black people without any respect."

CRITICAL DISCUSSION

Parks's courage and dignity made her a beloved national figure, and the critical reception of her autobiography reflects this affection and respect. Jack Greenberg, reviewing the book for the children's book section of the *New York Times,* described it as a "simply told and moving story" that "I want ... my ... grandchildren to read." Joseph Tomberlin, writing in the *Mississippi Quarterly,* called it "an important book as a firsthand account of the life and contributions of a genuine pioneering heroine." Robert Norrell of the *Georgia Historical Quarterly,* writing for a more academic audience, found *My Story* "less analytic than most scholars would want," asserting, "one wishes for more of her views on some of what happened later to her and 'her' movement."

It is hard to separate the legacy of *My Story* from the legacy of the civil rights pioneer herself. As Nancy Hobbs said in a *Salt Lake Tribune* review, "Her story has become history; now, with her own telling, fallacies have been corrected and emotions have been added." Parks's quietly resonant retelling of her life has become part of the literature of the civil rights movement. It has been an especially powerful tool of education because its style and content is accessible to young readers. As racial prejudice and discrimination have remained important social issues, Parks's memoir has become recommended reading in classrooms confronting the issue of racism.

Mainly viewed as young adult literature, *My Story* has not been the subject of ongoing scholarly analysis in the decades since its publication. However, it has continued to be viewed as an important primary source for researchers studying the civil rights era. Parks's composed, straightforward account of the internal workings of the Montgomery bus boycott and such organizations as the Brotherhood of Sleeping Car Porters, the National Association for the Advancement of Colored People, and the Alabama Voter's League has given historians and other academics reliable insights into a dynamic era of change. For example, in a 2003 article in *Agenda*, Pam Brooks cites Parks's perspective in *My Story* in analyzing the role of women in the human rights movements in the United States and South Africa.

BIBLIOGRAPHY

Sources

Greenberg, Jack. Rev. of *Rosa Parks: My Story*, by Rosa Parks with Jim Haskins. *New York Times* 2 Feb. 1992: BR30. Print.

Harrington, Walt. "A Person Who Wanted to Be Free." *Washington Post* 8 Oct. 1995: W.24. Print.

Hobbs, Nancy. "Books Tell Contributions of Women to Civil Rights and the Civil War." *Salt Lake Tribune* 18 Feb. 1992: A5. Print.

Norrell, Robert J. Rev. of *Rosa Parks: My Story*, by Rosa Parks with Jim Haskins. *Georgia Historical Quarterly* 76.2 (1992): 535–36. Print.

Tomberlin, Joseph A. "Rosa Parks: My Story." *Mississippi Quarterly* 47.1 (1993): 91+. Literature Resource Center. Web. 13 Nov. 2012.

Further Reading

Brooks, Pam. "'But Once They Are Organised, You Can Never Stop Them': 1950s Black Women in Montgomery and Johannesburg Defy Men and the State." *Agenda* 58 (2003): 84–97. Print.

Bryant, Jean Gould. "From the Margins to the Center: Southern Women's Activism, 1820–1970." *Florida Historical Quarterly* 77.4 (1999): 405–28.

Cohen, Daniel. Rev. of *Rosa Parks: My Story*, by Rosa Parks with Jim Haskins. *Smithsonian*. May 1993: 145+. General Reference Center GOLD. Web. 13 Nov. 2012.

Garrow, David J. "Hopelessly Hollow History: Revisionist Devaluing of Brown v. Board of Education." *Virginia Law Review* 80.1 (1994): 151–60. Print.

Parks, Rosa, with Gregory J. Reed. *Quiet Strength: The Faith, the Hope, and the Heart of the Woman Who Changed a Nation*. Grand Rapids, Mich.: Zondervan, 1994. Print.

AUDRE LORDE'S *ZAMI*: A NEW KIND OF AUTOBIOGRAPHY

Born in 1934, Audre Lorde was a young adult when Rosa Parks made her famous stand in Montgomery. Coming of age in New York City, the Caribbean American Lorde not only experienced racism but also isolation and homophobia as she gradually came to understand and embrace her identity as a lesbian. An accomplished writer, Lorde published her first volume of poetry in 1968. Soon after she ended a heterosexual marriage to Edwin Rollins and began a long-term relationship with Frances Clayton. In addition to being a nationally recognized poet and essayist and poet laureate of New York state from 1991 to 1992, Lorde became one of the most respected voices in the international lesbian community. She died of cancer on the island of St. Croix in 1992.

In 1982 Lorde recorded the pivotal experiences of her youth in her book *Zami: A New Spelling of My Name*. Lorde called *Zami* a "biomythography," meaning that the book blended fact, memory, poetry, and story to convey the essence of her life in a more sensually complete way than a traditional narrative. The book's title itself contains several levels of meaning. Lorde had asserted her identity early in life by changing the spelling of her name from Audrey to Audre. In addition, in the Caribbean patois, *zami* (an elision of *les amies*) is a name used for lesbians. Lorde's innovative autobiographical style was deeply personal, conveying emotional reality as well as the facts of her life.

Tina Gianoulis

The Story of My Life
An Afghan Girl on the Other Side of the Sky
Farah Ahmedi

✧ Key Facts

Time Period:
Early 21st Century

Relevant Historical Events:
Soviet war in Afghanistan; rise of the Taliban; Ahmedi's immigration to the United States

Nationality:
Afghan

Keywords:
women's writing; war; immigration

OVERVIEW

Published in 2005, *The Story of My Life: An Afghan Girl on the Other Side of the Sky* is a memoir written by Farah Ahmedi (with assistance from Tamim Ansary) that tells of the adversity she overcame growing up in warn-torn Afghanistan. Ahmedi was born in 1988, during Afghanistan's war with the Soviet Union, and went on to suffer great hardship: as a seven-year-old she lost her leg in a landmine explosion, and her father and sisters were killed by a bomb during her youth. In the book's ninth chapter, "Escape from Afghanistan," Ahmedi describes her difficult journey across the mountains along the Afghan border to Pakistan at the age of thirteen, with a prosthetic leg and her asthmatic mother. This chapter and the rest of the book convey Ahmedi's ability to beat the odds in pursuit of her dreams. In 2002 she and her mother made it to Chicago in the United States, where they experienced greater freedom than they had ever imagined.

At the encouragement of her sponsor, Alyce Litz, Ahmedi submitted her tale to the 2004 "Story of My Life" search on the ABC morning program *Good Morning America*. From approximately 6,000 entries, voters chose Ahmedi's piece as the winner. According to an *Authorlink* interview with Ahmedi, the book's publisher, Simon & Schuster, assigned a professional writer who spoke Farsi (Ahmedi's native language) to take down her story. *The Story of My Life* was met with significant acclaim, receiving enthusiastic reviews from newspapers such as the *Chicago Tribune* and *Chicago Sun-Times* and renowned authors such as Mary Karr and Mary Higgins Clark.

HISTORICAL AND LITERARY CONTEXT

Ahmedi's young life was relentlessly shadowed by war. She was born in Ghazni, near Kabul, as the conflict in Afghanistan between the mujahedeen and Soviets reached its peak. Still, Ahmedi was passionate about school, and in 1995, to avoid being tardy, she took a shortcut and stepped on the landmine that took her leg. She was flown to Germany, where she lived with her family for nearly two years while she recovered from the blast. Upon her return home, bombs were falling nearly every day in Kabul; one hit her family's house, killing her father and sisters. The Taliban had come into power by this point, and her brothers fled to escape being drafted into the military, leaving Ahmedi and her mother to fend for themselves. Ahmedi and her mother eventually escaped to Pakistan and then to the United States in 2002.

Ahmedi says that without the encouragement she received that she would not have shared her story. According to the book's prologue, when Litz saw an advertisement for the "Story of My Life" contest and prompted Ahmedi to enter it, Ahmedi responded by saying, "I'm not even nineteen years old, and I haven't achieved anything yet." However, Litz insisted that "with a life like mine, surviving itself was an achievement—just surviving." Even though Ahmedi did not totally agree with this statement, she decided to share her story because "it is not mine alone. It is the story of many people."

Following the terrorist attacks of September 11, 2001, *The Story of My Life* was one of many books that emerged depicting young women in the Muslim world. According to Gillian Whitlock, author of the essay "The Skin of the Burqa: Recent Life Narratives from Afghanistan," some of these narratives pose a complicated problem: whereas they provide powerful voices to feminist resistance, they also promote certain misunderstandings, including the burqa, a traditional garment worn by Islamic women, as necessarily and always being antifreedom. Books such as Saira Shah's *The Storyteller's Daughter* (2003), *Zoya's Story* (2002) by Zoya with John Follain and Rita Critofari, and Batya Yasgur's *Behind the Burqa: Our Life in Afganistan and How We Escaped to Freedom* (2002) engage compassion and fuel anti-Taliban sentiment, but they do so from a Western perspective and for a primarily Western audience.

Ahmedi's memoir has been embraced by U.S. language arts educational programs for upper grades. According to educator Ruth R. Caillouet, teaching after 9/11 requires a more culturally inclusive approach, and she uses *The Story of My Life,* along with *The Kite Runner* (2003) by Khaled Hosseini, to examine Afghanistan. In her essay "The Other Side of Terrorism and the Children of Afghanistan," Caillouet asserts, "Reading this book [*The Story of My Life*] gives students a deeper understanding of the complexities of Afghani society and culture."

THEMES AND STYLE

The central theme in Ahmedi's memoir, particularly in the chapter "Escape from Afghanistan," is the struggle to overcome adversity in the name of freedom and safety. Although Ahmedi and her mother knew that they needed to reach Quetta, Pakistan, the path there is perilous. Ahmedi writes, "From Jalalabad to the border, we would be on our own. As for getting across the border, no one knew what that entailed. As for making the journey from the border to Quetta, that was like asking how to get from one part of the moon to another part." They are alone and in restricted health, Ahmedi on an old prosthetic and her mother "rasping with every breath … [because] we had no medicine for her condition." Yet the two reach their destination.

Although Ahmedi had to be persuaded to tell her story, there is no sense that she shied from recounting the danger and challenges of her situation. She creates a narrative in which her triumph is all the more powerful by providing apt detail. For example, in describing the grim terror of the difficult bus ride to the border of Pakistan she tells how the passengers all carry plastic bags to contend with mass nausea on the trip. In every circumstance Ahmedi is always careful to give thanks for assistance. After failing to cross the border on their second night, they receive help from a family that has discovered a smugglers' hiking route to Pakistan. The father, Ghulam Ali, invites Ahmedi and her mother to join them. "I have known long periods of being no one," Ahmedi writes. "But then, without warning, a person like Ghulam Ali just turns up and says, 'I see you. I am on your side.' Strangers have been kind to me when it mattered most."

The memoir's language is both straightforward and natural, reflecting Ahmedi's growing command of English. The chapter "Escape from Afghanistan" begins with a letter from a relative in Quetta inviting Ahmedi and her mother to come to Pakistan and closes with the two joyously crossing the border. As Ahmedi writes, "We started laughing. We couldn't stop. We tried to stop our mouths with our palms, and we couldn't do it…. [Y]ou might as well say we had been in prison for thirty years and had suddenly been released—that was the kind of joy we felt." The book remains steadfastly focused on overcoming adversity, with the gratitude, hope, and happiness that come with it.

CRITICAL DISCUSSION

Among the thousands of entries, Ahmedi's was selected as one of three finalists. Voters made their picks on the *Good Morning America* website, and Ahmedi was declared the winner. A month later, in April 2005, her memoir was published. An additional printing of the book, under the new title *The Other Side of the Sky: A Memoir,* was released the same year and became a *New York Times* best seller. On the jacket of the book, the *Chicago Tribune* lauds it as a "poignant tale of survival" and the *Chicago Sun-Times* calls it "a remarkable journey."

Ahmedi's tale has proved to be a key addition to the significant body of work focused on the lives of Muslim women, written most often after they fled their home countries. Ahmedi's, however, may also play a unique role in disability studies. In an essay in *Disability Studies Quarterly,* Kristina R. Knoll writes that "the complex interweaving of topics, including cross-cultural perspectives of women's issues, nationality, class and racial privileging, religion and disability, would leave many disability scholars thirsting for more narratives with such explicit intersectionality of lived experiences."

Ahmedi's memoir has been celebrated in educational realms as a tool for multicultural literary studies, a testament to the vitality of its content. According to Clare Bradford in her essay "Representing Islam," some of the books in the same vein as Ahmedi's—including those by Suzanne Fisher Staples—are "marketed in a way that constructs the female Muslim subject as a unified, oppressed figure." Further, she contends that "the representations of oppression and of exoticism that permeate depictions of girls and women in *Shabanu* and *Haveli* [by Fisher] imply as their opposite Western women who are in charge of their own lives and who do not rely on the magnanimity of men." *The Story of My Life,* however, stands out as something different. A 2010 article by Allison Baer and Jacqueline N. Glasgow in the *Journal of Adolescent & Adult Literacy* mentions *The Story of My Life* alongside two novels about Muslim adolescents, *The Girl in the Tangerine Scarf* (2006) by Mohja Kahf and *Does My Head Look Big in This?* (2005) by Randa Abdel-Fattah. Baer and Glasgow laud all three books for their educational

Author Farah Ahmedi, right, shares her autobiography with First Lady Laura Bush, left, in a diplomatic reception at the White House in 2005. © KRISANNE JOHNSON/GETTY IMAGES

THE STORY OF MY LIFE IN THE CLASSROOM

The Story of My Life: An Afghan Girl on the Other Side of the Sky is often taught in high school and university world literature classes. For one teacher, the motivation to teach Farah Ahmedi's text was especially personal. Soon after the events of 9/11, Ruth Caillouet's son enlisted in the Louisiana National Guard and served a year in Afghanistan. Caillouet, now a professor at Clayton State University, spent that year worrying about her nineteen-year-old son. Since she knew nothing about the places where her son was stationed, such as Kandahar and Kabul, she started reading Afghani literature. She writes in a 2006 article in the *English Journal*, "My son was in Afghanistan, and in my need to find a way to cope, I turned to literature and teaching." All of this studying and worrying became the inspiration for her curriculum unit on the literature of Afghanistan.

Caillouet includes *The Story of My Life* in her class because it offers a glimpse into Afghani life and culture, one that she writes is "struggling for some semblance of normalcy." She also teaches the text because many of the descriptions are similar to those in her son's letters: "Things are quiet tonight on the tower," he writes. "I can hear the locals praying in the city now. They sing their prayers over a loud speaker at sun up. That means it's almost time for me to get relieved from guard duty." Caillouet juxtaposes her son's experiences in Afghanistan with the literature as a way of challenging her students' views on war and encouraging them to ponder deeper issues.

qualities, writing that they "provide readers with windows through which to experience views and cultures quite different from their own."

BIBLIOGRAPHY

Sources

Ahmedi, Farah, with Tamim Ansary. *The Other Side of the Sky: A Memoir.* New York: Simon Spotlight Entertainment, 2005. Print.

Baer, Allison, and Jacqueline N. Glasgow. "Negotiating Understanding through the Young Adult Literature of Muslim Cultures." *Journal of Adolescent & Adult Literacy* 54.1 (2010): 23–32. ERIC. Web. 17 Nov. 2012.

Bradford, Clare. "Representing Islam: Female Subjects in Suzanne Fisher Staples's Novels." *Children's Literature Association Quarterly* 32.1 (2007): 47–62. *Project Muse.* Web. 17 Nov. 2012.

Caillouet, Ruth R. "The Other Side of Terrorism and the Children of Afghanistan" *English Journal* 96.2 (2006): 28–33. *JSTOR.* Web. 16 Nov. 2012.

Knoll, Kristina R. Rev. of *The Story of My Life: An Afghan Girl on the Other Side of the Sky,* by Farah Ahmedi with Tamim Ansary. *Disabilities Studies Quarterly* 26.2 (2006). Web. 16 Nov. 2012.

Whitlock, Gillian. "The Skin of the Burqa: Recent Life Narratives from Afghanistan." *SEYFETTIN,* 19 Jan. 2007. *Wordpress.* Web. 23 Nov. 2012.

Further Reading

Kristof, Nicholas D., and Sheryl WuDunn. *Half the Sky: Turning Oppression into Opportunity for Women Worldwide.* New York: Knopf, 2009. Print.

Nafisi, Azar. *Reading Lolita in Tehran: A Memoir in Books.* New York: Random, 2003. Print.

Shah, Saira. *The Storyteller's Daughter.* New York: Knopf, 2003. Print.

Yasgur, Batya Swift. *Behind the Burqa: Our Life in Afghanistan and How We Escaped to Freedom.* Hoboken, N.J.: Wiley, 2002. Print.

Rachel Mindell

The Story of My Life
Helen Keller

Helen Keller

Key Facts

Time Period:
Early 20th Century

Relevant Historical Events:
Keller receives an education despite her disabilities

Nationality:
American

Keywords:
deaf-blindness; education; disability

OVERVIEW

Helen Keller's *The Story of My Life,* first published in book form in 1903, is an autobiographical account of Keller's life up to that point, with particular emphasis on her acquisition of language and subsequent intellectual development as a deaf and blind child. Beginning with her birth in Tuscumbia, Alabama, in 1880, Keller relates how she lost her sight and hearing to a childhood illness, resulting in several years of increasing distress and frustration as she struggled in vain to express herself. Her eventual success in overcoming the limitations of her disabilities and learning to communicate under the tutelage of her teacher and lifelong companion, Anne Sullivan, forms the centerpiece of the book, which follows Keller through her education at various deaf and blind schools, and eventually at Radcliffe College, where she began writing the autobiography. The book's compelling depiction of Keller's uncommon life served as an inspiring portrait of triumph over adversity, as well as a powerful work of advocacy for the education of blind and deaf individuals.

At the time *The Story of My Life* was published, Keller had already achieved considerable renown for her unusual life story, as deaf-blind people with her level of education were extremely rare. A great critical and financial success, the book served as an important and influential testament to the learning potential of deaf and blind children, who were frequently dismissed as uneducable because of their disabilities. By far Keller's most enduringly popular work, *The Story of My Life* is now considered one of the classic autobiographical accounts of the early twentieth century, contributing significantly to Keller's status as an iconic American figure.

HISTORICAL AND LITERARY CONTEXT

Keller's autobiography was unique in its status as a firsthand account of the education of a deaf-blind individual during an era when educational opportunities for disabled children in general were severely circumscribed in the United States. Despite a growing (but limited) number of resources and institutions for both deaf and blind students, attempts to teach disabled youth—particularly ones with Keller's dual impairment—were often regarded as a waste of time, and instead of receiving instruction tailored to their specific needs, such children were frequently given up as a lost cause and institutionalized. An important forbear to Helen Keller was Laura Bridgman, another deaf-blind child, whose successful education (as publicized by Charles Dickens) at the Perkins Institution for the Blind in Boston inspired Keller's parents in their pursuit of a proper education for their daughter.

The Story of My Life, written with the assistance of Anne Sullivan and her husband, John Macy, first appeared in periodic installments in 1902 in the *Ladies' Home Journal,* followed the next year by a book publication that also included a selection of Keller's letters and a long biographical essay by Macy that reproduced many of Sullivan's letters as well. By this time, Keller was already a widely renowned figure. Her unprecedented level of education, largely funded by philanthropic donations, provoked widespread interest, as well as a great deal of prejudiced skepticism about the legitimacy of her accomplishments. Her own account of her intellectual progress, along with the corroboration provided by the book's supplementary materials, served as an illustration of her story's veracity and implicitly as a validation of deaf-blind potential.

Because *The Story of My Life* is generally believed to be the first book—autobiographical or otherwise—written by a deaf-blind individual, it is in many ways without literary precedent, though it shares a long tradition of American autobiographical writing and is also part of the relatively small body of literature dealing with the education of children with disabilities. Dickens's 1842 travelogue *American Notes,* with its widely read account of Bridgman's education, is an example of this latter group, as is Macy's supplementary essay. Firsthand literary accounts from the perspective of the child in question, however, were largely nonexistent prior to Keller's text; its only real predecessor was Keller's own 1892 essay "My Life," written when she was twelve and thoroughly revised and expanded to make her later autobiography.

In the decades since its publication, Keller's autobiography has become one of the standard American narratives of triumph over adversity. In addition to serving as a precursor to countless subsequent memoirs of disability, it was the primary basis for William

Playbill for *Deliverance*, a 1919 silent film about the life of Helen Keller starring Keller, her teacher Anne Sullivan, and others. Keller also recounts her life in her autobiography *Helen Keller: The Story of My Life*. © TOPHAM/THE IMAGE WORKS

Gibson's 1957 teleplay *The Miracle Worker,* which quickly spawned its own adaptations and soon became the most widely known version of Keller's life. Keller herself went on to publish several further autobiographical volumes, including *The World I Live In* (1908), a detailed elaboration of her sensory experiences, and *Midstream* (1930), which documents her later life. None of these subsequent works achieved the popularity of her first book, however.

THEMES AND STYLE

A central theme of Keller's narrative is the crucial importance of knowledge and learning. This conviction is most pronounced in Keller's discussion of her acquisition of language; the breakthrough moment in Keller's education, when she associates the manually spelled letters of the word "water" with the feeling of water on her hand, is described as a moment of glorious revelation: "Somehow the mystery of language was revealed to me. I knew then that 'w-a-t-e-r' meant the wonderful cool something that was flowing over my hand. That living word awakened my soul, gave it light, hope, joy, set it free!" This inaugurates an enduring commitment to the pursuit of knowledge, a commitment that never flagged despite the various impediments imposed by Keller's disabilities: "There were barriers still, but barriers that could in time be swept away."

The Story of My Life, unusual among autobiographies for being published when the author was still in her early twenties, was written primarily in order to explain how Keller acquired the education for which she had become famous. Although the book touches on many aspects of Keller's life, including her friendships, travels, religious beliefs, and fondness for nature, the greatest degree of emphasis is placed on her schooling. She devotes considerable attention to the ways in which her own learning process differed from that of hearing and sighted children: "The conversation [a hearing child] hears in his home stimulates his mind and suggests topics and calls forth the spontaneous expression of his own thoughts. This natural exchange is denied to the deaf child." Keller's elaboration of her own tutelage provided a concrete explanation for what many saw as either a hoax or a miracle, demonstrating that deaf and blind children were not uneducable but merely required different teaching methods.

Stylistically, *The Story of My Life* is characterized by an upbeat, appreciative tone and a mannered, somewhat flowery turn of phrase. Much of the text consists of lavish praise for Keller's friends and benefactors—"in a thousand ways they have turned my limitations into beautiful privileges"—and though she is candid regarding the unhappy times in her life, including her troubles upon finding that she had inadvertently plagiarized a piece of fiction, the book's overall cadence is one of grateful elation. The expression of this elation is marked by frequent literary and biblical allusions, as when she concludes her discussion of her parents' successful attempts to find a teacher for her: "Thus I came up out of Egypt and stood before Sinai, and a power divine touched my spirit and gave it sight, so that I beheld many wonders."

CRITICAL DISCUSSION

The Story of My Life was published to relatively weak initial sales but, buoyed by positive critical notices, soon became a great commercial success. These notices, in many ways an extension of the copious media coverage Keller had received since Sullivan's original success, frequently focused on the uniqueness of Keller's situation and the book's largely unprecedented status as an autobiographical document. William Allan Neilson, writing in the *Atlantic Monthly,* exemplifies this tendency to emphasize the text's singular nature, praising the ingenuity of Sullivan's teaching methods and asserting that "the book is indeed unique. The story itself and the years of effort which have made its telling possible, the personality which it reveals, and the creation of that personality—these are things which,

PRIMARY SOURCE

EXCERPT FROM *THE STORY OF MY LIFE*

The most important day I remember in all my life is the one on which my teacher, Anne Mansfield Sullivan, came to me. I am filled with wonder when I consider the immeasurable contrasts between the two lives which it connects. It was the third of March, 1887, three months before I was seven years old.

On the afternoon of that eventful day, I stood on the porch, dumb, expectant. I guessed vaguely from my mother's signs and from the hurrying to and fro in the house that something unusual was about to happen, so I went to the door and waited on the steps. The afternoon sun penetrated the mass of honeysuckle that covered the porch, and fell on my upturned face. My fingers lingered almost unconsciously on the familiar leaves and blossoms which had just come forth to greet the sweet southern spring. I did not know what the future held of marvel or surprise for me. Anger and bitterness had preyed upon me continually for weeks and a deep languor had succeeded this passionate struggle.

Have you ever been at sea in a dense fog, when it seemed as if a tangible white darkness shut you in, and the great ship, tense and anxious, groped her way toward the shore with plummet and sounding-line, and you waited with beating heart for something to happen? I was like that ship before my education began, only I was without compass or sounding-line, and had no way of knowing how near the harbour was. "Light! give me light!" was the wordless cry of my soul, and the light of love shone on me in that very hour.

I felt approaching footsteps. I stretched out my hand as I supposed to my mother. Some one took it, and I was caught up and held close in the arms of her who had come to reveal all things to me, and, more than all things else, to love me.

The morning after my teacher came she led me into her room and gave me a doll. The little blind children at the Perkins Institution had sent it and Laura Bridgman had dressed it; but I did not know this until afterward. When I had played with it a little while, Miss Sullivan slowly spelled into my hand the word "d-o-l-l." I was at once interested in this finger play and tried to imitate it. When I finally succeeded in making the letters correctly I was flushed with childish pleasure and pride. Running downstairs to my mother I held up my hand and made the letters for doll. I did not know that I was spelling a word or even that words existed; I was simply making my fingers go in monkey-like imitation. In the days that followed I learned to spell in this uncomprehending way a great many words, among them *pin, hat, cup* and a few verbs like *sit, stand* and *walk*. But my teacher had been with me several weeks before I understood that everything has a name.

One day, while I was playing with my new doll, Miss Sullivan put my big rag doll into my lap also, spelled "d-o-l-l" and tried to make me understand that "d-o-l-l" applied to both. Earlier in the day we had had a tussle over the words "m-u-g" and "w-a-t-e-r." Miss Sullivan had tried to impress it upon me that "m-u-g" is *mug* and that "w-a-t-e-r" is *water*, but I persisted in confounding the two. In despair she had dropped the subject for the time, only to renew it at the first opportunity. I became impatient at her repeated attempts and, seizing the new doll, I dashed it upon the floor. I was keenly delighted when I felt the fragments of the broken doll at my feet. Neither sorrow nor regret followed my passionate outburst. I had not loved the doll. In the still, dark world in which I lived there was no strong sentiment of tenderness. I felt my teacher sweep the fragments to one side of the hearth, and I had a sense of satisfaction that the cause of my discomfort was removed. She brought me my hat, and I knew I was going out into the warm sunshine. This thought, if a wordless sensation may be called a thought, made me hop and skip with pleasure.

SOURCE: Keller, Helen. *The Story of My Life*. New York: Doubleday, Page & Company, 1905.

---

even when pondered, are apt to seem little short of miraculous."

The Story of My Life contributed significantly to the iconic status that Keller has since attained within U.S. history. Its narrative, further popularized by *The Miracle Worker*, has become one of the most well-known inspirational stories in the country's history, a legacy that has met with a mixed reception both from members of blind and deaf communities (particularly in light of Keller's controversial advocacy of speech lessons for the deaf) and from Keller herself, as public interest in her early life tended to overshadow her other writings as well as her social and political activism for various humanitarian and leftist causes. Liz Crow, in a 2000 article in *Disability & Society*, notes that Keller "struggled … to make public and be taken seriously for her opinions on anything other than impairment." Scholarship on the text frequently analyzes its relationship to this legacy.

Contemporary scholarship focusing exclusively on *The Story of My Life* is relatively uncommon, but the book is sometimes discussed in relation to the autobiographical genre, especially in light of its status as a seminal narrative of disability. Georgina Kleege's article "Helen Keller and 'The Empire of the Normal'" (2000) analyzes the book's use of sensory details, frequently drawn from aural and visual experience, in relation to the more accurate, narratively experimental rendition of deaf-blind experience in Keller's next book, *The World I Live In*, which "chafes at the shortcomings of the genre [Keller] helped to invent." Likewise, Marta L. Werner's

2010 article "Helen Keller and Anne Sullivan: Writing Otherwise" discusses the material specifics of Keller's autobiographical writing process, exploring the textual relationship between her collaborative inscription methods and her attempts to convey her own subjectivity.

BIBLIOGRAPHY

Sources

Crow, Liz. "Helen Keller: Rethinking the Problematic Icon." *Disability & Society* 15.6 (2000): 845–59. *Taylor & Francis Online*. Web. 29 Oct. 2012.

Keller, Helen. *The Story of My Life*. Ed. Roger Shattuck with Dorothy Herrmann. New York: W. W. Norton, 2003. Print.

Kleege, Georgina. "Helen Keller and 'The Empire of the Normal'." *American Quarterly* 52.2 (2000): 322–25. *JSTOR*. Web. 29 Oct. 2012.

Neilson, William Allan. Rev. of *The Story of My Life,* by Helen Keller. *Atlantic Monthly* 91 (1903): 842–44. Print.

Werner, Marta L. "Helen Keller and Anne Sullivan: Writing Otherwise." *Textual Cultures* 5.1 (2010): 1–45. *Project MUSE*. Web. 29 Oct. 2012.

Further Reading

Cohen, Paula Marantz. "Helen Keller and the American Myth." *Yale Review* 85.1 (1997): 1–20. Print.

Cressman, Jodi. "Helen Keller and the Mind's Eyewitness." *Western Humanities Review* 54.2 (2000): 108–23. Print.

Halliday, Sam. "Helen Keller, Henry James, and the Social Relations of Perception." *Criticism* 48.2 (2007): 175–201. Print.

Herrmann, Dorothy. *Helen Keller: A Life*. New York: A. Knopf, 1998. Print.

Hurst, Andrea. "Helen and Heidegger: Disabled Dasein, Language and Others." *South African Journal of Philosophy* 22.1 (2003): 97–112. Print.

Keller, Helen. *The World I Live In*. New York: Century, 1908. Print.

Kleege, Georgina. "The Helen Keller Who Still Matters." Rev. of *The Story of My Life,* by Helen Keller. *Raritan* 24.1 (2004): 100–12. Print.

Leiber, Justin. "Helen Keller as Cognitive Scientist." *Philosophical Psychology* 9.4 (1996): 419–40. Print.

Mills, Kevin. "Out of the Non-Reading Gaol: Valentine Cunningham, Helen Keller, and Hermeneutic Freedom." *Literature & Theology* 11.3 (1997): 254–69. Print.

Montgomery, Travis. "Radicalizing Reunion: Helen Keller's *The Story of My Life* and Reconciliation Romance." *Southern Literary Journal* 42.2 (2010): 34–51. Print.

James Overholtzer

This Boy's Life
Tobias Wolff

Key Facts

Time Period:
Late 20th Century

Relevant Historical Events:
Cold War; Wolff's experience of family instability

Nationality:
American

Keywords:
divorce; abuse; militarism

OVERVIEW

Tobias Wolff's 1989 memoir *This Boy's Life* chronicles the author's troubled family life from the age of ten in 1955 until the end of his adolescence in the 1960s. The first few chapters cover a brief period when Toby, or Jack (as he decides he wants to be called at one point), and his divorced mother, Caroline, move from Florida to Utah and then to the Seattle area in search of new economic opportunities. After this upheaval, the two settle into a more conventional family arrangement when Caroline marries Dwight and they move in with him and his children in Chinook, a small logging town outside of Seattle. From there, the memoir focuses largely on the interactions between Toby and Dwight, who turns out to be a controlling and abusive stepfather and husband. With Dwight in the picture, *This Boy's Life* becomes a story of troubled childhood or, as Wolff himself put it in a 1990 interview in *Contemporary Literature,* the story of a "kid very much on his own" in a dysfunctional household.

When *This Boy's Life* was published, Wolff had already established himself as a successful author of fiction and a university-level creative writing teacher. He had previously published two collections of short stories, *In the Garden of North America Martyrs* (1981) and *Back in the World* (1985), and he won the 1985 PEN/Faulkner Award for his novella *The Barracks Thief.* Wolff's literary career took shape after a stint in the army from 1964 to 1968 and an Oxford education he received following his military service. *This Boy's Life* was well received, and in 1993 Michael Caton-Jones directed a film adaptation starring Robert De Niro as Dwight and Leonardo DiCaprio as Toby. Wolff's memoir remains significant both for its well-crafted storyline and its insightful look at the troubles of youth.

HISTORICAL AND LITERARY CONTEXT

From its opening scene in 1955 to the time of its publication in 1989, *This Boy's Life* spans nearly the entire Cold War era. Wolff is a child of the post–World War II military buildup, the arms race against the Soviet Union, and U.S. efforts to defeat communism, and this political climate looms in the background of the memoir. Within this context, the scouting magazine *Boy's Life,* from which the title is drawn, and the heroic ideals of the scouting culture that the magazine promoted became important influences in Wolff's formative years. Wolff tells of how he fantasized about exchanging his dissatisfying situation for the valiant life of the soldiers he read about in the magazine. When asked about the book's title in his interview with *Contemporary Literature,* he reiterated the importance of these cultural ideals: "I meant to suggest an ironic discrepancy between the ideal boyhood portrayed in the magazine and my own experience."

Though Wolff does not make any explicit political commentary in *This Boy's Life,* the memoir responds in subtle ways to the Cold War era. Wolff served in Vietnam and experienced disillusionment with heroic ideals (an experience he wrote about in a 1994 memoir titled *In Pharaoh's Army*). When discussing *This Boy's Life* in the *Contemporary Literature* interview, he made it clear that his fascination with a heroic image of boyhood and the violence of his upbringing played an important role in his choice to join the military: "I wanted the reader to be aware … that the boyhood obsession with weapons has a terminus somewhere, that it ends in war. There's a logical progression in the kind of life that boys are encouraged to lead and dream of in this country. There's a lot of violence in [*This Boy's Life*]—a lot of male violence." This representation of male childhood was common to an entire generation of men who served during this era.

Wolff's memoir draws on a rich background of literary predecessors. Graham Greene's *A Sort of Life* (1971) served as a theoretical guide for Wolff on writing memoirs. Greene's book proposes that memoirs often fail because writers do not treat serious childhood events with appropriate gravity; thus, Wolff sought to avoid such trivializing in *This Boy's Life.* Ernest Hemingway was another influence, acting as a stylistic model. Wolff also admitted to accidentally stealing a line from Anton Chekhov's letters, and F. Scott Fitzgerald's *The Great Gatsby* (1925) informed his understanding of self-invention. Among contemporary American writers, Wolff's work bears similarities to other personal accounts of overcoming childhood adversity, such as those by Richard Rodriguez and Maya Angelou.

This Boy's Life is Wolff's best-known work. The memoir has been widely anthologized, and it also played an incidental role in the history of popular American cinema, launching the acting career of DiCaprio. Perhaps because of its exploration of the universal challenges of youth, *This Boy's Life* remains compelling for today's audiences.

THEMES AND STYLE

This Boy's Life deals most centrally with childhood longing for acceptance and a sense of belonging and the ways a child learns to adapt in their absence. Before the move to Chinook, Caroline gives Toby the final say over whether she will marry Dwight. The young boy's desire for a unified family appears poignantly when Wolff explains why he ultimately approved of the marriage: "Unlike my mother, I was fiercely conventional. I was tempted by the idea of belonging to a conventional family, and living in a house, and having a big brother and a couple of sisters." Things quickly sour with Dwight, who seeks to control Toby with odd and pointless tasks such as evenings shucking chestnuts that no one ever eats. At various times, Dwight berates and belittles Toby. He steals the money Toby earns from his paper route, and there are several serious physical confrontations. With this conventional home life having proved to be such a disappointing mirage, Toby searches widely for strategies of adjustment, such as engaging with the scouts. He openly defies his stepfather, dreams of flight, drinks and skips class with his "outlaw" friends in high school, and hones his skills at lying and other sophisticated forms of deceit. It is ultimately his talent for deception that provides him a way out of Chinook.

Though it would have been easy for Wolff to make *This Boy's Life* a condemnation of the adults with whom he grew up, his goals were focused on personal memory and good storytelling. When asked specifically in the *Contemporary Literature* interview why he wrote the book, he spoke of wanting to preserve his memories of youth: "I started out jotting things down about my childhood, because I felt them slipping away, and I wanted to have some sort of record." At the same time, Wolff's record of the past fulfilled another goal of providing an entertaining and insightful read to his audience: "Also, I recognized that my childhood made a good story. For years I had seen people perk up when I told them some of the things that happened when I was a kid." Wolff stays focused tightly on narrating these events, refraining from in-depth exposition.

The most prominent structural feature of *This Boy's Life* is the way Wolff separates the life of the child from that of the successful teacher and writer he became. With a few brief exceptions, the memoir restricts readers to the experiences of young Toby as he lived them. This structure, with only minimal "bridges" linking to the child's future, is a conscious choice, as Wolff seeks to preserve and reflect the fear and uncertainty of growing up. Wolff's language is plain, clear, and direct. As A. M. Homes puts it in his 1996 piece in *BOMB*, it is "the taut, trim, prose of an athlete."

CRITICAL DISCUSSION

The critical acclaim Wolff had begun to garner in the mid-1980s increased with his publication of *This Boy's Life*. The memoir received favorable reviews in such esteemed publications as the *New York Times* and the *Harvard Book Review*. The *Times*'s Christopher Lehmann-Haupt praised the book for being "clear" and "hypnotic," a text that teaches "us something new about the alienated world of childhood." The *Review*'s Michael Martone, impressed by Wolff's craftsmanship as a storyteller, called the book "profound and memorable," likening the author's storytelling achievement to the skills of a talented tailor.

The aesthetic legacy of *This Boy's Life* and of Wolff's work in general is in part tied to a literary movement in the 1980s known as Dirty Realism. In his profile of the author in the *Age*, Kevin Rabelais describes the importance of this movement, "which examined impoverished, often blue-collar, lives." Rabelais adds that "the work of Dirty Realists such as [Raymond] Carver, [Richard] Ford, Jayne Anne Phillips, Ann Beattie and Wolff injected a new energy into American writing." In addition to its place in this energizing movement, Wolff's text contributed to a literary trend of melding formal conventions of fiction and autobiography. Scholarly focus on *This Boy's Life* has given rise to a rich corpus of work on the fundamental questions about childhood that Wolff explores.

This corpus touches on a wide variety of literary, social, and psychological topics. Daniel D. Challener has examined *This Boy's Life* as part of his interdisciplinary study of the social and psychological workings of childhood resilience; Peter J. Bailey has studied Wolff's blending of fictional and autobiographic forms; and Marilyn Wesley included Wolff's memoir in her study of American adventure stories and male violence, *Violent Adventure: Contemporary Fiction by American Men*. She interprets Wolff's childhood memoir as one of the contemporary "challenges to the tradition that a young man grows up to inherit a fully formed, patriarchally transmitted culture."

BIBLIOGRAPHY

Sources

Bailey, Peter J. "'Why Not Tell the Truth?': The Autobiographies of Three Fiction Writers." *Critique* 32:4 (1991): 211–23. *Academic Search Premier*. Web. 19 Nov. 2012.

Challener, Daniel D. *Stories of Resilience in Childhood: The Narratives of Maya Angelou, Maxine Hong Kingston, Richard Rodriguez, John Edgar Wideman, and Tobias Wolff*. New York: Garland, 1997. Print.

Homes, A. M., and Tobias Wolff. "Tobias Wolff." *BOMB* 57 (1996): 14–17. *JSTOR*. Web. 19 Nov. 2012.

Lehmann-Haupt, Christopher. "Books of the Times: Through a Dark Boyhood to a Place in the Sun." *New York Times* 12 Jan. 1989: C25. *LexisNexis Academic*. Web. 19 Nov. 2012.

Lyons, Bonnie, Bill Oliver, and Tobias Wolff. "An Interview with Tobias Wolff." *Contemporary Literature* 31:1 (1990): 1–16. *JSTOR*. Web. 19 Nov. 2012.

Martone, Michael. "*This Boy's Life: A Memoir* by Tobias Wolff." *Harvard Book Review* 11–12 (1989): 9–10. *JSTOR*. Web. 19 Nov. 2012.

Rabalais, Kevin. "The Essential Wolff: Profile." *Age* 21 June 2008: A2. Books 26. *LexisNexis Academic*. Web 19 Nov. 2012.

Wesley, Marilyn. *Violent Adventure: Contemporary Fiction by American Men.* Charlottesville: University of Virginia Press, 2003. Print.

Wolff, Tobias. *This Boy's Life: A Memoir.* New York: Grove, 1989. Print.

Further Reading

Angelou, Maya. *I Know Why the Caged Bird Sings.* New York: Random House, 1969. Print.

Greene, Graham. *A Sort of Life.* New York: Simon and Schuster, 1971. Print

Lehman, Daniel. *Matters of Fact: Reading Nonfiction over the Edge.* Columbus: Ohio State University Press, 1997. Print.

Wolff, Geoffrey. *The Duke of Deception: Memories of My Father.* New York: Random House, 1979. Print.

Wolff, Tobias. *In Pharaoh's Army: Memories of the Lost War.* New York: Knopf, 1994. Print.

Nicholas Snead

FILM ADAPTATION OF *THIS BOY'S LIFE*

In 1993 director Michael Caton-Jones brought together acting legend Robert De Niro and up-and-coming teenager Leonardo DiCaprio for his film adaptation of *This Boy's Life*. The New York Film Critics Circle recognized DiCaprio's prowess, awarding him second place in its Best Supporting Actor category for his combined work in *This Boy's Life* and *What's Eating Gilbert Grape?*

The film version of Wolff's memoir is a faithful and captivating representation of the frayed family relationship between Toby and Dwight. De Niro offers a chilling performance as the abusive stepfather, especially in the way he mocks and belittles Toby, and DiCaprio convincingly conveys the frustrations of the lost and rebellious youth. In an interview in *Contemporary Literature,* Wolff discussed how he wanted his memoir to capture the violence inherent in idealistic representations of American boyhood. De Niro and DiCaprio bring this violence to life in the visual medium. The film version is particularly memorable for a scene in which Dwight teaches Toby the art of the "dry-gulch," his term for taking a cheap shot in a fight before an opponent expects it.

Up from Slavery
Booker T. Washington

Key Facts

Time Period:
Early 20th Century

Relevant Historical Events:
End of slavery in the United States; Reconstruction; Washington's "Atlanta Compromise"

Nationality:
American

Keywords:
racism; assimilation; integration

OVERVIEW

The second of three autobiographical works by prominent African American leader Booker T. Washington, *Up from Slavery* (1901) was first serialized in the *Outlook* journal, followed by publication in book format. Delineating Washington's life from his birth into slavery on a Virginia plantation to his career as one of the most prominent black educators of his day, *Up from Slavery* is not only autobiography but also a manifesto of the author's philosophy of racial advancement for black Americans. Writing largely for a northern white audience, he uses personal anecdotes and maxims to enliven descriptions of his early years of hard labor, his subsequent struggles to educate himself, and his ultimate devotion to black education and economic advancement. *Up from Slavery* was created with the assistance of sympathetic white ghostwriter Max Thrasher.

Published at a time historians would later label the "nadir" of race relations in the United States, *Up from Slavery* was generally received with enthusiasm by many white readers who found Washington's tone of compromise and limited aspiration reassuring. Some black activists, however, found the book's dismissal of suffrage and other civil rights disappointing and were angered by his seeming acceptance of black inferiority. Others of both races saw the author's approach as realistic in a time of overwhelming racial division and recognized his biography as a significant factor in white acceptance of any social progress for blacks.

HISTORICAL AND LITERARY CONTEXT

The latter half of the nineteenth century was a turbulent time in the United States for blacks, enslaved or free. The conflicting views of slavery in the North and the South had been a major issue in the divisive Civil War, which raged from 1861 to 1865. The Emancipation Proclamation, issued by President Abraham Lincoln on January 1, 1863, had ended the institution of slavery in the rebellious southern states, and the Thirteenth Amendment to the Constitution extended the ban throughout the nation. Integrating free blacks into U.S. society, however, was a far more complicated matter. The postwar Reconstruction period saw the passage of extensive civil rights legislation, including the Fourteenth and Fifteenth Amendments, which granted blacks citizenship and the right to vote, respectively. Once federal pressure was withdrawn, however, white-dominated southern governments began the process of reversing these gains. In order to escape increasing oppression, thousands of African Americans began to leave the South, seeking new opportunities in northern states such as Kansas, Missouri, Indiana, and Illinois. So many migrated in 1879 that the year was dubbed the "Great Exodus."

By the 1890s conditions for black Americans had become grim. The number of blacks murdered by white lynch mobs rose dramatically, peaking at 230 in 1892. In 1896 the Supreme Court handed down a far-reaching decision in *Plessy v. Ferguson,* which allowed exclusion of blacks from first-class railway cars and paved the way for an institutionalized system of segregation. In this atmosphere, Washington, already head of the Tuskegee Institute in Alabama and a leader in the black community, delivered a pivotal address at the 1895 International Exposition in Atlanta. His speech, sometimes called the Atlanta Compromise Address, soothed his mostly white audience with a call for tolerance and economic opportunity for blacks rather than true political and social equality. The address propelled Washington to national fame and gained him political influence unprecedented for a black American.

The intense racism of the late 1800s inspired a vigorous literature of dissent, especially among African American writers. The earliest black American literature had been the autobiographical writings of slaves, such as William Wells Brown's 1847 *Narrative* and Solomon Northup's 1853 *Twelve Years a Slave.* Other African American writers used the symbolic language of poetry to explore the pervasive effects of racism. One of these was Paul Laurence Dunbar, whose poem "Sympathy," published in 1899, contains the evocative line, "I know why the caged bird sings." Like Washington, black statesman Frederick Douglass used the story of his own life to examine society in his 1845 autobiography, *Narrative of the Life of Frederick Douglass.* Pioneering sociologist W. E. B. Du Bois approached the issue from a scientific point of view in his 1898 work *The Study of the Negro Problems,* and crusading editor Ida B. Wells launched a campaign against racist violence in her 1892 pamphlet *Southern Horrors: Lynch Law in All Its Phases.*

The serialized sections of *Up from Slavery* were greeted with enthusiasm by the mostly northern urban white readers of the *Outlook,* and many requested that individual sections be published in a single volume. Among those less appreciative of Washington's conciliatory tone was Du Bois, whose 1903 book of essays, *The Souls of Black Folk,* contains a critical chapter titled, "Of Mr. Booker T. Washington and Others." The two points of view represented by Washington and Du Bois—the pragmatic and the radical, respectively—have remained central to the discourse about racism into the twenty-first century.

THEMES AND STYLE

Washington's central thesis in *Up from Slavery* is that success for the black race will come through thrift, hard work, and "industrial education," or training in skilled trades. He writes, "I … learned to love labour … for the independence and self-reliance which the ability to do something which the world wants done brings." In a time of severe exploitation of black workers, he advocates land ownership and self-employment as far more achievable goals than securing political rights. "The wisest among my race understand that the agitation of questions of social equality is the extremest folly," he says, asserting that "political agitation drew the attention of our people away from the more fundamental matters of perfecting themselves in the industries … and in securing property." He vividly describes his own thirst for education ("I was on fire constantly with one ambition, and that was to go to Hampton.") and extols the values of the student who is "constantly making an effort through the industries to help himself." In one of the most frequently quoted passages, Washington calls for a sort of limited unity he maintains will benefit both races: "In all things that are purely social we can be as separate as the fingers, yet one as the hand in all things essential to mutual progress."

Writing for a white audience in *Up from Slavery,* Washington carefully engineers his life story to present an unthreatening portrait of black Americans, much as the authors of earlier slave narratives had done. He chooses a classic American format—the "rags-to-riches" story of a poor but honest youth whose hard work and dedication lead to success. In service of this goal, the author exaggerates some of the details of his life and presents himself almost exclusively in a staidly heroic light. This carries through to his portrayal of Tuskegee Institute, the college he helped found in Alabama. Washington works to convince his readers to support Tuskegee, where "the education of the Negro was not making him worthless, but … adding something to the wealth and comfort of the community."

Though Washington adopts a didactic tone throughout, he uses humor and subtlety as well. He captures the ambiguous status of the American slave by describing his own uncertain roots: "I suspect

Students of architectural and mechanical drawing at Tuskegee Normal and Industrial Institute during the 1890s. As the director of this all-black school in Alabama, which later became Tuskegee University, Booker T. Washington aimed to produce teachers who would encourage hard work, self-sufficiency, and the development of skills that would help black students achieve equality with other races. © NORTH WIND PICTURE ARCHIVES/ALAMY

ELIZABETH KECKLEY: *BEHIND THE SCENES*

The slave narrative was one of the most important genres of early African American literature, but few slaves came as close to the seat of power as did Elizabeth Hobbes Keckley, who published her memoir, *Behind the Scenes; or, Thirty Years a Slave and Four Years in the White House,* in 1868. Born into slavery in Virginia about 1818, Keckley suffered beatings and rape at the hands of her owners before finally arranging to buy her freedom in 1855. She was an accomplished dressmaker who not only was able to support her husband and child with her earnings but for several years was also the main support of the white family that owned her.

After gaining her freedom, she moved to Washington DC, where she became seamstress to a number of powerful families before taking a job as dressmaker for Mary Todd Lincoln, wife of the president. Keckley was loyal to Mrs. Lincoln, and when the first lady's financial situation deteriorated after the assassination of her husband, Keckley tried to help, first by organizing a sale of Mrs. Lincoln's clothing and then by writing her autobiography, which was, in part, a defense of her employer. The public was scandalized, however, by the public exposure of Mary Lincoln's difficulties, and Keckley soon found herself abandoned by the family she had tried to support. She died in poverty and obscurity in 1907, but her autobiography is still an important source of historical information about the lives of slaves and the internal workings of the Lincoln household.

I must have been born somewhere and at some time." It is through small observations that Washington gives his most devastating portrait of the slave's life: "It had never occurred to me that there was no period of my life that was devoted to play." The replacement of ancestral names with the names of owners is a primary symbol of enslavement, and Washington explores several facets of naming. "There was a feeling that 'John Hatcher' or 'Hatcher's John' was not the proper title by which to denote a freeman; and so in many cases 'John Hatcher' was changed to 'John S. Lincoln' … the initial 'S' standing for no name, it being simply a part of what the coloured man proudly called his 'entitles.'"

CRITICAL DISCUSSION

Up from Slavery was successful in its aims of promoting white sympathy for the endeavors of industrious black Americans. A 1901 review in the *New York Times* hails the book as a positive response to the many negative portrayals of blacks and calls it "a brave record" and "a means of encouragement and inspiration to all aspiring souls among his people." Much of the African American response was positive as well. L. E. Herron's review in the *Southern Workman* calls the book "a 'lesson in life' that … cannot fail to inspire and help."

In an early review in the *Dial,* Du Bois recognizes that Washington "intuitively grasped the spirit of the age," though his later writing charges, "Mr. Washington represents in Negro thought the old attitude of adjustment and submission."

Washington's editor Lyman Abbott called *Up from Slavery* "a valuable addition both to American history and to American literature" that "ought to be in every school library in the country." His words proved prescient, as Washington's autobiography has rarely been out of print since its publication and has been translated into eighteen languages. Its short-term effects were considerable, including inspiring wealthy northern philanthropist Andrew Carnegie to donate extensively to Tuskegee Institute and influencing young Marcus Garvey to take a leadership role in the black community. In the long term, *Up from Slavery* remains an important text for historians and students of the development of the African American community.

Some modern scholars view Washington's philosophy of compromise and acceptance as an artifact of his moment in history. His biographer Louis R. Harlan notes that Washington's death coincided with the beginning of the Great Migration of black workers from the South to the North, asserting, "Washington's racial philosophy, pragmatically adjusted to the limiting conditions of his own era, did not survive the change." In the century since the publication of *Up from Slavery,* critics have continued to analyze Washington's unique contribution to the understanding of slavery. One such critic is Susanna Ashton, who has examined the humor underlying the author's stern instruction. Others have challenged the view of Washington as encouraging black compliance. One example is biographer Robert J. Norrell, who saw in the author the modern value of placing "a premium on finding consensus and empathizing with other groups."

BIBLIOGRAPHY

Sources

Abbott, Lyman. "Booker T. Washington, Statesman." *Silhouettes of My Contemporaries.* Doubleday, 1921. 258–81. Rpt. in *Twentieth-Century Literary Criticism.* Ed. Dennis Poupard. Vol. 10. Detroit: Gale Research, 1983. *Literature Resource Center.* Web. 6 Nov. 2012.

Du Bois, W. E. B. "Of Mr. Booker T. Washington and Others." *The Souls of Black Folk: Essays and Sketches.* Chicago: McClurg, 1915. 41–59. Rpt. in *Twentieth-Century Literary Criticism.* Ed. Dennis Poupard. Vol. 10. Detroit: Gale Research, 1983. *Literature Resource Center.* Web. 8 Nov. 2012.

Harlan, Louis R. "Booker T. Washington." *Documenting the American South.* Durham, N.C.: University of North Carolina, n.d. Web. 8 Nov. 2012.

Herron, L. E. Rev. of *Up from Slavery,* by Booker T. Washington. *Southern Workman* 30.5 (1901): 320. Print.

Norrell, Robert J. Introduction. *Up from History: The Life of Booker T. Washington.* By Booker T. Washington. Cambridge, Mass.: Belknap, 2009. Print.

Rev. of *Up from Slavery,* by Booker T. Washington. *New York Times* 9 Mar. 1901: BR1. *ProQuest.* Web. 12 Nov. 2012.

Washington, Booker T., and W. Fitzhugh Brundage. *Up from Slavery: With Related Documents.* Boston: Bedford/St. Martin's, 2003. Print.

Further Reading

Ashton, Susanna. "Entitles: Booker T. Washington's Signs of Play." *Southern Literary Journal* 39.2 (2007): 1+. *Literature Resource Center.* Web. 6 Nov. 2012.

Bly, Antonio T. "Navigating the Print Line: Shaping Readers' Expectations in Booker T. Washington's Autobiographies." *Alabama Review* 61.3 (2008): 190+. *Literature Resource Center.* Web. 6 Nov. 2012.

Harlan, Louis R. *Booker T. Washington: The Making of a Black Leader, 1856–1901.* New York: Oxford University Press, 1972. Print.

Howells, W. D. "An Exemplary Citizen." *North American Review* 173.537 (1901): 280–88. Rpt. in *Twentieth-Century Literary Criticism.* Ed. Dennis Poupard. Vol. 10. Detroit: Gale Research, 1983. *Literature Resource Center.* Web. 6 Nov. 2012.

Mugleston, William. "Booker T. Washington: Educator and Race Leader." *American National Biography.* Oxford: Oxford University Press, 2000. Print.

Tina Gianoulis

THE WAY TO RAINY MOUNTAIN

N. Scott Momaday

Key Facts

Time Period:
Mid-20th Century

Relevant Historical Events:
American Indian movement; civil rights movement; Native American renaissance

Nationality:
American

Keywords:
Native American; AIM; civil rights

OVERVIEW

N. Scott Momaday's *The Way to Rainy Mountain* (1969) is a multifaceted narrative that juxtaposes the oral history of the Kiowa people with the author's own memories. In an intricate layering of genres, Momaday, an enrolled member of the Kiowa Tribe of Oklahoma, retells tribal myths and history, shares family stories and individual reminiscences, describes Kiowa landscapes and people, and recounts his own journey to locate his Indian identity and ancestors. Blending visual and verbal material, Momaday scatters eleven stark black-and-white illustrations drawn in the Kiowa artistic tradition by his father, Al Momaday, throughout the text.

By the time *The Way to Rainy Mountain* was published, the author had already gained prominence as one of the first Native American writers to achieve recognition with a wide audience. Born Navarro Scott Mammedaty in 1934 on the Kiowa reservation in Oklahoma, Momaday has been honored with many prestigious awards, from a Pulitzer Prize to the National Medal of Arts, but readers will not find these achievements in *The Way to Rainy Mountain*. Rather, the autobiography is a collective yet personal story that spans hundreds of years of Kiowa history, beginning with the tribe's mythical entrance into the world and following its historical migration from the northwestern United States to the Great Plains to southwestern Oklahoma. Momaday intertwines the tribe's journey with his own pilgrimage to the burial site of his grandmother at Rainy Mountain, a small knoll in Oklahoma sacred to the Kiowa. That he accomplishes all of this in the span of less than one hundred pages is a feat in itself.

HISTORICAL AND LITERARY CONTEXT

The 1960s and 1970s saw a resurgence of Pan-Indian efforts to gain political and cultural recognition, with increased visibility as a result of efforts including the founding of the American Indian Movement (AIM) in 1968 and the occupation of Alcatraz Island in San Francisco by AIM members in 1969. Writings by Native Americans had not enjoyed widespread acclaim in American culture until Momaday's *House Made of Dawn* (1969), the first and only work by a Native American to win a Pulitzer Prize. This recognition launched what scholar Kenneth Lincoln terms the "Native American Renaissance" (the title of his 1983 book), with a notable increase in the writing and publication of literature by American Indians and more widespread teaching of native literary texts in college courses.

The publication of *The Way to Rainy Mountain* occurred amid this political and social mobilization, in the same year that the groundbreaking manifesto *Custer Died for Our Sins*, by Vine Deloria Jr., a Standing Rock Sioux, burst onto the American scene. Momaday's narrative began as a collection of Kiowa stories he gathered by interviewing Kiowa elders and then collected in a privately published, hand-printed book, *The Journey of Tai-me* (1967), which Momaday calls its "archetype." In forming the text, he pieced together stories from Kiowa elders—translated to English by his father because Momaday does not speak Kiowa—and research from anthropological accounts, folklore archives, and historical documents, as well as his own reimagining of these sources.

In relation to the American autobiographical tradition, *The Way to Rainy Mountain* is an experimental mix of Western literary conventions and Kiowa oral traditions, and it calls to mind modernist experimentation with its layering of private and public stories and visual and written forms. Its focus on the Kiowa people rather than on Momaday himself challenges the very definition of autobiography as the self-authored story of the individual. Rather, its collective narrative, in which the author explores the individual in relation to the larger tribal community, is a hallmark of Native American autobiographical writing, which typically incorporates personal memories and family stories with tribal history.

The Way to Rainy Mountain, along with *House Made of Dawn*, is one of Momaday's finest achievements and considered by scholars to be his greatest contribution to world literature. Although he also published a second autobiographical work, *The Names: A Memoir* (1976), a more conventional autobiography, Momaday himself has called *The Way to Rainy Mountain* his favorite book, in part because it grew out of stories he had heard since childhood. According to Kendall Johnson in her essay in *Columbia Guide to American Indian Literatures of the United States Since 1945* (2006), these two texts have been "monumental in establishing twentieth-century Native autobiography." Momaday's work has impacted

A 1941 painting of Kiowas in the Great Plains by W. Langdon Kihn. N. Scott Momaday's *The Way to Rainy Mountain* incorporates Kiowa legends, their historical context, and Momaday's personal reflections. Momaday's father, Al Momaday, illustrated the book. © W. LANGDON KIHN/NATIONAL GEOGRAPHIC SOCIETY/CORBIS

subsequent autobiographical writings by Native Americans, particularly in its challenge to the boundaries of autobiography and its inclusion of visual elements to tell a communal story.

THEMES AND STYLE

The near-destruction of Kiowa culture by the early twentieth century figures prominently in *The Way to Rainy Mountain,* but the preservation of Kiowa myths and traditions, the chronicling of Kiowa history, and the designation of Kiowa geographies are equally notable themes. As Momaday writes in the epilogue, Kiowa culture "is within the reach of memory still, though tenuously now, and moreover it is even defined in a remarkably rich and living verbal tradition which demands to be preserved for its own sake." The search for Indian identity, the importance of ancestral ties, and a reciprocal relationship with the natural world are key themes the work shares with other Native American literary texts. *The Way to Rainy Mountain* also explores conceptual concerns, including the origins, power, and preservation of language; the nature of the sacred; and the role of the imagination in creating the self and the world.

The Way to Rainy Mountain has a distinctive structure of twenty-four tripartite sections. Each of these two-page sections is told in three voices using three discourses—distinguished on the page with three typefaces—coming from three epistemological positions: the mythical (Kiowa tribal and family stories), the historical (historical and anthropological explanations), and the personal (Momaday's memories of Kiowa people and landscapes). The first triad, for example, relates the Kiowa origin story, in which "the Kiowas came one by one into the world through a hollow log." The Kiowa are "a small tribe in number" because a pregnant woman got stuck in the log and "no one could get through." The people who came into the world called themselves *Kwuda,* "coming out." The historical part of this triad builds on the mythical by explaining the etymology of the word "Kwuda" and how the people came to be called "Kiowa." The twenty-four sections are divided among three major chapters named after stages of a journey, and the book is framed by two of Momaday's poems. This multi-genre text maintains narrative continuity with the parallels between the historic migration of the Kiowa people and Momaday's journey to reestablish his connection with the tribe. As the book progresses the distinctions among the three parts fade, and the unification of myth, history, and personal narrative constitute the journey, as Momaday explains in the prologue.

The potency of language and the sacredness of the word are reflected in the tone of *The Way to Rainy Mountain.* Momaday writes, "A word has power in and of itself. It comes from nothing into sound and meaning; it gives origin to all things." His diction is direct and his syntax straightforward, recalling the Kiowa oral storytelling tradition. The language is richly concentrated, evoking the lyric poetry Momaday favors in his writing. The narrative incorporates oral storytelling devices, including repetition of words and phrases, multiple voices, songs, and formulas of oral expression such as, "You know, everything had to begin, and this is how it was," "A long time ago," and "Once there was." *The Way to Rainy Mountain* has variously been labeled autoethnography, creative nonfiction, lyrical prose poem, collective memoir, autobiography com-

NATIVE AMERICAN AUTOBIOGRAPHICAL WRITING

The very project of autobiography to represent the self in writing is complicated for Native Americans, for whom the idea of self may differ from a Western conception, yet the autobiographical tradition dates back hundreds of years. Personal narratives by Native Americans predate the advent of writing, if oral and pictographic accounts prior to contact with European explorers are considered. Early American writing includes many Native American personal narratives compiled by European Americans, known as "as-told-to" accounts because they were related to and written down by European Americans rather than by their subjects. Perhaps the best known of these is *Black Elk Speaks* (1932), written by John G. Neihardt based on conversations with Black Elk (Oglala Sioux) and translated from Lakota by Black Elk's son.

The earliest known written autobiography by a Native American is "A Short Narrative of My Life," a 1768 narrative by the Reverend Samson Occom (1723–92), a Mohegan, although it should be noted that others may have been written but have been lost over time. Many subsequent autobiographical writings by Native Americans detail the authors' conversion to Christianity, in part because during the nineteenth century religious organizations largely dominated Indian education. The first full-length autobiography published by an American Indian is thought to be *A Son of the Forest* (1829) by William Apess (Pequot, 1798–1839), ironically a few years after James Fenimore Cooper published his misnamed novel *Last of the Mohicans* (1826).

bined with a nonfiction study of Kiowa culture, creation hymn, novel, and epic history, suggesting that the work transcends the boundaries of genre altogether.

CRITICAL DISCUSSION

At the time of publication, *The Way to Rainy Mountain* received brief mention in mainstream magazines such as the *New Yorker* and *Atlantic Monthly*. Most reviewers commented on the beauty of its writing and the significance of its structure. In his favorable 1970 review in *Western Humanities Review,* Roland Dickey notes, "The book hangs together like a constellation, its parts varying in distance and intensity. The spaces, the silences, invite the reader to reflect." Jeffrey Huntsman praises its physical layout and writing in his scholarly review of the book, writing, "Momaday's writing is typically spare, exact, poetical in ultimate simplicity and honesty of diction and in its effect on the reader."

Since its publication, *The Way to Rainy Mountain* has received critical acclaim for its efforts to preserve Kiowa tradition and portray Kiowa culture and for its innovative form. It is frequently taught in high schools and colleges. Scholars name Momaday a key voice in both native literatures and American literature. In *The People and the Word* (2005), a study of the history and impact of Native American nonfiction from the eighteenth to the late twentieth century, scholar Robert Allen Warrior declares Momaday "the single most visible American Indian literary author of the twentieth century." In recent years Momaday has come to be seen affectionately as "the dean of American Indian writers," due not only to his Pulitzer Prize but also his extraordinary publication in a wide range of literary forms.

Scholarly work on *The Way to Rainy Mountain* has focused on its structure and its themes—particularly the decline and preservation of Kiowa culture and the search for an Indian identity. In *N. Scott Momaday: The Cultural and Literary Background* (1985), Matthias Schubnell contextualizes the book in Momaday's oeuvre and suggests it provides the author "the recognition of what it means to feel himself a Kiowa in the modern American culture that displaced his ancestors." Kimberly Blaeser uses reader-response theory in her 1989 article to show that Momaday makes the reader a "co-creator of the literary work" through its form; its use of "unusual juxtaposition, contradiction, intentional gaps and ambiguity"; its physical layout; and its visual contrasts. In *Sending My Heart Back across the Years* (1992), Hertha Wong indicates that *The Way to Rainy Mountain* and other contemporaneous Indian autobiographies "reclaim pre-contact Native American notions of a communal self that is linked to the tribe, the land, and the cosmos" and combine it with a Western notion of individuality. In a 2011 article, Anna Brigido-Corachán compares *The Way to Rainy Mountain* to Mexican American writer Gloria Anzaldúa's *Borderlands/The Fontera* and sees a connection in the search for belonging and recognition within their ethnic communities and the broader American culture.

BIBLIOGRAPHY

Sources

Blaeser, Kimberly. "*The Way to Rainy Mountain*: Momaday's Work in Motion." *Narrative Chance: Postmodern Discourse on Native American Indian Literature.* Ed. Gerald Vizenor. Albuquerque: University of New Mexico Press, 1989. 39–54. Print.

Brigido-Corachán, Anna M. "Native Journeys of Self-Figuration: N. Scott Momaday's *The Way to Rainy Mountain* and Gloria Anzaldúa's *Borderlands/The Fontera.*" *Selves in Dialogue: A Transethnic Approach to American Life Writing.* Ed. Begoña Simal. New York: Rodopi, 2011. 109–32. *ebrary.* Web. 20 Nov. 2012.

Dickey, Roland F. Rev. of *The Way to Rainy Mountain,* by N. Scott Momaday. *Western Humanities Review.* 24.3 (1970): 290–91. Print.

Huntsman, Jeffrey F. Rev. of *The Way to Rainy Mountain,* by N. Scott Momaday. *Studies in American Indian Literatures, ASAIL Newsletter* 4.2 (1980): 20–21. Print.

Johnson, Kendall. "Imagining Self and Community in American Indian Autobiography." *Columbia Guide to American Indian Literatures of the United States*

Since 1945. Ed. Eric Cheyfitz. New York: Columbia University Press, 2006. 357–409. Web. 20 Nov. 2012.

Momaday, N. Scott. *The Way to Rainy Mountain*. Albuquerque: University of New Mexico Press, 1969. Print.

Schubnell, Matthias. *N. Scott Momaday: The Cultural and Literary Background*. Norman: University of Oklahoma Press, 1985. Print.

Warrior, Robert Allen. *The People and the Word: Reading Native Nonfiction*. Minneapolis: University of Minnesota Press, 2005. Web. 20 Nov. 2012.

Wong, Hertha D. *Sending My Heart Back across the Years: Tradition and Innovation in Native American Autobiography*. New York: Oxford University Press, 1992. Web. 20 Nov. 2012.

Further Reading

Dickinson-Brown, Robert. "The Art and Importance of N. Scott Momaday." *Southern Review* 14.1 (1978): 30–45.

Krupat, Arnold, ed. *Native American Autobiography: An Anthology*. Madison: University of Wisconsin Press, 1994. Print.

Lincoln, Kenneth. "Tai-Me to Rainy Mountain: The Makings of American Indian Literature." *American Indian Quarterly* 10.2 (1986): 101–17. *JSTOR*. Web. 20 Nov. 2012.

Momaday, N. Scott. "The Man Made of Words." *Indian Voices: The First Convocation of American Indian Scholars*. San Francisco: Indian Historian, 1970. 49–84. Print.

Momaday, N. Scott. *The Man Made of Words: Essays, Stories, Passages*. New York: St. Martin's, 1997. Print.

Roemer, Kenneth M. *Approaches to Teaching Momaday's "The Way to Rainy Mountain."* New York: MLA, 1989. Print.

Schubnell, Matthias, ed. *Conversations with N. Scott Momaday*. Jackson: University of Mississippi Press, 1997. Print.

Teuton, Christopher B. *Deep Waters: The Textual Continuum in American Indian Literature*. Lincoln: University of Nebraska Press, 2010. Print.

Trimble, Martha Scott. *N. Scott Momaday*. Boise: Boise State College, 1973.

Woodward, Charles L. *Ancestral Voice: Conversations with N. Scott Momaday*. Lincoln: University of Nebraska Press, 1989.

Alicia Kent

Between Cultures

The Abandoned Baobab: The Autobiography of a Senegalese Woman by Ken Bugul	61
The Autobiography of Charles Darwin by Charles Darwin	65
Chona: The Autobiography of a Papago Woman by Maria Chona and Ruth Underhill	69
The Color of Water: A Black Man's Tribute to His White Mother by James McBride	72
A Cross and a Star: Memoirs of a Jewish Girl in Chile by Marjorie Agosín	75
Dreams from My Father: A Story of Race and Inheritance by Barack Obama	78
The Interesting Narrative of the Life of Olaudah Equiano, or Gustavus Vassa, the African, Written by Himself by Olaudah Equiano	81
A Long Way from Home by Claude McKay	84
Meatless Days by Sara Suleri	87
Memoirs of an Arabian Princess from Zanzibar by Emily Ruete	90
My Life Story by Fadhma Aïth Mansour Amrouche	93
Prison Writings: My Life Is My Sun Dance by Leonard Peltier	96
Rites: A Guatemalan Boyhood by Victor Perera	99
Ten Thousand Sorrows: The Extraordinary Journey of a Korean War Orphan by Elizabeth Kim	102
The Travels of Marco Polo by Marco Polo	105
When I Was Puerto Rican by Esmeralda Santiago	108
The Wonderful Adventures of Mrs. Seacole in Many Lands by Mary Seacole	111
The Worlds of a Maasai Warrior: An Autobiography by Tepilit Ole Saitoti	114

THE ABANDONED BAOBAB
The Autobiography of a Senegalese Woman
Ken Bugul

OVERVIEW

First published in French as *Le Baobab fou* in 1982, *The Abandoned Baobab: The Autobiography of a Senegalese Woman* (1991) by Ken Bugul is a fictionalized account of the author's real-life experience as an abandoned and alienated African woman struggling to form a coherent sense of identity. Labeled an autobiographical novel, the work traces the author's difficult experience of being abandoned by her mother; being raised an orphan in her native Senegalese village; rejecting African culture in favor of a colonial education; and living in Brussels, where she fights against racism, drug use, depression, and sexual exploitation before reclaiming her African cultural heritage. Throughout the text Bugul explores the legacy of colonialism in a narrative that extends the conventional strictures of autobiographical narrative to explore a wider sociopolitical and historical context.

Ken Bugul is a pseudonym of Mariétou M'Baye, who disguised her identity for fear of the scandal that might erupt due to the book's frank disclosures about her sexual experiences. In her native Wolof language, the name Ken Bugul means "the person no one wants" and, therefore, emphasizes the book's pronounced theme of abandonment. Though the novel did prove controversial upon its initial Senegalese publication in French, it also helped launch Bugul's career as a critically acclaimed writer of deeply personal and profound explorations of the postcolonial experience. Today, *The Abandoned Baobab* is considered a landmark work of late-twentieth-century African writing.

HISTORICAL AND LITERARY CONTEXT

Through the framework of the author's personal struggles, *The Abandoned Baobab* explores the legacy of colonialism in Africa. This process began in the fifteenth century, when European powers started to explore and settle overseas lands, and expanded into Africa in the sixteenth century. It was not until the mid-nineteenth century, however, that Europeans began to explore, conquer, and settle inland Africa. In 1854 Bugul's native country, Senegal, was colonized by France. Over the rest of the late nineteenth century, the French aggressively expanded their colonial presence on the continent. Like other colonizers, the French justified their suppression of indigenous peoples, customs, and languages by arguing that they were civilizing the local population through the imposition of superior European culture and values on native populations. The result was a century of occupation and oppression in many African countries, including Senegal.

By the time *The Abandoned Baobab* was published, Senegal had achieved independence from France. After becoming an independent state in 1960, the country was led by its influential first president Léopold-Sédar Senghor, who was also an important poet. In the 1930s, with Aimé Césaire, Senghor helped form *négritude,* a literary movement that called for African writers to assert their native cultural heritage and denounce the devastation wrought by colonialism. Though the movement had died out by 1960s, *négritude* remained influential on African writers through the twentieth century, and its mark can be detected in *The Abandoned Baobab.* Like her protagonist, Bugul was born before Senegal achieved independence and left her homeland to study in Belgium. Her experience both as a colonized subject at home and as an outsider in a European colonial center was central to the autobiographical impulse that led to book.

The Abandoned Baobab is part of a long tradition that can be traced back to Bakary Diallo's *Force-Bonté* (1927), which is considered the earliest Senegalese Francophone novel. Like Bugul's work, *Force-Bonté* recounts its protagonist's travels from Africa to Europe and back, offering along the way an examination of the differences between the colonized and colonial worlds. Another important precedent of *The Abandoned Baobab* is Cheikh Hamidou Kane's *L'Aventure ambiguë* (1961; *Ambiguous Adventure,* 1963). Kane's novel also records a young African's move to Europe and his subsequent alienation, disaffection, and confusion.

The success of *The Abandoned Baobab,* as well as the therapeutic value it offered its author, led Bugul to write two more books that continued her autobiographical explorations. *Cendres et braises* (1994) and *Riwan ou le chemin de sable* (1999) completed a trilogy that extensively explored and documented the author's lived experience within an ambiguously fictional framework. After completing this sixteen-year investigation into her life and identity, Bugul seemingly turned away from the subject of herself.

Key Facts

Time Period:
Late 20th Century

Relevant Historical Events:
Achievement of Senegalese independence; end of colonialism in Africa

Nationality:
Senegalese

Keywords:
postcolonialism; feminism; alienation

Author Ken Bugul in Bamako, Mali, in 2002. © FREDERIC REGLAIN/GAMMA-RAPHO/GETTY IMAGES

However, as the scholar Patrick Corcoran writes in *The Cambridge Introduction to Francophone Literature*, "her later 'fictional' works naturally continue to draw on such experience, often exploring what for Ken Bugul herself were deeply personal issues."

THEMES AND STYLE

The central theme of *The Abandoned Baobab* is that the alienation of familial, cultural, and geographic exile can be healed by the act of autobiographical writing. Throughout the text, Bugul struggles to reconcile her past in Africa and her present in Europe, both of which are defined in her mind by the experience of trauma, abandonment, and detachment. The book begins with "Ken's Prehistory," a brief section in which a third-person narrator describes life in Bugul's home village before her birth. Bugul's ancestors arrive, a fire nearly destroys the village, and a baobab seed is planted. As Mildred Mortimer writes in *Journeys through the French African Novel* (1990), "Accidental and unforeseen, the three events foreshadow and mirror important moments in the protagonist's life: migration, near destruction, rebirth." After falling into a despair that leads her to the brink of suicide in Belgium, Bugul returns to the village and the baobab tree at the novel's end, thus completing a personal and narrative journey through the pangs of alienation.

Bugul's motivation for writing *The Abandoned Baobab* was largely personal and therapeutic. According to Mortimer, when discussing her initial impetus for writing the novel, Bugul has said, "I had not intended to write a book, but to bear witness to my life, to get it out, put it before me on paper; and that released me." Despite her ostensibly therapeutic reason for writing about her life, Bugul's text also reveals an intense desire to grapple with the effects of colonialism on the colonized. She writes, for example, that colonialism "had created the spiritual distortion that brought into existence the people stripped of their bearings." And yet, while she writes that "[c]olonialism undermined everything," she declares that she "refused to believe that colonialism was the only reason for it all." Although writing about her own life, the author's decisions to use a pseudonym and to label her work "fiction" are indicative of the ways in which larger social forces have determined not only Bugul's text but also the course of her difficult life.

Stylistically, *The Abandoned Baobab* is notable for its mix of straightforward narrative reportage and lyrical investigations of her story's larger themes. For much of the novel, Bugul describes her life in Belgium in plain terms: "I went to the bathroom, following the instruction I had been given the night before." She often, however, breaks from this voice to describe despairing search for meaning in the seemingly prosaic events of her life: "The sublime superimposes itself on the unreal and I was incapable of dreaming.... I'd arrived like the devil prepared to fight the adversary."

CRITICAL DISCUSSION

Upon publication in Senegal in 1984, *The Abandoned Baobab* was met with widespread acclaim and helped catalyze Bugul's ongoing career as one of Africa's most vital writers. When the novel was translated into English in 1991, it was met with effusive praise from scholars and critics. In the *New York Times*, for

PRIMARY SOURCE

EXCERPT FROM *THE ABANDONED BAOBAB: THE AUTOBIOGRAPHY OF A SENEGALESE WOMAN*

The mother was busy preparing the millet for the noon meal she was to take to the fields, to the father and the two older sons who had left for the day early in the morning.

It was the period in which the land was being worked for the next sowing of the millet and peanuts.

"Ma, give me some sugar," begged Codou, Fodé's sister.

The mother didn't hear a thing. Sitting on her goatskin mat, the calabash in the hollow between her strong thighs—thighs that had pulsated for so many reasons since the day that the father had come to ask for her hand in marriage—she held her head lowered over her water-drenched millet. While one hand steadied the calabash and the other did the kneading, with her legs uncovered, her chest naked, her breasts sagging like empty pouches, the mother had dozed off.

"Ma!" Codou put a hand on the mother's shoulder.

"Eh! What do you want?" With a start, the mother woke up. "Some sugar to put in the *ndiambâne*." Carelessly, Codou added, "Fodé took down the most beautiful fruit of the baobab tree."

The mother was exasperated.

"Ah, I've had just about enough of you. Come and help me here. Light the fire and bring me the pot."

As she picked up her calabash again, the mother continued her monologue: "Oh God, what did I ever do to deserve such a no-good daughter! All she does is spend her time running around with the boys in the village, chasing birds and wild rats."

Codou wanted to take advantage of this opportunity to get away.

"Oh no! That's enough, you stay right here, you evil child. First go and call Fodé Ndao. I asked him to cut the wood for me. Another good-for-nothing; I'm going to tell his father to take him along to the fields. Who has ever seen anything like it: a man who stays home. Isn't he almost eight? Go, go find him and get back here right away, you, you don't do anything, you aren't good for anything, you don't know how to do anything at all."

And once again the mother started to knead the millet.

Suddenly she stopped, called back Codou, who was slowly heading for the granary, while with her feet she playfully worked the fine sand that had bathed the footsteps of this Gouye family for a whole generation.

"Quick, come back here, something is biting my back. Hurry up, you lazy thing."

Codou retraced her steps, came closer to the mother, bent over her.

"Below there, oh you're so silly, I said between … on the side … and there…."

"But mother, I don't see anything, there's nothing there," Codou managed to say.

"You have such a nasty attitude." The mother seemed at her wit's end.

She let go of the calabash and, taking the broom, she scratched her back.

Codou had already turned around and was running to the granary. She found Fodé also scratching himself everywhere. The velvet casing that covered the husk of the fruit was itching.

"Ah Codou, at last, what were you doing? Where's the sugar?" He was talking to his sister while he continued his scratching.

"Of course, if you're going to stroke that fruit you're going to get it all over yourself. Fodé, Ma said no. She says you should come and cut the wood."

Codou was talking to her brother as if she were talking to herself.

"Fine. We'll make the *ndiambâne* later," Fodé reluctantly consoled himself. "I'll steal some sugar from Ma, I know where she keeps it."

And the day passed with its little moments of pleasure, moments of dozing, moments of dreaming, of working, of contemplating space, until the evening fell.

The father and the brothers returned from the fields at the same time that the herd was brought back by Mbougne, the shepherd, who took it to graze all day in the brush.

With the dusk, exhaustion came swooping down. Darkness enveloped all instincts and dreams.

The moment. The hour of silence. Darkness. Dreams. The world going to sleep.

SOURCE: Bugul, Ken. *The Abandoned Baobab: The Autobiography of a Senegalese Woman.* Trans. Marjolijn de Jager. Brooklyn, NY: Lawrence Hill, 1991.

---

example, the American fiction writer Norman Rush called the book "a salutary reminder of how difficult it is truly to cast a cold eye on what we are and on the obstacles we face in the attempt to make ourselves into something we would prefer to have been." Rush also notes the book's cultural distinctiveness: "To read this book fairly one must be willing to acclimate, to hold in mind the awareness that the correct referents for its style are the forms of African oral public art—village storytelling, griot performances, praise-poems."

In the years following its publication, Bugul's narrative attracted considerable attention from scholars.

AFRICAN AUTOBIOGRAPHY

Ken Bugul's *The Abandoned Baobab* exists within a much larger tradition of African autobiography. That tradition includes not only written texts but also oral accounts recorded by missionaries, anthropologists, journalists, and other outsiders. These transcribed life stories first began to be published in the 1930s and continued to appear through the twentieth century. In these accounts, the life of the storyteller is filtered through the experience, language, and bias of the recorder. Some of the earliest transcribed autobiographies to emerge from Africa were composed by missionaries who took the facts of a subject's life and fit them into the framework of Christian-conversion narratives. In this way, the lives of these first African autobiographers were co-opted by Westerners who used the facts of their subjects' experiences to convert people to Christianity.

Thus, the self-composed autobiographies of African writers represent, explicitly or implicitly, attempts to reclaim not only identity but also agency from the clutches of colonial influence. One of the first female Africans to write her own autobiography was the Nigerian Kofoworola Aina Moore. Her story, which was published in 1936 as part of the collection *Ten Africans,* explores the alienation and confusion that emerged from her experience as a native in colonized Africa and as an outsider in Europe. These are themes that recur repeatedly in *The Abandoned Baobab* as well as other African autobiographies.

Even as she continued to publish works of fiction and autobiography and won the Grand Prix Littéraire d'Afrique Noir in 2000 for *Riwan ou le chemin de sable, The Abandoned Baobab* has remained her most prominent work among English-language audiences and critics. Scholars have approached the work through a wide range of analytical frameworks, considering its value within the context of autobiographical, African, and women's writing.

Bugul's text is often read for the ways in which it subverts traditional generic conventions of autobiographical writing. In her essay "African 'Herstory': The Feminist Reader and the Autobiographical Voice," Nicki Hitchcott places *The Abandoned Baobab* alongside Aoua Kéita's *Femme d'Afrique* (1975) and Nafissatou Diallo's *De Tilène au Plateau* (1975), arguing that the three texts "rewrite the traditionally male, bourgeois genre of autobiography, and the extent to which they correspond to the structures and ideologies of feminist autobiography or confession." Hitchcott argues, too, that, of the three, Bugul's book "is the most vehement condemnation of the West, [yet] it is also the most explicitly feminist text." Commentators have also drawn attention to the conflicted relationship with colonization found in *The Abandoned Baobab*. The scholar Elisabeth Mudimbe-Boyi, for example, notes the "dialectic of rejection and belonging" at play in the work. Mudimbe-Boyi places Bugul's book alongside Simone Schwarz-Bart's novel *Ti Jean L'Horizon,* arguing that they "are an invitation to reject, or at least relativize, the homogenizing discourse of an immutable and eternal African past."

BIBLIOGRAPHY

Sources

Bugul, Ken. *The Abandoned Baobab: The Autobiography of a Senegalese Woman.* Trans. Marjolijn de Jager. Brooklyn: Lawrence Hill, 1991. Print.

Corcoran, Patrick. *The Cambridge Introduction to Francophone Literature.* New York: Cambridge University Press, 2007. Print.

Hitchcott, Nicki. "African 'Herstory': The Feminist Reader and the Autobiographical Voice." *Research in African Literature* 28.2 (1997): 16–33. *ProQuest.* Web. 13 Nov. 2012.

Mortimer, Mildred. *Journeys through the French African Novel.* Portsmouth, N.H.: Heinemann, 1990. Print.

Mudimbe-Boyi, Elisabeth. "The Poetics of Exile and Errancy in *Le Baobab fou* by Ken Bugul and *Ti Jean L'Horizon* by Simone Schwarz-Bart." *Yale French Studies* 83.2 (1993): 196–212. Print.

Rush, Norman. "The Woman in the Broken Mirror." Rev. of *The Abandoned Baobab: The Autobiography of a Senegalese Woman,* by Ken Bugul. *New York Times.* New York Times, 15 Dec. 1991. Web. 13 Nov. 2012.

Further Reading

Azodo, Ada Uzoamaka, and Jeanne-Sarah de Larquier, eds. *Emerging Perspectives on Ken Bugul: From Alternative Choices to Oppositional Practices.* Trenton, N.J.: Africa World, 2008. Print.

Felski, Rita. *Beyond Feminist Aesthetics.* London: Hutchinson Radius, 1989.

Jelinek, Estelle, ed. *Women's Autobiography: Essays in Criticism.* Bloomington: Indiana University Press, 1980.

Mielly, Michelle. "Filling the Continental Split: Subjective Emergence in Ken Bugul's *Le Baobab fou* and Sylvia Molloy's *En breve cárcel.*" *Comparative Literature* 54.1 (2002): 42–57. *JSTOR.* Web. 13 Nov. 2012.

Nnaemeka, Obioma. *The Politics of (M)Othering: Womanhood, Identity and Resistance in African Literature.* Florence: Routledge, 1997.

Thompson, Chantal P. "The Myth of the Garden of Eden and the Symbolism of the Baobab Tree in West African Literature." *Francophone Post-Colonial Cultures: Critical Essays.* Ed. Kamal Salhi. New York: Lexington, 2003. Print.

Theodore McDermott

The Autobiography of Charles Darwin

Charles Darwin

Key Facts

Time Period:
Late 19th Century

Relevant Historical Events:
Darwin's voyage on the *Beagle* (1831)

Nationality:
English

Keywords:
evolution; religion; science

OVERVIEW

The Autobiography of Charles Darwin (originally published in 1887, five years after his death, as part of *The Life and Letters of Charles Darwin*) served both as a chronicle of the genesis of Charles Darwin's concepts about evolution and as a more general cultural record. Darwin's theories, which changed how people viewed the natural world and their relation to it, had been thoroughly explained in texts such as *On the Origin of Species* and *The Descent of Man*, and his first published book, *Journal and Remarks 1832–1835*, chronicles all of the observations made while sailing on the *Beagle* that led him to first formulate the theory of natural selection. In *The Autobiography*, Darwin focuses primarily on his youth and traces the habits of mind and approaches to research that he believed were crucial to his success as a scientist. Additionally, his autobiography gives an account of the intellectual elite of Victorian times—Darwin was close friends with not only prominent scientists but also writers, historians, and sociologists—and reflects his views on controversial issues of the day, such as religion and slavery.

The immediate reaction to *The Autobiography* was muted, in great part because Darwin's family deliberately censored any information that might be considered controversial. In particular, at the request of his wife, Emma, the sections about Darwin's loss of religious faith were gathered in a separate chapter and the more outright statements of disbelief were removed. While Darwin was already well known at the time of his autobiography's publication, the initial version, which emphasized his hard work and modesty about his achievement, solidified his reputation as an ideal industrious Victorian gentleman whose virtues justified paying attention to his scientific theories.

HISTORICAL AND LITERARY CONTEXT

Darwin came of age at a time when scientific study was rapidly gaining access to new data and developing new ways of interpreting it. The growth of technologies of travel and colonialism created motivation for mapping and exploring new lands (*H.M.S. Beagle*, on which Darwin took his famous voyage in the early 1830s, was commissioned by the British government to chart South America for trading and colonizing purposes) and resulted in new data, which scientists struggled to explain and organize. Some of the works dealing with this explosion of new information and approaches greatly influenced Darwin. They included Thomas Malthus's *Essay on the Principles of Population* (1798), which used observations and mathematical models to prove that populations inevitably outgrew their resources and engaged in struggles for existence; William Paley's 1802 work *Natural Theology* (though Darwin came to disagree with Paley's argument that complex organisms and natural systems proved the existence of God); and Charles Lyell's *Principles of Geology* (1830), which used growing geological data to argue for uniformitarianism, or gradual change over time (a key component of Darwin's theories).

In 1875 a German editor approached Darwin, then sixty-six, asking him to write some biographical reminiscences. Darwin was already widely acknowledged as the most important scientist of the age and had little interest in further publicity, but the recent deaths of several of his scientific mentors, including Lyell, as well as the announcement of the upcoming birth of his first grandchild, encouraged him to think about his legacy. The memories were intended only for his family and not for wider publication. When, after his death, the memoir was published along with some of his selected letters, family members quarreled over what should or should not be included, particularly in terms of Darwin's frank assessments of how his developing understanding of natural selection made it impossible for him to believe in traditional religion. It was not until 1958 that a version was published that included all of the previously expurgated passages.

Darwin wrote at a time in which autobiographies were tremendously popular, and his followed many of the trends of the age. For instance, like John Henry Newman's *Apologia Pro Vita Sua* (1864), Darwin's book is measured and almost impersonal, in marked contrast to autobiographies of earlier ages, which were often religious and featured passionate admissions of spiritual guilt. *The Autobiography* also modestly recounts actions and emphasizes self-sacrifice and hard work. In their emphasis on these traits, Victorian autobiographies, including Darwin's, had much in common with both novels and popular self-help books, such as those written by Samuel Smiles.

The posthumous *Autobiography* had little effect on how Darwin or his theories were viewed. Nevertheless, even the infrequent mentions of religious doubt

Illustration by Ned M. Seidler featuring Charles Darwin and some of his subjects of study.
© NATIONAL GEOGRAPHIC IMAGE COLLECTION/THE BRIDGEMAN ART LIBRARY

that his family allowed to remain in the early versions were grasped upon by other atheists of the age and *The Autobiography* continues to be referenced by those interested in the relation between evolutionary world views and religious faith.

THEMES AND STYLE

The Autobiography primarily covers Darwin's younger years, through his voyage on the *Beagle*, and the way that his early habits of mind, as well as his experiences and associations, shaped his success in developing and popularizing the theory of evolution. He briefly mentions his wife and children, and he devotes one chapter to the years spent developing his theory and another to a history of all of his publications. For the most part, however, he focuses on the values of careful observation, reasoning from examples, passionate love for science, and "energetic industry and … concentrated attention." *The Autobiography* also allows Darwin to comment on larger social issues. Most notable are his musings on religion, which he admits he completely left behind as he grew older, terming it "a damnable doctrine."

Darwin also outlines the unique habits of mind and the methodologies that he saw as crucial to his scientific success. "It has sometimes been said," he wrote, "that the success of the 'Origin' proved 'that the subject was in the air' … I do not think that this is strictly true." *The Autobiography* attempts to quantify why he was successful in creating that theory, a success he attributed to "the love of science—unbounded patience in long reflecting over any subject—industry in observing and collecting facts—and a fair share of invention as well as of common-sense." In addition to asserting the originality of his approach, Darwin describes himself "as if I were a dead man … looking back at my own life" and mourns his loss of pleasure in art and aesthetics. These moments suggest that in reviewing his life, Darwin felt both the natural melancholy of old age and an awareness of the way in which his ideas about the natural world had irrevocably changed not only science but also emotional and intellectual approaches to the world.

Many of the chief stylistic techniques of *The Autobiography* can be attributed to the fact that it was originally intended solely as a record for family members. Thus Darwin frequently uses direct address and familiar references that he need not explain fully. Janet Browne writes that "the work embodies many of the charms and oddities of the English gentleman at home: polite, considerate, shy, and amusingly self-deprecating; and yet unable or unwilling to delve too far below the surface." Many of these traits can be seen in this memory from his college-era mania for collecting beetles:

> "It was the mere passion for collecting, for I did not dissect them and rarely compared their external characters with published descriptions, but got them named anyhow. I will give a proof of my zeal: one day, on tearing off some old bark, I saw two rare beetles and seized one in each hand; then I saw a third and new kind, which I could not bear to lose, so that I popped the one which I held in my right hand into my mouth. Alas! it ejected some intensely acrid fluid, which burnt my tongue so that I was forced to spit the beetle out, which was lost, as well as the third one."

CRITICAL DISCUSSION

Early reactions to *The Autobiography* solidified, as Browne put it in 2010, Darwin's reputation "as an industrious man for the industrial age. He was revered as an independent and indefatigable thinker, dedicated to his work and nobly overcoming illness." Some early reviewers did catch on to the hints of religious unorthodoxy allowed in the first versions: for instance, in an 1891 biography that drew upon *The Autobiography*, William Mawer took Darwin's atheism for granted. Browne argues that the 1958 version of *The Autobiography*, edited by Darwin's granddaughter Nora Barlow, marked a new phase in critical responses to the book in which "her commitment to disclosing the inner focus on the private records of a great thinker" reflected "a wider fascination with psychological development and … personal lives."

The Autobiography, in conjunction with many of Darwin's published letters and research notebooks, has given scholars a richer understanding of his methods and motivations. Historians of science turn to it to help trace what was remarkable about Darwin's approach. John Angus Campbell, a historian of science and rhetoric, argued in 1974 that *The Autobiography* offers a means of studying the habits of mind and worldview that propelled Darwin's scientific and communicative prowess. Among cultural and literary theorists, *The Autobiography* often serves as a means to examine Darwin's intentions, or the beliefs that shaped his theories. Biographers have also used the work in part to create, in the words of Adrian Desmond and James Moore, a "defiantly social" portrait of Darwin as a product of his times as much as a great scientific genius.

The Autobiography is often cited in general studies of the role of autobiography in Victorian times. Scholars note the ways in which it focuses on portraying a modest man of action rather than of feeling, whose life can be read as a "conversion story" of failure, or weakness, to success. John Sturrock argues that this conversion in Darwin's text can actually be read in light of his own famous theories: "Darwin imposes an evolutionary perspective, placing himself intermediately, as the living but transient link between the generations of his line." After the dissemination of Sigmund Freud's ideas and psychoanalytic theory, several critics have read *The Autobiography* as a clue to Darwin's psychological motivations. Carolyn Dever, for instance, focuses on the book's few references to Darwin's mother (who died when he was eight), arguing that "the 'mother's riddle' is, for Darwin, the secret of human origins."

BIBLIOGRAPHY

Sources

Browne, Janet. *Charles Darwin: The Power of Place*. New York: Knopf, 2003. Print.

DARWINMANIA

By the 1870s, Darwin was the most famous scientist in England. His name had become synonymous with the idea of evolution, although the theory owed its full development to the work of many other scientists, including Alfred Russel Wallace and Thomas Huxley. For the typical Victorian, however, "Darwinism" denoted the idea of evolution, as Darwin's name and image increasingly appeared throughout popular culture. Cartoons and caricatures frequently portrayed Darwin—with his distinctive long beard, heavy eyebrows, and broad, sloping skull—as an ape himself. Darwinism was referenced in not only newspapers and magazines, but also popular books (including a daily almanac with quotes from Darwin, romance novels such as *The Lancashire Wedding; or, Darwin Moralized*, and the children's story *What Mr. Darwin Saw*), art, and even a song (the piano duet "Darwinian Theory"). Product manufacturers also seized upon the theme; chemist G. W. Merchant, for instance, featured a Darwinian ape in an advertisement for its gargling oil, extolling it as "a liniment for man or beast." Through these popular representations of Darwin, his ideas were made available to a wide swath of society, not just the intellectual elite who had the time and resources to read heavy tomes on science.

———. "Making Darwin: Biography and the Changing Representations of Charles Darwin." *Journal of Interdisciplinary History* 40.3 (2010): 347–73. Web. EBSCOhost. 9 Sept. 2012.

Darwin, Charles. *The Autobiography of Charles Darwin, 1809–1882. With Original Omissions Restored*. Ed. Nora Barlow. London: Collins, 1958. Print.

Desmond, Adrian, and James Moore. "Transgressing Boundaries." *Journal of Victorian Culture* 3 (1998): 147–68. EBSCOhost. Web. 7 Sept. 2012.

Dever, Carolyn. *Death and the Mother from Dickens to Freud: Victorian Fiction and the Anxiety of Origins*. Cambridge: Cambridge University Press, 1998. Print.

Mawer, William. *Truth for Its Own Sake: The Story of Charles Darwin, Written for Young People*. London: Swan Sonnenschein, 1889. Print.

Sturrock, John. *The Language of Autobiography: Studies in the First Person Singular*. Cambridge: Cambridge University Press, 1993. Print.

Further Reading

Barros, Carolyn A. *Autobiography: Narrative of Transformation*. Ann Arbor: University of Michigan Press, 1998. Print.

Campbell, John Angus. "Nature, Religion and Emotional Response: A Reconsideration of Darwin's Affective Decline." *Victorian Studies* 18.2 (1974): 159–74. Web. EBSCOhost. 8 Sept. 2012.

Harley, Alexis. "Genesis, the Origin, and Darwin's Autobiographies." *Forum* 1.1 (2005). Web. 8 Sept. 2012.

Irvine, William. *Apes, Angels, and Victorians*. New York: McGraw-Hill, 1955. Print.

Levine, George. "'And if It Be a Pretty Woman All the Better'—Darwin and Sexual Selection." *Literature, Science, Psychoanalysis, 1830–1970: Essays in Honour of Gillian Beer.* Ed. Helen Small and Trudi Tate. New York: Oxford University Press, 2003. 37–51. Print.

———. *Darwin and the Novelists: Patterns of Science in Victorian Fiction.* Cambridge: Harvard University Press, 1988. Print.

Machann, Clinton. *The Genre of Autobiography in Victorian Literature.* Ann Arbor: University of Michigan Press, 1994. Print.

Neve, Michael. Introduction. *Charles Darwin: Autobiographies.* By Charles Darwin. Ed. Michael Neve and Sharon Messenger. London: Penguin, 2002. Print.

Rosenberg, John D. "Mr. Darwin Collects Himself." *Nineteenth-Century Lives.* Ed. Laurence S. Lockridge, John Maynard, and Donald D. Stone. Cambridge: Cambridge University Press, 1989. 82–111. Print.

Abigail Mann

Chona
The Autobiography of a Papago Woman
Maria Chona, Ruth Underhill

OVERVIEW

First published in 1936 as the forty-sixth issue of the Memoirs of the American Anthropological Association series, *The Autobiography of a Papago Woman* is the life story of ninety-year-old Native American Maria Chona. The text has come to be seen among anthropologists as a collaboration between Chona and editor and ethnographer Ruth Underhill, who shaped the narrative. In the text, Underhill and Chona provide details about coming of age, getting married, bearing and rearing children, and becoming a female healer in Papago culture (which today is referred to as Tohono O'odham culture). Chona, who was born in 1845 or 1846, lived through many cultural changes, including the drafting of the U.S.-Mexico border in 1853. Therefore, she focuses in her autobiography on the changes that she witnessed, including learning how to sew and wear clothes and how to use Western-style doors as opposed to the crawl entrances typical of grass houses the Tohono O'odham built.

Like other Native American autobiographies of the time, *Papago Woman* shows an interest in preserving cultural details, as many feared Native Americans traditions would be wiped out by boarding schools, Christianity, or other federal policies. After the autobiography was republished as a book in 1979, it was rediscovered and anthologized in several collections of Native American literature. Underhill notes in an introduction to the 1979 edition that she deliberately emphasized details that would seem banal to those brought up in Tohono O'odham culture but that would be fascinating to an outsider. Because of Underhill's dominant role in the authorship of *Papago Woman*, the text is as significant for its problematic status as an autobiography as it is for documenting Native American culture at an important time of transition.

HISTORICAL AND LITERARY CONTEXT

The U.S. government instituted the reservation system in the 1850s, placing the village in which Chona was raised at the center of the Tohono O'odham reservation, the second-largest Native American reservation in Arizona. Although the Tohono O'odham did not lose as much land, or suffer as many casualties, as tribes such as the Apache and Crow, they did not retain ultimate control over their water, a precious resource in the Southwest. Officials from the Bureau of Indian Affairs often failed to protect Tohono O'odham sources of water and in some cases actively assisted settlers' illegal acquisition of water sources. In addition, rights to the Colorado River were apportioned by the U.S. Congress in 1921 without consulting affected native communities. One of Chona's earliest memories is of her father waking her at dawn and sending her to run for water with the other girls "far, far up the hills and across the flat land to a place called Where the Water Whirls Around."

Chona related her narrative to Underhill in 1932, during the Great Depression, which exacerbated conditions for many Native Americans. During this period, Native American testimonies to U.S. Senate committees regarding the breach of treaties increasingly detailed the loss of Native American land and resources, including rivers and timber, which were pilfered by European Americans also suffering in the harsh economic climate.

By the 1930s, collaborative, or ethnographic, autobiographies such as *Papago Woman* had become fashionable. Lesser-known examples include Gilbert L. Wilson's *Waheenee: An Indian Girl's Story Told by Herself to Gilbert L. Wilson* (1927), which was in

❖ *Key Facts*

Time Period:
Mid-20th Century

Relevant Historical Events:
U.S. westward expansion; Chona and Underhill's interaction and collaboration

Nationality:
American

Keywords:
anthropology; feminism; Native Americans

Chona: The Autobiography of a Papago Woman tells the life history of Maria Chona of the southern Arizona Tohono O'odham (Papago) tribe. Depicted here is a Papago woman from approximately the same era, circa 1930s, as when author Ruth Underhill recorded Chona's life story. © CORBIS

PRIMARY SOURCE

EXCERPT FROM *THE AUTOBIOGRAPHY OF A PAPAGO WOMAN*

In the summer everyone came home to our village and we planted corn. The corn was once a man and he lured a woman away to sleep with him. She stayed a long time, and when she came home, she knew the songs that made the corn grow. So when the men all went to their meeting, this man did not go but he stayed at home hearing his wife sing. The men from the meeting came to speak to him. "Why are you absent?" "Because I am listening to my wife." "How can it be that a man can learn more from a woman than from talking with us? Let us hear her, too."

So she came to the men's meeting and she sat between the chief and her husband. "Sing." And she sang the corn songs.

At the first song those men began to sing. At the second, they danced. At the third, the women came out of the houses, creeping to the council house to listen to the singing. At the fourth, they were all dancing, inside the council house and outside, to that woman's singing.

We sang those songs as we put the corn into the earth, but it was the men who sang, for women do not do those things now. We stood ready with the corn kernels while the men sang, then we went down the field together, each woman behind a man. The man dropped his stick into the soft earth, thud! As deep as my hand is long. The woman dropped in four corn kernels and scraped her bare toes over that red earth to cover them.

Then the corn came up. The fair stalks, the thick root, the broad leaves.

> I saw the tassels waving in the wind
> And I whistled softly for joy.

My father used to sing that at night while the corn was growing.

I used to like it in the summer time when all our friends and relatives were around us. The houses were scattered all over the flat land; round brush houses like ours. In every house there were women grinding corn, and down by the wash there were men bending over the fields where the corn and beans and squash were growing.

> In the furrow
> At the corner
> The corn is growing green
> Growing green.

I used to hear those songs coming from the houses, because we were so happy in summer time. We had rain. Every morning the sky was bright and every afternoon the little white cloud stood over the mountains to the east. Everywhere by the washes you saw the centipedes that are a sign of rain. We call them a blessing, those centipedes. There were so many that you could shake your head and, pff! one would fall out of your hair. Now there are no more. That fine weather is gone.

SOURCE: Chona, Maria. *Papago Woman*. Ed. Ruth M. Underhill. *Memoirs of the American Anthropological Association*, no. 46, 1936.

---

actuality told by Waheenee's son to the anthropologist, and *Pretty-Shield: Medicine Woman of the Crows* (1932) by Frank Linderman. These texts share, to differing degrees, the mediations of their third-party translators and the alterations of the ethnographers.

Papago Woman, published in the year of Chona's death, brought Underhill academic success at Columbia University, where she was pursuing her doctoral work. At the time, it was a significant feat for a woman to garner respect in the field of anthropology. Underhill went on to write many books including *Singing for Power: The Song Magic of the Papago Indians of Southern Arizona* (1938) and *Red Man's Religion* (1965). For both of these books, she drew on information imparted to her by Chona regarding such aspects of Tohono O'odham life as the making of cactus liquor, ceremonies, songs, dances, medicine, and witchcraft. Anthropologist Kathleen M. Sands cites *Papago Woman* as one of her original inspirations for studying with the Tohono O'odham in the 1980s.

THEMES AND STYLE

The text takes as its theme Tohono O'odham traditions as they surround the individual events of Chona's life. Chona relates details, such as crawling out of doors to avoid Apache arrows, for the benefit of foreigners unfamiliar with the Tohono O'odham way of life. Indeed, Underhill notes that the memoir is "an Indian story told to satisfy whites rather than Indians." That Chona's immediate audience was a white woman is evident in her storytelling: "When I was nearly as tall as my mother, the thing happened to me which happens to all our women though I do not know if it does to the Whites; I never saw any signs. It is called menses." Chona, via Underhill, also comments on changes that reflect colonization, recollecting, "We did not know how to sew in those days."

Underhill's stated purpose for living with the Tohono O'odham and interviewing Chona was to come to a greater understanding of the culture. Underhill writes in her introduction, "Chona acted as informant, hostess, guide, and means of introduction to the various villages, in most of which she had relatives or descendants." By implicitly positioning herself as a guest or visitor, however, Underhill ignores her position of relative power as a white outsider, making such judgments as, "In this culture, there persists strongly the fear of women's impurity with all its consequent social adjustments." However, Sands in a 1998 article in *Studies in American Indian Literatures* argues that declaring Chona a victim of Underhill's condescension may not be correct. The questions Chona directs at Underhill regarding what happens in European American culture can be read as an empowered exploration of a foreign culture.

The style of *Papago Woman* is informal and conversational. Chona's memories are punctuated with instances of direct speech to Underhill: "Do you say that some girls might think of other things and not listen?" This fraternal tone presents the relationship between Underhill and Chona as an intimate, trusting one, though critics have argued that this is possibly a false assumption and that significant edits made by Underhill actually create this tone. Underhill's introduction claims that the formality with which she undertook her project, as well as her academic credentials, render her trustworthy to Native and European Americans alike. However, Sands argues that Underhill's "expressions of care and concern" actually may serve to "usurp the power of the Native narrator."

CRITICAL DISCUSSION

Little is known about the critical reception of Chona's autobiography when it was first published. When *Papago Woman* was released as a book in 1979, parts of it were quickly excerpted into a number of Native American literature anthologies, including anthropologist Arnold Krupat's frequently cited *For Those Who Come After: A Study of Native American Autobiography: An Anthology* (1985). Krupat praises the text not for its authenticity as an autobiography but as "a composite, collaborative production, made up of the words spoken by Chona, of the words of [Ella Lopez] Antone's translation, and, finally, of the words Underhill chose for the final text."

The text remained relevant enough to warrant a subsequent printing in 1985 by Waveland Press. Comparing it to other similar texts of its day, Michael E. Staub in a 1991 essay for *American Quarterly* counters those critics who note that Underhill "editorializes more than she records this Papago woman's life story." Staub commends Underhill's choices, focusing on the circuitousness and inconsistencies of Chona's narration: "Speech repeats, it also contradicts, just as speech often does in conversation. Underhill could have smoothed out these details, but these … reflect a search for a written form that approximates the workings of a voice sorting through the memories of a long life." Contemporary ethnographers and literary scholars continue to examine the text for how it conveys orality even in its written form.

Some contemporary scholars, Krupat and Sands among them, have examined the omissions of any discussion of the violence of colonialism in *Papago Woman*. Sands remarks in that "the dynamics of culture change … are often ignored in favor of narratives that focus exclusively on traditional life ways. They are … framed in the elegiac mode." In line with this critique is Helen Carr's 1996 book *Inventing the American Primitive,* in which she writes, "Underhill has chosen to emphasize the rituals and harmonies of Chona's life" rather than "relations with government officials." Hertha D. Wong in a 1987 article in *MELUS* writes that Chona mentions in the text Native American personal narratives that have long been overlooked. These include objects that stretch the European American idea of what constitutes a document, such as the baskets that Chona weaves, which would have carried her individual style.

BIBLIOGRAPHY

Sources

Carr, Helen. *Inventing the American Primitive: Politics, Gender and the Representation of Native American Literary Traditions, 1789–1936.* New York: New York University Press, 1996. Print.

Chona, Maria. *Papago Woman.* Ed. Ruth M. Underhill. New York: Holt, 1979. Print.

Krupat, Arnold. *For Those Who Come After: A Study of Native American Autobiography.* Berkeley: University of California Press, 1985. Print.

Sands, Kathleen M. "Narrative Resistance: Native American Collaborative Autobiography." *Studies in American Indian Literatures* 10.1 (1998): 1–18. *JSTOR.* Web. 23 Nov. 2012.

Staub, Michael E. "(Re)Collecting the Past: Writing Native American Speech." *American Quarterly* 43.3 (1991): 425–56. *JSTOR.* Web. 23 Nov. 2012.

Wong, Hertha D. "Pre-literate Native American Autobiography: Forms of Personal Narrative." *MELUS* 14.1 (1987): 17–32. *JSTOR.* Web. 23 Nov. 2012.

Further Reading

Bataille, Gretchen M., and Kathleen M. Sands. *American Indian Women: Telling Their Lives.* Lincoln: University of Nebraska Press, 1984. Print.

Colasurdo, Christine. "'Tell Me a Woman's Story': The Question of Gender in the Construction of *Waheenee, Pretty-Shield,* and *Papago Woman.*" *American Indian Quarterly* 21.3 (1997): 385–407. *JSTOR.* Web. 23 Nov. 2012.

Fowler, Shelli B., et al. "Negotiating Textual Terrain: A Conversation on Critical and Pedagogical Interventions in the Teaching of Ethnic Autobiography." *Frontiers* 17.2 (1996): 4–49. *JSTOR.* Web. 23 Nov. 2012.

Rios, Theodore, and Kathleen M. Sands. *Telling a Good One: The Process of a Native American Collaborative Autobiography.* Lincoln: University of Nebraska Press, 2000. Print.

Underhill, Ruth M. *Singing for Power: The Song Magic of the Papago Indians of Southern Arizona.* Berkeley: University of California Press, 1938. Print.

Caitlin Moore

THE COLOR OF WATER
A Black Man's Tribute to His White Mother
James McBride

Key Facts

Time Period:
Late 20th Century

Relevant Historical Events:
Increased awareness of multiculturalism

Nationality:
American

Keywords:
multiculturalism; Jewishness; race; identity

OVERVIEW

James McBride's *The Color of Water: A Black Man's Tribute to His White Mother* (1996) is the dual story of McBride's childhood and the life of his mother, Ruth McBride, née Ruchel Zylska. With eleven dark-skinned siblings, a black father, and a mother who elusively referred to herself as "light-skinned" and refused to discuss her racial origins or family background, McBride was, from an early age, preoccupied with issues of race and identity. Alternating stories about Ruth's early life as an Orthodox Jew in the American South with scenes from McBride's childhood in New York, *The Color of Water* depicts the complexities of racial and cultural affiliations in twentieth-century America, as well as the family bonds, by turns fraught and transcendent, that further shape human lives.

Written over a period of fourteen years from interviews conducted with his mother, *The Color of Water* appeared as part of the glut of memoir and autobiography published on the eve of the new millennium. The book, which was both critically acclaimed and commercially successful, helped clear the way for a variety of art, music, and literature produced by multiracial and multicultural writers, artists, and musicians, along with a developing critical discourse regarding "mixed roots," as seen, for example, in Danzy Senna's 1998 novel *Caucasia*.

HISTORICAL AND LITERARY CONTEXT

The dual stories of McBride and his mother reflect changing attitudes about interracial relationships and multiracial identities in the United States during the twentieth century. Born in Poland in 1921, Ruth was raised in a strict, Orthodox Jewish household in Virginia, a state where antimiscegenation laws were enforced until struck down by the U.S. Supreme Court's 1967 ruling in *Loving v. Virginia*. In that case, a white man and black woman were married in the District of Columbia and returned to their home in Virginia, where they were subsequently prosecuted under that state's law prohibiting interracial marriages. Antimiscegenation statues in slave states such as neighboring Maryland caused this entrenchment with its laws banning interracial marriage as early as the 1640s. The law was more equitable in New York, where Ruth settled in the 1940s with her first husband, who was black, and where McBride grew up. But prejudice against interracial relationships remained entrenched in both black and white communities, and the social position of multiracial children was often ambiguous.

The Color of Water began as a Mother's Day feature written by McBride in 1982, during his tenure at the *Boston Globe*. When McBride first approached his mother with the idea of turning her story into a full-length book, she was reluctant. According to the book's closing chapter, even after agreeing she would respond to her son's questions with the same admonishment delivered often in his childhood: "mind your own business." Still, the book that resulted from these interviews has been praised for its dual-voiced approach, with commentators noting that the convergence of the stories of mother and son give a more complete picture of each than might otherwise have been possible. Moreover, Ruth's voice adds credence to McBride's discussion of his roots, which was important in the 1990s, a period characterized by increased awareness of distinct cultural subgroups in the United States, and a demand by the reading public for more authentic accounts of the minority experience.

McBride's autobiography provides an interesting counterpoint to the "tragic mulatto" tradition in literature, which began with abolitionist novels such as William Wells Brown's *Clotel; or the President's Daughter: A Narrative of Slave Life in the United States* (1853) and continued into the twentieth century. Novels such as *Imitation of Life,* written by Jewish author Fannie Hurst, present multiracial characters as anguished by their divided identities, particularly insofar as they attempt to distance themselves from the black part of their heritage to "pass" as white. Black writers such as Langston Hughes, in his play *Mulatto* and in a poem by the same name, also deal with multiracial characters seeking to identify with their white bloodlines. These works link the disavowal of blackness to the dominance of whites but also to white prejudices reproduced in black communities, where lighter skinned, educated blacks commanded higher status than their darker peers. McBride's family, while firmly rooted in the black community, does not escape questions about racial identity, with outings involving Ruth and her children provoking stares and comments from white and black onlookers. *The Color of Water,* however, while describing the confusion and sometimes embarrassment these outings provoked, emphasizes the fact that Ruth's twelve children have been universally successful, their "mixed" parentage no barrier to happiness and achievement.

The Color of Water was an immediate success, occupying the best-seller list for one hundred weeks and contributing to the rise of "multiracial" as a viable marketing category for literature and autobiography. While books such as Shirlee Haizlip's *The Sweeter the Juice: A Family Memoir in Black and White* (1994) dealt with some of the same themes and preceded McBride's book by several years, *The Color of Water*'s massive commercial success contributed significantly to the explosion of the genre.

THEMES AND STYLE

The importance of family bonds is central to *The Color of Water* with issues of racial and cultural identity a secondary focus explored in the context of familial relationships. Indeed, the guiding figure in the family, Ruth is described as "chief surgeon for bruises," "war secretary," "religious consultant," "chief psychologist," and "financial adviser." "Matters involving race and identity," McBride adds, "she ignored." Many of the book's most engaging passages describe the rituals cementing the McBride children together—"we snuck into each other's rooms by night to trade secrets, argue, commiserate, spy, and continue chess games and monopoly games that had begun days earlier." Four siblings shared a clarinet "handing it off to one another in the hallway at school like halfbacks on a football team." By contrast, Ruth's description of her upbringing emphasizes her loveless family and time spent at her father's general store: "We had no family life. That store was our life."

The Color of Water grew out of McBride's need to learn about and understand his mother's life as a means of understanding his own place as "a black man with something of a Jewish soul." McBride describes growing up, first in the Red Hook Housing Projects and then in St. Albans, Queens, surrounded by brown-skinned people, including his own siblings. His mother was typically the only white person he would see in the neighborhood and at the Baptist church his mother and biological father had founded. Besides her light skin, McBride and his siblings noticed other oddities in his mother—that she drank tea from a glass and that she spoke Yiddish. Ruth refused to talk about herself, however, and McBride and his siblings "traded information on Mommy the way other people trade baseball cards." As an adult, the "dull ache" from his childhood uncertainty about his mother and his own identity became "a giant, roaring musical riff, screaming through my soul" and demanding an answer, which he ultimately sought to establish in writing *The Color of Water*.

McBride's book diverges from the typical autobiographical format as it establishes two voices—McBride's and Ruth's, which narrate alternating chapters through much of the book. Ruth's sections often elucidate parallel or puzzling experiences in her son's life. Chapter One, "Dead," describes Ruth's estrangement from her Jewish family in the simple opening declaration, "I'm dead." By contrast, the next chapter, "Bicycle," details Ruth's difference from the other mothers he knew as exemplified by the "huge old clunker" of a bike she road all over town, an activity McBride later realizes characterizes his mother's restlessness and desire to escape the unhappiness of her past.

CRITICAL DISCUSSION

The Color of Water was a critical and commercial success. Writing in the *New York Times,* H. Jack Geiger asserted, "The two stories, son's and mother's, beautifully juxtaposed, strike a graceful note at a time (we are constantly told) of racial polarization. Together, I think, they give new meaning to some tired phrases. Try 'multicultural' and, even more, 'family values.'" Other critics praised the book as a significant contribution to the literary dialogue about race. McBride won the Cleveland Foundation's Anisfield-Wolf Book Award, which recognizes works deemed to advance awareness of racism and cultural diversity in the United States.

Commentators have included *The Color of Water* as a benchmark when appraising the creation of "mixed race" as a category of experience that produces its own unique strands of art and literature. The late twentieth and early twenty-first centuries saw a proliferation of

James McBride, author of *The Color of Water,* at the 2008 Toronto International Film Festival. He was speaking at a press conference for the film adaptation of his novel *Miracle at St. Anna.* © LEONARD ADAM/WIREIMAGE

JEWISH IDENTITY IN *THE COLOR OF WATER*

The Color of Water draws its name from Ruth McBride's response to young James's questions about the color of God's spirit. "It doesn't have a color.... God is the color of water. Water doesn't have a color." While much of McBride's early confusion about his identity (and his mother's) centers on physical appearance, he is also confused by Ruth's occasional use of Yiddish, for instance, with Jewish shopkeepers.

As an adult, McBride refers to his "Jewish soul" and expresses curiosity and wonder at his mother's background and the manner in which she shed most vestiges of her cultural and religious upbringing when she left her family. McBride interprets Ruth's lifelong emphasis on education and her insistence on sending her children to predominately white, Jewish schools as evidence of lingering Jewish values and an attempt to retain part of her heritage. In terms of religion, however, Ruth renounced her Orthodox upbringing, commenting that there were "too many rules to follow, too many forbiddens." Indeed, Ruth was instrumental in helping her first husband, McBride's father, in founding a storefront Baptist church in Brooklyn and fully immersed herself and her family in the Christian faith.

mixed-race literature, music, and art, with organized festivals and celebrations of "mixedness" proliferating along with them. In an article for the *New York Times*, Felicia R. Lee notes that McBride views phenomena like the Mixed Roots festival at the Japanese American National Museum in Los Angeles "as part of the larger work of exploding stereotypes." Lee also describes the author's reservation "that parsing multiracial identity was quickly becoming a preoccupation of the well off." McBride continues, "Tiger Mom's kids are going to do just fine. I'm worried about the Korean woman married to the white guy who drives a beer truck and loses a job. No one is telling their story."

Little critical scholarship has focused on *The Color of Water*, perhaps in part due to the multiplicity of stories available for analysis, as well as rapidly changing views on multiracial literature since its publication. Published in 2002, Reginald Watson's essay "The Changing Face of Biraciality: The White/Jewish Mother as Tragic Mulatto Figure in James McBride's *The Color of Water* and Danzy Senna's *Caucasia*" posits McBride's and Senna's portraits of white/Jewish mothers in predominately black families/communities as a sort of new version of the mulatto, divorced from their pasts and "passing" as black. According to Watson, "The literary image of the mulatto is an image that no longer symbolizes just black and white. Now, when one thoroughly examines biracial literature ... the face of diversity represented by the mulatto is truly a face that reflects us all."

BIBLIOGRAPHY

Sources

Geiger, H. Jack. "Rachel and Her Children." *New York Times.* New York Times, 31 Mar. 1996. Web. 1 Nov. 2012.

Lee, Felicia R. "Pushing Boundaries, Mixed-Race Artists Gain Notice." *New York Times.* New York Times, 5 July 2011. Web. 1 Nov. 2012.

McBride, James. *The Color of Water.* New York: Penguin, 2006. Print.

Watson, Reginald. "The Changing Face of Biraciality: The White/Jewish Mother as Tragic Mulatto Figure in James McBride's *The Color of Water* and Danzy Senna's *Caucasia.*" *Obsidian III* 4.1 (2002): 101+. *Literature Resource Center.* Web. 31 Oct. 2012.

Further Reading

DeYoung, Curtiss Paul, Michael O. Emerson, George Yancey, and Karen Chai Kim. *United by Faith: The Multiracial Congregation as an Answer to the Problem of Race.* Oxford: Oxford University Press, 2003. Print.

Elam, Michele. *The Souls of Mixed Folk: Race, Politics, and Aesthetics in the New Millennium.* Stanford, CA: Stanford University Press, 2011. Print.

Ginsberg, Elaine K. *Passing and the Fictions of Identity.* Durham, NC: Duke University Press, 1996. Print.

Neal, Mark Anthony. *Soul Babies: Black Popular Culture and the Post-Soul Aesthetic.* New York: Routledge, 2002. Print.

O'Hearn, Claudia. *Half and Half: Writers on Growing Up Biracial and Bicultural.* New York: Pantheon, 1998. Print.

Senna, Danzy. "The Mulatto Millennium." *Utne Reader.* Ogden, Sept.–Oct. 1998. Web. 31 Oct. 2012.

Sollers, Werner. *Neither Black nor White yet Both: Thematic Explorations of Interracial Literature.* Cambridge: Harvard University Press, 1999. Print.

Daisy Gard

A Cross and a Star
Memoirs of a Jewish Girl in Chile
Marjorie Agosín

OVERVIEW

First published in Spanish in 1994, Marjorie Agosín's *A Cross and a Star: Memoirs of a Jewish Girl in Chile* (1995) tells of a Jewish family's experience in Chile in the years surrounding World War II. In a first-person narrative Agosín, who spent much of her childhood in Chile, recounts her mother's recollections of childhood and young adulthood in Osorno, of her extended Russian and Viennese family, and of the struggle of growing up as an immigrant in a culture hostile to Judaism. Through telling her mother's story, Agosín examines the dislocation, exile, prejudice, and otherness experienced by Jews in Chile. The transgressive style of the narrative, its blending and shifting voice, and its refusal to adhere to a traditional autobiographical mode allow it to speak to a universal Jewish experience of alienation and struggle.

Before *A Cross and a Star* was published, Jewish populations in Chile had established synagogues and cultural centers but still were often the victims of subtle anti-Semitism. Agosín, whose family immigrated to the United States when she was fourteen, visited Chile periodically and wrote the narrative in part to draw attention to the racism against Jews she witnessed there. Popular with readers in both the United States and Latin America, the memoir was met with particular interest by members of the diaspora. Today *A Cross and a Star* is considered an important work of Jewish–Latin American literature and a successful poetic experiment in autobiography.

HISTORICAL AND LITERARY CONTEXT

A Cross and a Star describes a unique period in the history of Jews in Chile. In the years leading up to World War II, a large number of Jewish refugees arrived in Latin America after fleeing the rising anti-Semitism in Europe. Concurrent to this migration was an increase of German colonization in Chile and burgeoning Chilean support of Adolf Hitler's Nazi regime. When Agosín's memoir was published, Jews in Chile were still struggling to survive in a culture driven by a strong anti-Semitic past and the Catholic Church. Meanwhile, in other Latin American countries, such as Argentina and Brazil, Jews were uniting to fight anti-Semitic sentiment, a movement that Agosín felt was lacking in Chile.

The memoir joined other works by Agosín that were written to document those people who had vanished. Agosín's family had fled Chile just before dictator Augusto Pinochet came to power. The mass disappearances that occurred under his regime gave rise to women in search of *los desaparecidos* (the disappeared ones). Agosín was motivated to become an activist, as well as tell the stories of the disappeared ones, a mission she continued in *A Cross and a Star*. The text memorializes the members of Agosín's family who disappeared in World War II and preserves her mother's recollections of her passage into adulthood. Agosín has referred to herself as a "moral historian," speaking for the voiceless victims of oppression in her family, Latin America, and elsewhere.

A Cross and a Star, although nontraditional in its execution, is part of a line of second- and third-generation immigrant memoirs and Judeo–Latin American autobiographies. It was preceded by Maxine Hong Kingston's *The Woman Warrior* (1976), which makes use of a similar style of blended perspective to portray the immigrant experience. Victor Perera's *Rites: A Guatemalan Boyhood* (1985) also relates the dislocating experience of growing up Jewish in Latin America. Meanwhile, Ana María Shua's *The Book of Memories* (1994) describes the Jewish–Latin American experience via a fictionalized account of the author's Polish family in Argentina during World War I.

A number of Judeo–Latin American and second-generation immigrant memoirs followed Agosín's book. In *Heading South, Looking North: A Bilingual Journey* (1998), Ariel Dorfman recalls his experience as a political refugee from Pinochet's Chile, his dislocation, and his search for a home. Oscar Hijuelos relates his experience as a second-generation Cuban immigrant in *Thoughts without Cigarettes: A Memoir* (2011). After *A Cross and a Star,* Agosín wrote more texts about her family's history and the immigrant experience, including *Always from Somewhere Else: A Memoir of My Chilean Jewish Father* (1998) and *Uncertain Travelers: Conversations with Jewish Women Immigrants to America* (1999).

THEMES AND STYLE

A Cross and a Star deals with themes of dislocation, oppression, and memory. Throughout the text Agosín

❖ **Key Facts**

Time Period:
Late 20th Century

Relevant Historical Events:
World War II; the persecution and exile of Jews from Europe; the rule of Pinochet in Chile

Nationality:
Chilean

Keywords:
anti-Semitism; Jewishness; exile

BETWEEN CULTURES

Jewish citizens from Chile and other South American countries in a 2000 protest against pro-Nazi groups. Marjorie Agosín discusses her experiences as a Jewish female in Chile and the United States in the 1997 memoir *A Cross and a Star*. © AP IMAGES/ SANTIAGO LLANQUIN

describes the particular challenges of being both Jewish and a refugee in a Catholic, anti-Semitic country. The text continually visits the experiences of her mother, Frida Halpern, with prejudice, describing incidents such as "the time when the German girls in Southern Chile snatched her dolls and made fun of her, or when they stoned her at the exit to the state school." Agosín also details the suffering of older generations that escaped from Nazi Germany and their complicated identities. For example, there is "grandmother Helena," who taught Frida to speak German—"that same language that obliged her to strip and to tie up her hair so as later to have it shaved off, that same language that forbade her to go to the cinema and to school, to touch the trees and go out into the street." Passages such as this illustrate the tensions between the religious, national, and linguistic identities of a Jewish refugee.

Agosín seeks to bring to light the Jewish-Chilean experience and to memorialize the silent histories of the oppressed. To achieve these goals, she strays from the conventional autobiographical form, switching between her own and her mother's perspective. Early in the book, Agosín writes of telling her mother's story: "I didn't invent anything, or perhaps I invented everything. Sometimes her voice mingles with my own in order to become entangled with the language of love." The text also speaks to the positive power of memory, as when the first-person Frida says that her "memory is also an immense meadow of bell-flowers and trains of refugees that approach and become transfigured by the pulse, the breath of a new life with songs of peace."

By continually changing perspectives, Agosín is able to imitate the fluid nature of memory.

A Cross and a Star is notable for its poetic style, atemporal organization, and aforementioned shifts in perspective. In her foreword to the 1997 edition of the memoir, Laura Riesco writes about the stylistic effect of Agosín's narration: "Agosín's attempt to write a memoir that is not her own but her mother's, and that is not only her mother's but also her own—a memoir in which the clear and defining lines of identity and truth in writing are put into question— places her in the vanguard of this century's literary thought."

CRITICAL DISCUSSION

Upon its initial publication, *A Cross and a Star* drew the attention of well-regarded Latin American writers and critics, as well as commentary from scholars interested in the Jewish–Latin American experience. The book garnered praise from noted writers Isabel Allende and Hijuelos, who, in a blurb on the back of a 1997 edition, called it "a beautiful tale of fortitude" and praised Agosín's "poetic prose." Naomi Lindstrom reviewed the English translation in 1998 in *World Literature Today*, offering commendation for Agosín's "special talent for fascinating readers with emotionally charged description" and stating that the book would "interest students of Latin American Jewish narrative."

In the years following its publication, the work has continued to be lauded as an important Jewish–Latin American text. In her 2009 essay "Introduction to and Bibliography of Central European Women's

Holocaust Life Writing in English," Louise Vasvári mentions Agosín's text as an important record of "the situation in Latin America where large numbers of survivors emigrated, yet there is no published corpus of such life writing." Agosín's attempt to document the Jewish–Latin American experience and her unique contribution to the autobiographical genre are of particular interest to scholars.

A Cross and a Star is often discussed for its representation of Jewish identity and its distinct interpretation of the memoir as a form. Florence Moorhead-Rosenberg, in her 2003 article in *Ciberletras: Revista de Crítica Literaria y de Cultura*, discusses how Agosín represents a Jewish identity that is "constructed and presented as a rebellious entity, in conflict, given the strong pressures of marginalization present in the surrounding society, which has to find a way to respond." In her introduction to the memoir, Celeste Kostopulos-Cooperman describes the unique effect of the fractured narrative, writing that the "'blue' vapours of the gas chambers seem to penetrate the multi-layered memories, fusing the destinies of the narrator-protagonist to those of her departed relatives."

THE GERMAN PRESENCE IN CHILE

During the mid-nineteenth century, Chile encouraged German immigration, hoping to populate rural provinces such as Valdivia and Chiloé with an industrious group of farmers and artisans. Leaders of the German colonization of southern Chile, including Bernardo Philippi, were determined to create colonies that would allow German immigrants to maintain their language and culture. The geographic isolation of many of the colonies helped to make this possible, and the colonists gradually increased in number while maintaining a German identity.

In *A Cross and a Star*, Marjorie Agosín writes of the considerable German presence and the accompanying anti-Semitism in southern Chile during World War II. Afterward, some war criminals fled from Germany to Chile to avoid prosecution. One such criminal was SS General Walter Rauff, who had designed and operated mobile gas chambers during the Nazi extermination of Jews. He was known to live in Puerto Provenir, Chile, under his own name. After West Germany requested Rauff's extradition in 1962, which the Chilean Supreme Court denied, he worked as a manager of a crab fishery in Punte Arenas. German-born evangelical preacher Paul Schaefer also fled to Chile following World War II and established Colonia Dignidad, later believed to be the location of a detention and torture center for enemies of Augusto Pinochet's regime.

BIBLIOGRAPHY

Sources

Agosín, Marjorie. *A Cross and a Star: Memoirs of a Jewish Girl in Chile.* Trans. Celeste Kostopulos-Cooperman. Berkshire, U.K.: Garnet, 1997. Print.

Donovan, Gregory, and Jeff Lodge. "Interview with Marjorie Agosín." *Blackbird*. Virginia Commonwealth University, 2004. Web. 2 Nov. 2012.

Kostopulos-Cooperman, Celeste. Introduction. *A Cross and a Star: Memoirs of a Jewish Girl in Chile.* By Marjorie Agosín. Berkshire, U.K.: Garnet, 1997. xxi–xxx. Print.

Lindstrom, Naomi. Rev. of *A Cross and A Star: Memoirs of a Jewish Girl in Chile,* by Marjorie Agosín. *World Literature Today* 72.1 (1998): 110–11. *JSTOR.* Web. 1 Nov. 2012.

Moorehead-Rosenberg, Florence. "La identidad usurpada: La memoria Judía en *A Cross and a Star* de Marjorie Agosín." *Ciberletras: Revista de Crítica Literaria y de Cultura* 10 (2003). *Fundación Dialnet.* Web. 2 Nov. 2012.

Riesco, Laura. Foreword. *A Cross and a Star: Memoirs of a Jewish Girl in Chile.* By Marjorie Agosín. Berkshire, U.K.: Garnet, 1997. vii–xx. Print.

Vasvári, Louise O. "Introduction to and Bibliography of Central European Women's Holocaust Life Writing in English." *New Work in Holocaust Studies* 11.1 (2009): 2–21. *CLCWeb.* Web. 2 Nov. 2012.

Further Reading

Agosín, Marjorie. "A Journey through Imagination and Memory: My Parents and I, between the Cross and the Star." *Judaism* 51.4 (2002): 419–29. *Academic Search Elite.* Web. 1 Nov. 2012.

Agosín, Marjorie, ed. *Memory, Oblivion, and Jewish Culture in Latin America.* Austin: University of Texas Press, 2005. Print.

Lesser, Jeffrey, and Raanan Rein, eds. *Rethinking Jewish–Latin Americans.* Albuquerque: University of New Mexico Press, 2008. Print.

Sheinin, David, and Lois Baer Barr, eds. *The Jewish Diaspora in Latin America: New Studies on History and Literature.* New York: Garland, 1996. Print.

Smith, Sidonie, and Julia Watson. "De/Colonization and the Politics of Discourse in Women's Autobiographical Practices." *De/Colonizing the Subject: The Politics of Gender in Women's Autobiography.* Ed. Sidonie Smith and Julia Watson. Minneapolis: University of Minnesota Press, 1992. xiii–xxxi. Print.

Kristen Gleason

Dreams from My Father
A Story of Race and Inheritance
Barack Obama

Key Facts

Time Period:
Late 20th Century

Relevant Historical Events:
Civil rights movement brings greater racial equality

Nationality:
American

Keywords:
identity; race; displacement

OVERVIEW

President Barack Obama's first book, *Dreams from My Father: A Story of Race and Inheritance,* was published in 1995. The "autobiography, memoir, family history, or something else," as Obama calls it in his introduction, narrates his experiences growing up with his mother and maternal grandparents in Hawaii. The work also details Obama's time with his mother and stepfather in Indonesia and follows his life through college, community organizing on Chicago's South Side, and finally his visit to Kenya to meet his father's family. By charting his own struggle to understand his African American identity and his relationship to a father mostly known through stories, memories, and one visit of a few weeks, Obama also maps the complex role of racial identity in an increasingly globalized United States.

Obama was first approached about writing *Dreams from My Father* after his election as the first black editor of the *Harvard Law Review*. The book received somewhat favorable reviews upon publication, but sales were lacking. Almost a decade later, Obama was tapped to give the keynote address at the 2004 Democratic National Convention as a candidate for the U.S. Senate from Illinois, and *Dreams from My Father* was reprinted. This time, the book sold millions of copies and topped the *New York Times* best-seller list. Although it was first published before Obama had begun to pursue a career in politics, he may have been considering a political career while he was drafting *Dreams from My Father,* and his 2004 convention speech aided the memoir in propelling him onto the national stage.

HISTORICAL AND LITERARY CONTEXT

Obama was born six years before the Supreme Court case *Loving v. Virginia* ruled antimiscegenation laws unconstitutional. Interracial marriage had never been illegal in Hawaii, but Obama's parents married at the heyday of the civil rights movement, and *Dreams from My Father* addresses the question of black identity and the experience of displacement in both black and white communities. Obama's white grandparents had raised him in Hawaii for part of his childhood, and he describes the arc of their lives in order to arrive at a diagnosis of the subtle ways race inflects everyday life. Peppering the story of his grandparents' move to Hawaii and his parents' marriage is the question, "But would they let their daughter *marry* one?" His grandparents welcomed Barack Sr. to the family, but young Barack nevertheless felt displacement and alienation as a multiracial child.

Obama's family history provides the initial circumstances for writing *Dreams from My Father*. His parents, Ann Dunham, of Wichita, Kansas, and Barack Obama Sr., a member of the Luo tribe in Kenya, met as students at the University of Hawaii. They separated when their son was two years old. Obama saw his father only once more, at the age of ten, when his father traveled to Hawaii to visit the family. Obama moved to Jakarta, Indonesia, with his mother and stepfather, Lolo Soetoro, when he was six years old, and they lived there until he was ten.

The classics that the young Obama devoured in his childhood bedroom inform the themes of *Dreams from My Father:* W. E. B. Du Bois's *Souls of Black Folk,* Richard Wright's *Native Son,* and Ralph Ellison's *Invisible Man.* One of the strongest influences on his memoir is *The Autobiography of Malcolm X,* written with Alex Haley. Haley's *Roots* also anticipates the search for family history that Obama undertakes, yet Obama's own return to Africa at the end of *Dreams from My Father* marks the distinction between his story and that of most enslaved Africans—Obama can trace his family history to African kings, while most descendants of New World slaves can find no records beyond a bill of sale. Obama recalls how deeply Malcolm X's autobiography influenced his own stance on racial politics and black identity, yet its black nationalist bent ultimately failed to satisfy him. Obama's discussion of Malcolm X, argues Daniel Stein in his essay in *European Journal of American Studies,* allows "him to claim the text as part of his literary ancestry while simultaneously providing him with a foil against which he can establish his post-black-nationalist position on race."

When paired with his 2006 political biography, *The Audacity of Hope, Dreams from My Father* lays the groundwork for Obama's political career. Although the latter was written, ostensibly, without a view toward political office, Obama began to record events in his daily life when he was attending Columbia University. His life story has framed nearly every important stump speech he has given, and from his career in the

Senate to his reelection to the presidency, he has consistently linked his own, transnational biography with a national history that he characterizes as a slow but relentless move toward a more perfect union.

THEMES AND STYLE

The central theme of *Dreams from My Father* is that the search for individual identity is inextricably linked to a broader sense of community. Like other African American memoirs, it takes up the issues of double consciousness, racial invisibility, and black nationalism, yet the book ultimately concludes that fundamental human connection can unite people from different races, countries, and even historical moments. Standing beside his father's grave, he explains that "the black life, the white life, the sense of abandonment I'd felt as a boy, the frustration and hope I'd witnessed in Chicago" were all "connected with this small plot of earth an ocean away.... The pain I felt was my father's pain. My questions were my brothers' questions. Their struggle, my birthright."

Although Obama seemingly set out to tell the tale of his unique upbringing and impressive achievements, one of his major purposes in writing *Dreams from My Father* was to weave a broad assessment of race in the United States into his individual narrative. His refusal to imagine his own story as separate from African American cultural heritage as well as sociopolitical reality, in fact, reflects the book's main theme. Obama writes that biblical stories "became our stories, my story," and that "our triumphs and trials became at once unique and universal, black and more than black." The book lays the groundwork for Obama's political identity, yet it also draws on conventions of nineteenth-century writing as well as twentieth-century iterations that repurpose tropes from the African American literary canon. Traditionally, such works have wrestled with the "problem" of African American identity, and *Dreams from My Father* develops a transnational version of the development of a stable black identity. Obama's understanding of hope in the progressive arc of U.S. history can be traced to Frederick Douglass's "What, to the Slave, Is the Fourth of July?" and Martin Luther King Jr.'s "I Have a Dream" speeches.

Dreams from My Father is marked by an unsentimental, conversational style. As a political biography, it must hew closely to verifiable fact. In his introduction, Obama explains that the book's dialogue is "necessarily an approximation" and that "some characters are composites of people I've known, and some events appear out of precise chronology." The autobiography opens with Obama, at the age of twenty-one, receiving the news of his father's death in a car accident via a call from an aunt in Kenya. The book ends with his first visit to Nairobi to meet his father's family. The text is organized into three sections, each of which highlights a different facet of Obama's arc of self-determination: "Origins," in which he describes his childhood and young adulthood; "Chicago," which details his work in the black community of Altgeld Gardens; and

Then-senator Barack Obama with daughter Sasha while on the campaign trail in 2007. © VISIONS OF AMERICA, LLC/ALAMY

"Kenya," where Obama comes to understand the connections between his life in the United States and his African heritage.

CRITICAL DISCUSSION

Although initial critical reception of the book was positive, relatively little attention was paid to it until its rerelease in 2004. Since then, academic discussion of *Dreams from My Father* has proliferated. Academics treat the book as a postmodern autobiography-memoir hybrid that also aligns itself with the African American literary tradition. The memoir has a candid, open approach to topics such as casual drug use and disillusionment with U.S. institutions. This attitude marks it as one of the most forthcoming presidential autobiographies. Some scholars have suggested that the full disclosure Obama provides through *Dreams from My Father* anticipated the vetting process he would have to undergo as a presidential candidate.

Since its publication, Obama's memoir has become considered one of the most literary presidential autobiographies. In her review for the *New York Times,* Michiko Kakutani calls *Dreams from My Father* "the most evocative, lyrical and candid autobiography written by a future president." Many reviewers have emphasized its inheritance of tropes from earlier African American memoirs. Colm Tóibín, for example, in his review for *New York Review of Books,* compares *Dreams from My Father* to James Baldwin's *Notes of a Native Son,* suggesting that although the terms of

BARACK OBAMA'S GRAMMYS

When an abridged version of *Dreams from My Father: A Story of Race and Inheritance* was recorded as an audiobook in 2005, Barack Obama followed in the footsteps of fellow public servants Bill and Hillary Clinton in choosing to lend his own voice to the recording. Telling his story in person allowed Obama to lend authenticity and immediacy to the production. When the audio version of *Dreams from My Father* was released, reviews were largely favorable, with commentators noting Obama's characteristic eloquence and likability. Writing for the London *Observer,* for example, Rachel Redford described the recording as "persuasive and engaging," noting that "Obama shares with other great rhetoricians the power to move and captivate his listeners."

The work garnered the 2006 Grammy Award for the Best Spoken Word Album. Obama also received a Grammy for the audiobook version of his second autobiographical work, *The Audacity of Hope: Thoughts on Reclaiming the American Dream,* in 2008—the same year he was elected to his first term as president of the United States. As Obama's popularity has grown, increased attention has been focused on his audiobook recordings, with listeners expressing particular delight in his often humorous imitations of the people he knew while growing up.

Obama's African American identity strike many as globalized and postmodern, he has nevertheless shared many experiences of African Americans who came of age in Harlem, Chicago, or the South.

According to many scholars, *Dreams from My Father* follows a long tradition of African American autobiography and fiction in exploring the color line and its effect on personal identity. In *A Home Elsewhere: Reading African American Classics in the Age of Obama* (2010), Robert Stepto argues that pivotal scenes in Obama's memoir employ images that recur in canonical African American literature. He argues, for instance, that when a young Obama begins attending the Punahou School and is teased for his African name and alienated as one of two black students, he is not only recalling a formative moment from his past but also making a literary reference to the "schoolroom" trope that emerged in the work of Du Bois and James Weldon Johnson. According to Stepto, this image represents the initial moment when a young black child realizes that he is racially marked. However, in his essay in *Dissent,* David Bradley argues that Obama significantly revises these tropes, as when Barack Obama Sr. is invited to speak to young Barack's class, who, enlightened, admire the father and begin to accept the son.

BIBLIOGRAPHY

Sources

Banita, Georgiana. "'Home Squared': Barack Obama's Transnational Self-Reliance." *Biography: An Interdisciplinary Quarterly* 33.1 (2010): 24–45. Print.

Bradley, David. "Misreading Obama." *Dissent* 57.4 (2010): 91–95. *Project MUSE.* Web. 27 Nov. 2012.

Kakutani, Michiko. "From Books, New President Found Voice." *New York Times.* New York Times, 18 Jan. 2009. Web. 27 Nov. 2012.

Obama, Barack. *Dreams from My Father: A Story of Race and Inheritance.* New York: Three Rivers, 2004. Print.

Redford, Rachel. "From Struggle to Resounding Triumph." Rev. of *Dreams from My Father,* by Barack Obama. *Observer.* Guardian News and Media, 15 Nov. 2008. Web. 18 Dec. 2012.

Stein, Daniel. "Barack Obama's *Dreams from My Father* and African American Literature." *European Journal of American Studies* 1. European Association for American Studies, 2011. Web. 27 Nov. 2012.

Stepto, Robert. *A Home Elsewhere: Reading African American Classics in the Age of Obama.* Cambridge: Harvard University Press, 2010. Print.

Tóibín, Colm. "James Baldwin & Barack Obama." *New York Review of Books.* New York Review of Books, 23 Oct. 2008. Web. 27 Nov. 2012.

Further Reading

Baillie, Justine. "From Margin to Centre: Postcolonial Identities and Barack Obama's *Dreams from My Father.*" *Life Writing* 8.3 (2011): 317–29. Print.

Foley, Barbara. "Rhetoric and Silence in Barack Obama's *Dreams from My Father.*" *Cultural Logic: An Electronic Journal of Marxist Theory and Practice* (2009): 1–46. Print.

Green, Tara T. *A Fatherless Child: Autobiographical Perspectives on African American Men.* Columbia: University of Missouri Press, 2009. Print.

Jones, Suzanne W. "The Obama Effect on American Discourse about Racial Identity: *Dreams from My Father* (and Mother), Barack Obama's Search for Self." *The Obama Effect: Multidisciplinary Renderings of the 2008 Campaign.* Ed. Heather E. Harris, Kimberly R. Moffitt, and Catherine R. Squires. Albany: State University of New York Press, 2010. 131–52. Print.

Kloppenberg, James. *Reading Obama: Dreams, Hope, and the American Political Tradition.* Princeton, N.J.: Princeton University Press, 2011. Print.

Mastey, David. "Slumming and/as Self-Making in Barack Obama's *Dreams from My Father.*" *Journal of Black Studies* 40.3. Sage Journals, 2010. Web. 27 Nov. 2012.

Rahming, Melvin B., and Delores P. Aldridge, eds. *Critical Essays on Barack Obama: Re-affirming the Hope, Re-vitalizing the Dream.* Newcastle upon Tyne, U.K.: Cambridge Scholars, 2012. Print.

Selzer, Linda F. "Barack Obama, the 2008 Presidential Election, and the New Cosmopolitanism: Figuring the Black Body." *MELUS* 35.4 (2010): 15–37. Print.

Senaha, Eijun. "Barack Obama and His-Story: Paradox of Hybridity and Masculinity in His Autoandrography." *Journal of the Graduate School of Letters* 4 (2009): 57–66. Print.

Walters, Ron. "Barack Obama and the Politics of Blackness." *Journal of Black Studies* Sept. 2007: 7–29. Web. 27 Nov. 2012.

Anna Ioanes

The Interesting Narrative of the Life of Olaudah Equiano, or Gustavus Vassa, the African, Written by Himself

Olaudah Equiano

OVERVIEW

The Interesting Narrative of the Life of Olaudah Equiano, or Gustavus Vassa, the African, Written by Himself, first published in 1794, tells the story of a man who began life in an Igbo village in present-day Nigeria and died a successful author and businessman in England. In the intervening years, Olaudah Equiano experienced slavery from various perspectives and ultimately became an advocate for the abolition of the Atlantic slave trade. Equiano's unique experience and perspective—African by birth, European by education—allowed him to comment on the slave system with an authority few of his contemporaries could command.

Equiano's narrative appeared as debate over the slave trade intensified in Britain. Slavery, never widespread in the British Isles, was effectively outlawed there in 1789 by the Mansfield decision, which forbade masters forcibly returning slaves they had brought to Britain to the colonies. However, Britons of all ranks, including the aristocracy and the leadership of the Anglican Church, remained heavily invested in the slave trade and the West Indian plantations it supported. Activists such as Thomas Clarkson increasingly denounced such investments as immoral. By providing a firsthand account of slave trading and slavery in the Americas, *The Interesting Narrative* supports the effort to abolish the Atlantic slave trade. Even after the abolition of slavery in the British Empire in 1838, the publication contributed to the antislavery movement in the United States, becoming a model for narratives written by American escapees from slavery, including Frederick Douglass and Harriet Jacobs.

HISTORICAL AND LITERARY CONTEXT

The Interesting Narrative was both a business venture and a political intervention. The 1780s witnessed increasing antislavery sentiment in England, with activists focusing on the abolition of the Atlantic slave trade, which they hoped would lead to better conditions for slaves in the British colonies and gradually to the disappearance of slavery. In London in 1787, a group of activists founded the Committee for Effecting Abolition of the Slave Trade and began distributing literature and sending speakers to other areas of the United Kingdom, focusing especially on port cities that benefited directly or indirectly from the slave trade.

Although Equiano had himself been involved in the slave trade as a free man, working on trading vessels in the years immediately after he purchased his freedom in 1766 and helping to buy and supervise slaves for a friend's plantation in Central America in the mid-1770s, by the late 1770s he was becoming increasingly committed to charitable works directed toward impoverished free blacks in Britain and to the abolition of the slave trade. The first edition of *The Interesting Narrative* incorporated a genre popular with British abolitionists of its day: the petition to Parliament, a form of political speech open even to those subjects who, like Equiano, did not have the right to vote.

Equiano's narrative is probably the most famous work by an eighteenth-century African Briton, but it was not the first. A number of British subjects of African descent, including James Albert Ukawsaw Gronniosaw, Phillis Wheatley, Ignatius Sancho, John Marrant, and Ottobah Cugoana, published literary and autobiographical works in the 1770s and 1780s. While Cugoana's 1787 *Thoughts and Sentiments on the Evil and Wicked Traffic of the Slavery and Commerce of the Human Species* was the only dedicated antislavery tract, all of the authors contributed to the abolitionist project by serving as examples of the intellectual potential and full humanity of people of African descent. Equiano also drew on other genres in crafting his story, including antislavery works by white Britons such as Clarkson, spiritual autobiography, travel literature, and white captivity narratives such as Mary Rowlandson's 1682 *Sovereignty and Goodness of God*.

Equiano published each of the nine editions of *The Interesting Narrative* by subscription, an approach that not only allowed him to fund the production of the volume but also created, via printed lists of subscribers, a visible political and literary network. Equiano's subscribers—over one thousand in all—include fellow

❖ *Key Facts*

Time Period:
Late 18th Century

Relevant Historical Events:
Growth of the Atlantic slave trade; rise of abolitionism

Nationality:
Nigerian

Keywords:
slavery; abolition; race

BETWEEN CULTURES

Author Olaudah Equiano circa 1790, around the time of the publication of his autobiography *The Interesting Narrative*. © UNIVERSAL IMAGES GROUP/GETTY IMAGES

African British writers and their sponsors, abolitionists, aristocrats, members of Parliament, businessmen, and other authors and intellectuals. Proceeds from the sale of the book helped ensure Equiano's financial independence and his status as a gentleman—an unusual achievement for an eighteenth-century British subject of African descent.

THEMES AND STYLE

As an African eventually assimilated into European culture, Equiano is able to present himself as a somewhat distanced participant observer in multiple social systems. Because he is kidnapped in early childhood, he can present his ignorance of and wonder at European customs and products, such as a reading and books, as natural to his age and situation, emphasizing that, like other children of the same age, he was curious and eager to learn. Equiano describes himself as a young man making his way in the world, "commenc[ing] merchant with sixpence," buying his own freedom, converting to Christianity, and observing life at sea and in the Americas from his newfound religious perspective before settling for good in England.

Throughout *The Interesting Narrative,* Equiano is intent on proving his own capabilities (and by extension those of other Africans) and illustrating the horrors of the slave system. His account of the Middle Passage—the journey in the overcrowded holds of ships traveling from the West Coast of Africa to the Americas during which many recently captured Africans died—was the first written from the perspective of a slave, and the horror of the scenes described is magnified by the innocence of the child-observer. Similarly,

Equiano's experience of slavery in multiple places—the West Indies, the United States, and at sea—allows him to provide evidence of the cruelty that the system in all its forms allows and often encourages, even as he recounts occasional instances of kind treatment that allowed him to acquire skills such as reading and to begin to use those skills to work toward freedom. The frontispiece of *The Interesting Narrative* portrays the person he eventually became: a man of clearly African descent, dressed in formal clothing appropriate to an English gentleman and holding in his hands an open Bible.

The structure of Equiano's story is unusual among slave narratives because it begins as well as ends with freedom. As Henry Louis Gates observes in *The Classic Slave Narratives* (2012), "the movement of [Equiano's] plot ... is from African freedom, through European enslavement, to Anglican freedom." This structure allows Equiano to contrast the relatively mild nature of African slavery with the far more harsh European American system. It also, as Vincent Carretta suggests in *Equiano, the African: Biography of a Self-Made Man* (2005), "implies that [Equiano's] own progress from pre-Christian to Christian can be paralleled by the potential development of Africa from its present spiritual condition to that of a fully Christian culture, a progress that would be as natural and preordained on a societal level as his has demonstrably already been on a personal level." In addition, Carretta writes, "Equiano explicitly argues that Africa can be brought into the European commercial world, as he has been."

CRITICAL DISCUSSION

Initial reception of *The Interesting Narrative* was generally favorable, with most reviewers concurring with the *General Magazine and Impartial Review*'s (1789) description of the book's likely political impact: "the reader, unless perchance he is either a West-India planter, or a Liverpool merchant, will find his humanity often severely wounded by the shameless barbarity practiced toward the author's hapless countrymen in all our colonies." Assessments of the work's literary quality were less enthusiastic but still approving. An author for the *Monthly Review* in 1789 speculates that Equiano must have received editorial help from an "English writer" to render the book "sufficiently well-written," while Mary Wollstonecraft in *Analytical Review* in 1789 judges the style to be uneven—"a few well written periods do not smoothly unite with the general tenor of the language." Nevertheless, she suggests that Equiano proved himself the intellectual equal of "the more general mass of men ... in a more civilized society" such as England.

In addition to supporting the contemporary British antislavery movement, Equiano's book became a model for later slave narratives. Black abolitionist and former slave Douglass repeats in his 1845 autobiography several of Equiano's tropes, including the parallel journeys toward literacy and freedom, and the subtitle "written by himself," which highlights the intellectual capabilities of the author and by extension others of African descent. Another black abolitionist, Jacobs, also includes the "written by herself" line on the title page of her slave narrative. While scholars continue to study *The Interesting Narrative* as a foundational text of its genre, more-recent work has considered it as a text arising from cross-cultural encounters in the Atlantic contact zone.

Attention to Equiano's self-construction as "the African" has generated critical controversy. Carretta draws on baptismal records and a ship's muster to argue that Equiano was born in South Carolina and invented his accounts of the Middle Passage and Igboland, where he claimed to have been born, to support contemporary antislavery arguments. Other scholars, including Paul Lovejoy, Catherine Obianuju Acholonu, and Gates, concur with Carretta's emphasis on Equiano's self-presentation but conclude that the author's account of his African childhood, though probably supplemented by later reading, is credible.

BIBLIOGRAPHY

Sources

Carretta, Vincent. *Equiano, The African: Biography of a Self-Made Man.* Athens: University of Georgia Press, 2005. Print.

Equiano, Olaudah. *The Interesting Narrative of the Life of Olaudah Equiano, or Gustavus Vassa, the African, Written by Himself.* Ed. Werner Sollors. New York: Norton, 2001. Print.

Gates, Henry Louis, Jr. Introduction. *The Classic Slave Narratives.* Ed. by Gates. New York: Signet, 2012. xi–xxx. Print.

Rev. of *The Interesting Narrative of the Life of Olaudah Equiano, or Gustavus Vassa, the African, Written by Himself,* by Olaudah Equiano. *General Magazine and Impartial Review* July 1789: n. pag. Rpt. in *The Interesting Narrative of the Life of Olaudah Equiano, or Gustavus Vassa, the African, Written by Himself.* Ed. Werner Sollors. New York: Norton, 2001. 295. Print.

Rev. of *The Interesting Narrative of the Life of Olaudah Equiano, or Gustavus Vassa, the African, Written by Himself,* by Olaudah Equiano. *Monthly Review* June 1789: 551. Rpt. in *The Interesting Narrative of the Life of Olaudah Equiano, or Gustavus Vassa, the African, Written by Himself.* Ed. Werner Sollors. New York: Norton, 2001. 296. Print.

W [Mary Wollstonecraft]. Rev. of *The Interesting Narrative of the Life of Olaudah Equiano, or Gustavus Vassa, the African, Written by Himself,* by Olaudah Equiano. *Analytical Review* 4 (1789): 27–28. Rpt. in *The Interesting Narrative of the Life of Olaudah Equiano, or Gustavus Vassa, the African, Written by Himself.* Ed. Werner Sollors. New York: Norton, 2001. 296–97. Print.

Further Reading

Acholonu, Catherine Obianuju. "The Igbo Roots of Olaudah Equiano." *Olaudah Equiano and the Igbo World: History, Society, and Atlantic Diaspora Connections.* Ed. Chima J. Korieh. Trenton, N.J.: Africa World Press, 2009. 49–66. Print.

———. *The Igbo Roots of Olaudah Equiano: A Linguistic and Anthropological Search.* Rev. ed. Abuja: Afa, 2007. Print.

Hochschild, Adam. *Bury the Chains: Prophets and Rebels in the Fight to Free an Empire's Slaves.* Boston: Houghton Mifflin, 2005. Print.

Lovejoy, Paul E. "Autobiography and Memory: Gustavus Vassa, Alias Olaudah Equiano, the African." *Slavery and Abolition* 27.3 (2006): 317–47. Academic Search Complete. Web. 23 Nov. 2012.

THE *ZONG* ATROCITY AND ITS AFTERMATH

In one of his first contributions to the antislavery movement, Equiano visited abolitionist Granville Sharp in March 1783 to direct Sharp's attention to a lawsuit being tried in London between the owners of the slave ship *Zong* and its insurers, who refused to pay a claim for 133 sick African captives thrown into the sea on the orders of Captain Luke Collingwood. Collingwood, aware that the insurance policy did not cover death of his human cargo by natural causes, used the pretext of a dwindling water supply—proven false by the ship's record and later testimony—to commit the murders in hopes of preserving his profits.

Sharp had already played an active role in the Mansfield decision and had tried to help Equiano rescue a friend, John Annis, from being returned to slavery in the Caribbean. Outraged by the story of the *Zong,* Sharp attempted to have the perpetrators tried for murder. While this attempt failed, letters he wrote to clergymen had some effect: one clergyman, Peter Peckard, decided to focus a Latin essay competition at the University of Cambridge on the legality of slavery. The winner, Thomas Clarkson, became a key member of the British abolitionist movement.

Cathy Saunders

A Long Way from Home
Claude McKay

Key Facts

Time Period:
Mid-20th Century

Relevant Historical Events:
New Negro movement; Harlem Renassiance; Great Depression

Nationality:
Jamaican

Keywords:
communism; travel; racism

OVERVIEW

Jamaican-born writer Claude McKay published his autobiographical *A Long Way from Home* in 1937, focusing on more than a dozen years of world travel, beginning with the end of World War I and continuing through 1934. Written in a conversational style, the book describes the countries he explored and casually introduces major figures in art and politics, such as George Bernard Shaw and Leon Trotsky, whom he met. His matter-of-fact tone shifts occasionally into vivid description and, toward the end of the book, incorporates some poems. McKay's autobiography makes little mention of his private and emotional life; instead, it defends his literary influences and political allegiances.

Shocked by the racism rampant in the United States when he arrived from Jamaica in 1912, McKay's 1919 sonnet, "If We Must Die," propelled him to fame and linked his name with the New Negro movement. This flowering of cultural and political ferment was dubbed the Harlem Renaissance for its center in New York City, where many of African descent had migrated. But McKay spent most of the 1920s, its peak period, away from Harlem, and wrote *A Long Way from Home* after his 1934 return to New York. The book was met with hostility by the influential Alain Locke and never received as much attention as McKay's fiction and poetry or other memoirs of this period. Recently, McKay's autobiography has contributed to a reevaluation of relationships among African Americans, the Communist Party, and the previously unacknowledged gay subculture of the Harlem Renaissance.

HISTORICAL AND LITERARY CONTEXT

McKay's narrative begins in 1918, during the first wave of the Great Migration of African Americans moving north from the more harshly racist South and the Caribbean region. Soldiers, both black and white, were returning home from World War I. Precipitated by a struggle for employment and fueled by the fear of the growing movement for racial equality that was incited by Russia's new Bolshevik government, white gangs were terrorizing African Americans in numerous cities. But Harlem, a neighborhood in Manhattan, became a haven for many African Americans, birthing a period of the activity in the arts as well as a rise in political consciousness. Jamaican Marcus Garvey's movement promoting black people's return to Africa found adherents, though others argued for the benefits of integration within the States.

By the time McKay began writing *A Long Way from Home* in 1935, the Great Depression had wreaked havoc on previously vibrant Harlem, and the Communist Party seemed the only viable movement focusing on racial equality. In Soviet Russia, McKay's blackness had been embraced and he had been honored. But the sum of his experiences in Russia, as well as with Marxists in London, revealed numerous flaws in communism, which he presented frankly in the book. He sought to reveal an alternative solution based on the minority communities he had observed in North Africa and Europe.

America's New Negro movement had produced fine examples of modernist art, literature, dance, and jazz, but it was a white writer, Carl Van Vechten, who first exposed Harlem to the broader public in a controversial 1926 novel. Meanwhile, McKay, abroad, wrote stories of Harlem and a novel, *Home to Harlem,* which reawakened the anger of those who wanted more flattering portraits of African American life. W. E. B. Du Bois wrote that he was "nauseated" by McKay's novel. In 1933 James Weldon Johnson penned the first autobiography by a black writer to be reviewed in the *New York Times.* A couple of years later, McKay applied for a grant to write his autobiography, stating that a "direct and unveiled treatment" would better clarify his political affiliations.

When *A Long Way from Home* came out in 1937, it was poorly received by prominent African Americans and radicals. McKay's name-dropping of white cultural icons showed an apparent disregard for the New Negro movement, and he unflinchingly depicted the power struggles and political correctness within the communist movement. His book received a fraction of the attention that Langston Hughes's 1940 autobiography *The Big Sea* would amass. But recent critics are discovering the value of his text's oblique angle to the complex interactions between the political and artistic movements of the time, as they seek to incorporate into the mix an understanding of McKay's homosexuality.

THEMES AND STYLE

The idea, stated on the book's first page, that "the spirit of the vagabond, the demon of some poets, had got hold of" McKay serves to explain his perpetual sense of himself as an outside observer. It is never clear whether "home" is in his original Jamaica, or Harlem, or some undiscovered place. Impressionistically describing his travels, his significant encounters, and the effect of these on his development as a poet and novelist, McKay wants black readers to take what good they can from "the benefits of modern civilization" while developing their own "group soul." He provides almost no personal or emotional information, as these are not relevant to his purpose.

McKay's autobiography justifies his period of travel in Europe, Africa, and the Soviet Union, countering those who saw this sojourn as an evasion of the fight for racial justice in the United States. His lengthy account of his Russian experience served to "clear up any 'mystery' that is entertained" about the visit. He describes being embraced as "the Negro Poet" by the people and government of Soviet Russia, silencing those who questioned his radical credibility and paving the way for his critique of American communism in his next novel, *Harlem: Negro Metropolis*. The minimization of his sexual relationships, except for a few superficial ones with women, and a mention of his posing nude for artists in Paris, supports his claim that he is "entirely unobsessed by sex" and unaffected by "Anglo-Saxon prudery," thus discrediting the racial consciousness of those who felt his fiction was too salacious.

The structure of *A Long Way from Home* is mostly chronological, beginning with the meeting that initiates his success as a poet in the United States. He uses this conversation with a white editor to briefly relate his youth in Jamaica and intellectual development. In the later part of the book, starting with the chapters on his Russian travels, McKay includes some of his poems after recounting the situation that inspired them. His style is straightforward, moving from simple sentences to more lavish description, such as when he describes the dancer Isadora Duncan, whose "face was a series of different masks. And her self was the embodiment of Greek tragedy, *un être* endowed with divinity." He displays his mastery of languages, his erudition, and his artistic sensibility in these and other passages.

CRITICAL DISCUSSION

The leading black intellectuals of the day excoriated the book. Writing in the *New Challenge*, a leftist black quarterly, Locke called McKay a "spiritual truant" who was "insincere and disloyal to every group with whom he had ever associated himself." Other negative reviews came from communists sensitive to the criticisms McKay made about some of the Soviet government's repressive policies. Though not all reviewers were harsh, there were few very positive critiques. J. S. Balch of the *St. Louis Post Dispatch* criticized the "old conception of the poet as apart from other men," which was McKay's recurring refrain when asked to fight for the cause. Stung by the expected attacks,

Author Claude McKay photographed in 1941.
© CORBIS

McKay may have been even angrier at a review pairing his work with an autobiography of jailed labor leader Angelo Herndon, as if all black radicals could be lumped together. In any case, *A Long Way from Home* sold poorly, and McKay had increasing difficulty getting his work published.

Though never receiving the attention of other notable autobiographies of the Harlem Renaissance, politically conservative readers have looked to *A Long Way from Home* for its explanation of the African American disillusionment with communism. Leftist critics, however, doubt the veracity of McKay's account, claiming he followed the party line far longer than the book suggests. Contemporary criticism approaches the text using the insights of queer theory to uncover the relationship between sexuality, colonialism, and black proletarianism.

More recent critics such as Gary Edward Holcomb argue that the complexity of McKay's relation to the political currents of the day "permits a reading of McKay's work that opens the door of his closet, both sexual and political … in a way that shows how the sexual is the political in McKay." Holcomb's essay in *MFS Modern Fiction Studies* examines the gaps in McKay's text to reveal a hidden homoerotic narrative, noting, for example, how a relationship with an alleged pickpocket makes much more sense if the pickpocket were actually a prostitute. Holcomb argues that McKay's autobiography is more ambiguous than it appears and that the author's representation of himself must be questioned.

CLAUDE MCKAY'S LETTERS TO WILLIAM A. BRADLEY

Additional autobiographical insights into Claude McKay's life and work can be found in his extensive correspondence with his literary agent, William A. Bradley. These letters, now part of the William A. Bradley Agency collection housed at the University of Texas at Austin, detail McKay's life and writing practices during the period in which he composed his best-known novel, *Home to Harlem* (1928). It was Bradley who initially encouraged McKay to expand his short story of the same title into a novel, and the letters between the two men chronicle its development over a few short months in 1927.

McKay's attachment to his story of life in Harlem in the years following World War I is evident in numerous letters. He explains in a February 1927 letter to Bradley, for example, that "I am having a picnic doing it." McKay's letters also describe how he drew on his own life experiences to develop the characters from several of his short stories into the more rounded characters of the novel. Later letters reveal the more exhausting process of writing the novel *Banjo* (1930) and detail McKay's financial struggles as well as emotional support offered by Bradley.

BIBLIOGRAPHY

Sources

Cooper, Wayne C. *Claude McKay: Rebel Sojourner in the Harlem Renaissance. A Biography.* Baton Rouge: Louisiana State University Press, 1987. *Google Books.* Web. 20 Nov. 2012.

Holcomb, Gary Edward. "Diaspora Cruises: Queer Black Proletarianism in Claude McKay's *A Long Way from Home.*" *MFS Modern Fiction Studies* 49.4 (2003): 714–45. *Project MUSE.* Web. 12 Nov. 2012.

McKay, Claude. *A Long Way from Home.* 1937. Ed. Gene Andrew Jarrett. New Brunswick, N.J.: Rutgers University Press, 2007. Print.

"McKay, Claude (1889–1948)." *Africa and the Americas: Culture, Politics, and History.* Santa Barbara, Calif.: ABC-CLIO, 2008. *Credo Reference.* Web. 15 Nov. 2012.

Further Reading

Cooper, Wayne F. Foreword. *Home to Harlem.* By Claude McKay. 1928. Boston: Northeastern University Press, 1987. Print.

Dawahare, Anthony. *Nationalism, Marxism, and African American Literature between the Wars: A New Pandora's Box.* Jackson: University of Mississippi Press, 2002. Print.

Holcomb, Gary Edward. *Claude McKay, Code Name Sasha: Queer Black Marxism and the Harlem Renaissance.* Gainesville: UP of Florida, 2007. Print.

Lowney, John. "Haiti and Black Transnationalism: Remapping the Migrant Geography of *Home to Harlem.*" *African American Review* 34.3 (2000): 413. *ProQuest.* Web.

McKay, Claude. *Complete Poems: Claude McKay.* Ed. William J. Maxwell. Urbana: University of Illinois Press, 2004. Print.

———. *Harlem: Negro Metropolis.* New York: E.P. Dutton, 1940. Print.

Smethurst, James E. *The New Red Negro: The Literary Left and African American Poetry, 1930–1936.* Oxford: Oxford University Press, 1999. Print.

Solomon, Mark. *The Cry Was Unity: Communists and African Americans, 1917–1936.* Jackson: University Press of Mississippi, 1998. Print.

Tillery, Tyrone. *Claude McKay: A Black Poet's Struggle for Identity.* Amherst: University of Massachusetts Press, 1992. Print.

Robin Morris

Meatless Days

Sara Suleri

OVERVIEW

First published in 1989, Sara Suleri's memoir *Meatless Days* combines personal and political history, recounting the author's childhood in the young nation of Pakistan. The work chronicles the small events of Suleri's youth, the deaths of her grandmother and sister, and her eventual immigration to the United States. Narrated in a nonlinear manner that relies on memory and connection rather than on chronology, the memoir examines the roles of religion, gender, family, and food (in particular, meat) in the creation and transformation of culture, as well as the ways in which family, culture, and nation affect the formation or loss of individual identity. The mixed nationalities and religions of her family—comprising a Muslim Pakistani father and grandmother, a Protestant Welsh mother, and four siblings—allow her to explore cultural mingling, loss, and change from a personal perspective.

Suleri wrote *Meatless Days* as an expatriate; she refers in the book to her "American retreat," the loss of her identification with place, and her sense of having betrayed her patriotic Pakistani father by leaving her homeland. The book met with immediate acclaim for its postcolonial themes and its revealing treatment of gender roles; it was also noted as a work of diasporic detachment and elegy. Examining as it does the impossibility of constructing simple selves or straightforward autobiographies in a decolonizing world, today it is considered an essential part of the postcolonial literary canon.

HISTORICAL AND LITERARY CONTEXT

Growing up in a decolonized nation, Suleri was inevitably touched by the aftermath of British rule. The 1947 partition of the former colony established Pakistan as a state independent from India because of religious tensions between Hindus and Muslims. Originally, Pakistan was composed of two geographically separate areas (East and West Pakistan) divided by more than 1,000 miles of northern India. Conflicts arose recurrently over territory, supremacy, and independence, with the disposition of the disputed province of Kashmir providing a particularly difficult problem. In 1971 East and West Pakistan separated, with East Pakistan becoming the nation of Bangladesh. Because her family was politically engaged in these transformations, Suleri was exposed to a mélange of religious and cultural traditions, and negotiating a complicated balance between Hindu, Muslim, and Christian practices forms a key concern of her memoir.

Suleri arrived in the United States in 1976 to pursue graduate studies. When she wrote *Meatless Days* in 1989, she had been a professor at Yale University for six years. U.S. relations with Pakistan were strained at the time. Whereas during the 1970s Pakistan was perceived as an ally against potentially socialist India, by the 1980s U.S. foreign policy reflected concerns about the country's nuclear ambitions. Suleri explores the impact of these shifts in the narrative of Pakistan in what she calls her "alternative history," creating a dialogue between her family's private life and the public sphere. Instead of attempting to "explain" the Third World to her audience, she tries to make history "register as immediately to the reader as it would to me." She refuses to present the developing world as an "otherness machine," insisting on the concurrent strangeness and familiarity that constitute life after decolonization.

Meatless Days forms part of a multidisciplinary study of issues facing postcolonial states and peoples. By the 1980s pressing questions about the effects of imperialism had arisen in sociology, political science, literary fiction, and memoir. Works that, like Suleri's, focus on Pakistan include British Indian author Salman Rushdie's historical novel *Midnight's Children* (1980), which gives a fictionalized account of the origins and early years of the country, and his novel *Shame* (1984), which deals with religious oppression there. Among feminist works, the poet Anita Desai's *In Custody* (1984) broke ground in theorizing about Pakistani gender roles, while Kamala Das's memoir *My Life* (1988) explores the world of the Indo-Pakistani woman artist. In academics the writings of Homi Bhabha and Gayatri Chakravorty Spivak analyze the unique difficulties of communication across postcolonial barriers. All of these authors were born in India, and all except Das have lived in the West.

The critical success of *Meatless Days* paved the way for a number of increasingly postmodern accounts of Indo-Pakistani diasporic life, including Arundhati Roy's novel *The God of Small Things* (1997) and Jhumpa Lahiri's short story collection *Interpreter of Maladies* (1999), both about Indians who contend with life in the United States. Suleri subsequently published the scholarly work *The Rhetoric of English*

❖ **Key Facts**

Time Period:
Late 20th Century

Relevant Historical Events:
British decolonization of India; partition; Pakistani nuclearization

Nationality:
Pakistani

Keywords:
postcolonialism; history; partition

India (1992), in which she evaluates colonial and postcolonial discourses ranging from those of eighteenth-century Irish statesman and philosopher Edmund Burke and nineteenth- and twentieth-century Anglo-Indian author Rudyard Kipling to contemporary writers Rushdie and Indo-Trinidadian-British novelist V. S. Naipaul. The often-cited text remains one of the eminent works of postcolonial scholarship. In 2003 she published her second memoir, *Boys Will Be Boys,* as an elegy for her father.

THEMES AND STYLE

Meatless Days centers on themes of connection (and its lack), not only through family, culture, and nation but also through memory and time. The memoir simultaneously portrays the life of an individual and the trajectory of a culture through history, enmeshing the personal and the political. Suleri writes of her desire to "lose the sense of the differentiated identity of history and myself." Indeed, the character Sara is often only indirectly revealed; Suleri relinquishes the position of protagonist to the people around her, demonstrating the interdependence of individuals within a society. In her examination of her parents' relationship, an embodiment of cross-cultural tensions, she finds it necessary to consider differences in nationality, language, religion, and gender simultaneously: "How can I bring them together in a room, that most reticent woman and that most demanding man? … Papa's powerful discourse would surround her night and day." Connections in *Meatless Days* are rarely simple or easy: Suleri's relationships with her siblings involve both affection and competition, and she is unable to resolve the contradictions between her two very different lives, one in Pakistan and one in the United States. Gender, in particular, both creates and destroys connections. Suleri writes that in leaving Pakistan she "gave up the company of women," but she also claims that "there are no women in the Third World," pointing to the disparity between lived experience and cultural stereotypes.

In *Meatless Days* Suleri confronts the challenge of articulating her perceptions of cultural difference. Through her narration of her early life, she explores the losses, ambivalences, and radical paradoxes of postcolonial identity. She has repeated encounters with the dissimilarities between herself and others and with her own feelings of alienation and confusion, and her narration frequently highlights issues of communication—as in her contemplation of her relationship to her cultural "mother tongue," Urdu, which her Welsh mother cannot speak. She encapsulates the problem at the heart of her memoir when she claims that her audience is "lost, and angry to be lost, and both of us must find some tokens of exchange for this failed conversation."

Suleri's style is nonlinear; the memoir's construction follows daydreams, conversations, and recollections, creating an experience rather than a chronology. Mental associations and shifts reflect the enigmatic functioning of memory. Sometimes the author refuses to record a memory, repressing it as the mind might. Of her sister Ifat's tragic death, for example, she writes, "In this story, Ifat will not die before our eyes: it could not be countenanced." In keeping with poststructuralist inquiry, Suleri acknowledges the power of narrative configuration to shape both identity and history; she also emphasizes the inevitable untrustworthiness of personal and institutional memory.

CRITICAL DISCUSSION

The initial response to *Meatless Days* was strong, consisting of mainly positive reviews from major postcolonial studies scholars. Henry Louis Gates Jr.'s "Remembrance of Things Pakistani" (1983) compares the work favorably with Rushdie's writings, celebrating Suleri as a "Proust in Pakistan." In "Memory, Identity, Patriarchy" (1993), Sangeeta Ray pairs the book with Sri Lankan Canadian novelist Michael Ondaatje's postmodern memoir *Running in the Family* (1982). Seizing on Suleri's unorthodox structure and deconstructive use of language, critics have also linked her memoir to Joan Didion's essay collection *Slouching towards Bethlehem* (1968), among other postmodern works. The story's fragmented form and emphasis on loss and disconnection have often led to its characterization as haunting, mournful, or elegiac. Some commentators have complained that Suleri is overly elitist and withdrawn in her portrayal of Pakistani culture and people.

Although it is not as well known as the works of Didion and Rushdie, *Meatless Days* remains a significant part of the postcolonial literary canon. According to scholar Michael Gorra, in a 1995 article in *Transition*, it takes an "autobiographical turn" that was common in the mid-1980s and early 1990s, a trend that resituated autobiographical authority in broader cultural contexts while simultaneously insisting on the importance of individual lives. *Meatless Days* is often taught at the postsecondary level, with scholars approaching the work through a variety of lenses, including identity studies, food studies, postcolonial feminism, and cultural anthropology.

Current academic criticism of *Meatless Days* can be grouped into two broad categories: postcolonial studies and studies of postmodern identity. In the journal *Signs* (1998), Shahnaz Khan uses the work as an example of the conflicting demands placed on modern Muslim women. In his 1997 essay in *Journal of Commonwealth Literature,* Oliver Lovesey examines the memoir's deconstruction of selfhood into something "multifarious and unstable." Other criticism has interpreted the book's images of food and the gendered body, particularly noting the grotesqueness with which Suleri often combines the two. A number of critics, including Samir Dayal and Inderpal Grewal, have developed a critique of *Meatless Days* that highlights the interaction of Suleri's positions of privilege and outsidership—as a member of the middle class and an émigré—with the postcolonial feminism of her project. As Dayal points out in his piece in *Between the Lines: South Asians and Postcoloniality* (1996), the postmodern opacity of the author's style is potentially exclusionary, limiting her audience to Western, educated readers.

BIBLIOGRAPHY

Sources

Dayal, Samir. "Style Is (Not) the Woman: Sara Suleri's *Meatless Days*." *Between the Lines: South Asians and Postcoloniality*. Ed. Deepika Bahri and Mary Vasudeva. Philadelphia: Temple University Press, 1996. 250–69. Print.

Gates, Henry Louis, Jr. "Remembrance of Things Pakistani: Sara Suleri Makes History." *Voice Literary Supplement* 81 (1989): 37–38. Print.

Gorra, Michael. "The Autobiographical Turn." *Transition* 68 (1995): 143–53. *JSTOR*. Web. 4 Oct. 2012.

Grewal, Inderpal. Rev. of *Meatless Days*, by Sara Suleri. *NWSA Journal* 2.3 (1990): 508–10. Print.

Lovesey, Oliver. "Postcolonial Self-Fashioning in Sara Suleri's *Meatless Days*." *Journal of Commonwealth Literature* 32.2 (1997): 35–46. Print.

Ray, Sangeeta. "Memory, Identity, Patriarchy: Projecting a Past in the Memoirs of Ondaatje and Suleri." *Modern Fiction Studies* 39 (1993): 37–58. *JSTOR*. Web. 4 Oct. 2012.

Suleri, Sara. Interview by Abbas Nasir and Umber Khairi. *Newsline* Jan. 1990: 152–55. Print.

———. *Meatless Days*. Chicago: University of Chicago Press, 1989. Print.

Further Reading

Aegerter, Lindsay Pentolfe. "A Pedagogy of Postcolonial Literature." *College Literature* 24.2 (1997): 142–50. Print.

Easthope, Antony. "Paradigm Lost and Paradigm Regained." *The State of Theory*. Ed. Richard Bradford. London: Routledge, 1993. 90–104. Print.

Khan, Shahnaz. "Muslim Women: Negotiations in the Third Space." *Signs* 23.2 (1998): 463–94. Print.

Malin, Jo. *The Voice of the Mother: Embedded Maternal Narratives in Twentieth-Century Women's Autobiographies*. Carbondale: Southern Illinois University Press, 2000. Print.

Mannur, Anita. "Culinary Nostalgia: Authenticity, Nationalism, and Diaspora." *MELUS* 32.4 (2007): 11–31. Web. *JSTOR*. 4 Oct. 2012.

MEAT IN *MEATLESS DAYS*

In diasporic and postcolonial cultures, the politics of food are complex. Sara Suleri's *Meatless Days* uses meat in a number of overlapping images, both literal and metaphorical, to represent cultural memory and transmission. Fasting and feasting are key facets of Pakistani religious observance, and abstention and eating form links between disparate characters and sections of Suleri's autobiography. For instance, conflicting ideas about butchery demonstrate the cultural divide between her Welsh mother and Pakistani grandmother, and Sara and her sister are dismayed to discover that *kapuras*, a Pakistani dish that they greatly enjoy, are not sweetbreads but cooked testicles. Food also functions as a metaphor for mourning: it "is what you bury in your body." After her mother's death Sara dreams of the body as "hunks of meat wrapped in cellophane."

Throughout the memoir meat symbolizes sex and gender differences, connecting women to each other through traditional work and women to men through sexuality. Suleri often calls readers' attention to the meatiness of bodies by focusing on skin, muscles, and joints. Both men's and women's bodies become edible; various parts are compared to grapes, shrimp, and pieces of meat, among other foods. Because of meat's multiple and contradictory connotations—of violence, death, nourishment, and celebration—it encapsulates Suleri's relationship to her homeland and its history.

Murtiza, Ghulam, and Abdul Baseer. "Sara Suleri's Feminist Stance in *Meatless Days*." *European Journal of Social Sciences* 25.4 (2011): 550–62. Print.

Oed, Anja. "Aspects of (Self-)Representation in Sara Suleri's *Meatless Days*; or, What Does It Mean to Write a Book beyond What It Is About?" *Hybridity and Postcolonialism: Twentieth-Century Indian Literature*. Ed. Monika Fludernik. Tübingen: Stauffenberg, 1998. 187–97. Print.

Ray, Krishnendu. "The Nation Betrayed: Or about Those Who Left." *Economic and Political Weekly* 38.26 (2003): 2722–29. Print.

Sutherland, Katherine G. "Land of Their Graves: Maternity, Mourning and Nation in Janet Frame, Sara Suleri, and Arundhati Roy." *Canadian Review of Comparative Literature/Revue Canadienne de Littérature Comparée* 1.30 (2003): 201–16. Print.

Carina Saxon

Memoirs of an Arabian Princess from Zanzibar

Emily Ruete

Key Facts

Time Period:
Late 19th Century

Relevant Historical Events:
European colonization of Africa; Ruete's move to Germany from Zanzibar

Nationality:
Tanzanian

Keywords:
colonialism; women's writing; alienation

OVERVIEW

First published in German in 1886, *Memoirs of an Arabian Princess* by Emily Ruete (1844–1924) is one of the first published autobiographies of an Arab woman. The book outlines Ruete's childhood in Zanzibar, where she was born Sayyida Salme; gives detailed descriptions of the royal family's customs; and tells of her marriage to Rudolph Heinrich Ruete, a German merchant. She concludes with an account of her involvement in Otto von Bismarck's nascent colonial activities. While she writes in the tradition of a European travel narrative, her African heritage allows her to describe exotic customs accurately and without hyperbole. Positioning herself as an observer who dissects attitudes and behaviors in both Zanzibar and Germany, Ruete praises Arab lifestyles and points out hypocrisy in European culture, especially attitudes toward women and slavery.

In the book's preface, Ruete explains that she published her memoirs to give her children an accurate account of her native culture. After her husband's death, Ruete was stranded in a German society that viewed her as an exotic outsider; she wrote and published *Memoirs* partly as an attempt to support herself. However, the book was not a financial nor a literary success, and her opinions, such as her argument that abolition left harmful social and economic gaps in eastern Africa, sometimes contradict current postcolonial scholarship. But for twenty-first-century readers, Ruete is a candid spokesperson for a group that had few public voices—nineteenth-century African and Arab women.

HISTORICAL AND LITERARY CONTEXT

Ruete's autobiography demonstrates a unique intersection between Eastern and Western cultures. Western attitudes toward the East had been strained since the fall of Constantinople in 1453 at the hands of Muslim Turks. Despite the historic antipathy to Muslims, Westerners renewed their interest in the commodities and customs of Muslim culture as new trading companies formed in the sixteenth century and functioned into the nineteenth century. Among other issues, contact via commerce forced Europeans to consider questions about slavery, women's rights, and religion.

In this climate, Ruete conveys insights of an Arab traveler in both Eastern and Western cultures, widening the typical European perspective of the time. For example, she confronts the question of women's roles. More than a century before Ruete's time, English poet and playwright John Dryden, along with other European authors, claimed that Muslim women were enslaved by Muslim men. Ruete thought this claim was preposterous. Whereas European women were not allowed to own property, Ruete had inherited plantations at the age of twelve upon her father's death. Yet she writes as an outcast of both cultures. Because she became pregnant out of wedlock, she was forced to leave Zanzibar; but because the German government did not recognize her claims to the aristocracy after her husband's death, she was an outsider in Europe as well. Thus, writing her memoirs was the only legitimate way she could attempt to vindicate herself.

As trade between East and West grew, European travel narratives began to be published that purported to give readers intimate knowledge of foreign food, clothing, religion, and politics. As a native observer of these "foreign" customs in Zanzibar, Ruete contradicted existing European assumptions. Both Ruete and Lady Mary Wortley Montagu, a British aristocrat who wrote about life in Turkey in the mid-eighteenth century, mock European travel writers who claim to have firsthand experience of harems and mosques but who have never actually stepped foot inside such establishments. Ruete's narrative, on the other hand, gives factual insight into the domestic life of a royal harem, Muslim festivals, and Arab slavery. Her autobiography includes careful descriptions of the leisurely lives of Arab nobility, which would have sounded exotic—perhaps even shocking—to European readers used to outsiders' sanitized versions of Muslim culture.

Memoirs of an Arabian Princess did not receive widespread attention upon its initial publication. One of the book's English translators, Lionel Strachey, wrote that it "attracted little interest, both the German and the English versions soon falling into obscurity and going out of print." Strachey attributed this failure to the fact that European colonialism in Africa had not yet become full-fledged. However, as interest in postcolonial theory in subsequent generations rose, Ruete's work achieved more notice, particularly with the 1992 publication of her collected memoirs and letters, published as *An Arabian Princess between Two Worlds,* edited by Emeri van Donzel.

THEMES AND STYLE

The main theme in Ruete's autobiography is her critical comparison of Zanzibar to Europe. Although ostensibly a work of the travel narrative genre, the book adopts the trope of the domestic harem story popular in European literature at the time. The first sixteen chapters focus on family life and include "Brother Majid Reaches His Majority"; "An Outdoor Butchery, Kitchen, and Larder"; and "Love of Arabs for Their Horses." Even here, though, cultural comparison is present: Ruete writes about the "Defects of European Education" and the "Duplicity of the British Government." Thus, through the lens of her childhood experience, she constantly critiques the European culture in which she lives as an adult.

Like other female autobiographers, Ruete writes "to bequeath" her memoirs to her children, for they "were not at first intended for the general public." Implicit in her writing, though, is her desire to regain her aristocratic position. She signs her preface, "Emily Ruete, nee Princess of Oman and Zanzibar." This gives her authority: whereas most travel authors could claim only secondhand acquaintance with the domestic life they claimed to describe, she can claim the glamour and experience of an exotic aristocracy. However, Ruete's claim to this title was troubled. Her brother, Sultan of Zanzibar, denied her claims. In telling her story, Ruete uncovers her brother's true nature and claims authority over other European authors by contesting how "highly Europeans praise the Sultan of Zanzibar's affability; the real truth may be judged from what I have written about him." Though she tells her story in hopes that she will be recognized as a princess, her rightful position remained unsettled. Thus, she combined autobiography with travel writing, managing to critique European and foreign cultures simultaneously in an effort to champion her cause.

Stylistically, the autobiography adopts the worldly tone of travel literature, giving the "facts" of Ruete's life, as she says in her preface. As Billie Melman writes in a review of van Donzel's edition, the work "is an interesting example of what might be called 'autoethnography,' in which colonized people represent themselves in colonizer's terms." Melman states that Ruete "shrewdly appropriates Orientalist conventions of representation" to respond to "Western representations of Middle Eastern women and the Middle East." For instance, she gives "Examples Disproving the 'Inferiority' of Oriental Women." Her shrewdness extends to the details of the royal baths; she writes that the religious rules regulating clothing worn to the baths are "obeyed only by the extremely pious." Her observations cut both ways, then, dissecting European misconceptions about women while pointing out hypocrisy in her own culture.

Sir Bartle Frere, a member of the British aristocracy and onetime governor of the Cape Colony. A visit from Frere is described in the last chapter of *Memoirs of an Arabian Princess from Zanzibar.*
© CLASSIC IMAGE/ALAMY

CRITICAL DISCUSSION

Memoirs of an Arabian Princess received little critical attention upon its initial publication in 1886. One notable exception is Oscar Wilde's 1888 review, published in *Woman's World.* Wilde cites long passages from *Memoirs* and praises Ruete's story for being "as instructive as history and as fascinating as fiction." With trenchant prescience, he writes that "no one who is interested in the social position of women in the East should fail to read these pleasantly-written memoirs." Despite this, Ruete's autobiography has little legacy as a work of literature in and of itself; it is most often analyzed in the context of the genres of travel narrative, harem stories, and ethno-autobiography.

Twenty years after its initial publication, Strachey's English-language edition included a note authenticating Ruete's existence as a historical figure. Ironically, though Ruete wrote during an era of international commerce, Strachey surmises that her autobiography was written before its time. On the other hand, Melman suspects that Ruete's ideas about European culture were "not likely to endear her to Western readers, and a great deal of what she had to say on slavery was censored." Melman also states that Ruete was "fully aware" that she was "a political embarrassment" to the Germans and the British.

An outpouring of book reviews accompanied the publication of van Donzel's edition in 1992, but little has been written about it since. Aside from two articles on transcultural interactions, published in 2008 and 2009, and its inclusion as a source in footnotes for historical studies, *Memoirs* has not often been included in scholarly discussions of gender, race, or cultural interaction in the late nineteenth century. Interestingly, Ruete has appeared as a figure in modern

AN ARABIAN PRINCESS'S PERSPECTIVE ON SLAVERY

In Emily Ruete's *Memoirs,* a modern reader might be struck by the author's apparently cavalier attitude toward slavery. In a chapter devoted to this subject, she describes the release of slaves from British masters as "ruinous" because it left people without means of earning a livelihood. As a consequence of British abolition, "our island now enjoyed the advantage of being enriched by the presence of a few thousand loafers, tramps, and thieves," Ruete writes. She also harshly criticizes the "humane anti-slavery apostles" who "held aloof" because they had "attained their object in freeing those poor wretches from the degradation of serfdom."

Ruete's understanding of the situation is partly linked to her religious concerns. Praising Arab slave owners who, she claims, make sure that their slaves are "assured of their maintenance," she asks, "Is every non-Christian a heartless rascal?" Like English writer Daniel Defoe, who describes slavery in Muslim countries as more merciful than in Europe, Ruete considers Arab slavery preferable to the hypocrisy of European Christians who abandoned emancipated slaves. Furthermore, Ruete's racial and economic status influence her claims. In some ways she echoes nineteenth-century southern U.S. rhetoric when she writes that "negroes are very lazy, and will not work voluntarily."

German fiction, including H. C. Buch's *Sansibar Blues* (2008). Yet Fedwa Malti-Douglas, in her review of van Donzel's edition, praised Ruete, claiming her memoir "should become a classic" with today's "critics voraciously consuming products on gender and women." She goes on to state that the work should "be required reading for all those interested in the Middle East, in Muslims in the West, in ethnography, and in transnational phenomena in general."

BIBLIOGRAPHY

Sources

Al-Rawi, Ahmed K. "The Portrayal of the East vs. the West in Lady Mary Montagu's *Letters* and Emily Ruete's *Memoirs.*" *Arab Studies Quarterly* 30.1 (2008): 15+. *Literature Resource Center.* Web. 20 Nov. 2012.

Malti-Douglas, Fedwa. Rev. of *An Arabian Princess between Two Worlds: Memoirs, Letters Home, Sequels to the Memoirs, Syrian Customs and Usages,* by Sayyida Salme/Emily Ruete. *Journal of the American Oriental Society* 116.4 (1996): 794. *Literature Resource Center.* Web. 20 Nov. 2012.

Melman, Billie. Rev. of *An Arabian Princess between Two Worlds: Memoirs, Letters Home, Sequels to the Memoirs, Syrian Customs and Usages,* by Sayyida Salme/Emily Ruete. *International Journal of Middle East Studies* 26.3 (1994): 525–27. Web. 20 Nov. 2012.

Ruete, Emily. *Memoirs of an Arabian Princess.* Trans. Lionel Strachey. New York: Doubleday, 1907. U of Pennsylvania. Web. 20 November 2012.

Ruete, Emily/Sayyida Salme. *An Arabian Princess between Two Worlds: Memoirs, Letters Home, Sequels to the Memoirs, Syrian Customs and Usages.* Ed. Emeri van Donzel. New York: Brill, 1993. Print.

Wilde, Oscar. Rev. of *Memoirs of an Arabian Princess,* by Emily Ruete. *Woman's World* Mar. 1888: 35–45. Print.

Further Reading

Bhacker, M. Reda. "Family Strife and Foreign Intervention: Causes in the Separation of Zanzibar from Oman: A Reappraisal." *Bulletin of the School of Oriental and African Studies* 54.2 (1991): 269–80. *Cambridge Journals Online.* Web. 20 Nov. 2012.

Gottsche, Dirk. "Hans Christoph Buch's *Sansibar Blues* and the Fascination of Cross-Cultural Experience in Contemporary German Historical Novels about Colonialism." *German Life & Letters* 65.1 (2012): 127–46. Print.

O'Mahony, Anthony. Rev. of *An Arabian Princess between Two Worlds: Memoirs, Letters Home, Sequels to the Memoirs, Syrian Customs and Usages,* by Sayyida Salme/Emily Ruete. *Bulletin of the School of Oriental and African Studies* 59.2 (1996): 353–54. *Cambridge Journals Online.* Web. 20 Nov. 2012.

Roy, Kate. "German-Islamic Literary Interperceptions in Works by Emily Ruete and Emine Sevgi Ozdamar." *Encounters with Islam in German Literature and Culture.* Rochester, N.Y.: Camden House, 2009. 166–80. Print.

Schneppen, Heinz. *Sayyida Salme/Emily Ruete: Between Zanzibar and Germany, between Islam and Christianity.* Dar es Salaam: National Museum of Tanzania, 1999. Print.

Evelyn Reynolds

My Life Story

Fadhma Aïth Mansour Amrouche

Key Facts

Time Period:
Mid-20th Century

Relevant Historical Events:
French colonial rule of Algeria; Amrouche's French education

Nationality:
Algerian

Keywords:
alienation; colonialism; immigration

OVERVIEW

Printed in French in 1968 and translated into English twenty years later, *Historie de ma vie* (*My Life Story*) by Fadhma Aïth Mansour Amrouche is the first memoir published by a Kabyle woman, giving voice to a rarely represented culture and documenting a life encompassing many identities under colonial rule. Written in plain and straightforward language, *My Life Story* details eighty years of Amrouche's life, including her illegitimate birth in Kabylia, a part of eastern Algeria; her education by French nuns; her marriage at age sixteen; and the experience of raising eight children in poverty. Throughout the text, Amrouche details the experiences of being an immigrant in Tunisia and France, a Christian in a Muslim region, and a woman educated in French literature in an Arab/Berber country, and the struggle to embody and preserve many identities.

Amrouche details life under French colonial rule and the devastating effects of the war for Algerian independence. Her memoir is also significant for being largely apolitical as a simple tale of one woman's life. Although she wrote most of the text in 1946, Amrouche's memoir was published posthumously in 1968, per her instructions, by her daughter, Marie-Louise, also known as Taos. The book became part of the growing movement to preserve Berber culture, in which Amrouche's son Jean and daughter Taos were involved, and provides a rare glimpse into a culture little understood by the Western world.

HISTORICAL AND LITERARY CONTEXT

Although *My Life Story* does not seek to make any political statement, the turbulent political structures of the time in which it was written are apparent. France took violent control of Algeria in 1830. By 1874 France had legal authority over Kabylia, with its power firmly entrenched by the time of Amrouche's birth in 1882 or 1883. Even before she was born, Amrouche, as she details in her memoir, was dependent upon an ability to maneuver between two authorities: the Kabyle culture, which sanctioned killing her mother for becoming pregnant as an unmarried widow, and French magistrates, whom she begged to protect her. Amrouche received a haphazard French education, making it more difficult for her to return to Berber life.

The majority of the text was written during one month in 1946 while Amrouche and her husband were living in Tunis. In 1962, while living with her daughter in Paris, Amrouche added an epilogue. At the time of the publication of *My Life Story*, Algeria had won its independence from France through a violent guerrilla campaign that Amrouche writes about in her epilogue. As a part of an effort to preserve Berber culture, Amrouche and her children had been translating traditional Kabyle songs into French. Her children, Jean and Taos, who were writers and Berber activists, urged Amrouche to write her life story. Taos was one of the founding members of the Berber Academy, a group dedicated to preserving Berber culture, in 1966, just two years before *My Life Story* appeared.

My Life Story is a seminal work. At the time of its publication, very few texts like it had ever been published. Amrouche's first language, Kabyle, did not become a written language until 1970. Although autobiographies were a tradition of the Islamic Middle Ages, Amrouche could not read the Arabic they were written in. Her primary influences appear to have been the Kabyle tradition of oral storytelling—her text meanders into small details and often interjects the Arabic word *Mektoub* (God's will be done)—as well as "the solitary romantic heroes of the 19th century French canon," as Carolyn Duffey writes in a 1995 essay in *Pacific Coast Philology*.

Amrouche's autobiography was influential to many, especially North African women and those interested in preserving and understanding Berber culture. Her writing influenced Jean and to a greater extent Taos, who later wrote an autobiographical novel, *Jacinthe Noir*; compiled an anthology of Kabyle songs and folklore; and became a successful singer of Kabyle songs in France. Another successful Algerian female writer and filmmaker, Assia Djebar, also was influenced by Amrouche's work and expressed interest in making a film about her life story. In 1988 Dorothy S. Blair translated *My Life Story* into English, which English-speaking scholars see today as an extraordinary document of a time and place that otherwise would have gone undocumented.

THEMES AND STYLE

The primary theme of *My Life Story* is the experience of living between cultures and what it means to be an

Marie-Louise "Taos" Amrouche, shown here in a 1975 photograph, was the daughter of Fadhma Amrouche and an author in her own right. She translated her mother's poems and traditional Berber songs. © SOPHIE BASSOULS/SYGMA/CORBIS

outsider. Amrouche begins life as an outsider, attending a French school to escape the cruelty of her village. At school she is called Marguerite, but later she is told that she cannot use that name since she has not been baptized. When she returns to her village, her education further cements her outsider status. She marries into a polygamous family and immigrates to Tunis, where she does not speak the language. As she writes on the final page of the 1946 draft, "[N]ever, in spite of the forty years I have spent in Tunisia, in spite of my basically French education, never have I been able to become a close friend of any French people, nor of Arabs … I remain forever the eternal exile, the woman who has never felt at home anywhere."

Amrouche wrote her autobiography at the urging of her children. She dedicated the larger portion, written in 1946, to her son Jean and then gave him the manuscript, telling him not to publish it until his father's death. As she writes on the final page of the manuscript, "I dedicate these pages to my son Jean … so that he may know what my mother and I suffered and laboured, in order that, one day, the Berber poet Jean Amrouche could be born." In 1962 Jean died and Amrouche wrote the epilogue to her autobiography, dedicating it to Taos, who eventually got the book published in 1968, a year after her mother's death. Before Amrouche's passing, she and her two children worked to translate traditional Berber songs and poems into French.

Amrouche's writing style is typically simple and straightforward, occasionally becoming rapturous when describing a particular memory, as if reacting right on the page to the story she is telling. Remembering a favorite stream near her school, she writes, "My stream! I cannot count the happy hours I spent beside you!" Amrouche also includes an account of a prophetic dream in which a large bird drops her in front of the hospital where she would later work. In the earliest sections, when her memory is haziest, she writes about herself in the third person, as if seeing her life from the outside: "I later learned that this child was me."

CRITICAL DISCUSSION

Upon its publication in France in 1968, *My Life Story* was generally acknowledged as an important work, especially by those interested in the preservation and study of Berber culture. Before the text was published in English, Charlotte H. Bruner translated an excerpt and included it in her book *Unwinding Threads: Writing by Women in Africa* (1985), cementing Amrouche's status as one of the most important female African writers of the twentieth century. After being translated into English in 1988, the book gained in readership and became a topic of renewed interest among scholars. A 1990 review by Suha Sabbagh in the *Women's Review of Books* calls it "a rare, uncritical view of Berber society."

Although the luster of the book's status as the first Kabyle memoir faded as more people from the region took up the pen, Amrouche's memoir continues to be regarded as important and unique. Blair in the introduction to the 1988 edition calls Amrouche's book "a classic" and states that although *My Life Story* is "a very simple story, simply told," Amrouche "was a remarkable woman … and it was a remarkable thing that she ever came to write the story of her life." Today scholarly interest in postcolonial women's writing and Berber culture have cemented Amrouche's place in literature.

My Life Story is often studied today because of the ways in which Amrouche is forced to cross complex cultural boundaries and embody multiple identities throughout her life, as well as the ways in which composition of the autobiography adds a complex layer to this identity. Duffey writes that Amrouche combines her Kabyle heritage and French religious education in constructing her story, notably "accept[ing] neither set of influences unquestioningly, often providing an oblique criticism of each by combining them." Although Amrouche's text is not political, some scholars have noticed her criticisms of polygamy and harsh Kabyle customs, as well as her surprise at "the enormous prestige enjoyed by representatives of the male sex, even the most unprepossessing."

BIBLIOGRAPHY

Sources

Amrouche, Fadhma. *My Life Story*. Trans. Dorothy S. Blair. London: Women's Press, 1988. Print.

Bruner, Charlotte H., ed. *Unwinding Threads: Writing by Women in Africa*. Portsmouth: Heinneman Educational Books, 1985. Print.

Duffey, Carolyn. "Berber Dreams, Colonialism and Couscous: The Competing Autobiographical Narratives of Fadhma Amrouche's *Histoire de ma vie*." *Pacific Coast Philology* 30.1 (1995): 68–81. *JSTOR*. Web. 30 Oct. 2012.

Needham, Anuradha Dingwaney. "At the Receiving End: Reading 'Third' World Texts in a 'First' World Context." *Women's Studies Quarterly* 18.3–4 (1990): 91–99. *JSTOR*. Web. 30 Oct. 2012.

Sabbagh, Suha. "Tales of Exile." Rev. of *My Life Story*, by Fadhma Amrouche, and *A Woman of Nazareth*, by Hala Deeb Jabbour. *Women's Review of Books* 7.10–11 (1990): 42–43. Print.

Further Reading

Badran, Margot, and Miriam Cooke, eds. *Opening the Gates: An Anthology of Arab Feminist Writing*. Bloomington: Indiana University Press 2004. Print.

Geesey, Patricia. "Collective Autobiography: Algerian Women and History in Assia Djebar's *L'amour, la fantasia*." *Dalhousie French Studies* 35 (1996): 153–67. *JSTOR*. Web. 30 Oct. 2012.

Goodman, Jane E. "Writing Empire, Underwriting Nation: Discursive Histories of Kabyle Berber Oral Texts." *American Ethnologist* 29.1 (2002): 86–122. *JSTOR*. Web. 30 Oct 2012.

Gregg, Gary S. "Culture, Personality, and the Multiplicity of Identity: Evidence from North African Life Narratives." *Ethos* 26.2 (1998): 120–52. *JSTOR*. Web. 30 Oct 2012.

McDougall, James. "Social Memories 'in the Flesh': War and Exile in Algerian Self-Writing." *Alif* 30 (2010): 34–56. *JSTOR*. Web. 30 Oct. 2012.

Merolla, Daniela. *Gender and Community in the Kabyle Literary Space: Cultural Strategies in the Oral and in the Written*. Leiden: Leiden U CNWS, 1996. Print.

Emily Jones

FADHMA AMROUCHE'S LITERARY OFFSPRING

Much of Fadhma Amrouche's text is devoted to the experience of being a mother and raising eight children in dire poverty. Two of her children, Jean and Marie-Louise, also known as Taos—who were instrumental in urging her to write her autobiography—became writers themselves. In the French introduction to *Histoire de ma vie*, according to Dorothy S. Blair's translation, Kateb Yacine calls Fadhma Amrouche "the mountain stream that fed the well of spring waters from which the poet Jean Amrouche and his sister Taos drew … the gift of poetry."

Jean was born in 1906 in Ighil Ali, Algeria. He moved to Paris and became one of the earliest and most important Algerian poets writing in French. He published three volumes of poetry and was also well known as a radio broadcaster and essayist. He died in 1962, before the publication of his mother's book. His sister, Taos, was born in 1913 in Tunis and was the Amrouche family's only daughter. She too became a writer after moving to Paris, writing novels and a collection of Berber folklore and songs. She also became a fairly successful singer of Kabyle folk songs and was responsible for the publication and coediting of her mother's book. Taos died in 1976 in France.

Prison Writings
My Life Is My Sun Dance
Leonard Peltier

Key Facts

Time Period:
Late 20th Century

Relevant Historical Events:
American Indian movement; Peltier's alleged murder of two FBI agents

Nationality:
American

Keywords:
American Indian movement; prison; racism

OVERVIEW

Prison Writings: My Life Is My Sun Dance (1999) is a firsthand account of the life and imprisonment of American Indian movement (AIM) activist Leonard Peltier, who is serving two consecutive life sentences in a maximum-security prison for the murder of two Federal Bureau of Investigation (FBI) agents. Peltier claims he is innocent. Despite the fame of his trial and the large number of activists protesting his conviction and continued imprisonment—after Peltier's conviction it was discovered that witness statements and ballistics evidence were fabricated—the author does not deal directly with the process by which he was convicted. Instead he gives the reader an account of his own experiences, in prison and growing up on reservations in the United States, and the spiritual significance of his pain and suffering for the sake of his people.

Published after several failed appeals and a growing public outcry from U.S. and international organizations over the injustice of Peltier's imprisonment, the book was instantly popular among his supporters. *Prison Writings* uncovers the spiritual significance in Peltier's difficult circumstances and ultimately urges forgiveness and healing, rather than vengeance and anger, by presenting his spiritual journey and inner thoughts about the experiences. By exposing Peltier as a wise and spiritual elder ready to tell his stories to future generations—and not as the "hardened criminal" the FBI claimed he was—the book encouraged his followers and generated further support for his efforts to have his sentence repealed.

HISTORICAL AND LITERARY CONTEXT

Peltier was convicted of killing Jack Coler and Ronald Williams, two FBI agents who were involved in a shootout at the Pine Ridge Reservation in South Dakota in 1975. The shootout occurred at the height of a series of conflicts between AIM and the FBI that began when AIM and Lakota activists seized the community of Wounded Knee in 1973 to protest corrupt tribal government and the failure of the national government to fulfill treaties. A previous trial of two suspects in the murders of Coler and Williams—Bob Robideau and Dino Butler—resulted in acquittal. Many of Peltier's supporters believe that he did not receive a fair trial because he was the last suspect available for the prosecution to charge with the crime. An appeal of the verdict in 1978 was denied despite the fact that one of the judges involved had a conflict of interest. Many prominent activists—including Archbishop Desmond Tutu of South Africa and the Dalai Lama of Tibet—believe Peltier was wrongly convicted in a trial rigged by institutional racism in the U.S. justice system.

Peltier wrote the autobiography in a prison cell, drawing on previous documents and writings of his own, with the assistance of an editor. An active member of AIM and a known supporter of First Nations rights and freedoms, Peltier had been arrested under false circumstances on other occasions before the murders. Those accusations, although they were without evidence, were again brought against him during the murder trial, along with fabricated evidence and statements from witnesses who later admitted that they had been threatened by the FBI. The difficulty Peltier discusses in the writing of his memoir reflects his overall treatment during his life and his imprisonment: he is effectively silenced by the judicial system for what he feels is the crime of being himself.

Peltier's literary influences included the oral histories passed on by the elders of his community and the religious ritual of the Sun Dance ceremony that he uses to frame his life and struggles. He also links his story to that of Nelson Mandela, especially the prison experiences outlined in Mandela's book *Long Walk to Freedom*. Peltier expresses his hope that his story will have a happy ending like Mandela's does and that one day he, too, may enjoy his life, his grandchildren, and his freedom.

While Peltier already had a large following of supporters rallying for his release from prison, his autobiography further influenced public support and became a tool that activists used to present Peltier in a positive manner. The autobiography includes frank discussion of the racism toward First Nations people during the 1970s and calls into question the validity of the judicial system that continues to keep Peltier behind bars. Inspired by *Prison Writings*, the 2004 documentary *Incident at Oglala* covers Peltier's story, from the manufactured evidence to the injustice of keeping him in prison.

THEMES AND STYLE

One of the main themes throughout *Prison Writings* is that Peltier's only crime is "being an Indian." He describes speaking his native language in boarding school when he knew he would be punished for it: "The first infraction in my criminal career was speaking my own language." Peltier is aware of his ethnicity and is proud of his people and his heritage, which allows him to see the spiritual significance of his suffering while in a maximum-security prison. The "crime" of his heritage, as he constructs it in the autobiography, is the result of centuries of warfare between the white and native populations in the United States. The book concludes, however, on a note of hope, suggesting that past differences can be overcome and a new age of healing can begin: "To heal would require a real effort, and a change of heart, from all of us."

The author repeatedly states that his purpose in writing his text was not to discuss documents and facts related to his trial and conviction, which has already been done by numerous individuals in several different media. Rather Peltier wishes to present himself to the reading audience in the context of the spiritual suffering experienced during the Sun Dance ceremony, believing that this can inspire change. The Sun Dance is a ritual that generates a sense of community and spiritual renewal through sacrifice and a demonstration of ethics. Sun Dancers are chosen warriors who dance for four days without food or water and who undergo tests of strength, including painfully piercing the flesh. Peltier uses the traditional ideas of the Sun Dance to contextualize his imprisonment in terms of suffering for the betterment of himself and his community: "Sun Dance is our religion, our strength. We take great pride in that strength, which enables us to resist pain, torture, any trial rather than betray the People." He writes in a personal manner that constructs a clear voice, giving the piece the feeling of an oral narrative passed down through the generations, another important component of the Sun Dance. In addition to prose text, Peltier includes poetry that expresses emotional states ranging from pain and loneliness to spiritual enlightenment.

Written in the first person, the text has the tone of a calm elder. The emotions range from sadness and despair to dark humor, sometimes in the same passage. After catching himself writing vengeful thoughts—which he quickly regrets—Peltier notices the dark humor in his current situation: "Somewhere, somehow, there's got to be something funny about all of this. Something horrendously funny. A wild cosmic joke on me, a real knee-slapper in some demonic heaven or hell." Stylistically this expression of emotion represents the human nature of the author of the autobiography, presenting his viewpoint in a positive and forgiving manner.

CRITICAL DISCUSSION

Prison Writings was initially met with praise for Peltier's ability to look past the injustices of his trial, already well documented in other sources, and instead focus on his personal interpretation of pain and misfortune within the spiritual framework of the Sun Dance. Janice Dunham called the book "inspiring" in her review in *Library Journal* because "Peltier focuses more strongly here on the story of his life and its meaning; drawing a parallel to his participation in the Sun Dance ceremony." Patricia Monaghan gave the book a similar review in her *Booklist* article, writing, "His own simple, eloquent compassion for his captors as well as himself makes this a remarkable and moving book."

Beyond the initial reviews of the book, Peltier's autobiography has drawn a large following of political supporters who, swayed by the its presentation of a sane and spiritually sound individual who is not a murderer by nature, feel his sentence should be repealed. In an essay in *The Praeger Handbook on Contemporary Issues in Native America*, Bruce Johansen describes Peltier's personality in much the same way Peltier presents himself in *Prison Writings:* "He seemed to have an affable manner and a ready smile, not the kind of guy you would find on a wanted poster at the post office." Johansen further claims that "he did not seem, to me, like a cop killer." The portrayal of Peltier as a sane and spiritual individual, instead of a deranged killer, adds to the political legacy of the book because of its associations with Peltier's alleged innocence.

Predominant trends in scholarship place this autobiography among a wealth of documents that support the activist motions to repeal Peltier's prison sentence. Dewi Ioan Ball and Jay Porter in *Fighting Words* (2009) use an excerpt from *Prison Writings* to accompany their collection of documents surrounding Peltier's case, including official documents from the trial—such as the forged affidavits of Myrtle Poor Bear, the chief witness—and appeals from influential sources such as Amnesty International. Ball and Porter state that Peltier "spoke cogently and eloquently about the biased actions and rulings of the judge during the duration of the trial and of being set up by the FBI and the judicial process."

Leonard Peltier in prison in 1986. He was convicted of murdering two FBI agents during a shootout on the Pine Ridge Reservation in 1975. © AP IMAGES/CLIFF SCHIAPPA

THE CURIOUS CASE OF ANNA MAE AQUASH

A close friend of Leonard Peltier and a fellow AIM activist was Mi'kmaq Anna Mae Aquash, whose mysterious death coincides with the Peltier trial. On February 24, 1976, a rancher on the Pine Ridge Reservation found her body on his ranch. Her autopsy concluded that she died of exposure; her hands were removed and sent to FBI headquarters for identification. She was buried in a churchyard as a "Jane Doe." A week later she was identified and exhumed, and a second autopsy, performed at the request of her family, revealed she had been shot in the back of the head, execution style, with a .32-caliber bullet. She was reburied with traditional rites as her murder investigation began.

In 2004 AIM affiliate Arlo Looking Cloud was convicted of murdering Aquash, with further trials in 2008 and 2009 convicting Dick Marshall and John Graham with charges related to the murder. Some political theorists believe that AIM leaders ordered Aquash's death because she knew Peltier was guilty of murder and was working as an informant for the FBI, revealing AIM secrets and financial sources. Peltier writes that these accusations cause him more pain than anything he has encountered in prison, and he believes the FBI conspired to kill Aquash and subsequently framed AIM activists in a similar manner to his own conviction because of her organizational and influential role in AIM activism.

Writing in *College Literature,* Elizabeth Rich also follows this line of thinking, mentioning the number of "artists, writers, and documentary filmmakers" who "seem to be attracted to Leonard Peltier's story" and generally present him as wrongfully accused.

BIBLIOGRAPHY

Sources

Ball, Dewi Ioan, and Jay Porter, eds. "Chapter Eleven: Leonard Peltier." *Fighting Words: Competing Voices from Native America.* Santa Barbara, Calif.: Greenwood, 2009. 249–87. Print.

Dunham, Janice. "Prison Writings: My Life Is My Sun Dance." *Library Journal* 15 June 1999: 97. *Literature Resource Center.* Web. 8 Nov. 2012.

Johansen, Bruce E. "Beyond a Reasonable Doubt: The Curious Conviction of Leonard Peltier." *The Praeger Handbook on Contemporary Issues in Native America: Volume 2: Legal, Cultural, and Environmental Revival.* Native America: Yesterday and Today. Westport, Conn.: Praeger, 2007. 197–208. Print.

Monaghan, Patricia. "Prison Writings: My Life Is My Sun Dance." *Booklist* 1 May 1999: 1573. *Literature Resource Center.* Web. 8 Nov. 2012.

Peltier, Leonard. *Prison Writings: My Life Is My Sun Dance.* Ed. Harvey Arden. New York: St. Martin's, 1999. Print.

Rich, Elizabeth. "'Remember Wounded Knee': AIM's Use of Metonymy in 21st Century Protest." *College Literature* 31.3 (2004): 70–91. *JSTOR.* Web. 12 Nov. 2012.

Further Reading

"Anna Mae Pictou Aquash." *Notable Native Americans.* Detroit: Gale, 1995. *Gale Biography in Context.* Web. 12 Nov. 2012.

Beasley, Conger, Jr. "Looking for Leonard Peltier." *North American Review* 283 (1998): 64–71. *JSTOR.* Web. 8 Nov. 2012.

"Chapter Twenty-Three: Leonard Peltier." *Imprisoned Intellectuals: America's Political Prisoners Write on Life, Liberation, and Rebellion.* Ed. Joy James. Lanham, Md.: Rowman & Littlefield, 2003. 311–20. Print.

Hendricks, Steve. *The Unquiet Grave: The FBI and the Struggle for the Soul of Indian Country.* New York: Thunder's Mouth, 2006. Print.

Incident at Oglala: The Leonard Peltier Story. Dir. Michael Apted. Lion's Gate, 2004. Film.

Mandela, Nelson. *Long Walk to Freedom: The Autobiography of Nelson Mandela.* Boston: Little, Brown, 1995. Print.

Meister, Mark, and Ann Burnett. "Rhetorical Exclusion in the Trial of Leonard Peltier." Spec. issue of *American Indian Quarterly* 28 (2004): 719–42. *JSTOR.* Web. 8 Nov. 2012.

Katherine Barker

RITES
A Guatemalan Boyhood
Victor Perera

OVERVIEW

Published in 1985, *Rites: A Guatemalan Boyhood* is a partially fictionalized account of author Victor Perera's boyhood in Guatemala. Perera describes growing up in Latin America as a Jewish youth, touching on the jarring experience of his second circumcision, his early fascination with the English language, and violent political upheavals in Guatemala. Throughout the text, he expresses ambivalence regarding his Jewish ancestry while detailing his family's immigrant struggles and internal conflicts. *Rites* offers a uniquely multicultural perspective on the years directly preceding the Guatemalan Civil War, which erupted in 1960 and produced countrywide massacres of indigenous populations and many human rights violations.

When *Rites* was published, Perera had already established himself as a writer passionately concerned with reporting on conditions in his native country, particularly the oppression and mass killings of Guatemala's indigenous populations. The book provides another important view of life in Guatemala, addressing themes relating to the diaspora: dislocation, identity, and prejudice. Though initially appreciated for its unique treatment of the Sephardic experience in Latin America, the memoir was also criticized for its personal focus. Today it is considered a significant contribution to Jewish–Latin American literature.

HISTORICAL AND LITERARY CONTEXT

Rites presents a highly personal impression of growing up in a Jewish family in Guatemala and of the political situation there during the 1940s. The text chronicles the overthrow of pro-American dictator Jorge Ubico following a civilian and student revolt and describes Perera's return visits to Guatemala in the 1980s. Despite a promising presidential election, the drafting of a new constitution, and increased indigenous activism, Guatemala in the early 1980s suffered from the same mass disappearances and killings that it had under earlier dictatorships. Subsequent presidencies were highly influenced by military intervention. In an afterword, however, Perera notes some positive developments in the political situation, including an uprising led by indigenous activist Rigoberta Menchú and the deposition of would-be dictator Jorge Serrano in 1993.

At the time of the publication of *Rites* in 1985, Perera was known to be a determined opponent to military rule in Guatemala. Living in the United States, he made use of his relative safety to comment on the chaos and death he observed in the country where he spent his youth. As Guatemala was still in the grips of violent leadership, the memoir was published with an author's note stating that "names, places, and details [had] been changed to protect the privacy of individuals living and the dead."

Rites is part of a tradition of Sephardic memoir, which includes Albert Cohen's *Book of My Mother* (1954). The book is also an important contribution to literature of minorities and the oppressed in Guatemala. In 1971, following a disturbing visit to Guatemala, Perera began to write critically about the political situation there, beginning with an article in the *New York Times Magazine* titled "Guatemala: Always La Violencia," which brought him threats from President Arana Osorio. Preceding *Rites* in its attempt to document the minority experience in Guatemala was Menchú's famous testimonial on the indigenous plight, *I, Rigoberta Menchú* (1983).

Perera's memoir helped establish his reputation as an important commentator on Guatemala and paved the way for other autobiographical accounts of civil rights abuses in Latin America. In the years following the text's publication, many first-person accounts of life in Guatemala surfaced, such as *Guatemala: Never Again!* (1998), a report on human rights abuses compiled by the Archdiocese of Guatemala, Bishop Juan Gerardi, who was murdered two days after the text's publication. Perera's book also contributed to the development of the Jewish–Latin American memoir, including Marjorie Agosín's *A Cross and a Star: Memoirs of a Jewish Girl in Chile* (1995). Perera went on to further explore his family's Sephardic heritage in *The Cross and the Pear Tree* (1996) and to comment on the violence of society in his native country in *Unfinished Conquest: The Guatemalan Tragedy* (1995).

THEMES AND STYLE

Central to Perera's memoir of growing up in a Jewish family in 1940s Guatemala are themes of violence, sex, and corruption. He introduces his complicated relationship with his heritage in the first scenes, which

❖ **Key Facts**

Time Period:
Late 20th Century

Relevant Historical Events:
Guatemalan Civil War; uprising of Menchú; violent unrest in Guatemala

Nationality:
Guatemalan

Keywords:
Judaism; revolution; immigration

BETWEEN CULTURES

Rites: A Guatemalan Boyhood outlines Victor Perera's childhood experiences as a Jew growing up in Guatemala. As a youth, Perera was enthusiastic about popular culture, including film icon John Wayne, depicted here. © MARKA/ALAMY

describe the pain of his second circumcision. The text examines the sexual violence of Guatemalan society as it plays out in the personal realm, as when the narrator hears his friend's father insist that his wife sleep with him despite the fact that "the little Jew is here" so that "he can know in this house a man fucks his wife as God intended. Now turn yourself or I'll rip your asshole." He also details the rising violence in Guatemala to which he was witness during a trip to visit his cousin, noting that "twenty to twenty-five corpses appeared every day on city streets" and "more and more Indians joined underground peasant unions and guerrilla groups, and appeared on anti-Communist 'death lists' in regional newspapers."

The text is motivated by a desire to uncover the reality of the turmoil in Guatemala that had begun to show itself in society as "*mala saña* … a condition beyond motives of revenge, beyond all considerations of ideology or personal horror … a rage in the marrow that carries everything in its wake." Perera's exploration of his family's story is an attempt to uncover motivations and histories previously unclear to him—and perhaps to remain so. Of his father's decision to move away from Jerusalem, Perera asks, "Why Guatemala? Father never explained this to my satisfaction." Perera's detailed record of impressions gathered as a child and an adult, about both his family and Guatemala, creates a narrative with both personal and universal implications.

Stylistically, *Rites* is distinguished by its inclusion of visceral detail, use of metaphor, and structure of related vignettes. Perera begins the memoir with a vivid recounting of his second circumcision, recalling the rabbi's appearance with imagistic language: "[He] bore on his back a sizable hump, but lightly, as if he was vain of it. He had raven eyes, thick brows…. From inside his beaked nose wiry hairs radiated like an insect's antennae." Perera writes in raw detail about a Lacondon Indian beggar named El Sincarne, describing how "his legs were crossed sticks, so that he had to swing along the sidewalk on his hands and buttocks" and noting his "cadaver face and his shoulder-length hair, which made his sex a puzzle."

CRITICAL DISCUSSION

Although not a best seller, *Rites* garnered positive reviews. The text was praised for its attempt to document not only the author's personal experiences but also the more universal experiences of minority populations in Guatemala. In an August 1986 review of the book in the *Nation*, Richard Elman asserted that it "records pain in a loving, fine, but nonetheless painful manner. It is the unfinished business of a man who got away but chose not to forget." Those who had negative comments about the text reacted to its brief treatment of some events; Stewart Kellerman of the *New York Times* stated in a July 1986 review that *Rites* is "a readable book … [that] leaves you feeling you've dined on hors d'oeuvres."

As the reality of Guatemala's political situation and human rights abuses became increasingly clear to international audiences in the 1990s, *Rites* began to garner more attention for its exploration of the social and political climate of the country during the 1940s. Perera's position on the inside and outside of Guatemalan society, the son of Jewish immigrants who later immigrated to the United States, earned him attention as the bearer of a distinct point of view on life in Guatemala. Scholars have approached his work in many ways, considering its value as a record of the second-generation immigrant experience, its contribution to the Judeo-Spanish tradition, and its importance as a testimony on Guatemala's social and historical development.

Rites has been read in conjunction with Maxine Hong Kingston's *The Woman Warrior* (1975) as a method of exploring the way a second-generation immigrant writer makes use of language and forms national identity. In his 1997 article "Nation, Family, and Language," Steven V. Hunsaker considers the way that language functions in these texts, stating, "Given the troubled use of nation by Perera and Kingston, the 'felt experiences' of creating oneself and restricting others through language clearly play a central role in the process of imagining one's place in a national community." Scholars also read the text as a confounding of the traditional immigrant narrative, finding Perera's story to be one of his Sephardism instead. In her 1998 article "The Burden and the Treasure," Ada Savin speaks of the memoir as Perera's attempt to "[unearth] the treasures lying dormant in his fruitful name."

BIBLIOGRAPHY

Sources

Elman, Richard. "Unfinished Business." Rev. of *Rites: A Guatemalan Boyhood*, by Victor Perera. *Nation* 16 Aug. 1986: 118–19. *Points of View Reference Center*. Web. 15 Nov. 2012.

Hunsaker, Steven V. "Nation, Family, and Language in Victor Perera's *Rites* and Maxine Hong Kingston's *The Woman Warrior*." *Biography* 20.4 (1997): 437–61. *Project MUSE*. Web. 15 Nov. 2012.

Kellerman, Stewart. "In Short: Nonfiction." Rev. of *Rites: A Guatemalan Boyhood*, by Victor Perera. *New York Times Book Review* 13 July 1986: 19. *Academic Search Complete*. Web. 15 Nov. 2012.

Perera, Victor. *Rites: A Guatemalan Boyhood*. San Francisco: Mercury House, 1985. Print.

Savin, Ada. "The Burden and the Treasure: Victor Perera's Sephardic Family Chronicle." *Prooftexts* 18.3 (1998): 225–37. *JSTOR*. Web. 15 Nov. 2012.

Further Reading

Archdiocese of Guatemala. *Guatemala: Never Again! The Official Report of the Human Rights Office*. New York: Orbis, 1999. Print.

Bejarano, Margalit, and Edna Aizenberg, eds. *Contemporary Sephardic Identity in the Americas: An Interdisciplinary Approach*. New York: Syracuse University Press, 2012. Print.

Grandin, Greg. *The Blood of Guatemala: A History of Race and Nation*. Durham, N.C.: Duke University Press, 2000. Print.

Perera, Victor. *Unfinished Conquest: The Guatemalan Tragedy*. Berkeley: University of California Press, 1995. Print.

GENERAL JORGE UBICO

In *Rites: A Guatemalan Boyhood*, Victor Perera states that "the presidency of General Jorge Ubico spanned the first ten years of my life. As I was growing up he came to represent not only the fatherly caudillo and Lord of the Manor, but quite literally the Man on the White Horse: Once a year, on his birthday, he paraded the length of Sexta Avenida on a magnificent prancing stallion." Nicknamed "Tata," or "Daddy," Ubico ruled Guatemala for thirteen years, from 1931 to 1944. His presidential victory in 1931 has been alleged to be the result of U.S. involvement, and shortly thereafter he began instituting authoritarian rule. He instituted a number of brutal laws, including the *Ley de Fuga*, or Law of Flight. Under this law, the police were allowed to seize citizens (often political enemies, exploited workers, or indigenous peasants) without a warrants and, following interrogations, release them, only to shoot them as they "fled."

When civil unrest developed as a result of his restriction of democratic activity, Ubico was overthrown by a civilian and student revolt. Following his deposition, he absconded with a sizable portion of the Guatemalan treasury and fled to New Orleans, Louisiana, where he died in 1946.

Stavans, Ilan, ed. *The Schocken Book of Modern Sephardic Literature*. New York: Schocken, 2005. Print.

Kristen Gleason

TEN THOUSAND SORROWS
The Extraordinary Journey of a Korean War Orphan
Elizabeth Kim

❖ **Key Facts**

Time Period:
Early 21st Century

Relevant Historical Events:
Korean War; growth in U.S. adoptions of Korean children

Nationality:
Korean/American

Keywords:
adoption; cultural identity; multiculturalism

OVERVIEW

Elizabeth Kim's *Ten Thousand Sorrows: The Extraordinary Journey of a Korean War Orphan,* first published in 2000, is recognized as the first memoir written by a Korean Amerasian to treat the subject of adoption of Korean children. The book follows Kim's life, from her happy time with Omma (Korean for "mommy") to her shattering time with an adoptive Fundamentalist family in the United States to a brutal early marriage to an abusive man. The story opens after Omma and the author have shared several tender years together. But life takes a horrific turn when Kim witnesses Omma's murder by her family for refusing to give up the mixed-race child. This is the only the beginning of Kim's misery, as the book then follows her shockingly brutal life and subsequent attempts to come to terms with those abuses. The memoir touches on themes worthy of its weighty subject matter: intercultural and interracial adoption, the mother-daughter relationship, cultural hypocrisy, religious fanaticism, physical and mental trauma and its consequences, and self-reconciliation.

Since the mid-nineteenth century, biracialism and biculturalism have stood as issues in ethnic American literature due to the nation's history of slavery, immigration, diasporic resettlement, overseas commerce, and war. Many Asian American writers have explored these themes through autobiography, using the format to share their life experiences as immigrants, refugees, or the "excluded Others" in the United States. *Ten Thousand Sorrows* represents a new chapter in that lengthy history—one with the added twist of the thorny issues involved with cross-cultural adoption. Upon its publication, the memoir received much positive comment from major reviewers. While the book remains popular with general audiences, it has not had much impact in the academic world.

HISTORICAL AND LITERARY CONTEXT

The United States established military bases in South Korea during the Korean War (1950–1953). The subsequent liaisons between Korean women and white and black American soldiers resulted in many mixed-race children. These children—and the mothers who brought them into the world—bumped against Korea's long tradition of racial purity. (Exacerbating the situation, most American fathers then abandoned their Amerasian children and returned home.) To escape the social stigma, families often placed these mixed-race children in orphanages. When international adoption of Korean orphans began in 1955, many were adopted by Western parents. Kim was one such child.

Kim's childhood of prejudice as an Amerasian in Korea was not unusual. She remembers being the object of scorn for the family and community—a typical fate for mixed-race children and their mothers. That Kim was put up for adoption was also typical of this story line (the murder of her mother, however, is not). As a memoir of adoption, *Ten Thousand Sorrows* illustrates the confusion an adoptee faces when she is exposed to a new culture, religion, and family life. Religion is an important part of Kim's life in the United States: her adoptive parents are fiercely religious fundamentalist Christians as is her eventual husband.

Ten Thousand Sorrows can be classified under the rubrics of both the literature of adoption and the literature of trauma. Literature boasts many adoption memoirs. Helen Doss's *The Family Nobody Wanted* (1954) tells the tale of a large family made up of international adoptees, while Betty Jean Lifton's *Twice Born: Memoirs of an Adopted Daughter* (1975) describes one woman's experience as an adoptee. Autobiographies of trauma generally recount an individual's experience of physical or mental duress and the subsequent attempt to reconcile a posttraumatic present with an unforgettable and haunting past. This arc—so similar to that of *Ten Thousand Sorrows*—is seen in Theresa Hak Kyung Cha's *Dictee* (1982) and Richard E. Kim's *Lost Names: Scenes from a Korean Boyhood* (1998).

Subsequent to the publication of Kim's memoir, several Korean Americans have written about adoption. *Once They Hear My Name: Korean Adoptees and Their Journeys toward Identity* (2008) presents the oral histories of nine Korean adoptees. Jane Jeong Trenka's *The Language of Blood* (2005) recounts her and her sister's experience as Korean adoptees in Minnesota; she describes their sense of not belonging in either American or Korean culture. In a more scholarly vein, Eleana J. Kim's *Adopted Territory: Transnational Korean*

Adoptees and the Politics of Belonging (2010) discusses adoptees' journeys in search of their cultural and biological origins. Despite the growing genre, Kim's *Ten Thousand Sorrows* remains unique for its Korean Amerasian authorship and the exploration of cross-cultural adoption into a fundamentalist Christian family.

THEMES AND STYLE

A major theme of Kim's memoir is her lost mother-daughter relationship. Significantly, she dedicates her book to Omma, who loved her unconditionally despite indigence, familial prejudice, and societal condemnation. This theme is readdressed toward the end of the memoir, after Kim gives birth to her daughter, Leigh. The book also explores the themes of racism and cultural alienation. Living in the United States, Kim faces prejudice and humiliation because her "Amerasian face was so disconcerting." Kim's own American grandmother is racist, assuming that anyone nonwhite is "barbaric." Kim's ultrareligious American parents constantly remind her of how sinful she is and how she will be punished by "God's wrath and retribution." Consequently, Kim suffers guilt, fear, and self-hatred. The memoir, however, also includes the themes of forgiveness and spiritual healing, as Kim in the end is able to find peace by reflecting upon her past "sorrows."

Kim also is clearly using memoir as an opportunity to develop a narrative voice and to define a sense of self, with the hope that self-reflection and self-expression will lead to self-actualization. Kim becomes "stronger" and more "human and alive" through recording her experiences and her responses to those experiences. Through her writing, she is working to transcend the self-loathing instilled by her adoptive parents' fundamentalist Christian obsession with guilt, sin, and damnation.

Ten Thousand Sorrows is primarily narrated chronologically, although the flow of the plot occasionally is interrupted by flashbacks. Stylistically, Kim sometimes inserts lines of poetry into the narrative—a practice that echoes the use of poetry and song that has been a feature of Korean literature for centuries. Kim effectively employs pathos and ethos to elicit the reader's moral outrage at the wrongs perpetrated, either consciously or subconsciously, by the people around her. She is careful to define her adoptive parents as individuals and their fundamentalist Christian faith as a cultural phenomenon. For instance, she writes, "Dad was a study in contrast" because "he was an innately kind and loving man who could punish me harshly for a sinful thought and then spend the night on his knees, in tears, praying for my soul." She also uses metaphors in her depiction of the setting around her parents' home—the treeless, barren, and arid area in which their house is located is similar to the stifling atmosphere within the house, so deprived of poetry and imagination: "Poetry didn't interest them at all—I don't know if they even recognized it."

Thatched house, Hahoe Folk Village, South Korea, November 2008. In her memoir *Ten Thousand Sorrows*, Elizabeth Kim recounts watching her grandfather and uncle hang her mother in the corner of their Korean hut. © MICHELE BURGESS/ ALAMY

CRITICAL DISCUSSION

Ten Thousand Sorrows, upon its release in 2000, enjoyed largely positive reception. According to Miseli Jeon, who reviewed the memoir in 2004 for *Canadian Literature,* Kim's sufferings derive not only from "cultural displacement and racism but also from the omnipresent misogynist ideology that underlies even such dissimilar cultures as Korean Confucianism and Christian Fundamentalism." Antoinette Brinkman of *Library Journal* in a 2000 review commends Kim for her "simple but powerful reportorial style that puts the events in even harsher focus."

Some critics have indicated problems with the memoir that need to be revisited. In a 2000 article in *Korea Herald,* Brian Myers, a Korean studies expert, roundly criticizes the book for its distortion of "Korean life, language and custom." He argues, for example, that the word *honhyol,* which Kim defines as an epithet for a "mixed race animal," actually is "a word used in polite conversation by educated Koreans." He also notes that some "inconsistencies" in the narrative arise because no specific "years, names, locations" are specified to create verisimilitude. (Kim explains in her book that she has no birth certificate nor name or location for her birth family.) Margaret Juhae Lee in a 2000 review for the *Nation* defends Kim against Myers's criticism, asserting that nonfiction "tends toward self-reflection rather than historicity or definitiveness in describing a specific culture of experience." She adds that the nature of memory is "slippery, fragmented and often unreliable." Nevertheless, she notes that Kim neglects "to describe adequately the state and processes of her own memory." Therefore, her memoir resembles "a work in progress, especially in the last sections, where it devolves into shards of self-help homilies."

Many reviewers have noted the large, complex issues raised by the work and how the text helps to contextualize some feminist and religious matters.

Donna Seaman in a 2000 article for *Booklist* states that Kim's memoir "will stand as blazing testimony in the battle against sexism, violence against women, and religious tyranny" and that her book is "an affirmation of the power of love and compassion." Jeon particularly addresses the killing of Kim's mother in her review and encourages readers to contextualize this atrocity within the "atrocities practiced worldwide in the name of cultural, religious, and racial purity." Despite these rich issues raised, the memoir has yet to attract significant comment and criticism beyond book reviews.

BIBLIOGRAPHY

Sources

Brinkman, Antoinette. Rev. of *Ten Thousand Sorrows: The Extraordinary Journey of a Korean War Orphan,* by Elizabeth Kim. *Library Journal* 15 June 2000: 102. Print.

Jeon, Miseli. "Multiculturalism?" Rev. of *Ten Thousand Sorrows: The Extraordinary Journey of a Korean War Orphan,* by Elizabeth Kim. *Canadian Literature* 181 (2004): 147–49. Print.

Kim, Elizabeth. *Ten Thousand Sorrows: The Extraordinary Journey of a Korean War Orphan.* New York: Doubleday, 2000. Print.

Lee, Margaret Juhae. "Korea's Fallout." Rev. of *Ten Thousand Sorrows: The Extraordinary Journey of a Korean War Orphan,* by Elizabeth Kim. *Nation* 25 Dec. 2000: 32–34. Print.

Myers, Brian. "'Memoir' Defames Korean Culture." Letter. *Korea Herald* 3 Sept. 2000. Web. 3 Dec. 2012.

Seaman, Donna. Rev. of *Ten Thousand Sorrows: The Extraordinary Journey of a Korean War Orphan,* by Elizabeth Kim. *Booklist* 1 Apr. 2000: 1411. Print.

Further Reading

Bergquist, Kathleen Ja Sook, et al., eds. *International Korean Adoption: A Fifty-Year History of Policy and Practice.* New York: Routledge, 2007. Print.

Brian, Kristi. *Reframing Transracial Adoption: Adopted Koreans, White Parents, and the Politics of Kinship.* Philadelphia: Temple University Press, 2012. Print.

Briggs, Laura. *Somebody's Children: The Politics of Transracial and Transnational Adoption.* Durham, N.C.: Duke University Press, 2012. Print.

Hearst, Alice. *Children and the Politics of Cultural Belonging.* New York: Cambridge University Press, 2012. Print.

Hübinette, Tobias. *The Korean Adoption Issue between Modernity and Coloniality: Transnational Adoption and Overseas Adoptees in Korean Popular Culture.* Saarbrücken, Germany: LAP, 2009. Print.

Kim, Eleana J. *Adopted Territory: Transnational Korean Adoptees and the Politics of Belonging.* Durham, N.C.: Duke University Press, 2010. Print.

Lee, Ellen, Marilyn Lammert, and Mary Anne Hess. *Once They Hear My Name: Korean Adoptees and Their Journeys toward Identity.* Silver Spring, Md.: Tamarisk Books, 2008. Print.

Tuan, Mia, and Jiannbin Lee Shiao. *Choosing Ethnicity, Negotiating Race: Korean Adoptees in America.* New York: Russell Sage Foundation, 2011. Print.

Quan Ha

The Travels of Marco Polo
Marco Polo

OVERVIEW

Written in 1298, *The Travels of Marco Polo* is one of the earliest and most broadly read Western accounts of travels to the Far East. Polo, the son of a Venetian merchant, records the story of his three-and-a-half-year journey to the court of Kublai Khan, where he served for seventeen years before embarking on his return trip. During those years of service, Polo traveled as an ambassador and fact finder for the khan, and *The Travels of Marco Polo* recounts Polo's discoveries and observations on his journeys to the farthest ends of the Mongol Empire. Throughout the narration he explores a wide range of topics, including the geography, peoples, customs, history, and flora and fauna of Asia. Written and published after his twenty-four year stay in the Far East, *The Travels of Marco Polo* is the most important text documenting the history of one of Europe's earliest and most broadly recognized explorers.

In 1298, only three years after his return from China, Polo joined a fleet of Venetians who sailed against their merchant adversaries, the Genoese, only to be captured and imprisoned. It was in this prison in Genoa, over a period of several months, that Polo penned his travelogue with the help of his cellmate, Rustichiello of Pisa. Immediately popular for its descriptions of strange and hitherto unknown places and peoples, *The Travels of Marco Polo* was often discredited as fictitious. Most scholars of the day gave it little credence, but among the unlearned public, the book was viewed as a report from an entirely new world.

HISTORICAL AND LITERARY CONTEXT

The Travels of Marco Polo offers an early glimpse of the Far East, when mercantile and missionary interest in the region was on the rise in Europe. Some of the earliest contact between East and West came with expansion of the Mongol Empire. Although the Mongols would not continuously occupy their extreme western territories, by 1241 the sons and grandsons of Genghis Khan had advanced the boundaries of their empire as far as northeastern Italy. Early missionaries, such as the Hungarian Dominican Julian and the Franciscan John of Pian del Carpine, had traveled as far as Mongolia, bringing back to the West a wealth of historical and cultural information. Trade also motivated contact with the East, as Italian merchants often traded with the Tartars between the Volga and the Caspian Sea.

Polo's account of his time in China was written in cooperation with Rustichiello, a professional writer with whom he shared a prison cell following their capture in the Battle of Curzola (1298), part of a brief war provoked by trade issues between two of Italy's most powerful mercantile city-states, Genoa and Venice. Polo had been commissioned as "Gentleman-Commander" on one of the vessels taken by the Genoese. Because the account was composed by the two men, the cooperative nature of the text has affected its reception as autobiography. Rustichiello was also the author of epic tales, and much of the romantic tone is derived from his literary style.

The Travels of Marco Polo draws on a long history of travelogues. In *Marco Polo's Asia* (1960), the scholar Leonardo Olschki traces Polo's literary precursors to two tendencies that dominated the secular society of the times: "the spirit of adventure," seen in the tales of Alexander the Great and in *Prester John's Letter on the Wonders of India* (1164), and the "characteristic didacticism of the great age of compilers, encyclopedists and preceptors," embodied best in Lorraine Guisson's *Image du monde,* which, much like *The Travels of Marco Polo,* seeks to instruct the uneducated about various regions of the world.

The popular success of Polo's narrative led to a proliferation of tales about the fantastical East, many of them characterized by fictional exaggeration, such as *The Voyage and Travels of Sir John Mandeville* (1356), in which an unknown author tells the tale of Mandeville's thirty years of travel. In more recent literary history, Italo Calvino published *Invisible Cities* (1972), an imaginative and fictional retelling of Polo's travels in which Polo, after various journeys throughout the Mongol Empire, narrates to Kublai Khan the discovery of different cities.

THEMES AND STYLE

Because *The Travels of Marco Polo* catalogs the sights and sounds of a broad geographical empire over a period of more than two decades, its central theme develops through accretion. The broad topical scope of the text, which ranges from the "breeds of horses and asses" found "in the province of Persia" to the number of presents brought to the khan on the "White Feast"

❖ **Key Facts**

Time Period:
Late 13th Century

Relevant Historical Events:
Polo travels to the Far East

Nationality:
Italian

Keywords:
travel; trade; exploration; China

BETWEEN CULTURES

This image from a fourteenth-century manuscript of *The Travels of Marco Polo* includes a depiction of Marco Polo leaving for China with his father and uncle as well as the places they visited.
© IVY CLOSE IMAGES/ ALAMY

of the New Year, suggests that the central theme is the variety, beauty, and breadth of the world. This thematic concern is announced in the prologue to the text, in which Polo urges those who are "desirous of knowing the diversities of races of mankind, as well as the diversities of kingdoms, provinces and regions of all parts of the East" to read his book.

The Travels of Marco Polo offers an explicit account of Polo's reasons for recording his journeys in the East. The narration, Polo writes, was driven by his "wishing in his secret thoughts that the things he had seen and heard should be made public … for the benefit of those who could not see them with their own eyes." Although he is at times boastful of his favored position with the great khan, the text is, for the most part, an impersonal autobiographical narrative, insomuch as the narrative lens focuses on the world that Polo encountered as opposed to his experience encountering such a world. Dozens of chapters are devoted, for example, to the khan, his courts, wives, residences, and hunting trips, while at the same time, Polo's name or even the first-person pronoun "I" seldom appears.

Stylistically *The Travels of Marco Polo* is distinguished by its objective tone. Despite a title that suggests a heroic adventure story, the work provides little in the way of action or event. The book does not attempt to present an accurate timeline or itinerary for any of Polo's journeys. Instead, the text offers detailed anthropological and geographic descriptions. In a passage on eastern Persia, for example, Polo describes the gems and stones that can be found in the mountains, the embroidery work of the women, and the cultural practice of falconry: "In the mountainous parts are bred the best falcons that anywhere take wing. They are smaller than the Peregrine falcon; reddish about the breast, belly and under the tail; and their flight is so swift that no bird can escape them."

CRITICAL DISCUSSION

Upon publication, *The Travels of Marco Polo* was an immediate success. Within its first twenty years in print, the book, which was originally published in French, appeared in Franco-Italian, Tuscan, Venetian, German, and Latin, a broad range of translations for a nonreligious text in the Middle Ages. However, the text was often misread as fiction, frequently in the style of the romantic epic. For example, John Larner, in *Marco Polo and the Discovery of the World* (1999), notes that in 1312 the Countess of Burgundy, Mahaut, copied and bound the text, describing it as "the romance of the Great Kahn." Others, such as the Dominican friar Francesco Pipino, vouched for the book's veracity. Larner also cites Pipino's introduction to his 1314 Latin translation, in which Pipino writes, "But lest the inexperienced Reader should regard as beyond belief the many strange and unheard of things that are related in sundry passages of this book, let all know Messer Marco Polo, the narrator for these marvels to be a most respectable, veracious and devout person."

In the centuries since its publication, *The Travels of Marco Polo* has contributed to Polo's reputation as one of history's greatest explorers. In his introduction to a 2001 edition of the text, Jason Goodwin declares that "Marco Polo stands unchallenged as the world's most famous traveler." He goes on to explain how different generations have read the text, noting that "Columbus used his copy as a guidebook," while others, such as the readers of *National Geographic*, view Polo's text as "a window into the world's wild places." Scholars have evaluated the work through a broad range of critical lenses, considering not only the value of its historical testimony but also its insights about the peoples of the Mongol Empire and its unique literary qualities.

Many commentators have focused on the nature of the text. Olschki disputes the commonly held view that Polo's narration is mercantile in nature, arguing that the Polos were lay apostles for the Roman Catholic Church and that Polo sought to give the book "the character of a religious mission." Others, such as Frances Wood in *Did Marco Polo Go to China?* (1996), question the veracity of Polo's claims, arguing that he traveled only as far as Persia and that his accounts of the Far East were reconstructed from other travelers' tales.

BIBLIOGRAPHY

Sources

Goodwin, Jason. Introduction. *The Travels of Marco Polo*. By Marco Polo. Ed. Manuel Komroff. New York: Modern Library, 2001. ix–xv. Print.

Larner, John. *Marco Polo and the Discovery of the World*. New Haven: Yale University Press, 1999. Print.

Olschki, Leonardo. *Marco Polo's Asia*. Berkeley: University of California Press, 1960. Print.

KUBLAI KHAN

In 1215, the year in which his father, Genghis Khan, seized control of Peking, Mongol leader Tolui and his wife, Sorghaghtani Beki, gave birth to a son named Kublai. Kublai was tutored in Chinese Buddhism and embraced many aspects of Chinese culture, including the language and government. He used many Chinese advisers to help him rule over his lands. Although he was not born to become the Khagan, or the supreme Mongol ruler, his brother Möngke's death in 1259 cleared the path for Kublai's ascent to power. In 1260 the Mongol barons gathered to elect their next leader. At the age of forty-five, Kublai became Kublai Khan, the sole ruler of the Mongol Empire.

After a three-and-a-half-year journey across Persia, along the Silk Road, through the Gobi desert, and into northern China, a twenty-year-old Marco Polo arrived at the court of the Great Khan accompanied by his father and uncle. Khan oversaw the Mongol Empire during an important transitional period, when the Mongols established a more sedentary, agricultural society, and for seventeen years Polo aided him in doing so. He was treated as an honored member of the noble household, and he became a trusted adviser to the khan, embarking on numerous fact-finding missions for the emperor.

Polo, Marco. *The Travels of Marco Polo*. Ed. Manuel Komroff. New York: Modern Library, 2001. Print.

Wood, Frances. "Did Marco Polo Go to China?" *Asian Affairs* 27.3 (1996): 296–304. *Taylor & Francis*. Web. 15 Oct. 2012.

Further Reading

Bergreen, Laurence. *Marco Polo: From Venice to Xanadu*. New York: Alfred A. Knopf, 2007. Print.

Calvino, Italo. *Invisible Cities*. New York: Harcourt Brace Jovanovich, 1974. Print.

Komroff, Manuel. *Contemporaries of Marco Polo*. New York: Dorsett, 1989. Print.

Rossabi, Morris. *Khubilai Khan: His Life and Times*. Berkeley: U of California P, 1988. *Ebsco Ebook Collection*. Web. 15 Oct. 2012.

Thurbon, Colin. *The Silk Road: Beyond the Celestial Kingdom*. New York: Simon & Schuster, 1989. Print.

Tolstoy, Alexandra. *The Last Secrets of the Silk Road: In the Footsteps of Marco Polo by Horse and Camel*. Guilford: Lyons, 2003. Print.

Greg Luther

WHEN I WAS PUERTO RICAN
Esmeralda Santiago

❖ **Key Facts**

Time Period:
Late 20th Century

Relevant Historical Events:
American colonization of Puerto Rico; Operation Bootstrap; Santiago's immigration to New York

Nationality:
Puerto Rican/American

Keywords:
colonialism; alienation; immigration

OVERVIEW

Esmeralda Santiago's first autobiography, *When I Was Puerto Rican* (1993), tells the story of the author's childhood in her native Puerto Rico and the adjustments she must make when she immigrates to New York City with her mother and siblings. Told in the first person by Negi (Santiago's childhood nickname, a diminutive of *negrita,* because her skin was dark), the memoir details Santiago's life from age four through thirteen, a tumultuous period that involves several moves between the Puerto Rican countryside and the urban center of San Juan before the family's final journey to the mainland United States. A feisty tomboy with a penetrating curiosity, Negi is both deeply attached to her Puerto Rican culture and an outsider constantly struggling to make sense of life's contradictions. Her observations of the world illuminate the small cataclysms of everyday life with humor, anger, and the pride of developing identity.

Published in the same year that a voters' referendum reaffirmed Puerto Rico's status as a U.S. territory, *When I Was Puerto Rican* was warmly received by critics as an eloquent expression of the Latino immigrant experience. Santiago's memoir of growing up in 1950s Puerto Rico and early 1960s New York is part of a growing genre of Hispanic American literature that explores complex issues of language, culture, and identity rooted in a history of colonialism.

HISTORICAL AND LITERARY CONTEXT

When I Was Puerto Rican is rooted in the island culture of Puerto Rico, which was settled by the Spanish shortly after its discovery by Christopher Columbus in 1493 and has never existed as an independent nation. In the aftermath of the Spanish-American War in 1898, Spain ceded possession of Puerto Rico to the United States, beginning a long and often contentious relationship between the two countries. In 1917 Puerto Ricans became U.S. citizens, and in 1947 they were allowed a measure of self-governance. However, some residents resisted what they viewed as Yankee imperialism. Though nationalist activists protested U.S. domination with violent attacks on the U.S. president and Congress in 1950 and 1954, U.S. control of Puerto Rico was never seriously threatened.

By the time Santiago's autobiography was published, Puerto Ricans had long enjoyed citizenship in a so-called floating nation, in which they could live in the mainland United States but maintain close ties with their homeland. Negi comes of age during the 1950s, a period of expanded U.S. economic and industrial exploitation of Puerto Rico that changed island life dramatically. This expansion began during World War II and increased with the 1948 implementation of Operation Bootstrap, through which low-paid workers in Puerto Rican factories produced goods for export to the United States. At the same time, depressed economic conditions in the islands led to an upsurge in immigration north.

Puerto Rico has a rich literary tradition that reflects the island nation's multifaceted colonial history. The beloved nationalist poet Luis Lloréns Torres (*Alturas de América,* 1940) so influenced Santiago that she uses one of his pastoral verses to begin her memoir. A number of writers have explored the Puerto Rican immigrant experience, including Ed Vega (*Mendoza's Dreams,* 1987) and Nicholasa Mohr (*In Nueva York,* 1988). Santiago's depiction of the particular challenges of a Puerto Rican girl caught between two worlds reflects the lives of other Latinas as well: Sandra Cisneros's *The House on Mango Street* (1984) is the coming-of-age story of a Mexican American girl, and Julia Alvarez's *How the Garcia Girls Lost Their Accents* (1991) explores the cross-cultural experiences of a Dominican American family through the eyes of four sisters.

Santiago's memoir is an important part of the rising tide of literature probing the political and personal consequences of cultural identity and assimilation. She followed *When I Was Puerto Rican* with two more memoirs continuing Negi's story into adulthood, *Almost a Woman* (1998) and *The Turkish Lover* (2004). As Latino immigration to the north continues to increase, other writers have followed Santiago in chronicling the resulting blend of cultures, including Iris Gomez in *Try to Remember* (2010), about Colombian immigrants, and Mary Romero in *The Maid's Daughter* (2011), an exploration of Chicana workers.

THEMES AND STYLE

The foundation of Santiago's narrative is the experience of the outsider. Negi lives in the uncomfortable space between identities and often feels she does not truly belong anywhere. "I sat at the door," she says, "and tried to keep one eye on my sisters and brother and another on what went on inside." She cannot fully embody either the rural peasant *jíbara* culture of her father or the urban sophistication her mother values. Negi is forced to face the essential truth that success in one culture often means loss in another. The book is above all a story of the development of a child into an adult, and Santiago flavors each rite of passage with Caribbean perspective, as when Negi describes the death of a friend's grandfather: "I held on to the wreath so that ... I could not fly up into the sky ... into the clouds where Don Berto's soul waited, machete in hand."

Santiago presents a vivid picture of childhood, which can be idyllic and ominous by turns. "What frightened [Mami] I became curious about, and what she found exciting terrified me." Though mainly written in chronological order, *When I Was Puerto Rican* begins and ends with Negi's adult perspective. The prologue, "How to Eat a Guava," uses the imagery of the sweet tropical fruit to symbolize that which has been lost by the expatriate. In Puerto Rico the guavas are sweet and red, though the children sometimes eat them green and sour, enjoying the intensity of their crunch. "I had my last guava the day we left Puerto Rico.... But this is autumn in New York, and I'm no longer a child.... I push my cart away, toward the apples and pears of my adulthood." This device offers assurance of Negi's survival while highlighting both the disappointments and the acceptance that have been required of her.

When I Was Puerto Rican is written in a vivid, lyrical style that mixes Spanish words liberally among the English. Puerto Rico is essentially a bilingual commonwealth, and this interplay of Spanish and English is one of the most important devices Santiago uses to impart her dual experience. Each chapter begins with a nod to Negi's peasant roots, a *dicho*, or folk saying, in both languages, such as, "*Escapé del trueno y di con el relámpago.* I ran from thunder and hit lightning." Though driven to perform well in school, Negi feels "disloyal for wanting to learn English" and determines not to "learn English so I don't become American." Her father responds with a clear definition of imperialism, "They expect us to do things their way, even in our country."

CRITICAL DISCUSSION

Upon its publication, *When I Was Puerto Rican* received positive critical reviews and quickly became popular with readers. Yvonne Sapia of the *Los Angeles Times* describes Santiago's writing as "stylistically fluid and finely detailed," saying the book "takes its unique place in contemporary Latino storytelling." Jeff Gundy of the *Georgia Review* writes that Santiago's "real accomplishment is to have woven details of place, family, and social life into a vividly moving portrait." A paperback edition of *When I Was Puerto Rican* was released in 1994, and the same year Santiago wrote a Spanish-language translation, *Cuando era Puertorriqueña*.

In the years since the publication of Santiago's first memoir, Latin American culture has become a growing part of U.S. culture. Writing in *Confluencia*, Gregory Stephens uses *When I Was Puerto Rican* as a prime example of the new genre of "U.S. Latino/a literature," which he views as "now a part of the cultural mainstream in the U.S." Santiago's work has become a mainstay on high school and college reading lists, and in 2008 Mount Holyoke College highlighted *When I Was Puerto Rican* in its "One Book Holyoke" program, which included adapting excerpts for a staged reading. In 2006 Santiago adapted the sequel, *Almost a Woman*, into a screenplay for a television movie.

The complex intermingling of cultures that has resulted from the colonization of Latin America and the resulting immigration of millions of Latinos to the United States is a topic of growing interest to literary scholars. Santiago's memoir, with its probing exploration of the many facets of identity, offers rich ground for study. Stephens analyzes the work as "an example of 'borderlands literature' that bridges Caribbean literatures and that of U.S. Latinos," while Joanna Marshall, writing in *MELUS*, examines Santiago's memoir as a series of complex "negotiations of shame, pride, and identity," especially focusing on the imagery of food as representative of cultural identity. The blending of cultures does not come without hardship, however, and

PIRI THOMAS: *DOWN THESE MEAN STREETS*

Like Esmeralda Santiago, John Peter (Piri) Thomas was dark skinned and thus given the affectionate nickname *negrito* by his mother. Unlike Santiago, Thomas felt the painful effects of racism even within his own family, where he was the only dark child of a Puerto Rican mother and Cuban father. Born in New York in 1928, Thomas grew up in Spanish Harlem with his parents and six siblings, always feeling like an outsider because of the color of his skin.

As a young man growing up with poverty, anger, and rejection, Thomas faced special challenges, and he responded by becoming a street fighter, mugger, and drug dealer, trying to build a tough reputation that would protect him. When his illegal activities landed him in jail, he completed his education and began to take solace in writing. In 1967 he published his memoir, *Down These Mean Streets,* one of the earliest first-person accounts of the Latino immigrant experience. Thomas's unflinching portrayal of life in the immigrant ghetto not only educated many Anglos about the Puerto Rican American experience, but it also inspired other Latino writers, such as poet Martin Espada, to share their own experiences. Following the success of *Down These Mean Streets,* Thomas published novels, plays, poems, and stories. His memoir is still widely read and studied.

Maria Szadziuk states in *Mosaic,* "In Santiago's story, although the narrative voice seems to have reached a certain kind of equilibrium, taking what she considers best for her from both cultures, there is still some bitterness and alienation."

BIBLIOGRAPHY

Sources

Gundy, Jeff. "How Others Have Lived Here." Rev. of *When I Was Puerto Rican,* by Esmeralda Santiago. *Georgia Review* 48 (1994): 391–400. Print.

Marshall, Joanna Barszewska. "'Boast Now, Chicken, Tomorrow You'll Be Stew': Pride, Shame, Food, and Hunger in the Memoirs of Esmeralda Santiago." *MELUS* 32.4 (2007): 47+. *Literature Resource Center.* Web. 5 Nov. 2012.

Sapia, Yvonne V. "The Americanization of Esmeralda." Rev. of *When I Was Puerto Rican,* by Esmeralda Santiago. *Los Angeles Times.* 26 Dec. 1993: 9. Print.

Schultermandl, Silvia. "Rewriting American Democracy: Language and Cultural (Dis)Locations in Esmeralda Santiago and Julia Alvarez." *Bilingual Review* 28.1 (2004): 3+. *Literature Resource Center.* Web. 5 Nov. 2012.

Stephens, Gregory. "*When I Was Puerto Rican* as Borderland Narrative: Bridging Caribbean and U.S. Latino Literature." *Confluencia: Revista Hispánica de Cultura y Literatura.* 25.1 (2009): 30+. *Literature Resource Center.* Web. 5 Nov. 2012.

Szadziuk, Maria. "Culture as Transition: Becoming a Woman in Bi-ethnic Space." *Mosaic* 32.3 (1999): 109–29. *Literature Resource Center.* Web. 5 Nov. 2012.

Further Reading

Castillo, Debra A. *Talking Back: Toward a Latin American Feminist Literary Criticism.* Ithaca, N.Y.: Cornell University Press, 1992. Print.

Flores, Juan. *Divided Borders: Essays on Puerto Rican Identity.* Houston: Arte Publico, 1993. Print.

Ruggieri, Colleen A. "Appreciating Ethnic Diversity with *When I Was Puerto Rican.*" *World of Literature* 91.5 (2002): 56–62. Print.

Santiago, Esmeralda. *Almost a Woman.* Reading, Mass.: Perseus, 1998.

———. *The Turkish Lover.* Cambridge, Mass.: Da Capo, 2004.

Torres-Robles, Carmen L. "Esmeralda Santiago: Hacia Una (Re)definicion de las Puertorriquenidad." *Bilingual Review/La Revista Bilingue* 23.3 (1998): 206–13. Print.

Vega, Marta Moreno, Marinieves Alba, and Yvette Modestin, eds. *Women Warriors of the Afro-Latina Diaspora.* Houston: Arte Publico, 2012.

Tina Gianoulis

The Wonderful Adventures of Mrs. Seacole in Many Lands

Mary Seacole

OVERVIEW

Mary Seacole's *The Wonderful Adventures of Mrs. Seacole in Many Lands* (1857), one of the first autobiographical works by a Caribbean woman, recounts a life of travel and enterprise unusual for the period. Seacole, who learned herbal medicine from her Jamaican mother and had experience treating cholera in Panama, journeys to the front lines to treat troops sickened during the Crimean War. Written to capitalize on her fame as a skilled caregiver and motherly friend to British soldiers, the book was Seagrove's attempt to replenish her depleted funds after the war ended.

Seacole's book was published after she returned to England from Balaklava. London newspapers had carried reports of her bravery during the war, and the public responded to her autobiography with interest. Seacole did not receive the attention paid to Florence Nightingale in the decades following her death, but her story was rediscovered in the twentieth century, and attempts have been made to recognize her efforts to improve conditions for soldiers during the war. While written for a British audience by a woman who had chosen to leave behind her native Jamaica, *The Wonderful Adventures of Mrs. Seacole in Many Lands* is now regarded as a seminal work in the history of Caribbean literature.

HISTORICAL AND LITERARY CONTEXT

Jamaica was conquered by the English in 1655 and became one of the empire's most valuable holdings because of its sugar cultivation. Slave labor, much of it provided by Africans, was widespread through the nineteenth century. During this time, many children were born as a result of interracial couplings, often between white masters and black slaves. Pressure from English abolitionists resulted in the outlawing of the Atlantic slave trade in 1807; the British Emancipation Act of 1834 freed slaves to choose their own employment and ostensibly gave them voting rights. After emancipation, Jamaican society remained divided along racial and class lines, with whites at the top and newly freed blacks at the bottom. "Free people of color," as they were commonly known, represented a more mobile segment of society, some of whom, like Seacole, were able to take advantage of opportunities in the new economy, achieving a measure of economic security, education, and independence.

Seacole lived an unusually free and accomplished life for a woman of her time yet was still subject to the prejudices of Victorian society, which judged her "a motherly yellow woman" unfit to serve in English aid organizations during the Crimean War. Having learned nursing from her mother and with experience treating cholera, she was set on joining British soldiers on the battlefront. Seacole financed her own trip to the Crimea, established the British Hotel in Balaklava (by various accounts a convalescent home or canteen-style food service catering to soldiers), and gained a reputation for her nursing skills and courage. When the war ended in 1856, she was almost penniless. Ignored by the government to which she had appealed for recompense, Seacole penned her autobiography in an attempt to recover the money she had invested in aid efforts and to afford herself the income necessary to travel and continue her work.

The Wonderful Adventures of Mrs. Seacole in Many Lands is often compared to Mary Prince's *The History of Mary Prince* (1831), a similarly groundbreaking record of a black Caribbean woman's life. In terms of content and purpose, the two books diverged significantly, however. Prince, who grew up as a slave in Bermuda and Antigua, recounted the abuses she suffered at the hands of her white masters. The book was used by British abolitionists working to outlaw slavery in the colonies.

Initially, *The Wonderful Adventures of Mrs. Seacole in Many Lands* had little significant literary impact; however, the work is often counted as anticipating elements in Caribbean autobiographical work and fiction over the next century. In particular, discussions of writers such as Jean Rhys and Jamaica Kincaid often reference Seacole's contribution to the project of defining black Caribbean women's experiences and identities in the face of overwhelming cultural marginalization.

THEMES AND STYLE

The Wonderful Adventures of Mrs. Seacole in Many Lands centers on Seacole's commitment "to be of service to those who need a woman's help." Indeed, her early life, marriage, and widowhood are dispatched in the first

❖ *Key Facts*

Time Period:
Mid-20th Century

Relevant Historical Events:
Crimean War; English colonization of Jamaica

Nationality:
Jamaican

Keywords:
colonialism; nursing; women's writing

A photograph of author Mary Seacole dated 1860. Born in Jamaica, she nursed British soldiers during the Crimean War. © AMORET TANNER/ALAMY

chapter, with the remainder of the book devoted to her various ventures, most prominently nursing cholera patients in Jamaica and Panama and then again near the battlefront in Balaklava during the Crimean War. In recounting these experiences, particularly her wartime ministrations to British soldiers, Seacole characterizes herself as a "motherly yellow woman" intent on nursing her "sons." In addition to nursing, she details various commercial endeavors, from her earliest attempts to sell "West Indian preserves and pickles" in England to her eventual construction and direction of the British Hotel.

Although Seacole's autobiography was principally an unabashed attempt to recoup expenses after the war ended and the clientele for her hotel disappeared, she demonstrates a secondary preoccupation with legitimizing a life that would have been deemed unconventional—and perhaps not entirely respectable—by the English middle class. Throughout the narrative Seacole describes her hard work and good intentions, including her attachment to England and its people, which ultimately benefited the injured and ill soldiers she nursed during the war. Having laid this groundwork, she concludes by detailing the ways in which her health and economic circumstances have suffered as a result of her service. As if anticipating criticism about the state of her finances, she asserts, "When I think of the few whom I failed to pay in full (and so far from blaming me some of them are now my firmest friends), I cannot help remembering also the many who profess themselves indebted to me." Similarly, Seacole diffuses potential criticism of her appropriation of masculine freedoms such as travel and entrepreneurialism by casting her activities as directed by a calling to help, a suitably feminine attitude.

The Wonderful Adventures of Mrs. Seacole in Many Lands is distinguished by a self-deprecating tone, which is often in marked contrast to Seacole's pride in the accomplishments she describes. She uses comments by others as a means of relating her skill, courage, and perseverance without seeming boastful, prefacing these testimonials with remarks such as "I am far from wishing to speak of this fact with any vanity or pride."

CRITICAL DISCUSSION

Seacole's autobiography was well received by critics and the reading public. *The Illustrated Times of London,* in addition to praising the book, announced a festival honoring Seacole, which, while well attended, did not raise the funds that Seacole and her supporters had hoped. Historians have suggested that Seacole was not truly recovered from financial ruin until 1867, when Queen Victoria became involved on her behalf.

Seacole's book, along with her story, faded into obscurity after her death but was rediscovered in the twentieth century. She has since become a potent symbol and subject of discussion in disciplines as diverse as nursing and postcolonial studies. In recent years, there has been a push for recognition of Seacole's contribution to the British effort during the Crimean War and, from some quarters, for crediting Seacole, alongside Nightingale, with making significant contributions to the foundation of modern nursing. *The Wonderful Adventures of Mrs. Seacole in Many Lands* continues to attract scholarship, particularly as the narrative lends itself to discussions of colonial and postcolonial identities, particularly focusing on race and gender.

Seacole's text is often considered the starting point for discussions of Caribbean autobiography. In her essay "The Enigma of Arrival: *The Wonderful Adventures of Mrs. Seacole in Many Lands,*" Sandra Paquet characterizes Seacole's work as an attempt by the author to define herself outside of her native Jamaica, "a coming home to a New World identity," contrasting this perspective with slave narratives such as Prince's, which long for "a return to the African and peasant heart of the Caribbean." Paul Baggett extends this discussion in "Caught between Homes: Mary Seacole and the Question of Cultural Identity," pointing out how "her narrative illustrates the contradictions involved in claiming an allegiance to a national homeland for one whose cultural and racial heritage cannot be circumscribed within a strictly nationalist discourse." Other work analyzes the strategies Seacole deploys to reconcile these contradictions. Amy Robinson's 1994 piece in *Feminist Studies* points out the author's appropriation of the language and attitudes of her audience—English gentlemen—as both parody and a way to assume a voice of authority by embodying their prejudices.

BIBLIOGRAPHY

Sources

Baggett, Paul. "Caught between Homes: Mary Seacole and the Question of Cultural Identity." *MaComère* 3 (2000): 45–56. Rpt. in *Nineteenth-Century Literature Criticism*. Ed. Russel Whitaker. Vol. 147. Detroit: Gale, 2005. *Literature Resource Center.* Web. 6 Nov. 2012.

Paquet, Sandra Pouchet. "The Enigma of Arrival: *The Wonderful Adventures of Mrs. Seacole in Many Lands.*" *African American Review* 26.4 (1992): 651–63. Rpt. in *Nineteenth-Century Literature Criticism*. Ed. Russel Whitaker. Vol. 147. Detroit: Gale, 2005. *Literature Resource Center.* Web. 7 Nov. 2012.

Robinson, Amy. "Authority and the Public Display of Identity: *Wonderful Adventures of Mrs. Seacole in Many Lands.*" *Feminist Studies* 20.3 (1994): 537–57. Rpt. in *Nineteenth-Century Literature Criticism*. Ed. Russel Whitaker. Vol. 147. Detroit: Gale, 2005. *Literature Resource Center.* Web. 6 Nov. 2012.

Seacole, Mary. *The Wonderful Adventures of Mrs. Seacole in Many Lands.* 1857. Penn Libraries. Web. 7 Nov. 2012.

Further Reading

Gunning, Sandra. "Traveling with Her Mother's Tastes: The Negotiation of Gender, Race, and Location in *Wonderful Adventures of Mrs. Seacole in Many Lands.*" *Signs* 26.4 (2001): 949–81. Rpt. in *Nineteenth-Century Literature Criticism*. Ed. Russel Whitaker. Vol. 147. Detroit: Gale, 2005. *Literature Resource Center.* Web. 7 Nov. 2012.

THE CRIMEAN WAR

The Crimean War began in 1854 when conflicts over the territories controlled by the declining Ottoman Empire reached a head. Ending a decades-long period of relative peace in Europe, the conflict embroiled England, France, Turkey, and Sardinia in a struggle with Russia for control of the Ottoman territories, particularly the Holy Land of modern-day Israel. The war had a high rate of casualties, although many of the deaths occurred not from battle wounds but from disease, poor sanitation, and lack of supplies in the military camps established in Turkey. Florence Nightingale, with whom Mary Seacole had originally hoped to travel to the front, famously worked to improve conditions in battlefront hospitals and, upon her return to England, prepared a lengthy report that she presented to a government commission investigating army health conditions.

The Crimean War is notable for being the first war from which dispatches were returned to England and reported to the public in newspapers. This from-the-battlefield reporting was instrumental in publicizing the deplorable living conditions and the rampant spread of disease in military encampments, which led to mobilization of aid efforts, including those spearheaded by both Nightingale and Seacole.

McKenna, Bernard. "'Fancies of Exclusive Possession': Validation and Dissociation in Mary Seacole's England and Caribbean." *Philological Quarterly* 76.2 (1997): 219–39. Rpt. in *Nineteenth-Century Literature Criticism*. Ed. Russel Whitaker. Vol. 147. Detroit: Gale, 2005. *Literature Resource Center.* Web. 7 Nov. 2012.

Prince, Mary. *The History of Mary Prince.* 1831. Rpt. New York: Penguin Books, 2004. Print.

Robinson, Jane. *Mary Seacole: The Most Famous Black Woman of the Victorian Age.* New York: Carroll and Graf, 2004. Print.

Silkü, Rezzan Kocaöner. "Wonderful Adventures: Transcending Liminality and Redefining Identity in Mary Jane Grant Seacole's Autobiography." *ARIEL* 39.1–2 (2008): 113+. *Literature Resource Center.* Web. 7 Nov. 2012.

Daisy Gard

The Worlds of a Maasai Warrior
An Autobiography
Tepilit Ole Saitoti

❖ Key Facts

Time Period:
Late 20th Century

Relevant Historical Events:
European colonization of Africa; banishment of Saitoti's Maasai people from the Serengeti National Park

Nationality:
Tanzanian

Keywords:
colonialism; alienation

OVERVIEW

Written by Tepilit Ole Saitoti, *The Worlds of a Maasai Warrior: An Autobiography* (1986) is the story of a Maasai man from Tanzania who is educated in Western schools and eventually travels to the United States. Saitoti tells of his childhood as a herder in the pastoral culture of the Maasai, detailing the death of his mother; bonding and strife among the boys of his kraal, or settlement; and his initial reluctance to attend a Western school. After returning home, Saitoti becomes a ranger in the Serengeti National Park, stars in a National Geographic documentary called *Man of the Serengeti* (1972), and travels out of Tanzania to Germany and the United States. Navigating the cultural differences between his seminomadic people and industrialized nations is a trial for Saitoti, but throughout his text he stresses that it is a skill his people need to learn if they are to survive.

By the time *The Worlds of a Maasai Warrior* was published, Saitoti had already experienced a level of success in the United States, working with painter/photographer Carol Beckwith on an art book collaboration titled *Maasai* (1980), which won the Anisfield-Wolf Book Award in race relations. His autobiography received favorable reviews and brought to light the desultory effects of the Kenyan and Tanzanian governments' land-use policy for Maasailand. In his autobiography he writes that he pursued a degree in creative writing specifically "to be able to write about my people and their culture."

HISTORICAL AND LITERARY CONTEXT

The Worlds of a Maasai Warrior compares the values of the Maasai to those of the Western world without privileging one over the other. The Anglo-German Agreement of July 1890 determined borders for the East African countries of Chad, Tanzania, Kenya, Cameroon, Ghana, and others. With this treaty, as anthropologist John Galaty explains in his introduction to the text, the Maasai's traditional pastoral lands were bisected by the boundary between Tanzania and Kenya, though it took some time for the Maasai to be affected by the new boundaries. Ultimately, they were violently removed from their land. In Saitoti's account of his childhood, he makes no mention of this history, instead telling of freely herding cattle, goats, and sheep. Although he lived through and was affected by colonialist practices, his autobiography suggests that the greatest danger to the Maasai's stock is the immediate threat of lions, hyenas, and other wild predators.

Saitoti was born two years before the Serengeti National Park was created in Tanzania in 1951. Subsequently, the Maasai were forced outside the park boundary. Over time, the removal of Saitoti's people from their traditional pastures took its toll; their wealth had always been in their herds, which they used as currency. Toward the end of Saitoti's time in the United States, he received a letter from his sister, who wrote that his family in Tanzania was "barely clinging to life" and that she "would have to write a whole volume" to name all of the cattle that had died.

The Worlds of a Maasai Warrior was the first published autobiography of a Maasai man, who arrived in the United States at a time when Western popular culture was being exposed to the Maasai through media such as the National Geographic special and Beckwith's photographs. Saitoti's experience, his close relationship with his family, and his acceptance of some Western cultural practices contradict the romantic narrative that authentic Maasai warriors were always proud, removed, and antiquated people. Saitoti had already emphasized the Maasai's ability to fluidly exist between their culture and Western culture in his master's thesis of proposed land use, "Peaceful Coexistence through Multiple Use: A Cultural-Ecological Study of the Maasai."

Saitoti's autobiography, with its emphasis on Maasai herding practices, family life, and initiation rituals, received good reviews and became a canonical text for anthropologists and ethnographers. *Unbound* (2006), the memoir of Nobel Prize–winner Wangari Maathai, also traces environmental policy in the region and the author's move to the United States for education—though Maathai did not come from a pastoral people and thus encountered less disparity between her culture and the West. The influence of *The Worlds of a Maasai Warrior* may be seen more clearly in *The Last Maasai Warriors* (2012), in which Wilson Meikuaya and Jackson Ntirkana trace the events of their childhoods as herders and eventually argue for the education of Maasai in Western schools so that they might better thrive under postcolonialism.

THEMES AND STYLE

Central to *The Worlds of a Maasai Warrior* are the consequences, both positive and negative, of cultural commingling. Eventually coming to disbelieve the power of Maasai medicine men, or *laibonok*, and that curses passed down through generations cause warriors to die, Saitoti advises his elders to "send [their] children to school" if they truly "are determined to live." However, Saitoti's view is not simplistic. In the United States he encounters a racial tension more stark than the one between the Maasai and nonnomadic people in Tanzania. He remembers dating a white woman in Boston and walking down the street with her, writing "we must have shown fear … we were virtually breathless by the time we entered the theater."

Saitoti's motivation for writing his autobiography is not only to publicize the culture of the Maasai but also to assert their ability to adjust to changes. From a young age, he learns that speaking other languages gives him access to new cultures and that this access brings his family a degree of economic prosperity. In order to barter at the market, he speaks Kiswahili instead of his native Maa. In his travels he becomes fluent in English and German. He maintains that his people can continue to celebrate their culture without having to completely "assimilate to contemporary modes of living." Worried that Maasai "livestock is diminishing as a result of … the creation of national parks by the governments of Kenya and Tanzania," he travels the world looking for people and resources that can help him resist the growing marginalization of his people.

The Worlds of a Maasai Warrior is novelistic in its tone. Dialogue illustrates early memories, overheard stories, tales passed down through generations, and myths. Saitoti highlights the similarities between the Maasai and the outside world, writing that some stories "were told for us to appreciate wise ancestry" whereas others "taught us to respect our parents unquestioningly." Aside from the slight digressions, Saitoti proceeds chronologically across a period spanning the last decade of colonialism and the first few decades of independence in Tanzania, or from the 1950s through the 1980s.

CRITICAL DISCUSSION

Early reviews of *The Worlds of a Maasai Warrior* were positive. In the *Times Literary Supplement* (1987), Chinweizu writes that the book is "a humorous, lighthearted account," adding that its strength rests in how "each culture is its own center, and no one is more valid than any other." Similarly, critic Robert Pini in *Africa Today* (1989) calls it "a warm and coherent story supported by his natural empathy and his ability to relate to changing cultures."

In spite of its originality, Saitoti's text received little critical attention. The book marked the end of his career as a writer; at the end of his narrative, he tells of moving back to Tanzania to care for his family following the death of his brother. Galaty remarks in his introduction to the text that the modern Maasai experience "transpires less between two worlds than within a complex social field constructed out of simple influences and possibilities … a mix of Maasai, Swahili and English languages, and an interplay of local, Islamic and Christian beliefs." Saitoti's book serves to change the facile image portrayed by the missionary Ludwig Krapf, who characterized the Maasai as strange and warlike. Contemporary scholarship also seeks to contradict the notion set forth by Krapf.

Recent scholarship often cites Galaty in lieu of Saitoti, though Galaty finds *The Worlds of a Maasai Warrior* to embody the tenets of "anthropology itself." Anthropologists have drawn on Saitoti's firsthand account when analyzing identity formation and globalization's impact on Maasailand. Dorothy L. Hodgson references Saitoti in her 1999 article in *Ethnology* to illuminate parental resistance to government policies, arguing that "when forced by the government to send at least one child to school, elders reportedly gave the son they liked the least." Saitoti reports fearing this was the case when he went to boarding school. His testimony

Maasai performing warrior dance, Tanzania, East Africa, March 5, 2009. Author Tepilit Ole Saitoti was born into a traditional Tanzania society in 1949. © SERGEY URYADNIKOV/ALAMY

SCHOOL FOR MAASAI WARRIORS

Maasai herders grow close to their domestic animals, building them separate kraals, fending off predators and thieves, and ushering the animals home from pasture before nightfall. These duties begin when the Maasai are children. In his autobiography, Tepilit Ole Saitoti recalls that his chores continued through inclement weather and that he once waited out a hailstorm with no shelter, only to have the hailstorm give way to a flash flood. In colonial times, children who performed the bulk of the herding were required to attend school. The government of Tanzania set a quota for pastoralist children and called on local chiefs to comply.

Saitoti, though he resisted being sent away from home, came to enjoy his education, realizing after graduating "that a desire for further schooling had slowly been burning" within him. By the time his book was published, Maasai boys made up 95 percent of the enrollment for schools in the Ngorongoro region, whereas girls were underrepresented at 5 percent. Although the elders of his kraal complained of such low standards that "a sixth grader cannot even write his own name," Saitoti nevertheless argued that exposure to education would better equip Maasai for the changes of globalization.

that he chose to be baptized against his father's wishes is also Hodgson's source for the assertion that "most parents refused to permit their sons to be baptized."

BIBLIOGRAPHY

Sources

Beckwith, Carol. "An Interview with Carol Beckwith." *African Arts* 18.4 (1985): 38–45. *JSTOR.* Web. 23 Nov. 2012.

Chinweizu. "Between Kraal and College." Rev. of *Worlds of a Maasai Warrior,* by Tepilit Ole Saitoti. *Times Literary Supplement* 14 Aug. 1987: 871. *Times Literary Supplement Historical Archive.* Web. 23 Nov. 2012.

Hodgson, Dorothy L. "'Once Intrepid Warriors': Modernity and the Production of Maasai Masculinities." *Ethnology* 38.2 (1999): 121–50. *JSTOR.* Web. 23 Nov. 2012.

Pini, Robert. "Worlds Apart: A Maasai's Encounter with the West." Rev. of *The Worlds of a Maasai Warrior: An Autobiography,* by Tepilit Ole Saitoti. *Africa Today* 36.2 (1989): 29–30. *JSTOR.* Web. 23 Nov. 2012.

Saitoti, Tepilit Ole. *The Worlds of a Maasai Warrior.* Berkeley: University of California Press, 1986. Print.

Further Reading

Galaty, John G. "Ceremony and Society: The Poetics of Maasai Ritual." *Man* 18.2 (1983): 361–82. *JSTOR.* Web. 23 Nov. 2012.

Hughes, Lotte. "Malice in Maasailand: The Historical Roots of Current Political Struggles." *African Affairs* 104.415 (2005): 207–24. *JSTOR.* Web. 23 Nov. 2012.

Igoe, Jim. "Becoming Indigenous Peoples: Difference, Inequality, and the Globalization of East African Identity Politics." *African Affairs* 105.420 (2006): 399–420. *JSTOR.* Web. 23 Nov. 2012.

Imperato, Pascal James. "Maasai." *African Arts* 14.3 (1981): 79–80. *JSTOR.* Web. 23 Nov. 2012.

Little, Peter D. "Maasai Identity on the Periphery." *American Anthropologist* 100.2 (1998): 444–57. *JSTOR.* Web. 23 Nov. 2012.

Smith, Andrew B. "Hunters on the Periphery: The Ideology of Social Hierarchies between Khoikhoi and Soaqua." *Kronos* 24 (1997): 9–17. *JSTOR.* Web. 23 Nov. 2012.

Caitlin Moore

Coming of Age

Angela's Ashes by Frank McCourt	119
Black Boy by Richard Wright	122
A Child's Christmas in Wales by Dylan Thomas	125
The Dark Child: The Autobiography of an African Boy by Camara Laye	128
The Education of Henry Adams by Henry Adams	132
An Egyptian Childhood by Taha Hussein	135
Fun Home: A Family Tragicomic by Alison Bechdel	139
Incidents in the Life of a Slave Girl, Written by Herself by Harriet A. Jacobs	142
Life on the Mississippi by Mark Twain	146
My Life Story by David Unaipon	149
My Revolutionary Years: The Autobiography of Madame Wei Tao-Ming by Cheng Yu-hsiu	152
Persepolis by Marjane Satrapi	155
Red Azalea by Anchee Min	158
Red Scarf Girl: A Memoir of the Cultural Revolution by Ji-li Jiang	161
Stop-Time by Frank Conroy	164
Under My Skin: Volume One of My Autobiography, to 1949 by Doris Lessing	167
The Unwanted by Kien Nguyen	170
The Woman Warrior: Memoirs of a Girlhood among Ghosts by Maxine Hong Kingston	173

Angela's Ashes
Frank McCourt

OVERVIEW

First published in 1996, Frank McCourt's *Angela's Ashes* is a memoir of a childhood spent in mid-twentieth-century Ireland. In the book, McCourt, who was born in Brooklyn, New York, in 1930 but moved to Ireland with his Irish parents at the age of four, describes his life in the slums of Limerick up to the age of nineteen, when he returned to the United States. The memoir contains details of life in Ireland, including an exploration of the pervasive influence of the Catholic Church and the crushing effects of poverty, in a nostalgic and humorous reflection on the country and its people.

An instant best seller, *Angela's Ashes* appealed in particular to Irish Americans and other members of the Irish diaspora who had left Ireland to find a better life or whose ancestors had done so. However, as Ireland in the 1990s attempted to present itself as a modern, sophisticated European nation, McCourt's memoir was seen by many as an unwelcome reminder of the country's history. Many in Limerick accused him of lying about, or at least misremembering, the past. Nevertheless, his colloquial take on the misery of an Irish Catholic childhood made the book especially appealing to older Irish Americans, who could identify with the author, helping to explain why so many young Irish men and women felt compelled to leave Ireland during the twentieth century.

HISTORICAL AND LITERARY CONTEXT

In the 1930s, the decade in which *Angela's Ashes* begins, Ireland was a largely agricultural country. However, its small farms were generally unable to support the families who worked them, and many rural migrants moved to towns and cities but failed to find work. Over the previous century, the country had endured famine, large-scale emigration, political and religious divisions, and civil war. In 1922 it finally emerged as an independent nation after a long and bitter struggle with the English. However, the partitioning of the island into northern and southern states divided, and in many cases militarized, the population, which nevertheless remained economically dependent on England and on trade with North America and Europe. Many Irish men left their families to find work, and many, like McCourt's alcoholic father, frittered away their earnings.

McCourt began writing sketches and fragments about his childhood after he retired in 1987 from a nearly thirty-year career as a New York City schoolteacher. The book grew out of anecdotes he had told his students in class; occasional pieces he wrote for the *Village Voice*; and the two-man play *A Couple of Blaguards*, which he wrote and performed with his brother Malachy. He began writing his memoir in earnest in 1994 and was initially told by an agent that nobody wanted to read Irish memoirs. When a writer friend finally persuaded another agent to read the book, it quickly found a publisher. In an interview published in the 2005 Harper Perennial paperback edition, McCourt notes that all of the people who helped him publish the book were women. He labels his acknowledgments as "a small hymn to an exaltation of women."

Angela's Ashes is part of a twentieth-century tradition of Irish memoirists, including Sean O'Casey, Frank O'Connor, and Sean O'Faolain. Most of these writers in their memoirs express a desire to unpick and understand the peculiarities of Irish life—and perhaps expose its iniquities and contradictions. As McCourt writes at the beginning of the book, his "was, of course, a miserable childhood…. Worse than the ordinary miserable childhood is the miserable Irish childhood, and worse yet is the miserable Irish Catholic childhood."

The international success of *Angela's Ashes* placed it at the center of a resurgence in the genre of the Irish memoir. Writers such as Nuala O'Faolin and McCourt's brother Malachy became prominent authors as Ireland's improving economic status and a growing interest in family history, driven by the Internet, fueled the global popularity of McCourt's memoir. McCourt produced two more books about his life before his death in 2009—*'Tis* (1999), a memoir about his life after he returned to New York, and *Teacher Man* (2005).

THEMES AND STYLE

The three main themes of *Angela's Ashes* are what McCourt describes in a 1997 television interview as the three main characteristics of Ireland and the Irish: nationalism, Catholicism, and emigration. Although the story is told in a humorous, and at times lighthearted, way, it illuminates a difficult chapter in Irish history and depicts a society divided by religion, wealth, and class. For example, McCourt describes how he went to school through the back lanes to

❖ *Key Facts*

Time Period:
Late 20th Century

Relevant Historical Events:
Achievement of Irish independence; author's childhood in Ireland

Nationality:
Irish American

Keywords:
poverty; Catholicism; coming-of-age

COMING OF AGE

Actor Joe Breen portrayed a young Frank McCourt in the film adaptation of *Angela's Ashes*, which was released in 2000. © HANDOUT/GETTY IMAGES

avoid "the respectable boys who go to the Christian Brothers' School, or the rich ones who go to the Jesuit School." The rich ones, he explains in a tone of controlled anger, will "take over the family business, run the government, run the world," while he and his brothers will only "deliver their groceries, or go to England to work on the building sites." Nevertheless, many of the slum dwellers are encouraged to be proud of Ireland: a neighbor tells the author, "Shakespeare is that good he must have been an Irishman."

McCourt wrote the book in retirement, with the encouragement of his wife and a number of friends who were writers or who worked in publishing, to express the pain and joys of growing up in poverty in mid-twentieth-century Ireland. The Angela of the book's title is McCourt's mother, who tries to hold her family together, despite the absence of her husband, in a crushing atmosphere of severe poverty, strict religious observance, and social segregation. In one memorable scene, McCourt and the other sons of laborers and the unemployed must join the archconfraternity, a society in which they sing hymns and hear sermons. Although he is made to attend these meetings, he is considered too poor to become an altar boy and is turned away by the priest, an episode that underlines the social oppressiveness of slum life.

Angela's Ashes is told in a colloquial style using Irish idioms, dialect, and inventive punctuation. In a 1996 *New York Times* article by Michiko Kakutani, McCourt is quoted as saying that after trying several different styles, he settled on writing the memoir as "a note to myself" and in doing so found his voice. The childlike narrator often stumbles over himself in his haste to get the story out. For example, he justifies stealing bread from the rich by reasoning "if I starve I'll never have the strength for my telegram boy job at the post office, which means I'll have no money to put back all the bread and milk and no way of saving to go to America and if I can't go to America I might as well jump into the Shannon."

CRITICAL DISCUSSION

Angela's Ashes became an immediate success and quickly transformed McCourt's life. The book, which spent 117 weeks atop the *New York Times* best-seller list, won a Pulitzer Prize in 1997. Easy to read and authentic, the memoir provoked surprise among readers that such poverty could exist in a supposedly modern Western nation. Many were horrified by the living conditions McCourt describes but charmed by his lack of bitterness and by his affection for Limerick's characters and eccentric personalities. Kakuchani calls it a "stunning memoir," describing its prose as "pictorial and tactile, lyrical but streetwise."

Although it is impossible to say whether *Angela's Ashes* triggered the explosion in popularity of Irish memoirs at the turn of the twenty-first century, McCourt's memoir was certainly the most popular. In 1999 it was made into a film, and in 2012 it debuted as a musical. However, McCourt was often blamed for the upsurge in "misery memoirs" in the early twenty-first century, when writers tried to outdo each other by telling stories of their awful childhood, and in Limerick local authors wrote books contradicting McCourt's descriptions of poverty. Nevertheless, the book has received enthusiastic scholarly attention and has been discussed in terms of memoir theory and identity formation, particularly with respect to the Irish emigrant identity.

Scholars have most often read *Angela's Ashes* as part of a tradition of Irish memoir that fictionalizes life through tragicomedy and themes of exile and simultaneously criticizes and celebrates Irish culture. Writing for *Anglia,* Peter Lenz suggests similarities between McCourt's writing style and the Irish oral tradition. Others scholars, such as Eric P. Levy in a 2002 essay for *Irish University Review,* have explored the formation of identity in the slums of Limerick by examining the "predicament of individuality" and the way individuality is suppressed through "fear of disgrace and desire for esteem." Writing in 2007 for the *Journal of Narrative Theory,* Shannon Forbes problematizes the text's identity as a memoir, using Lacanian analysis to unravel its facts/memories and "discuss the numerous, highly complex linguistic structures and narrative techniques at work."

BIBLIOGRAPHY

Sources

Forbes, Shannon. "Performative Identity Formation in Frank McCourt's *Angela's Ashes: A Memoir.*" *Journal of Narrative Theory* 37.3 (2007): 473–96. *Academic OneFile.* Web. 23 Nov. 2012.

Kakutani, Michiko. "Generous Memories of a Poor, Painful Childhood." *New York Times.* New York Times, 17 Sept. 1996. Web. 23 Nov. 2012.

Lenz, Peter. "'To Hell or to America?': Tragicomedy in Frank McCourt's *Angela's Ashes* and the Irish Literary Tradition." *Anglia* 118.3 (2000): 411–20. Print.

Levy, Eric P. "The Predicament of Individuality in *Angela's Ashes.*" *Irish University Review* 32.2 (2002): 259–72. *General OneFile.* Web. 23 Nov. 2012.

McCourt, Frank. *Angela's Ashes.* London: Harper Perennial, 2005. Print.

O'Brien, George. "The Last Word: Reflections on *Angela's Ashes.*" *New Perspectives on the Irish Diaspora.* Ed. Charles Fanning. Carbondale: Southern Illinois University Press, 2000. 236–49. Print.

Further Reading

Fanning, Charles, ed. *New Perspectives on the Irish Diaspora.* Carbondale: Southern Illinois University Press, 2000. 236–49. Print.

Foster, R. F. *The Irish Story: Telling Tales and Making It Up in Ireland.* Oxford: Oxford University Press, 2002. Print.

Harte, Liam. *The Literature of the Irish in Britain: Autobiography and Memoir, 1725–2001.* Basingstoke, U.K.: Palgrave Macmillan, 2009. Print.

Matiko, Beverly J. "Ritual and the Rhetoric of Repetition in *Angela's Ashes.*" *Michigan Academician* 32.3 (2000): 289. *General OneFile.* Web. 23 Nov. 2012.

McCourt, Frank. *'Tis: A Memoir.* New York: Simon and Schuster, 2000. Print.

O'Casey, Sean. *Autobiographies.* 2 vols. London: Papermac, 1992. Print.

O'Faolain, Nuala. *Are You Somebody?: The Life and Times of Nuala O'Faolain.* Dublin: New Island, 2000. Print.

Chris Routledge

BLACK BOY
Richard Wright

✢ Key Facts

Time Period:
Mid-20th Century

Relevant Historical Events:
Passage of Jim Crow laws; Wright's move from the South to Chicago

Nationality:
American

Keywords:
coming-of-age; racism; Jim Crow

OVERVIEW

Black Boy, Richard Wright's classic American autobiography about growing up as an African American in the Jim Crow South, first appeared in 1945, with later chapters published in 1977, and was compiled and published in its entirety in 1991. In the first section, "Southern Night," the author recounts his childhood experiences, from the time he accidentally set his house on fire at age four to just before he moved to Chicago as a young man, all the while struggling against racism (both overt and institutionalized) and poverty. The second section, "The Horror and the Glory," added after Wright's death and published as *American Hunger,* details Wright's experiences moving to Chicago, trying to become a writer, and becoming involved with the Communist Party.

Wright was already a successful author at the time of *Black Boy*'s publication. His debut novel, *Native Son,* became a best seller in 1940 and was the first book by an African American chosen for the Book-of-the-Month Club. *Black Boy,* also selected by the club, enjoyed even higher praise from reviewers than *Native Son,* becoming the fourth-best-selling nonfiction book of 1945. At that time, no African American writer had achieved such a large audience. Today Wright's book is regarded as a classic American autobiography as well as a book that raised consciousness about the evils of racism and paved the way for future black writers and civil rights leaders.

HISTORICAL AND LITERARY CONTEXT

Black Boy played an integral role in exposing the effects of racism to a mainstream audience. Although the 1945 edition of Wright's autobiography ends twenty years before its publication date, very little had changed for blacks in the South in terms of legal protection. In 1896, twelve years before Wright's birth, the *Plessy vs. Ferguson* judgment made segregation legal—a ruling that would stand until *Brown vs. Board of Education* in 1954. Jim Crow laws denied southern blacks many of their rights as citizens. As Wright describes in the second part of *Black Boy,* although the North was less segregated and less violent than the South, it was far from free of racial intolerance. Even as a successful author by 1945, Wright felt he had to use a lawyer as an arbitrator in buying a house to avoid racial discrimination.

Wright first called his manuscript "Black Confession," which he then changed to "American Hunger," later settling on the simplicity of *Black Boy*. The Book-of-the-Month Club was interested in only the first fourteen chapters of the book, which dealt with Wright's boyhood in Mississippi, so Harper and Brothers published a shortened version in 1945. The omission of the final chapters was contrary to Wright's wishes because he felt it made racism seem like a purely southern problem. He wrote in his journal that he believed members of the Communist Party had pressured the Book-of-the-Month Club to get these final sections dropped (he had left the party in 1944, prior to the book's publication). After *Black Boy* was released, Wright became something of a spokesperson for an entire generation of African Americans, appearing on radio programs and delivering lectures to decry racism.

Before *Black Boy* appeared, the primary form of mainstream African American autobiography was the slave narrative, such as those of Frederick Douglass and Booker T. Washington, among other, lesser-known autobiographical writings by African Americans in the eighteenth, nineteenth, and early twentieth centuries. James Weldon Johnson published the autobiography *Along This Way* in 1933, Langston Hughes wrote *The Big Sea* (1940), and Zora Neale Hurston released *Dust Tracks on a Road* in 1942, but none of these books had the commercial impact of *Black Boy*. As Wright describes in his autobiography, as a self-taught reader who had to sneak books past both his religious grandmother and a library that did not loan to blacks, his own early literary influences were many and included Joseph Conrad, Stephen Crane, Fyodor Dostoevsky, Theodore Dreiser, Henrik Ibsen, H. L. Mencken, Gertrude Stein, and Émile Zola.

Today Wright is regarded as one of the most influential African American writers of the twentieth century. He directly influenced many younger writers, including James Baldwin, Gwendolyn Brooks, Ralph Ellison, Lorraine Hansberry, Chester Himes, and Anne Petry. In the foreword to the sixtieth-anniversary edition of *Black Boy,* contemporary Pulitzer Prize winner Edward P. Jones recalls the excitement and amazement he felt when he read *Black Boy* in high school.

THEMES AND STYLE

Black Boy is a coming-of-age story about an African American in the midst of a society fundamentally designed to hamper the success of black Americans.

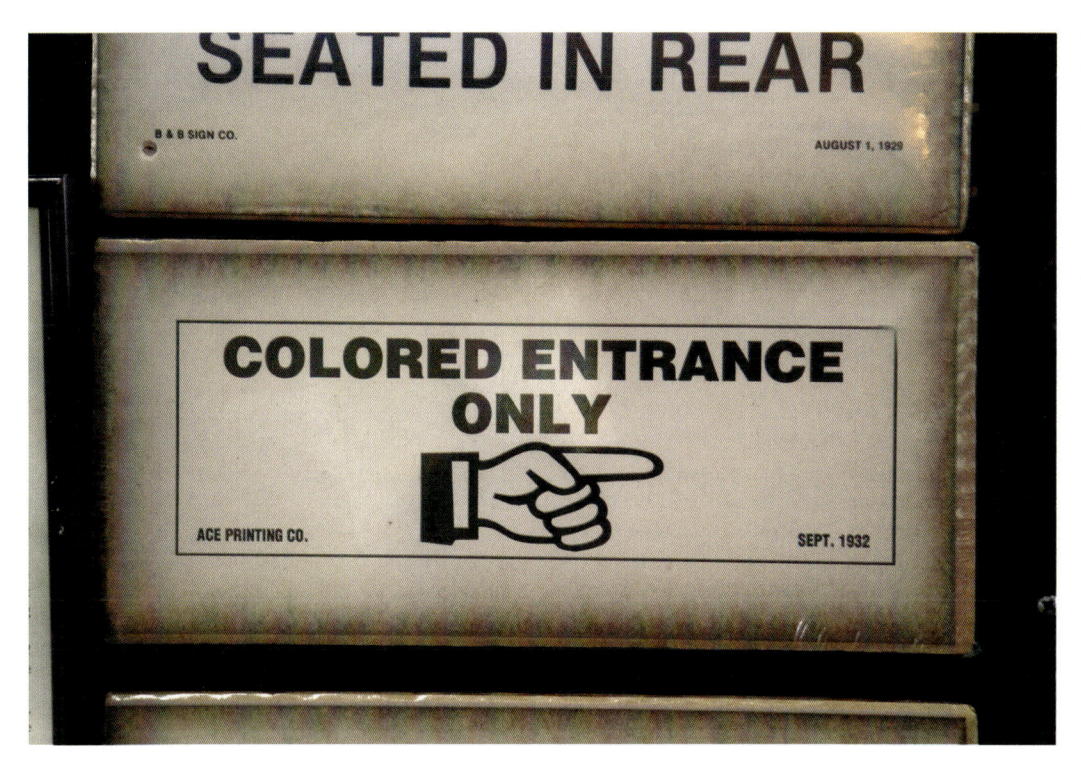

Examples of segregation signs on display at the Afro-American Music Fest in Detroit, Michigan. In his autobiography Black Boy, Richard Wright discusses the discrimination he faced. © CLARK BRENNAN/ALAMY

Wright describes the constant fear and humiliation of living as a black child in the South. As a very young boy, listening to tales of lynchings and mobs, Wright writes, "I had already grown to feel that there existed men against whom I was powerless, men who could violate my life at will." The text contains many examples of how his development as a writer and thinker was shaped by his dire circumstances and limited education, scrambling to grab any book he could get his hands on, and his financial and moral struggle to leave his family and the South. The later section of the book details Wright's struggles to make money during the Depression and his political and personal struggles with the Communist Party as he tried to find a community of his own that was not defined by race.

Wright had both political and personal reasons for writing *Black Boy*. Already an outspoken advocate against racism, he decided to write his autobiography after giving a talk at Fisk University in Nashville about growing up in a racist society. He was moved by the reaction of his audience and began to feel that his life story was worth telling. In writing his autobiography, he made many rhetorical decisions to sharpen the impact of his narrative. The story ends prior to his becoming a famous writer, instead ending (in both versions) in moments of uncertainty and struggle. Reviewers have criticized the author for fictionalizing parts of his experience, portraying his childhood as friendless, or omitting the fact that his mother made a decent living as a schoolteacher. Many scholars have questioned what it means to call something an "autobiography" and why Wright might have made certain untrue choices.

Far from a purely political or polemical text, however, *Black Boy* is a work of art in its own right, full of poetic, carefully chosen language, directly juxtaposing much of the horror and trauma of Wright's early childhood with hauntingly beautiful language. The text contains many parenthetical asides and digressions into sensory language, such as a lyrical passage recounting his experience of living with his grandmother, with pages of sentences beginning with "there was": "there was the drenching hospitality in the pervading smell of sweet magnolias … there was the drugged, sleepy feeling that came from sipping glasses of milk."

CRITICAL DISCUSSION

Black Boy was an enormous popular success and was viewed favorably by most critics, including being called a "remarkably fine book" by literary critic Lionel Trilling. One noted reviewer of the book was W. E. B. Du Bois, who called it "terribly overdrawn" and found the protagonist "self-centered to the exclusion of everybody and everything else." Mississippi Senator (and Ku Klux Klan member) Theodore Bilbo denounced the book on the floor of the Senate, calling it "the dirtiest, filthiest, lousiest, most obscene piece of writing" he had ever seen in print. William Faulkner wrote Wright a personal letter, saying that the content of *Black Boy* "needed to be said, and you said it well" but also noting that he believed *Native Son* had been a higher achievement.

Black Boy is seen today as a classic work of American autobiography, a near-canonical text still read in

AFTER *BLACK BOY*

Frustrated with the racial and social limitations of the United States, Richard Wright and his second wife and young daughter visited Paris in May 1946. A year earlier he had begun a correspondence with Gertrude Stein, who helped secure a visa for him; he would also become friends with Parisians Jean-Paul Sartre and Albert Camus. Wright, who had married a white woman, found the racial attitude of France refreshing. The Wrights would make Paris their permanent home a few years later.

Although Wright did not publish another book until 1953 (*The Outsider*), he tried other endeavors during his expatriate years, including writing the screenplay for and playing the teenage lead (at age forty-two) in an Argentinean film production of *Native Son*. He also wrote about his extensive travels to Africa, Asia, and Spain and published essays about communism. Wright continued to write and publish novels as well. A final, unfinished novel was published posthumously under the title *A Father's Law* in 2008. During the late 1950s Wright's marriage, finances, and health all collapsed. He died in 1960 at age fifty-two years from a heart attack stemming from dysentery he contracted during a visit to Africa.

classrooms. It has served as an inspiration for younger black writers as well as for many in the civil rights movement. As Hazel Rowley notes in *Richard Wright: The Life and Times*, Wright's influence is something that "every black American writer has to grapple with," and he is "a model to some and an anti-model to others." In particular, both Baldwin and Ellison were influenced by and consciously moved away from the influence of Wright. Wright himself found the weight of his achievement oppressive, and eight years passed before he wrote another novel. None of his future works would enjoy the enormous popularity of *Black Boy*.

Scholarship on *Black Boy* is extensive even today. Much of it has focused on authenticity and genre, examining the question of whether or not Wright's portrayal was accurate, whether it was representative for an entire race, and whether or not that matters. Timothy Adams tries to reconcile the authenticity and falsehood of *Black Boy* in his essay "Richard Wright: 'Wearing the Mask,'" arguing that although Wright sometimes "is deliberately false to historical truth, he seldom deviates from narrative truth." Some have criticized Wright for the stark political motives of his text, accusing him of portraying black life as too fundamentally bleak and joyless. In his essay in *The Omni-Americans* (1970), Albert Murray argues that Wright "regarded Negroes not as acquaintances and relatives to be identified against a very complex cultural background, but rather as human problems struggling to become people." Writing for *Antioch Review*, Ellison relates Wright's art to the African American tradition of blues music, explaining that trying to enjoy black culture in the midst of a hateful American culture would be like trying to enjoy "Beethoven's quartets" in a "Nazi prison." More recent scholarship has attempted to define Wright in a less rigid way, apart from the legacy of his classic works. Rowley states that critics have "made the man and his life into a statement" and that Wright "has been systematically trivialized and reduced."

BIBLIOGRAPHY

Sources

Adams, Timothy. "Richard Wright: 'Wearing the Mask'." *Richard Wright's Black Boy (American Hunger): A Casebook*. Ed. William L. Andrews and Douglas Edward Taylor. Oxford: Oxford University Press, 2003. Print.

Ellison, Ralph. "Richard Wright's Blues." *Antioch Review* 5.2 (1945): 198–211. *JSTOR*. Web. 14 Nov. 2012.

Moskowitz, Milton. "The Enduring Importance of Richard Wright." *Journal of Blacks in Higher Education* 59 (2008): 58–62. *JSTOR*. Web. 14 Nov. 2012.

Murray, Albert. "Identity, Diversity and the Mainstream." *The Omni-Americans*. New York: Outerbridge and Dienstfrey, 1970. Print.

Rowley, Hazel. *Richard Wright: The Life and Times*. Chicago: University of Chicago Press, 2008. Print.

Wallach, Jennifer Jensen. *Richard Wright: From Black Boy to World Citizen*. Chicago: Ivan R. Dee, 2010. Print.

Wright, Richard. *Black Boy*. Foreword by Edward P. Jones. New York: Harper Perennial, 1991. Print.

Further Reading

Bloom, Harold, ed. *Richard Wright's Black Boy*. New York: Chelsea House, 2006. Print.

Brewton, Butler E. *Richard Wright's Thematic Treatment of Women in Black Boy, Uncle Tom's Children, Native Son*. Bethesda, Md.: Academia, 2010. Print.

Craven, Alice Mikal, and William E. Dow, eds. *Richard Wright: New Readings in the 21st Century*. New York: Palgrave Macmillan, 2011. Print.

Fabre, Michel, and Ellen Wright, eds. *Richard Wright Reader*. Notes by Michael Fabre. New York: Harper and Row, 1978. Print.

Fabre, Michel. *The Unfinished Quest of Richard Wright*. Urbana: University of Illinois Press, 1993. Print.

Hakutani, Yoshinobu. "Creation of the Self in Richard Wright's Black Boy." *Black American Literature Forum* 19.2 (1985): 70–75. *JSTOR*. Web. 14 Nov. 2012.

Thaddeus, Janice. "The Metamorphosis of Richard Wright's Black Boy." *American Literature* 57.2 (1985): 199–214. *JSTOR*. Web. 14 Nov. 2012.

Ward, Jerry Washington, and Robert Butler. *The Richard Wright Encyclopedia*. Westport, Conn.: Greenwood, 2008. Print.

Webb, Constance. "What Next for Richard Wright?" *Phylon (1940–1956)* 10.2 (1949): 161–66. *JSTOR*. Web. 14 Nov. 2012.

Emily Jones

A Child's Christmas in Wales
Dylan Thomas

OVERVIEW

Dylan Thomas's *A Child's Christmas in Wales,* recorded in 1952 but not published until 1954, is a fictionalized autobiographical account of the author's childhood memories of Christmas. The text is unique for a nonnarrative structure that explores the emotions involved in remembering one's childhood and for its approach of generalizing memories rather than outlining them in chronological form. This writing style is related to the author's Welsh heritage, notably the Welsh history of oral narrative and memory that influenced his career as a poet and radio broadcaster.

The book is a compilation of two earlier works that were initially overshadowed by Thomas's poetry and longer prose narratives. Eventually, however, Thomas's fictionalized autobiography increased in popularity and became an emblem of the Christmas season. It has been reprinted often in illustrated children's books, broadcast over the radio and on television, and published in collections of Thomas's works. Although it still does not receive the same level of academic discussion as his poetry and fiction, *A Child's Christmas* remains a significant contribution to Thomas's canon because of the way it captures the sense of nostalgia surrounding Christmas.

HISTORICAL AND LITERARY CONTEXT

Born in 1914, shortly after the beginning of World War I, Thomas was raised in Swansea, a small town in rural Wales. Although his father was a teacher at the local grammar school, Thomas did not excel at his studies and ultimately dropped out of school in order to pursue poetry. In those early years, he published poems in numerous periodicals and magazines, including the *Sunday Referee* and *New Verse.* Thomas moved to London in 1934 and that year published his first collection of poems, which was titled *Eighteen Poems.* Thomas was influenced by the writings of James Joyce and developed an interest in the multiplicity of meanings a single word can hold. In addition, his Welsh heritage informed his writing career and underlies many of his works. Though he had his misgivings about Swansea because it was so far removed intellectually from the cultural hub of London, Thomas still felt a connection to it, which he explores in *A Child's Christmas.*

A Child's Christmas consists of two of Thomas's earlier works: a wartime radio broadcast, "Memories of Christmas" (1945), and a piece published in *Picture Post,* "Conversations about Christmas" (1947), neither of which had received much attention. He combined the two pieces in 1952 under the title *A Child's Christmas in Wales* when he was scheduled to make a phonograph recording of his poetry. The title stuck, and the new piece was published in *Quite Early One Morning* (1954), a collection of his work.

Although Thomas is best known for his poetry, he also achieved success through his radio broadcasts, for which he drew on the Welsh traditions of oral narrative and the concept of "remembrancing," whereby the very act of remembering an event is as important as the memory itself. Thomas felt disdain for London's trends in intellectual poetry, including the work of W. H. Auden. In reaction to writers such as Auden, Thomas mined his Welsh heritage as a way of raising his intellectual profile.

After Thomas's death in 1953, *A Child's Christmas* quickly became a holiday classic. His grasp of emotions and memory helped to make the piece extremely popular, as evidenced by its reproduction in many illustrated children's books and its broadcast on popular radio stations in London during the Christmas season. Although it received little literary attention at first, *A Child's Christmas* remains a beloved Christmas book today.

THEMES AND STYLE

The main focus of Thomas's memoir is the exploration of the emotions and memories associated with childhood Christmases. Thomas recalls throwing snowballs at his neighbor's cats, caroling with his siblings (which turns into an adventure with hippos and trolls), and enjoying the evening in the company of aunts and uncles. His narrative does not center on any particular Christmas; instead, it is a compilation of Thomas's memories and feelings. He begins by drawing attention to the multiplicity of his Christmas memories: "One Christmas was so much like another, in those years around the sea-town corner," so that "I can never remember whether it snowed for six days and six nights when I was twelve or whether it snowed for twelve days and twelve nights when I was six." This jumbling of emotions and images creates the nostalgic view of childhood for which *A Child's Christmas* is known.

Key Facts

Time Period:
Mid-20th Century

Relevant Historical Events:
Thomas combines two earlier works, "Memories of Christmas" and "Conversations about Christmas"

Nationality:
Welsh

Keywords:
nostalgia; Christmas; childhood

An illustration from the 1920s depicting a group of children singing Christmas carols. Dylan Thomas's *A Child's Christmas in Wales* is a nostalgic recollection of his own childhood Christmases. © MEDICI/ MARY EVANS/EVERETT COLLECTION

The genesis of *A Child's Christmas* was a commission by the BBC in 1945 to broadcast a warmhearted Christmas story that would bolster the spirits of listeners who had been ravaged by World War II. The story that resulted after he later combined the broadcast with his piece in *Picture Post* is not a typical autobiography and there is no narrative that brings unifying meaning to the author's life. Instead, the work explores the author's fond memories of all his childhood Christmases and presents them as an exploration of the act of remembering one's youth. The result is an examination of the feeling of Christmas rather than a narrative of specific events.

The book is divided into three sections, each rich in detail, that create vivid images and combine memory, imagination, and storytelling in the active recollection of childhood events. The first section occurs outside on Christmas Eve; the second is a conversation between a child and an adult about Christmases past; and the third is Christmas day itself, filled with relatives, food, song, and a few drinks "because it was only once a year." Thomas describes his Christmas Eve antics as such:

> But there were cats. Patient, cold and callous, our hands wrapped in socks, we waited to snowball the cats. Sleek and long as jaguars and horrible-whiskered, spitting and snarling, they would slink and sidle over the white back-garden walls, and the lynx-eyed hunters, Jim and I, fur-capped and moccasined trappers from Hudson Bay, off Mumbles Road, would hurl our deadly snowballs at the green of their eyes.

By inserting his current recollection that the location was "off Mumbles Road" into this description of childhood play, Thomas demonstrates his ability to combine his memories with the act of remembering.

CRITICAL DISCUSSION

Despite being overlooked by critics and the general public during Thomas's lifetime, *A Child's Christmas* was ultimately successful thanks to the endearing quality of Thomas's voice and the work's nostalgic take on childhood. A 1997 essay in *Literature and Its Times* reflects on the success of Thomas's recording of *A Child's Christmas*: "Though the record sold slowly at first, since Thomas's death in 1953 it has become his most famous recording. Its popularity has ensured that the story itself is still widely read." A 1978 review in *The Economist* notes that "the pleasure of this beautiful piece of prose is that it houses pure memory, unsoured by age."

The most lasting effect of Thomas's autobiography is the way it has triggered a sense of nostalgia among adult readers with its representation of Christmas through the eyes of a child. In "*A Child's Christmas in Wales:* Overview," Simon Baker writes about the "way in which Thomas holds the adult and childlike versions of reality in a perfect tension." According to the *Literature and Its Times* essay, Thomas's exploration of "the feelings and perceptions special to childhood," as interpreted "from the nostalgic point of view of an adult," is one of the work's most lasting triumphs.

Current trends in scholarship examine *A Child's Christmas* as an exemplary holiday narrative that touches the hearts of adults and children alike. Leslie Norris, in her foreword to a 1993 edition of Thomas's collected stories, calls *A Child's Christmas* "the best Christmas since Dickens," a "rich confection, as full as a Christmas stocking with gifts." In *Dylan Thomas*, Jacob Korg shares this view, writing that "*A Child's Christmas in Wales* has become a favourite holiday feature." Nevertheless, *A Child's Christmas* is of little interest to most literary scholars, who tend to focus on Thomas's weightier works.

BIBLIOGRAPHY

Sources

Baker, Simon. "*A Child's Christmas in Wales:* Overview." *Reference Guide to Short Fiction.* Ed. Noelle Watson. Detroit: St. James, 1994. *Literature Resource Center.* Web. 14 Nov. 2012.

Korg, Jacob. "Chapter 9: Thomas in Retrospect." *Dylan Thomas.* Ed. Jacob Korg. New York: Twayne, 1992. Twayne's English Authors Series 20. *The Twayne Authors Series.* Web. 14 Nov. 2012.

Norris, Leslie. Foreword. *The Collected Stories.* By Dylan Thomas. London: Dent, 1983. vii–xv. Print.

"Overview: 'A Child's Christmas in Wales.'" *Literature and Its Times: Profiles of 300 Notable Literary Works and the Historical Events that Influenced Them.* Ed. Joyce Moss and George Wilson. Vol. 3. Detroit: Gale, 1997. *Literature Resource Center.* Web. 14 Nov. 2012.

Thomas, Dylan. *A Child's Christmas in Wales.* 1954. Illus. Fritz Eichenberg. 1969. New York: New Directions, 1969. Print.

———. *The Love Letters of Dylan Thomas.* London: J. M. Dent, 2001. Print.

"When We Were Young." Rev. of *A Child's Christmas in Wales,* by Dylan Thomas. *The Economist* 23 Dec. 1978: 99. *The Economist Historical Archive.* Web. 15 Nov. 2012.

Further Reading

Ackerman, John. *Dylan Thomas: His Life and Work.* Oxford: Oxford University Press, 1964. Print.

Davis, James A. *Dylan Thomas's Places: Autobiographical and Literary Guide.* Swansea, U.K.: Christopher Davis, 1987. Print.

———. *A Reference Companion to Dylan Thomas.* Westport, Conn.: Greenwood, 1998. Print.

Dupuy, Marigny. "Another Side of Dylan." *New York Times Book Review,* 14 Nov. 2004: 28. *Literature Resource Center.* Web. 16 Nov. 2012.

Thomas, Dylan. "Reminiscences of Childhood." *Quite Early One Morning.* New York: New Directions, 1954. Print.

"Thomas, Dylan Marlais (1914–1953)." *Encyclopedia of World Biography.* Detroit: Gale, 1998. *Gale Biography in Context.* Web. 17 Nov. 2012.

Katherine Barker

THE LOVE LETTERS OF DYLAN THOMAS

Like many others of his generation, Dylan Thomas was a prolific letter writer. The poet's letters to the many women in his life, which were among his most eloquent and revealing, have recently been collected as *The Love Letters of Dylan Thomas* (2001). The letters are arranged in roughly chronological order by correspondent and prefaced by brief sketches of Thomas's relationship with each woman. The book opens with letters to Pamela Hansford Johnson, whom Thomas met while still in his teens, and continues with his correspondence to a diverse group of women, including his wife, Caitlin; the American writer Emily Holmes Coleman, a lover fourteen years his senior; Marged Howard-Stepney, whom, he recalls, "told me … to call on you when I was beaten down"; and Elizabeth Reitell, with whom he had an affair toward the end of his life and with whom he spent his final days.

Thomas's letters reveal his attachment to his wife, even as they expose his attempts to smooth over his numerous infidelities. For example, after Caitlin discovered a letter to Marged, he wrote, "That letter you saw was horrible, it was dirty and cadging and lying." The letters also offer significant insights into Thomas's life as a poet, his grueling reading tours in the United States, and his feelings about his craft.

THE DARK CHILD
The Autobiography of an African Boy
Camara Laye

❖ Key Facts

Time Period:
Mid-20th Century

Relevant Historical Events:
Laye studies in France; the négritude movement grows

Nationality:
Guinean

Keywords:
négritude; alienation; colonialism

OVERVIEW

Originally published in French as *L'Enfant Noir* (1953), *The Dark Child* is Camara Laye's lyrical autobiography of his childhood experience in the Guinean countryside and his high school years in the capital city Conakry. Crafted as a novel in which Laye appears as the character and narrator Fatoman, *The Dark Child* is divided into two parts. The first section is devoted to Fatoman's childhood, which he spends absorbing the Malinke culture in rural Kouroussa and neighboring Tindican, his mother's native village. In the second part, Fatoman begins his age of discovery and loss of innocence when he is sent to Conakry, Guinea's capital, at the age of fifteen to study at the École Georges Poiret. *The Dark Child* concludes with Fatoman receiving a scholarship to study in France. On the eve of his departure, Fatoman's father advises him, "Beware of ever deceiving anyone…. Be upright in thought and deed. And God shall be with you."

Upon publication, *The Dark Child* was hailed a classic and won Laye "instant acclaim and lasting respect as a limpid stylist," according to Eric Sellin in *World Literature Today*. Laye was awarded Le Prix Européen de l'Essai Charles Veillon for *The Dark Child* in 1954. Since its initial appearance and subsequent English translations, the work has become one of the most widely read pieces of African literature in French- and English-speaking nations. In the *French Review*, Jacques Bourgeacq explains that the text's wide appeal derives from its universal relevance, poetic language, nostalgic tone, and "the straightforwardness of its narrative style and the author's candid attitude, all these qualities resulting in a general impression of genuine simplicity." *The Dark Child* is regularly included in literary anthologies and taught in world literature courses.

HISTORICAL AND LITERARY CONTEXT

On January 1, 1928, in the ancient city of Kouroussa in Upper Guinea, Laye was born into a devout Muslim family belonging to the Malinke people—a historically important ethnic group distinguished by their artistic and cultural accomplishments. Founders of the Mali Empire, the Malinke once ruled over a large portion of West Africa, sharing their language and culture with neighboring ethnic groups for several centuries. Despite having adopted Islam as their official religion over time, the Malinke retained robust elements of pre-Islamic animist spiritual beliefs. Guinea was eventually conquered and administered by France, but Laye's tribal village was largely untouched by colonialism. Gerald Moore states in *Twelve African Writers* that "a city like [Laye's native village] was complex and self-sufficient enough to go very much on its own immemorial way. Its people … were not constantly obsessed with the alien presence of Europe in their midst."

Suffering from cultural alienation and loneliness, Laye began recording his childhood memories while studying at the Central School of Automobile Engineering in Argenteuil, a Parisian suburb. When his scholarship ran out, he had to abandon his studies and took a variety of manual-labor jobs to support himself. Despite the hardships, Laye took this time to become intimately acquainted with French art, literature, and music, while simultaneously exploring his African roots at the Musée de l'Homme. He also became closely affiliated with *négritude*—a movement for African cultural and artistic renaissance initiated in the 1930s by Léopold Senghor. Both *The Dark Child* and Laye's second novel, *The Radiance of the King* (1954), were significant contributions to the négritude movement. Laye's girlfriend, Marie Lorifo, joined him in France, and they were married in 1953—the same year *The Dark Child* was published.

Critics have consistently remarked upon the European influence on all of Laye's works, including *The Dark Child*. While some scholars draw parallels between *The Dark Child*'s coming-of-age story structure and Gustave Flaubert's *Sentimental Education: A Young Man's History* (1869), others note Laye's tendency of idealizing childhood in the manner of Jean-Jacques Rousseau. Although Laye's books follow European literary modes, his texts successfully incorporate and celebrate traditional African life and culture. In *The Writings of Camara Laye*, Adele King argues that the author transcends his cultural background and "belongs within the tradition of classic world literature, describing a personal and cultural dilemma in accents that speak to all mankind."

Regardless of the fact that Laye published only four books in his lifetime, he is "regarded by many critics of African literature as the continent's major

Francophone novelist," according to Charles R. Larson in the *Times Literary Supplement*. Laye's third book, *A Dream of Africa* (1966), is the sequel to *The Dark Child*. It begins with Fatoman returning home after six years in Europe. Although Fatoman is elated to be reunited with his family in his homeland, he realizes much has changed and people are "deeply marked" by the "harsh rigors of toilsome existence." It is a novel about disillusionment in which Fatoman discovers his country's serious political problems. While the country is on the brink of gaining independence from France, Fatoman warns, "Someone must say that though colonialism … was an evil thing for our country, the regime you are now introducing will be a catastrophe whose evil consequences will be felt for decades."

THEMES AND STYLE

Central to *The Dark Child* is the loss of innocence the narrator experiences as he moves from childhood to maturity. The first part of the book emphasizes the sacredness of all human activity and the importance of being part of a community. Feeling part of a whole is so integral to village life that when Fatoman's uncle moves too far ahead of the other farmhands during the annual harvest, he slows down, remarking to his nephew: "Don't forget that I must not get too far ahead of the others; it would offend them." The wonder and fantasy of the first section of the novel starkly contrast the harsh realities of Fatoman's adolescent years in Conakry. There, he suffers loneliness for the first time, experiences frustration when he is unable to attend his preferred school, sustains a wound that necessitates hospitalization, and witnesses the death of his friend Check. Fatoman's transformation during this time is best illustrated by his observation of the traditional healers attempting to cure Check: "I don't know whether Check had any great confidence in the medicine men. Probably not. By now we had spent too many years in school to have real faith."

Although Laye wrote *The Dark Child* to relieve the loneliness he felt while living on foreign soil, his autobiography poses important questions about the preservation of traditional ways of life that are eroding in the face of modernity. Laye was shocked by modern society and the omnipresence of twentieth-century technology in both Conakry and Paris. Of Conakry, Fatoman states, "This country, new to me, too new and too rugged, disturbed rather than enchanted me." In his essay "Camara Laye," John D. Conteh-Morgan remarks, "In symbolic terms, the narrator's departure for Conakry can be interpreted as a fall from the timeless world of grace and mythical experience into the time-bound universe of suffering and historical experience." This fall may explain why Laye spent the rest of his life studying and endeavoring to safeguard his African heritage. His final work, *The Guardian of the Word* (1978), was his attempt to preserve a rapidly declining oral art form.

Stylistically, *The Dark Child* has been widely praised for the quiet restraint of its prose. Moore states that it "is a unique book in many ways, written with a singular and gentle sincerity, yet with very conscious artistic skill." The first part of the book is not written in chronological order but rather follows Fatoman's recurring, habitual experiences: visiting Tindican, participating in festivals, watching his father work. The recounting of his early childhood is marked by poetic language, as is illustrated in the lyrical description of Tindican's annual harvest: "The long line of reapers hurled itself at the field and hewed it down…. They sang and they reaped. Singing in chorus, they reaped, voices and gestures in harmony." The second part of Laye's text gives way to more descriptive language and a linear progression as the narrator is torn from his harmonious universe and forced to live in a universe of modernity and rationality.

A 2001 photograph showing residents of Siguiri, Guinea, pumping water. Writer Camara Laye describes his childhood in Guinea in *The Dark Child: The Autobiography of an African Boy*.
© GREENSHOOTS COMMUNICATIONS/ ALAMY

CAMARA LAYE: RETURN TO AFRICA

After nine years in France with only a brief visit to Guinea in 1954, Camara Laye finally returned to Africa in 1956. However, he did not immediately take up residence in the country of his birth. Instead, he accepted various positions in Dahomey and Ghana, where he taught French and wrote a French news column. Laye returned to Guinea when it achieved independence from France in 1958. The break from diplomatic and economic ties with France created many difficulties for the young republic. Laye became an important figure in the newly independent Guinea, becoming ambassador to Ghana and then head of the Division of Economic Agreements in the Ministry of Foreign Affairs. He eventually became the associate director of the National Institute for Research and Documentation, which facilitated his personal research into the oral traditions of Upper Guinea.

Between 1958 and 1965 Laye had little time to devote to his writing. His literary endeavors were limited to writing a few radio plays, interviewing traditional sages, and presenting papers at the African literature conferences held in Senegal and Sierra Leone in 1963. By the mid-1960s he had become disillusioned and discouraged by Guinea's government, which was led by the radical nationalist leader Sékou Touré. A deteriorating economy led to a restless and occasionally conspiratorial population, which Touré stamped out through brutal repression. Fearing for his safety and disenchanted with the anti-intellectual character of Touré's regime, Laye went into exile in 1965, seeking political asylum in Dakar, Senegal. He became a researcher at the Insitut Fondamental d'Afrique Noire, where he was able to record traditional griots and study the folk culture of the Malinke people. Laye lived in Senegal until his death on February 4, 1980.

CRITICAL DISCUSSION

Many Western readers were instantly enamored of *The Dark Child*'s poetic representation of Africa and of Laye's spiritual vision. However, some African readers of the time criticized Laye for presenting Africa as overly idyllic in its rural simplicity and carefree innocence. They faulted the author for not speaking out against the harsh realities of colonialism and for "pandering to the folkloristic colonial stereotypes of eternal Africa," according to Conteh-Morgan. He quotes Cameroonian writer Mongo Beti as saying, "Laye closes his eyes stubbornly on the most basic reality.... Could he possibly have seen nothing but a peaceful, beautiful and motherly Africa? Is it imaginable that he did not once witness a single exaction by the colonial administration?"

Since its publication, *The Dark Child* has had a significant impact on the development of modern West African literature. In *The African Experience in Literature and Ideology*, Abiola Irele argues that *The Dark Child* is "the work that can with justice be regarded as having brought French African narrative prose finally into its own." Unlike the critics who argue that Laye did not do enough to condemn colonialism, Irele believes that *The Dark Child*'s celebration of the traditional African ways of life was "in fact a form of denial of the assumptions and explicit ideological outgrowth of the French colonial enterprise."

Regarded as an example of master craftsmanship of words, Laye's autobiographical work is often studied for its artistry. King calls *The Dark Child* "a carefully controlled story ... presented with economy and restraint.... A particular moment in Laye's life and in the history of Africa has been transformed into a minor classic, in which the autobiographical form has been raised to the level of art." Scholars regularly debate the vision expressed in Laye's carefully crafted language. Moore claims, "Laye does not proclaim his negritude or announce the coming dawn; he records what his childhood was, what was the quality and the depth of the life from which he sprang." Conteh-Morgan argues that the author's religious vision and idyllic portrayal of Africa "should be understood as the response of a man who recoiled in horror at what he saw as a dehumanizing and materialistic French society." He also states, "Laye, it is true, was not an overtly political writer. But to portray him as one who colluded in his people's subjugation (because his work is silent on it) is both to practice bad and dangerous logic and to misconceive the radical, even subversive character of his creative output."

BIBLIOGRAPHY

Sources

Bourgeacq, Jacques. "Camara Laye's *L'Enfant Noir* and the Mythical Verb." *French Review* 63.3 (1990): 503. *Literature Resource Center*. Detroit: Gale, 2012. *Literature Resource Center*. Web. 31 Oct. 2012.

"Camara Laye." *Contemporary Authors Online*. Detroit: Gale, 2003. *Literature Resource Center*. Web. 31 Oct. 2012.

Conteh-Morgan, John D. "Camara Laye." *African Writers*. Ed. C. Brian Cox. Vol. 1. New York: Charles Scribner's Sons, 1997. *Scribner Writers Series*. Web. 31 Oct. 2012.

Irele, Abiola. "Camara Laye." *The African Experience in Literature and Ideology*. Heinemann, 1981. *Contemporary Authors Online*. Detroit: Gale, 2003. *Literature Resource Center*. Web. 31 Oct. 2012.

King, Adele. "Camara Laye." *The Writings of Camara Laye*. Heinemann, 1980. *Contemporary Authors Online*. Detroit: Gale, 2003. *Literature Resource Center*. Web. 31 Oct. 2012.

Larson, Charles R. "Camara Laye." *Times Literary Supplement* 4 May 1967. *Contemporary Authors Online*. Detroit: Gale, 2003. *Literature Resource Center*. Web. 31 Oct. 2012.

Laye, Camara. *A Dream of Africa*. 1966. London: Collins, 1968. Print.

———. *The Dark Child*. 1954. New York: Farrar, Straus and Giroux, 1986. Print.

Moore, Gerald. "Camara Laye." *Twelve African Writers*. Bloomington: Indiana University Press, 1980.

Contemporary Authors Online. Detroit: Gale, 2003. *Literature Resource Center.* Web. 31 Oct. 2012.

Sellin, Eric. *World Literature Today* (Summer 1980). *Contemporary Authors Online.* Detroit: Gale, 2003. *Literature Resource Center.* Web. 31 Oct. 2012.

Ugbabe, Kanchana. "Camara Laye." *Contemporary African Writers.* Ed. Tanure Ojaide. Detroit: Gale, 2011. *Dictionary of Literary Biography* 360. *Literature Resource Center.* Web. 31 Oct. 2012.

Further Reading

Briere, Eloise A. "*L'Enfant Noir* by Camara Laye: Strategies in Teaching as African Text." *French Review* 55.6 (1982): 804–10. Print.

Burger, Roger A. "Decolonizing African Autobiography." *Research in African Literatures* 41.2 (2010): 32+. *Literature Resource Center.* Web. 31 Oct. 2012.

"Camara Laye (1928–)." *Contemporary Literary Criticism.* Ed. Carolyn Riley. Vol. 4. Detroit: Gale Research, 1975. 282–85. *Literature Criticism Online.* Web. 31 Oct. 2012.

"Camara Laye (1928–1980)." *Contemporary Literary Criticism.* Ed. Daniel G. Marowski, Roger Matuz, and Jane E. Neidhardt. Vol. 38. Detroit: Gale Research, 1986. 284–92. *Literature Criticism Online.* Web. 31 Oct. 2012.

Carroll, David. "Camara Laye's *The African Child*: A Reply." *African Literature Today* 5 (1973): 129–26. Print.

Edwards, Paul, and Kenneth Ramchand. "An African Sentimentalist: Camara Laye, *The African Child.*" *African Literature Today* 4 (1970): 37–53. Print.

Irele, Abiola. "In Search of Camara Laye." *Research in African Literatures* 37.1 (2006): 110–27. Print.

King, Adele. *Rereading Camara Laye.* Lincoln: University of Nebraska Press, 2002. Print.

Philipson, Robert. "Images of Colonized Childhood: Abrahams, Wright, Laye." *Literature of Africa and the African Continuum.* Ed. Jonathan Peters, Mildred P. Mortimer, and Russell V. Linnemann. Washington, D.C.: Three Continents, 1989: 75–81. Print.

Sow, Alioune. "Political Intuition and African Autobiographies of Childhood." *Biography* 33.3 (2010): 498+. *Literature Resource Center.* Web. 31 Oct. 2012.

Wehrs, Donald R. "Gendering the Subject and Engendering the Self: Mande Acculturation, Islamic Piety, and the Forging of Ethical Identity in Camara Laye's *L'Enfant Noir.*" *Modern Language Studies* 35.1 (2005): 7–27. Print.

Maggie Magno

The Education of Henry Adams
Henry Adams

✤ Key Facts

Time Period:
Early 20th Century

Relevant Historical Events:
Rapid change occurs during the Second Industrial Revolution; Adams leaves United States for Europe

Nationality:
American

Keywords:
politics; diplomacy; technology

OVERVIEW

Written in the third person and told from a highly sarcastic point of view, *The Education of Henry Adams*, published in 1918 after the author's death, recounts the struggle the journalist and historian experienced while coping with the arrival of the twentieth century. Adams, who was the grandson of U.S. president John Quincy Adams and great grandson of president John Adams, came of age during a time of intense scientific and technological change. The book expresses Adams's concern and apprehension about these rapid changes and introduces the term "dynamo" to describe this Second Industrial Revolution. He also criticizes an educational system that failed to prepare him for the modern, industrialized world.

Adams's critique of nineteenth-century educational practices was first privately published in 1907 and circulated among his closest friends. His treatise argues that his traditional education, which focused on history and classical literature, failed to prepare him for the major changes of the twentieth century. Adams, however, was no failure: he was a Harvard graduate who later taught history at Harvard for seven years; edited the *North American Review*; and wrote two novels, two biographies, and a nine-volume *History of the United States during the Administrations of Jefferson and Madison* (1889–91). Despite this success, he continued his self-education through independent reading and socializing with a broad group of friends, while maintaining that experience is the only true method of acclimating oneself to the fast-paced and increasingly mechanized world. After his death in 1918, *The Education of Henry Adams* was published commercially, and it received a Pulitzer Prize the following year. It has since been recognized as one of the most insightful works of autobiography in American literature.

HISTORICAL AND LITERARY CONTEXT

Adams's father, Charles Francis Adams, was the U.S. ambassador to Great Britain during the Civil War and a member of the U.S. House of Representatives. This lineage afforded Henry a number of privileges, including access to the best schools in the United States and the opportunity to travel the world as his father's secretary. Adams was keenly aware of the role his family had played in shaping American culture and politics; in his later years, however, he came to question the influence he and his family would have in the coming century. As a journalist in the 1870s and 1880s, he railed against what he perceived as corruption and backward thinking in American politics, but in pondering the need for reform he found that his privileged upbringing and classical education had failed to equip him with the proper framework for contextualizing the technological advancements and rapid changes in social organization that had so thoroughly altered the shape of democracy since the Civil War.

When *The Education* was first privately printed in 1907, new and miraculous inventions were being touted each year, ranging from the telegraph to the telephone, from the airplane to the automobile. The ways in which people communicated and conducted business were changing. Scientific discoveries, such as Albert Einstein's Theory of Relativity, led to a reevaluation of humanity's place in the cosmos, and political power was consolidated in the hands of a few empires even as nationalist independence movements were proliferating. In *The Education,* Adams complains that his education had focused too narrowly on the heroic individual in history and classical works from the literary canon rather than the broad social factors that were changing the world. That his education had been so focused on imparting the "facts" of the world when those facts seemed to be constantly changing left him disillusioned with formal educational practices, particularly in the subject of history. *The Education* also features a number of Adams's friends whom he considers particularly well suited for the twentieth century, including geologist and explorer Clarence King, described as someone who "saw ahead at least one generation further than the text-books."

The Education was written as a sequel to Adams's earlier work, *Mont-Saint-Michel and Chartres: A Study of Thirteenth-Century Unity* (1904), which posits that the architecture of medieval cathedrals reveals an underlying need to project a sense of unity and cohesion into a chaotic and dangerous world. *The Education,* then, can be seen as a similar attempt by Adams to determine his place in the seemingly infinite range of scientific advancements that had only served to make life less certain and more complicated. Adams was also influenced by a number of writers, including his friend Henry James. Noted for his psychological character studies, James is said to have based a number of works, including *Daisy Miller* (1878) and *The Portrait of a Lady* (1881), on Adams's wife, Marian. Like James, Adams attacks the Victorian world and its culture of self-assuredness by questioning the widely held assumption that the Anglo-American civilization represents a high point in the evolution of humankind.

Adams's ability to turn his experiences into a metaphor for an entire generation ensured that *The Education* would find a wide readership into the twenty-first century. As John Carlos Rowe writes in his introduction to *New Essays on* The Education of Henry Adams (1996), "Insofar as the 'Henry Adams' that combines both historical fact and imaginative perception appeals to several generations of readers, 'he' satisfies such readers by offering them a character of abstraction, the American Self." This technique of depicting a large swath of American history through the experiences of one or a handful of representative characters is evident in later works of historical fiction, such as John Dos Passos's *U.S.A. Trilogy* (1930–36) and E. L. Doctorow's *Ragtime* (1975).

THEMES AND STYLE

The central theme of Adams's autobiography is how his education failed to prepare him for an increasingly fragmented world that challenges every citizen to evolve into what Adams calls a "new American"—that is, "a child born of contact between the new and the old energies." These "new energies" are the advancements of science and technology—the symbolic dynamo—that continuously erodes the "old energies" of religion and morality as represented by the image of the Virgin Mary or the classical goddess Venus. Adams believes the battle between dynamo and Virgin had been won handily by the dynamo: "The force of the Virgin was still felt at Lourdes, and seemed to be as potent as X-rays; but in America neither Venus nor Virgin ever had value as force—at most as sentiment." Because science had destroyed the old certainties, and "the new [scientific] universe would know no law that could not be proved by its anti-law," one could no longer depend upon textbooks and teachers to gain knowledge of the universe and must instead rely on self-education and a "new social mind" that can accept contradiction and fragmentation as the norm.

Adams wrote *The Education* to show how inadequately he was prepared for modern life and to outline the qualities of "new Americans" that can prosper in the future. His third-person narrative and self-deprecating style make *The Education* read as one part paean to the old ways of the world and one part cautionary tale about the dangers of clinging to ideas that have proven illusory. He laments that the modern American "had turned his hand and mind to mechanics" and views such a disjointed and random society as "profoundly unmoral, and tend[ing] to discourage effort." But he takes from science the idea that concentrated energy must eventually dissipate and believes that the mindless push for progress and invention will one day cease or at least slow down enough to allow art and morality to reemerge in society.

The Education is notable for its critical, if often humorous, tone and third-person narration. Adams portrays himself and others of his generation as woefully unprepared to face the modern world ("[a]n average mind had succumbed already in 1850; it could no longer understand the problem in 1900") and decries the forces of science and industry for having "[torn] society to pieces and trampled it underfoot," calling himself "one of their earliest victims." Adams saw himself as unable to remove himself from his classical, northeastern values and become the self-made man he dreamt of becoming. As a result he (somewhat sarcastically) portrays himself as a failure and heaps scorn upon himself, his family (particularly his father), and his well-to-do contemporaries.

Statue of Abigail Adams with her son John Quincy Adams in Quincy, Massachusetts. Abigail Adams was the great-grandmother and John Quincy Adams the grandfather of writer and historian Henry Adams, who wrote about his life and American history in *The Education of Henry Adams*. © NORTH WIND PICTURE ARCHIVES/NORTH ALAMY

INDUSTRIALIZATION COMES TO AMERICA

In *The Education of Henry Adams,* Adams discusses his frustration in coming to terms with the Second Industrial Revolution. Also known as the Technological Revolution, this expansion of industry and technology took place in Western Europe, the United States, and Japan and lasted from the second half of the nineteenth century up to World War I. In the United States this revolution led to rapid economic growth and was marked by increased mechanization and improvements in transportation, such as the opening of the Transcontinental Railroad in 1869 and the U.S.-funded Panama Canal in 1914. The number of patents issued for new inventions increased from 36,000 in the years between 1800 and 1860 to 500,000 between 1860 and 1900.

By 1913, the United States produced one-third of the world's industrial products and had become a leader in technological advancements, thanks to visionaries such as Thomas Edison and Henry Ford. This era saw the rise of prominent businessmen such as John D. Rockefeller, Andrew Carnegie, and Cornelius Vanderbilt. A number of prominent companies that still exist in some form were founded at this time, including AT&T, Standard Oil, and General Electric. Despite Adams's anxieties over the consequences of industrialization, he correctly identified the dawn of the twentieth century as a new era, one that would put the United States at the forefront of the industrialized world.

CRITICAL DISCUSSION

Early reviews of *The Education* were almost unanimously positive, with the *North American Review* in 1918 calling it "deep enough and strong enough to be a Bible to some natures" and a *William and Mary Quarterly* reviewer describing it in 1919 as "a very interesting work by a brilliant member of a brilliant family." Adams's contemporary, Supreme Court justice Oliver Wendell Holmes Jr., notoriously disliked the author but praised his evocations of their shared boyhood in Boston. Historian Jackson Lears argues in his article "In Defense of Henry Adams" that Adams was simply a spokesman for an entire generation who had trouble adjusting to a changing world. *The Education of Henry Adams* won a Pulitzer Prize in 1919 and is considered by the Modern Library to be one of the top 100 English-language nonfiction books of the twentieth century.

Despite widespread critical and popular appreciation of *The Education,* the book was not published in an annotated scholarly edition until 1973, a fact that leads Rowe to express his amazement that "readers helped to turn a book of such difficult historical references into a classic in the several reading generations separating its private publication in 1907 and scholarly publication in 1973." This longevity underscores the fact that *The Education of Henry Adams* touches upon something that was as essential to the human condition then as it is now.

In 2007 multiple centennial versions of *The Education of Henry Adams* appeared along with renewed interest in his social commentary. Twentieth-century historians such as Van Wyck Brooks and Richard Hofstadter have tended to view Adams and *The Education* as an example of how the powerful, aristocratic families of the Northeast struggled with the decline of their social and political influence, but many more recent historians see Adams more as a character in history who struggled to adapt to the changing world and fashioned out of his failure to do so a riveting story of America's modernization.

BIBLIOGRAPHY

Sources

Adams, Henry. *The Education of Henry Adams: An Autobiography.* New York: Modern Library, 1999. Print.

Lears, T. J. Jackson. "In Defense of Henry Adams." *Wilson Quarterly* 7.4 (1983): 82–93. Print.

Rev. of *The Education of Henry Adams,* by Henry Adams. *North American Review* 208.757 (1918): 921–26. *JSTOR*. Web. 28 Nov. 2012.

Rev. of *The Education of Henry Adams,* by Henry Adams. *William and Mary Quarterly* 27.3 (1919): 213. *JSTOR*. Web. 28. Nov. 2012.

Rowe, John Carlos. Introduction. *New Essays on* The Education of Henry Adams. Cambridge: Cambridge University Press, 1996. 1–22. Print.

Samuels, Ernest. *Henry Adams.* Cambridge, Mass.: Belknap, 1995. Print.

Wills, Gary. *Henry Adams and the Making of America.* Boston: Houghton Mifflin, 2005. Print.

Further Reading

Adams, Richard C. "Henry Adams's Sympathetic Economy." *Journal of the Midwest Modern Language Association* 34.2 (2001): 29–50. Print.

Brookhiser, Richard. *Americas First Dynasty: The Adamses, 1735–1918.* New York: Free Press, 2002. Print.

O'Toole, Patricia. *The Five of Hearts: An Intimate Portrait of Henry Adams and His Friends, 1880–1918.* New York: Simon & Schuster, 2006. Print.

Pykstra, Natalie. *Clover Adams: A Gilded and Heartbreaking Life.* New York: Houghton Mifflin & Harcourt, 2012. Print.

Simpson, Brooks D. *The Political Education of Henry Adams.* Columbia: University of South Carolina Press, 1996. Print.

Rodney Harris

An Egyptian Childhood

Taha Hussein

OVERVIEW

First published serially in 1926 and 1927, *An Egyptian Childhood,* the first volume of the autobiography of Egyptian luminary Taha Hussein (1889–1973), is one of the best-known and most important works of modern Arabic fiction. Celebrated as a literary historian, social and education reformer, and author, Hussein (also often spelled "Husayn") is perhaps most famous for his work in modern literary criticism and the role he played in the birth of modern Arabic literature. He was the first to receive a PhD from the newly established Egyptian University, which would later become Cairo University; the first chair of Arabic literature at Cairo University; the first to receive the Egyptian state prize for literature; and the first Egyptian nominated for a Nobel Prize in Literature. Hussein spent several years studying in France, and he served as the president of the Arabic Language Academy and the Minister of Education in Egypt. Born into a poor Upper Egyptian family in 1889 in the early years of the British occupation, Hussein, the seventh of his father's thirteen children, was blind from an early age. *An Egyptian Childhood,* which follows the first thirteen years of Hussein's life (1889–1902), exposes the social norms and expectations that defined the life of the blind in Egypt at the turn of the twentieth century and demonstrates Hussein's defiance, from a young age, of these limitations.

Hussein wrote *An Egyptian Childhood* while caught up in controversy over his innovational work in literary history. Scholars have speculated that when he failed to undermine entrenched belief systems and intellectual perspectives through direct challenge, he turned to literature as a subtly subversive method of expression. *An Egyptian Childhood* was generally well received by critics, and it was translated into English in 1932. Hussein is known as the Dean of Arabic Literature, and his autobiography continues to occupy a central place in the field to this day.

HISTORICAL AND LITERARY CONTEXT

An Egyptian Childhood offers a picture of social, cultural, religious, and educational life in Upper Egypt at the turn of the twentieth century, during the early years of the British occupation, which began in 1882 and stretched until the 1952 Egyptian Revolution. The autobiography, told from the young protagonist's perspective, pays little attention to the contemporary political milieu, providing greater insight into the educational history of the period. In Upper Egypt, early learning took place at the *kuttab,* or Qur'an school, which emphasized basic Islamic education along with memorization of the Islamic holy book. The teachers of these classes were often blind—including the protagonist's own teacher—hinting at the path Hussein's life might have taken had he not rebelled against societal expectations. The autobiography ends with Hussein's first days at al-Azhar University, the center of Islamic learning, in Cairo, and reveals that religion, philology, and grammar were the fundamentals of education in turn-of-the-century Egypt.

With the outbreak of World War I in 1914, Egypt became a British protectorate and was placed under martial law. Although the 1919 Egyptian Revolution failed to end the protectorate, the British unilaterally declared Egyptian independence in 1922. However, the restrictive conditions outlined by the British made Egypt independent in name only. Despite the continuing British presence, a constitution was proclaimed in 1923 and the first parliamentary elections were held in 1924. In 1926, months before the first installment of *An Egyptian Childhood* appeared in Egyptian journal *al-Hilal,* Hussein's book on pre-Islamic poetry elicited sharp criticism by questioning traditional understandings of the field, and Hussein was accused of blasphemy for treating the Qur'an as a historical document. Egyptian journal *Al-Manar* charged that Hussein was "blind of both sight and mind," and he fled to France, where he dictated *An Egyptian Childhood* in just nine days. The childhood autobiography was immediately and immensely successful.

An Egyptian Childhood is part of a long Arabic autobiographical tradition, although the genre had fallen out of favor in the preceding generation. The text contains many of the common motifs of premodern Arabic autobiography, such as the incorporation of humorous childhood anecdotes even in works with an otherwise serious tone. The autobiographical tradition had been interrupted following the 1898 publication of Egyptian poet Ahmad Shawqi's *al-Shawqiyyat,* a poetry anthology that also included a short description of the poet's life. Discussion of the text itself became the forum for a broader intellectual debate over the literary innovation and cultural change that

❖ **Key Facts**

Time Period:
Mid-20th Century

Relevant Historical Events:
British colonial occupation of Egypt; failed Egyptian revolution of 1919

Nationality:
Egyptian

Keywords:
coming-of-age; colonialism; fiction

A boy fishing on a canal in the Nile Valley, Egypt. In An Egyptian Childhood, *Taha Hussein describes his boyhood experiences growing up along the Nile River.* © ERICH LESSING/ART RESOURCE, NY

characterized the nineteenth-century *nahda,* or "awakening," and Shawqi was denounced for having written a work perceived as self-praise rather than humbly allowing others to comment on his life and oeuvre. Early luminaries such as sixteenth-century jurist Jalal al-Din al-Suyuti had faced similar criticism. After *al-Shawqiyyat,* no more autobiographies were published in Arabic, although several were written, until Hussein's *An Egyptian Childhood* appeared.

In the wake of *An Egyptian Childhood*'s success, the Arabic autobiographical tradition regained its lost momentum, and Hussein's literary innovations influenced the course of its development. The genre flourished within Egypt in particular, encompassing Islamic reformer Rashid Rida's 1934 autobiography as well as Islamic feminist Huda Shaarawi's memoirs, written in the 1940s but first published in 1981. Hussein's text blurred the line between fiction and nonfiction by blending elements of the novel with autobiography, a technique widely imitated by later writers. Jabra Ibrahim Jabra uses this technique, for example, in *The First Well: A Bethlehem Boyhood* (1987). Today *An Egyptian Childhood* is required reading in many schools across the Arab world, and scholars continue to consider it one of the most important twentieth-century works of Arabic literature.

THEMES AND STYLE

Hussein's autobiography is a coming-of-age story centrally concerned with the protagonist's quiet refusal to let his inability to see define him or limit his life. The text traces the protagonist's discovery of his own blindness and explores the social and professional ramifications of the disability in Hussein's historical, economic, and cultural context. The protagonist feels "resentment" and, in time, "a silent, but heartfelt, grief" when he realizes that his brothers and sisters treat him with "a sympathy tainted with revulsion" because they "[see] what he [does] not see." At the age of nine the protagonist memorizes the Qur'an for the first time, although he will have to memorize it twice more before he retains it, and the escapades of this process form the bulk of the narrative. The blind sheikh who oversees his training offers a glimpse of the life Hussein is expected to lead. However, by the time the narrator first encounters the thirteen-year-old protagonist at al-Azhar, he is "conspicuous" but "[steps] unfalteringly and [does] not hesitate in his walk, and there [does] not appear on his face that darkness which usually covers the faces of the blind."

An Egyptian Childhood is related in the third-person voice by a narrator who recounts episodes from the life of a young blind boy, ostensibly Hussein, to the protagonist's nine-year-old daughter so that she, and of course the audience, will understand the challenges he has overcome and the importance of his accomplishments. The narrator tells the young girl, "Your father has spent every effort he possesses and has gone to almost unendurable pains to spare you the life he had when he was a lad." Hussein distinguishes between himself as author, himself as narrator, and himself as protagonist in the text, making it difficult to definitively determine if *An Egyptian Childhood* is autobiographical or a work of fiction. Neither the narrator nor the protagonist are ever named, with the narrator referring to the protagonist as "the lad," "the youth," or "our friend." However, it was not uncommon in the Arabic autobiographical tradition for writers to speak of themselves in the third person, and the authors of *Interpreting the Self: Autobiography in the Arabic Literary Tradition* (2001) argue that the inclusion of personal, potentially embarrassing anecdotes about the protagonist's childhood was a tool used to "establish the autobiographical authority of the text and mark it as distinct from a biography."

Consistent with Hussein's other writings, *An Egyptian Childhood* is notable for its skilled use of ornate language, and some scholars have credited its style for the text's enduring status as a classic. In *The Origins of Modern Arabic Fiction* (1997), Matti Moosa notes that "Taha Husayn's literary style will always be considered among the best in Arabic literature. In his fiction, however, this style seems to overwhelm the structure of the work and diminish the significance of the characters' actions." The autobiography is full of rich descriptions, and Hussein draws deeply from local superstitions and folk tales as well as from his own imagination. Describing the protagonist's perception of his surroundings as a young child, Hussein writes that the world of the nearby canal "was inhabited by various strange beings without number, among which were crocodiles which swallowed people in one mouthful, and also enchanted folk who lived under the water all the bright day and during the dark night."

CRITICAL DISCUSSION

Upon the serialized publication of *An Egyptian Childhood*, the text met with enormous popular and critical success. Writing in the *Bulletin of the School of Oriental Studies* in 1929, H. A. R. Gibb called *An Egyptian Childhood* "a work which is justly praised for its depth of feeling and for the truth of its descriptions, and has a good claim to be regarded as the finest work of art yet produced in modern Egyptian literature." Following the translation of *An Egyptian Childhood* into English, Roger Allen, reviewing the text in *World Literature Today*, noted that it had "long been considered the first great classic of modern Arabic prose literature."

Arabic autobiography and fiction began to flourish in the 1930s and 1940s, especially within Egypt, but *An Egyptian Childhood* maintained its canonical standing and remains today one of the most famous works of modern Arabic literature. Hussein's autobiography was adapted into a film in 1959 and made into a thirteen-episode television special in 1980. It has been translated into many languages, including French, Russian, Chinese, and Hebrew, and continues to attract scholarly attention in both Arabic and English.

Hussein's autobiography is often studied within the framework of literary history. The 2001 study *Interpreting the Self: Autobiography in the Arabic Literary Tradition*, edited by Dwight Reynolds, challenges the common assumptions that modern Arabic autobiography "has simply been 'borrowed' from the West" and that the genesis of *An Egyptian Childhood* can therefore be traced to the European tradition that Hussein encountered during his studies in France. Taking into consideration his "vast and intimate knowledge of pre-Islamic, classical, and medieval Arabic literature," the authors argue that "[w]hen viewed as part of the Arabic autobiographical tradition … his autobiography seems to be the culmination of a centuries-long chain of texts."

BATTLE DAYS

The Arabic title of Hussein's autobiography, *al-Ayyam*, literally translates as "The Days," and an English-language collection of his three autobiographical works, *An Egyptian Childhood, The Stream of Days,* and *A Passage to France*, was published under this title in 1997. However, "al-Ayyam" also evokes *Ayyam al-'Arab,* or the "Battle Days of the Arabs," a genre encompassing pre-Islamic oral accounts of intertribal conflict, as well as the corresponding poetry. These traditions differed between tribes and were passed down from generation to generation to preserve the narrative of heroism that would help shape collective identity.

As a literary historian, Hussein was certainly familiar with *Ayyam al-'Arab*. Translating the title of his childhood autobiography as "Battle Days" draws attention to several important features of the modern text. First, the work itself signals a shift from oral to written expression in the life of the blind author, who was forced to rely during the actual days of his childhood on orality. Second, while the "Battle Days of the Arabs" consisted of stories related with the goal of consolidating tribal identity, Hussein's "Battle Days" contains episodes that contributed to the development of his individual identity. Finally, physical heroism and strength in battle in pre-Islamic Arabia give way in *al-Ayyam* to intellectual bravery and the struggle against tradition.

Scholars have also been interested in *An Egyptian Childhood*'s treatment of blindness. Fedwa Malti-Douglas's *Blindness and Autobiography: Al-Ayyam of Taha Husayn* (1988), the first book-length English-language study on modern Arabic literature treating a single text, notes the tension between physical "personal blindness" and "social blindness," or "identification with the social category and the social roles of the blind," in the autobiography. Malti-Douglas questions readings of *An Egyptian Childhood* that insist it was born out of a straightforward desire to challenge tradition. She suggests instead that Hussein's lifelong defiance of the limitations of social blindness in Egypt drove his work.

BIBLIOGRAPHY

Sources

Allen, Roger. Rev. of *An Egyptian Childhood*, by Taha Hussein. *World Literature Today* 56.3 (1982): 566. Print.

Gibb, H. A. R. "Studies in Contemporary Arabic Literature." *Bulletin of the School of Oriental Studies, University of London* 5.3 (1929): 445–66. Print.

Malti-Douglas, Fedwa. *Blindness and Autobiography: Al-Ayyam of Taha Husayn.* Princeton, N.J.: Princeton University Press, 1988. Print.

Moosa, Matti. *The Origins of Modern Arabic Fiction.* 2nd ed. Boulder, Colo.: Lynne Rienner, 1997. Print.

Reynolds, Dwight F., ed. *Interpreting the Self: Autobiography in the Arabic Literary Tradition.* Berkeley: University of California Press, 2001. Print.

Further Reading

Hussein, Taha. *The Days.* Trans. E. H. Paxton, Wayment. Cairo: The American University in Cairo Press, 2001. Print.

———. *The Future of Culture in Egypt.* Trans. Sidney Glazer. New York: Octagon, 1975. Print.

Mahmoudi, Abdelrashid. *Taha Husain's Education: From the Azhar to the Sorbonne.* Richmond, U.K.: Curzon, 1998. Print.

Mitchell, Timothy. *Colonising Egypt.* Berkeley: University of California Press, 1991. Print.

Shaarawi, Huda. *Harem Years: The Memoirs of an Egyptian Feminist, 1879–1924.* Trans. Margot Badran. London: Virago, 1986. Print.

Allison Blecker

Fun Home
A Family Tragicomic
Alison Bechdel

OVERVIEW

Alison Bechdel's *Fun Home: A Family Tragicomic*, a graphic memoir published in 2006, tells the story of Bechdel's childhood in a small Pennsylvania town, focusing particularly on her relationship with her distant father, an English teacher, amateur historical restorer, and part-time funeral home director. Moving freely back and forth through time, the narrative depicts Bechdel's chilly upbringing and the complex, frequently dysfunctional relationships between her family members. A key development in Bechdel's coming of age is her discovery, shortly after coming out to her parents as a lesbian during her college years, that her father is a closeted gay man who has had multiple affairs with teenage boys, including some of his own high school students. The impact of this revelation, and of her father's subsequent death in a possible suicide, is a constant presence throughout Bechdel's ruminations on her upbringing.

One of a growing number of prominent gay- and lesbian-themed American comics published since the 1970s, *Fun Home* was also a high-profile example of the relatively new genre of autobiography in a graphic format. The book became a best seller and received widespread critical acclaim, despite the occasional controversy over its sexual themes and occasionally graphic sex scenes. It remains one of the most highly regarded autobiographical narratives published during the first decade of the new millennium, and its sophistication and thematic depth has contributed significantly to the increasing respectability of comics as a literary and artistic medium.

HISTORICAL AND LITERARY CONTEXT

In the decades leading up to the publication of *Fun Home*, issues of sexual orientation were often fraught with controversy and prejudice in the American consciousness. In many communities—especially small towns that lacked cohesive subcultural groups and diversity—homosexuality carried a debilitating social stigma, resulting in gay and lesbian individuals concealing, denying, or suppressing their sexual orientations. The U.S. military's "Don't Ask, Don't Tell" policy, which allowed gay and lesbian citizens to serve only if they kept their orientations undisclosed, gave official sanction to the perception of homosexuality as a dark secret to be concealed. Likewise, the ongoing debates about the validity of same-sex marriage, as well as acts of hate crime such as the torture and murder of gay University of Wyoming student Matthew Shepard in 1998, demonstrate the extent to which homosexuality was thought by many to be inherently illegitimate.

By the time *Fun Home* was published in 2006, cultural acceptance of homosexuality had advanced significantly, though it remained a controversial and divisive issue in many quarters. In many ways, Bechdel's memoir serves as a testament to the effects of past societal attitudes and prejudices on individual lives, especially in the sections dealing explicitly with her father Bruce's clandestine sexuality. The book also emphasizes the resonance and interconnections between different periods in the history of gay and lesbian experience through its recurring motif of Bechdel's desire for connection with the history of her deceased father, as well as through direct juxtapositions between her own sexual coming of age and Bruce's more tragic experience.

Bechdel's memoir emerged from a fertile milieu of autobiographical comics, as well as from a tradition of gay- and lesbian-themed comics, mostly from underground and alternative presses, that began to proliferate in the later decades of the twentieth century. Bechdel's own *Dykes to Watch Out For*, a biweekly comic strip begun in 1983, was a landmark in comics dealing with gay and lesbian themes, as was the work of Howard Cruse, whose 1995 graphic novel *Stuck Rubber Baby* was an avowed influence on Bechdel's memoir. Likewise, works such as Harvey Pekar's *American Splendor*, Art Spiegelman's *Maus*, and Marjane Satrapi's *Persepolis* all mined their authors' lives (and, in the case of *Maus*, the lives of the author's parents) for material, using the visual medium of comics as a platform for autobiographical reflections.

Fun Home brought Bechdel, already an author of renown in the comics field, greater mainstream recognition and further solidified the literary respectability of the graphic memoir genre. A part of the alternative comics tradition that emerged in the 1980s in the wake of the underground comix movement of the late 1960s and early 1970s, *Fun Home* also contributed to the ongoing commercial success and visibility of non-superhero comics. Introspective, autobiographical comics

❖ *Key Facts*

Time Period:
Early 21st Century

Relevant Historical Events:
Bechdel's father commits suicide; Bechdel comes out as a lesbian

Nationality:
American

Keywords:
lesbianism; alienation; graphic autobiography

COMING OF AGE

In her graphic novel Fun Home: A Family Tragicomic, *Alison Bechdel describes her father's obsession with restoring and decorating their large Victorian home. Depicted here is the sitting room of the Pines Inn in Pine Plains, New York, a restored Victorian mansion.* © ELLIOTT KAUFMAN/BEATEWORKS/CORBIS

continue to proliferate, and Bechdel herself published a second graphic memoir in 2012, titled *Are You My Mother?: A Comic Drama,* which focuses this time on Bechdel's relationship with her mother.

THEMES AND STYLE

A central theme of *Fun Home* is the effect of a person's sexual orientation on both personal development and family life. Bechdel sees Bruce's obsessively meticulous personality, manifested in his "monomaniacal restoration" of the family's large Victorian home, through the lens of his continual efforts to keep his secrets concealed. Speaking of her own burgeoning distaste for her father's ornamental aestheticism, Bechdel observes that "my father began to seem morally suspect to me long before I knew that he actually had a dark secret. He used his skillful artifice not to make things, but to make things appear to be what they were not." Her depiction of her own road to sexual maturity, emphasizing both its similarities and dissimilarities to her father's experiences, reaches a turning point with her decision to come out to her parents, followed by the revelation of her father's secrets. These personal disclosures contrast sharply with the secrecy and self-hatred dominating Bruce's life and foreground Bechdel's belief in publicly acknowledging one's own sexual orientation.

A primary inspiration for *Fun Home* was Bechdel's discovery of a photograph of one of her father's lovers. The artistic process prompted by this discovery allowed her to reflect on the events of her life and come to a fuller understanding of her relationship with her father. The book's recursive narrative structure demonstrates this intent: instead of presenting a straightforward chronological account of events, as in traditional autobiographies, she frequently revisits the same events from different perspectives, making it clear that the book was written not merely as a record of those events but as a sustained meditation on them. Archival documents, such as the aforementioned photograph and Bechdel's own diaries, are frequently incorporated into the text, often in ways that foreground the unreliability of historical reconstruction and autobiographical narrative: "By the end of November, my earnest daily entries had given way to the implicit lie of the blank page, and weeks at a time are left unrecorded."

Stylistically, *Fun Home* is marked by copious literary references, a fact that reflects the centrality of literature to the Bechdel family, as well as the family's emotional distance. Literature is the focus for the passionate emotional expression that the family cannot bestow on one another. For example, Bruce's youthful letters to his future wife are influenced by his reading of F. Scott Fitzgerald's biography: "Dad's letters to Mom, which had not been particularly demonstrative up to this point, began to grow lush with Fitzgeraldesque sentiment." Bechdel constantly uses literary works as a lens through which to examine her parents' experiences: "My parents are most real to me in fictional terms. And perhaps my cool aesthetic distance itself does more to convey the arctic climate of our family than any particular literary comparison." Likewise, her realization of her own sexual orientation occurs while reading, and her subsequent odyssey of self-discovery is explicitly bound up with her readings on homosexuality.

CRITICAL DISCUSSION

Fun Home met with popular and critical acclaim upon its publication. Reviews highlighted the book's literary complexity, noting Bechdel's formal ambition and careful interconnections of theme and literary resonance. Tom Gatti, writing in the London *Times*, wrote that "the text is a joy: as perceptive and intricate as the illustration. This must be one of the most literary comic books yet produced." Likewise, Sean Wilsey in the *New York Times Book Review* noted that Bechdel's "rich language and precise images combine to create a lush piece of work—a memoir where concision and detail are melded for maximum, obsessive density."

Since its initial publication, *Fun Home* has developed a reputation as a major work of graphic autobiography, joining such works as Spiegelman's *Maus* and Satrapi's *Persepolis* as one of the most well-regarded and widely read works within that genre. It remains by far Bechdel's most popular work, tending to overshadow her (generally well-received) prior and subsequent projects. It has also been the subject of a large amount of critical scholarship, much of which focuses on the text's queer and gender-related themes, as well as the ways in which the book's visual format contributes to its meaning and sets it apart from standard prose memoirs.

Scholarship on *Fun Home* tends to focus on its formal characteristics, pointing out the ways in which its treatment of autobiographical narrative is unique to the medium of comics. An example of this trend is Robyn Warhol's essay in *College Literature*, which analyzes the book in light of contemporary theories of narrative, observing that within the text "both the visual and the verbal subdivide into multiple separate and overlapping narrative tracks, creating narrative elements that 'work with' the space between image and words." Other criticism scrutinizes the book through a queer studies lens. Ann Cvetkovich's article in *Women's Studies Quarterly* analyzes Bechdel's use of archival material in order to "articulate how Bechdel uses this insurgent genre [i.e., graphic narrative] to provide a queer perspective that is missing from public discourse about both historical trauma and sexual politics."

BIBLIOGRAPHY

Sources

Bechdel, Alison. *Fun Home: A Family Tragicomic.* Boston: Houghton Mifflin, 2006. Print.

Cvetkovich, Ann. "Drawing the Archive in Alison Bechdel's *Fun Home.*" *Women's Studies Quarterly* 36.1–2 (2008): 111–28. *JSTOR*. Web. 22 Oct. 2012.

Gatti, Tom. Rev. of *Fun Home*, by Alison Bechdel. *Times.* Times Newspapers Limited, 16 Dec. 2006. Web. 22 Oct. 2012.

Warhol, Robyn. "The Space Between: A Narrative Approach to Alison Bechdel's *Fun Home.*" *College Literature* 38.3 (2011): 1–20. *MasterFILE Premier.* Web. 22 Oct. 2012.

Wilsey, Sean. "The Things They Buried." Rev. of *Fun Home*, by Alison Bechdel. *New York Times Book Review.* The New York Times Company, 18 Jun. 2006. Web. 14 Nov. 2012.

Further Reading

Bechdel, Alison. *Are You My Mother?: A Comic Drama.* Boston: Houghton Mifflin Harcourt, 2012. Print.

———. *The Essential Dykes to Watch Out For.* Boston: Houghton Mifflin Harcourt, 2008. Print.

Cruse, Howard. *Stuck Rubber Baby.* New York: Paradox, 1995. Print.

Fantasia, Annette. "The Paterian Bildungsroman Reenvisioned: 'Brain-Building' in Alison Bechdel's *Fun Home: A Family Tragicomic.*" *Criticism* 53.1 (2011): 83–97. Print.

Freedman, Ariela. "Drawing on Modernism in Alison Bechdel's *Fun Home.*" *Journal of Modern Literature* 32.4 (2009): 125–40. Print.

Lemberg, Jennifer. "Closing the Gap in Alison Bechdel's *Fun Home.*" *Women's Studies Quarterly* 36.1–2 (2008): 129–40. Print.

Scherr, Rebecca. "Queering the Family Album: The Re-orientation of Things in Alison Bechdel's *Fun Home.*" *Forum for World Literature Studies* 3.1 (2011): 40–51. Print.

Tolmie, Jane. "Modernism, Memory and Desire: Queer Cultural Production in Alison Bechdel's *Fun Home.*" *Topia* 22 (2009): 77–95. Print.

Watson, Julia. "Autographic Disclosures and Genealogies of Desire in Alison Bechdel's *Fun Home.*" *Biography* 31.1 (2008): 27–58. Print.

DYKES TO WATCH OUT FOR

Long before *Fun Home*'s publication, Bechdel had already attained considerable eminence within the alternative comics field, primarily on the strength of her long-running biweekly comic strip *Dykes to Watch Out For,* which she wrote and drew from 1983 to 2008. The strip, one of the first and most popular nationally syndicated comics to directly and regularly address queer concerns, follows the lives of a group of lesbian friends, documenting their evolving relationships, personal and professional travails, and reactions to contemporary issues and cultural trends.

The strip ran in dozens of independent gay and lesbian publications and was particularly appreciated for its overt engagement with social and political issues. Perhaps the most widely disseminated example of this engagement was an installment that introduced a sort of litmus test to evaluate the representation of female characters in films. This test has since come into wide use as a critical barometer and is now generally known as the "Bechdel test." The strip was suspended indefinitely in 2008 so that Bechdel could devote more time to completing *Are You My Mother?* but it remains one of the most venerable works of its kind, and the acclaim it accrued throughout its decades-long run paved the way for *Fun Home*'s massive success.

James Overholltzer

Incidents in the Life of a Slave Girl, Written by Herself

Harriet A. Jacobs

✤ *Key Facts*

Time Period:
Mid-20th Century

Relevant Historical Events:
Passage of the Fugitive Slave Law; growth of the abolition movement

Nationality:
American

Keywords:
abolitionism; slavery; feminism

OVERVIEW

Harriet A. Jacobs's *Incidents in the Life of a Slave Girl, Written by Herself,* first published in 1861, is one of the most important slave narratives written by a woman, and it played an important role in the abolitionist movement. Published four years before the Thirteenth Amendment ended slavery, Jacobs's autobiography advocates for equality under the law, irrespective of one's race, class, or gender. Aimed at stirring to action her white female audience in the North, *Incidents* presents slavery as a pervasive attack on domestic life, arguing that the power slave owners wielded over unprotected human beings led not only to fierce cruelty but also to unrestrained licentiousness that destroyed both white and black families. Unlike slave narratives published by men—such as *Narrative of the Life of Frederick Douglass* (1845), which values physical bravery—Jacobs's autobiography focuses on the feminine value of motherhood, showing the heroic efforts of an enslaved mother to protect her children.

Incidents is defined by the generic conventions that characterize literature about slave life, such as a focus on scenes of physical and psychological violence, including torture; accounts of the breaking up of families through the sale of children and spouses; a yearning for literacy and an even deeper yearning for freedom; observations on the moral depravity that ownership of human beings brings upon the owner; and accounts of triumphs over adversity. The work was sold in the Anti-Slavery Office in New York, and it allowed Jacobs to become even more involved in practical efforts of assisting runaway slaves.

HISTORICAL AND LITERARY CONTEXT

In the 1830s the northern states intensified their efforts to abolish slavery in the South. The abolitionist movement started within the churches: during a religious revivalism, an increasing number of Americans started believing that slavery was the product of sin. In 1833 the American Anti-Slavery Society was established. It recruited tens of thousands of members, religious or not. For a number of years, the society refused to accept women, who responded by starting their own local groups. Fugitive slaves soon joined the movement, and their testimony played a crucial role in its growth. The abolitionists' efforts included public lectures by whites and fugitive slaves (such as Douglass); newspapers (the white abolitionist Lydia Maria Child edited one for almost two years); and the purchase and distribution of copies of narratives of fugitive slaves and "gift books," such as Maria Weston Chapman and Julia Griffith's literary collections titled *The Liberty Bell,* which for several years were sold as part of fund-raising efforts. The germ of Jacobs's own narrative started as a series of letters to the *New York Daily Tribune* in 1853, in which she identified herself as "A Fugitive Slave" or "Fugitive."

When Jacobs's autobiography was published, it was standard practice to include a preface written by a white writer, who thus agreed to serve as a guarantor of the truthfulness of the account. *Incidents* included a preface by Child, who also helped Jacobs edit her story. She encouraged Jacobs to add a chapter on the Nat Turner insurrection and to end the autobiography on a personal note rather than a public chapter on the abolitionist John Brown. The preface attested to the trustworthiness of Jacobs's account, pointing out that her editorial interventions had been minimal. Child unabashedly draws attention to the "monstrous features" of slavery, especially sexual violence. Running the risk of being accused "of indecorum for presenting these pages to the public," Child points out that she does so "for the sake of my sisters in bondage," arguing that American women should not let mere delicacy be a deterrent for action.

Jacobs's autobiography follows in the footsteps of major slave narratives such as Olaudah Equiano's *The Interesting Narrative Life of Olaudah Equiano* (1789), Theodore Weld's *American Slavery as It Is* (1838), and the groundbreaking *Narrative of the Life of Frederick Douglass* (1845). *Incidents* appeared in print two years after another female author, Harriet E. Wilson, published *Our Nig* (1859); unlike Wilson's fictional narrative, which was largely overlooked by its intended black audience, Jacobs's account gained immediate recognition with black readers, precisely for its focus on real-life experience.

Incidents is a landmark in African American writing, and it left its imprint not only on the autobiographical genre but on fictional narratives as well. In the persona of Linda Brent, a fictional name Jacobs assumed in order to protect family and friends (her own name did not

A slave girl fans dinner guests on a Southern plantation in this hand-colored woodcut. After escaping from her life as a slave in North Carolina, Harriet Jacobs drew attention to the plight of women held in bondage, including sexual abuse and the sale of their children. © AP IMAGES/NORTH WIND PICTURE ARCHIVES

appear on the cover of the book), Jacobs constructs a resilient and highly articulate woman who values freedom, family, and community rather than a passive victim of seduction or aggression. *Incidents* may have influenced Frances Ellen Watkins Harper's *Iola Leroy; Or, Shadows Uplifted* (1892), a novel about a mixed-race woman and the social issues she faces in the antebellum South.

THEMES AND STYLE

The main theme in Jacobs's autobiography is the incalculable value of freedom. The narrative is an unwavering condemnation of slavery, denouncing its underpinnings in the ideology of white supremacy, patriarchal institutions, and willful distortions of Christianity. "My mistress had taught me the precepts of God's Word: 'Thou shall love thy neighbor as thyself,'" Jacobs points out. "But I was her slave, and I suppose she did not recognize me as her neighbor." Like *Narrative of the Life of Frederick Douglass*, *Incidents* expresses surprise that visitors coming from the free states could possibly imagine that slavery is "a beautiful patriarchal institution." In a series of rhetorical questions, Jacobs offers readers a graphic and highly effectual backdrop to her own story: "What does *he* [the visitor from the North] know … of mothers shrieking for their children, torn from their arms by slave traders? Of young girls dragged down into moral filth? Of pools of blood around the whipping post? … Of men screwed into cotton gins to die?"

Jacobs's purpose in writing *Incidents* was, as she states in the preface, to "add my testimony to that of abler pens…. Only by experience can any one realize how deep, and dark, and foul is that pit of abominations." She often addresses the reader directly in order to appeal to her audience's humanity and sense of justice and in anticipation of potential moral judgments directed at her: "If you want to be fully convinced of the abominations of slavery, go on a southern plantation, and call yourself a negro trader. Then there will be no concealment; and you will see and hear things that will seem to you impossible among human beings with immortal souls." Admitting that she had overstepped the moral standards of the time, Jacobs is extremely reticent in her account of her voluntary sexual liaison with a white neighbor. Her portrayal of her heroic struggle to protect her children from being sold into slavery, which included hiding in her grandmother's garret before her escape to the free northern states, is designed, in part, to atone for her sexual past. Nevertheless, although she asks her white female audience to overlook this episode in her life, she manages to integrate it in her overall struggle for freedom: "There is something akin to freedom in

PRIMARY SOURCE

EXCERPT FROM *INCIDENTS IN THE LIFE OF A SLAVE GIRL, WRITTEN BY HERSELF*

During the first years of my service in Dr. Flint's family, I was accustomed to share some indulgences with the children of my mistress. Though this seemed to me no more than right, I was grateful for it, and tried to merit the kindness by the faithful discharge of my duties. But I now entered on my fifteenth year—a sad epoch in the life of a slave girl. My master began to whisper foul words in my ear. Young as I was, I could not remain ignorant of their import. I tried to treat them with indifference or contempt. The master's age, my extreme youth, and the fear that his conduct would be reported to my grandmother, made him bear this treatment for many months. He was a crafty man, and resorted to many means to accomplish his purposes. Sometimes he had stormy, terrific ways, that made his victims tremble; sometimes he assumed a gentleness that he thought must surely subdue. Of the two, I preferred his stormy moods, although they left me trembling. He tried his utmost to corrupt the pure principles my grandmother had instilled. He peopled my young mind with unclean images, such as only a vile monster could think of. I turned from him with disgust and hatred. But he was my master. I was compelled to live under the same roof with him—where I saw a man forty years my senior daily violating the most sacred commandments of nature. He told me I was his property; that I must be subject to his will in all things. My soul revolted against the mean tyranny. But where could I turn for protection? No matter whether the slave girl be as black as ebony or as fair as her mistress. In either case, there is no shadow of law to protect her from insult, from violence, or even from death; all these are inflicted by fiends who bear the shape of men. The mistress, who ought to protect the helpless victim, has no other feelings towards her but those of jealousy and rage. The degradation, the wrongs, the vices, that grow out of slavery, are more than I can describe. They are greater than you would willingly believe. Surely, if you credited one half the truths that are told you concerning the helpless

having a lover who has no control over you, except that which he gains by kindness and attachment."

Incidents combines the structure of a slave narrative with the conventions of a sentimentalist novel, while showing that a former slave's coming-of-age narrative is also one of a loss of innocence. "I knew what I did, and I did it with deliberate calculation," she writes about her choice to have a sexual relationship, mournfully adding that slavery offered her no alternative. The language of the autobiography is rich with allusions and direct quotations from the Bible, which both expose the hypocrisy of slave owners' distortions of Christianity and offer the narrator a framework for understanding suffering and forgiveness. Some modern critics consider the tone to be morbid, but the narrative is in fact steeped in the vibrant energies of antebellum literature.

CRITICAL DISCUSSION

Incidents was immediately recognized as an important contribution to African American writing. In 1861 the *Weekly Anglo-African* hailed it as "the 'oft-told tale' of American slavery, in another and more revolting phase than that which is generally seen: More revolting," the reviewer argues, "because it is of the spirit and not the flesh," depicting "the terrible sufferings endured by and inflicted upon women, by a system which legalized concubinage, and offers a premium to licentiousness." The *National Anti-Slavery Standard* compared it to *Uncle Tom's Cabin*, while gently complaining about several instances of overt moralizing.

Ironically, the eloquence of Jacobs's narrative contributed to the oblivion into which it fell before the turn of the century. Many early-twentieth-century readers imagined that the autobiography was in fact a work of fiction by the editor (Child) or that it may have been based on Jacobs's life but had been written by Child herself. The autobiography was rediscovered in part during the civil rights movement, while doubts about its authorship still lingered. It was only in 1981, when Jacobs's letters became available, that Jean Fagan Yellin was able to certify beyond doubt that *Incidents* was, indeed, written by Jacobs, and thus fully restore it to critical and public acclaim.

Scholars continue to devote a great deal of attention to the choices that structure Jacobs's account of major episodes in her life. In an essay written in 2010, Novian Whitsitt speculates that Jacobs's elliptical account of her sexual past is based on the African American cultural tradition of "masking," which is a "technique of double meaning that allows the story teller to make accessible a hidden message only to those readers attuned to the secretive signs embedded within the story." Many critics, however, have focused on what Jacobs's narrative openly presents. Sally Gomaa's 2009 essay draws attention to the authors' skillful appropriation of the sentimental discourse of the time, which objectified the slave by focusing on the spectacle of the body in pain, in order to present herself as both spectacle and spectator, both object of slavery and empowered subject of her narrative as well millions suffering in this cruel bondage, you at the north would not help to tighten the yoke. You surely would refuse to do for the master, on your own soil, the mean and cruel work which trained bloodhounds and the lowest class of whites do for him at the south.

Every where the years bring to all enough of sin and sorrow; but in slavery the very dawn of life is darkened by these shadows. Even the little child, who is accustomed to wait on her mistress and her children, will learn, before she is twelve years old, why it is that her mistress hates such and such a one among the slaves. Perhaps the child's own mother is among those hated ones. She listens to violent outbreaks of jealous passion, and cannot help understanding what is the cause. She will become prematurely knowing in evil things. Soon she will learn to tremble when she hears her master's footfall. She will be compelled to realize that she is no longer a child. If God has bestowed beauty upon her, it will prove her greatest curse. That which commands admiration in the white woman only hastens the degradation of the female slave. I know that some are too much brutalized by slavery to feel the humiliation of their position; but many slaves feel it most acutely, and shrink from the memory of it. I cannot tell how much I suffered in the presence of these wrongs, nor how I am still pained by the retrospect. My master met me at every turn, reminding me that I belonged to him, and swearing by heaven and earth that he would compel me to submit to him. If I went out for a breath of fresh air, after a day of unwearied toil, his footsteps dogged me. If I knelt by my mother's grave, his dark shadow fell on me even there. The light heart which nature had given me became heavy with sad forebodings. The other slaves in my master's house noticed the change. Many of them pitied me; but none dared to ask the cause. They had no need to inquire. They knew too well the guilty practices under that roof; and they were aware that to speak of them was an offence that never went unpunished.

SOURCE: Jacobs, Harriet A. *Incidents in the Life of a Slave Girl, Written by Herself.* Ed. L. Maria Child. Boston: Published for the Author, 1861.

---

as her life. In a tribute to her life and writing, Jacobs's twentieth-century editor, Yellin, points out that Jacobs was "in [Ralph Waldo] Emerson's sense 'representative'; expressing the idea of the struggle for freedom, her life empowers others."

BIBLIOGRAPHY

Sources

Gomaa, Sally. "Writing to 'Virtuous' and 'Gentle' Readers: The Problem of Pain in Harriet Jacobs's *Incidents* and Harriet Wilson's *Sketches.*" *African American Review* 43.2–3 (2009): 371–81. *Project MUSE.* Web. 3 Dec. 2012.

Jacobs, Harriet A. *Incidents in the Life of a Slave Girl, Written by Herself.* Ed. Jean Fagan Yellin. Cambridge, Mass.: Belknap Press of Harvard University Press, 2009. Print.

Kreiger, Georgia. "Playing Dead: Harriet Jacobs's Survival Strategy in *Incidents in the Life of a Slave Girl.*" *African American Review* 42.3–4 (2008): 607–21. *Project MUSE.* Web. 3 Dec. 2012.

Stone, Andrea. "Interracial Sexual Abuse and Legal Subjectivity in Antebellum Law and Literature." *American Literature.* Durham, N.C.: Duke University Press, March 2009. Web. 3 Dec. 2012.

Whitsitt, Novian. "Reading between the Lines, the Black Cultural Tradition of Masking in Harriet Jacobs's *Incidents in the Life of a Slave Girl.*" *Frontiers* 31.1 (2010): 73–88. Print.

Further Reading

Berlin, Ira. *Generations of Captivity: A History of African-American Slaves.* Cambridge, Mass.: Harvard University Press, 2003. Print.

Fisch, Audrey, ed. *The Cambridge Companion to the African American Slave Narrative.* New York: Cambridge University Press, 2007. Print.

Foster, Frances Smith. *Written by Herself: Literary Production by African American Women, 1746–1892.* Bloomington: Indiana University Press, 1993. Print.

Franklin, John Hope, and Loren Schweninger. *Runaway Slaves: Rebels on the Plantation.* New York: Oxford University Press, 1999. Print.

Gould, Philip. *Barbaric Traffic: Commerce and Antislavery in the Eighteenth-Century Atlantic World.* Cambridge, Mass.: Harvard University Press, 2003. Print.

Johnson, Walter. *Soul by Soul: Life Inside the Antebellum Slave Market.* Cambridge, Mass.: Harvard University Press, 2000. Print.

Spillers, Hortense J., ed. *Black, White, and in Color: Essays on American Literature and Culture.* Chicago: University of Chicago Press, 2003. Print.

Yellin, Jean Fagan. *Harriet Jacobs: A Life.* New York: Basic, 2004. Print.

Zafar, Rafia. *We Wear the Mask: African Americans Write Literature, 1760–1870.* New York: Columbia University Press, 1997. Print.

Iona Patuleanu

Life on the Mississippi
Mark Twain

❖ Key Facts

Time Period:
Late 19th Century

Relevant Historical Events:
Civil War; Second Industrial Revolution; Twain's experience as a river boat pilot

Nationality:
American

Keywords:
history; Mississippi River; travelogue

OVERVIEW

Part autobiography and part history of the river and the times, *Life on the Mississippi* was first published in 1883 by Samuel Langhorne Clemens under his pseudonym, Mark Twain. The book is a remembrance of Twain's experiences as a steamboat pilot before the Civil War, a travelogue of his 1882 trip, and a commentary on the shifting ground of history, for which the river itself is a metaphor. The book's focus shifts from Twain's experiences to the people, places, sights, and sounds of the river, contextualizing his formative years as a river pilot within the variegated culture of the river.

In *Life on the Mississippi*, Twain returns to the river after a hiatus of twenty-one years to collect material to augment his popular "Old Times on the Mississippi," a series of sketches he had published in 1875 in the *Atlantic Monthly*. These sketches explored Twain's coming-of-age as a cub pilot in the years before the Civil War, and *Life on the Mississippi* grew from his long-standing desire to write a "standard work" (Twain's term) about the river. The first half of the book recaps his early days on the Mississippi, and the second part reads much like a travelogue, in which the successful author travels under an assumed name to gather stories about how river life has changed since his youth. *Life on the Mississippi* is considered important to understanding the development of Twain's authorial persona as well as his later novel, *Adventures of Huckleberry Finn* (1884).

HISTORICAL AND LITERARY CONTEXT

In the years between "Old Times on the Mississippi" and *Life on the Mississippi,* the Civil War, the second Industrial Revolution, and other factors had changed river life. The war halted river trade and travel for a time, and the Mississippi, vital for supply lines, was a key battleground. After the Civil War ended, advancements in transportation kept the steamboat culture of Twain's youth from wholly rising again. The Mississippi had changed its own course, swallowing towns such as Napoleon, Arkansas, and shifting state boundaries. Being faster, railroads took the majority of the tourist trade from steamboats, and the new tugboats, able to transport more goods more efficiently than steamboats, garnered a substantial amount of the shipping trade.

When *Life on the Mississippi* was published, Twain was already an established author, well known for humorous stories such as "The Celebrated Jumping Frog of Calaveras County" (1867) and his other travel writings. *The Innocents Abroad* (1869) documents Twain's "Grand Pleasure Excursion" aboard the retired Civil War ship USS *Quaker City* with a group of American tourists to France, the Mediterranean, and the Holy Land. *Roughing It* (1872) recounts Twain's stagecoach journey out West, his time as a prospector, and the beginnings of his career as a writer. *A Tramp Abroad* (1880) follows Twain and an imaginary companion, Mr. Harris, to Germany, Italy, and France. In many of these travelogues, the author plays with the role of the tourist and travel writer and satirizes touristic hubris and hypocrisy. Unsatisfied with "Old Times on the Mississippi," Twain stated in letters to his wife and mother that he intended to revisit the topic. During his research trip, he documented the changing culture and included narratives of those who had spent their lives on the river, such as that of a Confederate boat pilot.

Though there are not many autobiographies grounded in the Mississippi River, a long history of narratives of exploration in American literary history precedes *Life on the Mississippi*. Twain turned to several when writing the second half of his book, Horst Kruse reports, listing Charles Dickens's *American Notes* as well as Francis Parkman's *La Salle and the Discovery of the Great West* and *The Jesuits of North America* among Twain's resources.

In the afterword to the Oxford edition of *Life on the Mississippi*, Lawrence Howe notes that critic William Dean Howells had praised the book for its associative style. Howells suggests that the work was a precursor to the stream-of-consciousness structure that would predominate in later high modernist texts such as James Joyce's *Ulysses* (1922) and Virginia Woolf's *To the Lighthouse* (1927).

THEMES AND STYLE

Twain uses the Mississippi River as the backdrop for both his own coming-of-age and the coming-of-age of the United States. As a boat pilot, he can read the river like a book and understands that its history, like the river's banks themselves, are on tenuous ground. He begins with a partial history of the Mississippi's explorers, explaining Robert de La Salle's and Jacques

Marquette's land acquisitions. He then launches into a lengthy segment from the yet-to-be-published *Adventures of Huckleberry Finn,* known as the raftsman's chapter, which was cut from the final version of *Huckleberry Finn* and subsequently reinserted in twentieth-century editions of the book. It is only after introducing Huckleberry Finn that Twain begins his narrative. He transforms from a youth who dreams of the glories of traveling and the prestige of being a boat pilot to one who realizes that dream and then transcends it.

According to Twain's neighbor Joseph Twichell, as recounted by Howe, Twain wrote "Old Times on the Mississippi," the precursor to *Life on the Mississippi,* to give the *Atlantic Monthly* new material on a "virgin subject to hurl into a magazine." But he had always intended to write a longer work about the river. In this second work, Twain indelibly links the river to his life, commingling his own autobiography with stories of people he has met, grounding his narrative in his community. He also breaks convention by bifurcating his narrative. Both halves are retrospective, but the second half reflects on the former, perpetuating a sense of shifting identity. Twain also revisits the path he took repeatedly in his youth, proving his early claim that the Mississippi is an ever-changing book, always altered by what has come before and shaping the journey of those upon it.

Twain constructs his narrative along the same unsteady and shifting boundaries as the Mississippi itself, which enhances his changing perceptions and truths about life. Long-winded shaggy dog jokes, changing representations of characters—such as the pilot Mr. Brown—and tales of learning to pilot a steamship meet "historical history," local anecdotes, and information from secondary texts. Twain splits *Life on the Mississippi* at the point of his brother Henry's death in a ship explosion. The chapter describing the accident is of average length, but the next is less than a page long. Twain's remaining time as a pilot is summarized in a single short paragraph, followed by another summarizing other changes he faced in the intervening twenty-one years. By cutting off his early narrative so abruptly, Twain illustrates how his carefree youth ended with his brother's death.

CRITICAL DISCUSSION

An early reviewer for the *Daily Arkansas Gazette* falsely declared that "the demand for [*Life on the Mississippi*] is so large that it is almost impossible to supply it." While it sold well, it was not quite the blockbuster this reviewer claimed or that Twain had hoped. One early review published in the *St. Louis Globe-Democrat* lauded the work for being of local interest but doubted that the book would greatly interest those outside of the Mississippi River Valley. Another representative review from the same newspaper found *Life on the Mississippi* less funny than Twain's previous works and suspected it of "having been concocted in a cool, deliberate, business-like frame of mind," as if fulfilling a contract for humor.

As with most of Twain's works, the critical response to *Life on the Mississippi* has been wide ranging over subsequent generations. Kruse and others have responded to the accusations that the book was rushed and sloppy. Kruse defended Twain's work and detailed Twain's writing process, citing the many words the author himself excised as evidence that *Life on the Mississippi* is less slap-dash than had been believed. Because Twain incorporated the river into so many of his works—and into his pseudonym ("mark twain" is slang for a depth of two fathoms)—connecting Twain's experiences piloting and writing as Edgar Burde does in his 1978 *PMLA* article has also been common among Twain scholars. Burde argued that if "we look carefully at how Clemens mastered—and was mastered by—his steamboating experiences, we can … gain insights into the workings of his imagination and into his related problems of identity."

Because Twain finished *Adventures of Huckleberry Finn* shortly after *Life on the Mississippi,* many scholars have surmised that his research trip helped him finish

Mark Twain (Samuel L. Clemens), beloved American writer, caricatured as "America's Best Humorist " in an illustration by Joseph Keppler, 1885. © EVERETT COLLECTION/ALAMY

MARK TWAIN'S AUTOBIOGRAPHY: 175 YEARS IN THE MAKING

Though Mark Twain serialized "Chapters from My Autobiography" in the *North American Review* in 1906 and 1907, those sections told only part of his life's story. The rest would have to wait for publication, he decreed, for his death plus 100 years. Twain believed "only dead men can tell the truth in this world," and he was worried his personal and political vitriol would hurt and offend those near to him. He worried for good reason—as many found the unexpurgated text unflattering at best and full of bile at worst upon its long-awaited publication. Particularly shocking is his treatment of his secretary, Isabel Van Kleek Lyon, whom he calls a "forger, thief, drunkard, traitor and salacious slut" after a falling out.

Albert Bigelow Paine, Twain's friend and authorized biographer, and scholar Bernard DeVoto number among those who have published biographies of Twain, but many of the 5,000 pages Twain wrote or dictated to a stenographer in the years preceding his death have remained untouched. The University of California's Mark Twain Project has taken on the challenge of compiling, editing, and publishing the massive autobiography. The first of three volumes was published in November 2010 to mark Twain's 175th birthday and took twelve editors six years to complete.

the novel. Howe affirms that "all of the major studies of Twain's career mention *Life on the Mississippi*," but "most treat it in the course of discussing *Adventures of Huckleberry Finn*." In Walter Blair's essay "When Was *Huckleberry Finn* Written?" he disagrees with biographer Bernard DeVoto on the matter of the importance of *Life on the Mississippi* to *Huckleberry Finn*. Finding that Twain had produced nearly 400 pages of *Huckleberry Finn* by 1876, which he continued to revise over the course of seven years, Blair's stance has won many supporters. *Life on the Mississippi* is as much about the life of the river as it is a stereoscopic snapshot of Twain's life, his youth overlaid by his middle-aged reflection.

BIBLIOGRAPHY

Sources

Blair, Walter. "When Was *Huckleberry Finn* Written?" *American Literature* 30 (1958). JSTOR. Web. 12 Nov. 2012.

Burde, Edgar J. "Mark Twain: The Writer as Pilot." *PMLA* 93.5 (1978): 878–92. JSTOR. Web. 11 Nov. 2012.

Howe, Lawrence. Afterword. *Life on the Mississippi*. 1883. By Mark Twain. Ed. Shelley Fisher Fishkin. New York: Oxford University Press, 1996. 1–18. Print

———. For Further Reading. *Life on the Mississippi*. 1883. By Mark Twain. Ed. Shelley Fisher Fishkin. New York: Oxford University Press, 1996. 19–20. Print.

Kruse, Horst H. *Mark Twain and "Life on the Mississippi."* Amherst: University of Massachusetts Press, 1981. Print.

Morris, Willie. Introduction. *Life on the Mississippi*. 1883. By Mark Twain. Ed. Shelley Fisher Fishkin. New York: Oxford University Press, 1996. xxxi–lii. Print.

"New Books." Rev. of *Life on the Mississippi*, by Mark Twain. *St. Louis Globe-Democrat* 21 May 1883: 8. *19th Century U.S. Newspapers*. Web. 9 Nov. 2012.

Rev. of *Life on the Mississippi*, by Mark Twain. *Daily Arkansas Gazette* 13 May 1883: n.p. *19th Century U.S. Newspapers*. Web. 9 Nov. 2012.

Rohter, Larry. "Dead for a Century, Twain Says What He Means." *New York Times*. New York Times, 9 July 2010. Web. 10 Nov. 2012.

Sherwell, Philip. "Mark Twain Autobiography Creates a Stir." *Telegraph*. 13 Nov. 2010. *Telegraph*. Web. 10 Nov. 2012.

Twain, Mark. *Life on the Mississippi*. 1883. Ed. Shelley Fisher Fishkin. New York: Oxford University Press, 1996. Print.

Further Reading

Bridgman, Richard. *Traveling in Mark Twain*. Berkeley: University of California Press, 1987. Print.

Cox, James M. *Mark Twain: The Fate of Humor*. Princeton, N.J.: Princeton University Press, 1966. Print.

DeVoto, Bernard. Introduction. *Adventures of Huckleberry Finn*. By Mark Twain. New York: Limited Editions Club, 1942. Print.

———. "Noon and Dark." *Mark Twain at Work*. Ed. Bernard DeVoto. Cambridge, Mass.: Harvard University Press, 1942. 45–82. Print.

Ganzel, Dewey. "Twain, Travel Books, and *Life on the Mississippi*." *American Literature* 34.1 (1962): 40–55. JSTOR. Web. 10 Nov. 2012.

McCammack, Brian. "Competence, Power, and the Nostalgic Romance of Piloting in Mark Twain's *Life on the Mississippi*." *Southern Literary Journal* 38.2 (2006): 1–18. Print.

McIntire-Strasburg, Janice. "Mark Twain, Huck Finn, and the Geographical 'Memory' of a Nation." *Mark Twain's Geographical Imagination*. Ed. Joseph Alvarez. Newcastle upon Tyne, U.K.: Cambridge Scholars, 2009. 83–99. Print.

Katherine Bishop

My Life Story
David Unaipon

OVERVIEW

My Life Story (1951) is an autobiographical pamphlet penned by David Unaipon—an inventor, an evangelist, a public speaker, and the first published Australian Aboriginal writer. Unaipon's tale begins with his birth in 1872 "in a native wurley along the Banks of the River Murray at Tailem Bend" in Raukkan (Point McLeay), South Australia. In this vivid recollection of his youth, the author tells how he learned "the old ways" of the Ngarrindjeri people but also obtained a classical European education at the Point McLeay Mission. Unaipon fondly recalls his childhood at the mission and his adolescent years spent as a servant in the home of C. B. Snow, the first secretary of the Aborigines' Friends' Association (AFA). He saw his life's purpose as a continuation of the work of his father, who was "a good liaison officer between the black and white races."

Although Unaipon is now well known for his publications, he did not receive payment or proper recognition for his work during his lifetime, save for being awarded the Coronation Medal in 1953 for some of his achievements. Since his death in 1967, he has become a great legend and has inspired many works, including a professional ballet titled *Unaipon*, which was performed in 2004 at the Sydney Opera House. In 1988 the national David Unaipon Literary Award for Aboriginal and Torres Strait Islander writers was established, and the University of South Australia founded the annual David Unaipon Lecture. In 1995 the Australian Reserve Bank chose to commemorate Unaipon on the fifty-dollar note.

HISTORICAL AND LITERARY CONTEXT

Indigenous people belonging to 500 distinct groups occupied Australia for nearly 60,000 years before the British arrived in 1788. British colonization led to the shattering of the Aboriginal cultural heritage through the introduction of disease, the practice of resettlement, forced assimilation, and in some cases rape and murder. In 1834 the British government passed the Foundation Act, allowing British settlers to purchase freehold land in South Australia. The preamble to this act declared the entire area "waste and unoccupied," which essentially meant that the 8,000 Ngarrindjeri Aborigines living in the region legally ceased to exist.

My Life Story may never have come about without the AFA, which published the majority of Unaipon's writings, including his autobiography. Seeking to bring spiritual salvation to the Ngarrindjeri as well as train them for domestic labor, the AFA formed in 1859 and established the Point McLeay Mission in 1860. The mission appointed George Taplin to oversee its religious aspects. Unaipon's father, James, arrived at the mission in 1864; he was the first Aboriginal convert and worked closely with Taplin to further the institution's vision. By the time David was born in 1872, James had become the first Aboriginal missionary to the Ngarrindjeri. In addition to playing a critical role in David's education and writing career, the AFA supported his work as a public speaker and lay preacher.

Although anthropologists and ethnographers had collected and published indigenous oral narratives in the late nineteenth and early twentieth centuries, *My Life Story* is commonly understood to be the first Aboriginal autobiography. However, a 1934 manuscript exists in which Reuben Walker tells of his plight as a mixed-race child at Encounter Bay. In 1953 Unaipon added to his autobiographical sketch in the article "Leaves of Memory," which appeared in the *Aborigines' Friends' Association Annual Report No. 95*. Since Unaipon's pioneering publication, several prominent Aboriginal Australians have published their own autobiographies: tennis star Evonne Goolagong in 1973, the first Aboriginal federal parliamentarian Charlie Perkins in 1975, and boxer Keith B. Saunders in 1992 and 1998.

In the early 1920s Unaipon began studying and recording Aboriginal myths and legends. His work contributed to a greater understanding and preservation of Aboriginal culture in the face of white Australian prejudice. In 1930 W. Ramsay Smith published Unaipon's *Myths and Legends of the Australian Aboriginals* but did not give him the authorial credit. Unaipon dedicated much of his life to improving the living conditions and rights of Aborigines. He became his people's spokesperson and helped influence government Aboriginal policy. Aborigines became citizens of Australia in 1967, the year Unaipon died at age ninety-four. In addition to making significant contributions to literature, he was a skilled engineer and inventor who became fondly known as "Australia's Leonardo [da Vinci]."

❖ **Key Facts**

Time Period:
Mid-20th Century

Relevant Historical Events:
British colonization of Australia; passage of the Foundation Act; founding of the Aborigines' Friends' Association

Nationality:
Australian

Keywords:
aborigines; colonialism; religion

An Australian fifty-dollar bill featuring Ngarrindjeri Aboriginal David Unaipon, a writer, inventor, and preacher who wrote about his life in *My Life Story*. © CHRIS BUTLER/ALAMY

THEMES AND STYLE

As with many of Unaipon's works, *My Life Story* marries his Christian beliefs with his Aboriginal roots. His parents, he writes, were "full-blood aborigines" who lived "according to the customs of a primitive race." He vividly describes learning the ways of his people from the art of tracking animals to learning the best places to find birds' eggs. However, Unaipon also describes himself as "a product of missionary work." He argues that relations finally improved between the Aborigines and the white newcomers when the AFA sent Taplin to live among them. In 1934 the Aborigines' Progressive Association was formed to press for reform; in 1938 it organized the Day of Mourning, which Unaipon opposed. He writes in his autobiography, "I have carefully studied the plans adopted for the advancement of the aborigines, and I see no way out but in co-operation between the white and black races."

In *Remembering Aboriginal Heroes: Struggle, Identity and the Media*, John Ramsland and Christopher Gerald Mooney note that Unaipon wrote *My Life Story* "so as to shape his own biography." Up until this point, much had been written about or for Aborigines, but no Aborigines had published their own stories. When Unaipon wrote *My Life Story*, he was elderly but still active. Most of his writing was published in the 1920s and 1930s, though he composed many poems in the 1950s. Unaipon spent much of his energy in his later years working on his inventions.

The tone of Unaipon's work is strongly informed by his Christian upbringing. According to Adam Shoemaker in *Black Words, White Page*, Unaipon enjoyed reading the sermons of Thomas de Witt Talmage and Henry Drummond. Shoemaker asserts, "Unaipon emulated the elevated, sermonic prose style which characterized the work of these men." He goes on to state, "The analytical and synthetic approach of his more factual writing is indicative of a mind which was both questing and incisive." This facet of his style is particularly evident in Unaipon's description of his sheep-shearing invention: "I began by studying the machine used in sheep shearing for an Adelaide firm with a view to bringing about an improvement in its working. This I succeeded in doing and I obtained a patent for the same, but not being properly protected I lost financially any material gain arising from this discovery."

CRITICAL DISCUSSION

During Unaipon's lifetime, he was "hailed as proof of the success of white Australian society's civilising mission," according to John Alexander's "Following David Unaipon's Footsteps." Alexander writes that the press labeled Unaipon a "black genius" and "a human contradiction in terms." The first critical analysis of Unaipon's works did not appear until 1979, when John Beston wrote "David Unaipon: The First Aboriginal Writer." Beston argues that Unaipon's "Christianising of the legends somewhat obscures his strong underlying sense of Aboriginal identity" but that the author was faithful to his indigenous heritage above all else. "Unaipon," Beston writes, "was by no means a white man's puppet." Since then, scholars have questioned Beston's conclusion, saying he did not examine all of Unaipon's manuscripts or do sufficient digging into the AFA. As Shoemaker contends, Beston's conclusion "proceeds from false premises and ... is derived from research which was not comprehensive."

Other than Unaipon's published works, Aboriginal written literature did not become a distinct genre until the 1970s. Shoemaker's article, written in 1989, notes that Unaipon's works "were almost totally ignored until the 1970s and still deserve far more study than they have received." Alexander states that in the 1990s, after "a hiatus of fifty years, [Unaipon became] a symbol of the quest for Aboriginal reconciliation." He goes on to note, "Yet his endeavors sit uneasily within current Aboriginal aspirations for self-determination."

Modern critics continually question the marriage between Unaipon's Westernization and his Aboriginal heritage. Shoemaker poses the question, "Was Unaipon so fully indoctrinated into the Western Christian lifestyle that he renounced his independence and his Aboriginality?" He suggests that Unaipon "was so fully indoctrinated by the AFA that an Aboriginal world view was encouraged and permitted only so long as it did not conflict with Christian religious tenets." In *Ancient & Modern: Time, Culture and Indigenous Philosophy*, Stephen Muecke argues that Unaipon's cultivation of speech, dress, and Christian values came naturally to him and that Unaipon was "'growing' a new culture for himself and his people."

DAVID UNAIPON: FOLLOWING IN HIS FATHER'S FOOTSTEPS

David Unaipon was born on September 28, 1872, to James and Nymbulda Ngunaitponi (eventually anglicized as Unaipon). James was the first adult Christian at the Point McLeay Mission and the first of the "Taplin men," or traveling Aboriginal lay preachers. He also became the first Ngarrindjeri deacon in 1871. James held firmly to his Ngarrindjeri heritage. In *My Life Story*, Unaipon says his father "used his influence to persuade others to accept the Gospel." When the scriptures were translated into the Ngarrindjeri's native tongue, it was James's practice "to use this version in his visit to the native camps."

Like his father, Unaipon was educated by the Point McLeay missionaries. In *My Life Story*, he states that the Aborigines were "shattered by contact with white civilization." However, he also argues that Christian missions gave Aborigines "the inner Power to reconstruct their lives." In the eyes of the Aborigines' Friends' Association (AFA), Unaipon was the model Aboriginal citizen in his adoption of Christian values. He was fond of saying: "Look at me and you will see what the Bible can do." In *Black Words White Page: Aboriginal Literature 1929–1988*, Adam Shoemaker asserts, "As a writer, musician, inventor, and public speaker who was schooled in the classics, Unaipon must have seemed to the AFA a heaven-sent token of the worth of its policies, which were assimilationist many years before the concept became widely accepted throughout Australia."

BIBLIOGRAPHY

Sources

Alexander, John. "David Unaipon." *Australian Literature, 1788–1914.* Ed. Selina Samuels. Detroit: Gale, 2001. *Dictionary of Literary Biography.* Vol. 230. Literature Resource Center. Web. 11 Nov. 2012.

Alexander, John. "Following David Unaipon's Footsteps." *Journal of Australian Studies* 54–55 (1997): 22–29. Literature Resource Center. Web. 11 Nov. 2012.

Beston, John B. "David Unaipon: The First Aboriginal Writer." *Southerly* 3 (1979): 334–50. Print.

"David Unaipon." *Contemporary Authors Online.* Detroit: Gale, 2001. Literature Resource Center. Web. 11 Nov. 2012.

Mooney, Christopher Gerald, and John Ramsland. *Remembering Aboriginal Heroes: Struggle, Identity and the Media.* Melbourne: Brolga, 2006. Print.

Muecke, Stephen. *Ancient & Modern: Time, Culture and Indigenous Philosophy.* Sydney: University of New South Wales Press, 2004. Print.

Shoemaker, Adam. *Black Words, White Page: Aboriginal Literature 1929–1988.* St. Lucia: University of Queensland Press, 1989. Print.

Further Reading

Bell, Dianne. *Ngarrindjeri Wurruwarrin, A World That Is, Was and Will Be.* Melbourne: Spinifex, 1998. Print.

Berndt, R. M. *A World That Was: The Yaraldi of the Murray River and the Lakes.* Melbourne: Melbourne University Press, 1993. Print.

Carey, H. M. "'The Land of Byamee': K. Langloh Parker, David Unaipon, and Popular Aboriginality in the Assimilation Era." *Journal of Religious History* 22.2 (1998): 200–18. Print.

Heiss, Anita M. *Dhuuluu-Yala: O Talk Straight.* Canberra: Aboriginal Studies, 2003. Print.

Jones, Philip. "'A Curve Is a Line and a Line Is a Curve': Some of the Truth about David Unaipon." *Adelaide Review* 65 (1989): 10–11. Print.

Jones, Philip. "David Unaipon," *Australian Dictionary of Biography.* Volume 12. Ed. J. Ritchie. Melbourne: Melbourne University Press, 1990. 303–304. Print.

Muecke, Stephen. "'Between the Church and the Stage': David Unaipon at the Hobart Carnival, 1910." *University Technology Sydney Review* 6.1 (2000): 11–19. Print.

Willmot, Eric. "Dilemma of Mind." *The Inaugural David Unaipon Lecture.* Underdale: Kaurna Higher Education Centre, Aboriginal Studies Key Centre, University of South Australia, 1989. Print.

Maggie Magno

My Revolutionary Years
The Autobiography of Madame Wei Tao-Ming
Cheng Yu-hsiu

❖ *Key Facts*

Time Period:
Mid-20th Century

Relevant Historical Events:
World War II: Chinese military conflict with Japan; decline of the Manchu dynasty

Nationality:
Chinese

Keywords:
coming-of-age; women's writing; modernization

OVERVIEW

My Revolutionary Years: The Autobiography of Madame Wei Tao-Ming, written by Cheng Yu-hsiu (or Madame Wei Tao-Ming) in 1944, was among the first autobiographies penned by a Chinese woman in a position of power in the Chinese government during World War II. Madame Wei was one of the first female lawyers in Shanghai. She dreamed of launching a political party to represent women and of creating a bank especially for women. *My Revolutionary Years* describes the author's experiences growing up from "infant rebel" to powerful and respected woman during the late Manchu period. It opens with the author's recollection of the story of Mulan, the famous Chinese female warrior, which provides an example of how the structure of Madame Wei's family influenced her perspective and encouraged her revolutionary nature.

At the time *My Revolutionary Years* was published, the author's husband, Wei Tao Ming, was serving as the Chinese ambassador to the United States. Although this status afforded the couple some prominence, little is known about the initial reception of the book. Enduring interest in the work can be attributed in part to Madame Wei's drive to better her country, despite the limitations conventionally placed on her sex, and also to the availability of her other autobiographical writings, which help to ground the work. *My Revolutionary Years* is valued today for its insights into life during a volatile period of Chinese history and for its portrait of an unconventional woman who aspired to be a force in modernizing China.

HISTORICAL AND LITERARY CONTEXT

Madame Wei's autobiography describes the conditions of life in China during the World War II era, a time of intense warfare between China and Japan and a period during which China was undergoing modernization. The text covers a tumultuous period in which China was in its final years of dynastic rule, before it briefly embraced republicanism and finally became governed by the Communist Party. In the text, Madame Wei describes how the elevated status of her family contributed to her perspective and prepared her to assume a professional role at a time when such opportunities were rare for women. Likely because of her family's status, Madame Wei was granted the opportunity to complete a doctoral degree in law, which she received from the Sorbonne in Paris in July 1925. *My Revolutionary Years* delineates her experiences as one of the first female lawyers in China and describes in depth the decisions she made as a result of her various legal positions.

In 1944, when *My Revolutionary Years* first appeared, Madame Wei and her husband were living in the United States. While he served as an ambassador, she was active in charity organizations such as the United China Relief Fund and the China Aid Council. After returning to China following the war, she remained active in law and politics and was elected as a legislator in 1947. The couple immigrated to the United States in 1949, where Madame Wei lived until her death from cancer in 1959.

Prior to the publication of *My Revolutionary Years,* few autobiographies had examined the lives of girls and women in China. Madame Wei previously had written autobiographically in *A Girl from China* (1926; published under Soumay Tcheng, an Anglicized version of her maiden name). What few others did exist were generally written by political activists. Narratives about female revolutionaries such as Qiu Jin, one of the first female activists in China, would have set a precedent for the type of writing in which Madame Wei engaged. In looking for a strong female antecedent, she drew on the legend of Mulan, "a girl born sometime in the Sixth Century A.D." Raised by her father with the education and respect conventionally reserved for sons, Mulan famously disguised herself as a man in order to fight for the emperor. Madam Wei explains that as a young child on her mother's lap "I never grew tired of hearing about her and begged for the story over and over again" and notes that "Mulan meant as much to me as Boadicea or Joan of Arc means to any Western child." This influence is clearly felt in *My Revolutionary Years,* in which Madame Wei envisions herself as a modern Mulan who will defy gender expectations to attain personal freedom and out of love for her country and concern for its future.

Because Madame Wei had defied gender expectations and risen to a position of some power in China, the publication of her book marked a new era in the genre of autobiography. It helped to pave the way for the publication of other autobiographies by Chinese women. Another work from the same era, *The Girl with the White Flag* by Tomiko Higa, is about the author's girlhood during World War II. Like Madame Wei, Higa was exposed to and participated in political activism from a young age. She wrote her book around ten years after her experiences in 1945 (it was published in 1955); however, her book was not translated into English until 1991, after which time it was published as a young adult book in 1995. Another memoir by a Chinese woman, Ji-Li Jiang's *Red Scarf Girl* (1998), which chronicles the author's coming-of-age experiences in China during the Cultural Revolution (1966–76), has gained prominence in U.S. classrooms.

THEMES AND STYLE

Among the primary themes of *My Revolutionary Years* is that early life has a profound effect on personal development, establishing patterns that repeat throughout later life. Madame Wei describes her familial structure and offers a vivid portrayal of her grandmother, the dowager matriarch of her family. As she explains, men ostensibly had control based on their command over a family's presence in social spheres, yet women retained dominion in the domestic space. Madame Wei differentiates herself from her siblings by describing the traits she had in common with her grandmother; she also discusses how these similarities created clashes between them. The author portrays her expanding awareness of the conditions under which her family lived: an important member of the Manchu government, her father was estranged from her mother and likely kept a concubine (a customary practice in China at the time). However, Madame Wei's mother received little sympathy for her marital circumstances, as it was thought both by society and her family that she should just bear this situation. The author grounds her narrative in her initial discussion of the story of Mulan and its importance in her life. She describes identifying with the experiences of the female warrior who waged battle while preserving the secret of her sex. She ties the symbolic significance of this story to her own identity as a strong-willed and independent girl who, like Mulan, eschewed social conventions and expectations by asserting herself in ways generally expected of boys but not girls. When, for example, Madame Wei is betrothed in an arranged marriage, she sends a letter to her fiancé advising him to select a bride more suited to his interests, as she wanted to further her education abroad. No such action had ever been taken in a high-status Chinese family, and it caused her family to lose face. She describes how her childhood and adolescent experiences served as a foundation for her further defiance of convention in becoming a lawyer.

Madame Wei was aware of the obstacles she had overcome as a female. Even early in her life, she had taken steps to improve or better her surroundings. For example, when her mother and father were estranged, it was a young Madame Wei who convinced her mother to take the family to Peking. *My Revolutionary Years* describes their journey through a circuitous Asian route that included travels through Hong Kong. Once the family moved to Peking, she received a much more extensive formal education (more than girls customarily did at the time) because of her father; she also accompanied him almost constantly in his movement through the city. Based on this access, she gained a great deal of information and knowledge that she would not otherwise have. She saw autobiography as a means of recording the nuances of her experiences to provide future generations with an explicit record of the challenges she encountered and the decisions she made, both personally and professionally.

Madame Wei uses the first person to deliver an intimate and detailed description of how her identity emerged when she was a child. The book retains a crisp, formal, and authoritative style throughout, as she describes her experiences studying in a Christian school, then abroad in Japan and France. Through the use of the first-person perspective, she explains how her position of authority as a female impacted the way she interacted with her clients and her colleagues. Told from the perspective of Madame Wei's successful adult self, the text is imbued with an almost mythic quality,

Tcheng Yu-hsiu (Soumay Tcheng), author of *My Revolutionary Years*, in 1943, shortly before her memoir was published. At this time, her husband was serving as China's ambassador to the United States. © THOMAS D. MCAVOY/TIME LIFE PICTURES/GETTY IMAGES

MADAME WEI IN *GOOD HOUSEKEEPING*

In 1925 two passages from what would become *A Girl from China* were published in *Good Housekeeping* under the name Soumay Tcheng. Appearing in November and December, respectively, "The Story of a Young Woman Who Broke the Traditions of Centuries to Bring Freedom to Herself and Liberty to Her Native Land" and "The Dramatic Story of a Girl Who Risked Her Life to Free Her Country" describe some of the extraordinary events of Madame Wei's early life. The stories were transcribed by Mrs. John Van Vorst, whose introductory note describes Tcheng as "the leading spirit among the Chinese students in Paris."

The two-part sequence, which was accompanied by elaborate illustrations by John Richard Flanagan, chronicles how a young Madame Wei had thrown off the yoke of an arranged marriage and how she had elected instead to become a revolutionary on a number of fronts. Published with such articles as "The Hows and Whys of Making Butter Cakes" and "Gifts from the Kitchen," the passages also detail the specifics of the author's experiences as a courier of weapons and explosives between 1911 and 1913.

---

in the sense that her description makes the way her life unfolded seem almost ordained.

CRITICAL DISCUSSION

Not much has been written about the initial reaction to *My Revolutionary Years,* although the author's status as a prominent ambassador's wife marked it as unique and noteworthy. By the time the book was published, Madame Wei also commanded a strong reputation in her own right, as she had written about China's constitutionality and was active not only as a revolutionary prior to obtaining her law degree but also as an activist for women's rights, including voting. She had also founded a law firm with her husband and was the first Chinese lawyer to practice before the French courts in Shanghai. All of these elements of her background, coupled with the authoritative voice she uses in the text, helped to make it an international success.

Although it is not as well known or as frequently taught as more recent works such as *Red Scarf Girl,* Madame Wei's autobiography has endured through decades that have brought major social and political changes around the globe, a fact that attests to the enduring appeal of its message of female ambition and empowerment. *My Revolutionary Years* remains in print seventy years after its initial publication, and it has been translated into numerous languages. The work remains of historical interest for its account of Chinese life during an era of social and political change and of human interest for its account of a woman's family bonds and zeal to be a part of bringing change to her country.

The body of English-language criticism treating *My Revolutionary Years* is not extensive; it is discussed in scholarly conversations primarily for its value in revealing key details about the life of a female revolutionary and distinguished lawyer in China during its modern era. Some authors have discussed the contributions that Madame Wei made to the autobiographical genre, especially as her book represents a rare Asian voice. Other critics have commented on her lively portrayal of what it meant to be a revolutionary and, in particular, a female revolutionary at the young ages in which she participated in subversive organizations and movements. Other writings about her text and life have centered on her status as a renowned and accomplished female member of the legal profession during this period in Chinese history.

BIBLIOGRAPHY

Sources

Chin, Carol C. "Translating the New Woman: Chinese Feminists View the West, 1905–1915." *Gender and History* 18.3 (2006): 490–518. Print.

Ming, Madame Wei Tao. *My Revolutionary Years: The Autobiography of Madame Wei Tao-Ming.* New York: C. Scribner's Sons, 1944. Print.

Ng, Janet. *The Experience of Modernity: Chinese Autobiography of the Early Twentieth Century.* Ann Arbor: University of Michigan Press, 2003. Print.

Szto, Mary. "Gender and the Chinese Legal Profession in Historical Perspective: From Heaven and Earth to Rule of Woman?" *Selected Works of Mary Szto.* bepress, 2008. Web. 10 Dec. 2012.

Wong, Kevin Scott. *Americans First: Chinese Americans and the Second World War.* Cambridge, Mass.: Harvard University Press, 2005. Print.

Further Reading

Kagan, Richard C. "Ch'en Tu-hsiu's Unfinished Autobiography." *China Quarterly* 50 (1972): 295–314. Print.

Knechtges, David R. "Wit, Humor, and Satire in Early Chinese Literature." *Monumenta Serica* 29 (1970–71): 79–98. Print.

Larson, Wendy. *Literary Authority and the Modern Chinese Writer: Ambivalence and Autobiography.* Durham, N.C.: Duke University Press, 1991. Print.

Marr, David. "The 1920s Women's Rights Debates in Vietnam." *Journal of Asian Studies.* 35.3 (1976): 371–89. Print.

Wei, Karen T. *Women in China: A Selected and Annotated Bibliography.* Westport, Conn.: Greenwood, 1984. Print.

Grace Waitman

Persepolis
Marjane Satrapi

OVERVIEW

Written in French and initially published in four yearly volumes from 2000 to 2003, Marjane Satrapi's graphic memoir *Persepolis* is an autobiographical account of Satrapi's childhood and coming-of-age before, during, and after the Iranian Revolution of 1979. Using Satrapi's own privileged upbringing within an affluent, secular Iranian family—and her high school education in Vienna and subsequent return to Iran—as its narrative foundation, the memoir comments at length upon the social and cultural changes wrought by the deposition of the autocratic, Westernizing Shah Mohammed Reza Pahlavi and his replacement by Ayatollah Ruhollah Khomeini, supreme leader of the newly formed Islamic Republic of Iran. The effects of these changes upon the lives of ordinary Iranians, as well as those attending Iran's subsequent war with Iraq (1980–88), are illustrated by Satrapi's portrayal of her own experiences and those of her family, friends, and other compatriots up to her final departure from Iran in 1994 at the age of twenty-four.

Satrapi's first major work, *Persepolis* was published to great financial success and was soon translated into numerous other languages. One of a large number of expatriate autobiographical narratives about growing up under Iran's post-revolutionary fundamentalist regime, *Persepolis* was highly praised for the insight it gave into the realities of Iranian life in the late twentieth century. Frequently incorporated into high school and college curricula, it remains one of the most widely read examples of the Iranian memoir subgenre and among the most highly respected comic-book publications of the early twenty-first century.

HISTORICAL AND LITERARY CONTEXT

Much of *Persepolis* depicts Satrapi's personal experience of the actions of the new Iranian government in the wake of the 1979 Islamic Revolution. The relatively secular rulership of Mohammed Reza—whose reign was marked by numerous human rights abuses and a great degree of corruption as well as consistent efforts to modernize Iranian society along the lines of Western countries—gave way to a theocratic state whose laws emphasized traditional Islamic values, hence a new rule forbidding women from appearing in public without covering their hair. Meanwhile, a series of border disputes with Iraq precipitated a lengthy armed conflict that spanned most of the 1980s and exacted a heavy toll on the Iranian population and economy.

When the first installment of *Persepolis* appeared in 2000, about six years after Satrapi left Iran and moved to France, the Islamic Republic established by the revolution in 1979 had been in place for more than two decades. The effects of this shift on civilian life within Iran—and the realities of Iranian life in general—remained largely opaque to most Westerners, whose knowledge of Iran tended to consist mainly of extreme, adversarial incidents such as the hostage crisis at the U.S. embassy and the ayatollah's declaration of a *fatwa* against author Salman Rushdie in response to his authorship of a novel deemed blasphemous to Islam. Satrapi's memoir, with its relatively ordinary, down-to-earth depiction of life in Iran, functioned as a counterpoint to the extremism suggested by common Western perceptions of the country—perceptions she experienced firsthand during her time in Austria, which the narrative depicts in a way that suggests that prejudice and misogyny are hardly absent in ostensibly enlightened Western societies.

Around the turn of the twenty-first century, a sizable group of memoirs from former citizens of Iran were published in Western countries, shedding light on the revolutionary and post-revolutionary periods within Iran's history. Prominent examples of this trend include Azar Nafisi's *Reading Lolita in Tehran* (2003) and Roya Hakakian's *Journey to the Land of No* (2004), both of which, like *Persepolis*, devote considerable attention to the effects of post-revolutionary laws on the societal roles of women. *Persepolis* also emerged from a fertile tradition of autobiographical comics; a particularly important antecedent was the work of the French artist David B., who served as a mentor to Satrapi and whose own graphic memoir *Epileptic* exerted a substantial influence on the composition of *Persepolis*.

The financial and critical success of *Persepolis* contributed significantly to the commercial viability of expatriate Iranian memoirs as a whole as well as to the growing respectability of comics as a literary form. Diasporic memoirs of Iranian experience continued to proliferate over the next decade, and high-profile autobiographical comics became increasingly common. Satrapi herself continued to successfully mine her Iranian experiences for material, composing the more loosely autobiographical *Embroideries* (2005), about the sex lives of her family and friends, and *Chicken*

❖ **Key Facts**

Time Period:
Early 21st Century

Relevant Historical Events:
Iranian Revolution of 1979; Iran-Iraq War

Nationality:
Iranian

Keywords:
Islamism; revolution; exile

A still from the animated film version of Marjane Satrapi's *Persepolis*. © SONY PICTURES/ EVERETT COLLECTION

with *Plums* (2006), about the life and tragic death of her great-uncle. She also codirected a well-received *Persepolis* film adaptation in 2007.

THEMES AND STYLE

Central to *Persepolis* is an emphasis on the difficulty of reconciling a sense of Iranian cultural identity with a relatively secular, progressive upbringing and ideological background. Satrapi devotes considerable attention to illustrating how the onslaught of enforced fundamentalism following the revolution affected her personal growth; the book begins by describing how her coeducational French school was shut down in 1980 and female students were legally obligated to cover their heads—"we found ourselves veiled and separated from our friends"—resulting in a feeling of cultural dislocation that recurs throughout the text: "I really didn't know what to think about the veil. Deep down I was very religious but as a family we were very modern and avant-garde." Satrapi's feelings toward her Iranian background ebb and flow as the narrative progresses, eventually reaching a low point sometime after her family sends her to Austria to continue her education along with the admonition, "Don't ever forget who you are!" After a brief period of denying her own heritage, Satrapi takes this advice to heart, though she is ultimately unable to remain within Iran itself.

One of Satrapi's primary motivations for writing *Persepolis* was a desire to share a portrait of Iranian experience contrary to the country's frequently negative portrayal in other parts of the world. In a brief introductory note to the English-language edition, she states that post-revolutionary Iran "has been discussed mostly in connection with fundamentalism, fanaticism, and terrorism. As an Iranian who has lived more than half of my life in Iran, I know that this image is far from the truth." The narrative avoids implying that Satrapi's life as depicted in *Persepolis* is wholly representative of Iranians as a group—indeed, one chapter ends by juxtaposing a panel showing impoverished child army recruits exploding in a minefield with a panel showing Satrapi and her friends dancing at a party, thus emphasizing the degree to which Satrapi's wealth shielded her from many harsh aspects of Iranian life—but the genre of autobiography nonetheless allows Satrapi to offer her own life, in both its typical and atypical details, to combat common perceptions of Iran.

Persepolis is characterized by a simple, direct mode of expression in its prose and its illustrations. The narration and dialogue are seldom ornate or verbose, tending instead toward straightforward exposition and terse, emotionally charged sentences. In describing a hug with her mother during a visit to Austria, Satrapi, who had grown significantly taller in the nineteen months since her initial departure from Iran, writes, "It felt strange to take her in my arms. Our proportions had been reversed." The unadorned, almost epigrammatic tone of the writing is complemented by Satrapi's stark, black-and-white illustrative style, which avoids incidental details in favor of iconic simplicity. This emphasizes the book's autobiographical status as a document of its author's subjective memories rather than an exhaustively objective replication of historical fact.

CRITICAL DISCUSSION

Persepolis was a resounding success upon its initial release, quickly garnering strong sales, numerous awards, and largely positive reviews. Critics tended to praise the work as an informative and humanizing portrait of Iranian experience and a particularly impressive example of autobiographical comics, often comparing it to Art Spiegelman's seminal *Maus* narrative. Fernanda Eberstadt's review in the *New York Times* exemplifies the book's warm critical reception, hailing *Persepolis* as "one of the most delectable examples of a booming postmodern genre: autobiography by comic book" and applauding the work's evocative power: "Satrapi is adept at conveying the numbing cynicism induced by living in a city under siege both from Iraqi bombs and from a homegrown regime that uses the war as pretext to exterminate 'the enemy within.'"

In the years since its publication *Persepolis* has become one of the most widely read literary responses to the Iranian Revolution, significantly impacting Western readers' perception of that event. Its well-received film adaptation and frequent use as an assigned text in schools has ensured its continuing cultural influence, and in 2009 its art was used, with Satrapi's permission, as the basis for a brief comic protesting the results of that year's Iranian presidential election. Manuela Costantino, in a 2008 article in the *Canadian Review of American Studies*, observed that "because of its popularity, this graphic memoir can reach a large number of readers and shape their knowledge of Iran's culture and history and their understanding of cultural difference." Much recent scholarship on the text is devoted to analyzing the nature of this influence.

Scholarly writing on *Persepolis* frequently examines the text in relation to postcolonial theory and cultural studies, often discussing the ways in which larger issues of Eastern and Western culture are refracted by the narrative. A particularly noteworthy example is Nima Naghibi and Andrew O'Malley's 2005 article "Estranging the Familiar: 'East' and 'West' in Satrapi's *Persepolis*," which argues that, unlike *Reading Lolita in Tehran*, Satrapi's book "upsets the easy categories and distinctions that it appears to endorse: between the secular West and the threateningly religious East; between the oppressed and liberated woman (i.e., veiled and unveiled); between domestic and political/public." In support of this argument, the authors devote considerable analysis to the work's generic attributes as a comic, a focus shared by Hillary Chute's "The Texture of Retracing in Marjane Satrapi's *Persepolis*" (2008), which discusses the text's formal features in relation to its autobiographical project.

BIBLIOGRAPHY

Sources

Chute, Hillary. "The Texture of Retracing in Marjane Satrapi's *Persepolis*." *Women's Studies Quarterly* 36.1–2 (2008): 92–110. JSTOR. Web. 5 Nov. 2012.

Costantino, Manuela. "Marji: Popular Commix Heroine Breathing Life into the Writing of History." *Canadian Review of American Studies* 38.3 (2008): 429–47. Academic Search Complete. Web. 5 Nov. 2012.

Eberstadt, Fernanda. "God Looked Like Marx." Rev. of *Persepolis*, by Marjane Satrapi. *New York Times*. New York Times, 11 May 2003. Web. 5 Nov. 2012.

Naghibi, Nima, and Andrew O'Malley. "Estranging the Familiar: 'East' and 'West' in Satrapi's *Persepolis*." *English Studies in Canada* 31.2–3 (2005): 223–47. Academic Search Complete. Web. 5 Nov. 2012.

Satrapi, Marjane. *The Complete Persepolis*. Trans. Mattias Ripa and Blake Ferris. New York: Pantheon, 2007. Print.

Further Reading

B., David. *Epileptic*. Trans. Kim Thompson. New York: Pantheon, 2005. Print.

Chiu, Monica. "Sequencing and Contingent Individualism in the Graphic, Postcolonial Spaces of Satrapi's *Persepolis* and Okubo's *Citizen 13660*." *English Language Notes* 46.2 (2008): 99–114. Print.

Davis, Rocío G. "A Graphic Self: Comics as Autobiography in Marjane Satrapi's *Persepolis*." *Prose Studies* 27.3 (2005): 264–79. Print.

Elahi, Babak. "Frames and Mirrors in Marjane Satrapi's *Persepolis*." *Symploke* 15.1–2 (2007): 312–25. Print.

Hakakian, Roya. *Journey from the Land of No: A Girlhood Caught in Revolutionary Iran*. New York: Crown, 2004. Print.

Leservot, Typhaine. "Occidentalism: Rewriting the West in Marjane Satrapi's *Persépolis*." *French Forum* 36.1 (2011): 115–30. Print.

Malek, Amy. "Memoir as Iranian Exile Cultural Production: A Case Study of Marjane Satrapi's *Persepolis* Series." *Iranian Studies* 39.3 (2006): 353–80. Print.

Miller, Ann. "Marjane Satrapi's *Persepolis*: Eluding the Frames." *Esprit Createur* 51.1 (2011): 38–52. Print.

Nafisi, Azar. *Reading Lolita in Tehran: A Memoir in Books*. New York: Random House, 2003. Print.

READING LOLITA IN TEHRAN: A MEMOIR IN BOOKS

One of the most popular examples of Iranian women's autobiography to emerge around the turn of the twenty-first century was Azar Nafisi's best-selling 2003 memoir *Reading Lolita in Tehran*. Like *Persepolis*, Nafisi's text offers a personal recollection of the cultural turmoil surrounding the Iranian Revolution, the founding of Iran's Islamic Republic, and the subsequent Iran-Iraq war, with a particular emphasis on the ways in which women's lives were impacted by the repressive policies of the new regime.

Nafisi elaborates the difficulties she faced as a professor of English literature in post-revolutionary Iran, where she was eventually dismissed from her position at the University of Tehran in 1995 for refusing to wear a veil. Over the next two years she and seven of her female students gathered at her house every week to discuss works of Western literature. Nafisi's memoir, divided into four sections titled "Lolita," "Gatsby," "James," and "Austen," is framed around these discussions, which become a fulcrum for the group's efforts to make sense of contemporary Iranian life as well as serving as a form of cultural rebellion against the dictates of the Iranian government. The book ends with Nafisi's permanent emigration from Iran in 1997.

James Overholtzer

Red Azalea

Anchee Min

Key Facts

Time Period:
Late 20th Century

Relevant Historical Events:
Proletarian cultural revolution; Min's exile in the United States

Nationality:
China

Keywords:
Maoism; exile; revolution

OVERVIEW

Published in 1993, *Red Azalea* is Anchee Min's memoir of her life in China during the Great Proletarian Cultural Revolution (May 1966–October 1976), which was initiated and led by Mao Zedong. Min traces her early memories of the squalid living conditions, the Maoist propaganda, and her public denouncement of her teacher, as well as her sexual awakening for another woman, her lead role at the Shanghai Film Studio (overseen by Jiang Quing, Mao's wife), and her abrupt decision to move to the United States. The personal narrative is unique because Min not only acknowledges her victimization but also confesses to her ardent agency during the Cultural Revolution. Min occasionally interrupts the narrative in order to remind the reader that she writes with freedom in the United States, a country she had previously denounced.

Min composed her memoir in English during her first eight years of living in the United States, and some critics have identified it as part of a longstanding tradition of Asian expatriate writing. Min wrote the work in order to come to terms with her role in the Cultural Revolution. The publication was received with great enthusiasm, becoming an international best seller and earning a *New York Times* Notable Book award and many other honors. *Red Azalea* has influenced numerous Chinese American memoirs, and it is frequently taught at universities in programs that offer courses in gender and culture studies.

HISTORICAL AND LITERARY CONTEXT

Red Azalea offers a glimpse into China's Cultural Revolution, through which Mao intended to imbue the people with revolutionary fervor by attacking Chinese traditions. Propaganda, censorship, libricide, and the "cult of Mao" were ubiquitous. During these years, an estimated three million people were killed. Mao and his supporters imprisoned intellectuals, closed down universities, and removed senior party officials from office. Red Guards terrorized the people with their moral preoccupations, for example persecuting homosexuals. Mao demanded a return to the land, turning professional workers into physical laborers. He also remade gender norms by discouraging women from early marriage and forcing those in labor camps to behave and look like men.

On September 1, 1984, Min immigrated to the United States with the help of actress Joan Chen. From 1984 to 1992, Min composed *Red Azalea* in English. At the time of the book's publication, China's international profile was on the rise. The nation's bid for the 2000 Summer Olympics was denied, and the Chinese government subsequently threatened to boycott the 1996 Olympics and to resume its underground nuclear testing. Jiang Zemin had just become China's new president, coining the term "socialist market economy." This was four years after the Tiananmen Square massacre and four years before the political transfer of Hong Kong from England to China. The publication of Min's memoir provided many insights into a country that had piqued the interest of the world.

Red Azalea is part of a tradition of Chinese expatriate memoir writing. These personal narratives, in general, have provided inside information on twentieth-century China's political upheaval and have been popular in the West. In 1991 Jung Chang—a female Chinese expatriate living in England—published *Wild Swans:*

In *Red Azalea*, author Anchee Min describes her life in China under Mao Zedong, pictured here. While she initially embraces his form of communism, she later becomes disillusioned. © MICHAEL NICHOLSON/CORBIS

Three Daughters of China, a story about a family living through the turmoil of twentieth century China. It won the 1992 NCR Book Award, was named the 1993 British Book of the Year, and sold well more than ten million copies worldwide. *Wild Swans* stimulated international interest in China, helping to make *Red Azalea* attractive to publishers. Other notable Chinese expatriate writers include Gao Xingjian and Nien Cheng, who were both persecuted during the Cultural Revolution.

The success of *Red Azalea* led to a proliferation of personal narratives by Chinese expatriate women that recall their hardships during the Cultural Revolution. Among the most prominent of these is Anhua Gao's *To the Edge of the Sky* (2000). Like Min, Gao offers an inside perspective on the Cultural Revolution. Other successful memoirs published after *Red Azalea* include Ji-li Jiang's *Red Scarf Girl* (1998) and Adeline Yen Mah's *Falling Leaves* (1997). Min has written other books, including *Becoming Madame Mao* (2001), which documents the life of Mao's wife.

THEMES AND STYLE

The ideological enthusiasm behind Mao's Great Proletarian Cultural Revolution, and how it terrorized and brainwashed millions, is the central theme of *Red Azalea*. Throughout the memoir, Min offers examples of both Maoist propaganda and oppression. Min recalls her own agency: "I became a Mao activist in the district and won contests because I was able to recite the Little Red Book … I was able to recite all the librettos of the operas." Among these political operas, *The Red Lantern,* one of Min's favorites, begins, "My Dad is a pine tree, his will is strong. / A hero of indomitable spirit, he is a true Communist." Amid this Maoist enthusiasm, she recalls, "We often ran out of food by the end of the month. We would turn into starving animals … I drank water while longing for the day to end." As Min grows up, she describes the ways in which her life is controlled by the government, from forced labor to not being able to freely love another.

Min wrote her memoir in order to make more people aware of the Cultural Revolution's impact on the average Chinese citizen. However, the memoir also serves as a confession of her own involvement. The most powerful example is when Min publicly denounces her teacher—a Chinese American named Autumn Leaves—as a spy. Min recalls how for two hours a government secretary convinced her "that Autumn Leaves was a secret agent of the imperialists and was using teaching as a weapon to destroy our minds." Reflecting on her decision to censure Autumn Leaves, Min declares, "I was never forgiven … After the Revolution was over. It was after my begging for forgiveness, I heard the familiar hoarse voice say, I am sorry, I don't remember you. I don't think I ever had you as my student. It was at that meeting I learned the meaning of the word 'betrayal' as well as 'punishment.'"

ANCHEE MIN AND PEARL S. BUCK

In 1972, during the Cultural Revolution in China, Anchee Min was asked to denounce Pearl S. Buck as an "American cultural imperialist." Buck grew up in China and was the first American woman to win the Nobel Prize in Literature. Min complied, despite never having read Buck's magnum opus *The Good Earth* (1931). Years later, after the publication of *Red Azalea*, a fan gave Min a copy of Buck's book. In a 2011 interview with *BookBrowse*, Min confessed, "I read the book on a plane and burst into tears. I cried because I realized how beautifully Buck had told the story of the Chinese peasant … and that I was only one of a generation that had been indoctrinated to think poorly of Buck."

This led to the publication of Min's historical novel *Pearl of China* in 2011. She wrote the book in part, as she told *BookBrowse*, "to show how the relationship between Pearl Buck and China changed over time, just as mine had changed." As a Mao activist during the Cultural Revolution, Min condemned both the United States and Buck. In her 2005 preface to *Red Azalea,* she writes, "I wanted to tie grenades to my body and become a martyr by blowing up the Vietnam invaders, the Americans." Eventually, however, she came to understand the intense cultural indoctrination that took place during the Cultural Revolution.

Stylistically, *Red Azalea* is notable for its candor and its short, simple sentences. For example, Min writes, "I was an adult since the age of five. That was nothing unusual." In a 2003 *Time* magazine article, Lisa See comments, "Even though Min's English isn't perfect, that roughness is very refreshing." Min explains in a 1994 interview with Kathleen Wilson in *Contemporary Literary Criticism* that she learned to write by copying ancient Chinese opera scripts and that the poetry, compressed structure, and emotional intensity of the operas influenced her style. Min does not use direct dialogue because, as she explains in the *Contemporary Literary Criticism* interview, "[i]t sounds more Chinese." Also notable is the way in which Min anglicizes Chinese names; for example, her teacher is Autumn Leaves and her siblings are Blooming, Coral, and Space Conqueror.

CRITICAL DISCUSSION

Red Azalea was an overwhelming commercial success. It also was critically acclaimed, receiving excellent reviews from *Kirkus Reviews, Booklist,* the *New York Times Book Review,* and popular Chinese American women writers such as Amy Tan. Unlike *Wild Swans* and *The Kitchen God's Wife* (1991) by Tan, *Red Azalea* focuses on the later years of Mao's leadership during the Cultural Revolution. A big part of the memoir's success, according to Patti Duncan in her book *Tell This Silence* (2004), is "Min's resistance to official Chinese narratives of the Cultural Revolution."

In her preface to the 2005 edition of *Red Azalea*, Min explains that the book still holds great relevance because of the Chinese government's unwillingness to accept its mistakes and to change. Min condemns the Chinese government, which according to her calls the Cultural Revolution "Mao's tiny flaw," or an insignificant event that "should be forgotten." *Red Azalea* has continued to sell with vigor, thus making millions of people aware of what happened to ordinary Chinese citizens during the Cultural Revolution. Since the book's initial publication, critical interest has only increased.

Red Azalea is most often used in gender studies classes not only because of its overt homoeroticism but also because of the "de-gendering" of women during the Cultural Revolution. In a 1997 article for *College Literature,* Wendy Somerson explains how the Chinese Communist party de-gendered women by making them "look and behave as men did at that time. By encouraging women to wear the same dark clothes as men, short hair, and no make-up, the official doctrine suppressed women's traditional 'femininity.'" The effect of this was a unisex nation. In *Negotiating Identities* (2002), Helena Grice explores Western sexual stereotypes of Asian women and how publishing companies have exploited these to help sell works such as *Red Azalea*.

BIBLIOGRAPHY

Sources

"Anchee Min Talks about *Pearl of China*." *BookBrowse.* BookBrowse, 2011. Web. 18 Nov. 2012.

Duncan, Patti. *Tell This Silence: Asian American Women Writers and the Politics of Speech.* Iowa City: University of Iowa Press, 2004. Print.

Grice, Helena. *Negotiating Identities: An Introduction to Asian American Women's Writing.* Manchester, U.K.: Manchester University Press, 2002. Print.

Min, Anchee. *Red Azalea.* New York: Berkley Books, 2005. Print.

Somerson, Wendy. "Under the Mosquito Net: Space and Sexuality in *Red Azalea*." *College Literature* 24.1 (1997): 98–115. Print.

Wilson, Kathleen. Interview with Anchee Min. *Contemporary Literary Criticism* 86 (1994): 94–97. Print.

Further Reading

Chiu, Melissa, and Zheng Shengtian. *Art and China's Revolution.* New Haven, Conn.: Yale University Press, 2008. Print.

Grice, Helena. *Asian American Fiction, History and Life Writing.* New York: Routledge, 2009. Print.

Huang, Guiyou. *The Columbia Guide to Asian American Literature since 1945.* New York: Columbia University Press, 2006. Print.

Scott, A. O. "The Re-education of Anchee Min." *New York Times Magazine.* New York Times Magazine, 18 June 2000. Web. 18 Nov. 2012.

Wang, Annie. "A New Chapter." *Time.* Time, 20 Jan. 2003. Web. 18 Nov. 2012.

Ward, Elizabeth. "Anchee Min's Quiet Stiletto Stabs at Modern China." *Japan Times,* 12 March 1996: 16. Print.

Gregory Bach

RED SCARF GIRL
A Memoir of the Cultural Revolution
Ji-li Jiang

OVERVIEW

Red Scarf Girl: A Memoir of the Cultural Revolution (1997) is Ji-li Jiang's account of her childhood in China during the Cultural Revolution (1966–76). The narrative focuses on the internal conflict she experiences over her belief in Mao's revolution and its terrible consequences for her family. The memoir is told from the perspective of an innocent and intelligent young girl whose shock over revelations about her family's accrual of wealth, and the subsequent persecution of her and her family, further confuses her ideas about communism, righteousness, and her heritage. Jiang chooses this narrative perspective in order to free her story from the hardened judgments of an adult and imbue it with a sense of youthful idealism.

Jiang wrote her memoir after moving to the United States in 1984 to attend the University of Hawaii. Although she wanted *Red Scarf Girl* to be an inspiration for young readers struggling to make the right decisions in life, her primary objective was to teach American children about Chinese history and culture, which Jiang felt was lacking in her new country. The book was highly praised by critics and received numerous literary awards. Today it continues to be popular among adolescent girls.

HISTORICAL AND LITERARY CONTEXT

The Cultural Revolution was enacted by Mao Zedong, the Chinese Communist Party leader. It presented cultural reform to the people in terms of Marxist ideology, with a particular emphasis on class struggle. Due to opposition he faced within the party, Mao inspired China's student population, as well as the leaders of the People's Liberation Army, to take up his cause and pursue revolutionary change. The students formed the Red Guards, small vigilante organizations that were responsible for much destruction of property and many deaths during this time. The Red Guards destroyed anything that represented an old, capitalist culture and publicly degraded people thought to belong to the bourgeois class, including teachers, religious leaders, and actors. These people were publicly humiliated and often incurred violent beatings.

Jiang's memoir covers her adolescence and her experiences of the horrors of Mao's Cultural Revolution. Because her grandfather—who died when her father was seven years old—had been a landowner, Jiang's family was accused of exploiting people and was persecuted for being "bourgeois" due to the several "old culture" items it owned, including family photo albums, a stamp collection, and a mahogany bed frame. The family also had a housekeeper who, according to Jiang, was part of the family and could not find other employment. Although Jiang had been "brainwashed" into believing the ideas behind Mao's revolution, she did not understand how her family could be labeled as "bad" people deserving of public humiliation.

Red Scarf Girl is generally considered within two literary categories: the female adolescent memoir and Chinese literature about the Cultural Revolution. Jiang's book is often compared to memoirs such as Sue Saliba's *Watching Seagulls* (1997) and Tracey Porter's *Treasures in the Dust* (1999), both of which deal with young girls stoically facing life's challenges through their adolescent years. It also is similar to Feng Jicai's *Let One Hundred Flowers Bloom* (1996), which deals with historical events during the Cultural Revolution. Jiang was inspired to write her stories when she was given a copy of *Anne Frank: The Diary of a Young Girl* (1952) and was asked by her American friends to write her own memoir. Captivated by the childhood perceptions of Frank, Jiang decided to write her story from her perspective as a twelve-year-old, rather than as an adult recounting events with a critical eye.

After its publication, *Red Scarf Girl* received numerous honors, such as the Judy Lopez Memorial Award for Children's Literature, and was named as one of the best books of 1997 by *Publishers Weekly*. The book also had a significant cultural impact, exposing American children to Chinese culture and history. The book remains popular today among adolescent readers and continues to be lauded for its unique insights into a politically turbulent period for the Chinese.

THEMES AND STYLE

Red Scarf Girl centers on the internal conflict the author faces between her belief in Mao's revolution and the revolution's impact on her family. Jiang opens the memoir with several sayings she was taught in school, including, "Heaven and earth are great, but greater still is the kindness of the Communist Party;

❖ **Key Facts**

Time Period:
Late 20th Century

Relevant Historical Events:
Proletarian cultural revolution

Nationality:
China

Keywords:
Maoism; women's writing; revolution

Red Scarf Girl: A Memoir of the Cultural Revolution tells author Ji-li Jiang's story of survival during this time in Chinese history. Depicted here is a piece of government propaganda from the Cultural Revolution that was intended to encourage Chinese Communists to found a new standard of merit. © EVERETT COLLECTION INC/ALAMY

father and mother are dear, but dearer still is Chairman Mao." She admits to wholeheartedly believing in these slogans—later claiming she was brainwashed—and initially participated in actions to destroy the "Four Olds," which she defines as "old ideas, old culture, old customs, and old habits." Not until her dreams of success are crushed by the grim realities of the revolution does Jiang become caught in a web of confusion and humiliation, and she is overcome by a desire to do what she feels is fair.

The author's motivation for writing the text was to teach American children about the Cultural Revolution and her experiences of growing up in a different culture. She stresses in the book that she wanted to make the right decisions as a youth and now hopes to encourage her readers to do the same. She accomplishes this goal with a narrative voice that has been praised by critics for its innocence. "Why did Grandpa want to exploit people?" Jiang asks after learning that she cannot participate in the Red Successors, a student government in her school, because her grandfather was a landlord. Buying into the propaganda of the Communist party—including the notion that landlords are bad people—Jiang is constantly trying to balance her beliefs with her family's heritage.

The book is structured as a chronological narrative, with a tone that is initially calm and sure but quickly becomes sad, confused, and even disparate as the events unfold and Jiang's family becomes further persecuted for its bourgeois status. Jiang refrains from interjecting an analytical adult perspective into her narrative, as noted by Linda Brill Comerford in a 1997 *Publishers Weekly* review. Comerford lauds Jiang's "no-frills style in both speaking and writing," which "masterfully recreates the emotions she felt as a child 'brainwashed' into believing that her country had been saved by the grace of Chairman Mao."

CRITICAL DISCUSSION

Upon its publication, *Red Scarf Girl* received rave reviews for capturing the political milieu of China's Cultural Revolution from the unvarnished perspective of a child. Ilene Cooper's 1997 review in *Booklist* states, "Jiang's simple narrative voice is always true to the girl she was as events in China swirled into chaos." Comerford's *Publishers Weekly* review mentions the "passionate tone of this memoir" and Jiang's "undidactic approach," which invite "a thoughtful analysis of Ji-li's situation and beliefs."

As a book that provides an insightful look at Mao's Cultural Revolution, *Red Scarf Girl*'s legacy is secure. However, not all scholarship regards the narrator as a positive role model for adolescent girls. In a 1998 essay in *Journal for Adolescent and Adult Literacy,* Helen Harper examines Jiang's self-portrayal as a girl who stoically suffers for her beliefs instead of standing up for herself in a more active manner: "The passive stance taken by" the young Jiang in *Red Scarf Girl,* "while understandable considering the conditions, might have seemed less heroic if a male character were so positioned." Harper describes Jiang as "a 'good' girl suffering to do 'good' things for her family and country," a girl who focuses on "feminine suffering and endurance" rather than "active resistance."

Although Jiang's memoir is still widely read by adolescents, it inspires little attention from scholars. The most predominant trends in scholarship center on the quality of the prose and the book's ability to teach adolescent readers about Chinese history and society without seeming like a textbook. In a 1998 article in *Horn Book Magazine,* Roger Sutton examines *Red Scarf Girl*'s "rare and personal glimpse of the upheaval China suffered during the 1960s," in which the "breathlessness of the narration, tortures and triumphs related indiscriminately, gives the book immediacy if not subtlety." Both Sutton and Comerford marvel at how Jiang deftly handles difficult subject matter and makes it palatable to an adolescent audience.

BIBLIOGRAPHY

Sources

Comerford, Lynda Brill. "The Story of a Red Scarf Girl: A Talk with Ji-li Jiang." *Publishers Weekly* 10 Nov. 1997: 28. *Literature Resource Center.* Web. 18 Nov. 2012.

Cooper, Ilene. Rev. of *Red Scarf Girl: A Memoir of the Cultural Revolution,* by Ji-li Jiang. *Booklist* 1 Oct. 1997: 331. *Literature Resource Center.* Web. 18 Nov. 2012.

Harper, Helen. "Suffering Femininity: The Power and Pleasure of Young Adolescent Literature for Girls." *Journal for Adolescent and Adult Literacy* 42.2 (1998): 145–48. *JSTOR.* Web. 18 Nov. 2012.

Jiang, Ji-li. *Red Scarf Girl: A Memoir of the Cultural Revolution.* New York: HarperCollins, 1997. Print.

Rev. of *Red Scarf Girl: A Memoir of the Cultural Revolution,* by Ji-li Jiang. *Publishers Weekly* 28 July 1997: 75–77. *Literature Resource Center.* Web. 18 Nov. 2012.

Sutton, Roger. Rev. of *Red Scarf Girl: A Memoir of the Cultural Revolution,* by Ji-li Jiang. *Horn Book Magazine* Jan. 1998: 76. *Literature Resource Center.* Web. 18 Nov. 2012.

Further Reading

Daubier, Jean. *A History of the Chinese Cultural Revolution.* Trans. Richard Seaver. New York: Random House, 1974. Print.

"Ji-li Jiang." *Contemporary Authors Online.* Detroit: Gale, 2005. *Gale Biography in Context.* Web. 19 Nov. 2012.

Jiang, Ji-li. *Magical Monkey King: Mischief in Heaven.* New York: HarperCollins, 2004. Print.

Knight, Nick, and Colin Mackerras. "Cultural Revolution—China." *Encyclopedia of Modern Asia.* Ed. Karen Christensen and David Levinson. Vol. 2. New York: Scribner's, 2002. 221–25. *Gale World History in Context.* Web. 19 Nov. 2012.

"Mao Zedong." *Historic World Leaders.* Detroit: Gale, 1994. *Gale Biography in Context.* Web. 19 Nov. 2012.

Katherine Barker

JI-LI JIANG'S *MAGICAL MONKEY KING: MISCHIEF IN HEAVEN*

In order to further her goal of providing Western readers with knowledge about Eastern history and culture, Ji-li Jiang followed her publication of *Red Scarf Girl* with an illustrated children's book, *Magical Monkey King: Mischief in Heaven* (2004), which recounts traditional Chinese trickster stories. It tells the story of the beloved Chinese character Monkey and how he develops into Monkey King; charms Jade Emperor, the ruler of the universe; and overcomes adversity along the way. *Magical Monkey King* contains short chapters and illustrations that lend themselves to being read aloud in a group setting.

The book has been both a critical and commercial success. Many reviewers liken it to *Red Scarf Girl* because its discussion of traditional Chinese culture is directed at an American audience. Along with her continuing research and the development of her company, East West Exchange, the books promote Jiang's desire for an exchange between Eastern and Western nations that is aimed at improving cultural and political relations.

Stop-Time

Frank Conroy

❖ **Key Facts**

Time Period:
Mid-20th Century

Relevant Historical Events:
Conroy's experience at an experimental boarding school

Nationality:
American

Keywords:
avant-gardism; maturation

OVERVIEW

Published in 1967, Frank Conroy's memoir *Stop-Time* recounts incidents in the author's life between the ages of nine and eighteen. Conroy chronicles his coming-of-age in the 1940s, focusing on his relationship with his family, his experiences at the experimental Freemont boarding school, and his social and sexual maturation. *Stop-Time* examines questions of memory and narration, representing the disorganization and chaos of human recall by presenting the story of Conroy's life nonchronologically rather than as a clearly ordered portrait of maturation. The style and structure of *Stop-Time* address the relationship between memory, memoir, and fiction.

Conroy was born in New York City in 1936 to an American father and a Danish mother. He attended Haverford College in Pennsylvania, where he received a BA in 1958. *Stop-Time,* published when Conroy was only thirty-one, was seen by critics as a young man's book about his childhood, written when the recollections were still vivid and the emotions and experiences of youth still carried weight. Today the work is considered a key development in the form and style of the modern memoir, acknowledging the impossibility of life writing that is not constructed to appeal to an audience or that does not itself construct the narrative of the events and times it recounts.

HISTORICAL AND LITERARY CONTEXT

Although Conroy's birth year of 1936 allows readers to approximate when his memoir takes place, the work is notable for its refusal to draw attention to dates, reflecting what he sees as a child's ahistorical inhabitation of the moment. The Freemont boarding school in New York provides a memorable setting for key events in *Stop-Time.* Conroy describes life there as "a perpetual semi-hysterical holiday. We knew there were no limits in any direction…. Freedom was the key word. The atmosphere was heavy with the perfume of the nineteen-thirties—spurious agrarianism, sexual freedom (I was necking at the age of nine), sentimentalism, naiveté."

Stop-Time was Conroy's first publication. Before the book as a whole was published, five excerpts appeared in the *Partisan Review, New Yorker, Paris Review,* and *Urban Review* between 1965 and 1967 that were variously categorized as memoir, prose, and fiction. Despite enthusiasm from the editors at his book publisher, Viking Press, *Stop-Time* initially sold only 7,000 copies. In a 2004 interview with *Narrative,* Conroy reasoned that the work was fundamentally out of step with the era: "In the culture at the time, everything was drugs, and beatniks, the whole beginning of the revolution. And there I was with a sort of semiclassical book, and they didn't know whether it was fiction or nonfiction."

Stop-Time departs from conventional models of autobiography in several ways, most crucially in its refusal to offer the reader a kernel of understanding, a concluding moral. Conroy's work instead deals with the incomprehensible, with the ways that development occurs outside of human awareness. He has indicated that *The Autobiography of a Schizophrenic Girl* (1951) was a partial model for *Stop-Time.* In its blending of fact and fiction, *Stop-Time* has been compared to the works of James Joyce; Conroy also named Joyce as a stylistic influence, as well as George Orwell. In addition, critics have linked the work to the "mock autobiographies" of writers such as Gertrude Stein, Mary McCarthy, and Frederick Exley.

Despite its low sales figures, *Stop-Time* is seen as a paradigmatic work both of the childhood and avant-garde memoir. Conroy's disruption of narrative chronology and use of language to recreate remembered experiences and emotions have become key features of contemporary life writing. The names of Conroy's students at the University of Iowa Writers' Workshop—Jayne Anne Phillips, Stephanie Vaughn, Chris Offutt, Adam Haslett, Julie Orringer, and ZZ Packer, to name some—demonstrate the impact of his prose on the literary landscape. One student, Tom Grimes, published a memoir, *Mentor* (2010), about his experience working with Conroy.

THEMES AND STYLE

Conroy's themes include the emotional difficulties within a nuclear family, the attractions and complications of personal independence, and the role of reading in intellectual maturation. His father, who left the family when Conroy was "three or four," is an ambivalent figure in the text; he died young, and the author reports this with characteristically detached stoicism: "He showed me some books he had gotten to teach himself to draw. A few weeks later he died. He was six feet tall and at the end he weighed eighty-five pounds." The death of Conroy's father contrasts with the birth of his half-sister, whom he calls "the only complete and uncomplicated love in my life." Images of travel occur frequently throughout the text; cars, road trips, and walks provide metaphorical nonchronological linkages between the places, moments, and concerns of Conroy's youth. The work's title references a jazz term, signifying a pause intended for improvisation. This operates at two levels in Conroy's memoir, first indicating the interrupted and improvisatory act of narrated recollection and also referring to his stylistic interruption of chronology in his narrative form.

In his interview with *Narrative,* Conroy revealed his motivation for writing *Stop-Time:* having gone out to dinner with friends who had attended Ivy League colleges, Conroy "realized that they thought [his] background was the same as theirs. They didn't understand where [he] came from at all." Unlike many other autobiographical works, *Stop-Time* does not invest Conroy's young life with any particular significance. The memoir tells the story of his coming-of-age not because it is peculiar, important, or meaningful to anyone but the persons concerned; instead, it concerns, as Conroy writes, "passion recollected in tranquility." The reader is engaged merely by the intricacy of the author's recollections, the curious nonchronological nature of the narrative, and the impact and drama of Conroy's terse writing.

The memoir's prose style dramatizes the title's concern with the relationship of time to memory and recollection, shifting tenses and settings with equal swiftness. Conroy creates a fast pace, interspersing longer sentences with extremely short ones or with sentence fragments. In the prologue, for instance, he writes: "Fifty to sixty miles an hour through the empty streets of South London. No lights. Slamming in the gears, accelerating on every turn, winding up the big engine, my brain finally clean and white, washed out by the danger and the roar of the wind, I barreled into the countryside." His frequent use of lists and omission of conjunctions contributes to the book's rapid flow. He moves from past to present tenses within single paragraphs; additionally, tense shifts do not always correspond with narrative shifts between the 1940s and the 1960s, the writer's past and present. Conroy's nontraditional use of grammatical time demonstrates the truth of his dicta that "the act of concentrating on the writing and trying to write perfect sentences opens closed doors [in memory]."

CRITICAL DISCUSSION

Initial literary and critical responses to *Stop-Time* were favorable, as evidenced by its nomination for a National Book Award in 1967. A jacket blurb by acclaimed novelist William Styron praises the book for "its freshness, its wisdom and above all, in this day of youthful indulgence, its almost total lack of self-pity," and it also received favorable attention from author Norman Mailer. *Stop-Time* continued to attract literary interest for several years after its publication. Roger Sale's 1968 review in the *Hudson Review,* which places *Stop-Time* in the context of writing on memory, celebrates Conroy's vivid presentation of the objects and sensations of everyday life. While Walter Sullivan's 1969 piece for the *Sewanee Review,* "Fiction in a Dry Season: Some Signs of Hope," similarly praises *Stop-Time*'s stylish presentation of detail, it questions whether style alone is enough, concluding that "the whole seems less than the sum of its parts."

Conroy's innovations in memoir writing have been crucial to subsequent generations of authors, particularly through his work with the University of Iowa Writers' Workshop. He was director of the prestigious workshop from 1987 until his death in 2005, and under his stewardship, it stood for high culture, tight style, and avant-garde narrative strategies similar to those employed in *Stop-Time.* Conroy's writing has continued to attract critical attention, especially *Stop-Time,* which is seen as a key text in the development of the contemporary memoir genre. Academic criticism of his memoir has focused on its use of narrative technique to present biographical information; his stylistic innovations; and the vivid presence of objects, potentially metaphoric, in his presentation of the past.

Criticism such as Roger Ramsey's "The Illusion of Fiction in Frank Conroy's *Stop-Time*" has focused on parsing the relationship between literary narrative and biographical recollection. In his review for *Critique,* Timothy Dow Adams categorizes the book's genre as "mock autobiography," a literary simulation of the act of life writing. Other scholars have highlighted the intricacy

Frank Conroy, author of *Stop-Time*, in 2004. © AP IMAGES/CHARLIE NEIBERGALL

FRANK CONROY AND MUSIC

Stop-Time's title references a jazz term, a style of music with which Frank Conroy was intimately familiar. In addition to his literary works and career as a teacher, he was noted for his jazz piano talents. Conroy won a Grammy Award in 1986 and played with such major figures as Charles Mingus, Charlie Watts, and Bill Wyman. In his collection of essays *Dogs Bark, but the Caravan Rolls On* (2002), Conroy writes, "Jazz is American.... I believe the current renaissance will lead to a time when jazz is no longer marginalized, when artists working in jazz traditions will create work as strong as, and perhaps stronger than, the music that came out of the European tradition."

Music provided Conroy with a language for the intersection between external time and human memory and also served as the central thematic focus for the work he is perhaps best remembered for, his 1993 novel *Body and Soul*. The novel chronicles the history of Claude Rawlings, a virtuoso concert pianist who uses music to cushion the blows of his personal life. Reviewers of the book praised Conroy for his evocative narrative depiction of classical music, which was made possible by his deep knowledge of the art.

of *Stop-Time*'s use of metaphor and prose structure to represent memory. Likewise, Thomas Strychacz claims in the journal *Critique* that *Stop-Time* "demonstrates that we cling to form and structure in order to live and interpret lived experience, but it also suggests the danger of imposing patterns on actions and emotions."

BIBLIOGRAPHY

Sources

Adams, Timothy Dow. "'A Momentary Stay against Confusion': Frank Conroy's *Stop-Time*." *Critique* 27.3 (1986): 153. *MasterFILE Premier*. Web. 18 Nov. 2012.

Conroy, Frank. *Stop-Time*. New York: Viking, 1967. Print.

———. *Dogs Bark, but the Caravan Rolls On*. Boston: Houghton Mifflin, 2002. Print.

Crawford, Lacy. "Frank Conroy: An Interview." *Narrative* (2004): 1–31. Narrative. Web. 17 Nov. 2012.

Ramsey, Roger. "The Illusion of Fiction in Frank Conroy's *Stop-Time*." *Modern Fiction Studies* 20 (1974): 391–99. *MLA International Bibliography*. Web. 18 Nov. 2012.

Sale, Roger. "Seizing the Yesterday." *Hudson Review* 21.3 (1968): 546–52. Print.

Strychacz, Thomas F. "Controlling the 'Sloppiness of Things' in Frank Conroy's *Stop-Time*." *Critique* 29.1 (1987): 46. Print.

Sullivan, Walter. "Fiction in a Dry Season: Some Signs of Hope." *Sewanee Review* 77.1 (1969): 154–64. Print.

Further Reading

Bailey, Peter. "Notes on the Novel-as-Autobiography." *Genre: Forms of Discourse and Culture* 14.1 (1981): 79–93. *MLA International Bibliography*. Web. 18 Nov. 2012.

Baxter, Charles. *The Business of Memory: The Art of Remembering in an Age of Forgetting*. Vol. 3. New York: Graywolf, 1999. Print.

Coles, Robert. "Frank Conroy: Manchild in the Promised Land." *That Red Wheelbarrow* (1988): 110–14. *Essay and General Literature Index (H. W. Wilson)*. Web. 18 Nov. 2012.

Eakin, Paul John. "Living Autobiographically." *Biography* 28.1 (2005): 1–14. Print.

Grimes, Tom. *Mentor: A Memoir*. Portland: Tin House, 2010. Print.

Haegert, John. "Autobiography as Fiction: The Example of *Stop-Time*." *MFS Modern Fiction Studies* 3.4 (1987): 621–38. Print.

Workman, Mark E. "Narratable and Unnarratable Lives." *Western Folklore* (1992): 97–107. Print.

Carina Saxon

Under My Skin
Volume One of My Autobiography, to 1949
Doris Lessing

OVERVIEW

Under My Skin: Volume One of My Autobiography, to 1949 (1994), offers glimpses of Doris Lessing's experience growing up in Persia and southern Rhodesia during the waning years of the British Empire. The book ends with the author's move to England at age thirty with one of her three children in tow and the manuscript for her first novel in her suitcase. Her distrust of the autobiographical genre is evident throughout. While Lessing follows convention in *Under My Skin* to the extent that she attempts to provide truthful details about herself in loose chronological order, she devotes at least an equal amount of space to theoretical questions about the nature of truth and self. "If you try and claim your own life by writing an autobiography, at once you have to ask, But is this the truth?" Is there even such a thing as a self, she asks, given that people see life differently at different stages? Lessing frequently notes that her past fictions are truer than this current factual account. Along with her anecdotes and her examinations of the concept of self, the autobiography explores how humans are shaped by social rhythms, those larger historical forces outside their control.

When Lessing's autobiography was published, she was already considered one of the English language's most highly regarded writers of the twentieth century. Her novels had been published in multiple languages and had won many of Europe's prizes for literature. According to Lessing, *Under My Skin* was written partly in self-defense against unauthorized biographies and partly to satisfy her desire to make sense of aspects of her life that had always troubled her. The work was an instant success with devoted fans and literary critics alike and today is considered one of her greatest works.

HISTORICAL AND LITERARY CONTEXT

Under My Skin came out at a time when, as Lessing notes in the text, one could not write a literary autobiography without responding to questions about the nature of self. The term "postmodern" entered the lexicon of English literary criticism as early as the 1950s and by the 1970s had become a popular, if loosely defined, approach to writing. By the 1980s postmodernism and its attendant questions about self became central to memoirs, autobiographies, and personal essays of serious authors across the globe. The Czech writer Andrei Codrescu observes in an essay in *Autobiography and Postmodernism* (1995) that autobiography is composed of shifting frames of reference, reflecting the changes an author undergoes over time. Although Lessing derides questions on the nature of self as "rhetorical questions of the most tedious kind," she seems to have embraced the postmodern task with relish: "I read history with conditional respect. I have been involved a small way with big events, and know how quickly accounts of them become like cracked mirrors."

Under My Skin was not Lessing's first nonfiction account of her life. She wrote *Memoirs of a Survivor, An Attempt at an Autobiography* in 1975, when autobiography had fallen out of fashion. According to Lessing, neither her publishers nor the reading public showed much interest in the autobiographical aspect of the book. Foreign publishers left off the second part of the title and her English publishers did not include it in subsequent editions. When biography became marketable again during the early 1990s in England, Lessing had heard rumors that there were five American biographers working on her story, none of whom had asked permission. One had never even talked with her. She wrote *Under My Skin* in self-defense and followed it three years later with *Walking in the Shade: Volume Two of My Autobiography, 1949–1962*.

Under My Skin belongs to a tradition of literary memoirs such as James Baldwin's *Go Tell It on the Mountain* that not only give an account of the author's life but shed light on a culture, a historical moment, a place, a social or political issue, or some combination thereof. Descriptions of Lessing's mother's Liberty curtains hanging in the family's mud hut illustrate her desperation to stay in the middle class and exposes the class system in Britain, while stories of her amputee father's refusal to live in England after World War I represents a generation of British men who felt betrayed by their country. The lifestyles and mores of British citizens living in an African colony during the first half of the twentieth century are contrasted with the difficult lives of the Africans. Lessing's book also fits into the genre of postmodern autobiography that flourished during the 1990s. In his essay in the *Writer's*

❖ *Key Facts*

Time Period:
Late 20th Century

Relevant Historical Events:
British colonialism; decolonization; rise of postmodernism

Nationality:
South African

Keywords:
postmodernism; women's writing; postcolonialism

Author Doris Lessing at her home in London in 1994. © DAVID LEVENSON/ GETTY IMAGES

Chronicle, Hugh Ryan argues that perceptions of truth in literature changed dramatically after World War II and made it difficult for people who lived through that time to write with the conviction and clarity of their modernist predecessors. He notes, "The brutality of war tested the belief in perfection and progress. Authors tried to replicate for their readers the state of not knowing what was true or good." Other works representative of this genre include Annie Dillard's *The Writing Life* and Mario Vargas Llosa's *A Fish in the Water.*

The success of *Under My Skin* led to the publication of the second volume of her autobiography. Since 1994 Lessing has written several more novels, three collections of short stories, plays, and a graphic novel, along with personal essays including the collection *Time Bites* (2004). In 2007 she was awarded the Nobel Prize in Literature.

THEMES AND STYLE

The central theme of *Under My Skin* is whether the subject of an autobiography is a self, an intact unchanging person, or a postmodern subject who changes over time. Lessing writes, "Telling the truth or not telling it, and how much, is a lesser problem than the one of shifting perspectives, for you see your life differently at different stages, like climbing a mountain while the landscape changes with every turn in the path." She frequently comments on how she felt about a situation or a person at different ages. For example, as a young girl, Lessing saw her mother as the embodiment of everything she (Lessing) disliked. As a woman in her seventies writing her autobiography, she sees her mother as a tragic figure, courageous and dignified in the face of great disappointment. Her perceptions of herself have also undergone many changes: "Had I written this when I was thirty, it would have been a pretty combative document. In my forties, it would have been a wail of despair and guilt: oh my God, how could I have done this or that? Now I look back at that child, that girl, that young woman, with a more and more detached curiosity."

Although Lessing's stated reason for writing *Under My Skin* is self-defense, the text also reveals an intense personal desire to understand aspects of her life that have continued to trouble her. These include her relationship with her mother, her fascination with politics, the origins of her skepticism, her sexuality, and her fear of succumbing to what she labels the "nightmare repetition" of the past. She attempts to tease apart all the factors that made her who she is, looking at what it means to be a British citizen raised in a colony, the child of middle-class parents, a white person in a racist society, and a woman in a man's world and at how all of these factors combine to create the person. In a volume set between the end of World War I and the end of World War II, war is seen as an especially determinative factor. "We are all of us made by war, twisted and warped by war, but we seem to forget it."

Stylistically, Lessing's autobiography is remarkable for its vivid, intense, and often unsavory descriptions of childhood, which invite the reader not only to understand but to actually share the author's experience. Her language attempts to create the same sensations in the reader's mind that Lessing felt living through it. She opens chapter 3 with an image of herself as a small child: "A tiny thing among trampling, knocking careless giants who smell, who lean down towards you with great ugly hairy faces, showing big dirty teeth." Children experience the world much more viscerally than adults do, Lessing claims. Everything is experienced physically, first and foremost. Flavors explode in the mouth, smells beckon or repel. As we age, Lessing writes, we replace firsthand experience of the world with what we've been told to expect or been shown in pictures. "Children and grown-ups do not live in the same sensory world," she observes.

CRITICAL DISCUSSION

Scholars hailed *Under My Skin* as a welcome return to Lessing's earlier, more challenging style. Distinguished British novelist A. S. Byatt praised the book in the *Threepenny Review,* as did William Pritchard for the *Hudson Review.* Pritchard observes that the prose in *Under My Skin* has the kind of "relaxed power and delicacy" that had been absent from her work for twenty years. He continues that the first half of the book in particular "gets under the alert reader's skin." In her review of the autobiography for the *Women's Review of Books,* Ellen Cronan Rose agrees that the writing is most vivid in the first half. For Rose, the most interesting aspect of the autobiography is the way it documents the evolution of Lessing's interpretation of people and events in her life that she is "always trying to understand better." Critics also praised it for providing another window into the fascinating mind of the author.

If anything, the postmodern autobiography and memoir have increased in popularity in the two decades since the publication of *Under My Skin,* and the book continues to be read and examined by scholars. Areas of interest include information on Lessing's life and her approach to writing, as well as issues of gender, race, and class that are as relevant today as they were at the time the book was written. British novelist Hilary Mantel has called Lessing's autobiography her "greatest work of art."

Current scholarship on the text addresses issues connected to being white in colonial and postcolonial Africa. Typical of such scholarship is Julie Cairnie's 2007 *English Studies in Canada* article, in which she discusses the struggle that white women born in Africa have with the concept of home. They are perpetual outsiders no matter where they live. Cairnie argues that Lessing's choice to leave was an empathetic gesture. "In two of her texts written during and about the colonial period, *The Grass Is Singing* (1950) and *Under My Skin* (1994), Doris Lessing concentrates on the problem of white women and home, but she de-emphasizes that connection in the postcolonial period and turns her attention to the rights, responsibilities, and perils of black Zimbabweans and black Zimbabwean women in particular." Other scholars have criticized the recurring themes of madness and fate in Lessing's books as her way of deflecting group responsibility for the ravages of colonialism.

STORIES ABOUT CATS: DORIS LESSING'S ANIMAL NATURE

In *Under My Skin,* Doris Lessing reports that she cried longer and harder over the loss of her first cat than she did over the deaths of her parents or her brother. As a little girl, she became attached to a stray cat from the streets of Tehran, and when her family moved to Africa, she was forced to leave him behind. She was inconsolable. "For years the death of a cat plunged me into grief so terrible I had to regard myself as rather mad." Later she became attached to the cats on the African farm where she grew up. Her fascination with the fickle, demanding creatures has stayed with her through many changes in life, from the stone house in Persia to various flats in London.

Lessing has written three books on cats. *Particularly Cats* (1967), *Particularly Cats and Rufus the Survivor* (1993), and *The Old Age of El Magnifico* (2000). These are memoirs in which the author introduces the cats that have slunk and bullied and charmed their way into her life. She tells their stories through a mix of fiction and nonfiction, reveling in their exploits, rivalries, terrors, affections, ancient gestures, and learned behaviors. Her writings on cats have the effect of humanizing her.

BIBLIOGRAPHY

Sources

Byatt, A. S. "Out of Africa." Rev. of *Under My Skin,* by Doris Lessing. *Threepenny Review* 61 (1995): 15–16. *JSTOR.* Web. 6 Nov. 2012.

Cairnie, Julie. "Women and the Literature of Settlement and Plunder: Toward an Understanding of the Zimbabwean Land Crisis." *English Studies in Canada* 33.5 (2007): 165–88. *LION.* Web. 7 Nov. 2012.

Hargreaves, Tracy. "'… to find a Form That Accommodates the Mess': Truth Telling from Doris Lessing to B. S. Johnson." *Yearbook of English Studies* 42 (2012): 204–22. *LION.* Web. 7 Nov. 2012.

Lessing, Doris. *Under My Skin: Volume One of My Autobiography, to 1949.* London: HarperCollins, 1994. Print.

———. *Walking in the Shade: Volume Two of My Autobiography, 1949–1962.* London: HarperCollins, 1997. Print.

Pritchard, William H. "Looking Back at Lessing." Rev. of *Under My Skin,* by Doris Lessing. *Hudson Review* 48.2 (1995): 317–24. *LION.* Web. 6 Nov. 2012.

Rose, Ellen Cronan. "Somebody: But Who?" Rev. of *Under My Skin,* by Doris Lessing. *Women's Review of Books* 7.6 (1995): 11–12. *JSTOR.* Web. 6 Nov. 2012.

Ryan, Hugh. "The Postmodern Memoir." *Writer's Chronicle.* AWP, Mar.–Apr. 2012. Web. 8 Nov. 2012.

Further Reading

Bergland, Betty. "Postmodernism and the Autobiographical Subject: Reconstructing the 'Other.'" *Autobiography and Postmodernism.* Ed. Kathleen Ashley, Leigh Gilmore, and Gerald Peters. Amherst: University of Massachusetts Press, 1994. Print.

Greene, Gale. *Doris Lessing: The Poetics of Change.* Ann Arbor: University of Michigan Press, 1994. Print.

Klein, Carole. *Doris Lessing: A Biography.* New York: Carroll, 2000. Print.

Linfield, Susie. "Interview with Doris Lessing." *Salmagundi* 130–31 (2001): 59–74. *JSTOR.* Web. 7 Nov. 2012.

Reese, Christopher L. Rev. of *Doris Lessing: A Biography,* by Carole Klein. *World Literature Today* 75.2 (2001): 340–41. *JSTOR.* Web. 7 Nov. 2012.

Rowe, Margaret Roan. *Doris Lessing.* London: Macmillan, 1994. Print.

Rubenstein, Roberta. *Home Matters: Longing and Belonging, Nostalgia and Mourning in Women's Fiction.* New York: Palgrave, 2001. Print.

Kristin King-Ries

The Unwanted

Kien Nguyen

Key Facts

Time Period:
Early 21st Century

Relevant Historical Events:
Vietnam War; passage of the Amerasian Immigration Act

Nationality:
American

Keywords:
immigration; alienation; postwar trauma

OVERVIEW

In Vietnamese American literature, Kien Nguyen's *The Unwanted* (2001) stands as the first memoir recounting an Amerasian's traumatic childhood and painful adolescence in postwar Vietnam after the United States completely withdrew its troops in April 1975. The autobiography is told chronologically, opening with the narrator Kien's vivid memories of his fifth birthday and his family's affluence just three years prior to the end of the Vietnam War and concluding with his departure for the United States in the late 1980s. In postwar Vietnamese society, Kien's mixed-race background marks him as a target of discrimination and maltreatment because he represents the ignominious remnants of the past, or the "trash," left behind by the Americans. The author employs pathos effectively in the narrative, as he describes in vivid detail the realities of the life he had to live in postwar communist Vietnam, marked by corruption, poverty, social injustice, dehumanization, and oppression. These conditions aggravated the vicissitudes and calamities that Kien and his family were forced to endure.

After Vietnam was reunified in April 1975, people who had allied themselves with the former South Vietnamese government and/or the United States were under strict surveillance by the communists. Mothers of Amerasian children were considered degraded prostitutes who had immorally sold their bodies to the invaders. It was not until 1982, when the United States passed the Amerasian Immigration Act, that Amerasian children born between 1950 and 1982 could relocate to the United States with their families. When *The Unwanted* appeared in 2001, it received praise from reviewers, primarily due to its realistic portrayal of the social upheavals in postwar Vietnam and the human aspirations for equality and freedom.

HISTORICAL AND LITERARY CONTEXT

The Unwanted records the voice of an Amerasian child who was victimized by a racially discriminating communist society. There are no certain statistical data on Amerasians born during the Vietnam War, but it is estimated that more than 75,000 Amerasians and their relatives were granted entry into the United States in the late 1980s. Most were abandoned as children after their American fathers completed their military or contracted service and returned to the United States. Vietnamese women who were involved in romantic relationships or purely sexual affairs with U.S. soldiers usually were disdained for their apparent moral turpitude by a public that expected Vietnamese women to maintain purity in the Vietnamese bloodline. Generally, it was assumed that only a decadent woman would date or marry an American, partly due to the infamous reputation of U.S. soldiers, whose lasciviousness during the war was almost institutionalized. If mothers of Amerasians had been wealthy during the war, the communist regime classified them as "friends of the Americans," advocates of capitalism, and traitors to their country because they obviously had refused to join the national cause for liberation or function productively in the working class. Thus, in the postwar society, they and their mixed-race children faced animosity and discrimination from the local authorities and from many biased Vietnamese people.

Despite being published almost thirty years after the end of the Vietnam War, *The Unwanted* was received by an American public still obsessed with the war and its aftermath. Readers were familiar with literature written by U.S. combatants, who focused on personal war experiences and postwar trauma. Little was known, however, about the Vietnamese who could not escape Vietnam and, thus, had to suffer indignations under the communist regime because of their previous political affiliations. Likewise, the fate of Amerasians remained unknown, as they generally were rejected by both cultures. *The Unwanted,* on the one hand, condemns Vietnamese communism for its maltreatment of people—and particularly of Amerasian children—under its administration. On the other hand, it brings attention to the so-called "dust of life," or remnants, of the U.S. occupation in Vietnam, who sometimes were abandoned even by their mothers and families in postwar Vietnam.

The Unwanted can be classified under the rubric of literature of survival, which normally focuses on an individual's traumatic experience and the lengthy period of time it can take—sometimes twelve to fifteen years—for the victim to process and write about traumatic past experiences. Nguyen's autobiography can be grouped with the literature of trauma and survival written by preceding Vietnamese American memoirists, such as Tran Tri Vu's *Lost Years: My 1,632 Days in Vietnamese Reeducation Camps* (1989), Le Ly Hayslip's *When Heaven and*

Vietnamese villagers watch the arrival of American soldiers in a May 12, 1967, photograph. Kien Nguyen describes growing up in Vietnam with Vietnamese and American ancestry in *The Unwanted*. © BETTMANN/CORBIS

Earth Changed Places (1989), and Jade Ngoc Quang Huynh's *South Wind Changing* (1994). *The Unwanted* is the first childhood memoir written from an Amerasian perspective, but it shares many themes that previous memoirs present, especially those pertaining to social conditions prevailing in postwar Vietnam. Thus, the work is not only a personal account of childhood trauma but also a historical document about social realities in postwar Vietnam.

The publication of *The Unwanted* helps to justify the U.S. criticism of Vietnamese violations of human rights and, for better or worse, reinforces the biased portrayal of the communists as "jungle savages." Since the reunification of Vietnam in 1975, the United States has continuously raised concerns about the absence of justice, freedom, and democracy in Vietnam. Although Nguyen's memoir does not address his initial resettlement in the United States, it should be noted that Amerasians were unwelcomed by the American public, rejected by their American fathers, and generally discriminated against due to their mixed-raced identity. Often, the United States was not the dreamland that they had expected. Many were unable to find jobs due to their illiteracy, and some became gangsters. The Amerasians (America's "forgotten sons and daughters"), along with U.S. veterans (America's "ignored generation of returnees"), brought the war home.

THEMES AND STYLE

The Unwanted directly addresses Vietnamese racial discrimination, which derives from various cultural, historical, and political factors. Due to the country's long history of occupation by foreign forces—the Chinese, the French, the Japanese, and the Americans—many Vietnamese people traditionally did not approve either of interracial marriage or of romantic interludes. For instance, Kien's cousin, Tin, humiliates Kien with such obloquy as "a half-breed is a bastard child, usually the result from when a woman has slept with a foreigner." Kien's mother, Khuon, is degradingly called a "hooker" because it is thought that only through "prostitution" can a Vietnamese woman give birth to "half-breed" children.

Another major theme concerns the contradictions between communist propaganda and communist exercitation. This theme constitutes a thread that weaves its way throughout the book. Communist ideals and slogans seem to promote justice, equality, and happiness for all. However, in reality, privileges, opportunities, and recognitions devolve upon only a limited group of communist leaders and their relatives. Therefore, corruption, bribery, and usurpation are means through which communist authorities increase their personal wealth. In a conversation between Nguyen and his publisher, he said that he wrote the book as "therapy" for all the pain, suffering, and trauma he had experienced in Vietnam. Writing down his memories helped alleviate some of his deep-seated, negative feelings, such as "anger, sorrow, and regret." Nguyen also thought that, if he did not write about his past, "no other Vietnamese Amerasian would." *The Unwanted* serves, furthermore, as the author's attempt to understand his mother more truthfully rather than ideally. In writing the memoir, Nguyen quietly articulates his belief that a better future for the human race will arise only through an honest examination of past wrongdoings, so that people can "avoid repeating our past errors."

Nguyen skillfully uses suspense throughout the memoir to evoke the reader's curiosity and interest in the narrated events. He faces and overcomes many adversities, which makes the story of his survival both appealing and admirable. For example, he is sexually abused by his mother's live-in boyfriend, violently beaten by his cousins, discriminated against by his peers, and arrested by the police. Whenever an unfavorable incident happens to him or his family, he describes it so vividly that some readers have questioned the verisimilitude of the memoir and the reliability of his memory. Whether advertently or not, Nguyen successfully evokes his readers' emotions and empathy as he leads them past the stations along his life's journey, so fraught with "terror and repression, abuse and neglect, strength, and ultimately … survival."

CRITICAL DISCUSSION

The Unwanted received very positive reviews when it was released in 2001. Generally, Nguyen was commended for his beautiful and inspirational writing style, his compelling and dramatic storytelling techniques, and his successful portrayal of human valor and the will to survive. *Kirkus Reviews* affirms that "anyone looking for a firsthand insight into America's tangled relations with Vietnam will not be disappointed." Richard C. Kagan, who reviewed the memoir for the *Minneapolis Star Tribune,* concludes that the book is a "highly charged, episodic account of oppression, betrayal, and escape." Carol Memmott, reviewer for *USA Today,* draws attention to how the human mind is able to "call up painful details with extreme depth and clarity" and how successfully Nguyen "takes us into the heart and spirit of one person's undeserved and tragic childhood."

Nguyen's memoir often is expatiated within the corpus of biracial literature and the literature of trauma. Nathalie Huynh Chau Nguyen, in her comparative article on Euroasian/Amerasian perspectives, observes that "race, class, culture and politics all played their part in the adverse conditions experienced by Amerasians and their mothers in the postwar years." Rocío G. Davis notes that the protagonist Kien "negotiate[s] a process of racial ambivalence which exhausts the supposed fixity and impermeability of racial boundaries." Generally, issues such as the coming-of-age experience, childhood sexual abuse, mother-son relationships, identity crises, racial affiliations, and recent postcolonial discourse on hybridity draw scholarly attention to Nguyen's memoir.

Since 1975, the United States has accused Vietnam of human rights violations. *The Unwanted* reaffirms this criticism and implies that, although democracy and freedom do not exist in Vietnam, they do exist abundantly in the United States. This raises a question for postcolonial critics: Can the United States advertise its democracy to the world and exercise its role as the "global policeman" in many third-world countries based on such literary justification? Although *The Unwanted* is intentionally a personal memoir, it does carry political undertones—a common element among life narratives, which, by nature, can often be considered historical documents with certain political and emotionally charged messages.

BIBLIOGRAPHY

Sources

Davis, Rocío G. "Reading Asian American Biracial Autobiographies of Childhood: Norman Reyes' *Child of Two Worlds* and Kien Nguyen's *The Unwanted*." *Prose Studies: History, Theory, Criticism* 25.2 (2002): 79–101. Print.

Kagan, Richard C. "Book Recalls Burdens, Bias after Saigon Falls." Rev. of *The Unwanted,* by Kien Nguyen. *Minneapolis Star Tribune* 29 Apr. 2001. Print.

Memmott, Carol. "After Saigon Falls, Suffer the Amerasian Children." Rev. of *The Unwanted,* by Kien Nguyen. *USA Today* 5 Apr. 2001. Print.

Nguyen, Nathalie Huynh Chau. "Euroasian/Amerasian Perspectives: Kim Lefèvre's *Métisse Blanche* (White Métisse) and Kien Nguyen's *The Unwanted*." *Asian Studies Review* 29 (2005): 107–22. Print.

Rev. of *The Unwanted,* by Kien Nguyen. *Kirkus Reviews* 20 May 2010. Print.

Further Reading

Bass, Thomas A. *Vietnamerica: The War Comes Home.* New York: Soho, 1996. Print.

Davis, Rocío G. *Begin Here: Reading Asian North American Autobiographies of Childhood.* Honolulu: University of Hawai'i Press, 2007. Print.

DeBonis, Steven. *Children of the Enemy: Oral Histories of Vietnamese Amerasians and Their Mothers.* Jefferson, N.C.: McFarland, 1995. Print.

Freeman, James M. *Changing Identities: Vietnamese Americans 1975–1995.* Boston: Allyn and Bacon, 1995. Print.

Freeman, James M. *Hearts of Sorrow.* Palo Alto, Calif.: Stanford University Press, 1989. Print.

McKelvey, Robert S. *The Dust of Life, America's Children Abandoned in Vietnam.* Seattle: University of Washington Press, 1999. Print.

———. *A Gift of Barbed Wire: America's Allies Abandoned in South Vietnam.* Seattle: University of Washington Press, 2002. Print.

Memon, Wentz A. *Misplaced.* Frederick, Md.: PublishAmerica, 2007. Print.

Warren, Andrea. *Escape from Saigon: How a Vietnam War Orphan Became an American Boy.* New York: Square Fish, 2008. Print.

Yarborough, Trin. *Surviving Twice: Amerasian Children of the Vietnam War.* Washington, DC: Potomac, 2005. Print.

Quan Ha

THE WOMAN WARRIOR
Memoirs of a Girlhood among Ghosts
Maxine Hong Kingston

OVERVIEW

Maxine Hong Kingston's memoir *The Woman Warrior: Memoirs of a Girlhood among Ghosts* (1975) represents a significant contribution to the tradition of immigrant narratives. Blending vignettes from her own life with Chinese folktales and legends narrated by her mother, Kingston cultivates a style that emulates the distinctive syllabic and vocal characteristics of the Chinese language. She also plays with point of view, relaying her own perspective as a Chinese American in the first person; integrating the second person as a medium for sharing Chinese legends and tales; and employing the third person to communicate the speech patterns of her parents. *The Woman Warrior* reveals Kingston's struggle to reconcile her identity as a native-born American with her Chinese cultural heritage. The distinctive style and structure of the book reflect her somewhat schizophrenic experience of adapting to life in the United States while simultaneously trying to navigate her Chinese heritage.

Kingston's book is one of the first autobiographical accounts of the experiences of a Chinese American caught between two cultures—immersed in American life yet tethered to the practices and beliefs propagated by the country of her heritage. *The Woman Warrior* appeared at a time when writers were experimenting with the style and form of autobiography. As such, it garnered the interest of a wide spectrum of scholars, including those interested in postmodern narrative and those who concentrated on cultural marginalization and ostracism. Kingston's use of a multivocal narrative structure, which symbolized her own sense of displacement and alienation, resonated with readers. The initial reception of the book was overwhelmingly positive, and Kingston won the National Book Critics Circle Award for nonfiction in 1976.

HISTORICAL AND LITERARY CONTEXT

Kingston wrote *The Woman Warrior* during a period when authors were experimenting with innovative narrative styles and structures. She graduated from the University of California at Berkeley in 1962, around the time that the focus of literary studies began to expand to include more consciously the voices of people who had been previously marginalized. Amid the Black Power and feminist movements, women, African Americans, and writers from other ethnic groups were garnering academic attention. In addition, a new emphasis on how different theoretical schools could impact interpretations of literary writings was emerging. By the early 1970s autobiography as a genre was undergoing a radical evolution, allowing women and minorities to express themselves in creative ways. Kingston's text is part of a distinct subgenre of autobiography that describes the struggles of women belonging to ethnic minority groups.

At the time *The Woman Warrior* was published, American culture was full of stereotypes regarding Chinese Americans and Chinese culture. Chinese and, by extension, Chinese American women were widely perceived as silent, passive, and subservient. Kingston is credited with helping to challenge that myth through both her assertion of a bold narrative authority and her reinterpretation of the Chinese American woman as a warrior, an image influenced by both Chinese legend and American feminism. In subsequent works such as *China Men* (1980) and *Tripmaster Monkey* (1989), she challenges stereotypes of Chinese masculinity and of the Chinese immigrant experience in the United States.

In writing *The Woman Warrior*, Kingston was influenced by a broad range of texts and literary traditions, from Chinese folklore to American transcendentalism and European modernism. In a 1991 *American Literary History* interview with Shelley Fisher Fishkin, Kingston credits such diverse influences on her writing as Walt Whitman's poetry and Virginia Woolf's novel *Orlando*, about an ambiguous character who is sometimes a man and sometimes a woman. In writing *The Woman Warrior*, Kingston made use of innovative literary elements such as ambiguity and pluralism to communicate the anxiety and bewilderment involved in traversing two cultural spheres. Her use of postmodern techniques that incorporate the sense of instability is demonstrated by her choice to integrate first-, second-, and third-person voices into her writing. Through this approach, she is able to avoid establishing a stable narrative voice or an "I" with whom the reader can identify; instead, the reader experiences the same uncertainties that Kingston encountered while growing up.

❖ *Key Facts*

Time Period:
Late 20th Century

Relevant Historical Events:
Growth of cultural studies; Kingston's parent's emigration from China

Nationality:
American

Keywords:
immigration; identity; multiculturalism

Chinese ghost masks in Taiwan. In *The Woman Warrior: Memoirs of a Girlhood among Ghosts*, Maxine Hong Kingston discusses the "ghosts" of her Chinese heritage and American childhood.
© HENRY WESTHEIM PHOTOGRAPHY/ALAMY

Since the publication of *The Woman Warrior*, its usage in college and university courses has expanded exponentially. Because it treats numerous cultural and political issues, the book appears on women's studies and gender studies syllabi, on Asian American cultural and literary class reading lists, and in English literature classes. Her influence has been so broad that she is considered the preeminent literary voice and symbolic representative of the viewpoints of Chinese Americans. Her work, however, has been challenged by critics who have interpreted her writing as representing a universal Asian American perspective in a way that eradicates the differences between peoples of different countries of origin. Kingston has denied the validity of this interpretation of her work. In a global sense, her writing not only shifted the meaning and predominant structure of the autobiographical form but also ushered in an era in which Chinese American voices could be heard.

THEMES AND STYLE

The Woman Warrior examines the difficulties of forging personal identity as a woman caught between cultures. This theme is exhibited throughout the book's five chapters. The first two chapters, told in the third-person point of view, reveal Chinese folk legends that have impacted Kingston's perceptions of her heritage. The first of these chapters describes Kingston's aunt, who drowned herself after becoming pregnant during her husband's absence; subsequently, the woman's name was never uttered by the family because "it was as if she had never been born." The third chapter chronicles Kingston's mother's difficult life in China, tracing the impact that stories of life in China had on Kingston's perception of both her mother and herself while she was growing up. The fourth chapter traces the story of Kingston's mother's sister, whose life in China unfolded in a different fashion. The fifth chapter focuses on Kingston's experiences in the United States as a Chinese American and concentrates on her relationship with her mother. In this section, the author describes how she pushes the "deformed into [her] dreams, which [were] in Chinese, the language of impossible stories," acknowledging that she feels caught between the trappings of two contrastive and sometimes seemingly incompatible cultures.

Kingston wrote *The Woman Warrior* in stream-of-consciousness fragments, attempting to recreate, as accurately as possible, her own thought patterns. She coalesced and condensed these elements into coherent stories that she hoped would reflect the syllabic nuances of the Chinese language. She used imagery to make the stories and chapters as "American-friendly" as possible, perhaps to communicate her experiences more clearly to a broader reading audience. According to Paul Skenazy and Tera Martin's *Conversations with Maxine Hong Kingston* (1998), Kingston viewed herself as a translator, to the extent that she wished to "find an American language that would translate the speech of the people who are living their lives with the Chinese language." One of her strongest desires was for the book to be taken as a "corrective" to stereotypes of Chinese Americans and misperceptions concerning the nature of their experiences growing up in the United States.

Kingston utilizes postmodern narrative techniques by juxtaposing Chinese folktales with the events she relates from her own perspective. This format allows her to demonstrate the contradictions inherent in the two cultural spheres she inhabits and also to display the impact that narratives from her country of heritage had on her coming-of-age experiences. She incorporates the Chinese folktales to illustrate the unspoken and silenced elements of her family's history and to offer the characters of Chinese folklore as models through which to understand heritage and identity. The effects of her stylistic and structural choices are demonstrated most clearly in her first-person descriptions, such as when she observes, "Be careful what you say. It comes true. It comes true. I had to leave home in order to see the world logically, logic the new way of seeing. I learned to think that mysteries are for explanation…. Give me plastics, periodical tables, TV dinners with vegetables no more complex than peas mixed with diced carrots. Shine floodlights into dark corners: no ghosts." Kingston understood the lingering impact of language on perspective and realized that she had a greater familiarity with the more concrete and practical existence she experienced living in the United States, haunted though it might have been by the ghosts (both described and imagined) from her heritage.

CRITICAL DISCUSSION

The Woman Warrior was an immediate popular success when it was first published in 1975 and quickly attracted a substantial body of positive book reviews. Reviewing the book for the *Library Journal,* Sharon Wong described it as "beautifully written," while Jane Kramer's *New York Times* review lauded it as a "brilliant memoir," noting that it "shocks us out of our facile rhetoric, past the clichés of our obtuseness, back to the mystery of a stubbornly, utterly foreign sensibility."

Kingston's memoir stayed on the best-seller list for more than ten years. This success can be partially explained by the book's prevalence on university syllabi and by Kingston's status as an emblem to which women respond positively and enthusiastically. In the years following its publication, the book did, however, attract some controversy. Asian American scholar Frank Chin notably derided Kingston for misrepresenting aspects of Chinese culture and for seemingly accepting certain Western stereotypes about it. Other critics called into question the truth of many of Kingston's stories about her own life. Such controversies have ultimately served to further interest in the memoir, which has been the subject of an extensive body of critical work considering its statements about gender, immigrant life, narrative, and cultural inheritance.

Much of the most recent criticism on *The Woman Warrior* has focused on the text's relationship to the coming-of-age stories of other women straddling two cultures. Most notably, the text is often considered alongside several other roughly contemporaneous works of literature by women of color that emerged from the same cultural milieu, among them Toni Morrison's *The Bluest Eye* (1970) and Alice Walker's *The Color Purple* (1982). Like Kingston's memoir, these works of fiction attest to the challenges of constructing a single cohesive identity and navigating dual cultural traditions. Scholars have also considered the manner in which Kingston's autobiography represents a view of the United States unique to children of first-generation immigrants. Zhang Ya-Jie, a Chinese scholar who has spent time in the United States, explains in a 1986 article in *MELUS* that she initially found the text offensive to China's people and culture before coming to understand that the work is "after all, an American story, not a Chinese one." She goes on to note that the work "show[s] how a Chinese-American finds her own identity, how much she has to struggle through." Another group of critics has approached *The Warrior Woman* through the lens of statements that Kingston has made about her approach to writing. Most notably, commentators have explored how the text reflects Kingston's repeated assertion that she wants her writing to be accessible to a mainstream audience.

THE POLITICAL ACTIVISM OF MAXINE HONG KINGSTON

Although Maxine Hong Kingston initially resisted any conception of her writings as being political, her perspective on this issue has shifted over the course of her writing career. Soon after the initial publication of *The Woman Warrior*—which itself includes political content, especially in relation to the Vietnam War—she engaged in activism and openly supported the peace movement. She was also a self-proclaimed pacifist. As she gradually realized that the popularity of her writings gave her a powerful voice, she used her position to advocate for the use of art to foster peace around the world.

She also utilized her unofficial status as a spokesperson for the Chinese American perspective to offer her observations about the unique challenges that this group faces while living in the United States. In order to enact her role as a political activist in a positive manner, Kingston offered writing workshops to Vietnam veterans, whom she felt returned from their military experiences with stories that they needed to tell to be psychologically whole. These actions demonstrate her extreme dedication to the peace movement in terms of her overall goal to use her power to encourage pacifism across the globe.

BIBLIOGRAPHY

Sources

Fishkin, Shelley Fisher, and Maxine Hong Kingston. "Interview with Maxine Hong Kingston." *American Literary History* 3.4 (1991): 782–91. Print.

Huntley, Edelma D. *Maxine Hong Kingston: A Critical Companion.* Westport, Conn.: Greenwood, 2000. Print.

Kingston, Maxine Hong. *The Woman Warrior: Memoirs of a Girlhood among Ghosts.* New York: Vintage, 1975. Print.

Kramer, Jane. "On Being Chinese in China and America." Rev. of *The Woman Warrior,* by Maxine Hong Kingston. *New York Times* 7 Nov. 1976. Print.

Lim, Shirley Geok-lin. "Reading Back, Looking Forward: A Retrospective Interview with Maxine Hong Kingston." *MELUS* 33.1 (2008): 157–70. Print.

Skenazy, Paul, and Tera Martin. *Conversations with Maxine Hong Kingston.* Oxford: University Press of Mississippi, 1998. Print.

Wong, Sharon. Rev. of *The Warrior Woman,* by Maxine Hong Kingston. *Library Journal* 15 Sept. 1976: 1849. Print.

Zhang Ya-Jie. "A Chinese Woman's Response to Maxine Hong Kingston's *The Warrior Woman.*" *MELUS* 13.3–4 (1986): 103–07. Print.

Further Reading

Chin, Marilyn, and Maxine Hong Kingston. "A *Melus* Interview: Maxine Hong Kingston." *MELUS* 16.4 (1989): 57–74. Print.

Feng, Pin-chia. *The Female Bildungsroman by Toni Morrison and Maxine Hong Kingston: A Postmodern Reading.* New York: Peter Lang, 2000. Print.

Kim, Elaine H. "Defining Asian American Realities through Literature." *Cultural Critique* 6 (1987): 87–111. Print.

Lee, Y. S. "Type, Totality, and the Realism of Asian American Literature." *Modern Language Quarterly* 73.3 (2012): 415–32. Print.

Shan, Te-Hsing. "Life, Writing, and Peace: Reading Maxine Hong Kingston's *The Fifth Book of Peace.*" *Journal of Transnational American Studies* (2009): 1–22. Print.

Tokarczyk, Michelle M. *Class Definitions: On the Lives and Writings of Maxine Hong Kingston, Sandra Cisneros, and Dorothy Allison.* Selinsgrove, Pa.: Susquehanna University Press, 2008. Print.

Tsang, Venus. "Quack or Talk: Varieties of Storytelling and Identity Formation in Maxine Hong Kingston's *The Woman Warrior.*" *Imagining Home: Migrants and the Search for a New Belonging.* Ed. Diana Cavuoto Glenn. Kent Town, South Australia: Wakefield, 2011. Print.

Woo, Deborah. "Maxine Hong Kingston: The Ethnic Writer and the Burden of Dual Authenticity." *Amerasia Journal* 16.1 (1990): 173–200. Print.

Grace Waitman

Contemplation and Confession

The Autobiography of Ben Franklin by Benjamin Franklin	179
The Autobiography of Giambattista Vico by Giambattista Vico	183
The Autobiography of Malcolm X by Malcolm X	186
The Book of Margery Kempe by Margery Kempe	189
A Confession by Leo Tolstoy	193
Confessions by Augustine	196
Confessions by Jean-Jacques Rousseau	200
Darkness Visible by William Styron	204
Infidel by Ayaan Hirsi Ali	207
The Life by Teresa of Ávila	211
The Man Died: Prison Notes of Wole Soyinka by Wole Soyinka	214
The Meditations of the Emperor Marcus Aurelius Antoninus by Marcus Aurelius	218
Memoirs by Pablo Neruda	222
A Mountainous Journey: A Poet's Autobiography by Fadwa Tuqan	225
A True Relation of My Birth, Breeding, and Life by Margaret Cavendish	229
Walden; or, Life in the Woods by Henry David Thoreau	233

The Autobiography of Ben Franklin

Benjamin Franklin

OVERVIEW

First published in Paris in 1791 as *Memoires de la vie privée de Benjamin Franklin* and then in English in 1793 as *The Private Life of the Late Benjamin Franklin, LL.D.,* Benjamin Franklin's autobiography traces his rise to prominence in Philadelphia, as well as his thoughts and observations on literature, philosophy, and religion in colonial and revolutionary America. Franklin wrote the book, commonly known as *The Autobiography of Ben Franklin,* at various times and places. He penned the first section while in England in 1771, the second and third sections while representing the United States at the French Court in Paris between 1784 and 1785, and the final part after his return to Philadelphia in 1785. Because Franklin died before he was able to complete the work, his autobiography describes his life only until 1757, when he turned fifty-one years old, and thus does not discuss his later accomplishments as one of the Founding Fathers of the United States. Instead, it offers advice—primarily directed toward Franklin's son, William—on how to cultivate a well-rounded and worldly personality in what many see as a primer on personal conduct during the Revolutionary War era.

Franklin's autobiography first appeared in the wake of his death in 1790, well after he had gained fame throughout the Americas and Europe as a politician, an inventor, and a man of letters, and it was widely read. However, both the initial French and English editions were incomplete, containing only the first section. In 1818 Franklin's grandson, William Temple Franklin, published the first three sections in London. This remained the standard version until 1868, when U.S. statesman John Bigelow bought the original manuscript and published the full text. Since then, it has become one of the most influential early American texts as both a historical document and a collection of moral, spiritual, and practical guidance.

HISTORICAL AND LITERARY CONTEXT

The Autobiography of Ben Franklin provides insights into the changing world in which Franklin lived, and his globetrotting lifestyle made him well suited to take on such a task. Franklin had traveled and experienced more than most men of his time, visiting both the British and French royal courts. Despite having come from relatively little wealth and being largely self-educated, he was received by the European and early American elites on the strength of his reputation as an author, a scientist, and a respected public figure with honorary degrees from Harvard, Yale, William and Mary College, Oxford, and the University of St. Andrews.

At the time he began writing his autobiography in 1771, Franklin had already made a name for himself as an adept public speaker by successfully lobbying the British parliament on behalf of the Pennsylvania colony to repeal the Stamp Act of 1765. He set about recording the events of his life while vacationing in England, intending to provide his son William, who was serving as the colonial governor of New Jersey at the time, with some account of his genealogy and to describe the methods he took to achieve such high status so that they might "be imitated" by others. From 1776 to 1785 Franklin served as the U.S. ambassador to France, completing the second and third sections of his manuscript in the final years of his stay there. He began writing the fourth section toward the end of 1789, but it is very brief due to his death a few months later.

Franklin's weaving of moral and spiritual advice throughout the story of his rise to prominence can rightfully be viewed as a reflection of the early American religious climate. During the so-called Great Awakening of the 1730s and 1740s, a number of influential Protestant preachers, including Jonathan Edwards and George Whitefield, traveled throughout the colonies exhorting Christians to take more active roles in their religions and to put the teachings of the Bible into practice by performing good deeds in their communities. Though Franklin did not identify himself as a Christian, he did find immense value in the notion of personal redemption through self-education and public works.

Franklin and his revolutionary colleagues were certainly aware of the significance of their lives and activities, and a number of important figures from the era wrote memoirs or autobiographies to cement their legacies, though many of these works were not be published until decades after their deaths. Some of the more notable texts in this vein include Thomas Jefferson's *Autobiography, 1743–1790* (1821), Benjamin Rush's *Autobiography of Benjamin Rush: His "Travels through Life" Together with His "Commonplace Books"*

⁘ Key Facts

Time Period:
Late 18th Century

Relevant Historical Events:
American Revolutionary War

Nationality:
American

Keywords:
politics; colonialism; revolution

CONTEMPLATION AND CONFESSION

John Paul Jones and Benjamin Franklin at Louis XVI's Court, a nineteenth-century painting by Jean Leon Gerome Ferris. From 1776 to 1785 Franklin served as the U.S. ambassador to France. © SUPERSTOCK/GETTY IMAGES

for 1789–1813 (1948), and John Adams's *Diary and Autobiography* (1961). However, Franklin's text stands above other autobiographical works of the era in terms of literary value and sustained scholarly interest.

THEMES AND STYLE

The central theme of Franklin's autobiography is that regardless of background, anyone with the determination to lead a just and principled life can achieve greatness. The cornerstone of this argument is the author's insistence upon reading as much as possible across a wide variety of subjects in order to understand the ways of the world and what makes a virtuous life. He describes in the first section his youthful "improvement by constant study." At the beginning of the second section, he reprints a letter from a British diplomat named Benjamin Vaughan, who came across an early handwritten manuscript of the autobiography and urged Franklin to complete and publish the work, noting that it would provide "a noble rule and example of self-education."

Franklin was doubtlessly aware of how the story of his life and the lessons he had learned could influence not only his young son's future but also that of the fledgling nation. In many ways, his autobiography was crucial to initiating the notion of the American Dream, in which a person of modest means can achieve great wealth and esteem through hard work and determination alone. His story was a guide for individuals to achieve such status and for the United States as a whole to ascend to a position of influence in the international community. The idea of the "self-made" individual resonated strongly with early immigrants, many of whom arrived in the country with few material possessions and little social status. Ralph Waldo Emerson's "Self-Reliance" (1841) and "The American Scholar" (1841) draw upon this notion, as does abolitionist Frederick Douglass's "Self-Made Men" (1895). Henry Adams's Pulitzer Prize–winning autobiography *The Education of Henry Adams* (1918) makes a similar appeal for self-education, and powerful figures ranging from Henry Ford to Bill Gates have been celebrated as archetypal self-made Americans.

The Autobiography of Ben Franklin is written in a semiformal eighteenth-century style. Franklin's erudition and political background are readily apparent in his dense phrasing and use of obscure terminology, but the readability of the work does not suffer as a result, particularly in the wake of numerous scholarly and annotated modern editions that provide insights into

PRIMARY SOURCE

EXCERPT FROM *THE AUTOBIOGRAPHY OF BENJAMIN FRANKLIN*

Dear son: I have ever had pleasure in obtaining any little anecdotes of my ancestors. You may remember the inquiries I made among the remains of my relations when you were with me in England, and the journey I undertook for that purpose. Imagining it may be equally agreeable to you to know the circumstances of my life, many of which you are yet unacquainted with, and expecting the enjoyment of a week's uninterrupted leisure in my present country retirement, I sit down to write them for you. To which I have besides some other inducements. Having emerged from the poverty and obscurity in which I was born and bred, to a state of affluence and some degree of reputation in the world, and having gone so far through life with a considerable share of felicity, the conducing means I made use of, which with the blessing of God so well succeeded, my posterity may like to know, as they may find some of them suitable to their own situations, and therefore fit to be imitated.

That felicity, when I reflected on it, has induced me sometimes to say, that were it offered to my choice, I should have no objection to a repetition of the same life from its beginning, only asking the advantages authors have in a second edition to correct some faults of the first. So I might, besides correcting the faults, change some sinister accidents and events of it for others more favorable. But though this were denied, I should still accept the offer. Since such a repetition is not to be expected, the next thing most like living one's life over again seems to be a recollection of that life, and to make that recollection as durable as possible by putting it down in writing.

Hereby, too, I shall indulge the inclination so natural in old men, to be talking of themselves and their own past actions; and I shall indulge it without being tiresome to others, who, through respect to age, might conceive themselves obliged to give me a hearing, since this may be read or not as any one pleases. And, lastly (I may as well confess it, since my denial of it will be believed by nobody), perhaps I shall a good deal gratify my own vanity. Indeed, I scarce ever heard or saw the introductory words, "Without vanity I may say," & c., but some vain thing immediately followed. Most people dislike vanity in others, whatever share they have of it themselves; but I give it fair quarter wherever I meet with it, being persuaded that it is often productive of good to the possessor, and to others that are within his sphere of action; and therefore, in many cases, it would not be altogether absurd if a man were to thank God for his vanity among the other comforts of life.

And now I speak of thanking God, I desire with all humility to acknowledge that I owe the mentioned happiness of my past life to His kind providence, which lead me to the means I used and gave them success. My belief of this induces me to hope, though I must not presume, that the same goodness will still be exercised toward me, in continuing that happiness, or enabling me to bear a fatal reverse, which I may experience as others have done: the complexion of my future fortune being known to Him only in whose power it is to bless to us even our afflictions.

SOURCE: Franklin, Benjamin. *The Autobiography of Benjamin Franklin*. Ed. Charles W. Eliot. New York: PF Collier & Son, 1909.

---

some of the more difficult or antiquated language. The author is often quite humorous and self-deprecating, such as when he admits in the opening paragraphs that "I shall indulge the inclination so natural in old men, to be talking of themselves and their own past actions" and that "perhaps I shall a good deal gratify my own vanity." He also frequently turns his sharp wit against his friends and acquaintances, such as when he good-naturedly marvels at how the crowds "admir'd and respected" Whitefield despite "his common Abuse of them, by assuring them they were naturally *half Beasts and half Devils.*"

CRITICAL DISCUSSION

The Autobiography of Ben Franklin was among the first American works of literature to be widely read and taken seriously by a European audience, and it helped to buffer the nation from accusations of anti-intellectualism that persisted after the Revolutionary War. In an influential 1896 article titled "Sweetness and Light," written a year after Bigelow's complete edition of Franklin's autobiography was published, British poet and critic Matthew Arnold wrote that Franklin was "the very incarnation of sanity and clear sense." In the United States, the early reception to Franklin's work was enormously positive, helping to establish him as one of the nation's first literary, intellectual, and political heroes. As Gordon S. Wood writes in *The Americanization of Benjamin Franklin*, "Many people seemed to know his writings as well as they knew the Bible."

The longer-term reaction to the work was mixed. In his introduction to a 1906 edition of the autobiography, Frank Woodworth Pine describes it as "the interesting, human, and vividly told story of one of the wisest and most useful lives in our own history, and perhaps in any history." Mark Twain conveys a different opinion in his essay "The Late Benjamin Franklin" (1870), which he explains he wrote with the express purpose of "snub[ing] those pretentious maxims of his." Today, however, Franklin's autobiography is viewed as one of the most engaging and insightful documents of the emerging American national consciousness in the years after the Revolutionary War.

The Autobiography of Ben Franklin has remained popular with scholars and casual readers alike. It has been identified by some as a precursor to the self-help craze of the 1990s and by others (including Esmond Wright in his "The *Autobiography:* Fact or Fiction?") as an elaborate attempt by Franklin to secure his legacy by crafting a fascinating, if largely fabricated, literary persona. The 200th anniversary of Franklin's death in 1990 and the 300th anniversary of his birth in 2006 occasioned a number of new biographies and critical studies of his works. In 2006 Mark Skousen published *The Compleated* [sic] *Autobiography of Benjamin Franklin,* in which he tries to fill in the missing years from the autobiography by using a first-person style based on Franklin's authorial voice. Such offerings prove that the story of his rise to greatness from working-class roots is a foundational component of the American mythology.

BIBLIOGRAPHY

Sources

Arnold, Matthew. "Sweetness and Light." *Culture and Anarchy.* London: Thomas Nelson and Sons, 1869. Rpt. *Culture and Anarchy and Other Writings.* Ed. Stefan Collini. Cambridge: Cambridge University Press, 1993. 58–80. Print.

Franklin, Benjamin. *The Autobiography of Benjamin Franklin.* New York: Dover, 2008. Print.

Lawrence, D. H. "Benjamin Franklin." *Studies in Classic American Literature.* New York: T. Seltzer, 1923. 10–16. Print.

Pine, Frank Woodworth. Introduction. *Autobiography of Benjamin Franklin.* New York: Henry Holt, 1906. vii–xxi. Print.

Twain, Mark. "The Late Benjamin Franklin." *Galaxy* July 1870: 138–40. Print.

Wood, Gordon S. *The Americanization of Benjamin Franklin.* New York: Penguin, 2004. Print.

Wright, Esmond. "*The Autobiography:* Fact or Fiction?" *The Intellectual World of Benjamin Franklin.* Ed. Dilys Winegard. Philadelphia: University of Pennsylvania Press, 1990. 29–42. Print.

Further Reading

Arch, Stephen C. *After Franklin: The Emergence of Autobiography in Post-Revolutionary America, 1780–1830.* Hanover, N.H.: University Press of New England, 2001. Print.

Brands, H. W. *The First American: The Life and Times of Benjamin Franklin.* New York: Doubleday, 2000. Print.

Forde, Steven. "Benjamin Franklin's Autobiography and the Education of America." *American Political Science Review* 86.2 (1992): 257–368. Print.

Huang, Nian-Sheng. *Benjamin Franklin in American Thought and Culture: 1790–1990.* Philadelphia: American Philosophical Society, 1994. Print.

Isaacson, Walter. *Benjamin Franklin: An American Life.* New York: Simon & Schuster, 2004. Print.

McCormick, Blaine. *Ben Franklin: America's Original Entrepreneur: Franklin's Autobiography for Business Today.* Irvine, Calif.: Entrepreneur, 2008. Print.

Monaghan, E. Jennifer. *Learning to Read and Write in Colonial America.* Amherst: University of Massachusetts Press, 2005. Print.

Morgan, Edmund S. *Benjamin Franklin.* New Haven: Yale University Press, 2003. Print.

Jacob Schmitt

The Autobiography of Giambattista Vico

Giambattista Vico

OVERVIEW

First published in 1728, *The Autobiography of Giambattista Vico* is one of the best-known autobiographies to emerge from eighteenth-century Europe. Vico's autobiography is notable as one of the earliest to be organized around the theme of intellectual development. In the book, he traces his parentage and early memories; tells of his education; and focuses on early intellectual influences, which range from medieval logicians and metaphysicians such as Peter of Spain and Francisco Suárez to books of classical antiquity such as Aristotle's *Metaphysics* and Plato's dialogues. The autobiography also traces Vico's fascination with rhetoric, law, history, and poetry. By exhaustively detailing the author's intellectual interests, the autobiography serves the pedagogical aim of instructing the reader in the history of Western thought and provides insight into the formation of Vico's philosophical opus, *New Science,* whose composition coincided with that of the autobiography.

When the autobiography was published, Vico held a professorship in rhetoric at the University of Naples. The work was written in response to a request by Count Gian Artico di Porcía, who sought to publish a series of autobiographical narratives in the pages of the quarterly *Raccolta D'Opuscoli Scientifici e Filologici*. These intellectual autobiographies, written by creative scholars, would aid with "the advancement of learning in Italy our illustrious fatherland," according to Max Harold Fisch and Thomas Goddard Bergin in their definitive 1944 translation of Vico's autobiography. Unfortunately the series was never realized, and only Vico's autobiography, which served as a model, was published. Today *The Autobiography of Giambattista Vico* is considered an essential text of eighteenth-century thought that sheds light on the life of one of Italy's most significant philosophers.

HISTORICAL AND LITERARY CONTEXT

The Autobiography of Giambattista Vico criticizes the Cartesian rationalism prevalent in European thought during the late sixteenth century. In 1637 French philosopher René Descartes published his philosophical autobiographical treatise *Discourse on the Method,* which propounded skepticism toward accepted notions of the truth and the rational method of inquiry. According to Paul Archambault in a 2010 essay for *Symposium,* this "cult of Descartes" had become dominant among intellectuals by the early seventeenth century. In 1710 Vico wrote a refutation of Cartesian thought titled *Dell'antichissima sapienza italica,* which claims, according to Archambault, that "the Cartesians argue that mathematical sciences alone can contribute to the truth of the universe."

Vico composed his autobiography following a request by Count Gian Artico di Porcía, who envisioned a collection of autobiographies, or periautographies as they were called at the time, to serve as a tool of instruction for Italian students. According to Fisch and Bergin, the distinctive features of Porcía's project include "(a) its primarily pedagogical intent; (b) the representation of all the arts and sciences; (c) a uniform plan for all the autobiographies; and (d) a comprehensive critical supplement to the entire collection." The idea of such a collection had gained traction among many scholars in the early eighteenth century; its initial impetus may have come from the German philosopher Gottfried Wilhelm Leibniz. Although the collection of autobiographies was never realized, Vico's serves as a model of the form.

The Autobiography of Giambattista Vico is part of a long tradition of philosophical autobiographies beginning with St. Augustine's *Confessions* (c. 397 CE), which tells of Augustine's early life and illuminates many of his philosophical and theological ideas. However, Donald P. Verene in *The New Art of Autobiography: An Essay on* The Life of Giambattista Vico Written by Himself (1991) argues that Vico's autobiography differs because it is not a confession: "Through Augustine's adversities God is always the presence directing them toward the final end of the realization in Augustine's life of the Christian Truth…. In his autobiography, Vico portrays himself as making himself."

In the years following the publication of Vico's text, the philosophical autobiography became better established as a genre. *Ecce Homo,* written by German philosopher Friedrich Nietzsche in 1888 but not published until 1908, portrays Nietzsche's interpretation of his own philosophical development. In a 1994 essay for the *Personalist Forum,* David Parry argues that Nietzsche's autobiography is a refutation of the Cartesian self as posited in Descartes's *Discourse on the Method.* Several autobiographical collections, much as the one Porcía envisioned, have subsequently been

✤ **Key Facts**

Time Period:
Mid-18th Century

Relevant Historical Events:
Publication of Descartes's *Discourse on Method;* Count Gian Artico di Porcía requests Vico to write his autobiography

Nationality:
Italian

Keywords:
philosophy; intellectualism; pedagogy

Portrait of Giambattista Vico by Francesco Solimena. © LEEMAGE/GETTY IMAGES

published, such as the German series of philosophical autobiographies released under the name *Die Philosophie der Gegenwart in Selbstdarstellungen* (1920).

THEMES AND STYLE

The central theme of *The Autobiography of Giambattista Vico* is that the intellectual self is developed through the process of study and influence. Throughout the text, Vico offers a kind of intellectual genealogy, tracing how his study of and reaction to particular philosophical works determined his nature and the nature of his thought. He writes specifically of this philological intent: "With the candor proper to a historian, we shall narrate plainly and step by step the entire series of Vico's studies, in order that the proper and natural causes of his particular development as a man of letters may be known." By privileging historical discourse over Cartesian rationality, Vico seeks to reclaim the scholarly legitimacy of genealogical inquiry, which had suffered in the writings of modern philosophers such as Descartes and Blaise Pascal.

Although Vico ostensibly wrote the autobiography at the request of Porcía as a pedagogical document for the benefit of young Italian scholars, the text itself reveals a strong desire to catalog his own personal intellectual development. Part A of the autobiography was written immediately following one of Vico's greatest intellectual accomplishments, the completion of his first major philosophical work, which he called "the new science of the negative form." Part B was composed following his next philosophical accomplishment, the publication of *New Science*. The autobiography is an attempt to illustrate the origins of his philosophical inquiry and what distinguishes his ideas from those of his peers. Indeed, as Fisch and Bergin argue in their introduction to the autobiography, "Vico's original autobiography is thus to be read as the expression of his state of mind at the end of his two greatest creative efforts."

Stylistically, *The Autobiography of Giambattista Vico* is distinguished by its use of the third person and its formality, which cause the text to read more as a biographical work than as an autobiographical one. "Giambattista Vico," he begins, "was born in Naples in the year of 1670 of upright parents who left a good name after them." Aside from a few brief passages, the entire autobiography is written in the third person. By eliminating the subjective voice, Vico creates a highly impersonal autobiographical narrative that emphasizes the same scientific rigor he used to establish his philosophical genealogy.

CRITICAL DISCUSSION

The Autobiography of Giambattista Vico was published as a model for a planned series of autobiographies anthologized by Count Porcía. A brief assessment of the piece by Porcía was published alongside Vico's work, in which Porcía writes that Vico's autobiography is "better than any other so far received" and "will serve as a norm" for anyone seeking to publish an intellectual autobiography. Despite this initial praise, the work garnered limited attention within intellectual circles.

In the years following Vico's death, his reputation as a philosopher continued to grow. However, it was not the publication of the autobiography that led to this development but his philosophical magnum opus, *New Science,* which proved to be foundational to the history of philosophy. *The Autobiography of Giambattista Vico* has subsequently become an important text that serves to illuminate the origins and subjectivity of the philosophy expounded in *New Science,* and it has also proved influential in establishing the genre of the philosophical autobiography. Fisch and Bergin trace the influence of Vico's autobiography to works such as the American Philosophical Association's series Contemporary American Philosophy: Personal Statements, arguing that the idea and practice of intellectual autobiography has become "so familiar that it is difficult now to realize the novelty" of Porcía's proposal and Vico's work.

Scholars often read Vico's autobiography, as well as *New Science,* as a refutation of the tradition of philosophical rationalism initiated by Descartes's *Discourse on the Method*. Archambault argues that the autobiography was "written to combat the cult of Descartes, which was sweeping over Italy and all of Europe during the latter half of the seventeenth century and which favored the study of mathematical sciences to the detriment or outright elimination of the humanities." Parry ties Vico's work to the autobiographical elements of Nietzsche's writing, arguing that both authors' works present a distinct philosophical self-opposed to the one created by Descartes. Others scholars, such as Friedrich Meinecke and Isaiah Berlin, have focused on Vico's influence on the philosophy of history.

BIBLIOGRAPHY

Sources

Archambault, Paul J. "Vico and His Critics." *Symposium* 58.4 (2010): 248–69. *Taylor & Francis Online.* Web. 19 Nov. 2012.

Burke, Peter. *Vico.* Oxford: Oxford University Press, 1985. Print.

Miller, Cecilia. *Giambattista Vico: Imagination and Historical Knowledge.* New York: St. Martin's, 1993. Print.

Parry, David M. "Reconstructing the Self: Philosophical Autobiography in Vico and Nietzsche." *Personalist Forum* 10.2 (1994): 89–101. *JSTOR.* Web. 19 Nov. 2012.

Verene, Donald P. *The New Art of Autobiography: An Essay on* The Life of Giambattista Vico Written by Himself. Oxford: Clarendon, 1991. Print.

Vico, Giambattista. *The Autobiography of Giambattista Vico.* Trans. Max Harold Fisch and Thomas Goddard Bergin. Ithaca, N.Y.: Cornell University Press, 1944. Print.

Further Reading

Beckett, Samuel. "Dante … Bruno. Vico. Joyce." *Our Exagmination Round His Factification for Incamination of Work in Progress.* Norfolk, Conn.: New Directions, 1962. Print.

Croce, Benedetto. *The Philosophy of Giambattista Vico.* New York: Macmillan, 1913. Print.

Danesi, Marcel. *Giambattista Vico and Anglo-American Science.* Berlin: De Gruyter, 1994. Print.

Lilla, Mark. *G. B. Vico: The Making of an Anti-modern.* Cambridge: Harvard University Press, 1993. Print.

GIAMBATTISTA VICO'S *NEW SCIENCE*

First published in 1725, *New Science* is Giambattista Vico's major philosophical work. As Peter Burke writes in *Vico* (1985), "*New Science* is a book so stuffed full of ideas that it almost bursts at the seams. It is at once a study of history, philosophy, poetry, theology and law." The first version of the book, the so-called new science in negative form, was a criticism of existing philosophical theories, natural law systems, and utilitarian doctrines. However, the work was never published because Cardinal Lorenzo Corsini balked at the cost of publishing such a large tome and withdrew financial sponsorship. According to Max Harold Fisch and Thomas Goddard Bergin in their 1944 translation of *The Autobiography of Giambattista Vico,* this proved a good turn of events: "Within a few days it came to [Vico] with the force of inspiration that his 'negative' method had been a mistake; that by the employment of a positive method the work could be reduced to a fourth of its compass … the breaking of Corsini's promise was but one more dispensation of Providence." The shorter, positive version proved to be an important text in the philosophy of history and served as an influence on countless thinkers, even providing a temporal framework for James Joyce's *Finnegans Wake* (1939).

Mazzota, Giuseppe. *The New Map of the World: The Poetic Philosophy of Giambattista Vico.* Princeton, N.J.: Princeton University Press, 1999. Print.

Vico, Giambattista. *The New Science of Giambattista Vico.* Ithaca, N.Y.: Cornell University Press, 1984. Print.

Greg Luther

The Autobiography of Malcolm X
Malcolm X

Key Facts

Time Period:
Mid-20th Century

Relevant Historical Events:
Author's conversion to Islam; civil rights movement; establishment of the Black Muslims

Nationality:
American

Keywords:
civil rights; Islam; racism

OVERVIEW

Written by civil rights activist Malcolm X (born Malcolm Little) with the assistance of Alex Haley, *The Autobiography of Malcolm X* (1965) presents Malcolm's conversion to Islam after growing up as a violent black youth trapped in the racist society of mid-twentieth-century America. The book traces his life from his abusive childhood to his time in prison, his religious enlightenment, and the pilgrimage that would completely alter his beliefs, presenting him as a model for other black Americans to follow. The religious overtones of the latter half of the book and the author's manifest desire to better himself contradict popular media portrayals of him as an angry, dangerous activist determined to permanently separate black and white cultures. Nevertheless, Malcolm openly admits in the autobiography to this former version of himself and demonstrates, through his life story, how much an individual can change over a lifetime.

Published at the height of the civil rights movement in the United States, *The Autobiography of Malcolm X* received several awards for its presentation of the story of one of the movement's prominent leaders. Appearing shortly after Malcolm's assassination on February 21, 1965, the book had a major impact on activists of the day and significantly shaped black political thought. Today his autobiography is an important document about the political and religious transformation of the man himself and the history of the civil rights movement.

HISTORICAL AND LITERARY CONTEXT

Malcolm was born in 1925 into a racially divided society where he faced daily violence because of the color of his skin. Black Americans at the time were divided over how to improve their social and economic condition. The most prominent debate stemmed from a disagreement between black intellectuals W. E. B. Du Bois and Booker T. Washington. Du Bois argued for civil rights and political action, whereas Washington focused on self-improvement and racial uplift. During the 1920s and 1930s, leaders with more radical philosophies emerged, such as Jamaican political organizer Marcus Garvey, who promoted the return of blacks to Africa, and Elijah Muhammad, who in 1934 became leader of the Lost-Found Nation of Islam. Popularly known as the Black Muslims, this religious sect preached segregation and the belief that white people were devils.

By the time Malcolm, a member of Muhammad's Nation of Islam, began writing his autobiography in 1962, the organization had gained popularity in the black community. In order to promote the Nation of Islam and show how it had saved him from a life of crime, Malcolm dictated his life story to his editor, Haley, over a three-year period. Because of the time involved in the composition process, the autobiography covers the shift in Malcolm's ideas about religion and black rights and his official split from the Nation of Islam in 1964.

The Autobiography of Malcolm X generally falls into the category of American civil rights literature as a voice of opposition to prominent movement leaders such as Martin Luther King Jr., who advocated peace and integration. Malcolm's story also resembles the hagiography of a saint and is often compared to the life story of St. Augustine. In his *Dialogues,* Augustine chronicles his early life of sin, his realization of the glory of God, and his desire to inspire his audience to follow a proper, moral life. Malcolm's autobiography, much like Augustine's, also begins with his violent and criminal youth, describes his enlightenment in the religion of Islam, and follows his journey to better himself and his readers.

Published after Malcolm's death, the autobiography became a best seller and was regarded as a highly influential text. The book received the Anisfield-Wolf Book Award in 1966 and was adapted to film in 1992. It changed public opinion about Malcolm and his actions by drawing attention to his religious desire to become a better human being. Today *The Autobiography of Malcolm X* is considered an important text for its historical content and its discussion of an influential and unpredictable figure who was feared by whites and blacks alike during his time in the public eye.

THEMES AND STYLE

The main theme of *The Autobiography of Malcolm X* is that religious enlightenment can change a person who has been beaten down by racism and abuse. Malcolm opens his story with scenes of violence and bigotry, including a visit from the Ku Klux Klan to his parents' house. One of his "earliest vivid memories" is of white men burning down his house and his family's mad

As an outspoken leader in the Nation of Islam (a militant religious movement that encouraged black separatism), Malcolm X (right) influenced many black Americans to abandon Christianity and become Muslims. He was assassinated by members of the Nation of Islam after he left the group to become a Sunni Muslim. © PICTORIAL PRESS LTD/ ALAMY

panic to escape alive. He remembers accompanying his father to preach Garvey's "back to Africa" message, which deepened his sense of racial divide. Having the lightest skin among his siblings, he was often beaten by his mother—almost white herself and ashamed of her heritage—while his father, who was abusive toward his mother and siblings, favored him because of his light skin. In a world divided by race, Malcolm developed into a hardened and angry criminal before eventually finding religion. He explains how difficult his religious conversion was because of his past: "For evil to bend its knees, admitting its guilt, to implore the forgiveness of God, is the hardest thing in the world."

Malcolm writes in the text that he wanted to recount a story of religious enlightenment in order to provide a model for fellow black Americans to follow. He explains, "I would not spend an hour in the preparation of a book which had the ambition to perhaps titillate some readers. But I am spending many hours because the full story is the best way that I know to have it seen, and understood, that … the religion of Islam … completely changed my life." In the book, his incarceration and conversion are depicted as life-changing moments that he hopes will be recognized and emulated by readers.

The book is written as a chronological narrative from the perspective of Malcolm as an activist and a Muslim as he looks back on his life. Because of Haley's influence on the writing and editing process, scholars question how much of the narrative voice was imposed by Haley. Although Haley describes Malcolm's involvement and explains that the book was written in Malcolm's chosen style, the posthumous publication of the autobiography has left some readers questioning the influence Haley had, particularly on the overall organization of the book and the consistency of the diction.

CRITICAL DISCUSSION

The Autobiography of Malcolm X initially received excellent reviews that changed opinions of Malcolm on both sides of the racial divide. At first, news of Malcolm's death elicited mixed reaction, as described in *Contemporary Heroes and Heroines* (1992): "the White press took the opportunity to moralize that those who live by the sword die by it, while Black leaders acknowledged his moderating views and termed the loss of his brilliance and passion a setback for the civil rights movement." However, after the publication of the autobiography, "his message of Black unity, self-respect, and self-reliance truly began to strike a responsive chord." Barrett John Mandel in a 1972 essay in *Afro-American Studies* describes how the autobiography reveals Malcolm as "a man who spent the greater part of his life in learning how to be a human being, always working toward the goal of humanizing those around him."

ELIJAH MUHAMMAD AND THE BLACK MUSLIMS

Arguably the most influential man in Malcolm X's autobiography, Elijah Muhammad provided the religious enlightenment that brought Malcolm from imprisoned criminal to influential public leader of the Black Muslims. Muhammad also provided the catalyst for Malcolm's discovery of orthodox Islam and eventual realization that as the Nation of Islam's leader, Muhammad was a human being instead of a divinely chosen leader of people and messenger of Allah.

Born Elijah Poole in 1897 to two former slaves, Muhammad worked as a farmhand and had numerous odd jobs. He eventually moved to Detroit, where he met W. D. Fard, a door-to-door salesman and Islamic leader. After converting to Islam, Muhammad changed his last name—which was associated with his slave heritage—to Karriem and again to Muhammad when, after Fard's disappearance, he became leader of the Lost-Found Nation of Islam and the Messenger of Allah. Claiming that he was the last prophet, Muhammad believed that he would lead black Americans out of the oppression of slavery by associating white people with devils. However, after the assassination of Malcolm X, an act often attributed to Muhammad's Black Muslims, the Nation of Islam began to fall apart because of infighting and factionalism. Muhammad eventually succumbed to his failing health and his son took over leadership of what was left of the Black Muslim organization.

The book was a best seller for many years after its publication. Nancy Clasby in a 1974 essay for *Journal of Black Studies* notes the "universally acknowledged" praise of the work as "compelling and extraordinary." Part of the universal appeal of the book, Clasby writes, is its exploration of the development of the individual and the myth of national identity: "Deprived of an effective national myth, colonized man has had, in a sense, no biography which is not chartered and authorized by the oppressor." She notes that Malcolm "recognized and embodied" the "emergence of a new paradigm of human awareness among non-white peoples of the world," namely that they "make up three-quarters of the world's population."

Predominate trends in scholarship about the autobiography have examined the piece as a form of hagiographical writing—or writing that follows the expected patterns of a saint's life. Mandel follows this trend when he compares Malcolm's autobiography to "that of a sinner who becomes a saint, and the saint, like his Christian parallel, is a preacher." Josh Ozersky, in an essay in *Nonfiction Classics for Students: Presenting Analysis, Context, and Criticism on Nonfiction Works* (2002), also exemplifies this type of scholarship when he compares Malcolm's text to the dialogues of Augustine, a narrative style in which the "narrator would describe his sinful early days, his awakening at rock bottom, and finish on a triumphant note by describing his career as an apostle and reformed sinner." Some scholars reject this kind of theorizing, however, because it limits the scope of the work. For example, Paul Eakin in a 1976 essay for *Criticism* suggests that the limiting frame of hagiography "assumes that the narrative expresses a complete self" rather than the fragmented and continuously changing character of Malcolm X.

BIBLIOGRAPHY

Sources

Clasby, Nancy. "*The Autobiography of Malcolm X:* A Mythic Paradigm." *Journal of Black Studies* 5.1 (1974): 18–34. *JSTOR*. Web. 21 Nov. 2012.

Eakin, Paul John. "Malcolm X and the Limits of Autobiography." *Criticism* 18.3 (1976): 230–42. *JSTOR*. Web. 21 Nov. 2012.

Malcolm X. *The Autobiography of Malcolm X*. Ed. Alex Haley. New York: Ballantine, 1992. Web. 22 Nov. 2012.

"Malcolm X." *Contemporary Heroes and Heroines*. Vol. 2. Detroit: Gale, 1992. *Gale Biography in Context*. Web. 21 Nov. 2012.

Mandel, Barrett John. "The Didactic Achievement of Malcolm X's Autobiography." *Afro-American Studies* 2.4 (1972): 269–74. Rpt. in *Contemporary Literary Criticism. Literature Resource Center*. Web. 21 Nov. 2012.

Ozersky, Josh. "Critical Essay on *The Autobiography of Malcolm X*." *Nonfiction Classics for Students: Presenting Analysis, Context, and Criticism on Nonfiction Works*. Vol. 3. Ed. David M. Galens, Jennifer Smith, and Elizabeth Thomason. Detroit: Gale, 2002. *Literature Resource Center*. Web. 21 Nov. 2012.

Further Reading

"Elijah Muhammad." *Dictionary of American Biography*. New York: Scribner, 1994. *Gale Biography in Context*. Web. 22 Nov. 2012.

Marable, Manning. *Malcolm X: A Life of Reinvention*. New York: Penguin, 2011. Print.

Painter, Nell Irvin. "Malcolm X across the Genres." *American Historical Review* 98.2 (1993): 432–39. Rpt. in *Contemporary Literary Criticism. Literature Resource Center*. Web. 22 Nov. 2012.

Sanderson, Susan. "Critical Essay on *The Autobiography of Malcolm X*." *Nonfiction Classics for Students: Presenting Analysis, Context, and Criticism on Nonfiction Works*. Vol. 3. Ed. David M. Galens, Jennifer Smith, and Elizabeth Thomason. Detroit: Gale, 2002. *Literature Resource Center*. Web. 22 Nov. 2012.

Terrill, Robert E., ed. *The Cambridge Companion to Malcolm X*. Cambridge: Cambridge University Press, 2010. Print.

Katherine Barker

The Book of Margery Kempe
Margery Kempe

OVERVIEW

The Book of Margery Kempe, composed between 1436 and 1438, is an autobiographical work that describes the life and religious zeal of Margery Kempe, mystic of fifteenth-century England. The text boasts many unique qualities, not the least of which is its female authorship. To add to the unusual quality, Kempe was not a saint, nor was she even a particularly influential person in her time. Instead, she was an uneducated wife, mother, and merchant everywoman working to overcome her sins. Her spiritual journey demonstrates the intersection of ecclesiastical and secular life in late medieval England—particularly for women. Kempe spent her life juggling the desire to live a pious existence and the reality of her position as a married woman.

The Book of Margery Kempe is generally regarded as the first autobiography produced in English. However, the work was relatively unknown until the development of the printing press, at which point certain deeply religious passages became more available. These fragments—the only part of the work known for hundreds of years—presented Kempe as a saintly woman much like any of the other widely known female saints. When the full manuscript was discovered in 1934, however, a fuller picture came into focus: not just a sheltered mystic, Kempe was a psychologically complicated married woman of the middle class. The completed text was received with excitement for the mysteries it both cast and cleared up about women in late medieval England in general and about the peculiar character that was Kempe specifically.

HISTORICAL AND LITERARY CONTEXT

Christianity came to England with the Romans: the first churches were built in the second half of the fourth century. Over the next few centuries, England converted to Christianity. By Kempe's time in the late Middle Ages, Christianity played a major role in English people's everyday lives. The religious path was clear, and the institutionalized church made sure few strayed. Anyone going off course from ascribed Christian methods risked being labeled a "heretic," a capital offense and a charge Kempe narrowly escaped more than once. Kempe specifically belonged to the group of Christians practicing mysticism, a spiritual discipline that used intense contemplation and prayer as a route to a direct union with God.

Literacy rates in the later Middle Ages were low, and Kempe—despite being of a higher social class—was no exception. To capture the events of her life, she recited the story to a scribe, who then recorded it. As agreed, the text was published after Kempe's death, although it remained unknown until 1501 when publisher Wynken de Worde printed several sections. These highly religious excerpts presented Kempe as a holy woman similar to fourteenth-century English mystics such as Julian of Norwich, who makes an appearance in the work along with several other prominent Christian figures, including the Archbishop of Canterbury. Kempe's pilgrimages and visions of Jesus and Mary only added to this erroneous picture. Only after the full manuscript was discovered in 1934 did scholars realize that Kempe was drastically different. Indeed, she had not the quiet life of a cloistered mystic but rather had a husband and fourteen children. (While her children are largely unmentioned in the book, Margery's husband is a major character.)

Kempe wrote her story not as an autobiography—for no such genre existed—but to show others how God's mercy could fall upon even "sinful wretches" such as her. The literary influence for her story can be found in writings of saints and holy members of the church. Christian hagiography—the stories of the lives of the saints—provides both context and, to some extent, model for Kempe's story. Saintly models for some of the hagiographic elements found in *Margery Kempe* include the life of St. Catherine of Siena, who also experienced a sort of spiritual union with Christ.

Margery Kempe has caught the attention of modern scholars for two reasons: it provides rare insight into the daily lives of women in late medieval England, and it also documents the relationship between secular wives and ecclesiastical expectations. Scholars have interpreted the work in terms of psychoanalytic theory, religious hagiography, autobiography, feminism, and historical curiosity. Everything from Kempe's state of mind to her limited vocabulary has come under scrutiny by scholars in a modern attempt to gain understanding of a long-lost medieval world.

THEMES AND STYLE

The main theme of *Margery Kempe* is the entanglement between religious zeal, social obligations, and

❖ **Key Facts**

Time Period:
Mid-15th Century

Relevant Historical Events:
Kempe's struggle with sin and desire for saintliness

Nationality:
English

Keywords:
mysticism; women's writing; Middle Ages

CONTEMPLATION AND CONFESSION

Canterbury Pilgrims, an illustration from *The Siege of Thebes,* by John Lydgate (1370–1449). Like many people of her time, Margery Kempe completed pilgrimages to various holy sites in Europe and Asia.
© THE ART ARCHIVE/BRITISH LIBRARY

personal insecurities. Kempe's first vision of Christ comes after a bout of madness following the birth of her first child, during which she saw "devils opening their mouths all alight with burning flames of fire." Despite the warnings of her keepers, she is released and proves to be sane of mind. Kempe then spends the rest of her life struggling with her pride; her vanity; and her chastity, which she finally achieved after birthing fourteen children to her husband. One unforgivable (and unnamed) youthful sin for which Kempe never truly repents runs underneath every action she makes. She eventually does achieve spiritual enlightenment with the composition of her book about her life: "And often in the meantime, when this creature [Kempe] was in church, our Lord Jesus Christ with his glorious mother, and many saints as well, came into her soul and thanked her, saying that they were well pleased with the writing of this book."

The author's purpose in recording the details of her life is twofold. First, she wanted to provide other secular women with a model of how to worship Christ while fulfilling their social obligations. Second, she wanted to satisfy Christ himself, whom she felt desired her to write the book. She was approached to compose the events of her life when she devoted herself to God, but "she was warned in her spirit that she should not write so soon." It was not until "many years later" that "she was bidden in her spirit to write." And so she set out to pen "a short treatise and a comforting one for sinful wretches, in which they may have great solace and comfort for themselves, and understand the high and unspeakable mercy of our sovereign Saviour Jesus Christ."

Despite the religious tone of the book, the writing itself lacks the hagiographic outline associated with saintly lives, leaving the text disorganized and seeming uneducated. (Although certain hagiographical details occasionally appear, the work lacks the typical hagiography structure.) John Skinner, in his introduction to his 2000 edition of the text, notes the book is "impoverished in vocabulary while much of its structure remains obstinately repetitive." This likely reflects the uneducated nature of Kempe herself, although it could also be an indication of scribal intent or ability. Skinner explains: "We can never be certain how much of Margery's original narrative was moulded by her scribe."

CRITICAL DISCUSSION

The initial reaction to the discovery and subsequent publication of the entire work in 1934 was a mixture of excitement and confusion that generated a substantial body of criticism that continues to this day. Hope Emily Allen, a distinguished medievalist who was one of the first to read the full *Book of Margery Kempe* and construct a scholarly edition based on the manuscript, wrote to the *Times:* "It does give remarkably elevated spiritual passages, but they are interspersed with others highly fanatical, and with an immense number giving incidents of Margery's life." Justin McCann in his 1937 review of the work calls it "a complex book" that if read "as a contribution of [Christian] doctrine" is of little value. McCann suggests that when one looks at "the value of the book as a contribution of the literature of spiritual life," however, it then receives "a more favourable judgement."

Margery Kempe developed a legacy for its discussion of medieval religious practices from the perspective of a wife and mother. Feminist scholars note that it required a considerable leap (of courage as well as of faith) for a woman to believe her story was worth this kind of telling. Evelyn Underhill in her 1936 review of the book writes, "The discovery of the long-lost book of Margery Kempe of Lynn is an event almost equally important to students of mediaeval manners, and disconcerting to students of mediaeval mysticism." This is because the previous fragments printed by Wynken de Worde suggested "that Margery was a recluse and contemplative" along with many of her contemporary ascetics. Instead, Kempe was revealed to be "a vigorous and exuberant woman," to use Underhill's words, which continues to challenge scholarly opinions about the veracity of virgin saint narratives and the application of hagiographic tropes in the everyday lives of medieval people.

The wealth of scholarship generated in the wake of the 1934 discovery of the full text of *Margery Kempe* has taken many directions and includes many trends. One such approach looks at Kempe's attempts to fulfill her spiritual desires despite being a mother, merchant, and wife. Lisa Manter in "Savior of Her Desire" follows this trend: "The autobiographical materials provide a context that allows them to be viewed as attempts to resolve, within an imaginary realm, the discontinuities that plague her attempts to forge a coherent self-concept out of conflicting options." Another direction is to regard Kempe's book as a unique work that does not fit into the genres of hagiography or autobiography. Skinner exemplifies this trend when he states, "It would be wholly unhelpful to parade Margery Kempe's book before today's readers simply as autobiography" because "that genre had yet to be invented…. It would be unrealistic to anticipate the literary skills necessary for such an accomplishment in a woman who could neither read nor write."

MARGERY KEMPE AND THE WIFE OF BATH: GENDER DYNAMICS IN LATE MEDIEVAL ENGLAND

Margery Kempe's descriptions of her pilgrimages are often compared with the roughly contemporary stories of Geoffrey Chaucer in his *Canterbury Tales,* particularly the prologue and tale of the Wife of Bath. Both women came from the same class, traveled without their husbands, and were outspoken in their religious zeal. They also both balance their sexuality with their marital status, societal obligations, and religious ambitions. The two women provide interesting commentary about the interaction between married women and the church in late medieval England.

The women's differences, however, most interest scholars. The Wife of Bath was a fictional character created by Chaucer, a male writer. His narrative—along with the rest of the *Canterbury Tales*—received contemporary success and survives in numerous manuscripts. Kempe's story, on the other hand, is an account of a woman, by a woman. As such, it is based in female realities. Despite this (or because of it), the work was relatively unknown until the printing press in the sixteenth century and still was not discovered fully until recent history. For obvious reasons, *Margery Kempe* is believed to be the more accurate account for scholars to discern details about the lives of secular women in the late Middle Ages.

BIBLIOGRAPHY

Sources

Allen, Hope Emily. "A Medieval Work." *Times* (London) 27 Dec. 1934: 15. *Times Digital Archive.* Web. 13 Nov. 2012.

Kempe, Margery. *The Book of Margery Kempe.* Trans. B. A. Windeatt. London: Penguin, 2000. *ProQuest Information and Learning.* Web. 13 Nov. 2012.

Manter, Lisa. "The Savior of Her Desire: Margery Kempe's Passionate Gaze." *Exemplaria* 13.1 (2001): 39–66. Rpt. in *Literature Criticism from 1400 to 1800.* Vol. 145. Detroit: Gale, 2008. *Literature Resource Center.* Web. 13 Nov. 2012.

McCann, Justin. Rev. of *The Book of Margery Kempe,* by Margery Kempe. *Dublin Review* 200.400 (1937): 103–16. Rpt. in *Literature Criticism from 1400 to 1800.* Ed. James E. Person Jr. Vol. 6. Detroit: Gale, 1987. *Literature Resource Center.* Web. 13 Nov. 2012.

Skinner, John. Introduction. *The Book of Margery Kempe.* By Margery Kempe. Colorado Springs: Image Books, 1998. 1–11. Rpt. in *Literature Criticism from 1400 to 1800.* Vol. 56. Detroit: Gale, 2000. *Literature Resource Center.* Web. 13 Nov. 2012.

Underhill, Evelyn. "Margery Kempe." *Spectator* 157.5651 (1936): 642. Rpt. in *Literature Criticism from 1400 to 1800.* Ed. James E. Person Jr. Vol. 6. Detroit: Gale, 1987. *Literature Resource Center.* Web. 13 Nov. 2012.

Further Reading

Arnold, John H., and Katherine J. Lewis, eds. *A Companion to* The Book of Margery Kempe. Woodbridge, U.K.: D.S. Brewer, 2004. Print.

Castagna, Valentina. *Re-reading Margery Kempe in the 21st Century.* New York: Peter Lang, 2011. Print.

Chaucer, Geoffrey. *The Wife of Bath's Prologue and Tale.* Ed. Mark Allen, John H. Fisher, and Joseph Trahern. Norman: University of Oklahoma Press, 2012. Print.

Glenn, Cheryl. "Reexamining *The Book of Margery Kempe:* A Rhetoric of Autobiography." *Reclaiming Rhetorica: Women in the Rhetorical Tradition.* Ed. Andrea A. Lunsford. University of Pittsburgh Press, 1995. 53–68. Rpt. in *Literature Criticism from 1400 to 1800.* Vol. 56. Detroit: Gale, 2000. *Literature Resource Center.* Web. 14 Nov. 2012.

Harding, Wendy. "Body into Text: *The Book of Margery Kempe.*" *Feminist Approaches to the Body in Medieval Literature.* Ed. Linda Lomperis and Sarah Stanbury. University of Pennsylvania Press, 1993. 168–85. Rpt. in *Literature Criticism from 1400 to 1800.* Vol. 56. Detroit: Gale, 2000. *Literature Resource Center.* Web. 14 Nov. 2012.

Williams, Tara. *Inventing Womanhood: Gender and Language in Later Middle English Writing.* Columbus: Ohio State University Press, 2011. Print.

Katherine Barker

A Confession

Leo Tolstoy

OVERVIEW

Published in 1884, Leo Tolstoy's *A Confession* offers a stark account of the author's struggle with a nearly suicidal religious and existential crisis. Tolstoy traces the progress of the disenchantment that he experiences despite astounding success as a writer, his fortune, and his family. He saw that death brought an absolute annihilation that would render all of his achievements meaningless and thus drained life of its purpose. Repudiating his life as a landowner, soldier, and intellectual, he looks to peasants for insight into what he seeks. In them, he finds an attitude of acceptance and tranquility, which he admires. He is troubled, however, by the Russian Orthodox Church's exploitation of their humility and obedience. As he seeks to reconcile his doubt with his search for existential meaning, Tolstoy offers an autobiographical account with deep philosophical undertones.

When Tolstoy's text was published, he was the most prominent writer in Russia. Although his novel *Anna Karenina* had recently appeared to great acclaim, Tolstoy regretted having written the novel, dismissing it as trivial and wishing he could disown it. Tolstoy penned *A Confession* to perform a factual and rational analysis of the themes that he had explored in his fiction. He had long sought a form of Christianity that was free of the strictures and conventions of Russian Orthodoxy, which had long dominated Russian society. *A Confession* was initially banned in Russia owing to its controversial critique of religious institutions, and Tolstoy's continued critique of the church led to his excommunication in 1901. *A Confession*, which soon came to be admired within liberal Russian circles, is today considered among the most important philosophical and autobiographical works in world literature.

HISTORICAL AND LITERARY CONTEXT

Tolstoy wrote *A Confession* in response to his shifting perception of and role in Russia's move toward liberalism and modernism in the mid- to late nineteenth century. In the early part of the century, as many European nations began to initiate democratic reform and move toward constitutional forms of government, Russia became increasingly autocratic, particularly with the passage of the Fundamental Laws in 1832. This consolidation of imperial power led to unrest in the mid-1800s. In the 1850s, Tolstoy served as a soldier in the Russian army while also establishing himself as a writer. Upon his retirement from the military, Tolstoy, a landowner, devoted himself to the cause of freeing his serfs and giving them land, and in the 1860s he helped implement educational reform in Russia. His work for liberal causes was in keeping with a larger Russian move toward reform and modernization—a move that led to Czar Alexander II's Great Reforms in the 1860s and 1870s. These reforms led to the liberation of the serfs, to democratic reform, and to military modernization.

By the time Tolstoy began work on *A Confession*, however, he had lost all faith in the kinds of enlightened reform he had promoted, and he had turned instead to religion for solutions to the injustice and spiritual crisis he saw in society. Although this substantial change in perspective took place gradually over the course of Tolstoy's life, his reading of the German philosopher Arthur Schopenhauer in the late 1860s convinced Tolstoy that life was meaningless and evil. Despite his growing despair, Tolstoy began a new novel, *Anna Karenina*, in 1870 and completed it 1877. Despite its success and critical acclaim, Tolstoy fell into suicidal depression after its publication. After an extensive period of assessment of his life and views, he eventually discovered the will to live in profound religious faith, a process he documents in *A Confession*.

Tolstoy's *A Confession* belongs to a tradition of autobiographical writing that can be traced to St. Augustine's *Confessions*. Written around 397 CE, St. Augustine's *Confessions* was the first autobiographical work that documented its author's spiritual development rather than the events of his life. Like Augustine, Tolstoy recounts the story of his failure as a Christian as well as his struggle to become and remain a faithful disciple of God. Another important autobiographical precedent for Tolstoy's work was Jean-Jacques Rousseau's *Confessions*. Tolstoy drew also from Schopenhauer's *The World as Will and Representation*, completed in 1818, which triggered the spiritual crisis that motivated Tolstoy to find his faith.

Following *A Confession*, Tolstoy continued to write on religion, particularly about his own spiritual progression. In 1880 and 1881 he translated and bowdlerized the New Testament. The result was *Translation and Harmony of the Four Gospels*, a revision that

❖ **Key Facts**

Time Period:
Late 19th Century

Relevant Historical Events:
Tolstoy experiences religious and existential crisis; Russia institutes Great Reforms

Nationality:
Russian

Keywords:
Christianity; theology; faith

Author Leo Tolstoy in 1873, several years before *A Confession* was written. Portrait by Nicholas Kramskoy. © IGOR GOLOVNOV/ALAMY

reflected Tolstoy's conception of the "true" Christianity. He then wrote *Investigation of Dogmatic Theology* (1891) and *What I Believe* (1883), which offered the tenets of his idiosyncratic Christian faith. He continued to write on religion in *On Life* (1887), *The Kingdom of God* (1893), and *What Is Religion, and What Does Its Essence Consist Of?* (1902).

THEMES AND STYLE

The central theme of *A Confession* is that religious faith is an essential antidote to existential despair. Early in the text, Tolstoy charts the course of his rise to and disenchantment with worldly success. Eventually, Tolstoy writes, he came to the conclusion that "life is without meaning," and he was forced to confront the fundamental mysteries of existence. Tolstoy returned to the Russian Orthodox religion of his boyhood, but doing so entailed "unconsciously clos[ing] my eyes to the contradictions and obscurities in religious teaching." Confused by and skeptical of many church rituals, teachings, and policies, Tolstoy writes that he "envied the peasants their illiteracy and ignorance" for he could not forget his misgivings, no matter how certain he was of Christianity's essential truth. At the essay's end, Tolstoy remains conflicted but resolves to continue searching for answers: "My task is to find the truth and the falsehood and distinguish between them."

Tolstoy's reason for writing his *Confession* was the despair and confusion he experienced after achieving astonishing personal, professional, and artistic success. Early in the text, he writes of his pervasive, paralyzing doubt: "Contemplating the fame coming to me from my writings, I would say to myself, 'Fine, you're going to be more famous than Gogol, Pushkin, Shakespeare, Molière, or any other writer in the world…. What about it?" Unable to identify anything worth pursuing, he contemplated suicide, as he had "no wishes that seemed worth gratifying" and thus nothing to live for. Following a tradition of Christian conversion narratives, Tolstoy writes to illustrate the process of his successful struggle to find faith. Tolstoy, however, complicates this tradition of autobiographical writing by remaining shrouded in doubt at the text's end. By using autobiography to make a complicated theological argument, Tolstoy illustrates the personal element of his philosophical and religious concerns.

Stylistically, *A Confession* is notable for its mix of narrative and philosophical modes. By couching his religious progression in a linear, narrative form, Tolstoy engages the reader and allows his audience to follow the trajectory of his thought through its various oscillations. As part of that progression, Tolstoy leads his reader through various esoteric arguments about the meaning of existence. Referencing sources as diverse as Schopenhauer and the biblical King Solomon, he explores such concepts as "an infinite God, the sanctity of the soul, a link between human affairs and God, moral concepts of good and evil." In couching his philosophical interrogations in a narrative form, Tolstoy allows his audience to accompany him on his quest for answers.

CRITICAL DISCUSSION

Upon completion of *A Confession* in 1882, Tolstoy sought publication of the text in the Moscow journal *Russian Thought*. It was accepted by the journal and submitted to the Russian religious censor committee for approval. As related by Rosamund Bartlett in *Tolstoy: A Russian Life,* the committee concluded that "Tolstoy's attitude to Orthodoxy was disrespectful and so his article was therefore inadmissible." This edict was headline news in Russia, which only increased interest in the work. Copies were illicitly made and distributed, and the text was widely circulated and read. Despite (or because of) its being banned, Bartlett states that the text "reached a far wider readership than it would have done through the legitimate means of the 3,000-circulation *Russian Thought*." The work was not officially published until 1884 (in Geneva, Switzerland).

Tolstoy originally considered *A Confession* to be only an introduction to the first volume of a four-volume work. The first two volumes, *Investigation of Dogmatic Theology* and *Union and Translation of the Four Gospels,* remained unpublished at the time, but what Tolstoy envisioned would be the fourth volume was published as *What I Believe*. It is a summation of what the Russian Orthodox Church considered his heretical take on Christian truth. In 1901 the church excommunicated Tolstoy for his religious views. Those views, on the oppressive nature of religious systems and the wisdom of the poor, proved influential to a variety of twentieth-century figures, including Mohandas Gandhi and Vladimir Lenin. Scholars have approached the work through a wide range of analytical frameworks, considering its importance not only in religious but also literary, historical, philosophical, and autobiographical terms.

Much scholarship of Tolstoy's *Confession* has placed the work within a religious and historical context. In her foreword to Anthony Briggs's translation of *A Confession*, Helen Dunmore calls it "above all a very Russian piece of work, which falls into an historical context where Russians were trying to understand the social and political, moral and spiritual character of their nation, and were eagerly looking for change." Commentators also have considered the psychological origins of Tolstoy's autobiography. In "Does God Exist? A Clinical Study of the Religious Attitudes Expressed in Tolstoy's *Confession*," Daniel Rancour-Laferriere argues "that the very question of whether God exists or not in Tolstoy's mind is determined by a specific type of mood disorder." Noting its "exhibitionistic, narcissistic tinge," Rancour-Laferriere diagnoses Tolstoy with bipolar II disorder and cites this as the source of his "quasi-theological view of the world."

BIBLIOGRAPHY

Sources

Bartlett, Rosamund. *Tolstoy: A Russian Life*. New York: Houghton, 2011. Print.

Briggs, Anthony. *Brief Lives: Leo Tolstoy*. London: Hesperus, 2010. Print.

Dunmore, Helen. Foreword. *A Confession*. By Leo Tolstoy. Trans. Anthony Briggs. London: Hesperus, 2010. Print.

Rancour-Laferriere, Daniel. "Does God Exist? A Clinical Study of the Religious Attitudes Expressed in Tolstoy's *Confession*." *Slavic and East European Journal* 49.3 (2005): 445–73. *JSTOR*. Web. 18 Oct. 2012.

Further Reading

Boot, Alexander. *God and Man According to Tolstoy*. New York: Palgrave, 2009. Print.

Fodor, Alexander. *Tolstoy and the Russians: Reflections on a Relationship*. Ann Arbor, Mich.: Ardis, 1984. Print.

LEO TOLSTOY AND VLADIMIR CHERTKOV

During the last three decades of his life, from roughly 1880 until his death in 1910, Tolstoy obsessively immersed himself in the quest to discover religious truth and to abide by the truths he discovered. As of 1883, this quest was informed to a large degree by a religious seeker named Vladimir Chertkov. At the time of their meeting in Moscow, Chertkov was twenty-nine and Tolstoy was fifty-five. Chertkov grew up in an aristocratic family with close ties to Tsar Alexander II but, like Tolstoy, had grown disillusioned with the trappings of power and wealth. As a result, Chertkov devoted himself to freeing, educating, and empowering the peasants of his family's rural estate. He also had become involved in Christianity outside the Orthodox Church through his mother, a Protestant evangelist.

When Tolstoy and Chertkov met, they discovered their shared backgrounds and similar visions. As Tolstoy continued to write and examine his faith, he did so under the influence of his new friend. After Chertkov translated into English *What I Believe*, in which Tolstoy offered his religious and ethical creed, he Bartlett writes that he encouraged Tolstoy to "produce quality literature for the masses." As Chertkov became increasingly involved in the publication of Tolstoy's works and the course of Tolstoy's religious development, he came into conflict with Tolstoy's wife, Sonya, who fought to keep her family afloat despite her husband's growing devotion to asceticism and penury.

Gustafson, Richard F. *Leo Tolstoy: Resident and Stranger: A Study in Fiction and Theology*. Princeton, N.J.: Princeton University Press, 1986. Print.

Matual, David. *Tolstoy's Translations of the Gospels: A Critical Study*. Lewiston, N.Y.: Mellen, 1992. Print.

Medzhibovskaya, Inessa. *Tolstoy and the Religious Culture of His Time: A Biography of a Long Conversation*. Lanham, Md.: Lexington, 2008. Print.

Tolstoy, Leo. *Tolstoy's Letters*. New York: Scribner, 1978.

Wilson, A. N. *Tolstoy*. New York: Norton, 2001.

Theodore McDermott

Confessions

Augustine

Key Facts

Time Period:
Late 4th Century

Relevant Historical Events:
First Council of Nicaea; Augustine appointed Bishop of Hippo

Nationality:
Roman/Algerian

Keywords:
confession; Christianity; faith

OVERVIEW

Written in classical Latin and published around 397 CE, St. Augustine's *Confessions* is an early Christian work in which the author acknowledges his faith in God and confesses his sins. Drawing on scripture, philosophy, and classical rhetoric, Augustine addresses God in prayer with the utmost sincerity and sensitivity. He frequently quotes the Latin Bible, particularly the book of Psalms. *Confessions* is the main source of information on the life of Augustine, and in his later work *Retractions* he affirms that "books 1–10 of *Confessions* are written about me." The last three books (11–13) are less autobiographical and handle the philosophical issues of memory, time, and creation. Augustine's *Confessions* is a journey of self-discovery through which, by coming to know himself, he comes to know God.

By the time Augustine wrote *Confessions*, he had already composed numerous works, including *Soliloquies*, and he had recently been appointed bishop of Hippo, a Mediterranean port on the northern coast of Africa. He published *Confessions*, in part, to establish his identity in the relatively small community and to defend his position as bishop against his enemies. According to Augustine, *Confessions*—more than any of his other works—was received with enthusiasm, although some of his rivals took offense to the work. Pelagius, a contemporary ascetic theologian, condemned it for its denial of free will, and Pelagius's followers continued this attack for many years. Regarded by many as the first and finest autobiography ever written, *Confessions* has influenced countless philosophers and theologians and has inspired Christians and non-Christians alike for more than sixteen centuries.

HISTORICAL AND LITERARY CONTEXT

In the years after the death of Jesus, numerous Christian sects were making contradictory claims. Each group believed that it was upholding the teachings of Jesus and his apostles and thereby continuing the true apostolic tradition. Various gospels testified to their claims, including the four well-disseminated gospels of Matthew, Mark, Luke, and John and others such as the gospels of Thomas and of Mary Magdalene. In 325 CE the Roman emperor Constantine convened a council of bishops at Nicaea (now İznik, Turkey) to help the quest for orthodoxy. The Nicene Creed (which begins, "We believe in one God, the Father, the Almighty, maker of heaven and earth, of all that is, seen and unseen") together with a definitive list of canonical scriptures were eventually approved by the bishops and endorsed by Constantine for the purpose of establishing a universal, Christian church.

Bishop Valerius appointed Augustine bishop of Hippo in 396 CE, and Augustine published his *Confessions* the following year to defend his beliefs, which were under attack, and to explain his Manichaean past to the local community. Manichaeans were a Persian gnostic sect that taught the release of the spirit from matter through asceticism. Petilianus from the Donatist church, a rival Christian church in Africa, was accusing Augustine of being a secret Manichaean, while Secundinus, a Manichaean, was claiming that Augustine had left the sect because he was afraid of persecution. Others believed that Augustine's consecration as bishop violated the rules of the Council of Nicaea.

Many scholars claim that *Confessions* was the first autobiography ever written. The work is highly autobiographical but is ultimately unique in its character, being a mix of literary traditions. Nevertheless, *Confessions* resembles the book of Psalms (poems and hymns of worship) in both content and style. (Augustine had cherished and memorized all 150 psalms, and he cites many of them in *Confessions*.) The work also reflects the literary traditions of the *apologia* (a written defense of one's position or actions) and *commentarii* (notes/memoirs). Other influences include Marcus Tullius Cicero's *Hortensius* and the letters and sermons of Paul and Ambrose. The *Enneads*, by the ancient philosopher Plotinus, helped Augustine in formulating the Neoplatonic philosophical argument in *Confessions* that views the soul as being weighed down by a focus on the material world and needing help to see the true form of goodness and beauty of Christian doctrine. Augustine's earlier work *Soliloquies* is a philosophical self-examination in which he carries on an inner dialogue with himself; it anticipates his masterwork *Confessions* in which he addresses God rather than himself.

Augustine's *Confessions* has had an enormous impact on theologians, philosophers, and scholars since the Renaissance. Scholar Desiderius Erasmus produced an edition of Augustine's collected works in the early 1500s, and clergyman William Watts wrote one of the finest English translations in 1631. The work continued to inspire prominent thinkers, including Swiss-born French philosopher Jean-Jacques Rousseau, who wrote his own autobiographical self-examination, *Confessions,* which was published posthumously in 1782 and 1789, in two volumes. In the twentieth century, American psychologist William James and Austrian psychoanalyst Sigmund Freud took notable interest in the psychological aspects of Augustine's life. In the contemporary world, Augustine's *Confessions* is taught in a variety of university programs, from religious to rhetorical studies. Noted classical scholars such as James O'Donnell and Gillian Clark have provided vital up-to-date commentaries.

THEMES AND STYLE

The central theme of Augustine's *Confessions* explores humans' capacity to sin and their need for God's grace to free their will from sin in order to know God and attain salvation. According to Augustine's Neoplatonic philosophical view, sin is moving away from God and valuing material things. Augustine traces his own sins back to infancy: "Even then therefore did I something worthy to be blamed," such as cry for food and show jealousy. Concerning the episode of how he helped "rob" a pear tree, only to waste his loot by feeding it to hogs, he addresses God: "Surely thy law, O Lord, punishes thievery." He admits that he was "compelled neither by hunger nor poverty … nor cared I to enjoy the thing which I had stolen, but joying in the theft and sin itself." Augustine confesses to a variety of sins such as lustfulness, love of stage plays, and mocking the simplicity of the New Testament Greek language. He laments, "And behold I was now going on my thirtieth year, still sticking in the same clay; still possessed with a greediness of enjoying things present, they as fast flitting and wasting my soul; I still saying to myself, To-morrow I shall find it out."

Augustine's purpose for writing *Confessions* was to defend his position as bishop of Hippo against the slander of his foes. It was not written as a typical self-promoting memoir, which is evident by his direct address to God and his citing of scripture. Augustine selectively chooses his narrative to emphasize the meaning he thinks can be drawn from his life. So, whereas many autobiographical elements are missing, including information on personal relationships (he never provides the names of his best friend and his common-law wife, for example), he often discusses his mother as well as Ambrose, who both are crucial in guiding him to his eventual conversion. Noted American historian and writer Garry Wills, in discussing the scene in the baths of Tagaste, where Augustine feels that God has spoken to him through his mother, writes in his book *Augustine's Confessions* (2011) that "we are not in the realm of autobiography but of spiritual psychodrama." Yet *Confessions* is by far the most important source on Augustine's life, and in Book 10 Augustine concludes that "this is the fruit of my Confessions, not of what I have been, but of what I am."

The Conversion of St. Augustine, painted by Fra Angelico, depicts Augustine weeping in despair before he resolves to convert to Christianity. © MUSEE D'ART THOMAS HENRY, CHERBOURG, FRANCE/GIRAUDON/THE BRIDGEMAN ART LIBRARY

AFRICAN WANDERLUST

Augustine was born in Tagaste, Numidia (now Souk Ahras, Algeria), an ancient Berber kingdom, in 354 CE. North Africa had become a Roman province after the Phoenician city of Carthage was destroyed in 146 BCE. Although the Latin language and Roman mores predominated throughout the region, local cults still existed and aboriginal Berber was spoken in parts. Augustine attended primary school in Tagaste and then briefly studied at the university in Madaura. Madaura was the home of the novelist and orator Apuleius (flourished about 150 CE), who wrote the comic novel *The Golden Ass*—a conversion story, not unlike *Confessions,* in which the protagonist, lost in life's follies, ultimately discovers truth by becoming a priest of the Egyptian gods Isis and Osiris.

In 370 CE Augustine moved to Carthage and discovered Roman statesman Cicero's now lost work *Hortensius*—a treatise that promoted rhetoric and philosophy—upon which to some extent he would model his own writings. After four years, Augustine returned to Tagaste, but he went back to Carthage within the year to be an orator. Ever ambitious, he moved to Rome in 383 and then on to Milan to teach rhetoric in 384, where, ultimately, his conversion took place. Realizing the inanity of ambition, he eventually returned to Tagaste in 389. Augustine was appointed bishop of Hippo in 396, where he remained until his death in 430.

Stylistically, Augustine's *Confessions* resembles a lengthy prayer, because he directly addresses God in a laudatory tone throughout. He begins Book 1 with a quote from Psalms 147.5 (146.5 Vulgate): "Great art thou, O Lord, and greatly to be praised: great is thy power, and thy wisdom is infinite. And man, who being a part of what thou hast created, is desirous to praise thee." Augustine not only quotes the Psalms but also imitates them stylistically. Wills explains that "the most basic verse structure of the Psalms is a two line unit in which the second line repeats, reverses, or elaborates on the first one.... This pattern informs much of *Confessions,* its sighing replications, his way of turning a thought over and over. These give the book its air of slow reflection and inwardness." Augustine, trained as a rhetorician, understood the persuasive function of word choice and order. Some academics have claimed that *Confessions* is a rhetorical work because Augustine expects the listener to be changed after reading or hearing it. English scholar and historian Edward Gibbon, famed as the author of *The History of the Decline and Fall of the Roman Empire* (1776–1788), complained that Augustine's style "is usually clouded by false and affected rhetoric."

CRITICAL DISCUSSION

In *Retractationes* (426–427; *Reconsiderations*), Augustine notes that *Confessions* was his most widely read and favorably received book: "What others feel about it, let them find out on their own, though I know that it has pleased many of my fellows, and still does." Because of the rival Donatist church and its immense influence throughout North Africa, Augustine had opponents who were critical of the publication. In addition, Christian theologians and ascetics such as Pelagius and Julian of Eclanum attacked Augustine's theology, particularly for his denial of free will in *Confessions*. In his book *Augustine* (1985), scholar O'Donnell explains that these ascetics "were concerned that the value of their own self-denying way of life was undermined by what they saw as defeatist quietism."

Outside of canonical scripture, *Confessions* has been one of the most influential and widely read Christian works ever written. Although some scholars have pointed out that *Confessions* did suffer neglect in the Middle Ages, with Augustine's ecclesiological works such as *City of God* garnering more influence than *Confessions* in the religious communities, the work still retained its popularity. In his book *After Augustine* (2001), history and literature scholar Brian Stock demonstrates that *Confessions* "enjoyed a continuous readership throughout the Middle Ages and Renaissance." Since the Renaissance, it has become increasingly influential among academicians. Contemporary scholars have approached the work in a variety of ways; for example, they have provided valuable insights into its theological, historical, and autobiographical nature. The text is frequently used in the fields of philosophy, ethics, classics, religious studies, and rhetoric.

A predominant trend in recent scholarship has been the examination of rhetorical devices in Augustine's *Confessions*. Although Augustine presents rhetoric as deceptive and corrupting in *Confessions,* he nonetheless utilizes the art of persuasion throughout. In her commentary *Augustine: Confessions, Books I–IV,* classicist Clark has provided many insights into Augustine's rhetorical techniques. She writes that antithesis "is Augustine's favorite technique … antithesis is so frequent in all his writing that it seems rather to be the way he thinks." Other critics such as Annemare Kotze have explored the influence of Cicero's rhetorical work *Hortensius* on the expression of exhortative purpose throughout *Confessions*. This comparison has led to a better understanding of both Augustine and his purpose for writing *Confessions*.

BIBLIOGRAPHY

Sources

Augustine. *Confessions.* 2 vols. Trans. William Watts. Cambridge: Harvard University Press, 2000. Print.

Augustine. *The Retractions.* Vol. 60. Trans. Sister Mary Inez Bogan. Fathers of the Church. Washington, D.C.: Catholic University of America Press, 1999. Print.

Clark, Gillian. *Augustine: Confessions, Books I–IV.* Cambridge: Cambridge University Press, 1995. Print.

O'Donnell, James. *Augustine.* Boston: Hall, 1985. Print.

Stock, Brian. *After Augustine: The Meditative Reader and the Text.* Philadelphia: University of Pennsylvania Press, 2001. Print.

Wills, Garry. *Augustine's Confessions.* Princeton, N.J.: Princeton University Press, 2011. Print.

Further Reading

Bourke, Vernon. *Augustine's Love of Wisdom: An Introspective Philosophy.* West Lafayette, Ind.: Purdue University Press, 1992. Print.

Burton, Philip. *Language in the Confessions of Augustine.* Oxford: Oxford University Press, 2007. Print.

Ehrman, Bart. *Lost Christianities.* Oxford: Oxford University Press, 2003. Print.

Kotzé, Annemaré. *Augustine's Confessions: Communicative Purpose and Audience.* Boston: Brill, 2004. Print.

O'Connell, Robert. *Soundings in St. Augustine's Imagination.* New York: Fordham University Press, 1994. Print.

O'Donnell, James. *Augustine: Confessions.* Oxford: Clarendon, 1992. Print.

Pagels, Elaine. *The Gnostic Gospels.* New York: Random, 1979. Print.

Gregory Bach

Confessions

Jean-Jacques Rousseau

Key Facts

Time Period:
Late 18th Century

Relevant Historical Events:
Rousseau seeks to explain his personal philosophy

Nationality:
French

Keywords:
identity; philosophy; literary theory

OVERVIEW

Confessions, written by Jean-Jacques Rousseau and published posthumously in two volumes in 1782 and 1789, respectively, deals with the events and emotions in the author's life that define him as a person and that demonstrate his notion of the divided nature of identity: consisting of a separation among the self, the body, and the actions of an individual. Rousseau explores how each of these three components can operate independently of one another and lead to different states of mind in the individual. These qualities relate to Rousseau's writing career in philosophy and literature and his desire to find his lacking happiness by gaining control of all three aspects of his identity.

Rousseau wrote his autobiography toward the end of his literary career. He intended it to be a masterpiece of sorts that combined an honest examination of himself with his ideas about philosophy and literary theory without moralizing the events in his life with overarching meaning. Several chapters were released through public readings that left the audience in shocked silence and that left Rousseau feeling embarrassed and believing that he had not accomplished his purpose in writing the text. This silence was a result of the autobiography diverging from the expected forms of historical memoirs or Christian confessions, producing a rather revolutionary document in its style and content. Despite this reaction, however, Rousseau's *Confessions* proved to be a highly influential text that generated interest in the genre of autobiography and has created a wealth of critical scholarship that continues to this day.

HISTORICAL AND LITERARY CONTEXT

Rousseau's autobiography was composed after he had established himself in literary and philosophical realms as an accomplished writer and thinker. The act of composing an autobiography had historically been seen as one of two processes: either the confessions to God of thoughts and ideas that needed holy justification or the recording of memoirs in order to provide context for literary or theoretical writings. It was because of these expectations, based on the historical publications of these kinds of texts, that Rousseau's *Confessions* was met with stunned silence: Rousseau completely broke free from the historical trends surrounding autobiography and created the basis for a new genre of exploration of the self from an intimate perspective of personal transparency without stylistic artifice.

Confessions was the first of three full-length autobiographies written by Rousseau, and although several chapters were released in public readings in Paris, the text in its entirety was not published until well after the death of the author and the people who were featured in the narrative. The posthumous publication of the book was arranged by Rousseau, who did not follow the convention of disguising the names of people—whether they were presented in a positive or negative manner—which was something the contemporary audience thought was odd, unexpected, and ultimately disrespectful. The idea of writing an autobiography was not considered in itself to be a

CONTINUING THE STORY: ROUSSEAU'S *DIALOGUES* AND *REVERIES*

In addition to *Confessions,* Jean-Jacques Rousseau wrote two other autobiographical texts that proved to be quite different in style and content from his first discussion of his life. *Dialogues,* or *Rousseau, Judge of Jean-Jacques,* was published in 1772 and is structured as a fictional court hearing in which "Rousseau" and "the Frenchman" discuss "Jean-Jacques"—a notorious author—so that the criticisms leveled against the author could be handled judiciously. This is often considered to be the most strange of Rousseau's autobiographical texts, and the dark content constructs the theme of a conspiracy that can be found in sections of his second volume of *Confessions.*

The third and final work of autobiography, *Reveries of the Solitary Walker,* was written in the last two years of Rousseau's life, 1776–1778, and again presents a very different viewpoint than the other two texts. After the perceived contemporary failure of *Confessions* and *Dialogues,* Rousseau felt as though he could never reveal his true self to his reading audience. Thus *Reveries* is not addressed to a reader, as the previous two autobiographies are, but is instead addressed to Rousseau himself, suggesting that the writer has found peace in his memories and has focused on exploring the division of identity into the self, body, and actions not for the benefit of a reading audience but for his own personal pleasure.

completely foreign undertaking, especially considering the literary accomplishments of Rousseau, but the style and content of *Confessions* were unexpected by the audience because of their philosophical resonance and their style of complete transparency.

Confessions interacts with and was influenced by St. Augustine's text of the same name, although it is quite different in principle and content. Augustine wrote his confessions in terms of biblical scripture, demonstrating how the inner identity of the saint could be revealed only by God. Rousseau, however, discusses the presentation of himself as he feels he is, a concept that raises the necessary questions of a static self and the ability to act both in accordance with and in contrast to its moral principles.

The autobiography was immensely influential, providing the ideas of self-exploration and the definition of the self that would continue to be the basis for autobiographical writing throughout the romantic period and even into modern times. In addition to the wealth of scholarship discussing this work as a product of the Enlightenment, as a piece of philosophical writing, and as the inspiration for further advances in the autobiographical genre, the work itself has inspired specific autobiographical works including *The Prelude* (1850) by William Wordsworth, subtitled "The Growth of the Poet's Mind," which uses Rousseau's ideas about the self and self-examination through writing, and more modern texts such as *The Gulag Archipelago* (1973) by Aleksandr Solzhenitsyn, which paraphrases some key ideas from Rousseau's *Confessions*.

THEMES AND STYLE

The main theme running through *Confessions* is Rousseau's analysis of his life and memories as though there were two different versions of Rousseau: the character in the story and the essential self of the writer. While the division of identity into the self and the actions of an individual, which may operate independently of each other, is a fairly common viewpoint for modern autobiographical texts, it was an unprecedented division in Rousseau's text that shocked his intended audience and set the standard for later texts to follow. Rousseau clearly exemplifies this idea when discussing his recovery from a life-threatening injury: "This accident, which should have killed my body, killed only my passions, and I thank heaven each day for the happy effect it had on my soul." Here the division of the self takes on three different aspects: body, passions, and soul. When he is in control of all three, Rousseau is content in his autobiography. But the loss of control of any one of these components leads to an unbalanced and torn identity that searches for happiness.

Rousseau states his purpose for writing his autobiography in the very opening lines of the text: "I want to show my fellow men a man in all the truth of nature, and this man is to be myself." In presenting himself in this manner he exemplifies his philosophical theories about the natural man in society and the division of identity. While this text would establish many of the conventions of autobiographical writing that would be emulated by later writers, it was considered to be a deviation from all expectations at the time by attributing his actions and true identity to his own merits instead of placing the revelations of his character in the hands of God.

Because of the revolutionary ideas being discussed by Rousseau in *Confessions*, the style of the work is somewhat rambling and philosophical in tone. Written in two volumes and composed of twelve books in total, the autobiography is a lengthy project that covers multiple aspects of the writer's life, sometimes diverging into different themes and meanings. This further develops Rousseau's ideas about the division of identity and the development of an independent self. This organization and seemingly different yet interrelated themes has led many scholars, including Peter France in 1987, to classify this text as existing with "no single aim underlying the entire work," which suggests Rousseau was "moved more or less simultaneously by several different impulses." All of these impulses, however, "show a fascinating evolution in the enterprise of understanding the self and presenting it to the world."

Portrait of philosopher Jean-Jacques Rousseau, whose *Confessions* was published posthumously. © GL ARCHIVE/ALAMY

PRIMARY SOURCE

EXCERPT FROM *CONFESSIONS*

AFTER two years silence and patience, and notwithstanding my resolutions, I again take up my pen. Reader, suspend your judgment as to the reasons which force me to such a step: of these you can be no judge until you shall have read my book.

You have seen my youth pass away calmly without any great disappointments or remarkable prosperity. This was mostly owing to my ardent yet feeble nature, less prompt in undertaking than easy to discourage: quitting repose by violent agitations, but returning to it from lassitude and inclinations, and which, placing me in an idle and tranquil state for which alone I felt I was born, at a distance from the paths of great virtues and still further from those of great vices.

The first part of my confessions was written entirely from memory, and is consequently full of errors. As I am obliged to write the second part from memory also, the errors in it will probably be still more numerous. The remembrance of the finest portion of my years, passed with so much tranquility and innocence, has left in my heart a thousand charming impressions which I love to call to my recollection. Far from increasing that of my situation by these sorrowful reflections, I repel them as much as possible, and in this endeavor often succeed so well as to be unable to find them at will. This facility of forgetting my misfortunes is a consolation which Heaven has reserved to me in the midst of those which fate has one day to accumulate upon my head. My memory, which presents to me no objects but such as are agreeable, is the happy counterpoise of my terrified imagination, by which I foresee nothing but a cruel futurity.

All the papers I had collected to aid my recollection, and guide me in this undertaking, are no longer in my possession, nor can I ever again hope to regain them.

I have but one faithful guide on which I can depend: this is the chain of the sentiments by which the succession of my existence has been marked, and by these the events which have been either the cause or the effect of the manner of it. I easily forget my misfortunes, but I cannot forget my faults, and still less my virtuous sentiments. The remembrance of these is too dear to me ever to suffer them to be effaced from my mind. I may omit facts, transpose events, and fall into some errors of dates; but I cannot be deceived in what I have felt, nor in that which from sentiment I have done; and to relate this is the chief end of my present work. The real object of my confessions is to communicate an exact knowledge of what I interiorly am and have been in every situation of my life. I have promised the history of my mind, and to write it faithfully I have no need of other memoirs: to enter into my own heart, as I have hitherto done, will alone be sufficient.

SOURCE: Rousseau, Jean-Jacques. *Confessions*. London: Privately printed for the Members of the Aldus Society, 1903.

CRITICAL DISCUSSION

The initial reaction to the publication of *Confessions* was much like the response of the audience at the public readings during Rousseau's life: one of stunned silence from an unprepared audience. Catherine Beaudry in *The Role of the Reader* (1991) describes this contemporary reaction: "Not having anticipated the radical departure of the work from accepted conventions, the audience, overwhelmed, was incapable of expressing its reaction to the narrative." James Wilkinson expresses his disgust for the work in his 1817 article in the *North-American Review,* stating: "Vanity has seldom shewn itself in more perverse and reprehensible shapes, than when it has been thus occupied in giving to the world a self-exposure of disgraceful actions" such as presented by Rousseau in his "useless and disgusting *Confessions.*"

Despite its initial cold reception, *Confessions* has generated an abundance of critical scholarship, influenced many aspects of philosophy, and established many trends in autobiography that would become commonplace in the years following its publication. Ann Hartle in *The Modern Self* (1983) discusses how the "inner self which is a given for contemporary consciousness, a presupposition of our thinking about ourselves" was first expressed in this text and "is precisely what is at issue in Rousseau's *Confessions.*" Hartle outlines the importance of this establishment in Rousseau's autobiography: "The possibility of being so little like oneself, of being 'one and the same human being' and a 'totally different human being,' implies the self—a fixed self—which one can be like and not be like in one's actions." These ideas presented about the self and one's interaction with that self are the founding philosophical ideas that so heavily influenced the ascetic legacy of the text and set the groundwork for future trends in autobiography.

Predominate trends in scholarship discuss the influential nature of Rousseau's autobiography in terms of his philosophical revelations and his stylistic progressions within the genre itself. Ian Bell writes in his 1995 overview of *Confessions* that the "book remains one of the most influential and provocative texts in the Enlightenment and one of the formative early documents of European Romanticism." Felicity Baker also follows this trend when she writes in her 2000 discussion of Rousseau's autobiography that *Confessions* inspired "the demand for autobiography, from readers as well as writers," noting that this demand "increased along with the power and the freedom of individuals to write it."

BIBLIOGRAPHY

Sources

Baker, Felicity. "Autobiography as Non-fiction: Rousseau's Story of the Death of Claude Anet." *Eighteenth Century: Theory and Interpretation* 41.2 (2000): 141+. *Literature Resource Center*. Web. 4 Nov. 2012.

Beaudry, Catherine A. *The Role of the Reader in Rousseau's Confessions*. The Age of Revolution and Romanticism 2. New York: Peter Lang, 1991. Print.

Bell, Ian A. "The Confessions: Overview." *Reference Guide to World Literature*. Ed. Lesley Henderson. 2nd ed.

New York: St. James, 1995. *Literature Resource Center.* Web. 4 Nov. 2012.

France, Peter. *Rousseau: Confessions.* Cambridge: Cambridge University Press, 1987. Print.

Hartle, Ann. *The Modern Self in Rousseau's* Confessions: *A Reply to St. Augustine.* Notre Dame, Ind.: University of Notre Dame Press, 1983. Print.

Rousseau, Jean-Jacques. *Confessions.* 1782, 1789. Trans. Angela Scholar. Ed. Patrick Coleman. Oxford: Oxford University Press, 2000. Print.

Wilkinson, James. "Memoirs of My Own Times." *North-American Review and Miscellaneous Journal* 6.16 (1817): 78–109. *JSTOR.* Web. 5 Nov. 2012.

Further Reading

Havens, George R. *Jean-Jacques Rousseau.* Boston: Twayne, 1978. Print.

Kuhn, Bernhard. "Chapter 2: Natural Science and the Self in Rousseau's *Confessions.*" *Autobiography and Natural Science in the Age of Romanticism: Rousseau, Goethe, Thoreau.* Abingdon, U.K.: Ashgate, 2009. 23–42. *Ebrary.* Web. 5 Nov. 2012.

Mijolla, Elizabeth de. "Rousseau: *Confessions, Dialogues, Reveries.*" *Autobiographical Quests: Augustine, Montaigne, Rousseau, and Wordsworth.* 78–114. Charlottesville: University of Virginia Press, 1994. Print.

Solzhenitsyn, Aleksandr I. *The Gulag Archipelago, 1918–1956; An Experiment in Literary Investigation.* Trans. Thomas P. Whitney. New York: Harper & Row, 1974–1978. Print.

Starobinski, Jean. *Jean-Jacques Rousseau: Transparency and Obstruction.* Trans. Arthur Goldhammer. Chicago: University of Chicago Press, 1988. Print.

Wordsworth, William. "The Prelude, or, Growth of a Poet's Mind." 1850. *The Prelude.* Oxford: Woodstock, 1993. Print.

Katherine Barker

DARKNESS VISIBLE
William Styron

✣ **Key Facts**

Time Period:
Late 20th Century

Relevant Historical Events:
Stryon wins Prix mondial Cino Del Duca (Cino Del Duca World Prize, 1985)

Nationality:
American

Keywords:
clinical depression; suicide; authorship

OVERVIEW

Published in 1990, William Styron's *Darkness Visible: A Memoir of Madness* chronicles the author's successful battle against suicidal depression. Styron's account begins in 1985 in Paris, where he has gone to accept a literary prize and finds himself overwhelmed by depressive thoughts. He ruminates on the suicidal impulses and acts of various literary, artistic, and political icons, seeking clues to why some survive suicidal ideation while others do not. He then narrates the progress of his own mental illness from its onset to its exacerbation by problems with alcohol, leading to his hospitalization and recovery. Throughout the text, Styron interrogates depression's "impenetrable mystery." Ultimately, *Darkness Visible* raises doubt about the possibility for self-knowledge, even as Styron exhaustively recounts his search for answers.

When Styron's memoir was published, he was already a prominent novelist, most famous as the author of *The Confessions of Nat Turner* (1967), which was awarded the 1968 Pulitzer Prize for Fiction, and *Sophie's Choice* (1979), recipient of the 1980 American Book Award for Fiction. Styron first prepared the text that would become *Darkness Visible* as a lecture on affective disorders for the Johns Hopkins University School of Medicine's Psychiatry Department in May 1989. When a substantially expanded version of the address appeared later that year in *Vanity Fair*, it was widely acclaimed for the honest and public way it dealt with mental illness. Expanded again for its publication in book form, it continued to garner attention and praise. Today it is considered a groundbreaking work of memoir by an important twentieth-century American writer.

HISTORICAL AND LITERARY CONTEXT

Styron wrote *Darkness Visible* in response to contemporary attitudes toward and treatments of clinical depression. It counters the common popular conception of depression as a symptom of mental weakness or frailty. To explain his motivation, Styron points specifically to a November 1988 *New York Times* article in which various scholars and writers claimed that the Italian writer Primo Levi's 1987 suicide "demonstrated a frailty, a crumbling of character they were loath to accept." Styron characterizes this response as indicative of a larger cultural tendency to denigrate the victims of what is in fact a disease as biological as cancer. At the same time, he critiques doctors' tendency to medicate rather than holistically treat the illness. He writes of the many psychiatrists who "maintain their stubborn allegiance to pharmaceuticals" and uses his own negative experience of being prescribed the tranquilizer Halcion as an example.

The seed of Styron's memoir was a brief December 1988 *New York Times* op-ed he wrote in response to Levi's suicide. The article brought him the opportunity to participate in the Johns Hopkins symposium and write the lengthy *Vanity Fair* essay. For the expansion into a full-length book, Styron added the story of his illness's exacerbation in Paris and made other minor emendations. That the text was initially delivered as a medical school lecture lent it authority, and its appearance in *Vanity Fair* helped publicize it before it appeared in its final form. Although Styron had been a critically acclaimed writer since the publication of his first novel, *Lie Down in Darkness* (1951), his memoir's commercial success helped to considerably expand his readership.

Darkness Visible draws on an array of literary influences, many of which Styron discusses in the text. Among the most vital predecessors of his attitude toward his experience of despair were several works by the French writer Albert Camus, in particular the long essay *The Myth of Sisyphus*, which introduces Camus's existentialist philosophy. Styron quotes the text's opening line, which declares, "There is but one truly serious philosophical problem, and that is suicide." Styron expresses his own contemplation of suicide in these same terms, as "the fundamental question of philosophy." From Camus, Styron also derives his memoir's insistence that even "in the absence of hope we must still struggle to survive."

The success of Styron's groundbreaking account of personal struggle led to a proliferation of memoirs of depression. In 1995 the psychiatrist Kay Redfield Jamison published *An Unquiet Mind: A Memoir of Moods and Madness*, which combined the author's medical and personal experience with manic depression. Others who have been inspired by Styron's memoir include celebrities such as the actress Brooke Shields, who published *Down Came the Rain: My Journey through Postpartum Depression* in 2005, and writers such as Christopher Lukas, whose *Blue*

Genes: A Memoir of Loss and Survival (2008) explores the effects of his family history of suicide.

THEMES AND STYLE

The central theme of Styron's memoir is that, although the origins and outcomes of clinical depression are inexplicable, improved awareness of the condition can help combat its most drastic consequences. He explores the nature of his experience with depressive disorders alongside that of others—artistic people in particular—refusing to cast judgment on the afflicted. In lieu of claiming to know causes of or cures for illness, Styron offers a more limited case for hope as an antidote to despair. He writes, for example, that "one need not sound the false or inspirational note to stress the truth that depression is not the soul's annihilation; men and women who have recovered from the disease—and they are countless—bear witness to what is probably its only saving grace: it is conquerable."

Styron was motivated to pen his account not only by the onset of his own depression in 1985 but also by the criticism directed against Levi, a survivor of Auschwitz, for committing suicide. Styron was "appalled" that the faultfinders seemed "mystified and disappointed." In *Darkness Visible* he describes the frustration that drove him to write in the *Times* that "prevention of many suicides will continue to be hindered until there is a general awareness" of the suffering that precedes them and that "to the tragic legion who are compelled to destroy themselves there should be no more reproof attached than to the victims of terminal cancer." Although Styron probes deeply into the nature of his mental illness, he ultimately subverts conventional expectations of autobiographical writing by admitting his failure to come any conclusions, even tentative, about himself or his struggle.

Stylistically, *Darkness Visible* is notable for its mix of narrative, speculative, and intellectual modes. The text opens with a scene: "In Paris on a chilly evening late in October 1985 I first became fully aware that the struggle with the disorder in my mind—a struggle which had engaged me for several months—might have a fatal outcome." After an extended novelistic recounting of his experience in Paris, Styron provides his thoughts on the writing of Camus. He continues to move between many topics, including his life story; his views on art and writing; the biographies of Camus, the poet Randall Jarrell, the activist Abbie Hoffman, and others who have suffered from depression; and the medicinal treatment of mental illness and effectiveness of hospitalization in his own avoidance of suicide. In this way he offers a wide-ranging consideration of depression that exceeds the limitations of traditional memoir writing.

CRITICAL DISCUSSION

The initial *Vanity Fair* version of *Darkness Visible* drew strong responses. During the succeeding months readers sent Styron grateful letters expressing their appreciation for his frank discussion of such a challenging and thorny topic. The book was an immediate success, selling well and eliciting extensive admiration. Its popular success—it reached the top of the *New York Times* best-seller list—was accompanied by admiration from critics. In the *New York Times Book Review*, for example, Victoria Glendinning praises the book for its "tremendous writing" and notes that it speaks "not only for depressed people but to them."

A substantial body of scholarly criticism has considered the text in psychological and social terms. Following its publication, Styron's memoir was credited with bringing newfound attention to the realities of clinical depression and mental illness in general. Thomas J. Schoeneman, Katherine A. Schoeneman, and Selona Stallings write in the *Journal of Social and Clinical Psychology* (2004) that Styron's memoir "was embraced by both those who have and have not experienced it and by both lay and professional audiences." In placing his own experience within a larger social and medical context, Styron helped catalyze an understanding of mental illness not as weakness but as a biological problem that should rightly be considered as a medical impairment.

Critics also often cite Styron's memoir for the significance of its place in the literary world. As the scholar Lee Zimmerman writes in a 2007 issue of the journal *Biography*, "Although some depression narratives precede it, Styron's best-selling book more or less marks the launching point of the depression narrative as a definable and culturally important literary

Author William Styron in 1990, when he was promoting his autobiography Darkness Visible: A Memoir of Madness. *© AP IMAGES*

WILLIAM STYRON

Born in 1925 in the Hilton Village section of Newport News, Virginia, William Styron grew up with a father who suffered from depression; in addition, his mother died of cancer when he was a boy. He left home to attend college in North Carolina, first at Davidson College and then at Duke University. His education was interrupted when he enlisted in the Marine Corps and was called to service in 1944. He did not see combat during World War II, and upon his discharge in 1945, he began his first novel. When he was recalled to serve in Korea in 1951, the twenty-six-year-old Styron rushed to complete his manuscript, which appeared as *Lie Down in Darkness* to rave reviews and solid sales, launching his career.

After being discharged, again without experiencing combat, Styron went to Europe, where he helped found the *Paris Review* and married poet Rose Burgunder. The couple settled in Roxbury, Connecticut, and Styron continued to write. His subsequent novel, *Set This House on Fire* (1960), met with a poor reception. *The Confessions of Nat Turner* (1967) and *Sophie's Choice* (1979), Styron's next two novels, were widely lauded, though many African American critics took issue with what they saw as a racist portrayal of Turner, the leader of a famous 1831 slave rebellion. Styron produced several more essays and stories, but he did not publish another novel during his lifetime. He died in 2006 at the age of eighty-one, having struggled for most of his life with the depression he documented in *Darkness Visible*.

category." Some scholars have noted the book's unique artistic antecedents and influences. George E. Butler, for instance, draws connections between Styron's work and that of the German writer Johann Wolfgang von Goethe and the German composer Johannes Brahms. According to Butler, "Styron's allusion to the [Brahms composition] Alto Rhapsody places *Darkness Visible* within a tradition of despair explored by Goethe and Brahms, a tradition in which regeneration comes from the restoration of the individual's ties to the community."

BIBLIOGRAPHY

Sources

Butler, George E. "Goethe, Brahms, and William Styron's *Darkness Visible*." *Notes on Contemporary Literature* 39.2 (2009): n. pag. *Literature Resource Center*. Web. 10 Oct. 2012.

Glendinning, Victoria. "A Howling Tempest in the Brain." Rev. of *Darkness Visible: A Memoir of Madness*, by William Styron. *New York Times Book Review* 19 Aug. 1990: n. pag. *Academic Search Premier*. Web. 10 Oct. 2012.

Schoeneman, Thomas J., Katherine A. Schoeneman, and Selona Stallings. "'The Black Struggle': Metaphors of Depression in Styron's *Darkness Visible*." *Journal of Social and Clinical Psychology* 23.3 (2004): 325–46. *Academic Search Elite*. Web. 10 Oct. 2012.

Styron, William. *Darkness Visible: A Memoir of Madness*. New York: Random, 1990. Print.

Zimmerman, Lee. "Against Depression: Final Knowledge in Styron, Mairs, and Solomon." *Biography* 30.4 (2007): 465–90. *Project MUSE*. Web. 10 Oct. 2012.

Further Reading

Casciato, Arthur D., and James L. W. West III, eds. *Critical Essays on William Styron*. Boston: Hall, 1982. Print.

Coale, Samuel. *William Styron Revisited*. Boston: Twayne, 1991. Print.

Morris, Robert K., and Irving Malin, eds. *The Achievement of William Styron*. Athens: University of Georgia Press, 1975. Print.

Saari, Jon. Rev. of *Darkness Visible: A Memoir of Madness*, by William Styron. *Antioch Review* 49.1 (1991): 146–47. *JSTOR*. Web. 10 Oct. 2012.

Stern, Tina. "Border Narratives: Three First-Person Accounts of Depression." *Studies in the Literary Imagination* 36.2 (2003): 91–107. *EBSCOhost*. Web. 10 Oct. 2012.

Styron, Alexandra. *Reading My Father*. New York: Scribner, 2011. Print.

West, James L. W., III, ed. *Conversations with William Styron*. Jackson: UP of Mississippi, 1985. Print.

———. *William Styron, A Life*. New York: Random, 1998. Print.

Theodore McDermott

Infidel

Ayaan Hirsi Ali

OVERVIEW

Ayaan Hirsi Ali published *Infidel*, a memoir about her life as a Muslim, a refugee, a politician, and an activist, in 2007. The book describes Hirsi Ali's childhood in Somalia, Saudi Arabia, and Kenya; her controversial political career in Holland; and her move to the United States to work for a Washington think tank. She discusses how Islam shaped her life and how she fled to the Netherlands in 1992 to avoid an arranged marriage to a Canadian man. Although her mother considered her the least clever of her children, Hirsi Ali earned her master's degree in political science and was elected to parliament in Holland in 2003. Using her own life to illustrate how she believes Islam subjugates and persecutes women, Hirsi Ali paints an intimate portrait of the different worlds she has inhabited.

Hirsi Ali had already begun work on her memoir when in 2004 the Dutch filmmaker Theo van Gogh, whom she had collaborated with on a film about women's relationship to Islam and God, was murdered by a Muslim fundamentalist. She describes the Dutch government's attempt to protect her from death threats from Muslims offended by her outspokenness and her public criticism of Islam, which was part of her platform as a member of parliament. *Infidel* received wide recognition and was deemed "immensely important" by Salman Rushdie, himself a controversial figure in Islam, and drew criticism from those who felt it unfairly maligned all Muslims.

HISTORICAL AND LITERARY CONTEXT

Infidel is an indictment of the aspects of Islam that Hirsi Ali sees as not just holding women back in roles of ignorance and subservience but that also prevent Islam from reaching its full potential. While some women in Somalia, including two of the author's relatives, received an education and launched successful careers, Hirsi Ali asserts that most Somali women live under the auspices of increasingly strict Islam. For example, in discussing the custom of female circumcision, the author describes how she and her sister both underwent the process in 1974, when she was five and her sister was four. Later, working as a translator in Holland, Hirsi Ali witnessed a European medical team's horror at a woman's excision scar. In one of her press statements that drew protest from Muslims, Hirsi Ali pointed out that the prophet Muhammad, held in Islam to be the perfect human being, once married a nine-year-old girl.

Hirsi Ali's introduction to *Infidel* describes the atmosphere of mutual suspicion and diplomatic equivocation that characterized relations between the West and the Muslim world after the September 11, 2001, terrorist attacks. The book tracks the author's early experiences in Somalia, Ethiopia, and Saudi Arabia, including a beating by her Qur'an instructor that broke her skull. Her father, Hirsi Magan, helped found the Somali Salvation Democratic Front, a movement opposed to Somali dictator Mohamed Siad Barre, whose regime kept Magan imprisoned— he was a Columbia University-educated teacher—for the first few years of Hirsi Ali's life. After immigrating to Europe and becoming an advocate for Muslim women, Hirsi Ali befriended van Gogh and collaborated on the short film *Submission, Part 1* (2004). The film incited a strong Muslim backlash, and van Gogh was murdered in the streets of Amsterdam. Hirsi Ali describes how the killer "stabbed a five-page letter onto Theo's chest. The letter was addressed to me."

As a treatise on how some of the problems in Islamic countries are related to how Islam is interpreted, *Infidel* is similar to other critiques of African societies, such as Frantz Fanon's book *Les Damnés de la Terre* (1961; translated as *The Wretched of the Earth* [1963]), about postcolonial Algeria. Nurrudin Farah's novel *Sweet and Sour Milk* (1979) exposed Somalia's political and religious corruption, and the hypocrisy inherent to both. Novelist and poet Assia Djebar's novel *Women of Algiers in Their Apartment* (2002) explores three Muslim women in an Algeria newly independent from France. Looking at the broader context of Islam, Uganda-born Canadian scholar Irshad Manji's 2004 book *The Trouble with Islam Today* examines Islam's engagement with women, Judaism, and slavery.

Infidel spent more than thirty weeks on the *New York Times* best-seller list and spawned the biography *Ayaan the Tornado* (2006) by Sara Berkeljon and Hans Wansink, which explores Hirsi Ali's accomplishments as a member of the Dutch parliament, including sponsoring legislation that helped women who suffered genital excision or were victimized by domestic violence. Despite this, controversy continued. In May 2006 an opposition candidate questioned Hirsi

❖ Key Facts

Time Period:
Early 21st Century

Relevant Historical Events:
September 11 terrorist attacks; murder of Theo van Gogh; threats to Hirst Ali's life by Muslim extremists

Nationality:
Dutch/Somali

Keywords:
exile; Islam; extremism

CONTEMPLATION AND CONFESSION

Ayaan Hirsi Ali in 2007. In addition to writing *Infidel*, she also cowrote the controversial film *Submission, Part 1*, which led to the assassination of its director, Theo van Gogh.
© AP IMAGES/SHIHO FUKADA

Ali's Dutch citizenship on the grounds that she had provided a false name on her refugee application. She proved her legal name and had her citizenship restored in full, but nonetheless took a job in the United States after deciding against running for a second term in parliament.

THEMES AND STYLE

The central theme of Hirsi Ali's memoir is that too many women suffer under customs and rules that fail to serve the purpose for which they were designed, namely, the creation of healthy societies. Perhaps her most jarring example of this is the case of her mother. At the outset of the narrative, Hirsi Ali's mother is a self-empowered woman who managed to extract herself from an unhappy marriage. She then worked with the resistance movement that helped her second husband, Hirsi Ali's father, escape from prison. But she turned to a strict interpretation of Islam that grew stricter after Hirsi Ali's father left. Though she had protested her daughters' circumcisions, arranged unbeknownst to her by Hirsi Ali's grandmother, she succumbs to beating Hirsi Ali and her sister and subjecting them to shame. When Hirsi Ali begins menstruating, her mother calls her a "filthy prostitute."

Hirsi Ali's intention in writing *Infidel* was to explain why she came to the conclusions she did about Islam, appropriating for her title Islam's derogatory term for non-Muslims, "infidel." She dedicates the book to her family and "also to the millions and millions of Muslim women who have had to submit." As a young student of the Qur'an, she had learned that "true, deep submission: this is the meaning of Islam." Envisioning the work that became the film *Submission, Part 1,* Hirsi Ali realized that the new strain of fundamentalist Islam was successful because "the preachers used different kinds of media: videotapes of martyrs, cassette tapes of vivid sermons, websites reinforcing the message." She believes that "it is time for people who want to reform Islam to try the same techniques…. It's time now for satire, for art, for movies and books."

Hirsi Ali's storytelling focuses on tying the events of her life to the politics that shaped both the culture she came from and the one she chose as her home. She employs a novelist's eye for detail, as when her mother's half-sister proposes a husband for her: "Khadija's manner abruptly shifted. She leaned over the table, her eyes glittering, and cooed, 'But my dear, I have just the person for you!'" Even a menial job at a Dutch factory creates an opportunity for sociological analysis: "It was mutual xenophobia: the Dutch thought the Moroccans were lazy and unpleasant, and the Moroccans said the Dutch stank and dressed like whores. Both groups saw themselves as superior."

CRITICAL DISCUSSION

Infidel was interpreted by many in the Muslim community as an outright condemnation of the religion and of Muslim society. She has been accused of misunderstanding Islam, although Hirsi Ali maintains that what she hoped to do was start a discussion. The result was not unanticipated: "People called me an Uncle Tom, white on the inside, a traitor to my people," she wrote in *Infidel*. Her perspective as an African-born European politician was unique, and the book's scope was broader than other best-selling works treating similar themes, such as 2003's *Reading Lolita in Tehran*, by Iranian academic Azar Nafisi. William Grimes, reviewing *Infidel* in the *New York Times*, called it "brave, inspiring, and beautifully written" in "clear, vigorous prose." Wolfgang Schwanitz, writing in the *Middle East Journal*, deemed it "a breathtaking account by a seeker of truth. It is a powerful exposé of the failure of Muslim immigrants to be integrated into a predominantly non-Muslim Western European society."

Hirsi Ali's subsequent memoir, *Nomad*, failed to win the popular response of *Infidel*; a *New York Times* review by Nicholas Kristof of the second book argued that her approach was "antagonizing even more people," although scholar Richard Dawkins called Kristof's review "condescending." Nevertheless, *Infidel* continued to attract attention; a foreword by noted atheist Christopher Hitchens lent the book additional notoriety. Scholarly approaches to the work have considered it in light of theology, globalization, human rights issues, and shifting political identities affected by multiculturalism.

Hirsi Ali's memoir is often read alongside Ian Buruma's *Murder in Amsterdam: The Death of Theo van Gogh and the Limits of Tolerance* (2006) as a means of exploring the problems of Islamic communities' integration into Western societies. Comparing the two books in an article for *American Prospect*, Stephen Holmes observed that "Ali focuses on postcolonial guilt, moral relativism, and the melting away of European self-confidence" in analyzing European laissez-faire attitudes toward extremism in immigrant communities, while Buruma sees "a residual arrogance about the cultural, if not racial, superiority of Europeans." Scholars have also been interested in where *Infidel* fits into the Western taste for narratives of women entrapped by Muslim societies. Writing in the *Middle East Report*, Farzaneh Milani contrasts the idea of the Muslim woman as "the victim of an immobilizing faith" with "her representation in medieval European literature, where mainly male writers depicted her as a queen or a princess, often larger than life."

WORKING TOWARD CHANGE

In 2007 Ayaan Hirsi Ali set up her eponymous, New York-based AHA Foundation to raise awareness of honor violence, forced marriage, female genital mutilation, and Sharia law; to help those women affected; and to influence U.S. legislators to enact measures to protect women. In addition to gathering statistics and case studies, the foundation addresses the belief systems that lead families to harm women and girls. AHA promotes the view that people who perpetrate violence and coercion against women and girls often act with the conviction that they are carrying out God's will and doing what is right for their community and their families. However, the organization does understand that some of these customs have been passed down from generation to generation for centuries and are valuable markers of cultural identity.

The foundation's motto is "Investigate, Inform, Influence, Intervene." Its blog features coverage of the murder of twenty-year-old Jessica Modkad by her stepfather, who may have been sexually abusing her. Another post laments the fact that, while Great Britain has a national Forced Marriage Helpline, the United States does not—although the foundation is working to change that.

BIBLIOGRAPHY

Sources

Grimes, William. "No Rest for a Feminist Fighting Radical Islam." Rev. of *Infidel*, by Ayaan Hirsi Ali. *New York Times*. New York Times, 14 Feb. 2007. Web. 9 Nov. 2012.

Hirsi Ali, Ayaan. *Infidel*. New York: Simon & Schuster, 2007. Print.

Holmes, Stephen. "The European Dilemma." Rev. of *Infidel*, by Ayaan Hirsi Ali, and *Murder in Amsterdam*, by Ian Buruma. *American Prospect* 18.4 (2007): 43–47. Print.

Kristof, Nicholas. "The Gadfly." Rev. of *Nomad*, by Ayaan Hirsi Ali. *New York Times*. New York Time, 28 May 2010. Web. 9 Nov. 2012.

Milani, Farzaneh. "On Women's Captivity in the Muslim World." *Middle East Report* 246 (2008). 40–46. JSTOR. Web. 9 Nov. 2012.

Schwanitz, Wolfgang G. Rev. of *Infidel*, by Ayaan Hirsi Ali. *Middle East Journal* 61.3 (2007): 550–52. JSTOR. Web. 9 Nov. 2012.

Spruyt, Jan. "The Dutch Tornado Warning." Rev. of *Mijn vriheid: De autobiografie (My Freedom: The Autobiography)*, by Ayaan Hirsi Ali, and *De orkaan Ayaan (Ayaan the Tornado)*, by Sara Berkeljon and Hans Wansink. *Foreign Policy* 158 (2007): 90–93. JSTOR. Web. 9 Nov. 2012.

Further Reading

Asra, Nomani. *Standing Alone: An American Woman's Struggle for the Soul of Islam*. New York: HarperCollins, 2006. Print.

Dalrymple, Theodore. "Why She Abandoned Islam." Rev. of *Nomad*, by Ayaan Hirsi Ali. *Globe and Mail*. Globe and Mail, 21 May 2010. Web. 9 Nov. 2012.

Fanon, Frantz. *The Wretched of the Earth*. Trans. Constance Farrington. New York: Grove, 1963. Print.

Farah, Nurrudin. *Sweet and Sour Milk*. St. Paul: 1992. Print.

Hirsi Ali, Ayaan. *The Caged Virgin: An Emancipation Proclamation for Women and Islam*. New York: Simon & Schuster, 2002. Print.

Husseini, Rana. *Murder in the Name of Honor*. Oxford: Oneworld, 2009. Print.

Korteweg, Anna C. "The Sharia Debate in Ontario: Gender, Islam, and Representations of Muslim Women's Agency." *Gender and Society* 22.4 (2008): 434–54. *JSTOR.* Web. 9 Nov. 2012.

Manji, Irshad. *The Trouble with Islam Today.* Toronto: Vintage Canada. 2005. Print.

Nafisi, Azar. *Reading Lolita in Tehran.* New York: Random House, 2003. Print.

Sieg, Katrin. "*Black Virgins:* Sexuality and the Democratic Body in Europe." *New German Critique* 37.1 (2010): 109. *Duke Journals.* Web. 9 Nov. 2012.

Taoua, Phyllis. "Of Prisons and Freedom: Liberation in the Work of Assia Djebar." *World Literature Today.* U of Oklahoma, Nov. 2012. Web. 8 Nov. 2012.

Rebecca Rustin

THE LIFE
Teresa of Ávila

OVERVIEW

Written from 1562 to 1565 and published in 1588, *The Life* of St. Teresa of Ávila covers the first fifty years in the life of its author, a visionary Spanish nun who became instrumental in the reformation of the Carmelite religious order in the latter half of the sixteenth century. The book documents her spiritual development from early childhood, covering her adolescent preoccupation with worldly matters, her profession of monastic vows at the age of twenty, her various subsequent spiritual struggles and physical illnesses, and her beleaguered but ultimately successful efforts to establish an ascetic monastery based on reformist principles. She devotes particular attention to the divine visions she began to experience at the age of forty, elucidating the nature of these visions and the suspicion they aroused in many of her religious superiors and advisers. The book is thus an implicit argument, in the face of such animosity, for the religious validity of her spiritual approach and serves to legitimize her authority as a female religious mystic in relation to the authority of male clerics.

Written during a period of widespread religious controversy within the Roman Catholic world (as well as the omnipresent threat of the Spanish Inquisition), Teresa's *Life* met with varied reactions in both manuscript and book form. Some readers considered it to be evidence of heresy—at one point it was denounced as such to the Inquisition—but many found it both inspiring and useful in its detailed disquisitions on mental prayer and spiritual contemplation. It is now considered a classic of Christian mysticism and spiritual autobiography, and it is one of the most revered and widely read works in the history of Spanish literature.

HISTORICAL AND LITERARY CONTEXT

Teresa's *Life* is one of the major literary works of the Counter-Reformation of the sixteenth and seventeenth centuries. This movement was partly a response to the advent of the Reformation in 1517, which resulted in the public denunciation of many abuses, corruptions, and laxities within the clergy and established a new, highly influential school of religious practice—Protestantism—that served as an alternative (though Spain remained solidly Catholic). The Counter-Reformation, as codified during the Council of Trent (1545–1563), was a concerted effort to standardize Catholic doctrine, eliminating much of the corruption highlighted by Protestants and bringing the church back in line with its previous spiritual ideals. At the same time the movement denounced Protestant theological teachings and affirmed principles concerning sin and salvation, the nature of the sacraments, and the authority of the clergy, among other topics.

During the composition of Teresa's *Life*, which she wrote under the orders of her religious superiors, she founded the first of what turned out to be numerous reformed (or "discalced," referring to the clergy's lack of shoes) Carmelite monasteries, which was organized under considerably more austere principles than was Teresa's previous, unreformed (or "calced") convent, resulting in condemnation in many quarters. Teresa and her fellow mystics, with their emphasis on ascetic contemplation and true divine communion over empty ritual, contributed significantly to the Counter-Reformation, but their teachings were frequently criticized both by complacent clergy members opposed to reform and by pious Catholics concerned about the similarities between mysticism and Protestantism. Teresa's *Life* was in part a response to this opposition, which was also rooted in a long-standing clerical distrust of female mystics that predated the Reformation itself.

Teresa's narrative emerged from the literary tradition of spiritual autobiography inaugurated late in the fourth century by St. Augustine's *Confessions,* which Teresa references within her own text, and continued by works such as the autobiography of St. Ignatius of Loyola (1491–1556), another prominent Spanish figure of the Counter-Reformation. Teresa's *Life* may also be seen as a successor to such past accounts of mystic revelation as Julian of Norwich's *Showings* as well as *The Book of Margery Kempe,* the latter of which shares with Teresa's work a focus on the extent to which its author was subject to close scrutiny and suspicion as a result of her spiritual experiences.

One of the most renowned spiritual autobiographies of all time, Teresa's narrative contributed significantly to her eventual iconic status within Spanish literary and cultural history, an eminence which is now comparable to that of Miguel de Cervantes. The work itself prefigured a number of important later Carmelite mystic writings, most importantly those of Teresa's friend, protégé, and fellow reformer St. John of the Cross (1542–1591), whose poetry and prose likewise became a canonical part of mystic Christian literature. Teresa herself continued to draw upon her own

❖ *Key Facts*

Time Period:
Mid-16th Century

Relevant Historical Events:
Counter-Reformation; emergence of Protestantism

Nationality:
Spanish

Keywords:
spirituality; Counter-Reformation; monasticism

St. Teresa of Ávila depicted in a seventeenth-century painting at the Monastery of Santa María in Cañas, Spain. © MONASTERIO DE SANTA MARIA DE SAN SALVADOR, CANAS, SPAIN/ THE BRIDGEMAN ART LIBRARY

experiences for a number of subsequent writings, which included devotional instruction texts such as *The Way of Perfection* and the vision-inspired *Interior Castle*. Her *Life* remains widely read today and continues to serve as an inspiration for works within its genre.

THEMES AND STYLE

One of the principal themes of Teresa's *Life* is the importance of detachment from worldly concern in order to achieve communion with God in a monastic setting. She expresses considerable misgivings about the relaxed rules of modern convents and particularly about the ubiquity of unenclosed monastic houses—widely regarded as spiritually delinquent—in which visitors from outside the monastic community were regularly received: "This seems to me, as I say, a great pity; for, when a convent follows standards and allows recreations which belong to the world, and the obligations of the nuns are so ill understood, the Lord has perforce to call each of them individually, and not once but many times, if they are to be saved." She goes on to observe that "I cannot think why we should be astonished at all the evils which exist in the Church, when those who ought to be models on which all may pattern their virtues are annulling the work wrought in the religious Orders by the spirit of the saints of old."

Teresa's ostensible reason for writing the work is that she was ordered to do so, a fact she mentions repeatedly throughout the text in order to highlight her adherence to the monastic principles of obedience and humility, thus ameliorating the apparent egoism of writing a book about one's own life. However, another apparent motivation was a desire to comprehensively explain the nature of her spiritual journey, the legitimacy of which was regularly attacked by her religious opponents. A large part of Teresa's *Life* is devoted to a long, detailed anatomy of prayer, which she divides into four categories and discusses in terms of a garden metaphor: "And now I come to my point, which is the application of these four methods of watering by which the garden is to be kept fertile, for if it has no water it will be ruined. It has seemed possible to me in this way to explain something about the four degrees of prayer to which the Lord, of His goodness, has occasionally brought my soul." Her accounts of holy visions are similarly subject to careful elucidation.

Teresa's rhetorical style is marked by constant self-deprecation and overt professions of deference, which serve as a means of adhering to gender expectations and diffusing any threat to male ecclesiastical authority. The text is punctuated with encomiums to God's divine benevolence—"O my God, had I but understanding and learning and new words with which to exalt Thy works as my soul knows them!"—and Teresa repeatedly stresses his mercy in allowing someone as wicked as herself to enter into communion with him. Likewise, the book's various criticisms of the clerical establishment are always couched in terms that emphasize Teresa's inferiority, as when she notes that her own wretchedness made the spiritual danger of unenclosed convents far greater for her than for other nuns—"I did not realize that what was dangerous for me would not be so dangerous for others"—though she affirms that "the practice is never quite free from danger, because it is a waste of time." Similarly, the religious figures who condemn Teresa's visions as devilish possessions are always described in terms that stress their piety and venerability, and she scrupulously avoids attacking the character of anyone who opposes her.

CRITICAL DISCUSSION

Teresa's narrative attracted a wide range of reactions upon its completion in 1565, but those who read it generally saw it in a positive light. Rowan Williams, in his 1991 monograph on Teresa's work, notes, "Early reactions were favorable: Maestro Avila wrote (late in 1568) in encouraging terms, and the *letrados* who read the revised manuscript … agreed that it should be copied, though there was no question of its being distributed to a wider audience…. Only in 1574 did the work come directly under inquisitorial suspicion." The work was officially never found to contain heresy, though Cathleen Medwick points out in her 1999 biography that "after [Dr. Bernardino de] Carleval had acquired a following as a self-styled messiah, the Inquisition condemned him as a heretic, citing [Teresa's *Life*] as one of his most pernicious influences."

In the centuries since it was written, Teresa's *Life* has become a major Roman Catholic text. Its thoroughgoing advocacy for intense, ascetic religious contemplation as well as its affirmation of divine visitation served as a testament to the legitimacy of Carmelite reform and helped to consolidate the mystic tradition within Catholicism, while its various statements about the nature of prayer and holy vision made it a guiding text for countless subsequent believers and clergy members. Indeed, the majority of writing on the book thus far has been spiritual in nature—James V. Mirollo, writing in *Texas Studies in Literature and Language* in 1987, observes that "Teresa has more often than not been the subject of exclusively religious or pious rather than literary or cultural interests"—though academic criticism of the book has increased in recent decades.

Recent scholarship on Teresa's *Life* often examines the work in relation to both the autobiographical genre and its historical milieu. A noteworthy example is Elena Carrera's study *Teresa of Avila's Autobiography: Authority, Power and the Self in Mid-Sixteenth-Century Spain* (2005), which extensively analyzes the book's historical and literary context to show how the text "is particularly illustrative of the kind of complex works of social power and cultural authority which usually regulate the construction of the self." Likewise, many scholars discuss the work in relation to gender issues; an example is Carole Slade's *St. Teresa of Ávila: Author of a Heroic Life* (1995), which argues that the text conveys "Teresa's conviction, essentially feminist but based almost entirely on religious grounds, that the standard female life script did not coincide with the Christian life."

BIBLIOGRAPHY

Sources

Carrera, Elena. *Teresa of Ávila's Autobiography: Authority, Power and the Self in Mid-Sixteenth-Century Spain.* London: Legenda, 2005. Print.

Medwick, Cathleen. *Teresa of Ávila: The Progress of a Soul.* New York: Alfred A. Knopf, 1999. Print.

Mirollo, James V. "The Lives of Saints Teresa of Ávila and Benvenuto of Florence." *Texas Studies in Literature and Language* Spring 1987: 54–73. JSTOR. Web. 19 Nov. 2012.

Slade, Carole. *St. Teresa of Ávila: Author of a Heroic Life.* Berkeley: University of California Press, 1995. Print.

Teresa of Ávila. *The Life of Teresa of Jesus: The Autobiography of Teresa of Ávila.* Trans. and ed. E. Allison Peers. 1960. New York: Image, 1991. Print.

Williams, Rowan. *Teresa of Ávila.* London: Continuum, 1991. Print.

Further Reading

Bilinkoff, Jodi. *The Ávila of Saint Teresa: Religious Reform in a Sixteenth-Century City.* Ithaca, N.Y.: Cornell University Press, 1989. Print.

Brown, Kevin Smullin. "A Proposal of Saint Teresa de Ávila's Rhetorical Strategy in the Twentieth Chapter of *Libra de la Vida.*" *Journal of Romance Studies* 9.1 (2009): 19–29. Print.

Marcén, Elena Carrera. "*Honra,* Social Authority, and Their Ideological Contradictions: Teresa of Ávila's Views (1565)." *Hispanic Research Journal* 8.4 (2007): 307–17. Print.

Rhodes, Elizabeth. "Seasons with God and the World in Teresa of Ávila's *Book.*" *Studia Mystica* 22 (2001): 24–53. Print.

Teresa of Ávila. *Interior Castle.* Trans. and ed. E. Allison Peers. New York: Doubleday, 1961. Print.

Trillia, Raquel. "The Book of Her Life: Teresa of Ávila's Rhetoric of Implication." *Studia Mystica* 24 (2003): 104–46. Print.

Weber, Alison. *Teresa of Ávila and the Rhetoric of Femininity.* Princeton, N.J.: Princeton University Press, 1990. Print.

James Overholtzer

PRIMARY SOURCE

EXCERPT FROM *THE LIFE*

What I shall now describe was, I think something which began to do me great harm. I sometimes reflect how wrong it is of parents not to contrive that their children shall always, and in every way, see things which are good. My mother, as I have said, was very good herself, but, when I came to the age of reason, I copied her goodness very little, in fact hardly at all, and evil things did me a great deal of harm. She was fond of books of chivalry; and this pastime had not the ill effects on her that is had on me, because she never allowed them to interfere with her work. But we were always trying to make time to read them; and she permitted this, perhaps in order to stop herself from thinking of the great trials she suffered, and to keep her children occupied so that in other respects they should not go astray. This annoyed my father so much that we had to be careful lest he should see us reading these books. For myself, I began to make a habit of it, and this little fault which I saw in my mother began to cool my good desires and lead me to other kinds of wrongdoing. I thought there was nothing wrong in my wasting many hours, by day and by night, in this useless occupation, even though I had to hide it from my father. So excessively was I absorbed in it that I believe, unless I had a new book, I was never happy.

I began to deck myself out and to try to attract others by my appearance, taking great trouble with my hands and hair, using perfumes and all the vanities I could get—and there were a good many of them, for I was very fastidious. There was nothing wrong with my intentions, for I should never have wanted anyone to offend God because of me. This great and excessive fastidiousness about personal appearance, together with other practices which I thought were in no way sinful, lasted for many years: I see now how wrong they must have been. I had some cousins, who were the only people allowed to enter my father's house: he was very careful about this and I wish to God that he had been careful about my cousins too. For I now see the danger of intercourse, at an age when the virtues should be beginning to grow, with persons who, though ignorant of worldly vanity, arouse a desire for the world in others. These cousins were almost exactly of my own age or a little older than I. We always went about together; they were very fond of me; and I would keep our conversation on things that amused them and listen to the stories they told about their childish escapades and crazes, which were anything but edifying. What was worse, my soul began to incline to the thing that was the cause of all its trouble.

SOURCE: Teresa of Ávila. *The Complete Works of Saint Teresa of Jesus.* New York: Sheed & Ward, 1946.

THE MAN DIED
Prison Notes of Wole Soyinka
Wole Soyinka

❖ Key Facts

Time Period:
Mid-20th Century

Relevant Historical Events:
Nigerian Civil War; postcolonial turmoil; Soyinka's incarceration

Nationality:
Nigerian

Keywords:
civil war; postcolonialism; incarceration

OVERVIEW

The Man Died: Prison Notes of Wole Soyinka (1972) is a memoir of Soyinka's twenty-seven-month incarceration during the Nigerian Civil War (1967–1970) on false charges of conspiring with the Biafran separatists. The memoir is among the most famous of Soyinka's writings in his lifelong crusade against the abuses of power, which include more than twenty dramas, several collections of poetry and essays, novels, screen and radio plays, and other works of autobiography. A combination of autobiography, history, and political analysis, *The Man Died* is a moving personal record of one man's struggle to survive physical and psychological torture and a scathing public indictment of the corrupt and brutal military government of General Yakubu Gowon.

Compiled from his prison notes after his release in October 1969, *The Man Died* was originally published in England, where Soyinka had voluntarily exiled himself to escape the continued surveillance of the Gowon regime, which had emerged victorious in the civil war. The autobiography focused international attention on what Soyinka decried as "the genocide-consolidated dictatorship of the Army," and the author did not return to Nigeria until after Gowon's fall from power in 1975. Today, the book is viewed as an important precursor to Soyinka's later writings and political activities, which reverberate with themes of protest, affirmation, and human dignity. For his unswerving commitment to justice and liberty, in 1986 Soyinka became the first African to win the Nobel Prize in Literature.

HISTORICAL AND LITERARY CONTEXT

Soyinka's political activism was in response to successive postcolonial governments in Nigeria, which he attacked for purposely crippling the transition to democracy through the systemized corruption and exploitation that secured elitist rule. When the Republic of Nigeria declared its independence from Britain in 1960, the country consisted of a federation of three regions, with the Hausa ethnic group dominating in the North, the Yoruba in the West, and the Igbo in the East. A coup and countercoup in 1966 resulted in the massacre of thousands of Igbo living in the North. In retaliation, the military governor of the East proclaimed the region's secession from the federation and named it the Republic of Biafra in May 1967. Civil war ensued between the North and the West and the breakaway republic when federal military troops marched into Biafra to prevent the secession under orders from Nigeria's president, Gowon.

Soyinka, a Yoruba from the West and a professor of drama at the University of Ibadan, was opposed to the civil war but outraged by the slaughter of the Igbo. At the outbreak of hostilities, he traveled to Biafra in hopes of brokering a cease-fire between the separatists and the federal government. Upon his return in August 1967, he was arrested outside the University of Ifé by the Nigerian police, who accused him of helping Biafra secure fighter jets. He was held as a political prisoner until October 1969, though he was never formally charged or granted a trial. Placed in solitary confinement in a federal prison in Kaduna, Nigeria, for most of his detention and often denied basic human necessities, Soyinka created his own ink and scribbled notes on scraps of toilet paper, cigarette packages, and in between the lines of the few books he was allowed. Through the efforts of some sympathetic prison guards, a handful of Soyinka's letters and poems were released to the press while he was jailed, providing evidence that he was still alive. This added to his growing political and literary celebrity that had already reached international proportions by 1965, when the PEN writers' organization orchestrated Soyinka's previous release from prison on charges that he had broken into a radio station in western Nigeria at gunpoint to prevent the airing of false election results.

The Man Died forms part of a broad spectrum of literature produced in response to the Nigerian Civil War. This work and three others that Soyinka wrote on the basis of his prison notes—the poetry collection *A Shuttle in the Crypt* (1972), the novel *Season of Anomy* (1973), and the play *Madmen and Specialists* (1970)—are frequently compared with the wartime writings of other important Nigerian authors: the Igbo sympathizers Chinua Achebe and Christopher Okigbo; Ken Saro-Wiwa, who escaped from the eastern region to the federal side; and the government spokesperson and poet John Pepper Clark. Although written from

Wole Soyinka at home in Ibadan, Nigeria, in October 1969, a week after he was released from prison. He had been jailed for two years for his political dissent. © GETTY IMAGES

different perspectives, these works all portray the Nigerian Civil War as a watershed moment in the history of African decolonization and nation building.

More broadly, *The Man Died* is considered foundational to the African prison memoir, a genre that has had a significant impact on the international discourse about human rights and the persecution of dissenters. According to Biodun Jeyifo in *Wole Soyinka: Politics, Poetics and Postcolonialism* (2004), "*The Man Died* has the distinction … of being one of the earliest and perhaps the most powerful in a long line of prison writings of writer-activists in postcolonial African literature of which another great exemplar is [Kenyan author] Ngugi wa Thiong'o's *Detained: A Writer's Prison Diary*."

THEMES AND STYLE

The main theme of *The Man Died* is the moral imperative of human liberty. Soyinka rages against political intimidation and oppression, describing his own victimization in prison as well as the corrupt brutality of the Gowon administration and a legacy of colonialism that has perpetuated ethnic strife and abuses of power in Nigeria. Examples of barbarity, both inside and outside the prison walls, pervade the text. Soyinka is confined to a tiny cell and denied adequate food, clothing, and medical attention; authorities issue false press releases stating that he has confessed to aiding the Biafrans and that he has contracted syphilis; and rumors circulate that he will be killed in prison. Restrictions on talking, reading, and writing and the savagery of the prison guards cause Soyinka to doubt his human identity, and he suffers from hallucinations and paranoia. Yet, he transcends his personal anguish to document the horrors inflicted on the other prisoners, many of them Igbo, who are flogged, chained, and ruthlessly interrogated.

The Man Died represents Soyinka's attempt to balance personal indignation and humiliation with his social obligations as a committed artist. For Soyinka, silence is not an option. He writes, "The man dies in all who keep silent in the face of tyranny," and he likens his testimony to "a kind of chain-letter hung permanently on the leaden conscience of the world." Oliver Lovesey notes in a 1995 essay in *Research in African Literatures* that "Soyinka interrupts the relentless, deterministic narrative logic of the prison diary genre—what he names the 'indestructible continuum of ordeal-survival-affirmation'—with an extended meditation on Nigerian national identity." He further explains that "Soyinka's meditation … allows him to recover from his captors' control over his narrative, to connect his history to the nation's story, and to consider the future."

The prevailing tone of *The Man Died* is one of outrage at gross injustice. According to Peter Enahoro's

1973 essay in *Critical Perspectives on Wole Soyinka*, "Soyinka lays down his political thoughts in the manner of an enraged man pounding a table with his fists." The language is frequently inflammatory; Soyinka describes the military dictatorship as the "Nazi Gestapo" and compares Gowon to the Roman emperor Nero, "at the reactionary centre of the Nigerian leisurely classes fiddling away while the nation was burning." Portions of the memoir, however, depart from reportage and are more poetic; critics have described these sections as moving beyond the conventional limits of autobiography toward fictive narrative, as when Soyinka's tortured imagination produces a vision of the jail as a mythic underworld, where he exists as an Orpheus figure in conflict with two animalistic captors fashioned after Homer's cannibal Polyphemus and William Shakespeare's Caliban. Critics have also remarked on the spiritual intensity of stream-of-consciousness passages written when Soyinka was suffering from hallucinations and paranoia.

CRITICAL DISCUSSION

Outside Nigeria, *The Man Died* was widely hailed as a remarkable statement of self-worth and as an exposé of the atrocities against humanity committed by the military administration during the Nigeria Civil War. Authorities in Nigeria regarded the text as subversive; its sale was banned under the government of Muhammadu Buhari in the mid-1980s. In notices of *The Man Died* otherwise complimentary, charges of egocentrism were leveled against Soyinka. C. Tighe's 1976 review is typical: "I am not convinced that either *The Man Died* or *A Shuttle in the Crypt* were conceived purely as works of literature, or that they are solely memoirs of what contortions the human mind can be put to by inhuman oppressors. There is a strong element of self-advertisement, almost 'monument erecting', for the powers of his survival."

Since its first appearance, *The Man Died* has been reassessed in view of the whole of Soyinka's career. Scholars have observed that the author's criticism of the postcolonial leadership in Nigeria intensified after his term in prison. In *Dictionary of Literary Biography Yearbook 1986*, Thomas Hayes quotes Soyinka on his abiding concerns after the civil war: "My writing grows more and more preoccupied with the theme of the oppressive boot, the irrelevance of the color of the foot that wears it and the struggle for individuality." Scholars have also argued that *The Man Died* is the first of many works in which Soyinka articulated a metaphysical vision of social revolution based on the creative and destructive aspects of the Yoruba god Ogun.

The Man Died is frequently studied within the context of the African prison memoir. From this perspective, Soyinka's alleged egocentrism has been interpreted more sympathetically. Jeyifo argues that Soyinka's narrative voice "is probably without comparison in modern African literature in its completely unselfconscious and unembarrassed narration of the indissoluble identity of the author/narrator with the cause of Truth, Justice, and Humanity…. This is what gives Soyinka's assertion of the exceptionalism of his moral vision and political testament in this book, in spite of the unquestionably self-absorbed and self-inflated terms in which it is often expressed, convincing social validity." Lovesey considers *The Man Died* an important example of the manner in which the African prison diary has both reflected and shaped the process of postcolonial nation building: "The African prison diary brushes against the grain of official histories of the prisoner's activities; it rewrites official 'master narratives' of national history. In this sense Soyinka's meditation on his imprisonment and its writing, and his self-conscious reflection about the fate of the nation become an historical metanarrative. The progress of his personal humiliation recalls that of the 'humiliated nation' … under colonialism."

BIBLIOGRAPHY

Sources

Enahoro, Peter. Rev. of *The Man Died*, by Wole Soyinka. *Critical Perspectives on Wole Soyinka*. Ed. James Gibbs. Washington, D.C.: Three Continents, 1980. 239–40. Print.

Hayes, Thomas. "The 1986 Nobel Prize in Literature: Wole Soyinka." *Dictionary of Literary Biography Yearbook 1986*. Ed. J. M. Brook. Detroit: Gale, 1987. 3–18. *Dictionary of Literary Biography Complete Online*. Web. 4 Nov. 2012.

Jeyifo, Biodun. *Wole Soyinka: Politics, Poetics and Postcolonialism*. Cambridge: Cambridge University Press, 2004. Print.

Lovesey, Oliver. "Chained Letters: African Prison Diaries and 'National Allegory.'" *Research in African Literatures* 26.1 (1995): 31–45. *JSTOR*. Web. 7 Nov. 2012.

Soyinka, Wole. *The Man Died: Prison Notes of Wole Soyinka*. New York: Harper & Row, 1972. Print.

Tighe, C. "In Detentio Preventione in Aeternum: Soyinka's *A Shuttle in the Crypt*." *Critical Perspectives on Wole Soyinka*. Ed. James Gibbs. Washington, D.C.: Three Continents, 1980. 186–97. Print.

Further Reading

Amuta, Chidi. "The Ideological Content of Soyinka's War Writings." *African Studies Review* 29.3 (1986): 43–54. *JSTOR*. Web. 6 Nov. 2012.

Garuba, Harry. "'Predicting the Past': Soyinka's *The Man Died* and the Fiction of Memory." *An Introduction to the African Prose Narrative*. Ed. Lokangaka Losambe. Trenton, N.J.: Africa World, 2004. 199–208. Print.

Jaggi, Maya. "Lamenting Nigeria's Peculiar Mess." *World Policy Journal* 11.4 (1994–1995): 55–9. *JSTOR*. Web. 6 Nov. 2012.

Larson, Doran. "Toward a Prison Poetics." *College Literature* 37.3 (2010): 143–66. *Project MUSE*. Web. 29 Oct. 2012.

Ngugi wa Thiong'o. *Detained: A Writer's Prison Diary*. Oxford: Heinemann, 1981. Print.

Ogwude, Sophie Obiajulu. "Politics & Human Rights in Non-fiction Prison Literature." *War in African Literature Today.* Ed. Ernest N. Emenyonu. Ibadan: HEBN, 2008. Print.

Soyinka, Wole. *Madmen and Specialists.* London: Methuen, 1972. Print.

———. *Seasons of Anomy,* London: Rex Collings, 1973. Print.

———. *A Shuttle in the Crypt.* London: Rex Collings/ Methuen, 1972. Print.

Whitehead, Anne. "Journeying through Hell: Wole Soyinka, Trauma, and Postcolonial Nigeria." *Studies in the Novel* 40.1–2 (2008): 13–30. *Project MUSE.* Web. 29 Oct. 2012.

Janet Mullane

The Meditations of the Emperor Marcus Aurelius Antoninus

Marcus Aurelius

❖ **Key Facts**

Time Period:
Late 2nd Century

Relevant Historical Events:
Growth of Stoicism; growing prosperity of Rome

Nationality:
Roman

Keywords:
Stoicism; philosophy; Rome

OVERVIEW

First published around 180 CE, *The Meditations of the Emperor Marcus Aurelius Antoninus* is a contemplative work that the famous Roman emperor and Stoic philosopher wrote in twelve short books for his own moral enlightenment. *Meditations* is a collection of υπομνηματα (*commentarii* in Latin)—that is, personal notes that aid memory. The plain style of *Meditations* has both a sincerity and naturalness that is reminiscent of a diary, and Marcus frequently cites writers whom he admired. Although Latin was his native language, Marcus wrote *Meditations* in Greek because the technical language of Stoic theory did not have Latin equivalents. Stoic ideals aided the introspective Marcus Aurelius in his role as Roman emperor by providing moral guidance.

Marcus Aurelius—renowned philosopher and patron of learning—ruled as Roman emperor from 161 to 180 CE, and the initial reception of his *Meditations,* like that of many ancient writings, is mere guesswork. Marcus's contemporaries who documented his reign never mention *Meditations.* A study of the text suggests that *Meditations* was written over a period of years and then published around the time of Marcus's death in 180 CE, but the first mention of his work as a book is by the orator Themistius in 364 CE. Although the initial response to the publication appears quite modest, Marcus Aurelius's *Meditations* has had a tremendous impact on Western literary tradition, has served as primary source material for historians, and has been used as a treatise on Stoicism for nearly two millennia.

HISTORICAL AND LITERARY CONTEXT

At the time of Marcus's rule, religion and philosophy had been in a state of transition since the Hellenistic period. With the conquests of Alexander the Great, the city-state gave way to large impersonal kingdoms. This was a time of great change, especially for the elite of Greece, who now found themselves under outside rule. Many began to explore new religions that promised an afterlife, such as Christianity or the cult of Isis. Astrology, omens, thaumaturgy, and deification of individuals also became popular despite having been rejected for centuries. The most important Greek philosophic sect that arose during the Hellenistic era and continued with vigor under the Roman Empire was that of the Stoics. The basic tenet of Stoicism is the mastery of emotion by understanding what is and what is not within one's control. Stoics welcomed adversity as a test from God. Such tests were seen as a sign of divine favor. In *Meditations,* Marcus Aurelius denies his divine Status and strictly follows the moral code of stoicism.

The introspective Marcus Aurelius ruled the Roman Empire while it was arguably at its apex, and he wrote his *Meditations,* in part, during his military campaigning against the German tribes. The Roman Empire had "a widespread goodwill," M. Cary writes in *History of Rome,* continuing, "This salient feature of the period will be found on almost every page of M. Aurelius's *Meditations* … at a time when Rome was most powerful, its sense of *pietas* was also strongest." The second century CE was not a period of hedonism, but a time to reflect inward in order to minimize suffering and to better understand one's place in the larger world, as Marcus Aurelius's Stoic aphorisms disclose.

Many Roman emperors and generals wrote aide-mémoire (*commentarii*): Sulla's *Commentarii de Vita Sua,* Julius Caesar's *Commentarii de Bello Gallico,* and Augustus's *Res Gestae* are just a few. The titles of Book II ("Written among the Quadi on the River Gran") and Book III ("Written in Carnuntum") in *Meditations* suggest that Marcus Aurelius, like the others, wrote his meditations while on a military campaign. However, in contrast to the others, Marcus does not use rhetorical self-promotion. Instead, he castigates himself while discussing his private life. Literary and philosophical traditions that influenced the well-read emperor include diatribe, exhortation, Stoic philosophy, and the atomist theory of the Epicureans. He condemns poetry, rhetoric, and clever writing.

Marcus Aurelius's *Meditations* has had an enormous literary influence on Western culture. Among the works it has inspired are Frederick the Great's poem "Le Stoicien," Blaise Pascal's *Pensées,* and Antonio Guevara's *Golden Book of the Emperor Marcus Aurelius.* Captain John Smith and Cecil Rhodes are known to have carried a copy of *Meditations* throughout their life's adventures. Samuel Butler wrote with

THE MEDITATIONS OF THE EMPEROR MARCUS AURELIUS ANTONINUS

Marcus Aurelius Distributing Alms, painted by Joseph Marie Vien in 1765. © RMN-GRAND PALAIS/ART RESOURCE, NY

humor that Marcus Aurelius is more alive than most living people. In the contemporary world, Bill Clinton perused *Meditations* throughout his eight years of presidency, and the philosopher-warrior has been positively depicted in blockbuster movies such as *Gladiator*. Those who cannot find consolation in organized religion are sometimes attracted to Marcus Aurelius's practical spiritual guidance.

THEMES AND STYLE

The central theme of *Meditations* is that of the author exhorting himself toward moral enlightenment, just as the Greek title *ta eis eauton* ("Notes to Himself") suggests. The self-address makes the text autobiographical in nature, particularly Book I, in which Marcus acknowledges the influential people throughout his life. He writes, "From my grandfather Verus: the lessons of noble character and even temper." Although Marcus claims to "fall far short of philosophy," *Meditations* nonetheless resembles a Stoic treatise. For example, he expounds "Reflect like this: 'you are an old man, suffer this governing part of you no longer to be in bondage, no longer to be a puppet pulled by selfish impulse, no longer to be indignant with what is

CONTEMPLATION AND CONFESSION

MARCUS AURELIUS AND MARCUS CORNELIUS FRONTO

In 1815 Cardinal Angelo Mai discovered a *palimpsest codex* (a volume of manuscripts written over partly erased older manuscripts that are still sometimes legible) in the Ambrosian Library in Milan. It contained letters from the famous orator Marcus Cornelius Fronto and his many correspondents, one of whom was Marcus Aurelius. The letters between Marcus and Fronto, written between 139 CE and 148 CE, provide a fascinating biographical sketch of a young Marcus Aurelius. Unlike some ancient letters, they were not intended for publication. The letters pertain to everyday life, and Marcus's writing is exuberant and full of love for Fronto. The scholar Amy Richlin has attempted to discover if these are homoerotic love letters. She provides evidence for and against this idea. In Book I of his *Meditations,* Marcus Aurelius lists Fronto as someone to whom he is indebted: "From Fronto: to observe how vile a thing is the malice and caprice and hypocrisy of absolutism; and generally speaking that those whom we entitle 'Patricians' are somehow rather wanting in the natural affections." However, the last lines of "Letter 40" to Fronto show an entirely different style and outlook: "Good-bye my—what should I say? Whatever I say, it isn't enough—good-bye, my desire, <my light>, my pleasure." Richlin does not provide definite answers, but rather hopes to "open up a conversation."

allotted in the present or to suspect what is allotted in the future.'" As he sheds light on philosophy, philosophy sheds light on his life.

Marcus Aurelius wrote *Meditations* for himself alone. It resembles a private journal in which he expresses his innermost thoughts and cites the authors who inspired him, including Cato, Seneca, and Epictetus. Although Rome was at its peak, Marcus still dealt with the troubles of conspiracy, plague, and barbarian invasions. In response to the turbulence around him, his *Meditations* served to comfort him and enable him to rule justly. He writes, "Do things from outside break in to distract you? Give yourself time of quiet to learn some new good thing and cease to wander out of your course." Unlike the self-justifying and self-laudatory autobiographies of Julius Caesar and Emperor Augustus, which chronicle how they shaped the world, Marcus writes a more modern autobiography by showing how he is affected by the world. He does not intentionally write an autobiography, but rather composes a journal in order to take positive action. He writes, "Don't any more discuss at large what the good man is like, but be good."

Stylistically, *Meditations* is notable for its philosophical tone and unadorned style. For example, Marcus Aurelius writes, "How ridiculous and like a stranger to the world is he who is surprised at any one of the events of life." The tone is often exhortative, with Marcus beginning his thoughts with the phrase "always remember" more than forty times. Because it is a private journal, there is no obvious overall structure to the twelve books. Subjects abruptly change, stray thoughts interrupt, and repetitions abound without apparent reason. Marcus does not define terminology, nor does he explicate the historical moment. For example, he writes vaguely, "A spider is proud when he traps a fly, a man when he snares a leveret, another when he nets a sprat, another boars, another bears, another Sarmatian prisoners. If you test their sentiments, are they not bandits?" Historical sources document that Marcus defeated the Sarmatians around 175 CE, and so the reader realizes the significance of the nebulous thought: Marcus does not take pride in this type of achievement.

CRITICAL DISCUSSION

The initial reaction to Marcus Aurelius's *Meditations* is unknown. The first publication around the time of his death was most likely a small one. Although both Cassius Dio's *Historia Romana* (c. 200 CE) and the biographical text *Historia Augusta* (c. 300 CE) detail Marcus's life and reign, the first known mention of *Meditations* as a book was made by the orator Themistius in 364 CE. Emperor Julian—a contemporary of Themistius—may have known about the book's existence, and Arethas of Caesarea was known to have a copy at the end of the ninth century. The title *Meditations* was not attached to the text until the seventeenth century, by the English editors Méric Casaubon and Thomas Gataker.

Marcus Aurelius's *Meditations* has been admired for nearly two millennia. Because the tenets of Stoicism influenced early Christian thought and Marcus wrote with such ethical sincerity, William Faunce explains that "the medieval monks placed *Meditations* beside the New Testament and thought of Aurelius as possessing a mind naturally Christian." The first printed edition in the West was in 1559 by Zurich humanist Andreas Gesner, and the Italian cardinal Francesco Barberini spent many years translating and memorizing the text throughout the seventeenth century. By the seventeenth century the text was widely known, and it reached its height of popularity in the late nineteenth century. In the twentieth century, the text lost some of its popular appeal. R. B. Rutherford writes, "Marcus' book, once an accepted spiritual classic, is not much read nowadays, and literary criticism of his work is almost non-existent."

Although there is a lack of up-to-date translations, commentaries, and literary criticism of *Meditations,* there has been notable interest in the life of Marcus Aurelius. Anthony Birley and Frank McLynn have written two of the finest biographies. There has also been scholarly debate over Marcus's policy regarding early Christians. Christians are briefly mentioned in *Meditations* Book XI.3, and it has been argued that Marcus authorized two episodes of persecution. Most controversial is Thomas W. Africa's monograph "The Opium Addiction of Marcus Aurelius," in which the author attempts to prove Marcus's addiction to opium by scrutinizing *Meditations*. Scholar Pierre Hadot, however, refutes this idea in his *Philosophy as a Way of Life,* concluding that Africa's interpretation is "pure nonsense."

BIBLIOGRAPHY

Sources

Africa, Thomas W. "The Opium Addiction of Marcus Aurelius." *Journal of the History of Ideas* 22 (1961): 97–102. Print.

Carey, M. *History of Rome.* New York: St. Martin's, 1965. Print.

Faunce, William H. "Marcus Aurelius." *Autobiography in the Ancient World (B.C. 3800–A.D. 430).* Ed. Nicholas van Rijn. Honolulu: UP of the Pacific, 2002: xxv–xxviii. Print.

Hadot, Pierre. *Philosophy as a Way of Life.* Malden, Mass.: Blackwell, 1995. Print.

Marcus Aurelius. *The Meditations of the Emperor Marcus Aurelius Antoninus.* 2 vols. Ed. and trans. A. S. L. Farquharson. Oxford: Clarendon, 1944. Print.

Marcus Aurelius and Marcus Cornelius Fronto. *Marcus Aurelius in Love.* Ed. and trans. by Amy Richlin. Chicago: University of Chicago Press, 2006. Print.

Rutherford, R. B. *The Meditations of Marcus Aurelius: A Study.* Oxford: Clarendon, 1989. Print.

Further Reading

Birley, Anthony. *Marcus Aurelius: A Biography.* Rev. ed. New Haven: Yale University Press, 1987. Print.

Epictetus. *Enchiridion.* Trans. George Long. New York: Prometheus, 1991. Print.

Green, Peter. *Alexander to Actium: The Historical Evolution of the Hellenistic Age.* Berkeley: University of California Press, 1993. Print.

Hadot, Pierre. *The Inner Citadel.* Trans. Michael Chase. Cambridge: Harvard University Press, 1998. Print.

Hägg, Tomas. *The Art of Biography in Antiquity.* Cambridge: Cambridge University Press, 2012. Print.

McGing, Brian, and Judith Mossman, eds. *The Limits of Ancient Biography.* Swansea, Wales: Classical, 2006. Print.

McLynn, Frank. *Marcus Aurelius: Warrior, Philosopher, Emperor.* London: Bodley Head, 2009. Print.

Gregory Bach

Memoirs

Pablo Neruda

❖ Key Facts

Time Period:
Mid-20th Century

Relevant Historical Events:
Election of Salvador Allende; murder of Allende; Neruda's work as a consul

Nationality:
Chilean

Keywords:
communism; poetry; aesthetics

OVERVIEW

First published in 1974, *Confieso que he vivido: Memorias,* which was translated into English in 1977 and published as *Memoirs,* is a nonlinear, impressionistic record of Pablo Neruda's career as a poet and political activist. Neruda recalls his childhood in Temuco, Chile; his early development as a poet in Santiago; his time abroad as a Chilean consul; his lengthy relationship with the Communist Party; and his considerable achievements in the field of poetry, which include the Nobel Prize in Literature in 1971. Throughout *Memoirs,* Neruda insists that poetry should not be disconnected from the struggles of the people. Published shortly after Neruda's death, *Memoirs* expounds on the power of poetry in daily life and the importance of the poet in society; he writes that he is most proud of the social applications of his poetry and that he has "made people respect the occupation of poet [and] the profession of poetry."

Prior to publishing *Memoirs,* Neruda was involved in supporting the beleaguered, democratically elected Marxist Salvador Allende. The last section of his memoirs addresses this situation, condemning the military coup of 1973 and Allende's death, as well as U.S. intervention in Chilean politics. Neruda died in 1973, before the book was published, but much of the text had been composed in earlier decades and was edited after Neruda's death. Although initially received with some criticism due to its previously published content and sometimes hazy details, today the book stands as a record of his most famous achievements. *Memoirs* further cemented Neruda's reputation as one of the twentieth century's foremost poets.

HISTORICAL AND LITERARY CONTEXT

Memoirs offers a lengthy discussion of communism in Latin America and also traces Neruda's development as a poet and his relationships with artists such as Rafael Alberti and Ai Ch'ing in Europe and Asia during his time abroad. Neruda became more politically involved after experiencing the Spanish Civil War in 1936, in which his friend, the writer Federico García Lorca, was assassinated. Neruda returned to Chile, and in 1945 he was elected senator. He was later removed from office when communism was banned and fled to Buenos Aires. As a politician, he was sympathetic to the working class, miners, and underrepresented populations, a sentiment that often appeared in his poetry. By 1952 he had returned to Chile from Argentina, where he continued to advocate for the rights of the proletariat class. Neruda was nominated for the Chilean presidency in 1970 but withdrew his candidacy to support Allende.

Memoirs was prepared for publication by Neruda's third wife, Matilde Urrutia, and his friend Miguel Otero Silva, a Venezuelan writer and politician, following Neruda's death. The book is composed of previously published essays that appeared in the Brazilian magazine *O Cruzeiro Internacional* in 1962, segments of autobiographical poetry, and unpublished writing. In the preface, Neruda acknowledges the gaps in his recollections, which provides an explanation for the book's fragmented nature. The work's last section ends with Neruda accusing Augusto Pinochet, Chilean general and dictator, of betrayal by heading the military coup that overthrew Allende. Shortly after Neruda's death his houses in Santiago and Valparaíso were invaded and ransacked; the *Memoirs* manuscript went missing at this time but was later recovered.

Memoirs is part of a tradition in Chilean literature of authors tracing personal, social, and political memory through autobiography. Vicente Pérez Rosales's *Recuerdos del pasado* (1910) is a predecessor to Neruda's *Memoirs* in its explorations of Chilean natural history and social and cultural life. Gabriela Mistral, the first Chilean and first Latin American woman to receive the Nobel Prize in Literature wrote numerous works about her life in her native country in the generation before Neruda came to prominence. In *Memoirs,* Neruda praises his fellow writers, particularly those whose works speak to national origin and the conditions of life among the people, including Mistral. Of fellow communist and poet Paul Éluard, Neruda writes, "Poet of the highest kind of love, fire pure as noon, in France's most disastrous days he planted his heart in the center of his country and out of it came fire that was decisive in battle." Echoes of Neruda's *Memoirs* persist in modern Chilean autobiographies, including Isabel Allende's *Paula* (1995).

Memoirs helped advance the Latin American autobiographical tradition. Octavio Paz's *In Light of India* (1997) describes the Mexican poet's time as an ambassador in India, paralleling Neruda's recollections of his time as a consul in Ceylon and Burma. Other autobiographical writings of Latin American writers and activists have been published posthumously, including Adolfo Bioy Casares's *Rest for Travelers* (2001) and Che Guevara's *The Motorcycle Diaries* (1993).

THEMES AND STYLE

Throughout *Memoirs,* Neruda contemplates his political and social morality and his role as a poet in advancing that morality. While he does not delve into extended personal confessions, he is thoughtful about his role as a Chilean poet on the world stage. He declares his guiding principle: "I want to live in a world where no one is excommunicated…. I want to live in a world where beings are only human, with no other title than that." As a poet, he states that "the human crowd has been the lesson of my life. I can come to it with the born timidity of the poet, with the fear of the timid, but once I am in its midst, I feel transfigured. I am part of the essential majority. I am one more leaf on the great human tree." He returns, time and again, to the importance of being a poet of the people.

Neruda's motivations for writing his memoirs were both personal and political. He pens impassioned recollections of fellow writers, including Mistral and Pierre Reverdy, and scenes from his youth and political involvements, but he does not reveal a great deal about his personal life. In his preface he acknowledges the fallibility of his memory, writing that "many of the things I remember have blurred as I recalled them, they have crumbled to dust, like irreparably shattered glass." He goes on to describe his aim as poet of the people: "Perhaps I didn't live just in my self, perhaps I lived the lives of others." Neruda's avoidance of detailed confessions may be best explained via an anecdote from his memoir. He describes his reluctance to publish a book of poetry inspired by his new love Urrutia, for fear that it would upset his current wife, Delia del Carril, whom he was leaving. Instead of dwelling on personal revelations, Neruda focuses on recalling his wealth of experiences in the fields of literature and politics.

Memoirs is notable for its fragmented, nonlinear progression and poetic, sensual style. Portions of the memoir are taken from previously published essays, his book of poetry *Canto general* (1950), and *Memorial de isla negra* (1964). He injects italicized, stream of consciousness portions into the narrative. For example, Neruda describes his childhood love of nature: "The wild scent of the laurel, the dark scent of the boldo herb, enter my nostrils and flood my whole being…. The cypress of the Guaitecas blocks my way…. This is a vertical world." In characteristically imagistic prose, Neruda writes about a particular phrase of music, describing it as "build[ing] up in anguish like a Gothic structure … swayed by the rhythm that lifts a slender spire endlessly upward."

CRITICAL DISCUSSION

Memoirs was read widely and with interest as Neruda's first posthumous publication. Although acknowledged as an important contribution to his oeuvre, it drew some criticism because of its inclusion of previously published material. José Yglesias responded to the narrative's fractured nature in his *New York Times* review from 1977, stating that "Neruda must have written these marvelous, exasperating memoirs fitfully during the last decade of his life…. Neither his publishers nor his editors say so, but it would be one explanation for their discontinuity and unevenness."

The book survived some initial criticism to become an important volume in the body of work of one of the twentieth century's most renowned poets. Neruda's reputation as a poet dedicated to the support of the proletariat class in Chile was aided by *Memoirs*. Scholars have approached the work through a number of critical avenues, noting its value as a record of the political progression of one of literature's most famous communists, as well as a fascinating contemplation on life and literature by a world-famous poet.

Scholars often point to portions of Neruda's text to illuminate his success as a poet of the people. Kelly Austin's 2008 article in the *Comparatist* examines the section of his memoir titled "Yo, el Malacólogo" ("I, the Malacologist"), in which Neruda discusses his extensive shell collection in order to explore the tension between his material success and socialist ideology, noting that "by repeatedly placing at the forefront his role as collector (as donor), Neruda also transforms himself into a visitor to his own collection. He negotiates between the stances of having and not having…. In this way, he helps to illuminate the paradox inherent in his poetic practice and political critique." Scholars have also been interested in those sections of the memoir in which Neruda discusses the natural world. In his book *New World Poetics* (2007),

Chilean president Salvador Allende in 1973. The final section of Pablo Neruda's *Memoirs* was written after the coup that removed Allende, a friend of Neruda, from power. © BETTMANN/CORBIS

NERUDA IN THE FAR EAST

Between 1927 and 1932, Pablo Neruda lived in Burma, Ceylon, and Singapore, where he acted as Chilean consul, a title that bore little official responsibility. He speaks of his time in the Far East in the section of his *Memoirs* titled "Luminous Solitude," stating "Distance and a deep silence separated me from my world, and I could not bring myself to enter wholeheartedly the alien world around me." While he is thought to have written much of his famous book of poetry, *Residencia en la tierra,* in the Far East, gathering inspiration from his new surroundings, Neruda himself asserts that "I don't believe, then, that my poetry during this period reflected anything but the loneliness of an outsider transplanted to a violent, alien world."

While writing about his time in India and Asia, Neruda describes a variety of transformative experiences, including a parade of holy pilgrims, an elephant hunt, an obsessed lover, a pet mongoose, a temple filled with snakes, and a run-in with robbers. It was while traveling to Burma that he first met Jorge Luis Borges and César Vallejo, two important peers and rivals in Latin American letters; however, despite these literary encounters, his creative output dwindled as he moved on to Singapore. Finally, driven to distraction by his loneliness, he compulsively married a Dutch-Indonesian woman he called Maruca, to whom he never addressed a single love poem. He returned to Chile in 1932.

George B. Handley speaks of Neruda's meditation on nature as "one of the most important contributions of the century for its range of insights and remarkably prolific and sustained attention."

BIBLIOGRAPHY

Sources

Austin, Kelly. "'I Have Put All I Possess at the Disposal of the People's Struggle': Pablo Neruda as Collector, Translator, and Poet." *Comparatist* 32 (2008): 40–62. *Project MUSE.* Web. 18 Oct. 2012.

Handley, George B. *New World Poetics: Nature and the Adamic Imagination of Whitman, Neruda, and Walcott.* Georgia: University of Georgia Press, 2007. *ebrary.* Web. 18 Oct. 2012.

Neruda, Pablo. *Memoirs.* Trans. Hardie St. Martin. New York: Farrar, Straus & Giroux, 1977. Print.

Yglesias, José. "Braveries, Vanities, Passions." Rev. of *Memoirs,* by Pablo Neruda. *New York Times* 13 Mar. 1977: 3. *ProQuest Historical Newspapers.* Web. 18 Oct. 2012.

Further Reading

Dawes, Greg. *Verses against the Darkness: Pablo Neruda's Poetry and Politics.* Lewisburg, Pa.: Bucknell University Press, 2006. Print.

Feinstein, Adam. *Pablo Neruda: A Passion for Life.* New York: Bloomsbury, 2004. Print.

Lastarrias, José Victorino. *Literary Memoirs.* Ed. Frederick M. Nunn. Trans. R. Kelly Washbourne. Oxford: Oxford University Press, 2000. Print.

Stavans, Ilan, ed. *The Poetry of Pablo Neruda.* Trans. Miguel Algarín. New York: Farrar, Straus & Giroux, 2003. Print.

Urrutia, Matilde. *My Life with Pablo Neruda.* Trans. Alexandria Giardino. Stanford: California General Books, 2004. Print.

Kristen Gleason

A Mountainous Journey
A Poet's Autobiography
Fadwa Tuqan

Key Facts

Time Period:
Late 20th Century

Relevant Historical Events:
Establishment of Israel; Israeli-Palestinian conflict

Nationality:
Palestinian

Keywords:
politics; nationalism; Palestine; poetry

OVERVIEW

First published serially in 1978 and 1979, and then as a full-length book in 1985, *A Mountainous Journey: An Autobiography* by Fadwa Tuqan is one of the first personal accounts to be written by a Palestinian woman. Interweaving personal narrative with political history, the autobiography, published in Arabic as *A Mountainous Journey, a Difficult Journey,* follows the life of "Palestine's Outstanding Woman Poet" from her birth in 1917 to a prominent family in Nablus (in what is now the West Bank) to the outbreak of the 1967 Arab-Israeli War. The autobiography provides a critique of the patriarchal oppression that shaped Tuqan's life, as well as her poetic output, and reveals the inner conflict she experienced pre-1967 between her desire to portray her personal struggles as a woman in her poetry and external pressure to concentrate on the Palestinian national movement.

By the time *A Mountainous Journey* was published, Tuqan had achieved personal liberation, studying in England and moving into her own home, and her focus had shifted to the nationalist cause. Her involvement in the struggle was confirmed by the addition of an introduction by Palestinian "resistance poet" Samih al-Qasim to the full-length Arabic publication of *A Mountainous Journey*. When the text was translated into English in 1990, it was reframed as a feminist text, replacing al-Qasim's introduction with materials focusing on Tuqan's identity as a woman. Well received by scholars, the text has been praised for the unique perspective it provides, although some critics have noted its limited treatment of class and other sources of oppression as well as its shortcomings as a literary text. Tuqan died in 2003, but her autobiography remains an important social, historical, literary, and political document.

HISTORICAL AND LITERARY CONTEXT

A Mountainous Journey traces the history of Palestine from Tuqan's birth in 1917—the year the Balfour Declaration was issued conveying British support for the establishment of a Jewish national home in Palestine—until the Israeli occupation of the West Bank, including Tuqan's hometown of Nablus, in the 1967 Arab-Israeli War. Nablus is known as "Jabal al-Nar" (The Mountain of Fire) for its "tradition of struggle and dissent," and Tuqan's Arab nationalist father was imprisoned several times by the authorities that governed Palestine during the 1922–1948 British Mandate. In 1948 the State of Israel was established, and East Jerusalem and the West Bank, including Nablus, were annexed by Jordan. Although the women of Nablus had been involved in the political struggle since the start of the British Mandate, the period of unrest that began in 1948 ushered in a number of major social changes, such as the removal of the veil, that allowed bourgeois women to participate more actively in public life.

Following the 1967 Israeli occupation of the West Bank, Tuqan's poetry and writings increasingly reflected a sustained commitment to the Palestinian cause. A period of intense persecution and oppression of the Palestinians residing in the occupied territories began in 1977 with the election of Menachem Begin as prime minister of Israel and the ascendency of the Likud, a conservative political party, within the national government. Tuqan's autobiography was first serialized in 1978 and 1979, during the early years of Begin's settlement policy, which aimed to facilitate the annexation of the West Bank and the Gaza Strip and divide the Palestinian population through the settlement of a significant and strategically located Jewish population in the occupied territories. In 1987, two years after *A Mountainous Journey* was published as a book, the tension in the occupied territories led to the first Palestinian intifada, or uprising.

Although *A Mountainous Journey* is part of a long tradition of autobiography in Arabic literature that first began to flourish in the Middle Ages, the text can more narrowly be located within a sizable corpus of Palestinian "personal account literature" focused on the twentieth century that encompasses autobiographies, diaries, memoirs, and autobiographical fiction. In her foreword to the English translation of Tuqan's autobiography, Salma Khadra Jayyusi credits the post-1948 political reality with the rapid growth of the genre, attributing it to "the fact that a good part of the present world tries to dislodge the Palestinians and to deny the tragic facts of their recent experience." *A Mountainous Journey* also contributed to the development of a distinct body of Arab women's autobiography, such as Muslim feminist Huda

An aerial view of Nablus, where Fadwa Tuqan lived her life as described in Mountainous Journey. © WILLIAM KAREL/SYGMA/CORBIS

Shaarawi's *Harem Years: The Memoirs of an Egyptian Feminist, 1879–1924* (1981).

Numerous autobiographies written by Arab women appeared in the wake of *A Mountainous Journey*. Among the most prominent of these are Palestinian Mai Sayigh's *The Siege* (1988), Egyptian Nawal El Saadawi's *A Daughter of Isis* (1999), and Moroccan Fatima Mernissi's *Dreams of Trespass: Tales of a Harem Girlhood* (1994), written in English. Tuqan also followed *A Mountainous Journey* with a second autobiography about her post-1967 life titled *The Harder Journey* (1993), which is primarily concerned with the Israeli occupation.

THEMES AND STYLE

The central message of *A Mountainous Journey* is that struggle and adversity are surmountable and that poetry sustains the imprisoned, whether they are trapped in a cell or in "the prison of the house," although Tuqan confesses that the experience may limit personal poetic expression. The author paints a picture of her life inside the "bottled-up harem," where each of her female relatives "had been an old woman since the age of twenty-five," likening it to "a large coop filled with domesticated birds, content to peck the feed thrown to them, without argument." The oppressive patriarchy of the household eventually denies Tuqan access to the only intellectual, emotional, and spiritual outlets she has: school and nature. When her brother Ibrahim begins to teach her to read and compose poetry, urging her to become a true Palestinian poet by writing about the resistance, she finds that she is unable to move beyond her "personal feelings and sufferings." She is too concerned with her individual liberation as a woman to be able to write consistently about collective national liberation. This leads to feelings of guilt and inadequacy as well as anger, as when her father insists that Tuqan take Ibrahim's place as "the voice of the Palestinian people" after his death, even though she remains confined to the house: "How and with what right or logic does Father ask me to compose political poetry, when I am shut up inside these walls?"

Although Tuqan explains that she wrote *A Mountainous Journey* to provide hope for others upon similarly difficult life paths, her autobiographical impulse can also be traced to a more fundamental desire to assert her existence. The text opens with a description of a failed attempt by Tuqan's mother to abort her. She then shares that although her mother often related stories about her siblings, Tuqan was never included in these narrations. She was made to feel like a "nonentity." Penny Johnson, writing in the *Women's Review of Books* in 1991, asserts that "at its most powerful the autobiography is the story her mother didn't tell and, perhaps, the story Tuqan wanted to tell her mother but never could." Although the autobiography represents Tuqan's resistance to a world where her voice was silenced and her existence denied, her account is circumscribed by her continued modesty, evidenced by her coy accounts of her amorous relationships. She candidly reveals the psychological and emotional hardships she encounters but admits: "I have not completely removed the lid from my life's treasure chest."

The autobiography is notable for its use of poetic language, as well as its incorporation of letters, excerpts from poems and travel narratives by other authors, diary entries from 1966 through 1967, Tuqan's own poetry, and lists of classical and contemporary texts that the author encountered at different stages of her life. This personal literary history reveals the influence of other poets on her own writing, even describing the conditions and inspiration for the composition of some of her most well-known poems. However, Tuqan's inclusion of letters from male relatives and her reliance on male Palestinian writers for some of her descriptions of Nablus undercuts the female voice of the text.

CRITICAL DISCUSSION

Responses to *A Mountainous Journey* were mixed upon its translation into English, with some critics heralding its historical importance while others highlighted its shortcomings as a literary and social text. In her foreword to the English translation, Jayyusi recognizes "the book's importance as a testimony of Palestinian identity and rootedness" as well as "its great pathos as a work of literature that delineates, poignantly, the struggle of a gifted woman … who succeeds in forging her way to fame despite unbelievable difficulties." Joanna Kadi similarly praises Tuqan's critique of patriarchy in a 1992 review but criticizes her failure to adequately address other prevalent sources of oppression and discrimination, such as class, sexual orientation, and racism.

Although *A Mountainous Journey* was overshadowed by Tuqan's poetry, the autobiography continued to attract scholarly attention and critical acclaim in the years following its publication. Tuqan was warmly received by feminists in the Arab world, Israel, and the United States and remained popular among Palestinian nationalists. However, debate continued to surround her portrayal of men and patriarchy, with some critics arguing that *A Mountainous Journey* reinforced Western stereotypes about Arab society.

Scholars have explored Tuqan's relationship with her mother as presented in *A Mountainous Journey* within a range of analytical frameworks, considering its psychological, historical, and literary implications. In her introduction to the English translation of *A Mountainous Journey*, Fedwa Malti-Douglas performs a feminist close reading of several key passages. She argues that Tuqan's decision to open the text with a description of her mother's failed attempt to abort her subverts traditional autobiographical structure emphasizing the family, distinguishing Tuqan from her male predecessors, and "[liberating] her immediately from the psychological constraints of the traditional family." Stressing the psychological roots of the mother-daughter conflict, Dalya Abudi, in her 2011 study *Mothers and Daughters in Arab Women's Literature: The Family Frontier*, compares *A Mountainous Journey* to Mernissi's *Dreams of Trespass*. Abudi argues that due to their different relationships with their mothers, as well as their dissimilar harem experiences, as adults "Tuqan used her creative gift to set herself apart from the women in her family and her community, rejecting their traditional roles and ideals … , whereas Mernissi used her intellectual gift to become the spokesperson for the women in her family and her society, fighting tirelessly for their rights and freedom."

IBRAHIM TUQAN: THE POET OF PALESTINE

Fadwa Tuqan's brother Ibrahim took responsibility for her poetic education after she was forbidden to complete her schooling, and a close bond developed between them although Fadwa was haunted by accusations that Ibrahim had composed the poems published under her name. She was deeply affected by his death in 1941. She compares her grief to "the agony of orphanhood," and it inspired her to compose an elegy and pen a biography of his life called *My Brother Ibrahim* (1946).

Born in 1905, Ibrahim was one of the first Palestinian poets to write explicitly nationalistic poetry in the years leading up to and during the Arab Revolt, which began in 1936 in reaction to continued British governance of Palestine as well as widespread Jewish immigration to the area, and lasted until 1939. He resisted contemporary trends in poetry, preferring classical models, and his work appeared in newspapers, literary journals, and radio programs broadcast by the Palestine Broadcasting Service (PBS). Ibrahim headed the Arabic Section of the PBS until he was forced to resign in 1940 after being accused of promoting Palestinian nationalist sentiments. His poem "Mawtini," composed in the late 1930s, was set to music and became the unofficial national anthem of Palestine, popular across the Arab world. In 2004, following the fall of the Baathist regime of Saddam Hussein, it became the Iraqi national anthem.

BIBLIOGRAPHY

Sources

Abudi, Dalya. *Mothers and Daughters in Arab Women's Literature: The Family Frontier.* Boston: Brill, 2011. Print.

Jayyusi, Salma Khadra. "Mistress of the Two Gifts: Love and Pain." Foreword. *A Mountainous Journey: An Autobiography.* By Fadwa Tuqan. St. Paul, Minn.: Graywolf, 1990. vii–xiii. Print.

Johnson, Penny. "From Seclusion to Creation." Rev. of *A Mountainous Journey: An Autobiography*, by Fadwa Tuqan. *Women's Review of Books* 8.4 (1991): 11–12. Print.

Kadi, Joanna. "Finding Glimmers." Rev. of *A Mountainous Journey: An Autobiography*, by Fadwa Tuqan. *Bridges* 3.1 (1992): 164–67. Print.

Malti-Douglas, Fedwa. "A Palestinian Female Voice against Tradition." Introduction. *A Mountainous Journey: An Autobiography.* By Fadwa Tuqan. St. Paul, Minn.: Graywolf, 1990. 1–9. Print.

Further Reading

Al-Nowaihi, Magda M. "Resisting Silence in Arab Women's Autobiographies." *International Journal of Middle East Studies* 33.4 (2001): 477–502. Print.

Ashour, Radwa, Ferial J. Ghazoul, and Hasna Reda-Mekdashi, eds. *Arab Women Writers: A Critical Reference Guide, 1873–1999.* Cairo: American University in Cairo Press, 2008. Print.

Attar, Samar. "A Discovery Voyage of Self and Other: Fadwa Tuqan's Sojourn in England in the Early Sixties." *Debunking the Myths of Colonization: The Arabs and Europe.* Lanham, Md.: UP of America, 2010. 38–67. Print.

DeYoung, Terri. "Love, Death, and the Ghost of al-Khansā': The Modern Female Poetic Voice in Fadwā Ṭūqān's Elegies for Her Brother Ibrāhīm." *Tradition, Modernity, and Postmodernity in Arabic Literature: Essays in Honor of Professor Issa J. Boullata.* Ed. Kamal Abdel-Malek and Wael Hallaq. Leiden: Brill, 2000. 45–75. Print.

Mernissi, Fatima. *Dreams of Trespass: Tales of a Harem Girlhood.* Reading, Mass.: Addison-Wesley, 1994. Print.

Allison Blecker

A True Relation of My Birth, Breeding, and Life

Margaret Cavendish

OVERVIEW

Published as the final chapter of *Nature's Pictures Drawn by Fancy's Pencil to the Life* (1656), a collection of "feigned Stories," *A True Relation of My Birth, Breeding, and Life* by Margaret Cavendish was one of the earliest autobiographies published by a woman. The work offers a short account of Cavendish's childhood and upbringing alongside brief discussions of some of the more significant events in her life, including her introduction to her future husband, William Cavendish, then Marquis (later Duke) of Newcastle; their life in exile in the 1640s and 1650s; and her ultimately unsuccessful trip to England in an attempt to recoup funds from the sale of William's estates. Conscious of potential accusations of vanity, Cavendish nevertheless emphasizes her virtuous and chaste behavior toward her friends, family, and husband and links it to a principled education at the hands of her mother.

Cavendish wrote and published *A True Relation* while she was in exile in Antwerp, Belgium, in part to ensure that "after-Ages" accurately remembered her not only as the "daughter to one Master Lucas [her father]" and the "second wife to the Lord Marquis of Newcastle" but also as a famous writer in her own right. While there is little evidence for how *A True Relation* was initially received, Cavendish's lucid self-analysis (in particular, her descriptions of her contemplative habits), coupled with the text's desultory manner, may have irked some readers. In her biography *Mad Madge* (2003), Katie Whitaker cites a remark by Mary Evelyn (diarist John's wife), for example, that Cavendish's writings were "airy, empty, whimsical, and rambling." Nonetheless, *A True Relation* is today considered a crucial document of the English Civil War (1642–1651) period as well as an important early representative of the genre of female autobiography.

HISTORICAL AND LITERARY CONTEXT

A True Relation is peppered with allusions to what Cavendish calls an "unhappy" and "unnatural" war, a reference to the English Civil War that dominated her early adulthood. Unbeknownst to each other, both Cavendish and her future husband, William, were caught up in the nearly ten-year conflict between Parliamentarian and Royalist forces; she was a maid of honor to Queen Henrietta Maria, and he served as a general in the Royalist army. As the Parliamentarian forces began to gain the upper hand in 1644, England was no longer safe for the queen and her retinue, and she was forced to flee England in June for exile in France. With the exception of a trip to England in the early 1650s, Cavendish would spend the next sixteen years on the Continent with her husband.

Married to a former Royalist general and possessed of numerous Royalist connections herself (some of Cavendish's brothers had also fought against the Parliamentarian forces), Cavendish could not return to England permanently. Many of her early works, including *A True Relation,* were written and published while she and her husband were in exile in Antwerp. Although life there in the mid-1650s had its pleasantries (fraternization with other Royalist exiles, including the future king, Charles II, for example), and while Cavendish boldly declares in *A True Relation* that she and her husband were immune to their misfortunes ("Patience hath armed us, and misery hath tried us and finds us fortune-proof"), exile took its toll. Indeed, Cavendish's narrative frequently registers, albeit obliquely, the painful disruptions caused by the civil war and exile.

Nature's Pictures as a whole has much in common with Geoffrey Chaucer's *Canterbury Tales* and Giovanni Boccaccio's *Decameron,* but the literary antecedents of *A True Relation* are more difficult to define. Although at one point Cavendish compares her autobiographical project to the writings of Ovid and Julius Caesar, *A True Relation* is better situated within the developing mode of female autobiography. Her forerunners in the genre include Lady Grace Mildmay's autobiography (written sometime after 1617 and unpublished for many years) and Anne Collins's *Divine Songs and Meditacions* (1653), though both of these works are marked by a distinctively religious tone that Cavendish would largely abandon.

The notable departure of *A True Relation* from the religious emphasis of earlier autobiographies had a lasting influence on the genre as a whole, particularly for women in the later seventeenth century. In their decidedly secular cast, such works as *Memoirs*

❖ *Key Facts*

Time Period:
Mid-17th Century

Relevant Historical Events:
English Civil War; author's exile in Antwerp

Nationality:
English

Keywords:
exile; civil war; women's writing

Author Margaret Cavendish, Duchess of Newcastle, was known to be a prolific writer.
© MARY EVANS PICTURE LIBRARY/ALAMY

(1676) by Lady Ann Fanshawe, *Autobiography* (1670) by Alice Thornton, and *Memoirs* (1677–78) by Lady Anne Halkett, bear the unmistakable stamp of Cavendish's *A True Relation*. Cavendish's influence on the development of autobiography has been increasingly recognized as one of her most important contributions to English letters.

THEMES AND STYLE

The central theme of *A True Relation* is that the work is an absolutely true account of Cavendish's "birth, breeding, and life." As Gweno Williams points out in a 2002 essay, the word *truth* and the phrases "in truth" and "tis true" occur "at least" twenty times. Cavendish remarks toward the work's conclusion, "Neither did I intend this piece for to delight, but to divulge; not to please the fancy, but to tell the truth." Much of this "divulging," especially in the latter portion of *A True Relation,* takes the form of a description and vindication of Cavendish's shy, contemplative character. Late in the narrative, for example, Cavendish writes, "I being addicted from my childhood to contemplation rather than conversation, to solitariness rather than society [prefer] to write with the pen than work with the needle." More than just a character trait, Cavendish's shyness is a form of contemplation that in turn functions as a powerful, self-assertive gesture. For Cavendish, contemplation leads to writing and a quiet refusal to remain within traditionally feminine spheres of activity (here symbolized by needlework).

On account of the harsh criticism she endured during the early part of her authorial career and a fear that she might die and her husband remarry, Cavendish felt she was destined for historical oblivion; she wrote *A True Relation* in an attempt to ensure that a record of her life survived. In the epistle that precedes *A True Relation,* she anticipates a future "more just" to her "than the present," an era in which the record of her life might serve as an important supplement to any critical revaluation of her works, if not interesting in its own right. Because the text was written at a time when the generic constraints of autobiography had yet to be rigidly codified, Cavendish's attention to the basic facts of her life (her childhood, personality, and feelings) seems remarkably modern. Although unusually forthright when compared to her contemporaries (at one point she confesses to a speech difficulty), Cavendish was careful to omit potentially damaging details (the illegitimacy of her oldest brother, for example).

While *A True Relation* lacks any formal structure in the form of chapter breaks and the like, the work does follow a distinct trajectory, with the first two-thirds offering descriptions of Cavendish's childhood and time in exile and the final third presenting a characterization of the author. While the work is sometimes marked by a language of self-promotion ("I … wish myself the exactest of Nature's works"; "I am so well-bred"), Cavendish is quick to contradict such bold statements. Indeed, the work has often been characterized as a series of such oscillations. Thus, while Cavendish everywhere emphasizes her shy and retiring character, she also paints herself as an ambitious, assertive person: "I am very ambitious; yet 'tis neither for Beauty, Wit, Titles, Wealth or Power, but as they are steps to raise me to Fame's Tower, which is to live by remembrance in after-ages." Such displays of confidence in her art contrast markedly with her deprecation of her writing as mere "scribbling."

CRITICAL DISCUSSION

Early responses to *A True Relation* are sparse. While such works as *A Collection of Letters and Poems* (1678), an anthology of letters written to the Cavendishes, indicate that many people admired Cavendish's writings, the diaries of such men as Samuel Pepys offer a different perspective. Pepys, for example, refers to her as a "mad, conceited, ridiculous woman." Pepys's remarks are echoed in Cavendish's own confessed fears near the conclusion of *A True Relation,* where she hints at the possible reception of a work that violated the accepted standards of female authorship: "I hope my Readers, will not think me vain for writing my life."

When Cavendish issued a second edition of *Nature's Pictures* in 1671, she excluded *A True Relation,* for reasons still unclear. It remained out of print for many years, along with many of her other writings; while researching his *Memoirs of Several Ladies of Great Britain* (1752), for example, George Ballard had trouble locating Cavendish's works. The publication of a new edition in 1814 by Samuel Egerton Brydges, who notes that *Nature's Pictures* is full of "charm and amusement" and is sure to "entertain and instruct," marked the beginning of renewed interest in the work. Today the text is regarded as an important stepping-stone in the development of the female literary voice because of its presentation of Cavendish as, in Whitaker's words, an "individualistic woman who was not afraid to admit to her unfeminine … ambitions."

Issues of gender and genre (autobiography) have been at the forefront of modern critical interest in *A True Relation.* Thus, in "The 'Native Tongue' of the 'Authoress': The Mythical Structure of Margaret Cavendish's Autobiographical Narrative" (2003), Line Cottegnies notes that the work has been "hailed as one of the first narrative, nonreligious and nonhistorical autobiographies." Scholarly attention to Cavendish's generic innovation has been matched by studies focusing on her sophisticated relationship to gender. Mary Beth Rose, for instance, in her essay "Gender, Genre, and History: Seventeenth-Century English Women and the Art of Autobiography" (1986), describes a conflict between "self-assertion and self-denial," a desire both to transcend and to comply with a "Renaissance ideal of femininity." Elspeth Graham makes much the same point in *Genre and Women's Life Writing* (1989), noting a "vehemently asserted autonomy and dependent femininity." Studies of autobiography and gender have not been remiss in their attention to the political aspects of *A True Relation.* Rose, for example, describes the ways in which the chaos of the English Civil War made Cavendish's assertive foray into publishing possible, while Williams characterizes it as partly a "vindication of … the royalist cause."

THE BLAZING WORLD

While the exact reasons for Margaret Cavendish's withdrawal of her autobiography remain unclear, critics have pointed to the author's dispersal of autobiographical elements across many of her later writings as a potential explanation. Published in 1666 as part of her *Observations on Experimental Philosophy,* Cavendish's *A Description of the New World, Called the Blazing-World* is not only peppered with thinly veiled references to her own life and desires, but it also features a character named the Duchess of Newcastle.

Considered by many to be an early example of science fiction, *The Blazing World* describes a woman's journey from the "terrestrial world" to the wholly imaginary Blazing World, a realm of exceeding brightness, multicolored people, talking animals, and untold wealth. Cavendish's protagonist eventually becomes the empress of this world and leads an invasion back into the "real" world with the help of submarines, of all things. In one particularly poignant episode, the newly crowned empress hires the Duchess of Newcastle as her scribe, a revelatory plot development that is no doubt a reflection of Cavendish's own desire for literary fame. More than just transmuted autobiography, however, *The Blazing World* is also an early vindication of imaginative fiction and female authorship.

BIBLIOGRAPHY

Sources

Cavendish, Margaret. *Nature's Pictures Drawn by Fancy's Pencil to the Life.* London: J. Martin and J. Allestrye, 1656. *Early English Books Online.* Web. 10 Oct. 2012.

Cottegnies, Line. "The 'Native Tongue' of the 'Authoress': The Mythical Structure of Margaret Cavendish's Autobiographical Narrative." *Authorial Conquests: Essays on Genre in the Writings of Margaret Cavendish.* Ed. Cottegnies and Nancy Weitz. Cranbury, N.J.: Rosemont, 2003. 103–19. Print.

Graham, Elspeth. "Intersubjectivity, Intertextuality, and Form in the Self-Writings of Margaret Cavendish." *Genre and Women's Life Writing in Early Modern England.* Burlington, U.K.: Ashgate, 2007. Print.

Pepys, Samuel. *The Diary of Samuel Pepys: A New and Complete Transcription.* Ed. Robert Latham and William Matthews. London: HarperCollins, 2000. Print.

Rose, Mary Beth. "Gender, Genre, and History: Seventeenth-Century English Women and the Art of Autobiography." *Women in the Middle Ages and the Renaissance: Literary and Historical Perspectives.* Ed. by Rose. Syracuse, N.Y.: Syracuse University Press, 1986. 245–78. Print.

Whitaker, Katie. *Mad Madge: Margaret Cavendish, Duchess of Newcastle, Royalist, Writer, and Romantic.* London: Chatto & Windus, 2003. Print.

Williams, Gweno. "Margaret Cavendish, *A True Relation of My Birth, Breeding and Life.*" *A Companion to Early Modern Women's Writing.* Ed. Anita Pacheco. Malden, Mass.: Blackwell, 2002. 165–76. Print.

Further Reading

Battigelli, Anna. *Margaret Cavendish and the Exiles of the Mind.* Lexington: UP of Kentucky, 1998. Print.

Chalmers, Hero. "Dismantling the Myth of 'Mad Madge': The Cultural Context of Margaret Cavendish's Authorial Self-Presentation." *Women's Studies* 4.3 (1997): 323–40. Print.

Clucas, Stephen, ed. *A Princely Brave Woman: Essays on Margaret Cavendish, Duchess of Newcastle.* Aldershot, U.K.: Ashgate, 2003. Print.

Dowd, Michelle M., and Julie M. Eckerle, eds. *Genre and Women's Life Writing in Early Modern England.* Burlington, U.K.: Ashgate, 2007. Print.

Fitzmaurice, James. "Front Matter and the Physical Make-Up of *Nature's Pictures.*" *Women's Writing* 4.3 (1997): 353–67. Print.

Gardiner, Judith Kegan. "'Singularity of Self': Cavendish's *True Relation,* Narcissism, and the Gendering of Individualism." *Restoration: Studies in Literary Culture 1660–1700* 21.2 (1997): 52–65. Print.

Seelig, Sharon Cadman. "Shy Person to Blazing Empress." *Autobiography and Gender in Early Modern Literature: Reading Women's Lives, 1600–1680.* New York: Cambridge University Press, 2006. 131–53. Print.

Smith, Sidonie. "'The Ragged Rout of Self': Margaret Cavendish's *True Relation* and the Heroics of Self-Disclosure." *A Poetics of Women's Autobiography: Marginality and the Fiction of Self-Representation.* Bloomington: Indiana University Press, 1987. 84–101. Print.

Alex Covalciuc

Walden; or, Life in the Woods
Henry David Thoreau

OVERVIEW

Equal parts nature writing, social criticism, philosophical inquiry, and soul-searching autobiography, Henry David Thoreau's *Walden; or, Life in the Woods* (1854) is among the most revered works of American literature. Compiled mainly from journal entries written over a two-year stay in a single-room cabin that Thoreau built on the banks of Walden Pond near Concord, Massachusetts, *Walden* outlines the author's thoughts on the relationship between the modern individual, nature, and the divine over eighteen chapters organized by theme. Characterized by the author's distaste for the trappings and petty materialism of industrialized society, the work represents an experiment in living simply—or "deliberately," as Thoreau puts it—to achieve greater harmony between one's daily activities and the ultimate truths of the universe, the "secret of things."

Thoreau, a Concord native, was closely associated with a circle of like-minded New England writers, philosophers, and political activists known as the Transcendentalists, who viewed the natural world as a reflection of God's divine will and a sacred space for achieving a direct relationship with the sublime. Likewise, the Transcendentalists believed in the inherent goodness of the individual. *Walden* springs from Thoreau's attempt to put the principles of Transcendentalism into practice by shedding the trivial concerns of city life in pursuit of self-sufficiency and communion with nature. Despite slow initial sales, *Walden* has since been championed by a wide range of readers; its longevity may be attributed to the multifaceted and empowering nature of Thoreau's observations, which lend themselves to a variety of social, political, and academic worldviews.

HISTORICAL AND LITERARY CONTEXT

In many ways, *Walden* can be read as Thoreau's reaction to the social and political events of the mid-1800s. The United States, abuzz with a renewed sense of patriotism following its decisive defeat of the British in the War of 1812, entered an era of rampant expansionism and economic isolationism, spurring massive growth in manufacturing and technology and drastically changing the American way of life from rural and agricultural to urban and industrial. Two of the most notable technological developments of the 1800s, the telegraph and large-scale rail transport, greatly contributed to the country's westward expansion and modernization, but for Thoreau and others like him such advancements also served to alienate people from each other and the world around them. "We are in great haste to construct a magnetic telegraph from Maine to Texas; but Maine and Texas, it may be, have nothing important to communicate," he writes, later adding that "We do not ride upon the railroad; it rides upon us." Indeed, the Fitchburg Railroad company laid miles of railway throughout Massachusetts in the 1840s, greatly altering the landscape on the western end of Walden Pond in the years before Thoreau moved there.

Thoreau had always been something of an iconoclast, but it was not until he was befriended in 1837 by poet and philosopher Ralph Waldo Emerson, the intellectual leader of the Transcendentalist movement, that he would begin to organize his thoughts in the journals that provided the basis for the essays in *Walden*. In the early 1840s Thoreau published a number of well-received poems and essays in the *Dial*—the main publishing vehicle for a number of influential Transcendentalists, including Emerson, Bronson Alcott, Margaret Fuller, and William Ellery Channing. He subsequently built a small cabin on land owned by Emerson on the northern shore of Walden Pond a few miles outside of Concord. Thoreau took residence there on July 4, 1845, and lived in the cabin for just over two years, reading, writing, and refining his political and philosophical opinions in solitude but often returning to Concord to replenish his supplies and visit with friends and family. In September 1847 he left Walden Pond with the first of seven drafts of *Walden*, as well as the completed manuscript of another autobiographical work, *A Week on the Concord and Merrimack Rivers* (1849), which details a boating trip that Thoreau took with his brother, John, who died of tetanus in 1842.

Although none of Thoreau's works made him a literary celebrity during his lifetime, the publication of *Walden* in August 1854 did establish him as one of the most prominent, and accessible, Transcendentalist writers. Whereas Emerson had already expounded upon similar ideas in such well-known works as "Nature" (1836), "The Over-Soul" (1841), and "Self Reliance" (1841), *Walden* served to introduce readers

❖ *Key Facts*

Time Period:
Mid-19th Century

Relevant Historical Events:
Battle of Bunker Hill (1775); first American steam locomotive (1829); Panic of 1837

Nationality:
American

Keywords:
Transcendentalism; nature writing; urbanization; industrialism; philosophy

Replica of the simple cabin at Walden Pond near Concord, Massachusetts, where Henry David Thoreau lived from 1845 to 1847. © PRISMA BILDAGENTUR AG/ALAMY

to the practical application of such lofty ideals in one's own life, a subject that Thoreau had explored less successfully in *A Week on the Concord and Merrimack Rivers*. For many, Thoreau's experiment in *Walden* was quintessentially American in its mingling of mystical idealism with the gritty work of survival, going further in its elevation of personal experience than other nature-oriented works of American autobiography, such as Richard Henry Dana's *Two Years before the Mast* (1840) and Francis Parkman's *The Oregon Trail: Sketches of Prairie and Rocky-Mountain Life* (1849).

Thoreau's evocative documentation of the wildlife surrounding Walden Pond inspired a wave of American nature writers in the late nineteenth and early twentieth centuries. His wildlife observations also led later generations to deem him America's first environmentalist. But *Walden*'s influence is more far-reaching than that. In the years after Thoreau's death in 1862, prominent writers, including the poet Walt Whitman, naturalist John Muir, essayist and children's author E. B. White, and behavioral psychologist B. F. Skinner, made pilgrimages to Walden Pond to pay respect to the site that had fostered such a unique and fascinating American voice. Although Transcendentalism fell out of public favor at the turn of the twentieth century, a renewed focus on individual rights and resistance to conformity in the 1960s and 1970s led to a reevaluation of *Walden* as a defining work of American literature. Today it is often read alongside such rebellious works as Jack Kerouac's *On the Road* (1957) and Edward Abbey's *Desert Solitaire* (1968).

THEMES AND STYLE

The primary message of *Walden*, despite the dizzying (and sometimes contradictory) amount of aphorisms and advice that Thoreau offers in its eighteen chapters, is that life is simple and is complicated only by society's misplaced emphasis on busyness and wealth as a sign of productivity and worth. "Simplicity, simplicity, simplicity!" he writes, adding, "Why should we live with such hurry and waste of life?" Much of *Walden* details his labors in pursuit and support of a simple life—including charts and figures listing the supplies and costs involved in building the cabin, a chapter-long account of his work tending a bean field, and other descriptions of his efforts to maintain his cabin and keep himself warm and fed. Throughout the book Thoreau contrasts these self-sustaining labors with the labor-for-labor's-sake of industrial society. Whereas the majority of Americans in the nineteenth century saw the accumulation of wealth as the ultimate sign of self-worth, Thoreau argues in *Walden* that true worth stems from living in accordance with the higher laws of nature, something that can be accomplished only when one sets aside petty concerns. Thus, Thoreau's seemingly simple observations on the value inherent in the simple life he led at Walden Pond become something more akin to a revolutionary treatise advocating sweeping social reforms.

Thoreau's expansion of his private experience into the realm of public policy and conduct is seemingly at odds with the image he presents of himself as a world-weary hermit, and is achieved through a subtle use of persuasive rhetoric and structure to transform his autobiographical notes and observations into a rousing call to transform one's life and, ultimately, the American value system as a whole. "Thoreau liked to pretend that his book was a purely personal act of private communion," writes R. W. B. Lewis in *The American Adam*. "But that was part of his rhetoric, and *Walden* is a profoundly rhetorical book." Part of this effect stems from the fact that Thoreau heavily revised the *Walden* manuscript, nearly doubling its length in the years between 1846 and 1854. He gave *Walden* a greater sense of cohesiveness by condensing the narrative into a single year and organizing the chapters to reflect the passage of seasons within that year, so that it begins on the verge of fall—a kind of symbolic death—and ends in spring, signifying a rebirth. By moving his narrative away from the strictly autobiographical toward a more literary style, Thoreau managed to infuse the raw commentary of his journals with a sense of meaning that is at once personal and generalized. "The book begins to acquire mythic and archetypal dimensions," notes Robert Sattelmeyer in "The Remaking of *Walden*," with the end result being that it "becomes less topical and more universal in its reference."

The language of *Walden* also contributes to the universality of the work. Although Thoreau filled the book with concrete imagery—describing the sights, sounds, smells, textures, and tastes he encountered—nearly every image has a metaphorical or allegorical counterpart. A lake becomes "earth's eye" in which "the beholder measures the depth of his own nature"; the bean field becomes the site of self-cultivation, producing an "instant and immeasurable crop"; an elusive loon comes to signify the difficulty of Thoreau's search for truth when it "laugh[s] in derision of my efforts"; and a clash between red and black ants is likened to historical battles, including the American Revolution's Battle of Bunker Hill. Even one of Thoreau's earliest detractors, the poet James Russell Lowell, wrote that "there are sentences of his as perfect as anything in the language, and thoughts as clearly crystalized; his metaphors and images are always fresh from the soil." When Thoreau's language proves insufficient to elevate pure experience to the realm of spiritual truths, he often employs literary allusion, quoting from a diverse range of sources, including classical and contemporary poets, Hindu philosophers, and the Bible, to lend depth to his observations.

CRITICAL DISCUSSION

A long-standing rumor holds that *Walden*, like *A Week* before it, went largely unnoticed by Thoreau's contemporaries when it was published on August 9, 1854, and that it gained popularity only after the author's death in 1862. While it is true that sales were slow—publishers Ticknor and Fields did not sell out of the first printing until 1859 and did not issue a second printing until after Thoreau's death—Bradley P. Dean and Gary Scharnhorst reveal in "The Contemporary

BACK TO NATURE: UTOPIAN SOCIETIES OF THE 1840s

Henry David Thoreau was not the only American to reject industrial society in favor of a pastoral idyll in the mid-nineteenth century. Throughout the 1840s, a number of utopian societies—rural communities designed to be self-sufficient through subsistence farming and socialist-style cooperation between inhabitants—sprang up throughout the United States, particularly in New England. Two of the most notable of these experimental societies were known as Brook Farm and Fruitlands.

Brook Farm was established in 1841 by George Ripley and his wife, Sophia, in West Roxbury, Massachusetts, and Fruitlands was founded in 1843 in Harvard, Massachusetts, by Amos Bronson Alcott and Charles Lane. Inspired by Transcendentalist philosophy, members of these societies pooled their money, built large communal buildings, established schools, worked the land, and published journals espousing their ideals. Both were short lived—Brook Farm was disbanded in 1847 after a fire devastated the uninsured community, while residents of Fruitlands abandoned the experiment after a single harsh winter in 1843—but they did attract the attention of prominent Transcendentalist thinkers, including Thoreau. Ever the individualist, Thoreau noted in his journal after a visit to Brook Farm in 1841 that, "As for these communities—I think I had rather keep a bachelor's hall in Hell than go to board in Heaven."

Reception of *Walden*" that "*Walden* was more widely and favorably received by Thoreau's contemporaries than hitherto suspected," citing sixty-six reviews of the work's first printing, forty-six of which were "strongly favorable."

As the advancements of modernism became increasingly ubiquitous around the turn of the twentieth century, and two world wars pushed literary tastes away from romanticism and spiritual abstractions and toward fragmentary and nonlinear depictions of a world mired in chaos and despair, *Walden* all but disappeared from popular reading lists. While some prominent critics of the mid-twentieth century, including F. O. Matthiessen and White, continued to praise *Walden* as one of the greatest accomplishments in American letters, White was not alone in his observation in "Walden—1954" that "to admire the book is, in fact, something of an embarrassment, for the mass of men have an indistinct notion that its author was a sort of Nature Boy." Writing in 1962, Leo A. Bressler laments the lingering perception of Thoreau "as a kind of nineteenth century Nature Boy, a crank who managed to live on a few cents a day, a hermit who couldn't get along with his fellow man." He suggests that *Walden* is especially suited to the young and idealistic reader. Over the next several decades, coinciding with increased interest in the environment, civil liberties, and spiritualism, *Walden* came to be seen as a kind of multidimensional guidebook for American truth-seekers, nature lovers, freethinkers, and wanderers young and old. The 150th anniversary of the book's publication in 2004 saw a wave of critical appraisals and annotated editions of *Walden*, most heralding it as a foundational masterwork on which much of the American identity is built.

Critics approach the text from a variety of perspectives. Ecocritics such as Lawrence Buell focus on Thoreau's veneration of nature and subversion of the view that humanity sits atop the world hierarchy. Social critics analyze the portrayal of politics, labor, and economy as either an outright rejection or full-throated defense of American culture, while feminist critics such as Laura Dassow Walls argue that, despite its masculine imagery and language, *Walden* can be seen as an early feminist manifesto. Philosophers, including Stanley Cavell, have evaluated the implications of Thoreau's aphorisms for the establishment of a distinctly American brand of philosophy. Still others limit their attention to Thoreau's use of language and rhetoric to draw readers into the remote world of Walden Pond. Above all else, such a profusion of critical perspectives underscores the fact that *Walden* remains one of the most compelling and thought-provoking autobiographical works ever written.

BIBLIOGRAPHY

Sources

Bressler, Leo A. "*Walden*, Neglected American Classic." *English Journal* 51.1 (1962): 14–20. Print.

Dean, Bradley P., and Gary Scharnhorst. "The Contemporary Reception of *Walden*." *Studies in the American Renaissance*. Ed. Joel Myerson. Charlotte: UP of Virginia, 1990. 293–328. Print.

Lewis, R. W. B. "The Case against the Past." *The American Adam: Innocence, Tragedy and Tradition in the Nineteenth Century*. Chicago: University of Chicago Press, 1955. 13–27. Print.

Lowell, James Russell. "Thoreau." *Literary Essays*. Vol. 1. London: Houghton, 1893. 361–81.

Sattelmeyer, Robert. "The Remaking of *Walden*." *Writing the American Classics*. Ed. James Barbour and Tom Quirk. Chapel Hill: University of North Carolina Press, 1990. 53–78.

White, E. B. "*Walden*—1954." *Yale Review* 44 (1954): 13–22. Print.

Further Reading

Buell, Lawrence. *The Environmental Imagination: Thoreau, Nature Writing, and the Formation of American Culture*. Cambridge, Mass.: Belknap, 1995. Print.

Cafaro, Philip. *Thoreau's Living Ethics: "Walden" and the Pursuit of Virtue*. Athens: University of Georgia Press, 2004. Print.

Myerson, Joel, ed. *The Cambridge Companion to Henry David Thoreau*. Cambridge: Cambridge University Press, 1995. Print.

Petrulionis, Sandra Harbert, and Laura Dassow Walls, eds. *More Day to Dawn: Thoreau's "Walden" for the Twenty-First Century*. Amherst: University of Massachusetts Press, 2007. Print.

Ray, Robert B. *Walden x 40: Essays on Thoreau*. Bloomington: Indiana University Press, 2012. Print.

Robinson, David. *Natural Life: Thoreau's Worldly Transcendentalism*. Ithaca, N.Y.: Cornell University Press, 2004. Print.

Sayre, Robert F., ed. *New Essays on "Walden."* Cambridge: Cambridge University Press, 1992. Print.

Thoreau, Henry D., and Jeffrey S. Cramer. *Walden: A Fully Annotated Edition*. New Haven: Yale University Press, 2004. Print.

Jacob Schmitt

Theories

The Autobiographical Pact by Philippe Lejeune	239
An Autobiography, or The Story of My Experiments with Truth by Mohandas Gandhi	242
Autobiography: Essays Theoretical and Critical by James Olney	246
Bone Black: Memories of Girlhood by bell hooks	249
An Experiment in Autobiography by H. G. Wells	252
In the Presence of Absence by Mahmoud Darwish	255
Memories of a Catholic Girlhood by Mary McCarthy	258
"My Furthest-Back Person—'The African'" by Alex Haley	261
Praeterita by John Ruskin	264
Roland Barthes by Roland Barthes	267
Speak, Memory: An Autobiography Revisited by Vladimir Nabokov	270
To Be Young, Gifted and Black: An Informal Autobiography of Lorraine Hansberry by Lorraine Hansberry	273
Truth and Fiction Relating to My Life by Johann Wolfgang von Goethe	276
The Writing Life by Annie Dillard	279

The Autobiographical Pact
Philippe Lejeune

OVERVIEW

Philippe Lejeune's *Le Pacte autobiographique* (*The Autobiographical Pact*), published in Paris in 1975, is a collection of essays on the subject of autobiography, which he defines as a "retrospective narrative in prose that a real person makes of his/her own existence, when the emphasis is placed on that person's individual life, particularly on the history of that person's personality." It is a work of theory that attempts to establish rules—almost laws—for the genre. Lejeune takes the additional step of treating the topic of autobiography from the point of view of the reader rather than the author. Hence, the "pact" of the title is a crucial agreement between author and reader: the author avers that the author, narrator, and subject are all identical and that the narrative is as factual and truthful as possible, while the reader accepts this promise and places trust in the author's sincerity.

The timing of Lejeune's work is significant. After several decades in which critical thought had denied the centrality of authors, who had nearly been deconstructed out of their own texts, the individual life was poised to reappear as a fit topic for discourse because of the value of recounting of individual experiences. In *The Autobiographical Pact,* which insists upon the authenticity of the individual author, Lejeune creates a kind of alternate critical universe that has received considerable sympathetic attention.

HISTORICAL AND LITERARY CONTEXT

The principal historical context of Lejeune's work is the emergence of history itself—not as a literary form but as a valid and meaningful way of viewing the past. In the fifth century BCE in the Greek-speaking city-states ringing the Aegean Sea, a single self-identified individual—such as Herodotus of Halicarnassus or Thucydides, an Athenian—would make a record of past or ongoing events that aspired to verifiable factuality and correct chronology. These records were materially different from the legends, mythologies, epic poems, and religious narratives that had hitherto served as vehicles of common memories. The author's own life was not the principal subject, although if a personal experience illuminated the larger story, it would be included without apology. It was not until the Renaissance (1350–1600), however, that private individuals began writing the stories of their lives for posterity. The autobiography of Italian artist Benvenuto Cellini (1500–1571) stands out as an early, particularly colorful example of a personal narrative of someone who was neither an emperor nor a saint.

By the 1960s and 1970s, a breakup of the political and intellectual order that had unified Western culture after World War II created renewed interest in autobiography, to which Lejeune speaks in both *L'autobiographie en France* (*Autobiography in France,* 1971) and *The Autobiographical Pact.* In the face of the dominant Hegelianism of Western academic thought, there was also a revival of nominalism, a nagging heresy of the medieval world defined by historian Owen Chadwick in *The Reformation* (1964) as "the axiom that only the individual is real. Therefore it is impossible to frame syllogisms with a universal premise, since the 'universal' is only a collection of unique individuals."

In the 1950s and 1960s, literary critical theory in France was dominated by theories of language and literature derived from structuralism, which proposes treating literary works as expressions of, or reactions to, the social structures in which they are produced. During a slightly later period, academic studies of literature in the English-speaking world became mesmerized by the French theories, which tended to downgrade the importance of the individual author, and the study of literature became more the study of literary theory. By the time Lejeune published his first major work in 1971, the influence of structuralism was already waning in France.

The influence of Lejeune's work on the composition of autobiographies and memoirs has been minimal. However, the impact of *The Autobiographical Pact* and Lejeune's other writings on the study of autobiography in all its forms, including autobiographical fiction, has been great and lasting. Scholars of the form throughout Europe and the Americas now regularly cite Lejeune and aim his insights toward their own disciplines in hopes of illumination and clarification.

THEMES AND STYLE

The Autobiographical Pact seeks to define autobiographers as writers and also give meaning to their relationships with their readers. The "pact" of the title is a contract, in which the writer pledges that author, narrator, and subject are the same and that the narrative will be told as sincerely and honestly as possible.

❖ *Key Facts*

Time Period:
Late 20th Century

Relevant Historical Events:
Revival of nominalism; increased interest in autobiographical writing after World War II

Nationality:
French

Keywords:
literary criticism; theory

THEORIES

In *The Autobiographical Pact*, Philippe Lejeune was influenced by the ideas of French author Michel Butor, depicted here. Because of Butor, Lejeune examines "the use of personal pronouns in autobiography."
© INTERFOTO/ALAMY

The reader, in turn, pledges faith in the reasonable honesty of the telling. It follows that the reader cannot be professionally involved—such as, as a historian or lawyer—since no historian with integrity would take the word of a primary source on faith and no lawyer would take even sworn testimony as fact without rigorous cross-examination.

Apart from a refined but insatiable curiosity, Lejeune's principal motive seems to be to rehoist the flag of a separate, integrated authorial personality on the most stable and likely ground: the genre of autobiography. Yet, all is provisional: the author promises to be as honest as possible, and the reader agrees to read the text as if it were true. Lejeune writes, "I believe we can promise to tell the truth. I believe in the transparency of language … But of course it also happens that I believe the contrary … Telling the truth about the self, constituting the self as a complete subject—it is a fantasy. In spite of the fact that autobiography is impossible, this in no way prevents it from existing."

The structure of *The Autobiographical Pact* is largely that of data mining complemented by commentary. Lejeune had closely read most, if not all, of the literary autobiographies written in French. Thus, when he needs an example of a particular autobiographical trope, he has but to imagine a keyword and several passages immediately flash on the surface. The book proceeds as a series of searches for common properties to be used as parts of the definition of the form. When he hits a snag, when something does not fit, he shrugs and changes the terms of his search. His investment is in the writing itself, in the beauty of the individual voice.

CRITICAL DISCUSSION

The Autobiographical Pact was published in French in 1975 and has yet to be translated as a whole into English—perhaps because, while every culture with a literature produces autobiographies, Lejeune reads and thinks almost exclusively about those written in French. Deconstructionists and others of that bent have taken exception to many of his assertions and have rejected most of his premises, but French scholars have made room for him. *The Autobiographical Pact* quietly became a classic, and Lejeune, who has gradually expanded his turf to include most forms of nonfiction personal narrative (diaries and journals, letters, and so forth), has assumed the role of founding father in the realm of autobiographical studies.

Lejeune's work, and particularly *The Autobiographical Pact*, has drifted across the Atlantic. His version of theory—more description than hypothesis—has struck a chord among those who have found the works of authors such as Jacques Derrida, Michel Foucault, and Jacques Lacan to be, while undeniably brilliant, ultimately sterile and useless. Lejeune's most lasting legacy may be the work he has inspired in the United States and Canada. *The Autobiographical Pact* has acted like a time bomb: in the late 1990s and early 2000s, references to it began popping up in a wide variety of learned treatises.

It is not Lejeune's insight into any particular autobiography that makes his work of such high value to today's scholars but rather his invention of a new, fertile field of study, his immense and contagious sympathy for the enterprise of writing, and his uncanny gift for asking the right questions. Even those who, like Frédéric Regard, ultimately find Lejeune's framework to be too confining concede that *The Autobiographical Pact* is an indispensable tool for approaching the study of the personal narrative.

BIBLIOGRAPHY

Sources

Archambault, Paul J. "Autobiography and the Search for Transparency." *Symposium* 51.4 (1998): 231–46. *General OneFile*. Web. 23 Oct. 2012.

Chadwick, Owen. *Pelican History of the Church: The Reformation*. Vol. 3. Harmondsworth, U.K.: Penguin Books, 1964. Print.

Eakin, Paul John. *Touching the World: Reference in Autobiography*. Princeton, N. J.: Princeton University Press, 1992. Web. 21 Oct 2012.

Hoff, Ann K. "Bishop, the Autobiographical Pact, and Poetic Pedagogy." *CEA Forum* 35.2 (2006): n. pag. Web. 23 Oct. 2012.

Lejeune, Philippe. *Le Pacte autobiographique*. Paris: Seuil, 1975. Print.

Regard, Frédéric. "Autobiography & Geography: A Self-Arranging Question." *Reconstruction* 2.3 (2002): n. pag. Web. 24 Oct. 2012.

Further Reading

Braun, Rebecca. "'Mich in Variationen Erzahlen': Gunter Grass and the Ethics of Autobiography." *Modern Language Review* 103.4 (2008): 1051–66. *General OneFile*. Web. 25 Oct. 2012.

Egan, Susanna. "The Company She Keeps: Demidenko and the Problems of Imposture in Autobiography." *Australian Literary Studies* 21.4 (2004): 14–27. *General OneFile*. Web. 25 Oct. 2012.

Johnston, Georgia. "Counterfeit Perversion: Vita Sackville-West's *Portrait of a Marriage*." *Journal of Modern Literature* 28.1 (2004): 124–37. *General OneFile*. Web. 21 Oct. 2012.

Lejeune, Philippe. "How Do Diaries End?" *Biography* 24.1 (2001): 99. *General OneFile*. Web. 20 Oct. 2012.

Popkin, Jeremy D. "Coordinated Lives: Between Autobiography and Scholarship." *Biography* 24.4 (2001): 781–805. *General OneFile*. Web. 21 Oct. 2012.

"Return to Writing: Duras Becomes 'Duras.'" *Marguerite Duras Revisited*. Ed. Marilyn R. Schuster. New York: Twayne, 1993. 105–45. Twayne's World Authors Series 840. *Gale Virtual Reference Library*. Web. 25 Oct. 2012.

Gerald Carpenter

An Autobiography, or The Story of My Experiments with Truth

Mohandas Gandhi

❖ **Key Facts**

Time Period:
Mid-20th Century

Relevant Historical Events:
Institution of the Rowlatt Acts; British suppression of Indian independence movement; Gandhi is jailed

Nationality:
Indian

Keywords:
nonviolence; anticolonialism

OVERVIEW

First compiled into book form in 1927, *An Autobiography, or the Story of My Experiments with Truth* details Mohandas Gandhi's early life as well as his ideas of nonviolent noncooperation, which he called *satyagraha*. He recounts an anticolonialist attitude intricately linked with his Hindu faith from an early age. His socioreligious theories were shaped by his marriage at age thirteen; his law studies in London; his two decades in South Africa as an activist lawyer resisting oppressive government policies; and his final return to India, where he helped lead the movement for independence from the British *raj* (dominance). First published serially in a journal in which Gandhi had already been articulating his activist strategies, *An Autobiography* presents a humble account, humanizing a figure who had come to be called *mahatma* or "great soul."

Gandhi's chapters were widely read in their originals released in the journal *Navajivan* ("new life") at a time when he had already gained notoriety for leading the movement for home rule. Not only had he published a book under that title (*Hind Swaraj*) in 1909, but he had led boycotts of British products, organized local production of Indian cloth (*khadi*), and held considerable sway with the Indian Congress that he helped found. His autobiography is written in accessible language that rendered his nonviolent strategy comprehensible for the majority of Indians. The text has been useful for others committed to nonviolent civil disobedience, most notably Martin Luther King, Jr. during the U.S. civil rights movement.

HISTORICAL AND LITERARY CONTEXT

An Autobiography details Gandhi's experiences critiquing British rule at a time when open critique was increasingly perilous. In 1919 the British instituted the Rowlatt Acts, legislation that allowed the arrest and detainment without trial of anyone considered a subversive. In April of that same year, Gandhi called for a nationwide *hartal*, or day of fasting and prayer, meant to put a halt to all economic activity. In response to a demonstration in the city of Amritsar, the police shot and killed what Congress estimated to be 1,000 people. This violence led Gandhi to conclude that his movement was not yet organized enough and that he should scale back his nonviolence campaign until his ideas could be disseminated more widely in *Navajivan* as well as the magazine *Young India*. By this time he had also established his lifelong habit of traveling through the country to visit outlying villages and teach satyagraha.

From 1920 through 1922 Gandhi resumed his call for a massive noncooperation effort. He committed to wearing only khadi and to spinning his own cotton. His very appearance symbolized subversion in that it was a rejection of everything he found inherently Western, including dress. By 1922, 30,000 Indians were in jail for protesting the government, either by refusing to work for it or, as was the case with the tax resisters and boycotters, refusing to support it economically. Accused of sedition on March 10, 1922, Gandhi was sentenced to six years in jail (he would serve two), where he began to write his autobiography.

The concept of civil disobedience was not invented by Gandhi, though he played a major part in directing its practical and spiritual applications. While studying in London between 1888 and 1891, he was exposed to the ideas of three key figures: John Ruskin, who wrote *Unto This Last* (1860) and posited that what was good for the community was good for the individual; the Russian writer and pacifist Leo Tolstoy; and Henry David Thoreau, whose essay "Resistance to Civil Government" (1849; republished in 1866 as *Civil Disobedience*) argued that it was the citizenry's responsibility to critique undemocratic policies.

The intricate political maneuvers set out in *An Autobiography* were emulated in a number of subsequent socioreligious movements and their accompanying texts. The struggle for racial equality in the United States in the 1950s and 1960s saw the Montgomery bus boycott (1955), the March on Washington (1963), and the publication of King's essay "Letter from Birmingham Jail" (1963). Global justice movements—such as the protests in China that resulted in the march to Tiananmen Square in 1989 as well as the more recent Students for a Free Tibet—also implemented Gandhian tactics and offer contemporary insight into systems of oppression and subjugation.

Cover illustration from a French publication, *Le Petit Journal Illustre*, March 23, 1930. It depicts Mohandas Karamchand Gandhi urging the people of India to maintain their traditional culture and to resist the occupation of their country by the British Empire. © LEEMAGE/GETTY IMAGES

THEMES AND STYLE

Gandhi's autobiography centers on how to obtain spiritual enlightenment and truth, a task that for him was inseparable from Indian politics and independence. While detailing his relationship to *ahimsa,* a Sanskrit term meaning "to do no harm" that for Gandhi included taking vows of veganism, he offers visceral accounts of his body while fasting, marching, or otherwise under duress. This focus on the body demonstrates his ultimate control over his own life and death. Citing his refusal to "depend on outside authority" as his reason for abdicating meat and encouraging "self-purification" as a form of civil disobedience, Gandhi effectively convinced his audience that they already possessed the means for social change. Another tool that he highlights in the text is that of the spinning wheel. He describes organizing weavers, mills, storefronts, and community members to reduce economic dependence

PARTITION OF INDIA AND THE ASSASSINATION OF GANDHI

After World War II British authority on the subcontinent had been significantly weakened. India was also destabilized due to the infighting between different religious populations. Mohandas Gandhi's efforts to create Hindu-Muslim unity stalled as religious riots broke out in the state of Bengal in 1946. Gandhi traveled around the region, spreading his doctrine of nonviolence in an attempt to avert the conflicts. His efforts were largely ignored until, in 1947, he undertook a fast that he vowed to carry out "unto death," at which point both sides ceased their violence for a time.

Gandhi was firmly opposed to the partition of India that came with independence. As Pakistan formed a Muslim state and India formed a Hindu one, many citizens suddenly found themselves residing in countries that were hostile to their religion. The period was marked by mass exodus and displacement, in which Gandhi continued to preach religious tolerance. Religious fundamentalists, Hindus, Sikhs, and Muslims alike felt that his work toward building a coalition threatened their beliefs and, by extension, their nationhood. On January 30, 1948, while he was leading a prayer meeting, Gandhi was assassinated by a Hindu radical. India and Pakistan have been torn by periodic Hindu-Muslim violence ever since.

on Britain, where cloth was produced more cheaply. Gandhi explained to an Indian mill owner that the khadi movement would "provide employment to the semi-starved, semi-employed women of India."

The motivation for writing *An Autobiography* came not only from his hope of gaining independence for India but also from a desire to unite the Hindi and Muslim population and to eradicate the "untouchable" status from the caste system. Gandhi's book provides a blueprint for how other Indians could effect change in the bureaucratic and social justice arenas. Describing his exhaustive efforts persuading Congress to support the Muslim anti-imperialist movement, termed the Khalifat movement, Gandhi notes that they finally embraced "the adoption of non-co-operation for the sake of the Khalifat." He argues that "the only means for the declaration of Truth is *Ahimsa*," and it is with this argument that he causes Congress to "take upon themselves the responsibility of ridding Hinduism of the curse of untouchability." Believing that self-purification is the only path to changing the world, Gandhi utilizes the inherent self-reflection of the autobiographical genre, noting that "devotion to Truth has drawn me into the field of politics."

An Autobiography is structured around short, straightforward chapters that proceed in chronological order. In a style that is personal and informal, Gandhi endears himself to readers, edging his journalistic tones with self-deprecation and referring to himself as "imperfect and inadequate." Interwoven among the chapters' political stories are spiritual affirmations, such as "there is no other God than Truth," which spoke to the deeply religious Hindu population of India.

CRITICAL DISCUSSION

An Autobiography met with a warm, if somewhat patronizing, reception. Early criticism praised Gandhi's clear prose that focused on daily life. S. Radhakrishnan noted in 1939 that the text's playfulness reveals Gandhi as a "person endowed with the highest and most human qualities" who is "made more lovable by the consciousness of his own limitations and by an unfailing sense of humor." Similarly, the English novelist George Orwell, in his essay "Reflections on Gandhi" (1949), remarks that while he disagreed with Gandhi's political strategy in "a backwards, starving, overpopulated country," the autobiography "made a good impression." For Orwell *An Autobiography* demonstrated "that inside the saint, or near-saint, there was a very shrewd, able person."

An Autobiography continued to gain popularity after Gandhi was assassinated in 1948. As the West was exposed to more Eastern philosophy and religion, the text proved a perennially accessible one. Religious scholar Kay Koppedrayer, in her article "Gandhi's *Autobiography* as Commentary on the *Bhagavad Gītā*," interprets Gandhi's "actions and those of his well-chosen army of *satyagrahis* as lived examples of his understandings of the *Gita*'s teachings." Part of *An Autobiography*'s popularity was due also to the ongoing controversy regarding nonviolence and its use as a tool for marginalized communities. In his essay, Orwell outlined the debate that has characterized criticism since the autobiography's publication, claiming that for the British Gandhi "was an enemy, but since in every crisis he would exert himself to prevent violence—which from the British point of view meant preventing any effective action whatever—he could be regarded as our man." For its perspective regarding spirituality and politics, Gandhi's text has received scholarly treatments from the disciplines of religious, peace, and postcolonial studies.

Many scholars have read Gandhi's text against those of the postcolonial philosopher Frantz Fanon, especially *Black Skin, White Masks* (1952) and *The Wretched of the Earth* (1961), which advocate for violent resistance in the face of colonialism. Neil Howard's 2011 article in the *Journal of Pan African Studies* explains that Gandhi and Fanon were strong proponents of direct action, and both believed that the state would eventually have to acquiesce to the protests of the people. Howard shows their positions as potentially closer than scholars have previously thought, arguing that for "Fanon it was just a tragic fact that violence was unavoidable in the face of such deep and intransigent political and psychological repression."

BIBLIOGRAPHY

Sources

Erikson, Erik H. *Gandhi's Truth on the Origins of Militant Non-Violence.* New York: Norton, 1969. Print.

Gandhi, Mohandas. *An Autobiography, or the Story of My Experiments with Truth.* Boston: Beacon, 1957. Print.

Howard, Neil. "Freedom and Development in Historical Context: A Comparison of Gandhi and Fanon's Approaches to Liberation." *Journal of Pan African Studies* 4.7 (2011): 94. *Literature Resource Center.* Web. 6 Nov. 2012.

Koppedrayer, Kay. "Gandhi's *Autobiography* as Commentary on the *Bhagavad Gītā*." *International Journal of Hindu Studies* 6.1 (2002): 47–73. *JSTOR.* Web. 6 Nov. 2012.

Orwell, George. "Reflections on Gandhi." *Partisan Review* 6.1 (1949): 85–92. *Literature Criticism Online.* 3 Nov. 2012.

Radhakrishnan, S. *Mahatma Gandhi; Essays and Reflections on his Life and Work, Presented to Him on His Seventieth Birthday, October 2nd, 1939.* London: G. Allen & Unwin, 1949. Print.

Srinivasan, Vasanthi. "Community, Violence, and Peace: Aldo Leopold, Mohandas K. Gandhi, Martin Luther King, Jr., and Gautama the Buddha in the Twenty-first Century." *Philosophy East and West* 51.3 (2001): 425. *Literature Resource Center.* Web. 25 Oct. 2012.

Further Reading

Cortright, David. *Gandhi and Beyond: Nonviolence for a New Political Age.* 2nd ed. Boulder, Colo.: Paradigm, 2009. Print.

Dalton, Dennis. *Mahatma Gandhi: Nonviolent Power in Action.* 1993. New York: Columbia University Press, 2012. Print.

Hart, James G. "The Philosophy of Gandhi: A Study of His Basic Ideas." *Philosophy East and West* 44.1 (1994): 149. *Literature Resource Center.* Web. 25 Oct. 2012.

Lal, Vinay "The Gandhi Everyone Loves to Hate" *Economic and Political Weekly* 43.40: 55–64. *JSTOR.* Web. 26 Oct. 2012.

Perinbam, B. Marie. "Introduction: The Meaning of Violence." *Holy Violence: The Revolutionary Thought of Frantz Fanon: An Intellectual Biography.* Washington, D. C.: Three Continents, 1982. 5–14. Rpt. in *Twentieth-Century Literary Criticism.* Ed. Thomas J. Schoenberg. Vol. 188. Detroit: Gale, 2007. *Literature Resource Center.* Web. 26 Oct. 2012.

Sofri, Gianni. *Gandhi and India.* New York: Interlink, 1999. Print.

Caitlin Moore

Autobiography
Essays Theoretical and Critical
James Olney

Key Facts

Time Period:
Late 20th Century

Relevant Historical Events:
Increased study of the genre of autobiography

Nationality:
American

Keywords:
scholarship; gender; multiculturalism

OVERVIEW

Realizing that the 1970s had been formative to the critical study of the autobiography genre, James Olney edited and contributed to the 1980 collection *Autobiography: Essays Theoretical and Critical*. From the history of autobiography to its possible future, *Autobiography* features new and republished work on a variety of topics, including the impact of autobiography on the formation of U.S. history and identity, how gender intersects with the form of autobiography, and what makes an autobiography identifiable as such if there are few rules to the genre. Additionally, Olney and the other contributors question and discuss the provenance of selfhood, the validity of memory, the impact of style, the degree of fictiveness inherent to and acceptable in autobiography, and whether a "privileged access to experience" can be shared.

Olney's collection proved to be extremely influential among scholars. It brings together new work by Germaine Brée, Mary Mason, and Michael Sprinkler with republished essays by Elizabeth Bruss, James M. Cox, Paul John Eakin, and Barrett Mandel. The volume also contains Olney's translation of George Gusdorf's seminal 1956 essay "Conditions and Limits of Autobiography," which, Olney argues, chronologically began the critical foray into autobiography. Today the individual works in *Autobiography* are cited more frequently than the collection as a whole, but the book is still referred to as a formative step in the study of autobiography and is a valuable resource.

HISTORICAL AND LITERARY CONTEXT

In the introduction to *Autobiography: Essays Theoretical and Critical,* Olney ponders how to date the first autobiography and where the modern conception of the genre comes from. Early explorations into the critical implications of autobiography, which Olney cites as variously important, include Anna Robeson Burr's *The Autobiography: A Critical and Comparative Study* (1909), Wayne Shumaker's *English Autobiography: Its Emergence, Materials, and Forms* (1954), Gusdorf's 1956 article, and Roy Pascal's well-regarded *Design and Truth in Autobiography* (1960).

The same year *Autobiography* was published, other important works on autobiography appeared, including William Spengemann's *The Forms of Autobiography: Episodes in the History of a Literary Genre* and Estelle Jelinek's *Women's Autobiography: Essays in Criticism*. Olney himself suggests in *Autobiography* that the rise in autobiographies and autobiographical studies in and around 1980 comes from a "shift of attention from *bios* to *autos*—from the life to the self." This shift, he argues, "was largely responsible for opening things up and turning them in a philosophical, psychological, and literary direction." Moreover, he writes that various fields of study hinge on the "focalizing literature" of autobiography to translate the experiences at their center. The rise of interest in specializations such as American studies, African studies, women's studies, and black studies raised the profile of autobiographies because personal testimonies often reveal, as Olney puts it, the "experience and vision of a people."

Olney began critically examining autobiography in 1966. He published *Metaphors of Self: The Meaning of Autobiography* in 1972 and *Tell Me Africa: An Approach to African Literature* in 1973, heading a growing number of contemporaneous studies of autobiography. Related studies such as Elizabeth W. Bruss's *Autobiographical Acts* (1976) and Sidonie Smith's *Where I'm Bound: Patterns of Slavery and Freedom in Black American Autobiography* (1974) respond, Olney maintains in *Autobiography: Essays Theoretical and Critical,* to the importance of the self to contemporary society. This valuation of self led to an idea of autobiography that is an "endless, open-ended, labyrinthine antiautobiography" and to a student of autobiography who is a "vicarious autobiographer," or someone who writes and reads about the lives of others.

Since the publication of *Autobiography,* its essays have been widely cited. Meanwhile, Olney has continued to explore issues related to autobiography in works such as *Memory & Narrative: The Weave of Life Writing* (1998). He and several other authors featured in *Autobiography* remained active on the editorial board of autobiography-centric journals such as *a/b: Auto/Biography Studies,* which was founded in 1985. While scholars are still raising questions pertinent to the essence and execution of autobiography, shifts in technology and culture such as the rise of social media on the Internet have led to new ways of considering the genre.

THEMES AND STYLE

Though *Autobiography* is a fairly traditional anthology, it reflects Olney's assertion that "the student and reader of autobiographies … is a vicarious or closet autobiographer" who participates in a perpetually incomplete process of "self-creation" by reading and writing. The anthology begins with a discussion of what autobiography has been and develops through what it can be. The autobiography's potential includes the antiautobiography, as Germaine Brée calls it in her included essay, which avoids the completion of a story of selfhood. Completion and conclusions, Michel Leiris argues in his essay, are tantamount to death. The essays in *Autobiography*, Olney writes, serve as "widely various evidence" of the "mood of our time," which clings to the "open-endedness of autobiography that requires readers to continue the experience in their own lives," making the form of "antiautobiography" a boon rather than a bane.

Olney uses the collection to examine why, during this particular period in history, the autobiography has risen to prominence. While memoirs are an old form and the word "autobiography" even has some history, Olney writes in the introduction that autobiographical studies previously lacked a collection of scholarly essays for several reasons. First, critics were somewhat flummoxed by the generic slipperiness of autobiography until works such as Bruss's *Autobiographical Acts* began to more overtly delimit it as a literary form. Second, autobiographies were considered whole unto themselves so that, third, critical studies were viewed as superfluous. In his essay in the book, James M. Cox agrees with these assessments, remarking that "a collection of essays on autobiography would have been impossible as recently as a dozen years ago for the simple reason that the essays themselves did not exist."

Autobiography is what it claims to be—a collection of essays on autobiography—but it is also reflective of Olney as an author. He introduces the collection with the assertion that "literary criticism, too, can be seen as autobiography reluctant to come all the way out of the closet—that the literary critic, like Nietzsche's philosopher, is a closet autobiographer." As Rockwell Gray points out in his review of the collection in *Salmagundi,* "those who write about autobiography … do not usually reveal much of their personal involvement with the theme." Typically scholars rely on more conventional analytical practices and avoid the first-person "I" that Olney utilizes to guide the collection's introduction. Exactly how *Autobiography* is autobiographical for Olney is a less pellucid matter. However, his decision to end the book with Michael Sprinkler's essay on the production of selfhood through repetition and difference—which concludes with the assertion that in autobiography the "subject, self, and author collapse into the act of producing a text"—hints at his own authorial self-reflection within the collection's pages.

CRITICAL DISCUSSION

Autobiography was widely reviewed upon its publication, which made it a centerpiece of early discussions on autobiographical studies. Many reviewers praised the collection for its diverse subject matter and appeal, though others were less satisfied. Gray, for example, criticized the anthology for its exclusion of oral history and other "non-literary contexts," such as "group therapy sessions," while P. Rudnytsky of *World Literature Today* found it curious that no biographical (or autobiographical) information concerning its contributors was included. John N. Morris, writing in *Modern Philology,* questioned the claims of the essays and the collection as a whole, but he lauded the book's quest to understand how autobiography interacts with *zugehörigkeit* ("belonging"), as Barrett Mandel terms the sense of "subordination and obligation to shared truths" in his included essay.

Craig Werner begins his 1994 review of James Robert Payne's *Multicultural Autobiography: American Lives* with the assertion that "this excellent anthology of essays provides further evidence that James Olney's

Baseball pitcher Leroy "Satchel" Paige and Hal Lebovitz wrote Paige's 1948 autobiography *Pitchin' Man.* Autobiographies are the topic of the book *Autobiography: Essays Theoretical and Cultural,* edited by James Olney. © AP IMAGES/HARRIS LEWINE COLLECTION

THE POWER OF THREE IN *MEMORY AND NARRATIVE*

In his book *Memory and Narrative: The Weave of Life-Writing* (1998), James Olney continues the work he began in a 1981 paper, "Autobiography and the Narrative Imperative from St. Augustine to Samuel Beckett." The book won the 1999 Christian Gauss Award for Literary Scholarship and Criticism.

Memory and Narrative looks back at St. Augustine's focus on history before turning to Jean-Jacques Rousseau's feelings-centric texts to better understand the trajectory of contemporary (and often experimental) autobiography in authors such as Samuel Beckett, Franz Kafka, and Gertrude Stein. Olney's wide view centers on what he calls the "Trilogy Principle," the profound connection between beginnings, middles, and ends. He writes that "we foresee, we see, and we have seen—we look forward, we look at, and we look back—all through the operation of memory." The "Trilogy Principle" is "a single process that analysis would render in three stages that bear an inherently necessary relationship to one another such that any one would be incomplete without the other two." In other words, beginnings shape ends through connected middles, in individual autobiographies and within the genre's historical trajectory, so that without, say, Rousseau's achievement, "Augustine's would not be the beginning, Beckett's would not be the end."

classic anthology … ushered in a new era in the study of the genre" and heavily influenced the scholarship to come. Scholars such as Susanna Egan, who deems Olney "the father of autobiographical studies" in an essay in *Modern Philology*, share this sentiment. Even those who question Olney's anthology, such as Dagmar Barnouw, admit it inspired discussion and, at the very least, made Gusdorf's 1956 essay readily available.

Autobiography has rarely been discussed in recent scholarship beyond its pioneering role in expanding the range of what constitutes autobiography and how society understands selfhood. This contribution is generally viewed positively, but there are dissenters. Scholars such as Julie Rak find Olney's conflation of terms such as "autobiography," "memoir," and "life-writing" to be too broad and imprecise given the differing appeals of memoirs and autobiographies. Writing in *Genre*, Rak seeks to demarcate the genre of memoir from autobiography to better grasp "the changing relationship between ideas of selfhood and the role of public and private spheres in late capitalism."

BIBLIOGRAPHY

Sources

Barnouw, Dagmar. Rev. of *Autobiography: Essays Theoretical and Critical*, by James Olney. *German Quarterly* 54.3 (1981): 392–95. JSTOR. Web 22 Oct. 2012.

Egan, Susanna. Rev. of *Memory and Narrative: The Weave of Life-Writing*, by James Olney. *Modern Philology* 100.1 (2002): 164–67. JSTOR. Web. 24 Oct. 2012.

Gray, Rockwell. "Autobiography in Theory." Rev. of *Autobiography: Essays Theoretical and Critical*, by James Olney. *Salmagundi* 52–53 (1981): 175–87. JSTOR. Web. 22 Oct. 2012.

Morris, John N. Rev. of *Autobiography: Essays Theoretical and Critical*, by James Olney. *Modern Philology* 79.1 (1981): 114–19. JSTOR. Web. 22 Oct. 2012.

Rak, Julie. "Are Memoirs Autobiography?: A Consideration of Genre and Public Identity." *Genre* 37.3–4 (2004): 483–504. Duke University Press. Web. 23 Oct. 2012.

Rudnytsky, P. Rev. of *Autobiography: Essays Theoretical and Critical*, by James Olney. *World Literature Today* 55.1 (1981): 188. JSTOR. Web. 23 Oct. 2012.

Werner, Craig. Rev. of *Multicultural Autobiography: American Lives*, by James Robert Payne. *Journal of English and Germanic Philology* 93.1 (1994): 143–44. JSTOR. Web. 23 Oct. 2012.

Further Reading

Jelinek, Estelle C., ed. *Women's Autobiography: Essays in Criticism.* Bloomington: Indiana University Press, 1980. Print.

Olney, James. *Memory and Narrative: The Weave of Life-Writing.* Chicago: University of Chicago Press, 1998. Print.

Pascal, Roy. *Design and Truth in Autobiography.* Cambridge, Mass.: Harvard University Press, 1960. Print.

Paul, Jay. "What's the Use?: Critical Theory and the Study of Autobiography." *Biography* 10.1 (1987): 39–54. *Project MUSE*. Web. 24 Oct. 2012.

Payne, James Robert, ed. *Multicultural Autobiography: American Lives.* Knoxville: University of Tennessee Press, 1992. Print.

Spengemann, William C. *The Forms of Autobiography: Episodes in the History of a Literary Genre.* New Haven, Conn.: Yale University Press, 1980. Print.

Katherine Bishop

BONE BLACK
Memories of Girlhood
bell hooks

OVERVIEW

African American feminist scholar Gloria Jean Watkins published *Bone Black: Memories of Girlhood* under her pen name, bell hooks, in 1996. The autobiography is narrated sometimes in the first person, sometimes in the third, creating an impression of intimacy mixed with a hesitancy to get too close to the events remembered, as though the act of remembering might be overwhelming. Some of hooks's experiences are extremely painful. She describes feeling like an exile and an outcast in her own family, in addition to bearing the brunt of the nation's discomfort with race, as part of the first few waves of black students to be integrated with whites in the Kentucky public school system. Written as academic feminism began to look toward girlhood as an important area of study—and given that "white researchers" tend to evaluate attributes of black females such as self-esteem "based on values emerging from white experience"—hooks states at the outset that her intention is to contribute to the corpus of black girls' stories, beginning with her own: "Not enough is known about the experience of black girls in our society."

By the time *Bone Black* was published, hooks was an English professor at City College in New York City, as well as an established and outspoken, even controversial, cultural critic, poet, and scholar. Yet the memoir cleaves to the personal, matter-of-factly incorporating race politics both within the black community and in the context of black-white relations in the United States. The author folds questions of gender and sexuality into her life story while eliding major political events. Her autobiographical writing inclines more toward her work as a poet, and while some reviewers dismissed *Bone Black* as inaccessible and nonlinear, others welcomed its artistry. As an example of avant-garde memoir, the work stands alongside Roland Barthes's *Barthes by Barthes* (1977) as a keenly felt, impressionistic, fragmentary work of childhood reminiscence.

HISTORICAL AND LITERARY CONTEXT

Bone Black chronicles a coming-of-age in a politically volatile chapter of U.S. history. In 1954, when hooks was two, the U.S. Supreme Court ruled in the case *Brown vs. the Board of Education* that segregation of schools was unconstitutional. In 1956 nine southern states issued the "Southern Manifesto," declaring desegregation a threat to the social order. The year 1957 saw federal troops sent to Arkansas to protect black students attempting to integrate a white high school from violent mobs assembled outside. In the 1960s, as hooks attended her own Kentucky school under armed guard, President John F. Kennedy was elected and then assassinated; black civil rights champion Martin Luther King Jr. led nonviolent protests, won the Nobel Peace Prize, and in 1968 was also assassinated. The integration of the Kentucky school system was doomed to failure, and as late as the 1970s some Kentucky schools were still segregated.

In her foreword to *Bone Black,* hooks discusses the misunderstanding she has observed among her white peers in academia about the discrepancy between the way black women present themselves and the way they actually feel about themselves. Outspokenness, for example, is encouraged by parents and teachers in black communities, but an outspoken black girl does not necessarily think highly of herself, a type of nuance that requires, as hooks calls for, more autobiographical writing by black women in order to explain it. She has also suggested that the cultural "myth of the superstrong black woman" ought to be questioned, not only as a means of greater intercultural understanding but also to help heal the wounds hooks suspects the image hides. She places her preferred style for writing her own autobiography in the tradition of Audre Lorde's *Zami: A New Spelling of my Name* (1982), which Lorde called "biomythography," combining straight narrative with vivid and often abstract sense impressions.

Bone Black is classified in libraries alongside books by, and about, black luminaries such as Angela Davis, but it may also be seen as part of a broader tradition of feminist autobiography, such as Virginia Woolf's *Moments of Being* (1940); scholarly autobiography, such as Vladimir Nabokov's *Speak, Memory* (1951); and autobiography that deals with sexuality, such as Kathy Acker's works of the 1970s and 1980s. The black poet, memoirist, playwright, and scholar Maya Angelou, in her first memoir (she wrote five), *I Know Why the Caged Bird Sings* (1969), tells of her childhood in Arkansas, complete with many petty humiliations at the hands of those close to her, similar to the kind hooks describes.

✥ **Key Facts**

Time Period:
Late 20th Century

Relevant Historical Events:
Desegregation; civil rights movement

Nationality:
American

Keywords:
feminism; racism; avant-gardism

Author bell hooks photographed circa 1994. © BARRON CLAIBORNE/CORBIS

In addition to contributing to the record of black girls' experience, *Bone Black,* in its unapologetically freeform approach, may be seen as expressive of *écriture féminine,* a distinctly female way of writing proposed by 1970s feminists such as Hélène Cixous. Its nonlinear format and frank discussion of the female human body present a challenge to traditional, "masculine" writing, which tends to be more self-conscious, controlled, and unconcerned with female sexuality. In 1997 hooks published a second memoir, *Wounds of Passion: A Writing Life,* describing how the man she was romantically involved with both helped and hindered the writing of her first book, *Ain't I a Woman: Black Women and Feminism* (1981). Both works continue to be read alongside hooks's cultural criticism and poetry, which time and again draw on her own experiences to illuminate her understanding of the present.

THEMES AND STYLE

Bone Black touches on the various meanings of the color black, the strange chaos that permeates hooks's childhood home, and the different sources of solace and comfort she finds in the world around her. "Black is a woman's color," her mother tells her again and again, although hooks longs to wear it. In a high school art class, taught by "one of the few white teachers who do not keep black kids at arm's length," hooks learns, "Bone black is a black carbonaceous substance obtained by calcifying bones in closed vessels." Varying shades of blackness within her family arouse powerful emotions—a grandmother "who looks white" states that "a Black nigger is a no-good nigger." The leather strap used to whip children is black. The author adores the elderly; her "soot-black-skinned" maternal grandfather is particularly beloved. She recalls being "cuddled in his lap like a cat, hardly moving, hardly alive so near to the stillness of death was the bliss I knew in his arms."

Combining a deeply personal goal with her stated desire to tell at least one "story of black girlhood" in service to feminist scholarship, hooks writes in her foreword that she wants *Bone Black* to serve "as truth and myth—as poetic witness." Episodes read as dream visions, or fables, as when she befriends a green tree snake who helps her through an early childhood experience involving a pair of shoes she struggles to put on despite repeated punishment: "The green tree snake told her to take those shoes every day and put them on the trash, that maybe they would burn them along with all unwanted things." As an adolescent discovering her own body, it seems to hooks as though sexual pleasure is "reserved" for her brother: "The stained sheets that show signs of his having touched his body are flags of victory." In contrast, her sisters shame her for doing the same: "They watch her, waiting. They pull the covers quickly before she can free her hands." In such intensely personal revelations hooks courageously defies gender norms, both adding to the discourse of feminism and elaborating on her own understanding of her experience.

Bone Black eschews a stable narrative prose structure, shifting from first person to third person and back again, clearly identifying characters only occasionally, although it does follow a chronological progression from early childhood to adolescence. In a 1997 piece for *African American Review,* Evelyn Shockley calls *Bone Black* "a moving story, written in a vivid, incantatory prose." In one passage hooks laments the color of the rooms she shares with her sisters: "The upstairs rooms are painted pink. She hates the color pink. Grown-ups think it should be her favorite color. Pink innocence, pink dreams, pink the color of something alive but not quite allowed to be fully living."

CRITICAL DISCUSSION

When *Bone Black* was published, it met with mixed reviews. The *Kirkus Review*'s August 1996 issue noted, "The narrative voice is oddly disembodied, somehow disturbingly disengaged; there are moments of real force and pain here, but they are not sustained. A book of great intelligence, *Bone Black*'s power is somewhat diffused by this reticence of tone." In October 1996 *Publishers Weekly* declared that "her effort deserves close reading." The October 1996 issue of *Black Collegian* called it "a most soul-searching and tender work." Thulani Davis, in a December 1996 *New York Times* review, wrote that while the book was original, imitating neither traditional slave narrative nor the triumph-over-adversity style of Angelou and Malcolm X, it "seems trapped by an experiment in style."

Over the course of the latter half of the 1990s and through the first decade of the twenty-first century, autobiography continued to grow both as a field of study and as an active area in publishing. Southern women's voices in particular rang true with the reading public, as the popularity of memoirs by Jeanette Walls and Mary Karr demonstrated. After publishing her second memoir, *Wounds of Passion,* hooks continued her work as an academic, a cultural critic, and a journalist and also experimented with children's books. *Wounds of Passion* revisited some of the scenes described in *Bone Black,* such as the beating she received at the hands of her mother, and again used a shifting first-person/third-person format. Martha Nichols of the *Women's Review of Books* noted that the device "tends to call attention to itself" but that "when it works, hooks weaves together many voices—the black Southern sound of her childhood, adult hindsight, superheated poetic imagery—to create surprising juxtapositions." Her entire oeuvre continues to enthrall feminists, theorists of popular culture, and scholars of black America.

Reviewers continue to question hooks's methods in her autobiographical writing, particularly with regard to whether her aesthetic interventions contribute to a greater understanding of the text. In 1999, though praising *Bone Black*'s efficacy, *Callaloo* reviewer Steve Light experiences a certain disconnection, partially as a result of the intermittent use of the third-person narrator: "Is it that the writing, the authorial persona has underlined rather than transformed need, want, desire? Alas, yes … the third-person address … gives rise to a moralistic patina … which comes to demoralize the linguistic and prosodic mood." In hooks's idea of autobiography as a sort of personal myth-making and an attempt to heal, to mother, and to perhaps even "rewrite" herself, Susana Vega-González, writing in 2002 for the *Journal of English Studies,* recognizes hooks's affinity with the black lesbian poet Audre Lorde, who in 1984 wrote: "I have to learn to love myself before I can love you or accept your loving."

BIBLIOGRAPHY

Sources

Cooke, Claire. "Violently Silenced?: The Role of Violence in bell hooks' Development as a Writer." *Limina* 18 (2012). University of Western Australia. Web. 7 Dec. 2012.

Davis, Thulani. "Native Daughter." Rev. of *Bone Black,* by bell hooks. *New York Times* 15 Dec. 1996: BR32–34. *ProQuest.* Web. 16 Nov. 2012.

hooks, bell. *Bone Black: Memories of Girlhood.* New York: Holt, 1996. Print.

———. *Cultural Criticism and Transformation.* Northampton, Mass.: Media Education Foundation, 1997. *YouTube.* Web. 16 Nov. 2012.

Light, Steve. "Autobiographical Desire." Rev. of *Bone Black: Memories of Girlhood,* by bell hooks. *Callaloo* 22.1 (1999): 240–43. *JSTOR.* Web. 15 Nov. 2012.

WHAT DO YOU BELIEVE YOU DESERVE?

Having taught at both Yale University and City College in Harlem, New York City, bell hooks experienced a significant difference between the student body—but not in terms of intellectual ability. Many of the students she taught at Yale were white sons and daughters of privileged families who knew that they had a place in the world and that the education they were receiving at a prestigious university was going to solidify, perhaps even guarantee, that place. At City College, most of her students were black. Some already had children of their own, and many worked at menial jobs to help pay for their education. Between the students at Yale and the students at City College, hooks observed virtually no difference whatsoever in terms of intelligence. What she did see was a huge discrepancy in the students' sense of entitlement, of what they thought they deserved out of life, of their place in the world. Such confidence in the possibilities of the future she found tricky to teach—the black students seemed to have far fewer, and lower, expectations of their futures than the white students had.

Nelson, Corinne O. "New Books by Black Authors." *Black Collegian* 27.1 (1996): 12. *OmniFile.* Web. 16 Nov. 2012.

Nichols, Martha. "Good Girl, Bad Girl." Rev. of *Unafraid of the Dark: A Memoir,* by Rosemary L. Bray, and *Wounds of Passion: A Writing Life,* by bell hooks. *Women's Review of Books* 15.12 (1998): 16–18. *JSTOR.* Web. 16 Nov. 2012.

Rev. of *Bone Black,* by bell hooks. *Kirkus Reviews,* 15 Aug. 1996. Kirkus Reviews. Web. 16 Nov. 2012.

Rev. of *Bone Black,* by bell hooks. *Publishers Weekly,* 2 Oct. 1996. Publishers Weekly. Web. 16 Nov. 2012.

Shockley, Evelyn. Rev. of *Bone Black: Memories of Girlhood. African American Review* 31.3 (1997): 552–54. *JSTOR.* Web. 15 Nov. 2012.

Vega-González, Susana. "The Dialectics of Belonging in bell hooks' *Bone Black: Memories of Girlhood." Journal of English Studies* 3 (2001–02): 237–48. Print.

Further Reading

Andrews, William Leake. *Sisters of the Spirit: Three Black Women's Autobiographies of the Nineteenth Century.* Bloomington: Indiana University Press, 1986. *Google Books.* Web. 16 Nov. 2012.

Bryant, L., and Heather M. Clark, ed. "Writing Autobiography." *Essays on Writing.* New York: Longman, 2009. Print. 29–35.

Davidson, Maria del Guadalupe, and George Yancy, eds. *Critical Perspectives on bell hooks.* New York: Routledge, 2009. Print.

hooks, bell. *Killing Rage: Ending Racism.* New York: Holt, 1995. Print.

hooks, bell, and Cornel West. *Breaking Bread: Insurgent Black Intellectual Life.* Boston: South End, 1991. Print.

Karr, Mary. *The Liars' Club.* New York: Penguin, 1995. Print.

Rebecca Rustin

An Experiment in Autobiography

H. G. Wells

✣ Key Facts

Time Period:
Mid-20th Century

Relevant Historical Events:
Wells rejects convention and rises from the lower middle class

Nationality:
English

Keywords:
social class; education; Victorianism

OVERVIEW

Published in 1934, H. G. Wells's *An Experiment in Autobiography* tells of the author's rise from the lower middle class, his struggles with the restrictions of religion, and the development of his mind through what education he could obtain by means of his social position. Although it garnered critical acclaim, the book was also criticized for being too long, containing inconsistent prose, and lacking a central unifying theme. This last criticism is reflective of Wells's life and literary works in general: he is viewed by many scholars as a productive and interesting author in numerous genres but a true master of none.

Coming at the end of what many critics consider the most successful period in his intellectual career, *An Experiment in Autobiography* provides a background to the author's literary works and addresses many of the same issues as his novels, notably religion and spiritual fulfillment. The author is generally praised for his ability to critically analyze his own life and to portray even behavior considered socially undesirable or immature, such as his desire to fill the void left by his rejection of his mother's religion with the affections of numerous women. The work had a noticeable impact on scholars of Wells's work but was later overshadowed by the more interesting postscript *H. G. Wells in Love* (1984, edited by his son G. P. Wells), which deals directly with H. G.'s many romances and affairs.

HISTORICAL AND LITERARY CONTEXT

An Experiment in Autobiography provides a critical view of the social structures of Victorian society into which Wells was born. Wells examines the restrictions of class and spirituality during his childhood and how he was able to climb the social ladder through education. He begins with a study of his parents and ends with his ideas about an improved utopian state of world organization. Born into the lower middle class, Wells narrowly escaped the fate of his parents, who lived a life of moderate comfort obtained through hard work. He resented his mother's faith in God and believed religion was a tool designed to keep weak minds in their designated place in society. By rejecting Christianity and striving to overcome his social status, Wells proved that in the late nineteenth and early twentieth centuries, a person could improve his or her social standing.

At the time *An Experiment in Autobiography* was published, Wells was known for his voluminous literary output and his role in developing the scientific romance genre. Despite the number of novels and books he published, however, his oeuvre was generally considered to be lacking a masterpiece. His autobiography was, in part, designed to describe the unifying theory behind his writing and perhaps fulfill the role of masterpiece in the context of which all his other works could be studied. In discussing his own life, Wells could openly examine ideas about religion, class, and spiritual fulfillment that he had incorporated into his fictional writing.

Wells's autobiography was influenced by the theoretical discussions of psychoanalyst Carl Jung and by the explorations of spiritual fulfillment he had discussed in his own novels. He was particularly interested in Jung's idea of the persona and how it is not necessarily representative of a person but is rather a projection of how a person would like to be defined. In order to fully and frankly explore his life, Wells looks at his persona critically and intentionally recognizes its flaws as well as its positive qualities, ultimately deciding he is an average person who has led an interesting life.

Although *An Experiment in Autobiography* was recognized by scholars as providing the theoretical background to Wells's novels, it was not until the posthumous publication of his letters to Henry James (1958) and the postscript about his love affairs that critical interest in the work really peaked. Rarely discussed on its own, the book is generally viewed in relation to the more dramatic details of those later texts. In modern scholarship, it continues to be recognized as a backdrop for Wells's vast literary output and for the arresting details of his conflict with James and his numerous affairs.

THEMES AND STYLE

One of the main themes of Wells's lengthy autobiography is his struggle to overcome the restrictions of class in Victorian society: "This brain of mine came into existence and began to acquire reflexes and register impressions in a needy shabby home in a little town called Bromley in Kent," from which Wells began his efforts to do better than his parents and improve his social situation. To that end, he rejected his mother's devout faith, which he believed was designed to keep ignorant minds from questioning the rules of society. For Wells, religion was "a jumble up of miscellany of the old sacrificial and consolatory religions of the confused and unhappy townspeople of the early Empire" that was ultimately "silly" and damaging to the minds of believers. By rejecting religion—"I was born blasphemous and protesting"—Wells began the process of rejecting the restrictive lifestyle passed down by his parents.

Wells's objective is to present a complete picture of himself to his readers in order to bolster his reputation as a writer. He admits that although his work is passionate, it may not be excellent, and critics may only interact with portions of it to suit their needs. Nevertheless, Wells underscores his autobiography's relevance for his own soul searching as well as for that of his audience. "I have made the broad lines and conditions of the human outlook distinct and unmistakable for myself and for others," he writes. His ambition falls somewhat flat, however, as the lengthy and meandering discussion of his life yields no stunning conclusion or deep insight.

Stylistically, the work is filled with trifling details that prolong the narrative and distract the reader from its meaning or unifying purpose. In a 1934 review of the book in the *Times Literary Supplement,* Geoffrey West suggests that Wells's style "makes easy, pleasant reading" but "scarcely attempts to carry that totality of experience whose effective presentation might have made a great work of what one is inclined to call, so far, merely an interesting one." Indeed, in attempting to fill the void left by his rejection of his mother's religion, he fills his text—and his life—with needless frivolity.

CRITICAL DISCUSSION

Although initially met with praise from critics, *An Experiment in Autobiography* was never considered to be an outstanding example of Wells's writing. A 1935 review in the *English Journal* calls it "rich, intense, varied, and human" and compliments Wells's "refreshing frankness" in writing about "the rich life-story and dream of an adventurous thinker." West, meanwhile, says Wells "stopped short of what should really be the primary purpose of the autobiographer—to make real and immediate … the experience he dwells upon." Despite its positive qualities, Wells's autobiography failed to make an impact among contemporary reviewers as a work of literature.

After the publication of *H. G. Wells in Love* and of his correspondence with James, his autobiography became slightly more popular, though only in relation to these later texts. In "Paper Tiger," a 1985 review of Wells's autobiographical writings, Nancy Steffen-Fluhr demonstrates how these posthumous works interact with and enhance *An Experiment in Autobiography* and Wells's vision of himself: "Apparently Wells hoped to achieve posthumously, through the magic of book-binding, the psychic unity which had so eluded him in his life—to suture the story of his body to the story of his brain."

The predominant trends in scholarship on the book examine Wells's relationship with his mother and his inability to accept her unwavering religious devoutness. According to Richard Costa in "H. G. Wells: Life, Career, and Times," Sarah Wells "committed the one unpardonable sin in her son's cosmology: she had a 'set' mind about religion," which left H. G. feeling that if "he could not adhere to the furious deity to whom he was compelled to pray as a child, he sensed his need for something to fill the void, a God substitute." Penelope Quade, writing about Wells in *Extrapolation,* agrees: "Wells was not shy about sharing his opinions of religion and its effects on human behaviour and the tendencies of people to blindly adhere to their beliefs…. Wells perceives religion and the faith to which people cling to be a security blanket for the naïve."

"H. G. Wells Foreseeing Things," a cartoon portrait of the author by Max Beerbohm, published in *The Spectator* in February 1931. © THE PRINT COLLECTOR/ALAMY

H.G. WELLS IN LOVE: POSTSCRIPT TO *AN EXPERIMENT IN AUTOBIOGRAPHY*

In addition to *An Experiment in Autobiography*, H. G. Wells wrote a postscript, *H. G. Wells in Love: Postscript to* An Experiment in Autobiography, detailing his romances. He wished to have it added to the autobiography after his death (which occurred in 1946), and his son, G. P. Wells, published it as a separate book in 1984. The postscript enhanced the popularity of the autobiography.

In *H. G. Wells in Love,* Wells describes all the important women in his life and his relationships with them, including his wives—his cousin Isabel and later Amy Catherine Robbins, whom he called "Jane"—and his many mistresses, such as the British feminist Amber Reeves and the Russian noblewoman (and Maxim Gorky's common law wife) Moura Budberg. These and other women helped Wells develop his idea of the "lover-shadow," which he defines as the "subtle complex of expectation and hope" that all humans possess and which they seek to fulfill by taking on a lover. Whereas *An Experiment in Autobiography* deals with the development of Wells's *persona*, the postscript focuses on that of his lover-shadow.

BIBLIOGRAPHY

Sources

Costa, Richard Hauer. "Chapter 1: H. G. Wells: Life, Career, and Times." *H. G. Wells*. Boston: Twayne, 1985. *Twayne Authors Series*. Web. 25 Oct. 2012.

"In Brief Review." *English Journal* 24.1 (1935): 82–89. *JSTOR*. Web. 26 Oct. 2012.

Quade, Penelope. "Taming the Beast in the Name of the Father: *The Island of Dr. Moreau* and Wells's Critique of Society's Religious Molding." *Extrapolation* 48.2 (2007): 292–301. Rpt. in *Children's Literature Review*. Ed. Tom Burns. Vol. 133. Detroit: Gale, 2008. *Literature Resource Center*. Web. 25 Oct. 2012.

Steffen-Fluhr, Nancy. "Paper Tiger: Women and H. G. Wells." *Science Fiction Studies* 12.3 (1985): 311–29. *JSTOR*. Web. 25 Oct. 2012.

Wells, H. G. *An Experiment in Autobiography*. 2 vols. London: Victor Gollancz and Cresset, 1934. Print.

West, Geoffrey. "Mr. Wells's Autobiography." *Times Literary Supplement* 11 Oct. 1934: 685. *Times Literary Supplement Historical Archive*. Web. 26 Oct. 2012.

Further Reading

Atlas, James. "Experiment in Autobiography." *Atlantic* (Nov. 1984): 138+. *Literature Resource Center*. Web. 25 Oct. 2012.

Edel, Leon, and Gordon N. Ray, eds. *Henry James and H. G. Wells: A Record of Their Friendship, Their Debate on the Art of Fiction, and Their Quarrel*. Urbana: University of Illinois Press, 1958. Print.

"Herbert George Wells." *Encyclopedia of World Biography*. Detroit: Gale, 1998. *Gale Biography in Context*. Web. 28 Oct. 2012.

Huntington, John. *Critical Essays on H. G. Wells*. Boston: G. K. Hall, 1991. Print.

Scheick, William, J., ed. *The Critical Response to H. G. Wells*. Westport, Conn.: Greenwood, 1995. Print.

Wells, H. G. *H. G. Wells in Love: Postscript to* An Experiment in Autobiography. Ed. G. P. Wells. London: Faber and Faber, 1984. Print.

Katherine Barker

In the Presence of Absence
Mahmoud Darwish

OVERVIEW

In the Presence of Absence (2006; translated into English in 2011 by Sinan Antoon) is a prose elegy written by and for its author, Palestinian writer Mahmoud Darwish. The antithesis presented in the title is characteristic of the work's dominant motif of paradox: Darwish's meditation on death seems to suggest that it unifies or even overturns opposites. Similarly, a living poet can compose his own elegy—in a form neither strictly prose nor strictly verse—for audiences to consider before and after his or her death. The haunting presence of death—the great absence—in the work evokes Darwish's decades-long struggle with life-threatening heart problems, as well as his public life as a Palestinian poet born in 1941 who witnessed much of the upheaval in the region.

Although Darwish has been proclaimed to be, in American writer Joshua Cohen's words, "perhaps the foremost Palestinian poet of the last century," and his life was massively shaped by the political and military conflicts in the region, the context of *In the Presence of Absence* is arguably more personal than political, solidifying the autobiographical status of the work. In 1984 Darwish was diagnosed with a heart condition for which he underwent multiple surgeries (one necessitating resuscitation by electric shock) throughout the 1980s and 1990s. These experiences motivated his publication of this self-elegy two years before his death in Houston, Texas, in 2008 after another surgery. Already an acclaimed poet, Darwish published *In the Presence of Absence* to welcoming critics, although its long-term reception remains to be seen.

HISTORICAL AND LITERARY CONTEXT

Darwish's health problems were preceded by a life of transience. In 1948 he and his family fled from Palestine to Lebanon during the fighting that created the state of Israel. Although they returned to their homeland for a period, they were too late to be counted in the census and were denied citizenship, officially becoming "present absentee[s]." Throughout his life Darwish also lived in Russia, Egypt, Cyprus, Tunisia, and France. In Israel during the 1960s, he was repeatedly imprisoned or put under house arrest. Israel's government finally allowed him to settle in Ramallah in the West Bank in 1996, calling attention to the long historical "presence of his absence." Exile, tumult, and violence color *In the Presence of Absence* even as the work centralizes the personal catastrophe of Darwish's heart condition. As Antoon has noted, Darwish's "existence [is] intertwined with that of his exiled people." Insofar as "language is the only homeland," as Polish American author Czeslaw Milosz famously proclaimed, Darwish has become symbolic of his race, creating by his language a geography of exile.

In the Presence of Absence's publication was a heralded event in the Arab world. Darwish was living a contemplative life in Amman, Jordan, in a private apartment when he wrote his autobiography. Accordingly, the text is marked by what Professor Tetz Rooke describes in his 2008 article in the *Journal of Arabic and Islamic Studies* as embedded "dramatic episodes, such as that of the author's heart-failure, or … decisive moments in his life, like the flight from the home village in 1948; the expulsion of the PLO from Beirut in 1982; or the emotional return to Palestine after the peace agreement in 1993." In meditating on the abstraction of death, Darwish contemplates the particularities of his own life, composing an elegy that is also autobiography.

Self-elegy is a well-established form in Arabic literature, dating to pre-Islamic times. The Umayyad poet Malik ibn al-Rayb, who flourished in the seventh century, eulogized himself quite powerfully, and his work clearly influenced *In the Presence of Absence*. Darwish also includes intertextual references ranging from the Koran to Greek mythology to his own previous works. While his hybrid prose-poem form is indicative of his style and can be found in some of his other writings, including his earlier memoirs *Journal of an Ordinary Grief* (1973) and *Memory for Forgetfulness* (1987), Darwish also borrows from classical Arabic models, indicating both his "belonging and allegiance to the Arabic tradition" and its modernization in his hands.

In the Presence of Absence was well received in Arabic and has already inspired critical analyses in translation. Rooke, for example, argues that Darwish's 2008 death has increased the salience and power of his text. In his critical analysis titled "Martyrologies" (2011), Cohen ironically connects the poetics behind *In the Presence of Absence* to those of Abraham Sutzkever, a Yiddish poet, to make the larger point that "when you oppress a people, when you beat and rape and kill them, the literature they write will inevitably

✧ **Key Facts**

Time Period:
Early 21st Century

Relevant Historical Events:
Israeli-Palestinian conflict; Darwish's exile

Nationality:
Palestinian

Keywords:
death; poetry; exile

Palestinian poet Mahmoud Darwish. © REUVEN KOPICHINSKY/ASSOCIATED PRESS

resemble the literatures of other people who've been beaten, raped, and murdered." Cohen's use of Darwish as a representative Palestinian text speaks to his status as a national poet and to the prominence of *In the Presence of Absence*.

THEMES AND STYLE

A central theme of *In the Presence of Absence* is death, a farewell to Darwish's younger self (or selves, as the "you" of the text ages throughout). The work opens with a funeral scene, the corpse of which might be taken as the poet's younger self, or—as Rooke argues— as the poet's public persona, with the mourner as his private self. Either way, the I/you duality, "one in two and two in one," is present throughout the work. The fact that the speaker "is both the watching spectator and the watched protagonist in a seeming paradox" is, for Rooke, "the central narrative ploy of the work." The funeral scene likewise gets referenced throughout the text, with the last chapter beginning with the same words as the first, suggesting a cycle of eternal return that is in keeping with the work's paradoxical alignments and simultaneities.

Although *In the Presence of Absence* grapples intensely with Darwish's personal mortality, the text has also been construed by some critics as a political message or as a critique of the ways in which fame can make people unfamiliar to themselves. In addition, the work presents a meta-commentary on the power of poetry to heal wounds and unify opposites, the transcendence of word over world: poetry is both a means of political protest and a mode of personal expression and redemption. In focusing on language, Darwish experiments with it, stretching form beyond the limits of convention. Though his content is typical of autobiography, Darwish writes in neither prose nor poetry, in paragraphs rife with internal rhyme and alliteration, with verse fragments irregularly interspersed.

The most striking element of Darwish's style is his rampant use of juxtaposition, of "contradictions, dualities, and oppositions," according to Daniel Garrett in a 2012 review published in *Review of Contemporary Fiction*. Academic Manu Chander states in his 2012 article in *Literary Review* that "these pieces don't just capture the paradox of absence presence.... Rather, they reflect upon this paradox, continually confronting what it means to face what's not there." Perhaps being born so near the birth of the duality of Israeli-Palestinian relations, Darwish could not help but write in dualities. Even as he reveals their existence, however, he juxtaposes to suggest the subversion of binaries, forcing us to recognize the speciousness of opposites that can actually exist simultaneously. Another significant stylistic element, noted in particular by Rooke, is repetition, both thematic—as in Darwish's multiple returns to the funeral scene—and linguistic—as in his final chapter, constructed of a list of aphorisms in which the last word of each is picked up as the subject of the next.

CRITICAL DISCUSSION

Darwish's work was met with positive reviews. Antoon labored during the translation of the work to preserve elements such as rhyme, and he was nominated for the 2012 PEN translation prize for his efforts. Chander notes that "there is, to be sure, a kind of labor in following Darwish's journey.... The pieces here are rarely stirring, their images rarely startling." This concession is one of the few negative comments in reviews of the English translation. Yet Chander goes on to say that "even more rare is the casual phrase, the banal observation, or the ignorable moment," testifying to the power and poignancy of the text in an overall positive review characteristic of the work's reception.

The long-term resonance of *In the Presence of Absence* is difficult to predict; nevertheless, given Darwish's position as the national poet of Palestine, the text seems likely to have lasting political impact in spite of its personal themes. Even if the initial funeral scene of his work is meant to bid farewell to his "official," public self, this corpse remains more palpable in international memory than the private self Darwish preserves; in many contexts, because of his nationality as well as his life story, Darwish has become a political symbol, a legacy that will not be so easily eulogized.

The autobiographical tenor of *In the Presence of Absence* has been widely noted. As Chander mentions, Darwish "shows us a life of uncertainty and exile." Similarly, Garrett claims that "no ordinary language could match his experience of childhood exile, troublesome return, and prison, as well as friendship, love, and sensuality." Nevertheless, it is with faith in the strength of poetry that Darwish proceeds through his elegy. Rooke argues that "to deny the importance of the biographical dimension of Darwish's writing on the theme of his own death would ... be as rash as ignoring the political events of the Palestinian-Israeli conflict when reading his resistance poetry." *In the Presence of Absence* once again seems to unify apparently opposing forces: the politics of exile and the psychological processing of one's past.

BIBLIOGRAPHY

Sources

Chander, Manu Samriti. Rev. of *In the Presence of Absence*, by Mahmoud Darwish. *Literary Review* 55.2 (2012): 215–16. *Academic Search Premier*. Web. 15 Nov. 2012.

Cohen, Joshua. "Martyrologies." *Tablet Magazine* 17 Nov. 2011: n. pag. *General OneFile*. Web. 15 Nov. 2012.

Darwish, Mahmoud. *In the Presence of Absence*. Trans. Sinan Antoon. Brooklyn: Archipelago, 2011. Print.

LIFE, DEATH, AND COFFEE

Darwish was a coffee fanatic, although for him coffee and the ritual that accompanies it represents normalcy. In *Memory for Forgetfulness*, he describes living in Beirut during the Israeli invasion of Lebanon in 1982. His kitchen was open to sniper fire, and he describes, on the most violent day of the conflict, calculating whether he could make it into the kitchen to make coffee without being hit: "I measure the period between two shells. One second.... One second is not long enough to open the water bottle or pour the water into the coffee pot." He wishes for "a five-minute truce for the sake of coffee."

Over the course of these meditations, the drink comes to symbolize more than Darwish's "one and only goal"; it becomes defiance against the Israeli army: "Conquerors can do anything ... but they cannot root the aroma of coffee out of me. I shall make my coffee now. I will drink the coffee now ... that I may at least distinguish myself from a sheep and live one more day, or die, with the aroma of coffee all around me." Coffee, he continues, is "a journey," "a place," "geography." For this displaced poet, this "present absentee," coffee was just the kind of homeland he needed. It was a homeland he could carry with him.

Garrett, Daniel. Rev. of *In the Presence of Absence*, by Mahmoud Darwish. *Review of Contemporary Fiction* 32.1 (2012): 287–88. *Academic Search Premier*. Web. 15 Nov. 2012.

Rooke, Tetz. "*In the Presence of Absence*: Mahmoud Darwish's Testament." *Journal of Arabic and Islamic Studies* 8 (2008): 11–25. *Academic Search Premier*. Web. 15 Nov. 2012.

Further Reading

Cobham, Catherine. "From the Journals of Mahmoud Darwish 1941–2008." *GRANTA* Summer 2009: 108–10. *Academic Search Premier*. Web. 15 Nov. 2012.

Isaksen, Runo. *Literature and War: Conversations with Israeli and Palestinian Writers*. Trans. Kari Dickson. Northampton, Mass.: Olive Branch, 2009. Print.

Khader, Hassan. "Mahmoud Darwish: A Profile." *Palestine-Israel Journal of Politics, Economics & Culture* 15.3 (2008): 110–13. *Academic Search Premier*. Web. 15 Nov. 2012.

Nassar, Hala Khamis. *Mahmoud Darwish: Exile's Poet: Critical Essays*. Northampton, Mass.: Olive Branch, 2008. Print.

Siddiq, Muhammad. "Significant but Problematic Others: Negotiating 'Israelis' in the Works of Mahmoud Darwish." *Comparative Literature Studies* 47.4 (2010): 487–503. *Academic Search Premier*. Web. 15 Nov. 2012.

Wlizlo, Will. "To Thine Own Self." Rev. of *In the Presence of Absence*, by Mahmoud Darwish. *UTNE* Mar.–Apr. 2012: 85. *Academic Search Premier*. Web. 15 Nov. 2012.

Laura Johnson

Memories of a Catholic Girlhood

Mary McCarthy

Key Facts

Time Period:
Mid-20th Century

Relevant Historical Events:
Influenza pandemic of 1918; McCarthy being orphaned

Nationality:
American

Keywords:
orphanhood; Catholicism; pandemic

OVERVIEW

Mary McCarthy's *Memories of a Catholic Girlhood* (1957) is an account of the American author and critic's childhood in Minneapolis and Seattle. At times assuming the voice of her younger alter ego, McCarthy describes her moral and intellectual development, sketching her early life and providing commentary on the accuracy of her memories and the process of recreating them without giving in to the "temptation to invent." Known for incorporating thinly veiled autobiographic elements into her fiction, McCarthy attempts, in her autobiography, to sketch an honest self-portrait.

When McCarthy's book was published, she was a well-established essayist and critic who first made a name for herself with the New York Intellectuals, a group centered on the political and literary journal *Partisan Review.* Also a well-regarded novelist and short story writer whose friends and associates were fodder for her fiction, McCarthy's own story was greeted with interest and received favorable critical reviews. Widely considered to be McCarthy's best work, *Memories of a Catholic Girlhood* is notable not only for the light it casts on her creative preoccupations but also as a commentary on autobiography as a mode of expression distinct from but overlapping with fiction.

HISTORICAL AND LITERARY CONTEXT

The defining event in *Memories of a Catholic Girlhood* is the death of McCarthy's parents in the influenza pandemic of 1918. The pandemic, in which an estimated 675,000 people in the United States died, was, unlike other flu strains, especially deadly for adults in their prime, possibly due to a damaging overreaction of the mature immune system. McCarthy's parents died within a few days of each other, orphaning the six-year-old and her three younger siblings. Like many other flu orphans, the children were shunted between relatives, living first together with an abusive great uncle in Minneapolis and later separated, with McCarthy shipped off to her maternal grandparents in Seattle and her brothers remaining with various family members in the Midwest.

McCarthy published several stories based on her childhood experiences in periodicals such as the *New Yorker* and in a short story collection *Cast a Cold Eye* (1950), revised versions of which would appear as chapters in *Memories of a Catholic Girlhood.* Reviews of McCarthy's prior work frequently speculated about autobiographical elements in her fiction, and her repurposing of work that was formerly presented as fiction in the autobiography seemed to confirm such suppositions.

Though her essays were associated with and influenced by a number of literary traditions, most prominently that of the New York Intellectuals, McCarthy was singular in her approach to autobiography and her explicit discussion of the fictionalized elements of her text. In *Playing It Smart: New York Women Writers and Modern Magazine Culture* (2010), critic Katherine Keyser situates McCarthy among other young female writers, including Edna St. Vincent Millay and Dorothy Parker, who published in periodicals such as the *New Yorker* during the early part of their careers. These authors were also known for using satire and humor to undermine the fantasies of smart, urban career women that their work (and indeed existence as professional female writers in New York City) created for female readers. McCarthy, while disavowing feminism throughout her lifetime, was keen to expose the reality behind appearances. In this light, her contextualization of previously published chapters in her autobiography makes an interesting counterpoint to their initial appearance as stories or sketches in popular periodicals.

Memories of a Catholic Girlhood brought McCarthy her first real taste of critical and popular success, establishing her reputation as one of the preeminent American writers of the period. Often regarded as her best work, the book was followed in 1963 by the blockbuster novel *The Group,* which follows a set of friends from Vassar as they move into adulthood. Like her previous fiction, *The Group* was notable for containing elements of McCarthy's own life, including descriptions of marital disharmony resembling that of her first marriage to playwright Harold Johnsrud. McCarthy published several other novels, as well as numerous works of nonfiction, including literary criticism; political writing; and two additional works of autobiography, *How I Grew* (1987), which focuses on her teenage years and time at Vassar, and *Intellectual Memoirs: New York 1936–38,* detailing her postcollege life and early career writing for the *Nation* and the *New Republic.*

THEMES AND STYLE

McCarthy's autobiography examines the project of defining a personal history in the face of the knowledge that complete truth about one's life is in a sense unknowable. Throughout the text she relates incidents that illuminate her development, most importantly her orphanhood, which, she writes, has broken "the chain of recollection," leaving no one to verify or correct her earliest memories of herself and family life. Moreover, being an orphan created for her and for her brother, the actor Kevin McCarthy, "a burning interest in our past," a tendency that was reinforced by her Catholic education and its emphasis on history. While McCarthy acknowledges that she has sometimes forgotten and sometimes fictionalized elements of her story, she also emphasizes the care she has taken to get the basic truth of it right. Indeed, the inability to face the truth is, for McCarthy, a major source of pain in human life. Her paternal grandparents, for example, refused to see signs of the abuse and neglect of their grandchildren, writing a check every month for support but ignoring "our raw hands and scarecrow arms, our silence and our elderly faces."

Memories of a Catholic Girlhood is an attempt to reconstruct and retell the story of McCarthy's childhood, likely to satisfy the author's emotional and aesthetic needs. In her introduction to the work, she characterizes the approach that she and Kevin take to the past as being "like two amateur archeologists, falling on any new scrap of evidence, trying to fit it in, questioning our relations, belaboring our own memories." McCarthy frankly admits that being orphaned young has created the need to turn over and shape pieces of their family history. Without this shaping, they are left with formless "scraps." Writing about the benefits of a Catholic education, McCarthy suggests another motivation for her writing—that Catholicism had instilled in her "a conception of something prior to and beyond utility" and that, as a child, the church was her "only aesthetic outlet." As an adult, writing replaced prayer and communion as a means to find and make beauty.

The text is divided into chapters, most of which are followed by a brief commentary on the events McCarthy describes, pointing out inaccuracies or deliberate changes McCarthy has made for aesthetic reasons. Following "The Blackguard," for instance, which discusses the author's early fears for her Protestant grandfather's soul, she comments, "[T]he story is true in substance, but the details have been invented or guessed at." McCarthy introduces the final chapter, "Ask Me No Questions," in the commentary for the preceding story, "Yellowstone Park." Here she describes her rationale for saving discussion of her Grandmother Preston, a significant figure in her life, for the last chapter. Typifying McCarthy's overall approach to her autobiography, she introduces both a practical and an aesthetic reason for this arrangement. Her intensely private grandmother would have hated to be included in any memoir, so McCarthy refrained from writing about her until after her death. In addition, describing her grandmother—who, in her silence, secrets, and disconnection from her own Jewish roots, provides a foil for McCarthy's own frankness—is an aesthetic choice, maintaining tension through the text and adding punch as the book draws to a close.

Author Mary McCarthy in 1987. Her *Memories of a Catholic Girlhood* includes stories she wrote about her youth. © JULIO DONOSO/SYGMA/CORBIS

CRITICAL DISCUSSION

Memories of a Catholic Girlhood was published to largely favorable reviews. Charles Poore's critique in the *New York Times* was typical, praising McCarthy's "fine book" and calling the first chapter "one of the most stinging, brilliant and disturbing memoirs ever written by an American." Less favorable reviews tended to focus on the author's lack of warmth in her portrayal of other human beings and the sense that, while candid, McCarthy still holds readers at arm's length.

In the years since the book was published, the public's taste for memoir has increased, although more recent examples of the genre tend to blur the line between fiction and nonfiction that McCarthy's clarifications tried to keep in focus. Writing in the *New York Times*, memoirist Mary Karr recalls McCarthy's commitment to telling the truth and then laments that "in the decades since, objective truth (a phrase it's hard not to put quotes around) has lost power; subjective experience has gained authority. For many in my generation, Michael Herr's hallucinatory Vietnam memoir, *Dispatches*, has become a truer record of the war than the 'official' reports." For her part, Karr

THEORIES

MARY McCARTHY AND LILLIAN HELLMAN

Mary McCarthy was known for speaking her mind and at times alienating others, but her feud with fellow writer Lillian Hellman was unmatched either in intensity or in duration. Hellman, a commercially successful writer most known for her contributions to the stage and screen, ran in literary circles that overlapped with McCarthy's, and the two women at some point developed a mutual antipathy. Commentators have advanced various speculations as to its source, including a dispute over McCarthy's lover Philip Rahv, jealousy over career accomplishments—Hellman was more commercially successful while McCarthy was considered more literary—and even political differences dating back to the 1930s.

What is certain is that things came to a head when McCarthy, during a 1979 interview with Dick Cavett broadcast by PBS, declared that Hellman and her memoirs were overrated and that "every word she writes is a lie, including 'and' and 'the.'" Hellman, who had faced a number of accusations of fabrication in her memoirs, was furious and filed a $2.5 million lawsuit against McCarthy. The suit dragged on for five years, ending only with Hellman's death in 1984.

"want[s] to stay hamstrung by objective truth." Other critics also have focused on this aspect of McCarthy's work, with the majority of interest in the text focusing on her conception of autobiographic truth.

Scholars have approached this conception as it reveals McCarthy as an individual and reveals the sociological character of the United States during the mid-twentieth century. Barbara McKenzie, in her piece in *Mary McCarthy* (1966), traces the author's devotion to honesty, remarking that "Miss McCarthy in real life has had to struggle to be as truthful as she would like, a struggle heightened by a recognition of expediency and the accompanying subjugation of the 'whole' truth. These contradictory awarenesses help to explain both her preoccupation with honesty—in herself and in others—and her intense admiration of honesty where she finds it." Writing for *Criticism* in 2007, critic Michael Trask emphasizes the contemporary concept of authenticity rather than truth, asserting that McCarthy's interest in providing an authentic account of her life and family is a reaction against mass media and nascent consumer culture. For Trask, *Memories of a Catholic Girlhood* provides insight into "that transitional period whereby the conformist Cold War fifties gave way to the New Social Movements of the sixties." In this view, McCarthy's desire to be "authentic" exemplifies the notion, according to Trask, that "a pivotal and transformative feature of that era … was the advent of a dual rhetoric of intimacy and authenticity intended to guard against a means-oriented social world in which instrumentalism had become the social dominant at the expense of communal stability or individual integrity."

BIBLIOGRAPHY

Sources

Karr, Mary. "His So-Called Life." *New York Times*. New York Times, 15 Jan. 2006. Web. 12 Nov. 2012.

McCarthy, Mary. *Memories of a Catholic Girlhood*. New York: Harcourt Brace Jovanovich, 1957. Print.

McKenzie, Barbara. "Chapter 2: Childhood and the Distance of Time." *Mary McCarthy*. New York: Twayne, 1966. Print.

Poore, Charles. Rev. *Memories of a Catholic Girlhood*, by Mary McCarthy. "Books of the Times." *New York Times*. New York Times, 18 May 1957. Web. 12 Nov. 2012.

Trask, Michael. "In the Bathroom with Mary McCarthy: Theatricality, Deviance, and the Postwar Commitment to Realism." *Criticism* 49.1 (2007): 7+. *Literature Resource Center*. Web. 11 Nov. 2012.

Further Reading

Adams, Timothy Dow. *Telling Lies in American Autobiography*. Chapel Hill: University of North Carolina Press, 1990. Print.

Bloom, Alexander. *Prodigal Sons: The New York Intellectuals & Their World*. Oxford: Oxford University Press, 1986. Print.

Brightman, Carol. *Writing Dangerously: Mary McCarthy and Her World*. New York: C. Potter, 1992. Print.

Epstein, Joseph. "Mary McCarthy in Retrospect." *Commentary* 95.5 (1993): 41–47. Rpt. in *Contemporary Literary Criticism Select*. Detroit: Gale, 2008. *Literature Resource Center*. Web.

Gilmore, Leigh. "Policing Truth: Confession, Gender, and Autobiographical Authority." *Autobiography & Postmodernism*. Ed. Kathleen Ashley. Amherst: University of Massachusetts Press, 1994. 54–78. Rpt. in *Twentieth-Century Literary Criticism*. Vol. 222. Detroit: Gale, 2010. *Literature Resource Center*. Web. 11 Nov. 2012.

Keyser, Katherine. *Playing It Smart: New York Women Writers and Modern Magazine Culture*. New Brunswick, N.J.: Rutgers University Press, 2010. Print.

McCarthy, Mary. *How I Grew*. New York: Harcourt Brace Jovanovich, 1987. Print.

———. *Intellectual Memoirs: New York 1936–38*. New York: Harcourt Brace Jovanovich, 1992. Print.

Daisy Gard

"My Furthest-Back Person—'The African'"
Alex Haley

OVERVIEW

First published in the *New York Times* in 1972, the essay "My Furthest-Back Person—'The African'" is a recounting of Alex Haley's quest to trace branches of his family back to "the African" of his Grandma Palmer's stories. Slave traders, as the stories go, fell upon Kin-tay while he was out looking for wood to build a drum. Brought to "'Naplis" (Annapolis, Maryland) and sold to the Waller family of Virginia, "the African" holds an almost mythic significance as the "furthest-back" person in family history. As a self-taught writer who during his tenure in the Coast Guard had the title of Chief Journalist created solely for him, Haley valued his skill with the written word as a source of pride and identity. His research, which began in the decade following his retirement from the Coast Guard, offered him an opportunity to reconnect with his family after years of active duty. It also created the impetus for him to travel to Africa, a place to which he had long felt connected through family stories.

A need to shore up family relationships and to build a personal and cultural identity was evident in Americans of all colors following the turbulence of the 1960s. It was especially pointed for African Americans as they attempted to redefine themselves and their community in the years following the civil rights movement. Although Haley's essay was little noticed by critics, the novel that grew from its seeds, *Roots: The Saga of an American Family*, would become a blockbuster, making Haley the world's best-selling black writer and galvanizing a generation of Americans to explore the meaning of their own origins.

HISTORICAL AND LITERARY CONTEXT

For slaves in antebellum America, the separation of families was a reality of life. The agricultural boom between the American Revolution and the Civil War increased the internal demand for slaves. As a result, large numbers of slaves were transported to other states, a forced migration that separated kin groups and members of nuclear families. While some owners encouraged slave marriages, these were not legally binding, and it was not uncommon for partners to be separated through sale at the slave owner's whim. Men were most typically sold from family units, with many slave children growing up without knowing one or both parents. After the Civil War ended in 1865, some slaves sought family members through the Freedmen's Bureau or by advertising in periodicals. While some families were reunited during Reconstruction, many freed slaves remained cut off from living relatives and from their family history.

By 1972, when Haley's essay was published, the successes of the American civil rights movement in the 1950s and 1960s and the ongoing efforts of Black Power activists had helped legitimize the quest for an African American identity that acknowledged but was not defined by the past. "My Furthest-Back Person" raises the possibility of tracing and reclaiming individual family histories, despite the fragmenting force of slavery. In it, Haley recounts walking past the National Archives in Washington, D.C., on a Saturday morning in 1965 and being seized by an impulse to investigate his family tree. Excited by census details that confirmed the existence of people he knew through stories recounted on his grandmother's porch, Haley would undertake a research project tracing multiple generations of his family back to Kunta Kinte, the Kin-tay of his grandmother's stories, a slave who had been captured in Gambia and shipped to the United States on the *Lord Ligonier* in 1767.

Haley's essay displays some of the same preoccupations with black roots and the quest for a family identity evidenced in another fictionalized autobiography, James Baldwin's novel *Go Tell It on the Mountain* (1953). Baldwin's book follows the life of John Grimes, an African American boy growing up fatherless in Depression-era Harlem. John has a conversion experience and becomes heavily involved in a Pentecostal-style church. Baldwin also develops the story of several generations of John's family, who, through their migration from the south to the north after the Civil War, have become disconnected from the church and from the African traditions they had incorporated into their slave-quarter worship. Much like Haley's tracing of his family roots back to Africa, Baldwin's experiences as a young Pentecostal preacher became a means of linking himself to his family and his cultural past, and of forging a new identity in the process.

The most significant outgrowth of Haley's essay was his development of the concept into the best-selling novel *Roots*. A fictionalized version of Haley's search for information about his family's African origins, *Roots* garnered the National Book Award as well as a special Pulitzer Prize in 1976. The novel also stirred up a considerable amount of bad press for Haley, with two authors

Key Facts

Time Period:
Late 20th Century

Relevant Historical Events:
slavery (abolished 1865), American civil rights movement (1955–1968), Black Power movement (1960s and 1970s)

Nationality:
American

Keywords:
genealogy; slavery; family; Africa

Author Alex Haley in 1977. © BETTMANN/CORBIS

bringing copyright infringement suits; Harold Courlander, who claimed Haley copied extensively from his novel *The African*, and Margaret Walker Alexander, who accused him of copying from her book *Jubilee*. Haley settled the former case, blaming assistants for the contested passages, while the latter case was dismissed. Beyond these legal troubles, a number of critics also questioned the veracity of Haley's reported African lineage, along with historical details Haley describes in the novel.

THEMES AND STYLE

Central to "My Furthest-Back Person" is the notion that the oral history passed down on front porches and in living rooms forms the cornerstone of black genealogy and the cement between generations. Haley's essay recounts his boyhood experiences of sitting on his grandmother's porch in Henning, Tennessee, listening to "the story that had been passed down for generations." The story, often repeated and, as Haley grew into adulthood, often recalled, "diverted me up the Archives' steps," launching him on the quest to find his roots. Haley describes his excitement at finding the first recorded corroboration of his family stories and his desire to share it with the only surviving member of his grandmother's generation. This excitement, he says, echoes the delight he experienced as a boy when the adults would mention a long-dead family member who, in the story, "wasn't as big as *this* young 'un."

Having spent years researching his genealogy and traveling to Africa, purportedly finding in 1967 the village in Gambia from which Kunta Kinte was captured, Haley felt compelled to write about it, both as a personal act of claiming his identity and as an experience that would resonate with the many Americans descended from slaves. "Back home," he writes, "I knew that what I must write, really, was our black saga, where any individual's past is the essence of the millions'." Discussing his joyful reception by blood relatives in his country of origin, Haley describes breaking down in tears, a catharsis he wants to provide for others who knew "how we came in the seeds of our forefathers, captured, driven, beaten, inspected, bought, branded, chained in foul ships," because, "if you really knew, you needed weeping."

"My Furthest-Back Person" is structured and styled to emphasize the poignancy of homecoming. To that end, the dual stories of Haley's grandmother's porch and the village full of jubilant Africans wrap around the tale of Haley's search like an embrace. His boyhood memories are related in homey language: the storytelling on his grandmother's porch, he says, started "after the supper dishes had been washed" and, for the children, ended with "the whistling blur of lights of the Southbound Panama Limited train whooshing through Henning at 9:05 P.M." The stories themselves emphasize family by relating small but universal moments of bonding, as, for example, when Kin-tay walked his daughter Kizzy (Haley's great-great-great grandmother) around the plantation and "showed her different kinds of things, telling her what they were in his native tongue."

CRITICAL DISCUSSION

"My Furthest-Back Person" was published to little fanfare, with biographical and critical treatments of Haley and his work skipping from *The Autobiography of Malcolm X* (1965) to *Roots* (1976), both of which generated large bodies of criticism upon publication.

While "My Furthest-Back Person" garnered little attention in its own right, the impact of Haley's eleven-year project, which culminated in the publication of *Roots*, was significant. Interest in genealogy and its potential for individual and cultural self-discovery skyrocketed after *Roots*. Americans, both black and white, made attempts to fill in their family trees by poring over official records and interviewing family members. Moreover, the novel and its portrayal of the lives of slaves, particularly slavery's harrowing impact on nuclear families, sparked renewed discussion about race and justice in the United States. Still, some critics bely the notion that the popularity of *Roots* among a white audience reflected any real significant change in the way white America in the 1970s viewed African Americans. Writing in 1986, Michael Blayney suggested that the novel's "sentimental treatment of the family shifted attention away from political concerns toward heroic feats of individual characters." Further, "because the noble African, like the noble Indian before him, was extinct, white viewers felt free to sympathize and even identify with a set of non-white heroes." While *Roots* continues to be taught as a foundational text in some black studies programs and other college courses, it has not generated significant new scholarship in recent years.

The debate about Haley's fictionalization of the search for his tribal roots has died down as well, the general consensus echoing Deidre Carmody's reporting in the *New York Times* of the position held by many historians: "regardless of error, the historical essence of the work was truthful." Haley, who referred to his novel as "faction"—a fictionalized version of historical fact, likely agreed. In her overview of *Roots*, Jane Elizabeth Dougherty quotes Haley's contention that he was "just trying to give his people a myth to live by." Reflecting on this possibility, she concludes that "if one definition of myth is 'a useable version of the past,' Haley's saga certainly succeeds in overturning other myths about the Black American experience and giving African Americans a proud history."

BIBLIOGRAPHY

Sources

Blayney, Michael Steward. "*Roots* and the Noble Savage." *North Dakota Quarterly* 54.1 (1986): 1–17. Rpt. in *Twentieth-Century Literary Criticism*. Ed. Linda Pavlovski. Vol. 147. Detroit: Gale, 2004. *Literature Resource Center*. Web. 11 Oct. 2012.

Carmody, Deidre. "Haley Gets Special Pulitzer Prize." *New York Times*. New York Times, 11 Apr. 1977. Web. 11 Oct. 2012.

Dougherty, Jane Elizabeth. "Overview of 'Roots: The Saga of an American Family'." *Literature Resource Center*. Detroit: Gale, 2012. *Literature Resource Center*. Web. 11 Oct. 2012.

Gates, Henry Louis, Jr. *In Search of Our Roots*. New York: Crown, 2009. Print.

Haley, Alex. "My Furthest Back Person—The African." *New York Times*. New York Times, 16 July 1972. Web. 11 Oct. 2012.

Further Reading

Ball, Edward. *Slaves in the Family*. New York: Farrar, 1998. Print.

Gates, Henry Louis, Jr. *In Search of Our Roots: How 19 Extraordinary African Americans Reclaimed Their Past*. New York: Crown, 2009. Print.

Gerber, David A. "Haley's *Roots* and Our Own: An Inquiry into the Nature of a Popular Phenomenon." *Journal of Ethnic Studies* 5.3 (1977): 87–111. Rpt. in *Twentieth-Century Literary Criticism*. Ed. Linda Pavlovski. Vol. 147. Detroit: Gale, 2004. *Literature Resource Center*. Web. 11 Oct. 2012.

VOYAGES: THE TRANS-ATLANTIC SLAVE TRADE DATABASE

"My Furthest-Back Person" highlights some of the barriers to genealogical research that face descendants of slaves. Spearheaded by David Eltis, the Robert W. Woodruff Professor of History at Emory University, a massive international scholarly effort to help increase access to records of the slave trade was launched in 1990. The result was the open-access web resource *Voyages: The Trans-Atlantic Slave Trade Database*. The project, which is sponsored by Emory, Harvard's W. E. B. Du Bois Institute, and the National Endowment for the Humanities, seeks to help families, students, and researchers understand the history, scope, and global impacts of the slave trade. In his 2009 book *In Search of Our Roots*, Henry Louis Gates Jr. describes the database as "one of the most valuable and impressive historical research tools ever created."

Constructed from the logs of shipping companies, the database holds records from nearly 35,000 slave voyages made between 1514 and 1866. Project researchers estimate that this is roughly two-thirds of the total number made during that period. The database traces passages between Africa and Europe, North America, the Caribbean, and South America. The first direct voyage between Africa and the Americas was recorded in 1525; the last in 1867.

Haley, Alex. *Roots: The Saga of an American Family*. Garden City, N.Y.: Doubleday, 1976. Print.

Johnston, James H. *From Slave Ship to Harvard: Yarrow Mamout and the History of an African American Family*. New York: Fordham University Press, 2012. Print.

Washington, Booker T. *Up from Slavery*. Garden City, N.Y.: Doubleday, 1963. Print.

X, Malcolm, and Alex Haley. *The Autobiography of Malcolm X*. New York: Grove, 1965. Print.

Daisy Gard

Praeterita
John Ruskin

Key Facts

Time Period:
Late 19th Century

Relevant Historical Events:
Ruskin's mental breakdown; Ruskin's success as an art critic

Nationality:
English

Keywords:
aesthetics; art; mental illness

OVERVIEW

Published in twenty-eight installments between 1885 and 1889, *Praeterita* is the unfinished autobiography of John Ruskin (1819–1900), arguably the most important English art and social critic of his day. Writing near the end of his life during lucid periods of increasingly frail mental health, Ruskin purposefully excludes unhappy memories and avoids his quintessential tirades against false art and economic oppression. In the preface, he claims to have written *Praeterita*—which means "past" in Latin—frankly, garrulously, and at ease; speaking of what it gives me joy to remember … and passing in total silence things which I have no pleasure of reviewing." To this end, Ruskin attempts to present a paradisiacal version of his childhood, family life, travels, and aesthetic and spiritual educational experiences. However, as Elizabeth K. Helsinger notes in her essay in *Modern Philology, Praeterita* is "a strangely self-destructive autobiography…. [Ruskin] measures his achievements, professional and personal, and concludes he is a failure."

Far from being a failure, Ruskin is considered the Victorian era's leading art and social critic. He wrote more than forty books, several hundred essays, and numerous lectures in which he developed his theories regarding aesthetics, morality, and socioeconomic reform. Although his ideas were often controversial and at times aggressively rejected, Ruskin achieved intellectual eminence and influenced such thinkers as Leo Tolstoy and Bernard Shaw. Today he is remembered as among the greatest English prose stylists, producing works that were both eloquent and noteworthy.

HISTORICAL AND LITERARY CONTEXT

Ruskin was born in London on February 8, 1819, to first cousins John James and Margaret (Cock) Ruskin. Fiercely protective of their only child, Margaret and John James—a wealthy sherry merchant—were a powerful force in Ruskin's life, both encouraging and controlling their son's destiny. A strict disciplinarian and devout Christian, Margaret was responsible for her son's early education, much of which consisted of learning passages from the Scriptures. In 1823, the family moved to a house in the South London district of Herne Hill with gardens that became what Ruskin called his "little domain." Without friends his own age and permitted few toys, he had to rely on his imagination for amusement. "Steadily whipped if I was troublesome," he recalled, "I soon attained serene and secure methods of life and motion; and could pass my days contentedly in tracing the squares and comparing the colours of my carpet."

Ruskin launched his career as an art critic with the publication of *Modern Painters* in 1843, a lengthy treatise on aesthetics. He continued to write prolifically, publishing several more volumes of *Modern Painters* and a number of architectural studies. During the 1850s and 1860s, his writings shifted from aesthetics to social reform, his works now dominated by proposals for addressing socioeconomic inequalities for the poor and working class. While working as the Slade Professor of Fine Art at Oxford University, Ruskin began writing *Fors Clavigera* (1871–84), a monthly series that he hoped would instigate social reform. In 1878 he suffered a severe mental breakdown, followed by bouts of madness that plagued him for the rest of his life. He ceased writing *Fors* in 1884 to compose "some brief autobiography," which ultimately became the three-volume *Praeterita*.

Like many Victorian writers, Ruskin was uncomfortable with the direct exploration of self in literature and experimented with a different form of autobiography. According to Helsinger, "*Praeterita* is part of a shift in ways of viewing one's life which took place between [William] Wordsworth's *The Prelude* and [Walter] Pater's 'Conclusion' to *The Renaissance*." Whereas Wordsworth confidently views life as a single path from past to present, Pater sees it as "a tremulous wisp constantly reforming itself." Victorian poets such as Alfred, Lord Tennyson, and Robert Browning experimented with poetic structure to better explore selfhood, thus providing an alternative form of autobiography. Helsinger contends that in "both form and content they provide the closest contemporary parallels for *Praeterita*."

Ruskin planned *Praeterita* as three volumes consisting of twelve chapters each. However, by the time he began writing the third volume, his periods of lucidity were becoming less frequent, and he shortened the last volume to only four chapters. Although he lived until 1900, these final chapters form the last piece of writing Ruskin was able to complete. Modern critics categorize him as an astute observer of the culture and life of his time. His work also influenced other major authors. *Praeterita* prompted Marcel Proust to write his own lengthy reminiscence, *In Search of Lost Time,* which was published in seven parts between 1913 and 1927.

THEMES AND STYLE

Central to *Praeterita* is Ruskin's search for identity and the impact of the extreme isolation of his childhood on the formation of his adult life. Depicting his childhood as toyless and friendless, without even "companionable beasts" to enjoy, Ruskin recalls the "secluded years" spent in the "self-engrossed quiet of the Herne Hill life." By the time he turned twenty-one, he was "simply a little floppy and soppy tadpole, little more than a stomach with a tail to it, flattening and wriggling itself up the crystal ripples and in the pure sands of the spring-head of youth." Looking back as an old man on his eighteen-year-old self, he notes, "I find myself in nothing whatsoever changed. Some of me is dead, more of me stronger. I have learned a few things, forgotten many; in the total of me, I am but the same youth, disappointed and rheumatic."

Although Ruskin resolved "to set the facts down continuously," his autobiography fails to present his life as a linear progression. Indeed, the work is peppered with apologies for his narrative digressions. "Whether in the biography of a nation, or of a single person it is alike impossible to trace it steadily through successive years," he writes. "Some forces are failing while others strengthen, and most act irregularly, or else at uncorresponding periods of renewed enthusiasm after intervals of lassitude." Almost every chapter is titled after a location Ruskin frequently visited throughout his life, such as "The Simplon" or "L'Hotel du Mont Blanc." As he reminisces about his various visits to these significant places, the autobiography becomes "a history of continual return, of constant circling, a circumscription of a self identified with what it saw," Helsinger observes.

Like most of Ruskin's prolific works, *Praeterita* is marked by his mastery of prose style. In one notable passage, he eloquently describes the Rhone at Geneva: "But the Rhone flows like one lambent jewel; its surface is nowhere, its ethereal self is everywhere, the iridescent rush and translucent strength of its blue to the shore, and radiant to the depth." In his essay in *The Victorian Experience: The Prose Writers* (1982), Francis G. Townsend notes that Ruskin infuses "a spirit into the Rhone, as if the fluminal deities had returned, and the river is personified in a magnificent pathetic fallacy extended to almost inordinate length." The autobiography is frequently sprinkled with self-deprecating humor. For example, Ruskin compares his social ineptness to "a skate in an aquarium trying to get up the glass." "Ruskin's humor," writes Helsinger, "for all its deliberate grotesqueness, allows him to convey an important perception about himself while keeping 'morbid' introspection out of the autobiography."

Colorized photo portrait of author John Ruskin.
© LEBRECHT MUSIC AND ARTS PHOTO LIBRARY/ALAMY

CRITICAL DISCUSSION

R. H. Wilenski notes in *John Ruskin: An Introduction to Further Study of His Life and Work* (1933) that prominent artists and architects of the 1840s and 1850s criticized Ruskin's works. They considered him a pretentious amateur whose passion and eloquence could not compensate for his lack of artistic knowledge. Regardless, by the end of his life, Ruskin had gathered a great following and garnered praise from prominent literary figures such as Browning and Walt Whitman. Proust best summarizes the conflicting feelings regarding Ruskin's work, concluding that although his writings are "often stupid, fanatical, exasperating, false, and irritating," they are also "always praiseworthy and always great."

Early in the twentieth century, E. T. Cook and Alexander Wedderburn collected all of Ruskin's works into thirty-nine volumes to produce an edition titled *The Works of John Ruskin* (1903–12). They argue that *Praeterita* is "of all Ruskin's books, the most uniformly serene in temper." However influential Ruskin has been, Townsend contends that "despite his brilliant insights, and the marvelously acute observation of external fact on which those insights are based, his books will never again be widely read."

Yet many scholars today continue to study and appreciate Ruskin's extensive body of work, including *Praeterita,* and to investigate the nature of his autobiographical form. In *Nature's Covenant: Figures of Landscape in Ruskin* (1992), C. Stephen Finley writes, "It is more than simply true that *Praeterita* is a book of deaths, a book of mourning, and not merely the construction

PRIMARY SOURCE

EXCERPT FROM *PRAETERITA*

Walter Scott and Pope's Homer were reading of my own election, and my mother forced me, by steady daily toil, to learn long chapters of the Bible by heart; as well as to read it every syllable through, aloud, hard names and all, from Genesis to the Apocalypse, about once a year: and to that discipline—patient, accurate, and resolute—I owe, not only a knowledge of the book, which I find occasionally serviceable, but much of my general power of taking pains, and the best part of my taste in literature. From Walter Scott's novels I might easily, as I grew older, have fallen to other people's novels; and Pope might, perhaps, have led me to take Johnson's English, or Gibbon's, as types of language; but, once knowing the 32nd of Deuteronomy, the 119th Psalm, the 15th of 1st Corinthians, the Sermon on the Mount, and most of the Apocalypse, every syllable by heart, and having always a way of thinking with myself what words meant, it was not possible for me, even in the foolishest times of youth, to write entirely superficial or formal English; and the affectation of trying to write like Hooker and George Herbert was the most innocent I could have fallen into.

From my own chosen masters, then, Scott and Homer, I learned the Toryism which my best after-thought has only served to confirm.

That is to say, a most sincere love of kings, and dislike of everybody who attempted to disobey them. Only, both by Homer and Scott, I was taught strange ideas about kings, which I find for the present much obsolete; for, I perceived that both the author of the Iliad and the author of Waverley made their kings, or king-loving persons, do harder work than anybody else. Tydides or Idomeneus always killed twenty Trojans to other people's one, and Redgauntlet speared more salmon than any of the Solway fishermen, and—which was particularly a subject of admiration to me—I observed that they not only did more, but in proportion to their doings, got less than other people—nay, that the best of them were even ready to govern for nothing! and let their followers divide any quantity of spoil or profit. Of late it has seemed to me that the idea of a king has become exactly the contrary of this, and that it has been supposed the duty of superior persons generally to govern less, and get more, than anybody else. So that it was, perhaps, quite as well that in those early days my contemplation of existent kingship was a very distant one.

SOURCE: Ruskin, John. *Praeterita*. London: George Allen, 1907.

of a narrative of loss met by the greater compensation of rebirth and later gain. Even so, in the deepest sense, *Praeterita* is patterned upon spiritual autobiography." In *The Failing Distance: The Autobiographical Impulse of John Ruskin* (1975), Jay Fellows speculates that although Ruskin had an insistent autobiographical impulse, he feared introspection (as did many Victorians). Helsinger seems to agree, writing that *Praeterita* portrays "introspective journeying as isolated, self-involved, and finally fruitless: incapable of yielding a confident sense of self, or an exhilarating view of a purposeful life."

BIBLIOGRAPHY

Sources

Dziedzic, Nancy, ed. "John Ruskin (1819–1900)." *Twentieth-Century Literary Criticism*. Vol. 63. Detroit: Gale, 1996. 235–336. *Literature Criticism Online*. Web. 25 Nov. 2012

Fellows, Jay. *The Failing Distance: The Autobiographical Impulse of John Ruskin*. Baltimore: Johns Hopkins University Press, 1975. Print.

Finley, C. Stephen. *Nature's Covenant: Figures of Landscape in Ruskin*. University Park: Pennsylvania State University Press, 1992. Print.

Helsinger, Elizabeth K. "Ruskin and the Poets: Alterations in Autobiography." *Modern Philology* 74.2 (1976): 142–70. Print.

Pater, Walter. *The Renaissance: Studies in Art and Poetry*. London: Macmillan, 1888. Print.

Ruskin, John. *The Works of John Ruskin*. Ed. E. T. Cook and Alexander Wedderburn. London: George Allen, 1903–12. Print.

Townsend, Francis G. "On Reading John Ruskin." *The Victorian Experience: The Prose Writers*. Ed. Richard A. Levine. Athens: Ohio University Press, 1982. 150–73. Print.

Wilenski, R. H. *John Ruskin: An Introduction to Further Study in His Life and Work*. New York: Faber and Faber, 1933. Print.

Further Reading

Austin, Linda M. "*Praeterita*: In the Act of Rebellion." *Modern Language Quarterly* 48.1 (1987): 42–58. Print.

Caws, Mary Ann. "Against Completion: Ruskin's Drama of Dream, Lateness and Loss." *Sex and Death in Victorian Literature*. Ed. Regina Barreca. Bloomington: Indiana University Press, 1990. 107–19. Print.

Codell, Julie F. *The Victorian Artist: Artists' Life Writings in Britain, c. 1870–1910*. Cambridge: Cambridge University Press, 2003. Print.

Emerson, Sheila. *Ruskin: The Genesis of Invention*. Cambridge: Cambridge University Press, 1993. Print.

Finley, Stephen C. "Scott, Ruskin, and the Landscape of Autobiography." *Studies in Romanticism* 2.4 (1987): 549–72. Print.

Hewison, Robert. *John Ruskin*. London: Oxford University Press, 2007. Print.

Hilton, Tim. *John Ruskin: The Later Years*. New Haven, Conn.: Yale University Press, 2000. Print.

Kemp, Wolfgang. *The Desire of My Eyes: The Life and Work of John Ruskin*. New York: Farrar, Straus and Giroux, 1990. Print.

Peltason, Timothy. "Ruskin's Finale: Vision and Imagination in *Praeterita*." *ELH* 57.3 (1990): 665–84. Print.

Wheeler, Michael. *Ruskin and Environment: The Storm-Cloud of the Nineteenth Century*. Manchester, U.K.: Manchester University Press, 1995. Print.

Wheeler, Michael, and Nigel Whiteley. *The Lamp of Memory: Ruskin, Tradition, and Architecture*. Manchester, U.K.: Manchester University Press, 1992. Print.

Maggie Magno

Roland Barthes
Roland Barthes

OVERVIEW

First published in 1975 in French, *Roland Barthes* (1977) is a discussion within the genre of autobiography that departs radically from convention. In it, Roland Barthes, the author, attempts to separate himself from Barthes, the subject, by treating himself as an imaginary character in a novel. Paradoxically, the writer and the figure written about simultaneously are and are not the same. This attempt at separation gives rise to the humor and irony that exemplify the book, which is also characteristically fragmentary and disconnected. Its premise coincides with concepts in Barthes's theoretical works that define the subject of a text as a process rather than as a static entity, thus creating a sense of vitality and change in the protagonist or focus. He also explores the complications involved in composing an autobiography that both violates the traditional approach to autobiography and necessarily falls subject to its shortcomings.

At the time the book was published, Barthes had a reputation for his convoluted and often contradictory theories about literature, which were nevertheless brilliant in their ability to disrupt and alter traditionally structured habits of interpretation. The academic community was therefore stunned that he was willing to engage with such a time-honored form as autobiography, especially considering his well-documented dislike of the common use of biography as a key to meaning in an author's literary works. Although Barthes's autobiography was never considered his best text, critics embraced it for its embodiment of his theoretical ideas about language and the redundancy of authorship.

HISTORICAL AND LITERARY CONTEXT

Trends in autobiography in the 1960s and 1970s prescribed the use of a sequential narrative of events. A text was interpreted as a product of its author's experiences, which imbued it with an authorial "meaning" that was considered all important. Literary models at the time focused on structuralism, but Barthes's theoretical writing rejected the rigid narrative form and inherent meaning of the structuralist narrative, believing instead that a text is recreated—or "rewritten"—by the reader each time it is read. He was considered among the first poststructuralist theorists, although his work overflowed into other areas of literary theory, including semiotics and the structuralist theories he worked to subvert.

Roland Barthes was originally commissioned as part of the series Ecrivains de toujours, which featured biographies on influential literary authors titled "[name] *par lui-même.*" Barthes was a well-known academic and literary theorist who had previously published a text in the series treating the nineteenth-century French historian Jules Michelet titled *Michelet par lui-même* (1954; *Michelet,* 1987). To write a *par lui-même* about himself, however, was seen as a jest, especially considering his 1968 essay "The Death of the Author" that advocated locating meaning in language rather than in an author's historical or biographical origins. Barthes was serious, however, about both critiquing and revamping the structure of autobiography and its relation to the author.

In writing his autobiography, Barthes followed in the footsteps of his own theoretical work as well as being influenced by such theorists as the Swiss linguist Ferdinand de Saussure and French psychoanalyst Jacques Lacan. In the early twentieth century, Saussure had developed the notion of semiology, which distinguishes between the signifier (or "sign": the word or phrase) and the signified (the meaning or object it refers to). *Roland Barthes* incorporates the Saussurean notion that the association of text with author is arbitrary and meaningless; for Barthes, the subject of a text—including an autobiographical text—is nothing more than a product of language as interpreted by a reader. Lacan furthered Freud's ideas about the conscious and unconscious self and the id and ego as sections of the self. Barthes applies these philosophies as well: before presenting a series of images that do not portray him, he states, "I never look like myself" and explains that his id does not coincide with any image.

Roland Barthes was a popular read among literary critics and scholars alike, but its unique style and somewhat contradictory theoretical standpoint caused many to refrain from engaging with it publicly, especially given that Barthes's vast literary output provided plenty of other texts to study. Nevertheless, the author reviewed his own autobiography in *Quinzaine littéraire* (1975) under the title "Barthes puissance trois—Barthes critique le 'Barthes' de Barthes" ("'Barthes by Barthes' by Barthes"). In furthering his notion that the subject exists solely in the interpretative creativity of

❖ **Key Facts**

Time Period:
Late 20th Century

Relevant Historical Events:
Increased prominence of post-structuralism

Nationality:
French

Keywords:
literary theory; post-structuralism

Author and literary critic Roland Barthes in 1976. © BETTMANN/CORBIS

the reader, Barthes claims in the article that in reading his text, he can interpret his subject however he pleases—even though that subject is allegedly himself. After the publication of Barthes's autobiography, the genre gained popularity with both writers and scholars, who explored such aspects as the writing process itself and the problematic act of remembering, as Nathalie Sarraute did in *Enfance* (1983; *Childhood,* 1983).

THEMES AND STYLE

Roland Barthes declares false the assumption that the author of an autobiography determines the reader's understanding of the subject matter. This theme is evident in both the style and content of the book. The first of two sections contains photographs of Barthes as a child, a youth, and an adult and of various people, places, and things he finds of special interest. He provides accompanying phrases or paragraphs that account for his interest while intentionally avoiding references to his life. At the outset Barthes explains that the images "are the author's treat to himself, for finishing his book," adding that "what I shall say about each image will never be anything but imaginary." He then provides an alphabetical list of ideas that attract him, with a brief consideration of each, as well as an assortment of personal anecdotes. As a whole, the alphabetized fragments represent an exploration of his process in writing his autobiography. The anecdotes come with directives for reading: they "must all be considered as if spoken by a character in a novel." The subject thus comes into particularized "Being" as a function of the reader's particularized understanding.

Accepting the humorous intent in the commission, Barthes also took the opportunity to put his theories into practice. He turns himself into a process, disrupting any perception that he can be known. He writes (of himself), "He is troubled by any image of himself, suffers when he is named. He finds the perfection of a human relationship in this vacancy of the image." He must create some sense of himself, however, in order to construct a subject for his text. Barthes addresses this contradiction under the heading "Hypocrisy?": "Speaking of a text, he credits its author with not manipulating the reader [...] discovering that he himself does all he can to manipulate the reader." Charging conventional autobiography with crafting an identity that is necessarily false, Barthes proceeds to demonstrate that all texts, including his, manipulate. In "Roland Barthes, Reading, and Roleplay" (1991), James Seitz clarifies, "Barthes recognizes his desire to lead his readers in a certain direction; but the direction he leads is toward a space in which readers are left to their own devices."

Barthes's tone changes often, from academic to thoughtful to whimsical. His fragmentary discussions and personal observations create a unique style. The subjects and details he chooses reflect the development of his thoughts and explore his exploration of his own writing process. Under the heading "The fear of language," for example, Barthes records that "writing a certain text, he experiences a guilty emotion of jargon, as if he could not escape from a mad discourse no matter how individual he made his utterance: and what if all his life *he had chosen the wrong language?*" The alphabetical presentation of thoughts seems structurally rigid but results in an apparently random collection of items with no solid subject or internal meaning. Yielding his thoughts to language, Barthes features them as but aspects of a self open to a reader's interpretation.

CRITICAL DISCUSSION

Roland Barthes was met with surprise and praise for its ability to embody the very genre it problematized. In his 1977 review "Captured by Meanings," Frank Kermode describes the "privilege granted to the reader of this book" as the opportunity "to watch Barthes contemplating his own paradoxes, or contemplating himself contemplating them." A 1978 review by Roland Champagne lauds Barthes for "question[ing] the very nature of 'auto-bio-graphy' by giving us memoirs that expose the components of that word and the literary genre which it represents." In acknowledgment that some commentators did not take the book seriously, Kermode writes that it "is not the best testimony to the elegance and severity of Barthes's mind and the range of his intellectual achievement."

Roland Barthes gained a reputation as an "anti-autobiography," in the words of Christopher Prendergast in "The Open Text" (1980). Prendergast describes the work's particular resistance "to our intuitional orderings of the universe of knowledge," and he discusses the legacy of Barthes's book by saying that the work is "as much a set of problems and questions as anything else. The text of Barthes belongs to the living, to active inquiry, open debate, perpetual revision."

The main trend in scholarship surrounding the text recognizes it as an example of Barthes playing within his own theoretical constructs. In "Barthes as Text" (1981), George Wasserman argues that the author does not like images because "they are part of the bourgeois obsession with naming and adjectivizing things"; his autobiography is thus populated with inconsequential details that "are not intended to produce an image." Kermode comments on the self-examination inherent in a book that "is partly about the problem [Barthes] must have in writing it and partly about other and related problems such as the difference between what, as a writer, he thinks ought to be done and what in fact he does." In *Humanities Insights: Barthes* (2008), Mireille Ribière observes Barthes's willingness to challenge the principles of his own literary cohort; he "manages to breathe new life into the autobiographical genre, which all the innovative contemporary writers he had enthusiastically supported had carefully eschewed."

BIBLIOGRAPHY

Sources

Barthes, Roland. *Roland Barthes*. 1975. Trans. Richard Howard. New York: Noonday, 1977. Print.

Champagne, Roland A. Rev. of *Roland Barthes*, by Roland Barthes. *Modern Language Journal* 62.3 (1978): 147–48. *JSTOR*. Web. 22 Oct. 2012.

Kermode, Frank. "Captured by Meanings." *New York Times Book Review* 7 Aug. 1977: 13. Rpt. in *Contemporary Literary Criticism*. Ed. James P. Draper. Vol. 83. Detroit: Gale, 1994. *Literature Resource Center*. Web. 19 Oct. 2012.

Prendergast, Christopher. "The Open Text." *New Statesman* 25 Apr. 1980: 627–28. Rpt. in *Contemporary Literary Criticism*. Ed. Sharon R. Gunton and Daniel G. Stine. Vol. 24. Detroit: Gale, 1983. *Literature Resource Center*. Web. 19 Oct. 2012.

Ribière, Mireille. *Barthes*. London: Hodder, 2002. Print.

Seitz, James. "Roland Barthes, Reading, and Roleplay: Composition's Misguided Rejection of Fragmentary Texts." *College English* 53.7 (1991): 815–25. Print.

Wasserman, George R. "Barthes as Text." *Roland Barthes*. By Wasserman. Boston: Twayne, 1981. *Twayne Authors Series*. Web. 19 Oct. 2012. Twayne's World Authors Ser. 614.

ROLAND BARTHES AND "THE DEATH OF THE AUTHOR"

One of Roland Barthes's most influential and most notorious essays is "The Death of the Author" (1968). In it, he argues that applying historical or biographical details of authors' lives in interpreting their texts inhibits a productive and engaged reading. Barthes suggests that approaching a text with the notion that "the Author is dead" liberates the reading process from restrictions of instilled meaning, established identities, and preconceived notions of the text's origins.

In order to discuss the limitations of including authorial details in textual analysis, Barthes generates what he terms "Author"—with a capital "A"—and aligns the preconceived importance of the Author with God. In traditional forms of interpretation, this Author, according to Barthes's analysis, encodes a message in the text that the reader must uncover. By "killing" the Author—or focusing on the meanings inherent in the language and eschewing the Author—Barthes argues that the text can stand on its own merits and that the interpretation can change based on the reader's abilities, attitudes, experiences, and so forth.

Further Reading

Barthes, Roland. "Barthes puissance trois." *La quinzaine litteraire* 205 (1975): 3–5. Web. 6 Dec. 2012.

Burke, Sean. *The Death and Return of the Author: Criticism and Subjectivity in Barthes, Foucault and Derrida*. 3rd ed. Edinburgh: Edinburgh University Press, 2008. Print.

Calvet, Louis Jean. *Roland Barthes: A Biography*. Trans. Sarah Wykes. Bloomington: Indiana University Press, 1995. Print.

Connors, Clare. "The Author: Dead or Alive?" *English Review* 12.1 (2001): 17. *Literature Resource Center*. Web. 22 Oct. 2012.

Haustein, Katja. *Regarding Lost Time: Photography, Identity, and Affect in Proust, Benjamin, and Barthes*. London: Legenda, 2012. Print.

Hill, Leslie. "Roland Barthes: From Ideology to Event." *Radical Indecision: Barthes, Blanchot, Derrida, and the Future of Criticism*. Notre Dame, Ind.: University of Notre Dame Press, 2010. 71–154. Web. 22 Oct. 2012.

"Roland Barthes: 1915–1980." *The Norton Anthology of Theory and Criticism*. 2nd ed. Ed. Vincent B. Leitch. New York: Norton, 2010. 1316–20. Print.

Sarraute, Nathalie. *Enfance*. Paris: Gallimard, 1983. Print.

Sontag, Susan. Introduction. *A Barthes Reader*. Ed. Sontag. New York: Hill, 1982. Print.

Katherine Barker

Speak, Memory
An Autobiography Revisited
Vladimir Nabokov

✧ Key Facts

Time Period:
Mid-20th Century

Relevant Historical Events:
Russian Revolution of 1917; Nabokov's exile

Nationality:
Russian American

Keywords:
exile; revolution; self-consciousness

OVERVIEW

Vladimir Nabokov's 1951 autobiography, published in the United States as *Conclusive Evidence* and in London as *Speak, Memory*, presents a series of recollections about the first forty-one years of the author's life, concluding just prior to his immigration to the United States in 1940. A revised version was published in the United States in 1966 as *Speak, Memory: An Autobiography Revisited*. Written in a series of roughly chronological, self-contained chapters—each of which glides back and forth through time amid a recursive contemplation of some aspect of Nabokov's life—the book paints a nostalgic picture of the author's childhood in a wealthy, liberal household in prerevolutionary Russia and provides details of his subsequent education and other experiences when the family was forced into exile following the revolutions of 1917. Nabokov's dense, controlled, heavily detailed style reflects his intent to transcend the limitations of time and recapture his lost Russian past.

Written before Nabokov had become a major literary figure in the English-speaking world, *Speak, Memory* sold poorly upon its initial publication in 1951. In the decades since then, however, its reputation has significantly increased along with that of its author. It is now one of the most highly regarded autobiographical narratives of the twentieth century, noted for its nonlinear structure and emphasis on exhaustive contemplation over straightforward, sequential narrative. The book's preoccupation with the aesthetic virtues of style and evocation rather than the narrative events themselves prefigured many literary memoirs of the late twentieth and early twenty-first centuries.

HISTORICAL AND LITERARY CONTEXT

Nabokov's autobiography is particularly concerned with the profound changes, both in Russian society and in his own life, brought about by the Russian Revolutions of 1917. The first revolution, which occurred in February of that year, brought about the downfall of Tsar Nicholas II, replacing the Russian Empire with a republic under the control of the short-lived Russian Provisional Government, of which Nabokov's father was a member. This government was itself overthrown that October, when an armed insurrection placed political control in the hands of Vladimir Lenin's revolutionary Bolsheviks, inaugurating decades of communist rule in Russia and the Soviet Union. However, first this rule was consolidated through civil war that lasted for the next few years and forced Nabokov and his family to flee the country and settle in Europe.

Many of the chapters that constitute *Speak, Memory* were written from 1947 to 1950 and published as standalone essays in the *New Yorker*. Other chapters were written as early as the 1930s and likewise published in journals. During the 1940s Nabokov, who had already produced numerous Russian-language novels and achieved considerable renown in Russian émigré circles, was employed as a college professor in the United States. The memoir attempts to correct what Nabokov saw as the woefully misinformed perception of the October Revolution on the part of Western intellectuals swayed by Soviet propaganda. He argues that "despite the fundamentally inept and ferocious character of [the tsars'] rule, a freedom-loving Russian had had incomparably more means of expressing himself, and used to run incomparably less risk in doing so, than under Lenin."

Speak, Memory is part of a long tradition of Russian autobiographical literature and draws upon the modernist literary techniques that had emerged in recent decades in European writing. Noteworthy predecessors of Nabokov's book include Leo Tolstoy's meditative *A Confession* (1884) and the memoirs of Alexander Herzen and Nabokov's fellow émigré Ivan Bunin. Meanwhile, Nabokov's focus on recapturing past moments through sustained literary artifice bears the influence of time-obsessed modernist literature such as Marcel Proust's autobiographical novel *In Search of Lost Time* (1913–27), which shares with Nabokov's work a preoccupation with the intersection between memory and sensory experience.

Despite its lack of immediate impact, *Speak, Memory*'s self-consciousness and discursive style mark it as an important precursor of much of the literary autobiographical nonfiction that flourished in the 1950s and later. Nabokov's focus on individual memories and images, as opposed to telling a journalistic, sequential "story of his life," prefigures memoirs such as Frank Conroy's *Stop-Time* (1967), while his condemnation of Bolshevism, initially a somewhat controversial position within the Western intelligentsia, foreshadowed the subsequent publication of Nadezhda Mandlestam's *Hope against Hope* (1970) and other memoirs of Soviet repression. It remains widely read, both for its merits as an autobiography and for the insight it provides into the possible autobiographical inspirations of Nabokov's fiction.

THEMES AND STYLE

Central to Nabokov's text is a perception of time as a pervasive and imprisoning force whose corroding influence on the past can nevertheless be arrested and transcended through the diligent application of literary imagination. Near the beginning of his memoir, Nabokov traces his own sense of self-conscious identity back to the realization that his parents were older than he was—"I felt myself plunged abruptly into a radiant and mobile medium that was none other than the pure element of time"—and discusses his lifelong desire to escape the confines of temporal existence: "I have journeyed back in thought—with thought hopelessly tapering off as I went—to remote regions where I groped for some secret outlet only to discover that the prison of time is spherical and without exits." *Speak, Memory* is thus an attempt to circumvent time's dominion by carefully documenting the events of his own life, following the dictates of recurring themes and motifs rather than those of chronology.

Speak, Memory was primarily written in order to allow Nabokov to compose a sustained, exhaustive meditation on the various elements of his early life, many aspects of which were lost when his connection with Russia was severed. This meditation emphasizes the repetition of certain narrative threads throughout the author's past, hence the division of the book into chapters focusing mostly on specific topics (including his father, his mother, his lifelong hobby of collecting butterflies, his first childhood love experience, and his Russian tutors, among others) rather than on specific time periods, though the chapter-by-chapter progression is nonetheless roughly chronological. At one point, after describing how a friend of the family, the Russian Imperial minister of war, General Kuropatkin, used a handful of matches to amuse the young Nabokov, the author draws a connection to a later incident in which the same man, now in disguise and on the run from the Soviets, asks his father for a light. Of this connection, Nabokov notes that "what pleases me most is the match theme…. The following of such thematic designs through one's life should be, I think, the true purpose of autobiography."

Nabokov's text is characterized by a recursive narrative structure and a highly polished, meticulous prose style abounding in sensory detail. The author's emphasis on the "thematic designs" of his life creates a spiraling narrative progression, a fact Nabokov acknowledges late in the book with the introduction of the spiral as a symbol: "in spiral form, the circle,

Author Vladimir Nabokov in 1976. His *Speak, Memory: An Autobiography Revisited* describes his life from 1903 to 1940. © AP IMAGES

uncoiled, unwound, has ceased to be vicious; it has been set free." Within this structure, he frequently indulges in elaborate, heavily evocative sentences, as in the following description of his French governess's experience of waiting at a station platform, where "the door of the waiting room opens with a shuddering whine peculiar to nights of intense frost; a cloud of hot air rushes out, almost as profuse as the steam from the panting engine; and now our coachman Zahar takes over—a burly man in sheepskin with the leather outside, his huge gloves protruding from his scarlet sash into which he has stuffed them."

CRITICAL DISCUSSION

Speak, Memory was not a financial success upon its initial publication, despite a critical reception that was mostly positive. The book's stylistic qualities in particular attracted comment. Maurice Hindus, writing in the *Saturday Review,* called it "a beautiful and moving book" and asserted that "not since Joseph Conrad has a writer of Slav origin shown such a brilliant mastery of the subtleties and beauties of the English language." Meanwhile, Orville Prescott, in a less elated review for the *New York Times,* stated that the book was written "with subtlety and sensitivity, with tender nostalgia and with occasional flickers of almost stately irony," but complained that "Mr. Nabokov delights in a great many words formally draped over a minimum of matter. His prose is sometimes beautiful, more often laboriously self-conscious."

NABOKOV'S SYNESTHESIA

In *Speak, Memory: An Autobiography Revisited,* Vladimir Nabokov famously discusses his experiences of synesthesia, a congenital neurological condition in which unrelated sensations are involuntary combined. Nabokov experienced a particular kind of synesthesia, color-graphemic synesthesia, in which specific colors are perceived as properties of letters and numbers. In his memoir he describes how letters and letter sounds are colored in his mind's eye: "In the green group, there are alder-leaf *f,* the unripe apple of *p,* and pistachio *t.* Dull green, combined somehow with violet, is the best I can do for *w.*"

Nabokov relates his childhood discovery that his mother shared this trait after he complained to her that the colors on the alphabet blocks with which he was playing did not correspond properly with the letters. He also notes an awareness that his descriptions of these experiences might be off-putting to readers unfamiliar with such sensations. "The confessions of a synesthete," he writes, "must sound tedious and pretentious to those who are protected from such leakings and drafts by more solid walls than mine are." Although the condition is rare, several other notable artists have identified as synesthetes, among them composer Franz Liszt, musician Itzhak Perlman, and painter Wassily Kandinsky.

Despite these mixed beginnings, Nabokov's memoir has since become one of the most renowned of the twentieth century and a standout example of Russian émigré literature. The publication of the revised English edition in 1966, long after Nabokov had attained international notoriety on the basis of his controversial novel *Lolita* (1955), was much more successful, and sections of the book have frequently been excerpted for literature anthologies. It has attracted considerable scholarly interest for its uncommon handling of personal recollection, and as an autobiography the work has served as a means for scholars to draw connections between the author's life and his literary writings.

Scholarly writing that considers *Speak, Memory* as an independent work often analyzes its relationship to the conventions of autobiographical writing. Robert Alter, writing in the *Partisan Review* in 1991, examines Nabokov's highly controlled literary treatment of memory, drawing connections to Proust's concept of "involuntary memory" and asserting that "[Nabokov] often evinces a sense that he can actually stage a return to the past by a sufficiently deft and resourceful ordering of his prose medium. But there is also an aspect of Proustian involuntarism stalking this project of artful volition." Proust likewise figures into Matt Reed's 2000 article in *Clio,* which discusses Nabokov's aesthetic treatment of historical representation and his attempts to "find a way of both acknowledging the constructedness of the historical representation and the desires which motivate that work while preserving a connection to the past."

BIBLIOGRAPHY

Sources

Alter, Robert. "Nabokov and Memory." *Partisan Review* 58.4 (1991): 620–29. Rpt. in *Twentieth-Century Literary Criticism.* Ed. Linda Pavlovski and Scott T. Darga. Vol. 108. Detroit: Gale, 2001. *Literature Resources from Gale.* Web. 15 Nov. 2012.

Hindus, Maurice. "Gentle Russian Yesterdays." Rev. of *Conclusive Evidence,* by Vladimir Nabokov. *Saturday Review* 14 Apr. 1951: 29. Print.

Nabokov, Vladimir. *Speak, Memory: An Autobiography Revisited.* 1966. New York: Alfred A. Knopf, 1999. Print.

Prescott, Orville. Rev. of *Conclusive Evidence,* by Vladimir Nabokov. *New York Times.* New York Times, 23 Feb. 1951. Web. 15 Nov. 2012.

Reed, Matt. "*Homo Lepidopterist:* Nabokov and the Pursuit of Memory." *Clio* 29.3 (2000): 271–94. *Humanities Full Text (H.W. Wilson).* Web. 15 Nov. 2012.

Further Reading

Alexandrov, Vladimir E. *Nabokov's Otherworld.* Princeton, N.J.: Princeton University Press, 1991. Print.

Bontila, Ruxanda. "Shifting Relations in Nabokov's *Speak, Memory.*" *British and American Studies* 4.1 (1999): 67–72. Print.

Boyd, Brian. *Vladimir Nabokov: The Russian Years.* Princeton, N.J.: Princeton University Press, 1990. Print.

———. *Vladimir Nabokov: The American Years.* Princeton, N.J.: Princeton University Press, 1991. Print.

Diment, Galya. "Vladimir Nabokov and the Art of Autobiography." *Nabokov and His Fiction: New Perspectives.* Ed. Julian W. Connolly. Cambridge: Cambridge University Press, 1999. Print.

Gezari, Janet. "Chess Problems and Narrative Time in *Speak, Memory.*" *Biography* 10.2 (1987): 151–62. Print.

Green, Geoffrey. "Visions of a 'Perfect Past': Nabokov, Autobiography, Biography, and Fiction." *Nabokov Studies* 3 (1996): 89–100. Print.

Hägglund, Martin. "Chronophilia: Nabokov and the Time of Desire." *New Literary History* 37.2 (2006): 447–67. Print.

Moraru, Christian. "Time, Writing, and Ecstasy in *Speak, Memory:* Dramatizing the Proustian Project." *Nabokov Studies* 2 (1995): 173–90. Print.

Rosengrant, Judson. "Bilingual Style in Nabokov's Autobiography." *Style* 29.1 (1995): 108–27. Print.

Wood, Michael. *The Magician's Doubts: Nabokov and the Risks of Fiction.* Princeton, N.J.: Princeton University Press, 1994.

James Overholtzer

TO BE YOUNG, GIFTED AND BLACK
An Informal Autobiography of Lorraine Hansberry
Lorraine Hansberry

OVERVIEW

To Be Young, Gifted and Black: An Informal Autobiography of Lorraine Hansberry (1969), adapted by Hansberry's ex-husband, Robert Nemiroff, collects portions of the writer's plays; her unpublished autobiographic novel; and snippets of letters, journals, essays, poetry, and interviews. Organized into three sections that correspond in chronology and theme to her formative years, her artistic and political life, and her legacy, the book paints a portrait of Hansberry as an artist and an activist. From accounts of her early school days to her address to the winners of the United Negro College Fund writing contest—"write about *our* people: tell their story"—the work in *To Be Young, Gifted and Black* reveals a woman committed to a life of active engagement with ideas and with people.

Hansberry died in 1965 at the age of thirty-four, leaving behind a substantial amount of unpublished work as well as several plays, the most successful of which, *A Raisin in the Sun* (1959), was the first play by an African American woman to be produced on Broadway. It received the New York Drama Critics' Circle Award for best play of 1959. Hansberry's work reflects her upbringing in Depression-era Chicago, as well as her political commitment to the civil rights struggle that was snowballing during the period when she was coming of age. Full of the turmoil and hope of an important era of U.S. history, *To Be Young, Gifted and Black* is one of the most notable chronicles of the black experience in the shifting racial terrain of the mid-twentieth century.

HISTORICAL AND LITERARY CONTEXT

Following the Civil War, black Americans began to migrate to the Midwest seeking both new economic opportunities and a home free of the racist institutions still flourishing in the South. The Great Migration reflected hope for a better life, but conditions in midwestern cities such as Chicago were often grim, especially as the United States entered the Great Depression of the 1930s. Hansberry's family was considered well off by the standards of the day, but she was exposed to first poverty and then racism in the communities in which she lived. In 1938 her father, Carl, moved the family to an area of Chicago that was restricted to white people and subsequently fought a protracted court battle to stay there. While he eventually won the case, Hansberry recalled having been profoundly affected by the sometimes violent attacks of neighbors who wanted them to leave.

Much of the material in *To Be Young, Gifted and Black* was written in the 1950s and 1960s while Hansberry was living and working in New York City amid a group of young, politically minded writers and intellectuals. A significant portion of her subject matter, however, was rooted in her experiences growing up in Chicago, which, in a letter dated December 26, 1952, she calls "Dreiseresque," in reference to American novelist Theodore Dreiser's naturalist work. In her early years in New York, Hansberry worked as a writer for activist Paul Robeson's *Freedom* newspaper, further sharpening her focus on racial inequality. Her writing—letters, plays, and other prose collected in the book—reflects a journalist's eye for details and an activist's commitment to equality and social justice influenced by the developing civil rights movement.

While Hansberry spent most of her writing life in New York, her work is frequently placed with other writers of the Chicago Renaissance. By contrast with writers of the Harlem Renaissance, who focused on black pride and creativity, many of those centered in Chicago were more overtly political, dealing with the gritty realities of urban life, including violence and racism. Richard Wright's *Native Son* (1940), for example, chronicles the desperation and stunted development of the ghetto-bound Bigger Thomas and his family, themes that Hansberry would also explore in works such as *A Raisin in the Sun*.

The success of *A Raisin in the Sun*, which drew unprecedented numbers of black theatergoers when it opened on Broadway in 1959, laid the groundwork for the African American playwrights who would follow. Hansberry proved that a play rooted in the black experience was both commercially and critically viable. Playwrights such as August Wilson and Suzan Lori-Parks, both recipients of the Pulitzer Prize, have continued Hansberry's dramatic exploration of black family life, along with larger social and economic influences that shape individuals. Bruce Norris's 2010 play *Clybourne Park*, which responds to *A Raisin in the Sun* directly, describing events before and after Hansberry's play, also won the Pulitzer Prize.

Key Facts

Time Period:
Mid-20th Century

Relevant Historical Events:
Great Migration; development of the civil rights movement

Nationality:
American

Keywords:
activism; civil rights; migration

Author Lorraine Hansberry is at the center of this mural, titled *Singing in the Dark*, in the Little Five Points district of Atlanta, Georgia. © KRISTA ROSSOW/NATIONAL GEOGRAPHIC SOCIETY/CORBIS

THEMES AND STYLE

The struggle that defined Hansberry's life and art as presented in *To Be Young, Gifted and Black* was the development of a conscious view of the world that acknowledges both its beauty and the suffering of all who live. For Hansberry, the position of black Americans during the civil rights era was particularly advantageous for seeing and feeling both these dimensions of experience. This ability to see was what she seems to have been referring to when, addressing the winners of the United Negro College Fund's writing contest, she coined the phrase that Nemiroff would choose to title her autobiography. "The negro writer stands surrounded by the whirling elements of this world," she said in this address. "He stands neither on the fringe nor utterly involved: the prime observer waiting poised for inclusion." What Hansberry observed is offered in excerpts from various published and unpublished pieces of her writing. Some of these, notably *A Raisin in the Sun* and short autobiographical essays such as "Southside Summers" and "White Fur in the Depression," offer glimpses into black family life. Others, such as Hansberry's last staged play, *The Sign in Sidney Brustein's Window*, deal with the struggles faced by young adults attempting to grapple with relationship and career turmoil in the racially charged atmosphere of New York City during the civil rights era. Letters to Nemiroff written during the couple's marriage, which express Hansberry's loneliness and the insecurity she felt about her work, give a rare glimpse of her private emotions, which are otherwise relatively absent from the book.

In his foreword to *To Be Young, Gifted and Black*, Nemiroff states his intention to present a "self portrait" of Hansberry as a person and "as a prophetic chapter in the history of a people and of an age." The introduction by author James Baldwin, which is affectionately titled "Sweet Lorraine," emphasizes Hansberry's personality but, perhaps more prominently, her significance as a black artist. Hansberry, who died from cancer at the age of thirty-four, left behind a large amount of unpublished material, including parts of plays, an unfinished novel, and cabinets filled with notes and correspondence. Nemiroff's book is, on one level, a response to Hansberry's wishes, which are expressed in an undated fragment that closes the main body of the book: "If anything should happen—before 'tis done—may I trust that all commas and periods will be placed and someone will complete my thoughts. This last should be the least difficult—since there are so many who think as I do." Speaking in a 1974 interview in the *Back Bay Banner*, Nemiroff concurred: "I decided it was a major body of writing and I must find ways to get it out to the public. I saw it first as a legacy to the black community and secondly as a legacy to American literature and her generation."

Hansberry's book, both in structure and origin, is on the margins of the category autobiography. While the work is all Hansberry's, it was selected and compiled by Nemiroff, who had often been her sounding board as she was writing. Rather than a single narrative, the text comprises writing from a number of different sources and genres, including drama and fiction. Still, the text bears similarities to works that typify the genre, with vignettes from Hansberry's life and work in roughly chronological order and descriptions of her thoughts and feelings about her experiences. In her chapter on Hansberry in *The Twayne Authors Series*, scholar Anne Cheney writes of the book, "As the character of Hansberry intones selections from her journals, letters, and interviews, we are introduced to a young woman, brimming with hopes, disappointments, dreams, fears, and laughter. Not only does she become a vital human being, but she reveals—posthumously—the pattern of her entire career as a writer and a thinker."

CRITICAL DISCUSSION

To Be Young, Gifted and Black was expanded from a play by the same name, which had a highly successful run at New York's Cherry Lane Theater in 1969 and on its two-year national tour (1970–72). The book itself received little critical attention initially. In his 1980 essay on the author titled "Commitment amid Complexity," literary critic Steven Carter notes that *To Be Young, Gifted and Black* received "no review in the *New York Times* or any of the major new magazines and scholarly journals."

The phrase "to be young gifted and black" has entered popular culture in a number of ways. Singer Nina Simone used it to immortalize Hansberry's life. The lyrics by Weldon Irvine contain a message of hope that reflects the same in Hansberry's work: "Young, gifted and black / We must begin to tell our young / There's a world waiting for you / This is a quest that's just begun." The song proved enduring, with popular versions recorded by soul singers Donny Hathaway and Aretha Franklin, the latter of which won a Grammy Award in 1972. Discussions of issues faced by black students in education also make use of the phrase, which has become shorthand for a history of discrimination and struggle, as well as for the necessity of personal agency for a better future.

Cheney's chapter on Hansberry's autobiography is one of the few in-depth treatments of the text. She analyzes individual pieces from the book, with particular attention to Hansberry's drama. Assessing her dramatic legacy in relation to her life, Cheney writes, "Avoiding facile arguments of what a more timely death would have wrought, Lorraine Hansberry stands firmly in the very respectable ranks of Edward Albee, Lillian Hellman, and Thornton Wilder. The duality of her life—the conflict between upper-middle-class influence and black heritage and revolution—produced creative tension, which led to compelling works." Further, in both the play and the book, Cheney views Nemiroff's inclusion of "rapidly shifting scenes" and complex structure as being especially conducive to "causing us to confront the complexity, beauty, joy, and courage of black life."

LANGSTON HUGHES'S "HARLEM" AND *A RAISIN IN THE SUN*

The title for Hansberry's most famous play comes from the poem "Harlem" by Langston Hughes. Written in 1951, the opening stanza queries "What happens to a dream deferred? / Does it dry up / like a raisin in the sun?" Hughes's poem was published at a time when the dreams of black Americans, strong after slavery's end, had shrunk under the force of economic hardship and second-class citizenship. In Hansberry's play, this "dream deferred" is the dream of economic success and of homeownership. The Younger family, receiving a large insurance check, is split about how to use the money. They eventually purchase a house in a white neighborhood, only to have their new neighbors try to buy them out to keep the neighborhood white. Hansberry based the play on her own family's experiences in the 1930s, when neighbors tried to use Chicago's racially restrictive housing covenants to force the Hansberry family to move.

Hughes's poem famously ends with the lines that predicted the coming civil rights clashes—"Maybe it just sags / like a heavy load. / … or does it explode?" Hansberry's play does not end with an explosion but rather with an affirmation of sorts. The family patriarch, Walter, rejects the neighbor's buyout offer, stating that the family is proud of who they are and will give up neither their dream nor their home to satisfy small-minded prejudice.

BIBLIOGRAPHY

Sources

Bourne, Kay. "Nemiroff/Hansberry—Legacy to the Black Community." *Bay State Banner* 7 Mar. 1974. *ProQuest.* Web. 20 Nov. 2012.

Carter, Stephen. "Commitment amid Complexity: Lorraine Hansberry's Life in Action." *MELUS* 7.3 (1980): 39–53. Print.

Cheney, Anne. "The Human Race Concerns Me: To Be Young, Gifted and Black." *Lorraine Hansberry.* Boston: Twayne, 1984. *The Twayne Authors Series.* Web. 20 Nov. 2012.

Hansberry, Lorraine. *To Be Young, Gifted and Black.* New York: Signet, 2011. Print.

Nemiroff, Robert. Foreword and Postscript. *To Be Young Gifted and Black.* By Lorraine Hansberry. New York: Signet, 2011. Print.

Further Reading

Hansberry, Lorraine. *A Raisin in the Sun.* London: Methuen Drama, 2009. Print.

Keppel, Ben. *The Work of Democracy: Ralph Bunche, Kenneth B. Clark, Lorraine Hansberry, and the Cultural Politics of Race.* Cambridge, Mass.: Harvard University Press, 1995. Print.

Knupfer, Anne Meis. *The Chicago Black Renaissance and Women's Activism.* Urbana: University of Illinois Press, 2006. Print.

Scheader, Catherine. *Lorraine Hansberry: Playwright and Voice of Social Justice.* Springfield, N.J.: Enslow, 1998. Print.

Tracy, Steven. *Writers of the Black Chicago Renaissance.* Urbana: University of Illinois Press, 2011. Print.

Wilkerson, Margaret. "The Sighted Eyes and Feeling Heart of Lorraine Hansberry." *Black American Literature Forum* 17.1 (1983): 8–13. Print.

Daisy Gard

TRUTH AND FICTION RELATING TO MY LIFE

Johann Wolfgang von Goethe

✤ Key Facts

Time Period:
Early 20th Century

Relevant Historical Events:
Napoleonic wars; French Revolution; Enlightenment

Nationality:
German

Keywords:
enlightenment; literature; politics

OVERVIEW

Johann Wolfgang von Goethe's autobiography *Aus Meinem Leben: Dichtung und Wahrheit* (*Truth and Fiction Relating to My Life*), which describes the upbringing and early adulthood of one of Europe's most highly regarded intellectuals, was published in three installments during his lifetime (1811, 1812, and 1814) with a final volume appearing posthumously (1833). After detailing his early exposure to different languages and many fields of culture and learning, Goethe tells of how he studied law, dabbled in art, wrote poetry and his first novel, fell in love more than once, and experienced many other romantic entanglements and complex friendships. At a time of heightened intellectual activity in Europe that became known as the Enlightenment, Goethe occupied a unique vantage point as both a man of the arts and state-appointed official, and he trained his talented eye, both in his autobiography and elsewhere, on as many matters as possible.

Goethe was a prolific writer of poetry, plays, novels, and studies of science and art; an art school administrator; and a high-ranking official in the Duchy of Saxe-Weimar. *Truth and Fiction* describes, among other things, events in the Seven Years' War, Marie-Antoinette's stopover in Strasbourg on her way to marry King Louis XVI of France, and goings-on at the Weimar court. Goethe's autobiography was welcomed as a chronicle of an extraordinary life. Its sensibility and colorfully rendered episodes are echoed in later examples of autobiography and may also have influenced the nineteenth-century novel.

HISTORICAL AND LITERARY CONTEXT

By the time Goethe began to write his memoirs in 1811, European politics had been forever changed by events surrounding the French Revolution and the subsequent Napoleonic wars. The Seven Years' War, which had begun in 1756 when the author was seven, created tension in the Goethe family; Goethe's grandfather supported the Austrians, while his father was loyal to Prussia. Prussia's King Frederick II ("the Great") invaded Saxony, which was allied to Austria, France, Sweden, and Russia. Prussia's allies were Great Britain and Hanover. These alliances marked the "Great Revolution" in European diplomacy; previously, the British had been allied with Austria and the French with Prussia.

In 1806 Napoléon Bonaparte's armies sacked Weimar, where Goethe was living, but the French leader spared Goethe's house because he admired his work. That same year Goethe married the mother of his only child. As he undertook his autobiography in the years that followed, Goethe also wrote books about his travels in Italy (*Italian Journey,* 1816–17); verses in the manner of the Persian poet Hāfez (*The Parliament of East and West,* 1819); a sequel to his 1796 novel *Wilhelm Meister* (1821, finalized in 1829); various studies of art and science; and, in 1832, a second installment of his play *Faust* (1808).

Truth and Fiction may be seen as a species of *Künstler-Roman,* a type of novel that emerged during the German romantic period, notably in Ludwig Tieck's *Franz Sternbalds Wanderungen* (1798; *Franz Sternbald's Wanderings*), in which the main character's progress toward becoming a full-fledged artist or writer is chronicled. Though not a novel, Goethe's work is highly stylized, yet confessional, and blurs the boundaries between the genres of fiction and autobiography. The same has been observed of major Enlightenment figure Jean-Jacques Rousseau's autobiography *Confessions* (1882), in which Rousseau, like Goethe, recounts minute details of family life and the depth of his boyhood impressions. In *Theory of the Novel: A Historical Approach,* scholar Northrop Frye writes of *Confessions*: "The confession flows into the novel, and the mixture produces the fictional autobiography." Goethe's title *Truth and Fiction* seems to acknowledge this phenomenon.

Coming from an author as renowned as Goethe, the scope and sweep of *Truth and Fiction* made him "the first writer or artist to become a Public Celebrity," according to poet W. H. Auden in his foreword to *The Sorrows of Young Werther and Novella. Truth and Fiction* may have influenced Charles Dickens's major nineteenth-century works. Walter Pater's 1895 autobiographical work *The Child in the House* recalls Goethe's descriptions of boyhood in his grandmother's Frankfurt townhouse, and James Joyce's *Portrait of the Artist as a Young Man* (1916), with its highly subjective narrative describing the writer's development, may also be seen as following in the footsteps of Goethe's autobiography.

THEMES AND STYLE

If *Truth and Fiction* lacks an identifiably central theme, it makes up for it in bringing to the narrative kaleidoscope the many elements Goethe had at his disposal. The richness of his life is a perfect match for his desire and ability to describe everything in great detail. Almost nothing escapes him, and he encapsulates people with precision, noticing a local artist's "little, fat, good, but unpleasant-looking, wife, who would let him have no model but herself." Himself emblematic of the emotionally charged style of writing called *sturm und drang* (storm and stress), Goethe observes of William Shakespeare's *Hamlet,* newly fashionable in its mid-eighteenth-century German translation: "Hamlet and his soliloquies were spectres which haunted all the young minds ... [as] everybody fancied he had a right to be just as melancholy as the Prince of Denmark." As one who "observed everything accurately, noted it down industriously," he seems to operate at a slight remove from his experiences.

Goethe's motivation for writing his four volumes appears to have been to pay tribute to the experiences and people who shaped his life and intellect. In a preface attached to some eighteenth-century editions, Goethe writes that the project began when an editor asked him to put into context some twelve volumes of his poetry. Goethe quotes the letter in full, which asks that he provide "the states of life and feeling, which have supplied the materials.... Yield this favour to a small circle, and perhaps it will give rise to something that may be entertaining and useful to a larger one." Complying with the request, Goethe writes, he "laboured to set forth my internal impulses, external incitements, and the successive steps of my theoretic and practical advancement." His words reveal gratitude for the quality of his life, and the autobiography's generous proportions may be interpreted as thanks offered to his enthusiastic readership.

Truth and Fiction's learned and graceful style immediately marks it as the work of a great man, which Goethe sees no point in hiding. As though to "imply an individual in harmony with the cosmos," as scholar Dennis F. Mahoney puts it in *The Cambridge Companion to Goethe,* Goethe's first act as narrator of his own life story is to describe the astrological position of the planets at the moment of his birth. He does so if only to note that their "good aspects, which the astrologers managed subsequently to reckon very auspicious for me, may have been the causes of my preservation; for, through the unskillfulness of the midwife, I came into the world as dead."

CRITICAL DISCUSSION

Even before the final volume came out in 1833, *Truth and Fiction* enjoyed great success. In 1832, recounting an anecdote about Goethe and the dramatist and poet Friedrich Schiller (the two were great friends), the *Oriental Observer* of Calcutta, India, remarked on "that tone of cheerful gravity, combining the clearest insight with tolerance and kindly humour, to which no reader of his *Dichtung und Wahrheit* can be a stranger." (Schiller, for his part, is quoted in the Calcutta paper as saying, "I never like Goethe until he has had a bottle of champagne.") When the final volume did appear, it was also praised. London's *The Satirist; or, the True Censor of the Times* reviewed an English translation in 1849: "The books comprising the conclusion of the Autobiography are written in a very amusing, gossiping style. The recollections of Lavater, Zimmerman, Spinoza are very interesting."

Goethe's autobiography, as with his other writings, has been continuously read and studied since its initial publication. Thomas Mann, the Nobel Prize–winning German novelist and devoted scholar and editor of Goethe, believed the autobiography to be a superb example of the genre, mining it and *The Sorrows of Young Werther* (1774) for his 1939 biographical novel about Goethe, *Lotte in Weimar*. Critical interest in the work ranges from deciphering marginalia in a copy owned by Herman Melville and indexing biographical details to examining his verse and prose works for evidence of his vision of an ideal Germany.

Truth and Fiction has been useful to scholars as one of the most important examples of autobiography. Stephen A. Shapiro's 1968 *Comparative Literature Studies* essay is one of the first works to defend autobiography as an artistic undertaking, noting that Nobel Prize win-

Portrait of German playwright Johann Wolfgang von Goethe.
© ALFREDO DAGLI ORTI/ THE ART ARCHIVE AT ART RESOURCE, NY

PRIMARY SOURCE

EXCERPT FROM *TRUTH AND FICTION RELATING TO MY LIFE*

About the condition of German literature of those times so much has been written, and so exhaustively, that every one who takes any interest in it can be completely informed; in regard to it critics agree now pretty well; and what at present I intend to say piecemeal and disconnectedly concerning it, relates not so much to the way in which it was constituted in itself, as to its relation to me. I will therefore first speak of those things by which the public is particularly excited; of those two hereditary foes of all comfortable life, and of all cheerful, self-sufficient, living poetry,—I mean, satire and criticism.

In quiet times every one wants to live after his own fashion: the citizen will carry on his trade or his business, and enjoy the fruits of it afterward; thus will the author, too, willingly compose something, publish his labours, and, since he thinks he has done something good and useful, hope for praise, if not reward. In this tranquillity the citizen is disturbed by the satirist, the author by the critic; and peaceful society is thus put into a disagreeable agitation.

The literary epoch in which I was born was developed out of the preceding one by opposition. Germany, so long inundated by foreigners, interpenetrated by other nations, directed to foreign languages in learned and diplomatic transactions, could not possibly cultivate her own. Together with so many new ideas, innumerable foreign words were obtruded necessarily and unnecessarily upon her; and, even for objects already known, people were induced to make use of foreign expressions and turns of speech. The German, having run wild for nearly two hundred years in an unhappy tumultuary state, went to school with the French to learn manners, and with the Romans in order to express his thoughts with propriety. But this was to be done in the mother-tongue, when the literal application of those idioms, and their half-Germanisation, made both the social and business style ridiculous. Besides this, they adopted without moderation the similes of the southern languages, and employed them most extravagantly. In the same way they transferred the stately deportment of the prince-like citizens of Rome to the learned German small-town officers, and were at home nowhere, least of all with themselves.

But as in this epoch works of genius had already appeared, the German sense of freedom and joy also began to stir itself. This, accompanied by a genuine earnestness, insisted that men should write purely and naturally, without the intermixture of foreign words, and as common intelligible sense dictated. By these praiseworthy endeavours, however, the doors and gates were thrown open to an extended national insipidity, nay,—the dike was dug through by which the great deluge was shortly to rush in. Meanwhile, a stiff pedantry long stood its ground in all the four faculties, until at last, much later, it fled for refuge from one of them to another.

SOURCE: Goethe, Johann Wolfgang von. *Truth and Fiction Relating to My Life.* Trans. John Oxenford. London: Robertson, Ashford and Bentley, 1902.

ner André Gide looked to Goethe, Stendhal, Rousseau, Michel de Montaigne, and others before writing his own. In *The Cambridge Companion to Goethe,* Mahoney proposes that Goethe, hoping to educate his readership, structured his autobiography "as a school for further developing the type of active and well-disposed reader whom the narrator imagines as his ideal audience." This, writes Mahoney, shows "a morphology of growth that runs parallel to the development of German literature."

BIBLIOGRAPHY

Sources

Auden, W. H. "Foreword." *The Sorrows of Young Werther and Novella.* New York: Vintage, 1973. Print.

Carlyle, Thomas. "Schiller, Goethe, and Madame de Staël." *Fraser's Magazine for Town and Country, Vol. 5, February to July 1832.* London: J. Fraser, 1832. *Google Books.* Web. 21 Nov. 2012.

Godwin, Parke, J. H. Hopkins., Charles A. Dana, and J. S. Dwight, trans. and eds. *The Auto-biography of Goethe. Truth and Poetry: From My Life.* New York: Wiley and Putnam, 1846–47. *HathiTrust.* Web. 2 Nov. 2012.

Goethe, Johann Wolfgang von. *Truth and Fiction Relating to My Life.* Trans. John Oxenford. London: Robertson, Ashford and Bentley, 1902. Print.

McKeon, Michael, ed. *Theory of the Novel: A Historical Approach.* Baltimore: Johns Hopkins University Press, 2000. Print.

Perloff, Marjorie G. "The Autobiographical Mode of Goethe: *Dichtung und Wahrheit* and the Lyric Poems." *Comparative Literature Studies* 7.3 (1970). *JSTOR.* Web. 2 Nov. 2012.

Shapiro, Stephen A. "The Dark Continent of Literature: Autobiography." *Comparative Literature Studies* 5.4 (1968). *JSTOR.* Web. 2 Nov. 2012.

Sharpe, Lesley, ed., *The Cambridge Companion to Goethe.* Cambridge: Cambridge University Press, 2002. Print.

Further Reading

Berghahn, Klaus L., and Jost Hermand, eds. *Goethe in German-Jewish Culture.* Rochester, N.Y.: Camden House, 2001. Print.

Boyle, Nicholas. *Goethe: The Poet and the Age.* Vols. 1 and 2. Oxford: Clarendon, 1991. Print.

Burkhard, Henke, Susanne Kord, and Simon Richter, eds. *Unwrapping Goethe's Weimar.* Rochester, N.Y. Camden House, 1999. Print.

Goethe, Johann Wolfgang von. *Goethe's Works, 5 vols.* Ed. Hjalmar Hjorth Boyesen. Philadelphia: G. Barrie, 1885. *The Online Library of Liberty.* Web. 2 Nov. 2012.

Lewis, Tess. "Goethe's Perpetual Puberty." *Hudson Review.* 53.4 (2001). *JSTOR.* Web. 2 Nov. 2012.

Mann, Thomas, ed. *The Permanent Goethe.* New York: Dial, 1958. Print.

McIntosh, James. "Melville's Copy of Goethe's Autobiography and Travels." *Studies in the American Renaissance* (1984). *JSTOR.* Web. 2 Nov. 2012.

Rebecca Rustin

The Writing Life
Annie Dillard

OVERVIEW

Published in 1989, Annie Dillard's lyrical memoir *The Writing Life* is a collection of metaphors on writing as well as personal anecdotes and metaphysical explorations of what it means to live the life of a writer. Born Annie Doak in Pittsburgh in 1945, Dillard is perhaps best known for her essays on the natural world. She wrote the Pulitzer Prize–winning *Pilgrim at Tinker Creek* (1975), a collection of nonfiction essays, and her work has been reprinted in anthologies of personal-voice nature writing that include such authors as John Muir, Edward Abbey, and Barry Lopez. In *The Writing Life*, Dillard uses vivid, sparse language to describe her vocation in almost monastic terms; she explains that writing requires patience, deprivation, and courage, and it rewards with rare moments of ecstasy. Fifteen years and several books after the publication of *Pilgrim at Tinker Creek*, the author appears to have lost her sense of certainty. She expresses doubts about the importance of writing, saying, "The written word is weak. Many people prefer life to it." In the process of crafting her memoir, Dillard seeks out her former certainty by rediscovering what is sacred about the work. *The Writing Life* is a chronicle of that search.

Initially *The Writing Life* received mixed reviews, with some critics expressing disappointment in its apparent self-importance, while others found Dillard's details on the craft of writing insightful. At the time the work was published, the nature of the subject in autobiography and memoir was being reexamined and redefined. Dillard joins other authors in exploring the use of a subject other than the author/narrator in a personal narrative. Today *The Writing Life* is better known for its contribution to memoir writing than for its literary merits. It is widely cited in anthologies on literature, nature writing, spiritual essays, and scholarly works on pedagogy.

HISTORICAL AND LITERARY CONTEXT

The Writing Life is Dillard's third book on writing. Her first two, *Living by Fiction* and *Teaching a Stone to Talk*, were published in 1982. In *The Writing Life* she challenges would-be writers to approach their work with caution, citing the dangers and pitfalls that come with serious writing. Her memoir also meditates on the environment and spirituality and, therefore, attracted followers of her earlier works. Writers and academics from three different genres of writing—nonfiction, eco-criticism, and spiritual writing—had staked a claim on Dillard as one of their own. Later scholars would begin to study the work for its contribution to the genre of memoir.

The Writing Life was published two years after Dillard's more traditional memoir, *An American Childhood* (1987), and reviewers tend to overlook its memoir-like qualities. This is due, in part, to the fact that the publisher of *The Writing Life* promoted it as a book on writing and to Dillard's use of multiple voices, which broke the rules for memoir. As understanding of the genre began to change, *The Writing Life* appeared in lists of memoirs. Once classified as simple records of autobiographical events, memoirs were suddenly recognized as having the potential to be far more artful. Writers such as Paul Auster, who composed *The Invention of Loneliness* (1982), and Vivian Gornick, writer of *Fierce Attachments* (1987), drew on their skills as fiction writers to fashion their memoirs. Just as Auster and others experimented with perspective, Dillard engaged in interpreting and reinterpreting her experiences, telling them from varied perspectives.

Dillard's memoir is part of two traditions with long histories: autobiography/memoir and nonfiction essay. These genres were adapted by nineteenth-century American transcendentalists Henry David Thoreau and Ralph Waldo Emerson to address environmental devastation caused by the Industrial Revolution. Dillard's work came at a time of renewed environmental awareness ushered in by the creation of the U.S. Environmental Protection Agency in 1970. The essays in *The Writing Life* can be traced to the transcendentalists' style, which flourished in the 1980s. Another essayist in this tradition, Barry Lopez, won the National Book Award in 1986 for *Arctic Dreams,* a series of personal essays exploring the relationship between humans and their natural surroundings. Lopez's writing has a spiritual, dreamlike quality and shares with Dillard's work a fierce desire to capture the wildness and power of nature, with the threat of ecological disaster lurking in the shadows.

Dillard's memoir has been the subject of some harsh criticism, the harshest of which may have come from the author herself. On her official website, Dillard posted a biography written by her husband, Bob Richardson, which claims the author had repudiated

---

❖ *Key Facts*

Time Period:
Late 20th Century

Relevant Historical Events:
Growing prominence of creative nonfiction; birth of eco-criticism

Nationality:
American

Keywords:
women's writing; eco-criticism; pedagogy

THEORIES

Fall colors in Roanoke, Virginia. Acclaimed author Annie Dillard won the 1975 Pulitzer Prize for General Non-Fiction for her book *Pilgrim at Tinker Creek*, set in Virginia. © MIRA/ALAMY

nearly everything about *The Writing Life*. Even so, the work has inspired numerous memoirs, essays exploring spirituality and nature, literary scholarship, and texts on creative writing. Among the best known of these is Anne Lamott's *Bird by Bird: Some Instructions on Writing and Life* (1995), which is a personal narrative that offers writing tips and insights into the writing process. Dillard's slim volume also has been particularly influential in pedagogical scholarship on nonfiction essay writing and research.

THEMES AND STYLE

The main threads running through Dillard's memoir are how to write and the idea of the writing life as a kind of holy calling. She opens the book with a series of second-person instructions on how to work: "When you write, you lay out a line of words. The line of words becomes a miner's pick. You wield it, and it digs a path you follow." Her message is clear: there is one path, and that path is grueling labor. She questions whether she's made the right choice. She repeatedly poses the question, why write? "Why not shoot yourself, actually, rather than finish one more excellent manuscript on which to gag the world?" But Dillard also expresses ever-present reverence for the work. Writing is the greatest form of freedom, she says, and the closest a human being comes to understanding the absolute in nature.

Published fifteen years after Dillard's earliest works, *The Writing Life* is a memoir of an experienced writer slogging through an existential crisis: "This is why many experienced writers urge young men and women to learn a useful trade." Throughout the text she offers arguments against her chosen art. "Writing is a sorry excuse for life," she observes. Ultimately, though, it is clear that Dillard has decided to press on with the work she knows.

Stylistically, *The Writing Life* is notable for its poetic descriptions of nature. One of many examples comes from chapter 3. "The window looked out on a bit of sandflat overgrown with thick, varicolored mosses; there were a few small firs where the sandflat met the cobble beach; and there was the water." Also worth noting are the author's prayer-like expressions. She uses repetition to sound incantatory. In chapter 5 there are a series of paragraphs filled with questions. She asks "Why?" "Can?" "What?" over and over until the text begins to feel like a prayer. Finally, the book is notable for the way the author shifts voices, sliding seamlessly, if inexplicably, from one identity to the next. The narration moves among the instructive second person to the more intimate first person to a distant third person.

CRITICAL DISCUSSION

Initially, *The Writing Life* met with mixed reviews. Birdie MacLennan's article for the *Harvard Book Review* is on the more effusive end with its praise for the author's sensitivity and integrity in observing and crafting images of human experience. Malcolm Bradbury's 1992 review of the book for the *London Times Literary Supplement* deems it successful at describing writing as an activity, whereas Suzanne Berne from *Belles Lettres* (1990) damns with faint praise when she writes that the book is at its best when the writing is not strident or relentless. Sarah Maitland's review for the *New York Times* pronounces the book a failure, calling it "overwritten, self-important, and, therefore, unrevealing." In a 1990 critique for the *American Scholar*, Bruce Bawer claims *The Writing Life* is less about the author's sense of wonder than her need to show off.

In the decades since its publication, *The Writing Life* has attracted steady interest. In his 2006 book *The History Beat: How a Journalist Covers the Past*, Tony Horwitz calls it "a wonderful little book" on craft. Though *The Writing Life* has not achieved the iconic status of *Pilgrim at Tinker Creek*, Dillard's better-known works have helped to keep memoir in the public eye. Scholars have approached *The Writing Life* through a variety of analytical lenses: its importance as a work of phenomenology, through issues of gender politics in transcendentalism, its contributions to the memoir genre, and as a teaching tool for students of creative nonfiction who are studying the use of made-up personas in the personal essay. Dillard's text also has attracted its share of loyal followers among pedagogy scholars. An example can be found in John Creswell's book, *Research Design: Qualitative, Quantitative and Mixed Method Approaches,* in which he credits *The*

Writing Life with serving as inspiration for both his work and his life.

A recent trend in scholarship on *The Writing Life* is the idea that the author employs (or hides behind, depending on the perspective) a male voice in her ostensibly autobiographical work; her third-person narrator at times refers to the writer as "he." In chapter 3 she writes, "He finds himself inventing wholly new techniques." Writing for *Arizona Quarterly*, Richard Hardack argues that Dillard writes "consistently in the male persona and deploying a male epistemology. But she almost never confronts gender in her work."

BIBLIOGRAPHY

Sources

Auster, Paul. *The Invention of Solitude*. New York: Penguin, 1982. Print.

Bawer, Bruce. "Quiet—Author Suffering." Rev. of *The Writing Life*, by Annie Dillard. *American Scholar* 59.3 (1990): 445–49. *JSTOR*. Web. 30 Oct. 2012.

Berne, Suzanne. "The Lonely Life." Rev. of *The Writing Life*, by Annie Dillard. *Belles Lettres* 5 (1990): 6. *LION*. Web. 30 Oct. 2012.

Bradbury, Malcolm. "The Bridgeable Gap." Rev. of *The Writing Life*, by Annie Dillard. *Times Literary Supplement* 17 Jan. 1992: 8. *LION*. Web. 30 Oct. 2012.

Creswell, John. *Research Design: Qualitative, Quantitative and Mixed Method Approaches*. Thousand Oaks, Calif.: Sage, 2009. Print.

Enger, Leif. *Peace Like a River*. New York: Grove, 2001. Print.

Gornick, Vivian. *Fierce Attachments: A Memoir*. New York: MacMillan, 1987. Print.

Hardack, Richard. "'A Woman Need Not Be Sincere': Annie Dillard's Fictional Autobiographies and the Gender Politics of American Transcendentalism." *Arizona Quarterly* 64.30 (2008): 75–108. *LION*. Web. 30 Oct. 2012.

Hollcomb, Chris, and M. Jimmie Killingsworth. *Performing the Prose: The Study and Practice of Style in Composition*. Carbondale: Southern Illinois University Press, 2010. Print.

Lamott, Anne. *Bird by Bird*. New York: Anchor, 1994. Print.

MacLennan, Birdie. Rev. of *The Writing Life*, by Annie Dillard. *Harvard Book Review* 13.14 (1989): 22. *JSTOR*. Web. 30 Oct. 2012.

Maitland, Sarah. "Spend It All, Shoot It, Play It, Lose It." Rev. of *The Writing Life*, by Annie Dillard. *New York Times*. New York Times, 17 Sept. 1989. Web. 28 Nov. 2012.

McLean, Norman. *A River Runs through It*. Chicago: University of Chicago Press, 1976. Print.

TRANSCENDENTAL FICTION

If Annie Dillard and fellow creative nonfiction writers Barry Lopez, John McPhee, Edward Abbey, Wendell Barry, and others are heirs to the American tradition of transcendental essay writing, authors such as Norman McLean and Leif Enger are heirs to that tradition in the realm of fiction. Their novels incorporate transcendental themes and exhibit a pantheistic, romanticized reverence for nature that recalls the writing of Ralph Waldo Emerson and Henry David Thoreau. A passage from McLean's *A River Runs through It* (1976) illustrates the thread of idealized nature: "In the slanting sun of late afternoon the shadow of great branches reached across the river, and the trees took the river in their arms. The shadows continued up the bank, until they included us." In *Peace Like a River* (2001), Enger's belief in the spiritual power of language echoes the many prayerlike, poetic passages in Dillard's work: "The pulse of the country worked through my body until I recognized it as music. As language. And the language ran everywhere inside me."

Like Dillard's narrators, the characters in McLean and Enger find a stark, instructive beauty in stories from the Old Testament; they cling to Lazarus and Job for support. As one character from Enger's novel remarks about his father's relationship with his Bible, "Oh, but he worked that book; he held to it like a rope ladder."

Stone, Albert E. "Autobiography in American Culture: Looking Back at the 1970s." *American Studies International* 19.3–4 (1981): 3–14. *JSTOR*. Web. 28 Nov. 2012.

Further Reading

Bullough, Robert V., Jr., and Stefinee Pinnegar. "Guidelines in Autobiographical Forms of Self-Study Research." *Educational Researcher* 30.3 (2001): 13–21. *LION*. Web. 30 Oct. 2012.

Ireland, Julie A. "Annie Dillard's Ecstatic Phenomenology." *ISLE* 17.1 (2010): 23–34. *LION*. Web. 30 Oct. 2012.

Johnson, Sandra Humble. *The Space Between: Literary Epiphany in the Work of Annie Dillard*. Kent, Ohio: Kent State University Press, 1992. Print.

Moore, Dinty T. Rev. of *The Made-Up Self: Impersonating in the Personal Essay*, by Carl Klaus. *Fourth Generation* 13.1 (2011): 177–83. *LION*. Web. 30 Oct. 2012.

Slovic, Scott. *Seeking Awareness in American Nature Writing: Henry Thoreau, Annie Dillard, Edward Abbey, Wendell Berry and Barry Lopez*. Salt Lake City: University of Utah Press, 1992. Print.

Kristin King-Ries

WAR EXPERIENCES

An Arab-Syrian Gentleman and Warrior in the Period of the Crusades: Memoirs of Usāmah ibn Munqidh by Usāmah ibn Munqidh	285
An Autobiography, with Musings on Recent Events in India by Jawaharlal Nehru	289
Barefoot Gen: A Cartoon Story of Hiroshima by Keiji Nakazawa	293
Exiled Memories: A Cuban Childhood by Pablo Medina	296
Farewell to Manzanar by Jeanne Wakatsuki Houston and James D. Houston	299
Geronimo: His Own Story by Geronimo and S. M. Barrett	302
Golden Bones: An Extraordinary Journey from Hell in Cambodia to a New Life in America by Sichan Siv	306
The Invisible Thread by Yoshiko Uchida	309
A Long Way Gone: Memoirs of a Boy Soldier by Ishmael Beah	312
The Memoirs of Lady Anne Halkett by Lady Anne Halkett	315
Night by Elie Wiesel	318
Paekpom Ilchi: The Autobiography of Kim Ku by Kim Ku	322
The Sovereignty and Goodness of God by Mary Rowlandson	325
Testament of Youth by Vera Brittain	329
Wars I Have Seen by Gertrude Stein	332
When Heaven and Earth Changed Places: A Vietnamese Woman's Journey from War to Peace by Le Ly Hayslip and Jay Wurts	335
A Woman Soldier's Own Story by Xie Bingying	338

An Arab-Syrian Gentleman and Warrior in the Period of the Crusades

Memoirs of Usāmah ibn Munqidh

Usāmah ibn Munqidh

OVERVIEW

Written in Arabic at the end of the twelfth century, *An Arab-Syrian Gentleman and Warrior in the Period of the Crusades: Memoirs of Usāmah ibn Munqidh* is recognized in Western scholarship as one of the most important Arab Muslim narratives of the Crusades. First translated into English in 1929, Usāmah's memoirs provide a vital counterperspective to European accounts of the period. Through anecdotes, bits of poetry, and commentary, the text offers a social and cultural history of Egypt and Greater Syria, or *bilad al-sham,* a region encompassing modern-day Syria, Lebanon, Jordan, Palestine, and Israel, at the time of Saladin. The Arabic title of the text, *Kitab al-I'tibar,* can be translated as "learning by example," and Usāmah's memoirs, written at the end of his long life, are meant to be didactic as well as entertaining. Usāmah sets forth his own life in *An Arab-Syrian Gentleman* as a model for future generations, while stressing the idea that life is governed by divine will, and no individual action can alter fate.

When *An Arab-Syrian Gentleman* was translated into English, it was warmly received by critics who welcomed it as a significant addition to the historical record of the twelfth century. Scholars expressed particular interest in Usāmah's descriptions of the Franks, or Latin Christians, viewing his portrayal of their strange behavior and customs as a necessary counterpoint to European Crusader impressions of "the other." The text was also valued as a unique example of Arabic autobiography, although later studies have uncovered a strong Arabic autobiographical tradition, including a "cluster" of works by Usāmah's contemporaries. Today *An Arab-Syrian Gentleman* is still approached as a rich source for social, cultural, political, and science histories, although some scholars have begun to question its framing as autobiography, arguing that this characterization neglects its literary qualities while inviting scholars to read Usāmah's observations as both consistently truthful and representative of wider attitudes.

HISTORICAL AND LITERARY CONTEXT

An Arab-Syrian Gentleman provides an impressionistic military, political, social, and cultural history of Greater Syria and offers insight into the life of an elite Muslim nobility. In 1080 Usāmah's family, the Banu Munqidh, seized the small but strategically important city of Shayzar (in what is today northern Syria) from the Christian Byzantine Empire, and Usāmah was born there in 1095. Later that same year, Pope Urban II, responding to a plea from the Byzantine emperor Alexius Comnenus for help defending the borders of his empire against the advancing Seljuk Turks, issued a call to liberate Jerusalem and reconquer the Holy Land, beginning the First Crusade. By 1099 the Crusader armies had captured Jerusalem and established four Crusader states, including the nearby principality of Antioch, solidifying the Frankish presence in the region. An agreement reached by Usāmah's uncle, Sultan, delayed serious confrontation. As a child of noble birth, Usāmah studied grammar, calligraphy, and poetry, in addition to receiving a traditional Qur'anic education; acquired the combat skills that would serve him from a young age in frequent skirmishes with the Franks and other Arab tribes; and became an adept hunter, familiar with the habits of the lions, hyenas, and other wild animals that populated the region.

Usāmah wrote, or possibly dictated, his autobiography at the end of his life, when he was about ninety years old. Following his father's death in 1138, Sultan banished Usāmah from Shayzar. He fell into the employ of Mu'in al-Din Unur, the governor of Damascus, who charged him with negotiating an alliance with Jerusalem. Usāmah's journeys during this period provided much of the material for the sections of his autobiography dealing with the Franks. In the decades that followed, he held a series of diplomatic posts in Damascus and Cairo but was never able to establish a lasting relationship with a patron. His reputation as an "inveterate intriguer" and "mischief-maker" seems to have been well deserved, and he was repeatedly forced to resign his post or flee. In 1174 Usāmah was invited to the Damascus court of Saladin, the famous Counter-Crusader who unified Egypt and Greater Syria under his rule and established the Ayyubid dynasty. After just two years, however, Usāmah fell out of his favor and was pushed into retirement. It was at this time that he wrote his

Key Facts

Time Period:
Late 19th Century

Relevant Historical Events:
European colonization of Africa

Nationality:
German/Tanzanian

Keywords:
colonialism; women's rights; Arab culture

Loyset Liédet's fifteenth-century depiction of the Muslim leader Saladin at the Battle of Hattin, a key 1187 battle during the era of the Crusades. Usāmah ibn Munqidh recalls this era in his twelfth-century memoirs, *An Arab-Syrian Gentleman and Warrior in the Period of the Crusades*. © KHARBINE-TAPABOR/ THE ART ARCHIVE AT ART RESOURCE, NY

memoirs. He died in 1188, one year after Saladin reclaimed Jerusalem.

An Arab-Syrian Gentleman is part of a grouping of autobiographical texts written in Greater Syria at the turn of the thirteenth century, around the period of Saladin's rule. Many of the writers had personal connections to each other and to Saladin. The autobiography of historian and poet Umara al-Hakami al-Yamani, whom Saladin charged with treason and crucified in 1175, has been compared with Usāmah's memoirs for its literary style. Among the immediate successors of Usāmah's autobiography are *The Syrian Thunderbolt*, by Imad al-Din al-Katib al-Isfahani (d. 1201), which is framed as a biography of Saladin but focuses on Imad al-Din's own involvement in the sultan's affairs as his personal secretary.

Since its translation into English, *An Arab-Syrian Gentleman* has been considered one of the most important Arab Islamic counternarratives to European Christian accounts of the Crusades. The authors of *Interpreting the Self: Autobiography in the Arabic Literary Tradition* (2001) identify it as "one of the best-known medieval Arabic autobiographies in the West," and it occupies a central place in medieval scholarship on the region. Historians of science have mined the text for details about contemporary approaches to ecology and medicine, while other scholars have taken a broader view, utilizing it as a primary source for Arab-Islamic-centric reconstructions of the Crusades, as in Amin Maalouf's *The Crusades through Arab Eyes* (1983) and Carole Hillenbrand's *The Crusades: Islamic Perspectives* (1999).

THEMES AND STYLE

The central theme of Usāmah's memoirs is that the span of each man's life, as well as his personal successes and failures, are controlled solely by God: "Fate is an impregnable fortress." There is no shame in military defeat nor pride in victory because either outcome is attributed to divine will rather than "organization and planning" or "the number of troops and supporters." Cowardice and "over-cautiousness" will not prolong a man's life, just as bravery and reckless courage will not shorten it: "the duration of the life of a man is fixed and predetermined." Through anecdotes, Usāmah sought to impart these lessons to his readers. Even in his well-studied accounts of the Crusades, he credits God, "the author of all things," with the strange behavior of the Franks. Although the author goes on to complicate his initial descriptions of the Crusaders, he first exclaims: "When one comes to recount cases regarding the Franks, he cannot but glorify Allah (exalted is he!) and sanctify him, for he sees them as animals possessing the virtues of courage and fighting, but nothing else; just as animals have only the virtues of strength and carrying loads."

Although the only extant manuscript of *An Arab-Syrian Gentleman* is incomplete and the opening pages explaining the author's motivations for writing it have been lost, the text, composed when Usāmah was about ninety years old, reveals a desire to share the wisdom, values, and stories he acquired during the course of his long life. Notes at the end of the manuscript indicate that it was read by Usāmah's son, who in turn charged Usāmah's great-grandson with keeping the chain of transmission unbroken. The authors of *Interpreting the Self* stress that "the memoirs successfully ensured the transmission and perpetuation of a particular elite culture to [Usāmah's] progeny," preserving the memory of his own life as well as that of a specific "cultural group and class."

Stylistically, *An Arab-Syrian Gentleman* is notable for its informal style and associative organization of ideas. Having no chronological structure, the text relies instead on general themes to group anecdotes, meditations, and bits of poetry, a style that was common among Arabic literary works of the period. The informal language of Usāmah's memoirs, full of colloquialisms and grammatical errors, is incongruous given the author's elite education, reputation as a poet, and demonstrated love of literature. While some scholars blame a copyist, H. A. R. Gibb, writing for *Bulletin of the School of Oriental Studies,* interprets it as an accurate transcription of Usāmah's spoken Arabic, praising his scribe for creating a text in which "we can actually hear the man talking."

CRITICAL DISCUSSION

Upon the translation of *An Arab-Syrian Gentleman* into English, Western scholars emphasized its value as a historical document and welcomed the Arab Islamic voice it contributed to the field of Crusades studies, but they paid little attention to its literary value. In a 1930 review in the *Journal of the American Oriental Society,* James A. Montgomery hails Usāmah's memoirs as an important counternarrative: "To the student who knows the Crusades only through the Christian chronicles and the enthusiasm of the movement created in Europe and yet is indirectly informed on Islam, there is no better document than this by which to see the other side of the shield and to appreciate the spirit and character of the opponents of the Christian knights, themselves as knightly and in their own way as devout." Gibb similarly praises the text, asserting that it "[forms], to the Western reader, probably the most fascinating book in Arabic literature" and further identifying it as "the most valuable single source we possess for the social history of Syria at the time of the early Crusades."

THE POET OF THE AGE

The study and memorization of poetry were key components of elite education in the medieval Arab world, and Usāmah ibn Munqidh boasted that he had committed "twenty thousand verses of pre-Islamic poetry" to memory. It is not surprising, then, that in addition to his fame as a politician and warrior, Usāmah was a renowned poet. Historian Ibn Asakir, a contemporary of Usāmah, identified him as "the poet of the age" and said that his verse was "sweeter than honey and more to be relished than slumber after a prolonged period of vigilance."

Belle-lettrists writing in Arabic often incorporated poetry into their prose, using verse to bolster an argument or to illustrate a point. In this tradition, Usāmah included selections from his own poetry in his memoirs. For example, during his meditations on old age, Usāmah turns to lines he wrote several years earlier to describe his condition: "Destiny seems to have forgotten me, so that now I am like / An exhausted camel left by the caravan in the desert." Here, as in the framing prose text, he emphasizes once again that nothing can change "the hour of death," although he wishes he had died in battle rather than living a life "so prolonged that the revolving days have taken from me all the objects of pleasure."

In the years that followed, *An Arab-Syrian Gentleman* maintained its prominence even as the discovery of additional Arabic autobiographical accounts from the same and earlier periods undermined earlier claims to its singularity. Philip K. Hitti's translation was reprinted in 1987 and again in 2000. It remains, as Dana Sajdi remarked in a 2002–2003 review in the *Arab Studies Journal,* "an invaluable source" to the historian, "[offering] a rare and impressively wide view of lived history" in the form of an "infinitely lively narrative."

Although historians frequently utilize Usāmah's memoirs as a source, some have approached the text more critically, questioning its proper categorization as well as the prevalence of the author's observations and attitudes. Hillenbrand acknowledges the value of *An Arab-Syrian Gentleman and Warrior* in her 1999 *The Crusades: Islamic Perspectives* but cautions that it has "been overexploited, often rather too simplistically, by scholars, as if it is always appropriate to take it at its face value and as if no other evidence were available in the Islamic sources." She argues that because the text is work of *adab,* "a genre of Arabic literature … which aimed to please, divert and titillate its readers as well as to instruct them," and as such was "not bound by conventions to tell the 'truth,'" Usāmah's anecdotes and stories, particularly those about the Franks, should be approached with a degree of skepticism, as she does in her own study. In his essay in *The Middle Ages in Texts and Texture* (2011), Adnan Husain similarly seeks to correct the misconception that Usāmah's impressions of the Franks can be viewed straightforwardly as "a typical voice representing 'the other side.'" Instead, Husain asserts, "Usāmah's relations with and representations of the Latin Christians appear … , in some cases, unique to him" because they seem to have been based on "social differences within a horizon of elite warrior culture shared by both Christians and Muslims" that outweigh the religious differences most obvious to a contemporary audience.

BIBLIOGRAPHY

Sources

Gibb, H. A. R. Rev. of *An Arab-Syrian Gentleman and Warrior in the Period of the Crusades: The Memoirs of Usāmah ibn Munqidh,* by Usāmah ibn Munqidh. Trans. Philip K. Hitti. *Bulletin of the School of Oriental Studies* 6.4 (1932): 1003–11. Print.

Hillenbrand, Carole. *The Crusades: Islamic Perspectives.* Edinburgh: Edinburgh University Press, 1999. Print.

Husain, Adnan. "Wondrous Crusade Encounters: Usamah ibn Munqidh's *Book of Learning by Example.*" *The Middle Ages in Texts and Texture: Reflections on Medieval Sources.* Ed. Jason Glenn. Toronto: University of Toronto Press, 2011. 189–202. Print.

Montgomery, James A. Rev. of *An Arab-Syrian Gentleman and Warrior in the Period of the Crusades: The Memoirs of Usāmah ibn Munqidh,* by Usāmah ibn Munqidh (trans. Philip K. Hitti), and *The Origins of the Druze People and Religion with Extracts from Their Sacred Writings,* by Philip K. Hitti. *Journal of the American Oriental Society* 50 (1930): 261–63. Print.

Reynolds, Dwight F., ed. *Interpreting the Self: Autobiography in the Arabic Literary Tradition.* Berkeley: University of California Press, 2001. Print.

Sajdi, Dana. Rev. of *An Arab-Syrian Gentleman and Warrior in the Period of the Crusades: The Memoirs of Usāmah ibn Munqidh,* by Usāmah ibn Munqidh. Trans. Philip K. Hitti. *Arab Studies Journal* 11–12.1–2 (2003–04): 189–91. Print.

Further Reading

Christie, Niall. "Just a Bunch of Dirty Stories?: Women in the 'Memoirs' of Usamah Ibn Munqidh." *Eastward Bound: Travel and Travellers, 1050–1550.* Ed. Rosamund Allen. New York: Manchester University Press, 2004. 71–87. Print.

Cobb, Paul M. *Usama ibn Munqidh: Warrior-Poet of the Age of Crusades.* Oxford, U.K.: Oneworld, 2005. Print.

France, John, and William G. Zajac, eds. *The Crusades and Their Sources: Essays Presented to Bernard Hamilton.* Brookfield, U.K.: Ashgate, 1998. Print.

Ibn Jubayr. *The Travels of Ibn Jubayr.* Trans. R. J. C. Broadhurst. London: J. Cape, 1952. Print.

Maalouf, Amin. *The Crusades through Arab Eyes.* New York: Schocken, 1985. Print.

Allison Blecker

An Autobiography, with Musings on Recent Events in India

Jawaharlal Nehru

OVERVIEW

First published in 1936, Jawaharlal Nehru's *An Autobiography, with Musings on Recent Events in India* provides a firsthand account of the author's development into one of the most significant leaders of the Indian independence movement. Composed while Nehru was imprisoned by the British for his nationalist activism, the autobiography traces his progression from a childhood of privilege through his education in England to his deepening involvement in the struggle to free India from centuries of colonial rule. Central to the narrative is Nehru's conflicted relationship with Mohandas Gandhi, the most prominent advocate for Indian independence. Throughout the text, Nehru indicts not only British rule but also traditional Indian forms of government and religion. In their stead, he advocates for a peaceful revolution that will lead to a modern, independent, and socialist India. Though Nehru's autobiography purports to offer only an account of his "own mental development," the narrative of his life is so intertwined with the movement for Indian independence that his personal account becomes deeply political.

When Nehru's autobiography was published, his longtime alliance with Gandhi at the forefront of the Indian independence movement had begun to come undone. Whereas Gandhi perceived the movement as a personal and spiritual matter, Nehru saw it in purely political and social terms. In 1934, the year Nehru began his book, Gandhi left the Congress Party, which led the independence movement. *An Autobiography* describes Nehru's despair over Gandhi's departure, as well as the sources of their disagreement. Immediately popular with audiences interested in the life of such a prominent figure, the book helped Nehru assume leadership of the independence movement as Gandhi seemingly stepped away. Today his autobiography is considered an important firsthand account by the man who would become India's first prime minister.

HISTORICAL AND LITERARY CONTEXT

An Autobiography was composed during a period of great unrest in India, as the colonial order began to crack under pressure from a growing independence movement. In 1917 the colonial authorities announced that India would be encouraged to adopt self-governing institutions but would remain within the British Empire. Soon thereafter, however, the British in 1919 passed the Rowlatt Acts, which allowed the colonial government to detain prisoners without evidence. In response a renewed protest movement emerged, and nationwide work stoppages broke out in cities. Then, also in 1919, hundreds of peaceful protestors were massacred by the British general Reginald Dyer at Amritsar. The massacre and the government's callous response led to a loss of faith in the alleged good intentions of the British to allow self-governance. It also led to Gandhi's emergence as the leader of a nonviolent noncooperation movement for true Indian independence.

By the time Nehru's autobiography was published, he had spent some fifteen years engaged with Gandhi and other members of the Congress Party in the movement to free Indians from British rule. While initially a committed follower of Gandhi, Nehru began to move away from his mentor and to argue that socialist redistribution of wealth was integral to the movement's success. Gandhi, on the other hand, saw class struggle as inimical to the success of a unified independence movement. Despite their difference of opinion, Nehru participated in the Gandhi-led noncooperation movement as it ramped up in the early 1920s and intensified in the early 1930s. In 1930, after nearly a decade of intermittent strikes and other protest actions, Gandhi organized a 240-mile march to protest a British tax on salt. This protest strengthened the independence movement and led to a crackdown in which some forty thousand Indians, including Nehru, were imprisoned in 1932. When Nehru was released in 1934, he began to advocate increasingly for an Indian state based on Russian-style communism. He also deemed Gandhi's policy of nonviolence "inadequate" and called for revolution. Then, after a devastating earthquake in the province of Bihar, Nehru ruthlessly criticized the British response and was jailed again, for the seventh time, in February 1934. While imprisoned, he began his autobiography.

Nehru's autobiography is part of a tradition of anticolonialist writings that appeared during the Indian independence movement and that can be traced back to Gandhi's *Hind Swaraj*. Though Nehru's autobiography fundamentally argues against Gandhi's

❖ **Key Facts**

Time Period:
Mid-20th Century

Relevant Historical Events:
Growth of the Indian independence movement; Nehru's incarceration

Nationality:
Indian

Keywords:
colonialism; incarceration; socialism

Indian prime minister Jawaharlal Nehru in Delhi, 1947, with his grandson Rajiv Gandhi, who would become prime minister in 1984. © BETTMANN/CORBIS

notion that the independence movement was a moral rather than a political issue, the two share a deep concern with Indian nationalism. In 1933, a year before beginning his autobiography, Nehru published a pamphlet titled *Whither India?* In it, Nehru offers a Marxist account of Indian history and the Indian independence movement, asking, as quoted in Stanley Wolpert's *Nehru: A Tryst with Destiny* (1996), "Whither India? Surely to the great human goal of social and economic equality, to the ending of all exploitation of nation by nation and class by class, to national freedom with the framework of an international cooperative socialist world federation." This conception is central to the vision put forth a few years later, in Nehru's autobiography.

After its publication, *An Autobiography* proved to inspire a number of similar autobiographical writings. As the scholar Philip Holden argues in his 2005 essay in *Biography*, "In its mapping of individual onto national story, Nehru's text became the model for a series of national autobiographies written by the leaders of nations emerging from colonialism: Kwame Nkrumah's *Ghana* and Kenneth Kaunda's *Zambia Must Be Free*, for example, and later in the century, Nelson R. Mandela's *Long Walk to Freedom* and Lee Kuan Yew's retrospective *The Singapore Story*." The success of Nehru's autobiography also led to his own continued interrogation of his life story within a national context, as can be seen in his 1946 book *The Discovery of India*.

THEMES AND STYLE

The central theme of Nehru's autobiography is that the cause of Indian independence is worth the personal sacrifice and struggle that it requires. Throughout the text, Nehru refers to his own experience of deprivation and repeated imprisonment as fodder for his nationalist efforts as well as his socialist leanings. For him, this experience is instructive: "In prison one begins to appreciate the Marxian theory, that the State is really the coercive apparatus meant to enforce the will of a group that controls the government." Nehru uses his personal story of persecution to make a larger case for the extent and injustice of British repression in India and thus the need for popular resistance. This resistance, however, should not romanticize the precolonial past. Rather, it should acknowledge "the splendid gift" of science, which the British brought, and it should seek a path forward to modernity and prosperity. As Nehru writes, "Let us have done with the past and its bickering and face the future."

Nehru wrote his autobiography while imprisoned in the Dehru Dun jail from June 1934 to February 1935. As he writes in the book's preface, "The primary object in writing these pages was to occupy myself with a definite task, so necessary in the long solitudes of gaol life, as well as to review past events in India, with which I had been connected, to enable myself to think clearly about them." In addition to this deeply personal motivation, Nehru had a more public reason to write about his life: he hoped to demonstrate that his vision for India's future, rather than Gandhi's, was the right one. While acknowledging Gandhi's importance and virtue, Nehru expresses doubts about the effectiveness of nonviolence and the need "for some consistent philosophy of action which is both moral from the individual view-point and is at the same time socially effective." Written soon after Gandhi's departure from the Congress Party, Nehru's text uses an autobiographical narrative to demonstrate the shortcomings of Gandhi's spiritual rather than political conception of the independence and to make a pragmatic case for an industrialized and socialist Indian state.

Stylistically, Nehru's autobiography is notable for its mix of personal narrativizing and political theorizing. As the text moves between these modes, they become increasingly intertwined, so that the story of Nehru's life becomes an argument about the Indian independence movement. For example, his experience as a prisoner becomes a metaphor for India's own repression at the hands of the British. As Nehru writes of his time in Naini Tal prison, "A more sensible economic policy, more employment, more education would soon empty out our prisons. But of course to make that successful, a radical plan affecting the whole of our social fabric is essential." In this way his life experience is employed for his larger case about the nature of his political vision.

CRITICAL DISCUSSION

Upon publication, *An Autobiography* was an immediate and enduring success, selling well and eliciting extensive critical praise. Within the first few months of its appearance, the book was reprinted several times and garnered numerous glowing reviews. In the *Annals of the American Academy of Political and Social Science*, for example, Hans Kohn writes, "It is at the same time an outstanding book by its unusual human appeal and by the charm and the sincerity of the remarkable personality of the author, who combined with a rare power of expression a keen sensibility." Not all English-language reviewers were so flattering, however. In *International Affairs*, a reviewer faults Nehru for failing to mention "the state of anarchy which Nehru was active in fomenting, and the terrible strain imposed on the British officials in India of maintaining law and order against the insurgent forces of which he was the leader."

Following the autobiography's appearance, Nehru became increasingly prominent within the Indian independence movement. When in 1947 Britain at last granted India freedom, he became Indian's first prime minister. Guided by the same ideals he espoused in his autobiography, Nehru spent the next seventeen years leading the newly independent nation toward secularism, democracy, and socialism. Though not entirely successful, he did initiate Marxist economic policy, adopted a constitution that ensured equality, and worked to establish freedom of religion. Scholars have approached *An Autobiography* as an important document within the context of both the Indian independence movement and the broader twentieth-century anticolonialist struggle.

Nehru's autobiography continues to be read within the context of other anticolonial autobiographies. Holden calls *An Autobiography* a "paradigmatic text" for the way it sets up a framework for other anticolonial autobiographical writings that "map the disciplinary action of the nationalism movement on the chaos of the nation onto the protagonist's disciplining of a male body." In these texts, Holden writes, "a retrospective narrator shapes the events of the protagonist's life into a narrative of growth towards emancipation, just as nationalism itself is a narrative which remakes the past, populating it with national epics, national consciousness, national heroes before the nation is even thought of." Some commentators have questioned the text's effectiveness as a challenge to colonialism. In *Nationalist Thought and the Colonial World* (1993), Partha Chatterjee criticizes Nehru's autobiography for accepting "the very intellectual premises of 'modernity' upon which colonial domination was based."

BIBLIOGRAPHY

Sources

Chatterjee, Partha. *Nationalist Thought and the Colonial World: A Derivative Discourse?* Minneapolis: University of Minnesota Press, 1993. Print.

THE DISCOVERY OF INDIA

An Autobiography, with Musings on Recent Events in India was not the only book Jawaharlal Nehru penned in prison. In 1944, during his ninth and final stint in jail, he wrote a comprehensive work of Indian history, philosophy, and culture titled *The Discovery of India*. Jailed along with 60,000 other members of the Congress Party for his participation in the Quit India movement, which Gandhi catalyzed as an effort to achieve immediate independence, Nehru wrote of India's past in order to demonstrate the urgency for action in the present. As he writes, "Yet the past is ever with us and all that we are and that we have comes from the past.... To combine it with the present and extend it to the future, to break from where it cannot be so united, to make of all this the pulsating and vibrating material for thought and action—that is life."

Though primarily a work of history, *The Discovery of India* relies often on a personal approach. Of his approach, Nehru writes that "this is not going to be autobiography, though I am afraid the personal element will often be present." In fact, in the book's second chapter, Nehru picks up where *An Autobiography* leaves off: with his release from prison in 1935. As he proceeds, the facts of Nehru's life merge and intersect with the story he tells of the Indian nation and its fight to free itself from colonial rule.

Holden, Philip. "Other Modernities: National Autobiography and Globalization." *Biography* 28.1 (2005): 89–103. *Project MUSE*. Web. 19 Nov. 2012.

———. Rev. of *Autobiography, Travel and Postnational Identity: Gandhi, Nehru and Iqbal*, by Javed Majeed. *Biography* 30.3 (2007): 379–82. *Project MUSE*. Web. 20 Nov. 2012.

Kohn, Hans. Rev. of *An Autobiography*, by Jawaharlal Nehru. *Annals of the American Academy of Political and Social Science* 191 (1937): 274–75. *SAGE*. Web. 19 Nov. 2012.

Meston. Rev. of *An Autobiography, with Musings on Recent Events in India* and *India and the World*, by Jawaharlal Nehru. *International Affairs* 17.1 (1938): 132–34. *JSTOR*. Web. 19 Nov. 2012.

Nehru, Jawaharlal. *An Autobiography, with Musings on Recent Events in India*. Bombay: Allied, 1962. Print.

———. *The Discovery of India*. New York: Oxford University Press, 1994. Print.

Wolpert, Stanley. *Nehru: A Tryst with Destiny*. New York: Oxford University Press, 1996. Print.

Further Reading

Crocker, Walter. *Nehru: A Contemporary's Estimate*. London: Allen, 1979. Print.

Majeed, Javal. *Autobiography, Travel and Postnational Identity: Gandhi, Nehru and Iqbal*. Houndmills, U.K.: Palgrave, 2007. Print.

Mathai, M. O. *Reminiscences of the Nehru Age*. New Delhi: Vikas, 1978. Print.

Naik, M. K. "The Discovery of Nehru: A Study of Jawaharlal Nehru's Autobiography." *Perspectives on Indian Prose in English.* Ed. by Naik. Atlantic Highlands, N.J.: Humanities, 1982. Print.

Nanda, B. R. *Jawaharlal Nehru: Rebel and Statesman.* Delhi: Oxford University Press, 1995. Print.

Ramanan, Mohan. "Jawaharlal Nehru: The Writer as Maker of a Nation." *Literary Criterion* 32.3 (1996): 55–60. Print.

Stilz, Gerhard. "Experiments in Squaring the Ellipsis: A Critical Reading of the Autobiographies of Gandhi, Nehru, Chaudhuri and Anand." *New Perspectives in Indian Literature in English: Essays in Honour of Professor M. K. Naik.* Ed. C. R. Yaravintelimath, et al. New Delhi: Sterling, 1995. Print.

Zakaria, Rafiq, ed. *A Study of Nehru.* Calcutta: Rupa, 1989. Print.

Theodore McDermott

BAREFOOT GEN
A Cartoon Story of Hiroshima
Keiji Nakazawa

OVERVIEW

Originally published in Japan in 1973, Keiji Nakazawa's *Barefoot Gen: A Cartoon Story of Hiroshima* is a fictionalized autobiography in graphic novel form; the work recounts Nakazawa's survival of the U.S. nuclear attack on Hiroshima in August 1945. Told from the perspective of six-year-old Gen, the book traces the travails of his family in the months leading up to the bombing, ending with the death of his father and brother and the premature birth of his sister in the immediate aftermath of the blast. Nakazawa, who was en route to school when the bomb exploded, remembers what followed as "a living hell, the details of which remain etched in my brain as if it happened yesterday."

Comic books and graphic novels enjoyed a great deal of popularity in twentieth-century Japan, although *Barefoot Gen* marks the first significant graphic contribution to the tradition of literature written by survivors of the Hiroshima and Nagasaki attacks. Popular and well reviewed upon publication in Japan, the book has been translated into many languages (including English) and has exposed millions of readers to its compelling depiction of the horror of the atomic bomb. Spawning nine sequels, several animated adaptations, and 2011's prose *Hiroshima: The Autobiography of Barefoot Gen,* the work is widely considered to be groundbreaking in genre and a classic work of *hibakusha* (bomb survivor) literature.

HISTORICAL AND LITERARY CONTEXT

Keiji Nakazawa was six years old when the United States dropped a nuclear bomb on Hiroshima, where Nakazawa lived with his family. Although Germany had surrendered to the Allies on May 7, 1945, Japan's militaristic government vowed to fight on, ignoring the demand for surrender put forward in July's Potsdam Declaration. In response, the United States detonated the bomb over Hiroshima on August 6, 1945. The blast and subsequent fireball leveled 90 percent of the city, immediately killing some eighty thousand Japanese, many of them civilians. Those remaining suffered from radiation sickness and burns. Nakazawa's father, sister, and younger brother were killed. His mother, eight months pregnant, gave birth to a baby girl who survived a mere four months.

This devastation significantly impacted Nakazawa. Inspired by his sign-painter father to process his feeling through art, he spent much of his childhood drawing, and he eventually became a cartoonist. Japanese manga came of age along with Nakazawa, increasing in popularity during the postwar period. The adult Nakazawa worked at manga magazines, producing mainstream comics and working on personal projects about his war experiences on the side. In 1972 the editors of *Boy's Jump Monthly* asked each of their artists to produce an autobiographical comic. Nakazawa created a forty-five-page work called "I Saw It"; this piece became the basis for *Barefoot Gen.*

Barefoot Gen represents a unique intersection of *hibakusha* literature and manga. A number of firsthand accounts by survivors (who are also called *hibakusha*) emerged in the decades following the bombings. Michihiko Hachiya's *Hiroshima Diary: The Journal of a Japanese Physician August 6* along with Takashi Nagai's books *The Bells of Nagasaki* (1949) and *We of Nagasaki: The Story of Survivors in an Atomic Wasteland* (1951) all document the profound mental and physical effects on survivors. Meanwhile, manga also saw the influence of World War II and the A-bomb. Tezuka Osamu's long-running serial *Atom Boy,* for example, tells the story of a child robot, "Mighty Atom," who is abandoned by his scientist creator, evoking the many Japanese orphans who were a legacy of the bombings.

Barefoot Gen—with its humble beginnings as a magazine assignment—eventually grew to encompass ten volumes and inspired others working in the graphic novel medium, including Art Spiegelman. Spiegelman—who wrote the introduction to the 2004 English translation of *Barefoot Gen*—is famous for his graphic novel depiction of Nazi Germany. *Maus,* which tells the story of Spiegelman's Jewish father during the Holocaust, won a Pulitzer Prize in 1992. *Persepolis,* Marjane Satrapi's autobiographical account of the Islamic revolution in Iran, is another noteworthy example in the genre. Both *Maus* and *Persepolis* follow the trail blazed by Nakazawa: the graphic novel that addresses serious personal and political topics.

THEMES AND STYLE

In the author's note prefacing *Barefoot Gen,* Nakazawa states his goal of conveying to the reader "the

---

Key Facts

Time Period:
Mid-20th Century

Relevant Historical Events:
Nuclear attack on Hiroshima; World War II

Nationality:
Japanese

Keywords:
graphic autobiography; nuclear war; trauma

Japanese manga artist Keiji Nakazawa, author of *Barefoot Gen*. © LEBRECHT MUSIC AND ARTS PHOTO LIBRARY/ALAMY

preciousness of peace and the courage we need to live strongly, yet peacefully." Using bold artwork and blunt text, he depicts the horror of a nuclear blast and its immediate aftermath: the burned and melted skin, the trapped people, and the terror of the survivors. Nakazawa shows Gen, in his urgency to flee the fireball, trampling the dead and injured who cover the ground. Yet the theme on the brutalities of war begins even before the bombs fall: Gen's family is impacted by both the war itself and Japan's increasingly militaristic policies. "For poor people like us, this war doesn't do one bit of good," Gen's father notes. Indeed the family, like many others, is starving. Wartime pressures also force several of Gen's brothers into service and into the relative safety of the countryside. When Gen's father expresses his unpopular opinion against the government and how it is risking lives in a futile war, he is beaten and the children are harassed. As the book ends, Gen's mother, who has just given birth amid the rubble, holds his infant sister up to the sky and says, "When you grow up, you must never, ever let this happen again." His mother's hope echoes his father's wisdom from the book's opening: "The trampled wheat sends strong roots into the earth, endures frost, wind and snow, grows straight and tall … and one day bears fruit."

Nakazawa created *Barefoot Gen* as a means of conveying a message of peace and honoring his father and his mother. While not the conventional genre for autobiography, the graphic novel style offers visual and storytelling possibilities that other genres cannot match. Nakazawa's prefatory note states that he started drawing comics about Hiroshima as "a way to avenge my mother," who died of cancer in an A-bomb victims' hospital in 1966. On the one hand, this suggests that the comics are a way to vent his anger; on the other hand, the "vengeance" itself shows an attempt to constructively confront the forces—both Japanese and American—responsible for the war.

Nakazawa is unflinching in his look at the atrocities; he depicts the inhumanities of war in clear, undeniable black and white. He has said he hopes that people faced with such evidence will do what they can to promote peace and spare others such a future. The depictions of suffering are gruesome and affecting. Spiegelman, describing the power of Nakazawa's imagery, writes, "I've found myself remembering images and events from the *Gen* books with a clarity that makes them seem like memories from my own life."

CRITICAL DISCUSSION

Despite its harrowing content and critique of the Japanese government, *Barefoot Gen* was a critical and popular success when it appeared in Japan in 1973. Inspired by admiration for Nakazawa and his message, a group of volunteer translators formed Project Gen in 1976, with the aim of translating the book into other languages. The group hoped to expose generations of people, especially in the United States, to a visceral account of the consequences of nuclear warfare. The work, which was mostly ignored when it first appeared in English in 1987, drew largely positive reviews when rereleased in 2003. Jeff Zaleski, writing in *Publishers Weekly*, offered typical praise, calling the work "invaluable for the lessons it offers in history, humanity and compassion."

In the years since its publication, *Barefoot Gen* has gained substantial readership both in Japan and abroad, helping to bring the realities of nuclear war to new generations. Writing in the *Los Angeles Times*, Charles Solomon calls the text "hugely influential" and points out that "at a time when the threat of nuclear attack remains frighteningly high and Japan faces the crisis caused by the damaged reactors at Fukushima [following the 2011 earthquake and resulting tsunami], Nakazawa's story … takes on an added immediacy." Whether Nakazawa's message is fully heard in the West remains a subject of contention among scholars.

Commentary on the text has largely focused on *Barefoot Gen*'s political message rather than on its literary merits. Spiegelman raises the possibility that "by locating the causes of the bombings exclusively in the evils of Japanese militaristic nationalism rather than in the Realpolitik of Western racism and cold war power-jockeying, Nakazawa may make the work a little too pleasurable for American and British readers." In the essay "Flashforward Democracy: American Exceptionalism and the Atomic Bomb in *Barefoot Gen*," Christina Hong likewise suggests that by providing the audience with "a ground-level point of entry" to the Hiroshima bombing, Nakazawa allows the reader to identify with ordinary people, which in turn "enables a disavowal of the policy perspective behind the Hiroshima bombing." This perspective, Hong goes on to say, allows only "ersatz understanding" of the extent of the tragedy and the U.S. government's implication in it.

BIBLIOGRAPHY

Sources

Hong, Christine. "Flashforward Democracy: American Exceptionalism and the Atomic Bomb in *Barefoot Gen*." *Comparative Literature Studies* 46.1 (2009): 125–55. Print.

Nakazawa, Keiji. *Barefoot Gen: A Cartoon Story of Hiroshima.* San Francisco: Last Gasp, 2004. Print.

Solomon, Charles. "'Barefoot Gen': Keiji Nakazawa's Moving Autobiography Singed by Emotion." *Los Angeles Times.* Los Angeles Times, 3 June 2011. Web. 13 Nov. 2012.

Spiegelman, Art. "*Barefoot Gen:* Comics after the Bomb." Introduction. *Barefoot Gen: A Cartoon Story of Hiroshima.* By Keiji Nakazawa. San Francisco: Last Gasp, 2003. Print.

Zaleski, Jeff. Rev. of *Barefoot Gen*, by Keiji Nakazawa. *Publishers Weekly* 14 Jan. 2003: 55. Print.

Further Reading

Hachiya, Michihiko. *Hiroshima Diary: The Journal of a Japanese Physician, August 6–September 30, 1945.* Trans. and ed. Warner Wells. Chapel Hill: University of North Carolina Press, 1955. Print.

Motofumi, Asai. "*Barefoot Gen,* Japan, and I: The Hiroshima Legacy: An Interview with Nakazawa Keiji." *International Journal of Comic Art* 10.2 (2008): 308–27. Print.

Nagai, Takashi. *We of Nagasaki: The Story of Survivors in an Atomic Wasteland.* New York: Duell, 1951. Print.

Nakazawa, Keiji. *Hiroshima: The Autobiography of Barefoot Gen.* Ed. and trans. Richard H. Minear. Lanham, Md.: Rowman and Littlefield, 2011. Print.

Pellegrino, Charles R. *The Last Train from Hiroshima: The Survivors Look Back.* New York: Holt, 2010. Print.

Rosenbaum, Roman. "Graphic Depictions of the Asia-Pacific War." *Legacies of the Asia-Pacific War: The Yakeato Generation.* Ed. Roman Rosenbaum and Yasuko Claremont. New York: Routledge, 2011. Print.

Satrapi, Marjane. *Persepolis: The Story of a Childhood.* New York: Pantheon, 2003. Print.

Spiegelman, Art. *Maus: A Survivor's Tale.* New York: Pantheon, 1986. Print.

Takaki, Ronald. *Hiroshima: Why America Dropped the Atomic Bomb.* Boston: Little, Brown, 1995. Print.

HIROSHIMA: THE AUTOBIOGRAPHY OF BAREFOOT GEN

Keiji Nakazawa's prose autobiography, which was published in English in 2011, tells the writer's life story, including the process of writing *Barefoot Gen*. Although fictionalized in some respects, *Barefoot Gen* closely follows Nakazawa's own life. Most of the biographic details in the graphic novel match those in the autobiography, although it is also clear the author has taken artistic liberties in certain regards. One of the most important differences is in how Nakazawa finds out about the death of his family: in the autobiography, he hears the story of his brother's and father's deaths; in the graphic novel, Gen witnesses their demise. These changes are likely due to the demands of the genre, which required a more visual approach.

The editor of *Hiroshima: The Autobiography of Barefoot Gen*, Richard Minear, includes four-page sections of *Barefoot Gen* (as well as maps of Japan and the city of Hiroshima) between the chapters of Nakazawa's autobiography. These visuals provide the reader with a more complete depiction of the scale of destruction on the macro level as well as in human terms.

Daisy Gard

Exiled Memories
A Cuban Childhood
Pablo Medina

❖ **Key Facts**

Time Period:
Late 20th Century

Relevant Historical Events:
Castro's successful Cuban revolution; increase of Cuban emigration after communism

Nationality:
American/Cuban

Keywords:
communism; revolution; emigration

OVERVIEW

First published in 1990, Pablo Medina's *Exiled Memories: A Cuban Childhood* was one of the first memoirs to emerge from the Cuban diaspora. The book comprises essays describing the life of a middle-class boy growing up in 1950s Cuba and stories passed down through several generations of Medina's family. Medina's family left Cuba in 1960, and he was thrust into the foreign culture of the United States. *Exiled Memories* is the legacy of this journey, a reflection on a vanished childhood and an attempt to define home for a man who is neither fully Americanized nor "immaculately Cuban."

Medina's book was published after he had lived in the United States for almost twenty-five years. Created in part as a means of recording a family's "myths and folklore," *Exiled Memories* found an audience in several generations of Cuban Americans aware of the impending loss of culture as the first wave of immigrant parents and grandparents began to die. Initial reviews were positive but few—especially relative to the volume of critical attention focused on some of the more traditionally structured memoirs that would follow. Reissued in 2002 with a new chapter describing a visit to Cuba in 1999, the book remains a unique entry in the Cuban American literary canon.

HISTORICAL AND LITERARY CONTEXT

Fidel Castro's institution of a communist government was the defining event in the lives of many Cubans. Castro came to power in 1959, overthrowing Fulgencio Batista's military regime under the banner of democratic revolution. However, Castro instituted communist policies resulting in the nationalization of businesses and properties, censorship, and the persecution of citizens on the basis of ideological beliefs. Suffering economic hardship and fearing arrest, waves of Cubans began emigrating, many of them settling in the United States, primarily in Miami, Florida. While early immigrants tended to consider the move temporary, planning to return to Cuba once conditions became more favorable, Castro's government proved long lived, and many exiles became permanent residents of the United States.

By the 1980s Cuban American literature began to reflect this changing sensibility about the nature of exile and a longing to preserve memories of life in Cuba before Castro. Medina, who was born in Havana in 1948, left Cuba with his family and settled in New York in 1961. He was educated in the United States, earning a bachelor's in Spanish and a master's in English from Georgetown University. In 1976 he published his poetry collection *Pork Rind and Cuban Songs,* the first poetry collection by a Cuban American written in English. He also began teaching and writing essays. Although he had assimilated to American culture in many ways, he had difficulty reconciling his childhood in Cuba with his adult circumstances in the United States. Replying to a letter by a friend asking about his childhood, Medina began describing some of his memories. The letter eventually grew into *Exiled Memories.*

Immigrant autobiographies have a long tradition in the United States, although *Exiled Memories* is one of the first significant autobiographical works to emerge from the Cuban diaspora. Among the various strands of immigrant autobiography, writers fleeing countries during periods of war often focus on the idyllic characteristics of their prewar lives, especially writers who emigrated as children. In the tradition of Cuban autobiography dealing with Batista's years and Castro's repressive regime, Heberto Padilla's *Self-Portrait of the Other* (1988) provides an interesting counterpoint to Medina's work. Padilla, an influential Cuban poet and novelist, initially supported Castro's revolution but came to criticize the regime and was eventually imprisoned. He left Cuba in 1980.

Following Medina's book, a number of memoirs appeared that engage with themes of exile and Cuban identity. Many echo Medina's exploration of being caught between two cultures and his uncertainty regarding to which country he belongs. Examples include Gustavo Pérez Firmat's *Next Year in Cuba: A Cubano's Coming-of-Age in America* (1995), Virgil Suárez's *Spared Angola: Memories from a Cuban-American Childhood* (1997), Flor Fernández Barrios's *Blessed by Thunder: Memoir of a Cuban Girlhood* (1999), Evelio Grillo's *Black Cuban, Black American: A Memoir* (2000), National Book Award–winner *Waiting for Snow in Havana: Confessions of a Cuban Boy* (2003) by Carlos Eire, and Ruth Behar's *Traveling Heavy: A Memoir in between Journeys* (2013).

THEMES AND STYLE

Medina's autobiography is an attempt to answer the question, where is home? The book sifts through memories and family history dating back to the Cuban War of Independence. La Luisa, the farm of Medina's maternal grandfather, Fiquito, where the author whiled away many summers, figures prominently in the text. Medina recounts the violence of farm life—horse gelding, pig slaughter, Fiquito supervising work in the sugarcane fields with an ivory-handled pistol—but also the cooling breeze through the farmhouse and the nights of laughter around a lamp on the front porch. In addition to his own memories, Medina explores the family lore that has been passed down from previous generations, describing, for example, his grandfather Pablo's cosmopolitan residence in a tony suburb of Havana. In the final chapter, "Leaving," Medina seems to reach a conclusion: "I remember the family, their craziness, their resilience, their collective tongue wagging wildly at despair. … They have given me a home made of materials that nothing but death can breach."

Exiled Memories is both a record of a lost way of life, or a country that many Cubans construct only in memory, and an attempt to locate this lost Cuba alongside the present-day United States under the umbrella of personal identity. As a practical matter, Medina wants to leave a record of the Cuba of his childhood because "old folks of the family would not live forever" and someone must "chronicle our past for those generations who had never lived it." On a psychological level, as Medina tells Derek Alger in *Pif Magazine* in 2012, "They were wonderful stories about things I had experienced as a boy in Cuba … but they were holding me back in that my imagination was trapped in their web. … Let's say I was held captive by them. Once I wrote them down, however, those stories and experiences released their grasp on me."

In the preface to the 2002 edition, Medina describes his approach to autobiography as "anecdotal rather than chronological." *Exiled Memories* begins with an account of the author's arrival in New York and ends with an essay describing his departure from Cuba. In this manner, Medina plays with chronology to position himself as an adult and as an American remembering. His descriptions of people and places in Cuba include both a child's impression and an adult's critical reflection. For example, as a child, Medina saw Fiquito with his revolver as "a benevolent but firm *caudillo*" [leader]. As an adult, Fiquito is a more ambiguous figure, participating in the exploitation of the poor migrant workers, but also is fair and concerned with the health and well-being of everyone at La Luisa.

CRITICAL DISCUSSION

Exiled Memories was published to generally positive reviews. Typical was James Rhodes's 1990 essay in

Pablo Medina's memoir includes a description of his life as a child during the years that Fulgencio Batista, depicted here in a 1957 photograph, was president of Cuba and faced a rebellion led by Fidel Castro. © BETTMANN/CORBIS

Library Journal, which states that Medina "writes from the heart seeking to recapture what it means to be Cuban." Indeed, the autobiography touched off a series of others dealing with childhood memories of the diaspora, and the work is now considered an important part of the Cuban American literary canon.

Medina's autobiography and those that followed during the boom of Cuban American memoir writing in the 1990s raised the profile and cultural capital of Cuban American writers. In 2005 Medina, along with other Cuban writers, traveled to Cuba in support of writers and administrators attempting to establish libraries for books not officially approved by Castro's government. While Medina's activism and his fiction writing have received a fair amount of attention, little scholarship has addressed *Exiled Memories* as a standalone work.

Medina's text and the memoirs of his male compatriots have been placed alongside the narratives of Cuban American women dealing with similar issues of identity. In *Cuban American Literature of Exile: From Person to Person* (1998), scholar Isabel Alvarez-Borland analyzes the divergent consequences of being "between cultures" in men's and women's diasporic writing. Alvarez-Borland defines the "rhetorical task" of Medina and others as seeking "to give homogeneity to a social group's self-awareness of itself socially and culturally." However, "for the male writers this experience leads toward an unsettled view of the self and its relation to language; for the women authors the very separation from one's language and culture of origin becomes a step toward redefinition."

OPERATION PEDRO PAN

Operation Pedro Pan was a program funded by the U.S. government at the behest of the Catholic Welfare Bureau (today the Catholic Charities). The program provided a means for parents, fearing Fidel Castro's program of Marxist-Leninist indoctrination, to send their children to the United States to be educated. Running for two years (1960–1962,) the program brought more than fourteen thousand unaccompanied Cuban children to the United States, placing them with friends or relatives or in foster homes. As adults, some of those who had been in the program as children organized Operation Pedro Pan Group to make and preserve records of all those children involved. Social media has proven especially useful in helping these "Pedro Pans" to connect with each other and explore their shared history.

Operation Pedro Pan has at times been the subject of controversy. Castro, supported by a number of Cuban citizens, has contended that the operation was spearheaded by the Central Intelligence Agency in an attempt to spread fear and create opposition to Cuba's communist government, whose collectivization of property had negatively affected U.S. corporate interests. However, most accounts of the operation, while acknowledging the difficulties faced by children away from their families in a strange culture, point to positive outcomes for those who came to the United States through the program.

BIBLIOGRAPHY

Sources

Alger, Derek. Interview with Pablo Medina. *Pif Magazine.* Pif Magazine, 1 July 2012. Web. 17 Nov. 2012.

Alvarez-Borland, Isabel. *Cuban American Literature of Exile: From Person to Person.* Charlottesville: UP of Virginia, 1998. Print.

González, Rigoberto. "The Cuban Novels of Pablo Medina." *Los Angeles Review of Books.* Los Angeles Review of Books, 25 Sept. 2012. Web. 17 Nov. 2012.

Medina, Pablo. *Exiled Memories: A Cuban Childhood.* Austin: University of Texas Press, 1990. Print.

"Medina, Pablo (1948–)." *The Greenwood Encyclopedia of Latino Literature.* Ed. Nicolás Kanellos. Santa Barbara, Calif.: ABC-CLIO, 2008. *Credo Reference.* Web. 17 Nov. 2012.

Rhodes, James. "Exiled Memories." *Library Journal* 115.16 (1990): 98. Print.

Further Reading

Behar, Ruth. *Traveling Heavy: A Memoir in Between Journeys.* Durham: Duke University Press, 2013. Print.

Eire, Carlos. *Waiting for Snow in Havana.* New York: Free Press, 2003. Print.

Fernandez-Barios, Flor. *Blessed by Thunder: Memoir of a Cuban Girlhood.* Seattle: Seal, 1999. Print.

Firmat, Gustavo Perez. *Next Year in Cuba: A Cubano's Coming-of-Age in* America. Houston: Arte Público, 1995. Print.

Gracia, Jorge J. E., Lynette M. F. Bosch, and Isabel Alvarez Borland, eds. *Identity, Memory, and Diaspora: Voices of Cuban-American Artists, Writers, and Philosophers.* Albany: State University of New York Press, 2008. Print.

Grillo, Evelio. *Black Cuban, Black American: A Memoir.* Houston: Arte Público, 2000. Print.

López, Iraida H. "Reading Lives in Installments: Autobiographical Essays of Women from the Cuban Diaspora." *Cuban-American Literature and Art: Negotiating Identities.* Ed. Isabel Alvarez Borland and Lynette M. F. Bosch. Albany: State University of New York Press, 2009. Print.

Suárez, Virgil, and Delia Poey, eds. *Little Havana Blues: A Cuban-American Literature Anthology.* Houston: Arte Público, 1996. Print.

Daisy Gard

Farewell to Manzanar

Jeanne Wakatsuki Houston, James D. Houston

OVERVIEW

Farewell to Manzanar (1973), a memoir by Jeanne Wakatsuki Houston and her husband, James D. Houston, describes Jeanne's time in a Japanese American internment camp during World War II. In 1942—with the United States at war with Japan—seven-year-old Jeanne and her family were forcibly evacuated from their California home and relocated to Manzanar in the foothills of California's Eastern Sierras. The Wakatsukis and thousands of other Japanese Americans spent the next three years imprisoned behind barbed wire because the U.S. government doubted their loyalty. *Farewell to Manzanar* features a dual perspective: the eyes of a child experiencing the wrongful internment and the viewpoint of an adult coming to terms with its effect on her Japanese American identity.

Since its publication in 1973, *Farewell to Manzanar* has sold more than 1.5 million copies and has gone through more than sixty editions. Considered both a personal and a political memoir, it is one of the best-known pieces of Asian American literature and is part of many high school and college curriculums. Excerpts from the book appear in dozens of literature anthologies. In 1976 the Houstons adapted *Farewell to Manzanar* into a screenplay of the same name, winning both the Humanitas Prize and Christopher Award. The subsequent 1976 television movie version was the first Hollywood production with an all Japanese American cast.

HISTORICAL AND LITERARY CONTEXT

More than two years into World War II, the United States joined the conflict when the Imperial Japanese Navy bombed the naval base at Pearl Harbor, Hawaii, on December 7, 1941. Not only did the assault inspire great anger toward the Japanese, it also aroused suspicions about the loyalties of Japanese Americans. On February 19, 1942, President Franklin D. Roosevelt issued Executive Order 9066, which authorized the War Department to evacuate all Japanese Americans on the West Coast in the interest of national security. The order ultimately led to the relocation of 120,000 Japanese Americans (of which 70 percent were American-born citizens) to internment camps in the West and Southwest.

The Wakatsukis were among the first families to arrive and among the last to be released at the Manzanar camp. Deeply ashamed by the experience, Jeanne never shared this part of her life. After many years of marriage, however, she revealed the story to her husband, James, a writer. Believing this was a tale that every American should know, James encouraged Jeanne to write her recollections. Together they also painstakingly conducted historical research and interviewed Jeanne's family members and other former internees.

Farewell to Manzanar was one of the first to shed light on the Japanese American internment. Although Japanese Americans Miné Okubo and Monica Sone had earlier discussed the internment experience in their autobiographies—*Citizen 13660* and *Nisei Daughter*, respectively—*Farewell to Manzanar* was the first text to focus on the internment as the central event. *Los Angeles Times* contributor Ajay Singh described the "accessible and unsentimental work" as being important for first highlighting "a subject that had been largely ignored in popular histories."

Farewell to Manzanar continues to serve as an important cultural touchstone on the subject of the internments. Not only does the book hold a place in many school curricula, but the resulting movie does as well. In 2003 the film was given to every California public school and library as part of a curriculum focusing on civil rights. In lectures, Jeanne herself has emphasized the importance of her work in keeping the subject matter alive: "We as Americans cannot forget the injustices of history," the *St. Louis Post-Dispatch* cited her as saying. *Farewell to Manzanar* also launched Jeanne's career as a professional writer. She explored the postwar Asian American experience in *Beyond Manzanar: Views of Asian-American Womanhood* (1985), a collection of short stories and essays. She then revisited Manzanar in her first novel, *The Legend of Fire Horse Woman* (2003). She has received numerous awards, including the 2006 Award of Excellence from the Japanese American National Museum.

THEMES AND STYLE

Central to *Farewell to Manzanar* are the indignities of camp life and the effects imprisonment had on Jeanne, her family, and other internees. The conditions at the camp splintered families and caused people to fall ill and become emotionally drained. The camp experience was particularly difficult for Jeanne's father, Ko, who resorts

Key Facts

Time Period:
Mid-20th Century

Relevant Historical Events:
Japanese American internment; World War II

Nationality:
American

Keywords:
internment; ethnicity; civil rights

Author Jeanne Wakatsuki Houston reads from one of her works at a library in Salinas, California, in 2005. © AP IMAGES/THE SALINAS CALIFORNIAN, RICHARD GREEN

to drinking and violence when he is reunited with his family at Manzanar after a stint of false imprisonment in North Dakota. Jeanne states that the internment "brought [Ko] face to face with his own vulnerability, his own powerlessness. He had no rights, no home, no control over his own life." As one critic from the *New Yorker* noted, "Her father was too old to bend with the humiliations of the camp…. His story is at the heart of this book, and his daughter tells it with great dignity." Ko's troubles fragment the family, leading Jeanne to distance herself from both him and her family.

Jeanne initially intended to chronicle her family's history for her nieces and nephews. As painful memories were dredged up and the audience broadened, she acknowledged in the book's foreword that writing *Farewell to Manzanar* was "a way of coming to terms with the impact these years [had] on my entire life." Her memoir opens with the Pearl Harbor attack, an event that "snipped [our life] off, stopped it from becoming whatever else lay ahead." As Jeanne grows up, she recognizes the internment as the moment her family began to unravel and the point in time that she began to struggle with her identity as a Japanese American. At the end of *Farewell to Manzanar*, she comes full circle as she describes how she returned to the camp with her husband and children and found psychological closure. She concludes, "I had nearly outgrown the shame and the guilt and the sense of unworthiness."

Stylistically, *Farewell to Manzanar* is notable for accessibility. In "Beneath the Mask: Autobiographies of Japanese-American Women," her essay in *Women and Autobiography* (1999), Ann Rayson describes *Farewell to Manzanar* as "highly readable"; at the same time, Rayson notes that that the memoir "does not hesitate to confront the cultural conflict at the root of every Japanese-American's experience during World War II." Jeanne purposely chose to keep the text accessible. According to Singh, the author considers her memoir to be "not a sermon on political injustice nor an essay on the Constitution. It allows readers to enter the experience on the level of empathy."

CRITICAL DISCUSSION

Upon publication of *Farewell to Manzanar*, Jeanne became "quite unintentionally, a voice for a heretofore silent segment of society," according to a *Los Angeles Times* reviewer. In the *Saturday Review/World* review, Dorothy Rabinowitz praised the Houstons for recording "a tale of many complexities in a straightforward manner, a tale remarkably lacking in either self-pity or solemnity." A critic from the *New York Times Book Review* described *Farewell to Manzanar* as "a dramatic, telling account of one of the most reprehensible events in the history of America's treatment of minorities"; the review also criticized the book for failing to examine the broader political implications of the U.S. government's actions.

Farewell to Manzanar paved the way for the Japanese American World War II experience to become part of a national discussion. Artists continue to explore the effect internment has on the collective Japanese American psyche. The effects of the experience have been examined in autobiographical works such as those by Yoshiko Uchida and Akemi Kikumura. In 1988 each living survivor of the internment camps was awarded $20,000, and in 1990 President George H. W. Bush issued a public apology to survivors. Manzanar was named a National Historical Site in 1992. In addition to giving a voice to a silenced part of U.S. history, the Houstons' book opened a space for debate about what is permissible in the name of national safety—a pertinent topic in the era of homeland security.

Most media discussion about *Farewell to Manzanar* occurs in the form of book reviews. However, there is some scholarly work on the autobiography's value as both a political memoir and as a contribution to ethnic American and women's literature. Rayson calls *Farewell to Manzanar* an "act of self-revelation and exploration, the first contemporary version of the wartime Relocation experience." She argues that the memoir "influenced thousands of Japanese-Americans and gave national impetus to a new dialogue over the question of reparations." The *Encyclopedia of Feminist Literature* by Mary Ellen Snodgrass describes Houston as a "gentle feminist voice for humanity and inclusion" and praises her for capturing "from a woman's point of view the cruelties of American history."

BIBLIOGRAPHY

Sources

Houston, Jeanne Wakatsuki, and James D. Houston. *Farewell to Manzanar*. Boston: Houghton Mifflin, 1973. Print.

Rabinowitz, Dorothy. Rev. of *Farewell to Manzanar*, by Jeanne Wakatsuki Houston and James D. Houston. *Saturday Review/World* 6 Nov. 1973. "Jeanne Wakatsuki Houston." *Contemporary Authors Online*. Detroit: Gale, 2007. *Literature Resource Center*. Web. 3 Dec. 2012.

Rayson, Ann. "Beneath the Mask: Autobiographies of Japanese-American Women." *Women and Autobiography*. Ed. Martine Watson Brownley and Allison B. Kimmich. Wilmington, Del.: Scholarly Resources, 1999. 132–47. Web.

Rev. of *Farewell to Manzanar*, by Jeanne Wakatsuki Houston and James D. Houston. *Los Angeles Times*. Los Angeles Times, 15 Nov. 1984. Web. 3 Dec. 2012.

———. *New York Times Book Review*. New York Times, 13 Jan. 1974. Web. 3 Dec. 2012.

———. *New Yorker*. Condé Nast, 5 Nov. 1973. Web. 3 Dec. 2012.

Singh, Ajay. "The Lessons of History." *Los Angeles Times*. Los Angeles Times, 6 Nov. 2001. Web. 3 Dec. 2012.

Snodgrass, Mary Ellen. "Houston, Jeanne Wakatsuki (1934–)." *Encyclopedia of Feminist Literature*. New York: Facts On File, 2006. Print.

Toth, Sarah. "Students Revel in Visit with Author of Readmore Novel, *Farewell to Manzanar*." *St. Louis Post-Dispatch*. stltoday.com, 15 Apr. 2002. Web. 3 Dec. 2012.

Further Reading

Chappell, Virginia. "But Isn't This the Land of the Free?: Resistance and Discovery in Student Responses to *Farewell to Manzanar*." *Writing in Multicultural Settings*. Ed. Carol Severino, Johnella E. Butler, and Juan C. Guerra. New York: MLA, 1997. Print.

Houston, Jeanne Wakatsuki. *Beyond Manzanar: Views of Asian-American Womanhood*. Santa Barbara, Calif.: Capra, 1985. Print.

———. *The Legend of Fire Horse Woman*. New York: Kensington, 2003. Print.

JEANNE (TOYO) WAKATSUKI HOUSTON

On September 26, 1934, Jeanne Wakatsuki Houston was born in Inglewood, California, to George Ko and Riku (Sugai) Wakatsuki—first- and second-generation Japanese Americans, respectively. Father Ko was a fisherman, which put him under suspicion after the bombing of Pearl Harbor. The youngest of ten children, Jeanne spent her early childhood in Southern California until the family was relocated to Manzanar in 1942. Jeanne and her parents returned to Southern California at the close of the war in 1945 and lived there until moving to San Jose in 1952. (Most of her siblings moved east after the internment.) She attended San Jose State University, where she studied sociology and journalism; she graduated in 1956. Jeanne was the first in her family to earn a college degree.

Jeanne met James D. Houston while attending San Jose State University. They married in 1957 and had three children. James's stint in the air force led to a brief sojourn in England and France, where Jeanne studied French civilization at the Sorbonne in Paris. In addition to collaborating on *Farewell to Manzanar*, Jeanne worked with her husband on many other projects until his death in 2009. Although she has been lauded for other writings, *Farewell to Manzanar* is the author's best-known work. As of 2012 Jeanne continues to lecture in both university and community settings.

Moser, Linda Trinh. "Jeanne Wakatsuki Houston and James D. Houston." *Asian American Autobiographers: A Bio-bibliographical Critical Sourcebook*. Ed. Guiyou Huang. Westport Conn.: Greenwood, 2001. 127–33. Print.

Okamura, Raymond Y. "*Farewell to Manzanar*: A Case of Subliminal Racism." *Amerasia Journal* 3.2 (1976): 143–47. Print.

Okubo, Miné. *Citizen 13660*. New York: Columbia University Press, 1946. Print.

Sakurai, Patricia A. "The Politics of Possession: The Negotiation of Identity in *American Disguise, Homebase,* and *Farewell to Manzanar*." *Privileging Positions: The Sites of Asian American Studies*. Ed. Gary Y. Okihiro et al. Pullman: Washington State University Press, 1995. 157–70. Print.

Smith, Page. *Democracy on Trial: The Japanese American Evacuation and Relocation in World War II*. New York: Simon & Schuster, 1995. Print.

Tateishi, John, comp. *And Justice for All: An Oral History of the Japanese-American Detention Camps*. New York: Random House, 1984. Print.

Maggie Magno

Geronimo
His Own Story
Geronimo, S. M. Barrett

✦ Key Facts

Time Period:
Early 20th Century

Relevant Historical Events:
U.S. westward expansion; passage of the Indian Removal Act; Geronimo's surrender and removal to a reservation

Nationality:
American

Keywords:
Native American; westward expansion; reservation life

OVERVIEW

Geronimo: His Own Story (1906), by the Chiricahua Apache leader Geronimo, is one of the most important Native American accounts of life prior to and during the westward expansion of the United States. In his memoir, Geronimo tells the Apache origin myth and gives an account of his life, tracing his family origins, his experiences as a child, the battles he fought against both Mexicans and Americans from the 1860s until his surrender in 1886, and his ensuing life on the reservation. He also details his own struggles and search for revenge after his mother, wife, and children were slain in an attack by Mexican soldiers in 1859. Throughout the text Geronimo is steadfast in his indictment of the wrongs that the U.S. Army committed against his people, including broken treaties and surprise attacks, but he also offers a clear picture of the brutality of the raiding Apache tribes.

When the memoir was first published, Geronimo was being held as a prisoner of war on the Apache reservation in Fort Sills, Oklahoma. The work was composed with the aid of S. M. Barrett, who wrote President Theodore Roosevelt seeking permission for Geronimo to be allowed to give his account of the Apache conflict with the U.S. government. Although it was popular among readers curious about Native American life and customs, the book's readership was relatively limited. Today it is considered one of the most significant firsthand accounts of the conflicts between U.S. forces and Native American peoples during the westward expansion of the nineteenth century.

HISTORICAL AND LITERARY CONTEXT

In 1830 President Andrew Jackson signed the Indian Removal Act, which forced all Native Americans to be moved west of the Mississippi River; the land there was to belong to them, but following the acquisition of the Southwest during the Mexican-American War (1848), pioneering whites began to inhabit Apache territories in New Mexico and Arizona. Along with the history of conflict between the Apache and the United States, Geronimo's account details the enmity and violence between his tribe and Mexican soldiers based in Chihuahua and Sonora.

When Geronimo's autobiography was first published, it included introductory material by Barrett, in which he discusses his appeals to President Roosevelt and the process by which he compiled Geronimo's account. In the fall of 1905, after receiving permission from Roosevelt, Barrett employed Asa Daklugie, an educated Apache, to work as an interpreter and translator on the project. In the preface to the 1906 edition, Barrett states that it was his goal to "extend to Geronimo as a prisoner of war the courtesy due any captive, i.e., the right to state the causes which impelled him in his opposition to our civilization and laws." The scholar David Roberts, however, in *Once They Moved Like the Wind* (1993), argues that many of the "pivotal episodes" in Geronimo's life go unmentioned because Geronimo feared that "Barrett was a spy for the government, trying to trick him into making confessions for which he would be further punished."

Geronimo's autobiography draws on the tradition of Native American writings that arose during the conflicts of the nineteenth century, best exemplified by such works as *Life of Ma-ka-tai-me-she-kia-kiak, or Black Hawk,* which tells the life story of Black Hawk, a war chief of the Sauk and Fox who was imprisoned in Missouri following his defeat in the Black Hawk War of 1832. Although there is little to suggest that Geronimo was directly influenced by this work, *Geronimo: His Own Story* shares many of its thematic concerns, as well as the collaborative process of transcription and compilation. The structural arrangement of the autobiography also draws on the long tradition of oral storytelling within his tribe.

The success of Geronimo's autobiography led to the publication of other Native American narratives. Among the most prominent and best-known Native American autobiographies is *Black Elk Speaks* (1932), which gives Black Elk's account of his life as an Oglala Sioux, his participation in the Battle of the Little Bighorn in 1876, and his survival of the Massacre at Wounded Knee in 1890. Today *Geronimo: His Own Story* is considered not only an important historical document but also an influential piece of Native American literature.

THEMES AND STYLE

The central theme of Geronimo's book is that the U.S. government was unjust in the treatment of the Apache people in the second half of the nineteenth century

This portrait of Geronimo dates from 1903, shortly before the publication of *Geronimo: His Own Story.* © EVERETT COLLECTION INC/ALAMY

and that the violent resistance by the Apache was justified. Geronimo offers examples of these injustices throughout the text, from the massacre of the Apache at a supposedly peaceful conference at Fort Bowie to a broken treaty made by General Nelson Miles, the U.S. leader of the campaign against the Apache, who promised Geronimo a home on a reservation where his people could live together. Along with presenting Geronimo's political and historical opinions, the narrative serves to humanize the Apache in their struggle

SAMUEL CHAMBERLAIN'S MY CONFESSIONS: RECOLLECTIONS OF A ROGUE

Written primarily about his experiences in the Mexican-American War (1846–1848), Samuel Chamberlain's war memoir *My Confessions: Recollections of a Rogue* begins with the author's trip out West at the age of fifteen and chronicles his battles with the Apache and his amorous adventures on both sides of the border. Written between 1855 and 1861, the manuscript remained unpublished until it turned up in a Connecticut antique shop in the 1840s and was subsequently excerpted in *Life* magazine. Although much of the memoir strays far beyond the strictures of historical fact, it is still considered an important source for the Mexican-American War.

Late in the autobiography Chamberlain tells of taking up with the Glanton gang, a group of scalp hunters consisting of "Sonorans, Cherokee and Delaware Indians, French Canadians, Texans, Irishmen, a Negro and a full blooded Comanche." According to Chamberlain, the Mexican general José de Urrea was offering fifty dollars for every Apache scalp, and the gang sought to claim that money with scalps taken from the Apache as well as other more peaceful peoples. Chamberlain's account of his time with this marauding gang, led by John Glanton and "Judge" Holden, formed the historical basis for Cormac McCarthy's critically acclaimed novel *Blood Meridian* (1985).

with the United States. Geronimo records, for example, the brutality his people faced when U.S. soldiers launched a surprise attack: "They killed seven children, five women, and four warriors, captured all our supplies, blankets, horses, and clothing, and destroyed our tepees. We had nothing left; winter was beginning, and it was the coldest winter I ever knew."

Although Geronimo agreed to narrate his memoirs only if he was given monetary compensation, the text reveals a desire to chronicle his life and the history of his people. It proved to be a long process, but even as Geronimo tired of the endeavor of this collaborative composition, he kept his word to narrate his story to the transcribers because he had come to view it as a duty. The text shows his keen awareness of the historical dilemma his people were facing. "We are vanishing from the earth," he writes. "Yet I cannot think we are useless or Usen would not have created us." As his story develops, he depicts the U.S. encroachment upon historical Apache lands and the injustices and broken treaties the tribe suffered. Despite his attempts to decry these injustices, Geronimo's compromised position as a prisoner of war forced him to suppress certain details out of fear of punishment.

Stylistically, *Geronimo: His Own Story* is notable for its position in an oral storytelling tradition. In his introduction to a 1970 edition of the text, Frederick W. Turner III notes that "during the storytelling session Geronimo would range freely over the events of his life in the characteristic Indian manner. This manner consists of telling only that which seems to the teller important and telling it in the fashion and the order which seems to him appropriate." Turner includes this caveat, claiming that certain rearrangements might make for a more coherent story but that such a text would not be true to Geronimo's "aboriginal style."

CRITICAL DISCUSSION

Upon publication *Geronimo: His Own Story* was a moderate success, drawing reviews in national publications and a limited readership. It was considered an authentic and unique portrait; readers found it especially interesting because it was written by one of the country's best-known and most infamous Native Americans. Shortly after its publication, in November 1906, the *New York Times* ran a review titled "Geronimo: The Famous Apache Chief's Story of His Own Life," observing that there is "simplicity" and "eloquence" in the "sangfroid" of Geronimo's prose and claiming that "one does not often get as intimate a view of Indian life as is given in this book."

In the years following the American Indian Wars and the deportation of Native Americans to the reservations, the autobiography lost some of its popular appeal, but Geronimo's lasting presence as a cultural figure of rebellion and resistance has remained constant through the production of numerous children's books, biographies, and two films—*Geronimo* (1963) and *Geronimo: An American Legend* (1993). Scholars, however, continue to study Geronimo's original text through a variety of critical lenses that consider not only the value and veracity of its historical testimony but also its documentation of nineteenth-century racial politics.

Few scholars have focused exclusively on the text; most draw upon it as a document in the history of the U.S. conflict with the Apache between 1860 and 1886. Roberts sees the text as "invaluable" to the historical record but also as "unreliable." He argues that through its composition, Geronimo makes an "eloquent plea" to President Roosevelt that he be allowed to return to his homeland. In his dissertation *Geronimo Escapes: Envisioning Indianness in Modern America* (2011), Kevin Shupe examines how Geronimo's autobiography helped to shape the discourse whereby whites transmitted the "ideas of cultural difference that justified their intellectual and ideological understanding of Indians."

BIBLIOGRAPHY

Sources

Chamberlain, Samuel. *My Confession: The Recollections of a Rogue*. New York: Harper & Brothers, 1956. Print.

Geronimo. *Geronimo: His Own Story*. New York: Dutton, 1970. Print.

"Geronimo: The Famous Chief's Story of His Own Life." Rev. of *Geronimo: His Own Story*, by Geronimo. *New York Times* 17 Nov. 1906. *ProQuest Historical Newspapers*. Web. 2 Nov. 2012.

Roberts, David. *Once They Moved Like the Wind*. New York: Simon & Schuster, 1993. Print.

Shupe, Kevin D. "Geronimo Escapes: Envisioning Indianness in Modern America." Diss. George Mason U, 2011. *ProQuest*. Web. 2 Nov. 2012.

Turner, Frederick W., III. Introduction. *Geronimo: His Own Story*. By Geronimo. New York: Penguin, 1970. 3–36. Print.

Further Reading

Adams, Alexander. *Geronimo: A Biography*. New York: Putnam, 1971. Print.

Cole, D. C. *The Chiricahua Apache, 1846–1876: From War to Reservation*. Albuquerque: University of New Mexico Press, 1988. Print.

Gatewood, Charles B. *Lt. Charles Gatewood and His Apache Wars Memoir*. Lincoln: University of Nebraska Press, 2005. Print.

Griffen, William B. *Apaches at War and Peace: The Janos Presidio, 1750–1858*. Albuquerque: University of New Mexico Press, 1988. Print.

Kraft, Lewis. *Gatewood and Geronimo*. Albuquerque: University of New Mexico Press, 2000. Print.

Meadows, William C. *Kiowa, Apache, and Comanche Military Societies: Enduring Veterans, 1800 to Present*. Austin: University of Texas Press, 1999. Print.

Greg Luther

GOLDEN BONES
An Extraordinary Journey from Hell in Cambodia to a New Life in America
Sichan Siv

❖ **Key Facts**

Time Period:
Early 21st Century

Relevant Historical Events:
Reign of the Khmer Rouge; prosecution of Khmer Rouge officials

Nationality:
American/Cambodian

Keywords:
Khmer Rouge; American Dream; exile

OVERVIEW

Sichan Siv's *Golden Bones: An Extraordinary Journey from Hell in Cambodia to a New Life in America,* first published in 2008, is a Cambodian American's autobiography about survival under the Khmer Rouge and his subsequent realization of the American Dream. The book covers two distinct periods of Siv's life: the first focuses on his twenty-eight years in Cambodia (1948–1976), and the second recounts his journey in the United States from working as an apple-picking refugee in Connecticut to serving as a U.S. ambassador to the United Nations (1976–2006). The events in Siv's life are narrated chronologically: his happy childhood in an upper-middle-class family, his family's tragic fall due to political disfavor under Pol Pot's regime, his internment in Cambodia and escape to Thailand, and finally his rise to positions of leadership under the two George W. Bush administrations. His autobiography treats major themes found in diasporic literature, such as human survival, the need for recording cultural memory, the necessity of perseverance, and the achievement of the American Dream.

The years from 1975 to the late 1980s witnessed the arrival of various waves of Southeast Asian refugees and immigrants into the United States because of the Vietnam War, genocide in Cambodia, and political turbulence and oppression. Since the 1990s many of these refugees have written about their traumatic experiences in their homelands and their resettlement in the United States and other asylum-granting nations. Siv's autobiography was well received upon its publication and remains a testimony to the triumph of the human spirit over unimaginable adversity—though critics have pointed out that in its celebration of the United States it fails to acknowledge the U.S. role in enabling the Khmer Rouge to come to power.

HISTORICAL AND LITERARY CONTEXT

Under the rule of the Khmer Rouge in Cambodia, from 1975 through 1979, the communists under Pol Pot's totalitarian dictatorship committed atrocities, violated codes of international conduct and law, and exterminated more than two million people. During this period the Khmer Rouge tortured and murdered members of the upper class and the intelligentsia, detained and killed millions of peasants, and demolished religious and historical sites. Many of the Cambodians who escaped the regime were granted asylum in the United States or other Western countries due to international pressure, establishing diasporic Cambodian communities around the world. Even after the end of the Vietnam War and the Pol Pot era, Cambodia remains an impoverished country attempting to rise out of the ashes of its recent history.

Not until March 2003 did the United Nations and Cambodia agree to prosecute the top leaders of the Khmer Rouge in the International Court of Justice. By then, global indignation had intensified as documentary films, photographs of atrocious acts, and literature about Cambodia's "killing field" and genocidal policies became more accessible. Many survivors began to tell their stories of loss, separation, and victimization. Published at a time when the crimes committed by the Khmer Rouge were at the center of global attention, Siv's *Golden Bones* offers significant literary testimony about these atrocities and his hope for a brighter future.

In the late 1990s and the first decade of the twenty-first century, memoirs by Cambodian American authors gained significant attention. Dith Pran's *Children of Cambodia's Killing Fields: Memoirs by Survivors* (1997), Loung Ung's *First They Killed My Father: A Daughter of Cambodia Remembers* (2000), Chanrithy Him's *When Broken Glass Floats: Growing Up under the Khmer Rouge* (2001), and Haing Ngor's *Survival in the Killing Fields* (2003) all condemn the Khmer Rouge for its acts of inhumanity and brutality. Within the corpus of Southeast Asian American literature, which often is characterized by war, political turmoil, and diaspora, criticism of a dysfunctional, corrupt communist government and justification of life in exile are common. Many have written about how they overcame obstacles during their resettlement, describing how their diligence and optimism contributed to their success in the West.

Following the publication of *Golden Bones,* Siv was invited to lecture at various universities, conferences, and organizations. His story of survival and success remains a source of inspiration to many immigrants and refugees. He now works to help improve

Cambodia's education and economy and to promote a more global understanding of the country's long history and rich culture. His autobiography enriches the small corpus of Cambodian American literature and stands as a historical document that denounces the immorality of a regime founded upon fanaticism at a time when most of the world was preoccupied with other issues.

THEMES AND STYLE

Golden Bones treats themes of collective memory and diasporic assimilation. The tragedy that Siv and his family experience is the tragedy of the Cambodian. The autobiography condemns war, political fanaticism, and dictatorship and treats the nexus between the homeland and the asylum-granting country through a sense of ethno-national consciousness, especially through the author's commitment to the maintenance, restoration, and support of Cambodia. The second portion of the book reinforces the theme of the American Dream. The United States is depicted as a promised land of boundless opportunities that stands in stark contrast to Cambodia, a land in many ways deprived of hope: "Within a short time, I had been exposed to two extremes of modern civilization: the killing fields of Cambodia; and the world's most advanced society, the United States." He writes that in order to become a successful American, assimilation was key. He repeatedly reminds himself, "Forget the painful past and focus on the brighter future. Adapt and be adopted."

In the preface to *Golden Bones,* Siv states that, after his arrival in the United States in 1976, he often was asked about his plans for writing his life story. At the time he preferred not to "revisit a painful past" because he "was looking forward to building a new life." However, he finally realized that "the benefits of sharing the story would outweigh any temporary sadness," and he began writing the first chapter in March 2006. In a 2009 interview with Siv by Quan Manh Ha in *Southeast Review of Asian Studies,* Siv says that he wrote the book "to give some historical anecdotes" and that "producing the book entailed an educational process." Contextualizing *Golden Bones* within the conventions of most autobiographical writing, the book chronicles the author's journey from war to peace, from "hell" to "a beautiful country."

The two divisions in Siv's autobiography are titled "Cambodia" and "America." In the first part, the narrative is continuous, from his childhood to his escape from Cambodia. In the second part, he does not write much about his life during the Clinton administration; thus, there is a minor gap between the years 1992 and 2000. Despite the calamities and sufferings caused by the Khmer Rouge, Siv sometimes recounts events with a sense of humor. Several Khmer words and terms are used in the narrative, probably because they have no English equivalents, and Siv alludes to many names and sites that might be puzzling to readers unfamiliar with Cambodia's geography and history. As a Cambodian refugee writing in English, he relied on his wife, a Texas-born American, to help him edit the manuscript. He deigns to write about the adversities that must have affected him during his years in the United States, instead focusing on a Horatio Alger–style plot.

CRITICAL DISCUSSION

Generally, *Golden Bones* has been well received. However, the autobiography has failed to attract a body of criticism beyond book reviews. Most reviews of *Golden Bones* note the almost fairy-tale nature of the narrated events. For instance, Monirith Ly in a 2012 review in the *Journal of Southeast Asian American Education & Advancement* states, "*Golden Bones* is truly an inspiring book for any American, and especially for ambitious Americans from refugee and immigrant backgrounds."

However, reviewers have noted some shortcomings. A 2008 review in *Kirkus Reviews* calls the book an "uplifting saga" but points out two major flaws: Siv's overreliance on "cliché and oversimplified scenarios" and the lack of "logical transitions between scene shifts," which detracts readers' attention from the darker background against which the uplifting events occur. According to Sheldon Kelly in a 2008 review for *American Spectator,* Siv's autobiography "is more documented than finely written." Kelly compares Siv to a sleepwalker "holding his breath while skirting the snake pit of paralyzing memory."

Reviewers have focused on Siv's upper-middle-class background, which May-Lee Chai in *Asian Affairs* observes differentiates him from the majority of Cambodian survivors, who came primarily from working-class or peasant backgrounds. His elite educational and familial background was "critical to his success in the United States," Chai notes, though *Golden Bones* effectively portrays a "bygone era" in

Sichan Siv, left, and other members of the U.S. delegation listen to the minister for foreign affairs of Iraq, Naji Sabri, speaking at the United Nations (UN) General Assembly in New York on September 19, 2002. Siv, author of *Golden Bones,* served as an ambassador to the UN from 2001 to 2006. © AP IMAGES/ STUART RAMSON

Cambodia despite several "mundane" descriptions. Other scholars have pointed out that the work's commercial success lies in its wholesale affirmation of the American Dream and lack of criticism of the role the United States played in helping to bring the Khmer Rouge to power.

BIBLIOGRAPHY

Sources

Chai, May-Lee. Rev. of *Golden Bones: An Extraordinary Journey from Hell in Cambodia to a New Life in America,* by Sichan Siv. *Asian Affairs* 22 June 2009: 98–99. Print.

Ha, Quan Manh. Interview with Sichan Siv. *Southeast Review of Asian Studies* 31 (2009): 207–18. Print.

Kelly, Sheldon. "An American from Cambodia." *American Spectator* 41.8 (2008): 75–77. Print.

Ly, Monirith. Rev. of *Golden Bones: An Extraordinary Journey from Hell in Cambodia to a New Life in America,* by Sichan Siv. *Journal of Southeast Asian American Education & Advancement* 7 (2012): 1–4. Print.

Rev. of *Golden Bones: An Extraordinary Journey from Hell in Cambodia to a New Life in America,* by Sichan Siv. *Kirkus Reviews* 76.10 (2008): 81. Print.

Siv, Sichan. *Golden Bones: An Extraordinary Journey from Hell in Cambodia to a New Life in America.* New York: HarperCollins, 2008. Print.

Further Reading

Chon, Gina, and Sambath Thet. *Behind the Killing Fields: A Khmer Rouge Leader and One of His Victims.* Philadelphia: University of Pennsylvania Press, 2010. Print.

De Nike, Howard J., John B. Quigley, and Kenneth J. Robinson, eds. *Genocide in Cambodia: Documents from the Trial of Pol Pot and Ieng Sary.* Philadelphia: University of Pennsylvania Press, 2000. Print.

Hinton, Alexander Laban, and Robert Jay Lifton. *Why Did They Kill?: Cambodia in the Shadow of Genocide.* Berkeley: University of California Press, 2004. Print.

Kiernan, Ben. *The Pol Pot Regime: Race, Power, and Genocide in Cambodia under the Khmer Rouge, 1975–79.* 3rd ed. New Haven: Yale University Press, 2008. Print.

Schlund-Vials, Cathy J. *War, Genocide, and Justice: Cambodian American Memory Work.* Minneapolis: University of Minnesota Press, 2012. Print.

Tyner, James A. *The Killing of Cambodia: Geography, Genocide and the Unmaking of Space.* Surrey, U.K.: Ashgate, 2008. Print.

Quan Ha

THE INVISIBLE THREAD
Yoshiko Uchida

OVERVIEW

The Invisible Thread is the 1991 memoir of children's author and second-generation Japanese American Yoshiko Uchida. Following the Japanese navy's 1941 bombing of Pearl Harbor, Uchida and her family were forcibly moved from Berkeley, California, by the U.S. government along with 120,000 other West Coast Japanese Americans. The Uchidas were subsequently interned in a Utah concentration camp. Written in a plain style for young readers, the book falls roughly into two parts: the first documents a relatively idyllic childhood in Berkeley with her mother, father, and sister; the second tells the less happy story of the family's forced removal and internment.

Uchida's memoir is part of a growing literature on the forced relocation and internment of Japanese Americans in the Pacific Coast states when the United States was at war with Japan. As she makes clear, the racial discrimination that surfaced in this era had been long in the making: legislation in the early decades of the twentieth century made it increasingly difficult for Japanese nationals to immigrate to the United States and prohibited Japanese immigrants from becoming U.S. citizens. On the release of *The Invisible Thread*, reviewers praised Uchida for her insights into this fraught history of Japanese Americans, applauding in particular the lessons in diversity she afforded her young readers. Her memoir has since found acclaim among educators as a valuable classroom text for teaching the historical politics and ethics of U.S. race relations.

HISTORICAL AND LITERARY CONTEXT

The Invisible Thread describes an era in U.S. history when nationalist and sometimes racist assumptions informed the everyday attitudes of whites toward Japanese Americans—who, even when born on U.S. soil, were regarded as foreigners. The Japanese Imperial Navy's attack on the U.S. naval base at Pearl Harbor on December 7, 1941, exacerbated this racial division. Undertaken without a formal declaration of war, the attack, which resulted in the deaths of more than two thousand Americans, stunned the nation. Japan was in league with the Axis powers of Italy and Germany, who were already at war with the Allied countries of Britain, France, and the Soviet Union, among others. When President Franklin D. Roosevelt responded by declaring war on Japan, he brought the United States into World War II. The anti-Japanese backlash that ensued led directly to the government's relocation of people of Japanese ancestry from West Coast "exclusion zones" on the premise that they were a threat to national security. For Uchida, Pearl Harbor figures as the point at which implicit racial hostility was given concrete expression.

Published the year before her death, *The Invisible Thread* did not so much break new ground for Uchida as consolidate themes to which she had dedicated most of her life as a writer. Since the 1960s she had written in fiction and nonfiction about the internments, exposing the hardships that her parents' generation endured. Having already written an autobiography for an adult audience titled *Desert Exile: The Uprooting of a Japanese American Family* (1982), in choosing to retell her life story as a memoir for young adults, Uchida ended her career by making sure that upcoming generations would remember those who had struggled to be both Japanese and American in twentieth-century America.

The historical evacuations and internments that Uchida writes about have heavily influenced the production of Japanese American literature. One early comparable memoir is Monica Sone's 1953 *Nisei Daughter,* which tells a similar story of an idyllic Japanese American childhood disrupted by the attack on Pearl Harbor and the family's ensuing relocation to a camp in Idaho. Jeanne Wakatsuki Houston's 1973 autobiography *Farewell to Manzanar* also captures what the internments meant from the perspective of a young girl. A central subject for fiction since Shelley Ota's *Upon Their Shoulders* and John Okada's *No-No Boy* appeared in the 1950s, the plight of Japanese Americans in the camps continues to be taken up in novels such as Nina Revoyr's *Southland* (2003).

Uchida's achievement in *The Invisible Thread* is to bring the troubled political history of Japanese American race relations to young readers in a clear and relatable way. Accordingly, she has long been recognized as the author of teachable texts for the multicultural classroom in an age committed to increasing diversity awareness. In the decade before her death, the author received awards and honorable mentions from the *School Library Journal,* the Child Study Association of

Key Facts

Time Period:
Late 20th Century

Relevant Historical Events:
Japanese American internment; World War II

Nationality:
American

Keywords:
internment; racism; civil rights

WAR EXPERIENCES

Japanese and Japanese American women stand outside a barbershop in one of the U.S. war emergecy evacuation camps set up during World War II, Tule Lake Relocation Center, California, 1942/1943. Many Japanese Americans were interred in U.S. camps during the war for simply looking like the enemy. © UNIVERSAL HISTORY ARCHIVE/UIG/THE BRIDGEMAN ART LIBRARY

America, the San Mateo and San Francisco Reading Associations, and Friends of Children and Literature for her accessible explorations of Japanese and Japanese American culture and heritage.

THEMES AND STYLE

Uchida's main theme is the struggle of the Japanese American to feel at home in the United States without sacrificing her Japanese heritage. She tells how she and her sister Keiko as Nisei (second-generation Japanese Americans) initially rejected the Japanese language and culture kept alive by their Issei (first-generation) parents. Though made to feel like foreigners in the United States, they feel utterly out of place while visiting Japan, as if "thoroughly American inside." Only once she is grown up and given the opportunity of returning to Japan—on an education mission to collect folktales—does Uchida realize how Japan is a part of her. "In my eagerness to be accepted as an American during my youth," she confesses, "I had been pushing my Japaneseness aside. Now at last, I appreciated it and was proud of it."

In her epilogue, Uchida describes her writing in explicitly political terms, implicating her memoir as nothing less than a mission to safeguard democracy in the United States. "I find it painful to continue remembering and writing about it [the internments]," she says, "But I must. Because I want each new generation of Americans to know what once happened in our democracy. I want them to love and cherish the freedom that can be snatched away so quickly, even by their own country. Most of all, I ask them to be vigilant, so that such a tragedy will never happen to any group of people in America ever again." This adult call to vigilance contrasts with her childhood discovery that by writing in her notebook she could hold on to "the special magic of joyous moments" and find "comfort and solace" in writing in the face of disappointment. Taken together, these passages reveal Uchida's belief that the memoir is a powerful genre for remembering even the most painful moments and putting them to work in the express hope of transforming the ways in which Americans think about race and culture.

The Invisible Thread relies on a split structure. The first half gives a portrait of Uchida's family and its generous, hardworking, and happy life in Berkeley. Though she describes occasional racial tensions between white and Japanese Americans, these do not mar the delight of her childhood. The second half, however, is given to a much more critical tone, as it tells of her father's sudden detainment by the Federal Bureau of Investigation and the family's relocations first to Tanforan Racetracks, then to a camp under armed guard at Topaz in the Utah desert. A number of photographs appear in the pages between these two halves: they mostly reproduce family portraits taken at home and outside the camp but also include—significantly— pages from Uchida's childhood journals. She thus reminds readers of the central role given her writing in making sense of the history of her family and of the United States.

CRITICAL DISCUSSION

Initial reviews of *The Invisible Thread* typically praise Uchida's smooth, clear prose and her insights into the everyday life of her California childhood and the more surprising events of the relocation to the internment camps. Reviewers and scholars recognize in particular the memoir's merits and potentials as a teachable text. As *School Library Journal* critic Phyllis Graves put it, "for readers who don't know about the Japanese-American concentration camps, her book is an eye-opener….Uchida's story is thought-provoking and important for giving young people a firsthand account of our inhumanity to others."

Uchida's memoir of her wartime experiences is commonly acknowledged as an important work at the intersection of ethnic life-writing and children's literature. As scholars including Rocío G. Davis have noted, *The Invisible Thread* is recognized as a valuable text for teaching children about the making and breaking of cultural affiliations. In this sense, critics consider Uchida as a writer with potential for influencing young Americans to be attentive to history and to remember the lessons of the past. Scholars invoke her as an exemplary figure for discussing the ways in which ethnic writing, autobiography, and children's literature interrelate productively.

The Invisible Thread is a title that scholars regularly mention in passing but rarely take up exclusively. Davis is one of the few to treat it directly and extensively: she examines the memoir as an ethnic autobiography, a document informed by the Japanese American consciousness of being treated differently rubbing up against a perception of a white mainstream American culture. Scholars such as Jacqueline Glasgow have usefully compared Uchida's treatment of the internment of Japanese Americans with the works of Jeanne Wakatsuki Houston, Marcia Savin, Monica Sone, and Shizuye Takashima. Looking at the internments in the particular context of children's literature, Matthew Teorey points to *The Invisible Thread* as a work capable of "teaching interracial understanding and fellowship, historical truth, and cultural self-awareness."

BIBLIOGRAPHY

Sources

Davis, Rocío G. "Ethnic Autobiography as Children's Literature: Laurence Yep's *The Lost Garden* and Yoshiko Uchida's *The Invisible Thread*." *Children's Literature Association Quarterly* 28.2 (2003): 90–97. Print.

Glasgow, Jacqueline N. "Reconciling Memories of Internment Camp Experiences during WWII in Children's and Young Adult Literature." *Alan Review* 30.1 (2002): 41–45. Print.

PRESIDENTIAL PERSPECTIVES ON THE INTERNMENTS

It was President Franklin D. Roosevelt who, on February 19, 1942, signed the notorious Executive Order 9066 that gave U.S. military leaders the authority to designate military zones along the West Coast as "exclusion zones," from which they could exclude any or all persons at will. As it happened, they used it selectively to evict those of Japanese ancestry, corral them in "relocation centers," and then deport them to designated internment camps beyond the zones. It took more than thirty years before the U.S. government would officially acknowledge that the evacuations and internments entailed a flagrant disregard for constitutional rights.

In 1976 President Gerald Ford apologized and described the entire undertaking as a "national mistake." Some six years later, in 1982, President Jimmy Carter lent his signature to the creation of a Commission on Wartime Relocation and Internment of Civilians, which took three years to render the verdict that the incarcerations put into effect under Executive Order 9066 had indeed been unjustified. As Carter put it, what prevailed was "race prejudice, war hysteria, and a failure of political leadership." Later that decade, in 1988, President Ronald Reagan signed the Civil Liberties Act of 1988, which offered an official apology and distributed more than a billion dollars in compensation to the surviving camp internees.

Graves, Phyllis. "Uchida, Yoshiko. *The Invisible Thread*." *School Library Journal* 38 (1992): 144. Print.

Potucek, Susan C. "Using Children's Literature to Make History Come Alive: Discussing Prejudice and the Japanese Internment." *History Teacher* 28.4 (1995): 567–71. Print.

Teorey, Matthew. "Untangling Barbed Wire Attitudes: Internment Literature for Young Adults." *Children's Literature Association Quarterly* 33.3 (2008): 227–45. Print.

Further Reading

Chen, Fu-jen, and Su-lin Yu. "Reclaiming the Southwest: A Traumatic Space in the Japanese American Internment Narrative." *Journal of the Southwest* 47.4 (2005): 551–70. Print.

Davis, Rocío G. "Asian American Autobiography for Children: Critical Paradigms and Creative Practice." *Lion and the Unicorn* 30.2 (2006): 185–201. Print.

De Manuel, Dolores, and Rocío G. Davis. "Editors' Introduction: Critical Perspectives on Asian American Children's Literature." *Lion and the Unicorn* 30.2 (2006): v–xv. Print.

Trites, Roberta Seelinger. "Multiculturalism in Children's Literature." *Children's Literature Association Quarterly* 28.2 (2003): 66–67. Print.

David Aitchison

A LONG WAY GONE
Memoirs of a Boy Soldier
Ishmael Beah

❖ **Key Facts**

Time Period:
Early 21st Century

Relevant Historical Events:
Sierra Leone's civil war; Beah's experience as a child soldier

Nationality:
Sierra Leonean

Keywords:
child soldiers; war; Africa

OVERVIEW

First published in 2007, *A Long Way Gone: Memoirs of a Boy Soldier* details Ishmael Beah's experiences as a child pressed into war for three years in his native Sierra Leone as well as his rehabilitation back into society in the years following. Beginning with how his idyllic childhood was suddenly shattered by war, Beah documents the turmoil he faced upon being thrust into war and then again in being removed from it by UNICEF relief workers. Throughout the text Beah shares his experiences as a way to demonstrate the damages of warfare, especially on children.

Beah's memoir was published less than a decade after he was removed from Sierra Leone's civil war and only five years after the war's end in 2002. It joined an increasing number of texts raising awareness of the strife in his country. During this time countries such as Canada and the United States were encouraged to change their laws pertaining to gem importation due to reports from the United Nations and other organizations that connected the trade of diamonds to the civil war in Sierra Leone. The immense popularity of his memoir launched Beah to celebrity, and he continues to raise awareness of the impact of war on children.

HISTORICAL AND LITERARY CONTEXT

The civil war in Sierra Leone erupted in 1991, when the Revolutionary United Front (RUF) attempted to overthrow Joseph Momoh's government, and lasted until 2002. By the end more than fifty thousand people were dead and nearly a million more displaced. The former president of Liberia, Charles G. Taylor, was convicted of abetting the warlords; of crimes against humanity; and of war crimes in Sierra Leone's civil war including murder, slavery, and the use of child soldiers. Beah includes little of the detailed history of the war in his memoir, deciding instead to depict the war as he had understood it as a child—a blurry, poorly understood force that had been created by people far from him, as he told *The Daily Show*'s Jon Stewart in a 2007 interview.

Belinda Luscombe notes in *Time* magazine in February 2007, "We're at what might be called a cultural sweet spot for the African child soldier," referring to the trope of a "weaponized child" in pop culture that has become symbolic of "a situation gone rancid." However, those "kids-at-arms" do not control their own narrative as Beah does in *A Long Way Gone*. Another memoir of the war in Sierra Leone, also published in 2007, is *Black Man's Grave: Letters from Sierra Leone,* by Gary Stewart and John Amman. This work relies on testimony more than autobiography and on the perspective of adults rather than children. Beah's memoir uniquely combines these two popular elements to depict his experiences as a child soldier and a young man.

When it was released in 2007, *A Long Way Gone* joined a growing number of books written by Africans about their war experiences. However, many such books, such as Nobel Peace Prize–nominated activist Ken Saro-Wiwa's antiwar novel *Sozaboy* (1985), about the Biafran War, and Jean Hatzfeld's collection of testimonies on the Rwandan genocide, *Machete Season* (2006), do not speak as memoir or shared personal experience. Closest is writer and anthropologist Michael Jackson's 2004 *In Sierra Leone,* a collection of anecdotes and meditations on his own experiences and those of his friends during the Sierra Leone civil war. As these memoirs have spotlighted Sierra Leone's conflict, so too has the public's knowledge of it increased as the role of diamonds in the war has become better understood. In 2005 music artist Kanye West publicized diamonds' impact and their true cost in his Grammy Award–winning song "Diamonds from Sierra Leone," which was followed a year later by Edward Zwick's film *Blood Diamond,* a movie with a similar message.

A Long Way Gone was soon joined by other memoirs of childhood during wartime, including Thomas Buergenthal's *A Lucky Child: A Memoir of Surviving Auschwitz as a Young Boy* (2010) and L. A. Sherman's *Bengali Girls Don't: Memoirs of a Muslim Daughter* (2011), which retells Sherman's experiences during the Bangladesh liberation war. Additional memoirs of survivors of the Sierra Leone civil war followed, including Aminatta Forna's *The Devil That Danced on the Water: A Daughter's Memoir* (2010) and journalist Tim Butcher's *Chasing the Devil: On Foot through Africa's Killing Fields* (2011).

THEMES AND STYLE

A Long Way Gone is at heart an antiwar treatise. Beah shows how the cycle of revenge and mistrust breaks apart communities, doing as much damage as guns. "People stopped trusting each other, and every stranger became an enemy. Even people who knew you became extremely careful of how they related or spoke to you," he writes, describing how an old man warned him and his friends to "find safety before this untrustworthiness and fear cause someone to harm you." However, he is hopeful and praises human strength. No matter how far gone into violence or inhumanity one becomes, Beah argues, a return to society is possible, and people can rebuild themselves and their lives in the wake of devastation such as war.

Beah wrote *A Long Way Gone* with the goal of raising awareness of the recruitment of child soldiers and to try to dispel the notion that inhumane acts happen only to "other" people. Beah's story opens with an anecdote from high school, in which several of his American friends tell him they think that seeing "people running around with guns and shooting each other" as Beah did, is "Cool." In his 2008 essay for *Studies in the Novel,* Robert Eaglestone writes that the opening anecdote is a "frame [that] subverts what is to come." The naïveté of Beah's friends stands in stark opposition to his own too-mature understanding of it. He contrasts his friends' superficial understanding of war with a detailed account of the human price it extracts, dissuading his reader of any romantic notion of the glories of war. War should be avoided most of all, he argues, because of the effect it has on children. As he shows, it steals their childhoods. Speaking to the United Nations after his rehabilitation, he argued that the tumultuous effects of war on children are devastating, stating, "The problem that is affecting us children is the war that forces us to run away from our homes, lose our families, and aimlessly roam the forests."

Every section in the memoir—with the exception of those that describe Beah's time actually at war—contains flashbacks to his family life. He shows that memory and narrative have the power to provide strength. That his recollections of war are devoid of such memories highlights how removed his time in the war was from the rest of his life and exposes the divorcing of self that war can cause. As he describes his time as a soldier, instead of focusing on his memories as a source of inner strength, he details the drugs he was given to blot out his feelings as well as the sense of power he found externally in his gun. Yet his internal power is what saves him initially when he is lost and is also what helps pull him through rehabilitation, both by reminding him of his home and by helping him to confront his wartime actions. As Eaglestone argues, by using flashbacks during his recovery to share his most vivid memories of the war, "the text echoes the accounts of trauma that stress that the events are not experienced as they happen but only afterwards, in fragmentary and broken ways, as the self struggles to work through and reintegrate itself."

Author Ishmael Beah in 2007, the year his autobiography was published. © AURORA PHOTOS/ALAMY

CRITICAL DISCUSSION

A Long Way Gone met immediate acclaim as well as immediate censure. A dispute over Beah's credibility arose in part because of the uproar caused when James Frey's *A Million Little Pieces* (2003), a well-received account of extreme personal difficulties, had been so recently proven to be more fiction than memoir. After *A Long Way Gone*'s meteoric rise to the top of the best-seller lists, reporters for the *Australian* began printing the results of a series of investigations that they claimed invalidated many of the events and timelines Beah documents. Soon other sources, including the *Village Voice* and the *Sierra Eye,* began to question the accuracy of Beah's memoir. Beah and his publishers refute all such allegations, standing by the author's documentation and their right to label the book as nonfiction.

Since its release, *A Long Way Gone* has remained tremendously influential. A *New York Times* bestselling work, it garnered Beah the Quill Award for Best Debut Author in 2007, was named third in *Time* magazine's Top 10 Nonfiction books for 2007, and became the second selection for Starbucks' book program. In addition, it has become a staple in universities around the world, serving as the University of Iowa's selection for its 2008 One Community, One Book program. It is considered a prime example of both an "addiction-recovery" model and "African trauma literature," the latter a term Eaglestone argues against. Eaglestone maintains that Beah's memoir, like most cited examples

A LONG WAY BACK: MORE ON ISHMAEL BEAH

Ishmael Beah was born in Sierra Leone in 1980. After his town and country became ravaged by war, he was pressed into fighting in 1993. In 1995 he was rescued by UNICEF, removed from the conflict, and treated for drug addiction and trauma. After his rehabilitation he was one of two children chosen to represent Sierra Leone at the United Nations First International Children's Parliament, where he spoke on behalf of former child soldiers before he returned to Sierra Leone. Due to renewed violence in the area, he returned to the United States in 1998 and was adopted by Laura Simms, whom he had met at the United Nations. Beah finished high school at the United Nations International School in New York and graduated from Oberlin College with a bachelor's degree in political science in 2004.

After his memoir's release, Beah became UNICEF's advocate for Children Affected by War. A member of the Human Rights Watch Children's Rights Division Advisory Committee, he has spoken before the United Nations, the Council on Foreign Relations, and other non-governmental organization panels on the subject of war's effect on children. Further, he has created the Ishmael Beah Foundation, a thriving charity that works for the rehabilitation of children whose lives have been touched by war.

of the genre, is more than that overly homogenizing term indicates. Both antiwar activists and those looking to rehabilitate traumatized children have drawn on Beah's narrative to support their causes.

Additionally, *A Long Way Gone* is frequently discussed as a text about adolescence and maturity. Irina Kyulanova's 2010 piece in *Studies in the Novel* expands this point of view, arguing that Beah's memoir "construct[s] war as a deviant rite of passage" that must be reversed with a resocialization process. Instead of transforming from child to man, as in many war accounts, she argues that Beah must be transformed back into a child after his experiences so he can better become a man. Moreover, as Belinda Luscombe acknowledges in *Time* magazine, Beah's story is unique among the many depictions of children in wars because he is "a new breed; he's not just a victim but a perpetrator." Mark Sanders picks up this thread of guilt and culpability in his 2011 article in *Law and Literature*, debating how much of an excuse childhood should be in international courts dealing with crimes against humanity.

BIBLIOGRAPHY

Sources

Beah, Ishmael. *A Long Way Gone: Memoirs of a Boy Soldier.* New York: Farrar, Straus & Giroux. Print.

Eaglestone, Robert. "'You Would Not Add to My Suffering if You Knew What I Have Seen': Holocaust Testimony and Contemporary African Trauma Literature." *Studies in the Novel* 40.1–2 (2008): 72–85. JSTOR. Web. 30 Oct. 2012.

"Interview with Ishmael Beah." *The Daily Show with Jon Stewart.* Comedy Central, 14 Feb. 2007. Web. 28 Oct. 2012.

Kyulanova, Irina. "From Soldiers to Children: Undoing the Rite of Passage in Ishmael Beah's *A Long Way Gone* and Bernard Ashley's *Little Soldier.*" *Studies in the Novel* 42.1 (2010): 28–47. Project MUSE. Web. 30 Oct. 2012.

Luscombe, Belinda. "Pop Culture Finds Lost Boys." *Time.* Time, 2 Feb. 2007. Web. 29 Oct. 2012.

Sanders, Mark. "Culpability and Guilt: Child Soldiers in Fiction and Memoir." *Law and Literature* 23.2 (2011): 195–223. JSTOR. Web. 28 Oct. 2012.

Further Reading

Grass, Günter. *Peeling the Onion.* Trans. Michael Henry Helm. Orlando: Harcourt, 2007. Print.

Moran, Mary H. Rev. of *A Long Way Gone: Memoirs of a Boy Soldier,* by Ishmael Beah, and *Black Man's Grave: Letters from Sierra Leone,* by Gary Stewart and John Amman. *African Studies Review* 51.1 (2008): 197–99. JSTOR. Web. 27 Oct. 2012.

Sherman, Gabriel. "The Fog of Memoir: The Feud over the Truthfulness of Ishmael Beah's *A Long Way Gone.*" *Slate.* The Slate Group, 6 Mar. 2008. Web. 26 Oct. 2012.

Wessells, Michael. *Child Soldiers: From Violence to Protection.* Cambridge: Harvard University Press, 2007. Print.

Katherine Bishop

The Memoirs of Lady Anne Halkett
Lady Anne Halkett

OVERVIEW
Written between 1677 and 1678, *The Memoirs of Lady Anne Halkett* (or, *Autobiography of Lady Anne Halkett*) contains a firsthand account of the English Civil War (1642–1671) from the perspective of its pious and resourceful author. It presents a vivid picture of the challenges faced by an aristocratic woman without a steady income or strong family network during a time of intense political turmoil. Halkett demonstrates the intersections between her personal life and the civil war as she writes about her affair with Colonel Joseph Bampfield, with whom she collaborated to support King Charles II against Oliver Cromwell. However, Halkett's political action endangered her personal reputation. Thus her writing often attempts to justify her actions by using strategies from popular contemporary genres such as the literary romance. Throughout, Halkett portrays herself as an independent, discerning, moral woman who acts decisively to further the causes she holds dearest: Anglican Christianity and the English monarchy.

Originally composed as a private memoir, Halkett's autobiography was not published until 1875, nearly two hundred years after her death. Originally it was intended as a witness to her moral uprightness during the civil war, a time that created opportunities for many people to engage in intrigue and deception. By contrast, Halkett stresses her reliance on God and her righteousness throughout her experiences. In the centuries before it was published, *Memoirs* was overshadowed by Halkett's religious handbooks, but today it is considered an important example of seventeenth-century women's writing.

HISTORICAL AND LITERARY CONTEXT
Memoirs documents the ways in which the upheaval of the mid-seventeenth century influenced an individual's personal life. When Cromwell and his followers revolted against King Charles I in 1642, the English Civil War began. Since Halkett and her family were aristocrats, they joined other English nobles in supporting the king's cause. However, in 1649 King Charles was captured by the Scots, handed over to Cromwell, and beheaded. This initiated a period of suffering and displacement for many English aristocrats. Their goal became to restore the king's son, Charles II, to the throne, which they finally did in 1660.

When Halkett wrote *Memoirs* in the late 1670s, this political turmoil had largely ceased, allowing her to chronicle her participation in the Royalist cause as well as the failed relationships she had endured before she married Halkett. Among other events, she describes her collaboration with Bampfield to help the Duke of York, later King James II, escape from prison in 1648. Later she recounts her move to Edinburgh, where she met King Charles II. Surrounded by wounded soldiers, Halkett used her interest in medicine to alleviate their suffering, which gave her the opportunity to preach the need for repentance to her patients. When she married Sir James Halkett in 1656, she finally found financial and emotional stability, which gave her time to write.

During the civil war several female authors compiled accounts of their personal lives as they intersected with political circumstances. This group includes not only Halkett but also Lady Ann Fanshawe. Halkett mentions politics only when it influences her own experience; indeed, she focuses mainly on her personal struggles as she seeks the financial security and good reputation that would be conferred by a stable marriage. Although *Memoirs* evokes the vulnerable, lonely position that the war forced upon an unmarried aristocratic woman, it also demonstrates the possibilities for decisiveness and independence that such a chaotic time allowed. In this way Halkett's story parallels the work of contemporary female novelists such as Aphra Behn, who created highly emotional romantic plots ending in happy marriages. Halkett's religious tenor also echoes her seventeenth-century counterparts such as Anne Bradstreet, who composed poems that chronicled her individual emotional and spiritual growth.

Halkett's *Memoirs* was not published during her life, and after her death it remained obscure. If Halkett received any literary recognition it was for her religious work, which occupied twenty-one volumes, fourteen of which are still extant. Portions of these were published, including *Instructions for Youth*. Like *Memoirs*, Halkett's religious writings are marked by a desire for internal moral uprightness combined with a concern for practical, active living. Today, however, the autobiography has risen to prominence since it chronicles the emotional life of an individual during the civil war.

✧ Key Facts

Time Period:
Late 17th Century

Relevant Historical Events:
English Civil War

Nationality:
English

Keywords:
women's writing; moralism

Portrait of King Charles II by John Michael Wright. Upon learning of the restoration of Charles II to the English throne in the spring of 1660, Lady Anne Halkett was so overjoyed that she set aside one day a week for the rest of her life to praise God for the king's restoration. © NATIONAL PORTRAIT GALLERY, LONDON, UK/ THE BRIDGEMAN ART LIBRARY

THEMES AND STYLE

The autobiography's place as a war narrative derives from the fact that Halkett focuses on the dozen years during the interregnum, though she lived through most of the seventeenth century, from 1623 to 1699. By doing so, her autobiography exemplifies the trope of an unmarried, independent woman attempting to navigate the exigencies of war. More specifically it demonstrates the thematic tension between her desire to obey Christian principles and her romantic attachments, particularly to Bampfield. Halkett wishes to support the cause of God and the king, but when she falls in love with Bampfield her political activism becomes troubled. In addition, the narrative uses the royal family as a thematic strand to boost Halkett's reputation. Not only does she open by mentioning that her father was "Preceptor of Charles 1st" and her mother was "Lady of the Bedchamber to Queen Henrietta Maria," but she mentions every contact she had with royalty during the war.

Driven by these moral, emotional, and political concerns, Halkett constructed her text not so much as a personal diary but as an exoneration: she wishes to clear her reputation of any smears she accrued by her entanglement with Bampfield. Throughout the text, Halkett emphasizes her desire to live a righteous moral life consonant with her staunch Anglican beliefs. She opens *Memoirs* by stating that "since wee have an advocate with the Father of Christ the righteous, hee will plead for mee wherin I am inocentt and pardon wherin I have beene guiltty." If her human reader will not believe her, at least God will, but Halkett makes a strong argument for the rightness of her actions— if not in themselves then at least as she consistently sought to make wise decisions despite the culture of deception that surrounded her. Her mentions of her interactions with Charles II and James I also serve to clear her name, demonstrating the financial support and encouragement she received from these monarchs.

Stylistically, Halkett's *Memoirs* bends the conventions of autobiography to further her reputation. Instead of presenting her material via detached prose, she invites her reader's emotional participation in her life events. As Judith Kearns writes in her 2004 essay in *Texas Studies in Literature and Language,* Halkett addresses "'those who have experience' of melancholy vapours," proposing that they "will I hope have the more charity for mee when they consider what effects they have had upon themselves." Furthermore, Halkett introduces conventions from dramatic comedies, particularly the narrative arc of the suffering heroine who manages to find ultimate rest in a successful, fulfilling marriage. Kearns suggests that these strategies allow her to play up her "ingenuity and independence." Finally, Halkett's use of tropes from romantic adventure novels, such as moments of second sight; being rescued "from the gates of death"; and experiencing weird natural phenomena, including earthquakes, lends her autobiography dramatic appeal.

CRITICAL DISCUSSION

Memoirs was edited in 1857 by John Gough Nichols, who died before his edition was published. The work was completed by Samuel Rawson Gardiner. Apparently this edition had very little impact when it was published. In 1701, two years after Halkett died, an anonymous author, "S. C.," published a short biography of her alongside selections from her religious writings. These devotional texts were largely the only means by which Halkett was known as an author.

John Loftis, who edited an edition of *Memoirs* published in 1979, writes that Halkett's memoirs "have received less attention than their quality merits." In 1924 a biography of Halkett by L. M. Cumming was published in *Blackwood's Magazine.* Loftis writes that "its value is limited by the absence of citation of sources for the information provided." He also mentions a "comprehensive account of the *Memoirs*" by Margaret Bottrall published in 1958. Loftis's own edition combines Halkett's autobiography with the memoirs of Fanshawe. This was the only modern edition of *Memoirs* until Suzanne L. Trill's edition in 2007, which included an introduction and notes. The publication of Loftis's edition was followed by many scholarly works concerned with the tradition of women's autobiography. A tremendous outpouring of critical books and essays that used Halkett extensively occurred in the 1980s, involving scholars such as Sidonie Smith, Mary G. Mason, and Estelle Jelinek.

Recently the interest in women's writing in the seventeenth century and the development of memoir as a genre has been renewed. In 2000 Sheila Ottway published an essay that focused on the tension between public and private life in Halkett's autobiography. In 2007 Trill published a selection of Halkett's devotional writings, a supplement to *Memoirs*. As Sharon Seelig writes in her review of Trill's edition, these devotional writings "give a much broader sense of Halkett's interests: her considerable piety; her tendency, characteristic of her generation, to interpret events in the light of her religious beliefs; … her affinity with things Scottish as well as English; and her deep concern with political and ecclesiastical affairs." Perhaps most importantly these devotional texts fill in the time after *Memoirs*, giving the modern reader a glimpse into Halkett's life as wife, mother, and mourner for her children and husband.

BIBLIOGRAPHY

Sources

"Civil War and Revolution." *BBC History*. BBC, 2012. Web. 1 Nov. 2012.

Kearns, Judith. "Fashioning Innocence: Rhetorical Construction of Character in the *Memoirs of Anne, Lady Halkett*." *Texas Studies in Literature and Language* 46.3 (2004): 340+. *Literature Resource Center*. Web. 1 Nov. 2012.

Loftis, John, ed. *The Memoirs of Anne, Lady Halkett and Ann, Lady Fanshawe*. Oxford, U.K.: Clarendon, 1979. Print.

Seelig, Sharon. "Lady Anne Halkett: Selected Self-Writings." *Renaissance Quarterly* 61.2 (2008): 680+. *Literature Resource Center*. Web. 1 Nov. 2012.

Stevenson, David. "Halkett, Anne, Lady Halkett (1623–1699)." *Oxford Dictionary of National Biography*. Ed. Lawrence Goldman. Oxford: Oxford UP. Web. 1 Nov. 2012.

Further Reading

Cumming, L. M. "Anne, Lady Halkett." *Blackwood's Magazine* Nov. 1924: 654–76. Print.

Findley, Sandra, and Elaine Hobby. "Seventeenth-Century Women's Autobiography." *1642: Literature and Power in the Seventeenth Century*. Ed. Francis Barker. Essex: University of Essex, 1988. 11–36. Print.

Jelinek, Estelle. *The Tradition of Women's Autobiography: From Antiquity to the Present*. Boston: Twayne, 1986. Print.

Mason, Mary G. "The Other Voice: Autobiographies of Women Writers." *Autobiography: Essays Theoretical and Critical*. Ed. James Olney. Princeton, N.J.: Princeton University Press, 1980. 207–35. Print.

THE MEMOIRS OF LADY ANN FANSHAWE: WOMEN AND WAR EXPERIENCE

Alongside Lady Anne Halkett's *Memoirs*, Lady Ann Fanshawe's autobiography presents the toll taken by the Civil War on British aristocrats. Born in 1625, Fanshawe was the daughter of a noble house and enjoyed all the privileges of her status until 1640, when her mother died. Her father remarried and, two years later, openly supported Charles I. These events marked the beginning of the end for Fanshawe's family. Thus her *Memoirs* is to a great extent a work not of personal exoneration or spiritual testimony like Halkett's but instead an epitaph for British aristocratic families, both her own and her husband's.

During the Civil War Fanshawe's father was stripped of his titles, his wealth, and his land. Fanshawe writes that the only positive aspect of her life at this point was her marriage to Sir Richard Fanshawe, which lasted for twenty-two years and was extremely happy. Though she was often sick and pregnant, Fanshawe traveled with her husband around England and Europe as he fulfilled his duties to the British monarchs. After her husband's death in 1666, she devoted herself to providing for her children and writing. In this context she composed her autobiography to advise her children and to ensure that they remembered their distinguished father. Fanshawe died in 1680.

Ottway, Sheila. "Desiring Disencumbrance: The Representation of the Self in Autobiographical Writings by Seventeenth-Century English Women." Diss. University of Groningen, 1998. Print.

———. "They Only Lived Twice: Public and Private Selfhood in the Autobiographies of Anne, Lady Halkett and Colonel Joseph Bampfield." *Betraying Our Selves: Forms of Self-Representation in Early Modern English Texts*. Ed. Henk Dagstra, Sheila Ottway, and Helen Wilcox. New York: St. Martin's, 2000. 136–47. Print.

Person, James E., ed. "(Lady) Ann Fanshawe (1625–1680)." *Literature Criticism from 1400 to 1800*. Vol. 11. Detroit: Gale, 1990. *Literature Criticism Online*. Web. 1 Nov. 2012.

Smith, Sidonie. *A Poetics of Women's Autobiography: Marginality and the Fictions of Self-Representation*. Bloomington: Indiana University Press, 1987. Print.

Evelyn Reynolds

NIGHT
Elie Wiesel

✣ **Key Facts**

Time Period:
Mid-20th Century

Relevant Historical Events:
Holocaust; World War II

Nationality:
American/Romanian

Keywords:
Holocaust; Jewishness; Nazism

OVERVIEW

Elie Wiesel's *Night*—written in Yiddish and published in 1956, then substantially revised and shortened when Wiesel translated it for a 1958 French edition—is one of the most highly regarded and seminal examples of the autobiographical Holocaust narrative. Written in spare, emotionally weighted prose, the memoir relates the abrupt sequestration of Jews in Wiesel's small Transylvanian town of Sighet into a ghetto, followed by their forced removal in 1944 to the Auschwitz death camp, from which Wiesel was eventually transferred to camps at Buna and Buchenwald. The teenage Wiesel's profound spiritual despair at the realities of the Holocaust frames a grim, episodic narrative describing the horrors that Wiesel, his father, and their fellow inmates witness and endure at the hands of the Nazis until the arrival of U.S. forces at Buchenwald in April 1945. Wiesel's testimony stands as an enduring document of the atrocities perpetrated during the Holocaust, implicitly affirming the text's emphasis on the importance of bearing witness.

An important early memoir of the Jewish experience during the Holocaust, *Night* originally appeared in Buenos Aires in 1956 as part of a 176-book series of Yiddish war memoirs. Considered more as part of a larger collection than as an independent work, it attracted little notice outside the Yiddish-speaking world. Its subsequent French and English editions, though well received critically, were not commercially successful. The book greatly increased in renown over the next few decades, however, eventually becoming a massive best seller, a frequently assigned text in high school and college courses, and one of the single most widely read autobiographical accounts of the Holocaust experience. It remains a canonical work of Holocaust literature.

HISTORICAL AND LITERARY CONTEXT

Night is a horrific, personal document of the genocidal policies enacted against members of the Jewish population in German-occupied Europe before and during World War II. Following the advent of the Third Reich in 1933, Jews were subjected to numerous forms of persecution, including eugenics regulations designed to prevent them from reproducing; violent, state-sponsored mob attacks; and forced relocations to death and concentration camps. The beginning of the war in 1939 engendered the construction of many more camps and a renewed emphasis on incarcerating Jews within them, and in January 1942 the regime implemented Adolf Hitler's "Final Solution," calling for the systematic extermination of the Jewish race and resulting in the deaths of around six million Jews—a million of whom were probably killed earlier—between 1942 and the war's end in 1945.

Wiesel wrote his memoir, in its original incarnation, about ten years after the events depicted in the text, a time when relatively few autobiographical accounts from Holocaust survivors had come to global notice. The book's original Yiddish title—*Un di Velt Hot Geshvign,* which translates as "And the World Remained Silent"—suggests a global unwillingness to acknowledge the enormity of the genocide, and Wiesel was initially unable to generate publisher interest in his book outside the Yiddish readership for which it was originally composed. It was only with great difficulty that the writer François Mauriac, the Nobel laureate who persuaded Wiesel to translate the work into French, was able to get the translation published. In its wake, Wiesel became one of the most prominent advocates for Holocaust remembrance.

Night was an iconic early work in the tradition of autobiographical Holocaust writing that slowly began to emerge in the wake of World War II. An important contemporary account was Primo Levi's 1947 Auschwitz memoir *If This Is a Man,* which, like Wiesel's text, was published only with difficulty and sold poorly upon its initial release. Though first and foremost Jewish in its orientation, *Night* was also influenced by the writings of French existentialists—particularly the novelist and playwright Jean-Paul Sartre, under whom Wiesel studied at the Sorbonne—whose philosophical emphasis on alienation, meaninglessness, and absurdity can be observed in Wiesel's treatment of his own existential despair in the face of the Holocaust.

Though it was not a popular success upon its initial publication, *Night* served as an important predecessor to countless subsequent literary accounts of the Holocaust, autobiographical and otherwise. Books by other Holocaust survivors, such as Jean Améry, Tadeusz Borowski, and Imre Kertész, began to proliferate in the years and decades after *Night*'s publication, and Wiesel continued to discuss the Holocaust and its effects in his subsequent writings, publishing

Elie Wiesel at the Holocaust Memorial in Lyon, France, in 1987. Behind him is a photo of prisoners at the Buchenwald concentration camp in 1945, shortly after its liberation by Allied forces. Wiesel is pointing to himself in the photo. © AP IMAGES/LAURENT REBOURS

two thematic sequels, the novels *Dawn* (1960) and *Day* (1961), as well as several further autobiographical volumes dealing with his life after the war. In recent years *Night* is more widely read than it has ever been, and the current ubiquity of literary and popular narratives about the Holocaust (occasionally condemned by Wiesel as trivializing) owes much to seminal accounts such as *Night*.

THEMES AND STYLE

One of *Night*'s primary themes is the notion that the experience of the Holocaust utterly shattered previously held religious, philosophical, and societal formulations, replacing spirituality and civilization with nihilistic barbarism. Early in the text, Wiesel relates how, prior to his concentration camp experience, he was a deeply religious young man: "By day I studied Talmud and by night I would run to the synagogue to weep over the destruction of the Temple." Wiesel's faith is shaken by the horrors of Auschwitz—"I was alone, terribly alone in a world without God, without man"—and this loss of religious belief is accompanied by a breakdown of all standards of human behavior: Nazi officers burn babies alive, children turn against parents, and conventional values increasingly give way to either utter despair or an animalistic drive to survive at any cost. In a particularly chilling passage, Wiesel describes the murder of a father and son over a piece of bread: "His son searched him, took the crust of bread, and began to devour it. He didn't get far. Two men had been watching him. They jumped him. Others joined in. When they withdrew, there were two dead bodies lying next to me, the father and the son."

Wiesel wrote *Night* primarily to bear witness to the horrifying realities of the Holocaust, thus helping to ensure that its details are never forgotten or permitted to reoccur. This intent is reflected in the narrative's recurring motif of unheeded warnings and disregarded testimony; near the beginning of the book, Wiesel's mentor Moishe, recently escaped from the Gestapo, attempts to inform the Jews from Wiesel's town about the massacre he witnessed, but they dismiss him as a fantasist. *Night* is in many ways comparable to Moishe's story, and along with many other Holocaust narratives it seems intended as a dire testimony the world cannot afford to ignore. Many scholars believe that Wiesel's attempts to convey the deeper truth of the Holocaust may not be have been strictly factual and that much of *Night* is fictionalized to some degree. It is hence frequently referred to as an autobiographical novel rather than a memoir, much to Wiesel's chagrin.

Night is written in a plain, unadorned prose style that is used to narrate brief, emotionally charged vignettes. Wiesel's sentences tend to be short and rarely indulge in rhetorical flourishes or flowery description, instead describing his thoughts and the nightmarish events of the narrative in a simple, straightforward manner. This minimalist approach foregrounds the extremity of the book's content, such as when Wiesel discusses the hanging of two men and a child—"the two men were no longer alive. Their tongues were hanging out, swollen and bluish. But the third rope

WIESEL'S CAREER AFTER *NIGHT*

Since *Night*'s publication, Elie Wiesel has become a major public figure for his consistent advocacy on behalf of the victims of the Holocaust, as well as for speaking out on a wide variety of other concerns, including South African apartheid; the welfare of Israel; and various instances of modern ethnic warfare, including the Bosnian "ethnic cleansing" campaigns in the former Yugoslavia in the 1990s and the Darfur conflict in Sudan during the first decade of the twenty-first century. He has served on the governing board of various humanitarian organizations, and in addition to the Nobel Peace Prize, he has been awarded the Presidential Medal of Freedom and been inducted into the American Academy of Arts and Letters, among various other commendations.

He served as chairman of the Holocaust Memorial Council from 1978 to 1986 and is likewise the founding chairman of the United States Holocaust Memorial Museum. He also established the Elie Wiesel Foundation for Humanity, and his copious public statements on the subject have made him perhaps the most prominent Holocaust survivor in public life. As Ruth Franklin has observed, "by the 1980s he had virtually come to symbolize the Holocaust to many Americans." *Night* began this association, but it was only the beginning.

---

was still moving: the child, too light, was still breathing"—and ties this event to Wiesel's spiritual crisis by bluntly equating the hanging child with God, followed by a bleak, epigrammatic conclusion to the episode: "That night, the soup tasted of corpses."

CRITICAL DISCUSSION

Though *Night*'s initial non-Yiddish publication—in both French and English—was met with little commercial success, the book's critical reception was much more positive. Reviewers praised the memoir's moving evocation of appalling inhumanity, hailing the narrative as an especially powerful literary testament to the obscene reality of the Holocaust. Alfred Kazin's review in the *Reporter* exemplified the book's warm critical response, asserting that "in recounting these atrocious early experiences [Wiesel] makes one realize how difficult is it for a victim to do full justice to the facts." He singles out Wiesel's treatment of his own religious collapse as a particularly striking aspect of the work: "What makes his book unusual and gives it such a particular poignancy … is that it recounts the loss of his faith by an intensely religious young Jew who grew up in an Orthodox community of Transylvania." Kazin would later publicly take issue with the veracity of the hanging scene in *Night*.

Night's readership steadily expanded in the decades following its release, as the book became a prominent beneficiary of and a substantial contributor to the growing interest in Holocaust studies and remembrance. Writing in *Modern Judaism* in 1990, Richard Libowitz observes that "Elie Wiesel's *Night* and *The Diary of a Young Girl*, by Anne Frank, remained the most popular of [Holocaust] memoir materials" during the 1980s, a decade also marked by the bestowal, in 1986, of a Nobel Peace Prize upon Wiesel for the career of humanitarian testimony and advocacy that *Night* inaugurated. Recent scholarship on the work often focuses on how it functions as a memoir as well as its relationship to Holocaust writing as a whole.

Scholarly analysis of Wiesel's memoir frequently discusses its somewhat uncertain relationship to the autobiographical genre; Franklin's 2011 study *A Thousand Darknesses: Lies and Truth in Holocaust Fiction* exemplifies this tendency, asserting that "the book's poetic austerity comes at a cost to the literal truth. This cost, it must be said, does not detract in the least from *Night*'s validity as a Holocaust testimonial…. But it is worth recognizing that such a cost exists, if only to remind ourselves that no memoir can be at once an unerring representation of reality and a genuine artistic achievement." Other scholarship examines *Night* alongside other works about the Holocaust, as in Naomi Mandel's "Speaking Corpses and Spectral Spaces: Representing Testimony after the Holocaust" (1999), which incorporates *Night* into a discussion of the ways in which different works represent the act of bearing witness.

BIBLIOGRAPHY

Sources

Franklin, Ruth. *A Thousand Darknesses: Lies and Truth in Holocaust Fiction*. Oxford: Oxford University Press, 2011. Print.

Kazin, Alfred. "The Least of These." Rev. of *Night*, by Elie Wiesel. *Reporter* 27 Oct. 1960: 54–57. Print.

Libowitz, Richard. "Holocaust Studies." *Modern Judaism* 10.3 (1990): 271–81. *JSTOR*. Web. 10 Nov. 2012.

Mandel, Naomi. "Speaking Corpses and Spectral Spaces: Representing Testimony after the Holocaust." *Dialectical Anthropology* 24.3–4 (1999): 357–76. *Academic Search Complete*. Web. 10 Nov. 2012.

Wiesel, Elie. *Night*. Trans. Marion Wiesel. New York: Hill and Wang, 2006. Print.

Further Reading

Bloom, Harold, ed. *Elie Wiesel's* Night. Philadelphia: Chelsea House, 2001. Print.

Cohler, Bertram J. "Life Writing in the Shadow of the Shoah: Fathers and Sons in the Memoirs of Elie Wiesel and Leon Weliczker Wells." *Journal of Applied Psychoanalytic Studies* 7.1 (2010): 40–57. Print.

Fine, Ellen S. *Legacy of Night: The Literary Universe of Elie Wiesel*. Albany: State University of New York Press, 1982. Print.

Rosen, Alan, ed. *Approaches to Teaching Wiesel's* Night. New York: Modern Language Association of America, 2007. Print.

Roth, John K. "From Night to Twilight: A Philosopher's Reading of Elie Wiesel." *Religion & Literature* 24.1 (1992): 59–73. Print.

Schwarz, Daniel R. "The Ethics of Reading Wiesel's *Night*." *Style* 32.2 (1998): 221–42. Print.

Seidman, Naomi. "Elie Wiesel and the Scandal of Jewish Rage." *Jewish Social Studies* 3.1 (1996): 1–19. Print.

Suleiman, Susan Rubin. "Problems of Memory and Factuality in Recent Holocaust Memoirs: Wilkomirski/Wiesel." *Poetics Today* 21.3 (2000): 543–59. Print.

Sundquist, Eric J. "Witness without End?" *American Literary History* 19.1 (2007): 65–85. Print.

James Overholtzer

Paekpom Ilchi
The Autobiography of Kim Ku
Kim Ku

❖ *Key Facts*

Time Period:
Mid-20th Century

Relevant Historical Events:
Korean independence movement; World War II; division of Korea

Nationality:
South Korean

Keywords:
colonialism; independence; war

OVERVIEW

Paekpom Ilchi: The Autobiography of Kim Ku, published in 2000 and translated by Jongsoo Lee, is the first English-language publication of the autobiography of Korean nationalist Kim Ku (also often spelled as Kim Gu). Originally published in Korea in 1947, the English version is an invaluable resource for researchers of modern Korean history. The autobiography is divided into seven chapters that present the events of Kim's life in chronological order and is supplemented with a translator's introduction, historical notes, maps, photos, and an appendix. Kim's autobiography spans an extensive period, covering both world wars as well as the operations of the Korean Provisional Government (KPG) in China and the division of Korea following World War II. The autobiography reads as an inspirational story of a man who overcame countless obstacles to fight for the independence of his country.

Kim's original Korean-language autobiography was published in 1947, in the aftermath of World War II and the division of Korea that took effect in September 1945 and split the country into two occupied territories as part of the stipulations of Japan's unconditional surrender. (The United States administered the south half, the Soviet Union the north half.) Kim began to write his autobiography prior to World War II, upon being separated from his two young sons when he was forced to flee to China. He wanted to record his life story for them. *Paekpom Ilchi* received a warm reception by Koreans upon its initial publication and has remained popular there. Today, the book is regarded as an important resource for the study of the Korean independence movement and the history of modern Korea in general.

HISTORICAL AND LITERARY CONTEXT

At the turn of the twentieth century, Korea was marred by war and imperialism, caught between the political powers of Japan, China, and Russia. The Russo-Japanese War (1904–1905) eliminated Russia's presence in the country after China had already been expelled from Korea following the First Sino-Japanese War. After several treaties, Japan effectively annexed Korea in 1910, resulting in Japan's repressive imperialist rule over the country, which lasted until the end of World War II. Kim was involved in Japan-Korea political tensions from an early age, when he murdered a Japanese man in 1896 to avenge the Japanese Empire's assassination of Korea's Empress Myeongseong. Kim was jailed and tortured by the Japanese government for the crime, and upon escaping from prison, he sought refuge in a Buddhist temple. Throughout these years he fought for the education and enlightenment of the Korean people under the constant oppression of the Japanese government.

Kim's autobiography was published after the post–World War II division of Korea into northern and southern occupied zones. The KPG—in which Kim had been a leader—was dissolved prior to the country's split, and he returned to Korea and participated in negotiations in an attempt to avoid the division of his homeland. His autobiography includes a concluding statement that sums up his main objective in life: "If god asked me what was my wish, I would reply unhesitatingly, 'Korean independence.'" Published in a newly formed South Korean nation, *Paekpom Ilchi* increased Kim's celebrity throughout the country, yet it could have been motive for his assassination by Ahn Doo-hee only two years after its publication.

While it is difficult to discern what literary influences may have shaped Kim's work, the political ideals he presents in his autobiography were clearly influenced by the religions of Tonghak (Donghak), Confucianism, and Christianity. Kim was also likely influenced by Korean writing from the "Enlightenment" (*kaehwa*) period at the turn of the twentieth century, including the nationalist poetry of Han Yong Un, especially *Nimui Chimmuk* (*Silence of the Beloved*), a long poem that praises his homeland. The rhetoric employed in Kim's concluding chapter echoes the lyrical romanticism of the work of Han.

The success of Kim's autobiography, especially following his assassination two years after its publication, increased his fame. It brought much recognition to him posthumously, earning him the prestigious Republic of Korea Medal of Order of Merit for National Foundation and the Democratic People's Republic of Korea's National Reunification Prize. The later political statements of fellow KPG leaders such as Syngman Rhee, published in *Korea Flaming High, Excerpts from Statements by President Syngman Rhee in Crucial 1953* (1956), reflect ideals similar to those introduced by Kim in *Paekpom Ilchi*. Louise Yim's autobiography *My Forty Year Fight for Korea* (1951) tells of her experiences as a Korean rebel and adopts a nationalist rhetoric that is comparable to Kim's.

THEMES AND STYLE

In *Paekpom Ilchi*, Kim conveys his unwavering commitment to Korean independence through anti-Japanese activities, espousing broad democratic ideals to form his political foundation. He writes, "My political philosophy, summed up in one word, is freedom. The nation that we establish must be a nation of freedom…. I do not desire that our nation become a nation ruled by a dictatorship." The author writes in general terms of the ideals of freedom and independence, alluding to the repressive presence of Japan in his dismissal of dictatorships. He elaborates on this condemnation by drawing parallels between Korea's oppression under Japan and the cruel regimes of the German Nazis and Italian Fascists.

It appears that Kim initially began to write his autobiography while separated from his wife and two young children in Korea as a way of recording his personal and family histories. In his discussion of serving his people, Kim writes, "As a man belonging to a nation that has lost its independence, I lived the seventy years of my life in much shame, sorrow, and trouble…. I hope that our nation's young people, both male and female, will abandon the small and narrow thoughts of the past and become conscious of our people's great mission." The book reads as a message to Korean youth in general, although the author may have originally written it with his two sons in mind when employing the phrase "our nation's young people." Throughout the text, Kim constructs a message of hope and inspiration for future generations to carry on his struggle.

Paekpom Ilchi is notable for its straightforward, relatively formal narrative voice. Kim tells his story in the lexicon of an educated man, describing events in clear, succinct statements. In a passage where he recalls his introduction to the Tonghak religion, he writes, "I began to have curiosity about Tonghak and decided to visit them. As instructed by others, I did not eat any odorous foods, and I bathed clean and wore new clothing to go to see them. I heard that one could not be received otherwise." The author explains events chronologically, always employing a tone of respect in his dealings with those of other cultures or those superior to him. His detailed descriptions allow the reader to visualize his experiences, such as in this passage: "As I approached Mr. O's house, I could hear people reading something aloud. It was different from the tone of chanting Buddhist sutras or other poems and sounded rather like singing songs in harmony."

A statue of Kim Ku, located in Namsan Park in Seoul, South Korea.
© SANDRO LACARBONA/ ALAMY

CRITICAL DISCUSSION

While *Paekpom Ilchi* received a positive response from Koreans and quickly became a best seller, it is difficult to ascertain the reaction of critics since such scholarship is not available in English. One of the earliest books to address the autobiography is Chong-Sik Lee's *The Politics of Korean Nationalism* (1963). Lee cites *Paekpom Ilchi* extensively, using it as a historical source for his discussion of Korean nationalism and the KPG during Japanese occupation. The only extant English-language review of the book, published by Young Back Choi in 2002, praises it as "an interesting chronicle of events, observations, and personal reflections. It is full of out-of-the-ordinary episodes."

Kim has become a transnational Korean hero. His legacy is often found in different patriotic and educational events and activities both in Korea and abroad among Korean immigrant communities. For example, several essay contests in the United States have required students to engage with Kim's political philosophy. A brochure for a 2009 essay contest sponsored by the Korean Resource Center in the United States reads, "In commemoration of the 29th anniversary of 5.18 People's Uprising and the 60th anniversary of the death of Kim Ku, the Korean Resource Center (KRC) is sponsoring an essay contest to remember the spirit of civic participation and justice." Along similar lines, a 2012 Dream Scholarship Fund Application required contestants to write an essay that responds to Kim's statement "The Country I Want" (included

RESISTING JAPANESE OCCUPATION: THE KOREAN PROVISIONAL GOVERNMENT

The Korean Provisional Government (KPG) was an interim government organized in 1919 by Korean citizens in exile in Shanghai. The KPG was formed in reaction to increasingly severe Japanese suppression of Korean political demonstrations led by the March 1 Movement, which had issued a proclamation of Korea's independence from Japan in March 1919. Kim Ku, Syngman Rhee, and An Ch'ang-ho were among the leading members of the KPG. The establishment of the provisional government aided Korea in moving toward independence from Japan by forging important ties with different independence groups and governments abroad, even sending representatives to Europe and the United States to promote their cause. By 1922 many groups were unified under the KPG in their struggle for independence.

The influence of the KPG did not last long, however, and was soon weakened by Japan's violent suppression of nationalistic activities in Korea, as well as internal divisions within the coalition. Different KPG leaders sought support from opposing factions, splintering the provisional government's once-cohesive political interests. Upon Korea's liberation from Japan at the end of World War II, the KPG dissolved, and most of its members returned to Korea to participate in the formation of the newly established postcolonial Korean government.

in his autobiography). The majority of scholars regard *Paekpom Ilchi* as a valuable historical document.

Certain scholarship on Kim's autobiography, including Eugene Park's 2008 article "Status and 'Defunct' Offices in Early Modern Korea: The Case of Five Guards Generals (Owijang), 1864–1910," uses it to analyze the bureaucracy of the Korean military. Writes Park, "Compared to local elites, even more individuals that we may regard as chungin received Five Guards generalships…. A vivid portrayal of such an individual appears in the *Hidden Aspirations of Paekpom*—essentially an autobiography of Kim Ku … a famous Korean independence activist." Scholars such as Paul Beirne (*Su-Un and His World of Symbols: The Founder of Korea's First Indigenous Religion*, 2009), who are interested in the Tonghak religion, find insights in Kim's experiences with the religion that he documents in his autobiography.

BIBLIOGRAPHY

Sources

Beirne, Paul. *Su-Un and His World of Symbols: The Founder of Korea's First Indigenous Religion.* Burlington, U.K.: Ashgate, 2009. Print.

Choi, Young Back. Rev. of *Paekpom Ilchi: The Autobiography of Kim Ku*, by Kim Ku. *Journal of Asian Studies* 61.3 (2002): 1071–73. Print.

Kim, Ku. *Paekpom Ilchi: The Autobiography of Kim Ku.* Lanham, Md.: University Press of America, 2000. Print.

Lee, Chong-Sik. *The Politics of Korean Nationalism.* Berkeley: University of California Press, 1963. Print.

Park, Eugene. "Status and 'Defunct' Offices in Early Modern Korea: The Case of Five Guards Generals (Owijang), 1864–1910." *Journal of Social History* 41.3 (2008): 737–57. Print.

Further Reading

Ch'oe, Yong-ho, William De Bary, and Peter Lee, eds. *Sources of Korean Tradition: Volume 2: From the Sixteenth to the Twentieth Centuries.* New York: Columbia University Press, 2000. Print.

Kim, Sun Joo, ed. *The Northern Region of Korea: History, Identity, and Culture.* Seattle: Center for Korea Studies, University of Washington Press, 2010. Print.

Strauss, Barry, and David McCann. *War and Democracy: A Comparative Study of the Korean War and the Peloponnesian War.* Armonk, N.Y.: M.E. Sharpe, 2001. Print.

Yamamoto, Genzo, and Daniel Kim. "Navigating Multiple Modernities: Soon Hyun and the Envisioning of Korean/American Modernities." *Journal of Asian American Studies* 13.2 (2010): 127–62. Print.

Katrina White

The Sovereignty and Goodness of God
Mary Rowlandson

OVERVIEW

Mary Rowlandson's *The Sovereignty and Goodness of God* (1682) is a captivity narrative tracing the author's experiences as a prisoner of the Narragansett Indians during King Philip's War (1675–1676). Rowlandson and her three children were captured during a raid on their Lancaster, Massachusetts, home on February 10, 1675. The author was separated from her two older children soon after the attack. Her youngest, Sarah, was wounded and died eight days into the ordeal. Organized around a series of what Rowlandson calls "removes," the narrative chronicles her journey with her captors away from English civilization, her subsequent enslavement, her friendships with several kind Indians, and her ultimate release. As its title makes clear, the text emphasizes the strength that Rowlandson, the wife of a Puritan pastor, draws from her Christian faith during the ordeal. Although the narrative acknowledges the extraordinary nature of Rowlandson's experience, the tale is framed as one of Christian piety and repentance.

Due in part to its somewhat sensational subject matter, *The Sovereignty and Goodness of God* quickly gained broad readership in both the American colonies and England. Although female authorship was radical in Puritan society, Rowlandson's propriety was vouched for by famed minister Increase Mather, who wrote a *per amicum* (by a friend) preface to the book. Today the text is recognized as foundational to a tradition of American captivity narratives and is considered an important early reflection on Puritan beliefs, relationships between Native Americans and New England colonists, and the role of women in early American society.

HISTORICAL AND LITERARY CONTEXT

Written during a period of prolonged tensions between New England colonists and indigenous peoples, *The Sovereignty and Goodness of God* offers a commentary on the conflict that draws on Rowlandson's firsthand experiences and religious beliefs. Prior to the attack, the author and her husband enjoyed the social prominence afforded by his Harvard education and role as minister. The raid during which Rowlandson was captured was part of King Philip's War, a series of skirmishes between English colonists and a confederacy of Native American tribes from New England. The conflict began in the year of Rowlandson's capture and continued as late as 1678, although its end is sometimes dated to the death of its leader in August 1676. Known to the colonists as King Philip, Metacomet (1639–1676) was a Wampanoag chief who built a confederacy to defend Indian lands from European settlers. Rowlandson encountered Metacomet during her captivity. She describes him not as a savage but as a kind and thoughtful man who offered her tobacco and paid her to make a shirt and cap for his son.

By the time Rowlandson's narrative was published in 1782, King Philip's War had ended. Metacomet had been killed, his body desecrated, and his family sold into slavery. Although the colonists suffered heavy losses in the war, New England's indigenous population was decimated. In the decades that followed, colonists spread out over the region. Although *The Sovereignty and Goodness of God* is among the best-known autobiographical writings to emerge from colonial America, very little is known about its author's later life. Rowlandson suffered the death of her husband in 1678 and married Samuel Talcott the following year. Unaware of Rowlandson's marriage and subsequent name change, scholars once believed she died within several years of her release and possibly before the publication of her book. More recently, records have been uncovered suggesting that she actually lived until 1710 or 1711. Far more is known, however, about the months of her captivity than about the final three decades of her life.

The Sovereignty and Goodness of God is generally credited as one of the first major works published by a woman in America. Although a tradition of New World captivity narratives predates Rowlandson's text—among them Hernando de Escalante Fontaneda's 1575 account of his life among Florida's native population following a shipwreck—there is no evidence that she was aware of these texts. Her work is more clearly situated within a specific tradition of Puritan writings that includes Mather's *A Brief History of the War with the Indians in New England* (1676). The alternative title *A True History of the Captivity and Restoration of Mrs. Mary Rowlandson,* used for the work in England, reflects an attempt to play down the Puritan religious emphasis of the tale.

The success of Rowlandson's tale contributed to the tradition of captivity narratives that proliferated in the United States well into the nineteenth century. In a *Legacy* profile of the author, Rebecca Blevins Faery notes that the text "initiated and became the prototype

❖ **Key Facts**

Time Period:
Late 17th Century

Relevant Historical Events:
King Philip's War; colonization of America; Rowlandson's capture by Native Americans

Nationality:
American

Keywords:
colonialism; Native Americans; Christianity

WAR EXPERIENCES

An illustration depicting Nipmuc Indians raiding Brookfield, Massachusetts, during King Philip's War (also known as Metacomet's War or Metacomet's Rebellion) in 1675. Mary Rowlandson and her children were taken captive in a similar attack on Lancaster, Massachusetts, the same year.
© PRIVATE COLLECTION/ PETER NEWARK AMERICAN PICTURES/THE BRIDGEMAN ART LIBRARY

of innumerable subsequent stories of the white woman captured by Indians." Its influence can be traced in the spate of similar captivity narratives, among them those of Hannah Dustan (printed in Cotton Mather's *Magnalia Christi Americana*, 1702) and Mary Jemison (published by James Seaver as *The Life and Times of Mrs. Mary Jemison*, 1824).

THEMES AND STYLE

The central theme of *The Sovereignty and Goodness of God* is that faith in God's plan can bring peace even in the direst circumstances. Rowlandson describes nearly succumbing to her circumstances early in her ordeal, only to find that "the Lord renewed my strength still, and carried me along, that I might see more of His power." Although she relates continued struggles, particularly following the death of her daughter, an important turning point comes when one of her captors gives her a Bible obtained during another raid. That Bible, she explains, became "my guide by day, and my pillow by night." She credits her faith in God with saving her life by providing the comfort that allows her to remain silent and docile. A fellow captive, Goodwife Joslin, is vocal in her fear and desire for freedom and is consequently murdered by their captors. Rowlandson comes to see her ordeal as a test of faith and a reminder of the duty of Christian obedience. Generalizing from her own experiences, she goes so far as to suggest of the Native Americans that "God strengthened them to be a scourge to His people."

As a Puritan woman, Rowlandson broke with social and religious convention in claiming the authority to tell her own story. The published form of her text, prefaced by a statement by Mather and, in most early editions, followed by her husband's final sermon, reflects the difficulties she faced in asserting such authority. In addition to noting the need for male sanction, modern commentators have questioned the degree to which *The Sovereignty and Goodness of God* was edited or even shaped by the men whose texts accompanied hers. Unresolved questions regarding these men's involvement underscore problems of authenticity that plague women's autobiographical writings from the period.

The religious emphasis of Rowlandson's text is underscored by its earnest, formal tone and frequent inclusion of scripture. The author inserts passages from the Bible that apply to her own experience ("I may say as it is in Psalms 38. 5, 6. *My wounds stink and are corrupt, I am troubled, I am bowed down greatly, I go mourning all the day long*") or that bring strength during her captivity ("We opened the Bible, and lighted on Psal. 27, in which Psalm we especially took notice of that verse, *Wait on the Lord, be of good courage, and he shall strengthen thine heart, wait I say on the Lord*"). In her introduction to *The Sovereignty and Goodness of God* in *Women's Indian Captivity Narratives*, Kathryn Zabelle Derounian-Stodola notes stylistic aspects of the text that seem to have been borrowed from sermon conventions of the day. While such elements may be evidence of the influence of Rowlandson's husband and Mather, they also reflect the absolute centrality of religion to Puritan life. The structure that religion imposed on Rowlandson's captivity experience is reflected in the language that she uses to describe her captors. When detailing acts of violence, such as the raid, for example, she refers to the Native Americans in terms that underscore their separation from Christianity; they are "those merciless Heathen" or "hell-hounds."

CRITICAL DISCUSSION

The Sovereignty and Goodness of God was an immediate popular success. Published simultaneously in England and America, the book went through four editions in its first year. It remained popular in the decades that followed, as readers clamored for firsthand knowledge of Native Americans, their way of life, and their alleged barbarity. Rowlandson's perceived sexual vulnerability added to the appeal of the tale. The book's influence can be traced not only in the flourishing tradition of captivity narratives that followed hers in the marketplace but also in the prevalence of threatened women plots in popular fiction of the era.

After its initial success, the book slowly fell out of favor with readers and was largely forgotten by the end of the nineteenth century. During the twentieth century renewed scholarly attention was focused on the text, particularly by feminist and postcolonial critics, who saw its value as a statement about the role of

PRIMARY SOURCE

EXCERPT FROM *THE SOVEREIGNTY AND GOODNESS OF GOD*

On the tenth of February 1675, came the Indians with great numbers upon Lancaster: their first coming was about sunrising; hearing the noise of some guns, we looked out; several houses were burning, and the smoke ascending to heaven. There were five persons taken in one house; the father, and the mother and a sucking child, they knocked on the head; the other two they took and carried away alive. There were two others, who being out of their garrison upon some occasion were set upon; one was knocked on the head, the other escaped; another there was who running along was shot and wounded, and fell down; he begged of them his life, promising them money (as they told me) but they would not hearken to him but knocked him in head, and stripped him naked, and split open his bowels. Another, seeing many of the Indians about his barn, ventured and went out, but was quickly shot down. There were three others belonging to the same garrison who were killed; the Indians getting up upon the roof of the barn, had advantage to shoot down upon them over their fortification. Thus these murderous wretches went on, burning, and destroying before them.

At length they came and beset our own house, and quickly it was the dolefulest day that ever mine eyes saw. The house stood upon the edge of a hill; some of the Indians got behind the hill, others into the barn, and others behind anything that could shelter them; from all which places they shot against the house, so that the bullets seemed to fly like hail; and quickly they wounded one man among us, then another, and then a third. About two hours (according to my observation, in that amazing time) they had been about the house before they prevailed to fire it (which they did with flax and hemp, which they brought out of the barn, and there being no defense about the house, only two flankers at two opposite corners and one of them not finished); they fired it once and one ventured out and quenched it, but they quickly fired it again, and that took. Now is the dreadful hour come, that I have often heard of (in time of war, as it was the case of others), but now mine eyes see it. Some in our house were fighting for their lives, others wallowing in their blood, the house on fire over our heads, and the bloody heathen ready to knock us on the head, if we stirred out. Now might we hear mothers and children crying out for themselves, and one another, "Lord, what shall we do?" Then I took my children (and one of my sisters', hers) to go forth and leave the house: but as soon as we came to the door and appeared, the Indians shot so thick that the bullets rattled against the house, as if one had taken an handful of stones and threw them, so that we were fain to give back. We had six stout dogs belonging to our garrison, but none of them would stir, though another time, if any Indian had come to the door, they were ready to fly upon him and tear him down. The Lord hereby would make us the more acknowledge His hand, and to see that our help is always in Him. But out we must go, the fire increasing, and coming along behind us, roaring, and the Indians gaping before us with their guns, spears, and hatchets to devour us. No sooner were we out of the house, but my brother-in-law (being before wounded, in defending the house, in or near the throat) fell down dead, whereat the Indians scornfully shouted, and hallowed, and were presently upon him, stripping off his clothes, the bullets flying thick, one went through my side, and the same (as would seem) through the bowels and hand of my dear child in my arms. One of my elder sisters' children, named William, had then his leg broken, which the Indians perceiving, they knocked him on [his] head. Thus were we butchered by those merciless heathen, standing amazed, with the blood running down to our heels. My eldest sister being yet in the house, and seeing those woeful sights, the infidels hauling mothers one way, and children another, and some wallowing in their blood: and her elder son telling her that her son William was dead, and myself was wounded, she said, "And Lord, let me die with them," which was no sooner said, but she was struck with a bullet, and fell down dead over the threshold. I hope she is reaping the fruit of her good labors, being faithful to the service of God in her place.

SOURCE: Rowlandson, Mary. *Narrative of the Captivity and Restoration of Mrs. Mary Rowlandson.* Samuel Green, 1682.

---

women in colonial American society and the perception of racial and cultural differences that shaped it. *The Sovereignty and Goodness of God* has since been the subject of an extensive body of literary criticism that has examined its religious, gender, and racial politics.

Scholars have often focused on the issues of religious faith that are central to *The Sovereignty and Goodness of God*. Derounian-Stodola comments that Rowlandson "came to understand that affliction was a way to test, strain, and ultimately recharge her own personal spiritual complacency." Discussions of religion have also been tied to discussions of the text's complicated gender politics. Margaret H. Davis, in a 1992 article in *Early American Literature,* argues that Rowlandson's deference to her male captors originated in her Puritan beliefs, which required women to submit to male authority. She notes that Rowlandson is far less deferential to her female captors, "taking great pains to portray Indian women as cruel and capricious creatures." In a 2003 article in *Eighteenth-Century Studies,* Tiffany Potter further argues that the author is unable to consider the unique experiences of these women: "Rowlandson's work ultimately attempts to articulate indigenous femininity solely as a failure

THE TALE OF HANNAH DUSTAN

Like Mary Rowlandson, Hannah Dustan (1657–1736) gained fame as an Indian captive. Dustan was captured during a March 1697 raid on Haverhill, Massachusetts. The raid was carried out during King William's War, a conflict between the colonies of England and France, both allied with Native American tribes. Dustan's infant daughter was killed, and she and the infant's nurse were marched north with other captives. After weeks in captivity, Dustan led her fellow prisoners in a night-time revolt during which they killed and scalped their sleeping captors, including women and children. When they reached home, Dustan was given a sizable bounty. Today she is considered a folk hero by some, while others have protested the glorification of her violent acts.

Unlike Rowlandson, Dustan was wholly at the mercy of men to tell her story, which was shaped to their purposes. In *The Captive's Position* (2007), Teresa A. Toulouse notes that influential Puritan preacher Cotton Mather made use of Dustan's story "in three different venues at three different moments of political transition in Massachusetts." Mather first preached a sermon that included reference to Dustan's ordeal in 1697. The best known of Mather's treatments came in *Magnalia Christi Americana* (The Glorious Works of Christ in America). Published in 1702, it is credited with ensuring the enduring popularity of Dustan's tale.

---

to meet the English standard." Scholars continue to debate the degree to which Rowlandson's claiming of female authority is undercut by her conservative religious message and the framing, and perhaps shaping, of her text by powerful male figures.

BIBLIOGRAPHY

Sources

Davis, Margaret H. "Mary White Rowlandson's Self-Fashioning as Puritan Goodwife." *Early American Literature* 27.1 (1992): 49–60. Print.

Derounian-Stodola, Kathryn Zabelle. *Women's Indian Captivity Narratives*. New York: Penguin, 1998. Print.

Faery, Rebecca Blevins. "Mary Rowlandson." *Legacy* 12.2 (1995): 121–32. Print.

Potter, Tiffany. "Writing Indigenous Femininity: Mary Rowlandson's Narrative of Captivity." *Eighteenth-Century Studies* 36.2 (2003): 153–67. Print.

Rowlandson, Mary. *The Sovereignty and Goodness of God*. Ed. Neal Salisbury. Boston: Bedford, 1997. Print.

Toulouse, Teresa A. *The Captive's Position: Female Narrative, Male Identity, and Royal Authority in Colonial England*. Philadelphia: University of Pennsylvania Press, 2007. Print.

Further Reading

Andrews, William L., ed. *Journeys in New Worlds: Early American Women's Narratives*. Madison: University of Wisconsin Press, 1990. Print.

Armstrong, Nancy, and Leonard Tennenhouse. *The Imaginary Puritan: Literature, Intellectual Property, and the Origins of Personal Life*. Berkeley: University of California Press, 1992. Print.

Carroll, Lorrayne. "Captivity Literature." *The Oxford Handbook of Early American Literature*. Ed. Kevin J. Hayes. New York: Oxford University Press, 2008.

Lepore, Jill. *The Name of War: King Philip's War and the Origins of American Identity*. New York: Knopf, 1998. Print.

Mather, Increase. *A Brief History of the War with the Indians in New England*. London: Richard Chiswell, 1676. Print.

Namias, June. *White Captives: Gender and Ethnicity on the American Frontier*. Chapel Hill: University of North Carolina Press, 1993. Print.

Sayre, Gordon M., ed. *American Captivity Narratives*. New York: Houghton, 2000. Print.

Vaughan, Alden T., and Daniel K. Richter. "Crossing the Cultural Divide: Indians and New Englanders, 1605–1763." *Proceedings of the American Antiquarian Society* 90 (1980): 23–99. Print.

Greta Gard

Testament of Youth

Vera Brittain

OVERVIEW

Originally published in 1933, *Testament of Youth* is the first volume of British poet, novelist, and feminist Vera Brittain's autobiography. Running to six hundred pages, it covers the years from 1900 to 1925 and is one of the most celebrated accounts of World War I. It is also notable for having been written by a woman and for detailing women's experiences of the war, their contribution to the war effort, and the ways in which their lives were changed by the war. Based on diaries and letters from the period, the book is highly personal and emotive. For example, it conveys Brittain's intimate thoughts on falling in love with poet Roland Leighton and her deep grief after his death on the battlefield. Its intellectual range is much wider and more ambitious, however; it argues for a future in which youth is not wasted in wars and women have more opportunities to fulfill their potential.

When *Testament of Youth* was published, Brittain was already a poet, novelist, and noted public speaker at the League of Nations Union (a British arm of the post–World War I international League of Nations, which was established to further justice, security, and permanent peace). In the context of the fragile political situation in Europe in the early 1930s, the book served as a reminder of the way Brittain's generation had been exploited for the benefit of an older ruling elite and warned the current generation not to let this happen again. The entire first print run of three thousand copies sold in a matter of hours; the book made its author famous. A potent record of social change, in particular the struggle for women's rights, *Testament of Youth* remains Brittain's best-known work and is widely regarded as one of the most important memoirs of the early twentieth century.

HISTORICAL AND LITERARY CONTEXT

Testament of Youth is a frank and vivid description of World War I based on the author's experiences working as a Voluntary Aid Detachment (VAD) nurse in England, Malta, and France. The period covered by the book was the final stage in a slow transition from the Victorian to the modern era, a time of dramatic social and political change in Britain. Parliament was reformed; the 1916 Easter Rising in Ireland challenged British imperial power; women over the age of thirty were given the right to vote in 1918; and working-class political activism led to Ramsay MacDonald's election as the first Labour Party prime minister in 1924. When the war ended, much of the social deference that had figured so prominently in Victorian and Edwardian society was swept away. Many of Brittain's contemporaries, she writes, wanted nothing more than a life of hedonism and entertainment and no longer found relevance in the social and moral codes of the prewar world.

By the time the book was published, the flawed Treaty of Versailles, signed in 1919 with the aim of bringing lasting peace, was beginning to collapse, and German nationalism was once more a potent political force. Having tried to write her memoir several times in various forms since 1929, Brittain now pushed herself with (she states in her foreword) "a growing sense of urgency" in the face of Europe's mounting instability. The eventual book develops her thoughts about how the war had come to pass. As the pacifist views for which she later became famous took shape, she wrote as a reminder of the ordeals she and her contemporaries had been through, having been duped into sacrificing their lives to defend the interests of an ambivalent ruling class. Brittain had already established herself as a campaigner for women's rights, and the success of *Testament of Youth* on both sides of the Atlantic made her an important literary and public figure, giving her a platform to argue even more visibly for women's rights and world peace and against the rise of nationalism.

Testament of Youth was one of many British autobiographical and fictionalized accounts of the war published in the late 1920s and early 1930s. In England, where some towns and villages had actually lost an entire generation of men, "lost generation" literature flourished. Notable examples are Edmund Blunden's autobiography *Undertones of War* (1928), Siegfried Sassoon's novel *Memoirs of a Fox-Hunting Man* (1928), Robert Graves's autobiography *Goodbye to All That* (1929), and plays such as R. C. Sherriff's *Journey's End* and Irish writer Sean O'Casey's *The Silver Tassie*, both of which opened in London in 1929. Brittain's book was not the only one written by a woman about the war—Enid Bagnold's *A Diary without Dates* had described the life of a wartime nurse as early as 1917—but *Testament of Youth* is arguably the most accomplished, skillfully weaving personal struggles, trauma, and grief into a wider framework of social change.

❖ **Key Facts**

Time Period:
Mid-20th Century

Relevant Historical Events:
World War I; decline of Victorianism; growth of women's rights

Nationality:
English

Keywords:
women's rights; lost generation; war

Vera Brittain, author of *Testament of Youth*, photographed in 1934. © DAILY MAIL/REX/ALAMY

In addition to novels, poems, and many articles, Brittain published *Testament of Friendship* (1940), a biographical memoir of English writer and feminist Winifred Holtby, and *Testament of Experience* (1957), a further volume of autobiography. None had the impact of *Testament of Youth,* which was reissued by the feminist publishing house Virago in 1978—on the sixtieth anniversary of the end of World War I—and was successfully adapted for television as a BBC miniseries in 1979. In the 1980s it was also a recommended text on many high school literature syllabi in the United Kingdom.

THEMES AND STYLE
The main theme of *Testament of Youth* is the effect of World War I on the lives of the generation of young men and women who were directly involved in it. The narrative time span stretches from Brittain's middle-class childhood in Edwardian England to her marriage to the political scientist George Catlin in 1925. Much of the memoir focuses on her war work as nurse: she tells of time spent with dying men, dressing their wounds and dealing with rampant infection in unhygienic field hospitals. She describes tending to injured German prisoners at Étaples, knowing that only weeks earlier, they may have been trying to kill her only brother, Edward. Brittain also narrates the loss of four men who were close to her, including Edward and her fiancé, Leighton. It is from these tragic experiences that she draws her conclusion about the futility of fighting for "God, King, and Country," the "voracious trio" that had deprived her of "all that I valued most in life." She writes: "These shattered, dying boys and I were paying alike for a situation that none of us had desired or done anything to bring about."

Brittain's self-proclaimed aim was to remember the past in order to learn from it and, as she writes in her foreword, "mould the future." The juxtaposition of her personal experiences with major historical events illustrates a process of political awakening— the author's realization that the old narratives and ideologies with which her generation had grown up had become degenerate and corrupt. Everyday details, such as her prim and impractical nursing uniform, come to represent a fanciful and outdated Victorian worldview: "caps, collars, aprons, cuffs and waist-belts that accumulate germs and get lost." The story is as much about the way the war changed the world, and how it failed to do so, as it is about Brittain's own life. While the era brought new experiences and aspirations to her generation of women, the postwar world turned out to be one in which "survivors [were] not wanted."

Despite its radical politics and sometimes graphic subject matter, *Testament of Youth* is stylistically conventional. In a 2003 article in the London *Guardian,* Brittain's biographer Mark Bostridge notes that "despite the fact that she envisages herself as a modern woman, she remains at heart a Victorian." Following the author's trajectory chronologically from youthful hope and promise through grief, loss, and disillusionment to the steely, realistic adulthood of a damaged survivor, the book is punctuated with Latin quotations and poetic chapter headings. Despite resembling the constructions of an earlier civilization, its forward-looking sentiment is clearly and forcefully expressed: "The War was over; a new age was beginning; but the dead were dead and would never return." In her view of a world changed forever, Brittain anticipates the tenets of modernism.

CRITICAL DISCUSSION
Testament of Youth quickly became a best seller and a critical success. Although some commentators did not like Brittain's politics or her developing pacifism, and others complained that the book was excessively emotional, most found it compelling and dramatic. Reportedly, Virginia Woolf was unable to sleep until she had finished reading it. A reviewer in the *Times Literary Supplement* for August 31, 1933, wrote that "few people could have brought themselves to write such a chronicle. … Yet it was well worth doing—as a record of spiritual growth, as a memorial to sacrifices nobly made, and as a testimony to the horror and waste of war."

In the late 1930s, as another war in Europe became increasingly likely, Brittain's outspoken pacifism made her a popular speaker at peace rallies. None of her later writing received the continuing critical and popular attention accorded *Testament of Youth*. Besides studying its gender politics, its analysis of war, and its significance as cultural and historical commentary, scholars have also considered the book's importance as a form of autobiography in which personal experience is inescapably interwoven with large-scale historical events.

Testament of Youth has generally been read alongside the works of male war poets and writers as offering a "woman's perspective" on World War I. Brittain described it as an essentially gendered phenomenon in which the roles of men and women—and their capacity to fulfill them—were different and separate. In reference to *Testament of Youth* Richard Badenhausen suggests in "Mourning through Memoir" (2003) that since the 1980s the separation of women's experience of war from men's has seemed "necessarily limiting and potentially reductive." Brittain's autobiography has also been studied in the contexts of the histories of feminism and pacifism, class, trauma, and memory. In "Vera Brittain: Feminism, Pacifism, and the Problem of Class, 1900–1953" (1987), Yvonne Bennett concludes that the author had no real understanding of working-class concerns. Her ability to fight for such causes, for instance, came from her financial security and access to education. Andrea Peterson draws attention to Brittain's post-traumatic stress disorder in "Shell-Shocked in Somerville" (2004), and Ilya Parkins in "Feminist Witnessing and Social Difference" (2007) emphasizes the significance of Brittain's act of "voicing trauma" in the development of a "feminist theorization of remembrance."

BIBLIOGRAPHY

Sources

Badenhausen, Richard. "Mourning through Memoir: Trauma, Testimony, and Community in Vera Brittain's *Testament of Youth*." *Twentieth Century Literature* 49.4 (2003): 421. *Literature Resource Center*. Web. 5 Nov. 2012.

Bennett, Yvonne A. "Vera Brittain: Feminism, Pacifism, and the Problem of Class, 1900–1953." *Atlantis* 12.2 (1987): 18–23. *MLA International Bibliography*. Web. 5 Nov. 2012.

Bostridge, Mark. "The Making of a Peacenik." *Guardian* 30 Aug. 2003. Web. 5 Nov. 2012.

Brittain, Vera. *Testament of Youth*. London: Weidenfeld and Nicolson, 2009. Print.

Parkins, Ilya. "Feminist Witnessing and Social Difference: The Trauma of Heterosexual Otherness in Vera Brittain's *Testament of Youth*." *Women's Studies* 26.2 (2007): 95–116. Web. 5 Nov. 2012.

Peterson, Andrea. "Shell-Shocked in Somerville: Vera Brittain's Post-Traumatic Stress Disorder." *Gender and Warfare in the Twentieth Century: Textual*

Representations. Ed. Angela K. Smith. Manchester: Manchester University Press, 2004. 33–52. *MLA International Bibliography*. Web. 5 Nov. 2012.

Williams, Iolo. Rev. of *Testament of Youth*, by Vera Brittain. *Times Literary Supplement* 31 Aug. 1933: 571. *TLS Historical Archive*. Web. 6 Dec. 2012.

Further Reading

Albrinck, Meg. "Borderline Women: Gender Confusion in Vera Brittain's and Evadne Price's War Narratives." *Narrative* 6.3 (1998): 271–91. Print.

Berry, Paul, and Mark Bostridge. *Vera Brittain: A Life*. London: Virago, 2001. Print.

Bishop, Alan, and Mark Bostridge, eds. *Letters from a Lost Generation: The First World War Letters of Vera Brittain and Four Friends, Roland Leighton, Edward Brittain, Victor Richardson, Geoffrey Thurlow*. Boston: Northeastern University Press, 1999. Print.

Gorham, Deborah. *Vera Brittain: A Feminist Life*. Toronto: University of Toronto Press, 2000. Print.

Petersen, Andrea. "A Process of Redefinition: Vera Brittain's Autobiographical *Testaments*." *Inquiry: Critical Thinking across the Disciplines* 18.3 (1999): 63–80. Print.

Schwarz, Liane. "Vera Brittain's *Testament of Youth*: In Consideration of the Unentrenched Voice." *a/b: Auto/Biography Studies* 16.2 (2001): 237–55. *MLA International Bibliography*. Web. 5 Nov. 2012.

TESTAMENT OF FRIENDSHIP: VERA BRITTAIN AND WINIFRED HOLTBY

Testament of Friendship (1940), Vera Brittain's follow-up to *Testament of Youth*, traces the life of her close friend, journalist, and novelist Winifred Holtby. The two women met at Somerville College, Oxford, where both were students following World War I. After taking an initial dislike to each other, ostensibly because Holtby believed Brittain was a snob, the women formed a lifelong friendship. After graduation, Brittain and Holtby moved to London together to pursue their shared dream of authorship. The pair lived at 52 Doughty Street, where they launched their writing careers and were active in the women's rights movement. They became so close that Holtby lived for a time with Brittain, her husband, and their children. Brittain was Holtby's devoted companion as she battle the kidney disease that claimed her life in 1935. Following Holtby's death, Brittain edited her friend's final novel, *South Riding*, for publication in 1936. An expurgated edition of the two women's letters was published by Brittain in 1960.

Testament of Friendship chronicles Holtby's early life as well as the blossoming of her friendship with Brittain, the development of the women's individual writing careers, and their influences on each other's work. A new edition of the book was published by Virago in 2012.

Chris Routledge

WARS I HAVE SEEN

Gertrude Stein

Key Facts

Time Period:
Mid-20th Century

Relevant Historical Events:
German occupation of France; World War II; World War I; Spanish-American War

Nationality:
American

Keywords:
modernism; women's writing; occupation

OVERVIEW

First published in 1945, Gertrude Stein's *Wars I Have Seen* is a memoir of the author's experience as a civilian witness to war. Stein began composing the text in 1943, in the midst of World War II, as a means of documenting her experience in rural France during the German occupation. Though the book begins with Stein's birth, offers a brief account of her childhood, and covers her memories of the Spanish-American War and World War I, the narrative disproportionately focuses on her day-to-day life between 1943 and 1945. The memoir records Stein's attitudinal shift from resignation to bitterness and finally to relief when U.S. soldiers arrive to liberate France and announce the war's impending end. Because of its original form as a journal, *Wars I Have Seen* offers an unguarded and personal account that excludes much of the self-consciousness of Stein's other autobiographical writings.

When Stein's memoir was published, she was a prominent writer nearing the end of a long and distinguished career. Though she was known for her innovative and challenging prose style, *Wars I Have Seen* was plainer and more accessible than much of her previous work. It was also highly topical and offered a rare glimpse into the mundane reality of the recently ended World War II. As a result, it was a huge popular success and quickly became a best seller that received highly favorable reviews. In the twenty-first century, however, *Wars I Have Seen* is considered one of Stein's minor works and is valued primarily for its biographical information about one of modernism's most important writers.

HISTORICAL AND LITERARY CONTEXT

Wars I Have Seen responds to the conditions of French life during World War II, when the country was occupied by Germany. Though an American, Stein had lived in France since the turn of the twentieth century and considered herself at home there. In the prelude to the outbreak of war in the late 1930s, she was skeptical that Nazi Party leader Adolf Hitler would command his troops to attack France. When, in June 1940, the German army took Paris, Stein was living in the Rhône valley, in rural France, where she remained with her partner, Alice B. Toklas, for the rest of the war. At the time, Stein was at work on a novel, *Ida*, but found it difficult to continue amid the omnipresent threat of violence. Though she was granted passage to neutral Spain, she refused to go, preferring to remain in the village of Bilignin despite the presence of Nazi soldiers and the fact that she was a Jew.

By the time *Wars I Have Seen* was published in 1945, France had been liberated and the war had ended. Stein had begun the book as a daily journal two years before, in 1943, when she and Toklas moved from Bilignin to Culoz, a nearby village. The journal covers a period of fifteen months, during which time the German hold on France slowly loosened as the Allied forces gained military advantage and eventually ousted the Germans in 1944. In her journal Stein documents the arrival of U.S. soldiers at Culoz and the resulting celebrations that their appearance engenders. When the journal was assembled for publication as a memoir, the breaks between days were removed and the text appeared as one continuous document. Upon its publication in the immediate aftermath of the war, *Wars I Have Seen* offered a uniquely personal account of the day-to-day civilian experience of the conflict.

Stein's memoir was part of a fruitful, late-career exploration of autobiographical writing. As a prominent figure in the Paris avant-garde and a friend of many of modernism's most important figures, most notably cubist painter Pablo Picasso, Stein was often encouraged to write a memoir. She refused for many years, arguing that the form was an insufficient vehicle for her ambitious literary aims. In 1932, however, she relented and began *The Autobiography of Alice B. Toklas*. Though written from Toklas's perspective, the book almost exclusively narrates the events of Stein's life. From this first radical rethinking of "rules" of autobiography, Stein continued to expand the limitations of the form in works such as *Everybody's Autobiography* (1937), *Paris France* (1940), and finally *Wars I Have Seen*.

Wars I Have Seen became a great popular success and helped Stein reach a much broader audience. Unlike much of her previous work, which explored the deep interiority of human consciousness, this memoir looked outward to the world in a new way and offered a kind of journalistic account that was full of both human interest and information about the civilian war experience. As Stein biographer John Malcolm Brinnin writes in his 1959 book *The Third Rose*, "At a time when the fabulous adventures of war correspondents around the world were being turned out in one sensational book after another, her intimate, modest record of the realities of life under the occupation was fresh and welcome relief."

THEMES AND STYLE

The central theme of Stein's memoir is that, for civilian bystanders, the reality of life during war is essentially the same as life during peacetime: people remain primarily concerned with the mundane struggle to survive and find comfort. Throughout the text, Stein records the day-to-day events of Culoz, the tiny village where she lives with her partner, Toklas. Stein goes for walks, meets neighbors, laments the French bureaucracy, keeps up with radio reports of the war, and tells secondhand anecdotes about the French Resistance. For much of the memoir, Stein expresses her empathy with the German people, emphasizing the theme of the universality of experience. She even refuses to condemn Nazi anti-Semitism, despite her own Jewishness, which she never acknowledges. As it becomes increasingly clear that Allied victory is inevitable, however, Stein's impartiality fades and she enthusiastically anticipates the end of occupation and the arrival of U.S. troops.

Although Stein's reason for writing her memoir was ostensibly to document her life during wartime, the text also reveals a desire to make sense of her predicament as a Jew in a nation occupied by the Nazis. She began writing the journal that would become *Wars I Have Seen* in 1943, when she and Toklas moved from one rural French village to another. Stein decided to remain in France despite threats that she might be interned in a concentration camp. Though she and Toklas were advised to move to the safety of Switzerland, they refused. Stein's account of her life in Culoz indicates a desire to make sense of the struggle to continue living despite the threat of persecution and the reality of occupation. While the implications of her own Jewishness are not explicitly explored, she does attempt to understand the anti-Semitism that threatens her:

> There are such funny things, how can a nation that feels itself as strong as the Germans do be afraid of a small handful of people like the Jews, why it does seem funny, most strange and very funny, they must be afraid because … hate is fear, and why, what can they do to them, after all what can they do to them.

Stylistically, *Wars I Have Seen* is notable for its fragmented and repetitive openness. Though more conventional and linear than much of her other work, its prose style allows Stein to record the constant flux of consciousness and to capture the ways in which normal life proceeds despite the looming threat of war. In one notable passage, she writes:

> They have just been telling us over and over again that they are going to bombard all the railway stations and we are quite near a fairly important one, are we to be frightened or not we have not quite made up our minds, this afternoon there was an alert but nobody paid any particular attention but that was easy enough because nothing happened but anyway conversations went on.

CRITICAL DISCUSSION

Upon publication, *Wars I Have Seen* was an immediate popular and critical success, selling well and eliciting many admiring reviews. Ben Ray Redman wrote in the *Saturday Review of Literature* that "it is a good book, a very good book, and it would be a great pity if any readers were put off it by Gertrude Stein's reputation for willful obscurity." Though Redman's praise was typical and the book became a best seller, it was also subject to criticism. In *The Critical Response to Gertrude Stein* (2000), Kirk Curnutt notes that Djuna Barnes, in a review for the *Contemporary Jewish Record*, called the book sentimental and immodest.

After the end of World War II, Stein returned to Paris with Toklas and became a popular figure among U.S. soldiers stationed there as well as a celebrity among the French people. In *The Third Rose*, Brinnin writes that "as she went about on errands or walked her dog, always she was followed by an entourage that was apt to increase in number as it progressed." Among the U.S. soldiers, she became a kind of ambassador to French culture. Among the French, she was seen as a symbol of American kindness and openness. She gave public lectures, spoke at army functions, and even toured bases in occupied Germany. Her experience among the U.S. soldiers inspired her final novel, *Brewsie and Willie*.

Scholars continue to study *Wars I Have Seen* and to consider its literary value, its status as history, and its construction as autobiography. Many commentators have examined Stein's innovative approach to the generic expectations of autobiographical and historical writing. In "Gertrude Stein's War Autobiographies: Reception, History, and Dialogue" (2008), for example, Zofia Lesinska writes:

> The beginning of *Wars I Have Seen* communicates that in Stein's autobiographies, the projected image of the narrator is an intricate discursive compilation representing a plurality of voices which enter the authorial discourse…. Thus Stein's autobiographies cannot be read simply as the exposition of her own ideological position; what is far more interesting about her text is the representation of ideologies circulating France between 1939 and 1944.

Critics have also considered the book's exploration of identity within the larger context of modernism. Scholar Michael J. Hoffman, in *Gertrude Stein* (1976), argues that the book represents Stein's attempt "to sum up and explain her own struggle for identity and, by corollary, the struggle of all modern individuals for the same thing, individuals for whom she had always felt herself representative." Likewise, Stein's

THE AUTOBIOGRAPHY OF ALICE B. TOKLAS

Composed over the course of only six weeks in 1932 and published a year later, Gertrude Stein's book *The Autobiography of Alice B. Toklas* undermines many of the conventional expectations of autobiographical writing. From its title, the work appears to be a contradiction: an autobiography of someone who is not the text's author. In fact, however, it is even more complicated than that: it is a frequently inaccurate nonfiction account of Stein's life as narrated by Toklas, albeit written by Stein.

By assuming the voice of another to tell her own story, Stein employed the fundamental characteristic of autobiographical writing (the author as subject) to question the assumption that memoirs are necessarily honest, personal, and authentic. Her inversion of autobiographical form also led to a significant change in the style of her prose. Though her previous works were defined by a cubist form of composition that explored the extremes of syntactic fragmentation and repetition, *The Autobiography of Alice B. Toklas* was written in the plainer voice of Toklas, Stein's longtime partner. The book begins simply—"I was born in San Francisco, California"—and proceeds to offer firsthand accounts of the birth of modernism in Paris in the early twentieth century. Though criticized for its egocentrism and factual inaccuracies, the book was a best seller and is considered a groundbreaking work in the history of autobiographical writing.

alleged collaboration with the Nazi regime has played into the topic of identity and has been a frequent subject of discussion among scholars.

BIBLIOGRAPHY

Sources

Brinnin, John Malcolm. *The Third Rose: Gertrude Stein and Her World.* Boston: Little, Brown, 1959. Print.

Curnutt, Kirk. *The Critical Response to Gertrude Stein.* Westport, Conn.: Greenwood, 2000. Print.

Hoffman, Michael J. *Gertrude Stein.* Boston: Twayne, 1976. Print.

Lesinska, Zofia. "Gertrude Stein's War Autobiographies: Reception, History, and Dialogue." *Lit: Literature Interpretation Theory* 9:4 (2008): 313–42. Print.

Redman, Ben R. "The Importance of Being Earnest." Rev. of *Wars I Have Seen,* by Gertrude Stein. *Saturday Review of Literature* 10 Mar. 1945: 8. *Google Books.* Web. 28 Nov. 2012.

Stein, Gertrude. *Wars I Have Seen.* New York: Random House, 1945. Print.

Further Reading

Daniel, Lucy. *Gertrude Stein: Critical Lives.* London: Reaktion, 2009. Print.

Knapp, Bettina L. *Gertrude Stein.* New York: Continuum, 1990. Print.

Meyer, Steven. "Gertrude Stein." *Modernism and the New Criticism.* Ed. A. Walton Litz, Louis Menand, and Lawrence Rainey. Cambridge: Cambridge University Press, 2000. *Cambridge Histories Online.* Web. 25 Oct. 2012.

Neuman, Shirley, and Ira B. Nadel, eds. *Gertrude Stein and the Making of Literature.* Boston: Northeastern University Press, 1988. Print.

Mitrano, G. F. *Gertrude Stein: Woman without Qualities.* Burlington, U.K.: Ashgate, 2005. Print.

Rev. of *Wars I Have Seen,* by Gertrude Stein. *Washington Post* 18 Mar. 1945: S4. *ProQuest.* Web. 25 Oct. 2012.

Wagers, Kelly. "Gertrude Stein's 'Historical' Living." *Journal of Modern Literature* 31.3 (2008). *Project MUSE.* Web. 25 Oct. 2012.

Watson, Dana Cairns. *Gertrude Stein and the Essence of What Happens.* Nashville: Vanderbilt University Press, 2005. Print.

Will, Barbara. *Gertrude Stein, Modernism, and the Problem of "Genius."* Edinburgh: Edinburgh University Press, 2000. Print.

Theodore McDermott

WHEN HEAVEN AND EARTH CHANGED PLACES
A Vietnamese Woman's Journey from War to Peace

Le Ly Hayslip, Jay Wurts

OVERVIEW

Written by Le Ly Hayslip with Jay Wurts and published in 1989, *When Heaven and Earth Changed Places: A Vietnamese Woman's Journey from War to Peace* tells the story of a woman who survives war, escapes to build a new life in the United States, and finally returns to Vietnam to reunite with her family. Moving between the past and the present, the author revisits a childhood disrupted by the conflicting loyalties of colonial and civil wars and the compromises she must make to survive. However, that childhood is also grounded in the deep spiritual beliefs of her father and folklore that values patient endurance. Viewing her life story as process of healing, Hayslip is not defeated by her experiences but emerges with a message of compassion and understanding.

When Heaven and Earth Changed Places appeared fourteen years after the war in Vietnam ended, and many U.S. citizens were still grappling with the effects of the long and divisive conflict. Hayslip's narrative was not only one of the earliest accounts of the war from a Vietnamese point of view, but it was also a rare account of the experiences of a peasant woman. Her book gave American readers a new perspective on the war, and her empathetic tone made her story accessible even to those still defensive about U.S. involvement in Vietnam.

HISTORICAL AND LITERARY CONTEXT

Vietnam has been occupied through much of its history, first by neighboring Chinese and Mongols and later by the French, who took control in 1867. The Vietnamese people suffered under foreign rule—especially under the Japanese after World War II—until a resistance movement culminated in the defeat of the French in 1954. The country was partitioned, with the Chinese- and Soviet-supported Democratic Republic of Vietnam in the north and the Republic of South Vietnam backed by the United States and its Western allies. War soon broke out between conflicting factions in the two regions. By the late 1960s, hundreds of thousands of U.S. troops were enmeshed in a ground, air, and sea war in Vietnam that lasted until 1975.

Hayslip's memoir begins at two distinct historical moments: with her birth in 1949, in the midst of the war with the French, and in 1986, as she prepares to return to Vietnam to visit her remaining family. The French conflict introduces Hayslip to the terror of war; the Vietnamese civil war that follows teaches her about the moral ambiguities of combat; and the U.S. war sweeps her up in a struggle for survival that ends with her immigration to the United States. Hayslip's emigration is made possible by the U.S. soldier Ed Monroe, who marries her. Years later, after her children are grown, she decides to return to Vietnam in hopes of finding her mother, brother, and any other surviving family members. By the mid-1980s relations between the United States and Vietnam are still tense, though much of the shock and anguish has abated.

A rich body of literature arose examining the deep societal and personal consequences of the Vietnam conflict. Some of these, such as Ron Kovic's 1974 memoir *Born on the Fourth of July* and Tim O'Brien's 1978 novel *Going after Cacciato,* are soldiers' stories, while others, such as Bobbie Ann Mason's *In Country* (1985), explore the war's impact on U.S. civilians. In 1988 Duong Thu Huong's *Paradise of the Blind,* a critical look at the North Vietnamese victory, became the first Vietnamese book to be published in the United States. The next year Joanna C. Scott joined Hayslip in showing the Southeast Asian side of the conflict with her *Indochinese Refugees: Oral Histories from Laos, Cambodia, and Vietnam.* Another memoir, *Fallen Leaves,* published by Nguyen Thi Thu Lam in 1989, offers the perspective of the daughter of an upper-class family during the French and U.S. wars.

Hayslip's book was a landmark in several ways. One of the earliest English expressions of the Vietnamese perspective on the war, it was also a woman's story and uniquely resonant with feminists and other progressives. In 1993 Hayslip continued her story in a second memoir. Reprising some of the material in her first book, *Child of War, Woman of Peace* continues the story of Hayslip's life as a U.S. immigrant. That same year Vietnam veteran and Oscar-winning director Oliver Stone combined both books into the film *Heaven and Earth.*

THEMES AND STYLE

Hayslip's memoir explores war as a destructive force in the lives of ordinary people. "The war no longer

❖ *Key Facts*

Time Period:
Late 20th Century

Relevant Historical Events:
Vietnam War; increasing normalization of U.S.-Vietnamese relations

Nationality:
American/Vietnamese

Keywords:
exile; war; anticolonialism

Le Ly Hayslip, left, with director Oliver Stone, center, in 2007. Stone adapted Hayslip's autobiography, *When Heaven and Earth Changed Places*, into a film titled *Heaven and Earth* in 1993. At right is the director of the My Lai vestige site, Pham Thanh Cong. © AP IMAGES/DANG NGOC KHOA

seemed like a fight to see which side would prevail. Instead it had become a fight to see just how much and how far the Vietnam of my ancestors would be transformed," she writes. She honors the determination of ordinary people to survive: "Our job now, as it had always been, was to clean up and rebuild our lives with whatever the war had left us." In the face of war's devastation, ideological causes become unimportant, she explains: "Death and suffering, not people, become the enemy and anything that lives is your ally." Hayslip's own struggle to overcome the painful recollection of all she has experienced forms another important theme of her memoir. "Memories come quickly, stack up, and begin to weigh me down," she writes. Yet she remembers her father's words—"look those deepest, darkest, most terrible fears in the face and learn the lessons they've come to teach."

Hayslip's purpose is to promote compassion and understanding among those who were once on opposite sides of a war. She directs her message to Americans who fought on her nation's soil: "Anger can teach forgiveness, hate can teach us love, and war can teach us peace." The technique of switching from past to present gives the narrative immediacy and complexity. The reader knows from the beginning that the child Phung Thi Le Ly will survive to become the author Le Ly Hayslip, but that survival will be an intricate process. Hayslip's return to Vietnam finally reconciles both timelines; "by coming back to her place of landing, she completed the first circle of her life."

The dual timeline of *When Heaven and Earth Changed Places* is reflected in Hayslip's writing style. The 1986 sections are written in the form of a journal and have the ironic tone of experience. "'The Socialist Republic of Vietnam welcomes you,' [the greeter] says in voice that almost sounds as if it's true." Hayslip's early war-time recollections are written in the immediate voice of a child and are peppered with startling images ("a passing cloud of shrapnel"), unfamiliar sayings ("perfection is a slippery pig"), and incongruent imagery ("I folded up like a butterfly and pulled up my pants" she writes after her single experience of prostitution). She balances the despair of her youth with many references to Vietnamese folklore that prizes resilience and her Buddhist father, who told her that "your job is to stay alive … to live in peace and tend the shrine of our ancestors … and you will be worth more than any soldier who ever took up a sword."

CRITICAL DISCUSSION

Readers appreciated Hayslip's message of peace and tolerance. Judy Helfand wrote in the feminist journal *Off Our Backs* that "Le Ly offers an understanding of what it means to be a Vietnamese person who lived in the village we see being blown to pieces." David Shipler, reviewing the book for the *New York Times,* noted that Americans "have not cared to hear Vietnamese voices or look at ourselves through Vietnamese eyes." Lynne Bundesen of the *Los Angeles Times* complained of Hayslip's lack of specific historical detail but admitted that "as autobiography, this book is beyond criticism" and asserted that it "should be required reading in military colleges and in high schools and universities looking for broader, more personal interpretations of geo-politics." Among the Vietnamese American community, many of whom had opposed the North Vietnamese communists, some readers were angered by Hayslip's early support of the Viet Cong and viewed her book as opportunistic.

Decades after its publication, Hayslip's memoir is still viewed as a valuable portrayal of the effects of war on civilian populations, and especially on women. Her voice continues to be considered authoritative on both the consequences of war and the reconciliation of the self to traumatic experience. Still widely read in classrooms and book groups, *When Heaven and Earth Changed Places* has undergone several reprints and has been translated into seventeen languages.

When Heaven and Earth Changed Places has continued to be examined by scholars of the politics of war and colonization. In a 1997 piece in *Positions Asia Critique,* Viet Thanh Nguyen argues that Hayslip had changed the dialog about Vietnam by speaking out, thus altering the dialog wherein "Vietnamese bodies have been the silent spectacle on which American historical writing has been staged."

Hayslip's memoir, Nguyen states, has made her "representative of those anonymous millions of Vietnamese in whose name the war was fought by both sides." In her essay in *Haunting Violations, Feminist Criticism and the Crisis of the "Real"* (2001), Leslie Bow examines the memoir in terms of Hayslip's status as the "other" in the view of American readers: "Hayslip's story is a commodity in the glutted American media market on the war only to the extent that her race, gender, national, and class alterity would indicate that her account does not simply replay that of the journalist or soldier." Marion Gibson's 2004 essay "The War at Home: Family, Gender and Post-Colonial Issues in Three Vietnam War Texts," analyzes Hayslip's perspective as a woman whose "home and battlefield are identical, and identically an important test of family life."

BIBLIOGRAPHY

Sources

Bow, Leslie. "Third World Testimony in the Era of Globalization: Vietnam, Sexual Trauma, and Le Ly Hayslip's Art of Neutrality." *Haunting Violations, Feminist Criticism and the Crisis of the "Real."* Ed. Wendy Hesford and Wendy Kozol. Urbana: University of Illinois Press, 2001. 169–94. Print.

Bundesen, Lynne. "Vietnam: One Woman's Story." Rev. of *When Heaven and Earth Changed Places*, by Le Ly Hayslip with Jay Wurts. *Los Angeles Times* 25 June 1989: 4. *ProQuest.* Web. 28 Nov. 2012.

Gibson, Marion. "The War at Home: Family, Gender and Post-Colonial Issues in Three Vietnam War Texts." *Gender and Warfare in the Twentieth Century: Textual Representations.* Ed. Angela K. Smith. Manchester: Manchester UP; 2004. 154–73. Print.

Hayslip, Le Ly, with Jay Wurts. *When Heaven and Earth Changed Places.* New York: Doubleday, 1989. Print.

Helfand, Judy. "Woman in a War Zone." Rev. of *When Heaven and Earth Changed Places,* by Le Ly Hayslip with Jay Wurts. *Off Our Backs* 21.3 (1991): 22. *JSTOR.* Web. 28 Nov. 2012.

Nguyen, Viet Thanh. "Representing Reconciliation: Le Ly Hayslip and the Victimized Body." *Positions Asia Critique* 5.2 (1997): 605–42. Print.

Shipler, David K. "A Child's Tour of Duty." *New York Times Book Review* 25 June 1989. *General Reference Center GOLD.* Web. 16 Nov. 2012.

ANH DO: *THE HAPPIEST REFUGEE*

One of the most far-reaching results of the war in Vietnam was the flood of more than two million refugees who fled the country in its aftermath. Many, like Le Ly Hayslip, sought new lives in the United States, while others went to Britain, France, and Canada. Thousands of others, such as the family of Australian comedian Anh Do, fled in boats across the China Sea to Australia. In 2010 Do published a memoir of his family's experience titled *The Happiest Refugee: My Journey from Tragedy to Comedy.* Writing from his perspective as a popular Australian entertainer, Do traces his history from his parents' meeting during the uneasy days just after the war's end. When Do was only two his family and dozens of other refugees spent five days braving high seas, pirates, and the unknown in hopes of building a new life in Australia.

As is often the case for immigrants, the new life was not an easy one, and Do documents his mother's struggle to support the family and learn the customs of a new culture. Like Hayslip, Do maintains a positive tone of hope and gratitude as he depicts the often harsh immigrant experience. Also like Hayslip, Do's personal story ends, atypically, in celebrity, as he not only manages to survive the hardships of economic privation and culture shock but turns these experiences into the basis of a vibrant career as a comedian.

Further Reading

Christopher, Renny. "Le Ly Hayslip." *Asian American Writers. Dictionary of Literary Biography.* Vol. 312. Ed. Deborah L. Madsen. Detroit: Gale, 2005. *Literature Resource Center.* Web. 16 Nov. 2012.

Hallett, Brien. Rev. of *When Heaven and Earth Changed Places: A Vietnamese Woman's Journey from War to Peace,* by Le Ly Hayslip with Jay Wurts. *Manoa* 2.2 (1990): 194–95. Print.

Hayslip, Le Ly, with James Hayslip. *Child of War, Woman of Peace.* New York: Doubleday. 1993. Print.

Stephens, Rebecca L. "Distorted Reflections: Oliver Stone's *Heaven and Earth* and Le Ly Hayslip's *When Heaven and Earth Changed Places.*" *Centennial Review* 41.3 (1997). 661–69. Print.

Tina Gianoulis

A Woman Soldier's Own Story
Xie Bingying

Key Facts

Time Period:
Mid-20th Century

Relevant Historical Events:
End of the Manchu dynasty; the Long March; the emergence of Mao Zedong

Nationality:
Chinese

Keywords:
communism; women's writing; revolution

OVERVIEW

A Woman Soldier's Own Story, published in Chinese in 1936 with a second volume appearing ten years later, is the autobiography of feminist, teacher, essayist, novelist, and soldier Xie Bingying. Born in Hunan Province in 1906 just before the fall of the Qing dynasty, Xie was determined from an early age to have a better life than what had been laid out for her as an infant: she was to marry a son from a village family after having her feet bound (a brutal ancient practice meant to make women more attractive by keeping their feet very small). She eventually freed herself from her marital obligations, became a soldier, traveled, earned a living as a writer and teacher, became a mother, and held her own dying mother in her arms. Her daughter Lily Chia Brissman's translation (written with Barry Brissman and published in 2001) is the first English version to include Xie's second volume. In her preface, Xie writes: "My daughter Lily has worked closely with me to preserve the spirit and sense of my book as she has translated it into English."

Xie's literary aspirations were intermittently quashed by war. Her experience as a soldier in Chiang Kai-shek's Northern Expedition—a campaign against rogue warlords, with the aim of unifying China—was followed by multiple skirmishes with the anticommunist regime as a civilian. Xie subsequently worked with the women's division of the Chinese army in the war that followed the Japanese invasion of Manchuria in 1931. Today, *A Woman Soldier's Own Story* is considered to be a classic of Chinese literature.

HISTORICAL AND LITERARY CONTEXT

A Woman Soldier's Own Story is an indictment of a Chinese system that maintained a strict hierarchy of social classes. Women were expected to accept arranged marriages. Foot binding, the painful ritual to which Xie's mother attempted to submit her, was so common in rural society that those who had not had it done might have been asked, as Xie writes, "Is your mother dead?" Politically, China suffered disappointment when the 1919 Treaty of Versailles failed to return German-controlled "concessions"—commercial entities on Chinese soil—to China, and handed them to Japan. Outraged citizens protested, beginning with three thousand students in Peking (later called Beijing) on May 4, 1919, giving rise to the May Fourth Movement for political independence and social reform.

Sun Yat-sen, leader of China's Nationalist Party, called China a "hypo-colony," meaning it was under the influence of multiple foreign governments. He had been working with China's communists to unify the country, but after his death in 1925, Chiang, who eventually turned against communism, took over. In 1934, as Xie hid in the countryside after having been imprisoned on suspicion of leftist sympathies, 100,000 Chinese communists, including future leader Mao Zedong, fled their strongholds and embarked on the Long March, which lasted until 1936. While Xie's autobiography has been criticized for glossing over such events, it is still held dear by Chinese scholars and readers for its insider's view of a politically agitated period.

A Woman Soldier's Own Story is informed by China's long literary tradition, such as *The Peacocks Fly to the Southeast* from Han dynasty (206 BCE–220 CE), which is about a young woman who is forced by her family to divorce a man she loves and is pressed by her brother to remarry, finally choosing suicide as her only escape. Meanwhile, *Water Margins* (authorship uncertain), from approximately the sixteenth century, tells of the popular hero Song Jiang and his group of well-meaning bandits, who have been compared to Robin Hood and his merry men. Xie mentioned this book as a favorite, and *A Woman Soldier's Own Story* shows the influences of both tragic romance and forest adventure.

Xie's writings, including her autobiography, helped to propel a broader movement to liberate women in China. In 1936 feminist advocate and writer Bai Wei—whom Xie praised—came out with an autobiographical novel, *Tragic Life,* in which the protagonist's diseased body becomes an allegory for China itself. In 1940 Chinese publishing impresario Lin Yutang had his daughters translate Xie's writings for the U.S. market; the resulting *Girl Rebel* met with great success. In 1947 American readers welcomed *Autobiography of a Chinese Woman* by the physician Buwei Yang Chao. Also notable is the 1991 memoir *Ninety-Four Years of a Floating Life* by eminent and peripatetic scholar Su Xuelin.

THEMES AND STYLE

Xie's autobiography is infused with love of country and family, mixed with the powerful but often conflicting need to assert her individuality. Many of the author's

Terra-cotta soldier statues of women and children at a Beijing art gallery. The statues, by artist Marian Heyerdahl, are modeled after the famous terra-cotta soldiers in Xi'an, China, which date from the third century BCE. Writer Xie Bingying recounts her experiences in the Chinese military and other aspects of her life in *A Woman Soldier's Own Story*.
© AP IMAGES/ELIZABETH DALZIEL

experiences reflect her desire to see social change wash away the "shackles on my feet." For example, she runs away with a friend whose family is also trying to force her into an arranged marriage, but is caught by her mother and made to come home. As a soldier who is eager to succeed, Xie internalizes the concepts of militarism and does not critique them even when they contravene her literary pursuits. Later, unjustly imprisoned by the same regime for which she had fought, she is irked when one of her friends threatens to weep: "I disapproved of this. In military school we had all shouted the slogan 'Revolutionaries do not shed tears, only blood!' So why was he crying about this misfortune?"

As with her other works, Xie wrote her autobiography in order to survive—not just in terms of earning a living but also to maintain a semblance of order in her life. From an early age, she seizes on reading and writing as a means of liberation, of creating a space that is utterly hers. As her life becomes increasingly peripatetic and unstable, writing is a source of joy and sustenance. She falls in love with Qi, the father of her first child, because of his writing: "Qi wrote beautiful poems…. He wrote his letters in very small characters—almost like sesame seeds—and never scribbled…. I was intoxicated by his lovely poetry." Her pace of work is dizzying: "In Shanghai it took me less than three weeks to finish writing two books, *Young Wang Guocai* and *Letters to Youth*."

A Woman Soldier's Own Story reads as though its narrator is breathless, eager to get the story out before rushing off to the next major event of historic or life-altering proportions. She does admit to admiring Johann Wolfgang von Goethe's sentimental autobiographical novel *The Sorrows of Young Werther* (1787), and as Steven Levine notes in a 2001 article for *Library Journal*, "Xie was an idealist and a romantic given to florid writing that matches the impressive melodrama of her life." Indeed, even suicide is somewhat idealized: "Suicide is probably the best solution: a single moment of pain, then a lifetime of anguish is relieved," Xie writes while trapped in her parents' home trying to figure out how to avoid her unwanted arranged marriage. It is not the only time, nor is she the only character, to speak of suicide.

CRITICAL DISCUSSION

In the preface to the Brissmans' translation, Xie describes the initial reactions to her book: "Many newspapers in Shanghai and Nanjing [where Chiang Kai-shek had set up his government] gave the book favorable reviews when it appeared, calling it a sincere and truthful description of a young girl's struggle to educate herself and to rebel against suffocating feudal traditions." Scholar Weili Ye, writing in the *China Journal* in 2003, concurs that it "helped empower numerous younger Chinese women in their own struggles to achieve emancipation. In this respect, Xie Bingying's autobiography is a classic."

After the 1936 publication of the first volume of her autobiography, Xie continued to work alongside the Chinese military in the Sino-Japanese War. *New War Diary* (1938) offers more stories of her experience in the guise of a committed soldier—a situation that becomes her and, as more than one critic has noticed, creates an

SINO-JAPANESE RELATIONS

In September 2012 tensions between Japan and China erupted anew when a deal was brokered between the two nations calling for Japan to purchase territory known in China as Diaoyu and in Japan as Senkaku, a group of islands in the East China Sea that are thought to reside in the middle of a repository of oil, gas, and mineral resources. After the arrest by the Japanese of Chinese nationalists who staged a protest on the Senkaku/Diaoyu islands, further civilian demonstrations called for their release. In and around Shanghai, acts of aggression were committed against Japanese residents, and the outgoing Japanese ambassador's car was attacked as it made its way through the city. In Taiwan the islands are known as the Tiaoyutai, and anti-Japanese sentiment rose there as well, with protests against Japanese nationalization of the territory.

The two Sino-Japanese wars (1894–1895, 1937–1945) left a legacy of bitterness, particularly with respect to the disputed figures regarding an episode known as the Nanjing Massacre, in which 300,000 civilian Chinese perished, according to the Chinese. In 2007 a group of conservative Japanese members of parliament pronounced those numbers exaggerated.

image of a modern-day Mulan fighting as an independent woman. (*Mulan shi* is a folk ballad about a young girl who disguises herself as a boy and battles invading Huns on her father's behalf.) In a 2008 book titled *When "I" Was Born*, Jing M. Wang observes: "Xie Bingying's openly celebrated identity as a female soldier … moved a great stride beyond Mulan's assumed male disguise in order to qualify as a soldier." Scholars continue to examine the significance of *A Woman Soldier's Own Story* in terms of emerging ideas about women's place in society as China transitioned into the modern era.

Xie, as her autobiography recounts, was active in publishing, editing a women's journal and other works, including the 1945 anthology *Selected Autobiographies by Women Writers* (*Nu zuojia zizhuan xuanji*). That the anthology is sometimes read alongside Anne Frank's *Diary of a Young Girl*, written during World War II, is indicative of scholarly trends toward a more global perspective on history, with women's and girls' stories often providing surprising insights. In her 2002 review of Xie's autobiography in the *Women's Review of Books*, Gail Hershatter excuses the text's lack of concrete historical information while praising its personalized approach: "Her autobiography was written and published in a China controlled by the same Guomindang government responsible for the purge, the disbanding and the arrests. The silences in her book can be read as indicators of the perilous political environment in which Xie lived and worked."

BIBLIOGRAPHY

Sources

Hershatter, Gail. "Fighting for Her Life." Rev. of *A Woman Soldier's Own Story*, by Xie Bingying. *Women's Review of Books* 1 Feb. 2002. *AccessMyLibrary*. Web. 18 Nov. 2012.

Ip, Hung-Yok. "Fashioning Appearances: Feminine Beauty in Chinese Communist Revolutionary Culture." *Modern China* 29.3 (2003): 329–61. *JSTOR*. Web. 23 Nov. 2012.

Levine, Steven. Rev. of *A Woman Soldier's Own Story*, by Xie Bingying. *Library Journal* 15 Sept. 2001. *MyLibraryAccess*. Web. 18 Nov. 2012.

Liu, Jianmei. *Liu: Revolution Plus Love Cloth*. Honolulu: University of Hawaii Press, 2003. *Google Books*. Web. 23 Nov. 2012.

Wang, Jing M. *When "I" Was Born: Women's Autobiography in Modern China*. Madison: University of Wisconsin Press, 2008. *Google Books*. Web. 23 Nov. 2012.

Xie Bingying. *A Woman Soldier's Own Story*. Trans. Lily Chia Brissman and Barry Brissman. New York: Columbia University Press, 2001. Print.

Ye, Weili. Rev. of *A Woman Soldier's Own Story*, by Xie Bingying. *China Journal* 49 (2003): 228–30. *JSTOR*. Web. 18 Nov. 2012.

Further Reading

Chang, Jung. *Wild Swans: Three Daughters of China*. New York: Simon & Schuster, 1991. Print.

Dean, Britten. "British Informal Empire: The Case of China." *Journal of Commonwealth and Comparative Politics* 14.1 (1976): 64–81. *JSTOR*. Web. 18 Nov. 2012.

Feuerwerker, Yi-Tsi Mei. *Ding Ling's Fiction: Ideology and Narrative in Modern Chinese Literature*. Boston: Harvard University Press, 1982. Print.

Qian, Nanxiu. "Revitalizing the Xianyuan (Worthy Ladies) Tradition: Women in the 1898 Reforms." *Modern China* 29.4. *JSTOR*. Web. 23 Nov. 2012.

See, Lisa. *Snow Flower and the Secret Fan*. New York: Random House, 2005. Print.

Tanigawa, Michio. *Medieval Chinese Society and the Local "Community."* Trans. Joshua Fogel. Berkeley: University of California Press, 1985. *California Digital Library*. University of California. Web. 22 Nov. 2012.

Wang, Jing M., and Shirley Chang, eds. *Jumping through Hoops: Autobiographical Stories by Modern Chinese Women Writers*. Vancouver: University of British Columbia Press, 2002. Print.

Rebecca Rustin

Subject Index

Italic page numbers indicate illustrations. **Bold** page numbers and titles refer to main articles.

A

AAC. *See* Army Air Corps
Aaron, Daniel, **2:**271
Abandoned Baobab, The (Bugul), **1:61–64**
Abandonment, Bugul (Ken) on experience of, **1:**61–62
a/b: Auto/Biography Studies (journal), **1:**246
Abbey, Edward, *Desert Solitaire*, **1:**234
Abbey Theatre (Dublin), **2:**126, 128
Abbott, Lyman, **1:**52
Abdel-Fattah, Randa, *Does My Head Look Big in This?*, **1:**41–42
Abdo, Diya M., **3:**49
Abdul Hamid (Ottoman sultan), **2:**106
"Able-bodied," social construction of concept, **1:**8
Abolition, of slavery
    in Britain and British colonies, **1:**34, 81, 111, **3:**23
    in Cuba, **3:**7
    in U.S., **1:**33, 50
Abolitionist movement
    Adams (John Quincy) in, **2:**70
    in Britain, **1:**81–83, 111, **3:**23
    Douglass (Frederick) in, **1:**33
    Equiano (Olaudah) in, **1:**81–83
    Grimké (Charlotte Forten) in, **2:**29
    Higginson (Thomas Wentworth) in, **2:**238
    Jacobs (Harriet A.) in, **1:**142
    James (Henry) in, **2:**113
    Kemble (Fanny) in, **2:**335
    origins and rise of, **1:**142
    Prince (Mary) in, **3:**23, 25
    Ruete's (Emily) critique of, **1:**92
    "tragic mulatto" tradition in literature of, **1:**72
    in U.S. South vs. North, **1:**33
    Wheatley (Phillis) invoked in, **2:**45
Abootalebi, Ali R., **3:**220
Aboriginal Land Rights Act of 1976 (Australia), **3:**334
Aborigines, Australian
    Unaipon (David) on life as, **1:**149–151
    women, oral histories of, **3:**334–336
Aborigines' Friends' Association (AFA), **1:**149, 150, 151
Aborigines' Progressive Association, **1:**150
Abortion, in *A Mountainous Journey* (Tuqan), **1:**226, 227
About, Edmund, *Germaine*, **2:**115
Abouzeid, Leila, **3:**49
Abraham, Peter, **3:**251
Abraham Lincoln: A History (Nicolay and Hay), **3:**261–262
Abraham Lincoln: A Life (Burlingame), **3:**264
Abraham Lincoln: Complete Works (Nicolay and Hay), **3:**262

Abrams, Lynn
    A History of Everyday Life in Twentieth Century Scotland, **3:**173, 175
    Myth and Materiality in a Woman's World, **3:**175
    Oral History Theory, **3:173–175**, 179, 181, 285
    on *Women and Families* (Roberts), **3:**146
Abrash, Barbara, **3:**340
Abudi, Dalya, **1:**227
Abu Ghraib prison (Iraq), **3:**231
Account of Corsica (Boswell), **2:**328
Acculturation, in U.S., **1:**15–17. *See also* Assimilation
Accuracy. *See* Truth
Acebey, David, **3:**322
Achebe, Chinua, **1:**214
Acheson, Katherine O., **2:**64
Acker, Kathy, **1:**249
Acting career, of Kemble (Fanny), **2:**335–337
Actions, in identity, Rousseau (Jean-Jacques) on, **1:**200, 201
Acton, Carol, **2:**260, 261
Acts and Monuments, The (Day), **2:**97
Acts of Conscience (Taylor), **3:**227
Adamovich, Ales, **3:**282, 285
Adams, Abigail, **2:87**
    Adams's (John) correspondence with, **2:**316
    family of, **1:**133, **2:**69
    Letters of Mrs. Adams, **2:**87, 89
    "Letter to Her Daughter from the New White House," 2:87–90

SUBJECT INDEX

Adams, Ansel, **3:**102
Adams, Charles Francis, **1:**132, **2:**69, 87, 89
Adams, Henry
   The Education of Henry Adams, **1:**15, **132–134,** 180
   Mont-Saint-Michel and Chartres, **1:**132
Adams, John, **1:**132, **2:**69, 87, 316
Adams, John Quincy, **2:70**
   The Diary of John Quincy Adams, **2:69–71**
   family of, **1:**132, *133*
   Kemble's (Fanny) friendship with, **2:**335
Adams, Judith Porter, *Peacework,* **3:268–271**
Adams, Lauren, **2:**296
Adams, Marian, **1:**133
Adams, Percy, **2:**206
Adams, Timothy, **1:**124
Adams, Timothy Dow, **1:**165
Adler, Nanci, **3:**19
Adolescents
   as audience for *Go Ask Alice* (anonymous), **2:**294–296
   as audience for *Red Scarf Girl* (Jiang), **1:**161, 162
   drug use by, **2:**294–296
Adopted Territory (Kim), **1:**102–103
Adoption
   interracial/intercultural, **1:**102–104
   tradition of memoirs of, **1:**102
Adventures of Huckleberry Finn (Twain), **1:**146, 147–148
Advice
   in *The Autobiography of Ben Franklin* (Franklin), **1:**179
   in *Letters to a Young Poet* (Rilke), **2:**149–150
   in *Walden* (Thoreau), **1:**234
Aesthetics, Ruskin's (John) writings on, **1:**264
AFA. *See* Aborigines' Friends' Association
Afejuku, Tony, **3:**253
Affirmative action, in U.S.
   establishment and purpose of, **1:**15

   Rodriguez's (Richard) critique of, **1:**15, 16
   state bans on, **3:**20
Afghanistan
   Ahmedi (Farah) on life in, **1:**40–42
   Soviet war in, **1:**40, **3:**233
   Taliban in, rise of, **1:**40
   U.S. war in, **1:**42, **3:**207, 233
AFL. *See* American Federation of Labor
Africa. *See also specific countries*
   autobiographical tradition of, **1:**64
   borders in, establishment of, **1:**114
   colonial (*See* Africa, colonialism in)
   feminist autobiographies from, **1:**64
   Haley's (Alex) travels in, **1:**262
   idealization of, by Laye (Camara), **1:**130
   négritude movement in, **1:**61
   non–Africans' collaboration with authors of, **1:**64
   oral traditions of, **1:**64, **2:**242
   trauma literature of, **1:**313–314
   trickster stories of, **2:**3
Africa, colonialism in. *See also specific countries*
   Bugul (Ken) on legacy of, **1:**61–64
   cultural impacts of, **3:**141
   end of, **1:**3, 61
   in interior of continent, **3:**37
   Lessing (Doris) on experience of, **1:**167–169
   Nigerian Civil War and, **1:**215
   origins of, **1:**61, **3:**141, 251
Africa, Thomas W., **1:**221
African, The (Courlander), **1:**262
African American(s)
   citizenship for, **1:**50, **2:**38, 238
   in Civil War regiments, **2:**238–240, *239*
   communism among, **1:**3–5
   discrimination against (*See* Civil rights movement; Racism)
   family life of, **1:**273–275
   folklore of, **1:**9
   genealogy of, **1:**261–263
   in Great Depression, **3:**99
   Great Migration of, **1:**50, 52, 84, 273, **3:**99

   in interracial relationships, **1:**72–74
   Islam among, **1:**186–188
   lynchings of, **1:**18, 50
   masking tradition of, **1:**144
   in Reconstruction era, **1:**50
   as slaves (*See* Slave(s))
   in theater, rise of, **1:**273
   in Vietnam War, **3:**199–201
   voting rights for, **1:**50, **2:**238
   women (*See* African American women)
   in World War II, **3:**248–250
African American autobiographical writing. *See also* Slave narratives; *specific works and writers*
   by Angelou (Maya), **1:**18–20
   by Du Bois (W. E. B.), **1:**3–5
   by Grimké (Charlotte Forten), **2:**29–31
   by Haley (Alex), **1:**261–263
   by Hansberry (Lorraine), **1:**273–275
   by hooks (bell), **1:**249–251
   by Hurston (Zora Neale), **1:**9–11
   by King (Martin Luther, Jr.), **2:**32–34
   by Lorde (Audre), **2:**3–5
   by Malcolm X, **1:**186–188
   by McBride (James), **1:**72–74
   by McKay (Claude), **1:**84–86
   by Obama (Barack), **1:**78–80
   by Parks (Rosa), **1:**37–39
   as staple of African American literature, **1:**37
   tradition of, **3:**23–24
   by Wheatley (Phillis), **2:**44–46
   by Wright (Richard), **1:**122–124
African American identity. *See also* Multicultural and multiracial identities
   vs. feminist identity, of women, **2:**3
   Haley (Alex) on, **1:**261–263
   Obama (Barack) on, **1:**78–80
African American oral histories
   of civil rights movement, **3:**44–46, 99–101
   of Coe Ridge colony, **3:**90–92
   of Detroit, **3:**99–101

of higher education at white colleges, **3**:20–22
of Tuskegee Airmen, **3**:248–250
of Vietnam War veterans, **3**:199–201

African American Review (journal), **1**:250, **2**:5

African American women
Angelou (Maya) on lives of, **1**:18–19
in feminism, **1**:249, 250, **2**:3, 5
feminist vs. black identity of, **2**:3
hooks (bell) on lives of, **1**:249–250
as slaves, Jacobs (Harriet A.) on lives of, **1**:34, 35

African National Congress (ANC)
AIDS epidemic and, **3**:272, 274
establishment of, **2**:241
Luthuli (Albert) in, **1**:24, 25
Mandela (Nelson) in, **1**:27, 28, 29, **3**:242
Plaatje (Solomon Tshekisho) in, **2**:241

Africans in America (television miniseries), **3**:45
African Studies (journal), **3**:243
African Studies Review (journal), **3**:259
Africa Remembered (Curtin), **3**:141
Africa Today (journal), **1**:25, 115, **3**:142, 252
Afrikaners, **1**:27, **2**:241, **3**:242
Afro-American Studies (journal), **1**:187
Age (journal), **1**:48
Agenda (journal), **1**:39
Age of Illusion, The (Blythe), **3**:61
Agnew, Christopher S., **3**:126
Agosín, Marjorie
Always from Somewhere Else, **1**:75
A Cross and a Star, **1**:75–77, 99
Uncertain Travelers, **1**:75
Agrarian ideology, **2**:215
Agrarian reform movement, in Mexico, **3**:302–304
Agrarista movement, **3**:302–304
Agriculture, in England, oral histories of life in, **3**:59–61, 63–65
AHA Foundation, **1**:209
Ahimsa, **1**:243, 244

Ahmedi, Farah, *The Story of My Life,* **1**:40–42, *41*
Ahn Doo-hee, **1**:322
AIDS
emergence of, **3**:85
in South Africa, **1**:29, **3**:272–274
in U.S., **3**:85
AIDS Doctors (Oppenheimer and Bayer), **3**:272, 273, 274
Aiken, Katharine, **3**:339
AIM. *See* American Indian Movement
Ain't I a Woman (hooks), **1**:250
Airline industry, arbitration in, **3**:154
Ai Weiwei, **3**:301
Akazawa, Dennis, **3**:85
Akenfield: Portrait of an English Village (Blythe), **3**:59–62
Akharbach, Latifa, *Femmes et Politique,* **3**:47
Akhtar, Aasim Sajjad, **3**:178
Akiga's Story (East), **3**:141
Akiyama, Itsu, **3**:81
Alabama, Montgomery bus boycott in, **1**:20, 37, 38, 39, **2**:32, **3**:44, 45
Alan Paton Prize, for *Country of My Skull* (Krog), **3**:243
Albert (prince consort), **2**:209, 210
Alberti, Rafael, **1**:222
Alcatraz Island (San Francisco), AIM occupation of, **1**:54
Alcohol
in Appalachia, **3**:90, 91
in Idaho, **3**:95
Alcott, Amos Bronson, **1**:235
Alcott, Louisa May, **2**:223
Alexander, Elizabeth, **2**:4
Alexander, Harriet, **2**:340
Alexander, John, **1**:150, 151
Alexander, Margaret Walker, *Jubilee,* **1**:262
Alexander II (tsar of Russia), **1**:193, 195
Alexander the Great, **1**:105, 218
Alexandra Feodorovna, *The Last Diary of Tsaritsa Alexandra,* **2**:84–86, *85*
Alexievich, Svetlana
Boys in Zinc, **3**:285
Voices from Chernobyl, **3**:265, **282–286**

Alexis, Phil, **3**:108
Alexius Comnenus, **1**:285
Alger, Derek, **1**:297
Algeria
Amrouche (Fadhma Aïth Mansour) on life in, **1**:93–95
Feraoun (Mouloud) on life in, **2**:262–264
French colonial rule of, **1**:93–94, **2**:262–264
postcolonial, challenges facing, **2**:262
War of Independence in, **1**:93, **2**:262–264, *263*
Algerian War of Independence (1954–1962), **1**:93, **2**:262–264, *263*
Ali, Muhammad, **3**:44
Alienation
of Agosín (Marjorie), **1**:75
of American workers, **3**:343
of Amrouche (Fadhma Aïth Mansour), **1**:93–94
of Bugul (Ken), **1**:61–62
of Conrad (Joseph), **2**:192, 193
of Kim (Elizabeth), **1**:103
of Laye (Camara), **1**:128, 129
of Obama (Barack), **1**:78
of Ruete (Emily), **1**:90
of Santiago (Esmeralda), **1**:108–110
Alien Land Law of 1913 (California), **3**:195
ALIS. *See* Association du Locked-in Syndrome
All Change Here (Mitchison), **2**:235
Allen, Brooke, **2**:73
Allen, Harley, **3**:159
Allen, Hope Emily, **1**:191
Allen, Prudence, **2**:162
Allen, Roger, **1**:137
Allen, William Sheridan, *The Nazi Seizure of Power,* **3**:245
Allende, Isabel, **1**:76
Paula, **1**:222
Allende, Salvador, **1**:222, *223*
All God's Dangers (Rosengarten), **3**:73, 179
Allison, A. Lynn, **3**:290
Allison, Fred H., **3**:211

SUBJECT INDEX

Almayer's Folly (Conrad), **2:**192
Almost a Woman (Santiago), **1:**108, 109
Along Freedom Road (Cecelski), **3:**21
Along This Way (Johnson), **1:**13, 84, 122
Alonso, Harriet Hyman, **3:**270
'Alqam, Nabil, **2:**106
Alta California, oral histories of, **3:**114–116, *115*
Alter, Robert, **1:**272
Alternative Service Program, **3:**229
Alvarez, Julia, *How the Garcia Girls Lost Their Accents,* **1:**108
Alvarez-Borland, Isabel, **1:**297
Always a People (Kohn and Montell), **3:**107–109, 325
Always from Somewhere Else (Agosín), **1:**75
Al-Windawi, Mouayad, **2:**276
Al-Windawi, Thura, *Thura's Diary,* **2:**275–277
Amado, Jorge, **2:**8
Amador, José María, **3:**114–116
Amalric, Mathieu, **1:**7
Amanpour, Christiane, **2:**278
Ambrose, **1:**196, 197
Amerasian Immigration Act of 1982 (U.S.), **1:**170
America (journal), **2:**56, **3:**46, 309
America, Columbus's (Christopher) discovery of, **2:**201–203
American Anthropologist (journal), **3:**81, 142, 168, 320, 324
American Anti-Slavery Society, **1:**33, 142
American Arbitration Association, **3:**154
American autobiographical writing. *See also* African American(s); Asian American(s); Native American(s); *specific works and writers*
    by Adams (Abigail), **2:**87–90
    by Adams (Henry), **1:**132–134
    by Adams (John Quincy), **2:**69–71
    by Bechdel (Alison), **1:**139–141
    by Buck (Lucy), **2:**271–273
    by Carver (Jonathan), **2:**205–207
    by Chesnut (Mary Boykin Miller), **2:**250–252
    by Condict (Jemima), **2:**78–80
    by Conroy (Frank), **1:**164–166
    by Crèvecoeur (Michel-Guillaume Saint-Jean de), **2:**213–215
    by Dillard (Annie), **1:**279–281
    by Emerson (Ralph Waldo), **2:**139–141
    by Franklin (Benjamin), **1:**179–182
    by Gellhorn (Martha), **2:**101–103
    by Hawthorne (Nathaniel), **2:**223–225
    by Higginson (Thomas Wentworth), **2:**238–240
    by Houston (James D.), **1:**299–301
    by James (Henry), **2:**113–115
    by Jefferson (Thomas), **2:**316–318
    by Keller (Helen), **1:**43–46
    by Lee (Robert E.), **2:**38–40
    by McCarthy (Mary), **1:**258–260
    by McCourt (Frank), **1:**119–121
    by Medina (Pablo), **1:**296–298
    by Moore (Molly), **2:**278–280
    by Nabokov (Vladimir), **1:**270–272
    by Nin (Anaïs), **2:**123–125
    by O'Connor (Flannery), **2:**129–131
    by Olney (James), **1:**246–248
    by Plath (Sylvia), **2:**47–49
    by Poe (Edgar Allan), **2:**41–43
    by Rodriguez (Richard), **1:**15–17
    by Rowlandson (Mary), **1:**325–328
    by Santiago (Esmeralda), **1:**108–110
    by Sinor (Jennifer), **2:**163–165
    by Stanton (Elizabeth Cady), **1:**12–14
    by Stein (Gertrude), **1:**332–334
    by Stewart (Elinore Pruitt), **2:**91–93
    by Stone (Kate), **2:**244–246
    by Styron (William), **1:**204–206
    by Thoreau (Henry David), **1:**233–236
    by Twain (Mark), **1:**146–148
    by Ulrich (Laurel Thatcher), **2:**331–333
    by Wiesel (Elie), **1:**318–320
    by Williams (Tennessee), **2:**152–154
    by Wolff (Tobias), **1:**47–49
American Book Award
    for *Lakota Woman* (Brave Bird), **1:**23
    for *Sophie's Choice* (Styron), **1:**204
    for *The Unknown Internment* (Fox), **3:**225
American Cancer Society, **2:**3–4
American Childhood, An (Dillard), **1:**279
American Civil War (1861–1865)
    African American soldiers in, **2:**238–240, *239*
    Buck (Lucy) on life in South during, **2:**271–273
    Chesnut (Mary Boykin Miller) on life in South during, **2:**250–252
    conscientious objectors in, **3:**223
    diaries kept during, **2:**244, 271
    Douglass (Frederick) in, **1:**33
    Lee (Robert E.) in, **2:**38, 39–40
    Lincoln (Abraham) in, **3:**261
    slavery as issue in, **1:**50, **2:**38, 250
    start of, **2:**250, **3:**261
    Stone (Kate) on life in South during, **2:**244–246
American Dream
    Franklin (Benjamin) and, **1:**180
    Hispanic Americans' pursuit of, **3:**121, 122
    homesteading and, **2:**91
    Siv (Sichan) on, **1:**306, 307, 308
American Dreams (Terkel), **3:**300
American Ethnologist (journal), **3:**142
American Experience, The (television show), **3:**45
American Federation of Labor (AFL), **3:**328
American Historical Review (journal)
    on *Doña María's Story* (James), **3:**75
    on *The First Agraristas* (Craig), **3:**303
    on *Freedom Flyers* (Moye), **3:**249
    on *Hooligans or Rebels?* (Humphries), **3:**311

on *Survivors* (Miller and Miller), **3:**42

on *The Voice of the Past* (Thompson), **3:**188

on *Women in the Chinese Enlightenment* (Wang), **3:**148

American Indian Movement (AIM)
Brave Bird (Mary) in, **1:**21–23
FBI in conflicts with, **1:**96
occupation of Alcatraz by, **1:**54
occupation of Wounded Knee by, **1:**21, 22–23, 96
origins of, **1:**21, 54
Peltier (Leonard) in, **1:**96–98

American Indians. *See* Native American(s)

American Journal of Sociology, **3:**342

American Leaders in Nursing (Safeir), **3:**170

American Literary History (journal), **1:**173, **2:**4

American literature
disability studies on, **1:**8
realism in, rise of, **2:**240

American Mercury (journal), **2:**184

American Music (journal), **3:**133

American Notes (Dickens), **1:**43, 146, **2:**223

American oral histories. *See also* African American oral histories; Native American oral histories
of anarchists, **3:**3–5
of Appalachians, **3:**66–69, 86–89, 90–92
of coal miners, **3:**66–69, 96–98, 337–339
of colonial Californians, **3:**114–116
of draft resisters, **3:**221–223
of gay Asian Americans, **3:**83–85
on Great Depression, **3:**161–163
of Hispanic Americans, **3:**121–123, 131–133
of Idaho homesteaders, **3:**93–95
of Iraq War veterans, **3:**231–233
of Italian Americans, **3:**224–226
of IWW members, **3:**328–330
of Japanese American internees, **3:**80–81, 102–104, 195–198

of Japanese immigrants, first-generation, **3:**80–82
of Japanese war brides, **3:**127–130, *128*
of Jewish Americans, **3:**118–120
of labor arbitrators, **3:**153–155
of Lincoln (Abraham), **3:**261–264
of Los Alamos residents, **3:**239–241
of Mexican Americans, **3:**131–134
of nuns, **3:**308–310
of Nuremberg trial participants, **3:**293–295
origins of field, **3:**186
of Owens Valley residents, **3:**102–104
recognition of value of, **3:**20, 90
of teachers, **3:**77–79
of Tuskegee Airmen, **3:**248–250
on Vietnam War, **3:**199–201, 209–211, 221–223, 275–277
on war on poverty, **3:**254–256
of women coal miners, **3:**337–339
of women immigrants, **3:**305–307, *306*
of women peace activists, **3:**268–271
on workers' experiences, **3:**343–345
on World War II, **3:**202–204, 212–214, 224–226, 248–250

American Prospect (magazine), **1:**209

American Quarterly, **1:**71

American Revolutionary War (1775–1783)
Adams (John Quincy) on, **2:**69
autobiographies of era of, **1:**179–180
Condict (Jemima) on life during, **2:**78–80
conscientious objectors in, **3:**223
Crèvecoeur (Michel-Guillaume Saint-Jean de) on, **2:**213, 214
end of, **2:**69
Franklin (Benjamin) on, **1:**179
socioeconomic role of women after, **2:**331–332
start of, **2:**69
Wheatley's (Phillis) views on, **2:**44, 45

American Scholar (journal), **1:**280

"American Scholar, The" (Emerson), **1:**180

American Slave, The (Rawick), **1:**35

American Slavery as It Is (Weld), **1:**33, 142

American Sociological Review (journal), **3:**320

American Spectator (magazine), **1:**307

American Splendor (Pekar), **1:**139, **3:**330

American Studies (journal), **1:**35

American Theater (journal), **3:**213

American Transcendental Quarterly, **2:**141

American Woman Suffrage Association, **1:**12

American women. *See also* African American women
as coal miners, oral histories of, **3:**337–339
colonial, autobiographical writing by, **2:**78–79
education of, in eighteenth century, **2:**316–318
gender roles of, eighteenth-century, **2:**316
gender roles of, twentieth-century, **2:**47
as immigrants, oral histories of, **3:**305–307
Mexican American, oral histories of, **3:**131–133
as nuns, oral histories of, **3:**308–310
after Revolutionary War, socioeconomic role of, **2:**331–332
as teachers, oral histories of, **3:**77–79
in women's rights movement, **1:**12–14, **2:**47

Americas (journal), **3:**116

America's Invisible Gulags (Fox), **3:**226

AmeriCorps, **3:**254

Amerika (Kafka), **2:**120

Améry, Jean, **1:**318

Amidist Buddhism, **2:**59

Amistad (film), **2:**71

Amistad case, **2:**70, 71

SUBJECT INDEX

Amman, John, *Black Man's Grave*, **1**:312
Ammonds, Edith, **2**:91
Ammonds, Ida Mary, **2**:91
Among You Taking Notes (Mitchison), **2**:235–237
'Amr, Sa'di, **2**:104
'Amr, Sāmī, *A Young Palestinian's Diary*, **2**:104–106
Amritsar (India), massacre of 1919 in, **1**:242, 289
Amrouche, Fadhma Aïth Mansour, *My Life Story*, **1**:93–95
Amrouche, Jean, **1**:93, 94, 95
Amrouche, Taos (Mary-Louise), **1**:94
    Jacinthe Noir, **1**:93
    in *My Life Story* (Amrouche), **1**:93, 94, 95
Analytical Review (journal), **1**:82
Anarchism, in U.S., **3**:3–5
Anarchist Voices (Avrich), **3**:3–6
ANC. *See* African National Congress
An Ch'ang-ho, **1**:324
Andersen, Hans Christian, **2**:166
Andersen, Hendrik C., **2**:115
Anderson, Helen, **2**:60
Anderson, John Lee, **2**:220
Anderson, John Q., **2**:244
Anderson, Nan, **3**:92
Anderson, Stuart, **3**:170, 171
Anderson, Thomas P., **3**:207
Anderson, W. E. K., **2**:310, 311
And Justice for All (Tateishi), **3**:195–198, 224
Andonian, Aram, *The Memoirs of Naim Bey*, **3**:40
Andreas, Friedrich, **2**:151
Andreas-Salomé, Lou, **2**:149, 151
Andrew, Donna T., **2**:330
Angela's Ashes (McCourt), **1**:119–121
Angelico, Fra, **1**:197
Angelou, Maya, **1**:19
    I Know Why the Caged Bird Sings, **1**:18–20, 249
    "On the Pulse of the Morning," **1**:20
    A Song Flung Up to Heaven, **1**:18
    in tradition of Prince (Mary), **3**:24
    Wolff (Tobias) compared to, **1**:47

Anglia (journal), **1**:121
Anglicanism
    Book of Common Prayer in, **2**:98
    Edward VI in, **2**:97–99
    in English Civil War, **2**:26, 72, 256
    establishment of, **2**:72
    Methodism's rise and, **2**:195
    vs. Puritanism, **2**:26, 27
    rise of, **2**:97–98
    in slavery, **3**:23
    Wesley (John) in, **2**:195–196
    Woodforde (James) as clergyman in, **2**:287–289, *288*
Anglo–Boer War (1899–1902), **2**:241–243, *242*
Anglo–German Agreement (1890), **1**:114
Anglo-Iranian Oil Company, **3**:218
Anglorum Speculum, **2**:63–64
Angoff, Charles, **2**:184–185
Animal Farm (Orwell), **2**:117, *118*
Anisfield-Wolf Book Award
    for *The Autobiography of Malcolm X* (Malcolm X), **1**:186
    for *The Color of Water* (McBride), **1**:73
    for *Dust Tracks on a Road* (Hurston), **1**:9
    for *Maasai* (Beckwith and Saitoti), **1**:114
Aniwaya, Anigia Gltodi, **3**:326
Anna Karenina (Tolstoy), **1**:193
Annals of Ballitore, The (Leadbeater), **2**:157–159
Annals of the American Academy of Political and Social Science, **1**:291, **2**:7, 17, **3**:252
Anna of the Five Towns (Bennett), **2**:136
Anne Frank: The Diary of a Young Girl (Frank). *See Diary of Anne Frank, The* (Frank)
Anne of Denmark, **2**:62
Annie's Baby (Sparks), **2**:294
An Phoblacht (newspaper), **3**:316
Ansary, Tamim, **1**:40
Anselment, Raymond, **2**:258

Antelope's Strategy, The (Hatzfeld), **3**:258
Anthony, Joseph, **2**:261
Anthony, Susan B., **1**:12, 13
Anthropology
    in Africa, rise of, **3**:37
    Hurston's (Zora Neale) work in, **1**:9, 11
    Underhill's (Ruth) success in, **1**:70
    The Worlds of a Maasai Warrior (Saitoti) in, **1**:115
Antiautobiography
    Autobiography: Essays Theoretical and Critical (Olney) on, **1**:246, 247
    Roland Barthes (Barthes) as, **1**:268–269
Anticolonialism
    of Gandhi (Mohandas), **1**:242–244, 289
    of Nehru (Jawaharlal), **1**:289–291
Anti-Confucianism, **3**:124, 126
Antimiscegenation laws, U.S., **1**:72
Antioch Review (journal), **1**:124, **2**:221
Antiquarianism, **2**:177, 179
Antiretroviral therapy (ART), **3**:272, 273, 274
Anti-Semitism. *See also* Holocaust
    in Chile, Agosín (Marjorie) on, **1**:75
    in Germany, of Hitler (Adolf), **1**:31–32
    in Germany, Stein (Gertrude) on, **1**:333
    in Great Depression, **3**:118
Antiwar views. *See also* Pacifism; Peace activists
    of Sassoon (Siegfried), **2**:247, 248
    in *Strange Ground* (Maurer), **3**:275
    during Vietnam War, **3**:221, 222, 275, 277
Antoon, Sinan, **1**:255, 257
Antwerp (Belgium), Cavendish's (Margaret) exile in, **1**:229
ANZAC. *See* Australian and New Zealand Army Corp
"ANZAC Memories" (Thomson), **3**:177, 178
Anzaldúa, Gloria, *Borderlands/The Fontera*, **1**:56

Apache, Geronimo on, **1:**302–304
Apartheid, South African
    AIDS epidemic and, **3:**272
    end of, **1:**25, **3:**242
    establishment of, **1:**24, 27, **3:**242
    Luthuli (Albert) on, **1:**24–26
    Mandela (Nelson) on, **1:**27–29
    Truth and Reconciliation Commission on, **3:**242–244
Apess, William, *A Son of the Forest,* **1:**56, **3:**318
A/PLG. *See* Asian Pacific Lesbians and Gays
Apologia Pro Vita Sua (Newman), **1:**65
Appalachian Journal, **3:**92
Appalachian oral histories
    of African Americans of Coe Ridge, **3:**90–92
    of coal miners, **3:**66–69, 86, 87, *87, 91,* 96–98
    on culture, **3:**86–89
Appalachian Oral History Project, **3:**86–88
Appalachian stereotypes, **3:**68, 86, 96
Applegate, Wash, **3:**95
Apted, Michael, **3:**53
Aptheker, Herbert, **1:**3, 4
Apuleius of Madaura, *The Golden Ass,* **1:**198
Aquash, Mi'kmaq Anna Mae, **1:**98
Arab, Si Abderrahmane, **2:**262
Arab(s), racial profiling of, **3:**195, 197
Arabic autobiographical writing. *See also specific works and writers*
    by Al-Windawi (Thura), **2:**275–277
    by 'Amr (Sāmī), **2:**104–106
    by Darwish (Mahmoud), **1:**255–257
    by Ghazzawi ('Izzat), **2:**50–52
    by Hussein (Taha), **1:**135–137
    by Ruete (Emily), **1:**90–92
    tradition of, **1:**135–136, 137, 285, **2:**50
    by Tuqan (Fadwa), **1:**225–227
    by Usāmah ibn Munqidh, **1:**285–288
    by women, rise of, **1:**225–226

Arab–Israeli War (1967), **1:**225
Arab Revolt (1936–1939), **1:**227, **2:**104
Arab slavery, **1:**90, 92
Arab Studies Journal, **1:**287
Arab-Syrian Gentleman and Warrior in the Period of the Crusades, An (Usamah), **1:285–288**
Arafat, Yasser, **2:**50
Aragon, Louis, **2:**52
Arbitration, labor
    vs. mediation, **3:**155
    oral histories on development of, **3:**153–155
Arcadia (Stoppard), **2:**145
Archambault, Paul, **1:**183, 184
Archdiocese of Guatemala, **1:**99
Archer, W. H., **2:**191
Arctic (journal), **3:**139
Arctic Dreams (Lopez), **1:**279
Arden, Jane, **2:**109
ARENA. *See* National Republican Alliance
Arendt, Hannah, **2:**22, 121
Arethas of Caesarea, **1:**220
Are You My Mother? (Bechdel), **1:**140, 141
Argentina
    coup of 1943 in, **2:**220, **3:**73
    Guevara (Ernesto "Che") in, **2:**220–222
    Jews in, **1:**75
    labor movement in, oral histories of, **3:**73–75
    Peronism in, **3:**73–75
Arias, Arturo, **3:**165
Ariel (Plath), **2:**47
Aristocracy
    Chinese, **3:**124, 125
    French, **2:**306–307
    Japanese, **2:**297
Aristotle, **2:**96
Arizona
    coal mining in, **3:**11, 292
    Mexican American women in, oral histories of, **3:**131–133
    Navajo–Hopi land dispute in, oral histories of, **3:**10–12

Arizona Quarterly, **1:**281, **3:**201
Arkansas, Angelou (Maya) on life in, **1:**18
Arkansas Historical Quarterly, **3:**197
Arkin, Mark, **2:**337
Armed Forces & Society (journal), **3:**207
Armenian genocide, oral histories of, **3:**40–42, *41*
Armitage, Susan, **3:**191–192
Armstrong, Liahna, **2:**163, 164
Army Air Corps (AAC), U.S., Tuskegee Airmen in, **3:**248–250
Army Life in a Black Regiment (Higginson), **2:238–240**
Arnett, Edward, **3:**229
Arnold, Matthew, **1:**181, **2:**147
Arntzen, Sonja, **2:**297, 298, 299
Arranged marriage
    in China, **1:**153, 154, 338, 339, **2:**170
    in Montenegro, **3:**136, 137
ART. *See* Antiretroviral therapy
Art, of Bashkirtseff (Marie), **2:**306, *307,* 308
Art criticism, by Ruskin (John), **1:**264, 265
Arthur, Chester, **3:**10
Arthur, Emry, **3:**159
Arthur Ruppin (Ruppin), **2:**104
Arvin, Newton, **2:**114–115
Asa-Asa, Louis, **3:**24
Ascham, Roger, **2:**99
Ascherson, Neal, **2:**102
Ashkenazic Jews, **3:**118, 119
Ashmore, Susan Youngblood, *Carry It On,* **3:**254
Ashton, Susanna, **1:**52
Asia, Polo's (Marco) travels in, **1:**105–107. *See also* Southeast Asia; *specific countries*
Asian Affairs (journal), **1:**307
Asian American(s). *See also* Japanese American(s)
    gay, oral histories of, **3:**83–85, *84*
    racism against, **1:**103, 171
    stereotypes of, **1:**173, 174

SUBJECT INDEX

Asian American autobiographical writing. *See also specific works and writers*
    by Hayslip (Le Ly), **1:**335–337
    by Houston (Jeanne Wakatsuki), **1:**299–301
    by Kim (Elizabeth), **1:**102–104
    by Kingston (Maxine Hong), **1:**173–175
    by Min (Anchee), **1:**158–160
    by Nguyen (Kien), **1:**170–172
    by Siv (Sichan), **1:**306–308
    by Uchida (Yoshiko), **1:**309–311
Asian Pacific Lesbians and Gays (A/PLG), **3:**83, 84, 85
Asian Review of Books, **3:**16
Asian Studies Review (journal), **3:**148
As I Crossed a Bridge of Dreams (Sarashina), **2:189–191,** 290–291
Asisara, Lorenzo, **3:**114–116
Ask the Fellows Who Cut the Hay (Evans), **3:**59, **63–65**
Asleson, David, *Up the Swiftwater,* **3:**93
Assassination
    of Kennedy (John F.), **3:**254
    of Kim Ku, **1:**322
    of King (Martin Luther, Jr.), **1:**20
    of Lincoln (Abraham), **2:**246, **3:**261
    of Malcolm X, **1:**186, 188
Assimilation, in Australia, of Aborigines, **1:**149, 151, **3:**334
Assimilation, in U.S.
    of Japanese war brides, **3:**127
    of Native Americans, **3:**109
    oral histories of, **3:**305–307
    of refugees, **1:**307
    Rodriguez (Richard) on experience of, **1:**15–17
    Santiago (Esmeralda) on experience of, **1:**108
Association du Locked-in Syndrome (ALIS), **1:**7
Astell, Mary, *A Serious Proposal to the Ladies,* **2:**35
"As-told-to" accounts, of Native Americans, **1:**56
Atheism, of Darwin (Charles), **1:**65–67
Atlanta Compromise Address (Washington), **1:**50

Atlantic (magazine), **2:**335, **3:**61
Atlantic Monthly (magazine)
    Army Life in a Black Regiment (Higginson) in, **2:**238, 239–240
    Hawthorne's (Nathaniel) letters in, **2:**224
    Letters of a Woman Homesteader (Stewart) in, **2:**91, 92
    "Life in the Sea Islands" (Grimké) in, **2:**31
    Life on the Mississippi (Twain) in, **1:**146, 147
    on *The Story of My Life* (Keller), **1:**44
Atlantis (journal), **2:**131
Atom Boy (Osamu), **1:**293
Atomic weapons. *See* Nuclear weapons
At the Edge of the Abyss (Koker), **2:**253
"At the Home of Frederick Douglass" (Grimké), **2:**29
Audacity of Hope, The (Obama), **1:**78, 80
Auden, W. H., **1:**125, 276, **2:**147, 150
Audience
    adolescent, of *Go Ask Alice* (anonymous), **2:**294
    adolescent, of *Red Scarf Girl* (Jiang), **1:**161, 162
    authors' pact with, Lejeune (Philippe) on, **1:**239–240, **2:**174
    construction of memoirs to appeal to, **1:**164
    of *De Profundis* (Wilde), **2:**10
    European, of *Letters from an American Farmer* (Crèvecoeur), **2:**213, 214
    European, of *The Autobiography of Ben Franklin* (Franklin), **1:**181
    of letters, **2:**217
    white (*See* White audience)
    of *The Woman Warrior* (Kingston), **1:**174, 175
Audio adaptations, of *Dreams from My Father* (Obama), **1:**80
Augustine (saint), **1:197**
    City of God, **1:**198
    Confessions, **1:**183, 193, **196–199,** 201
    Dialogues, **1:**186

    An Interrupted Life (Hillesum) on, **2:**22, 24
    Malcolm X compared to, **1:**186, 188
    Olney (James) on, **1:**248
    Retractions, **1:**196, 198
    Soliloquies, **1:**196
    Teresa of Ávila influenced by, **1:**211
Augustus (Roman emperor), **1:**218, 220
"Auld Robin Gray" (Barnard), **2:**217, 218
Auschwitz and After (Delbo), **3:**34
Auschwitz concentration camp, **1:**318–320, **2:**22, **3:35,** 51
Ausgabe, Kritische, **2:**120
Auslander, Shalom, **2:**255
Aus Meinem Leben (Goethe). *See Truth and Fiction Relating to My Life* (Goethe)
Austen, Jane, **2:**133, 287, 289, 312
Auster, Paul, *The Invention of Loneliness,* **1:**279
Austin, Kelly, **1:**223
Australasian Journal of American Studies, **2:**30
Australia
    Aborigines of, **1:**149–151, **3:**334–336
    British colonial rule of, **1:**149
    Unaipon (David) on life in, **1:**149–151
    Vietnamese refugees in, **1:**337
    Warlpiri people of, oral histories of, **3:**334–336
    in World War I, **3:**177
Australian and New Zealand Army Corp (ANZAC), **3:**177
Australian Journal of French Studies, **2:**81
Australian Journal of International Affairs, **3:**207
Austria
    Jewish immigration to China from, **3:**14–16
    Satrapi (Marjane) in, **1:**155, 156
Authenticity. *See also* Truth
    of *Black Boy* (Wright), **1:**124

of *Memories of a Catholic Girlhood* (McCarthy), **1**:260
of *The Sovereignty and Goodness of God* (Rowlandson), **1**:326
of *A Woman in Berlin* (anonymous), **2**:282
Author(s)
    autobiography's relationship to, Barthes (Roland) on, **1**:267–268
    in pact with audience, Lejeune (Philippe) on, **1**:239–240, **2**:174
Authority, shared, in oral histories, **3**:179–181, 190
Authorship
    of *Chona* (Chona and Underhill), **1**:69
    of *Go Ask Alice* (anonymous), **2**:294
    of *Incidents in the Life of a Slave Girl* (Jacobs), **1**:144
    of *Journal of the First Voyage to America* (Columbus), **2**:201, 203
    of *Left Handed, Son of Old Man Hat* (Dyk), **3**:318, 319, 320
    meaning of, Barthes (Roland) on, **1**:267–269
    of *Mein Kampf* (Hitler), **1**:30, 32
    of oral histories, **3**:179
    of slave narratives, **1**:82–83
Autobiographical Pact, The (Lejeune), **1**:239–241
Autobiographical studies
    Barthes (Roland) in, **1**:267–269
    D'Israeli (Isaac) in, **2**:177–179
    Lejeune (Philippe) in, **1**:239–240, **2**:174–175
    Olney (James) in, **1**:246–248
    origins and rise of, **1**:239–240, 246–248, **2**:174
Autobiography. See also specific types and works
    author's relationship to, Barthes (Roland) on, **1**:267–268
    definition of, **1**:239
    literary criticism as form of, **1**:247
    vs. memoir, **1**:248, 279
    origins and rise of, **1**:239, 246
    rules for genre of, **1**:239, 246
Autobiography (Mill), **2**:16
Autobiography (Oliphant), **2**:335

Autobiography (Thornton), **1**:230
Autobiography, 1743–1790 (Jefferson), **1**:179, **2**:69
Autobiography, An, or The Story of My Experiments with Truth (Gandhi), **1**:24, 242–245
Autobiography, An, with Musings on Recent Events in India (Nehru), **1**:289–292
Autobiography and Postmodernism (journal), **1**:167
Autobiography: Essays Theoretical and Critical (Olney), **1**:246–248, 247
Autobiography in France (Lejeune), **1**:239, **2**:174
Autobiography of a Chinese Woman (Chao), **1**:338
Autobiography of Alice B. Toklas, The (Stein), **1**:332, 334
Autobiography of an Unknown Indian (Chaudhuri), **3**:251, 253
Autobiography of a Papago Woman, The (Underhill), **3**:318
Autobiography of a Runaway Slave (Barnet and Montejo). See *Biography of a Runaway Slave* (Barnet and Montejo)
Autobiography of a Schizophrenic Girl, The (Sechehaye), **1**:164
Autobiography of a Slave, The (Manzano), **3**:7
Autobiography of Ben Franklin, The (Franklin), **1**:179–182, **2**:213
Autobiography of Benjamin Rush (Rush), **1**:179–180
Autobiography of Charles Darwin, The (Darwin), **1**:65–68
Autobiography of Giambattista Vico, The (Vico), **1**:183–185
Autobiography of H.I.H. Soraya, The (Esfandiary), **3**:218
Autobiography of Malcolm X, The (Malcolm X), **1**:78, 186–188, **3**:44
Autobiography of W. E. B. Du Bois, The (Du Bois), **1**:3–5, 18
Autobiography of William Butler Yeats, The (Yeats), **2**:127–128
Autoethnography
    Dust Tracks on a Road (Hurston) as, **1**:11
    Memoirs of an Arabian Princess from Zanzibar (Ruete) as, **1**:91

The Way to Rainy Mountain (Momaday) as, **1**:55
Automobile industry
    automation of, **3**:343
    in Detroit, **3**:99, 100, 101
Auyero, Javier, *Contentious Lives*, **3**:268
Avant-garde memoirs
    Bone Black (hooks) as, **1**:249
    The Diary of Anaïs Nin (Nin) as, **2**:123
    Stop-Time (Conroy) as, **1**:164
Avary, Myrta Lockett, **2**:250, 251
Aventure ambiguë, L' (Kane), **1**:61
Avery, Genevieve, **3**:94
Avery, Oral, **3**:94
Aviation, U.S.
    naval, oral histories of, **3**:202–204
    Tuskegee Airmen in, oral histories of, **3**:248–250
Avrich, Karen, **3**:3
Avrich, Paul
    Anarchist Voices, **3**:3–6
    Sasha and Emma, **3**:3
Awards, book. See also Nobel prizes
    for *Abraham Lincoln: A Life* (Burlingame), **3**:264
    for *Akenfield* (Blythe), **3**:59
    for *Angela's Ashes* (McCourt), **1**:120
    for *The Audacity of Hope* (Obama), **1**:80
    for *The Autobiography of Malcolm X* (Malcolm X), **1**:186
    for *The Barracks Thief* (Wolff), **1**:47
    for *The Cancer Journals* (Lorde), **2**:5
    for *The Color of Water* (McBride), **1**:73
    for *The Confessions of Nat Turner* (Styron), **1**:204
    for *Country of My Skull* (Krog), **3**:243
    for *The Dark Child* (Laye), **1**:128
    for *Dreams from My Father* (Obama), **1**:80
    for *Dust Tracks on a Road* (Hurston), **1**:9
    for *The Education of Henry Adams* (Adams), **1**:132, 134

SUBJECT INDEX

Awards, book, *continued*
    for *"The Good War"* (Terkel), **3:**161, 212, 234, 279, 343
    for *House Made of Dawn* (Momaday), **1:**54
    for *The Invisible Thread* (Uchida), **1:**309–310
    for *Lakota Woman* (Brave Bird), **1:**23
    for *Letters Underway* (Ghazzawi), **2:**50
    for *A Long Way Gone* (Beah), **1:**313
    for *Maasai* (Beckwith and Saitoti), **1:**114
    for *Memory and Narrative* (Olney), **1:**248
    for *An Oral History of Abraham Lincoln* (Burlingame), **3:**261
    for *The Order Has Been Carried Out* (Portelli), **3:**265, 267
    for *Pilgrim at Tinker Creek* (Dillard), **1:**279
    for *Red Scarf Girl* (Jiang), **1:**161
    for *Riwan ou le chemin de sable* (Bugul), **1:**64
    for *Roots* (Haley), **1:**261
    for *Sophie's Choice* (Styron), **1:**204
    for *Thura's Diary* (Al-Windawi), **2:**275
    for *The Unknown Internment* (Fox), **3:**225
    for *Voices from Chernobyl* (Alexievich), **3:**282
    for *Wild Swans* (Chang), **1:**159
    for *The Woman Warrior* (Kingston), **1:**173
Axelrod, Steven Gould, **2:**48–49
Axford, Roger W., *Too Long Been Silent*, **3:**196
Ayres, Lew, **3:**228
Ayyam, al- (Hussein). *See Egyptian Childhood, An* (Hussein)
Ayyam al-'Arab, **1:**137
Azuma, Eiichiro, **3:**82

B

B., David, *Epileptic*, **1:**155
Baath party (Iraq), **2:**275, 276
Baba of Karo (Smith), **3:**141
Baby boomers
    drug use by, **2:**294
    Mexican American, **3:**133
    Soviet, oral histories of, **3:**331–333
    in workforce, **3:**343
Baby Doll (film), **2:**152
Back Bay Banner (periodical), **1:**274
Back in the World (Wolff), **1:**47
Bacon, Francis, **2:**66
Badenhausen, Richard, **1:**331
Baden-Powell, Robert, **2:**243
Bad War, The (Willenson), **3:**275
Baer, Allison, **1:**41–42
Baer, Elizabeth, **2:**271, 272, 273
Baer, Elizabeth R., **3:**36
Baez, Joan, **3:**159
Bagehot, Walter, **2:**35, 36
Baggett, Paul, "Caught between Homes," **1:**113
Baghdad (Iraq)
    in Iraq War, **2:**275–276, **3:**231
    Jewish immigration to China from, **3:**16
Baghdad Burning (Riverbend), **2:**275
Baghdad Burning II (Riverbend), **2:**275
Bagnold, Enid
    Brittain (Vera) compared to, **1:**329, **2:**259
    The Chalk Garden, **2:**259, 261
    The Chinese Prime Minister, **2:**261
    A Diary without Dates, **1:**329, **2:**259–261
    The Happy Foreigner, **2:**259
    National Velvet, **2:**259, 260, 261
    Sassoon (Siegfried) compared to, **2:**247
Bahr, Howard, *The Navajo as Seen by the Franciscans*, **3:**290
Bailer, Kermit G., **3:**100
Bailey, Kevin, **3:**187
Bailey, Peter J., **1:**48
Baillie, F. D., **2:**241
Bai Wei, *Tragic Life*, **1:**338
Baker, Alison, *Voices of Resistance*, **3:**47–49
Baker, Donald M., **3:**256
Baker, Felicity, **1:**202

Baker, Godfrey Evan, **2:**229
Baker, Ida, **2:**133
Baker, James T., **3:**162
Baker, Mark, *Nam,* **3:**199, 209, 210, 221, 231
Baker, Simon, **1:**126
Baker, William Massing, **2:**229
Bakgatla tribe, **2:**237
Bakhtiar, Shapour, **3:**220
Bakunin, Mikhail, **2:**120
Balaban, John, **3:**222
Balch, J. S., **1:**85
Baldick, Robert, **2:**81, 83
Baldwin, James
    Go Tell It on the Mountain, **1:**167, 261
    Notes of a Native Son, **1:**79–80
    on *To Be Young, Gifted and Black* (Hansberry), **1:**274
    Wright's (Richard) influence on, **1:**122, 124
Baldwin, Roger, **3:**329
Baldwin, William, **2:**99
Balkan Wars (1912–1913), **3:**135, 293, 294
Ball, Dewi Ioan, *Fighting Words*, **1:**97
Ballad of Reading Gaol, The (Wilde), **2:**9
Ballantyne, James, **2:**310
Ballard, Ephraim, **2:**333
Ballard, George, **1:**231
Ballard, Martha, **2:**331–333
Ballard, Molly, **3:**92
Ballent, Anahi, **3:**75
Ballet, inspired by Unaipon (David), **1:**149
Bampfield, Joseph, **1:**315, 316
Bancroft, Hubert H., **3:**114, 116
Banerjee, A., **2:**153
Bangarra Dance Theatre, **3:**335
Bangladesh, establishment of, **1:**87
Banjo (McKay), **1:**86
Banks, Ann, *First Person America*, **3:**161
Banks, Dennis, **1:**23
Banta, Martha, **2:**115
Bánzer, Hugo, **3:**322
Baobab fou, Le (Bugul). *See Abandoned Baobab, The* (Bugul)
Barbalet, Margaret, **3:**313

Barber, Denise, **3**:345
Barberini, Francesco, **1**:220
Barefoot Gen (Nakazawa), **1:293–295**
Barker, Eileen, **3**:41
Barker, Pat, **2**:248
Barlow, Joel, **2**:109
Barlow, Nora, **1**:67
Barmé, Geremie, **3**:288
Barnard, Anne, **2**:218
    "Auld Robin Gray," **2**:217, 218
    Journal of a Tour into the Interior, **2**:217, 218
    The Letters of Lady Anne Barnard to Henry Dundas, **2:217–219**
Barnes, Djuna, **1**:333
Barnes, Steven A., **3**:19
Barnet, Miguel, *Biography of a Runaway Slave*, **3:7, 7–9**
Barnouw, Dagmar, **1**:248
Barracks Thief, The (Wolff), **1**:47
Barre, Mohamed Siad, **1**:207
Barrel of a Pen (Ngũgĩ), **2**:12
Barrett, S. M., *Geronimo: His Own Story*, **1:302–305**
Barrio Boy (Galarza), **1**:15
Barrios de Chungara, Domitila
    Here Too, Domitila, **3**:322
    Let Me Speak!, **3**:74, **114–115**, **322–324**
Barry, Tom, *Guerilla Days in Ireland*, **3**:27
Barth, Karl, **2**:167
Barthes, Roland, **1:268**
    "The Death of the Author," **1**:267, 269
    Michelet par lui-même, **1**:267
    Roland Barthes, **1**:249, **267–269**
Bartlett, Rosamund, **1**:194, 195
Bashkirtseff, Marie
    The Journal of Marie Bashkirtseff, **2:306–308**
    The Last Confessions of Marie Bashkirtseff, **2**:306
    paintings of, **2**:306, *307*, 308
Baskin, John, *New Burlington*, **3**:86
Basler, Roy Prentice, *Collected Works of Abraham Lincoln*, **3**:262
Bass, Jonathan S., **2**:33–34
Bastien-Lepage, Jules, **2**:306

Bataille, Gretchen, **1**:23
Batchelor, Joy, **2:118**
Bates, Carl Murray, **3**:344
Bates, Edwin Morris, **2**:317
Batista, Ernesto, **2**:222
Batista, Fulgencio, **1**:296, *297*
Battlefields (television series), **3**:236
Battle of Valle Giula, The (Portelli), **3**:97, 157
Bauby, Jean-Dominique, *The Diving Bell and the Butterfly*, **1:6–8**
Baum, Geraldine, **2**:339
Baum, Oskar, **2**:120
Baum, Willa, **3**:188
Bauman, Janine, **3**:51
Baumel, Judith, *Double Jeopardy*, **3**:35
Baumgartner, Barbara, **3**:24–25
Bautista, Paul, **3**:85
Bawer, Bruce, **1**:280
Bayer, Ronald
    AIDS Doctors, **3**:272, 273, 274
    Shattered Dreams?, **3:272–274**
Beagle, H.M.S., **1**:65, 66
Beah, Ishmael, *A Long Way Gone*, **1:312–314**, *313*
Beamon, Mike, **3**:211
Bean, Thomas W., **2**:276
Bearden, Russell, **3**:197
Beatrice (princess), **2**:210
Beatty-Medina, Charles, *Contested Territories*, **3**:326
Beauchamp, Kathleen Mansfield. *See* Mansfield, Katherine
Beauchamp, Leslie, **2**:133, 135
Beaudry, Catherine, **1**:202
Bechdel, Alison
    Are You My Mother?, **1**:140, 141
    Dykes to Watch Out For, **1**:139, 141
    Fun Home, **1:139–141**, *140*
Bechdel, Bruce, **1**:139, 140
Bechdel test, **1**:141
Becker, Marshall Joseph, **3**:109
Beckham, Edward, **2**:27
Beckwith, Carol, *Maasai*, **1**:114
Becoming Madame Mao (Min), **1**:159
Bede, **3**:186
Bedoukian, Kerop, *The Urchin*, **3**:40
Beebe, Rose Marie

    The History of Alta California, **3**:115
    Testimonios, **3**:116
Beer and Revolution (Goyens), **3**:5
Beerbohm, Max, **1:253**, **2**:289
Beer brewing, in English villages, **3**:64
Beer Hall Putsch (1923), **1**:30
Beevor, Anthony, **2**:281, 282
Begging to Be Black (Krog), **3**:242
Begin, Menachem, **1**:225
Behar, Ruth
    on *Songs My Mother Sang to Me* (Preciado Martin), **3**:133
    Traveling Heavy, **1**:297
Behind the Burqa (Yasgur), **1**:40
Behind the Scenes (Keckley), **1**:52
Behn, Aphra, **1**:315, **2**:324
Beier, Lucinda McCray, *For Their Own Good*, **3:144–145**
Beik, Mildred Allen, **3**:67, 68, 95
Beineix, Jacques, **1**:6, 7
Beirne, Paul, **1**:324
Belarus
    censorship in, **3:282–284**
    Chernobyl nuclear disaster and, **3:282–284**
Belgium
    Bugul's (Ken) experience as African in, **1**:61–62
    Cavendish's (Margaret) exile in, **1**:229
    Congo as colony of, **2**:192–194
    Rwanda as colony of, **3**:257
    women miners in, **3**:337
Bell, Angelica, **2**:268
Bell, Anne Olivier, **2**:181–182
Bell, Clive, **2**:268
Bell, Ian, **1**:202
Bell, Vanessa, **2**:268
Bellanca, Mary Ellen, **2**:301
Belles Lettres (journal), **1**:280
Bell Jar, The (Plath), **2**:47
Bells of Nagasaki, The (Nagai), **1**:293
Beloved Land (Preciado Martin), **3**:131
Beltrán, Alberto, **3**:167
Benally, Malcolm D., *Bitter Water*, **3:10–13**
Benderman, Kevin, **3**:229

Benét, William Rose, **2:**185
Bengal
    British colonial rule of, **2:**328, **3:**253
    Mahomet (Dean) in, **2:**229–231
    religious riots of 1946 in, **1:**244
Bengali Girls Don't (Sherman), **1:**312
Bennett, Andrew, **2:**134
Bennett, Arnold, **2:137**
    Anna of the Five Towns, **2:**136
    Clayhanger trilogy, **2:**136, 137
    Hilda Lessways, **2:**138
    The Journals of Arnold Bennett, **2:136–138**
    Letters of Arnold Bennett, **2:**138
    A Man from the North, **2:**136
    The Old Wives' Tale, **2:**136
    Woolf (Virginia) on novels of, **2:**137, 138
Bennett, James, **3:**311–312, 313
Bennett, John, *Uqalurait,* **3:**107, **138–140**
Bennett, W. C., **3:**320
Bennett, Yvonne, **1:**331
Bentham, Jeremy, **2:**177
Benyon, Hew, **3:**54
Berber Academy, **1:**93
Berber culture
    in Morocco, **3:**47
    preservation of, **1:**93–95
Berber Dahir, **3:**47
Beresford, John, **2:**287
Bergen, Doris, **2:**24
Bergen-Belsen concentration camp, **2:**253, **3:**51
Bergin, Thomas Goddard, **1:**183, 184, 185
Bergreen, Laurence, **2:**203
Berisso (Argentina), oral history of life in, **3:**73–75
Berkeljon, Sara, **1:**207
Berkowitz, Leah, **2:**273
Berlin (Germany)
    Soviet occupation of, **2:**281–282
    Spandau prison in, **2:**54–56, 55
Berlin, Isaiah, **1:**185
Berlin Wall, fall of, **3:**247
Berman, Marshall, **3:**344–345

Bermuda, oral histories of slavery in, **3:23,** 23–25
Bernard, Gretchen Dobrott, **2:**131
Berne, Suzanne, **1:**280
Bernstein, Gail Eiseman, **3:**119
Bernstein, Irving, **3:**154
Berridge, Virginia, **3:**170, 171
Bertaux, Daniel, *Living through the Soviet System,* **3:**331
Bertraux-Wiame, Isabelle, **3:**188
Best, Nicholas, *Five Days That Shocked the World,* **3:**235
Beston, John, **1:**150–151
Beti, Mongo, **1:**130
Betts, Paul, **3:**247
Between Management and Labor (Friedman), **3:153–156,** 157
Bevan, Nye, **2:**235
Beverley, John, **3:**74
Beyond Manzanar (Houston), **1:**299
Bhabha, Homi, **1:**87
BIA. *See* Bureau of Indian Affairs
Biafran War, **1:**312
Biblical references
    in *Confessions* (Augustine), **1:**196
    in *An Interrupted Life* (Hillesum), **2:**22
    in *Jemima Condict* (Condict), **2:**79
    in *The Sovereignty and Goodness of God* (Rowlandson), **1:**326
    in *The Story of My Life* (Keller), **1:**44
Bicknell, Alexander, **2:**207
Biddle, Francis, **3:**224
Biel, Steven, **3:**4, 5
Bierce, Ambrose, **2:**240
Bigelow, John, **1:**179, 181
Biggs, Henry, **3:**99
Big Sea, The (Hughes), **1:**84, 122
Big Woods (Faulkner), **2:**215
Bilbo, Theodore, **1:**123
Bildungsroman, **1:**30, **2:**221
Bilingual education, in U.S., **1:**15–17
Bilingual Education Act of 1968 (U.S.), **1:**17
Billington, Ray Allen, **2:**29
Bingham, Caleb, *The Columbian Orator,* **1:**33–34
Binoche, Juliette, **3:**242

Biographies, origins and rise of, **2:**177, 178
Biography (journal), **1:**205, 290, **2:**77, 175, **3:**73, 233
Biography of a Runaway Slave (Barnet and Montejo), **3:7–9**
Biomythography, *Zami* (Lorde) as, **1:**9, 39, 249
Bioy Casares, Adolfo, *Rest for Travelers,* **1:**223
Biracial individuals. *See* Multiracial individuals
Bird, Stewart, *Solidarity Forever,* **3:328–330**
Bird by Bird (Lamott), **1:**280
Birley, Anthony, **1:**220
Birmingham News (newspaper), **2:**32
Birrell, Augustine, **2:**126
Bishop, Elizabeth, **2:**129
Bisisu, Mu'in, **2:**52
    Palestinian Notebooks, **2:**50
Bisky, Jens, **2:**281
Bismarck, Otto von, **1:**90
Bitsui, Roman, **3:**12
Bitter Water (Benally), **3:10–13**
Black (color), hooks (bell) on meanings of, **1:**250
Black Americans. *See* African American(s)
Black Bolshevik (Haywood), **1:**4
Black Boy (Wright), **1:122–124**
Black Chronicle, The (Hampton), **3:**44
Black Collegian (journal), **1:**250
Black Cuban, Black American (Grillo), **1:**296
Black Elk, Benjamin, **3:**110
Black Elk, Nicolas, *Black Elk Speaks,* **1:**21, 56, 302, **3:110–113,** *111,* 318
Black Elk Speaks (Black Elk and Neihardt), **1:**21, 56, 302, **3:110–113,** 318
Blackest Page in Modern History, The (Gibbons), **3:**40
Black Flame trilogy (Du Bois), **1:**5
Blackgoat, Roberta, **3:**292
Black Hawk, **1:**302
Black Hawk War (1832), **1:**302
"Black History, Oral History, and Genealogy" (Haley), **3:**186

Black identity. *See* African American identity

Black Man's Grave (Stewart and Amman), **1:**312

Black Mesa (Arizona)
    coal mining on, **3:**10, 292
    Navajo–Hopi land dispute in, oral histories of, **3:**10–12

Black Muslims, **1:**186, 188

Black nationalism
    of Du Bois (W. E. B.), **1:**4
    of Malcolm X, **1:**78
    Obama's (Barack) rejection of, **1:**78, 79

Black Panthers, **3:**200

Black Power movement, **1:**21

Blacks at Harvard (Sollors et al.), **3:**21

Black Unicorn, The (Lorde), **2:**4

Blackwood's Edinburgh Magazine, **3:**25

Blackwood's Magazine, **1:**316

Black Words, White Page (Shoemaker), **1:**150, 151

Black Worker in the Deep South (Hudson), **1:**3

Blaeser, Kimberly, **1:**56

Blair, Dorothy S., **1:**93, 94, 95

Blair, Hugh, **2:**109

Blair, Walter, **1:**148

Blake, Debra J., **3:**132, 133

Blake, Lillie Devereux, **2:**89

Blalock, Lucy Sadie Parks, **3:**108

Blaxhall (England), oral histories of life in, **3:**63–65

Blayney, Michael, **1:**262

Blessed by Thunder (Fernández Barrios), **1:**296

Blight, David W., **3:**266–267

Blindness
    of Hussein (Taha), **1:**135, 136, 137
    Keller (Helen) on experience of, **1:**43–46

Blithedale Romance, The (Hawthorne), **2:**225

Blixen, Karen, **2:**12

Blood, George, **2:**110

Blood Diamond (film), **1:**312

Blood Meridian (McCarthy), **1:**304

Blood of Spain (Fraser), **3:**176

Bloods: An Oral History of the Vietnam War by Black Veterans (Terry), **3:199–201**
    Everything We Had (Santoli) vs., **3:**210
    Strange Ground (Maurer) vs., **3:**275
    The Strength Not to Fight (Tollefson) vs., **3:**221
    Tears before the Rain (Engelmann) vs., **3:**279, 280
    What Was Asked of Us (Wood) vs., **3:**231, 232

Bloody Harlan (Taylor), **3:**96

Bloom, David, **2:**237

Bloom, Harold, **2:**139

Bloomsbury group, **2:**133, 180, 268–269

Blue, Martha
    Indian Trader, **3:**290, 291
    The Witch Purge of 1878, **3:290–292**

Blue Genes (Lukas), **1:**204–205

Blue Octavo Notebooks, The (Kafka), **2:**122

Blue Peter (periodical), **2:**193

Bluest Eye, The (Morrison), **1:**19, 175

Bluett, Thomas, *Some Memories of the Life of Job*, **3:**141

Blumenfeld, Yorick, **3:**61

Blunden, Edmund, *Undertones of War*, **1:**329

Blythe, Ronald
    The Age of Illusion, **3:**61
    Akenfield, **3:59–62**
    on *A Country Parson* (Woodforde), **2:**288, 289
    A Treasonable Growth, **3:**61
    The View in Winter, **3:**60

Boarding schools
    experimental, Conroy (Frank) on, **1:**164
    Native Americans at, **3:**109, 318

Boas, Franz, **1:**9, 11

Boat people, Vietnamese, **3:**280

Boccaccio, Giovanni, *Decameron*, **1:**229

Body(ies)
    able, social construction of, **1:**8
    of black women, **1:**18
    in identity, Rousseau (Jean-Jacques) on, **1:**200, 201
    meatiness of, Suleri (Sara) on, **1:**89

Body and Soul (Conroy), **1:**166

"Body Talk" (Spitzack), **3:**190

Boehmer, Elleke, **2:**241–242, 243

Boer War, Second. *See* Anglo–Boer War

Boer War, The (Churchill), **2:**241

Boer War Diary of Sol Plaatje, The (Plaatje), **2:241–243**

Boethius, *Consolation of Philosophy*, **2:**14

Bogart, Barbara Allen, *From Memory to History*, **3:**90

Boggs, Grace Lee, **3:**101

Boggs, James, **3:**99

Bohannon, Horace Augustus, **3:**249

Bohr, Niels, **3:**239

Bolívar, Antonio, **3:**169

Bolivia, oral histories of working-class women in, **3:**322–324, *323*

Bolshevik Revolution (1917), **2:**84, **3:**331

Bolshevism, **1:**270, 271

BOMB (magazine), **1:**48

Bone Black (hooks), **1:249–251**

Bonhoeffer, Dietrich, **2:**22

BookBrowse, **1:**159

Booklist (magazine)
    on *Freedom Flyers* (Moye), **3:**249
    on *Habits of Change* (Rogers), **3:**309
    on *Into the Jet Age* (Wooldridge), **3:**203
    on *Between Management and Labor* (Friedman), **3:**155
    on *Prison Writings* (Peltier), **1:**97
    on *Red Scarf Girl* (Jiang), **1:**162
    on *Ten Thousand Sorrows* (Kim), **1:**104
    on *Thura's Diary* (Al-Windawi), **2:**276
    on *Untold Tales, Unsung Heroes* (Moon), **3:**100
    on "*We Have Just Begun to Not Fight*" (Frazer and O'Sullivan), **3:**229
    on *Zlata's Diary* (Filipovic), **2:**339

Bookman (journal), **2:**194

Book of Common Prayer, **2:**98

Book of Margery Kempe, The (Kempe), **1:189–192,** 211, **2:**226

Book of Memories, The (Shua), **1:**75

Book of My Mother (Cohen), **1:**99

Book of the City of Ladies, The (Christine), **2:**162

Books Abroad (magazine), **2:**17

Books & Culture (journal), **3:**68

Books Ireland (journal), **2:**159, **3:**316

Boomer, Walter E., **2:**278–279, 280

Boorman, John, **3:**68, 242

Booth, Alison, **2:**210–211, 337

Booth, John Wilkes, **3:**261

Bootlegging. *See* Moonshine

Bootstrap, Operation, **1:**108

Borden, Mary, *The Forbidden Zone,* **2:**259

Borderlands literature, *When I Was Puerto Rican* (Santiago) as, **1:**109

Borderlands/The Fontera (Anzaldúa), **1:**56

Bordin, Guy, **3:**139–140

Boren, Mark Edelman, **2:**114

Borges, Jorge Luis, **1:**224

Bornat, Joanna
    on *Daring Hearts* (Brighton Ourstory), **3:**72
    Oral History, Health and Welfare, **3:170–172**

Born on the Fourth of July (Kovic), **1:**335, **3:**209

Borowski, Tadeusz, **1:**318

Bosnia, Filipovic (Zlata) on life in, **2:**338–340

Bosnian War (1992–1995), **2:**338–339

Bosnik, Anton, **3:**235

Bosque Redondo Reservation, **3:**10, 290, *291*

Bostdorff, Denise M., **2:**33

Bostock, Lisa, **3:**171

Boston College, **3:**29

Boston Globe (newspaper), **1:**16, 72

Bostonians, The (James), **2:**113

Boston Irish Reporter, **3:**29

Boston Tea Party, **2:79**

Bostridge, Mark, **1:**330, **2:**269

Boswell, James, **2:329**
    Account of Corsica, **2:**328
    The Journal of a Tour to the Hebrides, **2:**328
    Life of Samuel Johnson, **2:**177, 195, 309, 328, 329–330
    London Journal, **2:328–330**
    Woodforde (James) compared to, **2:**287, 288

Bosworth, Johnny, **3:**344

Botswana, Mitchison's (Naomi) visits to, **2:**237

Bottrall, Margaret, **1:**316

Bouhaddou, Saadia, **3:**48

Boundary 2 (journal), **2:**128

Bourgeacq, Jacques, **1:**128

Bourne, Edward, **2:**206

Boutcher, Warren, **2:**256

Bow, Leslie, **1:**337

Bowden, George, **2:**135

Bowe, John, *Gig,* **3:**343, 345

Bowe, Marisa, *Gig,* **3:**343, 345

Bowen, Elizabeth, **2:**101, 181
    The Death of the Heart, **2:**133

Bowker, Gordon, **2:**118

Bowring, Richard, **2:**290, 291, 292

Boyd, Belle, **2:**273

Boyer, Paul, *By the Bomb's Early Light,* **3:**239

Boyle, Kevin, **3:**101

Boyle, Robert, **2:**65

Boyle, Tony, **3:**98

Boy scouts, **1:**47, 48

Boys in Zinc (Alexievich), **3:**285

Boys' Life (magazine), **1:**47

Boys Will Be Boys (Suleri), **1:**88

Boyyd, Nan Alamilla, **3:**85

Bracken, John, **2:63**

Bradbury, Malcolm, **1:**280

Bradford, Clare, **1:**41

Bradford, Gamaliel, **2:**39, 314

Bradley, David, *Dissent,* **1:**80

Bradley, Ed, **3:**200

Bradley, William A., **1:**86

Bradstreet, Anne, **1:**315

Bragg, Melvyn, *Speak for England,* **3:**144

Brahms, Johannes, **1:**206

Brainwashing, in Cultural Revolution, **1:**161, 162

Branch, Michael P., **2:**214, 215

Braudel, Fernand, **3:**159

Brave Bird, Mary
    Lakota Woman, **1:21–23**
    Ohitika Woman, **1:**21, 23

Bravman, Bill, **3:**142

Brawne, Fanny, **2:**147

Braxton, Joanne, **1:**19

Braxton, Joanne M., **2:**31

Bray, William, **2:**65

Brazell, Karen, **2:**59, 60

Brazil
    de Jesus (Carolina Maria) on experience of poverty in, **2:**6–8
    Jews in, **1:**75

Breast cancer, Lorde's (Audre) battle with, **2:**3–5

Brée, Germaine, **1:**246, 247

Breen, Joe, **1:**120

Breidenbach, Bernhard von, *Peregrinationes in Montem Zion,* **2:**227

Brennan, William J., Jr., **3:**294

Brenner, Rachel, **2:**24

Brent, Jonathan, **2:**85–86

Breslau, Louise, **2:**306

Bressler, Leo A., **1:**235

Brewsie and Willie (Stein), **1:**333

Brewton, Vince, **1:**35

Breytenbach, Breyten, **3:**242

Brezhnev, Leonid, **3:**331

Bride of Lammermoor, The (Scott), **2:**209

Bridge, Horatio, **2:**223

Bridgman, Laura, **1:**43

Brief History of the War with the Indians in New England, A (Mather), **1:**325

Briggs, Anthony, **1:**195

Briggs, Asa, **3:**64

Briggs, Julia, **2:**182

Briggs, Kate, **2:**182

Briggsoth, Jean L., *Never in Anger,* **3:**138

Brighton (England), oral histories of gay life in, **3:**70–72, *71*

Brighton Gay Switchboard, **3:**72

Brighton Ourstory, *Daring Hearts,* **3**:70–72

Brigido-Corachán, Anna, **1**:56

Brill de Ramirez, Susan B., **3**:320

Brink, André, **1**:27, **3**:242

Brinker, William, **3**:277

Brinkman, Antoinette, **1**:103

Brinnin, John Malcolm, **1**:332–333

Brinson, Betsy, **3**:159, 266

Brissman, Barry, **1**:338, 339

Brissman, Lily Chia, **1**:338, 339

Bristol (England), oral histories of working-class youth in, **3**:311–313, *312*

Britain. *See also* England; Ireland; Scotland; Wales

    abolitionist movement in, **1**:81–83, 111, **3**:23

    abolition of slavery in, **1**:34, 81, 111, **3**:23

    African Britons in, **1**:81–82

    censorship of Irish history in, **3**:27, 28, 29

    class in (*See* Social class)

    education in, **2**:136, 320, **3**:311–313

    empire of (*See* British Empire)

    establishment of Great Britain (1707), **2**:328

    Franklin (Benjamin) in, **1**:179

    Great Depression in, **3**:53

    health-care industry of, **3**:170–172

    homosexuality in, ban on, **2**:9, 183, **3**:70

    industrialization of, **2**:16, 146, 300, **3**:59, 63

    Iranian relations with, **3**:218

    Irish Rebellion (1798) against, **2**:157, *158*, 159

    in Israel's establishment, **1**:225

    letter writing in, **2**:146, 217

    literacy in, rise of, **2**:136, 146, 320

    lost generation of, **1**:329

    Mahomet's (Dean) influence on culture of, **2**:230, 231

    Mass Observation Project in, **2**:235, 236, 237, 265, 266, 267

    nature writing in, golden age of, **2**:300

    Palestine under, **2**:104–106, **3**:14

    racism in, **2**:230

    religion in (*See* British religion)

    slave trade in, **1**:34, 81, 111

    social history of, Webb (Beatrice) on, **2**:16–18

    travel narratives in, popularity of, **2**:229

    Victorian (*See* Victorian era)

    wars of (*See specific wars*)

    women's rights movement in, **1**:329, 331, **2**:109

British Critic (journal), **2**:179

British Empire

    abolition of slavery in, **1**:34, 81, 111, **3**:23

    African countries in, **1**:167

    Australia in, **1**:149

    Egypt in, **1**:135

    during French Revolution, **2**:217, 218, 219

    India in (*See* India, British)

    Jamaica in, **1**:111

    Kenya in, **2**:12, **3**:141–143

    Nigeria in, **1**:214

    racism against people of color from, **2**:230

    Seven Years' War in expansion of, **2**:328

    South Africa in, **2**:217–219, 241–243

    Victorian era expansion of, **2**:16

    Zimbabwe (Rhodesia) in, **1**:167, **3**:251–253

British Journal of Aesthetics, **2**:128

British Journal of Education Studies, **3**:313

British Mandate for Palestine, **2**:104–106

British Medical Journal, **1**:6, 7–8

British monarchy. *See also* English Civil War; *specific rulers*

    in Renaissance, **2**:97–99

    Slingsby (Henry) on loyalty to, **2**:256–258

British Museum, **2**:183

British oral histories. *See also* English oral histories; Irish oral histories

    on health-care industry, **3**:170–172

    origins of field, **3**:186

    recognition of value of, **3**:64

    on World War II, **3**:234–236

British Petroleum, **3**:218

British religion. *See also* Anglicanism

    Catholicism, decline of, **2**:97, 99, 226

    Christianity, arrival of, **1**:189

    Great Awakening in, **2**:197

    Methodism, **2**:195–196

    Puritanism, **2**:72, 74

    Quakerism, **2**:26–28, 157–159

British women. *See* English women

Brittain, Vera, **1**:330

    Bagnold (Enid) compared to, **1**:329, **2**:259

    Mitchison (Naomi) compared to, **2**:235

    Sassoon (Siegfried) compared to, **2**:247

    Testament of Experience, **1**:330

    Testament of Friendship, **1**:330, 331

    Testament of Youth, **1**:329–331, **2**:247–248, 259, 269, **3**:176

Brittain, Victoria, **2**:14

Brod, Max, **2**:120, 121, 122

Brokenburn (Stone), **2**:244–246

Brooke, James, **2**:12

Brook Farm (utopian community), **1**:14, 235

Brookfield strike of 1970s, **3**:96

Brooklyn Historical Society, **3**:180

Brooks, Max, **3**:212

Brooks, Pam, **1**:39

Brooks, Van Wyck, **1**:134

Brothers: Black Soldiers in the Nam (Goff et al.), **3**:199

Broussard, Allen, **3**:21

Brown, C. G., **3**:173

Brown, Hume, **2**:309

Brown, James W., *Long Journey Home,* **3**:107, **325–327**

Brown, Jennifer S. H., **3**:109

Brown, John (abolitionist), **1**:33, **2**:29, 238

Brown, John (servant), **2**:209

SUBJECT INDEX

Brown, Joseph Epes, **3**:111
Brown, Patricia, **3**:338
Brown, William Wells
   Clotel, **1**:72
   Narrative, **1**:50
   The Negro in the American Rebellion, **2**:238
Browne, Janet, **1**:66, 67
Browne, Thomas, **2**:65, 67
Browning, Elizabeth Barrett, **2**:29
Browning, Orville H., **3**:263–264
Browning, Robert, **1**:264, 265
Brownmiller, Susan, **2**:283
Brown v. Board of Education, **1**:122, 249, **3**:44
Bruce, Edward Caledon, **2**:39
Bruce, Gary, *The Firm,* **3**:245–247
Bruckheimer, Jerry, **3**:345
Brugge, David M.
   The Navajo-Hopi Land Dispute, **3**:10
   "The Navajo Witch Purge of 1878," **3**:290
Bruner, Charlotte H., *Unwinding Threads,* **1**:94
Bruss, Elizabeth W., **1**:246
Bry, Theodor de, **2**:202
Bryant, Emma Spaulding, **2**:252
Bryant, Harold, **3**:201
Bryant, John Emory, **2**:252
Brydges, Samuel Egerton, **1**:231
Bryson, David, **3**:65
Buch, H. C., *Sansibar Blues,* **1**:92
Buchanan, John, **3**:177–178
Buchenwald concentration camp, **3**:51
Buck, Lucy
   Sad Earth, Sweet Heaven, **2**:271, 273
   Shadows on My Heart, **2**:38, 271–274
Buck, Neville, **2**:271
Buck, Pearl S., *The Good Earth,* **1**:159
Budberg, Moura, **1**:254
Buddhism, in Japan
   Murasaki Shikibu on, **2**:290, 291
   Nijo (Lady) as nun in, **2**:59, 60
   rise of, **2**:59, 61, 189
Buel, Joy Day, **2**:332

Buel, Richard, **2**:332
Buell, Lawrence, **1**:236
Bueno, Eva Paulino, **2**:8
Bueno, Fernanda, **2**:222
Buergenthal, Thomas, *A Lucky Child,* **1**:312
Buff, Truman, **3**:103
Buggery Act of 1533 (England), **3**:70
Bugul, Ken, **1**:62
   The Abandoned Baobab, **1**:61–64
   Cendres et braises, **1**:61
   Riwan ou le chemin de sable, **1**:61, 64
Buhari, Muhammadu, **1**:216
Buhle, Paul, **3**:159, 181, 330
Bui Tin, **3**:280
Bulletin of the School of Oriental Studies, **1**:137, 287
Bundeson, Lynne, **1**:336
Bunin, Ivan, **1**:270
Bunyan, John, *Grace Abounding to the Chief of Sinners,* **2**:26
Burawoy, Michael, **3**:342
Burde, Edgar, **1**:147
Bureau of Indian Affairs (BIA), U.S., **1**:69
Burgos-Debray, Elisabeth, **3**:114, 164, 165, 322
Burgunder, Rose, **1**:206
Burke, Bonaventure, **3**:310
Burke, Edmund, **1**:88, **2**:157, 158, 217
Burke, Peter, **1**:185
Burkett, B. G., **3**:201, 211
Burlingame, Michael
   Abraham Lincoln: A Life, **3**:264
   An Oral History of Abraham Lincoln, **3**:261–264
Burma, British colonial rule of, **2**:119
Burmese Days (Orwell), **2**:119
Burnett, Richard, **3**:159
Burney, Charles, **2**:312
Burney, Edward Francis, **2**:313
Burney, Fanny, **2**:313
   Diary and Letters of Madame D'Arblay, **2**:312, 314
   Evelina, **2**:312–313, 314
   Letters and Journals of Fanny Burney, **2**:312–315

   The Memoirs of Dr. Burney, **2**:312, 313
   Pope (Alexander) and, **2**:217
Burns, Anthony, **2**:29
Burns, Harry, **3**:95
Burns, Patrick, **3**:241
Burns, Robert, **2**:328
Burqas, **1**:40
Burr, Aaron, *The Private Journal of Aaron Burr,* **2**:88
Burr, Anna Robeson, **1**:246
Burroughs, Carolyn, **2**:337
Burroughs, John, **2**:141
Burson, Harold, **3**:294
Burst of Light, A (Lorde), **2**:3
Burton, Robert, **2**:177
Burton, Vicki Tolar, **2**:196
Buruma, Ian, *Murder in Amsterdam,* **1**:209
Bush, George H. W., **1**:300, **2**:278
Bush, George W., **1**:306, **2**:275
Bush, Laura, **1**:41
BusinessWeek (magazine), **3**:277
Butcher, Tim, *Chasing the Devil,* **1**:312
Bute, Lord, **2**:328
Butler, Dino, **1**:96
Butler, George E., **1**:206
Butler, Pierce Mease, **2**:335, 337
Butler, Samuel, **1**:218–219
Butor, Michel, **1**:240
Byatt, A. S., **1**:168
   Possession, **2**:77
Bykaw, Vasily, **3**:282
Byodoin Temple (Kyoto), **2**:298
Byrd, Jim, **3**:87
Byrd, Richard, **2**:280
Byron, George Gordon Noel, **2**:144
   Camino Real (Williams) on, **2**:154
   The Journal of Sir Walter Scott (Scott) on, **2**:309
   Kemble's (Fanny) friendship with, **2**:335
   Letters and Journals of Lord Byron, **2**:143–145, 309
   The Letters of John Keats (Keats) on, **2**:146
By the Bomb's Early Light (Boyer), **3**:239

C

Cadle, Tillman, **3:**158
Cady, Daniel, **1:**13
Caesar, Julius, **1:**218, 220
Caillouet, Ruth R., **1:**40–41, 42
Cain, William E., **1:**4–5
Caine, Barbara, **2:**17
Cairnie, Julie, **1:**169
Caldas (destroyer), **3:**183, 185
California
    affirmative action in, **3:**20
    African Americans in higher education in, **3:**20
    colonial, oral histories of, **3:**114–116
    gay Asian Americans in, oral histories of, **3:**83–85
    Gold Rush in, **3:**114
    immigrant land ownership in, restrictions on, **3:**195
    Italian American relocation in, **3:**224
    Japanese American internment in, **1:**299–301, **3:**102–104, 197
    missions of, **3:**114–116
    Owens Valley region of, oral histories of, **3:**102–104
    statehood for, **3:**114
California History (journal), **3:**225
California State University at Fullerton, Japanese American Oral History Project at, **3:**80, 102, 195
Californios
    definition of, **3:**114
    oral histories of, **3:**114–116
Californio Voices (Savage), **3:**114–117, 121
Calked Boots and Other Northwest Writings (Russell), **3:**93
Call, M. S., **1:**32
Callaloo (journal), **1:**5, 251, **3:**24
Callow, Simon, **2:**154
Calvino, Italo, *Invisible Cities*, **1:**105
Cambodia, under Khmer Rouge, Siv (Sichan) on life in, **1:**306–308
Cambodian Americans, Siv (Sichan) on experience of, **1:**306–308
Camden Society, **2:**226, 228

Cameron, David, **2:**261
Cameron, Samantha, **2:**261
Camino Real (Williams), **2:**154
Camp and Community (Garrett and Larson), **3:**102, 103–104
Campbell, John Angus, **1:**67
Campesinos, **3:**302–303
Camus, Albert
    Feraoun's (Mouloud) friendship with, **2:**262
    The Myth of Sisyphus, **1:**204
    Styron (William) influenced by, **1:**204, 205
    Wright's (Richard) friendship with, **1:**124
Canada
    oral histories of Inuits in, **3:**138–140, *139*
    U.S. draft evasion in, **3:**221
Canadian Book Review Annual, **3:**140
Canadian Journal of History, **2:**330, **3:**29
Canadian Literature (journal), **1:**103, **2:**175
Canadian Review of American Studies (journal), **1:**157
Cancer, Lorde's (Audre) battle with, **2:**3–5
Cancer Journals, The (Lorde), **2:**3–5
Cancian, Frank, **3:**168
Candor. *See also* Truth
    in *The Long Walk to Freedom* (Mandela), **1:**29
Caninius Rufus, **2:**95, 96
Canterbury Tales (Chaucer), **1:**191, 229
Canto general (Neruda), **1:**223
Cape of Good Hope, **2:**198, 199, 217, 218
Capitalism
    IWW's opposition to, **3:**328, 329
    working class in, **3:**53
Capital punishment. *See* Execution
Capital Times (newspaper), **2:**276
Capitulations of Santa Fé, **2:**201
Capote, Truman, **2:**152
Captivity narratives, **1:**81, 325–326
Caputo, John D., **2:**167
Caputo, Philip, *A Rumor of War,* **3:**209
Carboni, Sante, **3:**158

Cardanus, Hieronymus, **2:**98–99
Cárdenas, Lázaro, **3:**302, 303, *303,* 304
Carey, John, **2:**138
Caribbean autobiographical writing
    by McKay (Claude), **1:**84–86
    by Medina (Pablo), **1:**296–298
    by Santiago (Esmeralda), **1:**108–110
    by Seacole (Mary), **1:**111–113
Carlisle, Elizabeth Pendergast, **2:**332
Carlo Tresca (Pernicone), **3:**5
Carlson, Timothy, *Embedded,* **3:**276
Carlyle, Thomas, **2:**139–140, 144, 196, 310, 321
Carmelite religious order, **1:**211, 212
Carmody, Deidre, **1:**262
Carnegie, Andrew, **1:**52
Carranza, Venustiano, **3:**167
Carrera, Elena, **1:**213
Carretta, Vincent, **1:**82, 83, **2:**46
Carrier Warfare in the Pacific (Wooldridge), **3:**202–204
Carril, Delia del, **1:**223
Carrington, Dora, **2:**269
Carry It On (Ashmore), **3:**254
Carter, Jimmy, **1:**311, **3:**221
Carter, John, **1:**18
Carter, Ross S., *Those Devils in Baggy Pants,* **3:**212
Carter, Steven, **1:**274
Cartesian rationalism, **1:**183, 184
Carver, Jonathan
    The Journals of Jonathan Carver and Related Documents, **2:**205–208
    Travels through the Interior Parts of North America, **2:**205
Cary, Max, **1:**218, **2:**94, 95–96
Casada, James, **3:**252
Casaubon, Méric, **1:**220
Casey-Leininger, Charles F., **3:**100
Cash, Jean W., **2:**131
Caspar, C., **1:**31, 32
Cassius Dio, *Historia Romana,* **1:**220
Cast a Cold Eye (McCarthy), **1:**258
Castellanos, Miguel, **3:**206
Castle, The (Kafka), **2:**120
Castro, Fidel, **1:**296, 298, **2:**222, 280

Cat(s)
   in *A Country Parson* (Woodforde), **2:**289
   Lessing (Doris) on, **1:**169
Catherine of Siena (saint), **1:**189
Catholicism. *See also* Christian autobiographical writing
   Augustine in, **1:**196–198
   Boswell's (James) conversion to, **2:**329
   Counter-Reformation in, **1:**211
   in England, decline of, **2:**97, 99, 226
   in Ireland, **1:**119–120
   of McCarthy (Mary), **1:**259
   of Mexican American women, **3:**132
   nuns in, oral histories of, **3:**308–310
   of O'Connor (Flannery), **2:**129, 130
   Teresa of Ávila in, **1:**211–213
   Vatican II in, **3:**308, 309
   Williams's (Tennessee) conversion to, **2:**152
Catlett, Elizabeth, **2:**45
Catliln, George, **1:**330
Caton, William, **2:**26
Caton-Jones, Michael, **1:**47, 49
Catt, Carrie Chapman, **1:**12
Caucasia (Senna), **1:**72, 74
Caudill, Harry, *Night Comes to the Cumberlands*, **3:**66
"Caught between Homes" (Baggett), **1:**113
Caught in a Tornado (Ross), **3:**287
Cavell, Stanley, **1:**236
Cavendish, Margaret, **1:**230
   Clifford (Anne) compared to, **2:**62
   A Description of the New World, **1:**231
   Nature's Pictures Drawn by Fancy's Pencil to the Life, **1:**229, 231
   Osborne (Dorothy) compared to, **2:**324
   A True Relation of My Birth, Breeding, and Life, **1:**229–232
Cavendish, William, **1:**229
Cavett, Dick, **1:**260

CCP. *See* Chinese Communist Party
CDC. *See* Centers for Disease Control and Prevention
Cecelski, David, *Along Freedom Road*, **3:**21
Cecil, David, **2:**268
Cefkin, J. Leo, **3:**252
Cellini, Benvenuto, **1:**239
Cendrata, Lodovico, **2:**160
Cendres et braises (Bugul), **1:**61
Censorship
   in Belarus, **3:**282–284
   in Britain, **3:**27, 28, 29
   in China, **3:**287, 301
   in Kenya, **2:**14
   in Mexico, **3:**31, 32
   in Russia, **1:**193, 194
   in U.S., **1:**20, **2:**123, **3:**201
Centenary Edition of the Works of Nathaniel Hawthorne, The (Hawthorne), **2:**223
Centers for Disease Control and Prevention (CDC), U.S., **3:**85
Central Intelligence Agency (CIA), U.S., **1:**298, **3:**164
Century Magazine, **3:**261
CEP. *See* Coal Employment Project
Cereta, Laura, *Collected Letters of a Renaissance Feminist*, **2:**160–162
Cerro Gordo (California), **3:**103
Cervantes, Lorna Dee, **3:**133
Cervetto, Joe, **3:**225
Césaire, Aimé, **1:**61
Cha, Theresa Hak Kyung, *Dictee*, **1:**102
Chadwick, Owen, **1:**239
Chai, May-Lee, **1:**307–308
Chalk Garden, The (Bagnold), **2:**259, 261
Challener, Daniel D., **1:**48
Challenger, Melanie, **2:**338
Chalmers, Martin, **2:**304
Chamberlain, John, **1:**32
Chamberlain, Joseph, **2:**17
Chamberlain, Mary
   Fenwomen, **3:**61
   on *Women's Words* (Gluck and Patai), **3:**191
Chamberlain, Neville, **2:**265

Chamberlain, Samuel, *My Confessions*, **1:**304
Chamosa, Oscar, **3:**74, 75
Champagne, Roland, **1:**268, **2:**175
Chamula (Mexico), oral histories of indigenous people of, **3:**167–169
Chander, Manu, **1:**256, 257
Chandler, Sally, **3:**188
Chang, Gordon, **3:**81
Chang, Iris, **2:**19, 20
Chang, Jung, *Wild Swans*, **1:**158–159
Change of Tongue, A (Krog), **3:**242
Channing, Ellery, **2:**139
Chanthaphavong, Samaya L. S., **2:**299
Chao, Buwei Yang, *Autobiography of a Chinese Woman*, **1:**338
Chapelle, Dickey, *What's a Woman Doing Here?*, **2:**280
Chaplin, Charlie, **2:**183
Chaplin, Ralph, **3:**329
Chapman, James, **3:**234, 236
Chapman, Jedediah, **2:**79
Chapman, Maria Weston, *The Liberty Bell*, **1:**142
Character of England, A (Evelyn), **2:**65
Chardin, Jean-Baptiste-Siméon, **2:**110
Charles I (king of England)
   Eikon Basilike, **2:**256, 258
   in English Civil War, **1:**315, 317, **2:**26, 65, 72, 178, 256, 257, *257*
Charles II (king of England), **1:**316
   Evelyn (John) and, **2:**65
   Halkett (Anne), **1:**315, 316
   restoration of, **1:**315, **2:**26, 65, 72, 256, 258
Charlevoix, Pierre-François-Xavier de, *Journal of a Voyage to North-America*, **2:**205
Chasing the Devil (Butcher), **1:**312
Chatterjee, Partha, **1:**291
Chaucer, Geoffrey
   Canterbury Tales, **1:**191, 229
   The Letters of John Keats (Keats) on, **2:**146
Chaudhuri, Nirad C., *Autobiography of an Unknown Indian*, **3:**251, 253
Chavez, Cesar, **3:**133
Che: A Graphic Biography (Buhle and Rodriguez), **3:**330

Cheke, John, **2**:97

Chekhov, Anton, **1**:47, **2**:133

Chekisty (Dziak), **3**:245

Chen, Joan, **1**:158

Chen, Paul, **3**:84

Cheney, Anne, **1**:274, 275

Cheney, Dick, **2**:278

Cheng, Nien, **1**:159

Cheng Yu-hsiu (Madame Wei), **1**:153
  A Girl from China, **1**:152, 154
  My Revolutionary Years, **1:152–154**

Cherie (Goncourt), **2**:308

Chernobyl nuclear disaster (1986), **3**:282–285, *283*

Chertkov, Vladimir, **1**:195

Chesnut, Mary Boykin Miller
  A Diary from Dixie, **2:250–252**
  Mary Chesnut's Civil War, **2**:250, 251, 271
  The Private Mary Chesnut, **2**:250
  Stone (Kate) compared to, **2**:244, 246

Chew, Daglish, **3**:243

Chiang Kai-sheck, **1**:338

Chiapas (Mexico), oral histories of indigenous people of, **3**:167–169, *168*

Chiarello, Barbara, **2**:255

Chicago (Illinois)
  Hansberry (Lorraine) on life in, **1**:273, 275
  Haymarket Riot in, **3**:4
  race riots in, **3**:45
  Wright's (Richard) move to, **1**:122

Chicago Daily Tribune (newspaper), **2**:89

Chicago Renaissance, **1**:273

Chicago Sun-Times (newspaper), **1**:40, 41

Chicago Tribune (newspaper), **1**:23, 40, 41, **2**:121

Chicana women, oral histories of, **3**:131–133, *132*

Chicano, use of term, **3**:133

Chicano movement, **3**:133

Chicano studies, rise of, **3**:131–133

Chicken with Plums (Satrapi), **1:155–156**

Chigwedere, P., **3**:274

Child, Lydia Maria, **1**:142, 144

Childhood
  in Arabic autobiographies, **1**:135, 136
  idealization of, **1**:128
  treatment of, in memoirs, **1**:47
  during wartime, memoirs of, **1**:312–314

Child in the House, The (Pater), **1**:276

Child of the Dark (de Jesus), **2:6–8**, **3**:164, 322

Children
  of British working class, **3**:53–54, *54*, 311–313, *312*
  as casualties of Holocaust, **3**:36
  Cuban, immigration of, **1**:298
  interracial adoption of, **1**:102–104
  of Los Alamos, oral histories of, **3**:239–241
  as soldiers in Sierra Leone, **1**:312–314

Children of Los Alamos (Mason), **3:239–241**

Children of Sanchez (Lewis), **3**:31

Children's of Cambodia's Killing Fields (Pran), **1**:306

Childress, Lee, **3**:209

Child's Christmas in Wales, A (Thomas), **1:125–127**

Chile
  Agosín (Marjorie) on experience of Jews in, **1**:75–77
  autobiographical tradition of, **1**:222
  German immigration to, **1**:75, 77
  mass disappearances in, **1**:75
  military coup of 1973 in, **1**:222
  Neruda (Pablo) on life in, **1**:222–224

Chimurenga (Liberation) War, First (1896–1897), **3**:251

Chimurenga (Liberation) War, Second, **3**:251

Chin, Frank, **1**:175

China. *See also* Chinese autobiographical writing; Chinese oral histories
  arranged marriage in, **1**:153, 154, 338, 339, **2**:170
  censorship in, **3**:287, 301
  Confucianism in, **3**:124–126
  Cultural Revolution in (*See* Cultural Revolution)
  Du Bois (W. E. B.) and, **1**:3, 4
  dynastic rule of, end of, **3**:124, 126, 147
  establishment of republic, **2**:170, **3**:124, 126, 147, 299
  feminism in, rise of, **3**:147–149
  folklore of, **1**:173, 174
  foot binding in, **1**:338, **3**:147, 289
  Gandhi's (Mohandas) influence on protests in, **1**:242
  gender roles in, **1**:153, 158, 160, 338, **3**:147–149
  Great Leap Forward in, **3**:287, 299, 300
  Japanese invasion of (1931), **3**:215
  Japanese relations with, **1**:340, **3**:149
  Japan influenced by, in Heian period, **2**:189
  Jewish refugees in, oral histories of, **3**:14–16
  Kingston (Maxine Hong) on culture of, **1**:173–175
  Korean Provisional Government in, **1**:322, 324
  Long March in, **1**:338
  May Fourth Movement in, **1**:338, **3**:126, 147–149
  Nanking Massacre in, **1**:340, **2**:19–21
  Northern Expedition in, **1**:338
  Polo's (Marco) travels in, **1**:105, 106, 107
  Rabe (John) in, **2**:19–21
  Revolution of 1911–1912 in, **2**:170
  in Sino–Japanese Wars, **1**:322, 339, 340
  women of (*See* Chinese women)
  during World War II, **1**:152, 153, **3**:14–16

China Candid (Sang), **3**:299–300

China Daily News (newspaper), **3**:299

China Journal, **1**:339, **3**:149, 301

China Men (Kingston), **1**:173

China Remembers (Zhang and McLeod), **3**:301

Chinchilla, Norma, **3**:323

Chinese American(s)
- Kingston (Maxine Hong) on experience of, **1:**173–175
- Min (Anchee) on experience of, **1:**158–160
- stereotypes of, **1:**173, 174

Chinese autobiographical writing. *See also specific works and writers*
- by Cheng Yu-hsiu (Madame Wei), **1:**152–154
- expatriate, tradition of, **1:**158–159
- by Jiang (Ji-li), **1:**161–163
- by Lu Xun and Xu Guangping, **2:**170–172
- by Min (Anchee), **1:**158–160
- by women, rise of, **1:**152–153, 159, 338
- by Xie Bingying, **1:**338–340

Chinese Civil War (1927–1950), **3:**126

Chinese Communist Party (CCP). *See also* Cultural Revolution
- censorship by, **3:**301
- Cheng Yu-hsiu on, **1:**152
- Jiang (Ji-li) on, **1:**161, 162
- in liberation of women, **3:**147, 148
- Lu Xun and, **2:**170, 172
- oppression under, **1:**338
- origins and rise of, **2:**170, **3:**287

Chinese language
- Japanese writers' use of, **2:**290, 292
- in *The Woman Warrior* (Kingston), **1:**173, 174

Chinese Lives (Zhang and Sang), **3:**288, **299–301**

Chinese Missionaries Oral History Collection (Peake and Rosenbaum), **3:**299

Chinese oral histories
- on Cultural Revolution, **3:**287–289, 299–300
- of descendants of Confucius, **3:**124–126
- government influence on, **3:**301
- on life in late twentieth century, **3:**299–301, *300*
- of women in May Fourth Movement, **3:**147–149

Chinese Oral History Project (Columbia University), **3:**299

Chinese Prime Minister, The (Bagnold), **2:**261

Chinese Revolution (1911–1912), **2:**170

Chinese women
- in arranged marriages, **1:**153, 154, 338, 339, **2:**170
- autobiographies by, rise of, **1:**152–153, 159, 338
- feminism among, rise of, **3:**147–149
- foot binding of, **1:**338, **3:**147, 289
- gender roles of, **1:**153, 158, 160, 338, **3:**147–149
- in May Fourth Movement, oral histories of, **3:**147–149
- in military, **1:**338–340
- stereotypes of, **1:**173, **3:**147
- traditional treatment of, **3:**147
- in World War II, Cheng Yu-hsiu on, **1:**152–154
- Xie Bingying of lives of, **1:**338–340

Chineworth, Mary Alice, **3:309**

Ch'ing, Ai, **1:**222

Chinweizu, **1:**115

Chiricahua Apache, Geronimo on, **1:**302–304

Chisholm, Anne, **2:**269

Chittister, Joan, **3:**308

Choi, Samuel, **2:**314

Choi, Young Back, **1:**323

Choice (journal), **3:**19, 249, 255, 326, 332

Chona (Chona and Underhill), **1:69–71**

Chona, Maria, *Chona,* **1:**69–71

Chrisman, Laura, **2:**242

Christian autobiographical writing. *See also specific works and writers*
- by Augustine, **1:**196–198
- by Fox (George), **2:**26–28
- by Guylforde (Richarde), **2:**226–228
- by Kempe (Margery), **1:**189–191
- by Kierkegaard (Søren), **2:**166
- by Rowlandson (Mary), **1:**325–328
- by Teresa of Ávila, **1:**211–213
- by Tolstoy (Leo), **1:**193–195
- tradition of, **2:**166
- by Wesley (John), **2:**195–197

Christian Gauss Award, for *Memory and Narrative* (Olney), **1:**248

Christian Herald (periodical), **3:**110

Christianity. *See also specific denominations*
- in Crusades, **1:**285–288
- early history of, **1:**196
- in England, arrival of, **1:**189
- fundamentalist, **1:**102, 103
- Great Awakening in, **1:**179, **2:**197
- hostility between Islam and, after Crusades, **2:**226
- Kim Ku influenced by, **1:**322
- *The Letters of the Younger Pliny* (Pliny) in, **2:**94
- Marcus Aurelius on, **1:**220
- pilgrimages to Jerusalem in, **2:**226–228
- Protestant Reformation in, **1:**211
- slavery and, **1:**34, 144, **2:**44, 46
- Wells's (H. G.) rejection of, **1:**252–253

Christianity, conversion to
- by Africans, **1:**64
- by Australian Aborigines, **1:**149, 151
- by Equiano (Olaudah), **1:**82
- by Native Americans, **1:**56, **2:**46, **3:**114, 115

Christie, Agatha, **2:**259

Christine de Pisan, **2:**160, 162
- *The Book of the City of Ladies,* **2:**162

Christmas, Thomas (Dylan) on, **1:**125–126, *126*

Christopher, Neil, *Ilagiinniq,* **3:**138

Christopher Award, for *Thura's Diary* (Al-Windawi), **2:**275

Chronology, lack of. *See* Nonchronological order

Church, Thomas, **2:**196

Churches, origins of abolitionist movement in, **1:**142

Churchill, Caryl, *Top Girls,* **2:60**

Churchill, Ward, *Struggle for the Land,* **3:**10

Churchill, Winston
- *The Boer War,* **2:**241
- *Nella Last's War* (Last) on, **2:**265

Church of England. *See* Anglicanism
Church of the Brethren, **3:**223, 227
Chute, Hillary, **1:**157
CIA. *See* Central Intelligence Agency
Ciberletras (journal), **1:**77
Cicero, Marcus Tullius, **2:**94, 95
    Hortensius, **1:**196, 198
Cichy, Rose M., **3:**35
Cienfuegos, Camilo, **2:**222
Cimarróns, **3:**7
Circumcision
    female, Hirsi Ali (Ayaan) on, **1:**207
    male, Perera (Victor) on, **1:**99, 100
Cisneros, Sandra, *The House on Mango Street,* **1:**108
Citizen 13660 (Okubo), **1:**299
Citizenship, Australian, for Aborigines, **1:**149
Citizenship, U.S.
    for African Americans, **1:**50, **2:**38, 238
    for Japanese immigrants, **1:**309
    for Puerto Ricans, **1:**108
Citoyenne, La (newspaper), **2:**306
City College (New York City), **1:**249, 251
City of God (Augustine), **1:**198
Civil disobedience
    in India, by Gandhi (Mohandas), **1:**242, **2:**32
    in Palestinian intifada, first, **2:**50
    in U.S. civil rights movement, **2:**32–33, **3:**101
Civilian Public Service (CPS), U.S., **3:**227–229
Civilians
    in Iraq War, **2:**275, **3:**231, 232
    in Vietnam War, **1:**335–337
    in World War II, **1:**332–333, **3:**235
"Civilized" mind, theories of, **3:**37
Civil Liberties Act of 1988 (U.S.), **1:**311, **3:**197
Civil rights
    for African Americans (*See* Civil rights movement)
    for gays and lesbians, **3:**70, 72, 83–84
    for Native Americans, **1:**21, **3:**291, 292
    in Reconstruction era, **1:**50
Civil Rights Act of 1964 (U.S.), **1:**20, **3:**339
Civil rights movement, U.S.
    Angelou (Maya) in, **1:**18, 20
    civil disobedience in, **2:**32–33, **3:**101
    debate over approach to, **1:**186
    in Detroit, **3:**99–101
    disability studies and, **1:**8
    Du Bois (W. E. B.) in, **1:**3–4
    Gandhi's (Mohandas) influence on, **1:**242
    gradualist approach to, **2:**32–33
    Hansberry (Lorraine) in, **1:**273–275
    Jewish support for, **3:**118
    King (Martin Luther, Jr.) in, **2:**32–34
    Malcolm X in, **1:**186
    Montgomery bus boycott in, **1:**20, 37, 38, 39, **2:**32, **3:**44, 45
    oral histories of, **3:**44–46, 99–101
    origins and development of, **3:**44
    Parks (Rosa) in, **1:**37–39, **3:**101
    SCLC in, **1:**18, 20
    Vietnam War and, **3:**199, 200
    war on poverty and, **3:**254, 256
Civil war(s). *See specific countries*
Civil War Diary of Sarah Morgan, The (Morgan), **2:**271
Civil War History (journal), **2:**240, **3:**261
Cixous, Hélène, **1:**250, **2:**124
Clair, William, **2:**144
Clarissa (Richardson), **2:**301
Clark, Gillian, **1:**197, 198
Clark, John Pepper, **1:**214
Clark, Mary Higgins, **1:**40
Clarkson, Thomas, **1:**81, 83, **2:**75
Clary-Lemon, Jennifer, **3:**175
Clasby, Nancy, **1:**188
Class. *See* Social class
Classic Slave Narratives, The (Gates), **1:**82, 83
Clayhanger trilogy (Bennett), **2:**136, 137
Clayton, Frances, **1:**39
Clemens, Samuel Langhorne. *See* Twain, Mark
Clemm, Maria, **2:**41–43
Clifford, Anne, **2:**63
    The Diaries of Lady Anne Clifford, **2:**62–64
    "Knole Diary," **2:**62, 64
Clifford, D. J. H., **2:**62, 64
Clifford, Geraldine Jonçich, **3:**77
Clifford, James O., **3:**224
Cline, David, **3:**97, 98
Clinton, Bill, **1:**20, 219, **3:**166, 221
Clio (journal), **1:**272
Clive, Robert, **2:**178
Clodfelter, Mark, **3:**279
Clotel (Brown), **1:**72
Cloud Cuckoo Land (Mitchison), **2:**237
Clubbe, John, **2:**144, 145
Clybourne Park (Norris), **1:**273
Coal Employment Project (CEP), **3:**337, 339
Coal Hollow (Light and Light), **3:**66–69
Coal Miners' Wives (Giesen), **3:**337
Coal mining
    in Arizona, on Native American lands, **3:**10, *11,* 292
    in Kentucky, oral histories of, **3:**86–87, 96–98, *97,* 157
    in Ukraine, oral histories of, **3:**340–342
    in West Virginia, oral histories of, **3:**66–69, *67, 91*
    women in, oral histories of, **3:**337–339, *338*
Coburn, Carol, **3:**309
Codrescu, Andrei, **1:**167
Coe, Calvin, **3:**92
Coe, Joe, **3:**92
Coe, John, **3:**90
Coe, Little John, **3:**92
Coe, Samuel S., **3:**90
Coeckelbergh, Mark, **2:**168
Coe Ridge (Kentucky), oral histories of life in, **3:**90–92
Coetzee, J. M., **1:**27
Coeur d'Alene (Idaho), oral histories of life in, **3:**93, 95

SUBJECT INDEX

Coffee, **1:**257
Coffield, Frank, **3:**313
Cohen, Albert, *Book of My Mother,* **1:**99
Cohen, Eliot, **2:**279, 280
Cohen, Jacob, **3:**103
Cohen, J. M., **2:**203
Cohen, Joshua, **1:**255–256
Cohen, Lucy, **3:**122
Colaiaco, James A., **2:**33
Colby, Clara, **1:**12
Colby, William, **3:**279
Cold War
    Du Bois (W. E. B.) and, **1:**3
    Salvadoran Civil War in, **3:**205
    Soviet oral histories of, **3:**331–333
    in *This Boy's Life* (Wolff), **1:**47
    women's peace movement during, **3:**268
Cole, Lori E., **3:**191
Cole, Margaret I., **2:**16, 172
Coleman, Emily Holmes, **1:**127
Coler, Jack, **1:**96
Coleridge, Samuel Taylor
    Byron (George Gordon Noel) compared to, **2:**143
    Journals of Ralph Waldo Emerson (Emerson) on, **2:**141
    Literary Fund and, **2:**207
    The Rime of the Ancient Mariner, **3:**183
    Robinson (Henry Crabb) and, **2:**75
    Wordsworth (Dorothy) influenced by, **2:**300
Coleridge, Sara, *Memoirs and Letters of Sara Coleridge,* **2:**16
Collected Letters (Poe), **2:**41
Collected Letters of a Renaissance Feminist (Cereta), **2:**160–162
Collected Letters of Mary Wollstonecraft, The (Wollstonecraft), **2:**109–112
Collected Works of Abraham Lincoln (Basler), **3:**262
Collected Works of W. B. Yeats, The (Yeats), **2:**126, 128
Collective bargaining, arbitration in, **3:**153
Collective living, Stanton (Elizabeth Cady) on, **1:**14

Collective narratives, of Native Americans, **1:**54
Collective novels, **3:**282, 285
College Literature (journal), **1:**98, 141, 160, **2:**260, 261
Colleges, white, African Americans at, **3:**20–22
Collier's (magazine), **2:**103
Collingwood, Luke, **1:**83
Collins, Anne, *Divine Songs and Meditacions,* **1:**229
Collins, Michael, **3:**27
Collister, Peter, **2:**307
Colombia
    coup of 1953 in, **3:**183, 185
    oral history of shipwrecked sailor from, **3:**183–185, *184*
Colonialism. *See also* Africa, colonialism in; *specific countries*
    Fanon (Frantz) on violent resistance to, **1:**244, **2:**262
    Gandhi's (Mohandas) nonviolent resistance to, **1:**242–244
    Las Casas's (Bartolomé de) critique of, **2:**201, 202, 203
    Orwell's (George) critique of, **2:**119
Color
    hooks (bell) on meanings of, **1:**250
    Nabokov's (Vladimir) perception of, **1:**272
Colorado River, **1:**69
Color-graphemic synethesia, **1:**272
Color of Water, The (McBride), **1:**72–74
Color Purple, The (Walker), **1:**18, 175
Columbian Orator, The (Bingham), **1:**33–34
Columbia University
    Chinese Oral History Project, **3:**299
    Maurer (Harry) at, **3:**277
    Obama (Barack) at, **1:**78
Columbus, Christopher, **2:202**
    Gama (Vasco da) compared to, **2:**200
    Journal of the First Voyage to America, **2:201–204,** 205
    in Puerto Rico, **1:**108
Columbus, Ferdinand, **2:**203

Comaneci, Nadia, *Letters to a Young Gymnast,* **2:**150
Comaroff, John, **2:**241
Comerford, Linda Brill, **1:**162
Comerford, Maire, **3:**29
Comics
    autobiographical, **1:**139–140, 155–157
    gay- and lesbian-themed, **1:**139, 141
    Japanese, **1:**293–294
    on labor movement, **3:**330
Coming-of-age
    in *Angela's Ashes* (McCourt), **1:**119–121
    in *Black Boy* (Wright), **1:**122–124
    in *Bone Black* (hooks), **1:**249
    in *A Child's Christmas in Wales* (Thomas), **1:**125–127
    in *Chona* (Chona and Underhill), **1:**69
    in *The Dark Child* (Laye), **1:**128
    in *Dust Tracks on a Road* (Hurston), **1:**9
    in *The Education of Henry Adams* (Adams), **1:**132–134
    in *An Egyptian Childhood* (Hussein), **1:**136
    in *Fun Home* (Bechdel), **1:**139
    in *Incidents in the Life of a Slave Girl* (Jacobs), **1:**144
    in *Left Handed, Son of Old Man Hat* (Dyk), **3:**318, 319
    in *Life on the Mississippi* (Twain), **1:**146
    in *My Life Story* (Unaipon), **1:**149–151
    in *My Revolutionary Years* (Cheng), **1:**152–154
    in *Under My Skin* (Lessing), **1:**167–169
    in *Persepolis* (Satrapi), **1:**155–157
    in *Red Azalea* (Min), **1:**158–160
    in *Red Scarf Girl* (Jiang), **1:**161–163
    in *Stop-Time* (Conroy), **1:**164, 165
    in *The Unwanted* (Nguyen), **1:**170–172
    in *The Woman Warrior* (Kingston), **1:**174, 175

Coming of Age in Mississippi (Moody), **1:**37
Comitini, Patricia, **2:**301
Committee for Effecting Abolition of the Slave Trade, **1:**81
Committee for Peasant Unity, **3:**166
Commonplace books, **2:**140
Communication Studies (journal), **1:**14
Communism
    in Cambodia, under Khmer Rouge, **1:**306
    in Cuba, establishment of, **1:**296
    Du Bois's (W. E. B.) support for, **1:**3–5
    in East Germany, oppression under, **3:**245–246
    in India, Nehru's (Jawaharlal) advocacy for, **1:**289
    McKay's (Claude) support for, **1:**84, 85
    in Russia, establishment of, **1:**270
    U.S. containment policy on, **3:**205
    in Vietnam, postwar, **1:**170, 171
Communist Party, Chilean, **1:**222
Communist Party, Chinese. *See* Chinese Communist Party
Communist Party, East German, **3:**245
Communist Party, South African, **1:**27
Communist Party, U.S., **1:**3, 4, 122, 123
Community, sense of, among gay Asian Americans, **3:**83–85
Comparatist (journal), **1:**223
Comparative Literature Studies (journal), **1:**277
Comparative Studies of Society and History (journal), **3:**96
Complete Notebooks of Henry James, The (James), **2:113–116**
Complete Works of George Orwell (Orwell), **2:**117, 118
Computers and the Humanities (journal), **2:**203
Conan Doyle, Arthur
    The Great Boer War, **2:**241
    Partridge (Frances) and, **2:**269
Concentration camps. *See* Holocaust concentration camps
Conclusive Evidence (Nabokov). *See Speak, Memory* (Nabokov)

Concubines, in Japan, **2:**299
Condict, Jemima, *Jemima Condict,* **2:78–80**
Coney, Juliet, **2:**91, 92
Confederacy. *See* American Civil War
Confession, A (Tolstoy), **1:193–195,** 270
Confessions (Augustine), **1:196–199**
    The Autobiography of Giambattista Vico (Vico) vs., **1:**183
    The Autobiography of Malcolm X (Malcolm X) vs., **1:**186
    Confessions (Rousseau) influenced by, **1:**197, 201
    A Confession (Tolstoy) vs., **1:**193
    as first autobiography, **1:**196
    Teresa of Ávila influenced by, **1:**211
Confessions (Rousseau), **1:**193, 197, **200–203,** 276
Confessions of Lady Nijo (Nijo), **2:59–61**
Confessions of Nat Turner, The (Styron), **1:**204, 206
Confidence (James), **2:**114
Confieso que he vivido (Neruda). *See Memoirs* (Neruda)
Conflict Quarterly, **3:**277
Confluencia (journal), **1:**109
Confucianism, **3:**124–126
    gender roles in, **3:**147
    Kim Ku influenced by, **1:**322
    Kong Decheng on, **3:**124–126
    movements against, **3:**124, 126
    rituals of, **3:**124, 125
Confucius, **3:125**
    descendants of, **3:**124–126
Congo
    Belgian colonial rule of, **2:**192–194, *193*
    Conrad's (Joseph) travels in, **2:**192–194
Congo Diary, The (Conrad), **2:192–194**
Congress, Continental, **2:**69
Congress, U.S.
    gag rule on slavery in, **2:**70
    House Un-American Activities Committee of, **2:**152

    and water resources on reservations, **1:**69
Congress of Racial Equality, **2:**32
Congress Party (India), **1:**242, 289, 290, 291
Connally, John B., **3:**202, 203
Connecticut Gazette (newspaper), **2:**44
Conner, John, **2:**295
Conner, Valerie Jean, *The National War Labor Board,* **3:**153–154
Connolly, Cyril, **2:**235
Conquered, The (Mitchison), **2:**237
Conquest, Robert, **3:**19
Conrad, Joseph
    Almayer's Folly, **2:**192
    The Congo Diary, **2:192–194**
    Dogs Bark, **1:**166
    Heart of Darkness, **2:**192–193, 194
    Last Essays, **2:**193, 194
    Literary Fund and, **2:**207
    "An Outpost of Progress," **2:**192, 194
    "Up-river Book," **2:**194
Conrad, Peter, **2:**153–154
Conroy, Frank, **1:165**
    Body and Soul, **1:**166
    Stop-Time, **1:164–166,** 270
Conscientious objectors (COs)
    in Vietnam War, **3:**221–223, *222*
    in World War II, **2:**268–269, **3:**223, 227–229
Conscientious Objectors and the Second World War (Eller), **3:**227
Consciousness
    double, Obama (Barack) on, **1:**79
    in locked-in syndrome, **1:**6
    racial, Du Bois (W. E. B.) in advancement of, **1:**4
Consolation of Philosophy (Boethius), **2:**14
Constantine (Roman emperor), **1:**196
Constitution, Mexican, **3:**302
Constitutional amendments, U.S.
    Fifteenth, **1:**50, **2:**238
    Fourteenth, **1:**50
    Nineteenth, **1:**13
    Thirteenth, **1:**50

SUBJECT INDEX

Consumerism, rise of, before Great Depression, **3:**161
Containment policy, U.S., **3:**205
Conteh-Morgan, John D., **1:**129, 130
Contemporary Irish Traditional Narrative (Harvey), **3:**315
Contemporary Jewish Record (magazine), **1:**333
Contemporary Literary Criticism (journal), **1:**159
Contemporary Literature (journal), **1:**47, 48, 49
Contemporary Sociology (journal), **3:**303
Contentious Lives (Auyero), **3:**268
Contested Territories (Beatty-Medina and Rinehart), **3:**326
Continental Congress, **2:**69
Controlled Substances Act of 1970 (U.S.), **2:**294
Conversation in Religion & Theology (journal), **2:**195
Conversations with Myself (Mandela), **1:**27–28
Cony, Daniel, **2:**331, 332
Cook, E. T., **1:**265
Cook, Haruko Taya, *Japan at War*, **3:**215–217
Cook, Theodore F., *Japan at War*, **3:**215–217
Cooper, Ilene, **1:**162
Cooper, James Fenimore, *Last of the Mohicans*, **1:**56
Cooper, Laura, **3:**155
Coox, Alvin, **3:**216
Copenhagen (Frayn), **3:**239
Corcoran, Patrick, **1:**62
Corngold, Stanley, **2:**122
Corn King and the Spring Queen, The (Mitchison), **2:**237
Cornwell, Jocelyn, *Hard-Earned Lives*, **3:**170
Corr, Edwin G., **3:**205, 206
Correspondence. *See* Letter(s)
Corrigan, Felicitas, **2:**248
Corrigan, Philip, **3:**54
Corsini, Lorenzo, **1:**185
Cortizas, Nancy, **3:**122
Cory, Arthur M., **2:**141
COs. *See* Conscientious objectors

Costa, Richard, **1:**253
Costantino, Manuela, **1:**157
Cotnoir, Daniel, **3:**232
Cottage Dialogues among the Irish Peasantry (Leadbeater), **2:**157
Cottage Diaries, The (Leadbeater), **2:**157
Cottegnies, Line, **1:**231
Cottrell, Robert, **3:**229
Coulson, Robert, *Family Mediation*, **3:**154
Counterinsurgency, in Salvadoran Civil War, **3:**205, 206
Counter-Reformation, **1:**211
Count of Monte Christo, The (Dumas), **1:**6
Country of My Skull (Krog), **3:242–244**
Country Parson, A (Woodforde), **2:287–289**
Country Voices (Masumoto), **3:**224
Couple of Blaguards, A (McCourt), **1:**119
Courlander, Harold, *The African*, **1:**262
Courtney, Roger, *Palestinian Policeman*, **2:**104
Courts. *See* Judicial system; Supreme Court
Couser, G. Thomas, **2:**251
Coustillas, Pierre, **2:**320, 321
Coverdale, Linda, **3:**259
Coward, Noël, *The Noël Coward Diaries*, **2:**152
Cox, James M., **1:**246, 247
Cox, Virginia, **2:**161
CPS. *See* Civilian Public Service
Crabbe, George, **2:**158
Craig, Ann L.
  The First Agraristas, **3:**167, **302–304**
  Popular Movements and Political Change in Mexico, **3:**302
  Transforming State-Society Relations in Mexico, **3:**302
Crane, Hart, **2:**152
Crane, Stephen, **2:**240
Crangle, Sara, **2:**325–326
Cranmer, Thomas, **2:**97, 98
Cranston, Edwin A., **2:**190

Crapanzano, Vincent, *Tuhami*, **3:**47
Crashing Thunder (Radin), **3:**318
Crawford, Julie, **2:**63
Crawford, Miki Ward, *Japanese War Brides in America*, **3:127–130**
Creation stories
  Apache, **1:**302
  Kiowa, **1:**54, 55
Creswell, John, **1:**280–281
Crèvecoeur, Michel-Guillaume Saint-Jean de, *Letters from an American Farmer*, **2:213–216**
Crick, Francis, **3:**37
Crimean War (1853–1856), **1:**111–113
Criminal activity. *See* Hate crimes; War crimes
Crisis (journal), **1:**4
Crisp, Samuel, **2:**312–313
Critical Review (newspaper), **2:**206
Criticism. *See* Literary criticism
Criticism (journal), **1:**188, 260, **2:**8
Critique (journal), **1:**165, 166
Critofari, Rita, **1:**40
Croker, John, **2:**314
Cromwell, Oliver, **1:**315, **2:**26, 65, 72, 178, 256
Cross and a Star, A (Agosín), **1:75–77,** 99
Cross and the Pear Tree, The (Perera), **1:**99
Cross-cultural adoption, Kim (Elizabeth) on, **1:**102–104
Cross-cultural autobiographies
  The Abandoned Baobab (Bugul), **1:**61–64
  Chona (Chona and Underhill), **1:**69–71
  The Color of Water (McBride), **1:**72–74
  A Cross and a Star (Agosín), **1:**75–77
  The Dark Child (Laye), **1:**128–130
  Dreams from My Father (Obama), **1:**78–80
  Infidel (Hirsi Ali), **1:**207–209
  The Interesting Narrative of the Life of Olaudah Equiano (Equiano), **1:**81–83
  A Long Way from Home (McKay), **1:**84–86

Meatless Days (Suleri), **1:**87–89

Memoirs of an Arabian Princess from Zanzibar (Ruete), **1:**90–92

My Life Story (Amrouche), **1:**93–95

Prison Writings (Peltier), **1:**96–97

Rites: A Guatemalan Boyhood (Perera), **1:**99–101

Ten Thousand Sorrows (Kim), **1:**102–104

The Travels of Marco Polo (Polo), **1:**105–107

When I Was Puerto Rican (Santiago), **1:**108–110

The Woman Warrior (Kingston), **1:**173–175

The Wonderful Adventures of Mrs. Seacole (Seacole), **1:**111–113

The Worlds of a Maasai Warrior (Saitoti), **1:**114–116

Cross-cultural families. *See* Multicultural families

Cross-cultural identity. *See* Multicultural and multiracial identities

Crothers, A. Glenn, **3:**192

Crow, Liz, **1:**45

Crow Dog, Leonard, **1:**21

Crow Dog, Mary. *See* Brave Bird, Mary

Crowell, Sandra, *Up the Swiftwater*, **3:**93

Crowley, Stephen, **3:**341

Cruikshank, Julie, *Life Lived Like a Story*, **3:**320

Crusade in Europe (television show), **3:**234

Crusades, **1:**285–288, **2:**226

Cruse, Howard, *Stuck Rubber Baby*, **1:**139

Cruzeiro Internacional, O (magazine), **1:**222

Cry, the Beloved Country (Paton), **1:**27

Cuba
  immigration to U.S. from, **1:**296–298
  Medina (Pablo) on life in, **1:**296–297
  Motorcycle Diaries (Guevara) in, **2:**220
  Revolution in (*See* Cuban Revolution)
  runaway slaves in, oral histories of, **3:**7–9
  War of Independence in, **3:**7

Cuban American(s)
  autobiographical tradition of, **1:**296–297
  Medina (Pablo) on life as, **1:**296–298

Cuban identity, **1:**296–297

Cuban Revolution, **1:**296
  Chapelle's (Dickey) reporting on, **2:**280
  end of, **2:**222
  Guevara (Ernesto "Che") in, **2:**220, 221, 222

Cuban War of Independence (1895–1898), **3:**7

Cubilié, Anne, **3:**35

Cugoana, Ottobah, *Thoughts and Sentiments on the Evil and Wicked Traffic of the Slavery and Commerce of the Human Species*, **1:**81

Culman, Ernest, **3:**15

Cultural identity. *See also* Multicultural and multiracial identities
  of Korean American adoptees, **1:**102–103

Cultural Revolution (1966–1976)
  Cheng Yu-hsiu on, **1:**153
  Confucianism's rebirth after, **3:**124
  Jiang (Ji-li) on, **1:**161–162
  Kong Demao in, **3:**124–125
  Min (Anchee) on, **1:**158–160
  oral histories of, **3:**287–289, 299–300
  policies of, **3:**287, 299
  start of, **3:**287

Cultural studies, rise of, **1:**15

Cultural transmission, by Native Americans, **3:**107–109, 325–326

Culture. *See* Popular culture; *specific cultures*

Cumming, L. M., **1:**316

Cunningham, Valentine, **3:**59–60

Cuppy, Will, **2:**193–194

Curiosities of Literature (D'Israeli), **2:**177

Curious Journey (film), **3:**27, 28

Curious Journey (Griffith and O'Grady). *See Ireland's Unfinished Revolution* (Griffith and O'Grady)

Curnutt, Kirk, **1:**333

Curriculum Vitae (Klemperer), **2:**304, 305

Currie, Ruth Douglas, **2:**252

Curtin, Philip D., *Africa Remembered*, **3:**141

Curtis, Anthony, **2:**185

Custer, George, **3:**110

Custer Died for Our Sins (Deloria), **1:**54

Custis, Lemuel R., **3:**250

Cvetkovich, Ann, **1:**141

Cyprès, Jean-Philippe, *Women of Coal*, **3:**337

Czechoslovakia
  Kafka (Franz) on life in, **2:**120–122
  Prague Spring in, **3:**33

D

Daedalus (journal), **2:**122

Dahlgren, Dorothy, *In All the West No Place Like This*, **3:**93

Daily Arkansas Gazette (newspaper), **1:**147

Daily Show, The (television show), **1:**312

Daisy Miller (James), **1:**133, **2:**114

Daklugie, Asa, **1:**302

Dakota Territory, homesteaders in, **2:**163–164

Dalai Lama, **1:**96

Dale, Gareth, **3:**247

Dale, Stephen, **2:**231

Dalfiume, Richard M., *Desegregation of the U.S. Armed Forces*, **3:**248

Dallaire, Roméo, *Shake Hands with the Devil*, **3:**258

Dallaway, James, **2:**36

Dalrymple, William, **2:**231

Daly, Jane, **2:**229

Daly, Leo, **2:**159

Daly, Mary, *Gyn/Ecology*, **2:**3, 5

Dana, Richard Henry, *Two Years before the Mast*, **1:**234

Dancing, by teachers, ban on, **3:**78
Daniel, Samuel, **2:**62, 63, 256
Daniels, Roger, **3:**225–226
Danish autobiographical writing, by Kierkegaard (Søren), **2:**166–169
Danish national identity, **2:**166
Dantas, Audálio, **2:**6, 7
Dardis, Kimiko, **3:**128
Daring Hearts (Brighton Ourstory), **3:**70–72
Dark Child, The (Laye), **1:**128–131
Darkness Visible (Styron), **1:**204–206
Darkwater (Du Bois), **1:**3
Darley, Gillian, **2:**67
Darry, Walt, **3:**95
Darwaza, Muhammad 'Izzat, **2:**104
Darwin, Charles, **1:**66
   The Autobiography of Charles Darwin, **1:**65–68
   The Descent of Man, **1:**65
   Journal and Remarks 1832–1835, **1:**65
   London and the Life (Gissing) on, **2:**321
   On the Origin of Species, **1:**65
Darwin, Emma, **1:**65
Darwish, Mahmoud, **1:**256
   In the Presence of Absence, **1:**255–257
   Journal of an Ordinary Grief, **1:**255
   Letters Underway (Ghazzawi) on, **2:**50
   Memory for Forgetfulness, **1:**255, 257, **2:**50
Das, Kamala, *My Life,* **1:**87
Dash, G. A., *Oral History Project,* **3:**153
Dashkova, Ekaterina, *Memoirs of the Princess Daschkaw,* **2:**306
Daudet, Edmond, **2:**83
Daugherty, Rae, **3:**108
Daughter of Isis, A (Saadawi), **1:**226
Daughters of the Shtetl (Glenn), **3:**305
David, Deidre, **2:**336
Davidson, Gordon W., **2:**92
Davidson, Thomas, **2:**16
Davies, Andrew, **3:**311, 313
Davies, Catherine, **3:**73, 75
Davies, David J., **3:**289

Davin, Delia, **3:**299
Davis, Angela, *Modern Motherhood,* **3:**145
Davis, Ann Marie, **3:**128–129
Davis, Jefferson, **2:**250, *251*
Davis, Margaret H., **1:**327
Davis, Philip, **3:**318, 320
Davis, Rocío G., **1:**172, 311
Davis, Rodney O., *Herndon's Informants,* **3:**264
Davis, Susan Schaefer, **3:**48
Davis, Thulani, **1:**250
Davis, Varina, **2:**250, 251
Davison, Peter, **2:**117, 118–119
Dawes Act of 1887 (U.S.), **3:**107
Dawkins, Richard, **1:**209
Dawn (Wiesel), **1:**319
Dawson, Sarah Morgan, **2:**244, 246
Day (Wiesel), **1:**319
Day, John, *The Acts and Monuments,* **2:**97
Dayal, Samir, **1:**88–89
Daybooks, **2:**333
Days of Decision (Gioglio), **3:**221
Deacon, Florence, **3:**309
Deaf-blindness, **1:**43–46
Dean, Bradley P., **1:**235
Death
   in *The Congo Diary* (Conrad), **2:**193
   in *In the Presence of Absence* (Darwish), **1:**255–257
Death of Luigi Trastulli and Other Stories, The (Portelli), **3:**96, **157–160**
Death of Synge, The (Yeats), **2:**126, 127
"Death of the Author, The" (Barthes), **1:**267, 269
Death of the Heart, The (Bowen), **2:**133
Death penalty. *See* Execution
Death threats
   against Hirsi Ali (Ayaan), **1:**207
   against Rushdie (Salman), **1:**155
De Beer, Esmond S., **2:**65, 66
DeBlasio, Donna M., **3:**97
Decameron (Boccaccio), **1:**229
Declaration of Sentiments, The, **1:**12
Decolonising the Mind (Ngũgĩ), **2:**13

De Costa, Denise, **2:**24
Deering, Dorothy, **3:**345
Deffand, La Marquise du, **2:**268
Defoe, Daniel, **1:**92
   Journal of the Plague Year, **2:**174
   Robinson Crusoe, **3:**183
De Forest, William, *Miss Ravenel's Conversion,* **2:**240
Degen, Bill, **3:**94
Degler, Carl N., **2:**333
De Interpretatione (Demetrius), **2:**94
De Jesus, Carolina Maria, *Child of the Dark,* **2:**6–8, **3:**164, 322
De Klerk, Frederik Willem, **1:**27
Delaney, Lucy, *From the Darkness Cometh the Light,* **2:**250
Delaney, William, **2:**278, 279
Delaware Indians, oral histories of, **3:**107–109
Delaware Tribe in a Cherokee Nation (Obermeyer), **3:**326
Delbo, Charlotte, *Auschwitz and After,* **3:**34
Deleuze, Gilles, **2:**122
Del Giudice, Luisa, **3:**267
Deliverance (film), **3:**68
Deliverance (silent film), **1:**44
Dell'antichissima sapienza italica (Vico), **1:**183
Deloria, Vine, Jr., **3:**111
   Custer Died for Our Sins, **1:**54
Delta Airlines, **3:**154
Demetrius, *De Interpretatione,* **2:**94
Democracy, Du Bois (W. E. B.) on, **1:**4, 5
Democratic National Convention of 2004, **1:**78
Denetdale, Jennifer Nez, **3:**10, 12, 291
Deng Xiaoping, **3:**299
Denial
   as final phase of genocide, **3:**42
   of HIV-AIDS link, **3:**274
   of Holocaust, **3:**50
De Niro, Robert, **1:**47, 49
Denmark
   Kierkegaard (Søren) in, **2:**166–169
   national identity of, **2:**166
Denton, Kirk A., **2:**172

Depression (economic). *See* Great Depression
Depression (mood)
    Lincoln's (Abraham) struggle with, **3:**263
    rise of memoirs of, **1:**204–205
    Styron (William) on battle with, **1:**204–205
De Profundis (Wilde), **2:**9–11
De Quincey, Thomas, **2:**67, 140
Dernière impression, La (Haddad), **2:**262
Derounian-Stodola, Kathryn Zabelle, **1:**326, 327
Derrida, Jacques, **2:**167
Desai, Anita, *In Custody,* **1:**87
Descartes, René, *Discourse on the Method,* **1:**183, 184
Descent of Man, The (Darwin), **1:**65
Description of the New World, A (Cavendish), **1:**231
Desegregation of the U.S. Armed Forces (Dalfiume), **3:**248
Desert Exile (Uchida), **1:**309
Desert Solitaire (Abbey), **1:**234
Desert Storm, Operation. *See* Gulf War
Desmond, Adrian, **1:**67
Des Pres, Terrence, **2:**24
Destruction and Reconstruction (Taylor), **2:**250
Detained (Ngũgĩ), **1:**215, **2:**12–15
De Tilène au Plateau (Diallo), **1:**64
Detroit (Michigan)
    civil rights movement in, oral histories of, **3:**99–101
    migration of African Americans to, **3:**99
    race riots in, **3:**99, 100, *100,* 101
Detroit Lives (Mast), **3:**99
Detroit Summer, **3:**101
Detroit Urban League, **3:**99, 101
Detroit WestSiders, **3:**99
Deutschmann, David, **2:**220
De Valera, Eamon, **3:**27
De Veaux, Alexis, **2:**5
Dever, Carolyn, **1:**67
Devil on the Cross (Ngũgĩ), **2:**12, 13
Devil That Danced on the Water, The (Forna), **1:**312

DeVore, Irven, **3:**37
DeVoto, Bernard, **1:**148
DeWitt, John L., **3:**224
Dial (magazine), **1:**52, 233, **2:**92
Diallo, Bakary, *Force-Bonté,* **1:**61
Diallo, Nafissatou, *De Tilène au Plateau,* **1:**64
Dialogue and Armed Conflict (Roett and Smyth), **3:**205
Dialogues (Augustine), **1:**186
Dialogues (Rousseau), **1:**200
Diamonds, of Sierra Leone, **1:**312
Diaoyu/Senkaku (islands), **1:**340
Diaries. *See also specific works and writers*
    of American Civil War, **2:**244, 271
    British, in Mass Observation Project, **2:**235, 237
    D'Israeli (Isaac) on study of, **2:**177–179
    fictional, **2:**174
    Lejeune (Philippe) on study of, **2:**174–176
    posthumous publication of, **2:**174
    privacy as defining characteristic of, **2:**174
    rise in popularity of, **2:**65, 66, 120, 174, 177
    as source for biographies, **2:**177, 178
Diaries, 1915–1918 (Sassoon), **2:**247–249
Diaries, 1931–1949 (Orwell), **2:**117–119
Diaries of Beatrice Webb (Webb), **2:**16–18
Diaries of Franz Kafka, The (Kafka), **2:**120–122
Diaries of Lady Anne Clifford, The (Clifford), **2:**62–64
Diário da Noite (newspaper), **2:**6
Diary, Reminiscences and Correspondence of Henry Crabb Robinson (Robinson), **2:**75–77
Diary and Letters of Madame D'Arblay (Burney), **2:**312, 314
Diary from Dixie, A (Chesnut), **2:**250–252

Diary of a Madman (Gogol), **2:**174
Diary of Anaïs Nin, The (Nin), **2:**123–125
Diary of Anne Frank, The (Frank), **2:**253–255, *254*
    An Interrupted Life (Hillesum) vs., **2:**22
    Night (Wiesel) vs., **1:**320
    Red Scarf Girl (Jiang) inspired by, **1:**161
    Thura's Diary (Al-Windawi) vs., **2:**275, 277
    A Woman in Berlin (anonymous) vs., **2:**281
    A Woman Soldier's Own Story (Xie) vs., **1:**340
    Zlata's Diary (Filipovic) vs., **2:**338, 339, 340
Diary of a Nobody, The (Grossmith and Grossmith), **2:**174
Diary of John Evelyn, The (Evelyn), **2:**65–68, 72, 328
Diary of John Quincy Adams, The (Adams), **2:**69–71
Diary of Khalil al-Sakakini, The (Sakakini), **2:**104, 106
Diary of Lady Murasaki, The (Murasaki), **2:**59, 290–293
Diary of Robert Hooke, The (Hooke), **2:**72
Diary of Samuel Pepys, The (Pepys), **2:**72–74
    The Diary of John Evelyn (Evelyn) vs., **2:**65, 66, 72
    posthumous publication of, **2:**174, 328
    Scott (Walter) influenced by, **2:**309
Diary of Sir Henry Slingsby, The (Slingsby), **2:**256–258
Diary of Virginia Woolf, The (Woolf), **2:**133, 163, 180–182
Diary without Dates, A (Bagnold), **1:**329, **2:**259–261
Diary with Reminiscences of the War and Refugee Life in the Shenandoah Valley, A (McDonald), **2:**271
Dias, Bartolomeu, **2:**198, 199, 200
Díaz, Porfirio, **3:**167, 302, 303
Dib, Mohammed, **2:**262
DiCaprio, Leonardo, **1:**47, 49

SUBJECT INDEX

Dickens, Charles
   American Notes, **1:**43, 146, **2:**223
   Crèvecoeur (Michel-Guillaume Saint-Jean de) and, **2:**214
   The Diaries of Franz Kafka (Kafka) on, **2:**120
   Emerson (Ralph Waldo) and, **2:**140
   Goethe's (Johann Wolfgang von) influence on, **1:**276
   Journal of Katherine Mansfield (Mansfield) on, **2:**133
   London and the Life (Gissing) on, **2:**321
Dickey, Roland, **1:**56
Dickinson, Emily, **2:**238
Dictators, Latin American right-wing, rise of, **3:**185
Dictee (Cha), **1:**102
Didion, Joan, *Slouching towards Bethlehem,* **1:**88
Diet, of Gandhi (Mohandas), **1:**243. *See also* Food
Dieterich-Ward, Allen, **3:**96, 98
Dietrich, Marlene, **3:**295
Different Voices (Rittner and Roth), **3:**34
Dillard, Annie, **1:280**
   An American Childhood, **1:**279
   Living by Fiction, **1:**279
   Pilgrim at Tinker Creek, **1:**279
   Teaching a Stone to Talk, **1:**279
   The Writing Life, **1:**168, **279–281**
Dillard, Ernest, **3:**99–100
Diné. *See* Navajo
Di Porcía, Gian Artico, **1:**183, 184
Direct action, in civil rights movement, **2:**32–34
Dirrane, Bridget, **3:**316
Dirty Realism movement, **1:**48
Disabilities, people with
   Bauby (Jean-Dominique) on experience of, **1:**6–8
   education of, **1:**43, 44–45
   Keller (Helen) on experience of, **1:**43–46
   social construction of "able body" and, **1:**8
Disability & Society (journal), **1:**45
Disability literature, *The Diving Bell and the Butterfly* (Bauby) as, **1:**8
Disability studies, **1:**8, 41
Disability Studies Quarterly, **1:**41
"Disabled" (Owen), **1:**8
Disappearances, mass
   in Chile, **1:**75
   in Guatemala, **1:**99
Discourse on the Method (Descartes), **1:**183, 184
Discovery of India, The (Nehru), **1:**290, 291
Disease. *See specific diseases*
Dispatches (Herr), **1:**259, **3:**209
D'Israeli, Benjamin, **2:**177, 179
D'Israeli, Isaac
   Curiosities of Literature, **2:**177
   Miscellanies, **2:**177
   "Some Observations on Diaries, Self-Biography, and Self-Characters," **2:177–179**
Dissent (Bradley), **1:**80
DiStasi, Lawrence, *Una Storia Segreta,* **3:**224
Diurnal texts, **2:**163, 164
Divers Voyages Touching the Discoverie of America (Hakluyt), **2:**229
Divine Songs and Meditacions (Collins), **1:**229
Divine visions, of Teresa of Ávila, **1:**211, 212
Divine will, Usāmah ibn Munqidh on, **1:**285, 286
Diving Bell and the Butterfly, The (Bauby), **1:6–8**
Diving Bell and the Butterfly, The (film), **1:**6, 7
Division Street (Terkel), **3:**161, 299, 343
Divorce, in Heian period of Japan, **2:**299
Djebar, Assia, **1:**93
   Women of Algiers in Their Apartment, **1:**207
Do, Anh, *The Happiest Refugee,* **1:**337
Dobe region (Africa), oral histories of !Kung people of, **3:**37–38
Documentary films. *See also specific films*
   on Ballard (Martha), **2:**331
   on Delaware Indians, **3:**325
   on Holocaust, **3:**50, 52
   on Irish independence movement, **3:**27, 28
   on IWW, **3:**328
   on Navajo-Hopi land dispute, **3:**10, 11, 12
   on Peltier (Leonard), **1:**96
   on Saitoti (Tepilit Ole), **1:**114
   on Ukrainian coal miners, **3:**340
   on World War II, **3:**234
Documentary prose, in *Voices from Chernobyl* (Alexievich), **3:**282, 285
Dodd, Thomas J., **3:**294
Dodd, William E., **2:**251
Does My Head Look Big in This? (Abdel-Fattah), **1:**41–42
Dogs, in *A Country Parson* (Woodforde), **2:**288, 289
Dogs Bark (Conrad), **1:**166
Doi, Kochi, **2:**190, 290, 292
Doing Oral History (Ritchie), **3:**186, 294, 345
Doing Time for Peace (Riegle), **3:**229
Domesticity
   Stanton (Elizabeth Cady) on, **1:**13, 14
   Wordsworth (Dorothy) on, **2:**300, 301
Domestic Manners of the Americans (Trollope), **2:**223
Domestic violence
   in Islam, Hirsi Ali (Ayaan) on, **1:**207–209
   Malcolm X on experience of, **1:**187
   Wolff (Tobias) on experience of, **1:**47–49
Domingo, Jesús, **3:**169
Domingues, Francisco, **2:**200
Donald, David Herbert, **3:**263
Doña María's Story (James), **3:73–76**
Donbass region (Ukraine), oral histories of miners in, **3:**340–342
Donne, John, **2:**62
Donovan, Frances R., *The Schoolma'am,* **3:**77
Doody, Margret Anne, **2:**314

Doolittle, Hilda. *See* H.D.
Door, The (film), **3:**284
Dore, Elizabeth, **3:**75
Dorfman, Ariel, *Heading South, Looking North,* **1:**75
Doris Duke Indian Oral History Project, **3:**290
Doss, Helen, *The Family Nobody Wanted,* **1:**102
Dostoyevsky, Fyodor, **2:**22, 120, 133, 183, 184
Double consciousness, Obama (Barack) on, **1:**79
Double Jeopardy (Baumel), **3:**35
Dougherty, Jack, **3:**22
Dougherty, Jane Elizabeth, **1:**263
Douglas, Alfred, **2:**9–10
Douglas, David, **2:**309, 310
Douglass, Frederick, **1:**34. *See also Narrative of the Life of Frederick Douglass* (Douglass)
   Grimké (Charlotte Forten) influenced by, **2:**29
   Life and Times of Frederick Douglass, **1:**34
   My Bondage and My Freedom, **1:**34
   "Self-Made Men," **1:**180
   "What, to the Slave, Is the Fourth of July?," **1:**79
Dove Cottage (Grasmere), **2:**300, *301*
Down Came the Rain (Shields), **1:**204
Downing, Taylor, **3:**235, 236
Down These Mean Streets (Thomas), **1:**109
Draft, U.S. military, **3:**221–223
Drake, Barbara, **2:**172
Drake, Betsy, **2:**102
Dreaming of Sheep in Navajo Country (Weisiger), **3:**10
Dream of Africa, A (Laye), **1:**129
Dreams from My Father (Obama), **1:78–80**
Dreams of Trespass (Mernissi), **1:**226, 227
Dred Scott decision, **2:**38
Dreiser, Theodore, **1:**273, **2:**136
   Harlan Miners Speak, **3:**96
Drew, Bettina, **2:**338, 339, 340
Drinnon, Richard, **3:**320

Drugs
   adolescent use of, *Go Ask Alice* (anonymous) on, **2:**294–296
   in culture of 1960s, **2:**294
   U.S. war on, **2:**294
   Williams's (Tennessee) struggle with addiction to, **2:**152
Drummond, Henry, **1:**150
Dryden, John, **1:**90
D'Souza, Dinesh, **3:**166
Dube, John, **2:**241
Duberman, Martin, **1:**4
Dublin (Ireland)
   Abbey Theatre of, **2:**126, 128
   oral histories of life in, **3:**315, 317
Dublin Pub Life and Lore (Kearns), **3:**315, 317
Dublin Voices (Kearns), **3:**315
Du Bois, W. E. B., **1:**4
   The Autobiography of W. E. B. Du Bois, **1:3–5**, 18
   on *Black Boy* (Wright), **1:**123
   Black Flame trilogy, **1:**5
   Darkwater, **1:**3
   Dusk of Dawn, **1:**3, 4
   on *Home to Harlem* (McKay), **1:**84
   The Souls of Black Folk, **1:**4, 51
   The Study of the Negro Problem, **1:**50
   on *Up from Slavery* (Washington), **1:**51, 52
   and Washington (Booker T.), debate between, **1:**186
Dudley, David L., **1:**4
Duesberg, Peter, **3:**274
Duffey, Carolyn, **1:**93, 94
Dumas, Alexandre, *The Count of Monte Christo,* **1:**6
Dumm, Gary, *Students for a Democratic Society,* **3:**330
Dunbar, Paul Laurence, "Sympathy," **1:**50
Duncan, Isadora, **1:**85
Duncan, Patti, **1:**159
Duncan, Robert, **2:**123
Dundas, Henry, **2:**217–219
Dunham, Ann, **1:**78
Dunham, Janice, **1:**97

Dunmore, Helen, **1:**195
Dunn, Oliver, **2:**203
Dunnaway, Jen, **3:**201
Dunton, John, **2:**195
Duong Thu Huong, *Paradise of the Blind,* **1:**335
Duong Van Minh, **3:**280
Durham University Journal, **2:**185
Durrell, Lawrence, **2:**123
Duryea, Lyman C., **3:**206
Dusk of Dawn (Du Bois), **1:**3, 4
Dustan, Hannah, **1:**326, 328
Duston, Troy, **3:**20
Dust Tracks on a Road (Hurston), **1:9–11**, 18, 122
Dutch autobiographical writing
   by Hillesum (Etty), **2:**22–24
   by Hirsi Ali (Ayaan), **1:**207–209
Dyer, Geoff, **2:**81
Dyer, Reginald, **1:**289
Dyk, Ruth, **3:**319
Dyk, Walter, *Left Handed, Son of Old Man Hat,* **3:318–321**
Dykes to Watch Out For (Bechdel), **1:**139, 141
Dylan, Bob, **3:**159
Dziak, John, *Chekisty,* **3:**245

E

Eaglestone, Robert, **1:**313–314
Eakin, Paul John, **1:**188, 246
Early American Literature (journal), **1:**327
Earthquakes
   in China, **3:**301
   in Iran, **3:**220
East, Rupert, *Akiga's Story,* **3:**141
East Anglia (England), oral histories of village life in, **3:**59–61, *60*
Eastern California Museum (ECM), **3:**102
Easter Uprising of 1916 (Ireland), **3:**27, *28,* 315
East Germany, oral histories of Stasi in, **3:**245–247
East India Company, **2:**229–231
East of the Mediterranean (Munif), **2:**50

Easton, Celia A., **2**:289
East West Exchange, **1**:163
Eberstadt, Fernanda, **1**:156–157
Ecce Homo (Nietzsche), **1**:183
Echeverría, Luis, **3**:32
Eclectic Review (journal), **2**:178–179
ECM. *See* Eastern California Museum
Eco-criticism, **1**:279
Economic disparity
    industrialization in rise of, **2**:300
    among Native Americans, **3**:290
    in oral histories, **3**:190
Economic opportunity, for blacks in Reconstruction era, **1**:50
Economic Opportunity Act of 1964 (U.S.), **3**:254, *255*
Economic problems. *See* Finances, personal
Economic racism, **1**:4
Economics, of cancer, **2**:3–4, 5
Economist, The (weekly), **1**:126, **3**:300–301
Economy
    Britain, working class in, **3**:53
    Chinese, as socialist market, **1**:158
    German, after World War I, **1**:30, **3**:234
    Mexican, indigenous people in, **3**:168
Economy, U.S. *See also* Great Depression
    prosperity in, before Great Depression, **3**:161
    slavery in, **1**:33
    women in post-revolutionary, **2**:331–332
    after World War II, **3**:343
Écriture artiste, **2**:81, 83
Écriture féminine, **1**:250, **2**:124
Edel, Leon, **2**:113, 115
Edele, Mark, **3**:332
Edelstein, Tilden, **2**:239, 240
Edgeworth, Maria, **2**:157
Edinburgh Review (journal), **2**:35, 36, 73, 314
Editor & Publisher (magazine), **2**:279

Education
    Arab, poetry in, **1**:287
    in Britain, **2**:136, 320, **3**:311–313
    of children with disabilities, **1**:43, 44–45
    French, in Algeria, **1**:93, 94, **2**:262–263
    Islamic, in Egypt, **1**:135
    self-, Franklin (Benjamin) on, **1**:179, 180
    of women (*See* Education, of women)
Education, in U.S.
    Adams's (Henry) critique of, **1**:132–134
    affirmative action in, **1**:15
    of African Americans, at white colleges, **3**:20–22
    of African Americans, in Reconstruction, **1**:51
    anarchists' critique of, **3**:5
    bilingual, **1**:15–17
    at experimental boarding schools, **1**:164
    of Native Americans, at boarding schools, **3**:109, 318
    oral histories of teachers in, **3**:77–79
    racial quotas in, **3**:20
    Rodriguez (Richard) on, **1**:15–16
    school desegregation in, **1**:122, 249, **3**:44
    secondary, as compulsory, **3**:343
    of slaves, in preparation for emancipation, **2**:29–31, *30*
Education, of women
    in eighteenth-century Europe, **2**:35–36
    in eighteenth-century U.S., **2**:316–318
    in fifteenth-century Europe, **2**:160–161
    in Morocco, **3**:49
Education Act of 1870 (Britain), **3**:311
Educational Studies (journal), **3**:78
Education of Henry Adams, The (Adams), **1**:15, **132–134**, 180
Edwardian Childhoods (Thompson), **3**:312

Edwardians, The (Thompson), **3**:176, 186, 311
Edwards, Beatrice, *Places of Origin*, **3**:205
Edwards, Jonathan, **2**:197
Edwards, Louise, **3**:148–149
Edwards, Matilda, **3**:263
Edwards, Reginald, **3**:201
Edward VI (king of England), *The Literary Remains of Edward VI*, **2**:97–100, *98*
Edward VII (king of Great Britain), **2**:210
Edward VIII (king of Great Britain), **2**:235
Egan, Susanna, **1**:248
Eggers, Dave, *Voice of Witness*, **3**:161
Eglington, Lord, **2**:329
Egocentrism, Soyinka (Wole) accused of, **1**:216
Egotism, Romantic, **2**:177, 179
Egypt
    autobiographical tradition of, **1**:136
    British colonial rule of, **1**:135
    Hussein (Taha) on life in, **1**:135–137
    independence of (1922), **1**:135
    Islamic education in, **1**:135
    Revolution of 1919 in, **1**:135
    Revolution of 1952 in, **1**:135
    Usāmah ibn Munqidh on history of, **1**:285
Egyptian Childhood, An (Hussein), **1**:135–138
Eickelcamp, Ute, **3**:334
Eighteen Poems (Thomas), **1**:125
Eighteenth-Century Studies (journal), **1**:327
8 mars (journal), **3**:47
Eighty Years and More, Reminiscences 1815–1897 (Stanton), **1**:12–14
Eikon Basilike (Charles I), **2**:256, 258
Einstein, Albert, **3**:239
Eire, Carlos, *Waiting for Snow in Havana*, **1**:296–297
Eire-Ireland (journal), **2**:308
Ejército Zapatista de Liberación Nacional (EZLN), **3**:304

Ejido (land collective), **3:**302–304
Elaine Massacre (1919), **1:**18
Elementary Education Act of 1870 (Britain), **2:**136, 320
Elena, Eduardo, **3:**75
El Fassi, Malika, **3:**48
Elfenbein, Andrew, **2:**144, 145
ELH (journal), **2:**64
Eli (Sachs), **2:**255
Eliach, Yaffa, **3:**34
  Holocaust Oral History Manual, **3:**35
Eliot, T. S., **2:**147, 180
Elizabeth Cady Stanton as Revealed in Her Letters, Diary and Reminiscences (Stanton and Stanton), **1:**13
Elizabeth I (queen of England), **2:**62, 72, 99
Elle (magazine), **1:**6
Eller, Cynthia, *Conscientious Objectors and the Second World War*, **3:**227
Ellipses, Bagnold's (Enid) use of, **2:**260
Ellis, Henry, **2:**226
Ellis, Russ, **3:**21, 22
Ellison, Ralph, **1:**122, 124
Ellman, Richard, **2:**10
Ellwood, Thomas, **2:**26
Elman, Richard, **1:**100
Elon, Amos, **2:**304
El Salvador, oral histories of civil war in, **3:**205–208, *206*
El Salvador at War (Manwaring and Prisk), **3:205–208**
El Salvador: Testament of Terror (Fish and Sganga), **3:**206
Eltis, David, **1:**263
Eluard, Paul, **2:**52
Éluard, Paul, **1:**222
Emancipation Act of 1834 (Britain), **1:**111
Emancipation Proclamation of 1863 (U.S.), **1:**50, **3:**261
Embedded journalism, **2:**278–280
Embedded: The Media at War in Iraq (Katovsky and Carlson), **3:**276
Embroideries (Satrapi), **1:**155
Emergence of a UAW Local, The (Friedlander), **3:**153
Emerson, Everett, **2:**214

Emerson, Gloria, **2:**278
Emerson, Ralph Waldo, **2:140**
  "The American Scholar," **1:**180
  Dillard (Annie) influenced by, **1:**279
  Hawthorne (Nathaniel) and, **2:**139, 223
  James's (Henry) friendship with, **2:**113
  Journals of Ralph Waldo Emerson, **2:139–142**
  "Nature," **2:**141
  Robinson's (Henry Crabb) friendship with, **2:**75
  "Self-Reliance," **1:**180
  Thoreau (Henry David) and, **1:**233, **2:**139, 140
Emigration. *See* Immigration
Emms, Stephen, **2:**154
Emotions
  of Christmas, Thomas (Dylan) on, **1:**125–126
  in *The Diary of John Quincy Adams* (Adams), **2:**70
  in "Letter to Maria Clemm" (Poe), **2:**41–43
  in Stoicism, **1:**218
Empathy, in feminist oral history, **3:**190
Enahoro, Peter, **1:**215–216
Encomienda system, **2:**202, **3:**302
En 18 (Goncourt and Goncourt), **2:**82
Enemies among Us (Schmitz), **3:**224
"Enemy aliens," U.S. treatment of, **3:**224
Enfance (Sarraute), **1:**268
Enfant Noir, L' (Laye). *See Dark Child, The* (Laye)
Engel, Jeff, **3:**232
Engelmann, Larry, *Tears before the Rain*, **3:**210, 265, **279–281**
Engendering the Chinese Revolution (Gilmartin), **3:**147
Enger, Leif, **1:**281
  Peace Like a River, **1:**281
England. *See also* Britain; English autobiographical writing; English oral histories
  agriculture in, **3:**59–61, 63–65

  Bloomsbury group in, **2:**133, 180, 268–269
  Catholicism in, decline of, **2:**97, 99, 226
  Christianity in, arrival of, **1:**189
  homosexuality in, **3:**70–72
  Irish conquest by, **3:**315
  Lessing's (Doris) move to, **1:**167
  Mansfield's (Katherine) travels in, **2:**133, 135
  Victorian (*See* Victorian era)
  women of (*See* English women)
Engle, Paul, **2:**121
English, Kathy, **3:**233
English autobiographical writing. *See also specific works and writers*
  by Bagnold (Enid), **2:**259–261
  by Barnard (Anne), **2:**217–219
  by Bennett (Arnold), **2:**136–138
  by Brittain (Vera), **1:**329–331
  by Burney (Fanny), **2:**312–314
  by Byron (George Gordon Noel), **2:**143–145
  by Cavendish (Margaret), **1:**229–231
  by Clifford (Anne), **2:**62–64
  by Conrad (Joseph), **2:**192–194
  by Darwin (Charles), **1:**65–67
  by D'Israeli (Isaac), **2:**177–179
  by Edward VI, **2:**97–99
  by Equiano (Olaudah), **1:**81–83
  by Evelyn (John), **2:**65–67
  by Fox (George), **2:**26–28
  by Gissing (George), **2:**320–322
  by Guylforde (Richarde), **2:**226–228
  by Halkett (Anne), **1:**315–317
  by Keats (John), **2:**146–148
  by Kemble (Fanny), **2:**335–337
  by Kempe (Margery), **1:**189–191
  by Last (Nella), **2:**265–267
  by Lessing (Doris), **1:**167–169
  by Maugham (W. Somerset), **2:**183–185
  by Montagu (Mary Wortley), **2:**35–37
  by Orwell (George), **2:**117–119
  by Partridge (Frances), **2:**268–270

SUBJECT INDEX

English autobiographical writing, *continued*
    by Pepys (Samuel), **2:**72–74
    by Robinson (Henry Crabb), **2:**75–77
    in Romantic era, surge of, **2:**16
    by Ruskin (John), **1:**264–266
    by Sassoon (Siegfried), **2:**247–249
    by Slingsby (Henry), **2:**256–258
    by Victoria, **2:**209–211
    in Victorian era, traits of, **1:**65, 67
    by Webb (Beatrice), **2:**16–18
    by Wells (H. G.), **1:**252–254
    by Wesley (John), **2:**195–197
    by Wilde (Oscar), **2:**9–11
    by Wollstonecraft (Mary), **2:**109–111
    by Woodforde (James), **2:**287–289
    by Woolf (Virginia), **2:**180–182
    by Wordsworth (Dorothy), **2:**300–302
English Civil War (1642–1651)
    Anglicanism in, **2:**26, 72, 256
    Cavendish (Margaret) on life during, **1:**229, 231
    Evelyn (John) on life during, **2:**65
    Halkett (Anne) on life during, **1:**315–317
    Osborne (Dorothy) on life during, **2:**324
    Slingsby (Henry) in, **2:**256–258
English Historical Review (journal), **2:**17–18, **3:**313
English in Africa (journal), **2:**218
English Journal, **1:**16, 42, 253, **2:**254, **3:**345
English language
    The Book of Margery Kempe (Kempe) as first autobiography in, **1:**189
    in Puerto Rico, **1:**109
    in U.S. education, **1:**15, 16, 17
English Literature in Transition (journal), **2:**10
English oral histories
    of gays and lesbians, **3:**70–72
    of village life, **3:**59–61, 63–65
    of working-class women, **3:**144–146
    of working-class youth, **3:**311–313, *312*

English Studies in Canada (journal), **1:**169
English women
    eighteenth-century, Montagu (Mary Wortley) on opportunities for, **2:**35
    land inheritance by, Clifford (Anne) on, **2:**62–63, 64
    medieval, Kempe (Margery) on, **1:**189–191
    seventeenth-century, Clifford (Anne) on, **2:**62–64
    Victorian, Webb (Beatrice) on, **2:**16–18
    in workforce, entry of, **2:266, 3:**145
    working-class, oral histories of, **3:**144–146
    in World War I, **1:**329–331, **2:**259
"Enigma of Arrival, The" (Paquet), **1:**112–113
Enlightenment
    Goethe (Johann Wolfgang von) in, **1:**276
    Jefferson (Thomas) in, **2:**316
    Scottish contributions to, **2:**328
    Wollstonecraft (Mary) in, **2:**109
Enneads (Plotinus), **1:**196
Enright, Pat, **3:**159
Entrepreneurs, Hispanic American, oral histories of, **3:**121–123
Entrepreneurs in Cultural Context (Greenfield), **3:**121
Environmental costs, of coal mining, **3:**66, 67, 86
Environmental factors, in cancer, **2:**3
Enzensberger, Hans Magnus, **2:**282
Enzer, Hyman A., **2:**254
Epictetus, **2:**96
Epileptic (David B.), **1:**155
Epistulae familiares (Cereta). See *Collected Letters of a Renaissance Feminist* (Cereta)
Eppes, Elizabeth, **2:**316
Epstein, Joseph, **2:**185
Equal Accommodations Act of 1938 (Michigan), **3:**99
Equality. See Gender equality; Racial equality; Social equality
Equal Pay Act of 1963 (U.S.), **3:**339

Equiano, Olaudah, **1:82**
    The Interesting Narrative of the Life of Olaudah Equiano, **1:34, 81–83,** 142, **3:**23
    Wheatley (Phillis) compared to, **1:**81, **2:**44
Erasmus, Desiderius, **1:**196, **2:**98
Erbaugh, Mary S., **3:**301
Erdoes, Erich, **1:**23
Erdoes, Richard, **1:**21, 23
Ergas, Yasmine, **2:**23, 24
Escalante Fontaneda, Hernando de, **1:**325
Esfandiary, Soraya, *The Autobiography of H.I.H. Soraya,* **3:**218
Eskew, Glenn T., **3:**249–250
Eskimo, The (Weyer), **3:**138
Espada, Martin, **1:**109
Espectador, El (newspaper), **3:**183, 184, 185
Espionage, by Maugham (W. Somerset), **2:**183
Essais (Montaigne), **2:**72
Essay on the Principles of Population (Malthus), **1:**65
Essay to Revive the Antient Education of Gentlewomen, An (Makin), **2:**35
Essex (England), oral histories of working-class youth in, **3:**311–313, *312*
Estrangement (Yeats), **2:126–128**
Ethnic discrimination. See Anti-Semitism; Racism
Ethnic identity, assimilation and
    oral histories of, **3:**305
    Rodriguez (Richard) on, **1:**15–17
    Santiago (Esmeralda) on, **1:**108
Ethnicity, in *Dust Tracks on a Road* (Hurston), **1:**11
Ethnographic autobiography, Native American, **1:**69–70
Ethnography
    in *Doña María's Story* (James), **3:**73
    in *Juan the Chamula* (Pozas), **3:**167, 168
    in *Nisa* (Shostak), **3:**37–38
Ethnology (journal), **1:**115
Etter-Lewis, Gwendolyn, **3:**191
    My Soul Is My Own, **3:**21

Europe. *See also specific countries*
   The Autobiography of Ben Franklin (Franklin) in, **1:**181
   Bugul's (Ken) experience as African in, **1:**61–62
   colonies of (*See* Colonialism)
   gender roles in, eighteenth-century, **2:**35–37
   gender roles in, Renaissance, **2:**160–162
   instability in interwar period of, **1:**329
   James's (Henry) time in, **2:**113, 114
   Letters from an American Farmer (Crèvecoeur) in, **2:**213, 214
   querelle de femmes in early modern, **2:**160
   Ruete's (Emily) experience as African in, **1:**90–92
   student movements of 1968 in, **3:**33
   travel narratives of, **1:**90–91
   women of, vs. Muslim women, **1:**90
European Journal of American Studies, **1:**78
European Parliament, **3:**292
European Romantic Review (journal), **2:**301
Eusebius, **2:**94
Eustics, Ida Elrod, **1:**10
Evans, Elizabeth, **2:**78, 79, 80
Evans, George Ewart, *Ask the Fellows Who Cut the Hay,* **3:**59, **63–65**
Evans, Larry, **3:**340, 342
Evelina (Burney), **2:**312–313, 314
Evelyn, John, **2:**66
   Boswell (James) compared to, **2:**328
   A Character of England, **2:**65
   The Diary of John Evelyn, **2:65–68,** 72, 328
   Fumifugium, **2:**65
   Pepys (Samuel) compared to, **2:**65, 66, 72
   Sculptura, **2:**65
   Woodforde (James) compared to, **2:**287
Evelyn, Mary, **1:**229

Everybody's Autobiography (Stein), **1:**332
Everything We Had (Santoli), **3:**199, 201, **209–211,** 231, 275, 279
Evil spirits, *The Diary of Lady Murasaki* (Murasaki) on, **2:**292
Evolution, **1:**65–67
Ewen, Elizabeth, *Immigrant Women in the Land of Dollars,* **3:**305
Examiner (newspaper), **2:**146
Execution
   of Alexandra Feodorovna, **2:**84
   of Charles I, **2:**26, 65, 72, 178, 256, 257, *257*
   of Nazi war criminals, **2:**56
   of Slingsby (Henry), **2:**256, 257
Executive Order 8802, U.S., **3:**44, 248
Executive Order 9066, U.S., **1:**299, 311, **3:**104, 195, 224
Executive Order 9981, U.S., **3:**199, 249
Executive Order 11246, U.S., **3:**339
Exile
   Cavendish (Margaret) in, **1:**229
   Cubans in, **1:**296–297
   Darwish (Mahmoud) in, **1:**255
   Iranians in, **3:**218
   Jews in, **1:**75
   Laye (Camara) in, **1:**130
   Luthuli (Albert) in, **1:**24
   Nabokov (Vladimir) in, **1:**270
   Soyinka (Wole) in, **1:**214
Exiled Memories (Medina), **1:296–298**
Existentialism, Wiesel (Elie) influenced by, **1:**318
Exodus to Shanghai (Hochstadt), **3:14–16**
Experiment in Autobiography, An (Wells), **1:252–254**
Exploration, global
   by Columbus (Christopher), **2:**201–203
   by Gama (Vasco da), **2:**198–200
   tradition of narratives of, **2:**198–199
Exploration, of U.S. West, by Carver (Jonathan), **2:**205–207. *See also* Westward expansion
Expression, freedom of
   in China, **3:**301

   in South Africa, **1:**29
   in Soviet Union, **3:**333
Extraordinary Work of Ordinary Writing, The (Sinor), **2:163–165**
Extrapolation (journal), **1:**253
Extremist Islam. *See* Fundamentalist Islam
Eyes on the Prize (television series), **2:**34, **3:**44, 45, 46
Eyewitnesses at Nuremberg (Gaskin), **3:**293
EZLN. *See* Ejército Zapatista de Liberación Nacional

F

Fabian Society, **2:**16, 172, 235
Face of War, The (Gellhorn), **2:**102
Faces in a Mirror (Pahlavi), **3:**218
Fachinger, Petra, **1:**17
Faderman, Lillian, *Gay L.A.,* **3:**83–84
Fadiman, Jeffrey A.
   The Moment of Conquest, **3:**141
   An Oral History of Tribal Warfare, **3:**141
   South Africa's "Black" Market, **3:**142
   When We Began, There Were Witchmen, **3:**141–143
Faery, Rebecca Blevins, **1:**325–326
Faith. *See* Religious faith
Falk, Stanley, **3:**216
Fallen Leaves (Nguyen), **1:**335
Falling Leaves (Yen Mah), **1:**159
Fall of the Shah (Hoveyda), **3:**218
Familiar letters, **2:**217
Family(ies)
   African American, Hansberry's (Lorraine) depiction of, **1:**273–275
   Chinese, Cheng Yu-hsiu on, **1:**153
   dysfunctional, of Bechdel (Alison), **1:**139–140
   English working-class, oral histories of, **3:**144–146
   instability in, Wolff (Tobias) on, **1:**47–49
   multicultural (*See* Multicultural families)

Family Letters of Thomas Jefferson, The (Jefferson), **2**:317
Family Mediation (Coulson), **3**:154
Family Nobody Wanted, The (Doss), **1**:102
Famine
   in China, **3**:287, 299, 300
   in Ireland, **3**:27, 315
   in Ukraine, **3**:19
Fano, Claudio, **3**:266
Fanon, Frantz
   Feraoun (Mouloud) compared to, **2**:262, 263, 264
   Gandhi (Mohandas) compared to, **1**:244
   The Wretched of the Earth, **1**:207, **2**:263
Fanshawe, Ann, *Memoirs,* **1**:229–230, 315, 316, 317
Fanshawe, Richard, **1**:317
Farabundo Marti National Liberation Front (FMLN), **3**:205
Faragher, John Mack, **2**:91, 92
Farah, Nurrudin, *Sweet and Sour Milk,* **1**:207
Färberböck, Max, **2**:281
Fard, W. D., **1**:188
Far Eastern Economic Review (journal), **3**:288
Farewell to Arms, A (Hemingway), **2**:259
Farewell to Manzanar (Houston and Houston), **1:299–301**, 309
Farmanfarmian, Abolbashar, **3**:220
Farmer, James, *Lay Bare the Heart,* **3**:44
Farmer-Kaiser, Mary, **2**:246
Farming. *See* Agriculture
Farming the Home Place (Matsumoto), **3**:80
Farral, Fred, **3**:177
Farrison, Edward, **1**:11
Fassin, Didier, *When Bodies Remember,* **3**:272
Fast Horse, Lizzy, **1**:22
Father's Law, A (Wright), **1**:124
"Father's Legacy, A" (Slingsby), **2**:256, 257, 258
Fatwa, against Rushdie (Salman), **1**:155

Faulkner, William, **1**:123, **2**:152
   Big Woods, **2**:215
Faunce, William, **1**:220
Fausel, Nettie, **3**:103
Faust, Drew Gilpin, **2**:246, 271, 272
Faustine, La (Goncourt), **2**:308
Favelas (shantytowns), **2**:6–8, *7*
Fay, Frank, **2**:128
Fay, Willie, **2**:128
Fayer, Steve, *Voices of Freedom,* **3:44–46**
FBI. *See* Federal Bureau of Investigation
FDR. *See* Revolutionary Democratic Front
February Revolution (1917), **2**:84
Fedele, Cassandra, **2**:160
Federal Bureau of Investigation (FBI), **1**:96–98, **3**:224
Federal Writers' Project (FWP), **3**:22, 86, 161, 173, 179
Feinesser, Bronislawa, **3**:35
Feinman, Ilene, **3**:270
Felber, Lynette, **2**:124
Fellman, Michael, **2**:39
Fellows, Jay, **1**:266
Female circumcision, Hirsi Ali (Ayaan) on, **1**:207
Female Peronist Party (Argentina), **3**:75
Feminine writing style, vs. masculine writing style, **1**:250
Feminism
   black perspective in, need for, **1**:249, 250, **2**:3, 5
   in China, rise of, **3**:147–149
   in field of history, **3**:176, 177
   in field of oral history, **3**:190–192
   first-wave, **3**:268
   global rise of, **3**:37
   and interest in women's autobiographies, **1**:37
   in peace movement, **3**:268
   second-wave, **3**:268
   of *Walden* (Thoreau), **1**:236
   during World War II, Mitchison (Naomi) on, **2**:235–236
Feminist autobiographical writing
   The Abandoned Baobab (Bugul) as, **1**:64
   Bone Black (hooks) as, **1**:249–250

   Child of the Dark (de Jesus) as, **2**:6
   Collected Letters of a Renaissance Feminist (Cereta) as, **2**:160–162
   The Collected Letters of Mary Wollstonecraft (Wollstonecraft) as, **2**:109–111
   Diaries of Beatrice Webb (Webb) as, **2**:16, 18
   The Diaries of Lady Anne Clifford (Clifford) as, **2**:64
   The Diary of Anaïs Nin (Nin) as, **2**:124
   The Journal of Marie Bashkirtseff (Bashkirtseff) as, **2**:306
   Let Me Speak! (Viezzer and Barrios de Chungara) as, **3**:322–323
   Letters and Journals of Fanny Burney (Burney) as, **2**:313–314
   Letters of a Woman Homesteader (Stewart) as, **2**:91
   The Letters of Lady Anne Barnard to Henry Dundas (Barnard) as, **2**:218
   "Letter to Her Daughter" (Montagu) as, **2**:35–37
   Meatless Days (Suleri) as, **1**:88–89
   A Mountainous Journey (Tuqan) as, **1**:225, 227
   tradition of, **1**:249
   Women in the Mines (Moore) as, **3**:337, 338
Feminist science fiction, **2**:237
Feminist Studies (journal), **1**:113
Femme d'Afrique (Kéita), **1**:64
Femmes et Politique (Akharbach and Rerhaye), **3**:47
Feng Jicai
   Let One Hundred Flowers Bloom, **1**:161
   Ten Years of Madness, **3**:287
   The Three-Inch Golden Lotus, **3**:289
   Voices from the Whirlwind, **3:287–289**, 301
Fenwomen (Chamberlain), **3**:61
Feraoun, Mouloud
   Journal, 1955–1962, **2:262–264**
   The Poor Man's Son, **2**:262, 263, 264
Ferdinand (king of Spain), **2**:201
Ferman, Claudia, **3**:166

Fermi, Enrico, **3:**239
Fernández-Armesto, Felipe, **2:**200
Fernández Barrios, Flor, *Blessed by Thunder,* **1:**296
Ferrari, Christine, **2:**30
Ferrie, Pauline, **3:**29
Ferris, Ina, **2:**179
Ferris, Jean Leon Gerome, **1:180**
Fest, Joachim, **2:**55, 56
Feudalism, in China, **3:**124
Fiction
    in collective novels, **3:**282, 285
    in *An Egyptian Childhood* (Hussein), **1:**136
    in *Go Ask Alice* (anonymous), **2:**294
    in novels of manners, **2:**312
    science, **1:**231, **2:**237
    in *Stop-Time* (Conroy), **1:**164, 165
    transcendental, **1:**281
    in *Truth and Fiction Relating to My Life* (Goethe), **1:**276
Fictional diaries, **2:**174
Fielding, Henry, **2:**328
Fields, James T., **2:**224
Fierce Attachments (Gornick), **1:**279
Fifteenth Amendment, **1:**50, **2:**238
Fifth Column, The (Hemingway), **2:**102
Fighting Words (Ball and Porter), **1:**97
Filipovic, Alica, **2:**338
Filipovic, Malik, **2:**338
Filipovic, Zlata, *Zlata's Diary,* **2:**275, **338–340,** 339
Filippelli, Ronald L., **3:**329
Film adaptations. *See also* Documentary films; *specific films*
    of *Akenfield* (Blythe), **3:**59
    of *Angela's Ashes* (McCourt), **1:**120, *120*
    of *The Autobiography of Malcolm X* (Malcolm X), **1:**186
    of *Country of My Skull* (Krog), **3:**242
    of *The Diary of Anne Frank* (Frank), **2:**253, 254
    of *The Diving Bell and the Butterfly* (Bauby), **1:**6, 7, *7*
    of *An Egyptian Childhood* (Hussein), **1:**137
    of *Farewell to Manzanar* (Houston and Houston), **1:**299
    of *Geronimo* (Geronimo and Barrett), **1:**304
    of *The Good Man of Nanking* (Rabe), **2:**19
    of *Letters of a Woman Homesteader* (Stewart), **2:**91
    of *Motorcycle Diaries* (Guevara), **2:**220
    of *National Velvet* (Bagnold), **2:**261
    of *Native Son* (Wright), **1:**124
    of *Persepolis* (Satrapi), **1:**156, 157
    of *The Story of My Life* (Keller), **1:44**
    of *This Boy's Life* (Wolff), **1:**47, 49
    of *When Heaven and Earth Changed Places* (Hayslip), **1:**335, 336
    of Williams's (Tennessee) plays, **2:**152
    of *A Woman in Berlin* (anonymous), **2:**281
Finances, personal
    Poe's (Edgar Allan) preoccupation with, **2:**41–42
    Scott's (Walter) trouble with, **2:**309, 310
Finley, C. Stephen, **1:**265–266
Finn, Margot, **2:**289, 322
Finnegans Wake (Joyce), **1:**185
Firestone, Jennifer, **2:**150
Firestone, Shulamith, **3:**37
Firm, The (Bruce), **3:245–247**
First Agraristas, The (Craig), **3:167, 302–304**
First Household under Heaven, The (Meng), **3:**125
First Nations people. *See* Native American(s)
First Person America (Banks), **3:**161
First South Carolina Volunteers, **2:**238–240
First They Killed My Father (Ung), **1:**306
First Well, The (Jabra), **1:**136
Fisch, Max Harold, **1:**183, 184, 185
Fish, Joe, *El Salvador,* **3:**206
Fishburne, Laurence, **3:**249
Fishel, John T., *Uncomfortable Wars Revisited,* **3:**207
Fisher, Michael H., **2:**231
Fish in the Water, A (Vargas Llosa), **1:**168
Fishkin, Shelley Fisher, **1:**173
Fiss, Harry, **3:**295
FitzGerald, Edward, **2:**196
Fitzgerald, F. Scott, **1:**140
    The Great Gatsby, **1:**47
Fitzgerald, Robert, **2:**129, 131
Fitzgerald, Sally, **2:**129, 131
Fitzpatrick, David, *Politics and Irish Life,* **3:**27
Five Days That Shocked the World (Best), **3:**235
Flanagan, John Richard, **1:**154
Flaubert, Gustave, **2:**120, 268
    Letters, **2:**268
    Sentimental Education, **1:**128
Flaxman, John, **2:**77
Fleche, Andre, **2:**240
Fleishmann, Ulrich, **3:**8
Flenley, Paul, **3:**341–342
FLN. *See* National Liberation Front
Floating nation, Puerto Rico as, **1:**108
Florida, U.S. annexation of, **2:**69
Florio, John, **2:**256
Flu pandemic of 1918, **1:**258
Flynn, Sarah, **3:**44
FMLN. *See* Farabundo Marti National Liberation Front
Folklore
    African American, **1:**9
    Chinese, **1:**173, 174
Folk music, **3:**96, 157, 159
Follain, John, **1:**40
Fones-Wolf, Ken, **3:**97–98
Food
    in *A Country Parson* (Woodforde), **2:**288, 289
    diet of Gandhi (Mohandas), **1:**243
    in *Meatless Days* (Suleri), **1:**87, 88–89
    in *When I Was Puerto Rican* (Santiago), **1:**109
Foot, John, **3:**267
Foot binding, **1:**338, **3:**147, 289

Forbes, Andrew, **3:**102
Forbes, Shannon, **1:**121
Forbidden Zone, The (Borden), **2:**259
Force-Bonté (Diallo), **1:**61
Forced labor
    in China, **1:**158
    in Soviet Union (*See* Gulag system)
Ford, Gerald, **1:**311, **3:**221
Ford, Henry
    The International Jew, **1:**30, 32
    My Life and Work, **1:**30
Forefathers' Eve (Mickiewicz), **2:**192
Foreign Affairs (journal), **2:**279, **3:**246, 332
Forgiveness, in Truth and Reconciliation Commission, **3:**243, 244
Forna, Aminatta, *The Devil That Danced on the Water,* **1:**312
Forrester, Michael, *Tsuchino,* **3:**127–128
Fors Clavigera (Ruskin), **1:**264
Forster, E. M., **2:**180, 235
Forten, James, **2:**29
Forten, Richard, **2:**29
For Their Own Good (Beier), **3:**144–145
For Those Who Come After (Krupat), **1:**71
Fortnightly Review (magazine), **2:**82–83
For Whom the Bell Tolls (Hemingway), **2:**101
Fosse Ardeatine massacre (1944), oral histories of, **3:**265–267, *266*
Fossey, Diane, **3:**37
Foster, David, **2:**10
Foster, David William, **1:**17
Foster, Ollie, **3:**100
Foundation Act of 1934 (Britain), **1:**149
Fourie, Pieter, *The Politics of AIDS Denialism,* **3:**272
Fourteen Points (Wilson), **3:**29
Fourteenth Amendment, **1:**50
Fox, George, *Journal of George Fox,* **2:**26–28, *27*
Fox, Margaret, **2:**26
Fox, Stephen
    America's Invisible Gulags, **3:**226
    UnCivil Liberties, **3:**226

The Unknown Internment, **3:**215, **224–226**
Foxe, John, **2:**97, 98–99
Foy, Harriet D., **1:**10
France. *See also* French autobiographical writing
    Algeria as colony of, **1:**93–94, **2:**262–264
    Bashkirtseff (Marie) as immigrant in, **2:**306–308
    cultural decadence of, **2:**306–307
    Franklin (Benjamin) as ambassador to, **1:**179, *180*
    in French and Indian War, **2:**205
    Guinea as colony of, **1:**128, 129, 130
    Indochina as colony of, **3:**279
    Jefferson (Thomas) as diplomat in, **2:**316, 317–318
    Laye's (Camara) education in, **1:**128–129
    letter writing in, **2:**217
    literary critical theories of, **1:**239
    locked-in syndrome in literature of, **1:**6
    Morocco as protectorate of, **3:**47
    Nin's (Anaïs) life in, **2:**123
    Revolution in (*See* French Revolution)
    Senegal as colony of, **1:**61
    student movements of 1968 in, **3:**33
    Vietnam under, **1:**335, **3:**279
    Wollstonecraft's (Mary) travels in, **2:**109
    women's rights movement in, **2:**306
    in World War II, German occupation of, **1:**332–334
    Wright's (Richard) move to, **1:**124
France, Peter, **1:**201
Francis, Charles E., *The Tuskegee Airmen,* **3:**212
Francophone literature
    of Algeria, **2:**262, 264
    of Senegal, **1:**61
Frank, Anne, *The Diary of Anne Frank,* **2:253–255,** *254*
    An Interrupted Life (Hillesum) vs., **2:**22

Night (Wiesel) vs., **1:**320
Red Scarf Girl (Jiang) inspired by, **1:**161
Thura's Diary (Al-Windawi) vs., **2:**275, 277
A Woman in Berlin (anonymous) vs., **2:**281
A Woman Soldier's Own Story (Xie) vs., **1:**340
Zlata's Diary (Filipovic) vs., **2:**338, 339, 340
Frank, Dana, **3:**338
Frank, Leslie, *Witnesses to Nuremberg,* **3:293–295**
Frank, Margot, **2:**253, 255
Frank, Otto, **2:**253, 254, 255
Franklin, Aretha, **1:**274–275
Franklin, Benjamin, **1:**180
    The Autobiography of Ben Franklin, **1:**179–182, **2:**213
    Poor Richard's Almanac, **2:**88
    Shadows on My Heart (Buck) on, **2:**271
Franklin, Ruth, **1:**320
Franklin, USS, **3:**203
Franklin, William, **1:**179
Franklin, William Temple, **1:**179
Franks, in Crusades, **1:**285–288
Franz Sternbalds Wanderungen (Tieck), **1:**276
Fraser, Roland, *Blood of Spain,* **3:**176
Frasher, Burton, **3:**102
Frayn, Michael, *Copenhagen,* **3:**239
Frazer, Heather T., *"We Have Just Begun to Not Fight",* **3:227–230**
Frederick II (king of Prussia), **1:**276
Frederick the Great, "Le Stoïcien," **1:**218
Frediani, Alex, **3:**225
Fredrickson, George, **2:**240
Freedom
    of expression (*See* Expression)
    Mandela's (Nelson) conception of, **1:**28
    mental, in locked-in syndrome, **1:**6–7
    moral imperative of, Soyinka (Wole) on, **1:**215
    value of, Jacobs (Harriet A.) on, **1:**143–145

Freedom (newspaper), **1**:273
Freedom Charter of 1955 (South Africa), **1**:24, 25
Freedom Flyers (Moye), **3**:99, **248–250**
Freedom Writers Diary, The (Gruwell), **2**:338, 339, 340
Freeman, James M., **3**:279
Freemont boarding school, **1**:164
Free schools, **3**:5
Free will, Augustine on, **1**:196, 198
French Americans, **2**:213–215
French and Indian War (1754–1763), **2**:205, 213
French autobiographical writing. *See also specific works and writers*
 by Barthes (Roland), **1**:267–269
 by Bauby (Jean-Dominique), **1**:6–8
 by Goncourt (Edmond de and Jules de), **2**:81–83
 by Lejeune (Philippe), **1**:239–240, **2**:174–176
 by Rousseau (Jean-Jacques), **1**:200–202
French education, in Algeria, **1**:93, 94, **2**:262–263
French Review (journal), **1**:128
French Revolution (1789–1799)
 Armenian nationalists influenced by, **3**:40
 British Empire during, Barnard (Anne) on, **2**:217, 218, 219
 British views on, **2**:309
 Enlightenment ideas in, **2**:109
 Goethe (Johann Wolfgang von) and, **1**:276
 U.S. anarchists influenced by, **3**:3
French Studies (journal), **2**:307
Frere, Bartie, **1**:91
Freud, Sigmund
 Andreas-Salomé (Lou) and, **2**:151
 on Augustine, **1**:197
 Barthes's (Roland) use of ideas of, **1**:267
 Bloomsbury group's discussions of, **2**:268
 and Darwin's (Charles) motivations, **1**:67

 and diaries, rise of, **2**:120
 The Origin and Development of Psychoanalysis, **2**:175
Frey, James, *A Million Little Pieces*, **1**:313, **2**:296
Friedan, Betty, **3**:37
Friedlander, Peter, **3**:174
 The Emergence of a UAW Local, **3**:153
Friedman, Clara, *Between Management and Labor*, **3**:153–156, 157
Frisbie, Charlotte, **3**:12
Frisch, Michael
 in field of oral history, **3**:173, 174
 on *Hard Times* (Terkel), **3**:162
 "Oral History and the Digital Revolution," **3**:181
 Portraits in Steel, **3**:181
 A Shared Authority, **3**:173, **179–182**, 190, 192
Fritz, Germaine, **3**:309
From Baghdad to Brooklyn (Marshall), **3**:120
From Behind the Veil (Stepto), **1**:35
From Memory to History (Montell and Bogart), **3**:90
Frommer, Harvey
 Growing Up Jewish in America, **3**:118–120
 It Happened in Brooklyn, **3**:118
Frommer, Myrna Katz
 Growing Up Jewish in America, **3**:118–120
 It Happened in Brooklyn, **3**:118
From Rhodesia to Zimbabwe (Vambe), **3**:251
From the Darkness Cometh the Light (Delaney), **2**:250
Fronto, Marcus Cornelius, **1**:220
Fruitlands (utopian community), **1**:235
Fry, Amelia, **3**:188
Frye, Northrop, **1**:276
Fuchs, Esther, *Women and the Holocaust*, **3**:35
Fugitive Slave Act of 1850 (U.S.), **2**:29
Fugitive slaves
 in abolitionist movement, **1**:142
 oral histories of, **3**:7–9
 return of, **2**:29

Fujii, Lee Ann, **3**:259
Fujiwara no Kintō, **2**:189
Fujiwara no Michinaga, **2**:290, 292
Fujiwara Takayoshi, **2**:291
Fujiwara Teika, **2**:189
Fulbrook, Mary, **3**:246
Fulkerson, Richard, **2**:33
Fuller, Margaret, **2**:139
Fuller, William Robertson, **2**:241
Fullerton, Morton, **2**:113, 115
Fulton, William, **3**:276
Fumifugium (Evelyn), **2**:65
Fundamentalist Christianity, **1**:102, 103
Fundamentalist Islam, **1**:156, 208
Fun Home (Bechdel), **1**:139–141
Fur, Gunlög Maria, *A Nation of Women*, **3**:326
Furey, Hester, **3**:329
Fürst, Juliane, **3**:332
Furuseth, Owen, **3**:123
Fussell, Paul, **3**:61
FWP. *See* Federal Writers' Project

G

Gaelic League, **3**:27
Gaitán Ayala, Jorge Eliécer, **3**:185
Gaither, Frances, **2**:30
Galarza, Ernesto, *Barrio Boy*, **1**:15
Galaty, John, **1**:114, 115, **3**:142
Galbraith, John Kenneth, **3**:255
Galloway, Grace Growdon, **2**:79
Galsworthy, John, **2**:136
Galvin, John, **3**:206
Gama, Vasco da, *A Journal of the First Voyage of Vasco da Gama*, **2**:198–200, 199, 201
Gandhi, Mohandas, **1**:243
 An Autobiography, **1**:24, **242–245**
 civil disobedience by, **1**:242, **2**:32
 conscientious objectors influenced by, **3**:228
 Hind Swaraj, **1**:289
 Luthuli (Albert) influenced by, **1**:24
 Nehru's (Jawaharlal) relationship with, **1**:289–290, 291

Gandhi, Rajiv, **1:290**
Gangs, British youth, **3:**311–313
Gao, Anhua, *To the Edge of the Sky*, **1:**159
Gao Xingjian, **1:**159
GAP. *See* Gruppi di Azione Patriottica
Garceau, Dee, **2:**91, 92–93
García Lorca, Federico, **1:**222
García Márquez, Gabriel, *The Story of a Shipwrecked Sailor*, **3:183–185**
Gardiner, Samuel Rawson, **1:**316
Garff, Joakim, **2:**167–168
Garland, Anne Witte, *Women Activists*, **3:**268
Garland, Judy, **3:**295
Garnett, Anne, **2:**235
Garnett, Constance, **2:**268
Garrett, Daniel, **1:**256, 257
Garrett, Jessie, *Camp and Community*, **3:**102, 103–104
Garrison, William Lloyd, **1:**33, **2:**29
Garvey, Marcus, **1:**52, 84, 186, 187
Gary Convention of 1972, **3:**45
Gaskell, Elizabeth, **2:**143
Gaskin, Hilary, *Eyewitnesses at Nuremberg*, **3:**293
Gass, William H., **2:**149, 150
Gataker, Thomas, **1:**220
Gates, Henry Louis, Jr.
    The Classic Slave Narratives, **1:**82, 83
    In Search of Our Roots, **1:**263
    "Remembrance of Things Pakistani," **1:**88
    on Wheatley (Phillis), **2:**46
Gatten, Aileen, **2:**290, 292
Gatti, Tom, **1:**141
Gaulle, Charles de, **2:**262
Gay, Peter, **2:**304
Gay Caucus Book of the Year award, for *The Cancer Journals* (Lorde), **2:**5
Gay L.A. (Faderman and Timmons), **3:**83–84
Gay Liberation Front, **3:**72
Gay men. *See* Homosexuality
Gay rights movement, rise of
    in Britain, **3:**70, 72
    in U.S., **3:**83–84

Gay subculture, of Harlem Renaissance, **1:**84
Gay themes
    in comics, **1:**139, 141
    in *Hunger of Memory* (Rodriguez), **1:**17
Geertz, Clifford, **3:**74
Gehen-Bleiben (play), **2:304**
Geiger, H. Jack, **1:**73
Gelb, Norman, **2:**206
Gelles, Edith, **2:**89, 90
Gellhorn, Martha, **2:102**
    The Face of War, **2:**102
    Moore (Molly) and, **2:**278
    Selected Letters of Martha Gellhorn, **2:101–103**
    The Trouble I've Seen, **2:**101
Gellhorn, Walter, **3:**154, 155
Gender, in writing styles, **1:**250
Gender & History (journal), **3:**175
Gender discrimination, in coal mining, **3:**337, 339
Gender equality
    in Heian period of Japan, lack of, **2:**299
    Stanton (Elizabeth Cady) on, **1:**12, 13
Gender roles
    in Britain, **3:**144–146
    in China, **1:**153, 158, 160, 338, **3:**147–149
    in Europe, eighteenth-century, **2:**35–37
    in Europe, Renaissance, **2:**160–162
    in Iran, **1:**155
    in Ireland, **2:**157
    in Japan, **2:**60–61
    in Kenya, **3:**143
    in Montenegro, **3:**135, 136, 137
    in U.S., eighteenth-century, **2:**316
    in U.S., twentieth-century, **2:**47
    in World War I, **1:**331
Gender studies
    Red Azalea (Min) in, **1:**158, 160
    The Sovereignty and Goodness of God (Rowlandson) in, **1:**327
Genealogy, of Haley (Alex), **1:**261–263

General Allotment Act of 1887 (U.S.), **3:**107
General Magazine and Impartial Review, **1:**82
General Motors, **3:**343
Geneva Convention on the Laws and Custom of War (1949), **2:**56
Genghis Khan, **1:**105, 107
Genocide
    Armenian, **3:**40–42, *41*
    in Cambodia, **1:**306
    denial as final stage of, **3:**42
    in Guatemala, **3:**164
    in Nazi Germany (*See* Holocaust)
    in Rwanda, **1:**312, **3:**257–259, 293, 294
    in Ukraine, **3:**19
Genre (journal), **1:**248
"Gentlemen's Agreement" of 1907, **3:**80
Georgakas, Dan, *Solidarity Forever*, **3:328–330**
George, Keller, **3:**109
George, Susanne K., **2:**91–92, 93
George III (king of England), **2:**69, 328
Georgia, colonial, Wesley's (John) mission to, **2:**195, 196
Georgia Historical Quarterly, **1:**38
Georgia Review (journal), **1:**109
Georgia Weekly Telegraph (newspaper), **2:**38, 39
Gerardi, Juan, **1:**99
Géricault, Théodore, **2:144**
Gerlin, Valeria Mikhailovna, **3:**18
Germaine (About), **2:**115
German Americans, relocation in World War II, **3:**224, 226
German autobiographical writing.
    See also specific works and writers
    by Goethe (Johann Wolfgang von), **1:**276–278
    by Hitler (Adolf), **1:**30–32
    by Klemperer (Victor), **2:**303–305
    by Rabe (John), **2:**19–21
    by Rilke (Rainer Maria), **2:**149–151
    by Speer (Albert), **2:**54–56

German language, Nazi use of, **2**:303, 304, 305
German Romanticism, **2**:76
Germany. *See also* German autobiographical writing
    bildungsroman genre in, **1**:30
    economy of, **1**:30
    emigration to Chile from, **1**:75, 77
    Great Awakening in, **2**:197
    Künstler-Roman genre in, **1**:276
    nationalism in, **1**:30–32, 329, **2**:120, **3**:234
    Nazi (*See* Nazi Germany)
    reunification of, **3**:247
    Robinson's (Henry Crabb) travels in, **2**:75, 77
    Ruete's (Emily) move from Zanzibar to, **1**:90
    Stasi in, oral histories of, **3**:245–247
    student movements of 1968 in, **3**:33
    wars of (*See* specific wars)
Germany, Kent B., **3**:254
Geronimo (film), **1**:304
Geronimo, *Geronimo: His Own Story*, **1**:302–305, *303*
Geronimo: An American Legend (film), **1**:304
Geronimo: His Own Story (Geronimo and Barrett), **1**:302–305
Gerovitch, Slava, **3**:333
Gesner, Andreas, **1**:220
Gessen, Keith, **3**:282, 285
Getty, Serena, **2**:54–55
Gevisser, Mark, **3**:243
Gewen, Barry, **3**:213
Ghana (Nkrumah), **1**:290, **2**:12, 13
Ghana, Du Bois (W. E. B.) and, **1**:3, 4
Gharagozlou, Mary, **3**:220
Ghazzawi, 'Izzat
    Letters Underway, **2**:50–53
    The Woman Prisoner, **2**:50
Ghazzawi, Rami, **2**:50
Gheith, Jehanne M., *Gulag Voices*, **3**:17–19, 331
Ghent, Treaty of, **2**:69
Ghost Dance, **3**:110

Ghost masks, Chinese, **1**:174
Gibb, H. A. R., **1**:137, 287
Gibbon, Edward, **1**:198, **2**:37, 328
Gibbons, Herbert Adams, *The Blackest Page in Modern History*, **3**:40
Gibson, Marion, **1**:337
Gibson, Roy, **2**:95, 96
Gibson, William (playwright), **1**:43–44
Gibson, William Ford (novelist), **2**:145
Gide, André, **1**:278
    Log-book of the Coiners, **2**:180, 182
Giesen, Carol A. B., *Coal Miners' Wives*, **3**:337
Gig (Bowe and Bowe), **3**:343, 345
Gigliozzi, Liana, **3**:266
Gikandi, Simon, **2**:14
Gikuyu language, **2**:12, 13, 14
Gilbert, Sandra M., **2**:237
Gillette, Michael L., *Launching the War on Poverty*, **3**:254–256
Gillray, James, **2**:158
Gilman, Charlotte Perkins, **1**:14, **2**:324
Gilman, Richard, **2**:131
Gilmartin, Christina, **3**:149
Gilmartin, Elizabeth Kelley, *Engendering the Chinese Revolution*, **3**:147
Giltrow, Janet, **2**:207
Ginther, Ronald Debs, **3**:162
Gioglio, Gerald P., *Days of Decision*, **3**:221
Girl from China, A (Cheng), **1**:152, 154
Girl in the Tangerine Scarf, The (Kahf), **1**:41–42
Girl Rebel (Xie), **1**:338
Girl with the White Flag, The (Higa), **1**:153
Gissing, George
    London and the Life of Literature in Late Victorian England, **2**:320–323
    New Grub Street, **2**:320, 321, 322
Gittins, Diana, **3**:313
Gladiator (film), **1**:219
Gladstone, W. E., **2**:307
Glasgow, Jacqueline N., **1**:41–42, 311
Glasnost, **3**:282, 331, 333
Glass Menagerie, The (Williams), **2**:152

Glazier, Jack, **3**:141
Glenarvon (Lamb), **2**:145
Glendinning, Victoria, **1**:205
Glenn, Susan A., *Daughters of the Shtetl*, **3**:305
Glenny, William H., **3**:294
Globe & Mail (newspaper), **3**:119–120, 301
GLQ: A Journal of Lesbian and Gay Studies, **3**:72
Gluck, Sherna Berger
    Rosie the Riveter Revisited, **3**:224
    Women's Words, **3**:190–192
Go Ask Alice (anonymous), **2**:294–296
God, will of, Usāmah ibn Munqidh on, **1**:285, 286
Go-Daigo (Japanese emperor), **2**:61
Goddard, James Stanley, **2**:205, 207
God of Small Things, The (Roy), **1**:87
Godolphin, Margaret, **2**:66
Godwin, William, **2**:76, 109, 111
    Memoir, **2**:109
Goethe, Johann Wolfgang von, **1**:277
    Kafka (Franz) influenced by, **2**:120
    Kierkegaard's (Søren) critique of, **2**:166
    The Sorrows of Young Werther, **1**:276, 277, 339, **2**:166
    Styron (William) compared to, **1**:206
    Truth and Fiction Relating to My Life, **1**:276–278
    Wilhelm Meister's Apprenticeship, **1**:30
Goff, Stanley, *Brothers*, **3**:199
GoFukakusa (Japanese emperor), **2**:59, 60, 61
Gogh, Theo van, **1**:207, 209
Gogol, Nikolay, **2**:172
    Diary of a Madman, **2**:174
Going after Cacciato (O'Brien), **1**:335
Golb, Joel, **1**:32
Goldberg, Lina, **2**:295
Golden Ass, The (Apuleius), **1**:198
Goldenberg, Myrna, **3**:36
Golden Bones (Siv), **1**:306–308
Golden Book of the Emperor Marcus Aurelius (Guevara), **1**:218

SUBJECT INDEX

Goldensohn, Leon, *The Nuremberg Interviews,* **3:**293
Goldhagen, Daniel, **2:**304–305
Goldman, Emma, *Living My Life,* **3:**3
Gold Rush, California, **3:**114
Goldzwig, Steven R., **2:**33
Gomaa, Sally, **1:**144
Gomez, Iris, *Try to Remember,* **1:**108
Gómez, Laureano, **3:**183, 185
Gomez, Maximo, **3:**7
Goncourt, Edmond de
    Bashkirtseff (Marie) influenced by, **2:**306, 307–308
    Cherie, **2:**308
    En 18, **2:**82
    La Faustine, **2:**308
    Journal des Goncourt, **2:**81–83
Goncourt, Jules de
    En 18, **2:**82
    Journal des Goncourt, **2:**81–83
Gonne, Maud, **2:**127
Goodall, Jane, **3:**37
Goodbye to All That (Graves), **1:**329
Good Earth, The (Buck), **1:**159
Goodell, Stephen, **3:**254
Goodfriend, Joyce D., **2:**79
Good Housekeeping (magazine), **1:**154
"Good Man Is Hard to Find, A" (O'Connor), **2:**130
Good Man of Nanking, The (Rabe), **2:**19–21
Good Morning America (television show), **1:**40, 41
Goodrich, Chris, **1:**29, **3:**222
Goodrich, Frances, **2:**253
"Good War, The" (Terkel), **3:**212–214
    Bloods (Terry) vs., **3:**199
    Carrier Warfare in the Pacific (Wooldridge) vs., **3:**202
    Pulitzer Prize won by, **3:**161, 212, 234, 279, 343
    in rise of oral history, **3:**279
    The World at War (Holmes) vs., **3:**234
Goodwin, Jason, **1:**107
Good Wives (Ulrich), **2:**331–332
Goolagong, Evonne, **1:**149
Gorbachev, Mikhail, **3:**17, 282, 331, 333

Gordimer, Nadine, **1:**27
Gordon, Andrew, **3:**216
Gordon, Ann D., **1:**13
Gordon, Caroline, **2:**129
Gordon, Eleanor, **3:**175
Gordon, Ian, **2:**134
Gordon, Mary McDougall, **2:**79
Göring, Hermann, **3:**294
Gorky, Maxim, **1:**254
Gornick, Vivian, *Fierce Attachments,* **1:**279
Gorra, Michael, **1:**88
Gossamer Years, The (Michitsuna), **2:**189, 290, **297–299**
Gossen, Gary H., *Telling Maya Tales,* **3:**167
Go Tell It on the Mountain (Baldwin), **1:**167, 261
Gotlieb, Howard, **2:**101
Gottesmann, Christoph, **2:**282
Gougeon, Len, **2:**141
Gowon, Yakubu, **1:**214, 215, 216
Goyens, Tom, *Beer and Revolution,* **3:**5
Goyette, Gabriele, **1:**10
Graburn, Nelson, **3:**140
Grace Abounding to the Chief of Sinners (Bunyan), **2:**26
Graden, Dale, **3:**8
Graham, Elspeth, **1:**231
Graham, John, **1:**98
Grammy Award, for Obama's (Barack) audio adaptations, **1:**80
Granado, Alberto, **2:**220
Grandmothers, Mothers, and Daughters (Krause), **3:**305–307
Grand Prix Littéraire d'Afrique Noir, for *Riwan ou le chemin de sable* (Bugul), **1:**64
Grant, Duncan, **2:**268
Graphic autobiographies
    Barefoot Gen (Nakazawa), **1:**293–295
    Fun Home (Bechdel), **1:**139–141
    Persepolis (Satrapi), **1:**155–157
Grasmere (England), Dove Cottage in, **2:**300, *301*
Grasmere Journals (Wordsworth), **2:**16, **300–302**
Grass Is Singing, The (Lessing), **1:**169

Graulich, Melody, **2:**91, 92
Graves, Phyllis, **1:**311
Graves, Robert, **2:**248
    Goodbye to All That, **1:**329
Gray, Doris H., *Muslim Women on the Move,* **3:**48
Gray, Francine du Plessix, **2:**102
Gray, Rockwell, **1:**247
Gray, Thomas, **2:**146
Greasley, Philip, **3:**213
Great Awakening, **1:**179, **2:**197
Great Boer War, The (Conan Doyle), **2:**241
Great Britain. *See* Britain
Great Depression
    African Americans during, **3:**99
    in Appalachia, **3:**96
    in Britain, **3:**53
    end of, **3:**161
    global impact of, **3:**212
    in Harlem, **1:**84
    in Idaho, **3:**93, 94
    Jews during, **3:**118
    Native Americans during, **1:**69
    New Deal in, **3:**161 (*See also* Federal Writers' Project)
    oral histories of, **3:**86, 161–163, *162*
    start of, **3:**161, 212
    unemployment in, **3:**161, 212
Great Exodus (1879), **1:**50
Great Famine (Ireland), **3:**315
Great Famine of 1932–1933 (Ukraine), **3:**19
Great Gatsby, The (Fitzgerald), **1:**47
Great Lakes Review, **3:**213
Great Leap Forward, **3:**287, 299, 300
"Great Men" project, of Nevins (Allan), **3:**161, 173, 179, 181, 186
Great Migration, **1:**50, 52, 84, 273, **3:**99
Great Plains Quarterly, **2:**164
Great Proletarian Cultural Revolution. *See* Cultural Revolution
Great Reforms (Russia), **1:**193
Great Society, **3:**254
"Great Wall of China, The" (Kafka), **2:**120

Great War, The (television series), **3:**234, 236
Greece, ancient
    letter writing in, **2:**94
    slavery in, **2:**96
Green, Anna, **3:**175
Green, John, **2:**276
Green, Maia, **3:**142
Green, Roland, **3:**203
Greenberg, Jack, **1:**38
Greenberg, Martin, **2:**121
Greenberger, Evelyn B., **2:**141
Greene, Graham, **2:**130, 136, 152
    A Sort of Life, **1:**47
Greene, Janet Wells, **3:**97
Greenfield, Sidney, *Entrepreneurs in Cultural Context*, **3:**121
Greenwell, Regina, **3:**254
Greer, Germaine, **3:**37
Gregory, Horace, **2:**121
Gregory, Lady, **2:**126, 128
Grele, Ronald J., **3:**45, 51, 52, 174
Grewal, Inderpal, **1:**88–89
Grey, Jane, **2:**99
Grice, Helena, **1:**160
Griffith, Andy, **2:**295
Griffith, Elisabeth, **1:**13–14
Griffith, Julia, *The Liberty Bell*, **1:**142
Griffith, Kenneth, *Ireland's Unfinished Revolution*, **3:**27–30
Grillo, Evelio, *Black Cuban, Black American*, **1:**296
Grimes, Tom, *Mentor*, **1:**164
Grimes, William, **1:**209
Grimké, Angelina, **2:**31
Grimké, Angelina Weld, **2:**31
Grimké, Charlotte Forten
    "At the Home of Frederick Douglass," **2:**29
    The Extraordinary Work of Ordinary Writing (Sinor) compared to, **2:**163
    Higginson (Thomas Wentworth) and, **2:**29, 238
    The Journals of Charlotte Forten Grimké, **2:**29–31
    "Life in the Sea Islands," **2:**31
Grimké, Francis, **2:**31

Grimké, Sarah, **2:**31
Grindle, Merilee S., **3:**303
Griswold, Rufus W., **2:**41
Grob-Fitzgibbon, Benjamin, *The Irish Experience during the Second World War*, **3:**315–316
Gronniosaw, James Albert Ukawsaw, **1:**81, **2:**44
Grose, John Henry, *Voyage to the East Indies*, **2:**229
Gross, Robert, **1:**19
Grossman, Michele, **3:**335, 336
Grossmith brothers, *The Diary of a Nobody*, **2:**174
Grotius, Hugo, **2:**177
Group, The (McCarthy), **1:**258
Group Areas Act of 1950 (South Africa), **1:**24
Growing Up Jewish in America (Frommer and Frommer), **3:118–120**
Grundtvig, N. F. S., **2:**166
Gruppi di Azione Patriottica (GAP), **3:**265
Gruwell, Erin, *The Freedom Writers Diary*, **2:**338, 339, 340
Gu, Ming Dong, **2:**172
Guajardo, Paul, **1:**16
Guardian (newspaper), **1:**330, **2:**133, 154, **3:**243
Guardian of the Word, The (Laye), **1:**129
Guatemala
    Civil War of, **1:**99, **3:**164, 165–166
    human rights abuses in, **1:**99, 100, **3:**164–166
    indigenous populations of, massacres of, **1:**99, **3:**164
    indigenous populations of, oral histories of, **3:**164–166
    Perera (Victor) on life in, **1:**99–101
"Guatemala: Always La Violencia" (Perera), **1:**99
Guatemalan Civil War (1960–1996), **1:**99, **3:**164, 165–166
Guatemala: Never Again! (Archdiocese of Guatemala), **1:**99
Guattari, Félix, **2:**122
Guavas, **1:**109

Gubar, Susan, **2:**237
Gubarev, Vladimir, *Sarcophagus*, **3:**282, 284
Guerilla Days in Ireland (Barry), **3:**27
Guérin, Daniel, *No Gods, No Masters*, **3:**3
Guérin, Eugénie de, **2:**306
Guevara, Antonio, *Golden Book of the Emperor Marcus Aurelius*, **1:**218
Guevara, Ernesto "Che," **2:221**
    Che: A Graphic Biography (Buhle and Rodriguez) on, **3:**330
    Motorcycle Diaries, **1:**223, **2:220–222**
Guggenheim, Peggy, **2:**152
Guglielmo, Jennifer, *Living the Revolution*, **3:**5
Guiler, Hugh Parker, **2:**123
Guilt, in *Country of My Skull* (Krog), **3:**243
Guinea
    French colonial rule of, **1:**128, 129, 130
    independence of (1958), **1:**130
    Laye (Camara) on life in, **1:**128–130, *129*
Guisson, Lorraine, *Image du monde*, **1:**105
Guiteras-Holmes, Calixta, *Perils of the Soul*, **3:**167
Gulag Archipelago, The (Solzhenitsyn), **1:**201, **3:**17
Gulag system, oral histories of, **3:**17–19, *18*
Gulag Voices (Gheith and Jolluck), **3:17–19**, 331
Gulf War (1991), **2:**275, 278–280, *279*
Gulliford, Andrew, **3:**77
Gundy, Jeff, **1:**109
Gunning, Sarah Ogan, **3:**159
Gurewitsch, Brana
    Holocaust Oral History Manual, **3:**35
    Mothers, Sisters, Resisters, **3:34–36**
Gusdorf, George, **1:**246, 248
Gustavson, Andrea, **3:**162–163, 213
Guy, Josephine M., **2:**10
Guy Domville (James), **2:**114
Guylforde, John, **2:**228

SUBJECT INDEX

Guylforde, Richarde, *The Pylgrymage of Sir Richarde Guylforde*, **2:226–228**
Gyn/Ecology (Daly), **2:**3, 5

H

Ha, Quan Manh, **1:**307
Habit of Being, The (O'Connor), **2:129–132**
Habits of Change (Rogers), **3:308–310**
Habits of mind, Darwin (Charles) on, **1:**65–67
Habyarimana, Juvénal, **3:**257
Hachicho, Mohamad Ali, **2:**227, 228
Hachiya, Michihiko, *Hiroshima Diary*, **1:**293
Hackett, Albert, **2:**253
Haddad, Malek, *La Dernière impression*, **2:**262
Hadot, Pierre, **1:**221
Hagiographies
    The Autobiography of Malcolm X (Malcolm X) as, **1:**186, 188
    and *The Book of Margery Kempe* (Kempe), **1:**189, 190, 191
Hagood, Taylor, **1:**8
Hagopian, Patrick, **3:**201, 209, 211, 277
Haizlip, Shirlee, *The Sweeter the Juice*, **1:**73
Hakakian, Roya, *Journey to the Land of No*, **1:**155
Hakluyt, Richard, **2:**199
    Divers Voyages Touching the Discoverie of America, **2:**229
    The Principle Navigations, Voiages, Traffiques and Discoveries of the English Nation, **2:**229
Hakluyt Society, **2:**198, 199
Halas, John, **2:118**
Hale, Sondra, **3:**48–49, 191
Halevy, Irving, **3:**154–155
Haley, Alex, **1:262**
    "Black History, Oral History, and Genealogy," **3:**186
    "My Furthest-Back Person— 'The African,'" **1:261–263**
    Roots, **1:**18, 78, 261–263
    in writing of *The Autobiography of Malcolm X*, **1:**78, 186, 187, **3:**44

Halkett, Anne, *The Memoirs of Lady Anne Halkett*, **1:**230, **315–317**
Halkett, James, **1:**315
Hall, Betty Jean, **3:**339
Hall, Joan Wylie, **2:**153
Hall, Peter, **3:**59
Halperin, John, **2:**322
Halpern, Frida, **1:**76
Halsband, Robert, **2:**36
Hamdani, Abu Firas al-, **2:**52
Hamilton, J. Angus, *The Siege of Mafeking*, **2:**241
Hamilton, Paula, **3:**188
Hamilton, Robert A., **3:**294
Hamilton, William, **2:196**
Hamlet (Shakespeare), **1:**277
Hammon, Britton, **2:**44
Hammon, Jupiter, **2:**44
Hampton, Henry
    The Black Chronicle, **3:**44
    in *Eyes on the Prize* (television series), **2:**34
    Voices of Freedom, **3:44–46**
Hamsun, Knut, **2:**120
Handbook of Oral History, The (Humphries), **3:**313
Handley, George B., **1:**223–224
Han dynasty, Confucianism in, **3:**124
Hansberry, Lorraine, **1:**274
    A Raisin in the Sun, **1:**273, 274, 275
    The Sign in Sidney Brustein's Window, **1:**274
    To Be Young, Gifted and Black, **1:273–275**
Hansen, Arthur A., **3:**80–81, 197
    Japanese American World War II Evacuation Oral History Project, **3:**215
    Voices Long Silent, **3:**195
Han Yong Un, **1:**322
Hao Ping, **3:**289
Happiest Refugee, The (Do), **1:**337
Happy Foreigner, The (Bagnold), **2:**259
Haralson, Eric, **2:**115
Harbach, Patricia, **3:326**
Harbord, Gordon, **2:**249
Hardack, Richard, **1:**281

Hard-Earned Lives (Cornwell), **3:**170
Harder Journey, The (Tuqan), **1:**226
Hardships and Happy Times (Russell), **3:**93
Hard Times: An Oral History of the Great Depression (Terkel), **3:161–163,** 179, 199, **212,** 279, 343
Hardy, Thomas, **2:**136–137, 180, 181, 321
Harem Years (Shaarawi), **1:**225–226
Harlan, Louis R., **1:**52
Harlan County (Kentucky)
    oral histories of coal miners in, **3:**96–98, 157
    oral histories of working class in, **3:**157–159
Harlan County, USA (documentary), **3:**98
Harlan Miners Speak (Dreiser), **3:**96
Harlem, in Great Depression, **1:**84
"Harlem" (Hughes), **1:**275
Harlem: Negro Metropolis (McKay), **1:**85
Harlem Renaissance
    autobiographies of participants in, **1:**3
    vs. Chicago Renaissance, **1:**273
    Du Bois (W. E. B.) in, **1:**3
    gay subculture of, **1:**84
    Hurston (Zora Neale) in, **1:**9
    McKay (Claude) in, **1:**84–86
    origins of, **1:**84
Harling, Sean, **3:**28
Harman, Claire, **2:**313–314
Harney, Mary, **3:**315
Harper, Frances Ellen Watkins, *Iola Leroy*, **1:**143
Harper, Helen, **1:**162, **2:**276
Harries, Meirion, *Soldiers of the Sun*, **3:**215
Harries, Susie, *Soldiers of the Sun*, **3:**215
Harrington, Ann, **3:**309
Harris, Frank, **2:**261
Harris, Lillian Craig, **3:**126
Harrison, Thomas, **2:**235
Harrold, Charles, **2:**76
Hart, Frederick, **3:200**
Hart-Davis, Rupert, **2:**247, 248

382 THE LITERATURE OF AUTOBIOGRAPHICAL NARRATIVE ❖ VOLUME 1 ❖ AUTOBIOGRAPHY AND MEMOIR

Hartle, Ann, **1:**202
Harvard Book Review, **1:**48, 280
Harvard Iranian Oral History Project (HIOHP), **3:**218–220
Harvey, Clodagh Brennan, *Contemporary Irish Traditional Narrative,* **3:**315
Harvey, P., **3:**249
Harwood, Ronald, **1:**6
Haskins, Jim, *Rosa Parks: My Story,* **1:**37–39
Hassan, Kenja, **3:**12
Hastings, Selina, **2:**185
Hatch, Ozias M., **3:**263
Hatcher, Richard, **3:**45
Hate crimes, against gay men and lesbians, **1:**139
Hathaway, Donny, **1:**274
Hatherell, William, **2:**260
Hattin, Battle of (1187), **1:**286
Hatzfeld, Jean
    The Antelope's Strategy, **3:**258
    Life Laid Bare, **3:**258, 259
    Machete Season, **1:**312, **3:**257–260
Hauptman, L. M., **3:**326
Hausa people, **1:**214
Haushofer, Karl, **1:**32
Haviland, John B., **3:**169
Hawaii. *See* Pearl Harbor
Hawkesworth, E. C., **3:**135, 136, 137
Hawthorne, Julian, **2:**224
Hawthorne, Nathaniel
    The Blithedale Romance, **2:**225
    The Centenary Edition of the Works of Nathaniel Hawthorne, **2:**223
    Emerson (Ralph Waldo) and, **2:**139, 223
    The House of the Seven Gables, **2:**223–224
    James (Henry) and, **2:**113, 114, 115
    lost notebook of, **2:**224, 225
    The Love Letters of Nathaniel Hawthorne, **2:**225
    The Marble Faun, **2:**224, 225
    Notebooks and Letters, **2:**113, **223–225**
    Robinson (Henry Crabb) compared to, **2:**75
    The Scarlet Letter, **2:**223–224

Hawthorne, Sophia Peabody, **2:**223, 224, 225
Haxton, Frederick Gerald, **2:**183
Hay, John M., **3:**262
    Abraham Lincoln: A History, **3:**261–262
    Abraham Lincoln: Complete Works, **3:**262
    Letters of John Hay, **3:**263
    Lincoln and the Civil War Diaries and Letters of John Hay, **3:**262–263
Haydon, Benjamin, **2:**146
Hayes, Thomas, **1:**216
Hayls, John, **2:**73
Haymarket Riot (1886), **3:**4
Haynes, Katherine, **3:**344
Hays, Mary, **2:**109, 110
Hays, Megan, **3:**136–137
Hays, Rusel Everett, **3:**185
Hayslip, Le Ly, **1:336**
    When Heaven and Earth Changed Places, **1:**170–171, **335–337**
    Woman of Peace, **1:**335
Haywood, Harry, *Black Bolshevik,* **1:**4
Hazlitt, William, **2:**146
H.D. (Hilda Doolittle), **2:**123
Heading South, Looking North (Dorfman), **1:**75
Head of the Class (Morris), **3:20–22**
Head Start program, **3:**254
Healey, Mark, **3:**74
Health-care industry
    British, oral histories of, **3:**170–172
    South African, oral histories of, **3:**272–274
Health problems. *See also specific types*
    of Bauby (Jean-Dominique), **1:**6–8
    of Mansfield (Katherine), **2:**133, 134
    of Styron (William), **1:**204–205
Healy, George Peter Alexander, **2:**70
Heartland (film), **2:**91
Heart of Darkness (Conrad), **2:**192–193, 194
Heaven and Earth (film), **1:**335, *336*
Hecker, Earl, **3:**232

Heflin, Ruth J., **3:**112
Hegel, Georg Wilhelm Friedrich, **2:**166
Heian period (Japan)
    Michitsuna No Haha on life in, **2:**297–299
    Murasaki Shikibu on life in, **2:**290–292
    Nijo (Lady) on life in, **2:**60, 61
    Sarashina (Lady) on life in, **2:**189–191
Heilman, Anna, **3:**35
Heinemann Award, for *Akenfield* (Blythe), **3:**59
Heisenberg, Werner, **3:**239
Helfand, Judy, **1:**336
Helgeson, Jeffrey, **3:**255–256
Hélias, Pierre Jakez, *The Horse of Pride,* **3:**61
Heline, Oscar, **3:**162
Heller, Walter, **3:**254
Hellman, Lillian, **1:**260
Helms, Jessie, **2:**5
Helsinger, Elizabeth K., **1:**264, 265, 266
Helstern, Linda Lizut, **3:**12
Hemenway, Robert, **1:**9
Hemingway, Ernest
    A Farewell to Arms, **2:**259
    The Fifth Column, **2:**102
    For Whom the Bell Tolls, **2:**101
    Gellhorn's (Martha) marriage to, **2:**101, 102
    Notebooks (Williams) on, **2:**152
    The Sun Also Rises, **2:**259
    Wolff (Tobias) influenced by, **1:**47
Hemlow, Joyce, **2:**314
Henderson, John, **2:**96
Henderson, Thelton, **3:**20
Hendricks, Cecilia Hennel, **2:**91
Henige, David, **2:**203
Hennepin, Louis, *A New Discovery of a Vast Country in America,* **2:**205
Henrietta Maria (queen of England), **1:**229
Henry, Milton, **3:**248
Henry, Mona, **3:**316
Henry the Navigator, **2:**198
Henry VII (king of England), **2:**226, 228

SUBJECT INDEX

Henry VIII (king of England), **2:**72, 97, 226
Hensher, Philip, **2:**153
Hentges, Frank, **3:**162
Hentges, Rome, **3:**162
Henze, Hans Werner, **3:**7
Hepburn, James, **2:**138
Hepburn, Katharine, **2:**261
Here I Stand (Robeson), **1:**37
Here's to You, Jesus (Poniatowska), **3:**32
Heresy, Teresa of Ávila and, **1:**211, 212
Here Too, Domitila (Barrios de Chungara), **3:**322
Herman, David, **2:**128
Hermione, Countess of Ranfurly, **2:**235
Herndon, Angelo, **1:**85
Herndon's Informants (Wilson and Davis), **3:**264
Herodotus, **3:**186
Herr, Michael, *Dispatches,* **1:**259, **3:**209
Herrera, Spencer, **1:**17
Herron, L. E., **1:**52
Hershatter, Gail, **1:**340
Herzen, Alexander, **1:**270, **2:**120
Hess, Rudolph, **1:**32, **3:294**
Hester, Elizabeth, **2:**130–131
H-Ethnic (journal), **3:**8
Hevener, John W., *Which Side Are You On?,* **3:**96
Hewitt, David, **2:**311
Hewitt, Martin, **2:**66, 67
Heyerdahl, Marian, **1:339**
Heylin, Peter, **2:**99
Heyns, Michiel, **3:**243
Heywood, Christopher, **2:**242
Heywood, Thomas, **2:**162
H. G. Wells in Love (Wells), **1:**252, 253, 254
Hibakusha literature, **1:**293
Hibberd, Dominic, **2:**248, 249
Hibbert, Christopher, **2:**210
Hickey, Jim, **3:**316
Hickey, Margaret, *Irish Days,* **3:315–317**
Higa, Tomiko, *The Girl with the White Flag,* **1:**153
Higgins, Marguerite, **2:**278

Higginson, Thomas Wentworth
　Army Life in a Black Regiment, **2:238–240**
　Grimké (Charlotte Forten) and, **2:**29, 238
Hijuelos, Oscar, *Thoughts without Cigarettes,* **1:**75
Hikmet, Nazim, **2:**51
Hilda Lessways (Bennett), **2:**138
Hill, Joan, **3:**68
Hill, W. Nick, **3:**7, 8
"Hillbilly" culture, **3:**86
Hill Country Teacher (Manning), **3:77–79**
Hillenbrand, Carole, **1:**286, 287
Hillers, Marta, **2:**281
Hillesum, Etty
　An Interrupted Life, **2:22–25**
　The Letters and Diaries of Etty Hillesum, **2:**253
Him, Chanrithy, *When Broken Glass Floats,* **1:**306
Hinds, Hilary, **2:**27
Hind Swaraj (Gandhi), **1:**289
Hinduism, **1:**242, 244
Hindus, Maurice, **1:**271
Hinnant, Charles, **2:**329–330
Hinton, Deane, **3:**206
Hinton, James, **2:**267
Hintz, Carrie, **2:**326
HIOHP. *See* Harvard Iranian Oral History Project
Hipp, Daniel, **2:**249
Hirohito (emperor of Japan), **3:**215
Hiroshima (Japan), U.S. nuclear bombing of, **1:**293–294, **3:**239
Hiroshima Diary (Hachiya), **1:**293
Hiroshima: The Autobiography of Barefoot Gen (Nakazawa), **1:**293, 295
Hirsch, Jerrold, **3:**22, 192
Hirsch, Julia, **3:**306
Hirsi Ali, Ayaan, **1:208**
　Infidel, **1:**207–210
　Nomad, **1:**209
Hispanic-American Entrepreneur, The (Owsley), **3:121–123**
Hispanic American Historical Review (journal), **2:**7, **3:**122, 303, 323

Hispanic and Latino Americans
　as entrepreneurs, oral histories of, **3:**121–123
　Medina (Pablo) on experience of, **1:**296–298
　Santiago (Esmeralda) on experience of, **1:**108–110
　in South, **3:**123
　women, oral histories of, **3:**131–133
Historia Augusta, **1:**220
Historian (journal), **2:**231
Historia Romana (Cassius Dio), **1:**220
Historical Clarifications Commission, UN, **3:**166
Historical Journal of Film, Radio and Television, **3:**234
Historie de ma vie (Amrouche). *See My Life Story* (Amrouche)
History, field of. *See also* Oral histories
　Popular Memory Group's critique of, **3:**176–178
　role of oral histories in, **3:**281
History (journal), **2:**206, **3:**145
History and Theory (journal), **1:**26
History in Africa (journal), **1:**25
History of Alta California, The (Osio et al.), **3:**115
History of Education Quarterly, **3:**307
History of Everyday Life in Twentieth Century Scotland, A (Abrams), **3:**173, 175
History of Indies (Las Casas), **2:**201
History of Mary Prince, The (Prince), **1:**111, 113, **3:23–26**
History of the German Resistance (Hoffmann), **3:**245
History of Woman Suffrage (Stanton et al.), **1:**12
History Today (journal), **2:**200, **3:**246, 267
History Workshop Journal, **3:**54, 146, 173, 176, 209, 277
Hitchcott, Nicki, **1:**64
Hitchens, Christopher
　on Guevara (Ernesto "Che"), **2:**222
　on *Infidel* (Hirsi Ali), **1:**209
　Letters to a Young Contrarian, **2:**150
　on Orwell (George), **2:**117, 118, 119

Hitler, Adolf, **1:**31. *See also* Holocaust; Nazi Germany
    Chilean support for, **1:**75
    fall of Berlin and, **2:**281
    Final Solution of, **1:**318
    Mein Kampf, **1:**30–32
    Nella Last's War (Last) on, **2:**265
    Rabe's (John) letter on Nanking Massacre to, **2:**19, 21
    rise to power, **3:**14
    Speer's (Albert) relationship with, **2:**54, 55, 56
    Stein (Gertrude) on, **1:**332
    suicide of, **2:**281
Hitti, Philip K., **1:**287
HIV. *See* AIDS
Hoak, Dale, **2:**98, 99
Hobart, Mary, **2:**331
Hobbs, Nancy, **1:**38
Hobsbawm, Eric J., **2:**18
Hoby, Margaret, **2:**62
Hochstadt, Steve, *Exodus to Shanghai,* **3:**14–16
Hodgson, Dorothy L., **1:**115–116
Hoess, Rudolph, *My Soul,* **2:**54
Ho Feng-Shan, **3:**14
Hoffaman, Abraham, *Vision or Villainy,* **3:**102
Hoffe, Esther, **2:**122
Hoffman, Abbie, **1:**205
Hoffman, Michael J., **1:**333
Hoffman, Nancy, *Woman's "True" Profession,* **3:**77
Hoffmann, Peter, *History of the German Resistance,* **3:**245
Hofstadter, Richard, **1:**134
Hogarth Press, **2:**268
Hoggart, Richard
    The Uses of Literacy, **1:**16
    The Worst of Times, **3:**53
Holcomb, Gary Edward, **1:**85
Holden, Philip, **1:**290, 291
Holland. *See* Netherlands
Holland, Tom, **2:**145
Hollander, Tom, **2:**10
Holler, Clyde, **3:**112
Holmes, Amy J., **2:**244
Holmes, Henry Bry, **2:**245, 246

Holmes, Oliver Wendell, Jr., **1:**134
Holmes, Richard, *The World at War,* **3:**234–236, *235*
Holmes, Stephen, **1:**209
Holocaust
    denial of, **3:**50
    goal of, **3:**50
    Jewish immigration to escape, **1:**75, 76, **3:**14–16
    memorials to, **1:**319, **3:**51
    Nuremberg Laws in, **2:**253, **3:**14
    origins of, **3:**14, 34, 50
    rape in, **2:**283
    targets of, **3:**36, 50
    women survivors of, **3:**34–36
Holocaust autobiographies
    by Frank (Anne), **2:**253–255
    by Hillesum (Etty), **2:**22–24, 253
    by Klemperer (Victor), **2:**303–305
    by Nazis, **2:**54–56
    rise of, **1:**318
    by Wiesel (Elie), **1:**318–320
Holocaust concentration camps
    Auschwitz, **1:**318–320, **2:**22, **3:**35, 51
    Bergen-Belsen, **2:**253, **3:**51
    Buchenwald, **3:**51
    Mauthausen, **3:**51
    Westerbork, **2:**22–24, 253
Holocaust oral histories
    of American survivors and witnesses, **3:**50–52
    of Jewish refugees in China, **3:**14–16
    rise of, **3:**15, 34, 50
    of women survivors, **3:**34–36
    in *The World at War* (Holmes), **3:**235
Holocaust Oral History Manual (Gurewitsch and Eliach), **3:**35
Holoch, Adele, **2:**13
Holroyd, Michael, **2:**269
Holtby, Winifred, **1:**330, 331
    South Riding, **1:**331
Holton, Woody, **2:**90
Holy Club, **2:**195, 197
Holy Land, Guylforde's (Richarde) pilgrimage to, **2:**226–228

Homans, Margaret, **2:**211
Home Elsewhere, A (Stepto), **1:**80
Home Front, The (Satterfield), **3:**202
Homeland Security Department, U.S., **3:**245
Homes, A. M., **1:**48
Homestead Act of 1862 (U.S.), **2:**163, 165
Homesteading
    oral histories of, **3:**93–95
    Ray (Annie) on experience of, **2:**163–164
    Stewart (Elinore Pruitt) on experience of, **2:**91–93, *92*
Home to Harlem (McKay), **1:**84, 86
Homoeroticism
    in James's (Henry) novels, **2:**115
    in Marcus Aurelius's letters, **1:**220
    in *Red Azalea* (Min), **1:**160
Homosexuality
    of Bechdel (Alison), **1:**139, 140
    in Britain, legal ban on, **2:**9, 183, **3:**70
    in Britain, oral histories of, **3:**70–72
    Byron (George Gordon Noel) and, **2:**144
    Chinese persecution of, **1:**158
    in *Fun Home* (Bechdel), **1:**139–141
    gay rights movement, **3:**70, 72, 83–84
    in Harlem Renaissance, **1:**84
    in *Hunger of Memory* (Rodriguez), **1:**17
    James (Henry) and, **2:**115
    in *A Long Way from Home* (McKay), **1:**85
    of Lorde (Audre), **1:**39, **2:**3, 5
    of Maugham (W. Somerset), **2:**183, 185
    of McKay (Claude), **1:**84
    of Sassoon (Siegfried), **2:**247, 248
    in U.S., oral histories of, **3:**83–85
    U.S. attitudes toward, evolution of, **1:**139
    in U.S. military, **1:**139
    of Wilde (Oscar), **2:**9–10
    of Williams (Tennessee), **2:**152

SUBJECT INDEX

Hong, Christina, **1:**294
Hood River Issei, The (Tamura), **3:**80–82
Hooke, Robert, *The Diary of Robert Hooke*, **2:**72
hooks, bell, **1:**250
    Ain't I a Woman, **1:**250
    Bone Black, **1:**249–251
    Wounds of Passion, **1:**250, 251
Hooligan: A History of Respectable Fears (Pearson), **3:**312
Hooligans or Rebels? (Humphries), **3:**144, 311–314
Hooper, Charles, **1:**24
Hooper, Finley, **2:**96
Hooper, Sheila, **1:**24
Hooten, Elizabeth, **2:**26
Hope against Hope (Mandlestam), **1:**271
Hopi, in land dispute with Navajo, oral histories of, **3:**10–12
Hopkins, Anthony, **2:**71
Hopkins, Gerard Manley, **2:**147
Hopkinson, Amanda, **2:**221
Hopkinson, Francis, **2:**316
Hopkinson, Mrs. Thomas, **2:**316, 317
Horacek, Parson, **2:**149
Horn, Eva, **1:**32
Horn Book Magazine, **1:**162
Horniman, Annie, **2:**128
Horowitz, David, **3:**165
Horse of Pride, The (Hélias), **3:**61
Hortensius (Cicero), **1:**196, 198
Horwitz, Tony, **1:**280
Hosbawm, Eric, **3:**186
Hoskins, Katherine, **2:**115
Hospicio é Deus (Lopes Cançado), **2:**6
Hosseini, Khaled, *The Kite Runner*, **1:**40
Houlbrook, Matt, **3:**72
House Arrest (film), **1:**6, 7
Households, isolated vs. collective, Stanton (Elizabeth Cady) on, **1:**14
House Made of Dawn (Momaday), **1:**54
House of Confucius, The (Kong). *See In the Mansion of Confucius' Descendants* (Kong)

House of Representatives, U.S., gag rule on slavery in, **2:**70
House of Si Abd Allah, The (Munson), **3:**47
House of the Seven Gables, The (Hawthorne), **2:**223–224
House on Mango Street, The (Cisneros), **1:**108
House Un-American Activities Committee (HUAC), **2:**152
Housewife, 49 (television show), **2:**265
Houston, James D., *Farewell to Manzanar*, **1:**299–301
Houston, Jeanne Wakatsuki, **1:**300
    Beyond Manzanar, **1:**299
    Farewell to Manzanar, **1:**299–301, 309
    The Legend of Fire Horse Woman, **1:**299
Houston Chronicle (newspaper), **2:**85
Hoveyda, Abbas, **3:**218
Hoveyda, Fereydoun, *Fall of the Shah*, **3:**218
Howard, Maureen, **2:**48
Howard, Neil, **1:**244
Howard-Stepney, Marged, **1:**127
Howe, Barbara, **3:**68
Howe, Florence, *With Wings*, **1:**8
Howe, Lawrence, **1:**146, 147, 148
Howells, William Dean, **1:**146, **2:**239–240, **3:**261
Hower, Edward, **1:**23
How I Grew (McCarthy), **1:**258
Howkins, Alun, **3:**64–65
How the Garcia Girls Lost Their Accents (Alvarez), **1:**108
Hron, Madelaine, **3:**259
HUAC. *See* House Un-American Activities Committee
Huang Dinghui, **3:**148
Hubbell, J. L., **3:**290, 291
Hudson, Derek, **2:**77
Hudson, Hosea
    Black Worker in the Deep South, **1:**3
    The Narrative of Hosea Hudson, **1:**3–4
Hudson Review (journal), **1:**165, 168, **2:**115
Hughes, Barbara, **2:**159

Hughes, Langston
    The Big Sea, **1:**84, 122
    "Harlem," **1:**275
    I Wonder as I Wander, **1:**37
    Mulatto, **1:**72
Hughes, Ted, **2:**47, 48, 49
Human body. *See* Body
Humanism
    Cereta (Laura) in, **2:**160, 161
    Kierkegaard's (Søren) critique of, **2:**166, 167
Human rights
    "Letter from the Birmingham Jail" (King) as argument for, **2:**32
    universal, development of concept, **2:**316
Human rights abuses. *See also* Genocide
    in Cambodia, **1:**306
    in China, **1:**158, 161
    in Guatemala, **1:**99, 100, **3:**164–166
    in Iran, **1:**155
    in Iraq, **2:**275
    in Nazi Germany (*See* Holocaust)
    in Nigeria, **1:**214, 215, 216
    in Sierra Leone, **1:**312
    in South Africa, **3:**242
    in Ukraine, **3:**19
    in Vietnam, **1:**171, 172
Hume, David, **2:**328
Humor
    in *Angela's Ashes* (McCourt), **1:**119
    in *The Autobiography of Ben Franklin* (Franklin), **1:**181
    in *Confessions of Lady Nijo* (Nijo), **2:**60
    in *The Diary of Anne Frank* (Frank), **2:**253–254, 255
    in *Journals of Ralph Waldo Emerson* (Emerson), **2:**141
    in "Letter to Her Daughter from the New White House" (Adams), **2:**87
    in *Life on the Mississippi* (Twain), **1:**147
    in *Praeterita* (Ruskin), **1:**265
    in *Prison Writings* (Peltier), **1:**97

in *Selected Letters of Martha Gellhorn* (Gellhorn), **2:**102

in *Up from Slavery* (Washington), **1:**51–52

in *A Woman in Berlin* (anonymous), **2:**282

Humphrey, Carol Sue, **2:**318

Humphries, Stephen

   The Handbook of Oral History, **3:**313

   Hooligans or Rebels?, **3:**144, 311–314

   on *The World at War* (Holmes), **3:**235

Hunger of Memory (Rodriguez), **1:**15–17, 47

Hunsaker, Steven V., **1:**100

Hunt, Evelyn, **3:**269

Hunt, Leigh, **2:**143, 144, 146

Hunt, Richard, **3:**277

Hunt, Swanee, *This Was Not Our War,* **3:**268

Huntington, Countess of, **2:**44, 46

Huntsman, Jeffrey, **1:**56

Hurst, Fannie, **1:**10

   Imitation of Life, **1:**72

Hurston, Zora Neale

   Angelou (Maya) inspired by, **1:**18

   Dust Tracks on a Road, **1:**9–11, 18, 122

   Mules and Men, **1:**9

   Polk County, **1:**10

   Seraph on the Suwanee, **1:**9

   Tell My Horse, **1:**9, 11

   Their Eyes Were Watching God, **1:**11

   in tradition of Prince (Mary), **3:**24

Hurvitz, Yair, **2:**50

Husain, Adnan, **1:**287–288

Husayn, Taha. *See* Hussein, Taha

Hussain, Soofia, **3:**81

Hussein, Saddam, **2:**275, 276, 278, 279

Hussein, Taha, *An Egyptian Childhood,* **1:**135–138

Hutchinson, Mary, **2:**300

Hutchisson, James M., **2:**42

Hutu people, **3:**257–259, *258*

Huxley, Elspeth, **2:**12

Huxley, Thomas, **1:**67

Huynh, Jade Ngoc Quang, *South Wind Changing,* **1:**171

Hyde-Lees, Georgie, **2:**126

Hypocrisy

   in American Revolution, **2:**44, 45

   in European culture, **1:**90

   in slavery, **1:**34, 144, **2:**44, 45, 46

I

I, Rigoberta Menchú (Menchú), **3:**164–166

   Californio Voices (Savage) vs., **3:**114

   Child of the Dark (de Jesus) vs., **2:**8

   Doña María's Story (James) vs., **3:**73–74

   Let Me Speak! (Viezzer and Barrios de Chungara) vs., **3:**322

   Rites: A Guatemalan Boyhood (Perera) vs., **1:**99

   Women's Words (Gluck and Patai) on, **3:**191

IAD. *See* Institute for Aboriginal Development

I Am Rosa Parks (Parks), **1:**38

Ibn Asakir, **1:**287

Ibrahim, Christy Thompson, **1:**8

I Can Almost See the Lights of Home (Portelli), **3:**265–266

Ichijō (emperor of Japan), **2:**290, 291, 292

Ida (Stein), **1:**332

Idaho, oral histories of life in, **3:**93–95, *94*

Idealization

   of Africa, by Laye (Camara), **1:**130

   of childhood, by Laye (Camara), **1:**128

   of colonial America, by Crèvecoeur (Michel-Guillaume Saint-Jean de), **2:**213–215

Identity. *See also* Ethnic identity; Multicultural and multiracial identities; National identity; *specific groups*

   divided nature of, Rousseau (Jean-Jacques) on, **1:**200–202

   language in, role of, **1:**15–17, **3:**108, 109

   postcolonial, **1:**87–89

Identity formation

   in *Angela's Ashes* (McCourt), **1:**121

   in *Dust Tracks on a Road* (Hurston), **1:**11

   of Irish immigrants, **1:**121

   in *Journal, 1955–1962* (Feraoun), **2:**262–263

   in *The Journals of Charlotte Forten Grimké* (Grimké), **2:**31

   in *Praeterita* (Ruskin), **1:**265

   in *Wars I Have Seen* (Stein), **1:**333–334

Identity politics

   Columbus's (Christopher) legacy and, **2:**203

   cultural studies and, **1:**15

   disability studies and, **1:**8

   Rodriguez's (Richard) critique of, **1:**15–16

IEDs. *See* Improvised explosive devices

If This Is a Man (Levi), **1:**318

"If We Must Die" (McKay), **1:**84

Igbo people, **1:**214, 215

Ignatius of Loyola (saint), **1:**211

"I Have a Dream" (King), **1:**79, **2:**32

I Know Why the Caged Bird Sings (Angelou), **1:**18–20, 249

Ilagiinniq (Tulugarjuk and Christopher), **3:**138

Ill-Fated People, An (Vambe), **3:**251–253

Illinois, Lincoln's (Abraham) life and career in, **3:**261, 263. *See also* Chicago

Illness. *See* Health problems

Illustrated Times of London, **1:**112

Imad al-Din al-Katib al-Isfahani, *The Syrian Thunderbolt,* **1:**286

Image du monde (Guisson), **1:**105

Images and Conversations (Preciado Martin), **3:**121

Imitation of Life (Hurst), **1:**72

Imlay, Gilbert, **2:**111

Immigrant Women in the Land of Dollars (Ewen), **3:**305

SUBJECT INDEX

Immigration
    to Australia, from Vietnam, **1:**337
    to Chile, from Germany, **1:**75, 77
    to France, by Bashkirtseff (Marie), **2:**306–308
    from Ireland, **1:**119
    to Ireland, by Mahomet (Dean), **2:**229
    Jewish (*See* Jewish immigration)
Immigration, to U.S.
    by Agosín (Marjorie), **1:**75
    by Ahmedi (Farah), **1:**40, 41
    by Cheng Yu-hsiu, **1:**152
    Cuban, **1:**296–298
    by Hayslip (Le Ly), **1:**335
    Japanese, **1:**309, **3:**80–82, 127–129, 195
    Jewish, **3:**14, 118, 120
    Latin American, **1:**108–110, **3:**121
    by Medina (Pablo), **1:**296, 297
    by Min (Anchee), **1:**158
    by Nabokov (Vladimir), **1:**270
    by Nguyen (Kien), **1:**170, 171
    oral histories of, **3:**80–82, 305–307
    by Santiago (Esmeralda), **1:**108–110
    by Siv (Sichan), **1:**306, 307
    Southeast Asian, **1:**170, 171, 306–307, 337
    by Suleri (Sara), **1:**87
    after Vietnam War, **1:**170, 171, 337
Immigration Act of 1924 (U.S.), **3:**80, 127, 195
Immigration Act of 1982, Amerasian (U.S.), **1:**170
Immigration and Nationality Act of 1952 (U.S.), **3:**127
Immigration Reform and Control Act of 1986 (U.S.), **3:**121
Impeachment, of Johnson (Andrew), **1:**5
Imprisonment
    of Fox (George), **2:**26
    of Gandhi (Mohandas), **1:**242
    of Ghazzawi ('Izzat), **2:**50
    of Khomeini (Ruhollah), **3:**218, 219
    of Kong Demao, **3:**124
    of Mandela (Nelson), **1:**24, 27–29, **3:**242
    of Nehru (Jawaharlal), **1:**289, 290, 291
    of Ngũgĩ wa Thiong'o, **2:**12–14, *13*
    of Peltier (Leonard), **1:**96–98
    of Polo (Marco), **1:**105
    in Soviet Gulag system, oral histories of, **3:**17–19
    of Soyinka (Wole), **1:**214–216
    of Speer (Albert), **2:**54–56
    of Wilde (Oscar), **2:**9–10
Improvised explosive devices (IEDs), **3:**233
Inada, Lawson Fusao, *Only What We Could Carry,* **3:**80
In All the West No Place Like This (Kincaid and Dahlgren), **3:**93
Incarceration. *See* Imprisonment
Incest, Nin's (Anaïs) experience of, **2:**124
Incident at Oglala (documentary), **1:**96
Incidents in the Life of a Slave Girl (Jacobs), **1:142–145**
    autobiographies inspired by, **1:**18
    A Diary from Dixie (Chesnut) vs., **2:**250
    Equiano's (Olaudah) influence on, **1:**83
    The Journals of Charlotte Forten Grimké (Grimké) vs., **2:**29
    Narrative of the Life of Frederick Douglass (Douglass) vs., **1:**34, 35, 142, 143
In Country (Mason), **1:**335
In Custody (Desai), **1:**87
Independent (newspaper), **2:**239, 269, 276, **3:**316
Indexicality, **2:**267
India
    British partition of (1947), **1:**87, 244
    food of, in Britain, **2:**230, 231
    Gama's (Vasco da) first voyage to, **2:**198–200
    under Mogul Empire, **2:**229
    nationalism in, **1:**289–290

India, British colonial rule of
    Chaudhuri (Nirad C.) on life under, **3:**253
    East India Company in, **2:**229
    end of (1947), **1:**87, 244
    establishment of, **2:**229, 328
    Gandhi (Mohandas) in movement against, **1:**242–244, 289–290
    legacy of, **1:**87–89
    Mahomet (Dean) on culture of, **2:**229–231
    Nehru (Jawaharlal) in movement against, **1:**289–291
Indiana Magazine of History, **3:**109
Indian nationalism, **1:**289–290
Indian Removal Act of 1830 (U.S.), **1:**302, **3:**107
Indian Reorganization Act of 1934 (U.S.), **3:**107
Indian Territory, **3:**325
Indian Trader (Blue), **3:**290, 291
Indigenous people. *See also specific countries and groups*
    Columbus's (Christopher) encounters with, **2:**201, 202, *202*
    Gama's (Vasco da) encounters with, **2:**199
Individual actions, in identity, Rousseau (Jean-Jacques) on, **1:**200, 201
Individuals
    authors as, Lejeune (Philippe) on value of, **1:**239
    in Romantic era, focus on, **2:**16
    "self-made," **1:**180
Indochina, French colonial rule of, **3:**279
Indochinese Refugees (Scott), **1:**335
Indoctrination, in Cultural Revolution, **1:**159, 161, 162
Indonesia, Obama (Barack) in, **1:**78
Industrialization
    in Argentina, **3:**73
    and international labor movement, **3:**157
    in Soviet Union, **3:**17
    of U.S., Thoreau (Henry David) on, **1:**233
Industrialization, in Britain
    of agriculture, **3:**59, 63

in concepts of progress, **2:**146
economic inequality in, **2:**300
social inequality in, **2:**16
Industrial Revolution, Second
    Adams (Henry) on, **1:**132, 134
    Twain (Mark) and, **1:**146
Industrial Workers of the World
    (IWW), **3:**329
    establishment of, **3:**328
    oral histories of, **3:**328–330
    working conditions improved by, **3:**93
Infidel (Hirsi Ali), **1:207–210**
Influenza pandemic of 1918, **1:**258
Ingle, H. Larry, **2:**26, 28
Inheritance law, English, women in, **2:**62–63, 64
In Her Own Words (Morantz), **3:**170
In Light of India (Paz), **1:**222–223
Inman, Henry, **2:336**
In My Country (film), **3:**242
Innocence, loss of
    in *The Dark Child* (Laye), **1:**129
    in *Incidents in the Life of a Slave Girl* (Jacobs), **1:**144
Innocents Abroad, The (Twain), **1:**146
Innovations, in autobiographical writing
    of Cavendish (Margaret), **1:**230, 231
    of Conroy (Frank), **1:**165
    of Hussein (Taha), **1:**135–136
    of Kingston (Maxine Hong), **1:**173
    of Pepys (Samuel), **2:**72
    of Rousseau (Jean-Jacques), **1:**200–202
    of Stein (Gertrude), **1:**332, 333, 334
In Pharaoh's Army (Wolff), **1:**47
In Search of Lost Time (Proust), **1:**265, 270
In Search of Our Roots (Gates), **1:**263
Inside the Third Reich (Speer), **2:**54
In Sierra Leone (Jackson), **1:**312
Institute for Aboriginal Development (IAD), **3:**334, 336
Insurgencies
    in Iraq War, **3:**231, 232, 233

in Salvadoran Civil War, **3:**205, 206, 207
Insurrection Act of 1796 (Britain), **2:**159
Intellectual development, in *The Autobiography of Giambattista Vico* (Vico), **1:**183–185
Intellectual Memoirs (McCarthy), **1:**258
Intercultural adoption, Kim (Elizabeth) on, **1:**102–104
Interesting Narrative of the Life of Olaudah Equiano, The (Equiano), **1:34, 81–83,** 142, **3:**23
Interior, U.S. Department of, **3:**11
Interior Castle (Teresa of Ávila), **1:**212
International Affairs (journal), **1:**25, 291
International Court of Justice, **1:**306
International Jew, The (Ford), **1:**30, 32
International Journal of African Historical Studies, **3:**142, 252
International Journal of Middle East Studies, **3:**220
International Law Commission, UN, **2:**56
International Migration Review (journal), **3:**81, 225
International Review (journal), **2:**70
International Review of Social Research (journal), **3:**320
International Women's Conference, **3:**322
International Women's Year Tribunal, **3:**322
International Workingmen's Association, **3:**3
Internment. *See* Japanese American internment
Interpreter of Maladies (Lahiri), **1:**87
Interpreting the Self (Reynolds), **1:**136, 137, 286, 287
Interracial adoption, Kim (Elizabeth) on, **1:**102–104
Interracial relationships
    in Appalachia, **3:**92
    in Korean War, **1:**102
    McBride (James) on, **1:**72–74
    U.S. attitudes toward, **1:**72–74
    in U.S. postwar occupation of Japan, **3:**127–129

U.S. Supreme Court on, **1:**72, 78
Vietnamese attitudes toward, **1:**170, 171
in Vietnam War, **1:**170
Interrupted Life, An (Hillesum), **2:22–25**
Intertexts (journal), **3:**116
"Interviewing Women" (Oakley), **3:**190
Interviews. *See* Oral histories
In the Cities of the South (Seabrook), **3:**54
In the Combat Zone (Marshall), **3:**221, 279
In the Garden of North American Martyrs (Wolff), **1:**47
In the Mansion of Confucius' Descendants (Kong and Ke), **3:124–126,** 299
In the Presence of Absence (Darwish), **1:255–257**
Intifada, first, **1:**225, **2:**50–52
Into the Jet Age (Wooldridge), **3:**203
Introspection, Ruskin's (John) fear of, **1:**265, 266
Inuits, oral histories of, **3:**138–140, *139*
Inuktitut language, **3:**138, 139–140
Invention of Loneliness, The (Auster), **1:**279
Investigation of Dogmatic Theology (Tolstoy), **1:**194
Invisible Cities (Calvino), **1:**105
Invisible Soldier, The (Motley), **3:**212
Invisible Thread, The (Uchida), **1:309–311**
Iola Leroy (Harper), **1:**143
Iowa, labor movement in, **3:**153
Iran
    coup of 1953 in, **3:**218
    in Iran–Iraq War, **1:**155, 157
    Islam in, **1:**155, 156
    oral histories of political history of, **3:**218–220
    Revolution of 1979 in, **1:**155, 157, **3:**218, 220
    Satrapi (Marjane) on life in, **1:**155–157
    uprising of 1963 in, **3:**218, 219
    White Revolution in, **3:**218
    women's rights in, **3:**218

SUBJECT INDEX

Iranian Studies (journal), **3:**219
Iran–Iraq War (1980–1988), **1:**155, 157
Iraq. *See also* Iraq War
    in Gulf War, **2:**275, 278–280
    in Iran–Iraq War, **1:**155, 157
IraqGirl: Diary of a Teenage Girl in Iraq, **2:**275
Iraq Veterans against the War, **3:**232
Iraq War (2003–2011), **2:**276
    Al-Windawi (Thura) on experience of, **2:**275–276
    embedded journalists in, **2:**278, 280
    vs. Salvadoran Civil War, **3:**207
    U.S. veterans of, oral histories of, **3:**231–233, *232*
Ireland
    Catholicism in, **1:**119–120
    Civil War in, **3:**27, 315
    Easter Uprising in, **3:**27, 315
    English conquest of, **3:**315
    famine in, **3:**27, 315
    gender roles in, **2:**157
    independence movement in, **3:**27–29
    independence of (1922), **1:**119, **3:**315
    Leadbeater (Mary) on life in, **2:**157–159
    Mahomet's (Dean) move to, **2:**229
    McCourt (Frank) on life in, **1:**119–121
    nationalism in, **1:**119, **2:**127, 128, **3:**315
    oral histories of, **3:**27–29, 315–317
    oral traditions of, **1:**121
    poverty in, **1:**119–121
    Quakerism in, **2:**157–159
    Rebellion of 1798 in, **2:**157, *158,* 159
    War of Independence in, **3:**27–29, 315
    Yeats (William Butler) on life in, **2:**126–128
Ireland's Unfinished Revolution (Griffith and O'Grady), **3:**27–30
Irele, Abiola, **1:**130

Irish Americans, McCourt (Frank) on experience of, **1:**119–121
Irish autobiographical writing
    by Leadbeater (Mary), **2:**157–159
    rise in popularity of, **1:**119, 120
    tradition of, **1:**119, 121
    by Yeats (William Butler), **2:**126–128
Irish Civil War (1922–1923), **3:**27, 315
Irish Days (Hickey), **3:315–317**
Irish Experience during the Second World War, The (Grob-Fitzgibbon), **3:**315–316
Irish identity, **1:**121
Irish nationalism, **1:**119, **2:**127, 128, **3:**315
Irish National Theatre Society, **2:**128
Irish oral histories
    on life in twentieth century, **3:**315–317
    on War of Independence, **3:**27–29
Irish Rebellion (1798), **2:**157, *158,* 159
Irish Republican Brotherhood, **3:**27
Irish University Review (journal), **1:**121
Irish Voice (newspaper), **3:**29
Irish War of Independence (1919–1921), **3:**27–29, 315
Irizarry, Estelle, **2:**203
Irvine, Weldon, **1:**274
Isabella of Castille, **2:**201
Isani, Mukhtar Ali, **2:**45
Isay, David, **3:**174
Isca, Valerio, **3:**5
Isham, Ralph Hayward, **2:**330
Isherwood, Christopher, *The World in the Evening,* **2:**152
Islam. *See also* Muslim *entries*
    fundamentalist, **1:**156, 208
    Hirsi Ali's (Ayaan) critique of, **1:**207–209
    in Iran, **1:**155, 156
    Malcolm X's conversion to, **1:**186–188
    violence against women in, **1:**207–209
Islamic education, in Egypt, **1:**135
Isocrates, *To Nicocles,* **2:**94

Isolation
    of households, Stanton (Elizabeth Cady) on, **1:**14
    personal, Hawthorne (Nathaniel) on, **2:**223, 224
Israel
    establishment of (1948), **1:**225, 255, **2:**104, **3:**118
    Palestinian territories occupied by, **1:**225, **2:**50, *51*
Israeli–Palestinian conflict, **1:**225, 255, 257, **2:**50–52
Issei, **3:**80–82
Italian Americans, relocation during World War II, oral histories of, **3:**224–226
Italian autobiographical writing
    by Cereta (Laura), **2:**160–162
    by Polo (Marco), **1:**105–107
    by Vico (Giambattista), **1:**183–185
Italian oral histories
    on Fosse Ardeatine massacre, **3:**265–267
    on working class, **3:**157–159
Italian Quattrocentro, **2:**160
Italy. *See also* Italian autobiographical writing
    education of women in, **2:**160–161
    Fosse Ardeatine massacre in, **3:**265–267
    labor movement in, **3:**157–159, *158*
    Montagu's (Mary Wortley) move to, **2:**35
    Nazi occupation of, **3:**265–267
    Renaissance, women in, **2:**160–162
    working class in, **3:**157–159
It Happened in Brooklyn (Frommer and Frommer), **3:**118
It Happened to Nancy (Sparks), **2:**294
Iverson, Peter, **3:**291
Iwakoshi, Miyo, **3:**82
I Will Bear Witness (Klemperer), **2:303–305**
I Will Marry When I Want (Ngũgĩ), **2:**12
I Wonder as I Wander (Hughes), **1:**37
IWW. *See* Industrial Workers of the World
Izumi Shikibu, **2:**189, 190, 290

J

Jabra, Jabra Ibrahim, *The First Well*, **1**:136
Jacinthe Noir (Amrouche), **1**:93
Jack, Peter Monro, **2**:149
Jacka, Tamara, **3**:301
Jackson, Andrew, **1**:302, **2**:335
Jackson, Anna, **2**:134, 135
Jackson, Ernest, **2**:263
Jackson, Jamie Smith, **2:295**
Jackson, Michael, *In Sierra Leone*, **1**:312
Jackson, Molly, **3**:157
Jackson, Samuel L., **3**:242
Jackson, Timothy P., **2**:24
Jackson-Schebetta, Lisa, **2**:102
JACL. *See* Japanese American Citizens League
Jacobs, Harriet A., *Incidents in the Life of a Slave Girl*, **1:142–145**, *143*
   autobiographies inspired by, **1**:18
   A Diary from Dixie (Chesnut) vs., **2**:250
   Equiano's (Olaudah) influence on, **1**:83
   The Journals of Charlotte Forten Grimké (Grimké) vs., **2**:29
   Narrative of the Life of Frederick Douglass (Douglass) vs., **1**:34, 35, 142, 143
Jacobsen, Jens Peter, **2**:149
Jacob's Room (Woolf), **2**:138
Jaffer, Zubeida, **3**:243
Jamaica
   English colonial rule of, **1**:111
   McKay's (Claude) youth in, **1**:84, 85
   slavery in, **1**:111
Jamaican autobiographical writing
   by McKay (Claude), **1**:84–86
   by Seacole (Mary), **1**:111–113
James, Alice, **2**:113
James, Daniel, *Doña María's Story*, **3**:73–76
James, Henry, **2**:114
   Adams (Henry) influenced by, **1**:132–133
   The Bostonians, **2**:113

The Complete Notebooks of Henry James, **2:113–116**
   Confidence, **2**:114
   Daisy Miller, **1**:133, **2**:114
   Gellhorn (Martha) on, **2**:101
   Guy Domville, **2**:114
   on *Journal des Goncourt* (Goncourt and Goncourt), **2**:82–83
   Kemble's (Fanny) friendship with, **2**:335, 336
   The Notebooks of Henry James, **2**:113, 114, 115
   The Portrait of a Lady, **1**:133, **2**:113
   Roderick Hudson, **2**:114
   The Spoils of Poynton, **2**:115
   Wells's (H. G.) letters to, **1**:252, 253
   The Wings of the Dove, **2**:113, 115
James, William, **1**:197, **2**:113
James I (king of England), **1**:316, **2**:62
James II (king of England), **1**:315
Jameson, Anna, **2**:335
Jamison, Kay Redfield, *An Unquiet Mind*, **1**:204
Japan. *See also* Japanese autobiographical writing
   Buddhism in (*See* Buddhism)
   China invaded by (1931), **3**:215
   Chinese relations with, **1**:340, **3**:149
   gender roles in, **2**:60–61
   Heian period in (*See* Heian period)
   hibakusha literature of, **1**:293
   immigration to U.S. from, **1**:309, **3**:80–82, 127–129, 195
   Kamakura period in, **2**:59–61
   Korea under rule of, **1**:322–324
   marriage in, **2**:297–299
   Mongol invasions of, **2**:59
   in Nanking Massacre, **1**:340, **2**:19–21
   Nara period in, **2**:189
   nationalism in, **3**:234
   in Russo–Japanese War, **1**:322, **3**:234
   in Sino–Japanese Wars, **1**:322, 339, 340, **3**:234
   in World War II, oral histories of, **3**:127–129, 215–217 (*See also* World War II)

Japan at War (Cook and Cook), **3:215–217**
Japanese, Nazis & Jews (Kranzler), **3**:15
Japanese American(s)
   autobiographical tradition of, **1**:299, 309
   first-generation, oral histories of, **3**:80–82
   Houston (Jeanne Wakatsuki) on experience of, **1**:299–301
   internment of (*See* Japanese American internment)
   Japanese war brides, oral histories of, **3**:127–129, *128*
   racism against, **1**:309, **3**:81, 82, 127, 195
   Uchida (Yoshiko) on experience of, **1**:309–311
Japanese American Citizens League (JACL), **3**:197
Japanese American internment, **1:310, 3:196**
   establishment of policy, **1**:299, 311, **3**:104, 195
   Houston (Jeanne Wakatsuki) on experience of, **1**:299–301
   Italian American relocation and, **3**:224
   at Manzanar, **1**:299–301, **3**:102–104, 197, *225*
   oral histories of, **3**:80–81, 102–104, 195–197
   reparations for, **3**:195, 197
   Uchida (Yoshiko) on experience of, **1**:309–311
Japanese American Oral History Project, **3**:80, 102, 195
Japanese American World War II Evacuation Oral History Project (Hansen), **3**:215
Japanese autobiographical writing. *See also specific works and writers*
   by Michitsuna No Haha, **2**:297–299
   by Murasaki Shikibu, **2**:290–292
   by Nakazawa (Keiji), **1**:293–295
   by Nijo (Lady), **2**:59–61
   by Sarashina (Lady), **2**:189–191
   by women, tradition of, **2**:59, 60

Japanese War Brides in America (Crawford et al.), **3:**127–130
Japan-Russia Treaty of Peace, **3:**234
Jarrell, Randall, **1:**205
Jaspers, Karl, **2:**167
Jawhariyyeh, Wasif, **2:**104
Jay's Journal (Sparks), **2:**294
Jayyusi, Salma Khadra, **1:**225, 227
Jazz
    and *Stop-Time* (Conroy), **1:**165, 166
    Terkel's (Louis "Studs") writing style compared to, **3:**214
Jefferson, Alexander, **3:**249
Jefferson, Lucy, **2:**316
Jefferson, Martha, **2:**316–318
Jefferson, Mary, **2:**316
Jefferson, Thomas, **2:**317
    Autobiography, 1743–1790, **1:**179, **2:**69
    on coal in Appalachia, **3:**86
    Crèvecoeur (Michel-Guillaume Saint-Jean de) and, **2:**213, 215
    The Family Letters of Thomas Jefferson, **2:**317
    Letters from Jefferson to His Daughter, **2:**38, **316–319**
    Notes on the State of Virginia, **2:**45, 215
    on Wheatley's (Phillis) poetry, **2:**45
Jeffrey, Francis, **2:**35, 36, 73
Jelinek, Estelle, **1:**246
Jelmek, Estelle C., **1:**14
Jemima Condict (Condict), **2:**78–80
Jemison, Mary, **1:**326
Jenner, W. J. F., **3:**299
Jennings, Humphrey, **2:**235
Jeon, Miseli, **1:**103, 104
Jerome, **2:**94
Jerusalem, **2:**227
    under British Mandate, 'Amr (Sāmī) on, **2:**104, 105, *105*
    Guylforde's (Richarde) pilgrimage to, **2:**226–228
    secular education in, **2:**106
Jessee, Erin, **3:**180
Jesus, Carolina Maria de. *See* De Jesus, Carolina Maria

Jew(s)
    anarchism among, **3:**3
    in Chile, **1:**75–77
    in Guatemala, **1:**99–100
    in interracial relationships, **1:**72–74
    prejudice against (*See* Anti-Semitism)
    The Protocols of the Elder of Zion on conspiracy of, **1:**32
    in World War II (*See* Holocaust)
Jewel of the Desert (Taylor), **3:**80
Jewish American Committee, **3:**118
Jewish autobiographical writing. *See also specific works and writers*
    by Agosín (Marjorie), **1:**75–77
    by D'Israeli (Isaac), **2:**177, 179
    by Frank (Anne), **2:**253–255
    by Hillesum (Etty), **2:**22–24
    by Kafka (Franz), **2:**120–122
    by Klemperer (Victor), **2:**303–305
    by Perera (Victor), **1:**99–101
    by Stein (Gertrude), **1:**332, 333
    by Wiesel (Elie), **1:**318–320
Jewish Community of North Minneapolis, The (Lewin), **3:**50
Jewish identity
    of Jewish Americans, **3:**119
    of Jewish refugees, **1:**75–77
Jewish immigration
    to China, **3:**14–16
    to Latin America, **1:**75, 76, *76*
    to Palestine, **2:**105, **3:**14
    to U.S., **3:**14, 118, 120
Jewish oral histories. *See also* Holocaust oral histories
    of anarchists, **3:**3
    of U.S. life, **3:**118–120
Jewish Social Studies (journal), **1:**31
Jeyifo, Biodun, **1:**215, 216
Jiang, Ji-li
    Magical Monkey King, **1:**163
    Red Scarf Girl, **1:**153, 154, 159, **161–163**
Jiang Quing, **1:**158
Jiang Zemin, **1:**158
Jim Crow laws. *See* Racial segregation

Job Corps, **3:**254
Johansen, Bruce, **1:**97
John, Augustus Edwin, **2:127**
John II (king of Portugal), **2:**198
John of the Cross (saint), **1:**211
Johnson, Andrew, **1:**5
Johnson, Arvid, **3:**94
Johnson, Charles, **1:**10
Johnson, David, **2:**219, **3:**143
Johnson, E. D. H., **2:**300
Johnson, James Weldon, *Along This Way*, **1:**13, 84, 122
Johnson, Josephine, **2:**152
Johnson, Kendall, **1:**54, **2:**115
Johnson, Lyndon Baines, **3:**254–256, 255
Johnson, Martin, **3:**261, 264
Johnson, Pamela Hansford, **1:**127
Johnson, Penny, **1:**226
Johnson, Richard, *Making History*, **3:**176, 177
Johnson, Robert David, **3:**254
Johnson, Samuel
    on *Evelina* (Burney), **2:**313
    letters of, **2:**217
    Life of Samuel Johnson (Boswell) on, **2:**177, 195, 309, 328, 329–330
    on *Turkish Embassy Letters* (Montagu), **2:**37
Johnson, Tom, **3:**200, 338
Johnsrud, Harold, **1:**258
Jolluck, Katherine R., *Gulag Voices*, **3:17–19**, 331
Jolote, Juan Pérez, **3:**167–169
Jones, Bob, **3:**5
Jones, Catherine, **2:**311
Jones, Edward P., **1:**122
Jones, John Paul, **1:180**
Jones, J. William, **2:**38, 39
Jones, Lu Ann, **3:**135–136, 137
Jones, Roderick, **2:**261
Jörgensen, Beth Ellen, **3:**31, 32
Josephson, Paul, **3:**285
Journal(s). *See also specific works and writers*
    Lejeune (Philippe) on study of, **2:**174–175

rise in popularity of, in England, **2:**177
of ships' captains, Spanish law on, **2:**201
as source for biographies, **2:**177, 178

Journal, 1955–1962 (Feraoun), **2:262–264**

Journal and Remarks 1832–1835 (Darwin), **1:**65

Journal des Goncourt (Goncourt and Goncourt), **2:81–83**

Journal for Early Modern Cultural Studies, **2:**199

Journal for the Scientific Study of Religion, **3:**41

Journalism
African Americans in, **3:**199–200
Gellhorn's (Martha) career in, **2:**101–102
on hooliganism in Britain, **3:**312
literary, in Enlightenment England, **2:**328
Moore's (Molly) career in, **2:**278–280
Orwell's (George) work in, **2:**117

Journal of Acquired Immune Deficiency Syndromes, **3:**274

Journal of Adolescent & Adult Literacy, **1:**41, 162, **2:**276

Journal of American Ethnic History, **3:**5, 81, 306, 320

Journal of American Folklore, **3:**88, 91, 109

Journal of American History
on *And Justice for All* (Tateishi), **3:**197
on *Bloods* (Terry), **3:**201
on *Brokenburn* (Stone), **2:**246
on *Children of Los Alamos* (Mason), **3:**240
on *The Death of Luigi Trastulli* (Portelli), **3:**159
on *Freedom Flyers* (Moye), **3:**249
on *Habits of Change* (Rogers), **3:**309
on *Head of the Class* (Morris), **3:**22
on *Hill Country Teacher* (Manning), **3:**77
on *The Hispanic-American Entrepreneur* (Owsley), **3:**122
on *The Hood River Issei* (Tamura), **3:**80
on *Launching the War on Poverty* (Gillette), **3:**254
on *A Midwife's Tale* (Ulrich), **2:**333
on *Our Appalachia* (Shackelford and Weinberg), **3:**87
on *Peacework* (Adams), **3:**269
on *A Shared Authority* (Frisch), **3:**181
on *Solidarity Forever* (Bird et al.), **3:**329
on *They Say in Harlan County* (Portelli), **3:**98
on *"We Have Just Begun to Not Fight"* (Frazer and O'Sullivan), **3:**229

Journal of American Studies, **3:**5, 163, 213

Journal of an Ordinary Grief (Darwish), **1:**255

Journal of Appalachian Studies, **3:**68

Journal of Arabic and Islamic Studies, **1:**255

Journal of a Residence in America (Kemble), **2:**335, 336

Journal of a Residence on a Georgian Plantation (Kemble), **2:**335, 336, 337

Journal of Asian American Studies, **3:**84, 85

Journal of Asian and African Studies, **3:**148

Journal of Asian Studies, **3:**148, 280, 281

Journal of a Tour into the Interior (Barnard), **2:**217, 218

Journal of a Tour to the Hebrides, The (Boswell), **2:**328

Journal of a Voyage to North-America (Charlevoix), **2:**205

Journal of Black Studies, **1:**5, 188

Journal of Canadian Studies, **3:**181

Journal of Commonwealth Literature, **1:**88

Journal of Conflict Studies, **3:**207

Journal of Contemporary History, **3:**35

Journal of English Studies, **1:**251

Journal of Family History, **2:**91, **3:**126

Journal of Folklore Research Reviews, **3:**12, 326

Journal of General Education, **3:**345

Journal of George Fox (Fox), **2:26–28**

Journal of Ideology, **3:**291

Journal of Japanese Studies, **2:**60, **3:**216

Journal of John Woolman, The (Woolman), **2:**213

Journal of Jules Renard, The (Renard), **2:**183

Journal of Katherine Mansfield (Mansfield), **2:133–135**

Journal of Literary Studies, **1:**29

Journal of Madam Knight, The (Knight), **2:**78

Journal of Magellan's Voyage (Pigafetta), **2:**201

Journal of Marie Bashkirtseff, The (Bashkirtseff), **2:306–308**

Journal of Military History, **3:**116, 216

Journal of Modern African Studies, **1:**26

Journal of Modern History, **3:**19

Journal of Modern Literature, **1:**17, **2:**122, 269

Journal of Narrative Theory, **1:**121

Journal of Negro History, **1:**11, **2:**45

Journal of New Zealand Literature, **2:**134

Journal of Pan African Studies, **1:**244

Journal of Sir Walter Scott, The (Scott), **2:**67, **309–311**

Journal of Social and Clinical Psychology, **1:**205

Journal of Social Archaeology, **3:**116

Journal of Social History, **3:**75, 145, 311

Journal of Southeast Asian American Education and Advancement, **1:**307

Journal of Southern History, **3:**78, 91, 96, 261

Journal of the American Oriental Society, **1:**287

Journal of the First Voyage of Vasco da Gama, A (Author Unknown), **2:198–200,** 201

Journal of the First Voyage to America (Columbus), **2:201–204,** 205

Journal of the History of Medicine and Applied Science, **3:**272

Journal of the History of Sexuality, **3:**84

Journal of the Midwest Modern Language Association, **3:**329

Journal of the Plague Year (Defoe), **2:**174

SUBJECT INDEX

Journal of the Royal Anthropological Institute, **3:**142
Journal of Women's History, **3:**136
Journals of Arnold Bennett, The (Bennett), **2:**136–138
Journals of Charlotte Forten Grimké, The (Grimké), **2:**29–31
Journals of John Wesley (Wesley), **2:**195–197
Journals of Jonathan Carver and Related Documents, The (Carver), **2:**205–208
Journals of Ralph Waldo Emerson (Emerson), **2:**139–142
Journals of Søren Kierkegaard (Kierkegaard), **2:**166–169
Journey of Tai-me, The (Momaday), **1:**54
Journey's End (Sherriff), **1:**329
Journey to the Land of No (Hakakian), **1:**155
Jouvenel, Bertrand de, **2:**102
Joyce, James
    Conroy (Frank) influenced by, **1:**164
    Evelyn's (John) influence on, **2:**67
    Finnegans Wake, **1:**185
    Goethe's (Johann Wolfgang von) influence on, **1:**276
    Literary Fund and, **2:**207
    Portrait of the Artist as a Young Man, **1:**276, **2:**126
    Thomas (Dylan) influenced by, **1:**125
    Ulysses, **1:**146, **2:**67, 180
    Vico's (Giambattista) influence on, **1:**185
    Woolf's (Virginia) critique of, **2:**180
Joye, Harlon, *Living Atlanta,* **3:**44
Juan Pérez Jolote (Pozas). *See Juan the Chamula* (Pozas)
Juan the Chamula (Pozas), **3:**167–169
Jubilee (Alexander), **1:**262
Judaism. *See* Jew(s)
Judas Kiss, The (play), **2:**10
Judgment at Nuremberg (film), **3:**295
Judicial system, U.S. *See also* Supreme Court

    racism of, in Peltier's (Leonard) trial, **1:**96
Judy Lopez Memorial Award for Children's Literature, for *Red Scarf Girl* (Jiang), **1:**161
Julian (Roman emperor), **1:**220
Julian of Eclanum, **1:**198
Julian of Norwich, **1:**189
    Showings, **1:**211
Jung, Carl, **1:**252, **3:**111
Junod, Violaine, **1:**25
Justice Department, U.S., **3:**224

K

Kabyle culture, preservation of, **1:**93–95
Kadi, Joanna, **1:**227
Kafka, Franz, **2:**121
    Amerika, **2:**120
    The Blue Octavo Notebooks, **2:**122
    The Castle, **2:**120
    The Diaries of Franz Kafka, **2:**120–122
    "The Great Wall of China," **2:**120
    The Trial, **2:**120, 121–122
Kagan, Richard C., **1:**172
Kagero Diary, The (Michitsuna). *See Gossamer Years, The* (Michitsuna)
Kahf, Mohja, *The Girl in the Tangerine Scarf,* **1:**41–42
Kahn, Ava, **3:**51–52
Kahn-Levitt, Laurie, **2:**331
Kakutani, Michiko, **1:**79, 120, **3:**183, 184, 185, 201
Kalvelage, Lisa Schmidt, **3:**269
Kamakura period (Japan), Nijo (Lady) on life in, **2:**59–61
Kameyama (Japanese emperor), **2:**59
Kana writing, **2:**290, 292
Kandinsky, Wassily, **1:**272
Kane, Cheikh Hamidou, *L'Aventure ambiguë,* **1:**61
Kanon, Joseph, **2:**282
KANU. *See* Kenya African National Union
Kaori Hayashi, Katie, *Japanese War Brides in America,* **3:**127–130

Kaplan, Morris, **3:**72
Kappus, Franz Xaver, **2:**149–150
Kapungu, Leonard T., *The United Nations and Economic Sanctions against Rhodesia,* **3:**251
Karkabi, Barbara, **2:**85
Karlsen, Carol F., **2:**333
Karr, Mary, **1:**40, 251, 259–260
Karush, Matthew, **3:**74, 75
Kashiwahara, Ken, **3:**280
Kashmir, dispute over, **1:**87
Katherine Mansfield Notebooks, The (Mansfield), **2:**133, 134
Katovsky, Bill, *Embedded,* **3:**276
Katz, Kimberly, **2:**104, 105, 106
Kaunda, Kenneth, *Zambia Must Be Free,* **1:**290
Kazan, Elia, **2:**152
Kazin, Alfred, **1:**320, **2:**47
Kearney, Michael, **3:**303
Kearns, Judith, **1:**316
Kearns, Kevin C.
    Dublin Pub Life and Lore, **3:**315, 317
    Dublin Voices, **3:**315
Keats, George, **2:**147
Keats, John, **2:**147
    The Letters of John Keats, **2:**146–148
    Life, Letters, and Literary Remains, **2:**146
    Selected Letters, **2:**146
Keckley, Elizabeth Hobbes, *Behind the Scenes,* **1:**52
Keenan, Edward N., **3:**219
Keene, Donald, **2:**191
Kehagia, Angie, **2:**124–125
Kéita, Aoua, *Femme d'Afrique,* **1:**64
Keitel, Wilhelm, **2:**54
Ke Lan, *In the Mansion of Confucius' Descendants,* **3:**124–126, 299
Keller, Bill, **1:**28, 29
Keller, Helen, **1:**44
    Midstream, **1:**44
    "My Life," **1:**43
    The Story of My Life, **1:**43–46
    The World I Live In, **1:**44, 45
Kellerman, Stewart, **1:**100

Kelley, James E., Jr., **2**:203
Kelly, Debra, **2**:263–264
Kelly, Éamon, **3**:315
Kelly, Orrin, **3**:162
Kelly, Sheldon, **1**:307
Kemble, Charles, **2**:335
Kemble, Fanny, **2:336**
   Journal of a Residence in America, **2**:335, 336
   Journal of a Residence on a Georgian Plantation, **2**:335, 336, 337
   "An Old Woman's Gossip," **2**:335
   Records of a Girlhood, **2:335–337**
   A Year of Consolation, **2**:336
Kemp, Lysander, **3**:167, 168
Kempe, Margery, *The Book of Margery Kempe,* **1:189–192,** 211, **2**:226
Kendall-Smith, Malcolm, **3**:229
Kennedy, John F., **2**:32, **3**:254
Kennedy, Randall, *Blacks at Harvard,* **3**:21
Kentucky
   coal mining in, oral histories of, **3**:86–87, 96–98, *97,* 157
   Coe Ridge community in, oral histories of, **3**:90–92
   school desegregation in, **1**:249
   working class in, oral histories of, **3**:157–159
Kenya
   borders of, establishment of, **1**:114
   British colonial rule of, **2**:12, **3**:141–143
   independence of (1963), **2**:12, **3**:141
   Mau Mau rebellion in, **2**:12
   Meru people of, oral histories of, **3**:141–143, *142*
   Ngũgĩ wa Thiong'o on life in, **2**:12–14
   Obama's (Barack) visits to, **1**:78, 79
Kenya African National Union (KANU), **2**:12
Kenyatta, Jomu, **2**:12
Keppel-Jones, Arthur, **3**:252
Keppler, Joseph, **1:147**
Kermode, Frank, **1**:268, 269
Kerouac, Jack, *On the Road,* **1**:234
Kerr, Walter, **2**:154

Kertész, Imre, **1**:318
Kesselman, Wendy, **2**:253
Kessler, Lauren, *Stubborn Twig,* **3**:80
Keynes, John Maynard, **2**:180
Keyser, Katherine, **1**:258
KGB, Stasi modeled on, **3**:245
Khalid, Robina Josephine, **2**:5
Khalifat movement, **1**:244
Khan, Shahnaz, **1**:88
Khashan, 'Abd al-Karim, **2**:52
Khmer Rouge, **1**:306–308
Khomeini, Ruhollah, **1**:155, **3**:218, 219
Khrushchev, Nikita, **3**:331, 333
Kidder, Annemarie S., **2**:149
Kiehr, Kathy, **3:187**
Kierkegaard, Søren, *Journals of Søren Kierkegaard,* **2:166–169,** *167*
Kihn, W. Langdon, **1**:55
Kikumura, Akemi, **1**:300
Kilani, Sami, *Three Minus One,* **2**:52
Kilinc, Ibrahim, **3**:219
Killam, Douglas, **2**:14
Kilvert, Francis, **2**:287, 288
Kim, Eleana J., *Adopted Territory,* **1**:102–103
Kim, Elizabeth, *Ten Thousand Sorrows,* **1:102–104,** *103*
Kim, Richard E., *Lost Names,* **1**:102
Kim Gu. *See* Kim Ku
Kim Ku, *Paekpom Ilchi,* **1:322–324,** *323*
Kimura, Saeko, **2**:61
Kincaid, Jamaica, **1**:111
Kincaid, Simone Carbonneau, *In All the West No Place Like This,* **3**:93
Kindersley, Jemima, *Letters from the Island of Teneriffe,* **2**:229
King, Adele, **1**:128, 130
King, Clarence, **1**:132
King, Florence, **2**:331
King, Martin Luther, Jr., **2:33**
   assassination of, **1**:20
   Gandhi's (Mohandas) influence on, **1**:242
   "I Have a Dream," **1**:79, **2**:32
   "Letter from the Birmingham Jail," **2:32–34**

   vs. Malcolm X, approaches of, **1**:186
   national holiday celebrating, **1**:37, **2**:33
   in SCLC, **1**:20, **2**:32, 34
   Voices of Freedom (Hampton and Fayer) on, **3**:44
King, Mary Elizabeth, **2**:52
King, Peter, **2**:24
King, R. W., **2**:76–77
King Lear (Shakespeare), **2**:147
King Philip's War (1675–1676), **1**:325–328, *326*
Kingsley, Mary, *Travels in West Africa,* **2**:335
Kingston, Maxine Hong
   China Men, **1**:173
   Tripmaster Monkey, **1**:173
   The Woman Warrior, **1**:75, 100, **173–176**
Kinnell, Galway, **2**:150
Kinsington (London), **2:321**
Kiowa Tribe, Momaday (N. Scott) on history of, **1**:54–56
Kipling, Rudyard, **1**:88, **2**:192
Kirkus Reviews (magazine)
   on *Bone Black* (hooks), **1**:250
   on *Golden Bones* (Siv), **1**:307
   on *Growing Up Jewish in America* (Frommer and Frommer), **3**:119
   on *Machete Season* (Hatzfeld), **3**:259
   on *Spandau* (Speer), **2**:56
   on *Strange Ground* (Maurer), **3**:277
   on *The Strength Not to Fight* (Tollefson), **3**:222
   on *Tears before the Rain* (Engelmann), **3**:280
   on *The Unwanted* (Nguyen), **1**:172
Kirsch, Jonathan, **2**:279, **3**:45
Kitab al-I'tibar (Usamah). *See Arab-Syrian Gentleman and Warrior in the Period of the Crusades, An* (Usamah)
Kite Runner, The (Hosseini), **1**:40
Ki Tsurayuki, **2**:191
Klæstrup, Peter, **2:167**
Klaus, Ida, **3**:155
Klee, Paul, **2**:120

SUBJECT INDEX

Kleege, Georgina, **1**:45

Klein, Josephine, *Samples from English Culture,* **3**:144

Klemperer, Eva, **2**:303, 305

Klemperer, Victor
    Curriculum Vitae, **2**:304, 305
    I Will Bear Witness, **2:303–305**
    The Lesser Evil, **2**:304
    Lingua Tertii Imperii (LTI), **2**:304, 305

Klinkhammer, Stephen, **3**:209

Klotter, James C., **3**:88

Kluckhohn, Clyde, **3**:290

Klum, Heidi, **3**:345

K'Meyer, Tracy E., **3**:192, 309

Knight, Sarah Kemble, *The Journal of Madam Knight,* **2**:78

Knight, William Angus, **2**:300

Kniss, Lloy, **3**:229

"Knole Diary" (Clifford), **2**:62, 64

Knoll, Kristina R., **1**:41

Ko, Dorothy, **3**:147

Koch, Grace, **3**:335, 336

Koch, John T., **3**:29

Koegel, John, **3**:133

Kohbieter, Gérard, **3**:15

Kohn, Alfred, **3**:15

Kohn, Hans, **1**:291

Kohn, Rita T.
    Always a People, **3:107–109**, 325
    Long Journey Home, **3**:107, **325–327**

Koker, David, *At the Edge of the Abyss,* **2**:253

Kong Decheng, **3**:124

Kong Demao, *In the Mansion of Confucius' Descendants,* **3:124–126**, 299

Konile, Notrose Nobomvu, **3**:242

Konner, Melvin, **3**:37

Konrad Wallenrod (Mickiewicz), **2**:192

Koppedrayer, Kay, **1**:244

Kopple, Barbara, **3**:98

Korea
    division of (1945), **1**:322
    independence movement in, **1**:322–324
    interracial children in, **1**:102

    Japanese imperialist rule of, **1**:322–324
    Kim Ku on life in, **1**:322–324

Korea Herald (newspaper), **1**:103

Korean Americans, Kim (Elizabeth) on experience of, **1**:102–104

Korean Provisional Government (KPG), **1**:322–324

Korean War (1950–1953), **1**:102, **3**:199

Korg, Jacob, **1**:126, **2**:322

Kornbluh, Joyce L, *Rocking the Boat,* **3**:337

Kostopulos-Cooperman, Celeste, **1**:77

Kotkin, Stephen, **3**:341

Kotze, Annemare, **1**:198

Kovic, Ron, *Born on the Fourth of July,* **1**:335, **3**:209

Kovner, Sarah, *Occupying Power,* **3**:128

Kozol, Jonathon, *Letters to a Young Teacher,* **2**:150

KPG. *See* Korean Provisional Government

Kramer, Jane, **1**:175

Kramer, Samuel, **2**:94

Kramer, Stanley, **3**:295

Kramskoy, Nicholas, **1**:194

Kranzler, David, *Japanese, Nazis & Jews,* **3**:15

Krapf, Ludwig, **1**:115

Krause, Corinne Azen, *Grandmothers, Mothers, and Daughters,* **3:305–307**

Kreider, Robert, *Sourcebook,* **3**:227

Kresh, Joseph, **2**:121

Kristof, Nicholas, **1**:209

Krog, Antjie
    Begging to Be Black, **3**:242
    A Change of Tongue, **3**:242
    Country of My Skull, **3:242–244**
    There Was This Goat, **3**:242

Kropotkin, Peter, **2**:120

Krowl, Michelle, **2**:273

Krupat, Arnold, *For Those Who Come After,* **1**:71

Kruse, Horst, **1**:146, 147

Kublai Khan, **1**:105, 106, 107

Kuhn, Clifford, *Living Atlanta,* **3**:44

Kukis, Mark, **3**:212

Ku Klux Klan, **1**:186–187

Kumashiro, Kevin, *Restoried Selves,* **3**:83

!Kung people, oral histories of, **3**:37–38

Kunin, Aaron, **2**:64

Künstler, Mort, **2**:273

Künstler-Roman, **1**:276

Kushner, Tony, **3**:235

Kusmer, Kenneth, **3**:87–88

Kuwait, in Gulf War (1991), **2**:278–280

Kwong, Luke S. K., **3**:301

Kyalanova, Irina, **1**:314

Kyoto (Japan), **2**:59, 61, 189, 290, 297, *298*

L

Labor, forced
    in China, **1**:158
    in Soviet Union (*See* Gulag system)

Labor arbitration, oral histories of, **3**:153–155

Labor History (journal), **3**:341

Labor movement, oral histories of
    arbitration in, **3**:153–155
    in Argentina, **3**:73–75
    in Bolivia, **3**:322–324
    in Idaho, **3**:93
    in Iowa, **3**:153
    in Italy, **3**:157–159, *158*
    by IWW members, **3**:328–330
    in Kentucky, **3**:96–98, 157–159
    in Michigan, **3**:99, 101
    tradition of, **3**:153, 157

Labor Party (Argentina), **3**:73

Labor strikes
    by coal miners, **3**:96–98
    by IWW, **3**:328

Labor Studies Journal, **3**:68

Labour (journal), **3**:338

Labour History (journal), **3**:177, 313

Labour History Review (journal), **3**:64, 341

Labour Party (Britain), **2**:16

Lacan, Jacques, **1**:267, **3**:188

Ladies' Home Journal, **1**:43

Ladjevardi, Habib
Memoirs of Fatemeh Pakravan, **3:**218–220
Memoirs of Prince Hamid Kadjar, **3:**219
Memoirs of Shapour Bakhtiar, **3:**220

Lady Murasaki Shu (Murasaki), **2:**291
LaFarge, Oliver, **3:**318
Laffont, Robert, **2:**338
La Forte, Robert S., *Remembering Pearl Harbor,* **3:**202
Lagos de Moreno (Mexico), land redistribution movement in, **3:**302–303
Lahiri, Jhumpa, *Interpreter of Maladies,* **1:**87
Lahontan, Baron de, *New Voyages to North-America,* **2:**205
Lakota Sioux
Black Elk on life as, **3:**110–113
Brave Bird (Mary) on life as, **1:**21–23, 22
Lakota Woman (Brave Bird), **1:**21–23
Lalla Aicha (princess of Morocco), **3:**49
Lamb, Caroline, **2:**143, 145
Glenarvon, **2:**145
Lamb, Charles, **2:**75
Lamb, Mary Ellen, **2:**64
Lame Deer, **1:**23
Lamentation of a Sinner (Parr), **2:**97
Lamott, Anne, *Bird by Bird,* **1:**280
Lampert, Jo, **3:**336
Lampkins, Robert, **3:**87
Lampman, Robert, **3:**255
La Navidad, **2:**203
Lancashire (England), **3:**64
Lancaster, Burt, **3:**295
Land
of Australian Aborigines, **1:**149, **3:**334–335
British, inheritance by women, **2:**62–63, 64
of Maasai people, **1:**114
Mexican, redistribution of, **3:**302–304
of Native Americans, **1:**302, **3:**10–12, 110

U.S., restrictions on immigrant ownership of, **3:**195
of VaShawasha people, **3:**251
Landlord's Friend, The (Leadbeater), **2:**157
Land Ordinance of 1785 (U.S.), **2:**163
Land redistribution movement, in Mexico, **3:**302–304
Lane, Charles, **1:**235
Lane, James B., **3:**161
Langbauer, Laurie, **2:**209, 211
Langer, Lawrence, **2:**24
Langford, Rachel, **2:**174
Langhamer, Claire, **3:**146
Language(s)
acquisition of, by Keller (Helen), **1:**44
in identity, **1:**15–17, **3:**108, 109
power of, Momaday (N. Scott) on, **1:**55
in U.S. education, **1:**15, 16
Language of Blood, The (Trenka), **1:**102
La Niña (ship), **2:**203
Lanzmann, Claude, **3:**50, 52
La Pinta (ship), **2:**203
Larcius Macedo, **2:**96
Larg, D. G., **2:**77
Larner, John, **1:**107
Larson, Charles R., **1:**129
Larson, Ronald, *Camp and Community,* **3:**102, 103–104
Larson, Wendy, **3:**148
La Salle, Robert de, **1:**146–147
Las Casas, Bartolomé de
History of Indies, **2:**201
Journal of the First Voyage to America (Columbus) assembled by, **2:**201–203, 205
A Short Account of the Destruction of the Indies, **2:**201
Lassner, Phyllis, **2:**269
Last, Clifford, **2:**265, 266
Last, Nella
Mitchison (Naomi) compared to, **2:**235
Nella Last's Peace, **2:**265
Nella Last's War, **2:**265–267
Last, William, **2:**265

Last Confessions of Marie Bashkirtseff, The (Bashkirtseff), **2:**306
Last Diary of Tsaritsa Alexandra, The (Alexandra), **2:**84–86
Last Essays (Conrad), **2:**193, 194
Last Maasai Warrior, The (Meikuaya and Ntirkana), **1:**114
Last Man, The (Shelley), **2:**145
Last of the Mohicans (Cooper), **1:**56
"Late Benjamin Franklin, The" (Twain), **1:**181–182
Latimer, Hugh, **2:**97
Latin America. *See also specific countries*
Agosín (Marjorie) on experience of Jews in, **1:**75–77
autobiographical tradition of, **1:**222–223
culture of, in U.S. culture, **1:**109
Guevara's (Ernesto "Che") journey through, **2:**220–222
immigration to U.S. from, **1:**108–110, **3:**121
Perera (Victor) on experience of Jews in, **1:**99–100
poverty in, **2:**220–221
right-wing dictators in, rise of, **3:**185
testimonios of (*See* Testimonios)
Latin American Perspectives (journal), **3:**323
Latino Americans. *See* Hispanic and Latino Americans
Lau, Peter, **3:**22
Launching the War on Poverty (Gillette), **3:**254–256
La Viers, Henry, **3:**87
Lavrin, Asunción, **3:**323
Law and Literature (journal), **1:**314
Lawlor, Bruce, **3:**210
Law of Flight (Guatemala), **1:**101
Lawrence, D. H., **2:**123, 136, 152, 207, 213
Lawtoo, Nidesh, **1:**16–17
Lay Bare the Heart (Farmer), **3:**44
Laye, Camara
The Dark Child, **1:**128–131
A Dream of Africa, **1:**129
The Guardian of the Word, **1:**129
The Radiance of the King, **1:**128

Lazraq, Zhor, **3:**48
Leadbeater, Betsy, **2:**157–158
Leadbeater, Lydia, **2:**158
Leadbeater, Mary
   The Annals of Ballitore, **2:**157–159
   Cottage Dialogues among the Irish Peasantry, **2:**157
   The Cottage Diaries, **2:**157
   The Landlord's Friend, **2:**157
   Tales for Cottagers, **2:**157
Leadbeater, William, **2:**157
Leading the Way (Santoli), **3:**210
League of Nations, **3:**257
League of Nations Union, **1:**329
Lears, Jackson, **1:**134
Leaves from the Journal of Our Life in the Highlands (Victoria), **2:**209–212
"Leaves of Memory" (Unaipon), **1:**149
Lebovitz, Hal, **1:**247
Lecar, Mike, **3:**119
Ledoux, Charles Alexandre Picard, **2:**184
Ledy, Cheik, **1:**28
Lee, Chong-Sik, **1:**323
Lee, Ellen, *Once They Hear My Name,* **1:**102
Lee, Felicia R., **1:**74
Lee, Hannah, **3:**16
Lee, Hermione, **2:**133, 134
Lee, Jennie, **2:**235
Lee, Joan Faung Jean, *Oral Histories of First to Fourth Generation Americans,* **3:**83
Lee, Jongsoo, **1:**322
Lee, Leo Ou-Fan, **2:**172
Lee, Margaret Juhae, **1:**103
Lee, Mary, **2:**38
Lee, Maryat, **2:**129, 131
Lee, Mary Custis, **2:**40
Lee, Richard, **3:**37
Lee, Robert E., **2:**39
   Buck (Lucy) and, **2:**273
   "Letter to His Son," **2:**38–40
Lee, Susan Savage, **2:**153
Lee Kuan Yew, *The Singapore Story,* **1:**290

Leepson, Marc, **3:**211
Leeson, David, **3:**29
Lefevre, Mike, **3:**345
Left Handed, *Left Handed, Son of Old Man Hat,* **3:**318–321
Left Handed, Son of Old Man Hat (Left Handed and Dyk), **3:**318–321
Legacy (journal), **2:**29
Legend of Fire Horse Woman, The (Houston), **1:**299
Legislation. *See specific laws*
Legvold, Robert, **3:**246, 332
LeHeew, Justin, **3:**232
Lehmann-Haupt, Christopher, **1:**48
Leibniz, Gottfried Wilhelm, **1:**183
Leigh, Augusta, **2:**143
Leighton, Frederic, **2:**335
Leighton, Roland, **1:**329, 330
Leipzig war crimes trials (1921), **3:**293
Leiris, Michel, **1:**247
Lejeune, Philippe
   The Autobiographical Pact, **1:**239–241
   Autobiography in France, **1:**239, **2:**174
   Me Too, **2:**174
   On Diary, **2:**174, 175
   "Practice of the Private Journal," **2:**174–176
Lenape. *See* Delaware Indians
L'Enfant, Pierre, **2:**87
Lenin, Vladimir, **1:**270, **3:**331
Lenta, Margaret, **2:**218
Lenz, Peter, **1:**121
Leonard, Karen, **3:**81
Leon Montiel, Livia, **3:**131
Leopold II (king of Belgium), **2:**192
Leppmann, Wolfgang, **2:**149
Lesbians. *See* Homosexuality
Lesinska, Zofia, **1:**333
Lesser Evil, The (Klemperer), **2:**304
Lessing, Doris, **1:**168
   The Grass Is Singing, **1:**169
   Memoirs of a Survivor, **1:**167
   Under My Skin, **1:**167–169
   Walking in the Shade, **1:**167
Le Sueur, James, **2:**263, 264

Let Me Speak! (Viezzer and Barrios de Chungara), **3:**74, 114–115, **322–324**
Let My People Go (Luthuli), **1:24–26**
Let One Hundred Flowers Bloom (Feng), **1:**161
Letter(s), writing of. *See also specific works and writers*
   in Britain, art of, **2:**146, 217
   consideration of audience in, **2:**217
   early history of, **2:**94
   in France, **2:**217
   manuals on, **2:**217
   in U.S., as social convention, **2:**223
"Letter from the Birmingham Jail" (King), **2:32–34**
Letters and Diaries of Etty Hillesum, The (Hillesum), **2:**253
Letters and Journals of Fanny Burney (Burney), **2:312–315**
Letters and Journals of Lord Byron (Byron), **2:143–145,** 309
Letters between Two (Lu and Xu), **2:170–173**
Letters from an American Farmer (Crèvecoeur), **2:213–216**
Letters from Jefferson to His Daughter (Jefferson), **2:**38, **316–319**
Letters from the Island of Teneriffe (Kindersley), **2:**229
Letters Home (Plath), **2:47–49**
Letters of Arnold Bennett (Bennett), **2:**138
Letters of a Woman Homesteader (Stewart), **2:91–93**
Letters of John Hay (Hay), **3:**263
Letters of John Keats, The (Keats), **2:146–148**
Letters of Lady Anne Barnard to Henry Dundas, The (Barnard), **2:217–219**
Letters of Mrs. Adams (Adams), **2:**87, 89
Letters of Rainer Maria Rilke (Rilke), **2:**150
Letters of Sidney and Beatrice Webb, The (Webb and Webb), **2:**172
Letters of the Younger Pliny, The (Pliny), **2:94–96**

Letters on an Elk Hunt (Stewart), **2**:91
Letters on God and Letters to a Young Woman (Rilke), **2**:149
Letters to a Young Contrarian (Hitchens), **2**:150
Letters to a Young Gymnast (Comaneci), **2**:150
Letters to a Young Novelist (Vargas Llosa), **2**:150
Letters to a Young Poet (Rilke), **2**:149–151
Letters to a Young Teacher (Kozol), **2**:150
Letters Underway (Ghazzawi), **2**:50–53
Letters Written during a Short Residence in Sweden, Norway, and Denmark (Wollstonecraft), **2**:111
"Letter to Her Daughter" (Montagu), **2**:35–37
"Letter to Her Daughter from the New White House" (Adams), **2**:87–90
"Letter to His Daughter" (Jefferson), **2**:38
"Letter to His Son" (Lee), **2**:38–40
"Letter to Maria Clemm" (Poe), **2**:41–43
"Letter to the Reverend Samson Occom" (Wheatley), **2**:44–46
Let the People Decide (Moye), **3**:249
Lettsom, John Coakley, **2**:207
Leung, Laifong, *Morning Sun*, **3**:301
Levi, Primo
    If This Is a Man, **1**:318
    suicide of, **1**:204, 205
Levin, Meyer, **2**:253
Levin, Susan M., **2**:301
Levine, Robert, **2**:7–8
Levine, Steven, **1**:339, **3**:288
Lévi-Strauss, Claude, *Tristes Tropiques*, **3**:37
Levy, Eric P., **1**:121
Lewalski, Barbara, **2**:64
Lewin, Recha, **3**:50
Lewin, Rhoda
    The Jewish Community of North Minneapolis, **3**:50
    Witnesses to the Holocaust, **3**:50–52

Lewis, Jane, **2**:18
Lewis, Oscar
    Children of Sanchez, **3**:31
    Pedro Martinez, **3**:31
Lewis, R. W. B., **1**:235
Lewy, Guenter, **3**:42
Ley, Robert, **3**:293–294
Ley de Fuga (Guatemala), **1**:101
Liberalism, in Russia, rise of, **1**:193
Liberator (newspaper), **1**:33, 35, **2**:29, 31, 45
Liberty Bell, The (Chapman and Griffith), **1**:142
Libowitz, Richard, **1**:320
Library Journal
    on *Exiled Memories* (Medina), **1**:297
    on *Mothers, Sisters, Resisters* (Gurewitsch), **3**:35
    on *Prison Writings* (Peltier), **1**:97
    on *Solidarity Forever* (Bird et al.), **3**:329
    on *Ten Thousand Sorrows* (Kim), **1**:103
    on *Voices from the Whirlwind* (Feng), **3**:288
    on *A Woman at War* (Moore), **2**:279
    on *A Woman Soldier's Own Story* (Xie), **1**:339
    on *The Woman Warrior* (Kingston), **1**:175
Lieberman, Thorney, **3**:66
Liédet, Loyset, 1:286
Lie Down in Darkness (Styron), **1**:204, 206
Life (magazine), **1**:304, **3**:61
Life, Letters, and Literary Remains (Keats), **2**:146
Life, The (Teresa of Ávila), **1:211–213**
Life and Times of Frederick Douglass (Douglass), **1**:34
Life for Africa, A (Mitchison), **2**:237
"Life in the Sea Islands" (Grimké), **2**:31
Life Laid Bare (Hatzfeld), **3**:258, 259
Life Lived Like a Story (Cruikshank), **3**:320
Life of Samuel Johnson (Boswell), **2**:177, 195, 309, 328, 329–330

Life on the Mississippi (Twain), **1:146–148**
Life under a Cloud (Winkler), **3**:239
Life-writing movement, of Aborigines, **3**:334
Lifton, Betty Jean, *Twice Born*, **1**:102
"Ligeia" (Poe), **3**:38
Light, Kenneth
    Coal Hollow, **3:66–69**
    Valley of Shadows and Dreams, **3**:67
Light, Melanie
    Coal Hollow, **3:66–69**
    Valley of Shadows and Dreams, **3**:67
Light, Steve, **1**:251
Likud party (Israel), **1**:225, **2**:52
Lincoln, Abraham, **3**:262
    and African American soldiers, **2**:240
    assassination of, **2**:246, **3**:261
    election of, **2**:38, 250
    Emancipation Proclamation of, **1**:50, **3**:261
    Homestead Act under, **2**:164
    oral history of life of, **3**:261–264
    views on slavery, **2**:38
Lincoln, Kenneth, **1**:54
Lincoln, Mary Todd, **1**:52, **3**:261, 263, 264
Lincoln, Robert Todd, **3**:261, 262, 263
Lincoln and the Civil War Diaries and Letters of John Hay (Hay), **3**:262–263
Lincoln Prize, for *Abraham Lincoln: A Life* (Burlingame), **3**:264
Linderman, Frank, *Pretty-Shield*, **1**:70
Lindstrom, Naomi, **1**:76
Lingua Tertii Imperii (LTI) (Klemperer), **2**:304, 305
Linguistic autobiographies, *Hunger of Memory* (Rodriguez) as, **1**:17
Linneaus, Carl, **2**:300
Linton, Sherri LaVie, **1:10**
Lin Yutang, **1**:338
Lionnet, Françoise, **1**:11
Lipsitz, George, **3**:191
LIS Organization, **1**:7
Liszt, Franz, **1**:272

Literacy
- in Britain, rise of, **2:**136, 146, 320
- in Middle Ages, **1:**189
- in *Narrative of the Life of Frederick Douglass* (Douglass), **1:**35
- and slave narratives, **1:**35

Literary autobiographies. *See also specific works and writers*
- Lejeune (Philippe) on study of, **2:**174
- religious struggle in, **2:**26
- self as topic in, **1:**167

Literary criticism
- Bennett's (Arnold) career in, **2:**136
- disability studies in, **1:**8
- as form of autobiography, **1:**247
- French theories in, **1:**239
- by Hawthorne (Nathaniel), **2:**223–224
- Hussein's (Taha) career in, **1:**135
- by Maugham (W. Somerset), **2:**183
- poststructuralism in, **1:**267
- structuralism in, **1:**239, 267
- by Woolf (Virginia), **2:**137, 138, 180

Literary Fund, **2:**207

Literary references
- in *De Profundis* (Wilde), **2:**9
- in *Fun Home* (Bechdel), **1:**140, 141
- in *Walden* (Thoreau), **1:**235

Literary Remains of Edward VI, The (Edward VI), **2:97–100**

Literary Review (journal), **1:**256

Literary theory, Barthes's (Roland) work in, **1:**267

Literature and Medicine (journal), **1:**7, 8

Lithuania, Jewish immigration to China from, **3:**16

Little Big Horn, Battle of (1876), **3:**110

Litz, Alyce, **1:**40

Liu Xiaobo, **3:**301

Lives of Others, The (film), **3:**245

Living Atlanta (Kuhn et al.), **3:**44

Living by Fiction (Dillard), **1:**279

Living My Life (Goldman), **3:**3

Living the Revolution (Guglielmo), **3:**5

Living through the Soviet System (Bertaux et al.), **3:**331

Lloréns Torres, Luis, **1:**108

Lloyd, Constance, **2:**9

Lloyd's Evening Post, **2:**196

Lobato, Mirta Zaida, **3:**74, 75

Locke, Alain, **1:**84, 85

Locke, John, **2:**140

Locked-in syndrome, **1:**6–8

Lockhart, John Gibson, **2:**143, 144
- *Memoirs of the Life of Sir Walter Scott*, **2:**309, 310

Lockhart, Sophia Scott, **2:**309

Loftis, John, **1:**316

Logan, Andy, **3:**295

Log-book of the Coiners (Gide), **2:**180, 182

Logging industry, in Idaho, **3:**93

Loisel, Clary, **3:**33

Lomax, Alan, **1:**9

Lomax, Dana Teen, **2:**150

Lombardi, Irma, **3:**329

Lomov, Nikolai, **3:**235

London (England)
- Boswell's (James) move to, **2:**328
- Great Fire of, **2:**73
- Kinsington district in, **2:**321
- literary journalism in, **2:**328

London and the Life of Literature in Late Victorian England (Gissing), **2:320–323**

London Journal (Boswell), **2:328–330**

London Review of Books, **2:**14

London School of Economics and Political Science, **2:**16, 172

Long, Huey, **1:**5

Long, Janet Nakamarra, **3:**107, 335

Long, Judith, **2:**92

Long, Lisa, **2:**29, 31

Longfellow, Henry Wadsworth, **2:**223

Long Journey Home (Brown and Kohn), **3:**107, **325–327**

Long Journey Home (documentary), **3:**325

Long March, **1:**338

Long Walk to Freedom, The (Mandela), **1:**25, **27–29**, 96, 290

Long Way from Home, A (McKay), **1:84–86**

Long Way Gone, A (Beah), **1:312–314**

Looking Cloud, Arlo, **1:**98

Look up for Yes (Tavalaro), **1:**6

Lopes Cançado, Maura, *Hospicio é Deus*, **2:**6

Lopez, Barry, *Arctic Dreams*, **1:**279

Lorde, Audre, **2:**4
- *The Black Unicorn*, **2:**4
- *A Burst of Light*, **2:**3
- *The Cancer Journals*, **2:3–5**
- hooks (bell) compared to, **1:**249, 251
- Hurston's (Zora Neale) influence on, **1:**9
- in tradition of Prince (Mary), **3:**24
- *Zami*, **1:**9, 37, 39, 249, **2:**5

Lorifo, Marie, **1:**128

Lori-Parks, Suzan, **1:**273

Lort, Michael, **2:**313

Los Alamos (New Mexico), oral histories of, **3:**239–241

Los Angeles (California)
- gay Asian Americans in, **3:**83–85
- water resources for, **3:**102, 103

Los Angeles Times (newspaper)
- on *Barefoot Gen* (Nakazawa), **1:**294
- on *Diaries, 1931–1949* (Orwell), **2:**118
- on *A Diary without Dates* (Bagnold), **2:**260
- on *Farewell to Manzanar* (Houston and Houston), **1:**299, 300
- on *The Long Walk to Freedom* (Mandela), **1:**29
- on *The Strength Not to Fight* (Tollefson), **3:**222
- on *Voices of Freedom* (Hampton and Fayer), **3:**45
- on *When Heaven and Earth Changed Places* (Hayslip), **1:**336
- on *When I Was Puerto Rican* (Santiago), **1:**109
- on *A Woman at War* (Moore), **2:**279
- on *Zlata's Diary* (Filipovic), **2:**339

Lost-Found Nation of Islam. *See* Black Muslims

Lost generation, **1:**329

Lost Names (Kim), **1:**102

Lost Years (Vu), **1:**170

Lotte in Weimar (Mann), **1**:277

Louisiana
  during Civil War, Stone (Kate) on life in, **2**:244–246, *245*
  Hispanic American entrepreneurs in, oral histories of, **3**:121–123
  U.S. purchase of, **2**:69

Louis XVI (king of France), **2**:213

Love Carried Me Home (Miller), **3**:35

Lovejoy, David, **2**:27

Love Letters of Dorothy Osborne to Sir William Temple, The (Osborne), **2:324–327**

Love Letters of Dylan Thomas, The (Thomas), **1**:127

Love Letters of Nathaniel Hawthorne, The (Hawthorne), **2**:225

Lovesey, Oliver, **1**:88, 215, 216

Loving v. Virginia, **1**:72, 78

Lowell, Amy, **2**:190, 292

Lowell, James Russell, **1**:235

Lowell, Robert, **2**:129

Lowenthal, Cynthia, **2**:36, 37

"Low-intensity" conflicts, **3**:207

Loyalty
  in Japanese American internment, **3**:196
  to monarchy, Slingsby (Henry) on, **2**:256–258

Lozano, Connie, **3**:103

LSD, **2**:295

Lucas, E. V., **2**:10

Lucassen, Jan, **3**:75

Lucky Child, A (Buergenthal), **1**:312

Lugo, Catherine, **3**:88

Luis, Keridwen, **3**:38

Luis, William, **3**:8

Lukas, Christopher, *Blue Genes*, **1**:204–205

Lu Lihua, **3**:148

Luna, Rachael, **3**:78

Luongo, Katherine, **3**:143

Lupus, **2**:129

Luscombe, Belinda, **1**:312, 314

Luthuli, Albert, **1**:24
  Let My People Go, **1**:24–26
  "Our Struggles for Progress," **1**:25
  "We Don't Want Crumbs," **1**:25

Lu Xiuyuan, **3**:288

Lu Xun, *Letters between Two*, **2**:170–173, *171*

Ly, Monirith, **1**:307

Lydgate, John, **1:190**

Lydston, Stub, **3**:103

Lyell, Charles, *Principles of Geology*, **1**:65

Lynch, Claire, **3**:316–317

Lynchings, **1**:18, 50

Lynd, Alice, *Rank and File*, **3**:179

Lynd, Staughton, *Rank and File*, **3**:179

Lynn, Kenneth, **2**:251

Lyon, Isabel Van Kleek, **1**:148

M

Maalouf, Amin, **1**:286

Maasai (Beckwith and Saitoti), **1**:114

Maasai people, Saitoti (Tepilit Ole) on experience of, **1**:114–116, *115*

Maathai, Wangari, *Unbound*, **1**:114

Macaulay, Thomas Babington, **2**:144, 314, 329

MacCarthy, Desmond, **2**:268

MacCarthy, Molly, **2**:268

MacDonald, John, **3**:139

MacDonald, Ramsay, **2**:17

MacEoin, Uinseann, *Survivors*, **3**:27, 315

Machete Season (Hatzfeld), **1**:312, **3:257–260**

MacKenzie, Jeanne, **2**:16, 17

MacKenzie, Norman, **2**:16, 17, 172

MacLane, Mary, **2**:306

MacLennan, Birdie, **1**:280

Macqueen, James, **3**:25

Macy, John, **1**:43

Maddocks, Melvin, **3**:61

Maddy-Weitzman, Bruce, **3**:49

Madero, Francisco, **3**:167

Madge, Charles, **2**:235

Madison, James, **2**:316

Madison, R. D., **2**:240

Madmen and Specialists (Soyinka), **1**:214

Madsen, Kim, **3**:174–175

Mafeking, siege of (1899–1900), **2**:241–243

Magan, Hirsi, **1**:207

Magellan, Ferdinand, **2**:201

Magical Monkey King (Jiang), **1**:163

Mahomet, Dean, *The Travels of Dean Mahomet*, **2**:229–232

Mahoney, Dennis F., **1**:277, 278

Mai, Angelo, **1**:220

Maid's Daughter, The (Romero), **1**:108

Maier, Joseph, **3**:295

Mail and Guardian (newspaper), **3**:243

Mailer, Norman, **1**:165

Maitland, Sarah, **1**:280

Makin, Bathsua, *An Essay to Revive the Antient Education of Gentlewomen*, **2**:35

Making History (Johnson et al.), **3**:176, 177

Making of a Gay Asian Community, The (Wat), **3:83–85**

Making of Modern London, The (television series), **3**:313

Makley, Charlene, **3**:288–289

Malan, Daniel François, **1**:27

Malan, Rian, *My Traitor's Heart*, **3**:242

Malcolmson, Patricia, **2**:265

Malcolmson, Robert, **2**:265

Malcolm X, *The Autobiography of Malcolm X*, **1**:78, **186–188**, *187*, **3**:44

Malik ibn al-Rayb, **1**:255

Malingre, Rose, **2**:83

Malinke people, **1**:128, 130

Mallon, Thomas, **1**:7

Malone, Edmond, **2**:330

Malthus, Thomas, *Essay on the Principles of Population*, **1**:65

Malti-Douglas, Fedwa, **1**:92, 137, 227

Mammeri, Mouloud, **2**:262

Man (journal), **3**:168

Manalansan, Martin F., IV, **3**:83, 84, 85

Manar, Al- (journal), **1**:135

Manchester (England), oral histories of working-class youth in, **3**:311–313, *312*

Manchu dynasty, **1**:152, 153

Manchurian Incident (1931), **3**:215

Mandel, Barrett John, **1**:187, 246, 247

Mandel, Naomi, **1**:320

SUBJECT INDEX

Mandela, Nelson, **1:28**
    AIDS epidemic and, **3:**272, *273*
    Conversations with Myself, **1:**27–28
    imprisonment of, **1:**24, 27–29, **3:**242
    The Long Walk to Freedom, **1:**25, **27–29**, 96, 290
Mandela, Winnie, **1:**28, 29
Mandeville, John, *The Travels of Sir John Mandeville,* **2:**198, 227
Man Died, The (Soyinka), **1:214–217**, **2:**12, 14
Mandlestam, Nadezhda, *Hope against Hope,* **1:**271
Man from the North, A (Bennett), **2:**136
Manga (Japanese comics), **1:**293
Manhattan Project, oral histories of, **3:**239–240
Manichaeans, **1:**196
Manji, Irshad, *The Trouble with Islam Today,* **1:**207
Mann, Abby, **3:**295
Mann, Thomas, *Lotte in Weimar,* **1:**277
Manning, Bradley, **3:**229
Manning, Diane, *Hill Country Teacher,* **3:77–79**
"Man of Constant Sorrow" (song), **3:**159
Man of the Serengeti (documentary), **1:**114
Mansart Builds a School (Du Bois), **1:**5
Mansfield, Katherine, **2:134**
    Bashkirtseff's (Marie) influence on, **2:**306
    Journal of Katherine Mansfield, **2:133–135**
    The Katherine Mansfield Notebooks, **2:**133, 134
    Partridge (Frances) compared to, **2:**269
    Scrapbook of Katherine Mansfield, **2:**134
    A Writer's Diary (Woolf) on, **2:**180
Mansfield decision (1789, Britain), **1:**81, 83, **3:**23
Mantel, Hilary, **1:**169
Manter, Lisa, **1:**191
Manuel I (king of Portugal), **2:**198, 199

Manwaring, Max G.
    El Salvador at War, **3:205–208**
    Small Wars & Insurgencies, **3:**206
    Uncomfortable Wars, **3:**207
    Uncomfortable Wars Revisited, **3:**207
Manzanar (Wehrey), **3:**102
Manzanar internment camp (California), **1:**299–301, **3:**102–104, 197, *225*
Manzano, Juan Francisco, *The Autobiography of a Slave,* **3:**7
Mao Zedong, **1:**158, **3:**288. *See also* Cultural Revolution
    death of, **3:**299
    in Long March, **1:**338
    Lu Xun and, **2:**170
    rise to power, **3:**287
Mapes, Elizabeth A., **2:**254
Mara, Michael, **2:**61
Marble Faun, The (Hawthorne), **2:**224, 225
Marcello, Ronald E., *Remembering Pearl Harbor,* **3:**202
Marchand, Leslie A., **2:**144
Marchesi, Ilaria, **2:**96
March 1 Movement (Korea), **1:**324
March on Washington (1963), **1:**20
Marcus, Eric, *The Struggle for Gay and Lesbian Equal Rights,* **3:**83
Marcus, Jane, **2:**17
Marcus Aurelius, *The Meditations of the Emperor Marcus Aurelius Antoninus,* **1:218–221**, *219*
Marek, Kurt, **2:**282
Margaret (princess), **2:**152
Marie, Adrien, **2:82**
Marijuana, **2:**295
Maritime literature, tradition of, **3:**183
Mark, Thomas, **2:**126
Mark Twain Project, **1:**148
Marquette, Jacques, **1:**146–147
Marrant, John, **1:**81
Marriage
    arranged, in China, **1:**153, 154, 338, 339, **2:**170
    arranged, in Montenegro, **3:**136, 137
    in eighteenth century, limitations of, **2:**35, 36

    forced, **1:**209
    in Heian period of Japan, **2:**297–299
    interracial (*See* Interracial relationships)
    Osborne's (Dorothy) ideas about, **2:**324–325
    Pepys's (Samuel) depiction of, accuracy of, **2:**73
    same-sex, **1:**139
    of women teachers in U.S., ban on, **3:**78, 79
Marse Chan (Page), **2:**250
Marsh, Dawn, **3:**326
Marshall, Dick, **1:**98
Marshall, Jack, *From Baghdad to Brooklyn,* **3:**120
Marshall, Joanna, **1:**109
Marshall, Kathryn, *In the Combat Zone,* **3:**221, 279
Martin, Isabella, **2:**250, 251
Martin, Keavy, *Stories in a New Skin,* **3:**138
Martin, Ramela, *Out of Darkness,* **3:**40
Martin, Tera, **1:**174
Martineau, Harriet, **2:**29, 335
Martone, Michael, **1:**48
Martyn, Edward, **2:**128
Marwick, Arthur, **3:**234
Marxism
    in Cultural Revolution, **1:**161
    of Guevara (Ernesto "Che"), **2:**220
Mary Chesnut's Civil War (Chesnut), **2:**250, 251, 271
Mary I (queen of England), **2:**98, 99
Mary II (queen of England), **2:**324, 325
Maryland, interracial marriage in, **1:**72
Masculine writing style, vs. feminine writing style, **1:**250
Masculinity, in *Journal of George Fox* (Fox), **2:**27
Masking, African American tradition of, **1:**144
Masks, Chinese ghost, **1:**174
Mason, Bobbie Ann, *In Country,* **1:**335
Mason, Katrina, *Children of Los Alamos,* **3:239–241**
Mason, Keith, **2:**206

Mason, Mary, **1:**246

Mason, Terry, **3:**344

Massacre in Mexico (Poniatowska), **3:**31–33

Massey, Mary Elizabeth, **2:**246

Mass Observation Project, **2:**235, 236, 237, 265, 266, 267

Masson, David, **2:**310–311

Masson, Madeleine, **2:**218

Mast, Robert, *Detroit Lives,* **3:**99

Mastectomies, **2:**3

Masumoto, David Mas, *Country Voices,* **3:**224

Matagari (Ngũgĩ), **2:**14

Mather, Cotton, **1:**326, 328

Mather, Increase, **1:**325, 326

    A Brief History of the War with the Indians in New England, **1:**325

Matrilineal culture, of Navajo, **3:**318

Matsumoto, Valerie, *Farming the Home Place,* **3:**80

Mattachine Society, **3:**83

Matthews, William, **2:**65

Matthiessen, F. O., **1:**235, **2:**113, 114, 115

Maturation, Conroy (Frank) on experience of, **1:**164

Maugham, Robin, **2:**185

Maugham, W. Somerset, **2:**184

    Bennett (Arnold) compared to, **2:**136

    The Razor's Edge, **2:**185

    The Summing Up, **2:**183

    A Writer's Notebook, **2:**183–185

Mau Mau rebellion, **2:**12

Maunsell, Jerome, **2:**122

Maupassant, Guy de, **2:**113, 183, 306

Maurer, Harry

    Not Working, **3:**277

    Sex: An Oral History, **3:**276, 277

    Strange Ground, **3:**275–278

    Webs of Power, **3:**277

Mauriac, François, **1:**318, **2:**130

Maus (Spiegelman), **1:**139, 141, 156, 293

Mauthausen concentration camp, **3:**51

Mawer, William, **1:**67

"Mawtini" (Tuqan), **1:**227

Mayans, **3:**166, 167

Mayer, Henry, **3:**45

May Fourth (New Culture) Movement (China), **1:**338, **3:**126, 147–149, 148

Mayo, John, **3:**87

M'Baye, Mariétou. *See* Bugul, Ken

Mbeki, Thabo, **1:**29, **3:**272, 274

McBride, James, *The Color of Water,* **1:**72–74, *73*

McBride, Ruth, **1:**72–74

McCabe, Dabney, **2:**39

McCann, Justin, **1:**191

McCarthy, Cormac, *Blood Meridian,* **1:**304

McCarthy, Justin, **3:**42

McCarthy, Kevin, **1:**259

McCarthy, Mary, **1:**259

    Cast a Cold Eye, **1:**258

    The Group, **1:**258

    How I Grew, **1:**258

    Intellectual Memoirs, **1:**258

    Memories of a Catholic Girlhood, **1:**258–260

McCloy, John, **3:**234

McColloch, Mark, **3:**329

McCombs, Edward, **3:**291

McCourt, Angela, **1:**120

McCourt, Frank

    Angela's Ashes, **1:**119–121

    A Couple of Blaguards, **1:**119

    Teacher Man, **1:**119

    'Tis, **1:**119

McCourt, Malachy, **1:**119

McCulloch, Mark, **3:**247

McDonald, Cornelia Peake, *A Diary with Reminiscences of the War and Refugee Life in the Shenandoah Valley,* **2:**271

McDonald, F. W., **2:**196

McDonough, A. R., **2:**336

McDougall, Bonnie S., **2:**171, 172

McElroy, John Harmon, **2:**214, 215

McGill, Robert, **2:**131

McKay, Claude, **1:**85

    Banjo, **1:**86

    Harlem: Negro Metropolis, **1:**85

    Home to Harlem, **1:**84, 86

    "If We Must Die," **1:**84

    A Long Way from Home, **1:**84–86

McKay, Nellie, **1:**10, 11

McKee, Guian A., **3:**254, 256

McKelvey, Tara, **3:**233

McKenzie, Barbara, **1:**260

McKinney, Gordon B., **3:**92

McLean, Norman, *A River Runs through It,* **1:**281

McLeod, Calum, *China Remembers,* **3:**301

McLynn, Frank, **1:**220

McNeil, Linda, **3:**78

McNeill, Laurie, **2:**175

McPherson, Dolly, **1:**20

McPherson, Robert S., **3:**12

    Navajo Land, Navajo Culture, **3:**10

Mead, Margaret, **1:**9

Meatless Days (Suleri), **1:**87–89

Meatpacking industry, in Argentina, **3:**73–75

Medeiros-Lichem, María Teresa, **3:**32

Media coverage. *See* Journalism; War correspondents

Mediation, vs. arbitration, **3:**155

Medical conditions. *See* Health problems; *specific conditions*

Medicine

    British, oral histories of, **3:**170–172

    midwifery in, **2:**331–333, *332*

    technological advances in, **3:**170

Medieval era. *See* Middle Ages

Medina, Pablo

    Exiled Memories, **1:**296–298

    Pork Rind and Cuban Songs, **1:**296

Meditations of the Emperor Marcus Aurelius Antoninus, The (Marcus Aurelius), **1:**218–221

Medwick, Cathleen, **1:**212

Mee, Jon, **2:**146, 147

Meikuaya, Wilson, *The Last Maasai Warrior,* **1:**114

Meinecke, Friedrich, **1:**185

Mein Kampf (Hitler), **1:**30–32

Melancholy, in *Confessions of Lady Nijo* (Nijo), **2:**60

Melhuish, Mary, **3:**311

Melman, Billie, **1:**91

MELUS (journal), **1:**17, 71, 109, 175

Melville, Herman, **1:**277, **2:**215, 223, 224

    Moby Dick, **2:**224

Memmott, Carol, **1:**172

Memoir. *See also specific works and writers*

    vs. autobiography, **1:**248, 279

    construction of, to appeal to audience, **1:**164

Memoir (Godwin), **2:**109

Memoir Club, **2:**182

Memoirs (Fanshawe), **1:**229–230, 315, 316, 317

Memoirs (Neruda), **1:222–224**

Memoirs (Scott), **2:**309

Memoirs (Williams), **2:**152, 153

Memoirs and Letters of Sara Coleridge (Coleridge), **2:**16

Memoirs of a Fox-Hunting Man (Sassoon), **1:**329, **2:**247

Memoirs of an Arabian Princess from Zanzibar (Ruete), **1:90–92**

Memoirs of a Spacewoman (Mitchison), **2:**237

Memoirs of a Survivor (Lessing), **1:**167

Memoirs of Dr. Burney, The (Burney), **2:**312, 313

Memoirs of Fatemeh Pakravan (Ladjevardi), **3:218–220**

Memoirs of Lady Anne Halkett, The (Halkett), **1:**230, **315–317**

Memoirs of Naim Bey, The (Andonian), **3:**40

Memoirs of Prince Hamid Kadjar (Ladjevardi), **3:**219

Memoirs of Shapour Bakhtiar (Ladjevardi), **3:**220

Memoirs of the Life of Sir Walter Scott (Lockhart), **2:**309, 310

Memoirs of the Princess Daschkaw (Dashkova), **2:**306

Memorial de isla negra (Neruda), **1:**223

Memories of a Catholic Girlhood (McCarthy), **1:258–260**

Memory(ies)

    of Christmas, Thomas (Dylan) on, **1:**125–126

    enigmatic nature of, Suleri (Sara) on, **1:**87, 88

    fluid nature of, Agosín (Marjorie) on, **1:**75–76

    in locked-in syndrome, Bauby (Jean-Dominique) on, **1:**6–7

    in oral history field, **3:**176–178, 186

    of survivors of Armenian genocide, reliability of, **3:**42

    and time, Conroy (Frank) on, **1:**164, 165, 166

    and time, Nabokov (Vladimir) on, **1:**271, 272

    of witnesses, Portelli (Alessandro) on, **3:**265, 266

Memory and Narrative (Olney), **1:**246, 248

Memory for Forgetfulness (Darwish), **1:**255, 257, **2:**50

Memory Studies (journal), **3:**98

Menchú, Rigoberta, *I, Rigoberta Menchú,* **3:**164–166, *165*

    Californio Voices (Savage) vs., **3:**114

    Child of the Dark (de Jesus) vs., **2:**8

    Doña María's Story (James) vs., **3:**73–74

    Let Me Speak! (Viezzer and Barrios de Chungara) vs., **3:**322

    Rites: A Guatemalan Boyhood (Perera) vs., **1:**99

    Women's Words (Gluck and Patai) on, **3:**191

Mencken, H. L., **2:**137

Mendibil, Claude, **1:**6, 7

Meng Jixin, *The First Household under Heaven,* **3:**125

Mennonites, **3:**223, 227

Mental freedom, in locked-in syndrome, **1:**6–7

Mental illness

    of Ruskin (John), **1:**264

    Styron (William) on struggle with, **1:**204–205

Mentor (Grimes), **1:**164

Merchant, G. W., **1:**67

Mercier, Laurie, **3:**81

Meredith, George, **2:**320

Merlo, Frank, **2:**153

Mernissi, Fatima, *Dreams of Trespass,* **1:**226, 227

Mersky, Peter, **3:**203

Meru people, oral histories of, **3:**141–143, *142*

Meschia, Karen, **2:**237

Mesopotamia, letter writing in, **2:**94

Messerschmidt, J. W., **2:**282

Metacomet, **1:**325

Metaphors of Self (Olney), **1:**246

Meth, Rose, **3:**35

Methodism, **2:**195–196

Me Too (Lejeune), **2:**174

Mexican Americans

    Rodriguez (Richard) on experience of, **1:**15–17

    women, oral histories of, **3:**131–134, *132*

Mexican-American War (1846–1848), **1:**304

Mexican Indians, oral histories of, **3:**167–169

Mexican oral histories

    on agrarian reform movement, **3:**302–304

    of indigenous people, **3:**167–169

    on Tlatelolco massacre of 1968, **3:**31–33

Mexican Revolution (1910–1920), **3:**167, 302

Mexico

    agrarian reform movement in, **3:**302–304

    California as colony of, **3:**114

    constitution of, **3:**302

    indigenous people of, **3:**167–169, 304

    Revolution of 1910–1920 in, **3:**167, 302

    Tlatelolco massacre of 1968 in, **3:**31–33

Meyer, Melissa, *The Politics of AIDS Denialism,* **3:**272

Meyers, Gladys Peterson, **3:**78

MFS Modern Fiction Studies (journal), **1:**85

Mhudi (Plaatje), **2:**241, 243

Michaels, Walter Benn, *The Trouble with Diversity,* **1:**16

Michelet, Jules, **1:**267
Michelet par lui-même (Barthes), **1:**267
Michigan. *See* Detroit
Michigan Equal Accommodations Act of 1938, **3:**99
Michigan Historical Review (journal), **2:**207, **3:**100
Michilimackinac, Fort, **2:**205–207, *206*
Michi's Memories (Tamura), **3:**127
Michitsuna No Haha, *The Gossamer Years,* **2:**189, 290, **297–299**
Mickiewicz, Adam
    Forefathers' Eve, **2:**192
    Konrad Wallenrod, **2:**192
Middle Ages
    Christianity in, **1:**189
    Confessions (Augustine) in, **1:**198
    Kempe (Margery) on life in, **1:**189–191
    literacy in, **1:**189
    pilgrimages in, **1:190,** 191, **2:**226
Middle class, English
    expansion of, **2:**177
    Last (Nella) on life of, **2:**265
    Pepys (Samuel) on life of, **2:**72
    Victoria and, **2:**209, 211
    Woodforde (James) on life of, **2:**287–288
Middle East Journal, **1:**209, **3:**49, 219
Middle East Report, **1:**209
Middle East Studies Association Bulletin, **3:**48, 220
Middle Passage, **1:**82, 83
Midgley, Peter, **2:**242
Midnight's Children (Rushdie), **1:**87
Midstream (Keller), **1:**44
Midwest Book Review, **3:**263
Midwifery, **2:**331–333, *332*
Midwife's Tale, A (Ulrich), **2:331–334**
Midwives of the Future (Ware), **3:**308
Mieder, Wolfgang, **2:**305
Mielke, Erich, **3:246**
Migration, of African Americans within U.S., **1:**50, 52, 84, 273. *See also* Immigration
Mihailovic, Draza, **3:**135
Milani, Abbas, *The Persian Sphinx,* **3:**218, 219
Milani, Farzaneh, **1:**209

Milburn, Clara, **2:**235
    Mrs. Milburn's Diary, **2:**265
Mildmay, Grace, **1:**229
Miles, Jack, **2:**339
Miles, Nelson, **1:**303
Milich, Zorka, *A Stranger's Supper,* **3:135–137**
Military, Australian, in World War I, **3:**177
Military, Chinese, women in, **1:**338–340
Military, Colombian, **3:**183–185
Military, U.S. *See also* Veterans; *specific wars*
    African Americans in, **2:**238–240, **3:**199–201, 248–250
    desegregation of, **3:**199, 248, 249
    draft in, **3:**221–223
    homosexuality in, **1:**139
    Japanese Americans in, **3:**196
    Japanese war brides and, **3:**127–129, *128*
    journalists embedded with, **2:**278–280
    Korean American children of, **1:**102
    racism in, **3:**44, 199–201, 248–250
    slaves as soldiers in, **2:**238–240
    Styron (William) in, **1:**206
    Vietnamese American children of, **1:**170
    Wolff (Tobias) in, **1:**47
Military Review (journal), **3:**233
Militia groups, in Scotland, **2:**309
Mill, James, **2:**177
Mill, John Stuart, *Autobiography,* **2:**16
Millay, Edna St. Vincent, **1:**258
Miller, Anita, **2:**138
Miller, Donald E., *Survivors,* **3:40–43,** 50
Miller, Henry, **2:**123, 124
    Tropic of Cancer, **2:**123
Miller, Jack, **3:**329
Miller, Joy E., *Love Carried Me Home,* **3:**35
Miller, June, **2:**124
Miller, Lorna Touryan, *Survivors,* **3:40–43,** 50

Miller, Michele, **3:**233
Miller, William Lee, **2:**71
Millett, Kate, **3:**37
Mill Hunk Herald (magazine), **3:**342
Milligan, Don, **3:**71–72
Million Little Pieces, A (Frey), **1:**313, **2:**296
Milosz, Czeslaw, **1:**255
Milton, John, **2:**140, 146
Min, Anchee
    Becoming Madame Mao, **1:**159
    Pearl of China, **1:**159
    Red Azalea, **1:158–160**
Minamoto no Rinshi, **2:**290, 292
Minamoto no Yoritomo, **2:**61
Minear, Richard, **1:**295
Mine of Her Own, A (Zanjani), **3:**337
Mining. *See also* Coal mining
    in Bolivia, oral histories of, **3:**322–324
    prohibitions on women in, **3:**337
    in Ukraine, oral histories of, **3:**340–342
Mining Cultures (Murphy), **3:**337
Minneapolis Star Tribune (newspaper), **1:**172
Minnesota History (journal), **3:**51
Minorities Research Group, **3:**70
Minority groups. *See* Assimilation; *specific groups*
Minority Report to the Commission of the Poor Law (Webb), **2:**16
Minus, Ed, **2:**269
Miracle Worker, The (teleplay), **1:**44, 45
Miranda, Deborah A., **3:**116
Mirollo, James V., **1:**213
Mirow, Kurt Rudolf, *Webs of Power,* **3:**277
Mirra, Carl, *Soldiers and Citizens,* **3:**231–232
Mirsky, Jonathan, **3:**280, 288
Miscellanies (D'Israeli), **2:**177
Misery memoirs, *Angela's Ashes* (McCourt) as, **1:**120–121
Missing Pages (Terry), **3:**199–200
Missionary work
    in colonial California, **3:**114–116
    in Great Awakening, **2:**197
    of Wesley (John), **2:**195–196

Mississippi Quarterly, **1:**35, 38, **2:**42
Mississippi River, Twain (Mark) on, **1:**146–147
Mississippi Valley Historical Review (journal), **2:**92
Missouri Compromise (1820), **1:**33
Miss Ravenel's Conversion (De Forest), **2:**240
Mistral, Gabriela, **1:**222, 223
Mitchell, Stephen, **2:**149
Mitchell, Virginia R., **3:**307
Mitchison, Clemency, **2:**235, 236
Mitchison, Naomi, *Among You Taking Notes,* **2:**235–237, 236
Mitford, John, **2:**143
Mitford, Mary Russell, *Our Village,* **3:**59
Mitson, Betty E., *Voices Long Silent,* **3:**195
Mittler, Barbara, **3:**148
Miyata Waichirō, **2:**191
MK. *See* Umkhonto we Sizwe
Mkhize, Sibongiseni, **1:**26
Mlambo, Eshmael, *Rhodesia,* **3:**251
MLN (journal), **3:**8
Moby Dick (Melville), **2:**224
Mock autobiographies, *Stop-Time* (Conroy) as, **1:**164, 165
Modern Asia Studies (journal), **2:**198, 200
Modern Drama (journal), **2:**102
Modern Fiction Studies (journal), **3:**74, 243
Modernism
    Bagnold (Enid) in, **2:**261
    Bennett (Arnold) in, **2:**136, 138
    Brittain (Vera) in, **1:**330
    Lu Xun in, **2:**172
    Nin (Anaïs) in, **2:**123
    origins and rise of, **2:**180
    Stein (Gertrude) in, **1:**332, 333, 334
    vs. traditionalism, Woolf (Virginia) on, **2:**138
    Woolf (Virginia) in, **2:**180
Modernization
    in Iran, rise of, **3:**218
    in Russia, rise of, **1:**193
    in U.S., Thoreau's (Henry David) critique of, **1:**233

Modern Judaism (journal), **1:**320
Modern Language Journal, **3:**301
Modern Motherhood (Davis), **3:**145
Modern Painters (Ruskin), **1:**264
Modern Philology (journal), **1:**247, 248, 264
Modern schools, **3:**5
Modisane, Bloke, **3:**251
Modkad, Jessica, **1:**209
Mogul Empire, **2:**229, *230*
Mohammed Reza Pahlavi (shah of Iran), **1:**155, **3:**218, *219*
    The Shah's Story, **3:**218
Mohammed V (sultan of Morocco), **3:**47, 49
Mohegan tribe, **1:**56, **2:**44, 46
Mohr, Nicholasa, **1:**108
Moi, Daniel arap, **2:**12, 14
Moira, Fran, **2:**4
Momaday, Al, **1:**54, 55
Momaday, N. Scott
    House Made of Dawn, **1:**54
    The Journey of Tai-me, **1:**54
    The Names: A Memoir, **1:**54
    The Way to Rainy Mountain, **1:**54–57, *55*
Moment of Conquest, The (Fadiman), **3:**141
Moments of Being (Woolf), **1:**249, **2:**182
Momoh, Joseph, **1:**312
Monaghan, Patricia, **1:**97
Monarchy. *See* British monarchy
Monasticism
    Teresa of Ávila on, **1:**211–213
    in U.S., oral histories of, **3:**308–310
Mondor, Colleen, **3:**249
Money. *See* Finances
Möngke Khan, **1:**107
Mongol Empire, **1:**105–107, **2:**59
Monroe, Ed, **1:**335
Montagu, Edward Wortley, **2:**35
Montagu, Mary Wortley, **2:**36
    audience of letters of, **2:**217
    "Letter to Her Daughter," **2:**35–37
    Ruete (Emily) compared to, **1:**90
    Turkish Embassy Letters, **2:**35, 37

Montaigne, Michel de, **2:**62, 256, 257
    Essais, **2:**72
Monteiro, Anthony, **1:**5
Montejo, Esteban, *Biography of a Runaway Slave,* **3:**7–9
Montell, William Lynwood
    Always a People, **3:**107–109, 325
    From Memory to History, **3:**90
    The Saga of Coe Ridge, **3:**90–92
Montenegro, oral histories of women of, **3:**135–137, *136*
Montgomery, James A., **1:**287
Montgomery bus boycott (1955), **1:**20, 37, 38, 39, **2:**32, **3:**44, 45
Monthly Review (journal), **1:**82
Montoya, Maria, **3:**133
Mont-Saint-Michel and Chartres (Adams), **1:**132
Moody, Anne, *Coming of Age in Mississippi,* **1:**37
Moon, Elaine Latzman, *Untold Tales, Unsung Heroes,* **3:**99–101
Moon, in Japanese poetry, **2:**191
Mooney, Christopher Gerald, **1:**150
Moonshine
    in Appalachia, **3:**90, 91
    in Idaho, **3:**95
Moore, Dorothy, **2:**333
Moore, Elijah, **2:**333
Moore, G. E., **2:**268
Moore, Gerald, **1:**128, 129
Moore, James, **1:**67
Moore, Kofoworola Aina, **1:**64
Moore, Marat, *Women in the Mines,* **3:**157, 328, **337–339**
Moore, Molly, *A Woman at War,* **2:**278–280
Moore, Thomas, **2:**143, 144
Moorehead, Caroline, **2:**101, 102
Moorhead-Rosenberg, Florence, **1:**77
Moosa, Matti, **1:**137
Moral Economy of AIDS in South Africa, The (Nattrass), **3:**272
Morality
    Conrad's (Joseph) concern with, **2:**192, 193
    Neruda (Pablo) on poetry and, **1:**223

Morantz, Regina, *In Her Own Words,* **3:**170

Mora-Torres, Gregorio, **3:**114, 115, 116

Moravians, **2:**196, 197

More Leaves from the Journal of Our Life in the Highlands (Victoria), **2:**209

Morello, Ruth, **2:**95, 96

Moreno Franglinal, Manuel, *The Sugarmill,* **3:**7

Morgan, Sarah, *The Civil War Diary of Sarah Morgan,* **2:**271

Morgan, Ted, **2:**56

Morgan, Winifred, **1:**35

Morgenthau, Henry, Jr., **3:**293

Morgenthau Plan, **3:**293

Morley, Christopher, **2:**330

Morley, Edith, **2:**77

Mormino, Gary R., **3:**191

Morning Sun (Leung), **3:**301

Moroccan Soul, The (Segalla), **3:**48

Morocco, oral histories of women in independence movement of, **3:**47–49, 48

Morris, Gabrielle, *Head of the Class,* **3:**20–22

Morris, Ivan, **2:**190

Morris, John N., **1:**247

Morris, Margaret Hill, **2:**80

Morrison, Toni, *The Bluest Eye,* **1:**19, 175

Morse, Richard M., **2:**7

Mort, John, **3:**100

Mortensen, Peter, **2:**163, 164, 165

Mortimer, Mildred, **1:**62

Mortimer, Raymond, **2:**268

Mosaic (journal), **1:**110, **3:**320

Mosby, John Singleton, *War Reminiscences,* **2:**250

Moss, William W., **3:**125–126, 213

Mossadegh, Mohammad, **3:**218, 219

Mostow, Joshua, **2:**292

Mother and Son (Seabrook), **3:**55

Mother-daughter relationships

in *A Mountainous Journey* (Tuqan), **1:**226, 227

in Plath's (Sylvia) writings, **2:**47–49

in *Ten Thousand Sorrows* (Kim), **1:**102 104

Motherhood

Jacobs (Harriet A.) on, **1:**142

Stanton (Elizabeth Cady) on, **1:**13

Mothers, Sisters, Resisters (Gurewitsch), **3:**34–36

Motley, Mary Penick, *The Invisible Soldier,* **3:**212

Motoori Noringa, **2:**190

Motorcycle Diaries (Guevara), **1:**223, **2:**220–222

Motsa, Zodwa, **1:**29

Mouffe, Barbara S., **2:**224

Moujahide, Ghalia, **3:**48

Moulton, Seth, **3:**231

Mountain, Carolyn, **3:**122, 123

Mountainous Journey, A (Tuqan), **1:**225–228

Mount Holyoke College, **1:**109

Mount Kenya, oral histories of Meru people of, **3:**141–143

Mount Vesuvius, eruption of, **2:**94, 95

Mourão, Manuela, **2:**199, 200

Movies. *See* Film adaptations; *specific movies*

Moving Out (Spence), **2:**163

Moya, Jose C., **3:**75

Moye, J. Todd

Freedom Flyers, **3:**99, **248–250**

Let the People Decide, **3:**249

Mpolweni, Nosisi, *There Was This Goat,* **3:**242

Mrs. Milburn's Diary (Milburn), **2:**265

Mrs. Miniver (film), **2:**265

Ms. magazine, **1:**11

Mudimbe-Boyi, Elisabeth, **1:**64

Muecke, Stephen, **1:**151

Muhammad, Elijah, **1:**186, 188

Muhlen, Norbert, **2:**56

Muhlenfeld, Elisabeth, **2:**250, 251

Mu'in al-Din Unur, **1:**285

Muir, John (naturalist), **1:**234

Muir, John (Vietnam veteran), **3:**209

Mujahidin, **3:**233

Mulan (legendary figure), **1:**152, 153, 340

Mulatto (Hughes), **1:**72

Mulattos

Jewish–black, **1:**74

as "tragic," in literary tradition, **1:**72

Mules and Men (Hurston), **1:**9

Mulford, Jeremy, **2:**266

Mullan, Fitzhugh, **3:**274

Muller, Bobby, **3:**232, 233

Muller, James, **3:**273

Mullin, Janet E., **2:**289

Mullins, Emer, **3:**29

Multicultural and multiracial identities

Kim (Elizabeth) on, **1:**102–103

Kingston (Maxine Hong) on, **1:**173–175

McBride (James) on, **1:**72–74

Nguyen (Kien) on, **1:**170

Obama (Barack) on, **1:**78–80

Santiago (Esmeralda) on, **1:**108–110

Suleri (Sara) on, **1:**87–88

"tragic mulatto" tradition and, **1:**72

Multicultural Autobiography (Payne), **1:**247–248

Multicultural families

Kim (Elizabeth) on, **1:**102–103

McBride (James) on, **1:**72–74

Obama (Barack) on, **1:**78–80

Suleri (Sara) on, **1:**87–88

Multiculturalism

academic debate over, **1:**16

and Columbus's (Christopher) legacy, **2:**203

Multicultural literary studies, *The Story of My Life* (Ahmedi) in, **1:**40–42

Multiracial individuals, racism against

in Korea, **1:**102

in Vietnam, **1:**170, 171

Multiracial literature, rise of, **1:**73–74

Munck, Ronnie, **3:**29

Munif, Abdelrahman, *East of the Mediterranean,* **2:**50

Munns, Jessica, **2:**67

Munson, Henry, Jr., *The House of Si Abd Allah,* **3:**47

Murao, Helen, **3:**197

SUBJECT INDEX

Murasaki Shikibu, **2:190**
    The Diary of Lady Murasaki, **2:**59, **290–293**
    Lady Murasaki Shu, **2:**291
    Michitsuna No Haha in family of, **2:**297
    The Tale of Genji, **2:**59, 60, 189, 190, 290–292, *291*
Murder in Amsterdam (Buruma), **1:**209
Murdock, Kenneth B., **2:**113, 114, 115
Murphy, Caryle, **2:**278
Murphy, Mary, **2:**17
    Mining Cultures, **3:**337
Murray, Albert, *The Omni-Americans,* **1:**124
Murray, John, **2:**143
Murry, John Middleton, **2:**133, 134, 135
Museum of North Idaho, **3:**93, 95
Music
    Conroy (Frank) on, **1:**166
    folk music revival of 1960s, **3:**96
    in Japanese American internment camps, **3:**104
    of labor movement, **3:**329
    of Mexican American women, **3:**131–133
    of working class, **3:**157, 159
Muslim(s)
    African American, **1:**186–188
    in conflict with Christians, after Crusades, **2:**226
    in conflict with Hindus, in India, **1:**244
    of India, **1:**244, **2:**230
    Malinke people as, **1:**128
    racial profiling of, in U.S., **3:**195, 197
    slavery in countries of, **1:**90, 92
Muslim autobiographical writing. *See also specific works and writers*
    by Ahmedi (Farah), **1:**40–42
    by Hirsi Ali (Ayaan), **1:**207–209
    by Laye (Camara), **1:**128–130
    by Malcolm X, **1:**186–188
    by Usāmah ibn Munqidh, **1:**285–288
Muslim women
    Ahmedi (Farah) on experience of, **1:**40–42
    circumcision of, **1:**207
    vs. European women, roles of, **1:**90
    Hirsi Ali (Ayaan) on mistreatment of, **1:**207–209
    Ruete (Emily) on rights and roles of, **1:**90–92
    Western biases in narratives depicting, **1:**40, 41
    Western misconceptions about, **1:**90, 91
Muslim Women on the Move (Gray), **3:**48
My Apprenticeship (Webb), **2:**17
My Bondage and My Freedom (Douglass), **1:**34
My Brother Ibrahim (Tuqan), **1:**227
My Confessions (Chamberlain), **1:**304
Myers, Brian, **1:**103
Myers, Constance, **3:**87
Myerson, Joel, **2:**224, 225
My Forty Year Fight for Korea (Yim), **1:**323
"My Furthest-Back Person— 'The African'" (Haley), **1:261–263**
My Life (Das), **1:**87
"My Life" (Keller), **1:**43
My Life and Work (Ford), **1:**30
My Life Story (Amrouche), **1:93–95**
My Life Story (Unaipon), **1:149–151**
Myrdal, Jan, *Report from a Chinese Village,* **3:**299
My Revolutionary Years (Cheng), **1:152–154**
My Soul (Hoess), **2:**54
My Soul Is My Own (Etter-Lewis), **3:**21
Mystery and Manners (O'Connor), **2:**131
Mysticism
    of Kempe (Margery), **1:**189–191
    of Teresa of Ávila, **1:**211–213
Myth and Materiality in a Woman's World (Abrams), **3:**175
Myth of Sisyphus, The (Camus), **1:**204
Mythology
    of Aborigines, **1:**149
    of Kiowas, **1:**54–56
    of Navajo, **3:**320

Myths and Legends of the Australian Aboriginals (Unaipon), **1:**149
My Traitor's Heart (Malan), **3:**242

N

NAACP. *See* National Association for the Advancement of Colored People
Nablus (West Bank), **1:**225, *226*
Nabokov, Vladimir, **1:271**
    Speak, Memory, **1:**249, 270
    Speak, Memory: An Autobiography Revisited, **1:270–272**
Nadeau, Remi, *The Water Seekers,* **3:**102
Nafisi, Azar, *Reading Lolita in Tehran,* **1:**155, 157, 209
NAFTA. *See* North American Free Trade Agreement
Nagai, Takashi
    The Bells of Nagasaki, **1:**293
    We of Nagasaki, **1:**293
Nagasaki (Japan), U.S. nuclear bombing of, **3:**239
Nagel, Paul C., **2:**71
Naghibi, Nima, **1:**157
Naipaul, V. S., **1:**88
Najder, Zdzisław, **2:**192
Nakazawa, Keiji, **1:294**
    Barefoot Gen, **1:293–295**
    Hiroshima, **1:**293, 295
Nam (Baker), **3:**199, 209, 210, 221, 231
Names, of slaves, **1:**52
Names, The: A Memoir (Momaday), **1:**54
Nanking (Nanjing) Massacre (1937)
    Rabe's (John) account of, **2:**19–21
    Sino–Japanese relations after, **1:**340
Napangardi, Georgina, **3:**107, 335
Napoleon (Scott), **2:**310
Napoléon Bonaparte, **1:**276, **2:**217
Napoleonic wars, **1:**276
Napoleon III, **2:**82
Narain, Mona, **2:**231
Nara period (Japan), **2:**189
Narrative (Brown), **1:**50
Narrative (journal), **1:**164, 165

Narrative of Hosea Hudson, The (Hudson), **1:**3–4

Narrative of Sojourner Truth (Truth), **1:**37

Narrative of the Life and Travels of Mrs. Nancy Prince (Prince), **3:**24

Narrative of the Life of Frederick Douglass (Douglass), **1:**33–36

   Eighty Years and More (Stanton) vs., **1:**12

   Equiano's (Olaudah) influence on, **1:**82–83

   Incidents in the Life of a Slave Girl (Jacobs) vs., **1:**34, 35, 142, 143

   Up from Slavery (Washington) vs., **1:**50

Narrative point of view (perspective)

   in *The Autobiography of Giambattista Vico* (Vico), **1:**184

   in *Bone Black* (hooks), **1:**249, 250, 251

   in *A Cross and a Star* (Agosín), **1:**76

   in *The Woman Warrior* (Kingston), **1:**173

   in *The Writing Life* (Dillard), **1:**280, 281

Narrative voice

   of *Angela's Ashes* (McCourt), **1:**120

   of *The Autobiography of Malcolm X* (Malcolm X), **1:**187

   of *Bone Black* (hooks), **1:**250

   of *The Color of Water* (McBride), **1:**73

   of *A Cross and a Star* (Agosín), **1:**76

   of *The Education of Henry Adams* (Adams), **1:**133

   of *An Egyptian Childhood* (Hussein), **1:**136

   of *Go Ask Alice* (anonymous), **2:**295

   of *I Know Why the Caged Bird Sings* (Angelou), **1:**18, 19

   of *Lakota Woman* (Brave Bird), **1:**23

   of *My Revolutionary Years* (Cheng), **1:**153

   of *Nella Last's War* (Last), **2:**266

   of *Paekpom Ilchi* (Kim), **1:**323

   of *Red Scarf Girl* (Jiang), **1:**161, 162

   of *Ten Thousand Sorrows* (Kim), **1:**103

   of *When Heaven and Earth Changed Places* (Hayslip), **1:**336

   of *The Woman Warrior* (Kingston), **1:**173

   of *The Writing Life* (Dillard), **1:**281

Nasar, Sylvia, **2:**18

Nash, Charles Elventon, *The History of Augusta*, **2:**331, 333

Nash, Christine, **3:**61

Nash, John, **3:**61

Nash, Philip Tajitsu, **3:**197

Nassiri, Nematollah, **3:**219

Nation (magazine), **1:**100, 103, 258, **2:**92, 102

Nation, Michael, **3:**211

National Academy of Arbitrators, **3:**153

National American Women's Suffrage Association (NAWSA), **1:**12, 13

National Anti-Slavery Standard (newspaper), **1:**144

National Association for the Advancement of Colored People (NAACP)

   on anti-lynching legislation, **1:**18

   in civil rights movement, **3:**44

   Du Bois (W. E. B.) in, **1:**4

   establishment of, **3:**44

   in military desegregation, **3:**248

National Book Award, for *Roots* (Haley), **1:**261

National Book Critics Circle Award

   for *Voices from Chernobyl* (Alexievich), **3:**282

   for *The Woman Warrior* (Kingston), **1:**173

National Geographic, **1:**114

National Health Service (Britain), **3:**170

National identity

   Danish, **2:**166

   Portuguese, **2:**199–200

Nationalism

   Armenian, **3:**40

   black, **1:**4, 78, 79

   British, **2:**219

   Chinese, **2:**170

   German, **1:**30–32, 329, **2:**120, **3:**234

   Indian, **1:**289–290

   Irish, **1:**119, **2:**127, 128, **3:**315

   Japanese, **3:**234

   Moroccan, **3:**47–49

   Palestinian, **1:**225, 227

   Puerto Rican, **1:**108

Nationalist Party (China), **1:**338

Nationalization

   in Cuba, **1:**296

   in Iran, **3:**218

National Liberation Front (FLN) (Algeria), **2:**262

National Party (South Africa), **1:**24, 27, **3:**242

National Republican Alliance (ARENA), **3:**205

National Savings Movement (Britain), **3:**145

National security, U.S.

   East German Stasi and, **3:**245

   racism and, **3:**195, 197

National Socialist German Workers' Party, **1:**30. *See also* Nazi Germany

National Velvet (Bagnold), **2:**259, 260, 261

National War Labor Board, The (Conner), **3:**153–154

National War Labor Board (NWLB), U.S., **3:**153–154

National Woman Suffrage Association, **1:**12

Nation of Islam. *See* Black Muslims

Nation of Women, A (Fur), **3:**326

Native American(s)

   in AIM (*See* American Indian Movement)

   Carver's (Jonathan) encounters with, **2:**205, 206, 207

   civil rights of, **1:**21, **3:**291, 292

   Columbus's (Christopher) encounters with, **2:**202

   conversion to Christianity, **1:**56, **2:**46, **3:**114, 115

   cultural transmission by, **3:**107–109, 325–326

   education of, at boarding schools, **3:**109, 318

SUBJECT INDEX

Native American(s), *continued*
    forced removal of, **1**:302, **3**:290, *291,* 318, 325, 327
    in King Philip's War, **1**:325–328, *326*
    oral traditions of, **1**:21, 54, 55, 96, 302, 304, **3**:138
    in Pan-Indian movement, **1**:54
    racism against, **1**:96
    religion of, **3**:110–112
    U.S. treaties with, **1**:69, **3**:107, 110, 290, 327
    U.S. wars with, **1**:302–304, **3**:110
Native American autobiographical writing. *See also specific works and writers*
    by Brave Bird (Mary), **1**:21–23
    by Chona (Maria), **1**:69–71
    in collective narratives vs. autobiographies, **1**:54
    by Geronimo, **1**:302–304
    by Momaday (N. Scott), **1**:54–56
    non–Native writers' collaboration in, **1**:21, 23, 56, 69–70
    by Peltier (Leonard), **1**:96–98
    rise of, **1**:54
    tradition of, **1**:54, 56, **3**:110, 318, 320
Native American identity
    language in, **3**:108, 109
    search for, **1**:22, 55, 56
Native American oral histories
    from Alta California, **3**:114–116, *115*
    of Black Elk, **3**:110–113
    of Delaware Indians, **3**:107–109
    of Inuits, **3**:138–140
    of Left Handed, **3**:318–320
    of Navajo, **3**:10–12, 290–292, 318–320
    from Owens Valley (California), **3**:102, 103
    of Woodland Indians, **3**:107–109
Native American renaissance, **1**:54
Native American reservations
    Brave Bird (Mary) on life on, **1**:21
    Chona (Maria) on life on, **1**:69
    economic disparities in, **3**:290
    establishment of system of, **1**:69, 302, **3**:318

    Geronimo on life on, **1**:302
    Navajo, **3**:10–12, 290–291, 318
    Navajo–Hope land dispute in, **3**:10–12
    Peltier (Leonard) on life on, **1**:96
    social change in, **3**:290
    water resources of, **1**:69, **3**:11
Native Land Act of 1913 (South Africa), **2**:241
Native Life in South Africa (Plaatje), **2**:241, 242, 243
Native Son (Wright), **1**:122, 123, 273
NATO, demonstrations against, **3**:157, 158
Nattrass, Nicoli, *The Moral Economy of AIDS in South Africa,* **3**:272
Natural History (journal), **3**:38
Naturalistic diction, in *Notebooks and Letters* (Hawthorne), **2**:224
Natural philosophy, **2**:300
Natural selection, **1**:65
Natural Theology (Paley), **1**:65
Natural world
    British writing on, golden age of, **2**:300
    Dillard's (Annie) essays on, **1**:279
    Neruda's (Pablo) love of, **1**:223–224
    Thoreau (Henry David) on, **1**:233–236
    in transcendental fiction, **1**:281
    Wordsworth's (Dorothy) descriptions of, **2**:300–302
"Nature" (Emerson), **2**:141
Nature's Pictures Drawn by Fancy's Pencil to the Life (Cavendish), **1**:229, 231
Naudowessee tribe, **2**:206
Navajivan (journal), **1**:242
Navajo, **3**:319
    in land dispute with Hopi, oral histories of, **3**:10–12
    Left Handed on life of, oral history of, **3**:318–320
    "Long Walk" of, **3**:290, *291*
    matrilineal culture of, **3**:318
    origins of, **3**:318
    witch purge of 1878 among, oral histories of, **3**:290–292
Navajo as Seen by the Franciscans, The (Bahr), **3**:290

Navajo-Hopi Land Dispute, The (Brugge), **3**:10
Navajo-Hopi Settlement Act of 1974 (U.S.), **3**:10
Navajo Land, Navajo Culture (McPherson), **3**:10
Navajo language, **3**:11, 12
Navajos, The (Underhill), **3**:290
Navajo Times (newspaper), **3**:12
"Navajo Witch Purge of 1878, The" (Brugge), **3**:290
Naval Aviation News, **3**:203
Navarrete, Martín Fernández de, **2**:201
Navy, Colombian, **3**:183–185
Navy, U.S., in World War II, oral histories of, **3**:202–204, *203*
NAWSA. *See* National American Women's Suffrage Association
Naylor, James, **2**:26
Naylor, Phillip, **2**:263
Nazi Germany. *See also* Holocaust
    autobiographies written after end of, **2**:54
    bombardment of Britain by, **2**:265, 269, 270
    Chilean support for, **1**:75
    establishment of, **3**:14
    extent of conquest by, **3**:14
    fall of, **2**:281–282
    Fosse Ardeatine massacre by, **3**:265–267
    France occupied by, **1**:332–334
    Italy occupied by, **3**:265–267
    Klemperer (Victor) on rise of, **2**:303–305
    Nanking Massacre and, **2**:19, 20, 21
    Netherlands occupied by, **2**:22–24, 253–255
    Speer's (Albert) role in, **2**:54–56
    war crimes of, **1**:77, **2**:54–56, **3**:293–295
Nazi Seizure of Power, The (Allen), **3**:245
NCR Book Award, for *Wild Swans* (Chang), **1**:159
Neal, R. S., **3**:178
Ned, Annie, **3**:320
Nedjma (Yacine), **2**:262

Neeson, Liam, **2:**10
Negative capability, **2:**146, 147
Négritude movement, **1:**61, 128
Negro in the American Rebellion, The (Brown), **2:**238
Nehru, Jawaharlal, **1:290**
    An Autobiography, with Musings on Recent Events in India, **1:289–292**
    The Discovery of India, **1:**290, 291
    Whither India?, **1:**290
Neihardt, John G., *Black Elk Speaks,* **1:**21, 56, 302, **3:110–113**, 318
Neilson, William Allan, **1:**44–45
Nella Last's Peace (Last), **2:**265
Nella Last's War (Last), **2:265–267**
Nelson, Edward, **3:**51
Nelson, Truman, **1:**4
Nemiroff, Robert, **1:**273, 274, 275
Neoliberalism, in Argentina, rise of, **3:**74
Neoplatonism, of Augustine, **1:**196, 197
Neruda, Pablo
    Canto general, **1:**223
    Memoirs, **1:222–224**
    Memorial de isla negra, **1:**223
Nesbitt, Gussie, **3:**45
Netherlands
    colonialism of, Barnard's (Anne) critique of, **2:**218
    Hillesum (Etty) on life in, **2:**22–24
    Hirsi Ali (Ayaan) on life in, **1:**207–209
    Nazi occupation of, **2:**22–24, 253–255
Neubauer, Carol, **1:**18
Never in Anger (Briggsoth), **3:**138
Nevins, Allan
    on *The Diary of John Quincy Adams* (Adams), **2:**70
    "Great Men" project of, **3:**161, 173, 179, 181, 186
    influence on oral history field, **3:**37, 173
New Age (journal), **1:**25
New Burlington (Baskin), **3:**86
New Challenge (journal), **1:**85
New Criterion (journal), **2:**73, 185, 337

New Culture Movement. *See* May Fourth Movement
New Deal, **3:**161. *See also* Federal Writers' Project
New Discovery of a Vast Country in America, A (Hennepin), **2:**205
Newell, Esther Pollack, **3:**269
New England Quarterly, **2:**114
New German Critique (journal), **1:**32
New Grub Street (Gissing), **2:**320, 321, 322
New Harmony (utopian community), **1:**14
Newman, Andrew, *On Records,* **3:**326
Newman, John Henry, *Apologia Pro Vita Sua,* **1:**65
New Mexico
    Bosque Redondo Reservation in, **3:**10, 290, *291*
    oral histories of development of atom bomb in, **3:**239–241
New Negro movement, **1:**84. *See also* Harlem Renaissance
New Orleans (Louisiana), oral histories of Hispanic American entrepreneurs in, **3:**121–123, *122*
New Republic (magazine), **1:**4, 258, **2:**150, 340, **3:**61
New Science (Vico), **1:**183, 184, 185
New Statesman (journal), **3:**59
New Statesman & Society (journal), **2:**221
Newsweek (magazine), **1:**19
New Voyages to North-America (Lahontan), **2:**205
New War Diary (Xie), **1:**339–340
New West Indian Guide (journal), **3:**7, 8
New Woman, **2:**259
New World, Columbus's (Christopher) discovery of, **2:**201–203
New York (state), interracial marriage in, **1:**72
New York City. *See also* Harlem Renaissance
    African American migration to, **1:**84
    City College in, **1:**249, 251
    in Great Depression, **1:**84
    Hansberry (Lorraine) on life in, **1:**273

    Jews living in, **3:**118, 119, *119*, 120
New York Daily Tribune (newspaper), **1:**142
New Yorker (magazine), **1:**258, 270, 300
New York Intellectuals, **1:**258
New York Post (newspaper), **3:**165
New York Review of Books, **1:**7, 79, **3:**60, 165, 280, 288
New York Times (newspaper)
    on *The Abandoned Baobab* (Bugul), **1:**62–63
    on *Along This Way* (Johnson), **1:**84
    on *Angela's Ashes* (McCourt), **1:**120
    on *Bloods* (Terry), **3:**201
    on *Bone Black* (hooks), **1:**250
    on *The Color of Water* (McBride), **1:**73, 74
    on *Diaries of Beatrice Webb* (Webb), **2:**17
    on *The Diaries of Franz Kafka* (Kafka), **2:**121
    on *A Diary from Dixie* (Chesnut), **2:**251
    on *The Diary of Anne Frank* (Frank), **2:**253
    on *The Diary of John Quincy Adams* (Adams), **2:**70
    on *The Diary of Samuel Pepys* (Pepys), **2:**73
    on *Dreams from My Father* (Obama), **1:**79
    on *Everything We Had* (Santoli), **3:**211
    on *Geronimo* (Geronimo and Barrett), **1:**304
    on *Hard Times* (Terkel), **3:**162
    on *Hunger of Memory* (Rodriguez), **1:**16
    on *Infidel* (Hirsi Ali), **1:**209
    on *Letters to a Young Poet* (Rilke), **2:**149
    on Levi's (Primo) suicide, **1:**204, 205
    on *London and the Life* (Gissing), **2:**322
    on *The Long Walk to Freedom* (Mandela), **1:**28, 29
    on *Mein Kampf* (Hitler), **1:**32

SUBJECT INDEX

New York Times (newspaper), **continued**
- on *Memoirs* (Neruda), **1:**223
- on *Memories of a Catholic Girlhood* (McCarthy), **1:**259
- on *Motorcycle Diaries* (Guevara), **2:**220
- "My Furthest-Back Person—'The African'" (Haley) in, **1:**261
- on *Our Appalachia* (Shackelford and Weinberg), **3:**87
- on *Persepolis* (Satrapi), **1:**156–157
- on *Red Azalea* (Min), **1:**158
- on *Rites: A Guatemalan Boyhood* (Perera), **1:**100
- on *Roots* (Haley), **1:**262
- on *Rosa Parks: My Story* (Parks and Haskins), **1:**38
- on *Selected Letters of Martha Gellhorn* (Gellhorn), **2:**102
- on *Shoah* (film), **3:**52
- on *Speak, Memory* (Nabokov), **1:**271
- on *The Story of a Shipwrecked Sailor* (García Márquez), **3:**183
- on *This Boy's Life* (Wolff), **1:**48
- on *Up from Slavery* (Washington), **1:**52
- on *When Heaven and Earth Changed Places* (Hayslip), **1:**336
- on *Witnesses to Nuremberg* (Stave et al.), **3:**294
- on *A Woman in Berlin* (anonymous), **2:**282
- on *The Woman Warrior* (Kingston), **1:**175
- on *Working* (Terkel), **3:**344
- on *The Writing Life* (Dillard), **1:**280

New York Times Book Review
- on *Chinese Lives* (Zhang and Sang), **3:**301
- on *Darkness Visible* (Styron), **1:**205
- on *A Diary without Dates* (Bagnold), **2:**260
- on *Dust Tracks on a Road* (Hurston), **1:**10–11
- on *Farewell to Manzanar* (Houston and Houston), **1:**300
- on *Fun Home* (Bechdel), **1:**141
- on *The Good Man of Nanking* (Rabe), **2:**20
- on "*The Good War*" (Terkel), **3:**213
- on *The Habit of Being* (O'Connor), **2:**131
- on *The Journals of Charlotte Forten Grimké* (Grimké), **2:**30
- on *Letters Home* (Plath), **2:**48
- on *A Midwife's Tale* (Ulrich), **2:**333
- on *The Travels of Dean Mahomet* (Mahomet), **2:**231
- on *Voices of Freedom* (Hampton and Fayer), **3:**45
- on *What Was Asked of Us* (Wood), **3:**233
- on *A Writer's Diary* (Woolf), **2:**181
- on *Zlata's Diary* (Filipovic), **2:**339

New York Times Magazine, **1:**99
New Zealand, Mansfield (Katherine) on life in, **2:**133–135
Next Year in Cuba (Pérez Firmat), **1:**296
Ng, Wendy, **3:**81
Ngarrindjeri people, **1:**149, 151
Ngor, Haing, *Survival in the Killing Fields,* **1:**306
Ngũgĩ wa Mirii, **2:**12
Ngũgĩ wa Thiong'o
- *Barrel of a Pen,* **2:**12
- *Decolonising the Mind,* **2:**13
- *Detained: A Writer's Prison Diary,* **1:**215, **2:**12–15
- *Devil on the Cross,* **2:**12, 13
- *I Will Marry When I Want,* **2:**12
- *Matagari,* **2:**14
- *Petals of Blood,* **2:**12

Nguyen, Kien, *The Unwanted,* **1:**170–172
Nguyen, Nathalie Huynh Chau, **1:**172
Nguyen, Viet Thanh, **1:**336–337
Nguyen Thi Thu Lam, *Fallen Leaves,* **1:**335
Nicene Creed, **1:**196
Nicholas II (tsar of Russia), **1:**270, **2:**84, 85
Nichols, John Gough, **1:**316, **2:**97, 99
Nichols, Julie, **2:**164
Nichols, Madaline W., **2:**7
Nichols, Martha, **1:**251
Nichols-Ledermann, Deborah, **3:**325, 326
Nicholson-Preuss, Mari, **3:**246

Nicolay, Helen, **3:**263
Nicolay, Helena, **3:**263
Nicolay, John G., **3:262**
- *Abraham Lincoln: A History,* **3:**261–262
- *Abraham Lincoln: Complete Works,* **3:**262
- in *An Oral History of Abraham Lincoln* (Burlingame), **3:**261–264
Nicolay, John Jacob, **3:**263
Nies, Judith, **3:**292
Nietzsche, Friedrich
- Andreas-Salomé (Lou) and, **2:**151
- *Ecce Homo,* **1:**183
- Vico (Giambattista) compared to, **1:**183, 184–185
Nigeria
- Civil War of, **1:**214–216
- Equiano (Olaudah) in, **1:**81–83
- independence of (1960), **1:**214
- postcolonial governments of, **1:**214–216
- Soyinka (Wole) on life in, **1:**214–216
Nigerian Civil War (1967–1970), **1:**214–216
Night (Wiesel), **1:318–321**
Night Comes to the Cumberlands (Caudill), **3:**66
Nightingale, Florence, **1:**111, 112, 113
Nijo, Lady, *Confessions of Lady Nijo,* **2:59–61**
Nikki genre, **2:**191
Nilsen, Alleen Pace, **2:**294, 295
Nin, Anaïs, **2:124**
- Bashkirtseff's (Marie) influence on, **2:**306
- *The Diary of Anaïs Nin,* **2:123–125**
- *The Extraordinary Work of Ordinary Writing* (Sinor) compared to, **2:**163
Nineteen Eighty-Four (Orwell), **2:**117, 118, 255
Nineteenth Amendment, **1:**13
Nineteenth Century (journal), **2:**307
Ninety-Four Years of a Floating Life (Su), **1:**338

SUBJECT INDEX

Nisa: The Life and Words of a !Kung Woman (Shostak), **3:**37–39
Nisei Daughter (Sone), **1:**299, 309
Nisei Soldiers Break Their Silence (Tamura), **3:**80
Nixon, Richard, **1:**21, **2:**294, **3:**279
Nkrumah, Kwame, **1:**4
    Ghana, **1:**290, **2:**12, 13
Nobel prizes
    to Buck (Pearl S.), **1:**159
    to García Márquez (Gabriel), **3:**183
    to King (Martin Luther, Jr.), **2:**32
    to Lessing (Doris), **1:**168
    to Luthuli (Albert), **1:**25
    to Maathai (Wangari), **1:**114
    to Mandela (Nelson), **1:**29
    to Menchú (Rigoberta), **3:**164, 165, 166
    to Mistral (Gabriela), **1:**222
    to Neruda (Pablo), **1:**222
    to Soyinka (Wole), **1:**214
    to Wiesel (Elie), **1:**320
Noche de Tlatelolco, La (Poniatowska). *See Massacre in Mexico* (Poniatowska)
Noël Coward Diaries, The (Coward), **2:**152
No Future without Forgiveness (Tutu), **3:**244
No Gods, No Masters (Guérin), **3:**3
Nolan, Janet, **3:**269
Nomad (Hirsi Ali), **1:**209
Nominalism, **1:**239
Nomura, Mary, **3:**104
Nonchronological order
    in *The Dark Child* (Laye), **1:**129
    in *Stop-Time* (Conroy), **1:**164, 165
Nonfiction essays, tradition of, **1:**279
No-No Boy (Okada), **1:**309
Nonviolent movements
    in India, Gandhi (Mohandas) in, **1:**242–244, 289–290
    in South Africa, against apartheid, **1:**24–26
    in U.S., King (Martin Luther, Jr.) in, **2:**32–34
Noonan, Lucille Brody, **3:**119
Norma Rae (film), **3:**98

Norrell, Robert J., **1:**38, 52
Norris, Bruce, *Clybourne Park,* **1:**273
Norris, Leslie, **1:**126
Norris, Randall, *Women of Coal,* **3:**337
North, James W., **2:**333
North, U.S.
    abolitionism in, **1:**33
    in Civil War (*See* American Civil War)
    Great Migration to, **1:**50, 52, 84, 273, **3:**99
    racial segregation in, **3:**250
    racism in, **1:**122
North American Free Trade Agreement (NAFTA), **3:**304
North American Review (journal), **1:**132, 134, 148, 202, **2:**89, 336
North Carolina, oral histories of coal mining in, **3:**86–87
Northern Expedition, **1:**338
Northern Ireland
    conflict over, **3:**27
    establishment of, **1:**119
North Fork of the Coeur d'Alene River (Russell), **3:**93
North Korea, establishment of (1945), **1:**322
Northside Chronicle, **3:**342
Northup, Solomon, *Twelve Years a Slave,* **1:**50
North Vietnam, establishment of (1954), **1:**335, **3:**279. *See also* Vietnam War
Norton, M. D. Herter, **2:**149
Norton, W. W., **2:**150
Nostalgia
    for Christmas, Thomas (Dylan) on, **1:**125, 126
    for English rural landscapes, **3:**63
    of Ukrainian miners, **3:**340, 341
Notarianni, Philip, **3:**225
Notebooks (Williams), **2:152–154**
Notebooks* and *Letters (Hawthorne), **2:**113, **223–225**
Notebooks of Henry James, The (James), **2:**113, 114, 115
Notes of a Native Son (Baldwin), **1:**79–80

Notes on the State of Virginia (Jefferson), **2:**45, 215
Not Working (Maurer), **3:**277
Novel(s). *See also* Fiction
    collective, **3:**282, 285
    of manners, **2:**312
Ntirkana, Jackson, *The Last Maasai Warrior,* **1:**114
Nuclear disaster, Chernobyl, **3:**282–285
Nuclear weapons
    movement against, **3:**239, 268, 269
    Pakistani, **1:**87
    U.S. development of, oral histories of, **3:**239–241
    U.S. use of, in World War II, **1:**293–294
Nunavut (Canada), oral histories of Inuits in, **3:**138–140, *139*
Nungarrayi, Molly, **3:**336
Nungarrayi, Rosie, **3:**335
Nuns, American, oral histories of, **3:**308–310
Nuremberg Interviews, The (Goldensohn), **3:**293
Nuremberg Laws of 1935 (Germany), **2:**253, **3:**14
Nuremberg Rallies, **1:**31
Nuremberg trials (1945–1946), **3:**294
    critics of, **2:**56
    oral histories of, **3:**293–295
    outcome of, **2:**56
    Speer (Albert) in, **2:**54, 56
Nursing
    in Crimean War, **1:**111–113
    in World War I, **1:**329, 330, **2:**259–261, *260*
NWLB. *See* National War Labor Board
NWSA Journal, **3:**338

O

OAH Magazine of History, **3:**101
Oakley, Ann
    "Interviewing Women," **3:**190
    The Sociology of Housework, **3:**144

Obama, Barack, **1:**79
    The Audacity of Hope, **1:**78, 80
    Dreams from My Father, **1:78–80**
    King's (Martin Luther, Jr.) influence on, **2:**33

Obama, Barack, Sr., **1:**78, 79, 80

Obama, Sasha, **1:**79

Obermeyer, Brice, *Delaware Tribe in a Cherokee Nation,* **3:**326

O'Brien, Glen, **3:**316

O'Brien, Tim, **3:**201
    Going after Cacciato, **1:**335

O Brother Where Art Thou (film), **3:**159

Observer (newspaper), **1:**80, **2:**153, **3:**235, 236

O'Casey, Sean, **1:**119, **3:**27
    The Silver Tassie, **1:**329

Ocasio-Melendez, Marcial, **3:**122

Occom, Samson
    "A Short Narrative of My Life," **1:**56
    Wheatley's (Phillis) letter to, **2:44–46**

Occupying Power (Kovner), **3:**128

"Occupy" movement, **3:**328

O'Connor, Flannery, **2:**130
    "A Good Man Is Hard to Find," **2:**130
    The Habit of Being, **2:129–132**
    Mystery and Manners, **2:**131

O'Connor, Frank, **1:**119

O'Connor, K. C., **3:**19, 332

October Revolution (1917), **1:**270

O'Donnell, James, **1:**197, 198

O'Faolain, Sean, **1:**119

O'Faolin, Nuala, **1:**119

O'Farrell, Brigid, *Rocking the Boat,* **3:**337

Ofer, Dalia, **3:**35

Offences Against the Person Act of 1861 (Britain), **3:**70

Off Our Backs (magazine), **1:**336, **2:**4

Oglala Sioux. See Lakota Sioux

O'Grady, Sean, **3:**316

O'Grady, Timothy, *Ireland's Unfinished Revolution,* **3:27–30**

Ogun (deity), **1:**216

O'Hara, Daniel, **2:**128

O'Hara, John, **2:**137

Ohio History (journal), **3:**326

Ohitika Woman (Brave Bird), **1:**21, 23

Oil industry, in Iran, **3:**218

Okada, John, *No-No Boy,* **1:**309

Okigbo, Christopher, **1:**214

Okihiro, Gary Y., **3:**197

Oklahoma, forced relocation of Delaware Indians to, **3:**325

Okubo, Miné, *Citizen 13660,* **1:**299

"Old Times on the Mississippi" (Twain), **1:**146

Old Wives' Tale, The (Bennett), **2:**136

"Old Woman's Gossip, An" (Kemble), **2:**335

Oliphant, Margaret, **2:**210
    Autobiography, **2:**335

Olive Schreiner Prize, for *Country of My Skull* (Krog), **3:**243

Olivier, Gerrit, **3:**243

Olivieri, Giovanni, **2:**160

Olney, James
    Autobiography: Essays Theoretical and Critical, **1:246–248,** *247*
    Memory and Narrative, **1:**246, 248
    Metaphors of Self, **1:**246
    Tell Me Africa, **1:**246

Olschki, Leonardo, **1:**105, 107

Olson, Ray, **3:**229

Olympica, Nazaria, **2:**160, 161

Olympics, **1:**158, **3:**32

O'Malley, Andrew, **1:**157

O'Malley, Ernie, *The Singing Flame,* **3:**27

Ombudsman, origin of term, **3:**154

Omni-Americans, The (Murray), **1:**124

Omori, Annie Shepley, **2:**190, 290, 292

O'Nan, Stewart, **3:**211

"On Being Brought from Africa to America" (Wheatley), **2:**46

Once They Hear My Name (Lee et al.), **1:**102

Ondaatje, Michael, *Running in the Family,* **1:**88

On Diary (Lejeune), **2:**174, 175

One Day in the Life of Ivan Denisovich (Solzhenitsyn), **3:**17

O'Neill, Eugene, **2:**152

O'Neill, Kevin, **2:**159

O'Neill, Michael, **3:**55

Only What We Could Carry (Inada), **3:**80

Ono Kazuko, **3:**149

On Records (Newman), **3:**326

On the Origin of Species (Darwin), **1:**65

"On the Pulse of the Morning" (Angelou), **1:**20

On the Road (Kerouac), **1:**234

Opequon, Battle of (1862), **2:**272

Operas, Chinese, **1:**159

Operation Bootstrap, **1:**108

Operation Desert Storm. See Gulf War

Operation Pedro Pan, **1:**298

Opium, Marcus Aurelius and, **1:**221

Oppenheimer, Gerald M.
    AIDS Doctors, **3:**272, 273, 274
    Shattered Dreams?, **3:272–274**

Oppenheimer, J. Robert, **3:**240, *240,* 241

Oppenheimer, Peter, **3:240**

Oppenheimer, Toni, **3:240**

Opper, Frederick, **3:**4

Oppression
    communist, in China, **1:**338
    of indigenous people of Guatemala, **3:164–166**
    political, in East Germany, **3:245–246**
    racial, Angelou (Maya) on, **1:**18

Oral American Historians Magazine, **3:**21

Oral contraceptives, **3:**170, *171*

Oral histories. *See also specific works and writers*
    Abrams (Lynn) on theory of, **3:173–175**
    audio vs. print recording of, **3:**65
    class differences in collection of, **3:**177
    definitions of, **3:**97, 158, 285
    economic disparities in collection of, **3:**190
    evaluation of reliability of, **3:**281
    four forms of, **3:**174
    Frisch (Michael) on shared authority in, **3:179–181,** 190

guidelines for collecting, **3:**187 188, 313
internationalization of, **3:**129
motivations for collecting, **3:**135
origins and development of field, **3:**37, 157, 173, 179–181, 186
Popular Memory Group on need for, **3:**176–178
Portelli (Alessandro) in field of, **3:**159, 173, 267
as primary sources in field of history, **3:**281
recognition of value of, **3:**20, 64, 90, 173, 186
as social change agent, **3:**86, 186, 187
subjectivity in, **3:**162, 173, 186
technological advances in, **3:**181
Thompson (Paul) on value of, **3:**186–189, 209
of women, feminist approach to, **3:**190–192

Oral Histories of First to Fourth Generation Americans (Lee), **3:**83

Oral History (journal)
 "ANZAC Memories" (Thomson) in, **3:**177, 178
 on *Daring Hearts* (Brighton Ourstory), **3:**72
 on *The Death of Luigi Trastulli* (Portelli), **3:**159
 on *Ireland's Unfinished Revolution* (Griffith and O'Grady), **3:**29
 "popular memory" issue of, **3:**177, 178
 on *The Voice of the Past* (Thompson), **3:**188
 on *Women's Words* (Gluck and Patai), **3:**192
 on *Working-Class Childhood* (Seabrook), **3:**54
 on *The World at War* (Holmes), **3:**235

Oral History, Health and Welfare (Bornat et al.), **3:**170–172

"Oral History and the Digital Revolution" (Frisch), **3:**181

Oral History Association Book Award, for *The Order Has Been Carried Out* (Portelli), **3:**265, 267

Oral History of Abraham Lincoln, An (Burlingame), **3:**261 264

Oral History of Tribal Warfare, An (Fadiman), **3:**141

Oral History Project: The Early Days of Labor Arbitration (Dash), **3:**153

Oral History Reader, The (Perks and Thomson), **3:**173, 178, 179, 181

Oral History Review (journal)
 on *Always a People* (Kohn and Montell), **3:**109
 on *And Justice for All* (Tateishi), **3:**197
 on *Children of Los Alamos* (Mason), **3:**240
 on *Chinese Lives* (Zhang and Sang), **3:**301
 on *Coal Hollow* (Light and Light), **3:**67
 on *The Death of Luigi Trastulli* (Portelli), **3:**159
 on *El Salvador at War* (Manwaring and Prisk), **3:**207
 on *Everything We Had* (Santoli), **3:**210, 211
 on *The Firm* (Bruce), **3:**246
 on *The First Agraristas* (Craig), **3:**303
 on *"The Good War"* (Terkel), **3:**213
 on *Habits of Change* (Rogers), **3:**309
 on *The Hispanic-American Entrepreneur* (Owsley), **3:**122
 on *In the Mansion of Confucius' Descendants* (Kong and Ke), **3:**125
 on *Japan at War* (Cook and Cook), **3:**216
 on *Japanese War Brides in America* (Crawford et al.), **3:**128, 129
 on *Long Journey Home* (Brown and Kohn), **3:**326
 on *Oral History Theory* (Abrams), **3:**174
 on *The Order Has Been Carried Out* (Portelli), **3:**266
 on *Peacework* (Adams), **3:**269
 on *A Shared Authority* (Frisch), **3:**179, 180, 181
 on *Shattered Dreams?* (Oppenheimer and Bayer), **3:**273
 on *The Strength Not to Fight* (Tollefson), **3:**223
 on *Survivors* (Miller and Miller), **3:**41
 on *Swiftwater People* (Russell), **3:**95
 on *They Say in Harlan County* (Portelli), **3:**97
 Thomson (Alistair) in, **3:**135
 on *The Voice of the Past* (Thompson), **3:**188
 on *Voices from this Long Brown Land* (Wehrey), **3:**103
 on *Witnesses to Nuremberg* (Stave et al.), **3:**294
 on *Witnesses to the Holocaust* (Lewin), **3:**51
 on *Women in the Mines* (Moore), **3:**339
 on *Women's Words* (Gluck and Patai), **3:**191

Oral History Society, **3:**65, 170, 172
Oral History Society (journal), **3:**5
Oral History Theory (Abrams), **3:173–175,** 179, 181, 285

Oral traditions
 African, **1:**64, **2:**242
 African American, **1:**262
 Irish, **1:**121
 Kabyle, **1:**93
 Native American, **1:**21, 54, 55, 96, 302, 304, **3:**138
 VaShawasha, **3:**251, 252
 Welsh, **1:**125

Oratorical autobiography, *Eighty Years and More* (Stanton) as, **1:**14
Ordeal of Mansart, The (Du Bois), **1:**5
Order Has Been Carried Out, The (Portelli), **3:**158**, 265–267**
Oregon, Japanese immigrants in, **3:**80–82, *81*
Oregon Historical Quarterly, **3:**82
Oregon Trail, The (Parkman), **1:**234
Oregon Treaty (1846), **2:**69
Organisation de l'Armee Secrete, **2:**262
Organization of American Historians: Magazine of History, **3:**277
Oriental Observer (periodical), **1:**277
Origin and Development of Psychoanalysis, The (Freud), **2:**175

Origin myths. *See* Creation stories
Orlando (Woolf), **1:**173, **2:**64, 181
Orleck, Annelise, *Storming Caesars Palace,* **3:**254
Orphans
    of influenza pandemic, **1:**258
    Kim (Elizabeth) as, **1:**102
    Korean, **1:**102
    McCarthy (Mary) as, **1:**259
Orthodox Jews, **3:**16
Orwell, George
    Animal Farm, **2:**117, *118*
    on *An Autobiography* (Gandhi), **1:**244
    Burmese Days, **2:**119
    Complete Works of George Orwell, **2:**117, 118
    Conroy (Frank) influenced by, **1:**164
    Diaries, 1931–1949, **2:117–119**
    Nineteen Eighty-Four, **2:**117, 118, 255
    The Road to Wigan Pier, **2:**117, **3:**66
Osamu, Tezuka, *Atom Boy,* **1:**293
Osborne, Dorothy, *The Love Letters of Dorothy Osborne to Sir William Temple,* **2:324–327**
Osio, Antonio María, *The History of Alta California,* **3:**115
Oslo Accords (1993), **2:**50, 52
Osorio, Arana, **1:**99
Osterud, Nancy Gray, **3:**135–136, 137
O'Sullivan, John, *"We Have Just Begun to Not Fight",* **3:227–230**
Osur, Alan M., **3:**249
Ota, Shelley, *Upon Their Shoulders,* **1:**309
Otero Silva, Miguel, **1:**222
O'Toole, Sean, **2:**115
Ottoman Empire
    in Armenian genocide, **3:**40–42
    in Crimean War, **1:**113
    Jewish immigration to China from, **3:**16
    Young Turk Revolution in, **2:**106
Ottway, Sheila, **1:**316–317
Ou, Li, **2:**147

Our Appalachia (Shackelford and Weinberg), **3:**66, **86–89**
Our Nig (Wilson), **1:**142
Our Partnership (Webb), **2:**17, 172
OurStory Scotland, **3:**70
"Our Struggles for Progress" (Luthuli), **1:**25
Our Village (Mitford), **3:**59
Outlook (journal), **1:**50, 51, **3:**119
Out of Darkness (Martin), **3:**40
"Outpost of Progress, An" (Conrad), **2:**192, 194
Outsider literature, *The Cancer Journals* (Lorde) as, **2:**3
Overboe, James, **1:**8
Overland Monthly and Out West Magazine, **2:**127
Owen, Robert Dale, **1:**14
Owen, Wilfred
    "Disabled," **1:**8
    Sassoon (Siegfried) and, **2:**247, 248
Owens Valley, The (Wehrey), **3:**102
Owens Valley (California), oral histories of, **3:**102–104, *103*
Owsley, Beatrice Rodriguez, *The Hispanic-American Entrepreneur,* **3:121–123**
Oxford University, **2:**287
Ozersky, Josh, **1:**188
Oziewicz, Stanley, **3:**301

P

PAC. *See* Pan African Congress
Pace, Michael, **3:**326
Pacheco, José Emilio, **3:**31, 32
Pacific Coast Philology (journal), **1:**93
Pacific Historical Review (journal), **3:**148, 225
Pacific Review (journal), **3:**126
Pacifism. *See also* Conscientious objectors
    of Brittain (Vera), **1:**329–331, **2:**269
    of Kingston (Maxine Hong), **1:**175
    of Partridge (Frances), **2:**268–269

Pacifist's War, A (Partridge), **2:268–270**
Pack, Sam, **3:**320
Packer, George, **2:**322
Pacte autobiographique, Le (Lejeune). *See Autobiographical Pact, The* (Lejeune)
Paderni, Paola, **3:**149
Padilla, Herberto, *Self-Portrait of the Other,* **1:**296
Padilla, Tanalis, **3:**303
Paekpom Ilchi (Kim), **1:322–324**
Page, Thomas Nelson, *Marse Chan,* **2:**250
Pahlavi, Ashraf, *Faces in a Mirror,* **3:**218
Paige, Leroy "Satchel," **1:**247
Paine, Albert Bigelow, **1:**148
Painter, Nell Irvin, **1:**3–4
Paintings, by Bashkirtseff (Marie), **2:**306, *307,* 308
Paiute tribe, **3:**102, 103
Pakistan
    Ahmedi's (Farah) escape from Afghanistan to, **1:**40, 41
    establishment of (1947), **1:**87, 244
    legacy of colonialism in, **1:**87–89
    Suleri (Sara) on life in, **1:**87–89
    U.S. relations with, **1:**87
Pakravan, Fatemeh, *Memoirs of Fatemeh Pakravan,* **3:**218–220
Pakravan, Hassan, **3:**218–220
Pakravan, Saïdeh, **3:**218
Palestine, under British Mandate
    'Amr (Sāmī) on life in, **2:**104–106
    Jewish immigration to, **2:**105, **3:**14
Palestine Broadcasting Service (PBS), **1:**227
Palestine-Israel Journal of Politics, Economics, and Culture, **2:**50
Palestine Liberation Organization (PLO), **2:**50
Palestinian autobiographical writing. *See also specific works and writers*
    by 'Amr (Sāmī), **2:**104–106
    by Darwish (Mahmoud), **1:**255–257
    by Ghazzawi ('Izzat), **2:**50–52
    tradition of, **1:**225–226, **2:**50, 104
    by Tuqan (Fadwa), **1:**225–227

Palestinian–Israeli conflict. *See* Israeli–Palestinian conflict

Palestinian nationalism, **1:**225, 227

Palestinian Notebooks (Bisisu), **2:**50

Palestinian Policeman (Courtney), **2:**104

Palestinian statehood, calls for, **2:**50, 52

Palestinian territories, Israeli occupation of, **1:**225, **2:**50, *51*

Paley, William, *Natural Theology,* **1:**65

Pall Mall Gazette (newspaper), **2:**83

Palmer, Michele, *Witnesses to Nuremberg,* **3:293–295**

Pan African Congress (PAC), **1:**25

Pan-Indian movement, **1:**54

Papago culture, Chona (Maria) on life in, **1:69,** 69–71

Paquet, Sandra, "The Enigma of Arrival," **1:**112–113

Paradise of the Blind (Duong), **1:**335

Paradox, in *In the Presence of Absence* (Darwish), **1:**255, 256

Paranoia, in East Germany, **3:**245

Paretskaya, Anna, **3:**332

Paris (France)
    American expatriates in, **2:**101
    Gellhorn (Martha) in, **2:**101
    nineteenth-century, Goncourts (Jules and Edmond de) on life in, **2:**81–83
    Wright's (Richard) move to, **1:**124

Paris, Treaty of (1783), **2:**69

Paris Commune of 1871, **3:**3

Paris France (Stein), **1:**332

Park, Eugene, **1:**324

Parker, Dorothy, **1:**258, **2:**133, 134

Parker, John, **2:**205, 206, 207

Parkins, Ilya, **1:**331

Parkman, Francis, **1:**146
    The Oregon Trail, **1:**234

Parks, Rosa, **1:38, 3:45**
    and civil rights movement in Detroit, **3:**101
    I Am Rosa Parks, **1:**38
    Quiet Strength, **1:**38
    Rosa Parks: My Story, **1:**19, **37–39**

Parliament, British
    in English Civil War (*See* English Civil War)
    on women miners, **3:**337

Parliament, European, **3:**292

Parr, Joy, **3:**181

Parr, Katherine, **2:**97, 99
    Lamentation of a Sinner, **2:**97

Parrington, Vernon, **2:**213

Parry, David, **1:**183, 184–185

Parry, Edward Abbott, **2:**324, 325

Parsons, Daniel, **2:**256, 257–258

Parsons, Neil, **2:**241

Partido Independiente de Color (PIC), **3:**8

Partido Revolucionario Institucional, **3:**303

Partisan Review (journal), **1:**258, 272

Partridge, Frances, *A Pacifist's War,* **2:268–270,** *269*

Partridge, Ralph, **2:**268, 269

Pascal, Blaise, *Pensées,* **1:**218

Pascal, Roy, **1:**246

Passerini, Luisa, **3:**74, 159, 173

"Passing"
    as black, **1:**74
    as white, **1:**72

Pass Laws Act of 1952 (South Africa), **1:**24, 25

Patai, Daphne, *Women's Words,* **3:190–192**

Pater, Walter, **1:**264, **2:**183, 184
    The Child in the House, **1:**276

Patmore, Coventry, **2:**147

Paton, Alan, *Cry, the Beloved Country,* **1:**27

Patriarchy
    Italian Renaissance, **2:**160
    in Montenegro, **3:**135, 136, 137
    Palestinian, Tuqan's (Fadwa) critique of, **1:**226, 227

Patriotism. *See also* Nationalism
    British, of Barnard (Anne), **2:**217, 218, 219

Patterson, David, **2:**24

Paul, Moses, **2:**46

Paula (Allende), **1:**222

Payn, Graham, **2:**152

Payne, Ethel, **3:**199–200

Payne, James Robert, *Multicultural Autobiography,* **1:**247–248

Paz, Octavio, **3:**32
    In Light of India, **1:**222–223

PBS. *See* Palestine Broadcasting Service

Peabody Western Coal Company, **3:**11

Peace activists, women, oral histories of, **3:**268–271

Peace Like a River (Enger), **1:**281

Peacework (Adams), **3:268–271**

Peacocks Fly to the Southeast, The, **1:**338

Peake, Cyrus H., *Chinese Missionaries Oral History Collection,* **3:**299

Pearce, Jenny, *Promised Land,* **3:**205–206

Pearl Harbor, Japanese bombing of, **1:**299, 300, 309, **3:**195, 202, 212, 215, 234

Pearlman, Elihu, **2:**73

Pearl of China (Min), **1:**159

Pearse, Patrick, **3:**27

Pearson, Geoffrey, *Hooligan,* **3:**312

Pechonick, Paula Martin, **3:**326

Peckard, Peter, **1:**83

Pedersen, David, **3:**207

Pedro Martinez (Lewis), **3:**31

Pedro Pan, Operation, **1:**298

Peer pressure, *Go Ask Alice* (anonymous) on, **2:**295

Pekar, Harvey
    American Splendor, **1:**139, **3:**330
    Students for a Democratic Society, **3:**330
    Studs Turkel's Working, **3:**330

Pelagius, **1:**196, 198

Peled-Elhanan, Nurit, **2:**50–51

Peltier, Leonard, *Prison Writings,* **1:96–98,** *97*

PEN/Faulkner Award, for *The Barracks Thief* (Wolff), **1:**47

Penn, William, **2:**26, **3:**327

Pennsylvania
    Ukraine compared to, **3:**340, 342
    women immigrants in, oral histories of, **3:**305–307

Pennsylvania History (journal), **2:**79, **3:**191, 306

Pensées (Pascal), **1:**218
Pepys, Samuel, **2:73**
    Boswell (James) compared to, **2:**328
    The Diary of Samuel Pepys, **2:**72–74, 174, 309, 328
    Evelyn (John) compared to, **2:**65, 66, 72
    on *A True Relation of My Birth, Breeding, and Life* (Cavendish), **1:**230
Percy, Walker, **2:**129
Peregrinationes in Montem Zion (Breidenbach), **2:**227
Perera, Victor
    The Cross and the Pear Tree, **1:**99
    "Guatemala: Always La Violencia," **1:**99
    Rites: A Guatemalan Boyhood, **1:**75, **99–101**
    Unfinished Conquest, **1:**99
Perestroika, **3:**17, 331
Perestroika from Below (documentary), **3:**340
Pérez Firmat, Gustavo, *Next Year in Cuba,* **1:**296
Pérez Rosales, Vicente, *Recuerdos del pasado,* **1:**222
Perils of the Soul (Guiteras-Holmes), **3:**167
Perissinotto, Giorgio, **3:**116
Perkins, Charlie, **1:**149
Perks, Robert
    Oral History, Health and Welfare, **3:170–172**
    The Oral History Reader, **3:**173, 178, 179, 181
Perlman, Itzhak, **1:**272
Perloff, Marjorie, **2:**150
Pernicone, Nunzio, *Carlo Tresca,* **3:**5
Perón, Eva, **3:**73, *74,* 75
Perón, Juan, **2:**220, **3:**73, 75
Peronism, **3:**73–75
Perrucci, Robert, **3:**207
Perry, Lorry, **2:**175
Perry, Yaakov, **1:**17
Persecution, of Jews. *See* Holocaust
Persepolis (Satrapi), **1:**139, 141, **155–157,** *156,* 293

Persia
    Lessing (Doris) on life in, **1:**167
    Polo's (Marco) travels in, **1:**106, 107
Persian Gulf War (1991). *See* Gulf War
Persian Sphinx, The (Milani), **3:**218, 219
Persona, Wells (H. G.) on, **1:**252
Personal finances. *See* Finances
Personalist Forum (journal), **1:**183
Personality and Individual Differences (journal), **2:**124
Perspective. *See* Narrative point of view
Petals of Blood (Ngũgĩ), **2:**12
Peters, H. F., **2:**150
Peterson, Andrea, **1:**331
Petilianus, **1:**196
Peyser, Seymour, **3:**293–294
Phaler, Karl, **3:**209
Pham Thanh Cong, **1:336**
Pham Van Xinh, **3:**281
Phelps, Elizabeth Porter, **2:**332
Philadelphia Inquirer (newspaper), **3:**222
Philadelphia Jewish Voice (journal), **3:**16
Philippi, Bernardo, **1:**77
Phillips, Bruce "Utah," **3:**329
Phillips, Richard, **2:**35
Phillips, Wendell, **1:**33
Phillpotts, Eden, **2:**137
Philosophical autobiographies
    The Autobiography of Giambattista Vico (Vico) as, **1:**183–185
    Confessions (Rousseau) as, **1:**200–202
    Journals of Søren Kierkegaard (Kierkegaard) as, **2:**166–168
    Meditations (Marcus Aurelius) as, **1:**218–221
    tradition of, **1:**183–184
Philosophy, natural, **2:**300
Philosophy and Social Criticism (journal), **2:**168
Philosophy East and West (journal), **3:**148
Photography
    in *Coal Hollow* (Light and Light), **3:**66, 67

    in *Long Journey Home* (Brown and Kohn), **3:**326
    in oral history field, **3:**181
    in *Solidarity Forever* (Bird et al.), **3:**329
Phylon (journal), **2:**33
PIC. *See* Partido Independiente de Color
Picasso, Pablo, **1:**332
Picture of Dorian Gray, The (Wilde), **2:**9
Pierce, Franklin, **2:**223
Piercy, Marge, **2:**4
Pif Magazine, **1:**297
Pigafetta, Antonio, *Journal of Magellan's Voyage,* **2:**201
Pignalosa, Giovanni, **3:**159
Pilgrimages
    of Guylforde (Richarde), **2:**226–228
    in Middle Ages, **1:190,** 191, **2:**226
    tradition of narratives of, **2:**198–199, 226
Pilgrim at Tinker Creek (Dillard), **1:**279
Pillow Book, The (Sei), **2:**59, 189, 190, 290
Pine, Frank Woodworth, **1:**181
Pine Ridge Reservation (South Dakota)
    AIM occupation of Wounded Knee at, **1:**21, 22–23, 96
    Peltier (Leonard) in shootout at, **1:**96
Pini, Robert, **1:**115
Pinochet, Augusto, **1:**75, 77, 222, **3:**185
Piper, Jane, **3:**276, 277
Pipino, Francesco, **1:**107
Pitt, William, the Elder, **2:**328
Pitt, William, the Younger, **2:**217
Pitt-Rivers, Julian, **3:**168, 169
Pittsburgh (Pennsylvania)
    Ukraine compared to, **3:**340, 342
    women immigrants in, oral histories of, **3:**305–307
Pittsburgh Courier (newspaper), **3:**248
Pittsfield Free Press, **3:**263
Plaatje, Solomon Tshekisho
    The Boer War Diary of Sol Plaatje, **2:241–243**

Mhudi, **2:**241, 243

Native Life in South Africa, **2:**241, 242, 243

Places of Origin (Edwards and Siebentritt), **3:**205

Plagiarism. *See also* Authorship

    Carver (Jonathan) accused of, **2:**205, 206, 207

    Cereta (Laura) accused of, **2:**160

    by Mahomet (Dean), **2:**229

Plain, Gill, **2:**237

Plassey, Battle of (1757), **2:**229

Plath, Aurelia Schober, **2:**47–49

Plath, Sylvia, **2:48**

    Ariel, **2:**47

    The Bell Jar, **2:**47

    Letters Home, **2:**47–49

    The Unabridged Journals of Sylvia Plath, **2:**49

Plath, Warren, **2:**47

Plato, *Seventh Letter,* **2:**94

Plessy v. Ferguson, **1:**37, 50, 122

Pliny the Elder, **2:**94, 96

Pliny the Younger, *The Letters of the Younger Pliny,* **2:94–96,** 95

PLO. *See* Palestine Liberation Organization

Plöckinger, Othmar, **1:**32

Plotinus, *Enneads,* **1:**196

Plum, Fred, **1:**6

Plumstead, A. W., **2:**215

Plunka, Gene A., **2:**255

PMLA (journal), **1:**147, **2:**63

Poddar, Prem, **3:**143

Poe, Edgar Allan, **2:42**

    Collected Letters, **2:**41

    "Letter to Maria Clemm," **2:41–43**

    "Ligeia," **3:**38

Poe, Neilson, **2:**41–42

Poe, Virginia Clemm, **2:**41–43

Poems on Various Subjects (Wheatley), **2:**44

Poetic style

    of *Black Boy* (Wright), **1:**123

    of *Child of the Dark* (de Jesus), **2:**6, 7

    of *A Cross and a Star* (Agosín), **1:**76

    of *The Dark Child* (Laye), **1:**128, 129

    of *The Journals of Charlotte Forten Grimké* (Grimké), **2:**30

    of *Memoirs* (Neruda), **1:**223

    of *A Mountainous Journey* (Tuqan), **1:**227

    of *Narrative of the Life of Frederick Douglass* (Douglass), **1:**35

    of *The Way to Rainy Mountain* (Momaday), **1:**55

    of *The Writing Life* (Dillard), **1:**280

Poetique (journal), **2:**174

Poetry. *See also specific poets*

    in *Confessions of Lady Nijo* (Nijo), **2:**59, 60

    Japanese *waka,* **2:**189, 191, 292

    in *Letters Underway* (Ghazzawi), **2:**51–52

    in medieval Arab education, **1:**287

    on racism, effects of, **1:**50

    Romantic, **2:**143, 146

    social role of, Neruda (Pablo) on, **1:**222, 223

    in *Ten Thousand Sorrows* (Kim), **1:**103

    in *When I Was Puerto Rican* (Santiago), **1:**108

Point of view. *See* Narrative point of view

Pokagon, Simon, *Queen of the Woods,* **3:**110

Poland

    Jewish immigration to China from, **3:**16

    Russian occupation of, **2:**192

Police, East German. *See* Stasi

Polish American Studies (journal), **3:**307

Polish autobiographical writing, by Conrad (Joseph), **2:**192–194

Politeness, in letter writing, **2:**217

Political activism

    of Douglass (Frederick), **1:**34, 35

    of Kingston (Maxine Hong), **1:**175

    of Soyinka (Wole), **1:**214

Political autobiography, *Dreams from My Father* (Obama) as, **1:**78–80

Political development

    of Guevara (Ernesto "Che"), **2:**220–222

    of Lu Xun, **2:**170–172

Political parties. *See specific parties*

Politics and Irish Life (Fitzpatrick), **3:**27

Politics of AIDS Denialism, The (Fourie and Meyer), **3:**272

Polk County (Hurston), **1:**10

Pollard, Edward, **2:**39

Pollin, Burton R., **2:**41, 42

Pollitt, Katha, **2:**124

Polner, Murray, **3:**16

Polo, Marco, *The Travels of Marco Polo,* **1:105–107,** *106,* **2:**198, 201

Pol Pot, **1:**306

Pommelier, Alfred, **3:**344

Pompeii, destruction of, **2:**94, 95

Poniatowska, Elena, **3:32**

    Here's to You, Jesus, **3:**32

    Massacre in Mexico, **3:**31–33

Poole, Elijah. *See* Muhammad, Elijah

Pooley, William V., **2:**92

Poor Bear, Myrtle, **1:**97

Poore, Charles, **1:**259

Poor Man's Son, The (Feraoun), **2:**262, 263, 264

Poor Richard's Almanac (Franklin), **2:**88

Pope, Alexander, **2:**146, 217, 328

Popkin, Jeremy D., **2:**174, 175

Popular culture

    Boswell (James) in, **2:**328

    Byron (George Gordon Noel) in, **2:**145

    Darwin (Charles) in, **1:**67

    Guevara (Ernesto "Che") in, **2:**221

Popular Memory Group, "Popular Memory: Theory, Politics, Method," **3:**176–178

"Popular Memory: Theory, Politics, Method" (Popular Memory Group), **3:176–178**

Popular Movements and Political Change in Mexico (Craig), **3:**302

Pork Rind and Cuban Songs (Medina), **1:**296

Porte, Joel, **2:**140

SUBJECT INDEX

Portelli, Alessandro
    The Battle of Valle Giula, **3:**97, 157
    The Death of Luigi Trastulli, **3:**96, **157–160**
    in field of oral history, **3:**159, 173
    I Can Almost See the Lights of Home, **3:**265–266
    The Order Has Been Carried Out, **3:**158, **265–267**
    They Say in Harlan County, **3:**87, **96–98,** 158
Porter, Jay, *Fighting Words,* **1:**97
Porter, Katherine Anne, **2:**152
Porter, Tracey, *Treasures in the Dust,* **1:**161
Porterfield, Amanda, **3:**112
Portrait of a Lady, The (James), **1:**133, **2:**113
Portrait of the Artist as a Young Man (Joyce), **1:**276, **2:**126
Portraits in Steel (Frisch), **3:**181
Port Royal Experiment, **2:**29–31
Portugal
    colonial power of, origins of, **2:**198
    Gama's (Vasco da) exploration for, **2:**198–200
    national identity of, **2:**199–200
Portuguese Studies (journal), **2:**200
Positions Asia Critique (journal), **1:**336
Positions: East Asia Cultures Critique (journal), **2:**292
Posner, Jerome B., **1:**6
Possession (Byatt), **2:**77
Postcolonial identity, **1:**87–89
Postcolonialism
    in *Meatless Days* (Suleri), **1:**87–89
    Orwell (George) in, **2:**119
Postcolonial studies
    The Boer War Diary of Sol Plaatje (Plaatje) in, **2:**243
    The Letters of Lady Anne Barnard to Henry Dundas (Barnard) in, **2:**218–219
    Memoirs of an Arabian Princess from Zanzibar (Ruete) in, **1:**90–91
    My Life Story (Amrouche) in, **1:**94
    The Unwanted (Nguyen) in, **1:**172
    The Wonderful Adventures of Mrs. Seacole (Seacole) in, **1:**112

Postman, Neil, **3:**119
Postmodern, origins of term, **1:**167
Postmodern autobiography
    Dreams from My Father (Obama) as, **1:**79
    Meatless Days (Suleri) as, **1:**87–89
    Under My Skin (Lessing) as, **1:**167–169
    The Woman Warrior (Kingston) as, **1:**173, 174
Postmodernism
    Kierkegaard's (Søren) influence on, **2:**167
    origins and rise of, **1:**167
    self in, **1:**167
    truth in, **1:**168
Poststructuralism, **1:**267
Potawatomi tribe, **3:**110
Potter, Hillary, **3:**122
Potter, Martha Beatrice. *See* Webb, Beatrice
Potter, Tiffany, **1:**327–328
Pottle, Frederick, **2:**328
Pound, Ezra, **2:**126
Poverty
    difficulty of defining, **3:**255
    primary, **3:**53
Poverty, in Britain
    in English villages, **3:**59
    McCourt (Frank) on, **1:**119–121
    in Victorian era, **2:**16
    among working class, **3:**53
Poverty, in Latin America
    in Brazil, de Jesus (Carolina Maria) on, **2:**6–8
    in Guatemala, Menchú (Rigoberta) on, **3:**164–165
    Guevara (Ernesto "Che") on, **2:**220–221
Poverty, in U.S.
    among coal miners, **3:**66, 67
    war on, oral histories of, **3:**254–256
    Wright (Richard) on, **1:**122
Powell, Enoch, **3:**186
Powell, Malea, **3:**109
Powers, Lyall H., **2:**113, 115
Powers, William, **3:**111–112

Powwows, **3:108**
Pozas, Ricardo, *Juan the Chamula,* **3:167–169**
Pozzetta, George, **3:**225
"Practice of the Private Journal" (Lejeune), **2:174–176**
Praeterita (Ruskin), **1:264–266**
Pragmatism, of Washington (Booker T.), **1:**51, 52
Prague (Czechoslovakia), Kafka (Franz) on life in, **2:**120–122
Prague Spring (1968), **3:**33
Pran, Dith, *Children's of Cambodia's Killing Fields,* **1:**306
Pratt, Mary Louise, **3:**166
Pratt, Richard Henry, **3:**109
Preciado Martin, Patricia
    Beloved Land, **3:**131
    Images and Conversations, **3:**121
    Songs My Mother Sang to Me, **3:131–134,** 302
Preece, Harold, **1:**10
Prejudice. *See also* Anti-Semitism; Racism
    against homosexuality, **1:**139
Prelude, The (Wordsworth), **1:**201, 264, **2:**302
Prendergast, Christopher, **1:**268–269
Prescott, Orville, **1:**271
Presidential elections, U.S.
    of 1860, **3:**261
    of 1992, **3:**221
Presidential oral histories
    of Johnson (Lyndon Baines), **3:**254–256
    of Lincoln (Abraham), **3:**261–264
    tradition of, **3:**254
Presidential Studies Quarterly, **2:**33, **3:**263
Presidios, of California, **3:**114–116
Press coverage. *See* Journalism; War correspondents
Prester John's Letter on the Wonders of India, **1:**105
Pretty-Shield (Linderman), **1:**70
Pride, cultural, of Woodland Indians, **3:**108, 109
Priestley, J. B., **2:**137
Primary poverty, **3:**53

SUBJECT INDEX

"Primitive" mind, theories of, **3:**37
Primm, Alex T., **3:**326
Prince, Mary, *The History of Mary Prince,* **1:**111, 113, **3:**23–26
Prince, Nancy, *Narrative of the Life and Travels of Mrs. Nancy Prince,* **3:**24
Principle Navigations, Voiages, Traffiques and Discoveries of the English Nation, The (Hakluyt), **2:**229
Principles of Geology (Lyell), **1:**65
Pringle, Thomas, **3:**23, 24–25
Printz, Mike, **3:**225
Prisk, Court, *El Salvador at War,* **3:**205–208
Prison. *See* Imprisonment
Prison narratives, Arabic tradition of, **2:**50. *See also specific works*
Prison Writings (Peltier), **1:**96–98
Pritchard, William, **1:**168
Pritchett, V. S., **3:**60
Privacy
    of diaries, as defining characteristic, **2:**174
    under East German Stasi, **3:**245
    James's (Henry) concern with, **2:**114, 115
    of Kierkegaard (Søren), violation of, **2:**166, 167
    in *Letters between Two* (Lu and Xu), **2:**171
    Maugham's (W. Somerset) concern with, **2:**183, 185
Private Journal of Aaron Burr, The (Burr), **2:**88
Private Mary Chesnut, The (Chesnut), **2:**250
Prix Européen de l'Essai Charles Veillon, Le, for *The Dark Child* (Laye), **1:**128
Prix Goncourt, establishment of, **2:**82
Profiling, racial, **3:**195, 197
Progoff, Ira, **2:**123
Progress
    industrialization in Keats's (John) concept of, **2:**146
    national, Emerson (Ralph Waldo) on, **2:**139, 140
Prohibition, in Idaho, **3:**95

Prohibition of Mixed Marriages Act of 1949 (South Africa), **1:**27
Project Gen, **1:**294
Proletarian Cultural Revolution. *See* Cultural Revolution
Promised Land (Pearce), **3:**205–206
Propaganda
    British, in World War II, **2:**270
    in Cultural Revolution of China, **1:**158, 159, *162*
    Orwell (George) on, **2:**117, 118
    Soviet, in World War II, **2:**282
    in Vietnam, **1:**171
Proposition 209 (California), **3:**20
Prose, Francine, **2:**231, 339, 340
Protection of State Information Bill (South Africa), **1:**29
Protestantism. *See also specific types*
    origins of, **1:**211
    rise of, in England, **2:**97–99
Protestant Reformation, **1:**211, **2:**72, 166
Protocols of the Elder of Zion, The, **1:**32
Proust, Marcel
    In Search of Lost Time, **1:**265, 270
    and *Speak, Memory* (Nabokov), **1:**272
Prouty, Olive Higgins, **2:**47
Psalms, book of, **1:**196, 198
Pseudonyms
    Bugul (Ken) as, **1:**61, 62
    Twain (Mark) as, **1:**146, 147
Psychoanalysis
    Nin's (Anaïs) experience with, **2:**123
    and rise of diaries, **2:**120
Public Historian (journal), **3:**68, 97
Publishers Weekly
    on *Barefoot Gen* (Nakazawa), **1:**294
    on *Bone Black* (hooks), **1:**250
    on *Carrier Warfare in the Pacific* (Wooldridge), **3:**203
    on *Growing Up Jewish in America* (Frommer and Frommer), **3:**119
    on *In the Cities of the South* (Seabrook), **3:**54

    on *Red Scarf Girl* (Jiang), **1:**161, 162
    on *A Stranger's Supper* (Milich), **3:**136
    on *A Woman at War* (Moore), **2:**279
    on *Zlata's Diary* (Filipovic), **2:**339
Puck (magazine), **3:**4
Puerto Rico
    Santiago (Esmeralda) on life in, **1:**108–110
    Spanish colonial rule of, **1:**108
    as U.S. territory, **1:**108
Pulitzer Prize
    for *Angela's Ashes* (McCourt), **1:**120
    for *The Confessions of Nat Turner* (Styron), **1:**204
    for *The Education of Henry Adams* (Adams), **1:**132, 134
    for *"The Good War"* (Terkel), **3:**161, 212, 234, 279, 343
    for *House Made of Dawn* (Momaday), **1:**54
    for *Maus* (Spiegelman), **1:**293
    for *A Midwife's Tale* (Ulrich), **2:**331
    for *Pilgrim at Tinker Creek* (Dillard), **1:**279
    for *Roots* (Haley), **1:**261
Puritanism
    in Britain, **2:**72, 74
    in U.S., **1:**325–327
Purves, Bill, **3:**16
Pushkin, Aleksandr, **2:**143
Pylgrymage of Sir Richarde Guylforde, The (Guylforde), **2:**226–228
Pynson, Richard, **2:**227

Q

Qa'ida, al-, **2:**275
Qasim, Samih al-, **1:**225
Qawuqji, Fawzi al-, **2:**104
Qing dynasty (China), **3:**147
Qiu Jin, **1:**152
Quade, Penelope, **1:**253
Quadriplegia, **1:**6–8

Quakerism
- conscientious objection in, **3:**223, 227
- of Fox (George), **2:**26–28
- of Leadbeater (Mary), **2:**157–159
- origins of, **2:**26–28, 157
- persecution of, **2:**26–28
- women's role in, **2:**28, 157

Quan, Adan, **2:**221
Quarterly Journal of Speech, **2:**33
Quarterly Review, **2:**309, 314
Queen of the Woods (Pokagon), **3:**110
Queer studies
- *Daring Hearts* (Brighton Ourstory) in, **3:**70
- *Fun Home* (Bechdel) in, **1:**141
- *Hunger of Memory* (Rodriguez) in, **1:**17
- *A Long Way from Home* (McKay) in, **1:**85

Querelle de femmes, **2:**160
Quiche tribe, **3:**164, 165
Quiet Strength (Parks), **1:**38
Quigley, Kathy, **3:**309
Quinn, Arthur Hobson, **2:**42
Quintilian, **2:**95
Quintus, **2:**94
Quinzaine litteraire (journal), **1:**267
Quite Early One Morning (Thomas), **1:**125
Quit India movement, **1:**291
Qur'an, Hussein's (Taha) study of, **1:**135, 136

R

Rabe, John, *The Good Man of Nanking,* **2:**19–21, *20*
Rabelais, Kevin, **1:**48
Rabin, Yitzhak, **2:**50
Rabinowitz, Dorothy, **1:**300
Race
- development of concept of, **2:**200
- in education, Rodriguez (Richard) on, **1:**15–16
- sociology of, Du Bois (W. E. B.) on, **1:**5

Race relations, in U.S.
- Du Bois (W. E. B.) on, **1:**3–5
- Hurston (Zora Neale) on, **1:**9
- in military, in Vietnam War era, **3:**199–201
- in Reconstruction era, **1:**50–52
- Washington (Booker T.) on, **1:**50–52

Race riots
- in Chicago, **3:**45
- in Detroit, **3:**99, 100, *100,* 101

Racial consciousness, Du Bois (W. E. B.) in advancement of, **1:**4
Racial equality
- Communist Party on, **1:**84
- Washington (Booker T.) on, **1:**50, 51

Racial identity. *See* African American identity; Multicultural and multiracial identities
Racial oppression, Angelou (Maya) on, **1:**18
Racial profiling, of Arab and Muslim Americans, **3:**195, 197
Racial purity
- in Korea, **1:**102
- in Vietnam, **1:**170

Racial quotas, in U.S. higher education, **3:**20
Racial segregation, in South Africa. *See* Apartheid
Racial segregation, in U.S.
- *de jure* vs. *de facto,* **3:**20
- in Detroit, oral histories of, **3:**99–100
- in higher education, **3:**20
- hooks (bell) on end of, **1:**249
- institutionalization of, **1:**37, 50, 122, **3:**44
- in military, end of, **3:**199, 248, 249
- in North vs. South, **3:**250
- Parks (Rosa) on experience of, **1:**37–39
- in schools, end of, **1:**122, 249, **3:**44
- Supreme Court on, **1:**37, 50, 122, 249, **3:**44
- Wright (Richard) on experience of, **1:**122–124, *123*

Racial tropes, in *Dreams from My Father* (Obama), **1:**80
Racism
- in Australia, against Aborigines, **1:**149
- in Britain, **2:**230
- in Chile, against Jews, **1:**75–77
- in Korea, against multiracial individuals, **1:**102
- in South Africa, under apartheid, **1:**24–26, 27–29
- in Vietnam, against multiracial individuals, **1:**170, 171

Racism, in U.S.
- Angelou (Maya) on experience of, **1:**18–19
- Du Bois (W. E. B.) on pervasiveness of, **1:**3–5
- gradualist approach to, King (Martin Luther, Jr.) on, **2:**32–33
- Hansberry (Lorraine) on experience of, **1:**273
- in higher education, oral histories of, **3:**20–22
- hooks (bell) on experience of, **1:**249–250
- against Italian Americans, **3:**224–226
- against Japanese Americans, **1:**309, **3:**81, 82, 127, 195
- against Korean Americans, **1:**103
- Malcolm X on experience of, **1:**186–187
- in military, **3:**44, 199–201, 248–250
- in national security policy, **3:**195, 197
- against Native Americans, **1:**96
- in North vs. South, **1:**122
- Parks (Rosa) on experience of, **1:**37–39
- in Peltier's (Leonard) trial, **1:**96
- in Reconstruction era, **1:**50
- against Vietnamese Americans, **1:**171
- Wright (Richard) on experience of, **1:**122–124

Radar, development of, **3:**202
Radcliffe College, **1:**43
Radhakrishnan, S., **1:**244

Radiance of the King, The (Laye), **1:**128
Radicalism, in U.S., history of, **3:**328–329
Radin, Paul, *Crashing Thunder,* **3:**318
Radio broadcasts, of Thomas (Dylan), **1:**125, 126
Raftery, Judith, **3:**307
Rahv, Philip, **1:**260
Railroads, U.S.
    expansion of, **1:**233
    racial segregation in, **3:**250
Rainbow, Edward, **2:**63
Raines, Edgar F., Jr., **3:**229
Raisin in the Sun, A (Hansberry), **1:**273, 274, 275
Rak, Julie, **1:**248, **2:**174, 175
Raleigh, Donald J.
    Russia's Sputnik Generation, **3:**331, 332, 333
    Soviet Baby Boomers, **3:331–333**
Ramey, Delphia, **3:**87
Ramose, Mogobe B., **3:**253
Ramsdell, Lea, **1:**17
Ramsey, Roger, **1:**165
Ramsland, John, **1:**150
Ranching, in U.S. West, **2:**91–93
Rancour-Laferriere, Daniel, **1:**195
Randolph, A. Philip, **3:**248
Rank, Otto, **2:**123
Rank and File: Histories of Working Class Organizers (Lynd and Lynd), **3:**179
Raoul, Valerie, **1:**7, **2:**307
Rape
    in *I Know Why the Caged Bird Sings* (Angelou), **1:**18, 19
    in *A Woman in Berlin* (anonymous), **2:**281–282
    in World War II, **2:**281–283
Raphael, Jody, **2:**282
Rappaport, Helen, **2:**210
Rasputin, Grigori, **2:**85, 86
Ratele, Kopano, *There Was This Goat,* **3:**242
Rationalism
    Cartesian, **1:**183, 184
    Kierkegaard's (Søren) critique of, **2:**166, 167
Rauff, Walter, **1:**77

Rauwerda, A. M., **3:**25
Ravel, Maurice, **2:**137
Ravenstein, Ernest, **2:**199
Rawick, George P., *The American Slave,* **1:**35
Rawlings, Claude, **1:**166
Ray, Annie, **2:**163–165
Ray, Charles, **2:**163, 164
Ray, Sangeeta, **1:**88
Raynaud, Claudine, **1:**9, 11
Rayson, Ann, **1:**300–301
Razor's Edge, The (Maugham), **2:**185
Read, Florence, **1:**4
Read, J., *Speaking Our Minds,* **3:**170
Reading Lolita in Tehran (Nafisi), **1:**155, 157, 209
Reagan, Ronald, **1:**37, 311, **2:**32–33
Realism
    in American literature, rise of, **2:**240
    in depictions of war, **2:**240
Recession, agricultural, in Britain, **3:**59, 61
Reconstruction era, **1:**50–52, **2:**238, 252
Records of a Girlhood (Kemble), **2:335–337**
Recuerdos del pasado (Pérez Rosales), **1:**222
Red Air Fighter, The (Richthofen), **1:**30
Red Azalea (Min), **1:158–160**
Red Buffalo (journal), **3:**162, 179
Redford, Rachel, **1:**80
Red Guards (China), **1:**158, 161, **3:**287, 288, 289
Red Lantern, The (opera), **1:**159
Redman, Ben Ray, **1:**333
Red Man's Religion (Underhill), **1:**70
Red Mirror, The (Wen), **3:**287
Redmond, Lucille, **2:**159, **3:**316
Red Power movement, **1:**21
Red Scarf Girl (Jiang), **1:**153, 154, 159, **161–163**
Reed, Matt, **1:**272
Reel, A. Frank, **3:**294
Reese, Florence, **3:**98
Reeves, Amber, **1:**254
Reeves, Ambrose, **1:**25

Reformation. *See* Protestant Reformation
Refugees
    Jewish, **1:**75–77, **3:**14–16
    Southeast Asian, **1:**306–307, 337
Regard, Frédéric, **1:**240
Regents of the University of California v. Bakke, **3:**20
Region (journal), **3:**332
Reich-Ranicki, Marcel, **2:**304
Reidy, Joseph, **3:**200–201
Reitell, Elizabeth, **1:**127
Relief of Mafeking, The (Young), **2:**241
Religion. *See also specific religions*
    in abolitionist movement, **1:**142
    in conscientious objection, **3:**221, 223, 227, 228
    theological certainty in, Robinson (Henry Crabb) on, **2:**76
    tradition of autobiographies of, **1:**193, 211
    women's roles in, Stanton (Elizabeth Cady) on, **1:**12
Religious faith
    Darwin's (Charles) loss of, **1:**65–67
    struggles with, in literary autobiographies, **2:**26
    Wiesel's (Elie) loss of, **1:**319–320
Religious Life in a New Millennium (Schneiders), **3:**308
Relocation law (Public Law 93–531), **3:**11
Remembering Pearl Harbor (La Forte and Marcello), **3:**202
Remembrance
    Clifford (Anne) on, **2:**62, 63
    Wiesel (Elie) on, **1:**318
"Remembrance of Things Pakistani" (Gates), **1:**88
Rementer, James A., **3:**325, 326
Remini, Robert V., **2:**71
Renaissance
    English monarchy in, **2:**97–99
    origins of autobiography in, **1:**239
    rise of diaries in, **2:**120
    women's role in, **2:**160–162
Renard, Jules, *The Journal of Jules Renard,* **2:**183

SUBJECT INDEX

Reparations
    for Japanese American internment, **3:**195, 197
    for World War I, **1:**30
Reporter (journal), **1:**320
Report from a Chinese Village (Myrdal), **3:**299
Report of the Departmental Committee on Homosexual Offences and Prostitution (1957), **3:**70
Rerhaye, Narjis, *Femmes et Politique,* **3:**47
Research in African Literatures (journal), **1:**215, **2:**14, 263, **3:**253
Reservations. *See* Native American reservations
"Resistance to Civil Government" (Thoreau), **1:**242
Rest for Travelers (Bioy Casares), **1:**223
Restoration (England), **2:**65, 72, 73
Restoration and 18th Century Theatre Research (journal), **2:**337
Restored Selves (Kumashiro), **3:**83
Retractions (Augustine), **1:**196, 198
Return to Nisa (Shostak), **3:**38
Reuss, Richard A., **3:**91
Revelli, Nuto, *The World of the Defeated,* **3:**61
Reverdy, Pierre, **1:**223
Reveries of the Solitary Walker (Rousseau), **1:**200
Reveries over Childhood and Youth (Yeats), **2:**126, 127
Review of Contemporary Fiction (journal), **1:**256
Review of English Studies (journal), **2:**77
Review of Religious Research (journal), **3:**309
Reviews in American History (journal), **3:**4, 87, 116
Revolutionary Democratic Front (FDR), **3:**205
Revolutionary United Front (RUF), **1:**312
Revolutionary War, American. *See* American Revolutionary War
Revoyr, Nina, *Southland,* **1:**309
Reynolds, Dwight F., *Interpreting the Self,* **1:**136, 137, 286, 287
Reynolds, Harriet, **2:**224

Reynolds, J., *Speaking Our Minds,* **3:**170
Reynolds, John Hamilton, **2:**146
Reynolds, William James, **2:**224
Rhee, Syngman, **1:**323, 324
Rhetoric, of Augustine, **1:**198
Rhetoric of English India, The (Suleri), **1:**87–88
Rhetoric Review (journal), **2:**30
Rhodes, Cecil, **1:**218, **3:**251
Rhodes, James, **1:**297
Rhodes, Richard, **3:**162, 241
Rhodesia
    British colonial rule of, **1:**167, **3:**251–253
    Lessing (Doris) on life in, **1:**167
Rhodesia (Mlambo), **3:**251
Rhys, Jean, **1:**111
Ribière, Mireille, **1:**269
Rice, Howard C., **2:**215
Rice, Judith A., **3:**261, 263
Rice, Julian, **1:**23
Rice bars, **3:**83, 84
Rich, Adrienne, **2:**3
Rich, Elizabeth, **1:**98
Richard III (king of England), **2:**228
Richards, Cynthia D., **2:**111
Richardson, Bob, **1:**279–280
Richardson, Dorothy, **2:**123
Richardson, Jonathan, **2:36**
Richardson, Karl Spence, **2:**163
Richardson, Robert D., **2:**141
Richardson, Samuel, **2:**328
    Clarissa, **2:**301
Richardson, Sue, **2:**271
Richlin, Amy, **1:**220
Richthofen, Manfred von, *The Red Air Fighter,* **1:**30
Rick, Dorothy, **3:**5
Rickard, W., **3:**273
Ricosti, Neide, **2:**8
Rida, Rashid, **1:**136
Ridley, Glynis, **2:**67
Rieff, Davic, **2:**340
Riegle, Rosalie, *Doing Time for Peace,* **3:**229
Riesco, Laura, **1:**76

Rife, Flora, **3:**87
Rigaur, Gerd, **2:304**
Rightist movements, Hitler's (Adolf) influence on, **1:**30, 32
Right-wing dictators, Latin American, rise of, **3:**185
Rigney, Anne, **2:**311
Rilke, Rainer Maria, **2:150**
    An Interrupted Life (Hillesum) on, **2:**22
    Letters of Rainer Maria Rilke, **2:**150
    Letters on God and Letters to a Young Woman, **2:**149
    Letters to a Young Poet, **2:149–151**
    Notebooks (Williams) on, **2:**152
Rilke, Ruth, **2:**149
Rime of the Ancient Mariner, The (Coleridge), **3:**183
Rinehart, Melissa, *Contested Territories,* **3:**326
Ringelheim, Joan, **3:**35–36
Ripley, George, **1:**235
Ripley, Sophia, **1:**235
Ritchie, Donald
    on *Between Management and Labor* (Friedman), **3:**155
    Doing Oral History, **3:**186, 294, 345
    on *Head of the Class* (Morris), **3:**21
    on *Witnesses to Nuremberg* (Stave et al.), **3:**294
Rites: A Guatemalan Boyhood (Perera), **1:**75, **99–101**
Ritter, Evelyn J., **3:**107
Rittner, Carol, *Different Voices,* **3:**34
Ritts, Morton, **3:**120
Ritualism, Chinese, **3:**124, 125
Rivas, Gladys C., **3:**207
Rive, Richard, *Writing Black,* **1:**25
Rivera, José, **2:**220
Riverbend
    Baghdad Burning, **2:**275
    Baghdad Burning II, **2:**275
River Runs through It, A (McLean), **1:**281
Rivers, W. H. R., **2:**248
Riwan ou le chemin de sable (Bugul), **1:**61, 64

Roach, John, **3**:250

Road to Wigan Pier, The (Orwell), **2**:117, **3**:66

Robbins, Amy Catherine, **1**:254

Roberts, Adam, **2**:33

Roberts, David, **1**:302, 304

Roberts, Elizabeth
    in *Oral History, Health and Welfare* (Bornat et al.), **3**:171
    in origins of oral history, **3**:64
    A Woman's Place, **3**:144, 145, 146
    Women and Families, **3:144–146**

Roberts, Nesta, **3**:54

Roberts, Rosemary, **3**:124, 125

Roberts, Sasha, **2**:325

Robeson, Paul, **1**:273
    Here I Stand, **1**:37

Robideau, Bob, **1**:96

Robin, Diana, **2**:160

Robinson, A. M. Lewin, **2**:217

Robinson, Amy, **1**:113

Robinson, Henry Crabb, *Diary, Reminiscences and Correspondence of Henry Crabb Robinson*, **2:75–77**

Robinson, Jo Ann Gibson, **1**:37

Robinson, Jo Ann O., **3**:223

Robinson Crusoe (Defoe), **3**:183

Robles, Emmanuel, **2**:262, 263

Rock Burst (Russell), **3**:93, 95

Rocking the Boat (O'Farrell and Kornbluh), **3**:337

Rocky Mountain Review (journal), **2**:153

Roderick Hudson (James), **2**:114

Rodier, Katharine, **2**:31

Rodin, Auguste, **2**:149

Rodina, Nina Ivanovna, **3**:18

Rodríguez, Andrés, **2**:146, 147

Rodriguez, Richard, *Hunger of Memory*, **1:15–17**, 47

Rodriguez, Spain, *Che: A Graphic Biography*, **3**:330

Roessel, Monty, **3**:291

Roett, Riordan, *Dialogue and Armed Conflict*, **3**:205

Rogers, Byron, **2**:102

Rogers, Carole Garibaldi, *Habits of Change*, **3:308–310**

Rogers, Katharine, **2**:37

Rogers, Robert, **2**:205, 207

Rogers, Seth, **2**:31

Rogovin, Milton, **3**:181

Rohlmann, Monika, **3**:140

Rohrbach, Augusta, **2**:252

Rohter, Larry, **2**:220

Rojas Pinilla, Gustavo, **3**:183, 184, 185

Roland Barthes (Barthes), **1**:249, **267–269**

Roldán, María, **3**:73–75

Rolle, Andrew, **3**:225

Rollins, Edwin, **1**:39

Roman autobiographical writing
    by Augustine, **1**:196–198
    by Marcus Aurelius, **1**:218–221
    by Pliny the Younger, **2**:94–96

Roman Empire, under Marcus Aurelius, **1**:218–221

Romanov dynasty (Russia), **2**:84–86

Romanticism
    Byron (George Gordon Noel) in, **2**:143
    D'Israeli's (Isaac) influence on, **2**:179
    egotism in, **2**:177, 179
    German, **2**:76
    Keats (John) in, **2**:146
    surge of autobiographies in era of, **2**:16, 177

Romantic relationships
    in *An Interrupted Life* (Hillesum), **2**:22, 24
    of Wells (H. G.), **1**:252, 253, 254

Romantic Review (journal), **2**:175

Rome, ancient
    under Marcus Aurelius, **1**:218–221
    Pliny the Younger on history of, **2**:94–96
    slavery in, **2**:96

Rome (Italy), Fosse Ardeatine massacre in, **3**:265–267

Romero, Mary, *The Maid's Daughter*, **1**:108

Rooke, Tetz, **1**:255, 256, 257

Roosevelt, Eleanor, **2**:101, 103, 254, **3**:248

Roosevelt, Franklin D.
    African American votes for, **3**:44
    Great Depression and, **3**:161, 212
    Italian American relocation under, **3**:224–226
    Japanese American internment under, **1**:299, 309, 311, **3**:104, 195
    labor arbitration under, **3**:153
    Manhattan Project under, **3**:239
    on Morgenthau Plan, **3**:293
    racism in military under, **3**:44, 248

Roosevelt, Kermit, **2**:220

Roosevelt, Theodore
    Geronimo and, **1**:302, 304
    in Japan-Russia Treaty of Peace, **3**:234
    Through the Brazilian Wilderness, **2**:220

Roots (Haley), **1**:18, 78, 261–263

Roque Ramirez, Horatio, **3**:85

Rosa Parks: My Story (Parks and Haskins), **1**:19, **37–39**

Roscoe, Adrian, **3**:252–253

Rose, Ellen Cronon, **1**:169

Rose, Jacqueline, **2**:49

Rose, Mary Beth, **1**:231

Rose, Michael E., **3**:145

Roseberry, William, **3**:324

Rose Hill (Wolcott), **3**:86

Roseman, Mark, **3**:35

Rosen, Edgar, **2**:17

Rosenbaum, Arthur L., *Chinese Missionaries Oral History Collection*, **3**:299

Rosenfeld, Maya, **2**:52

Rosengarten, Theodore, *All God's Dangers*, **3**:73, 179

Rosenthal, Anton, **3**:329

Rosenwald, Lawrence Alan, **2**:140, 141

Rosianus Geminus, **2**:96

Rosie the Riveter Revisited (Gluck), **3**:224

Ross, David, **3**:209, 210

Ross, Ellen, **3**:145

Ross, James, *Caught in a Tornado*, **3**:287

Ross, Robert, **2**:9, 10

Ross, Sarah Gwyneth, **2**:160

SUBJECT INDEX

Roth, John, *Different Voices,* **3:**34
Rothchild, Sylvia, *Voices of the Holocaust,* **3:**50
Rotkirch, Anna, *Living through the Soviet System,* **3:**331
Roughing It (Twain), **1:**146
Rouse, David, **3:**155
Rousseau, Jean-Jacques, **1:201**
　　Boswell (James) and, **2:**329
　　Confessions, **1:**193, 197, **200–203,** 276
　　Dialogues, **1:**200
　　Laye (Camara) compared to, on childhood, **1:**128
　　Olney (James) on, **1:**248
　　Reveries of the Solitary Walker, **1:**200
　　U.S. anarchists influenced by, **3:**3
Rowe, John Carlos, **1:**133, 134
Rowlandson, Mary, *The Sovereignty and Goodness of God,* **1:**81, **325–328,** **3:**24
Rowlatt Acts of 1919 (Britain), **1:**242, 289
Rowley, Hazel, **1:**124
Rowley, Susan, *Uqalurait,* **3:**107, **138–140**
Rowntree, Seebohm, **3:**53
Roy, Arundhati, *The God of Small Things,* **1:**87
Royal Literary Fund, **2:**207
Royal Society, **2:**65
RPF. *See* Rwandan Patriotic Front
Ruark, Robert, **2:**12
Ruch, Barbara, **2:**61
Rudnytsky, P., **1:**247
Ruete, Emily, *Memoirs of an Arabian Princess from Zanzibar,* **1:90–92**
Ruete, Rudolph Heinrich, **1:**90
RUF. *See* Revolutionary United Front
Ruiz, Vicki L., **3:**303
Rule and Exercises of Holy Living and Dying (Taylor), **2:**195
"Rule of taste," **2:**189
Rumor of War, A (Caputo), **3:**209
Running in the Family (Ondaatje), **1:**88
Rupert, Harry Cramer, **2:**93
Ruppin, Arthur, *Arthur Ruppin,* **2:**104

Rural England
　　depopulation of, **3:**59
　　oral histories of life in, **3:**59–61, 63–65
Rural Ireland, oral histories of life in, **3:315–317,** *316*
Rural women, tradition of oral histories of, **3:**135–136
Rush, Benjamin, *Autobiography of Benjamin Rush,* **1:**179–180
Rush, Norman, **1:**63
Rushdie, Salman
　　fatwa against, **1:**155
　　on *Infidel* (Hirsi Ali), **1:**207
　　Midnight's Children, **1:**87
　　Shame, **1:**87
　　Suleri (Sue) and, **1:**88
Rusk, Dean, **3:**279
Ruskin, John, **1:265**
　　Fors Clavigera, **1:**264
　　Modern Painters, **1:**264
　　Praeterita, **1:264–266**
　　Unto This Last, **1:**242
　　The Works of John Ruskin, **1:**265
Ruskin, John James, **1:**264
Ruskin, Margaret (Cock), **1:**264
Russell, Bert
　　Calked Boots and Other Northwest Writings, **3:**93
　　Hardships and Happy Times, **3:**93
　　North Fork of the Coeur d'Alene River, **3:**93
　　Rock Burst, **3:**93, 95
　　The Sawdust Dream, **3:**93
　　Swiftwater People, **3:93–95**
Russell, George, **2:**126, 128
Russell, Marie, **3:**93, 95
Russia. *See also* Soviet Union
　　Alexandra Feodorovna on life in, **2:**84–86
　　autobiographical tradition of, **1:**270
　　Bolshevik Revolution in, **2:**84, **3:**331
　　censorship in, **1:**193, 194
　　communism in, establishment of, **1:**270
　　February Revolution in, **2:**84

Great Reforms in, **1:**193
Jewish immigration to China from, **3:**16
liberalism in, rise of, **1:**193
Maugham's (W. Somerset) travels in, **2:**183, 184
Nabokov (Vladimir) on life in, **1:**270–272
October Revolution in, **1:**270
Poland occupied by, **2:**192
Revolution of 1917 in, **1:**270
Romanov dynasty in, end of, **2:**84–86
in Russo–Japanese War, **1:**322
Tolstoy (Leo) on life in, **1:**193–195
Russian Americans, Nabokov (Vladimir) as, **1:**270–272
Russian Orthodox Church, **1:**193, 194
Russian Review (journal), **3:**285, 333
Russian Revolution (1917), **1:**270
Russian Thought (journal), **1:**194
Russia's Sputnik Generation (Raleigh), **3:**331, 332, 333
Russo–Japanese War (1904–1905), **1:**322, **3:**234
Rustichiello of Pisa, **1:**105, **2:**201
Rustin, Bayard, **1:**20
Rutherford, R. B., **1:**220
Rwanda, Belgian colonial rule of, **3:**257
Rwandan genocide
　　oral histories of, **1:**312, **3:**257–259
　　war crimes trials after, **3:**293, 294
Rwandan Patriotic Front (RPF), **3:**257
Rwililiza, Innocent, **3:**257, 259
Ryan, Allan A., Jr., **3:**294
Ryan, Hugh, **1:**168
Ryerson, Richard Alan, **2:**90

S

Saadawi, Nawal El, *A Daughter of Isis,* **1:**226
Sabbagh, Suha, **1:**94
SABC. *See* South African Broadcasting Corporation
Sabor, Peter, **2:**314
Sachs, Nelly, *Eli,* **2:**255

Sackville, Margaret, **2:**64
Sackville-West, Vita, **2:**62, 64, 181
SACP. *See* South African Communist Party
Sad Earth, Sweet Heaven (Buck), **2:**271, 273
Sadler, Thomas, **2:**75, 77
Saemann, Karyn, **2:**276
Safeir, Gwendolen, *American Leaders in Nursing,* **3:**170
Safer, Morley, **3:**279
Safundi (journal), **3:**243
Saga of Coe Ridge, The (Montell), **3:90–92**
Sago mine disaster of 2006 (West Virginia), **3:**66, 67
Saigon, fall of, **3:**209, 279, *280*
Saints. *See also specific saints*
    lives of (*See* Hagiographies)
    relics of, **2:**226
Saint-Simon, Duc de, **2:**174
Saitoti, Tepilit Ole
    Maasai, **1:**114
    The Worlds of a Maasai Warrior, **1:114–116**
Sajdi, Dana, **1:**287
Sakakini, Khalil al-, *The Diary of Khalil al-Sakakini,* **2:**104, 106
Saladin, **1:**285–286, *286*
Salama, Gwen, **3:**45
Salamini, Heather Fowler, **3:**303
Salazar, Claudia, **3:**191
Sale, Roger, **1:**165
Salemi, Esmail, **3:**218
Saliba, Sue, *Watching Seagulls,* **1:**161
Salisbury, Richard, **3:**207
Salles, Walter, **2:**220
Salm, Arthur, **3:**67
Salmagundi (journal), **1:**247
Salme, Sayyida. *See* Ruete, Emily
Salomé (Wilde), **2:**183
Salter, Andrea, **2:**267
Salter, John R., Jr., **3:**329
Salter, Michael, **3:**294
Salt Lake Tribune (newspaper), **1:**38
Salvadoran Civil War, oral histories of, **3:**205–208, *206*
Same-sex marriage, **1:**139

Samkange, Stanlake, **3:**251
Samples from English Culture (Klein), **3:**144
Sampson, Anthony, **1:**27
Samway, Patrick H., **3:**45–46
Sánchez, Rosaura, **3:**114, 116
    Telling Identities, **3:**115, 121–122
Sancho, Ignatius, **1:**81, **2:**44
Sand, Georges, **2:**82
Sanders, Mark, **1:**314, **3:**243
Sanders, Robert, *Brothers,* **3:**199
Sanders, Valerie, **2:**336
San Diego Union-Tribune (newspaper), **3:**67
Sandos, James A., **3:**116
Sands, Kathleen M., **1:**70, 71
Sandul, Paul, **3:**188
Sang Ye
    China Candid, **3:**299–300
    Chinese Lives, **3:**288, **299–301**
Sansibar Blues (Buch), **1:**92
Sansom, George, **2:**189
Santa Fe, USS, **3:203**
Santa María (ship), **2:**203
Santiago, Esmeralda
    Almost a Woman, **1:**108, 109
    The Turkish Lover, **1:**108
    When I Was Puerto Rican, **1:108–110**
Santoli, Al
    Everything We Had, **3:**199, 201, **209–211,** 231, 275, 279
    Leading the Way, **3:**210
    To Bear Any Burden, **3:**210
Santoni, Pedro, **3:**116
Santrouschitz, Hermine, **2:**253
Sao Paulo (Brazil), de Jesus (Carolina Maria) on favelas of, **2:**6–8
Sapia, Yvonne, **1:**109
Sarajevo (Bosnia), Bosnian War in, **2:**338–340
Sarashina, Lady
    As I Crossed a Bridge of Dreams, **2:189–191,** 290–291
    Michitsuna No Haha as aunt of, **2:**297
Sarashina Diary. See As I Crossed a Bridge of Dreams

Sarcasm, in *The Education of Henry Adams* (Adams), **1:**132, 133
Sarcophagus (Gubarev), **3:**282, 284
Sargent, John Singer, **2:**114
Saro-Wiwa, Ken, **1:**214
    Sozaboy, **1:**312
Sarra, Edith, **2:**191, 299
Sarraute, Nathalie, *Enfance,* **1:**268
Sartre, Jean-Paul, **1:**124, 318, **2:**152, 167
Sasha and Emma (Avrich), **3:**3
Sassoon, Siegfried, **2:247**
    on *A Country Parson* (Woodforde), **2:**287, 289
    Diaries, 1915–1918, **2:247–249**
    Memoirs of a Fox-Hunting Man, **1:**329, **2:**247
    Orwell (George) compared to, **2:**117
    Sherston's Progress, **2:**247
Satire, in "Letter to the Reverend Samson Occom" (Wheatley), **2:**44, 45
Satirist, The (newspaper), **1:**277
Satrapi, Marjane
    Chicken with Plums, **1:**155–156
    Embroideries, **1:**155
    Persepolis, **1:**139, 141, **155–157,** *156,* 293
Sattelmeyer, Robert, **1:**235
Satterfield, Archie, *The Home Front,* **3:**202
Saturday Evening Post (magazine), **2:**250
Saturday Review (magazine), **1:**271, **2:**185, **3:**318
Saturday Review of Literature (magazine), **1:**333
Saturday Review/World (magazine), **1:**300
Satyagraha, **1:**242
Saudi Arabia, in Gulf War, **2:**278, 279
Saunders, Anna, **3:**247
Saunders, Keith B., **1:**149
Saunders, Loraine, **2:**118–119
Saussure, Ferdinand de, **1:**267
Savage, Priscilla, **3:**64
Savage, Thomas, *Californio Voices,* **3:114–117,** 121

SUBJECT INDEX

SAVAK, **3**:219
Savicheva, Tanya, **2**:277
Savin, Ada, **1**:100
Savoye, Jeffrey A., **2**:41
Sawdust Dream, The (Russell), **3**:93
Saxton, Marsha, *With Wings*, **1**:8
Sayigh, Mai, *The Siege*, **1**:226
Sayre, Robert, **2**:207
Scalp hunters, **1**:304
Scammell, G. V., **2**:198, 200
Scandinavia, Wollstonecraft's (Mary) travels in, **2**:111
Scaphandre et le papillon, Le (Bauby). See *Diving Bell and the Butterfly, The* (Bauby)
Scarlet Letter, The (Hawthorne), **2**:223–224
Scar literature, *Voices from the Whirlwind* (Feng) as, **3**:287
Schaefer, Paul, **1**:77
Schapera, Isaac, **2**:242
Scharnhorst, Gary, **1**:235
Schayegh, Cyrus, **3**:220
Schiller, Friedrich, **1**:277
Schimpf, Albrecht, **3**:235
Schmelz, Peter J., **3**:333
Schmidt, Matthias, **2**:54
Schmidt, Rob, **3**:68
Schmitz, John Eric, *Enemies among Us*, **3**:224
Schnabel, Julian, **1**:6
Schneider, Karen, **2**:269
Schneiders, Sandra Marie, *Religious Life in a New Millennium*, **3**:308
Schoeneman, Katherine A., **1**:205
Schoeneman, Thomas J., **1**:205
Schonbrun, Eva, **3**:35
School Library Journal, **1**:311, **3**:45, 225
Schoolma'am, The (Donovan), **3**:77
Schools. *See* Education
Schopenhauer, Arthur, **1**:193, 194
    The World as Will and Representation, **1**:193
Schrager, Samuel, **3**:329
Schreiber, Harry, **3**:21
Schubnell, Matthias, **1**:56
Schulkind, Jeanne, **2**:182
Schulman, Nicole, *Wobblies!*, **3**:330

Schuth, Katarina, **3**:309
Schwanitz, Wolfgang, **1**:209
Schwartz, Matthew, **2**:96
Schwarz-Bart, Simone, *Ti Jean L'Horizon*, **1**:64
Schwarzkopf, Norman, **2**:279
Scibetta, Barbara, *War Brides of World War II*, **3**:127
Science, Darwin (Charles) on success in, **1**:65–67
Science and Engineering Ethics (journal), **2**:168
Science fiction
    by Cavendish (Margaret), **1**:231
    feminist, **2**:237
SCLC. *See* Southern Christian Leadership Conference
Scotland. *See also* Scottish autobiographical writing
    in Enlightenment, contributions of, **2**:328
    in establishment of Great Britain, **2**:328
    militia groups in, **2**:309
    oral histories of life in, **3**:173, 175
    Victoria's visits to Highlands of, **2**:209–211
    during World War II, Mitchison (Naomi) on life in, **2**:235–237
Scott, David, **2**:258
Scott, Joanna C., *Indochinese Refugees*, **1**:335
Scott, Margaret, **2**:133, 134
Scott, Rebecca, **3**:68
Scott, Shaunna L., *Two Sides to Everything*, **3**:96
Scott, Walter, **2**:310
    "Auld Robin Gray" (Barnard) and, **2**:217
    The Bride of Lammermoor, **2**:209
    The Journal of Sir Walter Scott, **2**:67, **309–311**
    Kemble's (Fanny) friendship with, **2**:335
    Memoirs, **2**:309
    Napoleon, **2**:310
    Shadows on My Heart (Buck) on, **2**:271
    Waverly, **2**:309

Scottish autobiographical writing
    by Boswell (James), **2**:328–330
    by Mitchison (Naomi), **2**:235–237
    by Scott (Walter), **2**:309–311
Scottish Geographical Magazine, **2**:198
Scottish Historical Review (journal), **2**:236, 288–289, **3**:146
Scott-Moncrieff, G., **2**:329
Scrapbook of Katherine Mansfield (Mansfield), **2**:134
Scribner, Charles, **2**:101
Scribner, Doris, **3**:282, 285
Scribner's Monthly, **2**:114
Scrots, Guillaume, **2**:98
Sculptura (Evelyn), **2**:65
Seabrook, Jeremy
    In the Cities of the South, **3**:54
    Mother and Son, **3**:55
    Unemployment, **3**:54
    The Unprivileged, **3**:55
    Working-Class Childhood, **3**:53–55
Seacole, Mary, *The Wonderful Adventures of Mrs. Seacole in Many Lands*, **1**:111–113, *112*
Seaman, Donna, **1**:104, **2**:339
Season of Anomy (Soyinka), **1**:214
Seaver, Paul S., **2**:74
Secession, Lee's (Robert E.) views on, **2**:38, 39
Sechehaye, Marguerite, *The Autobiography of a Schizophrenic Girl*, **1**:164
Second Common Reader (Woolf), **2**:289
Secundinus, **1**:196
Sedgwick, Ellery, **2**:91
See, Lisa, **1**:159
Seeger v. United States, **3**:223
Seelig, Sharon, **1**:317
Seelig, Sharon Cadman, **2**:64
Segalla, Spencer D., *The Moroccan Soul*, **3**:48
Segregation. *See* Racial segregation; Sexual segregation
Seidensticker, Edward, **2**:297, 298, 299
Seidler, Ned M., **1**:66

Sei Shōnagon
  The Diary of Lady Murasaki (Murasaki) on, **2:**290, 291
  Michitsuna No Haha in family of, **2:**297
  The Pillow Book, **2:**59, 189, 190, 290
Seitz, James, **1:**268
Selected Autobiographies by Women Writers (Xie), **1:**340
Selected Letters (Keats), **2:**146
Selected Letters of Martha Gellhorn (Gellhorn), **2:101–103**
Selective Service, U.S., **3:**221, 227, 229
Self. *See also* Identity
  Hurston's (Zora Neale) views on, **1:**9, 10
  in identity, Rousseau (Jean-Jacques) on, **1:**200–202
  importance in society, and rise of autobiographies, **1:**246
  Lessing (Doris) on nature of, **1:**167, 168
  Native American vs. Western conceptions of, **1:**56
  in postmodernism, **1:**167
Self-actualization, in *Ten Thousand Sorrows* (Kim), **1:**103
Self-doubt, of Hawthorne (Nathaniel), **2:**223–224
Self-education, Franklin (Benjamin) on, **1:**179, 180
Self-elegy, of Darwish (Mahmoud), **1:**255–257
Self-Help (Smiles), **2:**310
Self-help books, *The Autobiography of Ben Franklin* (Franklin) as precursor to, **1:**182
Self-knowledge, Styron's (William) struggle for, **1:**204
"Self-made" individuals, Franklin (Benjamin) and, **1:**180
"Self-Made Men" (Douglass), **1:**180
Self-Portrait of the Other (Padilla), **1:**296
"Self-Reliance" (Emerson), **1:**180
Selkirk, Andrew, **3:**183
Sellin, Eric, **1:**128, **2:**263
Selochan, Viberto, **3:**207
Selznick, Irene Mayer, **2:**261
Seme, Pixley ka Isaka, **2:**241

Semiology, **1:**267
Sending My Heart Back across the Years (Wong), **1:**56
Seneca, **2:**94, 96
Seneca Falls Convention (1848), **1:**12
Senegal
  Bugul (Ken) on life in, **1:**61–64
  French colonial rule of, **1:**61
  independence of (1960), **1:**61
Senesh, Hannah, **2:**22
Senghor, Léopold-Sédar, **1:**61, 128
Senkaku/Diaoyu (islands), **1:**340
Senkewicz, Robert M.
  The History of Alta California, **3:**115
  Testimonios, **3:**116
Senna, Danzy, *Caucasia,* **1:**72, 74
Sentimental Education (Flaubert), **1:**128
"Separate but equal" doctrine
  end of, **3:**44
  establishment of, **1:**37, 50
Sephardic Jews
  in Guatemala, **1:**99–100
  immigration to U.S., **3:**118, 120
September 11, 2001, terrorist attacks
  East German Stasi and, **3:**245
  Hirsi Ali (Ayaan) on aftermath of, **1:**207
  national security after, **3:**195, 197, 245
  racial profiling after, **3:**195, 197
  The Story of My Life (Ahmedi) after, **1:**40
  U.S.-led invasion of Iraq after, **2:**275
Septicus Clarus, **2:**95
Seraph on the Suwanee (Hurston), **1:**9
Serbs, in Bosnian War, **2:**338
Serengeti National Park, **1:**114
Serious Proposal to the Ladies, A (Astell), **2:**35
Serrano, Jorge, **1:**99
Sestigers, **3:**242
Seton, William, **2:**213
Set This House on Fire (Styron), **1:**206
Seutonius Tranquillus, **2:**94
Seventh Letter (Plato), **2:**94

Seven Years' War (1754–1763), **1:**276, **2:**205, 328
Sévigné, Madame de, **2:**35
Sewanee Review (journal), **1:**165, **2:**76, 153, 269
Seward, Anna, **2:**217
Sex: An Oral History (Maurer), **3:**276, 277
Sexual activity
  adolescent, *Go Ask Alice* (anonymous) on, **2:**294
  in *The Diary of Anaïs Nin* (Nin), **2:**123
  in Japan, in Kamakura period, **2:**60–61
  in *Nisa* (Shostak), **3:**37, 38
Sexual discrimination
  in China, **3:**148
  in coal mining, **3:**337, 339
Sexuality, of African American women
  Angelou (Maya) on, **1:**18
  hooks (bell) on, **1:**250
  Jacobs (Harriet A.) on, **1:**143–144
Sexual orientation. *See* Homosexuality
Sexual segregation, among Meru people, **3:**143
Sexual violence, in Guatemala, **1:**100. *See also* Rape
Sforza, Ascanio Maria, **2:**160, 161
Sganga, Cristina, *El Salvador,* **3:**206
Shaarawi, Huda, **1:**136
  Harem Years, **1:**225–226
Shackelford, Laurel, *Our Appalachia,* **3:**66, **86–89**
Shackleton, Abraham, **2:**157
Shackleton, Elizabeth, **2:**157
Shackleton, Richard, **2:**157
Shadows on My Heart (Buck), **2:38, 271–274**
Shaffer, Deborah, *Solidarity Forever,* **3:328–330**
Shah, Saira, *The Storyteller's Daughter,* **1:**40
Shah's Story, The (Mohammed Reza), **3:**218
Shaka (Zulu leader), **1:**25
Shake Hands with the Devil (Dallaire), **3:**258

Shakespeare, William
- *Hamlet,* **1:**277
- *Journal of Katherine Mansfield* (Mansfield) on, **2:**133
- *Journals of Ralph Waldo Emerson* (Emerson) on, **2:**140
- Kemble's (Fanny) performances of, **2:**337
- *King Lear,* **2:**147
- *The Letters of John Keats* (Keats) on, **2:**146
- pilgrimage narratives used by, **2:**226
- *Two Gentlemen of Verona,* **2:**226, 228

Shame (Rushdie), **1:**87
Shamuyarira, Nathan, **3:**251
Shanghai (China), oral histories of Jewish refugees in, **3:**14–16, *15*
Shapin, Steven, **3:**240
Shapiro, Judith, **3:**301
Shapiro, Karin, **3:**272
Shapiro, Stephen A., **1:**277–278
Shared Authority, A (Frisch), **3:**173, **179–182,** 190, 192
Sharma, Govind, **2:**14
Sharp, Granville, **1:**83
Shattered Dreams? (Oppenheimer and Bayer), **3:272–274**
Shaw, George Bernard, **1:**84, **2:**16, 17, 128
Shaw, Nate, **3:**73
Shawqi, Ahmad, *al-Shawqiyyat,* **1:**135–136
Shawqiyyat, al- (Shawqi), **1:**135–136
Sheard, S., **3:**171
Shelley, Mary, *The Last Man,* **2:**145
Shelley, Percy Bysshe, **2:**143, 145, 146, 154
Shell shock, **2:**247, 248
Shepard, Alex, **3:**175
Shepard, Matthew, **1:**139
Sheridan, Dorothy, **2:**236
Sheridan, Richard Brinsley, **1:**34, **2:**217
Sherman, Beatrice, **1:**10–11
Sherman, L. A., *Bengali Girls Don't,* **1:**312
Sherman, William T., **3:**290
Sherriff, R. C., *Journey's End,* **1:**329

Sherry, Norman, **2:**194
Sherston's Progress (Sassoon), **2:**247
Sherwin-White, A. N., **2:**95
Shi, Shumei, **2:**172
Shields, Brooke, *Down Came the Rain,* **1:**204
Shinoda, Paul, **3:**196
Shipler, David, **1:**336
Shirane, Haruo, **2:**59
Shirinian, Lorne, **3:**42
Shizuo, Tanisuga, **3:**216
Shoah (film), **3:**50, 52
Shockley, Evelyn, **1:**250
Shoemaker, Adam, *Black Words, White Page,* **1:**150, 151
Shona people, **3:**251, *252*
Shopes, Linda, **3:**98, 181
Short, John, **2:**167
Short, William, **2:**213
Short Account of the Destruction of the Indies, A (Las Casas), **2:**201
"Short Narrative of My Life, A" (Occom), **1:**56
Shōshi (empress of Japan), **2:**290, 291, 292
Shostak, Marjorie
- *Nisa,* **3:37–39**
- *Return to Nisa,* **3:**38

Showings (Julian of Norwich), **1:**211
Shrader, Charles R., **3:**210
Shrier, Helene, **3:**119, 120
Shriver, Robert Sargent, Jr., **3:**254, 256
Shua, María, *The Book of Memories,* **1:**75
Shukert, Elfreida, *War Brides of World War II,* **3:**127
Shumaker, Wayne, **1:**246
Shuman, Amy, **3:**159
Shupe, Kevin, **1:**304
Shuttle in the Crypt, A (Soyinka), **1:**214
Sidney, Angela, **3:**320
Siebentritt, Gretta Tovar, *Places of Origin,* **3:**205
Siege, The (Sayigh), **1:**226
Siegelbaum, Lewis H., *Workers of the Donbass Speak,* **3:**157, **340–342**
Siege of Mafeking, The (Hamilton), **2:**241

Siemens, **2:**19
Sierra Eye (magazine), **1:**313
Sierra Leone
- Beah (Ishmael) on life in, **1:**312–314
- civil war of, **1:**312–314

Siglo XX (Bolivia), **3:**322
Siglo XX Housewives Committee, **3:**322
Sign in Sidney Brustein's Window, The (Hansberry), **1:**274
Sign language, Warlpiri, **3:**335–336
Signs (journal), **1:**88
Silver Tassie, The (O'Casey), **1:**329
Silvester, Christopher, **2:**276
Sim, Lorraine, **2:**269
Simmons, Allan H., **2:**194
Simms, Laura, **1:**314
Simone, Nina, **1:**274
Simplicity, Thoreau's (Henry David) advocacy of, **1:**233, 234
Simpson, Carol Chung, **3:**127
Simpson, Wallis, **2:**235
Sin, struggle with
- Augustine on, **1:**196–198
- Kempe (Margery) on, **1:**189, 190

Sindall, Rob, *Street Violence in the Nineteenth Century,* **3:**312
Singapore, Neruda (Pablo) in, **1:**224
Singapore Story, The (Lee), **1:**290
Singh, Ajay, **1:**299, 300
Singh, Amar, **2:**231
Singh, Amardeep, **2:**231
Singh, Nikky-Guninder Kaur, **2:**185
Singing Flame, The (O'Malley), **3:**27
Singing for Power (Underhill), **1:**70
Singletary, Otis A., **2:**245
Sino–Japanese War, First (1894–1895), **1:**322, 340, **3:**234
Sino–Japanese War, Second (1937–1945), **1:**339, 340
Sino-Judaic Institute, **3:**16
Sinor, Jennifer, *The Extraordinary Work of Ordinary Writing,* **2:163–165**
Sioux. *See* Lakota Sioux
Sisterhood, in oral history field, **3:**190
Sithole, Jabulani, **1:**26
Sithole, Ndabaningi, **3:**251

SUBJECT INDEX

Siv, Sichan, *Golden Bones,* **1**:306–308, *307*
Skenazy, Paul, **1**:174
Skin color, hooks (bell) on meanings of, **1**:250
Skinner, B. F., **1**:234
Skinner, John, **1**:190, 191
Skousen, Mark, **1**:182
Slade, Carole, **1**:213
Slantchev, Brantislav, **2**:299
Slave(s)
    as Civil War soldiers, **2**:238–240
    education of, in preparation for emancipation, **2**:29–31, *30*
    former, oral histories of, **3**:23–25
    genealogy of, **1**:261–263
    Jacobs (Harriet A.) on families of, **1**:142–143
    naming of, **1**:52
    rebellions by, **2**:238
    runaway, oral histories of, **3**:7–9
    separation of families of, **1**:261, 262
Slave narratives. *See also specific works and writers*
    authorship of, **1**:82–83
    Behind the Scenes (Keckley) as, **1**:52
    A Diary from Dixie (Chesnut) compared to, **2**:250
    Incidents in the Life of a Slave Girl (Jacobs) as, **1**:18, 34, 35, 142–145
    The Interesting Narrative of the Life of Olaudah Equiano (Equiano) as, **1**:34, 81–83, 142
    The Journals of Charlotte Forten Grimké (Grimké) vs., **2**:29
    modern autobiographies inspired by, **1**:18, 37
    Narrative (Brown) as, **1**:50
    Narrative of the Life of Frederick Douglass (Douglass) as, **1**:33–35
    Twelve Years a Slave (Northup) as, **1**:50
    Up from Slavery (Washington) as, **1**:50–52
    WPA collection of, **1**:35
Slave owners
    effects of slavery on, Douglass (Frederick) on, **1**:34

    naming of slaves by, Washington (Booker T.) on, **1**:52
    power of, Jacobs (Harriet A.) on, **1**:142
Slavery. *See also* Abolitionist movement
    Adams (John Quincy) on debate over, **2**:69, 70, 71
    in ancient Greece and Rome, **2**:96
    Arab vs. Western institution of, **1**:90, 92
    in Bermuda, oral histories of, **3**:23–25
    British abolition of, **1**:81, **3**:23
    Chesnut (Mary Boykin Miller) on, **2**:251
    Christianity and, **1**:34, 144, **2**:44, 46
    as Civil War issue, **1**:50, **2**:38, 250
    in Cuba, oral histories of, **3**:7–9
    Cuban abolition of, **3**:7
    Douglass's (Frederick) critique of, **1**:33–35
    Equiano's (Olaudah) critique of, **1**:81–83
    Jacobs's (Harriet A.) critique of, **1**:142–145
    in Jamaica, **1**:111
    Kemble's (Fanny) critique of, **2**:335
    Lincoln's (Abraham) views on, **2**:38
    Ruete (Emily) on, **1**:90, 92
    Stone (Kate) on, **2**:245
    U.S. abolition of, **1**:50
    Wheatley's (Phillis) critique of, **2**:44–46
Slave trade
    British abolition of, **1**:34, 111, **3**:23
    British debate over, **1**:81
    Equiano's (Olaudah) critique of, **1**:81–83
    increase in access to records of, **1**:263
    U.S. abolition of, **1**:33
Slavic Review (journal), **3**:332
Slavonic and East European Studies (journal), **3**:135
Sleeper, Jim, **3**:119

Slingsby, Henry
    The Diary of Sir Henry Slingsby, **2**:256–258
    "A Father's Legacy," **2**:256, 257, 258
Slouching towards Bethlehem (Didion), **1**:88
Small, Ian, **2**:9, 10
Small, Meredith, **3**:38
Small Talk (Mitchison), **2**:235
Small War (1895–1898), **3**:7. *See also* Spanish–American War
Small Wars & Insurgencies (Manwaring), **3**:206
Smiles, Samuel, **1**:65
    Self-Help, **2**:310
Smith, Abigail Adams, **2**:87–90
Smith, Adam, **2**:328
    Wealth of Nations, **2**:200
Smith, Angela K., **2**:18, 261
Smith, Betty, **2**:251
Smith, Bruce, **3**:177–178
Smith, Charlotte, **2**:300
Smith, Clark, *Brothers,* **3**:199
Smith, David Lee, **3**:108
Smith, Donald, **2**:236
Smith, Ethel Day, **3**:338
Smith, Gail K., **2**:331
Smith, Gayle, **3**:210
Smith, Geoffrey, **3**:229
Smith, Graham, **3**:171
Smith, Heather, **3**:123
Smith, John (captain), **1**:218
Smith, Joseph, **2**:178
Smith, Kitty, **3**:320
Smith, Mary F., *Baba of Karo,* **3**:141
Smith, Nadia Clare, **2**:308
Smith, Sidonie, **1**:246
Smith, Stevie, **2**:235
Smith, Thomas, **3**:345
Smith, W. Ramsay, **1**:149
Smith College, **2**:47
Smollett, Tobias, **2**:37, 328
Smyth, Frank, *Dialogue and Armed Conflict,* **3**:205
Snodgrass, Mary Ellen, **1**:301
Snow, C. B., **1**:149

Snow, Edward, **2:**150, 151
Snow, William, **2:**39
Sobukwe, Robert, **1:**25
Social change
    in Appalachia, **3:**86
    in English villages, **3:**59–61, 63–64
    in English working class, **3:**53, 144
    on Native American reservations, **3:**290
    oral histories as agent for, **3:**86, 186, 187
Social class divisions. *See also* Middle class; Working class
    in Brazil, **2:**6, 7
    in Britain, **1:**252–253, **2:**259
    in China, **1:**338, **3:**299
    in collection of oral histories, **3:**177
    in India, **1:**244, 289
    in Ireland, **1:**119–120
    in U.S., **3:**328
Social construction, of "able-bodied," **1:**8
Social equality
    in Britain, in Victorian era, **1:**252, **2:**16
    in U.S., affirmative action and, **1:**15, 16
Social History (journal), **3:**149, 176, 178
Socialism
    in field of history, **3:**176, 177
    in India, Nehru's (Jawaharlal) advocacy of, **1:**289, 290, 291
    in labor movement, **3:**157
    in *The Voice of the Past* (Thompson), **3:**186, 188
    during World War II, Mitchison (Naomi) on, **2:**235
Socialist market economy, of China, **1:**158
Social mobility, in Britain, **1:**252–253
Social reform
    in Brazil, **2:**6
    in Britain, **1:**264, 329, **2:**16
Social Studies of Science (journal), **3:**240
Social welfare, in Britain, oral histories of, **3:**170–172

Society
    poetry in, Neruda (Pablo) on, **1:**222, 223
    self in, and rise of autobiographies, **1:**246
Society of Friends. *See* Quakerism
Society of United Irishmen, **2:**159
Sociological Theory (journal), **3:**332
Sociology
    of race, Du Bois (W. E. B.) on, **1:**5
    Webb's (Beatrice) career in, **2:**16, 17
Sociology of Housework, The (Oakley), **3:**144
Soetoro, Lolo, **1:**78
Soldiers and Citizens (Mirra), **3:**231–232
Soldiers of the Sun (Harries and Harries), **3:**215
Solidarity and Survival (Stromquist), **3:**153
Solidarity Forever (Bird et al.), **3:328–330**
"Solidarity Forever" (song), **3:**329
Soliloquies (Augustine), **1:**196
Solimena, Francesco, **1:184**
Sollors, Werner, *Blacks at Harvard*, **3:**21
Solomon, Charles, **1:**294
Solomon, Martha, **1:**14
Solotaroff-Enzer, Sandra, **2:**254
Solzhenitsyn, Aleksandr
    The Gulag Archipelago, **1:**201, **3:**17
    One Day in the Life of Ivan Denisovich, **3:**17
Somalia
    Hirsi Ali (Ayaan) on life in, **1:**207–209
    interpretation of Islam in, **1:**207
    women in, treatment of, **1:**207
Somali Salvation Democratic Front, **1:**207
Some Memories of the Life of Job (Bluett), **3:**141
"Some Observations on Diaries, Self-Biography, and Self-Characters" (D'Israeli), **2:177–179**
Somerson, Wendy, **1:**160
Sommer, Barbara, **3:**109
Somoza Debayle, Anastasio, **3:**185

Sone, Monica, *Nisei Daughter*, **1:**299, 309
Song Flung Up to Heaven, A (Angelou), **1:**18
Songs My Mother Sang to Me (Preciado Martin), **3:131–134,** 302
Son of Old Man Hat (Left Handed and Dyk). *See* Left Handed, *Son of Old Man Hat* (Left Handed and Dyk)
Son of the Forest, A (Apess), **1:**56, **3:**318
Sontag, Susan, **2:**122
Sophie's Choice (Styron), **1:**204, 206, **3:**36
Sorghaghtani Beki, **1:**107
Sorin, Gerald, **3:**5
Sorrel, Lorraine, **2:**4
Sorrows of Young Werther, The (Goethe), **1:**276, 277, 339, **2:**166
Sort of Life, A (Greene), **1:**47
Soul, Augustine on, **1:**196
Souls of Black Folk, The (Du Bois), **1:**4, 51
Sourcebook (Kreider), **3:**227
South, U.S.
    abolitionism in, **1:**33
    Angelou (Maya) on life in, **1:**18–20
    in Civil War (*See* American Civil War)
    Great Migration out of, **1:**50, 52, 84, 273, **3:**99
    Latino Americans in, **3:**123
    lynchings in, **1:**18, 50
    racial segregation in, vs. North, **3:**250
    racism in, vs. North, **1:**122
    Reconstruction era in, **1:**50–52, **2:**238, 252
    slavery in economy of, **1:**33
    Wright (Richard) on life in, **1:**122–124
South Africa. *See also* South African autobiographical writing
    AIDS in, **1:**29, **3:**272–274
    Anglo–Boer War in, **2:**241–243
    apartheid in (*See* Apartheid)
    British colonial rule of, Barnard (Anne) on life under, **2:**217–219
    British colonial rule of, establishment of, **2:**241–243

freedom of expression in, **1:**29
Truth and Reconciliation Commission of, **3:**242–244
unification of (1910), **2:**241, 242
South African autobiographical writing. *See also specific works and writers*
by Lessing (Doris), **1:**167–169
by Luthuli (Albert), **1:**24–26
by Mandela (Nelson), **1:**27–29
by Plaatje (Solomon Tshekisho), **2:**241–243
South African Broadcasting Corporation (SABC), **3:**242
South African Communist Party (SACP), **1:**27
South African Native National Congress, **2:**241
South African oral histories
on AIDS epidemic, **3:**272–274
on Truth and Reconciliation Commission, **3:**242–244
South African War. *See* Anglo–Boer War
South Africa's "Black" Market (Fadiman), **3:**142
South Carolina, during Civil War, Chesnut (Mary Boykin Miller) on, **2:**250–252
South Central Review (journal), **2:**255
South Dakota. *See* Pine Ridge Reservation; Wounded Knee
Southeast Asia. *See also specific countries*
immigration to U.S. from, **1:**170, 171, 306
refugees from, **1:**306–307, 337
Southeast Review of Asian Studies (journal), **1:**307
Southern Christian Leadership Conference (SCLC)
Angelou (Maya) in, **1:**18, 20
establishment of, **1:**20
King (Martin Luther, Jr.) in, **1:**20, **2:**32, 34
Southern Command, U.S., **3:**205, 207
Southern Horrors (Wells), **1:**50
Southern Literary Journal, **2:**131
Southern Literary Messenger (magazine), **2:**41
Southern Manifesto (1956), **1:**249

Southern Workman (journal), **1:**52
Southey, Robert, **2:**66–67, 196
South Korea
establishment of (1945), **1:**322
Kim Ku on life in, **1:**322–324
Southland (Revoyr), **1:**309
South Riding (Holtby), **1:**331
South Vietnam. *See also* Vietnam War
establishment of (1954), **1:**335, **3:**279
fall of, oral histories of, **3:**279–281
U.S. military involvement in, origins of, **3:**279
Southwestern American Literature (journal), **3:**12
Southwestern Historical Quarterly, **2:**245, **3:**255
South Wind Changing (Huynh), **1:**171
Sovereignty and Goodness of God, The (Rowlandson), **1:**81, **325–328**, **3:**24
Soviet Baby Boomers (Raleigh), **3:331–333**
Soviet Union. *See also* Russia
Afghan war with, **1:**40, **3:**233
baby boomers of, oral histories of, **3:**331–333
Berlin occupied by, **2:**281–282
Chernobyl nuclear disaster in, **3:**282–285
collapse of, **3:**282, 331, 333, 340
Du Bois (W. E. B.) and, **1:**3, 4
establishment of, **3:**331
glasnost in, **3:**282, 331, 333
Gulag system in, oral histories of, **3:**17–19
industrialization in, **3:**17
KGB of, Stasi modeled on, **3:**245
McKay's (Claude) reception in, **1:**84, 85
perestroika in, **3:**17, 331
Sowden, Benjamin, **2:**37
Soyinka, Wole, **1:**215
Madmen and Specialists, **1:**214
The Man Died, **1:214–217**, **2:**12, 14
Season of Anomy, **1:**214
A Shuttle in the Crypt, **1:**214
Sozaboy (Saro-Wiwa), **1:**312
Spacks, Patricia Meyer, **2:**35

Spain
California as colony of, **3:**114
colonial power of, origins of, **2:**201, 202
Columbus's (Christopher) exploration for, **2:**201–203
in Cuban War of Independence, **3:**7
Morocco as protectorate of, **3:**47
Puerto Rico as colony of, **1:**108
in Ten Years' War, **3:**7
Teresa of Ávila in, **1:**211–213
Spandau (Speer), **2:54–56**
Spandau prison (Berlin), **2:**54–56, 55
Spanish–American War (1898), **1:**108, 332, **3:**7
Spanish Civil War (1936–1939)
Gellhorn's (Martha) reporting on, **2:**101–103
Guevara (Ernesto "Che") influenced by, **2:**220
Neruda's (Pablo) experience in, **1:**222
Spanish Inquisition, **1:**211
Spanish language
in identity, **1:**15–17
in Puerto Rico, **1:**109
in U.S. education, **1:**15, 16, 17
Spared Angola (Suárez), **1:**296
Sparks, Beatrice
Annie's Baby, **2:**294
as author of *Go Ask Alice* (anonymous), **2:**294–296
It Happened to Nancy, **2:**294
Jay's Journal, **2:**294
Spartacus (magazine), **3:**70
Speak, Memory (Nabokov), **1:**249, 270
Speak, Memory: An Autobiography Revisited (Nabokov), **1:270–272**
Speak for England (Bragg), **3:**144
Speaking Our Minds (Read and Reynolds), **3:**170
Spear, Thomas, **3:**143
Spectator (magazine), **2:**102, 231, 328, **3:**59, 235
Spector, Scott, **2:**122
Speer, Albert
Inside the Third Reich, **2:**54
Spandau, **2:**54–56
in *The World at War* (Holmes), **3:**235

SUBJECT INDEX

Spence, Polly, *Moving Out,* **2:**163
Spencer, Terence, **2:**228
Spender, Stephen, **2:236**
Spengemann, William, **1:**246
Spenser, Edmund, **2:**62, 146
Spiegelman, Art
 Maus, **1:**139, 141, 156, 293
 Nakazawa's (Keiji) influence on, **1:**293, 294
Spielberg, Steven, **2:**71
Spier, Julius, **2:**22
Spion Kop, Battle of (1900), **2:242**
Spiritual fulfillment, Wells (H. G.) on, **1:**252
Spiritual suffering, Peltier (Leonard) on, **1:**96, 97
Spitzack, Carole J., "Body Talk," **3:**190
Spivak, Gayatri Chakravorty, **1:**87
Spoils of Poynton, The (James), **2:**115
Spokesman Review (newspaper), **3:**95
Spratt, Margaret, **3:**306–307
Sprinkler, Michael, **1:**246, 247
Stacey, Judith, **3:**191
Staël, Madame de, **2:**75–76
Staempfle, Bernhard, **1:**32
Stalin, Joseph, **3:332**
 Gulag system under, **3:**17, 18, 19
 Khrushchev (Nikita) on, **3:**333
 oral histories about life under, **3:**340, 341
 rise to power, **3:**331
Stalingrad, Battle of (1942–1943), **2:**281
Stallings, Selona, **1:**205
Stallworthy, John, **2:**248
Stalp, Marybeth, **3:**309
Stanford University, **1:**15, *16*
Stanton, Elizabeth Cady, **1:13**
 Eighty Years and More, **1:12–14**
 History of Woman Suffrage, **1:**12
 The Woman's Bible, **1:**12, 13
Stanton, Harriot, **1:**13
Stanton, Henry, **1:**13
Stanton, Theodore, **1:**13
Staples, Suzanne Fisher, **1:**41
Starfield, Jane, **2:**242
Stark, Arthur, **3:**155
Starr, Louis M., **3:**186, 188

Starr, Roger, **3:**61
Stasi, oral histories of, **3:**245–247
Staten, Henry, **1:**16–17
Staub, Michael E., **1:**71
Stavanger International Prize for Freedom of Expression, for *Letters Underway* (Ghazzawi), **2:**50
Stave, Bruce M., *Witnesses to Nuremberg,* **3:293–295**
St. Clair, David, **2:**6
Steel Shavings (magazine), **3:**161
Steelworkers Trilogy, **3:**153
Steer, George, **2:**101
Steffen-Fluhr, Nancy, **1:**253
Stein, Daniel, **1:**78
Stein, Emmanuel, **3:**154
Stein, Gertrude
 The Autobiography of Alice B. Toklas, **1:**332, 334
 Brewsie and Willie, **1:**333
 Everybody's Autobiography, **1:**332
 Ida, **1:**332
 Paris France, **1:**332
 Wars I Have Seen, **1:332–334**
 Wright's (Richard) friendship with, **1:**124
Steinhoff, Johannes, *Voices from the Third Reich,* **3:**215
Stelzig, Eugene, **2:**77
Stengel, Richard, **1:**28
Stephens, Gregory, **1:**109
Stepto, Robert B.
 From Behind the Veil, **1:**35
 A Home Elsewhere, **1:**80
Stereotypes
 of Appalachian culture, **3:**68, 86, 96
 of Chinese Americans, **1:**173, 174
 of Chinese women, **1:**173, **3:**147
 of Japanese war brides, **3:**128
 of Japan in World War II, **3:**215
 of Mexican Americans, **3:**131, 133
Sterling, Bruce, **2:**145
Sterne, Laurence, **2:**328
Stevens, Ayako, **3:**128
Stevens, Elizabeth Zofchak, **3:**338
Stevenson, Adlai, **2:**101
Stevenson, Brenda, **2:**29, 30, 31

Stevenson, Robert Louis, **2:**73
Stewart, Clyde, **2:**91
Stewart, Elinore Pruitt
 Letters of a Woman Homesteader, **2:91–93**
 Letters on an Elk Hunt, **2:**91
Stewart, Gary, *Black Man's Grave,* **1:**312
Stewart, Henry C., **1:**8
Stewart, Jon, **1:**312
Stewart, Randall, **2:**225
Stille, Alexander, **3:**159
Still Ready (film), **3:**48
Stizia, Lorraine, **3:**192
St. John, J. Hector. *See* Crèvecoeur, Michel-Guillaume Saint-Jean de
St. Louis Globe-Democrat (newspaper), **1:**147
St. Louis Post Dispatch (newspaper), **1:**85, 299
Stock, Brian, **1:**198
Stock market, U.S., 1929 crash of, **3:**161, 212
Stock Reduction Act (U.S.), **3:**318
"Stoicien, Le" (Frederick the Great), **1:**218
Stoicism, **1:**218–221
Stoll, David, **3:**164, 165, 166
Stone, Albert E., **2:**213, 214
Stone, Harlan Fiske, **2:**56
Stone, Kate, *Brokenburn,* **2:244–246**
Stone, Norman, **2:**85
Stone, Oliver, **1:**335, *336*
Stone, William, **2:**244, 246
Stoppard, Tom, *Arcadia,* **2:**145
Stop-Time (Conroy), **1:164–166,** 270
Stories in a New Skin (Martin), **3:**138
Storming Caesars Palace (Orleck), **3:**254
StoryCorps, **3:**174, 345
Story of a Shipwrecked Sailor, The (García Márquez), **3:183–185**
Story of My Life, The: An Afghan Girl on the Other Side of the Sky (Ahmedi), **1:40–42**
Story of My Life, The: Helen Keller (Keller), **1:43–46**
Story of My Life and Work, The (Washington), **1:**37
Storyteller's Daughter, The (Shah), **1:**40

Storytelling traditions
  German, **1:**30
  Irish, **3:**315
  Native American, **1:**21, 22, 55, 302, 304, **3:**320
Stowe, Harriet Beecher, **2:**143
  Uncle Tom's Cabin, **1:**33, 144
Strachey, Alix, **2:**268
Strachey, James, **2:**268
Strachey, Julia, **2:**268
Strachey, Lionel, **1:**90, 91
Strachey, Lytton, **2:**268
Strange Ground (Maurer), **3:275–278**
Stranger's Supper, A (Milich), **3:135–137**
Strata (journal), **3:**174
Stream-of-consciousness
  A Diary without Dates (Bagnold) compared to, **2:**260
  Life on the Mississippi (Twain) as precursor to, **1:**146
  in *The Man Died* (Soyinka), **1:**216
  in *Memoirs* (Neruda), **1:**223
  in *The Woman Warrior* (Kingston), **1:**174
Street, Brian, **2:**237
Streetcar Named Desire, A (film), **2:**152
Streetcar Named Desire, A (Williams), **2:**152
Street Violence in the Nineteenth Century (Sindall), **3:**312
Strength Not to Fight, The (Tollefson), **3:221–223,** 227, 276
Strickland, Susanna, **3:**23, 24, 25
Strikes. *See* Labor strikes
Strindberg, August, **2:**120
Strobel, Larry, *When the Mill Whistle Blew,* **3:**93
Stromquist, Shelton, *Solidarity and Survival,* **3:**153
Strong, Pauline, **3:**320
Strottman, Theresa, **3:**240
Strozier, Charles B., **3:**263–264
Structuralism, **1:**239, 267
Struggle for Gay and Lesbian Equal Rights, The (Marcus), **3:**83
Struggle for the Land (Churchill), **3:**10
Strychacz, Thomas, **1:**166

Stuart, John T., **3:**261
Stubborn Twig (Kessler), **3:**80
Stuck Rubber Baby (Cruse), **1:**139
Students
  in Cultural Revolution, **1:**161
  deferments for, in Vietnam War, **3:**221
  in movements of 1968, **3:**31–33
Students for a Democratic Society (Buhle et al.), **3:**330
Studies in American Indian Literatures (journal), **1:**23, 70, **3:**109
Studies in English Literature (journal), **2:**231
Studies in the Novel (journal), **1:**313, 314
Studs Turkel Program, The (radio show), **3:**161
Studs Turkel's Working (Buhle and Pekar), **3:**330
Study of the Negro Problem, The (Du Bois), **1:**50
Sturgis, Caroline, **2:**139
Sturgis, Howard, **2:**115
Sturrock, John, **1:**67
Styron, William, **1:**205
  The Confessions of Nat Turner, **1:**204, 206
  Darkness Visible, **1:204–206**
  Lie Down in Darkness, **1:**204, 206
  Set This House on Fire, **1:**206
  Sophie's Choice, **1:**204, 206, **3:**36
  on *Stop-Time* (Conroy), **1:**165
Suárez, Virgil, *Spared Angola,* **1:**296
Subjectivity, in oral histories, **3:**162, 173, 186
Submission, in Islam, Hirsi Ali (Ayaan) on, **1:**208
Submission, Part 1 (film), **1:**207, 208
Suenaga, Shizuko, *Japanese War Brides in America,* **3:127–130**
Suffolk (England), oral histories of village life in, **3:**59–61, 63–65
Suffrage. *See* Voting rights
Sugarmill, The (Moreno Franginal), **3:**7
Sugawara no Michizane, **2:**189
Sugawara no Takasue, daughter of. *See* Sarashina, Lady
Sugiman, Pamela, **3:**178

Suicide
  of Hitler (Adolf), **2:**281
  of Levi (Primo), **1:**204, 205
  of Plath (Sylvia), **2:**47
  Styron's (William) battle with, **1:**204–205
  of Woolf (Virginia), **2:**268
  Xie Bingying's idealization of, **1:**339
Sukhu, Gopal, **3:**288
Suleri, Sara
  Boys Will Be Boys, **1:**88
  Meatless Days, **1:87–89**
  The Rhetoric of English India, **1:**87–88
Sullivan, Anne, **1:**43–46
Sullivan, Walter, **1:**165
Sully, Thomas, **2:**317
Sumerians, letter writing by, **2:**94
Summerfield, Penny, **2:**237, **3:**336
Summers, Carol, **3:**253
Summerskill, Edith, **2:**235
Summing Up, The (Maugham), **2:**183
Sumner, Fort. *See* Bosque Redondo Reservation
Sun Also Rises, The (Hemingway), **2:**259
Sun Dance ceremony, **1:**23, 96, 97
Sunday Times (newspaper), **2:**85
Sunrise Tomorrow (Mitchison), **2:**237
Sun Yat-sen, **1:**338, **2:**170
Suppression of Communism Act of 1950 (South Africa), **1:**27
Supreme Court, U.S.
  Amistad case in, **2:**70, 71
  on conscientious objectors, **3:**223
  on interracial marriage, **1:**72, 78
  on labor arbitration, **3:**153
  on racial quotas in higher education, **3:**20
  on racial segregation, **1:**37, 50, 122, 249, **3:**44
  on slavery, **2:**38
Survival, literature of
  The Story of a Shipwrecked Sailor (García Márquez) as, **3:**183–185
  They Say in Harlan County (Portelli) as, **3:**96–97
  The Unwanted (Nguyen) as, **1:**170

SUBJECT INDEX

Survival in the Killing Fields (Ngor), **1:**306
Surviving the Slaughter (Umutesi), **3:**258
Survivors: An Oral History of the Armenian Genocide (Miller and Miller), **3:**40–43, 50
Survivors: The Story of Ireland's Struggle (MacEoin), **3:**27, 315
Suter, Thomas, **2:**271
Sutherland, John, **2:**311
Sutherland, Sibyl, **3:**78
Sutton, Roger, **1:**162
Sutzkever, Abraham, **1:**255
Su Xuelin, *Ninety-Four Years of a Floating Life,* **1:**338
Suyeoshi, Amy, **3:**84
Suzuki, Mihoko, **2:**64
Sweeney, Joseph, **3:**29
Sweet and Sour Milk (Farah), **1:**207
Sweeter the Juice, The (Haizlip), **1:**73
Swiftwater People (Russell), **3:**93–95
Swinburne, Algernon Charles, **2:**82, 147
Swinnerton, Frank, **2:**138
Symmachus, **2:**94–95
Symons, Julian, **2:**42–43
"Sympathy" (Dunbar), **1:**50
Symposium (journal), **1:**183
Synethesia, **1:**272
Synge, John Millington, **2:**126, 128
Syria, Greater, Usāmah ibn Munqidh on history of, **1:**285–286
Syrian Thunderbolt, The (Imad al-Din), **1:**286
Syrkin, Marie, **2:**22–23, 24
Szadziuk, Maria, **1:**110

T

Taccola, Mariano, **2:161**
Tacitus, Cornelius, **2:**94, **3:**186
Taggart, Cynthia, **3:**95
Taine, Hippolyte, **2:**82
Taino people, **2:202**
Tait's Edinburgh Magazine, **2:**178
Takaki, Shintaro, **3:**82
Takasue's daughter. *See* Sarashina, Lady

Takeshita, Ben, **3:**196
Takooshian, Harold, **3:**41
Talcott, Samuel, **1:**325
Tale of Genji, The (Murasaki), **2:**59, 60, 189, 190, 290–292, *291*
Tales for Cottagers (Leadbeater), **2:**157
Taliban, rise of, **1:**40
Talking to Myself (Terkel), **3:**214
Tallichet, Suzanne E., **3:**338–339
Talmadge, Herman, **1:**5
Talmage, Thomas de Witt, **1:**150
Tamai Kōsuke, **2:**189, 190–191
Tamari, Salim, **2:**104, 105, 106
Tamura, Keiki, *Michi's Memories,* **3:**127
Tamura, Linda
  The Hood River Issei, **3:80–82**
  Nisei Soldiers Break Their Silence, **3:**80
Tan, Amy, **1:**159
Tanzania
  establishment of borders of, **1:**114
  Ruete (Emily) on life in, **1:**90–92
  Saitoti (Tepilit Ole) on life in, **1:**114–116
Taplin, George, **1:**149, 150
Tappes, Shelton, **3:**101
Tarhan, Mehmet, **3:**229
Tatars, **3:**17, 19
Tateishi, John, *And Justice for All,* **3:195–198,** 224
Tateishi, Yuri, **3:**197
Tavalaro, Julia, *Look up for Yes,* **1:**6
Taylor, Barbara, **2:**111
Taylor, Charles G., **1:**312
Taylor, Craig, **3:**59, 60, 61
Taylor, Elizabeth, **2:**261
Taylor, Ethel Barol, **3:**269, 270–271
Taylor, Jeremy, *Rule and Exercises of Holy Living and Dying,* **2:**195
Taylor, Paul F., *Bloody Harlan,* **3:**96
Taylor, Phyllis, **3:**119
Taylor, Richard, *Destruction and Reconstruction,* **2:**250
Taylor, Sandra, *Jewel of the Desert,* **3:**80
Taylor, Steven J., *Acts of Conscience,* **3:**227
Taylor, Telford, **3:**212
Taylor, Vic, **3:**103

Tchaikovsky, Pyotr Ilyich, **2:**143
Tcheng, Soumay. *See* Cheng Yu-hsiu
Teacher Man (McCourt), **1:**119
Teachers, U.S., oral histories of, **3:**77–79
Teachers College Record (periodical), **3:**77
Teaching a Stone to Talk (Dillard), **1:**279
Tears before the Rain (Engelmann), **3:**210, 265, **279–281**
Tebutt, Melanie, **3:**178
Technological advances
  Adams (Henry) on, **1:**132–134
  in agriculture, in England, **3:**59, 63
  Emerson (Ralph Waldo) on, **2:**139
  in medicine, **3:**170
  in oral history field, **3:**181
  Thoreau (Henry David) on, **1:**233
  in World War I, **2:**180
Technological Revolution, **1:**134
Teel, Witcher, **3:**78
Teenagers. *See* Adolescents
Telegraph (newspaper), **1:**7–8, **2:**153, 261
Telegraph, invention of, **1:**233
Television adaptations. *See also specific programs*
  of *Go Ask Alice* (anonymous), **2:**294, *295*
  of *Nella Last's War* (Last), **2:**265, 266
  of *Testament of Experience* (Brittain), **1:**330
  of *Working* (Terkel), **3:**343
Telling Identities (Sánchez), **3:**115, 121–122
Telling Maya Tales (Gossen), **3:**167
Tell Me Africa (Olney), **1:**246
Tell My Horse (Hurston), **1:**9, 11
Temple, Mary "Minny," **2:**113
Temple, William, **2:**324–327
Ten Africans (collected stories), **1:**64
"Tenir un journal" (Lejeune). *See* "Practice of the Private Journal" (Lejeune)
Tennyson, Alfred, **1:**264, **2:**140, 271, 335
Ten Thousand Sorrows (Kim), **1:102–104**

Ten Years of Madness (Feng), **3:**287
Ten Years' War (1868–1878), **3:**7
Teorey, Matthew, **1:**311
Teresa of Ávila, **1:212**
   Interior Castle, **1:**212
   The Life, **1:211–213**
   The Way of Perfection, **1:**212
Terkel, Louis "Studs," **3:**213, *344*
   on *AIDS Doctors* (Oppenheimer and Bayer), **3:**274
   American Dreams, **3:**300
   Chinese Lives (Zhang and Sang) inspired by, **3:**299, 300
   Division Street, **3:**161, 299, 343
   "The Good War", **3:**161, 199, 202, **212–214,** 234, 343
   Hard Times, **3:161–163,** 179, 199, 212, 279, 343
   in origins and rise of oral history, **3:**173, 179, 279, 345
   Talking to Myself, **3:**214
   Touch and Go, **3:**214
   Working, **3:**161, 300, **343–345**
Terni (Italy), oral histories of working class in, **3:**157–159
Terrorism. *See* September 11 terrorist attacks
Terry, Ellen, **2:**335
Terry, Wallace, *Missing Pages,* **3:**199–200. *See also Bloods* (Terry)
Tertullian, **2:**94
Testament of Experience (Brittain), **1:**330
Testament of Friendship (Brittain), **1:**330, 331
Testament of Youth (Brittain), **1:329–331, 2:**247–248, 259, 269, **3:**176
Testimonios. *See also specific works*
   definition of, **3:**7, 322
   origins of, **3:**7
   tradition of, **3:**73–74, 114–115, 164, 322
Testimonios: Early California Through the Eyes of Women (Senkewicz and Beebe), **3:**116
Testimony Films, **3:**313
Tet Offensive (1968), **3:**275
Texas, oral histories of teachers in, **3:**77–79, *78*

Texas Studies in Literature and Language (journal), **1:**213, 316
Textual Cultures (journal), **2:**252
Textual Practice (journal), **2:**182
Thackeray, William, **2:**335
   Vanity Fair, **2:**312
Thames Television, **3:**234
Theater, Hansberry's (Lorraine) writing for, **1:**273–275
Theatre History Studies (journal), **2:**153
Their Eyes Were Watching God (Hurston), **1:**11
Thelen, David, **3:**181
Themistius (orator), **1:**218, 220
Theobald, Paul, **3:**78
Theoharis, Jeanne, **3:**101
Theological Studies (journal), **3:**309
Theology. *See* Religion
Thérèse Raquin (Zola), **1:**6
There Was This Goat (Krog et al.), **3:**242
These Are Our Lives (Federal Writers' Project), **3:**86
They Say in Harlan County (Portelli), **3:**87, **96–98,** 158
Thirteenth Amendment, **1:**50
This Boy's Life (Wolff), **1:47–49**
This Was Not Our War (Hunt), **3:**268
Thomas, Caitlin, **1:**127
Thomas, David, **2:**247, 248
Thomas, Dylan
   A Child's Christmas in Wales, **1:125–127**
   Eighteen Poems, **1:**125
   The Love Letters of Dylan Thomas, **1:**127
   Quite Early One Morning, **1:**125
Thomas, John Peter (Piri), *Down These Mean Streets,* **1:**109
Thompson, Dorothy, **2:**278
Thompson, Paul
   on *Akenfield* (Blythe), **3:**59–61
   on *The Death of Luigi Trastulli* (Portelli), **3:**159
   The Edwardians, **3:**176, 186, 311
   Hooligans or Rebels? (Humphries) influenced by, **3:**311–312
   on *In the Mansion of Confucius' Descendants* (Kong and Ke), **3:**126

   Living through the Soviet System, **3:**331
   Oral History, Health and Welfare, **3:170–172**
   on *The Saga of Coe Ridge* (Montell), **3:**92
   Vietnam War literature influenced by, **3:**209
   The Voice of the Past, **3:**59–61, 92, **186–189,** 209, 311–312
Thompson, Stephen, **3:**126
Thompson, Thea, *Edwardian Childhoods,* **3:**312
Thomson, Alistair
   "ANZAC Memories," **3:**177, 178
   on internationalization of oral history, **3:**129
   The Oral History Reader, **3:**173, 178, 179, 181
   on origins of oral history, **3:**135
   on Portelli (Alessandro), **3:**267
   on *The Voice of the Past* (Thompson), **3:**188
   on *Women's Words* (Gluck and Patai), **3:**192
Thomson, David, **3:**65
Thorberg, Raymond, **2:**115
Thoreau, Henry David, **1:**234
   conscientious objectors influenced by, **3:**228
   Dillard (Annie) influenced by, **1:**279
   Emerson (Ralph Waldo) and, **1:**233, **2:**139, 140
   Gandhi (Mohandas) influenced by, **1:**242
   Hawthorne (Nathaniel) and, **2:**223
   James (Henry) compared to, **2:**115
   "Resistance to Civil Government," **1:**242
   Walden, **1:233–236, 2:**140, 215
   A Week on the Concord and Merrimack Rivers, **1:**233, 234, 235, **2:**140
Thoreau, John, **1:**233
Thornbrough, Emma Lou, **3:**91
Thornhill, James, **2:325**
Thornton, Alice, *Autobiography,* **1:**230
Thornton, Margaret Bradham, **2:**153, 154

Thornton, Michael, **2**:261
Thorpe, Charles, **3**:240
Those Devils in Baggy Pants (Carter), **3**:212
Thoughts and Sentiments on the Evil and Wicked Traffic of the Slavery and Commerce of the Human Species (Cugoana), **1**:81
Thoughts without Cigarettes (Hijuelos), **1**:75
Thrasher, Max, **1**:50
Thrasher, Sesali Storm, **3**:233
Three-Inch Golden Lotus, The (Feng), **3**:289
Three Minus One (Kilani), **2**:52
Threepenny Review (journal), **1**:168
Through the Brazilian Wilderness (Roosevelt), **2**:220
Thura's Diary (Al-Windawi), **2**:275–277
Tieck, Ludwig, *Franz Sternbalds Wanderungen*, **1**:276
Tiefenbrun, Susan, **2**:33
Tighe, C., **1**:216
Ti Jean L'Horizon (Schwarz-Bart), **1**:64
Tiller, Emma, **3**:162
Tilley, M. P., **2**:228
Tilton, Theodore, **2**:239
Time (magazine)
    on *Bloods* (Terry), **3**:201
    on *I, Rigoberta Menchú* (Menchú), **3**:165
    on *A Long Way Gone* (Beah), **1**:312, 313, 314
    on *Red Azalea* (Min), **1**:159
    Terry (Wallace) at, **3**:199
Time, and memory
    Conroy (Frank) on, **1**:164, 165, 166
    Nabokov (Vladimir) on, **1**:271, 272
Times Higher Education (magazine), **3**:247
Times Literary Supplement
    on *Akenfield* (Blythe), **3**:59, 61
    on *A Country Parson* (Woodforde), **2**:288
    on *The Dark Child* (Laye), **1**:129
    on *De Profundis* (Wilde), **2**:10

    on *Diaries, 1915–1918* (Sassoon), **2**:248
    on *An Experiment in Autobiography* (Wells), **1**:253
    on *The Journals of Jonathan Carver and Related Documents* (Carver), **2**:206
    on *Testament of Youth* (Brittain), **1**:330
    on *Working-Class Childhood* (Seabrook), **3**:54
    on *The Worlds of a Maasai Warrior* (Saitoti), **1**:115
    on *The Writing Life* (Dillard), **1**:280
Times of London (newspaper), **1**:32, 141, 191, **2**:75, 275
Timmons, Stuart, *Gay L.A.,* **3**:83–84
Tin mining, in Bolivia, oral histories of, **3**:322–324
Tippett, Mehetable, **2**:213
'Tis (McCourt), **1**:119
Tishler, Jennifer, **3**:285
Titcomb, Caldwell, *Blacks at Harvard,* **3**:21
Tito, **3**:135
Titon, Jeff, **3**:88
Tlatelolco massacre of 1968 (Mexico), **3**:31–33
To Bear Any Burden (Santoli), **3**:210
To Be Young, Gifted and Black (Hansberry), **1**:273–275
Tocqueville, Alexis de, **2**:214
Todd, Janet, **2**:109, 110, 111
"To His Excellency General Washington" (Wheatley), **2**:44
Tohono O'odham culture, Chona (Maria) on life in, **1**:69–71
Tóibín, Colm, **1**:79–80
Toilet paper, prisoners writing on, **1**:214, **2**:12, 13, 54
Toki, Tanaka, **3**:216
Toklas, Alice B., **1**:332, 333, 334
Tollefson, James W., *The Strength Not to Fight,* **3**:221–223, 227, 276
Tolstoy, Leo, **1**:194
    Anna Karenina, **1**:193
    A Confession, **1**:193–195, 270
    conscientious objectors influenced by, **3**:228

    Gandhi (Mohandas) influenced by, **1**:242
    Investigation of Dogmatic Theology, **1**:194
    Kafka (Franz) influenced by, **2**:120
    Rilke (Rainer Maria) and, **2**:151
    Translation and Harmony of the Four Gospels, **1**:193–194
    What I Believe, **1**:194, 195
Tolstoy, Sonya, **1**:195
Tolui Khan, **1**:107
Tomalin, Claire, **2**:73
Tomasini, Giacomo Filippo, **2**:160, 161
Tomberlin, Joseph, **1**:38
Tomko, Steve, **3**:87
Tommaso da Milano, **2**:160
Tomorrow (magazine), **1**:10
Tompkins, Sally, **2**:273
Tone, Theobald Wolfe, **2**:159
Tonghak religion, Kim Ku influenced by, **1**:322, 323, 324
To Nicocles (Isocrates), **2**:94
Tonna, Charlotte, **2**:335
Tonomura, Hitomi, **2**:61
Too Long Been Silent (Axford), **3**:196
Top Girls (Churchill), **2**:60
Torkington, Richard, **2**:227
Totah, Khalil, **2**:106
To the Edge of the Sky (Gao), **1**:159
To the Lighthouse (Woolf), **1**:146
Touch and Go (Terkel), **3**:214
Toulouse, Teresa A., **1**:328
Touré, Sékou, **1**:130
Towazugatari (Nijo). *See Confessions of Lady Nijo* (Nijo)
Townsend, Francis G., **1**:265
Townsend, Sue, **2**:338
Trade, between West and East
    expansion of, **1**:90, 105
    Gama's (Vasco da) exploration and, **2**:198–200
Trade routes, in colonial U.S., **2**:205
Tragic Life (Bai), **1**:338
"Tragic mulatto" tradition, **1**:72
Trail of Broken Tears Caravan (1972), **1**:21
Trajan (Roman emperor), **2**:94
Tramp Abroad, A (Twain), **1**:146

Transcendental fiction, **1:**281
Transcendentalism
    Dillard (Annie) influenced by, **1:**279
    Emerson (Ralph Waldo) in, **2:**140
    James's (Henry) views on, **2:**113
    Thoreau (Henry David) in, **1:**233–236
    utopian societies inspired by, **1:**235
Transforming State-Society Relations in Mexico (Craig), **3:**302
Transition (journal), **1:**88
Translation and Harmony of the Four Gospels (Tolstoy), **1:**193–194
Transnational autobiography, *Dreams from My Father* (Obama) as, **1:**79
Trask, Michael, **1:**260
Trastulli, Luigi, **3:**157, 158
Trauma, autobiographies of
    by Africans, **1:**313–314
    definition of, **1:**102
    Ten Thousand Sorrows (Kim) as, **1:**102
    The Unwanted (Nguyen) as, **1:**170–171, 172
Traveling Heavy (Behar), **1:**297
Travel narratives. *See also specific works and writers*
    The Autobiography of Ben Franklin (Franklin) as, **1:**179
    borrowing from other sources in, **2:**227, 229
    Life on the Mississippi (Twain) as, **1:**146–147
    A Long Way from Home (McKay) as, **1:**84–86
    Memoirs of an Arabian Princess from Zanzibar (Ruete) as, **1:**90–92
    Motorcycle Diaries (Guevara) as, **2:**220–221
    The Pylgrymage of Sir Richarde Guylforde (Guylforde) as, **2:**226–228
    rise in popularity of, **1:**90, **2:**229
    The Travels of Dean Mahomet (Mahomet) as, **2:**229–231
    The Travels of Marco Polo (Polo) as, **1:**105–107
    Western biases in, **1:**90

The Wonderful Adventures of Mrs. Seacole (Seacole) as, **1:**111
Travels in West Africa (Kingsley), **2:**335
Travels of Dean Mahomet, The (Mahomet), **2:**229–232
Travels of Marco Polo, The (Polo), **1:**105–107, *106*, **2:**198, 201
Travels of Sir John Mandeville, The (Mandeville), **2:**198, 227
Travels through the Interior Parts of North America (Carver), **2:**205
TRC. *See* Truth and Reconciliation Commission
Treadwell, James, **2:**179
Treason
    Slingsby (Henry) convicted of, **2:**257, 258
    in Treason Trials of South Africa, **1:**24
Treasonable Growth, A (Blythe), **3:**61
Treasures in the Dust (Porter), **1:**161
Treaties. *See specific treaties*
Treister, Kenneth, **3:**51
Trelawney, Edward John, **2:**143, 154
Trembling of the Veil, The (Yeats), **2:**126, 127
Trench warfare, in World War I, **2:**247
Trenka, Jane Jeong, *The Language of Blood*, **1:**102
Trent, Council of, **1:**211
Trevelyan, G. O., **2:**143
Trial, The (Kafka), **2:**120, 121–122
Trials
    of anarchists, **3:**4
    Nuremberg, **2:**54, 56, **3:**293–295
    of Peltier (Leonard), **1:**96
    Treason, of South Africa, **1:**24
    of Wilde (Oscar), **2:**9, 183, 185
Tribune Books, **2:**338
Tricknor, William D., **2:**224
Trickster stories
    African, **2:**3
    Chinese, **1:**163
Trill, Suzanne L., **1:**316, 317
Trilling, Lionel, **1:**123
Trilogy Principle, **1:**248
Trimmer, Sarah, **2:**300
Triple Alliance (1668), **2:**324

Tripmaster Monkey (Kingston), **1:**173
Trippa, Elchide, **3:**158
Tristes Tropiques (Lévi-Strauss), **3:**37
Troide, Lars, **2:**314
Trollope, Anthony, **2:**101, 320
Trollope, Frances, *Domestic Manners of the Americans*, **2:**223
Tropes, racial, in *Dreams from My Father* (Obama), **1:**80
Tropic of Cancer (Miller), **2:**123
Trotsky, Leon, **1:**84, **2:**172
Trouble I've Seen, The (Gellhorn), **2:**101
Troubles, The (Ireland), **3:**27, 29
Trouble with Diversity, The (Michaels), **1:**16
Trouble with Islam Today, The (Manji), **1:**207
True Relation of My Birth, Breeding, and Life, A (Cavendish), **1:**229–232
Truman, Harry, **3:**199, 248, 249, 293
Trumpener, Katie, **2:**305
Truth
    authors' pact regarding, Lejeune (Philippe) on, **1:**239–240, **2:**174
    of *Biography of a Runaway Slave* (Barnet and Montejo), **3:**8
    of *Bloods* (Terry), **3:**199, 201
    in Cartesian rationalism, **1:**183
    of *Dust Tracks on a Road* (Hurston), **1:**9–11
    of *Everything We Had* (Santoli), **3:**211
    of *Go Ask Alice* (anonymous), **2:**294, 295
    of *The Good Man of Nanking* (Rabe), **2:**19, 20–21
    of *The History of Mary Prince* (Prince), **3:**25
    of *I, Rigoberta Menchú* (Menchú), **3:**164, 165–166
    of *The Journal of Marie Bashkirtseff* (Bashkirtseff), **2:**307
    of *Journal of the First Voyage to America* (Columbus), **2:**203
    Lessing (Doris) on nature of, **1:**167
    of *Letters of a Woman Homesteader* (Stewart), **2:**92
    of *A Long Way from Home* (McKay), **1:**85

SUBJECT INDEX

Truth, *continued*
 of *A Long Way Gone* (Beah), **1:**313
 in *Memories of a Catholic Girlhood* (McCarthy), **1:**259–260
 of *A Million Little Pieces* (Frey), **2:**296
 of *Night* (Wiesel), **1:**319, 320
 in postmodernism, **1:**168
 of *Roots* (Haley), **1:**262
 of *Spandau* (Speer), **2:**54–55
 of *Survivors* (Miller and Miller), **3:**42
 of *Ten Thousand Sorrows* (Kim), **1:**103
 of *The Travels of Marco Polo* (Polo), **1:**107
 of *A True Relation of My Birth, Breeding, and Life* (Cavendish), **1:**230
 of *The Unwanted* (Nguyen), **1:**172
 of *A Woman in Berlin* (anonymous), **2:**281, 282
 of *The Woman Warrior* (Kingston), **1:**175
 of *Zlata's Diary* (Filipovic), **2:**340
Truth, Sojourner, *Narrative of Sojourner Truth,* **1:**37
Truth and Fiction Relating to My Life (Goethe), **1:**276–278
Truth and Reconciliation Commission (TRC), oral histories of, **3:**242–244
Try to Remember (Gomez), **1:**108
Tso, Mae, **3:**11
Tsuchino (Forrester), **3:**127–128
Tsukamoto, Mary, **3:**197
Tuberculosis
 Bashkirtseff's (Marie) struggle with, **2:**306, 307, 308
 Mansfield's (Katherine) struggle with, **2:**133
Tubman, Harriet, **2:**29
Tuchman, Barbara, **3:**186
Tuhami (Crapanzano), **3:**47
Tulsa Studies in Women's Literature (journal), **2:**111, 124
Tulugarjuk, Leo, *Ilagiinniq,* **3:**138
Tunisia, Amrouche (Fadhma Aïth Mansour) in, **1:**93, 94

Tuqan, Fadwa
 The Harder Journey, **1:**226
 A Mountainous Journey, **1:225–228**
 My Brother Ibrahim, **1:**227
Tuqan, Ibrahim, **1:**226, 227
Turgenev, Ivan, **2:**183
Turkey
 Armenian genocide denied by, **3:**40, 42
 in Crimean War, **1:**113
Turkish Embassy Letters (Montagu), **2:**35, 37
Turkish Lover, The (Santiago), **1:**108
Turner, D. R., **3:**255
Turner, Frederick W., III, **1:**304
Turner, J. M. W., **2:**143
Turner, Nat, **1:**206, **2:**238
Tuskegee Airmen, oral histories of, **3:**248–250
Tuskegee Airmen, The (film), **3:249**
Tuskegee Airmen, The (Francis), **3:**212
Tuskegee Institute, **1:**50, 51, *51,* 52
Tute, James, **2:**205
Tutsi people, **3:**257–259
Tutu, Desmond
 No Future without Forgiveness, **3:**244
 on Peltier's (Leonard) imprisonment, **1:**96
 in Truth and Reconciliation Commission, **3:243,** 244
Twain, Henry, **1:**147
Twain, Mark, **1:147**
 Adventures of Huckleberry Finn, **1:**146, 147–148
 The Innocents Abroad, **1:**146
 "The Late Benjamin Franklin," **1:**181–182
 Life on the Mississippi, **1:146–148**
 "Old Times on the Mississippi," **1:**146
 in realist movement, **2:**240
 Roughing It, **1:**146
 A Tramp Abroad, **1:**146
Twelve Years a Slave (Northup), **1:**50
Twentieth-Century Literary Criticism (journal), **2:**24
Twentieth Century Literature (journal), **2:**134

27 Wagons Full of Cotton (Williams), **2:**152
Twice Born (Lifton), **1:**102
Twichell, Joseph, **1:**147
Two Gentlemen of Verona (Shakespeare), **2:**226, 228
Two Sides to Everything (Scott), **3:**96
Two Years before the Mast (Dana), **1:**234
Ty, Eleanor, **2:**111
Tyminski, Dan, **3:**159
Tyndale, William, **2:**97
Typhus, in German concentration camps, **2:**253
Tzotzil language, **3:**167

U

UAW. *See* United Automobile Workers
Ubico, Jorge, **1:**99, 101
UC. *See* University of California
Uchida, Yoshiko, **1:**300
 Desert Exile, **1:**309
 The Invisible Thread, **1:309–311**
UDI. *See* Unilateral Declaration of Independence
Ukraine
 Bashkirtseff's (Marie) emigration to France from, **2:**306–308
 Chernobyl nuclear disaster in, **3:**282–285
 Great Famine of 1932–1933 in, **3:**19
 independence of (1991), **3:**340
 miners in, oral histories of, **3:**340–342, *341*
Ulin, David, **2:**118
Ulrich, Laurel Thatcher
 Good Wives, **2:**331–332
 A Midwife's Tale, **2:331–334**
Ulysses (Joyce), **1:**146, **2:**67, 180
Umara al-Hakami al-Yamani, **1:**286
Umkhonto we Sizwe (MK), **1:**27
Umutesi, Marie Béatrice, *Surviving the Slaughter,* **3:**258
UMW. *See* United Mine Workers
UMWA. *See* United Mine Workers of America
UN. *See* United Nations

SUBJECT INDEX

Unabridged Journals of Sylvia Plath, The (Plath), **2:**49
Unaipon (ballet), **1:**149
Unaipon, David, **1:150**
    "Leaves of Memory," **1:**149
    My Life Story, **1:149–151**
    Myths and Legends of the Australian Aboriginals, **1:**149
Unaipon, James, **1:**149, 151
Una Storia Segreta (DiStasi), **3:**224
Unbound (Maathai), **1:**114
Uncertain Travelers (Agosín), **1:**75
UnCivil Liberties (Fox), **3:**226
Uncle Tom's Cabin (Stowe), **1:**33, 144
Uncomfortable Wars (Manwaring), **3:**207
Uncomfortable Wars Revisited (Manwaring and Fishel), **3:**207
Underhill, Evelyn, **1:**191
Underhill, Ruth
    The Autobiography of a Papago Woman, **3:**318
    Chona, **1:69–71**
    The Navajos, **3:**290
    Red Man's Religion, **1:**70
    Singing for Power, **1:**70
Under My Skin (Lessing), **1:167–169**
Undertones of War (Blunden), **1:**329
Underwood, Thomas, *Blacks at Harvard,* **3:**21
Unemployment (Seabrook), **3:**54
Unemployment, during Great Depression, **3:**161, 212
UNESCO, **3:**334
Unfinished Conquest (Perera), **1:**99
Ung, Loung, *First They Killed My Father,* **1:**306
Unger, Harlow Giles, **2:**71
Ungo, Guillermo M., **3:**205
UNICEF, **1:**312, 314, **2:**338
Uniformitarianism, **1:**65
Unilateral Declaration of Independence (UDI), **3:**251
Union Maids (film), **3:**179
Union of Automobile Workers, **3:**99
Unions. *See* Labor movement
Unitarian movement, in England, **2:**76
United Automobile Workers (UAW), **3:**153

United Kingdom. *See* Britain
United Mine Workers (UMW), **3:**98
United Mine Workers of America (UMWA), **3:**337, 339
United Nations (UN)
    First International Children's Parliament at, **1:**314
    Historical Clarifications Commission of, **3:**166
    International Law Commission of, **2:**56
    in International Women's Year Tribunal, **3:**322
    on Iraqi invasion of Kuwait, **2:**278
    on Rwandan genocide, **3:**257, 258
    Siv (Sichan) as U.S. ambassador to, **1:**306, *307*
    on workers' rights, **3:**157
United Nations and Economic Sanctions against Rhodesia, The (Kapungu), **3:**251
United Nations Children's Fund (UNICEF), **1:**312, 314, **2:**338
United Nations Educational, Scientific and Cultural Organization (UNESCO), **3:**334
United Negro College Fund, **1:**273, 274
United States. *See also* American *entries*
    anarchism in, **3:**3–5
    censorship in, **1:**20, **2:**123
    Cheng Yu-hsiu in, **1:**152
    coal mining in, **3:**66–69, 86, 87, 96–98, 157
    colonial era of (*See* United States, colonial)
    containment policy of, **3:**205
    economy of (*See* Economy)
    education in (*See* Education)
    expansion of (*See* Westward expansion)
    flu pandemic of 1918 in, **1:**258
    gender roles in, eighteenth-century, **2:**316
    gender roles in, twentieth-century, **2:**47
    in Guatemalan Civil War, **3:**166
    homosexuality in, attitudes toward, **1:**139
    immigration to (*See* Immigration)

    industrialization of, **1:**233
    interracial adoption in, **1:**102–104
    interracial relationships in, attitudes toward, **1:**72–74
    labor movement in (*See* Labor movement)
    Latin American culture in, **1:**109
    letter writing in, **2:**223
    midwifery in, **2:**331–333
    minorities in (*See* Assimilation; Civil rights; *specific groups*)
    national progress of, Emerson (Ralph Waldo) on, **2:**139, 140
    Native American treaties with, **1:**69, **3:**107, 110, 290, 327
    nuclear weapons of, **1:**293–294, **3:**239–241
    Pakistani relations with, **1:**87
    poverty in, **1:**122, **3:**66, 67, 254–256
    presidential election of 1860 in, **3:**261
    presidential election of 1992 in, **3:**221
    Puerto Rico as territory of, **1:**108
    Puritanism in, **1:**325–327
    Reconstruction in, **1:**50–52, **2:**238
    Saitoti's (Tepilit Ole) education in, **1:**114, 115
    in Salvadoran Civil War, **3:**205–207
    slavery in (*See* Slavery)
    on Vietnamese human rights violations, **1:**171, 172
    Vietnamese relations with, **1:**335
    wars of (*See* Military; *specific wars*)
    women of (*See* American women)
United States, colonial
    Afro-Atlantic writers in, **2:**44
    in Alta California, **3:**114–116
    Condict (Jemima) on life in, **2:**78–80
    Crèvecoeur (Michel-Guillaume Saint-Jean de) on life in, **2:**213–215
    French and Indian War in, **2:**205, 213
    Great Awakening in, **1:**179, **2:**197
    idealization of, **2:**213–215
    King Philip's War in, **1:**325–328

SUBJECT INDEX

United States, colonial, *continued*
    Rowlandson (Mary) on life in, **1:**325–328
    Wesley's (John) mission to, **2:**195, 196
    women's autobiographical writing in, **2:**78–79
University of California (UC), Mark Twain Project of, **1:**148
University of California at Berkeley, **3:**21
    African Americans at, oral histories of, **3:**20–22
    student movements of 1968 at, **3:**33
University of Iowa Writers' Workshop, **1:**164, 165
University of London, **2:**77
University of Nairobi, **2:**12, 13
University of Pennsylvania, **2:**275, 276
University of Toronto Quarterly, **3:**140
Unknown Internment, The (Fox), **3:**215, **224–226**
Unlawful Organizations Act of 1960 (South Africa), **1:**25
Unprivileged, The (Seabrook), **3:**55
Unquiet Mind, An (Jamison), **1:**204
Untold Tales, Unsung Heroes (Moon), **3:99–101**
Unto This Last (Ruskin), **1:**242
Unwanted, The (Nguyen), **1:170–172**
Unwinding Threads (Bruner), **1:**94
Up (documentary series), **3:**53
Upcott, William, **2:**65
Updike, John, **3:**59–60
Up from Slavery (Washington), **1:**3, 15, **50–53**
Upon Their Shoulders (Ota), **1:**309
"Up-river Book" (Conrad), **2:**194
Up the Swiftwater (Crowell and Aleson), **3:**93
Uqalurait (Bennett and Rowley), **3:**107, **138–140**
Urban Anthropology (journal), **3:**122
Urban II (pope), **1:**285
Urchin, The (Bedoukian), **3:**40
Urey, Harold, **3:**239
Urogi (witchcraft), among Meru people, **3:**141–143

Urrea, José de, **1:**304
Urrutia, Matilde, **1:**222, 223
Ury, Marian, **2:**60, 292
Usāmah ibn Munqidh, *An Arab-Syrian Gentleman and Warrior in the Period of the Crusades,* **1:285–288**
USA Today (newspaper), **1:**172
U.S. Catholic Historian (journal), **3:**309
Uses of Literacy, The (Hoggart), **1:**16
Utopian societies, **1:**14, 235
Utopian Studies (journal), **2:**255

V

Vaarzon-Morel, Petronella, *Warlpiri Women's Voices,* **3:**107, **334–336**
VAD. *See* Voluntary Aid Detachment
Valerius (bishop), **1:**196
Valéry, Paul, **2:**150
Vallejo, César, **1:**224
Valley of Shadows and Dreams (Light and Light), **3:**67
Vambe, Lawrence Chinyani
    From Rhodesia to Zimbabwe, **3:**251
    An Ill-Fated People, **3:**251–253
Van Brunt, H. L., **3:**87
Vance, Kevin, **2:**40
Van Derlinder, Jean, **3:**291
Van der Veen, Jon, **3:**181
Van Donzel, Emeri, **1:**91, 92
Van Horssen, Jessica, **3:**181
Vanity Fair (magazine), **1:**204, 205, **2:**118
Vanity Fair (Thackeray), **2:**312
Van Orman, Richard A., **3:**91
Van Vechten, Carl, **1:**84
Van Vorst, Mrs. John, **1:**154
Vanzan, Anna, **3:**219
Vargas Llosa, Mario
    A Fish in the Water, **1:**168
    Letters to a Young Novelist, **2:**150
VaShawasha people, oral histories of, **3:**251–253
Vasquez, Jose "Pepe," **3:**122
Vasvári, Louise, **1:**76–77
Vatican Council, Second (Vatican II), **3:**308, 309

Vaughan, Benjamin, **1:**180
Vega, Ed, **1:**108
Vega, Jaime, **2:**222
Vega-González, Susana, **1:**251
Veganism, of Gandhi (Mohandas), **1:**243
Velasco, Luis Alejandro, **3:**183–185
Velho, Álvaro, **2:**198
Velikova, Rumiana, **1:**5
Venice, Republic of, **2:**198
Veracity. *See* Truth
Verene, Donald P., **1:**183
Verisimilitude. *See* Truth
Versailles, Treaty of (1919)
    Chinese disappointment with, **1:**338, **3:**126, 147, 149
    Germany after, **1:**30, **3:**234
Vesey, Denmark, **2:**238
Vesuvius, Mount, eruption of, **2:**94, 95
Veterans, oral histories of
    by African Americans, **3:**199–201, 248–250
    from Iraq War, **3:**231–233, *232*
    from Vietnam War, **3:**199–201, 209–211, 275–277
    from World War II, **3:**202–204, 248–250
Veterans History Project, **3:**128
Vettini, Amanda, **3:**171–172
Viareggio Book Prize, for *The Order Has Been Carried Out* (Portelli), **3:**265
Vico, Giambattista, **1:**184
    The Autobiography of Giambattista Vico, **1:183–185**
    Dell'antichissima sapienza italica, **1:**183
    New Science, **1:**183, 184, 185
Victoria (queen of Great Britain), **2:**210
    expansion of empire under, **2:**16
    Leaves from the Journal of Our Life in the Highlands, **2:209–212**
    More Leaves from the Journal of Our Life in the Highlands, **2:**209
    Seacole (Mary) and, **1:**112
Victorian era (1837–1901)
    autobiographies in, traits of, **1:**65, 67

biographies in, approach to, **2:**143
end of, **1:**329–330
expansion of empire in, **2:**16
Gissing (George) on culture of, **2:**320–322
literary marketplace of, **2:**320–322
social inequality in, **1:**252, **2:**16
social mobility in, barriers to, **1:**252
social reform at end of, **1:**329, **2:**16
women in, Webb (Beatrice) on, **2:**16–18
working-class youth in, **3:**311–312
Victorian Literature and Culture (journal), **2:**210
Victorian Studies (journal), **2:**17, 322, 337, **3:**313
Victory at Sea (television show), **3:**234
Vidal, Gore, **2:**152, 153
Videla, Jorge Rafael, **3:**185
Vien, Joseph Marie, **1:219**
Vietnam
French rule of, **1:**335, **3:**279
history of occupations of, **1:**335
partition of (1954), **1:**335
postwar social conditions in, **1:**170–172
racism against multiracial individuals in, **1:**170, 171
reunification of (1975), **1:**170, 171
U.S. relations with, **1:**335
in Vietnam War, oral histories of, **3:**279–281
Vietnamese American(s)
autobiographical tradition of, **1:**170–171
Hayslip (Le Ly) on experience of, **1:**335–337
Nguyen (Kien) on experience of, **1:**170–172
racism against, **1:**171
Vietnam Veterans Memorial, **3:200,** 223
Vietnam Veterans Memorial Fund, **3:**223
Vietnam War, **1:171, 3:210**
antiwar movement against, **3:**221, 222, *269,* 275, 277

conscientious objectors in, **3:**221–223
and drug use, rise of, **2:**294
escalation under Johnson (Lyndon Baines), **3:**254, 256
fall of Saigon in, **3:**209
fall of South Vietnam in, **3:**279–281
Hayslip (Le Ly) on life during, **1:**335–337
literature on consequences of, **1:**335
media coverage of, **2:**280, **3:**199
mistakes made in, **3:**275–276
Nguyen (Kien) on life after, **1:**170–172
refugees from, **1:**306, 337
start of, **1:**335, **3:**275, 279
Tet Offensive in, **3:**275
U.S. entry into, **1:**335, **3:**209, 275
U.S. withdrawal from, **3:**275, 279
Vietnam War oral histories
by African American veterans, **3:**199–201
by American civilians, **3:**275–277, *276*
by American veterans, **3:**199–201, 275–277
by conscientious objectors, **3:**221–223
on fall of South Vietnam, **3:**279–281
by Vietnamese civilians and veterans, **3:**279–281
View in Winter, The (Blythe), **3:**60
Viezzer, Moema, *Let Me Speak!,* **3:**74, 114–115, **322–324**
Vigne, Thea, **3:**311
Villa, Pancho, **3:**167, 302
Village Voice (newspaper), **1:**119, 313
Vindication of the Rights of Women, A (Wollstonecraft), **2:**314
Violence
in British gangs, **3:**311–313
domestic (*See* Domestic violence)
in Guatemala, Perera (Victor) on, **1:**99–100
in Israeli–Palestinian conflict, Ghazzawi ('Izzat) on, **2:**50–51

sexual, in Guatemala, **1:**100 (*See also* Rape)
against women, in Islam, **1:**207–209
Violence against Women (journal), **2:**282
Violent Adventure (Wesley), **1:**48
Virginia
in Civil War, **2:**38
coal mining in, oral histories of, **3:**86–87
interracial marriage in, **1:**72
Virginia Magazine of History and Biography, **2:**38
Virginia Quarterly Review, **2:**137
Vision or Villainy (Hoffaman), **3:**102
Visions, divine, of Teresa of Ávila, **1:**211, 212
VISTA. *See* Volunteers in Service to America
Visual elements, in *The Way to Rainy Mountain* (Momaday), **1:**54, 55, *55*
Vitier, Cintio, **2:**220
Vizgalova, Irina, **3:**332
Voice. *See* Narrative voice
Voice of the Past, The (Thompson), **3:186–189**
on *Akenfield* (Blythe), **3:**59–61
Hooligans or Rebels? (Humphries) influenced by, **3:**311–312
on *The Saga of Coe Ridge* (Montell), **3:**92
Vietnam War literature influenced by, **3:**209
Voice of Witness (Eggers and Vollen), **3:**161
Voices from Chernobyl (Alexievich), **3:265, 282–286**
Voices from the Grave (film), **3:**29
Voices from the Third Reich (Steinhoff), **3:**215
Voices from the Whirlwind (Feng), **3:287–289,** 301
Voices from this Long Brown Land (Wehrey), **3:102–104**
Voices Long Silent (Hansen and Mitson), **3:**195
Voices of Freedom (Hampton and Fayer), **3:44–46**
Voices of Resistance (Baker), **3:47–49**

SUBJECT INDEX

Voices of the Holocaust (Rothchild), **3:**50
Vollen, Lola, *Voice of Witness,* **3:**161
Voltaire, **2:**37, 329
Voluntary Aid Detachment (VAD), **1:**329, **2:**259–261
Volunteers in Service to America (VISTA), **3:**254
Vo Nguyen Giap, **3:**279
Voss, Barbara L., **3:**116
Voter registration drives, **1:**20
Voting rights
    for African Americans, **1:**50, **2:**238
    for women, **1:**12, 13, 14
Voting Rights Act of 1965 (U.S.), **1:**20
Voyage and Travels of Sir John Mandeville, The, **1:**105
Voyages: The Trans-Atlantic Slave Trade Database, **1:**263
Voyage to the East Indies (Grose), **2:**229
V-2 rockets, **2:**270
Vu, Tran Tri, *Lost Years,* **1:**170
Vuic, Kara Dixon, **3:**277

W

Wada, Ernest, **3:**85
Wagenknecht, Edward, **2:**137
Waggoner, Hyatt, **2:**225
Waheenee (Wilson), **1:**69–70
Wainwright, Loudon, **3:**213
Waiting for Snow in Havana (Eire), **1:**296–297
Waka (Japanese poems), **2:**189, 191, 292
Wakatsuki, George Ko, **1:**300, 301
Wakatsuki, Riku, **1:**301
Wakefield, Priscilla, **2:**300
Wakeman, Stephen H., **2:**224
Walden (Thoreau), **1:233–236,** **2:**140, 215
Waldron, Philip, **2:**134
Waldsteicher, David, **2:**45
Wales, Thomas (Dylan) on life in, **1:**125–126
Walker, Alice
    Angelou's (Maya) influence on, **1:**18–19
    The Color Purple, **1:**18, 175

    on Hurston (Zora Neale), **1:**11
    The Way Forward Is with a Broken Heart, **1:**18–19
Walker, Pierre, **1:**20
Walker, Reuben, **1:**149
Walker, Robert, **2:66**
Walking in the Shade (Lessing), **1:**167
Walking Purchase of 1737, **3:**327
Walkowitz, Daniel J., *Workers of the Donbass Speak,* **3:**157, **340–342**
Wall, Irwin, **2:**263
Wallace, Alfred Russel, **1:**67
Wallace, John R., **2:**191
Waller, P. J., **3:**313
Wallington, Nehemiah, **2:**74
Walls, Jeanette, **1:**251
Walls, Laura Dassow, **1:**236
Wall Street Journal, **2:**20, **3:**164
Walmsley, Jan, *Oral History, Health and Welfare,* **3:170–172**
Walpole, Horace, **2:**97, 146, 195, 196
Walpole, Hugh, **2:**115
Walton, Edith, **2:**260
Walton, John, *Western Times and Water Wars,* **3:**102
Walton, Martin, **3:**28
Wang, Jing M., **1:**340
Wang Zheng, *Women in the Chinese Enlightenment,* **3:147–149**
Wansink, Hans, **1:**207
War(s). *See also specific wars*
    childhood during, memoirs of, **1:**312–314
    "low-intensity," **3:**207
    realism in depictions of, **2:**240
War brides, Japanese, **3:**127–129, *128*
War Brides of World War II (Shukert and Scibetta), **3:**127
War correspondents
    Chapelle (Dickey) as, **2:**280
    Gellhorn (Martha) as, **2:**101–103
    in Gulf War, **2:**278–280
    in Iraq War, **2:**278, 280
    in Vietnam War, **2:**280, **3:**199
War crimes
    in Sierra Leone civil war, **1:**312
    in World War II, **1:**77, **2:**54–56, **3:**293–295

Ward, Fumiko, **3:**128
Ward, Hiley, **2:**279
War Department, U.S., **3:**248
Wardle, Ralph M., **2:**109, 111
Ware, Ann Patrick, *Midwives of the Future,* **3:**308
Warhol, Robyn, **1:**141
Warlpiri people, oral histories of, **3:**334–336
Warlpiri sign language, **3:**335–336
Warlpiri Women's Voices (Vaarzon-Morel), **3:**107, **334–336**
Warner, Edith, **3:**241
Warner, Fara, **2:**20
War of 1812, **1:**233, **2:**69
War on drugs, U.S., **2:**294
War on poverty, U.S., **3:**254–256
War Reminiscences (Mosby), **2:**250
Warrior, Robert Allen, **1:**56
Wars I Have Seen (Stein), **1:332–334**
War Walks (television series), **3:**236
Washington, Booker T.
    and Du Bois (W. E. B.), debate between, **1:**186
    The Story of My Life and Work, **1:**37
    Up from Slavery, **1:**3, 15, **50–53**
Washington, D.C.
    Adams (Abigail) on life in, **2:**87–90
    establishment of, **2:**87
Washington, George, **2:**44, 87
Washington Post (newspaper), **1:**16, **2:**56, 278, 331
Washington Post Book World, **3:**213
Washington Times (newspaper), **2:**40
Wasserman, George, **1:**269
Waswo, Richard, **2:**309–310
Wat, Eric, *The Making of a Gay Asian Community,* **3:83–85**
Watching Seagulls (Saliba), **1:**161
Watergate scandal, **3:**279
Waterloo, Battle of (1815), **2:**312
Water Margins (Chinese novel), **1:**338
Water resources
    in Australia, **3:**334
    in California, **3:**102, 103
    on Native American reservations, **1:**69, **3:**11

Waters, Chris, **3:**72
Waters, Ethel, **1:**10
Water Seekers, The (Nadeau), **3:**102
Watkins, Gloria Jean. *See* hooks, bell
Watson, James, **3:**37
Watson, Nora, **3:**343
Watson, Reginald, **1:**74
Wattenberg, Miriam, **2:**253
Watts, William, **1:**196
Waverly (Scott), **2:**309
Way Forward Is with a Broken Heart, The (Walker), **1:**18–19
Wayne, John, **1:100**
Way of Perfection, The (Teresa of Ávila), **1:**212
Way to Rainy Mountain, The (Momaday), **1:54–57,** *55*
Wealth
 in Ireland, **1:**119–120
 of Native Americans, **3:**290
Wealth of Nations (Smith), **2:**200
Weapons of mass destruction (WMD), in Iraq, **2:**275
Webb, Beatrice
 Diaries of Beatrice Webb, **2:16–18**
 The Letters of Sidney and Beatrice Webb, **2:**172
 Minority Report to the Commission of the Poor Law, **2:**16
 My Apprenticeship, **2:**17
 Our Partnership, **2:**17, 172
Webb, Richard Davis, **2:**157–158
Webb, Sidney, **2:**16, 17, 172
Webs of Power (Maurer and Mirow), **3:**277
Webster, Daniel, **2:**75
Webster, Robert, **2:**195
Wedderburn, Alexander, **1:**265
"We Don't Want Crumbs" (Luthuli), **1:**25
Weekly Anglo-African, **1:**144
Week on the Concord and Merrimack Rivers, A (Thoreau), **1:**233, 234, 235, **2:**140
Weglyn, Michi, *Years of Infamy,* **3:**212
"We Have Just Begun to Not Fight" (Frazer and O'Sullivan), **3:227–230**
Wehrey, Jane
 Manzanar, **3:**102

The Owens Valley, **3:**102
 Voices from this Long Brown Land, **3:102–104**
Weil, Simone, **2:**22, 24
Weinberg, Bill, *Our Appalachia,* **3:**66, **86–89**
Weinberg, Sidney J., **3:**163
Weinberg, Sydney Stahl, *The World of Our Mothers,* **3:**305
Weiner, Marli, **2:**273
Weise, Robert, **3:**96, 97
Weisiger, Marsha L., *Dreaming of Sheep in Navajo Country,* **3:**10
Weiss, Brad, **3:**142–143
Weiss, Cora, **3:**269
Weiss, Gillian, **3:**334
Wei Tao-Ming, **1:**152, 154
Wei Tao-Ming, Madame. *See* Cheng Yu-hsiu
Weitzman, Lenore J., **3:**35
Welcher, Jeanne K., **2:**67
Weld, Theodore, *American Slavery as It Is,* **1:**33, 142
Wellcome Trust, **3:**170
Wellesley, Arthur, **2:**217
Wells, G. P., **1:**252, 254
Wells, H. G., **1:253**
 Bennett (Arnold) compared to, **2:**136
 on *A Diary without Dates* (Bagnold), **2:**260
 An Experiment in Autobiography, **1:252–254**
 Gellhorn (Martha) and, **2:**101
 H. G. Wells in Love, **1:**252, 253, 254
 letters of, **1:**252, 253
 London and the Life (Gissing) on, **2:**320
 Woolf (Virginia) on novels of, **2:**138
 A Writer's Notebook (Maugham) on, **2:**183
Wells, Ida B., *Southern Horrors,* **1:**50
Wells, Sarah, **1:**253
Welsh, Michael, **3:**240
Welsh autobiographical writing, by Thomas (Dylan), **1:**125–127
Welsh v. United States, **3:**223

Wen, Chihua, *The Red Mirror,* **3:**287
We of Nagasaki (Nagai), **1:**293
Werfel, Franz, **2:**120
Werner, Craig, **1:**247–248
Werner, Marta L., **1:**45–46
Wesley, Charles, **2:**195
Wesley, John, *Journals of John Wesley,* **2:195–197,** *196*
Wesley, Marilyn, *Violent Adventure,* **1:**48
West, E. Bernard, *Living Atlanta,* **3:**44
West, Geoffrey, **1:**253
West, Kanye, **1:**312
West, Russell, **2:**174
West, U.S., Carver's (Jonathan) exploration of, **2:**205–207. *See also* Westward expansion
West Bank, **2:**51
 Darwish (Mahmoud) in, **1:**255
 Israeli occupation of, **1:**225
 Tuqan (Fadwa) on life in, **1:**225
Westerbork concentration camp, **2:**22–24, *23,* 253
Western Folklore (journal), **2:**92
Western Historical Quarterly, **2:**163, **3:**12, 133, 225
Western Humanities Review (journal), **1:**56
Western Times and Water Wars (Walton), **3:**102
Westfall, Joseph, **2:**168
Westfall, Suzanne, **2:**99
West Indies
 Columbus's (Christopher) voyage to, **2:**201–203, *202*
 slavery in, **3:**23–25
Westoff, Clara, **2:**151
West Virginia
 coal mining in, **3:**66–69, *67, 91*
 colonial era in, **3:**66
 statehood for, **3:**66
Westward expansion, U.S.
 Adams (John Quincy) on history of, **2:**69
 Black Elk on experience of, **3:**110
 Chona (Maria) on experience of, **1:**69
 Emerson (Ralph Waldo) on potential of, **2:**139

SUBJECT INDEX

Westward expansion, U.S., *continued*
   Geronimo on experience of, **1:**302–304
   Ray (Annie) on experience of, **2:**163–164
   Stewart (Elinore Pruitt) on experience of, **2:**91–93, *92*
   Thoreau's (Henry David) critique of, **1:**233
Wey, William, **2:**226
Weyer, Edward Moffat, *The Eskimo*, **3:**138
Wharton, Edith, **2:**113
"What, to the Slave, Is the Fourth of July?" (Douglass), **1:**79
What I Believe (Tolstoy), **1:**194, 195
What's a Woman Doing Here? (Chapelle), **2:**280
What Was Asked of Us (Wood), **3:231–233**, 276
Wheatley, Phillis, **2:**45
   Equiano (Olaudah) compared to, **1:**81, **2:**44
   "Letter to the Reverend Samson Occom," **2:**44–46
   "On Being Brought from Africa to America," **2:**46
   Poems on Various Subjects, **2:**44
   Prince (Mary) compared to, **3:**23
   "To His Excellency General Washington," **2:**44
Wheatley, Susanna, **2:**44, 46
Wheelock, Eleazar, **2:**46
Whelan-Stewart, Wendy, **2:**49
When Bodies Remember (Fassin), **3:**272
When Broken Glass Floats (Him), **1:**306
When Heaven and Earth Changed Places (Hayslip), **1:170–171, 335–337**
When I Was Puerto Rican (Santiago), **1:108–110**
When the Mill Whistle Blew (Strobel), **3:**93
When We Began, There Were Witchmen (Fadiman), **3:141–143**
Which Side Are You On? (Hevener), **3:**96
Whitaker, Katie, **1:**229
White, E. B., **1:**234, 235

White, Gilbert, **2:**300
White, Jerry, **3:**54
White, Mike, **2:**255
White, Raymond O., **3:**107, 108
White, Thomas Willis, **2:**41
White audience
   of *Dust Tracks on a Road* (Hurston), **1:**9, 11
   of *Incidents in the Life of a Slave Girl* (Jacobs), **1:**142, 143
   of "Letter from the Birmingham Jail" (King), **2:**33
   of *Up from Slavery* (Washington), **1:**50–52
White colleges, African Americans at, **3:**20–22
Whitefield, George, **2:**46, 197
White Revolution (Iran), **3:**218
Whitesinger, Pauline, **3:**11
Whither India? (Nehru), **1:**290
Whitley, Glenna, **3:**201, 211
Whitlock, Gillian, **1:**40, **3:**25
Whitman, Walt, **1:**173, 234, 265
Whitsitt, Novian, **1:**144
Whittier, John Greenleaf, **2:**29
Wickert, Erwin, **2:**19
Widder, Keith, **2:**207
Wiesel, Elie, **1:319**
   Dawn, **1:**319
   Day, **1:**319
   Night, **1:318–321**
Wiggins, Sarah Woodfolk, **2:**246
WikiLeaks, **3:**229
Wilburn, Oleson, **3:**92
Wilde, Oscar
   The Ballad of Reading Gaol, **2:**9
   De Profundis, **2:**9–11
   indecency trial of, **2:**9, 183, 185
   Maugham (W. Somerset) influenced by, **2:**183, 184, 185
   on *Memoirs of an Arabian Princess from Zanzibar* (Ruete), **1:**91
   The Picture of Dorian Gray, **2:**9
   Salomé, **2:**183
Wilde-Menozzi, Wallis, **2:**255
Wild Swans (Chang), **1:**158–159
Wilenski, R. H., **1:**265
Wilford, Hugh, **3:**5

Wilhelm Meister's Apprenticeship (Goethe), **1:**30
Wilkins, William Henry, **2:**217
Wilkinson, Edmund L., **3:**248–249
Wilkinson, James, **1:**202
Wilkinson, Jane, **2:**14
Will. *See* Divine will; Free will
Will, Herman, **3:**228
Willenson, Kim, *The Bad War*, **3:**275
William and Mary Quarterly, **1:**134
William of Orange, **2:**324, *325*
Williams, Ben Ames, **2:**250
Williams, Bill, **3:**186
Williams, David, **2:**207
Williams, Gweno, **1:**230, 231
Williams, Lynne, **3:**175
Williams, Ronald, **1:**96
Williams, Rowan, **1:**212
Williams, Tennessee, **2:153**
   Camino Real, **2:**154
   The Glass Menagerie, **2:**152
   Memoirs, **2:**152, 153
   Notebooks, **2:**152–154
   A Streetcar Named Desire, **2:**152
   27 Wagons Full of Cotton, **2:**152
Willis, Lord, **2:**236
Willison, George, **2:**329
Wills, Garry, **1:**197, 198
WILPF. *See* Women's International League for Peace and Freedom
Wilsey, Sean, **1:**141
Wilson, August, **1:**273
Wilson, Bee, **2:**289
Wilson, Douglas L., *Herndon's Informants*, **3:**264
Wilson, Edmund, **2:**246
Wilson, Gilbert L., *Waheenee*, **1:**69–70
Wilson, Harriet E., *Our Nig*, **1:**142
Wilson, Jean Moorcroft, **2:**249
Wilson, Kathleen, **1:**159
Wilson, Sonia, **2:**81, 307
Wilson, Woodrow, **3:**29, 153
Winder, Robert, **3:**59, 61
Windham, William, **2:**217
Winfrey, Oprah, **2:**296
Wing, Sandra Koa, **2:**265, 267

Wings of the Dove, The (James), **2:**113, 115
Winkler, Allan, *Life under a Cloud*, **3:**239
Winkler, Michael, **2:**151
Winn, Mathew, **3:**233
Winter, Naomi, **2:**27
Winter Soldier (Iraq Veterans against the War), **3:**232
Winterthur Portfolio (journal), **3:**320
Wirzba, Norman, **3:**67–68
Wisconsin Magazine of History, **3:**329
Wise, Christopher, **1:**23
Wise, R. Todd, **1:**23
Wister, Sally, **2:**78–79
Witchcraft
    among Meru, **3:**141–143
    among Navajo, **3:**290–291
Witch Purge of 1878, The (Blue), **3:**290–292
With Wings (Saxton and Howe), **1:**8
Witke, Roxanne, **3:**147
Witnesses, memory of, **3:**265, 266
Witnesses to Nuremberg (Stave et al.), **3:**293–295
Witnesses to the Holocaust (Lewin), **3:**50–52
WMD. *See* Weapons of mass destruction
Wobblies, **3:**93, 328–330
Wobblies, The (documentary), **3:**328
Wobblies!: A Graphic History (Buhle and Schulman), **3:**330
Woerner, Fred F., **3:**205
Wolcott, Reed, *Rose Hill,* **3:**86
Wolf, Benjamin, **3:**155
Wolfe, Charles, **3:**159
Wolff, Tobias
    Back in the World, **1:**47
    The Barracks Thief, **1:**47
    In Pharaoh's Army, **1:**47
    In the Garden of North American Martyrs, **1:**47
    This Boy's Life, **1:**47–49
Wolford, John B., **3:**266
Wolfson, Susan, **2:**147
Wollett, Jan, **3:**280
Wollstonecraft, Mary
    The Collected Letters of Mary Wollstonecraft, **2:**109–112
    on *The Interesting Narrative of the Life of Olaudah Equiano* (Equiano), **1:**82
    Letters Written during a Short Residence in Sweden, Norway, and Denmark, **2:**111
    A Vindication of the Rights of Women, **2:**314
Wolpert, Stanley, **1:**290
Woman (periodical), **2:**136
Woman at War, A (Moore), **2:**278–280
Woman in Berlin, A (anonymous), **2:**281–283
Woman of Peace (Hayslip), **1:**335
Woman Prisoner, The (Ghazzawi), **2:**50
Woman's Bible, The (Stanton), **1:**12, 13
Woman Soldier's Own Story, A (Xie), **1:**338–340
Woman's Place, A (Roberts), **3:**144, 145, 146
Woman's "True" Profession (Hoffman), **3:**77
Woman's World (magazine), **1:**91
Woman Warrior, The (Kingston), **1:**75, 100, **173–176**
Women. *See also specific countries, ethnicities, and religions*
    in abolitionist movement, **1:**142
    education of (*See* Education)
    oral histories of, feminist approach to, **3:**190–192, *191*
    religious roles of, Stanton (Elizabeth Cady) on, **1:**12
    Renaissance, **2:**160–162
    social roles of (*See* Gender roles)
Women Activists (Garland), **3:**268
Women and Families (Roberts), **3:**144–146
Women and the Holocaust (Fuchs), **3:**35
Women in the Chinese Enlightenment (Wang), **3:**147–149
Women in the Mines (Moore), **3:**157, 328, **337–339**
Women of Algiers in Their Apartment (Djebar), **1:**207
Women of Coal (Norris and Cyprès), **3:**337
Women religious, oral histories of, **3:**308–310
Women's International Congress, **3:**268
Women's International League for Peace and Freedom (WILPF), **3:**268, 269, 270
Women's Peace Oral History Project, **3:**268–270
Women's Review of Books (journal)
    on *Bone Black* (hooks), **1:**251
    on *A Mountainous Journey* (Tuqan), **1:**226
    on *My Life Story* (Amrouche), **1:**94
    on *Songs My Mother Sang to Me* (Preciado Martin), **3:**133
    on *Under My Skin* (Lessing), **1:**169
    on *Voices of Resistance* (Baker), **3:**48
    on *A Woman Soldier's Own Story* (Xie), **1:**340
    on *Women in the Mines* (Moore), **3:**338
Women's rights movement. *See also* Feminism
    in Britain, **1:**329, 331, **2:**109
    in China, **1:**338
    in France, **2:**306
    in Iran, **3:**218
    in U.S., **1:**12–14, **2:**47
Women's studies, *Letters of a Woman Homesteader* (Stewart) in, **2:**91
Women's Studies Quarterly, **1:**141
Women Strike for Peace (WSP), **3:**268
Women's Voluntary Service, **2:**265
Women's Words (Gluck and Patai), **3:**190–192
Women's Writing (journal), **2:**325
Wonderful Adventures of Mrs. Seacole in Many Lands, The (Seacole), **1:**111–113
Wong, Alan, **3:**181
Wong, Hertha D., **1:**71
    Sending My Heart Back across the Years, **1:**56
Wong, Sharon, **1:**175
Wood, Frances, **1:**107
Wood, Gordon S., **1:**181
Wood, John, **3:**25
Wood, Trish, *What Was Asked of Us,* **3:231–233,** 276

SUBJECT INDEX

Woodforde, Anna Maria, **2:**289

Woodforde, James, *A Country Parson,* **2:287–289**

Woodland Indians, oral histories of, **3:**107–109, *108*

Woodley, Arthur E., Jr., **3:**200

Woodson, Dorothy C., **1:**25

Woodward, Comer Vann, **2:**250, 251

Woodworth-Nay, Laura, **3:**12

Wooldridge, E. T.
  Carrier Warfare in the Pacific, **3:202–204**
  Into the Jet Age, **3:**203

Woolf, Leonard, **2:**180, 181, 182, 235, 268

Woolf, Virginia, **2:181**
  on Bennett's (Arnold) novels, **2:**137, 138
  in Bloomsbury group, **2:**180, 268
  Clifford (Anne) as inspiration for, **2:**64
  on *A Country Parson* (Woodforde), **2:**287, 288, 289
  Diaries of Beatrice Webb (Webb) on, **2:**16
  on *The Diary of John Evelyn* (Evelyn), **2:**66, 67
  The Diary of Virginia Woolf, **2:**133, 163, 180–182
  Hogarth Press of, **2:**268
  Jacob's Room, **2:**138
  Kingston (Maxine Hong) influenced by, **1:**173
  Moments of Being, **1:**249, **2:**182
  Nin (Anaïs) compared to, **2:**123
  Orlando, **1:**173, **2:**64, 181
  on Osborne (Dorothy), **2:**324, 325
  A Pacifist's War (Partridge) on, **2:**268
  Second Common Reader, **2:**289
  suicide of, **2:**268
  on *Testament of Youth* (Brittain), **1:**330
  To the Lighthouse, **1:**146
  A Writer's Diary, **2:180–182**

Woolman, John, *The Journal of John Woolman,* **2:**213

Worde, Wynken de, **1:**189, 191

Wordsworth, Christopher, **2:**301

Wordsworth, Dorothy
  Grasmere Journals, **2:**16, **300–302**
  Osborne (Dorothy) compared to, **2:**324

Wordsworth, William
  Byron (George Gordon Noel) compared to, **2:**143
  Grasmere Journals (Wordsworth) and, **2:**300–302
  Journals of Ralph Waldo Emerson (Emerson) on, **2:**141
  Keats (John) and, **2:**146
  The Prelude, **1:**201, 264, **2:**302
  Robinson (Henry Crabb) and, **2:**75

Workers of the Donbass Speak (Siegelbaum and Walkowitz), **3:**157, **340–342**

Workforce, English women's entry into, **2:**266, **3:**145

Work in America report, **3:**343

Working (Terkel), **3:**161, 300, **343–345**

Working class
  in Bolivia, oral histories of women in, **3:**322–324
  in Italy and Kentucky, oral histories of, **3:**157–159
  in Ukraine, oral histories of, **3:**340–342

Working class, in Britain
  education of, **3:**311–313
  social change in, **3:**53, 144
  in Victorian era, **2:**16
  women in, oral histories of, **3:**144–146
  youth in, oral histories of, **3:**53–54, 311–313

Working-Class Childhood (Seabrook), **3:53–55**

Works of John Ruskin, The (Ruskin), **1:**265

Works Progress Administration (WPA), **1:**35, **3:**99

World Affairs (journal), **1:**32

World as Will and Representation, The (Schopenhauer), **1:**193

World at War, The (Holmes), **3:234–236**

World at War, The (television series), **3:**234, 236

World I Live In, The (Keller), **1:**44, 45

World in the Evening, The (Isherwood), **2:**152

World Literature Today (journal), **1:**76, 128, 137, 247, **2:**191

World of Our Mothers, The (Weinberg), **3:**305

World of the Defeated, The (Revelli), **3:**61

Worlds of a Maasai Warrior, The (Saitoti), **1:114–116**

Worlds of Color (Du Bois), **1:**5

World Today (journal), **2:**33

World War I
  Australian military in, **3:**177
  Bagnold's (Enid) service in, **2:**259–261
  conscientious objectors in, **3:**223
  in England, Brittain (Vera) on life during, **1:**329–331, **3:**176
  Germany after defeat in, **1:**30, **3:**234
  Japanese nationalism after, **3:**234
  lost generation of, **1:**329
  Mansfield's (Katherine) writing during, **2:**133
  in modernism, rise of, **2:**180
  nursing in, **1:**329, 330, **2:**259–261, *260*
  Sassoon's (Siegfried) service in, **2:**247–249
  Stein (Gertrude) on experience of, **1:**332
  technological advances in, **2:**180
  war crimes trials after, **3:**293
  women's experience of, **1:**329–331, **2:**259

World War II. *See also* Holocaust; Japanese American internment; Nazi Germany
  autobiographies after, rise of interest in, **1:**239
  China during, **1:**152, 153, **3:**14–16
  conscientious objectors in, **2:**268–269, **3:**223, 227–229
  and *Dust Tracks on a Road* (Hurston), changes to, **1:**9
  end of, **2:**281, **3:**239

England during, Last (Nella) on life in, **2:**265–267
England during, Partridge (Frances) on life in, **2:**268–269
in France, Stein (Gertrude) on experience of, **1:**332–334
Gellhorn's (Martha) reporting on, **2:**101–103
German bombardment of Britain in, **2:**265, 269, 270
German occupation of France in, **1:**332–334
in Germany, Klemperer (Victor) on experience of, **2:**303–305
Iran in, **3:**218
Italian American relocation in, **3:**224–226
Italy in, Nazi occupation of, **3:**265–267
Japanese bombing of Pearl Harbor in, **1:**299, 300, 309, **3:**195, 202, 212, 215, 234
Japanese names for, **3:**215
Korea after, division of, **1:**322
Nuremberg trials after, **2:**54, 56, **3:**293–295
oral histories of (*See* World War II oral histories)
Palestine during, **2:**104
propaganda in, **2:**117, 118, 270, *282*
rape in, **2:**281–283
Scotland during, Mitchison (Naomi) on life in, **2:**235–237
Soviet occupation of Berlin in, **2:**281–282
start of, **3:**215, 234
U.S. entry into, **1:**299, 309, **3:**161, 202, 212, 234
U.S. liberation of France in, **1:**332, 333
U.S. naval aviation in, **3:**202–204
U.S. occupation of Japan after, **3:**127–129
U.S. use of nuclear weapons in, **1:**293–294, **3:**239
war crimes in, **1:**77, **2:**54–56, **3:**293–295
women's autobiographical writing during, **2:**235, 237

World War II oral histories. *See also* Holocaust oral histories
international, **3:**234–236
Italian, **3:**265–267
Japanese, **3:**127–129, 215–217
World War II oral histories, U.S.
by conscientious objectors, **3:**227–230
by Italian Americans, **3:**224–226
by Japanese Americans, **3:**80–81, 102–104, 195–197
by naval veterans, **3:**202–204
by ordinary people, **3:**212–214
by Tuskegee Airmen, **3:**248–250
by war brides, **3:**127–129
Worst of Times, The (Hoggart), **3:**53
Wotton, Edward, **2:**256
Wounded, literature of the, *Voices from the Whirlwind* (Feng) as, **3:**287
Wounded Knee (South Dakota)
AIM occupation of (1973), **1:**21, 22–23, 96
massacre at (1890), **3:**110, 111
Wounds of Passion (hooks), **1:**250, 251
WPA. *See* Works Progress Administration
Wren, Christopher, **2:**65
Wretched of the Earth, The (Fanon), **1:**207, **2:**263
Wright, Esmond, **1:**182
Wright, John Michael, **1:316**
Wright, Richard
Black Boy, **1:**122–124
A Father's Law, **1:**124
Native Son, **1:**122, 123, 273
Writer's Chronicle (journal), **1:**167–168
Writer's Diary, A (Woolf), **2:**180–182
Writer's Notebook, A (Maugham), **2:**183–185
Writing
Dillard (Annie) on vocation of, **1:**279–281
Gissing's (George) struggle to earn living with, **2:**320, 321
Mansfield (Katherine) on process of, **2:**133
Poe's (Edgar Allan) struggle to earn living with, **2:**41

Woolf (Virginia) on process of, **2:**180–182
Writing Black (Rive), **1:**25
Writing Life, The (Dillard), **1:168, 279–281**
Wrong Turn (film), **3:**68
Wroth, Mary, **2:**62
WSP. *See* Women Strike for Peace
Wudunn, Sheryl, **2:**20–21
Wunyabari, Maloba, **3:**142
Wurts, Jay, **1:**335
Wyman, Leland, **3:**320
Wynn, Antony, **3:**220
Wyoming, homesteaders in, **2:**91–93, *92*

X

X, Malcolm. *See* Malcolm X
Xavier, Silvia, **2:**30
Xie Bingying
Girl Rebel, **1:**338
New War Diary, **1:**339–340
Selected Autobiographies by Women Writers, **1:**340
A Woman Soldier's Own Story, **1:338–340**
Xu Guangping, *Letters between Two,* **2:170–173**
Xu Xin, **2:**20

Y

Yablonski, Jock, **3:**98
Yacine, Kateb, **1:**95
Nedjma, **2:**262
Yaddo artists' colony, **2:**129
Yale Law Journal, **3:**197
Yale Review (periodical), **2:**193
Yale University, **1:**251
Yamamoto, Tak, **3:**84
Yardley, Jonathan, **3:**213
Yasgur, Batya, *Behind the Burqa,* **1:**40
Yasutomi, Shigeyoshi, **3:**129
Ye, Weili, **1:**339, **3:**149
Yearbook of English Studies, **2:**322
Year of Consolation, A (Kemble), **2:**336

SUBJECT INDEX

Years of Infamy (Weglyn), **3:**212
Yeats, Elizabeth, **2:**126
Yeats, William Butler, **2:127**
   The Autobiography of William Butler Yeats, **2:**127–128
   The Collected Works of W. B. Yeats, **2:**126, 128
   The Death of Synge, **2:**126, 127
   Estrangement, **2:126–128**
   Reveries over Childhood and Youth, **2:**126, 127
   The Trembling of the Veil, **2:**126, 127
Yellin, Jean Fagan, **1:**144, 145
Yen Mah, Adeline, *Falling Leaves,* **1:**159
Yglesias, José, **1:**223
Yiddish language, *Night* (Wiesel) in, **1:**318
Yim, Louise, *My Forty Year Fight for Korea,* **1:**323
Yoda, Tomiko, **2:**292
Yoruba people, **1:**214, 216
Yoselevska, Rivka, **3:**235
You May Well Ask (Mitchison), **2:**235
Young, Andrew, **3:**45
Young, Filson, *The Relief of Mafeking,* **2:**241
Young, Jennifer Rene, **2:**45
Young, John Wesley, **2:**305
Young, Marilyn, **3:**280, 281

Young Palestinian's Diary, A ('Amr), **2:104–106**
Young Turk Revolution (1908), **2:**106
Young Turks, **3:**40
Youth. *See* Adolescents; Children
Yurechko, John, **2:**279
Yurovsky, Yakov, **2:**84

Z

Zahn, Gordon, **3:**228
Zaleski, Jeff, **1:**294
Zambia Must Be Free (Kaunda), **1:**290
Zami (Lorde), **1:**9, 37, 39, 249, **2:**5
Zane, Paolo, **2:**161
Zanjani, Sally Springmeyer, *A Mine of Her Own,* **3:**337
Zanzibar, Ruete (Emily) on life in, **1:**90–92
Zapata, Emiliano, **3:**302, 303, 304
Zapatistas, **3:**304
Zen Buddhism, **2:**59, 61
Zerbini, Euricledes, **2:**6
Zeuske, Michael, **3:**7, 8, 9
Zhang Kijian, *China Remembers,* **3:**301
Zhang Xinxin, *Chinese Lives,* **3:**288, 299–301
Zhang Ya-Jie, **1:**175
Zhu Su'e, **3:**148
Ziegler, Philip, **2:**266, **3:**235

Zimbabwe
   British colonial rule of, **1:**167, **3:**251–253
   VaShawasha people of, oral histories of, **3:**251–253
Zimmerman, Lee, **1:**205–206
Zinzendorf, Nikolaus Ludwig von, **2:**197
Zionism, Palestinian views on, **2:**104, 105, 106
Zlata's Diary (Filipovic), **2:275, 338–340**
Zola, Émile
   Bashkirtseff (Marie) influenced by, **2:**306
   The Complete Notebooks of Henry James (James) on, **2:**113
   Journal des Goncourt (Goncourt and Goncourt) and, **2:**82, 83
   Thérèse Raquin, **1:**6
Zong (slave ship), **1:**83
Zora Neale Hurston: Jump at the Sun (documentary), **1:**18
Zorzi, Rosella Mamoli, **2:**115
Zoya, *Zoya's Story,* **1:**40
Zoya's Story (Zoya), **1:**40
Zuma, Jacob, **1:**29
Zunes, Stephen, **1:**25–26
Zunigha, Curtis, **3:**108
Zwick, Edward, **1:**312
Zylska, Ruchel. *See* McBride, Ruth

Author Index

The author index includes author names represented in *The Literature of Autobiographical Narrative*. Numbers in **Bold** indicate volume, with page numbers following after colons.

A

Abrams, Lynn, **3**: 173
Adams, Abigail, **2**: 87
Adams, Henry, **1**: 132
Adams, John Quincy, **2**: 69
Adams, Judith Porter, **3**: 268
Agosín, Marjorie, **1**: 75
Ahmedi, Farah, **1**: 40
Alexievich, Svetlana, **3**: 282
Al-Windawi, Thura, **2**: 275
Amr, Sāmī, **2**: 104
Amrouche, Fadhma Aïth Mansour, **1**: 93
Angelou, Maya, **1**: 18
Augustine, **1**: 196
Aurelius, Marcus, **1**: 218
Avrich, Paul, **3**: 3

B

Bagnold, Enid, **2**: 259
Baker, Alison, **3**: 47
Barnard, Anne, **2**: 217
Barnet, Miguel, **3**: 7
Barrett, S. M., **1**: 302
Barrios de Chungara, Domitila, **3**: 322
Barthes, Roland, **1**: 267
Bashkirtseff, Marie, **2**: 306
Bauby, Jean-Dominique, **1**: 6
Bayer, Ronald, **3**: 272
Beah, Ishmael, **1**: 312
Bechdel, Alison, **1**: 139
Benally, Malcolm D., **3**: 10
Bennett, Arnold, **2**: 136
Bennett, John, **3**: 138
Bird, Stewart, **3**: 328
Black Elk, **3**: 110
Blue, Martha, **3**: 290
Blythe, Ronald, **3**: 59
Bornat, Joanna, **3**: 170
Boswell, James, **2**: 328
Brighton Ourstory, **3**: 70
Brittain, Vera, **1**: 329
Brown, James W., **3**: 325
Bruce, Gary, **3**: 245
Buck, Lucy, **2**: 271
Bugul, Ken, **1**: 61
Burlingame, Michael, **3**: 261
Burney, Fanny, **2**: 312
Byron, George Gordon Noel, **2**: 143

C

Carver, Jonathan, **2**: 205
Cavendish, Margaret, **1**: 229
Cereta, Laura, **2**: 160
Cheng Yu-hsiu, **1**: 152
Chesnut, Mary Boykin Miller, **2**: 250
Chona, Maria, **1**: 69
Clifford, Anne, **2**: 62
Columbus, Christopher, **2**: 201
Condict, Jemima, **2**: 78
Conrad, Joseph, **2**: 192
Conroy, Frank, **1**: 164
Cook, Haruko Taya, **3**: 215
Cook, Theodore F., **3**: 215
Craig, Ann L., **3**: 302
Crawford, Miki Ward, **3**: 127
Crèvecoeur, Michel-Guillaume Saint-Jean de, **2**: 213

D

Darwin, Charles, **1**: 65
Darwish, Mahmoud, **1**: 255
De Jesus, Carolina Maria, **2**: 6
Dillard, Annie, **1**: 279
D'Israeli, Isaac, **2**: 177
Dog, Mary Crow, **1**: 21
Douglass, Frederick, **1**: 33
Du Bois, W. E. B., **1**: 3
Dyk, Walter, **3**: 318

E

Edward VI, **2**: 97
Emerson, Ralph Waldo, **2**: 139
Engelmann, Larry, **3**: 279
Equiano, Olaudah, **1**: 81
Evans, George Ewart, **3**: 63
Evelyn, John, **2**: 65

F

Fadiman, Jeffrey A., **3**: 141
Fayer, Steve, **3**: 44
Feng Jicai, **3**: 287

AUTHOR INDEX

Feodorovna, Alexandra, **2**: 84
Feraoun, Mouloud, **2**: 262
Filipovic, Zlata, **2**: 338
Fox, George, **2**: 26
Fox, Stephen, **3**: 224
Frank, Anne, **2**: 253
Frank, Leslie, **3**: 293
Franklin, Benjamin, **1**: 179
Frazer, Heather T., **3**: 227
Friedman, Clara, **3**: 153
Frisch, Michael, **3**: 179
Frommer, Harvey, **3**: 118
Frommer, Myrna Katz, **3**: 118

G

Gandhi, Mohandas, **1**: 242
García Márquez, Gabriel, **3**: 183
Gellhorn, Martha, **2**: 101
Georgakas, Dan, **3**: 328
Geronimo, **1**: 302
Ghazzawi, 'Izzat, **2**: 50
Gheith, Jehanne M., **3**: 17
Gillette, Michael L., **3**: 254
Gissing, George, **2**: 320
Gluck, Sherna Berger, **3**: 190
Goethe, Johann Wolfgang von, **1**: 276
Goncourt, Edmond de, **2**: 81
Goncourt, Jules de, **2**: 81
Griffith, Kenneth, **3**: 27
Grimké, Charlotte Forten, **2**: 29
Guevara, Ernesto "Che," **2**: 220
Gurewitsch, Brana, **3**: 34
Guylforde, Richarde, **2**: 226

H

Haley, Alex, **1**: 261
Halkett, Lady Anne, **1**: 315
Hampton, Henry, **3**: 44
Hansberry, Lorraine, **1**: 273
Haskins, Jim, **1**: 37
Hatzfeld, Jean, **3**: 257
Hawthorne, Nathaniel, **2**: 223
Hayashi, Katie Kaori, **3**: 127

Hayslip, Le Ly, **1**: 335
Hickey, Margaret, **3**: 315
Higginson, Thomas Wentworth, **2**: 238
Hillesum, Etty, **2**: 22
Hirsi Ali, Ayaan, **1**: 207
Hitler, Adolf, **1**: 30
Hochstadt, Steve, **3**: 14
Holmes, Richard, **3**: 234
hooks, bell, **1**: 249
Houston, James D., **1**: 299
Houston, Jeanne Wakatsuki, **1**: 299
Humphries, Stephen, **3**: 311
Hurston, Zora Neale, **1**: 9
Hussein, Taha, **1**: 135

J

Jacobs, Harriet A., **1**: 142
James, Daniel, **3**: 73
James, Henry, **2**: 113
Jefferson, Thomas, **2**: 316
Jiang, Ji-li, **1**: 161
Jolluck, Katherine R., **3**: 17

K

Kafka, Franz, **2**: 120
Keats, John, **2**: 146
Ke Lan, **3**: 124
Keller, Helen, **1**: 43
Kemble, Fanny, **2**: 335
Kempe, Margery, **1**: 189
Kierkegaard, Søren, **2**: 166
Kim, Elizabeth, **1**: 102
Kim Ku, **1**: 322
King, Martin Luther, Jr., **2**: 32
Kingston, Maxine Hong, **1**: 173
Klemperer, Victor, **2**: 303
Kohn, Rita, **3**: 107, 325
Kong Demao, **3**: 124
Krause, Corinne Azen, **3**: 305
Krog, Antjie, **3**: 242

L

Ladjevardi, Habib, **3**: 218
Last, Nella, **2**: 265
Laye, Camara, **1**: 128
Leadbeater, Mary, **2**: 157
Lee, Robert E., **2**: 38
Left Handed, **3**: 318
Lejeune, Philippe, **1**: 239, **2**: 174
Lessing, Doris, **1**: 167
Lewin, Rhoda, **3**: 50
Light, Kenneth, **3**: 66
Light, Melanie, **3**: 66
Lorde, Audre, **2**: 3
Luthuli, Albert, **1**: 24
Lu Xun, **2**: 170

M

Mahomet, Dean, **2**: 05
Malcolm X, **1**: 186
Mandela, Nelson, **1**: 27
Manning, Diane, **3**: 77
Mansfield, Katherine, **2**: 133
Manwaring, Max G., **3**: 205
Martin, Patricia Preciado, **3**: 131
Mason, Katrina, **3**: 239
Maugham, W. Somerset, **2**: 183
Maurer, Harry, **3**: 275
McBride, James, **1**: 72
McCarthy, Mary, **1**: 258
McCourt, Frank, **1**: 119
McKay, Claude, **1**: 84
Medina, Pablo, **1**: 296
Menchú, Rigoberta, **3**: 164
Michitsuna No Haha, **2**: 297
Milich, Zorka, **3**: 135
Miller, Donald E., **3**: 40
Miller, Lorna Touryan, **3**: 40
Min, Anchee, **1**: 158
Mitchison, Naomi, **2**: 235
Momaday, N. Scott, **1**: 54
Montagu, Lady Mary Wortley, **2**: 35
Montejo, Esteban, **3**: 7

Montell, William Lynwood, **3**: 90, 107
Moon, Elaine Latzman, **3**: 99
Moore, Marat, **3**: 337
Moore, Molly, **2**: 278
Morris, Gabrielle, **3**: 20
Moye, J. Todd, **3**: 248

N

Nabokov, Vladimir, **1**: 270
Nakazawa, Keiji, **1**: 293
Neihardt, John G., **3**: 110
Nehru, Jawaharlal, **1**: 289
Neruda, Pablo, **1**: 222
Nguyen, Kien, **1**: 170
Nijo, Lady, **2**: 59
Nin, Anaïs, **2**: 123

O

Obama, Barack, **1**: 78
O'Conner, Flannery, **2**: 129
O'Grady, Timothy, **3**: 27
Olney, James, **1**: 246
Oppenheimer, Gerald M., **3**: 272
Orwell, George, **2**: 117
Osborne, Dorothy, **2**: 324
O'Sullivan, John, **3**: 227
Owsley, Beatrice Rodriguez, **3**: 121

P

Palmer, Michele, **3**: 293
Patai, Daphne, **3**: 190
Parks, Rosa, **1**: 37
Partridge, Frances, **2**: 268
Peltier, Leonard, **1**: 96
Pepys, Samuel, **2**: 72
Perera, Victor, **1**: 99
Perks, Robert, **3**: 170
Plaatje, Solomon Tshekisho, **2**: 241
Plath, Sylvia, **2**: 47
Pliny the Younger, **2**: 94
Poe, Edgar Allan, **2**: 41

Polo, Marco, **1**: 105
Poniatowska, Elena, **3**: 31
Popular Memory Group, **3**: 176
Portelli, Alessandro, **3**: 96, 157, 265
Pozas, Ricardo, **3**: 167
Prince, Mary, **3**: 23
Prisk, Court, **3**: 205

R

Rabe, John, **2**: 19
Raleigh, Donald J., **3**: 331
Rilke, Rainer Maria, **2**: 149
Roberts, Elizabeth, **3**: 144
Robinson, Henry Crabb, **2**: 75
Rodriguez, Richard, **1**: 15
Rogers, Carole Garibaldi, **3**: 308
Rousseau, Jean-Jacques, **1**: 200
Rowlandson, Mary, **1**: 325
Rowley, Susan, **3**: 138
Ruete, Emily, **1**: 90
Ruskin, John, **1**: 264
Russell, Bert, **3**: 93

S

Saitoti, Tepilit Ole, **1**: 114
Sang Ye, **3**: 299
Santiago, Esmeralda, **1**: 108
Santoli, Al, **3**: 209
Sarashina, Lady, **2**: 189
Sassoon, Siegfried, **2**: 247
Satrapi, Marjane, **1**: 155
Savage, Thomas, **3**: 114
Scott, Sir Walter, **2**: 309
Seabrook, Jeremy, **3**: 5301
Seacole, Mary, **1**: 111
Shackelford, Laurel, **3**: 86
Shaffer, Deborah, **3**: 328
Shikibu, Lady Murasaki, **2**: 290
Shostak, Marjorie, **3**: 37
Siegelbaum, Lewis H., **3**: 340
Sinor, Jennifer, **2**: 163
Siv, Sichan, **1**: 306
Slingsby, Sir Henry, **2**: 256

Soyinka, Wole, **1**: 214
Speer, Albert, **2**: 54
Stanton, Elizabeth Cady, **1**: 12
Stave, Bruce M., **3**: 293
Stein, Gertrude, **1**: 332
Stewart, Elinore Pruitt, **2**: 91
Stone, Kate, **2**: 244
Styron, William, **1**: 204
Suenaga, Shizuko, **3**: 127
Suleri, Sara, **1**: 87

T

Tamura, Linda, **3**: 80
Tateishi, John, **3**: 195
Teresa of Ávila, **1**: 211
Terkel, Louis "Studs," **3**: 161, 212, 343
Terry, Wallace, **3**: 199
Thiong'o, Ngũgĩ wa, **2**: 12
Thomas, Dylan, **1**: 125
Thompson, Paul, **3**: 170, 186
Thoreau, Henry David, **1**: 233
Tollefson, James W., **3**: 221
Tolstoy, Leo, **1**: 193
Tuqan, Fadwa, **1**: 225
Twain, Mark, **1**: 146

U

Uchida, Yoshiko, **1**: 309
Ulrich, Laurel Thatcher, **2**: 331
Unaipon, David, **1**: 149
Underhill, Ruth, **1**: 69
Usāmah ibn Munqidh, **1**: 285

V

Vaarzon-Morel, Petronella, **3**: 334
Vambe, Lawrence Chinyani, **3**: 251
Vico, Giambattista, **1**: 183
Victoria, Queen, **2**: 209
Viezzer, Moema, **3**: 322

AUTHOR INDEX

W

Walkowitz, Daniel J., **3**: 340
Walmsley, Jan, **3**: 170
Wang Zheng, **3**: 147
Washington, Booker T., **1**: 50
Wat, Eric, **3**: 83
Webb, Beatrice, **2**: 16
Wehrey, Jane, **3**: 102
Weinberg, Bill, **3**: 86
Wells, H. G., **1**: 252
Wesley, John, **2**: 195
Wheatley, Phillis, **2**: 44
Wiesel, Elie, **1**: 318
Wilde, Oscar, **2**: 9
Williams, Tennessee, **2**: 152
Wolff, Tobias, **1**: 47
Wollstonecraft, Mary, **2**: 109
Wood, Trish, **3**: 231
Woodforde, James, **2**: 287
Wooldridge, E. T., **3**: 202
Woolf, Virginia, **2**: 180
Wordsworth, Dorothy, **2**: 300
Wright, Richard, **1**: 122
Wurts, Jay, **1**: 335

X

Xie Bingying, **1**: 338
Xu Guangping, **2**: 170

Y

Yeats, William Butler, **2**: 126

Z

Zhang Xinxin, **3**: 299

Title Index

The title index includes works that are represented in *The Literature of Autobiographical Narrative*. Bolded numbers refer to volumes, with page numbers following colons.

A

Abandoned Baobab, The: The Autobiography of a Senegalese Woman [Ken Bugul], **1**: 61

Akenfield: Portrait of an English Village [Ronald Blythe], **3**: 59

Always a People: Oral Histories of Contemporary Woodland Indians [Rita Kohn and William Lynwood Montell], **3**: 107

Among You Taking Notes: The Wartime Diary of Naomi Mitchison, 1939–1945 [Naomi Mitchison], **2**: 235

Anarchist Voices: An Oral History of Anarchism in America [Paul Avrich], **3**: 3

And Justice for All: An Oral History of the Japanese American Detention Camps [John Tateishi], **3**: 195

Angela's Ashes [Frank McCourt], **1**: 119

Annals of Ballitore, The [Mary Leadbeater], **2**: 157

Arab-Syrian Gentleman and Warrior in the Period of the Crusades, An: Memoirs of Usāmah ibn Munqidh [Usāmah ibn Munqidh], **1**: 285

Army Life in a Black Regiment [Thomas Wentworth Higginson], **2**: 238

As I Crossed a Bridge of Dreams [Lady Sarashina], **2**: 189

Ask the Fellows Who Cut the Hay [George Ewart Evans], **3**: 63

Autobiographical Pact, The [Philippe Lejeune], **1**: 239

Autobiography, An, or The Story of My Experiments with Truth [Mohandas Gandhi], **1**: 242

Autobiography, An, with Musings on Recent Events in India [Jawaharlal Nehru], **1**: 289

Autobiography: Essays Theoretical and Critical [James Olney], **1**: 246

Autobiography of Ben Franklin, The [Benjamin Franklin], **1**: 179

Autobiography of Charles Darwin, The [Charles Darwin], **1**: 65

Autobiography of Giambattista Vico, The [Giambattista Vico], **1**: 183

Autobiography of Malcolm X, The [Malcolm X], **1**: 186

Autobiography of W. E. B. Du Bois, The: A Soliloquy on Viewing My Life from the Last Decade of Its First Century [W. E. B. Du Bois], **1**: 3

B

Barefoot Gen: A Cartoon Story of Hiroshima [Keiji Nakazawa], **1**: 293

Between Management and Labor: Oral Histories of Arbitration [Clara Friedman], **3**: 153

Biography of a Runaway Slave [Miguel Barnet and Esteban Montejo], **3**: 7

Bitter Water: Diné Oral Histories of the Navajo-Hopi Land Dispute [Malcolm D. Benally], **3**: 10

Black Boy [Richard Wright], **1**: 122

Black Elk Speaks: Being the Life Story of a Holy Man of the Oglala Sioux [Black Elk and John G. Neihardt], **3**: 110

Bloods: An Oral History of the Vietnam War by Black Veterans [Wallace Terry], **3**: 199

Boer War Diary of Sol Plaatje, The: An African at Mafeking [Solomon Tshekisho Plaatje], **2**: 241

Bone Black: Memories of Girlhood [bell hooks], **1**: 249

Book of Margery Kempe, The [Margery Kempe], **1**: 189

Brokenburn: The Journal of Kate Stone, 1861–1868 [Kate Stone], **2**: 244

C

Californio Voices: The Oral Memoirs of José María Amador and Lorenzo Asisara [Thomas Savage], **3**: 114

Cancer Journals, The [Audre Lorde], **2**: 3

Carrier Warfare in the Pacific: An Oral History Collection [E. T. Wooldridge], **3**: 202

Child of the Dark: The Diary of Carolina Maria de Jesus [Carolina Maria de Jesus], **2**: 6

Children of Los Alamos: An Oral History of the Town Where the Atomic Bomb Began [Katrina Mason], **3**: 239

TITLE INDEX

Child's Christmas in Wales, A [Dylan Thomas], **1**: 125

Chinese Lives: An Oral History of Contemporary China [Zhang Xinxin and Sang Ye], **3**: 299

Chona: The Autobiography of a Papago Woman [Maria Chona and Ruth Underhill], **1**: 69

Coal Hollow: Photographs and Oral Histories [Kenneth Light and Melanie Light], **3**: 66

Collected Letters of a Renaissance Feminist [Laura Cereta], **2**: 160

Collected Letters of Mary Wollstonecraft, The [Mary Wollstonecraft], **2**: 109

Color of Water, The: A Black Man's Tribute to His White Mother [James McBride], **1**: 72

Complete Notebooks of Henry James, The [Henry James], **2**: 113

Confession, A [Leo Tolstoy], **1**: 193

Confessions [Augustine], **1**: 196

Confessions [Jean-Jacques Rousseau], **1**: 200

Confessions of Lady Nijō [Lady Nijō], **2**: 59

Congo Diary, The [Joseph Conrad], **2**: 192

Country of My Skull: Guilt, Sorrow, and the Limits of Forgiveness in the New South Africa [Antjie Krog], **3**: 242

Country Parson, A: James Woodforde's Diary, 1759–1802 [James Woodforde], **2**: 287

Cross and a Star, A: Memoirs of a Jewish Girl in Chile [Marjorie Agosín], **1**: 75

D

Daring Hearts: Lesbian and Gay Lives of the 50s and 60s Brighton [Brighton Ourstory], **3**: 70

Dark Child, The: The Autobiography of an African Boy [Camara Laye], **1**: 128

Darkness Visible [William Styron], **1**: 204

Death of Luigi Trastulli and Other Stories, The [Alessandro Portelli], **3**: 157

De Profundis [Oscar Wilde], **2**: 9

Detained: A Writer's Prison Diary [Ngũgĩ wa Thiong'o], **2**: 12

Diaries, 1915–1918 [Siegfried Sassoon], **2**: 247

Diaries, 1931–1949 [George Orwell], **2**: 117

Diaries of Beatrice Webb [Beatrice Webb], **2**: 16

Diaries of Franz Kafka, The [Franz Kafka], **2**: 120

Diaries of Lady Anne Clifford, The [Lady Anne Clifford], **2**: 62

Diary, Reminiscences and Correspondence of Henry Crabb Robinson, Barrister-at-Law [Henry Crabb Robinson], **2**: 75

Diary from Dixie, A [Mary Boykin Miller Chesnut], **2**: 250

Diary of Anaïs Nin, The [Anaïs Nin], **2**: 123

Diary of Anne Frank, The [Anne Frank], **2**: 253

Diary of John Evelyn, The [John Evelyn], **2**: 65

Diary of John Quincy Adams, The [John Quincy Adams], **2**: 69

Diary of Lady Murasaki, The [Lady Murasaki Shikibu], **2**: 290

Diary of Samuel Pepys, The [Samuel Pepys], **2**: 72

Diary of Sir Henry Slingsby, The [Sir Henry Slingsby], **2**: 256

Diary without Dates, A [Enid Bagnold], **2**: 259

Diving Bell and the Butterfly, The [Jean-Dominique Bauby], **1**: 6

Doña María's Story: Life History, Memory and Political Identity [Daniel James], **3**: 73

Dreams from My Father: A Story of Race and Inheritance [Barack Obama], **1**: 78

Dust Tracks on a Road [Zora Neale Hurston], **1**: 9

E

Education of Henry Adams, The [Henry Adams], **1**: 132

Egyptian Childhood, An [Taha Hussein], **1**: 135

Eighty Years and More, Reminiscences 1815–1897 [Elizabeth Cady Stanton], **1**: 12

El Salvador at War: An Oral History of Conflict from the 1979 Insurrection to the Present [Max G. Manwaring and Court Prisk], **3**: 205

Estrangement, Being Some Fifty Extracts from a Diary Kept in 1909 [William Butler Yeats], **2**: 126

Everything We Had [Al Santoli], **3**: 209

Exiled Memories: A Cuban Childhood [Pablo Medina], **1**: 296

Exodus to Shanghai: Stories of Escape from the Third Reich [Steve Hochstadt], **3**: 14

Experiment in Autobiography, An [H. G. Wells], **1**: 252

Extraordinary Work of Ordinary Writing, The: Annie Ray's Diary [Jennifer Sinor], **2**: 163

F

Farewell to Manzanar [Jeanne Wakatsuki Houston and James D. Houston], **1**: 299

Firm: The Inside Story of the Stasi, The [Gary Bruce], **3**: 245

First Agraristas, The: An Oral History of a Mexican Agrarian Reform Movement [Ann L. Craig], **3**: 302

Freedom Flyers: The Tuskegee Airmen of World War II [J. Todd Moye], **3**: 248

Fun Home: A Family Tragicomic [Alison Bechdel], **1**: 139

G

Geronimo: His Own Story [Geronimo and S. M. Barrett], **1**: 302

Go Ask Alice [Anonymous], **2**: 294

Golden Bones: An Extraordinary Journey from Hell in Cambodia to a New Life in America [Sichan Siv], **1**: 306

Good Man of Nanking, The: The Diaries of John Rabe [John Rabe], **2**: 19

"Good War, The": An Oral History of World War II [Louis "Studs" Terkel], **3**: 212

Gossamer Years, The [Michitsuna No Haha], **2**: 297

Grandmothers, Mothers, and Daughters: Oral Histories of Three Generations of Ethnic American Women [Corinne Azen Krause], **3**: 305

Grasmere Journals [Dorothy Wordsworth], **2**: 300

Growing Up Jewish in America [Myrna Katz Frommer and Harvey Frommer], **3**: 118

Gulag Voices: Oral Histories of Soviet Incarceration and Exile [Jehanne M. Gheith and Katherine R. Jolluck], **3**: 17

H

Habit of Being, The: Letters of Flannery O'Connor [Flannery O'Conner], **2**: 129

Habits of Change: An Oral History of American Nuns [Carole Garibaldi Rogers], **3**: 308

Hard Times: An Oral History of the Great Depression [Louis "Studs" Terkel], **3**: 161

Head of the Class: An Oral History of African American Achievement in Higher Education and Beyond [Gabrielle Morris], **3**: 20

Hill Country Teacher: Oral Histories from the One-Room School and Beyond [Diane Manning], **3**: 77

Hispanic-American Entrepreneur, The: An Oral History of the American Dream [Beatrice Rodriguez Owsley], **3**: 121

History of Mary Prince, a West Indian Slave, Related by Herself, The [Mary Prince], **3**: 23

Hood River Issei, The: An Oral History of Japanese Settlers in Oregon's Hood River Valley [Linda Tamura], **3**: 80

Hooligans or Rebels?: An Oral History of Working-Class Childhood and Youth, 1889–1939 [Stephen Humphries], **3**: 311

Hunger of Memory: The Education of Richard Rodriguez [Richard Rodriguez], **1**: 15

I

I, Rigoberta Menchú: An Indian Woman in Guatemala [Rigoberta Menchú], **3**: 164

I Know Why the Caged Bird Sings [Maya Angelou], **1**: 18

Ill-Fated People, An: Zimbabwe before and after Rhodes [Lawrence Chinyani Vambe], **3**: 251

Incidents in the Life of a Slave Girl, Written by Herself [Harriet A. Jacobs], **1**: 142

Infidel [Ayaan Hirsi Ali], **1**: 207

Interesting Narrative of the Life of Olaudah Equiano, The, or Gustavus Vassa, the African, Written by Himself [Olaudah Equiano], **1**: 81

Interrupted Life, An: The Diaries of Etty Hillesum [Etty Hillesum], **2**: 22

In the Mansion of Confucius' Descendants: An Oral History [Kong Demao and Ke Lan], **3**: 124

In the Presence of Absence [Mahmoud Darwish], **1**: 255

Invisible Thread, The [Yoshiko Uchida], **1**: 309

Ireland's Unfinished Revolution: An Oral History [Kenneth Griffith and Timothy O'Grady], **3**: 27

Irish Days: Oral Histories of the Twentieth Century [Margaret Hickey], **3**: 315

I Will Bear Witness: A Diary of the Nazi Years, 1933–1945 [Victor Klemperer], **2**: 303

J

Japan at War: An Oral History [Haruko Taya Cook and Theodore F. Cook], **3**: 215

Japanese War Brides in America: An Oral History [Miki Ward Crawford, Katie Kaori Hayashi, and Shizuko Suenaga], **3**: 127

Jemima Condict: Her Book, Being a Transcript of the Diary of an Essex County Maid during the Revolutionary War [Jemima Condict], **2**: 78

Journal, 1955–1962: Reflections on the French-Algerian War [Mouloud Feraoun], **2**: 262

Journal des Goncourt: Mémoires de la vie littéraire [Jules de Goncourt and Edmond de Goncourt], **2**: 81

Journal of George Fox [George Fox], **2**: 26

Journal of Katherine Mansfield [Katherine Mansfield], **2**: 133

Journal of Marie Bashkirtseff, The [Marie Bashkirtseff], **2**: 306

Journal of Sir Walter Scott, The [Sir Walter Scott], **2**: 309

Journal of the First Voyage of Vasco da Gama, 1497–1499, A [Author Unknown], **2**: 201

Journal of the First Voyage to America [Christopher Columbus], **2**: 201

Journals of Arnold Bennett, 1896–1928, The [Arnold Bennett], **2**: 136

Journals of Charlotte Forten Grimké, The [Charlotte Forten Grimké], **2**: 29

Journals of John Wesley [John Wesley], **2**: 195

Journals of Jonathan Carver and Related Documents, 1766–1770, The [Jonathan Carver], **2**: 205

Journals of Ralph Waldo Emerson [Ralph Waldo Emerson], **2**: 139

Journals of Søren Kierkegaard [Søren Kierkegaard], **2**: 166

Juan the Chamula: An Ethnological Re-creation of the Life of a Mexican Indian [Ricardo Pozas], **3**: 167

L

Lakota Woman [Mary Crow Dog], **1**: 21

Last Diary of Tsaritsa Alexandra, The [Alexandra Feodorovna], **2**: 84

Launching the War on Poverty: An Oral History [Michael L. Gillette], **3**: 254

Leaves from the Journal of Our Life in the Highlands, from 1848 to 1861 [Queen Victoria], **2**: 209

Left Handed, Son of Old Man Hat: A Navajo Autobiography [Left Handed and Walter Dyk], **3**: 318

Let Me Speak!: Testimony of Domitila, a Woman of the Bolivian Mines [Moema Viezzer and Domitila Barrios de Chungara], **3**: 322

Let My People Go [Albert Luthuli], **1**: 24

"Letter from the Birmingham Jail" [Martin Luther King Jr.], **2**: 32

Letters and Journals of Fanny Burney [Fanny Burney], **2**: 312

TITLE INDEX

Letters and Journals of Lord Byron, with Notices of His Life [George Gordon Noel Byron], **2**: 143

Letters between Two [Lu Xun and Xu Guangping], **2**: 170

Letters from an American Farmer [Michel-Guillaume Saint-Jean de Crévecoeur], **2**: 213

Letters from Jefferson to His Daughter [Thomas Jefferson], **2**: 316

Letters Home [Sylvia Plath], **2**: 47

Letters of a Woman Homesteader [Elinore Pruitt Stewart], **2**: 91

Letters of John Keats, 1814–1821, The [John Keats], **2**: 146

Letters of Lady Anne Barnard to Henry Dundas, from Cape and Elsewhere, The [Anne Barnard], **2**: 217

Letters of the Younger Pliny, The [Pliny the Younger], **2**: 94

Letters to a Young Poet [Rainer Maria Rilke], **2**: 149

Letters Underway ['Izzat Ghazzawi], **2**: 50

"Letter to Her Daughter" [Lady Mary Wortley Montagu], **2**: 35

"Letter to Her Daughter from the New White House" [Abigail Adams], **2**: 87

"Letter to His Son" [Robert E. Lee], **2**: 38

"Letter to Maria Clemm" [Edgar Allan Poe], **2**: 41

"Letter to the Reverend Samson Occom" [Phillis Wheatley], **2**: 44

Life, The [Teresa of Ávila], **1**: 211

Life on the Mississippi [Mark Twain], **1**: 146

Literary Remains of Edward VI, The [Edward VI], **2**: 97

London and the Life of Literature in Late Victorian England: The Diary of George Gissing, Novelist [George Gissing], **2**: 320

London Journal, 1762–1763 [James Boswell], **2**: 328

Long Journey Home: Oral Histories of Contemporary Delaware Indians [James W. Brown and Rita T. Kohn], **3**: 325

Long Walk to Freedom, The [Nelson Mandela], **1**: 27

Long Way from Home, A [Claude McKay], **1**: 84

Long Way Gone, A: Memoirs of a Boy Soldier [Ishmael Beah], **1**: 312

Love Letters of Dorothy Osborne to Sir Wiliam Temple, 1652–54, The [Dorothy Osborne], **2**: 324

M

Machete Season: The Killers in Rwanda Speak [Jean Hatzfeld], **3**: 257

Making of a Gay Asian Community, The: An Oral History of Pre-AIDS Los Angeles [Eric Wat], **3**: 83

Man Died, The: Prison Notes of Wole Soyinka [Wole Soyinka], **1**: 214

Massacre in Mexico [Elena Poniatowska], **3**: 31

Meatless Days [Sara Suleri], **1**: 87

Meditations of the Emperor Marcus Aurelius Antoninus, The [Marcus Aurelius], **1**: 218

Mein Kampf [Adolf Hitler], **1**: 30

Memoirs [Pablo Neruda], **1**: 222

Memoirs of an Arabian Princess from Zanzibar [Emily Ruete], **1**: 90

Memoirs of Fatemeh Pakravan [Habib Ladjevardi], **3**: 218

Memoirs of Lady Anne Halkett, The [Lady Anne Halkett], **1**: 315

Memories of a Catholic Girlhood [Mary McCarthy], **1**: 258

Midwife's Tale, A: The Life of Martha Ballard, Based on Her Diary, 1785–1812 [Laurel Thatcher Ulrich], **2**: 331

Mothers, Sisters, Resisters: Oral Histories of Women Who Survived the Holocaust [Brana Gurewitsch], **3**: 34

Motorcycle Diaries [Ernesto "Che" Guevara], **2**: 220

Mountainous Journey, A: A Poet's Autobiography [Fadwa Tuqan], **1**: 225

"My Furthest-Back Person—'The African'" [Alex Haley], **1**: 261

My Life Story [Fadhma Aïth Mansour Amrouche], **1**: 93

My Life Story [David Unaipon], **1**: 149

My Revolutionary Years: The Autobiography of Madame Wei Tao-Ming [Cheng Yu-hsiu], **1**: 152

N

Narrative of the Life of Frederick Douglass [Frederick Douglass], **1**: 33

Nella Last's War: The Second World War Diaries of Housewife, 49 [Nella Last], **2**: 265

Night [Elie Wiesel], **1**: 318

Nisa: The Life and Words of a !Kung Woman [Marjorie Shostak], **3**: 37

Notebooks [Tennessee Williams], **2**: 152

Notebooks and *Letters* [Nathaniel Hawthorne], **2**: 223

O

Oral History, Health and Welfare [Joanna Bornat, Robert Perks, Paul Thompson, and Jan Walmsley], **3**: 170

Oral History of Abraham Lincoln, An: John G. Nicolay's Interviews and Essays [Michael Burlingame], **3**: 261

Oral History Theory [Lynn Abrams], **3**: 173

Order Has Been Carried Out, The: History, Memory, and Meaning of a Nazi Massacre in Rome [Alessandro Portelli], **3**: 265

Our Appalachia [Laurel Shackelford and Bill Weinberg], **3**: 86

P

Pacifist's War, A: Diaries 1939–1945 [Frances Partridge], **2**: 268

Paekpom Ilchi: The Autobiography of Kim Ku [Kim Ku], **1**: 322

Peacework: Oral Histories of Women Peace Activists [Judith Porter Adams], **3**: 268

Persepolis [Marjane Satrapi], **1**: 155

"Popular Memory: Theory, Politics, Method" [Popular Memory Group], **3**: 176

"Practice of the Private Journal" [Philippe Lejeune], **2**: 174

Praeterita [John Ruskin], **1**: 264

Prison Writings: My Life Is My Sun Dance [Leonard Peltier], **1**: 96

Pylgrymage of Sir Richarde Guylforde, The [Richarde Guylforde], **2**: 226

R

Records of a Girlhood [Fanny Kemble], **2**: 335

Red Azalea [Anchee Min], **1**: 158

Red Scarf Girl: A Memoir of the Cultural Revolution [Ji-li Jiang], **1**: 161

Rites: A Guatemalan Boyhood [Victor Perera], **1**: 99

Roland Barthes [Roland Barthes], **1**: 267

Rosa Parks: My Story [Rosa Parks and Jim Haskins], **1**: 37

S

Saga of Coe Ridge, The: A Study in Oral History [William Lynwood Montell], **3**: 90

Selected Letters of Martha Gellhorn [Martha Gellhorn], **2**: 101

Shadows on My Heart: The Civil War Diary of Lucy Rebecca Buck of Virginia [Lucy Buck], **2**: 271

Shared Authority, A: Essays on the Craft and Meaning of Oral and Public History [Michael Frisch], **3**: 179

Shattered Dreams?: An Oral History of the South African AIDS Epidemic [Gerald M. Oppenheimer and Ronald Bayer], **3**: 272

Solidarity Forever: An Oral History of the IWW [Stewart Bird, Dan Georgakas, and Deborah Shaffer], **3**: 328

"Some Observations on Diaries, Self-Biography, and Self-Characters" [Isaac D'Israeli], **2**: 177

Songs My Mother Sang to Me: An Oral History of Mexican American Women [Patricia Preciado Martin], **3**: 131

Sovereignty and Goodness of God, The [Mary Rowlandson], **1**: 325

Soviet Baby Boomers: An Oral History of Russia's Cold War Generation [Donald J. Raleigh], **3**: 331

Spandau: The Secret Diaries [Albert Speer], **2**: 54

Speak, Memory: An Autobiography Revisited [Vladimir Nabokov], **1**: 270

Stop-Time [Frank Conroy], **1**: 164

Story of a Shipwrecked Sailor, The [Gabriel García Márquez], **3**: 183

Story of My Life, The: An Afghan Girl on the Other Side of the Sky [Farah Ahmedi], **1**: 40

Story of My Life, The: Helen Keller [Helen Keller], **1**: 43

Strange Ground: Americans in Vietnam 1945–1975: An Oral History [Harry Maurer], **3**: 275

Stranger's Supper, A: An Oral History of Centenarian Women in Montenegro [Zorka Milich], **3**: 135

Strength Not to Fight, The: An Oral History of Conscientious Objectors of the Vietnam War [James W. Tollefson], **3**: 221

Survivors: An Oral History of the Armenian Genocide [Donald E. Miller and Lorna Touryan Miller], **3**: 40

Swiftwater People: Lives of Old Timers on the Upper St. Joe & St. Maries Rivers [Bert Russell], **3**: 93

T

Tears before the Rain: An Oral History of the Fall of South Vietnam [Larry Engelmann], **3**: 279

Ten Thousand Sorrows: The Extraordinary Journey of a Korean War Orphan [Elizabeth Kim], **1**: 102

Testament of Youth [Vera Brittain], **1**: 329

They Say in Harlan County: An Oral History [Alessandro Portelli] **3**: 96

This Boy's Life [Tobias Wolff], **1**: 47

Thura's Diary: A Young Girl's Life in War-Torn Baghdad [Thura Al-Windawi], **2**: 275

To Be Young, Gifted and Black: An Informal Autobiography of Lorraine Hansberry [Lorraine Hansberry], **1**: 273

Travels of Dean Mahomet, a Native of Patna in Bengal, through Several Parts of India, While in the Service of the Honourable the East India Company Written by Himself, in a Series of Letters to a Friend, The [Dean Mahomet], **2**: 229

Travels of Marco Polo, The [Marco Polo], **1**: 105

True Relation of My Birth, Breeding, and Life, A [Margaret Cavendish], **1**: 229

Truth and Fiction Relating to My Life [Johann Wolfgang von Goethe], **1**: 276

U

Under My Skin: Volume One of My Autobiography, to 1949 [Doris Lessing], **1**: 167

Unknown Internment, The: An Oral History of the Relocation of Italian Americans during World War II [Stephen Fox], **3**: 224

Untold Tales, Unsung Heroes: An Oral History of Detroit's African-American Community, 1918–1967 [Elaine Latzman Moon], **3**: 99

Unwanted, The [Kien Nguyen], **1**: 170

Up from Slavery [Booker T. Washington], **1**: 50

Uqalurait: An Oral History of Nunavut [John Bennett and Susan Rowley], **3**: 138

V

Voice of the Past, The: Oral History [Paul Thompson], **3**: 186

Voices from Chernobyl: The Oral History of a Nuclear Disaster [Svetlana Alexievich], **3**: 282

Voices from the Whirlwind: An Oral History of the Chinese Cultural Revolution [Feng Jicai], **3**: 287

Voices from this Long Brown Land: Oral Recollections of Owens Valley Lives and Manzanar Pasts [Jane Wehrey], **3**: 102

Voices of Freedom: An Oral History of the Civil Rights Movement from the 1950s through the 1980s [Henry Hampton and Steve Fayer], **3**: 44

Voices of Resistance: Oral Histories of Moroccan Women [Allison Baker], **3**: 47

TITLE INDEX

W

Walden; or, Life in the Woods [Henry David Thoreau], **1**: 233

Warlpiri Women's Voices: Our Lives, Our History [Petronella Vaarzon-Morel], **3**: 334

Wars I Have Seen [Gertrude Stein], **1**: 332

Way to Rainy Mountain, The [N. Scott Momaday], **1**: 54

"We Have Just Begun to Not Fight": An Oral History of Conscientious Objectors in Civilian Public Service during World War II [Heather T. Frazer and John O'Sullivan], **3**: 227

What Was Asked of Us: An Oral History of the Iraq War by the Soldiers Who Fought It [Trish Wood], **3**: 231

When Heaven and Earth Changed Places: A Vietnamese Woman's Journey from War to Peace [Le Ly Hayslip and Jay Wurts], **1**: 335

When I Was Puerto Rican [Esmeralda Santiago], **1**: 108

When We Began, There Were Witchmen: An Oral History from Mount Kenya [Jeffrey A. Fadiman], **3**: 141

Witch Purge of 1878, The: Oral and Documentary History in the Early Navajo Reservation Years [Martha Blue], **3**: 290

Witnesses to Nuremberg: An Oral History of American Participants at the War Crimes Trials [Bruce M. Stave, Michele Palmer, and Leslie Frank], **3**: 293

Witnesses to the Holocaust: An Oral History [Rhoda Lewin], **3**: 50

Woman at War, A [Molly Moore], **2**: 278

Woman in Berlin, A: Eight Weeks in the Conquered City: A Diary [Anonymous], **2**: 281

Woman Soldier's Own Story, A [Xie Bingying], **1**: 338

Woman Warrior, The: Memoirs of a Girlhood among Ghosts [Maxine Hong Kingston], **1**: 173

Women and Families: An Oral History, 1940–1970 [Elizabeth Roberts], **3**: 144

Women in the Chinese Enlightenment: Oral and Textual Histories [Wang Zheng], **3**: 14703

Women in the Mines: Stories of Life and Work [Marat Moore], **3**: 337

Women's Words [Sherna Berger Gluck and Daphne Patai], **3**: 190

Wonderful Adventures of Mrs. Seacole in Many Lands, The [Mary Seacole], **1**: 111

Workers of the Donbass Speak: Survival and Identity in the New Ukraine, 1989–1992 [Lewis H. Siegelbaum and Daniel J. Walkowitz], **3**: 340

Working: People Talk about What They Do All Day and How They Feel about What They Do [Louis "Studs" Terkel], **3**: 343

Working-Class Childhood: An Oral History [Jeremy Seabrook], **3**: 5301

World at War, The [Richard Holmes], **3**: 234

Worlds of a Maasai Warrior, The: An Autobiography [Tepilit Ole Saitoti], **1**: 114

Writer's Diary, A [Virginia Woolf], **2**: 180

Writer's Notebook, A [W. Somerset Maugham], **2**: 183

Writing Life, The [Annie Dillard], **1**: 279

Y

Young Palestinian's Diary, 1941–1945, A: The Life of Sāmī 'Amr [Sāmī 'Amr], **2**: 104

Z

Zlata's Diary: A Child's Life in Sarajevo [Zlata Filipovic], **2**: 338